WORLD ENCYCLOPEDIA OF PEACE

(SECOND EDITION)

WORLD ENCYCLOPEDIA OF PEACE

(SECOND EDITION)

VOLUME II

Honorary Editor-in-Chief

Javier Perez De Cuellar

Editor-in-Chief

Young Seek Choue

 **OCEANA PUBLICATIONS, INC.®**
NEW YORK

•

 **SEOUL PRESS**

World Encyclopedia of Peace (Second Edition)

Published in the United States of America in 1999 and distributed exclusively throughout the world, except in Korea, by
Oceana Publications Inc.
75 Main Street
Dobbs Ferry, New York 10522
Phone: (914) 693-8100
Fax: (914) 693-0402

ISBN: 0-379-21400-8 (Volume II)
ISBN: 0-379-21398-2 (Set)

Library of Congress Cataloging-in-Publication Data

World encyclopedia of peace / honorary editor-in-chief, Javier
Perez de Cuellar, editor-in-chief, Young Seek Choue. -- 2nd ed.
    p. cm.
    Includes bibliographical references and indexes.
    ISBN 0-379-21398-2 (clothbound set : alk. paper)
    1. Peace Encyclopedias. I. Perez de Cuellar, Javier, 1920-
II. Young Seek Choue, 1921-
JZ5533 .W67 1999
327.1'03--dc21   99-34811
                                                                CIP

Published simultaneously in the Republic of Korea in 1999 by
Seoul Press
Jin Wang Kim, Publisher
Room 303, Jeodong Bldg., 7-2, Jeodong, Chung-ku
Seoul 100-032, Korea
Phone: (02) 2275-6566
Fax: (02) 2278-2551

ISBN: 89-7225-098-8   94330 (Volume II)
ISBN: 89-7225-096-1 (Set)

Printed in the Republic of Korea by Seoul Press

D

Dante, Alighieri

Dante, Alighieri (1265-1321) is hailed as one of the most profound poetic geniuses of the Western world. Born in Florence, on the Italian peninsula, he is best known for his lengthy allegorical poem, the *Divine Comedy,* in which he describes a journey through hell, purgatory, and paradise. This work is usually regarded as the most beautiful and comprehensive expression of medieval Christian civilization. It was probably begun after Dante's exile from his native Florence in 1301, an exile resulting from the poet's involvement in the turbulent politics of that deeply divided city. It was not completed until shortly before Dante's death in Ravenna some 20 years later.

Florence, and for that matter all Europe, was torn by violent conflict throughout most of Dante's life; indeed his own later years were saddened and embittered by exile because of this strife. Not surprisingly, Dante turned his formidable intelligence to the problem of the cause and cure of human warfare. The *Divine Comedy* contains numerous bitter condemnations of violence and of those who Dante felt were responsible for causing it. His ideas on war and peace, however, appear more clearly in two prose treatises: *Il Convivio* [The Banquet], probably written between 1304 and 1307, and *Monarchia* [On Monarchy], written around 1312.

Dante maintained in these works that the distinguishing characteristic of humankind is reason, and that therefore the goal of all human striving is to lead a rational life. Such a life he held to be possible only in the state of peace. Warfare, with its bloodshed and destruction, Dante considered the very antithesis of a rational existence. All human institutions have goals, and the highest goal of all political institutions is to provide the people living under their authority with peace. "Peace," he wrote, "is the target at which all shafts are sped."

Dante argued passionately that the only form of government which could really guarantee peace would be a world government. He saw the entire human race as a single community, bound together by its common longing for a rational life, hence by a common interest in peace. Since every community must have a leader to organize and direct it, it followed that the entire human race should be subject to the authority of a single ruler. This ruler, since he already controlled everything, would never be tempted to make war to increase his power or possessions. Everyone else, living under his iron authority, would lack the power to start a war. Only thus, concluded Dante, could man's greed, lust, and pride be restrained, and war prevented.

Dante showed that this was more than an abstract fancy for him by going on to justify subjection to a particular ruler, the head of the Holy Roman Empire, as a religious obligation. Dante reasoned that God had first given the rightful authority to rule the human race to the ancient Roman Empire. He asserted that God shows us His will by intervening in human affairs, and that the history of the Roman Empire contained numerous examples of divine guidance. Without such guidance Rome could never have won so many wars and been so successful at bringing so many people under its authority.

Dante also argued that the birth of Christ within the Roman Empire was an unmistakable sign of God's approval of its authority. Even Christ's death at the hands of Roman authorities indicated to Dante that God was telling us that the Roman Empire is the rightful government of the entire world. For Christ to have truly redeemed all men by his death, reasoned Dante, his punishment on the cross had to have been decreed by a legitimate authority. Otherwise, he would simply have been the victim of individuals' ill-will. Hence, concluded Dante, the authority of the Roman Caesars must have been ordained by God as legitimate.

Dante rejected the argument that the papacy was the rightful heir of Roman authority, maintaining that it was instead the Holy Roman Emperor to whom all the kings and principalities of the world should subject themselves. The papacy's power, he insisted, lay only in the spiritual, not the political domain. Indeed, it appears that his *Monarchia* was inspired by the abortive attempt of the Holy Roman Emperor, Henry VII, to restore imperial power in Italy.

Even as Dante wrote, however, the rising power of such territorial entities as England, France, and the various German and Italian states were making a mockery of his hopes for the political unity and peace of Christendom. His longing for world government as a guarantor of peace would later be echoed by such thinkers as Sully, Rousseau, and Kant. At the dawn of the fourteenth century, though, his ideas appeared to be hopelessly out of touch with reality.

See also: *Henri IV*; *Kant, Immanuel*; *Peace in the Middle Ages*; *Perpetual Peace*; *Rousseau, Jean-Jacques*

Bibliography —————————————————————————

Bergin T G 1976 *Dante*. Greenwood, Westport, Connecticut
Chubb T C 1966 *Dante and his World*. Little, Brown, Boston, Massachusetts
Dante 1950 *Monarchia*. Florence. [1972 *Monarchy*. Garland, New York]
Davis C T 1957 *Dante and the Idea of Rome*.
D'Entreves A P 1965 *Dante as a Political Thinker*. Clarendon, Oxford
Gilbert A H 1971 *Dante's Conception of Justice*. AMS Press, New York
Hemleben S J 1943 *Plans for World Peace Through Six Centuries*. University of Chicago Press, Chicago, Illinois

GARRETT L. McAINSH

Daudet, Alphonse

Alphonse Daudet's deep awareness of human motivations, his irony (sometimes tolerant and sometimes otherwise), his humor, his sentimentality, even his at times excessive pathos, have endeared this writer to generations of readers. His humane view of the world and those who live in it, devoid of Zola's scientism and utopianism, continue to attract those for whom other Naturalists have little appeal. His penetrating insights into mankind's behavior, however compassionate, never helped him understand war, however, and the events he witnessed during the Franco-Prussian War precluded his ever becoming a peace advocate.

Daudet was born in Nîmes on May 12, 1840. A notable historian, his older brother Ernest had an honorable career as a novelist but was content to live in the shadow of his more renowned younger brother. The boys were born into a substantial, conservative middle class family, attached to the dethroned Bourbons. Experiencing business reverses, the father, Vincent Daudet, soon moved to Lyon, where he prospered no more than he had done in Nîmes and where his sons were reared in straitened circumstances. Alphonse proved to be a gifted student, reading voraciously and, at a very early age, trying his hand at creative writing. To complete his studies, he worked in 1856 and 1857 as a *maître d'internat* at the Collège d'Alars. Few were the reward for such hard labor, and soon all he wanted to do was escape. In November 1857, with a few poems he had written but without taking his *baccalauréat*, he did so, going to Paris, where Ernest had preceded him two months earlier and was making his début as a journalist. Essentially, it was Ernest's modest income that sup-

ported both brothers for several years. These poor, sometimes happy, sometimes sad years would later be recreated in the novel *Le Petit Chose*. As for Ernest, in 1861 he was named editor for the Corps Législatif, moving to the Senate in 1869. He had at last found security.

For Alphonse, the early years in Paris were bohemian years, largely spent in that Latin Quarter he would evoke so lovingly in *Les Rois en exil*. In salons and cafés he met various writers and nascent orators, some destined to leave their mark on French political and cultural life. It was in such company that the handsome young Southerner met the artists' model Marie Rieu and became her lover. There ensued a stormy liaison, punctuated with quarrels and short-lived reconciliations, that lasted intermittently until 1860. With Marie, Daudet knew a kind of world he would describe much later in *Sapho*, the heroine of which is an artists' model. Meanwhile Daudet published his first book, a collection of poems called *Les Amoureuses*. It was dedicated to Marie Rieu, whose name would disappear in subsequent editions.

Even before its publication in *Les Amoureuses*, one of Daudet's poems, "Les Prunes," was being recited in different salons. One evening in 1860, after it had appeared in print, it was recited at the Tuleries Palace. Empress Eugénie liked it and asked the Emperor's brother, the Comte (future Duc) de Morny, if he knew the author. Morny, president of the Corps Législatif, did not. However, remembering the Empress' enthusiasm, he later sent for the poet and, taken with the young man, offered him a position as his secretary. Daudet admitted that he was a Bourbonist, but when the statesman urbanely declared that it made no difference, he accepted the job. Thus, until Morny died in 1865, his material needs were taken care of and he could begin to prepare seriously for his career as a man of letters. At Morny's death he was ready to earn his living exclusively as a writer.

Daudet's health, never robust, had been weakened by Paris' cold, damp climate and his own excesses. In the autumn of 1861 he was advised to take a cure in warmer climes, and from November to February he traveled in Algeria. The following winter, for the same reasons, he was in Corsica. In 1863 and 1864 he rested in the sunshine of his native Provence. In addition to *Impressions et souvenirs* (1862), his travels provided material for future stories and novels. On January 27, 1867 he married Julia Allard and, with his bride, visited Provence again. Thereafter the couple would reside now in Paris, now in the village of Champrosay. Methodical and gifted with words, Julia Allard was to become a respected author in her own right. The Daudets' two sons Léon and Lucien were to be writers as well.

The Second Empire survived the Duc de Morny by only a few years. When the early defeats of the Franco-Prussian War in late summer 1870 made it possible for the Empire's republican opposition, long hungry for power, to seize control, the regime came to an inglorious end that it did not deserve. France's new leaders were men Daudet had no reason to trust, but his patriotism did not waver. When the war came, as we shall see, he waited, watched, hoped, and even participated in as much as circumstances and his health permitted. However, his most productive period, inaugurated with the novel *Fromont jeune et Risler aîné* and the novelas *Les Femmes d'aritstes* in 1874, was to come after the war.

Daudet's health remained a serious concern. In 1884 it became more problematic than ever. From that year onward, the author was the victim of unrelenting pain, his condition eventually being diagnosed as locomotor ataxy. Publicly he attributed his ailment to the privations he had endured while serving his literary novitiate. In his own mind, he was convinced that it was due to his dissipation during those years. He kept a journal of his illness as well as of his thoughts and impressions, a journal which, under the title *La Doulou*, was not published until 1929. Although he remained busy, his health continued to decline over the next thirteen years, so that, for those who knew him well, it should have come as no surprise when he dropped dead at the dinner table on the evening of December 18, 1897.

For most readers, Daudet's fame rests chiefly on the short stories, but, as was true of so many of his French contemporaries, the writer's first book was a collection of poems. Entitled *Les Amoureuses*, it came out in 1858 when the author was eighteen. Several poems, such as "Les Prunes" and "Les Cerisiers" interested readers and reviewers. Several others, such as "L'Oiseau bleu" and "Nature impassible," are noteworthy as well. The volume was rather well received. It earned the poet no money, however, nor did *La Double Conversion, conte en vers*, which appeared in 1861. Meanwhile, Daudet turned to journalism, writing articles and stories for *Le Monde illustré, Le Musée de famille, Le Figaro, Paris-Journal*, and *La Revue fantaisiste*. *Le Petit Chaperon rouge* (1861) is a series of articles written for *Le Figaro*. Even when he attained success as an author, Daudet never gave up writing for periodicals entirely. In addition to his work at *Le Figaro*, he wrote for *L'Evénement, L'Illustration, La Nouvelle Revue, Le Petit Moniteur, Le Musée universal, Le Soir, Le Parti national*, and *Le Bulletin français*, to name a few.

Was Daudet beginning to suspect around 1860 and 1861 that poetry was not to be his best medium? Perhaps so. One of his earliest prose ventures had been the tale "Audiberte," which came out in installments in *Paris-Journal* during the summer of 1859. The *Letters de mon moulin*, the collection of short stories that was to make his reputation, started appearing in *L'Evénement* on August 18, 1866. With *L'Evénement's* incorporation into *Le Figaro*, the stories resumed after a short hiatus in *Le Figaro*. Best remembered among the stories are "La Mule du pape," "La Chèvre de M. Seguin," "L'Elixir du révérend père Gaucher," "Le Secret de Maître Corneille," and "Le Sous-préfet aux champs." When the stories appeared in book form in 1869, several others had been added, including "L'Arlésienne." Charm and gentle humor characterize these narratives, except for those that, like "L'Arlésienne," have a quiet, touching poignancy.

A year after the *Lettres de mon moulin*, the Franco-Prussian War caused an upheaval in Daudet's life, although it inspired several works, the most memorable of which is the *Contes du lundi*, another collection of short stories. Of these the most popular has always been "La Dernière Classe," a sad tale about the deep emotion of teacher, pupils, and townspeople when M. Hamel conducts the last class he or anyone else will be allowed to teach, in French, at an Alsatian town which the Prussians have occupied and where the new classroom idiom henceforth will have to be German. "Le Nouveau Maître," a sequel to this story, appeared in *Contes et récits* (1873). The *Contes du lundi*, unlike the *Lettres de mon moulin*, are sad or else ironic, sarcastic, or vituperative.

In spite of the popular appeal the short stories have always had, some of Daudet's best writing is to be found in the novels. Treating a multitude of topics, they spring from a wide variety of moods and are expressed in a plethora of rich tones. Daudet's first real novel, *Le Petit Chose*, was autobiographical and had been started during a stay in the Midi in 1866. Laid aside and polished later, it was not published until 1866. With both humor and pathos, it recounts Daudet's childhood and adolescence, including the difficult period at the Collège d'Alais. Initially *Fromont jeune et Risler aîné*, the author's best novel, came out as a serial in *Le Bien Public* from March to June 1874 and was then published, later that same year, in book form. Set in a hardworking Paris milieu, this powerful narrative is the story of a vicious woman whose insecurities and meanness drive her to wreck the lives of all who have been kind to her as she has risen economically and socially. In the author's own day and later, *Fromont jeune*, like a number of other Daudet stories and novels, has been compared, with some justification, to those of Dickens. Probably, however, the novel's leading woman character, Sidonie Chèbe, has more in common with Thackeray's Becky Sharp (*Vanity Fair*). The novel was a great success and had numerous printings and editions.

Finished in 1875, published in 1876, *Jack* was Daudet's next novel, and it recreates the short, sad career of a frail lad Daudet had known and befriended and who, abandoned by his worthless mother and her lover, had died of lung disease. Before publication, the novel had been serialized in *Le Petit Moniteur*. *Le Nabob*, first published in *Le Temps*, followed in 1877. For quite some time Daudet had wanted to write a novel about the Second Empire, and this was it. Thinly disguised, various celebrities of the era, including the Duc de Morny, drift through its pages and bring it to life. The novel's success was immediate and enormous both in France and abroad. Soon the author was at work on *Les Rois en exil*, a novel about an exiled, playboy king and his heroic wife and pathetic little son. Like its predecessor, it was serialized in *Le Temps*, then appeared in the bookstores. It was another success. Still another was *Numa Roumestan*, portraying an unscrupulous southern politician who is dishonest in politics and equally dishonest toward his admirable wife, who happens to be a Northerner. The novel came out in 1881 after the usual installment publication in a newspaper, *L'Illustration*. *L'Evangéliste*, denouncing religious fanaticism, took its place with the other novels in 1883. *Sapho*, in 1884, is laid in that artists' bohemia that

Daudet had once known so well and on which, now, he passed harsh judgment. Daudet had decided never to seek admission into the Académie Française. It was just as well. One of his next novels, *L'Immortel* (1888), would have kept him out, ridiculing as it does both the Academy and Academicians and castigating the means some writers use to become members.

In addition to these very serious ones, Daudet wrote a triad of novels the hero of which is an ebullient, irrepressible, comic Southerner named Tartarin, from the town of Tarascon. Daudet inaugurated the series with *Tartarin de Tarascon* (1870). Tartarin's adventures so amused readers that *Tartarin sur les Alpes* (1885) and *Port-Tarascon* (1890) were written to keep the beloved creation in the public eye.

Most of Daudet's novels as well as several of the short stories were made into plays, all staged with varying degrees of success. In addition, there were plays that, instead of being adaptations, were written directly for the stage. Two of these date from the beginning of Daudet's career, when the apprentice writer may have hoped to establish himself as essentially a dramatist. His first play, *La Dernière Idole*, in collaboration with Ernest L'Epine, was written in 1861 and performed the following February. It was a resounding success. His next play, *Les Absents* (1863), was not. Much later *La Lutte pour la vie* (1889) pointed out the dangers of scientism, as did *L'Obstacle* (1890). Daudet also wrote theatre criticism, and his *Entre les frises et la rampe*, published in 1894, is for the most part a collection of drama reviews he had written for the *Journal officiel*. In addition, he tried his hand at opera libretti. With music by Emile Pessard, *Le Char*, produced at the Opéra Comique in 1878, was written with Paul Arène's collaboration. *Sapho*, with Jules Massenet's score, dates from 1897. Daudet also wrote a number of personal reminiscences, among them *premier voyage, premier mensonge*, which Mme Daudet published in 1900; *Souvenirs d'un homme de lettres* (1888); and *Trente ans de Paris* (1888). Aside from short stories, in collections mentioned earlier, that have an appeal for children as well as for adults, Daudet's work contains a certain amount of children's literature as such. *Les Cigognes* (1884) is representative. Another children's book is *Les Petits Robinsons des caves ou le siège de Paris raconté par une petite fille de huit ans*, which appeared in 1872. Mme Daudet may have had a hand in writing it.

When the Franco-Prussian War broke out in July 1870, Daudet and his family were at their country house in Champrosay. From the start, things went badly for France. Later Daudet would evoke in "La

Mort de Chauvin" (*Contes du lundi*) "the whole series of disasters, which, for us, made this sad month of August a long nightmare, as it were, hardly interrupted." Around the first of September, the Daudets returned to Paris. It was to a Paris quite different from the one they had left. News of Napoleon III's surrender at Sedan on 2 September traveled fast. When it reached Paris, the Second Empire was doomed. Daudet had seen the men of the Second Empire at close hand and had not been too impressed with them. But when he saw the self-seeking incompetents who, in the name of democracy, seized power on 4 September he was disheartened, and it must have occurred to him that the chances of a victorious outcome were now slim indeed. There were, of course, the optimists, unable to believe that, whoever was at the controls, France was vulnerable. In his short story "*Le Siège de Berlin*," Daudet shows us a retired colonel who had served under Napoleon I. Elderly and in fragile health, he has learned of the war, and, to sustain his morale, he is told each day how much progress the French have made as they push onward toward the Prussian capital. This is all a charitable lie, needless to say. When he learns the truth, that the Prussians are actually at the gates of Paris, the bitter news kills him.

When the Daudets returned to the city, the Prussian armies, advancing rapidly, were reaching its outskirts. Soon the long, terrible siege began. Daudet, barely recovered from a broken leg, joined the National Guard and saw action on the Marne River and on the Paris ramparts. During the ordeal, Paris starved, hoped, endured, and, on January 28, 1871, ultimately surrendered. German troops marched into the city, and Daudet was once more a civilian. In March the Commune with its reckless, doctrinaire zealots, crazed with unworkable ideals and a zest for arson, seized power. The insurrectionists moved Daudet to both contempt and horror as its "terrible" leaders expounded on the need "to kill, to shoot in the name of morality."[1] The Third Republic government retreated to Versailles, and for two months, while the Germans looked on, a civil war raged. With his family Daudet fled to Versailles. There, finding the mood and attitude of those in power not much more to his liking than what he had seen in Paris, he went back to Champrosay. Both house and village were a shambles, but he settled in and remained until the horrors were over, even when destructive German soldiers were quartered in his house. Angry, hurt, humiliated, Daudet had a great deal to say about his own and France's awesome experience. While the Germans' "harsh," "barbarous" language was distasteful to him, their drunkenness, their stealing, their vandalism repelled him much more as he watched it, unable to prevent or halt it. "And to think," he wrote, "that France is at the mercy of these brutes!"[2]

Robert Helmont, an essentially autobiographical novel, recounts the author's experiences and vents his sorrow and rage as he coped with the invaders on the one hand and, on the other, listened to the Versaillais' bombardment of Paris a few miles away. The *Lettres à un absent* are addressed to Daudet's friend and collaborator Paul Arène, on active duty with the army at the time. For the most part, this account of Paris during the siege and the Commune is made up of articles and short stories that appeared in *Le Soir* in 1871, the book coming out later the same year. While Daudet considered France a "warlike" country[3], he nevertheless declared in it that "war is the saddest, most stupid thing in the world."[4] If he despised the Third Republic's "dictators" and those military leaders who had not been equal to the opposition they faced, he nonetheless loved and pitied the common French soldier who did his best whatever the odds. Such a soldier he presented in "Le Porte-drapeau," for example. Nor did he fail to hold up to the public's admiration the patriotism and valor of older citizens who wanted to do their part. In "Le Mauvais Zouave" he showed a blacksmith who, at the age of fifty-five, volunteered for active duty (*Contes du lundi*).

To sum up, Daudet hated war and said as much. Especially after the Second Empire's overthrow, France's leaders inspired in him meagre confidence. Yet, once France had invaders on its soil, he joined the National Guard, although the state of his health would have exempted him from military service. The war with Prussia and the French civil war that ensued left him profoundly distressed. He continued to read about and discuss the war for the remainder of his life, and, as we have seen, he wrote a great deal about it. While the war experience prompted him to hope that such things would never be repeated, it was far from making him a proponent of peace. However, such things were indeed to be repeated. Also a writer but much less famous than his father, Léon Daudet would live to see World War I and describe its unspeakable inhumanity and destruction in such works as *Les Horreurs de la guerre* (1928) and *La Guerre totale* (1918).

Notes ——————————————————

1. Alphonse Daudet, *Notes sur la vie in OEuvres complètes illustrées*, XVI (Paris: Librairie de France, 1929), 18.

2. Robert Helmont, *Journal d'un solitaire 1870-1871* in *OEuvres complètes illustrées*, V (Paris: Librairie de France, 1929), 19.

3. See G.V. Dobie, *Alphonse Daudet* (London: Thomas Nelson and Sons, 1949), p. 167.

4. *Lettres à un absent* in *OEuvres complètes illustrées*, III (Paris: Librairie de France, 1930), 26.

Bibliography ———————————————

Becker C 1994 "Daudet, la guerre, la commune," *Ecrire la Commune. Témoignages, récits, et romans.* Editions du Lérot, Tusson
Benoît-Guyod G 1947 *Alphonse Daudet, son temps, son oeuvre.* Jules taillandier, Paris
Bornecque J H 1951 *Les Années d'apprentissage d'Alphonse Daudet.* Nizet, Paris
Dobie G V 1949 *Alphonse Daudet.* Thomas Nelson and Sons, London
Fricker E 1937 *Alphonse Daudet et la société du Second Empire.* Boccard, Paris
Roche A V 1976 *Alphonse Daudet.* Twayne Publishers, Boston
Sachs M 1965 *The Career of Alphonse Daudet.* Harvard University Press, Cambridge

HARRY REDMAN, JR.

Davies, David

David Davies, or Lord Davies as he became in 1932, was prominent between the two world wars as an advocate of the League of Nations (see *League of Nations*) and specifically of an International Police Force as a means of preventing war. This article considers his career in respect of his concern for peace, examines his leading ideas, and attempts critically to assess them.

The grandson of a Welsh industrial pioneer, David Davies (1880-1944) inherited great wealth and formidable personal energy. He also curiously combined the moral values of Welsh nonconformity with the tastes of the landed gentry, and was, for example, on the one hand a militant teetotaller and philanthropist, and on the other a passionate fox-hunter and big-game hunter. Indeed, one is tempted to see in his idea of swiftly "putting down" aggressors by a mobile force the working out of both his philanthropic and his hunting instincts.

The First World War, as for others of his generation, was a traumatic experience for Davies. Upon its outbreak he threw himself into the task of raising a volunteer battalion, which he commanded on the Western Front from December 1915 until June 1916 when Lloyd George enlisted him, as a fellow Welsh Liberal Member of Parliament, to serve as his parliamentary private secretary. At the end of the war, horrified by the waste and carnage he had experienced, he resolved to do all in his power to ensure that such a catastrophe should never recur.

His first endeavor, in 1919, was to found at the College of Wales in Aberystwyth, as a memorial to the students of the college who had fallen in the war, a Chair for the systematic study of international political relations with particular emphasis upon the promotion of peace. This was a brilliant academic innovation, and to Davies must go the credit of having set up the world's first Chair of International Politics (or International Relations) and so started a new discipline of study which is now to be found in universities the world over.

The Aberystwyth Chair was also designed to increase understanding of the League of Nations and give intellectual support to the League idea. Indeed, in 1922 David Davies gave it the name "The Woodrow Wilson Chair" in honor of the League's foremost founder and advocate (see Nobel Peace Prize Laureates: *Woodrow Wilson*). But he was also deeply conscious that the League as an institution needed the wholehearted support of public opinion within the democratic states which then largely constituted its membership. Hence he was in the forefront of setting up the League of Nations Union (of which he became vice-president), and in the following year, 1919, attended in Paris a conference from which emerged the International Federation of League of Nations Societies. He was also the dominant spirit in the Welsh Council of the League of Nations Union, and in 1938 provided it with an imposing headquarters in the Temple of Peace in Cardiff.

Despite this championship, the League of Nations Covenant did not go nearly far enough in Davies's opinion. He desired a much stronger League Council capable of taking swift and resolute action against any aggressor. The first step, he thought, should be to persuade the United States to enter the League through working upon American public opinion. One such effort was the presentation in Washington of an appeal signed by 400,000 Welsh women to the representatives of 20 million American women, Mrs. Eleanor Roosevelt being one of the hostesses. But this Lysistrata-like gesture achieved little tangible result.

By the end of the 1920s Davies had become convinced that the League of Nations as it stood was incapable of preventing a recurrence of war. The solution, he concluded, was simple: there must be an impartial Tribunal to settle international disputes, together with an International Police Force to carry out, and if necessary impose, its decisions. He had convinced himself; it but remained to convince the world.

Davies set about campaigning for his idea with the energy and total dedication that he brought to all his causes. Although virtually new to authorship, he rapidly produced a large book on the subject: *The Problem of the Twentieth Century*, published in 1930. He toured the United States in 1931 but was disappointed at the lack of response. The following year he accepted a peerage from Ramsay MacDonald in order to better publicize his ideas. Also in 1932 he founded, and heavily subsidized "The New Commonwealth," a movement which, with its journal of the same name, was designed both to promote the idea of an International Tribunal and Police Force and to undertake the necessary propaganda and research. Many of those who were committed to strengthening the League of Nations—Churchill (see *Churchill, Winston*), Macmillan, Archbishop Temple, and others—associated themselves with the movement. In 1934 Lord Davies (as he now was) travelled through Hitler's Germany and even managed to establish a branch of The New Commonwealth there.

Meanwhile the limp behavior of the League of Nations—or rather of its leading members—in the face of growing threats to world peace, filled him with despair and contempt. He campaigned with vigor against Japan's seizure of Manchuria, and Sir John Simon's "spineless acquiescence" at Geneva. In 1935-36 he protested vehemently when the League failed to take effective action against Italy over the invasion of Abyssinia. In 1938 he vainly tried to raise an international air force to assist the Chinese against Japan. Like Churchill, he was assiduous in his warnings, expressed frequently and forcefully in Parliament and the press, about Hitler's aggressive intent. When the former Soviet Union attacked Finland, in 1939, he organized a Finnish Aid Committee and later visited the country with a view to arranging the arrival of a British Brigade. As the weak and the neutral fell before the *Realpolitik* of the mighty, he considered that in his warnings about the fate of a world lacking an all-powerful International Police Force he had been amply vindicated by events.

What, in detail, were his ideas? They are set out in the 800 page *Problem of the Twentieth Century* and are further elaborated in several of his subsequent publications, notably the posthumous *Seven Pillars of Peace* (1945). Fundamentally, in his view, the Covenant of the League of Nations did not go far

enough in the direction of international government and order. What was wanted, he maintained, was a new League, or Commonwealth, founded upon different principles. Whereas the Council of the League had been weakened by the addition of insignificant states, the new Executive would be a business-like body consisting of the Great Powers with a number of second-rank Powers serving on a rotative basis. The unanimity principle which had so hamstrung the League would be replaced by a two-thirds majority vote. Should a dispute arise, it would be settled by the International Court if it was justiciable, and by an Equity Tribunal consisting of impartial and disinterested experts if it was not. Once the decision of the Tribunal had been accepted by the Council and Assembly, it would be binding on the parties, and any refusal to accept it would be met by sanctions, ultimately of force (see *International Law; International Court of Justice*).

The military sanction would be exercised by an International Police Force consisting of quotas of men and armaments drawn from the member states. It would need to be more powerful than any member state or any combination of nonmember states. Should a clear case of aggression (see *Aggression*) occur, the Police Force would be instantly deployed. Once international order had been ensured by such means, claimed Lord Davies, states would no longer need armed forces beyond their requirements for preserving internal peace. The consequent shedding of so great an expense should be welcome to all.

Ideas of this character, which E. H. Carr has categorized as "utopian" (Carr 1939), concerned not with what is, but with what should be, proved attractive to many intellectuals and philanthropists in the period between the two world wars, though rarely to those engaged in the business of government. Yet although some of Lord Davies's ideas now look eccentric or even bizarre—he argued, for example, that the International Police Force should be given a monopoly of submarines, bombers, tanks, and poison gas, together with Palestine to base them in—it would be unfair to dismiss his schemes as simply those of a misguided enthusiast. The Lytton Commission, appointed by the League in 1931 to report upon the Manchurian dispute, showed how an Equity Tribunal could operate, and the United Nations Security Council (see *Status and Role of the United Nations*), aside from the veto, had much in common with Davies's strengthened Executive—as the Charter's provision for armed forces to be made available recalled his quota system. And as for his idea that aggression should be met with swift counteraction, this was at length realized when

North Korea invaded South Korea in 1950; the United Nations' response was "Daviesonian" in its speed, scale, and effectiveness.

Nonetheless, such examples only go to show how far removed from reality, and practicality, the Davies solution was. For the recommendations of the Lytton Commission, although unanimously adopted by the League Assembly, were not, and indeed could not be, enforced; the Security Council has not yet received its armed forces and Military Staff Committee from the major Powers; and Korea was a "one-off" exercise made possible only through the temporary Soviet boycott of the Council's proceedings.

At first sight the international coalition formed against Iraq following its seizure of Kuwait in August 1990, together with 'Operation Desert Storm,' the air offensive which swiftly destroyed the aggressor's power to resist, appear to have come nearer to a realization of Lord Davies's ideas than anything that has so far occurred. Yet the response to Kuwait, overwhelmingly American as in Korea, in reality reflected the individual interests of many powers which over this issue happened to converge; it was far remove from the basic Davies idea that aggression should be countered by an International Police Force directed by a world authority motivated by principles of natural justice and acting independently of any particular state (see *Collective Security and Collective Self-defense*).

In truth no state, despite all the arguments marshalled in Lord Davies's tomes as to what is "reasonable" and "rational," would be prepared to surrender control of its own destiny to a body like an International Executive armed with an all-powerful Police Force. Central to Lord Davies's thesis is the "domestic analogy"—how, in domestic society, justice is upheld and order maintained by the courts and the police, or how the United States, for example, achieved a single authority out of 13 sovereign colonies—but this is the main philosophical flaw in his thinking. The world is in no way like domestic society, or the United States, a country whose people had so much in common to start with, or even like Western Europe, now integrating up to a point.

It was more natural to think so in the 1920s and early 1930s, however, than it would be now. Then most of the world was dominated by the Western democracies, and gave the illusion of having more homogeneity and potential harmony than in truth it possessed; the brief international impact of Wilsonian liberalism—the final flicker of the Enlightenment—did the rest. Today we are much more conscious than was Lord Davies's generation of the ferocious ideological and nationalistic maelstrom that the world in fact is; and if we are more sophisticated than we were about understanding and having to cope with it, for that we have in part to thank David Davies—not for his ideas about peace, but for his having pioneered, in 1919, the systematic and scientific study of international politics.

See also: *World Order; World Government; Cold War; Peacekeeping Forces; United Nations Peacekeeping Operations*

Bibliography ———————————————————

Carr E H 1939 *The Twenty Years' Crisis 1919-1939*. Macmillan, London

Davies D 1930 *The Problem of the Twentieth Century: A Study in International Relationships*. Ernest Benn, London

Davies D 1932 *Suicide or Sanity? An Examination of the Proposals before the Geneva Disarmament Conference: The Case for an International Police Force*. Williams and Norgate, London

Davies D (Lord) 1934 *Force*. Ernest Benn, London

Davies D (Lord) 1936 *Nearing the Abyss*. Constable, London

Davies D (Lord) 1945 *The Seven Pillars of Peace*. Longmans, London

Lewis P 1977 *Biographical Sketch of David Davies (Topsawyer) 1818-1890 and His Grandson David Davies (1st Baron Davies) 1880-1944*. Peter Lewis, Milford Hall, Newtown

Long D, Wilson P (eds.) 1995 *Thinkers of the Twenty Years' Crisis*. Clarendon Press, Oxford, Chap. 3, 'David Davies and the Enforcement of Peace

New Commonwealth, 1936 *The Functions of an International Equity Tribunal*. The New Commonwealth, London

New Commonwealth, 1939 *Air Force for the Peace Front*. Peace Book Company, London

Porter B (ed.) 1972 *The Aberystwyth Papers: International Politics 1919-1969*. Oxford University Press, London, Chaps. 2, 4, App. 1

BRIAN E. PORTER

Declaration of the Rights of Man

The term "Declaration of the Rights of Man" refers to those manifestos which seek to protect fundamental or natural human rights. The basic elements of fundamental human rights may be described as liberty, equality, and the dignity of life.

The origins of this ideal of the inalienable rights that each human being possesses can be traced back to antiquity. There has always been a basic emotion of respect for natural human rights, but it was in the course of the civil revolutions of the eighteenth century that a more systematic theory took shape. The American and French revolutions especially, had an enormous impact on the creation and development of the modern ideal of human rights. The American Declaration of Independence (1776), the Virginia Declaration of Rights (1776), and the French Declaration of the Rights of Man and of the Citizen (1789), exemplify the development of these rights.

The chief aim of these documents was the attainment of the rights to liberty, property, security, and to resist oppression.

The contents of such declarations continued to change gradually, with the emergence of the criticism that hitherto, that is, during the civil revolutions, they did not appeal for the natural rights of all but in reality pleaded only for the rights of the bourgeoisie. In addition, those declarations which asserted freedom from state interference led to the development of free economic activities and gave birth to the progress of capitalism. Thus they also entailed the rise of many evils such as the wide gap between rich and poor, and human alienation. Though political freedom is guaranteed in these declarations, suffrage was limited only to the wealthy and in reality not granted to the poorer classes, such as laborers and peasants.

As a result, a system of justice became necessary in order to free people from these evils. To the authors of such criticism, justice meant that the laborers and the peasantry must have a substantial and concrete influence on government instead of merely the nominal and abstract freedoms asserted in these declarations. They demanded complete equality for all and the necessary measures that would permit the state to intervene in economic activities (see *Justice and Peace*).

It could be said that the Russian Revolution of 1917, following the American and French precedents, tried to meet these new demands. The Bolsheviks in Russia condemned the French Declaration of Rights and its limitations as mere tools for the establishment and preservation of bourgeois supremacy, causing them to issue in January 1918, the Declaration of the Rights of Workers and Exploited Peoples. But in the Russian constitution of 1918, we can find no traditional wording asserting natural rights similar to that in the constitutions of France and the United States. The Bolsheviks had no concern with securing

civil freedom or preventing interference with fundamental rights by the public authorities. Their aim was to guarantee the rights of the working people and to accomplish the nationalization of major production industries. It was the Soviet constitution of 1936 that guaranteed not only fundamental social rights such as working rights, the right to receive education, and so on, but also various civil rights such as freedom of religion, expression, association, and residence.

Another type of declaration of human rights, different from those mentioned above, was the Weimar Constitution of Germany in 1919. It declared the rights to organize, to work, and to life, as the fundamental rights of the working person.

After the Second World War, the ideal of humanism came to occupy a central place in declarations of human rights. This was primarily a result of resistance to the suppression of human rights under fascism. In addition to this, it is also a product of the internationalization or cosmopolitanization of human rights which made its appearance with the development of international exchanges and the rise of developing countries. In 1945, the Charter of the United Nations was announced as a document which declares the necessity of the preservation of human rights and justice on the international level. It contains a reaffirmation of "faith in fundamental human rights in the dignity and worth of the human person, in the equal rights of men and women and of nations large and small." One of the aims of the United Nations is "promoting and encouraging respect for human rights" and "assisting in the realization of human rights and fundamental freedoms." For the attainment of these aims, the United Nations and the instruments adopted under its auspices have played various roles. Specifically, the Charter of the United Nations vests responsibility for the guarantee of human rights in the General Assembly and, under the General Assembly's authority, in the Economic and Social Council (ECOSOC). The Trusteeship Council is concerned with human rights in trust territories, and the Security Council can take jurisdiction over human rights questions when it holds that international peace and security are endangered.

An international organ, the Commission of Human Rights, was also established upon the provisions of the United Nations Charter, proclaiming the Universal Declaration of Human Rights in 1948 which insists on safeguards for human rights based on humanism.

The Charter of the United Nations and the Universal Declaration of Human Rights have inspired action for the international protection of human rights within two important regions of the world. The first area is the European Convention for the Protection of Human Rights and Fundamental Freedoms, agreed upon in 1950; and the second is the American Convention on Human Rights (also called the Pact of San Jose, Costa Rica), adopted in 1969. Both are regional developments in the field of human rights, and have established specialized courts on human rights.

In the latter half of the twentieth century, the Declaration of the Rights of Man has gained ground as a universal value not only within individual countries, but also in the international arena. It is proper that respect for human rights should be the core of peace and culture, especially when we consider that peace means not only the absence of war and violence, both personal and social, but also the promotion of a harmonious, functional, cooperative, and well-integrated society. Whatever meaning we may give to the word "peace," the respect for human rights is an absolute prerequisite.

However, the Universal Declaration of Human Rights faces some formidable obstacles. First, it carries only a symbolic effect, lacking legal force. It is very difficult for the declaration itself to exercise any real influence upon society. Second, the balance between esteem for the international provisions of human rights and the domestic jurisdiction clause is very difficult to honor. Human rights have traditionally come within the domestic jurisdiction of sovereign states. Thus even if the United Nations asserts the necessity of safeguards for human rights in member states, there are limitations on its effect. For example, the General Assembly and other United Nations organs have repeatedly dealt with human rights developments occurring within individual states, such as the racial conflict in South Africa, and forced labor in Eastern Europe. But the United Nations is not always able to exercise its power effectively to solve these problems because of the preservation of national sovereignty.

See also: *Human Rights and Peace: International Bill of Human Rights*

Bibliography ————————————

Becker C L 1942 *The Declaration of Independence.* Knopf, New York

Dicey A V 1959 *Introduction to the Study of the Law of the Constitution,* 10th edn. London

Laski J H 1971 *The Rise of European Liberalism: An Essay in Interpretation.* Unwin, London

Hobbes T 1904 *Leviathan.* G P Putnam's Sons, New York

Jellineck G 1895 *Die Erklärung der Menschen-und Bürgerrechte.* Max Farrand [1901 *The Declaration of the Rights of Man and Citizens.* Holt, New York]

Locke J, Hume D, Rousseau J J 1948 *Social Contract.* Oxford University Press, London

Marx K, Engles F 1977 *Communist Manifesto.* Progress Publishers, Moscow

Sabine G H 1950 *A History of Political Theory,* rev. edn. Holt, New York

United Nations 1967 *Human Rights: A Compilation of International Instruments of the United Nations.* United Nations, New York

United Nations *The United National Yearbook on Human Rights.* (published annually since 1946) United Nations, New York

TADASHIGE TAKAMURA

Democracy and Foreign Policy

Foreign policy is to some extent an expression of a country's character, and in the case of democratic states their political characteristics are demonstrated in several ways. As related to foreign policy, democracy may be thought of as:

(a) a method of formulating foreign policy with an emphasis on the relationship of governmental leadership and public opinion;

(b) advocacy for the adoption by others of democratic norms and practices;

(c) promulgation of democracy through supportive or subversive intervention in other countries by a democratic state and components of its society;

(d) the imposition of democracy by force on conquered peoples; and

(e) the use of democratic-like practices which express the fundamental values of a democratic society in the conduct of its foreign relations.

Democratic governance consists of practices and procedures designed to make government officials responsive to the general public. These practices include free and open debate, mass media free from government control but with extensive access to information to provide to the public, access for individuals and groups to office holders, review and supervision of the executive by the legislature, an independent judiciary, elections in which multiple political parties may offer alternatives, and other procedures that ensure that public opinion is heard and felt in government policies. Usually, political leaders shape and greatly influence public opinion through legislative and diplomatic initiatives as well as by advocating their policies in public discourse and private meetings.

Most commonly, debate and discussion about foreign policy occur through political party activity, parliamentary processes, and the elite press and mass media of communication. Sometimes, however, mass movements protesting against public policy or advocating change act through marches, demonstrations, and other means of unmediated petitioning of governments.

Public debate about foreign policy tends to be conducted by elites—government and political leaders, scholars, interest-group speakers, researchers, and mass media elites—who write and speak before an attentive public, a portion of the citizenry which is knowledgeable about and interested in foreign affairs. The largest portion of the public, however, tends to be inattentive and less informed about international relations and thus tends to react to events and symbols in terms of unstructured moods. With the complexity of the relationship between public opinion and governmental leadership, there is considerable scope for interaction. There is, as well, dispute about the proper role that public opinion should play in the formulation of policy.

Like some other kinds of countries, democracies sometimes advocate that others adopt the values and practices peculiar to their form of government. A premium tends to be placed on elections, particularly as a means of bringing to office political leaders who hold democratic values. Because democracy includes a conception that individuals have intrinsic rights not dependent upon governments, democrats sometimes advocate to other governments that they treat their citizens in conformity with standards derived from the formulation of basic human rights. Such advocacy has been extended to international conferences and organizations in an attempt to gain broad agreement to human rights standards. One example of this is the Universal Declaration of Human Rights adopted by the United Nations General Assembly in 1948 (see *International Bill of Human Rights*), and another resulted in the inclusion of human rights provisions in the Helsinki agreements of 1975 among the European and North American states that attended the Conference on Security and Cooperation in Europe (see *Organization on Security and Cooperation in Europe (OSCE)*).

Promulgation of democracy through subversion and/or supportive intervention in foreign countries is conducted both by governments and by other constituents of plural societies. Many foreign aid programs have aimed at strengthening governments which either foster democratic practices or which are allied with democratic governments. Moreover, governments sometimes use subsidies to such institutions as labor unions, newspapers, and opposition political parties to help to create or strengthen pluralistic societies. Supportive intervention is also provided by other units; for example, labor unions send both funds and personnel to other countries to strengthen free labor there, corporations subsidize and support sympathetic forces, and political parties give help in organizing and campaigning to parties in other countries that share a similar ideological outlook.

Governments sometimes use subversion to undermine regimes which are thought to be antidemocratic. The United States in the post-1945 period has been particularly active through the Central Intelligence Agency (CIA). This kind of activity has become very controversial in the United States, partly because it is based upon contradictory premises. The problem may be illustrated by the "destabilization" of Chile between 1970 and 1973. Chile was a democratic country, but the United States interfered in 1970, trying to prevent the election of Salvador Allende Gossens as president. When that effort failed, the US governments sought through trade and credit sanctions as well as clandestine support for opposition groups to destabilize the Allende government, which led eventually to its overthrow in a military *coup d'état*. The justification by advocates of the US interventionist policy was that, although Allende was elected through democratic procedures, as a Marxist he was dedicated to creating a regime that was not based upon democratic values and therefore would end procedural democracy. In this case, then, there was a contradiction between the definitions of democracy as procedures and as moral values. Critics retort that the use of antidemocratic procedures in itself violates the values of democracy, particularly when aimed against a viable democratic polity. They also point out that the end result in the Chilean case, and in other cases as well, tends to be the opposite of what was intended; whereas Chile had been a democratic state until 1973, it became thereafter a military dictatorship (see *Intervention*).

The two outstanding cases of imposing democracy by force on conquered peoples are the former Federal Republic of Germany and Japan. At the end of the Second World War the occupiers, led by the United

States, decided to change the institutional arrangements and the political cultures of the two states and societies. Thus, in each case, there was fashioned a polity that included parliamentary forms of government, protection of individual rights, and educational systems designed to teach democratic values rather than authoritarian ones. Additionally, in the case of the former Federal Republic of Germany cartelization of industry was ended, and in the case of Japan land reform and equality for women were inaugurated. These reforms were not completed before the United States chose to emphasize security concerns regarding the former Soviet Union and drew the former Federal Republic of Germany and Japan into alliances with itself.

The last meaning to be given to democracy and foreign policy is the use of democratic-like practices which express the fundamental moral values of a democratic society in peace and war (see *Global Ethics, Human Rights Laws and Democratic Governance*). This is a standard which democratic politics impose upon themselves rather than upon others. While not entirely precise, the conception includes using force only as a last resort; employing diplomacy in an attempt to harmonize interests; respecting elections and concomitant freedoms of speech, assembly, and association; and respecting basic human rights and extending tolerance to others. In addition, the conception entails acting in conformity with and on behalf of fundamental democratic values of freedom, equality and fraternity. An important part of the debate in the United States about the Vietnam war dealt with the betrayal of its own values by the US government through its actions in Southeast Asia.

Following the ideas of Immanuel Kant (1970) (see *Kant, Immanuel*), some writers (Doyl 1983, 1986; Russett 1993) hold to a position of liberal or democratic peace theory. They argue that liberal or democratic states maintain a separate peace and do not engage in war with one another, implying that as more states become democratic war in the international system diminishes. Others (Layne 1994; Gowa 1995) dispute this view.

Alexis de Tocqueville (1959) thought that democracies were ill-equipped to conduct foreign policy, and many others have carried this theme forward by arguing that democracies are at a disadvantage in competing with authoritarian states. Those who hold such sentiments often argue that democracies, therefore, need to adopt the practices of their adversaries in their foreign policy. On the other hand, James Bryce (1921) thought that democracies chose ends as wisely as other kinds of polities even though they

might suffer from some disadvantages of means. Woodrow Wilson (see Nobel Peace Prize Laureates: *Woodrow Wilson*) thought that democracies were superior and attempted to give new meaning to democracy by projecting certain ideas such as "open covenants openly arrived at" onto international politics. More recently, Samuel Huntington (1981) has noted the paradox of democracy and foreign policy, for democracy as a domestic political system is rendered safer and more secure by the extension of dominant power in the world, yet power domination is mostly antithetical to democratic concepts of equality and liberty.

The relation of democracy and foreign policy to the issue of peace and war, therefore, is not settled. One view holds that war is caused by evil leaders and that popular control would make war less likely. On the other hand, the popular mood varies, and public opinion is sometimes more belligerent than leadership opinion. What is clear from both of these positions is that democracy does afford through debate and accountability a corrective for erroneous policies. Ultimately, foreign policy involves the use of power (see *Power*), and the issue is whether power is used to maintain and promote democratic values. Often these are best promoted by peaceful means, but, occasionally, war may be the appropriate or perhaps the only defense of these values.

See also: *Intercultural Relations and Peace Studies; Peace and Democracy*

Bibliography ————————————————

Bryce J 1921 *Modern Democracies*. Macmillan, New York

Doyle M 1983 Kant, liberal legacies and foreign affairs. *Philosophy and Public Affairs* (Summer/Fall)

Doyle M 1986 Liberalism and world politics. *American Political Science Review* 80 (December)

Gowa J 1995 Democratic states and international disputes. *Int'l Organization* 49 (Summer)

Huntington S P 1981 *American Politics: The Promise of Disharmony*. Harvard, Cambridge, Massachusetts

Kant I 1971 *Kant's Political Writings*. Reiss H (ed.) Nisbet H B (trans). Cambridge University Press, Cambridge

Layne C 1994 Kant of Cant: The myth of the democratic peace. *Int'l Security* 19 (Fall)

Linz J J, Stepan A (eds.) 1978 *The Breakdown of Democratic Regimes*. Johns Hopkins University Press, Baltimore, Maryland

Montgomery J D 1957 *Forced to be Free: The Artificial Revolution in Germany and Japan*. Chicago University Press, Chicago

Pearson L B 1955 *Democracy in World Politics*. Princeton University Press, Princeton, New Jersey

Pennock J R 1979 *Democratic Political Theory*. Princeton University Press, Princeton, New Jersey

Russett B 1993 *Grasping the Democratic Peace*. Princeton University Press, Princeton, New Jersey

Sartori G 1962 *Democratic Theory*. Wayne State University Press, Detroit, Michigan

Schumpeter J 1950 *Capitalism, Socialism and Democracy*. Harper and Row, New York

de Tocqueville A 1959 *Democracy in America*. Vintage Press, New York

Waltz K N 1967 *Foreign Policy and Democratic Politics: The American and British Experience*. Little, Brown and Company, Boston

HOWARD H. LENTNER

Democratization, An Agenda for

1. Introduction: Democratization and Democracy

Democratization is a process which leads to a more open, more participatory, less authoritarian society. Democracy is a system of government which embodies, in a variety of institutions and mechanisms, the ideal of political power based on the will of the people.

In places from Latin America to Africa, Europe and Asia, numbers of authoritarian regimes have given way to democratic forces, increasingly responsive governments and increasingly open societies. Many States and their peoples have embarked upon a process of democratization for the first time. Others have moved to restore their democratic roots.

The basic idea of democracy is today gaining adherents across cultural, social and economic lines. While the definition of democracy is an increasingly important subject of debate within and among societies, the practice of democracy is increasingly regarded as essential to progress on a wide range of human concerns and to the protection of human rights (see *Human Rights and Peace*).

Both democratization and democracy raise difficult questions of prioritization and timing. It is therefore not surprising that the acceleration of democratization and the renaissance of the idea of democracy have met with some resistance. On the practical level, the world has seen some slowing and erosion in democratization processes and, in some cases, reversals. On the normative level, resistance has arisen which in some cases seeks to cloak authoritarianism in claims of cultural differences and in others reflects the undeniable fact that there is no one model of democratization or democracy suitable to all societies. The reality is that individual societies decide if and when to begin democratization. Throughout the process, each society decides its nature and its pace. The starting point from which a society commences democratization will bear greatly on such decisions. Like the process of democratization, democracy can take many forms and evolve through many phases, depending on the particular characteristics and circumstances of societies. And, in every society, the persistence of democracy itself requires an ongoing process of political renewal and development (see *Social Progress and Human Survival*).

The phenomenon of democratization has had a marked impact on the United Nations. Just as newly independent States turned to the United Nations for support during the era of decolonization, so today, following another wave of accessions to statehood and political independence, Member States are turning to the United Nations for support in democratization. While this has been most visible in the requests for electoral assistance received since 1989 from more than 60 States—nearly one third of the Organization's membership—virtually no area of United Nations activity has been left untouched. The peacekeeping mandates entrusted to the United Nations now often include both the restoration of democracy and the protection of human rights (see *United Nations Peacekeeping*). United Nations departments, agencies and programmes have been called upon to help States draft constitutions, create independent systems for the administration of justice, provide police forces that respect and enforce the rule of law, depoliticize military establishments and establish national institutions for the promotion and protection of human rights. They also have been asked by many States engaged in democratization to help encourage and facilitate the active participation of citizens in political processes, and to foster the emergence of a productive civil society, including responsible and independent communications media (see *Peacekeeping Forces*).

These operational activities were the subject of a report requested of the Secretary-General by the General Assembly in its resolution 49/30 of December 7,

1994. My report, "Support by the United Nations system of the efforts of Governments to promote and consolidate new or restored democracies" (A/50/332 and Corr. 1), was presented to the Assembly on August 7, 1995. The General Assembly welcomed my report in its resolution 50/133 of December 20, 1995 and requested me to prepare a second report on the same subject, which I accordingly presented on October 18, 1996 (A/51/512). Beyond operational assistance, there is a growing interest among Member States in the democratization of the United Nations itself (see *United Nations Reform: Historical and Contemporary Perspective*). At the Special Commemorative Meeting of the General Assembly held from October 22 to 24, 1995 on the occasion of the fiftieth anniversary of the United Nations, nearly every speaker, including 128 heads of State or Government, addressed this important issue.

Reflecting on these realities—the fact of democratization, the request for the United Nations involvement and the interest in widening the scope of democratization—I believe the time has come for a deeper consideration of the idea in all its ramifications and possibilities. I discern four components of such an attempt: an emerging consensus on democracy and its practical importance; the foundation for United Nations concern with democratization and the role envisaged for it; the new momentum for, and the resultant expansion in, United Nations support for democratization; and a new dimension of this support—democratization at the international level.

I offer the present paper in the hope that it may deepen understanding of United Nations efforts in favour of democratization and intensify debate on future international action in this area. To address the subjects of democratization and democracy does not imply a change in the respect that the United Nations vows for the sovereignty of States or in the principle of non-intervention in internal affairs set out in Article 2, paragraph 7, of the Charter of the United Nations. To the contrary, the founding Purposes and Principles of the United Nations are the very basis of the present reflection (see *United Nations Charter*).

The United Nations is not alone in supporting democratization. The past decade has brought a proliferation of actors engaged in this effort, which has fast become a massive global enterprise. These actors include international and regional intergovernmental organizations; individual States; parliamentarians; non-governmental organizations from the local to the global levels; and private actors such as legal professionals, the media, academics, private institutions and civic associations, including ethnic, cultural and religious groups. Taken together, they represent a vast spectrum of perspectives, expertise, approaches and techniques. The consideration of democratization offered in the present paper focuses on the United Nations as one such actor, albeit unique in character. Thus, from the outset, it is essential to be clear about the particular aim and distinct role of the United Nations in democratization.

The United Nations is, by design and definition, universal and impartial. While democratization is a new force in world affairs, and while democracy can and should be assimilated by all cultures and traditions, it is not for the United Nations to offer a model of democratization or democracy or to promote democracy in a specific case. Indeed, to do so could be counter-productive to the process of democratization which, in order to take root and to flourish, must derive from the society itself. Each society must be able to choose the form, pace and character of its democratization process. Imposition of foreign models not only contravenes the Charter principle of non-intervention in internal affairs (see *Intervention*), it may also generate resentment among both the Government and the public, which may in turn feed internal forces inimical to democratization and to the idea of democracy.

Therefore, the United Nations does not aim to persuade democratizing States to apply external models or borrow extraneous forms of government. Rather, the United Nations aims to help each State pursue its own particular path. Understanding democratization as a process calling for wide-ranging action, the United Nations aims to support democratizing States in a variety of processes and experiences. Its role in favour of democratization in a particular State is understood and carried out as one of assistance and advice.

The United Nations possesses a foundation and a responsibility to serve its Member States in democratization, yet it must receive a formal request before it can assist Member States in their democratization processes. United Nations activities and responsibilities in the area of democratization thus parallel and complement those in development: to provide and help coordinate assistance to those who request it, and to seek a strengthened context in which those requesting and those responding may achieve success.

Democratization is predominantly a new area for technical assistance. Traditionally, technical assistance has been provided in the context of economic and social development, with the main emphasis on building and strengthening physical infrastructure and the executive arm of the Government; assistance in governance beyond that was made virtually impossible by the political climate throughout most of the United Nations history. While the United Nations still provides technical assistance in those areas, the wave of economic and political transitions witnessed in the post-Cold War period has led Member States to reorient their requests for technical assistance towards areas more relevant to democratization, broadly defined (see *Democracy and Foreign Policy*).

The United Nations strengthens the context for support to democratization through information-gathering and awareness-raising and by offering Member States and the wider international community a universally legitimate global forum for dialogue, debate and consensus-building. Through the United Nations, multilateral agreements can be reached—whether embodied in the form of non-binding norms, internationally recognized standards or binding obligations—which help to define a common political and legal framework for action. Indeed, it is to a certain extent through the forum of the United Nations that a consensus on democracy and its practical importance has begun to take shape.

2. An Emerging Consensus

Over the last half century, the meaning of democracy has shifted considerably in world affairs. In 1945, democracy was a clear concept as defined by the Allied nations in opposition to fascism. With the onset of the Cold War, democracy came to be propounded from two perspectives, East and West. As the third world took its place on the international stage, its members strove to find their own methods of government, appropriate to their needs, providing in the process alternative perspectives on democracy. Today, the rapidly changing global scene has set the age-old concept of democracy in a new light. While differences in the economic, social, cultural and historical circumstances of the world's societies mean that differences will continue between democracy as viewed by one society and democracy as viewed by another, democracy is increasingly being recognized as a response to a wide range of human concerns and as essential to the protection of human rights.

This is not to say that democracy is without its detractors. In some quarters, the charge is made that there can be no democracy in times of trouble or war, that democracy itself leads to disorder, that democracy diminishes efficiency, that democracy violates minority and community rights, and that democracy must wait until development is fully achieved. However, whatever evidence critics of democracy can find in support of these claims must not be allowed

to conceal a deeper truth: democracy contributes to preserving peace and security, securing justice and human rights, and promoting economic and social development (see *Peace and Democracy*).

Democratic institutions and processes channel competing interests into arenas of discourse and provide means of compromise which can be respected by all participants in debates, thereby minimizing the risk that differences or disputes will erupt into armed conflict or confrontation. Because democratic Governments are freely chosen by their citizens and held accountable through periodic and genuine elections and other mechanisms, they are more likely to promote and respect the rule of law, respect individual and minority rights, cope effectively with social conflict, absorb migrant populations and respond to the needs of marginalized groups. They are therefore less likely to abuse their power against the peoples of their own State territories. Democracy within States thus fosters the evolution of the social contract upon which lasting peace can be built. In this way, a culture of democracy is fundamentally a culture of peace.

Democratic institutions and processes within States may likewise be conducive to peace among States. The accountability and transparency of democratic Governments to their own citizens, who understandably may be highly cautious about war, as it is they who will have to bear its risks and burdens, may help to restrain recourse to military conflict with other States. The legitimacy conferred upon democratically elected Governments commands the respect of the peoples of other democratic States and fosters expectations of negotiation, compromise and the rule of law in international relations. When States sharing a culture of democracy are involved in a dispute, the transparency of their regimes may help to prevent accidents, avoid reactions based on emotion or fear and reduce the likelihood of surprise attack.

Lacking the legitimacy or real support offered by free elections, authoritarian Governments all too often have recourse to intimidation and violence in order to suppress internal dissent. They tend to reject institutions such as a free press and an independent judiciary which provide the transparency and accountability necessary to discourage such governmental manipulation of citizens (see *Social Conflicts and Peace*). The resulting atmosphere of oppression and tension, felt in neighbouring countries, can heighten the fear of war. It is for this reason that the Charter declares that one of the first purposes of the United Nations is "to take effective collective measures for the prevention and removal of threats to the peace."[1] Threatened by the resentment of their own people, non-democratic Governments may also be more likely to incite hostilities against other States in order to justify their suppression of internal dissent or forge a basis for national unity.

It is true that the introduction of democratic practices into formerly authoritarian or war-torn States may contribute to civil conflict by opening channels for free expression, including the expression of hatred. Free and fair elections can be followed by the suppression of those defeated. There is also a danger that strengthening civil society without also addressing State capacity may undermine governability or overwhelm the State. Especially for Governments in underdeveloped countries, which are typically engaged full time in the provision of basic human needs for their populations, the risks to stability that may arise in the early stages of democratization may make them reluctant to continue democratization or even to begin the process at all.

These difficult questions of prioritization and timing suggest several important lessons. First and foremost, it is essential that each State itself decide the form, pace and character of its democratization process (see *State Responsibility*). This suggests a fundamental prerequisite for democratization: the existence of a State which is able and is willing not only to create the conditions for free and fair elections, but also to support the development and maintenance of the institutions necessary for the ongoing practice of democratic politics. Second, democratization must begin with an effort to create a culture of democracy—a political culture, which is fundamentally non-violent and in which no one party or group expects to win or lose all the time. Such a culture is built upon a societal consensus not about policy, but about the process and framework of democratic political life: that the will of the people is the basis of governmental authority; that all individuals have a right to take part in government; that there shall be periodic and genuine elections; that power changes hands through popular suffrage rather than intimidation or force; that political opponents and minorities have a right to express their views; and that there can be loyal and legal opposition to the Government in power. Third, democratization must seek to achieve institutional balance between the State and civil society. Finally, support for democratization must be coupled with support for development in order that socio-economic as well as civil and political rights are respected. Although development can take place without democracy, there is no evidence that the breakthrough to development requires an authoritarian regime. There is, however, ample evidence sug-

gesting that, over the long term, democracy is an ingredient for both sustainable development and lasting peace (see *Human Rights and Environmental Rights: Their Sustainable Development Compatibility*). Moreover, the globalization of economic activity and communications has generated pressures for democratization and human rights.

In today's world, freedom of thought, the impetus to creativity and the will to involvement are all critical to economic, social and cultural progress, and they are best fostered and protected within democratic systems (see *Idea of a Liberal Democratic Peace*). In this sense, the economic act of privatization can be as well a political act, enabling greater human creativity and participation. The best way to cultivate a citizen's readiness to participate in the development of his or her country, to arouse that person's energy, imagination and commitment, is by recognizing and respecting human dignity and human rights. The material means of progress can be acquired, but human resources—skilled, spirited and inventive workers—are indispensable, as is the enrichment found through mutual dialogue and the free interchange of ideas. In this way, a culture of democracy, marked by communication, dialogue and openness to the ideas and activities of the world, helps to foster a culture of development.

Democracy is not an affirmation of the individual at the expense of the community; it is through democracy that individual and collective rights, the rights of persons and the rights of peoples, can be reconciled. Many different balances can be struck between the rights of individuals and the rights of the community within the context of democratic politics. Democratic processes are the most reliable way to ensure that these balances are genuinely reflective of a people's broader culture, which, in every society, must itself serve as the ballast for the healthy functioning of democracy.

Democracy today is receiving widespread acknowledgement for its capacity to foster good governance, which is perhaps the single most important development variable within the control of individual States. By providing legitimacy for government and encouraging people's participation in decision-making on the issues that affect their lives, democratic processes contribute to the effectiveness of State policies and development strategies. Democratic institutions and practices foster the governmental accountability and transparency necessary to deter national and transnational crime and corruption and encourage increased responsiveness to popular concerns. In development, they increase the likelihood that State goals reflect broad societal concerns and that government is sensitive to the societal and environmental costs of its development policies.

Non-democratic States over time tend to generate conditions inimical to development: politicized military rule; a weak middle class; a population constrained to silence; prohibitions on travel; censorship; restrictions on the practice of religion or imposition of religious obligations; and pervasive and often institutionalized corruption. Without democratic institutions to channel popular pressures for development and reform, popular unrest and instability will result. The reality is that no State can long remain just or free, and thus also have the potential to pursue a successful and sustainable development strategy, if its citizens are prohibited from participating actively and substantially in its political processes and economic, social and cultural development (see *Equitable Equality: Gandhian Concept*). Increasingly, it is from this perspective that democracy is being seen today—as a practical necessity.

3. The Foundation for Action

The consensus that is currently taking shape on the practical importance of democracy finds the United Nations well placed to respond to the requests of its Member States for assistance in democratization.

At the time of the United Nations founding in 1945, as the Second World War was drawing to a close, the overriding aim was to prevent the recurrence of global conflict. With the creation of the United Nations, the founders began a second experiment in democratic international organization, building upon the League of Nations and the logic of its Covenant, framed in the aftermath of the First World War (see *League of Nations*). The Covenant had been intended to guard against the dangers of thwarted nationalism through respect for self-determination; to transcend the dangerous reliance on power balances through a shared system of security; to reverse the arms race through disarmament; and to replace secret treaties with open, international diplomacy. Democracy within and among States was understood as the binding element of these efforts. It would preserve the sovereignty and political independence of nations, by allowing individuals to exercise their fundamental right to political participation, and of peoples, by allowing them to exercise their fundamental right to self-determination. It would foster State participation in democratic international organizations and processes and in collective security arrangements. It would also encourage respect for the rule of law within and

among States. The same understanding of democracy underpins the Charter of the United Nations. Within the original framework of the Charter, democracy was understood as essential to efforts to prevent future aggression, and to support the sovereign State as the basic guarantor of human rights, the basic mechanism for solving national problems and the basic element of a peaceful and cooperative international system.

The word "democracy" does not appear in the Charter. However, with the opening words of that document, "We the Peoples of the United Nations," the founders invoked the most fundamental principle of democracy, rooting the sovereign authority of the Member States, and thus the legitimacy of the Organization which they were to compose, in the will of their peoples. The Charter offers a vision of democratic States and democracy among them that both derives from and aims to realize the founders' "faith in fundamental human rights, in the dignity and worth of the human person, in the equal rights of men and women and of nations large and small."[2] Their commitment to democracy shows in the stated Purposes of the United Nations to promote respect for the principle of equal rights and self-determination of peoples[3] and for human rights and fundamental freedoms for all without discrimination.[4] It is further revealed in the stated Principle of the United Nations that "the Organization is based on the principle of the sovereign equality of its Members."[5]

The Universal Declaration of Human Rights (see *International Bill of Human Rights*), adopted unanimously by the General Assembly in 1948,[6] elaborates upon this original commitment to democracy. The Universal Declaration proclaims the right of all individuals to take part in government, to have equal access to public service, and to vote and be elected. It further states that "the will of the people shall be the basis of authority of government," and that "this will shall be expressed in periodic and genuine elections which shall be by universal and equal suffrage and shall be held by secret vote or by equivalent free voting procedures."[7] It also declares the right to equality before the law, to freedom of opinion and expression, and to freedom of peaceful assembly and association.

The Declaration on the Granting of Independence to Colonial Countries and Peoples, adopted by the General Assembly in 1960,[8] strongly reaffirmed the right of all peoples to self-determination (see *Self-determination*) and declared that, "by virtue of that right [all peoples] freely determine their political status and freely pursue their economic, social and cultural development."[9] The Declaration also called for "immediate steps" to "be taken, in Trust and Non-

Self-Governing Territories or all other territories which have not yet attained independence, to transfer all powers to the peoples of those Territories, without any conditions or reservations, in accordance with their freely expressed will and desire, without any distinction as to race, creed or colour, in order to enable them to enjoy complete independence and freedom."[10]

Taken together, these three primary documents, the Charter of the United Nations, the Universal Declaration of Human Rights and the Declaration on the Granting of Independence to Colonial Countries and Peoples, provide a clear and solid foundation for a United Nations role and responsibility in democratization.

Soon after the birth of the Organization, however, the onset of the Cold War effectively truncated United Nations support for its Member States in democratization. On one side of the global ideological confrontation were States which claimed to have peace and democracy at home, and which supported peoples' calls for self-determination and democratization abroad (see *Cold War*). Yet those States often misappropriated the name of democracy and acted in drastically undemocratic ways. On the other side were States which endeavoured to maintain peace and democracy at home and to promote those objectives within other States. Yet those States often supported authoritarian regimes, on the grounds that those regimes opposed communism and defended market freedoms, or used non-democratic means to achieve their foreign policy goals. The actions of both sides seemed to suggest a belief that peace and democracy within States could be achieved by war and non-democracy among States.

The Cold War thus interrupted the project of democratic international organization begun by the founders. Throughout the decades of this confrontation, many of the major decisions of international peace and security were taken outside the United Nations and managed within the context of a non-democratic system, the bipolar system. The principle of self-determination was usurped and manipulated. International law became a casualty. The bright prospects for democracy within and among States soon faded to a faint glow.

Nonetheless, during that time the United Nations was active in keeping international organization alive, in promoting and facilitating decolonization, in easing the transition of newly independent peoples into the international State system, in promoting economic and social development, in building human rights machinery and in defending international law.

The principle of self-determination was reaffirmed not only in the Declaration on the Granting of Independence to Colonial Countries and Peoples but also in the International Covenants on Civil and Political Rights and on Economic, Social and Cultural Rights,[11] which both entered into force in 1976, the latter Covenant making clear that economic, social and cultural rights stand on an equal basis with civil and political rights. The International Covenant on Civil and Political Rights in its Article 25 reaffirmed and made binding respect for the right of all individuals to take part in public affairs, to vote and be elected in periodic and genuine elections, and to have equal access to public service. It did the same for other basic human rights critical to the achievement of genuine electoral processes and democratic government, such as freedom of expression, of information, of assembly, of association and movement, and freedom from intimidation.

The foundation for a United Nations role in democratization was thus fortified even during the global contest of the Cold War. As the era of super-Power confrontation was coming to an end and the drive for democratization gained momentum, there emerged a fresh prospect for the pursuit of the Charter's original goals, and for offering assistance in democratization.

4. An Evolving United Nations Role

The new acclaim for democracy and growing recognition of United Nations potential in democratization have been reflected most obviously in the General Assembly's increased attention in recent years to enhancing the effectiveness of the principle of periodic and genuine elections. In its resolutions on this matter, which has appeared annually on its agenda since 1988, the Assembly has reasserted the foundation for a United Nations role in democratization by explicitly reaffirming the relevant principles, purposes and rights articulated in the Charter of the United Nations, the Universal Declaration of Human Rights and the International Covenant on Civil and Political Rights. In a related series of resolutions on respect for the principles of national sovereignty and non-interference in the internal affairs of States in their electoral processes (see *Non-intervention and Non-interference*), the Assembly has explicitly recalled its resolution containing the Declaration on the Granting of Independence to Colonial Countries and Peoples.

The General Assembly also has placed a dual emphasis on democracy as an ideal and as an essential ingredient for progress. In its resolution 43/157 of December 8, 1988, reaffirming that the will of the people, expressed in periodic and genuine elections, shall be the basis of authority of government, the General Assembly stressed that, "as a matter of practical experience, the right of everyone to take part in the government of his or her country is a crucial factor in the effective enjoyment of a wide range of other human rights and fundamental freedoms, embracing political, economic, social, and cultural rights."

This series of General Assembly resolutions, together with the respondent reports submitted by myself and other relevant United Nations entities, illustrates the ongoing process of dialogue, assessment, debate and reform in the area of electoral assistance that has emerged in response to the rising tide of interest in democratization and requests for United Nations support. This process has been influenced and received added impetus from the dialogue taking place in international conferences, particularly the World Conference on Human Rights, which was convened by the United Nations in Vienna in June 1993, and the First and Second International Conferences of New or Restored Democracies, held respectively at Manila in June 1988, with 13 countries participating, and at Managua in July 1994, with 74 countries participating. The result has been the establishment of a Focal Point for Electoral Assistance Requests within the United Nations Department of Political Affairs, along with an Electoral Assistance Division; the establishment of various trust funds for electoral assistance; the creation of a global Electoral Assistance Information Network, coordinated by the Electoral Assistance Division, in which an increasing number of intergovernmental, non-governmental and private organizations are participating; and, on the operational level, the refinement of procedures and design of new approaches to electoral assistance.

The evolution of this reform process in the electoral field has coincided with a major reorientation of Member States' requests for technical assistance in institution-building, evident in the expanding interest of the United Nations agencies and programmes in the social dimension of development and in the question of governance. The scope of requests for assistance made by Member States has broadened, and now encompasses assistance provided before, during and after the holding of elections in order to "ensure the continuation and consolidation of democratization processes in Member States requesting assistance."[12]

It is on the availability of such assistance from the United Nations system, and following on a request made in the Managua Plan of Action,[13] that the General Assembly requested me to prepare the August 7, 1995 report, "Support by the United Nations system

of the efforts of Governments to promote and consolidate new or restored democracies."[14] That report, as well as the October 18, 1996 report of the same title,[15] details the range of available assistance, from assistance in the creation of a political culture in which democratization can take root, to assistance in democratic elections, to assistance in building institutions which support democratization.

The reports emphasize that democratization must have indigenous support if it is to take root within a society. The United Nations assists Member States in building such support by helping to promote a culture of democracy. With its impartiality and universal legitimacy, and its Charter-based purpose of promoting human rights and fundamental freedoms for all, the United Nations is uniquely placed to provide such assistance.

Assistance in creating a culture of democracy can take many forms and often is provided in the context of electoral assistance, although it is and need not be limited to that context. In Cambodia (1993) and El Salvador (1994), the United Nations helped the parties to conduct a fair electoral campaign—free from partisan intimidation—through diplomacy, civic education programmes and efforts to ensure fair access to the media (see Nobel Peace Prize Laureates: *United Nations Peacekeeping Forces*). In Mozambique (1994), the United Nations has helped transform the Resistência Nacional de Moçambique (RENAMO) into a political party and facilitated the country's transition from a one-party to a multi-party system. In many other countries around the world, United Nations programmes for the return of refugees and displaced persons to their home territories constitute a major contribution to the re-creation of a polity within which democratization may be seriously contemplated.

Support for a culture of democracy has proved critical to success in holding free and fair elections in which all actors in society—government officials, political leaders, parliamentarians, judicial officials, police and military forces and individual citizens—play their accorded roles. Moreover, it has proved critical to ensuring that electoral results are respected and that there is widespread support among all actors for the continued practice of democratic politics beyond a first referendum or election. In this regard, should a political stalemate or crisis at some point occur which threatens to derail the democratization process or to interrupt the practice of democratic politics, the United Nations should be ready to serve as a neutral and confidential mediator to try to facilitate a peaceful and satisfying resolution of the dispute. The request of the parties concerned is a prerequisite.

This same emphasis on the continuation and consolidation of democratization processes has guided the United Nations refinement of procedures and design of new approaches in the field of electoral assistance, although the purpose of elections themselves must not be to decide on whether or not democratization will go forward but to elect a legitimate Government. The United Nations offers electoral assistance which aims to build both confidence in democratic political processes and long-term national capacity to conduct periodic and genuine elections. The United Nations endeavours to help States construct an electoral process and an electoral infrastructure using appropriate technology. Where possible, it assists in the creation of a national network for electoral observation, which encourages the participation of national political parties and nongovernmental organizations and thereby strengthens simultaneously national capacity and the base of support for continued democratization.

Beyond fostering a culture of democracy and holding democratic elections lies the evident and crucial need to prepare, and to continually renew and strengthen, the institutional ground in which democratization can take shape. The United Nations provides a wide variety of assistance in this area, encompassing much of its operational work in development and human rights, and focusing on both State institutions and the institutions of civil society. As stressed in my two reports, the United Nations offers assistance in institution-building for democratization that encompasses far more than helping Member States to create democratic structures of government, or to strengthen existing ones. United Nations assistance in institution-building also involves helping to improve accountability and transparency, to build national capacity and to reform the civil service—in a word, good governance. It involves institutional support for the rule of law, in which United Nations departments, agencies and programmes help States to reform and strengthen legal and judicial systems, to build human rights institutions, including those of a humanitarian character, to create police and military forces respectful of human rights and the rule of law, to provide police forces that enforce the rule of law and to depoliticize military establishments. Finally, United Nations assistance in this area involves institution-building for social development, such as helping to create independent trade unions or to promote the full integration of women into all aspects of political, social, cultural and economic life—a task of particular importance to the consolidation of democratization.

The entire range of United Nations assistance, from support for a culture of democracy to assistance in institution-building for democratization, may well be understood as a key component of peace-building. Peace-building is a new approach which emphasizes that in order to achieve lasting peace, the effort to prevent, control and resolve conflicts must include action to address the underlying economic, social, cultural, humanitarian and political roots of conflict and to strengthen the foundations for development (see *Peacebuilding from Below*).

The proliferation of actors engaged in such activities supporting democratization has on the whole been a positive trend. Requesting States and their peoples, which themselves represent a wide diversity of circumstances, characteristics and priorities, are being offered a rich variety of perspectives, capacities, approaches and techniques from which to choose. Yet with this proliferation of actors and activity there also comes the risk of confusion, waste and duplication of effort. As in the field of development, the United Nations today can help to rationalize and harmonize the multiplicity of public and private efforts worldwide in the field of democratization.

To illustrate, in cases where the United Nations has been entrusted with a peacemaking or peacekeeping mandate to help bring about national reconciliation and democratic consolidation, the establishment of informal, ad hoc groups of States to support the United Nations in that effort has served to harmonize diplomatic initiatives and to achieve, among other aims, a coordinated approach in promoting a culture of democracy. Such has been the case, for example, with the "Friends of the Secretary-General for El Salvador," the "Friends of the Secretary-General for Guatemala" and the "Friends of the Secretary-General for Haiti", where the United Nations and the Organization of American States have deployed a joint civilian human rights mission (see *Civilian-based Defense*).

In electoral assistance, lack of coordination among international actors risks far more than waste and duplication. Conflicting advice from technical consultants, over-funding of or inordinate attention to particular electoral components to the detriment of others, and lack of unity in assessments by electoral observers, whether made before, during or after an election, are all possible results. Each can carry potentially severe consequences for the overall electoral effort.

The United Nations Focal Point for Electoral Assistance Requests, the Under-Secretary-General for Political Affairs, helps to ensure coordination among the primary United Nations units active in the electoral field. Among all international actors in the electoral field, coordination is served by ongoing United Nations activities, such as the maintenance of the global Electoral Assistance Information Network, the publication and dissemination of guidelines and handbooks on electoral assistance, and the convening of workshops and seminars with various governmental, intergovernmental and non-governmental partners of the United Nations in electoral assistance. On the operational level, the United Nations can provide an umbrella framework for communication and coordination. Where possible, the United Nations has fostered joint operations with regional intergovernmental organizations. Such field cooperation has brought positive results for the requesting States, assisting organizations and relevant donors, and bodes well for enhanced coordination in the future.

In institution-building for democratization, the task of coordination among international actors is substantially more complex and difficult than in the electoral field. Institution-building for democratization not only involves a far larger and more diverse group of actors; it is a newer and wider area of international activity which, unlike electoral assistance, lacks a precise organizational focus. Coordination of international actors is essential to avoid waste and duplication and, more importantly, to avoid conflicting advice from technical consultants, programmes working at cross purposes and over-funding of or inordinate attention to particular aspects of the democratization process to the detriment of others; the last could lead in turn to an imbalance between the capacities of State and civic institutions. Any or all of these results could undermine the overall effort to consolidate democratization.

The United Nations is well placed to facilitate coordination among international actors engaged in institution-building for democratization. The United Nations maintains a global network of regional economic and social commissions and country offices. The global mandate of the United Nations spans economic, social, security, political, humanitarian and human rights issues, which is why the United Nations is active across virtually the full range of issues relevant to democratization and can help integrate these issues into a wider effort linking peacekeeping, refugee assistance, relief efforts, reconstruction and development. Finally, the United Nations itself accounts for many of the international actors engaged in institution-building for democratization.

The United Nations serves coordination in institution-building by strengthening coordination within its own organizational framework and within the United Nations system as a whole. The Administrative Committee on Coordination, chaired by the Secretary-General and composed of the executive heads of all the United Nations programmes and specialized agencies, including the Bretton Woods institutions, works to foster an effective division of labour within the United Nations system and to promote joint initiatives towards common objectives. An important part of this effort is the United Nations resident coordinator system, designed to promote effective coordination among all economic and social actors at the country level. In the context of peacekeeping, this coordinating role is fulfilled by the Special Representative of the Secretary-General in command of the operation. This coordination effort within the United Nations system already allows for and encourages the participation of non-United Nations actors, both governmental and non-governmental. Through this effort can be developed an expanding network for information-sharing, policy development and programme cooperation in democratization support. In this context, post-election needs-assessment missions aimed at recommending programmes that might contribute to democratic consolidation could be a useful basis for formulating coordinated approaches and joint initiatives among international actors. Such missions are now offered by the United Nations Electoral Assistance Division in accordance with General Assembly resolution 48/131 of December 20, 1993.

For the United Nations, the task of fostering communication and coordination among international actors in democratization assistance goes hand in hand with the effort to strengthen the international context for such assistance. Towards this end, the convening of international conferences has proved to be an effective mechanism.

With the United Nations Conference on Environment and Development, held at Rio de Janeiro in June 1992, the United Nations began a series of international conferences that have brought together not only all States, but also relevant non-governmental organizations and other representatives of civil society to focus on interlocking economic and social issues by considering their impact on the human person and human communities. At Rio, the focus was on sustainable development and the necessity for a new and equitable partnership among all States, developed and developing, and between government and civil society at all levels. At Vienna (June 1993), the world turned its attention to human rights and, in particular, to the mutually reinforcing relationship between democracy, development and the respect for human rights. At Cairo (September 1994), the focus was on population and development, linking demographic change to development policies. At Copenhagen (March 1995), the age-old problems of poverty, unemployment and social disintegration were considered as global problems requiring global attention. At Beijing (September 1995), the advancement of women was discussed as a key to progress in the search for equality, development and peace. At Midrand, South Africa (May 1996), trade and development were addressed in the context of globalization and liberalization, and at Istanbul (June 1996), the focus was on human settlements and the problems of development in cities (see *United Nations: Achievements and Agenda*).

Taken together, these conferences evidence an emerging global consensus on democracy itself and, more clearly, on an array of issues directly and indirectly relevant to democratization. This consensus is being translated into international norms, agreements and specific commitments, integrated by Member States into national priorities and supported by the United Nations and others through operational activities.

Through international conferences and in other ways, such as the resumed fiftieth session of the General Assembly on public administration and development (April 15-19, 1996), the United Nations fosters a supportive international environment for democratizing States—and, indeed, for all democracies, new and long-established—which encourages consolidation of democratization while helping to guard against erosion, reversal or abandonment of democratic politics.

Yet, the objective to create a supportive international environment for democracy and democratizing States requires expanded effort. If the new phenomenon of democratization within States is to be fully understood, and its progress certainly advanced, it must be considered in its full international context.

This means recognizing, as in 1945, the positive relationship between democracy and the functioning of the international system. The logic of the Charter is today made manifest as United Nations support for democratization helps to prevent aggression and to foster the construction and maintenance of viable and independent States as the basic guarantors of human rights, the basic mechanisms for solving national problems and the basic elements of a peaceful and cooperative international system.

This relationship has evolved since 1945. The reality of globalization and the new world environment now require democratization at the international level, so that democratization within States can take root, so that the problems brought on by globalization which affect all States may be more effectively solved and so that a new, stable and equitable international system can be constructed in place of the bipolar system so recently swept away.

5. Democratization at the International Level

Democratization internationally is necessary on three interrelated fronts. The established system of the United Nations itself has far to go before fulfilling to the extent possible the democratic potential of its present design, and in transforming those structures which are insufficiently democratic. The participation of new actors on the international scene is an acknowledged fact; providing them with agreed means of participation in the formal system, heretofore primarily the province of States, is a new task of our time. A third challenge will be to achieve a culture of democracy internationally. This will not only require a society of States committed to democratic principles and processes; it will also demand an enlarged international civil society deeply involved in democratic institutions, whether State, inter-State or supra-State, private or quasi-private; committed to democratic practices, procedures and political pluralism; and composed of peoples ingrained with those habits of openness, fairness and tolerance that have been associated with democracy since ancient times.

There are of course substantial differences between democratization at the international level and democratization within States. At the international level there are international organizations and institutions, and international decision-making and international law, but there is no international structure equivalent to that of State government. International society is both a society of States and a society of individual persons. Nonetheless, the concept of democratization as a process which can create a more open, more participatory, less authoritarian society applies both nationally and internationally.

There are likewise substantial differences between the ideas of national democracy and international democracy. Growing recognition of the practical importance of democracy within States has nevertheless contributed to growing recognition of the practical importance of democracy among States and generated increased demand for democratization internationally.

Individual involvement in the political process enhances the accountability and responsiveness of government. Governments which are responsive and accountable are likely to be stable and to promote peace. Many internal conflicts stem from the belief, justified or not, that the State does not represent all groups in society or that it seeks to impose an exclusive ideology. Democracy is the way to mediate the various social interests in a particular community. In the international community, it is the way to promote the participation of all actors and to provide a possibility to solve conflicts by dialogue rather than by force of arms. The process of democratization internationally can therefore help promote peaceful relations among States (see *Internationalization*).

With participation, economic and social development become meaningful and establish deeper roots. Building democratic institutions at the State level helps to ensure that the priorities of diverse social groups are considered in the formulation of development strategies. In the international economic system, democracy can mean that the relationship between developed and developing States is one not of assistance but of cooperation. Instead of chronic reliance on emergency relief, the concerns of developed and developing States can be mediated in conferences and other United Nations intergovernmental consultations, which also engage relevant non-State actors. Democratization, therefore, can help guarantee that, through the United Nations, the poorest countries will have an ever growing voice in the international system. It can help ensure that the international system does not leave a vast portion of the world to fend for itself but truly promotes the integration and participation of all peoples.

If democratization is the most reliable way to legitimize and improve national governance, it is also the most reliable way to legitimize and improve international organization, making it more open and responsive by increasing participation, more efficient by allowing for burden-sharing and more effective by allowing for comparative advantage and greater creativity. Moreover, just like democratization within States, democratization at the international level is based on and aims to promote the dignity and worth of the individual human being and the fundamental equality of all persons and of all peoples.

The new world environment has strengthened this fundamental link between democratization nationally and internationally. Once, decision-making in global affairs could have only a limited effect on the internal affairs of States and the daily lives of their peoples. Today, decisions concerning global matters carry with them far-reaching domestic consequences, blurring the lines between international and domestic policy. In this way, unrepresentative decisions on global issues can run counter to democratization

within a State and undermine a people's commitment to it. Thus, democratization within States may fail to take root unless democratization extends to the international arena.

Decisions at the global level are going to increase because the problems which can only be solved globally are going to multiply (see *Globalization*). Already, States everywhere increasingly confront forces far beyond the control of any one State or even group of States. Some of these forces are irresistible, such as the globalization of economic activity and communications. These forces, although predominantly positive in effect, affect societies unevenly, can seem accountable to no one and are creating opportunities for a host of transnational criminal activities, from illegal arms transfers to the laundering of profits from the narcotic trade. Environmental pressures are similarly irresistible and create global problems. States can also be substantially affected by another State's domestic decisions in regard to finance or the environment and by the decisions of local authorities and private actors. It is not the forces themselves that are new but their increasing scale and level of influence upon the State.

These global forces can feed and interact with forces exerted upon States from below. Increased access to communications media, particularly radio, television and film, raise awareness of problems and opportunities and lead people everywhere to demand more accountability, more representation and more participation in governance—more control over their future and more say in the decisions that affect their lives. Global forces can also be a source of individual insecurity, social disarray and dangerous fragmentation, creating fertile ground for fanaticism, ethnocentrism and isolationism (see *Role of Europe in the Management of Global Problems*).

All this means that the requirements of political governance are extending beyond State borders, even as States feel new pressures from below. Democracy within the State will diminish in importance if the process of democratization does not move forward at the international level. For if a State today is to acquire or retain the capacity to provide an enabling environment for its citizens, it must extend its influence to those factors beyond its unilateral control which help to determine the conditions of life within it. Such an extension of sovereignty will be possible and legitimate only to the extent that it rests upon mechanisms of democratic accountability. For all States, democratization at the international level has become an indispensable mechanism for global problem-solving in a way that is accountable and acceptable to all and with the participation of all concerned. Dominance by one country or group of countries must over time evolve into a democratic international system in which all countries can participate, along with new non-State actors involved in international affairs.

There are signs that such a process is already taking place. As States have confronted popular demands to deal with economic, security and environmental issues that evade effective action on a strictly national basis, they have increasingly found themselves seeking solutions through cooperative arrangements and participation in regional and international intergovernmental organizations (see *Regionalism, Economic Security and Peace: The Asia Pacific*). Such organizations are proliferating and the scope of their activities is broadening, thereby fostering democratic principles and participation at the international level. At the same time, new channels of political expression and activity for individual citizens are developing outside governmental structures but inside the public sphere once considered the virtually exclusive province of government; the proliferation of non-governmental organizations from the local to the global and the expansion of activity through international political associations, or "political internationals," both make clear the deficiencies of existing governmental structures in the face of global change (see *Non-governmental Organizations (NGOs)*). The overall result is that globalization is creating chains of interlocking decisions and political associations which link different levels of political representation. In other words, what is emerging are de facto linkages extending from individual citizens all the way to international organizations, grappling with global problems and prospects. The forces at work in the world today are thus demanding and enabling an unprecedented democratization of international politics and decision-making.

The United Nations has recognized and supported this process of democratization internationally. Its advancement deserves to become a leading priority in world affairs. But before discussing how the United Nations and others can further this process, it is essential to be clear about the nature of the political "system" that is to be democratized.

The "system" in which the world operates is by its very name "international." However, as observed above, the States which are its basic components increasingly must operate in the midst of global as well as internal forces. Moreover, "international relations"—not relations among nations but relations among sovereign States—are increasingly shaped not

only by the States themselves but also by an expanding array of non-State actors on the "international" scene, ranging all the way from individual persons to civic associations, non-governmental organizations, local authorities, private multinational business, academia, the media, parliamentarians and regional and international intergovernmental organizations (see *Interdependence, International*).

These changes have come to the fore largely because of the quick succession of historical events which the world has witnessed in recent years. The fall of the Berlin Wall and the end of Cold War and of East-West antagonism shattered the ideological screen which concealed the complex reality of international relations and precipitated the collapse of the bipolar system. Although reference is commonly made to the "international system," in reality a new international system, with a new structure for international stability and cooperation, has yet to emerge (see *Peace, Systems View of*). The most legitimate, effective and responsive way to build such a system—taking into account not only geopolitical issues, but economic behaviour and social and cultural aspirations—is by democratizing the structures and mechanisms already in place.

5.1 Member States

The first priority in this effort must be a fundamental change on the part of the Member States themselves. Despite all the pressures affecting State sovereignty in our time, the concept of sovereignty remains essential for rendering unequal power equal and for making international organization possible; States remain the most important actors of all, and will continue to be the fundamental building blocks of the international system (see *State, Theory of the*). Yet today only a small proportion of States play their full role on the world stage. Some States, small in size or population, exercise influence far beyond their objective attributes of power. Other States possessing vast power refrain from international involvement commensurate with their strength. Of course, domestic political and constitutional constraints are involved, but the first and greatest step forward in democratization internationally must be increased attention to and engagement with international affairs by all States Members of the United Nations, as an application of the concept of sovereignty.

With this step must come a commitment on the part of all States not only to engage in dialogue and debate but also to discourage isolationism, to oppose unilateralism, to accept decisions reached democratically, to refrain from using force illegitimately, to oppose aggression, to promote and respect the rule of law in international relations and to maintain a general spirit of solidarity, cooperation and community. Unless the majority of Member States have the political will to pay attention to global affairs as they do to national affairs, the democratization of international relations will not succeed.

5.2 New Actors

Next is the integration of new non-State actors, who are undeniably of increasing influence in world affairs, into existing international structures and mechanisms. There is a great diversity of such actors. They participate in different ways and in different degrees, more effectively within organizations and associations. The vast majority are in the North, and among them are the key actors in the process of globalization: the transnational entities involved in business and finance, which can cooperate closely with the Governments of the countries in which they are based (see *Multinational Corporations and Peace*). The degree and nature of the loss of sovereignty brought on by globalization therefore differs between the States of the North and the States of the South. Increasing the participation of the new actors in international institutions must not be allowed to accentuate the gap between North and South. Just as democratization within a State must include an effort to empower citizens to participate in their own political process, so must democratization internationally include an effort to empower all States—developed or developing, North or South, rich or poor—to participate in the international political system, of which they are all a part.

The United Nations is fundamentally and from its inception an Organization of sovereign States. Yet it also has from its inception offered its Member States an indispensable mechanism for cooperation with actors, both governmental and non-governmental, functioning outside the United Nations. The creation in 1945 of an International Intergovernmental Organization with provisions for cooperating not only with other such organizations—such as the specialized agencies formally brought into the United Nations system under the aegis of Article 57 of the Charter—but also with regional and non-governmental organizations, was a major achievement. Specifically, Chapter VIII of the Charter is devoted entirely to United Nations cooperation with regional organizations and arrangements in the maintenance of international peace and security. Article 71 of the Charter empowers the Economic and Social Council to make arrangements for consultation with non-governmental organizations active in its area of competence.

Within these provisions and the general framework of the Charter, the United Nations has made great strides in expanding dialogue and practical cooperation with the new actors as their influence on and importance to world affairs has grown. Nonetheless, the discussions on United Nations reform have not dealt adequately with the issue of their integration. It is crucial that in the future they do. Towards this end, the paragraphs below address several of the new actors in turn, outlining the special features which make their integration essential, their present level of involvement in the United Nations and its work, and suggestions to stimulate discussion on the question of their integration into the formal United Nations system. The suggestions touch upon a variety of steps towards deeper integration that could be taken by the United Nations Secretariat, by Member States, either individually or through the intergovernmental machinery of the United Nations, by the actor in question or, most often, by some combination of the aforementioned, acting jointly. Substantively, the steps primarily fall along three main lines, each of which stresses integration as a way to give the new actors a voice in the United Nations: a voice that can be a contribution to problem-solving; a voice on matters before the United Nations, not limited to the situation of each actor; and an avenue of expression to the international community on the prospects, problems and requirements of the sectors that these actors represent.

5.3 Regional Organizations

The upsurge in activity through regional organizations in the last decade, and especially since the end of the Cold War, has challenged the community of States to develop the new regionalism not as a resurgent "spheres of influence" but as a healthy complement to internationalism. Moreover, at a time of increasing demand but decreasing resources within the United Nations for international action, the potential of regional groups to contribute political, diplomatic, financial, material and military resources has taken on even greater importance. Especially in the area of international development assistance and cooperation, where donor fatigue and indifference have set in, and in peace-enforcement, where the United Nations at present has no capacity, regional groups are for the United Nations increasingly important potential partners whose cooperation could be engaged (see *Integration, Regional*).

Many regional intergovernmental organizations participate as permanent observers in the sessions and work of the General Assembly. Regional groups have long cooperated with the United Nations in the development field through the United Nations regional economic and social commissions, established in the earliest years of the Organization. Only in the vastly changed circumstances of the post-Cold War years has the United Nations been able to explore new forms of cooperation with regional groups in the maintenance of international peace and security and to delegate responsibility in particular cases to States and organizations of the regions concerned. Under the flexible framework provided by Chapter VIII of the Charter, different forms of United Nations/regional cooperation have developed: consultations, diplomatic support, operational support, co-deployment and joint operations. In August 1994 and again in February 1996, I convened at United Nations Headquarters a high-level meeting with regional organizations that have cooperated with the United Nations in peace and security, to examine patterns of and principles for improving cooperation, and to explore the potential for expanded cooperation in the future.

The integration of regional organizations into the United Nations system is a cornerstone of democratization internationally (see *Global Integration*). To build upon this basis, consideration should be given to holding regular meetings at United Nations Headquarters every year or every two years between the Secretariat and regional organizations cooperating with the United Nations in peace and security. The pivotal role of regional organizations in democratizing development should be enhanced by opening channels to the regional level for the views of those at the local level, and by reducing bureaucratic obstacles to the flow or volume of assistance; the United Nations regional economic and social commissions are well placed to contribute to such an effort. Regionalism should be strengthened internationally through United Nations-sponsored agreements on horizontal, interregional connections in all areas of endeavour.

5.4 Non-governmental Organizations

In the last few decades the number of non-governmental organizations (NGOs) has grown at an astonishing rate—the number of international non-governmental organizations alone having risen from roughly 1,300 in 1960 to over 36,000 in 1995—and their functional scope has expanded considerably. The thousands of NGOs that operate today, from the grassroots to the global level, represent a wide diversity in size, statute, field of activity, methods, means and objectives. However, all are self-governing, private

institutions engaged in the pursuit of public purposes outside the formal apparatus of the State. Such organizations are taking on an increasingly important role in world affairs by carrying the voices and needs of the smallest communities to international attention, forging contacts between citizens' groups across the world and offering citizens direct channels of participation in world affairs. To international organizations, non-governmental organizations can bring not only strengthened legitimacy but also field experience and expertise across a vast array of human concerns, as well as a valuable capacity for information-gathering and dissemination. Non-governmental organizations are proving extremely powerful in fighting isolationism (see *Isolationism*) and indifference among both Governments and citizens, and in mobilizing public opinion and support, especially financial support and donor assistance.

Some 200 non-governmental organizations were present at the 1945 United Nations Conference on International Organization at San Francisco, where the Charter of the United Nations was agreed and signed. Since that time, the United Nations-NGO partnership has grown into a global network, encompassing some 1,600 non-governmental organizations in consultative status with the Economic and Social Council under Article 71 of the Charter, some 1,500 associated with the United Nations Department of Public Information, and the many other non-governmental organizations affiliated with United Nations offices and agencies in every part of the world. On the legislative/policy-making side, NGO participation in United Nations work is most advanced in the human rights and treaty bodies, with NGO involvement also having been critical to the establishment of those bodies. Less advanced but moving definitively forward is NGO participation in legislation and policy-making in the economic and social field. Recognizing the vital role played by non-governmental organizations at the Earth Summit (Rio de Janeiro, June 1992), the Programmes of Action adopted there, Agenda 21,[16] provides for NGO participation in the Commission on Sustainable Development established for its follow-up. Agenda 21 encourages the entire United Nations system and all intergovernmental organizations to review and report on ways of enhancing NGO participation in policy design, decision-making, implementation and evaluation. The momentum generated by Rio for strengthened NGO participation has been carried forward in subsequent conferences and led, among other outcomes, to the adoption by the Economic and Social Council in July 1996 of a new resolution on the consultative relationship between the United Nations and non-governmental organizations.[17] On the operational level, NGO participation is most advanced in humanitarian emergencies, but it is also substantial in the development field, where NGO participation is facilitated by the United Nations Non-Governmental Liaison Service at Geneva and by various NGO committees and advisory bodies established by United Nations departments and agencies (see *Human Rights and Environmental Rights: Their Sustainable Development Compatibility*).

To deepen further the democratizing potential of the NGO phenomenon, non-governmental organizations and other representatives of civil society (including those addressed specifically below) should be invited to participate in Member State delegations on a regular basis. The Open-ended High-level Working Group on the Strengthening of the United Nations System has suggested that consideration be given to the establishment of a "civil society forum". In addition, the Conference of Non-Governmental Organizations in Consultative Status with the Economic and Social Council should be empowered to make more precise and operational recommendations for the consideration of the Council and to help ensure that the non-governmental organizations in such status are representative and of recognized utility.

Each of the actors discussed below is already represented in some way through non-governmental organizations in consultative status with the Economic and Social Council. Therefore, participation via the Economic and Social Council should deepen on all fronts if these actors obtain some formalized or semi-formalized connection with the Council.

5.5 Parliamentarians

Parliamentarians, as the directly elected representatives of their constituents, are for international organizations an essential link to international public opinion. Without such a link it has become extremely difficult to build recognition, understanding and support for international efforts, especially in recent years as those efforts have become more complex and the international environment more uncertain. At the same time, by carrying the views and concerns of their constituents to the international arena, parliamentarians offer a direct channel for increasing the legitimacy, responsiveness and effectiveness of international organizations. Situated between citizens of States and the community of States, and by definition committed to dialogue, discussion and agreement, parliamentarians are a direct and motive force for democratization at the international level.

Parliamentarians have participated in the work of the United Nations in a variety of ways. Acting both individually and in concert, they have cooperated with the United Nations in the field across the full range of support for democratization. At the United Nations, they have engaged in informal consultations with the Secretariat, participated in Member State delegations, contributed to preparations for international conferences and fostered international dialogue by occasionally convening their own conferences at the United Nations through the Inter-Parliamentary Union, the world organization of parliamentarians. The Inter-Parliamentary Union has long had consultative status with the Economic and Social Council. Following a request of the General Assembly in its resolution 50/15 of November 15, 1995, I concluded in July 1996 an agreement on cooperation between the United Nations and the Inter-Parliamentary Union[18] which will strengthen that cooperation and give it "a new and adequate framework." As Secretary-General, I also continued to meet with parliamentarians and members of state legislatures, upon their request, during my official visits to Member States, as do my Special Envoys and Special Representatives and other representatives of the United Nations system.

To consolidate and take further advantage of the contributions of parliamentarians as a factor of democratization internationally, Member States should consider: encouraging and facilitating the closer involvement of parliamentarians in United Nations efforts to provide international support for democratization within States; establishing a continuing committee or commission on the United Nations within their national parliaments; and urging the Inter-Parliamentary Union to convene every three years at a United Nations location in order to foster international dialogue and debate on the United Nations and issues before the United Nations and its Member States.

5.6 Local Authorities

While today's major challenges are undeniably global in character, it is at the local level where their impact is felt most directly, which is why local authorities, such as mayors and metropolitan officials, have become notably more active on global issues and, in some cases, collectively organized across countries on matters of common concern. Local participation enhances the legitimacy and effectiveness of global decisions by helping to ensure that those decisions emerge from the realities of local life and are supported by local action. Yet vigorous and effective local governance is essential not only to global problem-solving: by contributing to health and sustainable human settlements, it is also essential to international peace and security in the broadest sense. With the global trend towards urbanization, human settlements increasingly will be urban settlements. Already, the city is where global problems converge and where their interconnections are most apparent; mass migration, overpopulation, natural disasters, air and water pollution, land degradation, the rights of women and children, minority rights, unemployment, poverty and social disaffection are just some of the prime examples (see *Human Security*). At the same time, however, the city may also be the place where a sound basis for solving these problems can be built, for of all human settlements, cities are best placed to foster dialogue and diversity, to engender community and a spirit of civic engagement while also opening windows to the world. Mayors and metropolitan authorities have therefore become indispensable agents for social integration within and among cities and thus within and among States.

Since the Earth Summit, where local authorities were identified as one of the "major groups" of society responsible for sustainable development, the involvement of local authorities in United Nations efforts has advanced considerably. Following the Summit, a Local Agenda 21 initiative was launched by the International Council for Local Environmental Initiatives, whose members are cities and towns actively promoting participatory development processes at the local level. Mayors and metropolitan authorities participate in the work of the Commission on Sustainable Development and many exchange information and consult informally with the Commission's secretariat. Mayors and metropolitan authorities have also mobilized in support of the United Nations Framework Convention on Climate Change and contribute to its Conference of Parties. The organizational framework for the United Nations Conference on Human Settlements (Habitat II) allowed for a more formalized involvement of local authorities. In the area of operational activities for development, programmes requested by Member States increasingly involve United Nations cooperation with local authorities. In the peace and security sphere, many local authorities support United Nations efforts through "sister cities" and other such cooperation and cultural exchange programmes, and many cities have declared themselves nuclear-weapon-free zones. Cities have also been strongly supportive of the United Nations by hosting international gatherings and events and by providing homes to the many United Nations offices around the world.

To strengthen local frameworks for global problem-solving and deepen the involvement of local authorities in the United Nations system, consideration should be given to instructing United Nations resident coordinators to maintain regular dialogue with local authorities, making the interaction an integral part of the work, at the country level, on operational activities for development. The possibility of establishing a joint committee of concerned Secretariat entities and apex organizations of local authorities should be examined; such a committee would serve to raise awareness and promote exchange of experiences among local authorities and could be established along the lines of the Committee for the Promotion and Advancement of Cooperatives, which brings together the United Nations Secretariat, United Nations agencies and international non-governmental organizations to promote and coordinate assistance to cooperatives and is financed by contributions from its members. Member States should also consider a more formalized involvement of local authorities through the establishment of a small subsidiary body of the Commission on Sustainable Development, which would contribute regularly to the work of the Commission and to other relevant United Nations bodies.

5.7 Academia

At this time of profound change, academia, including universities, research institutes and public policy centres, has taken on increased importance in world affairs by helping to uncover the dimensions of change and to construct an intellectual platform upon which future efforts may be built. By expanding the flow of ideas, academia has become increasingly powerful in encouraging public participation in national and international dialogue on the future and, more importantly, in shaping that dialogue. Thus, by its very nature, academia also contributes to democratization. At the same time, academia is providing important new evidence on the complementarity among peace, development and democracy, and on the contribution of international organizations to all three.

Many academic groups have engaged in informal consultations with the Secretariat and United Nations departments, agencies and programmes. They have also participated in practical assistance programmes. The United Nations itself has several research centres and institutes, as well as its own United Nations University, which promotes scholarly debate, research and training across the range of issues relevant to the operation and efforts of international organizations. The Academic Council on the United Nations System, established by scholars, teachers and practitioners from around the world active in the work and study of international organizations, fosters dialogue and cooperation between academia and the various components of the United Nations system.

To enable the widest range of the world's peoples to benefit from advances in thought and research, and to give greater recognition to the views and needs of academic institutions and enterprises, consideration should be given to expanding informal consultations with academia across the United Nations system in order to facilitate the contribution of individual scholars, scientists and research institutions to United Nations projects and problem-solving. Integrating the programme of work of the United Nations University with the overall work of the United Nations system would be an important contribution towards that end, as would the inclusion by the periodic conferences of academic disciplines of panels or programmes involving United Nations practitioners (see *Peace and Governance Programme of the United Nations University*). The United Nations University and its subsidiary institutions should be strengthened to forge stronger links between academics and research institutions in the North and the South, with a view to fostering global networks where this might not otherwise be easily accomplished. Member States should consider offering a United Nations centre as the venue for academic gatherings to discuss the problems and prospects of research universities and institutions related to the work of that centre. These could serve both substantive scholarship and the capacity of academia to play a more direct role in world affairs.

5.8 Business and Industry

Business and industry today has more power over the future of the global economy and the environment than any Government or organization of Governments. The cooperation of business and industry, whether informal producers, small or medium-sized enterprises or large-scale corporations, is critical to the achievement of development that is both socially and environmentally sustainable. Transnational or multinational corporations in particular—which are today estimated to be 40,000 in number, controlling some 250,000 foreign affiliates worth approximately $2.6 trillion in book value and accounting for some one third of world private-sector productive assets—are playing an extremely important role in economic development. This occurs not only through foreign

direct investment in transitional and developing economies but also through the transfer of technology and skills and the stimulation of host country business enterprise. Moreover, and most importantly, by increasingly integrating the various functions of production across State borders, and as the world's main investors, traders, transferrers of technology and movers of people across borders, transnational corporations are today driving the emergence of an integrated international production system (see *Transnationalism*). A development agent and a positive factor for social integration within and among States, the private business sector—especially transnational business—must be recognized as an integral player in international organization and more closely involved in international decision-making.

While business and industry has become increasingly important for shaping the world economy, the United Nations has become increasingly important for shaping the environment in which business and industry operates. United Nations efforts for peace help to maintain a stable environment in which business and industry can flourish. Less well known is the significant role played by the United Nations system in establishing the regulatory framework in which business and industry acts internationally. This is done, for example, by the World Trade Organization (see *World Trade Organization (WTO)*) in trade and intellectual property rights, by the International Monetary Fund in financial transactions and by the United Nations Environment Programme, the International Labour Organization and many other United Nations programmes and specialized agencies. United Nations entities also set industry guidelines and standards and offer policy analysis and technical assistance to Member States in improving their business and industry-related policies, infrastructure and institutional framework. While United Nations efforts having an important bearing on business are extensive, interaction between the two is at present sporadic, primarily informal and not reflective of the influential role that has been achieved by business and industry in international affairs. The only major exception to this is the International Labour Organization, which brings together in its General Conference Member States represented by delegates from government, employers and workers, each of which are entitled to vote individually on all matters. The need and, in today's more open and increasingly globalized environment, the possibility now exists to transform the role of business and industry within the United Nations into that of an active partnership in pursuit of common objectives. In this regard, the role played by business and industry at the Earth Summit and its continuing participation in the work of the Commission on Sustainable Development are foundations upon which to build. The same can be said of the pioneering efforts under way towards linking international organizations, both governmental and non-governmental, with national and private multinational banks in order to provide the funds and services which small and medium-sized entrepreneurs in transitional and developing countries require for sustainable development activities.

To further the widest possible mutually beneficial involvement of business and industry in the work of the United Nations, consideration should be given to establishing both a roster of United Nations technical and managerial personnel for temporary assignment to business and industry and a roster of business and industry executives and technical personnel for United Nations technical assistance activities. The effort to build the latter roster could be made in conjunction with an initiative to expand the United Nations Volunteers programme to encourage business and industry executives to engage in United Nations work and, *inter alia*, to join in early-stage planning for post-conflict peace-building, with the aim of encouraging foreign investment to facilitate recovery and reconstruction. Member States should also explore the expansion of the tripartite representational structure of the International Labour Organization to other parts of the United Nations system. Also to be considered is the expansion of United Nations efforts to achieve agreement on key issues required for a favourable environment for business, such as uniform commercial codes and intellectual property and accounting standards, and to deal with transnational problems, such as crime and corruption, which inhibit both good governance and good business.

5.9 The Media

Responsible and independent global communications media can engage Governments and people in global affairs and enable them to be informed, to discuss and debate, and to express positions on the issues of the day. In this way, the global communications revolution and the global wave of democratization are mutually reinforcing: a free press is a vehicle for democratization; democratization promotes the open society in which a free press can flourish. However, in this age of instant information and near total communication, the media have become not only the major venue for dialogue and debate within and among States, but also, definitively, an international actor with a distinct role on the international stage.

The media can help keep international politics open, responsive and accountable. Without that essential link to the world public, organizations such as the United Nations would be nothing more than forums for the mutual mutterings of national and international bureaucracies. At the same time, the media itself, especially through the immensely powerful imagery of television and film, have the ability to set the terms of international debate and to shape world public opinion. Through the issues, peoples and places they choose to highlight—or to ignore—the media today have enormous influence over the international agenda. If this influence is to be constructive and effective, the media must focus not only on the drama of conflict and confrontation in certain areas of the world, but on the global pattern of violence and the broader economic, social, political and humanitarian issues that dominate the international community's long-term agenda.

The United Nations has an obligation to protect the independence and freedom of news organizations and to defend the right of all peoples, as set out in Article 19 of the Universal Declaration of Human Rights,[19] to the freedom of opinion and expression, including the freedom "to seek, receive and impart information and ideas through any media and regardless of frontiers." The United Nations Educational, Scientific and Cultural Organization (UNESCO), along with various news organizations, has endorsed a Charter for a Free Press, committed to the unfettered flow of news and information both within and across national borders. Through UNESCO, the Department of Public Information of the Secretariat and various other entities, the United Nations offers its Member States support for the development of free, responsible and independent communications media. While striving to promote responsible and independent communications media worldwide, the United Nations also endeavours, without intruding on that independence, to engage the cooperation of the media by making information about the United Nations and its work easily accessible to the media, and through it, to non-governmental organizations and the public at large.

While the media are a powerful force for democratization, efforts to involve them closely with the international system would contravene their highest principles of independence and objectivity. At the same time, however, thought should be given to the many issues which have arisen with the vast new role of the media in global affairs, issues which affect not only people, cultures and Governments but the media themselves. Among steps to be considered could be:

endeavours by the United Nations and its Member States to offer greater transparency and access to world media; strengthening the information capacity of United Nations operations to help focus media interest and attention on international problems at risk of international neglect; and consideration by the General Assembly's Committee on Information of the establishment of a forum where members of the media, if they choose, and without compromising their independence, could report to the international community on the state of the media.

Integrating these new actors into the daily practice of international politics and decision-making will not be a simple task. In some cases, where involvement is relatively limited and where the actor is of a most private nature, the path towards deeper integration may not at this time be clear. But whether or not Member States confront this challenge, these new actors will continue to influence the shape of the new international system as it emerges through the gradual construction of new rules and procedures (see *Internationalization*). Only a concerted effort to take account of these actors will pave the way for the major structural changes now being contemplated.

The benefits of such an approach to reform are seen most clearly in the United Nations practice of convening special international conferences and summits. By organizing such gatherings, the United Nations has created issue-based constituencies and provided conditions under which declarations are being reached that are akin to general referendums on transnational issues. The democratic nature of these conferences contributes to the legitimacy and effectiveness of the programmes of action they are producing. Through the series of global conferences on interlocking economic and social issues, the United Nations has been providing an ongoing democratic process through which a new international consensus on and framework for development can be built. The process has given new direction to the reform and strengthening of the United Nations development machinery, which has advanced considerably, particularly in the past year. This makes manifest the critical relationship between engaging with the new actors on the international scene and reforming the architecture for international relations, the third step in promoting democratization internationally.

5.10 The Architecture of the United Nations

By promoting democratization within its own architecture, the United Nations, as the world's largest and most inclusive organization of Governments, can make a major contribution to democratization at the international level. Since entering office, I have made democratization a guiding objective of Secretariat reform, as evidenced, for example, in the decentralization of decision-making that has already been enacted.

This reform needs to be advanced by reform in the United Nations intergovernmental machinery, for which democratization can also serve as a guiding objective. There is a clear need to move towards intergovernmental machinery that is less fragmented, better able to affect global forces and more open to civil society. There is also a clear need for an Organization in which all principal organs function in the balance and harmony contemplated by the Charter. This means an Organization which operates more consistently at the political level, with a clear sense of its comparative advantages and priorities, conscious of the linkages among all dimensions of its mission, and equipped with mandates and resources that are effectively matched.

The General Assembly is the embodiment of the United Nations universality and the cornerstone of representation and participation within the United Nations system, today bringing together 185 Member States on the basis of sovereign equality and democratic principles, along with several permanent observers. Improvements in the functioning of the Assembly have been a major focus of the Open-ended High-level Working Group on the Strengthening of the United Nations System. I see the Assembly performing on a continuing basis the role that the special international conferences have been playing in recent years, addressing comprehensively, and at the highest political level, the major global issues facing the international community, and fostering national and international commitments. Each session on a particular theme could consolidate and follow through on earlier meetings and set the agenda for work that lies ahead. The Assembly's role should be one of synthesis and overall policy assessment and coordination vis-à-vis the membership as well as the United Nations system.

The strengthening of the Economic and Social Council has been a long-standing item on the reform agenda. It received special attention in the Halifax Summit Communiqué of the Group of Seven major industrialized nations in June 1995[20] and has been considered over the past few years by two working groups. The General Assembly has acted, in its resolution 50/227 of May 24, 1996, to reinforce significantly the coordinating role of the Economic and Social Council. Equally important, in the resolution the General Assembly also instructed the Council to undertake further reviews of its functional and regional commissions and its expert groups. The resolution thus set the stage not only for greater balance in the functioning of the Assembly and the Council, but also for a further streamlining and strengthening of the intergovernmental machinery in the economic and social field. With a view towards the continuing revitalization of the Economic and Social Council, I see three priority requirements: more regular and formalized participation in the work of the Council by the new actors on the global scene; ministerial participation, and increasing involvement of the new actors, in the high-level segment; and a decision to bring the reforms initiated so far in relation to operational activities a step further, so as to enable the Economic and Social Council to exercise an effective role of governance over all the operational funds and programmes of the Organization.

Enhancing the General Assembly and the Economic and Social Council should help to correct the growing imbalance in the functioning, responsibilities and authority of those organs and of the Security Council. At the same time, the new international environment and the marked expansion in the level and scope of Security Council activity call for the reform of its membership, procedure and working methods, towards a more efficient, representative and open body.

The question of Security Council reform is the focus of ongoing debate in the General Assembly through its working group on the matter and other Council-related issues.[21] Member States have welcomed the positive steps taken thus far to improve the flow of information between the Council and the membership at large and to increase the participation of States not members of the Council, especially troop-contributing countries, in Council debates. Progress on the more complex and difficult issue of Security Council membership and voting procedures has been slow. However, the reports of the working group and the remarks made during the Special Commemorative Meeting of the General Assembly, held from October 22 to 24, 1995, reveal an emerging consensus on a number of important points. Most Member States seem to concur that the present size and composition of the Security Council are no longer representative of the general membership of the United Nations or of geopolitical realities. Bearing in mind the need for manageability, most also seem to agree that more effective, equitable and representative participation in the Security Council could be achieved by increasing the overall number of its seats. Once full consensus is reached, the question will ultimately be resolved by the Member States

through the processes set out in the Charter, as in 1965 when the membership of the Council was expanded from 11 to 15 by Charter amendment and the minimum number of votes needed for the Council to act was raised from 7 to 9.

The vision and the will required to bring about the changes currently being contemplated concerning the composition, the procedure and the working methods of the Security Council will not be easy to achieve, as balancing capacity to contribute with geo-political representation will be one of the most difficult obstacles to overcome, but transformation in some form may become essential for the future success of the Council and for the Organization itself. The achievement of those changes would be a major contribution to the realization of a United Nations Organization in which each element plays its full and proper role (see *Status and Role of the United Nations*).

A fundamental part of this effort must be to encourage and facilitate the use of the International Court of Justice (see *International Court of Justice*). The Charter envisions the Court as an integral component of the peacemaking apparatus of the United Nations as a whole, through its roles in arbitration and the peaceful settlement of disputes. In this regard, the establishment by the Security Council in 1994 of a United Nations Observer Group to monitor, at the request of the parties, the implementation of the Court's judgment in the case concerning the *Territorial Dispute (Libyan Arab Jamahiriya/Chad),*[22] has created an impressive precedent, which shows much promise for international law and its functioning in an increasingly integrated United Nations system.

All Member States should accept the general jurisdiction of the Court without exception; where domestic constraints prevent this, States should provide a list of the matters they are willing to submit to the Court. The dispute settlement clauses of treaties should permit the exercise of the Court's jurisdiction. The Security Council, under Articles 36 and 37 of the Charter, can recommend that Member States submit disputes to the International Court of Justice. I have on several occasions urged that the Secretary-General be authorized by the General Assembly, pursuant to Article 96 of the Charter, to turn to the Court for advisory opinions, providing a legal dimension to his diplomatic efforts to resolve disputes. Beyond this, the General Assembly should not hesitate to draw upon that same Article in referring to the Court questions concerning the consistency of resolutions adopted by United Nations bodies with the Charter of the United Nations.

With the International Court of Justice as one of its

principal organs, and as the world body of sovereign States, the United Nations provides the forum and the mechanism for the advancement of international law and jurisdiction (see *International Law*). This aspect of United Nations endeavours deserves wider recognition and attention from its Member States, not least because international law is another essential aspect of the United Nations architecture which holds enormous potential for democratization at the international level. International law promotes mutual respect among States and peoples, provides a rigorous analytical framework for approaching problems of mutual concern and offers a powerful basis for multilateral action. As such, it is a powerful tool for democratization. At the same time, democratization internationally will strengthen respect for international law. Democratic processes are designed to accommodate diversity. Democratic processes at the international level therefore provide the best way to reconcile the different legal systems of States. With continued democratization internationally, one can contemplate the eventual creation of a common international legal system, not to replace national legal systems, but to serve in certain kinds of cases as a core institution of democratic cooperation within and among States.

The establishment of the International Tribunal for the Law of the Sea, and the actions of the Security Council establishing international tribunals on war crimes committed in the former Yugoslavia and in Rwanda, are important steps towards the effective rule of law in international affairs. The next step must be the further expansion of international jurisdiction. The General Assembly in 1994 created an ad hoc committee to consider the establishment of a permanent international criminal court, based upon a report and draft statute prepared by the International Law Commission.[23] The Assembly has since established a preparatory committee to prepare a draft convention for such a court that could be considered at an international conference of plenipotentiaries.[24] This momentum must not be lost. The establishment of an international criminal court would be a monumental advance, affording, at last, genuine international jurisdictional protection to some of the world's major legal achievements. The benefits would be manifold, enforcing fundamental human rights and, through the prospect of enforcing individual criminal responsibility for grave international crimes, deterring their commission (see *International Criminal Laws*).

This area of United Nations activity, promoting democratization internationally, exemplifies the seamless connection between the United Nations roles in peace-building at the State level and in the maintenance of the international system. As is apparent in the diversity of new actors to be accounted for and in the changes in architecture to be addressed, this task of the United Nations has become increasingly complex in recent years. It amounts to nothing less than managing the construction of a new international system in an increasingly globalized environment, marked by a rapidly expanding array of non-State actors. It amounts to nothing less than peace-building at the international level, in the aftermath of the Cold War.

6. Conclusion: Toward an Agenda for Democratization

In June 1992, at the request of the Security Council, I issued "An Agenda for Peace,"[25] in which I emphasized the need for a comprehensive approach to peace and security, incorporating preventive diplomacy, peacemaking, peacekeeping and peace-building. I also drew the attention of the international community, in the report, to the reality that peace and development could no longer be regarded as separate undertakings (see *Peace and Social Development*).

In May 1994, at the request of the General Assembly, I produced a companion report to "An Agenda for Peace," entitled "An Agenda for Development,"[26] in which I presented development as a multidimensional enterprise that involves far more than economic growth. Development efforts have to be guided by a new understanding of the different dimensions of development, one of which is democracy as good governance.

The present paper has been motivated by the evident desire for democratization, not only within States, but also among them and throughout the international system. It has been rooted in the conviction that peace, development and democracy are inextricably linked. While recognizing that the relations between these three great concepts remain a matter of controversy, this paper, in a sense, completes my reflections on "An Agenda for Peace" and "An Agenda for Development" and is offered in the hope it will motivate intensified international debate on the two agendas and contribute to the necessary construction of a third essential agenda, an agenda for democratization.

At the heart of this debate will be the difficult questions, raised by democratization, of prioritization and timing among peace, development and democracy, questions which have been a constant concern throughout this paper. In some cases, peace, development and democracy have been pursued simultaneously. Such was the case in Cambodia, El Salvador and Mozambique, where United Nations efforts in support of democratization served as a link between conflict resolution, on the one hand, and reconstruction and development, on the other.

In other cases, however, the joint pursuit of these goals has proved more difficult than expected, at times contributing to political instability, social disarray and economic disappointment. These experiences have brought to the fore the main question of prioritization: whether democratization requires as a precondition the achievement within a nation of a certain level of peace and development.

Peace can be seen as essential, for without some degree of peace, neither development nor democracy is possible. Yet both development and democracy are essential if peace is to endure. The articulation between development and democracy is more complex. Experience has shown that development can take place without democracy. However, there is little to suggest that development requires an authoritarian regime and much to suggest that, over the long term, democracy is an essential ingredient for sustainable development. At the same time, development is an essential ingredient for true democracy so that, beyond formal equality, all members of society are empowered to participate in their own political system.

The present paper does not pretend to provide an easy answer to the questions of prioritization and timing that have arisen with the new wave of democratization. Rather, it seeks, by drawing out the lessons of experience, to help shape a platform of understanding upon which solutions can be built. Foremost among these lessons is that there is no one model of democratization or democracy suitable to all societies. The path adopted by each society depends upon its historical circumstances, economic situation, and the political will and commitment of its members.

Realism imposes prioritization upon States. Each State must be free to determine for itself its priorities for the welfare of its people. This prioritization, however, should only be applied over the short term and cannot serve States as a pretext for the neglect of any one of the three objectives of peace, development and democracy.

Given the potential dangers of democratization, a cautious approach is understandable and, in fact, necessary. However, with this caution must come the crucial recognition that these dangers can be reduced. Lessons learned about democratization over the past few years suggest ways in which democratization can

be undertaken more safely and effectively, and more certainly advanced. Democratization requires a comprehensive approach, addressing not only the holding of free and fair elections, but also the construction of a political culture of democracy and the development and maintenance of institutions to support the ongoing practice of democratic politics. Democratization must seek to achieve a balance between the institutions of the State and the institutions of civil society. In order to succeed over time, democratization within States must also be supported by a process of democratization among States and throughout the international system.

Democratization internationally brings with it its own set of problems of prioritization and timing. Democratization internationally, as this paper has sought to show, can be a contribution to peace and development. However, there is a concern that international efforts to deal with the outbreak of conflict may detract attention and resources away from development cooperation and democratization support. Between development and democratization the articulation is, here again, more complex. Democratization internationally can serve the cause of social equity and be a powerful tool for addressing the alarming socio-economic gap between North and South. At the same time, however, democratization internationally may itself require the reduction of the North-South gap, so that all States are empowered to participate in the international political system, to which they all belong. This latter concern goes beyond the question of resources available for State participation. If democratization internationally is to include the increased participation of new non-State actors, the fact that the vast majority of these actors today come from the North must be considered.

With its global mandate and as the world's most inclusive global forum, the United Nations role in democratization is, in a sense, to help States and the international community deal with the questions of prioritization and timing as they arise both nationally and internationally. Through the United Nations, the three great goals of peace, development and democracy can receive the comprehensive treatment they deserve.

The United Nations project in democratic international organization, begun some 50 years ago, has gained new momentum. Yet significant obstacles remain. The disruptions and distortions of recent decades must be overcome. The original understandings of 1945 must be restored and hard-won wisdom readily applied. Disillusion created by the manifest difficulties of creating a new international system must be surmounted. The wave of democratization must be seen in its full context, as a movement of global extent and requiring integration of all levels of world affairs.

While democratization must take place at all levels of human society—local, national, regional and global—the special power of democratization lies in its logic, which flows from the individual human person, the one irreducible entity in world affairs and the logical source of all human rights. At the same time that democratization will rely upon individual commitment to flourish, democratization will foster the conditions necessary for the individual to flourish. Beyond all the obstacles lie bright prospects for the future.

See also: *United Nations Governance; United Nations Peacekeeping Operations; United Nations and the Myth of the Unity of Mankind*

Notes ——————————————————

1. Charter of the United Nations, Article 1, paragraph 1.
2. Ibid., preamble.
3. Ibid., Article 1, paragraph 2, and Article 55.
4. Ibid., Article 1, paragraph 3, and Article 55.
5. Ibid., Article 2, paragraph 1.
6. General Assembly resolution 217 A (III).
7. Ibid., article 21, paragraph 3.
8. General Assembly resolution 1514 (XV).
9. Ibid., article 2.
10. Ibid., article 5.
11. General Assembly resolution 2200 A (XXI).
12. General Assembly resolution 48/131, para. 4.
13. A/49/713, annex II.
14. A/50/332.
15. A/51/512.
16. *Report of the United Nations Conference on Environment and Development, Rio de Janeiro, 3-14 June 1992*, vol. I, *Resolutions Adopted by the Conference* (United Nations publication, Sales No. E. 93. I. 8 and corrigendum), resolution 1, annex II.
17. Economic and Social Council resolution 1996/31.
18. A/51/402, annex
19. General Assembly resolution 217 A (III).
20. A/50/254-S/1995/501, annex I, paragraph 36.
21. Open-ended Working Group on the Question of Equitable Representation on and Increase in the Membership of the Security Council and Other Matters related to the Security Council.
22. *I. C. J. Reports* 1994, p. 6.
23. See *Official Records of the General Assembly, Forty-ninth Session, Supplement No. 10* (A/49/10), chap. II. B. I.
24. See ibid., *Fifty-first Session, Supplement No. 22*, vols. I and II.
25. A/47/277-S/24111.
26. A/48/935.

BOUTROS BOUTROS-GHALI

Détente

Détente, the French noun meaning relaxation, designates in diplomatic terminology a condition of reduced tensions and lowered levels of threat or conflict between two or more states. Policies of détente refer to those actions and agreements which are designed to reduce conflict and improve mutual relations. In contrast to entente, which suggests overlapping and common interests, policy coordination, and possibly alliance, détente does not necessarily imply shared interests beyond the mutual desire to avoid war, crises, and high levels of tensions and threat.

Historically, policies of détente have been accompanied by treaties or understandings which establish certain "rules of the game" to which states should adhere in conducting their mutual relations. These have delineated boundaries or spheres of influence, reinforced norms such as noninterference in other states' internal affairs, and enunciated general principles that would guide the conduct of diplomacy. A recent example would be the Camp David agreements and the subsequent Egypt-Israeli peace treaty (1979) which not only settled some territorial issues, but also prescribed modalities for conducting future Israeli-Egyptian relations.(see *Camp David Accords*)

The term détente, however, has been used primarily to describe Soviet-American-West European relations in the late 1960s and early 1970s. The governments of a number of North Atlantic Treaty Organization (NATO) (see *North Atlantic Treaty Organization (NATO)*) and Warsaw Pact members undertook numerous initiatives to try to reduce East-West conflict in general, and the possibilities of nuclear war in particular (see *East-West Conflict*). The Soviets, though acknowledging some of the commonly understood meanings of détente, emphasized instead concepts such as the "relaxation of tensions" and "peaceful coexistence." While these ideas are not incompatible with détente, Soviet and Western interpretations of their actual policy implications differed considerably.

The origins of East-West détente go back at least to the Cuban missile crisis of 1962, when the former Soviet Union and the United States came close to engaging in nuclear war. The dangers of that crisis compelled both sides to acknowledge that they shared a common interest in avoiding future confrontations that could result in escalation, and possibly in nuclear exchanges. Whatever the fundamental differences between the two Superpowers on philosophical questions and territorial issues, they recognized that their nuclear capabilities had reached the point where their use, should deterrence fail, would mean mutual devastation.

Following the dramatic events of October 1962, the two Superpowers negotiated a series of treaties and conventions that placed limited forms of control on some of the most dangerous manifestations of the Cold War (see *Cold War*). These included the establishment of the direct "hot line" between the White House and the Kremlin to make certain there can be instantaneous and clear communication between leaders in crisis situations; the treaty to ban atmospheric testing of nuclear devices; the Non-proliferation Treaty (see *Non-Proliferation Treaty (NPT)*); and numerous initiatives by the former Soviet Union to organize a Pan-European conference to settle outstanding issues on the Continent and to devise explicit "rules of the game" for the conduct of diplomatic relations.

The Nixon Administration in Washington (1968-75) raised détente to the status of official policy for the long-range management of Soviet-American relations. Henry Kissinger, the American Secretary of State during President Nixon's second term, articulated a theory (1974) that would provide guidelines for his diplomacy vis-à-vis the Soviet Union. He developed the hypothesis that the more an adversary is enmeshed in relationships that provide concrete rewards, the less likely it is to pursue adventurous and hostile policies. The United States negotiated a number of bilateral agreements with the Soviet Union in areas such as cultural relations, trade, scientific cooperation, and arms control, through which rewards were made potentially available to the Soviets. Should the Soviets fail to moderate their policies and in various way challenge American interests abroad, the rewards could be withdrawn. In brief, the theory held that a situation of increased Soviet-American interdependence could be manipulated in a manner to reduce threats, to complicate Soviet decision making in terms of raising the costs of hostile policies, and to demonstrate that advantages such as technology transfers and lucrative trade could be the reward for Soviet moderation.

The Soviet interpretation of peaceful coexistence (see *Peaceful Coexistence*) and relaxation of tensions was considerably different. While Secretary Brezhnev emphasized the necessity for peaceful relations with capitalist states in his speeches and Party con-

gress pronouncements, he and his subordinates repeatedly emphasized that peaceful coexistence did not mean any form of philosophical rapprochement between capitalism and socialism. It emphatically did not require abandonment of measures to promote the advance of socialism. Propaganda, agitation, assistance to fraternal parties, and material and moral support for national liberation movements and other revolutionary parties would continue as before. The role of the Soviet Union as the central inspiration and source of support for socialist and progressive forces around the world would not change. Peaceful coexistence, according to Soviet leaders' statements, meant only that the Soviet Union would promote friendly and mutually profitable relations with capitalist states in order to reduce the likelihood of direct confrontations and nuclear war (see *Marxist-Leninist Concepts of Peace and Peaceful Coexistence*). The Soviets saw nothing incompatible between the desire to improve diplomatic relations with the West, while at the same time engaging in their traditional revolutionary activities abroad. While they accepted American initiatives to create more interdependence, they never acknowledged that rewards and punishments could be manipulated successfully in order to change the main lines of traditional Soviet interventionary activities abroad. These diverging interpretations ultimately led to the collapse of détente.

The diplomatic negotiations launched in the decade of détente resulted in an impressive array of treaties, agreements, and accords, all designed to reduces risks and dangers associated with Cold War crises and nuclear weapons. There were in particular five important Soviet-American agreements that provided a framework of guidelines for the conduct of mutual relations and for reducing the growing arms competition. The Strategic Arms Limitation Talks (SALT) treaty of 1972 placed limits on the numbers of intercontinental ballistic missile (ICBM) launchers, and included an agreement to limit the deployment of antiballistic missile systems, thereby circumventing a new dimension of the arms race. At the May 1972 Nixon-Brezhnev summit meetings in Moscow, the two parties signed the Basic Principles Agreement which called for peaceful coexistence (a phrase the Americans would rather have avoided), and confirmed the parties' commitment to "prevent the development of situations capable of causing a dangerous escalation of their relations . . . ." They also agreed to exercise restraint in their mutual relations and to negotiate and settle differences by peaceful means. Most important—and notably ignored in their subsequent relations—the former Soviet Union and the United States acknowledged that "efforts to obtain unilateral advantages at the expense of the other . . . are inconsistent with the objectives" of maintaining peace and stability. At the summit meeting of June 1973, the two leaders signed a further document, the Agreement on the Prevention of Nuclear War, in which they reiterated their obligation to cooperate in crisis prevention, and to engage in consultations in dangerous situations. There was a further commitment to do everything possible to avoid nuclear war. The intent of both agreements was not only to collaborate to manage crises, but also to prevent them.

A further agreement was signed to put an end to harassment of naval exercises by each other's airplanes, and to avoid hazardous incidents at sea. However, the capstone of the détente process was the SALT II treaty which placed new ceilings on the numbers of strategic missile launchers and provided guidelines for the introduction of new weapons systems. The treaty did not require actual arms reductions, but its supporters claimed that its limits would prevent the Superpowers from indulging in an ever-more costly arms race. Although the terms of the treaty were generally adhered to by both parties, the document was never submitted to the United States Senate for approval and thus did not constitute a binding treaty.

There were, in addition, significant agreement between the former Soviet Union and other powers. Bilateral accords with France and Canada established the principle of consultations with their governments during diplomatic crises. The perennial issue of Berlin was satisfactorily resolved in the early 1970s (see *Ostpolitik*), and, finally, the long multilateral negotiations that led to the signing of the Final Act of the Conferences on Security and Cooperation in Europe (CSCE) in 1975 culminated in a significant undertaking to expand East-West relations in Europe (*see Helsinki Process*).

The Helsinki Final Act, as it has come to be known, included a statement of principle to guide mutual relations among the thirty-five participating states. These principles included the prohibition of interference in each other's internal affairs, of the use or threat of force to change existing states boundaries, and positive commitments to settle disputes and conflicts by peaceful means. The Final Act also designed "confidence-building" measures in the military realm, provided for mutual notification of military maneuvers and exercises involving more than 25,000 personnel, mutual exchange of observers at such exercises, and other provisions that would prevent any signatory from anticipating that an ordinary

military exercise was in fact an attempt to intimidate or to prepare for war. The Final Act also provided means for increasing East-West trade, communications, and cultural exchanges. The most contentious parts of the agreement touched upon issues of human rights, family reunification, and emigration.

The Final Act was the most comprehensive product of détente, and pointed in the direction of a considerable expansion of East-West contacts. Unfortunately, since it did not deal with the critical issues of military confrontation between the North Atlantic Treaty Organization (NATO) and the Warsaw Pact, it was destined to have only negligible influence on the overall character of East-West relations. Indeed, by emphasizing issues where fundamental philosophical incompatibilities persisted, such as human rights, the Final Act in some cases raised the level of conflict.

By the late 1970s the era of détente had come to an end. The major parties had signed a series of agreements, but they had not come to a common understanding regarding what forms of foreign policy behavior were appropriate to a regime of détente. The Americans assumed that détente defined the limits of interventionary behavior on a global basis (see *Intervention*). Despite the treaties and pronouncements prohibiting provocative challenges against the interests of the other state, and the agreements to consult in times of crisis, there was no explicit prohibition against the sorts of policies which the Soviets described as aid to fraternal countries and parties. In the mid-1970s the former Soviet Union intervened on behalf of revolutionary parties and regimes in Angola, Mozambique, Ethiopia, and the People's Democratic Republic of Yemen, culminating in the armed invasion of Afghanistan in December 1979. From the Western perspective, the latter action was fatal to détente. It demonstrated that whatever the Soviet undertakings on nuclear issues and on Pan-European relations, it would not hesitate to use armed force in other areas of the world.

From the Soviet point of view, détente or peaceful coexistence was seriously undermined by American and Western European efforts to intervene on behalf of human rights groups in the former Soviet Union, Czechoslovakia, and Poland. Although the question of human rights had become a matter of international scrutiny and monitoring, as provided for in the Helsinki Final Act, the Soviets and their allies insisted that the principle of noninterference in internal affairs overrode any concerns a foreign government might have with the way the socialist states deal with their populations. The issue remained at an impasse: Moscow and the governments of the other socialist states saw Western efforts on behalf of human rights as attempts to subvert their regimes.

Moreover, according to the Soviets, the United States never followed up on the Basic Principles Agreement, which had explicitly referred to the former Soviet Union as an equal to the United States. American administrations had apparently regarded the agreement as platitudinous, and never acknowledged publicly that the former Soviet Union had rights as an equal partner to become involved in all diplomatic problems on the international agenda. The Soviets, who had argued that détente was made possible by the rough military and diplomatic parity of the two Superpowers (the Americans could thus no longer resort to nuclear blackmail or intervene with impunity on the side of counter revolution in the Third World), complained that in fact the United States was not prepared to deal with them as an equal. Kissinger's deliberate exclusion of the former Soviet Union in Middle East negotiations, and American rapprochement with the People's Republic of China in the 1970s also challenged the Soviets. Throughout the 1970s, in the Soviet view, the United States reneged on the undertakings of the 1972 and 1973 summit meetings, and they believed that President Reagan's explicit policy of reestablishing American military paramountcy could not be reconciled with the rules of the game developed during the decade of détente.

Although vestiges of détente remained in the follow-up conferences to the CSCE (Belgrade 1978, Madrid 1981, Stockholm 1983), and some progress was made in developing military confidence-building measures, most of the official rules did not survive the 1970s. Afghanistan, the Solidarity uprising in Poland, and the continued buildup of Soviet military forces have as proof to most Western observers that the former Soviet Union shared no common interests with the West except the avoidance of nuclear war. In the last years of the Carter Administration and throughout President Reagan's first term, the vocabulary and actions of détente were formally jetisoned. American policy became increasingly confrontational, emphasizing a combination of tough rhetoric and a massive buildup of American military capabilities. The former Soviet Union, while still paying lip service to the notion of peaceful coexistence, displayed few of the forms of moderation anticipated by Dr. Kissinger.

Policies of détente, where there is a common understanding of the "rules of the game," may enhance peace and reduce conflict and irritations between states. However, where there is no common understanding or where vital interests remain fundamentally incompatible, treaties, conferences, declarations, and covenants such as those of the 1960s and 1970s will likely be insufficient to bring about more than a temporary improvement in relations. The essential ingredient for a successful policy of détente is genuine changes in the interests and objectives of the states involved, to the point where they are mutually compatible across a broad range of issues. While the détente of the 1970s had left a residue of arms control agreements and confidence-building measures in Europe, it will be remembered more for atmospherics than for any fundamental changes in the foreign behavior of the major powers.

See also: *International Conflicts, De-escalation of; Peaceful Coexistence; Security and Cooperation in Europe; Conflict Resolution, History of; East-West Conflict*

Bibliography

Aćimović L 1981 *Problems of Security and Cooperation in Europe.* Sijthoff and Nordhoff, Alphen an de Rijn

Andren N, Birnbaum K E (eds.) 1980 *Belgrade and Beyond: The CSCE Process in Perspective.* Sijthoff, Alphen an den Rijn

Brezhnev L I 1981 *Report of the CPSU Central Committee to the 26th Congress of the Communist Party of the Soviet Union and the Party's Tasks in the Fields of Domestic and Foreign Policy.* Crosscurrents Press, New York

Deporte A W 1975 *Europe Between the Superpowers.* Yale University Press, New Haven, Connecticut

Ferraris L G et al. 1975 *Report on a Negotiation: Helsinki-Geneva-Helsinki.* Sijthoff and Nordhoff, Alphen an den Rijn

George A et al. 1983 *Managing US-Soviet Rivalry: Problems of Crisis Prevention.* Westview, Boulder, Colorado

Griffiths W E 1978 *The Ostpolitik of the Federal Republic of Germany.* MIT Press, Cambridge, Massachusetts

Hyland W G *Soviet-American Relations: A New Cold War?* Rand Corporation, Santa Monica, California

Kissinger H 1974 Détente with the Soviet Union: The reality of competition and the imperative of cooperation, *Dept. State Bull,* 14 Oct 1974, Washington, DC

Kissinger H 1979 *The White House Years.* Little, Brown, Boston, Massachusetts

Lavigne M 1979 *Les Relations economiques est-ouest.* Presses Universitaires de France, Paris

Trofimenko H 1981 America, Russia, and the Third World. *Foreign Affairs* 59(5)

K. J. HOLSTI

Deterrence

When discussing deterrence it is important to distinguish between the theories of deterrence and the strategy of deterrence. The former pertains to the logical postulates of deterrence and the assumptions on which they are based. The latter is an attempt to apply deterrence to real world conflicts. Deterrence, in theory and practice, is an attempt to influence another actor's assessment of its interests. It seeks to prevent an undesired behavior by convincing the party who may be contemplating it that the cost will exceed any possible gain. Deterrence presupposes that decisions are made in response to some kind of rational cost-benefit calculus, that this calculus can be successfully manipulated from the outside, and that the best way to do this is to increase the cost side of the ledger. Different scholars have developed their own variants of deterrence theory. All of them, however, are based on these assumptions.

Another important distinction is between general and immediate deterrence (Morgan 1983). General deterrence is based on the existing power relationship and attempts to prevent an adversary from seriously considering any kind of military challenge because of its expected adverse consequences. Immediate deterrence is specific; it attempts to forestall an anticipated challenge to a well-defined and publicized commitment. Because cases of immediate deterrence are easier to identify, most research has sought to explain their outcomes. But analyses of immediate deterrence that ignore its relationship to general deterrence offer a biased assessment of its success rate and an incomplete picture of the conditions and processes that account for its outcome.

The strategy of deterrence has given rise to its own literature about how it is best accomplished. The first wave of this theory, almost entirely deductive in nature, was developed in the 1950s and 1960s by such scholars as Bernard Brodie (1959), William Kaufmann (1954), and Thomas Schelling (1966). Most of these works stressed the importance of imparting credibility to commitments and explored various mechanisms leaders could exploit toward this end. The literature of this period is often referred to as classical deterrence theory (Jervis 1979).

Some political scientists and historians consider deterrence an efficacious strategy. Huth and Russett (1984 and 1988) have compiled a highly controversial data set of alleged deterrence encounters and have used it to test hypotheses about successful immediate deterrence. Kenneth Waltz (1993) and John Gaddis (1997) maintain that general nuclear deterrence has kept the peace between the superpowers (see *Nuclear Deterrence, Doctrine of*).

From the beginning, deterrence theory and strategy has spawned critiques. The most interesting are those that evaluate deterrence strategy in light of empirical evidence from historical cases. The works of Milburn (1959), Snyder and Diesing (1977), George and Smoke (1974) and Lebow (1981) are representative. Milburn and George and Smoke argued that deterrence might be made more efficacious if threats of punishment were accompanied by promises of reward for acceptable behavior. George and Smoke and Snyder and Diesing sought to divorce from its Cold War context and root it in a less politically specific theory of initiation.

Empirical analyses of deterrence had implications for the postulates of deterrence theory. On the basis of their case studies, George and Smoke (1974) argued for a broader formulation of rational choice. They hoped that this would enable the theory to incorporate domestic political concerns and other factors affecting foreign policy behavior that deterrence theory had not previously taken into account.

Janice Gross Stein and Ned Lebow (Lebow 1981; Jervis, Lebow and Stein 1984; Lebow and Stein 1987) have developed a more extensive critique of immediate deterrence that has three interlocking components: the political, psychological, and practical. Based on the study of numerous historical cases they contend that political and practical factors interact with psychological processes to multiply the obstacles to successful prediction of state behavior and successful conflict management (see *Deterrence*).

The political component concerns the motivation behind foreign policy challenges. Deterrence is unabashedly a theory of opportunity. Adversaries are assumed to seek opportunities to make gains and pounce when they find them. Case studies of actual conflicts point to an alternative explanation for resorts to force, which Lebow and Stein term a theory of "need." Strategic vulnerabilities and domestic political needs often constitute incentives to use force. When leaders become desperate, they may resort to force even when the military balance is unfavorable and there are no grounds for doubting adversarial resolve. Deterrence may be an inappropriate and dangerous strategy in these circumstances. For if leaders are driven less by the prospect of gain than they are by the fear of loss, deterrent policies can provoke the very behavior they are designed to forestall by intensifying the pressures on the challenger to act.

The psychological component is also related to the motivation behind deterrence challenges. To the extent that policymakers believe in the necessity of challenging commitments of their adversaries, they become predisposed to see their objectives as attainable. When this happens, motivated bias can be pronounced and take the form of distorted threat assessments and insensitivity to warnings that the policies to which our leaders are committed are likely to end in disaster. Policymakers can convince themselves, despite evidence to the contrary, that they can challenge an important adversarial commitment without provoking war. Because they know the extent to which they themselves are powerless to back down, they expect their adversaries to accommodate them by doing so. Policymakers may also seek comfort in the illusion that their country will emerge victorious at little cost to itself if the crisis gets out of hand and leads to war. Deterrence can thus be defeated by wishful thinking.

The practical component of the Lebow and Stein critique highlights the distorting effects of cognitive biases and heuristics, political and cultural barriers to empathy, and the differing cognitive contexts the deterrer and would-be challengers are apt to use to frame and interpret signals. Problems of this kind are not unique to deterrence; they are embedded in the very structure of international relations. They nevertheless constitute particularly severe impediments to deterrence because of a deterrer's need to understand the world as it appears to the leaders of a would-be challenger in order to manipulate effectively its cost-benefit calculus. Failure to do this accurately can result in deterrent policies that actually succeed in making the proscribed behavior more attractive to a challenger.

The first two components of this critique challenge core assumptions of deterrence theory. The third component is directed more at the strategy of deterrence, but it also has implications for deterrence theory. If the strategy of deterrence is so often unsuccessful because of all of the practical difficulties associated with its implementation, then the theory of deterrence must be judged a poor guide to action.

For many years, empirical research on deterrence, whether qualitative or quantitative, drew primarily on cases of immediate, conventional deterrence. Beginning in the late 1980s evidence on Soviet and Chinese foreign policy began to become available and it became possible for the first time to reconstruct critical Soviet-American and Sino-American deterrence encounters, and to make some observations about the role of general deterrence in these relationships.

Research on the Cuban missile crisis, the Soviet-American crisis arising out of the 1973 Middle East War, and the two Taiwan Straits crises of 1954 and 1958 tend to confirm the findings of critics of conventional deterrence. So does research on general nuclear deterrence. Zhang (1992), Hough (1994), and Lebow and Stein (1994) find that deterrers do worry about their reputations and the credibility of commitments, but that the targets of deterrence rarely question their adversary's resolve. For this reason efforts to communicate resolve were often perceived as a gratuitously aggressive behavior and sometimes provoked the kind of challenges they were designed to prevent. In doing so, the strategy of deterrence helped to provoke the Cuban missile and Taiwan Straits crises and to prolong the Soviet-American and Sino-American conflicts.

Based on the study of Soviet-American relations in the Khrushchev and Brezhnev eras, Lebow and Stein offer the following conclusions about the role of general nuclear deterrence: a) Leaders who try to exploit real or imagined nuclear advantages for political gain are not likely to succeed; b) Credible nuclear threats are very difficult to make; c) Nuclear threats are fraught with risk; d) Strategic build-ups are more likely to provoke than to restrain adversaries because of their impact on the domestic balance of political power in the target state; e) Nuclear deterrence is robust when leaders on both sides fear war and are aware of each other's fears.

War-fighting, MAD, and finite deterrence all mistakenly equate stability with specific arms configurations. More important than the distribution of nuclear capabilities, or leaders' estimates of relative nuclear advantage, is their judgment of an adversary's intentions. The Cuban missile crisis was a critical turning point in Soviet-American relations because it convinced Kennedy and Khrushchev, and some of their most important advisors as well, that their adversary was as committed as they were to avoiding nuclear war. This mutually acknowledged fear of war made the other side's nuclear capabilities less threatening and paved the way for the first arms control agreements (see *Arms Control, Evolution of*).

By no means did all American and Soviet leaders share this interpretation. Large segments of the national security elites of both superpowers continued to regard their adversary as implacably hostile and willing to use nuclear weapons. Even when Brezhnev and Nixon acknowledged the other's fear of war, they used the umbrella of nuclear deterrence to compete vigorously for unilateral gain. Western militants did not begin to change their estimate of

Soviet intentions until Gorbachev (see Nobel Peace Prize Laureates: *Mikhail S. Gorbachev*) made clear his commitment to ending the arms race and the Cold War.

The drawbacks to deterrence that we identify do not lead us to conclude that it should be discarded. Rather, scholars and statesmen must recognize the limits and inherent unpredictability of deterrence and make greater use of other strategies of conflict prevention and management.

See also: *Conflict: Inherent and Contingent Theories; Cold War; East-West Conflict*

Bibliography

Brodie B 1959 The anatomy of deterrence. *World Politics* 11(January)
Chang G H 1990 *Friends and Enemies: The United States, China, and the Soviet Union, 1948-1972.* Stanford University Press, Stanford
Gaddis J L 1997 *We Now Know: Rethinking Cold War History.* Oxford University Press, Oxford
George A L, Smoke R 1974 *Deterrence in American Foreign Policy: Theory and Practice.* Columbia University Press, New York
Herring E 1995 *Danger and Opportunity: Explaining International Crisis Outcomes.* Manchester University Press, Manchester
Holloway D 1994 *Stalin and the Bomb.* Yale University Press, New Haven
Huth P, Russett B 1984 What makes deterrence work? Cases from 1900 to 1980. *World Politics* 36
Huth P, Russett B 1988 Deterrence Failure and Crisis Escalation. *World Politics* 32
Hopf T 1994 *Peripheral Visions: Deterrence Theory and American Foreign Policy in the Third World, 1965-1999.* University of Michigan Press, Ann Arbor
Huth P, Russett B 1984. What makes deterrence work? Cases from 1900 to 1980. *World Politics* 36(4)
Jervis R 1979 Deterrence theory revisited. *World Politics* 31
Jervis R, Lebow R N, Stein J G 1985 *Psychology and Deterrence.* John Hopkins University Press, Baltimore
Kaufmann W W 1954 *The Requirements of Deterrence.* Center of International Studies, Princeton
Lebow R N 1981 *Between Peace and War: The Nature of International Crisis.* John Hopkins University Press, Baltimore
Lebow R N, Stein J G 1987a Beyond deterrence. *J. Social Issues* 4
Lebow R N, Stein J 1994 *We All Lost the Cold War.* Princeton University Press, Princeton
Mercer J 1996 *Reputation and International Politics.* Cornell University Press, Ithaca
Milburn T W 1959 What constitutes effective deterrence? *J. Conflict Resolution* 3
Morgan P M 1983 *Deterrence: A Conceptual Analysis*, rev. edn. Sage Library of Social Science, Beverly Hills
Richardson J L 1994 *Crisis Diplomacy: The Great Powers since the Mid-Nineteenth Century.* Cambridge University Press, Cambridge
Schelling T 1966 *Arms and Influence.* Yale University Press, New Haven
Tetlock P E 1987 Testing deterrence theory: Some conceptual and methodological issues. *J. Social Issues* 43(4)
Waltz K 1993 The Stability of a Bipolar World. *Int'l Security* 18
Zhang S H 1992 *Deterrence and Strategic Culture: Chinese-American Confrontations, 1949-1958.* Cornell University Press, Ithaca

RICHARD NED LEBOW

Development: Cultural Dimensions

Perhaps the most important new phenomenon in the international approach to, and views on, culture and cultural policies since the Eurocult Conference in 1970 is that the notion of cultural development is no longer looked upon as sufficient for determining events and tasks, but it is rather the cultural dimension of development that is used as a comprehensive fundamental dimension.

1. A New Concept of Development

The change is not simply a reversal of the order of terms, but there is a new concept that apparently underlies the new term. On studying the cultural dimension of universal social development, culture itself has to be studied from a wider and more general angle. This change of approach meets the requirements of our age, corresponding to the spirit of the 1970s and, presumably, also of the 1980s, that is, of the decades that have—more imperatively than ever—put the development of the whole of humankind into the focus of the public thinking of the world. The evolution of the Third World, concern with the problems of the developing and of the poorly developed countries, their increasing role in international politico-economic life, and the economic difficulties threatening the further progress of developed countries—all these problems together indicate that one of the most important tasks of the human world is to ensure the possibility of further development in a form that offers genuine possibilities for further development even to the most backward countries.

Development interpreted in this sense is, naturally, a very complex notion incorporating a number of serious subproblems. Several factors are to be distinguished: first of all economic, social, political, and cultural development, that is, factors that are inseparably interconnected. The indispensable role of culture has become more and more apparent in this system of factors. Many economists and planning experts thought initially that development depended merely on creating appropriate economic conditions, yet in recent decades the view is gaining ground that economic growth cannot be explained by economic causes alone. There exists a "residuum" that is inexplicable by using merely economic arguments: the source of this residual part is culture, the "human factor," the "human capital."

The recognition of the role of "human capital" is, naturally, not the product of the twentieth century alone. This idea emerged with particular emphasis through economists who tried to find out how a nation could fight its way out of backwardness. One of these economists in the nineteenth century was Friedrich List who emphasized that the welfare of a nation did not depend merely on what it produced but also on how it did it, that is, under what cultural conditions and with how much knowledge and organization. Another was the Hungarian Zoltán Széchenyi who, in the first half of the nineteenth century, fought hard for the progress of the Hungarian people and who stressed the decisive role of the "multitude of educated human brains" as a factor equal to the development of economic life.

We can therefore say that in general the emphasis upon the cultural dimension of development was fed by two great ideas, tasks, or programs: the liquidation of backwardness and the practical implementation of democracy.

2. General Implications

The development of culture exerts its impact upon general social and economic development through several large "linkage systems." Culture powerfully affects the evolution of the concrete situation of the following factors:

(a) The capacities of the workers in performing labor processes,

(b) The state of general organization of labor and production,

(c) The evolution of processes of innovation and adaptation to the new,

(d) The development of a mode of life, of a lifestyle, including that of the individual's relation to work,

(e) Consumers' habits,

(f) Free time according to the wider interpretation of "leisure,"

(g) Growing awareness of our relation to the community, to society, and of "identity" with society.

These organic and fundamental links penetrate all sectors of economic life. In other words, socio-economico-cultural development is to be handled as a unity wherein the various branches are merely partial ingredients.

In times of economic growth it is important to ensure that culture has its appropriate share in universal development for the sake of future evolution. When growth slackens or stops, culture runs the risk of getting into a more unfavorable situation than is necessary. This, however, would be a short-sighted policy because its detrimental consequences will manifest themselves later in a serious form. One cannot strive to develop every field of culture in a significant degree yet—without permitting any regression from the levels achieved—we have to determine the most important tasks that deserve exceptional support and create new resources by regrouping forces, by developing cultural democracy, and by an emphatic development of the cultural activities of the community.

3. Implications for Peace

The realization of the role of culture does not only determine cultural policy in the strict sense of the term but also has a wide impact on the whole of social life. Culture has a predominant function in achieving and maintaining peace. The relationship is a reciprocal one: the development and the evolution of culture does not only require peace but also orientates millions of people toward peace, while at the same time peace promotes people's inclination to acquire cultural values. And the more solid are the foundations of peace, the stronger its stimulative effect.

The internationalism of culture acts in the same direction. The culture of every country, of every nation, develops under national conditions, yet the universal values in it become international, that is, suitable for interpretation and assimilation by other nations. In the course of the past centuries formerly isolated cultural regions have become so closely interlinked that today we have good reasons to speak about world culture, including world literature, and world science. International cultural, scientific, and artistic life, as well as the permanent and organic exchange of cultural values, have become a reality. This process is one of the most important manifestations of peaceful coexistence and cooperation, a consolidating factor of preserving peace in the world.

See also: *Cosmopolitanism; Cultural Democracy; Cultural Roots of Peace*

IVÁN VITÁNYI

DIE WAFFEN nieder!

Die Waffen nieder! [Lay Down Your Arms!] by Baroness Bertha von Suttner, published in 1889, was called "*The Uncle Tom's Cabin* of the peace movement." Tolstoy wrote to compliment her: "The abolition of slavery was preceded by a famous novel written by a woman . . . May God grant that the abolition of war will follow on your novel."

Such was not to be the case, but the novel was timely, it struck a responsive chord among legions of readers, it had its converts, and it brought the author into active participation in the young international peace movement. It remains a historic document of prime importance, evidencing the growing consciousness of war's inconsistency with the increasing physical unification of the world and with the general belief in progress.

The Baroness was a well-known writer in the German-speaking world where she had already published novels of social criticism and studies on current problems, which showed the influence of Darwin, Spencer, and Buckle. She had come to believe that "war was an institution handed down to us by the barbarians and to be removed by civilization," when she learned "by accident" that there was a peace society in England that was working to that very end. She decided to make her contribution to the cause by writing a novel of a woman who lost her beloved through war.

Following the example of her library idol, Emile Zola (see *Zola, Emile*), the Baroness prepared herself to describe realistically the battlefields of the wars between 1859 and 1870-71 by examining the reports of army surgeons and Red Cross workers. What had been a theoretical opposition to war now became a passionate condemnation, and through the pages of the novel she conveyed both.

Central to the theme is a love story, modelled on Suttner's own happy marriage, and her husband sat for the portrait of the hero. Martha von Tilling, who tells the story, is, like the Baroness herself, an Austrian aristocrat, who is led through a series of tragic circumstances designed to highlight the opposition of the destructiveness of war to the beauties of love. The horrors of war are set in counterpoint to well-worn pronouncements on the military virtues, while the petty origins of the wars that brought such suffering are mockingly laid bare in satirical narration of diplomatic history. Interwoven throughout are dialogues on the merits and disadvantages of war, with the opponents given the benefit of Suttner's favorite philosophers and writers, while the defenders are unthinking traditionalists.

She sent the manuscript for serialization to magazine editors who had been asking her for material, only to receive rejection notices with comments such as "it would offend many of our readers." The Baroness finally prevailed on the publisher of her earlier work to issue an edition of 1,000 copies. These were quickly snapped up and there had to be new printings—in the first 15 years, 37 times in Germany alone. When the last popular edition was published in Germany in 1914 in 200,000 copies, the novel had been translated into 16 languages. It has been estimated that it reached altogether a total of more than one million readers.

As a result of this unexpected success, the Baroness, who had thought to serve the peace movement only by her pen, now became one of its international leaders. (see *Peace Movements of the Nineteenth Century*). The novel recruited supporters, including most of the members of Sutter's new Austrian Peace Society, and also Alfred Hermann Fried, a young publisher in Berlin, who became her closest collaborator. Her friend, Alfred Nobel, wrote to congratulate her in a typically witty turn of phrase, saying that she should not declare "Lay Down Your Arms!" because "you make use of weapons yourself, and your weapons—the charm of your style and the nobility of your ideas—have a far greater range than the hellish weapons of war." This started Nobel on the course that led to the establishment of the Nobel Peace Prize (see *Nobel Peace Prizes*).

What made *Die Waffen nieder!* such a phenomenal success? Everybody loves a love story, and this one is set in circles of high society in Vienna, Berlin, and Paris, a milieu remote and fascinating to so many of the novel's readers. It is a very human story, told in the first person with authentic detail by the author who herself moved in those circles, and whose battlefield descriptions, based on careful research, have the ring of truth. Indeed, many readers were so convinced that the story of Martha von Tilling was actually the life story of the Baroness herself that they were surprised to learn that the Baroness von Suttner had not been executed by the Paris Communards in 1871.

To the sophisticated reader today, the novel seems too sentimental, the dialogue tedious, and most of the characters shallow. Artistically, it was no work of high literary quality. Nor was *Uncle Tom's Cabin* for that matter. Each of these propagandistic novels came just at the right historical moment to evoke such a remarkable response.

Suttner's readers, for the most part, were willing to listen to her message, clothed as it was in an interesting story, but they were not stirred to action against war. In 1914, when the Baroness died, the peace movement was still a small movement of little influence. All too soon the horrors of the world wars of this century would dwarf into insignificance the inhumanities of wars past that the Baroness had described so well.

The novel remains, however, a testament to the life work of a great woman, who, almost from the moment when she wrote the words of Martha von Tilling's son on the last page of the novel, devoted all her efforts to the purpose she has him formulate: "the ennobling of humanity."

See also: *Nobel Peace Prizes; Tolstoy, Leo;* Nobel Peace Prize Laureates: *Bertha von Suttner; Alfred Fried*

Bibliography ————————————————

Braker R 1991 *Weapons of Women Writers. Bertha von Suttner's "Die Waffen nieder!" as Political Literature in the Tradition of Harriet Beecher Stowe's "Uncle Tom's Cabin."* New York

Kelly A 1991 Film as antiwar propaganda. Lay down your arms (1914). *Peace & Change: A Journal of Peace Research* 16

Suttner B von 1889 *Die Waffen nieder! Eine Lebensgeschichte* Dresden [1892 *"Ground Arms!" The Story of a Life.* Chicago, Illinois; 1894 *Lay Down Your Arms: The Autobiography of Martha von Tilling,* 2nd edn, London (reprinted 1972 Garland Library of War and Peace, New York)]

Suttner B von 1907 How I Wrote, "Lay Down Your Arms." *Among the World's Peacemakers.* New York, (reprinted 1972 Garland Library of War and Peace, New York)

IRWIN ABRAMS

Diplomatic Recognition

When two governments exchange ambassadors, they engage in diplomatic recognition of their respective states and of the regimes ruling in the states. So long as governments recognize each other, they can engage in normal diplomacy in the family of nations.

New nation-states as well as revolutionary regimes coming to power in long-established countries are, therefore, understandably eager to secure diplomatic recognition on a wide basis. But various considerations often delay diplomatic recognition of such states.

Methods for according international recognition are not firmly established under international law. Recognition implies that a state can and will abide by international law and thus can be a party to a lawsuit. The declarative theory of recognition argues that states have rights before they are recognized, such as the right of self-defense and the right to organize their own political systems as they wish; thus, recognition simply means an acceptance of the personality of a state (Hackworth 1940 pp. 166-68). The constitutive theory argues that a state's rights under international law begin with diplomatic recognition from other countries; the quick recognition of Israel by the United States in 1948 is an example of the application of this theory, as the United States was eager to claim that any aggression against Israel would be a violation of international law.

One problem with the constitutive theory is that unrecognized states might be free to violate international law. A second problem is that it is unclear how many older states must extend diplomatic recognition in order for a new state or regime to be considered a member of the family of nations. The question of individual versus collective recognition is therefore raised.

When the Bolsheviks unseated the czardom of Imperial Russia in 1917, many countries refused to extend diplomatic recognition to the new regime. The United States, similarly, has denied diplomatic recognition to new governments in Latin America so as to encourage dissidents to continue internal strife until a more "legitimate" regime could establish itself. In 1932 this legitimacy principle, as a part of the constitutive theory of recognition, was elevated to the level of a formal "doctrine." United States Secretary of State Henry Stimson refused to recognize the state of Manchukuo, established in 1931 by Japan in Manchuria, on the grounds that the new government had been set up in violation of international law. Known as the Stimson Doctrine, the League of Nations subsequently adopted a similar position, and only El Salvador, Germany, Hungary, Italy, and Japan exchanged ambassadors with Manchukuo.

In the case of individual recognition, a government decides for itself when and whether to exchange ambassadors with another government. Sometimes negotiations are conducted in third-country locations to resolve any problems concerning unsettled claims before recognition is accorded. The establishment of Brunei as an independent state in 1984 was followed by general individual recognition throughout the world, for example.

In the case of collective recognition, a state becomes a member of the world polity by an act of the international community as a whole. While the Treaty of Versailles extended collective recognition to the new state of Czechoslovakia in 1919, the League of Nations denied admission—and thus collective recognition—to Liechtenstein in 1920 on the basis that the small state had contracted out some of the attributes of sovereignty (customs, diplomatic representation, postal and telecommunication services) to other countries.

Some efforts to accord collective recognition have been attempted by regional blocs of states. Diplomatic recognition of the Palestine Liberation Organization (PLO) by the Arab states is one such effort.

One authority on international law has enumerated a list of all members of the international community as well as 22 "entities of doubtful or unusual legal status" (Bishop 1971 pp. 330-33). Between 1971 and 1984 the status of 11 of these entities was so clarified that they would probably not appear on his list today. Although Berlin is included as one of the doubtful 22, he does not list Germany.

Small and Singer (1982 pp. 47-50) list 176 members of the interstate system between 1816 and 1980. One of their criteria for system membership is that a state must be recognized by two major powers (Britain and France before 1920, any two thereafter) (p. 40). After 1920 they add a second criterion—membership in the League of Nations or United Nations (p. 41). But they include the two Koreas, and they exclude Byelorussia and the Ukraine (members) on the basis of a third criterion—whether the country controls its own foreign policy (p. 42).

In earlier attempts to list members of the international system, Singer and Small (1966) developed a scale of "status" or "rank" for each member of the world community. Giving three points to every ambassador assigned to a country, two points for missions headed by ministers (or ministers-resident or envoys), and one point for diplomatic representation only by a *chargé d'affaires*, they find that England and France topped the list between 1817 and 1879; Germany replaced England from 1884 to 1894, and the United States first appeared in the top two in 1909. Their effort was restricted to measuring a state's international prestige, it could also be used for other purposes, such as determining at what point individual recognitions have become the collective will of the international community.

See also: *Ambassadors*

Bibliography ————————————————————

Bishop W W Jr 1971 *International Law*, 3rd edn. Little, Brown, Boston, Massachusetts
Hackworth G H 1940-44 *Principles of International Law*. Government Printing Office, Washington, DC
Singer J, Small M 1966 The composition and status ordering of the international system: 1815-1940. *World Politics* XVIII
Small M, Singer J D 1982 *Resort to Arms: International and Civil Wars, 1816-1980*. Sage, Beverly Hills, California

MICHAEL HAAS

Disarmament and Development

Within the United Nations (UN) and its related organ, the Conference on Disarmament (CD), the attempt to establish an institutional linkage between disarmament and development has a long history. It was first raised by countries in the South, but the principle has since found widespread support within the UN membership, both North and South. As early as 1950 a draft resolution was submitted by India to the General Assembly which recommended the establishment of a peace fund for development, to be financed by the savings from disarmament. Since then there has been a plethora of proposals, both on the principle and the detail of establishing such a link.

The examination of such a linkage began formally within the UN in 1960. A resolution of the General Assembly (Resolution no. 1516 (XV)) asked the Secretary-General to examine the economic and social consequences of disarmament. It requested an examination of the effects at a national level, within different economic systems and in countries at differing levels of development, the likely effects upon demand, world trade, and the possible structural imbalances which would be caused within and between nations following disarmament.

The request for this study followed the adoption during the previous (14th) session of the General Assembly of General and Complete Disarmament as the fundamental goal of future disarmament initiatives and negotiations. In this respect the request to the Secretary-General was an attempt to promote this goal through planning and policy prescription. It was a policy-related document in two senses. First, it was an examination of the likely effects of disarmament on the world economy; adverse effects and distortions had to be predicted and ways of overcoming them worked out in advance. Second, it was an attempt to counterbalance the negative aspects of armament with a positive alternative—"the utilization of resources released by disarmament for the purpose of economic and social development, in particular of the under-developed countries" (General Assembly Resolution no. 1516 (XV)). This was based upon a common sense equation; the enormous amount of the world's resources which are spent on armaments are a waste and would be better spent on development efforts.

This, in essence, has remained the motive for establishing an institutional link between disarmament and development within the UN. The political starting point of the debate was the basic premise that, in the words of Inga Thorsson (the former Swedish disarmament minister and key architect of the debate), "it is wrong to squander resources on armaments while the basic needs of so many people remain unmet." Fundamental to the belief that disarmament and development can be intertwined is the assumption that throughout the world, but particular-

ly in the North, military expenditure is too high, individual countries are "overarmed," and a reallocation of resources would improve rather than degrade the prevailing system of international security. Furthermore, the creation of a link between disarmament and development was also intended to create a "disarmament dividend" which was designed to ensure that the resources released by the disarmament process would be directed toward social and economic development, particularly in developing nations.

This same formula can be seen in almost all other United Nations reports on the subject. *The Economic and Social Consequences of Disarmament,* published in 1962, concluded that only a fraction of arms spending need be reallocated to have a significant beneficial effect upon development. A 1972 report entitled *Economic and Social Consequences of the Arms Race and of Military Expenditure* stated that major disarmament measures would "make a fundamental change in the prospects for economic and social development." Another report in the same year called *Disarmament and Development* struck a less enthusiastic chord when it concluded that "national and international efforts to promote development should neither be postponed or allowed to lag merely because disarmament is slow."

This note of caution stemmed from the fact that during the 1970s the UN had made a formal link between the Second Development Decade and the First Disarmament Decade (UN General Assembly Resolution No. 2026 (XXIV)), a link which was repeated for the 1980s (UN Resolution No. 35/46). Whilst it was hoped that the linkage would provide a stimulus for disarmament and the reduction of military expenditure it was also necessary to ensure that slow progress in disarmament should not become an excuse for lackluster efforts to achieve development. On the positive side of the coin, the linking of disarmament and development made the case for each more persuasive. Obversely, however, the UN approach took no account of the adverse effect of the existing pattern and nature of armament upon development efforts. Outside the UN system, few took the disarmament and development issue seriously except at the moral level.

The acceptance of the link between armament and underdevelopment was the major change in emphasis which came with the most recent and thorough UN report on the subject, *The Relationship between Disarmament and Development*, published in 1982. It has become known as the Thorsson Report—Inga Thorsson chaired the group which compiled the report, based upon the commissioned studies of a group of experts. The report concentrates upon a substantiation of the global opportunity cost of armament and concludes that

> the world can either continue to pursue the arms race with characteristic vigour, or it can move consciously and with deliberate speed towards a more sustainable world order. *It cannot do both* . . . . The arms race and underdevelopment are not two problems; they are one. They must be solved together or neither will ever be solved. (emphasis added)

To this end the report presents a series of alternative scenarios up to the year 2000 which stress the likely adverse effects upon development of continuing with the present arms race.

The Thorsson Report takes the establishment of a New International Economic Order (NIEO) (see *New International Economic Order*) as the basis for future development in developing nations. Central to the NIEO is a new international system which focuses in particular upon the inequalities between North and South. Thorsson identifies on two levels the importance of disarmament to the establishment of a NIEO. First, disarmament would permit the creation of an international security regime based upon the principles of cooperation and mutual accommodation between states to replace the present system which works so much to the disadvantage of the weaker states. Long-term security interests, she argues, would be far better served by such a change. Second, disarmament is important because of the range of key resources it would release. Many commentators have argued that the arms race stifles economic growth because it competes for resources, particularly in land, minerals, and energy which are then directed into unproductive areas (see *Economics of Disarmament: Certain Premises*). Equally important is that research and development efforts, upon which growth and progress depend, are dominated by the military organizations of the rich countries. The example of the arms trade is a case in point. Whilst a high level of technology is transferred from North to South, the skills and opportunities to achieve innovation in technology are not. In this instance at least the technology gap between North and South is becoming wider.

Another significant inclusion in the Thorsson Report is a substantial discussion on arms conversion (see *Arms Conversion*); the redeployment of the resources, skills, and capacity currently utilized by the defense industries to socially useful production. The importance of conversion in this context is a firm recognition of the industrial and economic dislocation which would occur in the wake of disarmament (see *Economics of Disarmament and Conversion*). As with the earlier UN reports, the aim is to anticipate and circumvent objections and areas of resistance to a reversal of the arms race.

But, the fundamental failing of the Thorsson Report echoes the failings of its predecessors—the burden of the arms race is still exclusively focused upon the North. To the extent that the individual and aggregated defense expenditures of the developed countries far exceed those of the developing countries, this emphasis is understandable. But, at the same time, the exclusion of developing countries' military expenditure ignores a significant factor which makes the link between disarmament and development so vital. This is the negative effect which past and existing levels of military expenditure (and by implication militarization) in developing countries have had upon nation building in general and the direction and pace of development in particular. Certainly, the report does consider the adverse effects of a hostile strategic environment, actual or perceived, and the resultant diversion of resources away from development. But, no consideration is given to the political and economic effects at the domestic level resulting from a high level of militarization and the inevitable effects upon the nature and direction of development (see *Militarism and Militarization*). But it would be wrong to assume that this omission is an oversight. In effect what has been left unstated is the result of the inherent limitations of what can be achieved from the UN system. In every area of the UN's work for disarmament, the member countries tend to block, frustrate, and filibuster when negotiations reach the matters of substance.

A common theme running through all efforts to link disarmament with development has been the attempt to establish some form of institutional arrangement for the reallocation of resources released by disarmament. These proposals have most commonly taken the form of a fund for development to be financed from the resources released by disarmament. In addition to the first proposal, which came from India in 1950, there have been many others. In 1955 the French proposed an International Fund for Development and Mutual Assistance—individual states would reduce their military spending by a percentage which would increase every year. It was, therefore, a proposal to achieve disarmament through the reduction of military budgets. One significant feature of the French proposal was the stipulation that 75 percent of the funds released would be spent in the donor country.

A Soviet proposal made in 1956 and repeated with more detail in 1958 suggested a special fund for development assistance. As a starting point, the Soviets suggested that the United States, the former Soviet Union, the United Kingdom, and France should reduce their military spending by l0-15 percent and should invite other countries to do the same. In 1958 Brazil proposed an Industrial Conversion and Economic Development Fund which would receive not less than 20 percent of the resources released through disarmament. In 1973 the UN General Assembly adopted a resolution calling for a reduction of 10 percent in the military budgets of the permanent members of the Security Council, with other major spenders urged to participate; 10 percent of that reduction would then be allocated to development efforts. This was initially seen as a one-off reduction in the military spending of the states involved (General Assembly Resolution 3039 A (XXVIII)).

There have been many other such proposals in recent years. The one which received the greatest attention in the Thorsson Report was a French proposal made at the First Special Session of the UN General Assembly on Disarmament (1978) to establish an International Disarmament Fund for Development which would be managed by a new specialist UN agency. It was further suggested that this agency in itself would be a concrete way of emphasizing the link between disarmament and development. Elaborations on this proposal suggested that the major contributors to the fund should be the most developed and largest military spenders whilst the recipients should be the least developed and smallest military spenders. Furthermore, the proposal envisaged an initial, catalytic endowment of US $1 billion to the fund. It was the French proposal which the Thorsson Report considered the most appealing. The endowment in itself would greatly aid the development efforts of the poorest countries. But behind this enthusiasm lay an acceptance that the "disarmament dividend" approach suffered from an obvious failing—a distinct lack of disarmament. Furthermore, the various proposals have not been encouraged by any attempts at unilateral action.

The Thorsson Report also studied two other possible approaches. First, voluntary contributions could play an important role—many of the expert studies upon which the report was based and the creation of the UN World Disarmament Campaign were financed in this way. The second approach was a tax on defense spending to finance such a fund. The Brandt report, *North-South: A Programme for Survival*, published in 1980, suggests a new world development fund to be financed out of an automatic tax upon military spending and the arms trade. But the report is skeptical about this second possibility, not least because it would depend upon a continuation, rather than a cessation, of the arms race. In sum the report regards the disarmament dividend approach as the most attractive proposal, despite its failings.

The undoubted quality of the Thorsson Report is marred by a prescriptive conclusion which has clear limitations. The author herself admits as much when she reflects that, "at a time when progress on disarmament and development issues is minimal and seemingly beset by major differences in viewpoint, conflicting interests and lack of political impetus, proposals for a new disarmament fund for development, which would link the two issues, seems audacious . . . ." Furthermore, the level of enthusiasm for the linking of disarmament and development issue displayed during the two Special Sessions on disarmament in 1978 and 1982 notwithstanding, the issue has remained marginal to both thinking and action in mainstream development and to the conduct of disarmament and arms control negotiations.

It has never been difficult to criticize the foundations upon which the disarmament and development debate is based. In all too many instances the key debating points seemed broad, pious, and occasionally irrelevant. Certainly, a considerable amount of energy and effort has gone unrewarded and in all likelihood this will continue to be the case. The vision of the major military powers forgoing successive generations of armaments and directing the resources saved into funds for Third World development is unequivocally utopian. For both now and the foreseeable future, disarmament—as opposed to armament limitation or control—is not on the agenda. In the present climate the agenda is well-booked by talks about talks, to be followed by talks about remit, to be followed by possible agreements which will do much to improve the climate of international affairs but little to reverse the arms race. Within the UN itself the disarmament machinery will continue to be incessantly compromised by the aggressive delivery of negative and irreconcilable political statements.

Judged by the standards of outside observers, the attempt to link disarmament and development has been a failure. But it should not be forgotten that the United Nations is a unique and complex institution in which all manner of entrenched political conflicts are played out in many subtle ways. The disarmament and development debate should also be seen as a part of this milieu; within the United Nations the disarmament and development debate has served an important purpose. To begin with it has reiterated the strong moral imperative in the disarmament process. Furthermore, it may be argued that the issue had a hidden role and performed a valuable function in keeping alive the ultimate goal of General and Complete Disarmament (GCD). During the 1960s, at a time when the Superpowers were moving away from a declared policy of disarmament to one of arms control (see *Arms Control, Evolution of*), the disarmament and development thesis came of age. In addition, by linking disarmament to development the United Nations attempted to retain its role as a potential broker of a common security system. Implicit in this role is the concept of the guarantee of security without the threatened or actual resort to arms or war.

In the event, rather than becoming a potential source of funds for development, arms control has become an institution of the arms race. Disarmament became a marginal consideration and with it the concept of a common security system has faded as a central tenet within the United Nations. But by actively linking disarmament with development an attempt was made to keep alive the issues of disarmament and common security. It was symbolic of exactly what was at stake in the demand for disarmament and highlighted the opportunistic realism of the arms controllers. Indeed, this aspect gained increased significance as the number of nonaligned developing countries increased in both the United Nations itself and the CD. Within the CD these states have joined forces with the neutral countries of Europe and function together as the Group of 21 Neutral and Nonaligned Countries. A primary goal of this coalition had been to shift the emphasis of international politics away from the prevailing East-West axis to one which would strive to redress the imbalance between North and South. In this respect, disarmament for development became a powerful metaphor.

Of late the head of steam which built up under the West European peace movement appears to have reduced. Although not mutually exclusive, there has been a commensurate rise in interest in the problems of militarization in developing countries. In reality, the impetus and momentum for disarmament in developing countries will not come from these quarters. Disarmament will only become a reality when political conditions permit a definition of security which approximates something altogether different than it connotes at present—an unbridled reliance upon advanced military technology. But, nevertheless, the limited and less obvious role of the attempts to link disarmament and development should not go unrecognized.

Contrary to popular belief, the post-Cold War world has not been less armed. The superpower rivalry over, power aspirants have unleashed designs of arm acquisition, not only in conventional but more so in strategic terms. The countries of Southeast Asia, for example, have mostly embarked on arm acquisition programs. North Korea had been desirous of acquiring nuclear weapons. Of late, India and Pakistan blasted nuclear tests in violation of the CTBT. These countries are, ironically, home to millions of economically disenfranchised people. The rationality of disarmament and development is, thus, severely tested.

See also: *Militarism and Militarization; North-South Conflict; Thorsson, Inga*

Bibliography

Eccles P 1983 *Disarmament and Development: The Vital Links.* Irish Commission for Peace and Justice, Dublin
Graham M, Jolly R, Smith C (eds.) 1986 *Disarmament and World Development,* 2nd edn. Pergamon Press, Oxford
Smith C, Graham M 1985 Disarmament and . . . what? A new perspective for the disarmament and development debate, *IDS Bulletin* 16 (4)
United Nations 1982 The relationship between disarmament and development. *Disarmament Study Series* No. 5, United Nations, New York

MAC GRAHAM; CHRIS SMITH; PEDRO B. BERNALDEZ

Domino Theory

The "domino theory" was based on a figure of speech used by American president Dwight D. Eisenhower in the spring of 1954 to justify American aid to the French in their struggle against the Vietminh in Indochina. Eisenhower and his aides had become convinced of the necessity of preventing the communist-led Vietminh from gaining control of Indochina, but realized that they needed to convince the public, both in the United States and throughout the noncommunist world, that the struggle in Southeast Asia was of crucial importance. This problem was given urgency by the fact that the French, about to suffer a disastrous defeat at Dien Bien Phu, could not be expected to hold on much longer without even more massive infusions of American aid. Thus, at a Press conference on April 7, 1954, Eisenhower welcomed a reporter's question on his goals in Indochina. He responded by saying:

> You have . . . the "falling domino" principle. You have a row of dominos set up, you knock over the first one, and what will happen to the last one is the certainty that it will go over very quickly . . . . But when we come to the possible sequence of events, the loss of Indochina, of Burma, of Thailand, of the Malay Peninsula and Indonesia . . . you are talking really about millions and millions and millions of people.
> Finally, the geographical position achieved . . . turns the . . . island defensive chain of Japan, Formosa, of the Philippines and to the southward; it moves in to threaten Australia and New Zealand. It takes away . . . that region that Japan must have as a trading area, forcing Japan toward the Communist areas in order to live. So, the possible consequences of a Communist takeover in Indochina are just incalculable to the free world.

This belief that a communist victory in Indochina would lead inexorably to more communist victories elsewhere in Asia had actually been the basis of America's Indochina policy since the late 1940s. What Eisenhower did, in other words, was to give a new name to an already existing and widely accepted fear, rather than to formulate a new conceptual underpinning for United States policy.

Within a few months of Eisenhower's press conference, his administration began to back away from the implications of the domino theory by accepting the Geneva compromise, whereby communist control of North Vietnam was given international recognition. It was argued that this settlement would buy time in which the other nations of southern Asia could become strong enough to resist communist pressure, thereby nullifying the Domino Theory's grim predictions. Nonetheless, the domino metaphor and the fears which it verbalized were resurrected when former South Vietnam became threatened by communist insurrection during the late 1950s, and were used by the United States government to justify its ever-deepening involvement in that tragic struggle. President Johnson, for example, claimed in the early 1960s that, "the battle against communism must be joined in Southeast Asia . . . or the United

States, inevitably, must surrender the Pacific and take up our defenses on our own shores." Similarly, a few years later his successor as president, Richard Nixon, told critics of his administration's commitment to Vietnam to "go talk to the dominos," that is, to the noncommunist nations near Vietnam.

From its inception, the Domino Theory has been highly controversial. Many observers insist that the fall of former South Vietnam to the communists in 1975, and of Laos and Cambodia a short time later, proves the validity of the theory. However, while the other countries of Southeast Asia are beset with many serious problems, they do not now appear to be particularly vulnerable to communist subversion or attack. Moreover, what problems they do have appear to originate in their own internal difficulties rather than in the communist takeover of Indochina.

Critics of the Domino Theory charge that it is based on the dubious assumption that communism is a global monolith pursuing a centrally directed, coherent expansionist policy. It implies that it is external pressure from neighboring communist countries which is the major factor in creating communist unrest within a country. Many experts complain that the Domino Theory woefully underestimates the indigenous causes of communism's popularity in many parts of Asia. They point out that there were specific factors behind the popularity of communism in Indochina which do not exist in most of the other countries mentioned by Eisenhower and other proponents of the Domino Theory.

Bibliography ————————————————

Fifield R H 1973 *Americans in Southeast Asia.* Crowell, New York

Fitzgerald F 1972 *Fire in the Lake: The Vietnamese and the Americans in Vietnam.* Random House, New York

Graebner N A 1977 *Cold War Diplomacy.* Van Nostrand, New York

Kolko G 1969 *The Roots of American Foreign Policy.* Beacon Press, Boston, Massachusetts

Lyon P 1974 *Eisenhower: Portrait of the Hero.* Little, Brown, Boston

GARRETT L. MCAINSH

Donne, John

First as Reader in Divinity to the Benchers of Lincoln's Inn (1616-22) and then as Dean of St. Paul's Cathedral, Donne became one of the most celebrated

preachers in England, and arguably the most searching expositor of theodicy in English prior to John Milton. As such, he reflected frequently on peace "since *good* and *bad, peace* and *anguish, life* and *death* proceed from him, who is *Shaddai*, the almighty God" (Potter and Simpson III, Sermon 8, 255-57, p. 194; hereafter by volume, sermon, first line and page number). He speaks with consistent Christian orthodoxy of (as he put it in one characteristic place) "the Cross of Christ, which is the Ensign of the universal Peace of this world, and the means of the eternal Peace of the next" (I, 2, 9, p. 168).

Within the context of the sermons, which are the most fruitful focus for the purpose of this article, he draws on St. Augustine for conceptions of peace and war (as well as for other things). No pacifist, he believed that war may be just and necessary for a Christian state in that state's defense against aggression. In a time of great fear of Spanish invasion, in 1626, he averred: "Ambition is their religion . . . . Things being now, I say, in this state, with these men, since wee heare that Drums beat in every field abroad, it becomes us also to returne to the brasing and beating of our Drums in the Pulpit too . . ." (VII, 6, 83, p. 166). At approximately the same period, he remarked in a prefatory letter to King Charles I that "Wee are in Times when the way to *Peace* is *Warre*, but my Profession leades not me to *those Warres*" (VII, 2, p. 72).

But as an Augustinian and Renaissance worldling, he knew the issue to be more complex than that, realized that the *civitas terrena* can interpenetrate the *civitas dei* in various ways. A decade or so earlier, in his *Essays in Divinity*, he meditated on the story in Exodus of the Israelites' deliverance from Egyptian bondage into the promised land. In effect, he defines a warlike version of peace antithetical to his concept of true peace, in life under Pharaoh, "such an oppressor, as would neither let them go, nor live there . . . one who increased their labours and diminished their numbers . . . one who would neither allow them to be Naturals, nor Aliens (p. 73)." He reflects, not unlike Milton's Samson, on the demoralizing effects of murderous slavery: "So soon did a dejection make them call their former *bondage, rest*" and how God had to train them by degrees to a divinely destined war (p. 77). "Peace," he insists to a London congregation (probably in 1624) "is a blessed state, but it must be the peace of God" (X, 8, 253, p. 185).

He exhibits, too, a not unusual Renaissance sense of mutability and vicissitude in the *civitas terrena*, although he seems not to feel quite so anxiously threatened by destructive change as Spenser had felt:

If we could imagine a blessing of peace without permanency, we might call a nights sleepe, though in the midst of an Army, peace: but it is onely provision for the permanency and continuance, that makes these blessings blessings. To thinke of, to provide against famine, and sicknesse, and warre, that is the blessing of plenty, and health, and peace. One of Christs principall titles was, that he was *Princeps pacis*, and yet this prince of peace sayes . . . . I came not to bring you peace, not such a peace as should bring them security against all warre . . . . If God cast a firebrand of warre, upon a State accustomed to peace, it burnes the more desperately, by their former security. (III, 2, 407, p. 84)

Donne uses *security* in the sense usual then, close to *complacency*. But one quotation at length can perhaps best sketch his awareness of what he conceives as a continuum, from large, distant wars to immediate microwars of strife, banditry, and street crime:

For the first temporall blessing of peace, we may consider the lovelinesse, the amiablenesse of that, if we looke upon the horror and gastlinesse of warre: either *in Effigie*, in that picture of warre, which is drawn in every leafe of our own Chronicles, in the blood of so many Princes, and noble families, or if we look upon warre it selfe, at that distance where it cannot hurt us, as God had formerly kindled it amongst our neighbours, and as he hath transferred it now to remoter Nations, whilest we enjoy yet a Goshen in the midst of all those Egypts. In all Cities, disorderly and facinorous men, covet to draw themselves into the skirts and suburbs of those Cities, that so they may be the nearer the spoyle, which they make upon passengers. In all Kingdomes that border upon other Kingdomes, and in Islands which have no other border but the Sea, particular men, who by dwelling in those skirts and borders, may make their profit of spoile, delight in hostility, and have an adversenesse and detestation of peace: but it is not so whithin: they who till the earth, and breed up cattell, and imploy their industry upon Gods creatures, according to Gods ordinance, feele the benefit and apprehend the sweetnesse, and pray for the continuance of peace. (III, 2, 297, p. 81)

Twentieth century readers of this might suppose Donne undervalues the psychological elements of civil violence—the have nots acting out rancor and hostility against the haves, against privilege, or property, or symbolic persons. But we recognize that inwardly troubled persons assail the very tranquility of those around them, and Donne insists on that point as central.

This veteran of military, polemical, diplomatic, and civil contention, this relentless psychologist, insists most centrally of all that peace and war—whether for justice or oppression—come out of the choices made from the hearts of individuals. To a Whitehall congregation including James I himself, in 1620, Donne voices first praise that the King is "a Peace-maker, and a Peace-preserver both at home and abroad" and then speaks warningly: "Persons who are preferred for service in the warre, prove often suspicious to the Prince" (III, 2, 267, 321, p. 80, 82). He means "may well be suspected by the king." It is an implicit caution not to overtrust war-mongers. Similarly, he speaks on a later occasion of princes and laws perverted and subverted. His concession that "Tis true, we are governed by a peaceable, and a just law" (III, 8, 304, p. 195) is an implicit warning and reproach to any Stuart king. Donne the sometime lawyer is suggesting that it is chiefly the rule of law which hedges against strife and injustice, more than kingship.

But the motive for oppression and unjust strife, he always insists, is some breach of charity: "where there is one enemy, there is no peace" (IV, 1, 220, p. 51); "We cannot promise you peace with God, without a war in yourselves . . ." (IX, 16, 126, p. 353). He preached a whole Christmas sermon on Colossians 1. 19-20 about spiritual peace as roughly the kind of untemptedness amid temptations which Milton anatomizes in *Paradise Regained* (IV, 11). Again, he closes a sermon with the hope that his congregation may depart the "Table" of the Eucharist "in the peace of the Church . . . without uncharitablenesse towards others" (VII, 11, 733, p. 299; see also III, 7, 523, 543, pp. 185, 186).

He accepts the implications of commitment to a God of peace, for example when he expands approvingly on Ephesians 2, 14, about contention between Jew and Gentile: "'He is our peace,' says the Apostle, and hath made 'of both one, and hath broken the stop of the partition wall'" (II, 3, 579, p. 110). He recognizes, too, that peace and war are not simple reciprocals of one another (like up and down). The variations in diction in one passage in particular, given his characteristic care with words, suggest a degree of categorical difference: "I am farre from giving fire to them that desire warre. *Peace* in this world, is a pretious *Earnest*, and a faire and lovely *Type* of the everlasting peace of the world to come: And warre in this world, is a shrewd and fearefull *Embleme* of the everlasting discord and tumult, and torment of the world to come: And therefore, our *Blessed God*, blesse us with this externall, and this internall, and make that lead to an eternall peace" (IV, 7, 199, p. 182). A *type* in ordinary seventeenth century usage is an event or entity in time which stands as a metaphor for a greater thing later in time.

Like the noun *earnest* (as in *earnest money*), it emphasizes orderly relationship. An *emblem* is primarily a visual design. It may be, as here figuratively, an ugly picture; but in any case, it emphasizes rather coolly static conceptualization. Nor are the associations of *fair* and *lovely* quite squarely opposite those of *fearful* and *shrewd*. The last, in seventeenth century usage, tends to mean not merely "discerning," but "probing, in an unpleasant way," and is sometimes associated with "shrewish."

The humbling consideration, never far from the center of Donne's consciousness, is the fallen state of the world, and with it the risky, tentative, contingent aspect of all human projects. Hence the word *pretend* when he interprets what Christians seek when they pray "Thy kingdom come": "This is the blessed state that wee pretend to, in the Kingdome of God in this life; Peace in the State, peace in the Church, peace in our Conscience" (III, 4, 494, p. 127). What the posture and attitude of prayer imply in practical, ethical, and political terms may not be altogether clear. But praying for internal or external peace certainly contrasts with imposing "peace" with arrogant violence.

At the same time that Donne is humbly conscious of human tendencies to self-deception and misdoing, he is hopeful and buoyant. The hope grows not only from his lively Anglican sense of Redemption and grace but from his pervasive sense of all men as wayfarers. Insofar as life is a journey (ideally, for him, to "heavenly Jerusalem"), then the scenes and circumstances of life are stations on that journey, and our actions are steps or mis-steps. And by so much our choices and efforts are critically important. He addresses a prayerful injunction to his congregation rightly to constitute their circumstance along that "way":

enrich thy selfe with that blessed Legacy, his Peace. Let whole world be in thy consideration as one house; and then consider in that, in the peacefull harmony of creatures, in the peacefull succession, and connexion of causes, and effects, the peace of Nature. Let this Kingdome, where God hath blessed thee with a being, be the Gallery, the best roome of that house, and consider in the two walls of that Gallery, the Church and the State, the peace of a royall, and a religious Wisedome; let thine owne family be a Cabinet in this Gallery, and finde in all the boxes thereof, in the severall duties of Wife, and Children, and servants, the peace of vertue, and of the father and mother of all vertues, active discretion, passive obedience; and then lastly, let thine owne bosome be the secret box, and reserve in this Cabinet, and find there the peace of conscience, and truelie thou has the best Jewell in the best Cabinet, and that in the best Gallery of the best house that can be had, peace with the Creature, peace in the Church, peace in the State, peace in thy house, peace in thy heart, is a faire Modell, and a lovely designe even of the heavenly Jerusalem which is *Visio pacis*, where there is no object but peace. And therefore the holy Ghost to intimate to the US, that happy perfectnesse, which wee shall have at last, and not till then, chooses the Metaphor of an enemy, and enmity, to avert us from looking for true peace from any thing that presents it selfe in the way. (IV, 135, p. 49)

Animating this, and countless other addresses to "beloved" congregation and to himself, in sermons, and to himself in "Satyre III" and "Divine Poems," is the Augustinian concern with love. For Donne as for Augustine, the very heart of the peace issue, as of every other important human issue, is right love. That is, greatest love must attach only to that which is most truly and greatly worthy of it, lesser degrees of love only to lesser objects.

Bibliography ————————————————

Bald R C 1970 *John Donne: A Life*. Oxford University Press, Oxford

Carrithers G 1972 *Donne at Sermons: A Christian Existential World*. SUNY Press Albany, New York

Potter R, Simpson E M (eds.) 1953-62 *The Sermons of John Donne*, 10 Vols. University of California Press, Berkeley and Los Angeles, California

Reeves T D 1981 *Annotated Index to the Sermons of John Donne*, Vol. 3. Index to Topics. "Elizabethan and Renaissance Studies 95" of Salzburg Studies in English Literature. Institut für Anglistic und Amerikanistic, Salzburg

Roberts J R 1982 *John Donne: An Annotated Bibliography of Modern Criticism, 1968-1978*. University of Missouri Press, Columbia, Missouri

Simpson E M (ed.) 1952 *Essays in Divinity*. Clarendon Press, Oxford

GALE H. CARRITHERS

Dubois, Pierre

Pierre Dubois (c.1250-c.1320) was a lawyer and publicist in the service of Philip IV, one of France's most outstanding medieval monarchs. He was a valuable proponent of Philip IV's policies, writing a number of pamphlets defending the royal position in Philip's quarrels with the Templar order, with the papacy, and with numerous other foes. In his most famous pamphlet, *De Recuperatione Terre Sancte* [The recovery of the Holy Land], written around 1306, Dubois developed one of the earliest recorded plans for achieving a general European peace. No pacifist, Dubois urged such a peace as a necessary prerequisite for the reconquest of the Holy Land from the Moslems.

Traditional pleas for European unity took the position that all European states were not really sovereign, but instead were subject to the ultimate authority of the papacy or the Holy Roman Empire. Dubois rejected the idea that the popes should wield political power, and argued that the concept of subjection to the Holy Roman Empire was anachronistic. The emperors, he pointed out, had become too weak to lead Europe. Instead, the Europeans should unite under the leadership of the strongest ruler they had, his own master, the king of France. Peace would come to Europe, he maintained, if all Christian states would ally themselves with one another under French leadership. He urged that such an alliance should

include a binding oath taken by all rulers, swearing that they would keep the peace with one another. To help maintain this peace, he proposed that a permanent court be established to peacefully adjudicate any disputes which might arise and that a council be set up whereby common problems and concerns could be amicably discussed. This council, said Dubois, should be empowered to institute various sanctions, including military retaliation, against any state which broke the peace.

These proposals had no discernible effect on their time, as the European rulers continued to go about the business of making war on one another. Echoes of Dubois's ideas, however, were to appear in numerous plans for peace in coming centuries. Dubois is significant in that he was the first European thinker to propose an international court of arbitration as a means of resolving disputes without war (see *International Judicial Settlement*). In addition, unlike earlier thinkers, not to mention his more famous Italian contemporary, Dante (see *Dante, Alighieri*), he recognized that Europe's division into sovereign states was definitive. Rather than pursue the chimera of peace through political unity under the authority of one all-encompassing European state, Dubois concentrated on finding ways in which the existing sovereign states could live together without war.

See also: *Peace in the Middle Ages*

Bibliography ——————————————

Burns D 1917 A medieval internationalist: Pierre Dubois. *Monist* 27
Dubois P 1956 *The Recovery of the Holy Land*. Columbia University Press, New York

Hemleben S J 1943 *Plans for World Peace Through Six Centuries*. University of Chicago Press, Chicago, Illinois
Power E 1967 Pierre Dubois and the domination of France. In: Hearnshaw F J C (ed.) 1967 *The Social and Political Ideas of Some Great Medieval Thinkers*. Barnes and Noble, New York

GARRETT L. MCAINSH

Dulles, John Foster

John Foster Dulles (1888-1959), fifty-second American Secretary of State, almost seemed destined by virtue of family, education, and experience to become involved in diplomacy. His grandfather, John W. Foster, served as Secretary of State under President Benjamin Harrison, and his uncle, Robert Lansing, held that position in the Wilson Administration. While a student Dulles attended the Hague Conference of 1907 as a private secretary to his grandfather, a member of the Chinese delegation. Dulles' senior thesis at Princeton won him a fellowship to study at the Sorbonne in Paris with the philosopher Henri Bergson. After law school and military service during the First World War, he was appointed to the American delegation at the Versailles Conference.

During the interwar period Dulles practiced law, rising to head of the prestigious New York firm of Sullivan and Cromwell in 1927. Much of his work involved international law, providing ample opportunities for travel abroad. His analyses of international issues such as German reparations frequently appeared in print. During the 1930s Dulles took part in several major conferences of intellectuals on questions of war and peace, and his own writings took on an increasingly theoretical and philosophical tone. In 1939 he published *War, Peace and Change*, a philosophical treatise that linked human nature, domestic political processes, attributes of the international system, and war. Starting from the premise that change is inherent in the universe, Dulles' analysis devoted considerable attention to rigidities in the international system that prevent peaceful accommodation between the "dynamic" (have-not) and "static" (have) nations. Selected passages in the book were later cited, somewhat unfairly, by critics as indicating that Dulles harbored sympathies for the "dynamic" nations that were challenging the post-Versailles *status quo:* Germany, Japan, and Italy. Although Dulles had admired Woodrow Wilson (see Nobel Peace Prize Laureates: *Woodrow Wilson*) and had taken an increasingly active lay role in church efforts to maintain peace, he

warned against moralism in international affairs. As late as 1938 he wrote, "Every tendency to identify the Kingdom of God with a particular structure of society or economic mechanism must result in moral confusion for those who maintain the system and disillusionment for those who suffer from its limitations."

During the Second World War Dulles served as the Chairman of the Commission to Study the Basis of a Just and Durable Peace. In that and other positions he played a significant role in generating public support for American participation in the United Nations. Dulles also emerged as an important figure in the Republican Party. In 1940 he supported his fellow New Yorker, Governor Thomas Dewey, for the Republican presidential nomination. Four years later Dewey won the nomination. As Dewey's chief foreign policy spokesman during the campaign, Dulles joined with Secretary of State Cordell Hull in an agreement to keep the United Nations from becoming a partisan issue. The Hull-Dulles agreement is often cited as the origin of bipartisanship in postwar American foreign policy.

After Dewey's defeat, Dulles served the Truman Administration as a member of the American delegation in several meetings of the Council of Foreign Ministers. In 1948 Dewey was again nominated for the presidency and it was generally believed that Dulles would become Secretary of State. However, President Truman defeated Dewey in a startling upset. A few months later Dewey appointed Dulles to a vacant seat in the Senate but he lost a bitterly contested election to retain it.

During the following months Dulles wrote his second major book, *War or Peace*. Whereas his analysis a decade earlier had warned against excessive moralism, finding the major causes of war in the international system itself, *War or Peace* located the source of contemporary international conflict in the ambitions of the former Soviet Union which, in turn, derived from the atheistic nature of its society and ideology. Dulles also continued to serve the Truman

Administration in various capacities, most notably in guiding the complex negotiations on the Japanese Peace Treaty.

The 1952 presidential election, resulting in a landslide victory for Dwight D. Eisenhower, finally brought Dulles an appointment as Secretary of State. Although the dour Dulles differed in a number of respects from the President and he never joined the circle of Eisenhower's intimate friends, they developed an effective working relationship. Dulles understood the importance of his direct access to the President and, unlike some of his predecessors (e.g., Lansing and Hull) or successors (e.g., William Rogers and Cyrus Vance) he ensured that members of the White House staff did not compete effectively for influence with Eisenhower.

Whereas contemporary observers often depicted Eisenhower as a somewhat passive President who acceded to Dulles' initiatives in foreign and defense policy, scholarship based on recently opened archives has tended to portray the President as an astute and effective leader. Nevertheless, Dulles' importance as a foreign policy leader remains beyond question. Some aspects of his policy may be summarized very briefly.

(a) Dulles was consistently skeptical of Soviet foreign policy goals. He displayed little enthusiasm for "summitry," including the meeting of heads of state in Geneva in 1955. He dismissed the sincerity of various Soviet "peace offensives" by Stalin's successors, fearing that Western allies and public opinion would conclude, prematurely, that the Cold War was over.

(b) Although he had called for American recognition of the People's Republic of China prior to the Korean War in 1950, Dulles adamantly pursued a nonrecognition policy while Secretary of State. This reflected in part the state of American public opinion during the 1950s, but there is no indication that his private views differed on the issue.

(c) The "New Look" in defense policy, announced in 1954, reflected some ideas that Dulles had developed before assuming office in 1953. Sharing Eisenhower's fiscal conservatism and distaste for large standing armies in peacetime, Dulles proposed greater reliance on nuclear weapons and reduction of conventional forces to maintain deterrence, while reducing costs.

(d) Dulles is generally credited as having been an astute negotiator in private, but he often created controversies and political difficulties with his public pronouncements. Moralistic rhetoric and phrases such as "go to the brink," "Soviet collapse," "neutralism is immoral," and "agonizing reappraisal," as well as a penchant for taking credit for foreign policy successes while sharing the blame for failures, caused critics to question his skills as a diplomat. Dulles' rather erratic behavior during the Suez crisis of 1956 perhaps represented the nadir of his term as Secretary of State. On the other hand he was much more effective in dealing with the dangerous German and Berlin issues.

During the dual crises over Suez and Hungary in 1956 Dulles was stricken with cancer. In 1959 the malignancy recurred, forcing his resignation in April. He died on May 24, 1959.

Bibliography

Ambrose S E 1984 *Eisenhower: The President*. Simon and Schuster, New York

Dulles J F 1939 *War, Peace and Change*. Harper, New York

Dulles J F 1950 *War or Peace*. Macmillan, New York

Gross P 1994 *Gentleman Spy: The Life of Allen Dulles*. Houghton Mifflin, Boston

Immerman R (ed.) 1990 *John Foster Dulles and the Diplomacy of the Cold War*. Princeton University Press, Princeton, NJ

Holsti O R 1962 The belief system and national images. *J. Conflict Resolution* 6

Hoopes T 1973 *The Devil and John Foster Dulles*. Atlantic Monthly Press, Boston, Massachusetts

OLE R. HOLSTI

Dumas Pere, Alexandre

Alexandre Dumas' grandfather, Alexandre Davy, Sieur de La Pailleterie (1714-86), had a right to be addressed as "marquess," a title his grandson seldom availed himself of. He lived for a time in Santo Domingo, producing several children there by a slave woman, Cessette Dumas. Returning to France, he was soon followed by an eighteen-year-old son, Thomas Alexandre, who seems to have been something of a favorite with him. Born in 1762, Thomas Alexandre enlisted in the army under the name Dumas in 1786. With the French Revolution, rapid promotions came his way, and in 1793 he was a general. Politically he was a republican, which is not unrelated, no doubt, to the fact that his ambitious commander, General Napoleon Bonaparte, took a pronounced dislike to him. Leaving Egypt in 1799, he fell into the hands of the Neapolitans and was clapped in prison. Exchanged in 1801, he was never allowed to return to active service. He and his wife, with Mme Dumas' parents, lived modestly in Villers-Cotterets, where Alexandre, the future writer, was born on July 24, 1802. General Dumas died less than four years later, leaving a son devoted to his memory.

On her husband's death, Mme Dumas found herself penniless. Nevertheless, young Alexandre somehow managed to attend school, declined to become a priest, and, with his fine handwriting, eventually obtained work in Paris as a clerk in the Duc d'Orléans' employ. Soon, in his spare time, he was writing plays. When the Duc d'Orléans became King Louis Philippe in 1830, Dumas, despite his inherited republican convictions, kept on very good terms with several members of the royal family. By a curious coincidence, the new queen was a daughter of that King of Naples who had once put his father in prison.

Meanwhile, Dumas' plays were being staged and acclaimed, and soon their author was a celebrity. He traveled extensively, led an exhausting social life, and steadily turned out an incredible number of plays, novels, and other books, all radiating their author's boundless, robust vitality. This vitality carried over into the writer's personal life, which was filled with a staggering procession of mistresses, most of them women of the theatre. By one of the earliest, Catherine Lebay, he had a son, Alexandre Dumas Fils, who one day would become a famous dramatist. There were other children as well, all with different mothers. All but ordered to do so by the Crown Prince, Dumas married one mistress, Ida Ferrier. A mistress was one thing, but a wife was quite another. When the marriage collapsed, as it inevitably did, Mme Dumas retired to Italy, living there as the Marquise de La Pailleterie.

Dumas did not know how to handle money. Generous with others and with himself, he made and squandered millions. His grandiose schemes, such as the newspapers he founded, all came to nothing, as did his Théâtre Historique. Opening on February 20, 1847, it closed its doors on October 16, 1850. The writer's showy home, the Château de Monte-Cristo, was built at this time, and this too Dumas lost. In 1852 he was bankrupt. Undaunted, he continued to earn huge sums

but was nonetheless virtually penniless when a stroke killed him on December 5, 1870. On the heels of the initial French disasters in the Franco-Prussian War, he had left his Paris apartment and gone to stay with his son and grandchildren near Dieppe. Even though he had tried to be, he had never been elected to the Académie Française. Alexandre Dumas Fils became a member in 1874.

With Hugo's startlingly provocative verse drama *Hernani* the French Romantics won the stage in 1830. Would *Hernani* have been the triumph it was, however, had it not been for a Dumas prose drama the year before? Very possibly it would not. On February 11, 1829, the Comédie Française public witnessed the initial performance of the history play, *Henri III et sa cour*, which was an enormous success. A month after *Hernani* Dumas had another electrifying success with a verse play, *Christine*, another history play. Dumas' poetry was not as good as his prose, but audiences did not seem to notice.

Other triumphs awaited Dumas. The next one, with a contemporary setting rather than an historical one, was *Antony*, which treats adultery sympathetically. As usual, the dramatist was admirably seconded by a splendid cast. The play opened on May 3, 1831, with Marie Dorval and Pierre Bocage in the leading roles. Later the same year came *Charles VII chez ses grands vassaux*. With it, as with the even more important *La Tour de Nesle*, Dumas returned to romanticized history, situating his plots in the medieval period then so popular with French reading and theatre-going audiences. *La Tour de Nesle*, with Mlle George and Pierre Bocage in the principal roles, was produced at the Porte St-Martin on may 29, 1832. As with Dumas' other period plays, it takes liberties with historical reality but much more than compensates for this with its swift action and with the excitement the play generates.

In 1822 a troupe of English actors visited Paris and performed at the Porte St-Martin, where they were roundly booed. Five years later the literary climate was changing, and another company, one that included Harriet Smithson, Kemble, Macready, and Kean, played to thunderous applause at the Odéon. Pierre Bocage and Marie Dorval had been impressed. Mlle Mars had attended performances and observed the foreign actors' technique. Another avid spectator had been Dumas, who vowed to revitalize the French theatre, giving it plays as full of movement, action, and passion as those the visitors were staging. He succeeded. Indeed, so taken had he been with the English actors that, nearly a decade after their Paris visit, he wrote a play about one of them, Edmund Kean, who had died in 1833. *Kean ou désordre et génie* (1836) was presented at the Théâtre des Variétés, with Frédérick Lemaître, whom Dumas considered the best actor of the day, playing the role of Kean. The play was another hit. Another of Dumas' contemporary plays is *Richard Darlington* (1831). Though less successful, *Napoléon Bonaparte* (1831), still another of Dumas' modern plays, should be mentioned, if for no other reason than because it demonstrates the writer's admiration for a military hero.

Dumas turned out many other dramas, almost too numerous even to list. His success as a playwright notwithstanding, very early in his career he turned his attention to the novel as well. While in his theatre he blazed new trails, with his novels what he essentially did was apply to French prose a technique he learned from reading Sir Walter Scott. He did not, to be sure, invent the French historical novel—Mme de La Fayette had already done it—but he gave it new life and a new orientation. Unlike Mme de La Fayette, he was but little interested in subtle character analyses. But what his novels lack in probing studies of motivation they more than make up for with their heroes' and heroines' torrid love affairs, their innumerable credibility-stretching adventures, and their hairbreadth escapes. Dumas' fiction, with sweeping, virtuoso brushstrokes, paints a vast historical fresco. It stretches from the Middle Ages, represented by such novels as *Isabel de Bavière* (1835), to the author's own times as seen in *Les Mohicans de Paris* (1854-55), a tableau of Restoration life and manners, and *Les Louves de Machecoul* (1858), dealing with the Duchesse de Berry's unsuccessful effort to overthrow the July Monarchy and secure the French throne for her son.

One of Dumas' most famous novels is *Les Trois Mousquetaires*, which takes place during the reign of Louis XIII. Using raw materials found mostly in Gatien de Courtilz de Sandras' *Mémoires de M. d'Artagnan* (1700) and Tallemant des Réaux' *Historiettes* (published 1834), he transformed them into a spirited tale that thrilled its readers when, originally, it appeared in installments in *Le Siècle* and again when it came out as an eight-volume book in 1844.

A liberal in politics, Dumas nevertheless was alive to the horror of the French Revolution and took a highly conservative attitude in presenting it to his readers. Louis XVI, Marie Antoinette, and their courtiers, real and imaginary, appear as sensitive, attractive characters in *Joseph Balsamo* (1846-48), *Le Collier de la reine* (1849-50), *Le Chevalier de Maison-Rouge* (1845-46), *Ange Pitou* (1851), and *La Comtesse de Charny* (1852-55).

After *Les Trois Mousquetaires* Dumas' other surest claim to renown is *Le Comte de Monte-Cristo* (1844-45), which spans the Bourbon Restoration period and most of the July Monarchy. First as a popular serial in the *Journal des débats*, then in book form (18 volumes), it enjoyed a phenomenal success and still does. If *Les Trois Mousquetaires* had been a novel about love and adventure, this one was about love and revenge. The public took to it immediately, guaranteeing it a place, along with *Les Trois Mousquetaires*, as one of the author's two masterpieces. Anticipating the practice of Daudet, the Goncourt brothers, and Zola, Dumas adapted these two novels, and many of the others as well, for the stage or permitted other dramatists to do so.

In Dumas' historical plays and fiction one must not look for accuracy in matters of detail—the author was far too busy for that and, besides, he was temperamentally unsuited to this kind of work. Nor should one be bothered by an occasional anachronism. What *is* important is the vitality, the momentum, the remarkable, sustained sense of history that underlies the monumental achievement the author accomplished. Whether concerned with history or not, Dumas' theatre and fiction both reveal the same vigor, the same exuberant, powerful imagination, the same intensity and verve. In both genres the male characters are men of action, and often the women are cast in the same mould. The thing that really distinguishes this writer's theatre from his fiction is that, whereas the plays generally have unhappy endings (at least the serious plays), in the novels the heroes and heroines survive and get a better chance to translate their laudable aspirations into realities. Dumas had become famous as a playwright. His novels made him even more famous.

For many of his plays and novels Dumas had collaborators, including Gérard de Nerval. On the whole, these aids were happy enough to acquire experience and considered that they were well treated and well paid. Far from misusing his collaborators' labors, Dumas often frankly acknowledged them, and, even when he did not, whatever ideas, scenarios, or rough drafts those he worked with handed him, he touched up or rewrote, so that all of the works appearing under his name bear the unmistakable stamp of his particular genius. Sometimes his name did not appear at all on collaboration works, as is the case with Nerval's *Léo Burckart*.

Apart from his novels and plays, his most enduring contributions to literature, Dumas wrote quite a few works in other genres. He tried his hand at poetry but wisely realized that this was not his true medium and turned to prose. Traveling widely, he published a considerable amount of travel literature, including the *Impressions de voyage en Suisse* (1835), which had an enormous appeal. A gifted cook, he wrote a *Grand Dictionnaire de cuisine*, published after his death (1873). He loved animals and for a time kept various pets, which led to his writing an *Histoire de mes bêtes* (1858). History, serving as an indispensable backdrop for most of his theatre and prose, interested him for its own sake, and he wrote a number of volumes of more or less pure history, among them *Gaule et France* (1833), *Louis XIV et son siècle* (1844-45), *La Régence* (1849), *Louis XV* (1849), *Louis XVI* (1850-51), *Napoléon* (1840), and *Le Dernier Roi* or *Histoire de la vie politique et privée de Louis Philippe* (1852). Since he died shortly after its overthrow, he had no opportunity to prepare a history of the Second Empire. Some of Dumas' personal recollections, exciting but often unreliable, are recorded in *Comment je devins auteur dramatique*, which first appeared in the *Revue des Deux Mondes* in 1833 and then later with the first volume of his theatre, and in *Mes Mémoires* (1852-54), which breaks off in the 1830s. Like almost all writers of his day, Dumas went in for a certain amount of journalism and even established several short-lived periodicals: *Le Mois* (1848), *Le Mousquetaire* (1852), *Le Monte-Cristo* (1857), *D'Artagnan* (1868), and others.

Dumas was not a man of peace. His father, the General, he considered a remarkable man (his name appears on the Arch of Triumph in Paris). In *Mes Mémoires* Dumas praises him, recounts his exploits in France, Italy, and Egypt, and justifies his conduct. He points out with pride that the Austrians called General Dumas "the black devil" and tells how, returning exhausted after a military engagement he told a comrade, "I killed so many, so many." Displeased that the General had had to retire to civilian life in 1801, he blamed those who, not appreciating him as a soldier or else too timid to intercede with Napoleon on his behalf, allowed his abilities to be wasted. Dumas notes that, in dying, his father expressed the hope that the French armies would continue to be victorious. Had General Dumas been permitted to continue his military career, would his son have followed in his footsteps? It is possible.

Dumas glorified war. Despite resenting the Emperor's ill treatment of his father, Dumas viewed Napoleon as a great man and devoted several works to his life and career, including the play *Napoliéon Bonaparte*. Many of Dumas' most spectacular heroes are soldiers. Readers applaud as the Three Musketeers, skilled swordsmen in the service of King Louis XIII, rout their adversaries, Cardinal de Richelieu's Guards, and as the Whites and the Blues (*Les Blancs et les bleus*) battle one another fiercely in the interests of the French Republic or in the interests of its foes. Dumas was well aware that war was a terrible thing, but at the same time he looked upon it as a glorious one. Of Charles Nodier, whom he made a character in *Les Blancs et les bleus* and who has just witnessed a military action, he commented that the young man "had seen the poetic side, the movement, the fire, the smoke; but, from where he was, distance had concealed the details from him." Soon "he was going to see the hideous side, the agony, the stillness, the death; he was finally going to enter bloody reality."

Although he had not chosen a military career, on several occasions circumstances nevertheless thrust Dumas into the thick of a certain amount of military activity. At the time of the July Monarchy and again when the Revolution of 1848 broke out, he participated in the street fighting. In 1860, as Giuseppe Garibaldi was campaigning to unite Italy under King Victor Emmanuel of Piedmont, Dumas rushed into the fray, whipping up the insurgents' enthusiasm and procuring them arms and having the incidental pleasure of seeing the Neapolitan Bourbons, who had imprisoned his father in 1799, dethroned and driven into exile. Having already translated Garibaldi's memoirs, he now promoted the revolutionaries' cause by writing *I Borboni di Napoli* and founding, in Naples, a newspaper he called the *Indipendente*, further contributing to the movement with *Les Garibaldiens* (1861) and *La San Pelice* (1864-65). Clearly Dumas was not a peace proponent. If, however, war is unavoidable, perhaps his contemporaries should have listened to his prophetic warning when, noting Prussia's defeat of Austria at the Battle of Sadowa (1860) and her annexation of Hanover, he called attention to the threat the ambitious Germans posed for France. *La Terreur prussienne*, a novel published in 1868, sounded an alarm that, heeded, could have caused France to be better prepared when the disastrous war with Prussia came two years later.

Bibliography

Clouard H 1955 *Alexandre Dumas*. Albin Michel, Paris

Hemmings F W J 1979 *Alexandre Dumas, the King of Romance*. Charles Scribner's Sons, New York

Henry G 1976 *Monte Cristo ou l'extraordinaire aventure des ancêtres d'Alexandre Dumas*. Perrin, Paris

Maurois A 1957 *Les Trois Dumas*. Hachette, Paris Trans. (1957) as The Titans. Greenwood Press, Westport

Ross M 1981 *Alexandre Dumas*. David & Charles, London

Schopp C 1985 *Alexandre Dumas, le génie de la vie*. Mazarine, Paris trans 1988 as *Alexandre Dumas, Genius of life*. Franklin Watts, New York and Toronto

HARRY REDMAN, JR.

E

Eastern Europe, Transformation of

The delimitation of the area of "Eastern Europe"—covering several geographically, historically and culturally differentiated regions—remains a subject of vigorous debate. Especially the status of some former Soviet republics (the Baltic states, for example) is not fully clear. However, it seems justified to adopt the widely applied general meaning of Eastern Europe as a political shorthand for the states which used to be ruled by communist parties after the Second World War, that is: Albania, Bulgaria, Czechoslovakia (now the Czech and Slovak Republics), Hungary, Poland, Romania, and (former) Yugoslavia.

1. The Peaceful Change

The quick collapse of most of the communist governments in Eastern Europe, constituted the first link of a chain of occurrences which led to the end of the Cold War. In a few years the collapse brought about proclamation of *The London Declaration on a Transformed North Atlantic Alliance*, which called for political consultation between NATO and the Warsaw Pact (July 1990); international accord for the reunification of Germany (October 1990); signing of *The Conventional Forces in Europe Treaty* (CFE) by 22 countries of the Warsaw Pact and NATO together with adoption of *The Charter of Paris for a New Europe* during the CSCE Summit Meeting (November 1990); dissolution of the military and political structures of the Warsaw Pact (March and July 1991); decline of the Soviet Union (December 1991); and finally—the withdrawal of the Soviet/Russian army from the former Warsaw pact countries (completed in 1993).

The Eastern Europe's processes of transformation, preceded by Mikhail Gorbachev's "new thinking," "perestroika" [rebuilding] and "glastnost" [openness] in the Soviet Union, began in 1989 (see *Glasnost and Perestroika*). Several dramatic events happened that year: in Poland—the triumph of democratic opposition in parliamentary election, in June, and then accession to an office of the Prime Minister by the Solidarity candidate, Tadeusz Mazowiecki, in August; in Hungary—removal of the communist party monopoly on power from the constitution and proclamation of a free republic by acting President Matyas Szuros, in October; in the German Democratic Republic (that is, Eastern Germany)—resignation of the leader of the communist party Erich Honecker and opening of the Berlin Wall, in November; in Bulgaria—stepping down of the communist Todor Zhivkov who had ran the country since 1954, in November; in Czechoslovakia—quitting of the communist leadership, in November, and election of Vaclav Havel, renowned playwright and leader of a civic movement, for presidency, in December; in Romania—overthrowing and execution of Nicolae Ceausescu, the infamous national Stalinist dictator for 24 years, in December. Taken together, those events were usually referred to as the "Autumn of Nations." However, it is difficult to recognize such an expression as a proper one. The very term 'Autumn' suggests decline, fall, rather than revival of the East European nations, which was the case.

Only the Romanian changes were accompanied by bloodshed, caused mainly by fights provoked by the secret police (Securitate). In other countries strikes and huge mass protests led by the democratic movements brought down communist leadership in a peaceful way. The Polish example of "round table" negotiations offered to the Solidarity labor movement by a communist government and the ideas of nonviolence professed by the former have to be cited here. All these stunning developments made up a rare real-life laboratory for social sciences. Literally in front of the world's eyes Eastern Europe was going through unprecedented processes of peaceful transformation of political, economic and social structures. Putting it into the peace research language: on vast areas of Europe *the structural, indirect violence was eliminated without resort to direct violence and armed force* (the tragedy of civil war and policy of "ethnic cleansing" in Yugoslavia is a special case).

2. Dilemmas of Transformation

Under those circumstances the new major trends in Eastern Europe arose. In response to strong social pressure and guided by liberal ideas, the post-communist governments initiated democratic and free market-oriented reforms. The security policy of the East European states was reoriented and gradually turned to the West. The so-called Euro-Atlantic option became a priority. The option was expected to provide necessary means of national defense, ensure economic assistance and facilitate civilizational development, and finally—confirm the irreversible nature of the transformation.

Four great, interrelated dilemmas—or paradoxes—appeared while the transformation of Eastern Europe was moving forward. Their substance could be reduced to the following question: the old system has lost, indeed, but is it justified to speak about the success of the new solutions?

First, *the political, economic and social changes in progress are too deep and extensive to make a reversal of the historical process possible. On the other hand, there is a mounting sense of how distant the goal still is and how scant are the guarantees of success.* There are many reasons for this. The factor that once unified society—the exhilaration of the victory—has disappeared, and the role of anti-communism as the binding agent of the old opposition elites has waned. The economic and social costs of transformation are high, among them inflation, unemployment and widening stratification which is giving rise to counterclaims by large social groups. The tasks of governments are becoming more complicated as they are forced to fill out the slogans of parliamentary democracy and market economics with real programs.

Second, the new elites in the East European states have discovered on coming to power that *not all the problems they face are legacies of communism which will "automatically" vanish in the process of transformation, thus more sophisticated strategies are needed to eliminate them.* The economic arrears are the result not only of planned economies, state ownership and inefficient management, but also of centuries of retardation in Eastern Europe. The acute deficiencies in political culture spring not only from authoritarian forms of government during the recent half century but also from the difficult history of this part of Europe. The same applies to the ethnic disputes and conflicts; these were 'frozen' by the 50 years of totalitarianism rather than precipitated by them.

Third, after the transitional period characterized by temporary arrangements and partial solutions, *the*

East European nations aspired to the status of matured democracies and states of law. In most of them, the political system became subject to the democratic cycle of parliamentary elections and changing of governments. *However, it still happens that the rules of democracy, especially respect for democratic procedures of coming to power and quitting, are questioned.* Moreover, the remnants of communism and conflict potential that still exists in the countries which are delayed in reforming their political system and economy, result in a second wave of mass protests, turmoil and sudden changes of government or even violence, civil war and chaos (the new Yugoslavia, Bulgaria, Albania, 1996/97).

The contradictory impulses emanating from the international environment contribute to the fourth of the dilemmas. *Having helped to bring the era of bipolarity to an end and remove the risk of full-scale nuclear war, the East European states find themselves occupying a "security vacuum."* Adding to their sense of diminished security are the weakness of the existing 'European architecture' and the number of "classic," geographically localized conflicts there (Balkans' tensions, open conflicts and armed struggles; the questions of Hungarian minorities in Romania, Slovakia, Ukraine and new Yugoslavia; the Polish concerns about the Russian enclave of Kaliningrad). The indisputable contribution of the West to the fall of communism and the encouraging signals it sent out raised expectations of swift admission to Western integration structures. Its long-lasting restraint has left them unfulfilled.

3. In Search of a Model

The peculiarities of the transformation of Eastern Europe may be presented in the shape of a "stability triangle." It grasps relations between a political sphere—consolidating democracy and freedom, an economic sphere—establishing market economy and achieving prosperity, and a sphere of security—ensuring sovereignty and protection of national identity (see Fig. 1).

Realization of economic reform in the East European states requires political initiative and protection. Dissatisfaction of society caused by the costs of the reforms turns against politicians who introduce them and leads to the changes of government. Democratization of political system and successful development of economy contribute to the establishment of a mechanism for internal conflict resolution (see *Peace and Democracy*). Achievement of political and economic goals of transformation is difficult, if not impossible,

Figure 1
Stability triangle

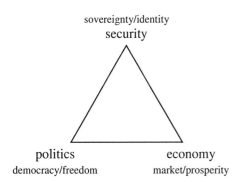

sovereignty/identity
security

politics economy
democracy/freedom market/prosperity

without the assistance of external security policy that adds to the domestic capabilities of a given state. That is why the considered and balanced improvement in *all spheres* of transformation is necessary to provide long-term stability for Eastern Europe.

But the task is even harder. The early transformations of this century remained within the framework of the existing system (Brynt and Mokrzycki 1994). The post communist system in most cases has a revolutionary character. Moreover, it is expressed simultaneously in several domains (Góralczyk in Góralczyk, Kostecki and Zukrowska 1995 pp. 143-56). Therefore the transformation of Eastern Europe assumes in fact a *multidimensional* revolution (see Fig. 2).

One can notice, then, that the search for a paradigm of transformation in Eastern Europe is a difficult task. Such a paradigm must encompass a unique and complex process "on the move" and consist of both destructive (elimination of communist system) and constructive (building of a new society) components.

4. Lessons for Peace Research

The transformation of Eastern Europe affects various components of peace research. The starting point for the discussion should be that—as Dieter Senghaas [1991: 18] expressed it—"With the collapse of communism in Eastern Europe and the trend now being followed in the [former—W.K.] Soviet Union, the original content of the conflict between East and West has evaporated: the East-West conflict is dead at its core." It means, first and foremost, that events in Eastern Europe and subsequent European development dealt a definite blow to the bipolar pattern of world forces (the movement from bipolar to multipolar international system has been going on for years). Instead, another form of competition has grown stronger—that between forces of integration and fragmentation in the international environment (globalism versus regionalism, pan-nationalism versus ethnonationalism, ecumenical approach versus sectarianism etc.). That means that peace research has *to encompass larger number of variables within the framework of its theory and analysis.*

As a consequence, the old strategies for sparing the world a disastrous large-scale armed conflict between East and West—either drafted or analyzed within the scope of peace research—have now become rather outdated, although the ideas of nuclear-free zones, arms limitation, peaceful coexistence etc., can be implemented in other territories. The peace research community has got an opportunity *to focus on strategies for building peace through multilateral and comprehensive international cooperation* (see *Emerging Tool Chest for Peace Builder*). In effect more stress may have to be put on "positive peace" and the

Figure 2
Multidimensional revolution

Challenge	Response (path of development)
Democratization	From totalitarianism into parliamentary democracy and the rule of law
Marketization	Replacement of planned economy by market mechanisms
Privatization	Transition from "public" (state) to private property
Civil society building	From "state as an instrument in hands of the ruling class" to the society based on human rights, ethical considerations and identification with common interest
A mentality change	Attempts to replace passive and self-centred attitudes by responsibility sharing, tolerance towards dissimilarity and pro-ecological postures
Shaping of national identity	From "socialist internationalism" back to Europe, commitment to protection of national minorities' rights and—in some cases—establishment of new independent states
Reconstruction of international environment	From Soviet bloc and Cold War divisions to good-neighbourly relations and desire of membership in (West) European structures

impact of international interdependencies as foundations of peaceful relations among the nations (see *Internationalization*). Special attention can be paid to the international organizations which provide the institutional environment for approaches to many peace-related issues. In sum, today peace researchers have to think not only how to lower and diffuse tensions but also—even more carefully—how to build confidence in international relations.

Third, the very concept of a relationship between structural violence and direct violence assumes a new content (see *Structural Violence and the Definition of Conflict*). It is true that transformation of Eastern Europe has set in motion democratic mechanisms in that part of the continent. At the same time it has "unfrozen" many conflicts, which had for dozens of years been kept under the lid (see *Ethnic Conflict and International Relations*). One example was the war in the former Yugoslavia, which—as Håkan Wiberg (1993 p. 21) says—"was a European microcosm: virtually all boundaries in Europe have gone through it" (East/West, Catholic/Orthodox, Moslem/ Christian, North/South). The main potential areas of conflicts are the disputes related to the question of national minorities in Eastern Europe, their identity, rights and duties (not to mention several dramatic events on the territory of what used to be the Soviet Union). The transformation of Eastern Europe also keeps awakening ever new tensions, particularly over economic problems, which reflect the gap between the needs and aspirations of the societies and the chances for their satisfaction. The task for peace research is then *to see whether and how democratic mechanisms can cope with the threats coming from nationalisms and attitudes of reclaim*, or, putting it in other words, whether they could prevent the peaceful revolution of early 1990s from boiling over into an armed struggle and chaos (as in Albania, 1997), and whether other countries of Europe might contribute to that effect. Also, the questions of the different techniques of conflict prevention and crisis management should be analyzed more extensively (see *Crisis Management*). So for peace research the question is and remains: how to establish and maintain peace both between the nations and within them.

Fourth and finally, the end of the Cold War means that peace may no longer be seen as the necessity of preserving the *status quo*. A guarantee of peace no longer is the commonly felt fear of a "hot" war, or the notorious balance of power. The image of "enemy" has changed, although not completely disappeared. Transformation of Eastern Europe and the recent pan-European processes confirmed that peace is a dynamic pattern of various social processes. They have to be controlled somehow but surely not by force; rather an accord supported by every sovereign party concerned should be the basis for such an attempt. Therefore peace research is facing a need t*o produce cognitive tools that will match the new substantial tasks concerning the post-Cold War developments*. Efforts to work out the model of Eastern Europe's revolution and search for a paradigm of transformation are but a part of such an endeavor.

See also: *Cold War; East-West Conflict; Evolutionary Movement toward Peace; Nonviolence; Security and Cooperation in Europe*

Bibliography ———————————————————

Ash T G 1990 Eastern Europe. The year of truth. *The New York Review of Books* 15 (February)

Banac I (ed.) 1992 *Eastern Europe in Revolution*. Cornel University Press, Ithaca and London

Balcerowicz L 1995 *Socialism, Capitalism, Transformation*. Central European University, Budapest, London, New York

Beyme K von 1996 *Transition to Democracy in Eastern Europe*. Macmillan, London

Bryant Ch G A, Mokrzycki E (eds.) 1994 *The New Great Transformation? Change and Continuity in East-Central Europe*. Routlege, London and New York

Clague Ch, Rausser G C (eds.) 1992 *The Emergence of Market Economies in Eastern Europe*. Blackwell, Oxford

Derlien H-U, Szablowski G J (eds.) 1993 *Regime Transition, Elites and Bureaucracies in Eastern Europe*. Blackwell, Oxford

Eberwein W 1992 *Transformation Process in Eastern Europe. Perspectives from the Modelling Laboratory*. Lang, Frankfurt

Góralczyk B, Kostecki W, Żukrowska K 1995 *In Pursuit of Europe. Transformations of Post-Communist States 1989-1994*. Institute for Political Studies, Warsaw

Keen M F, Mucha J L (eds.) 1993 *Eastern Europe in Transformation. The Impact on Sociology*. Greenwood Press, Westport

Ramet S P 1991 *Social Currents in Eastern Europe. The Sources and the Meaning of the Great Transformation*. Duke University Press, Durham

Schöplflin G 1993 *Politics in Eastern Europe*. Blackwell, Oxford

Senghaas D 1991 Peace research on threshold of the 1990s. In: K Gert (ed.) *Searching for Peace after the Cold War*. Frankfurt/Main, PRIF Reports

Staniszkis J 1992 *The Ontology of Socialism*. Oxford University Press/Clarendon Press

Wiberg H 1993 European peace research in the 1990s. In: J Balázs, H Wiberg (eds.) *Peace Research for the 1990s.* Akadémiai Kiadó, Budapest

Wnuk-Lipiński E (ed.) 1995 *After Communism. A Multidisci-* *plinary Approach to Radical Social Change.* Institute for Political Studies, Warsaw

WOJCIECH KOSTECKI

East-West Conflict

The phrase "East-West conflict" was often used interchangeably with the term "Cold War" to describe the intense hostility which developed between the Western allies and the former Soviet Union in the years following the defeat of Nazi Germany in 1945. The phrase has also been used to describe the wider competition for world power in the twentieth century that arose between the democratic countries of the "West" (dominated since 1945 by the United States) and the communist world of the "East" (led by the former Soviet Union, following the Bolshevik Revolution). The East-West conflict dominated international politics after the Second World War, until the fall of communism throughout Eastern Europe during 1989 and the subsequent disintegration of the former Soviet Union in 1991. Though the characteristic ideological and military features of the Cold War competition have disappeared, the legacy of the East-West conflict continues to overshadow discussion about the future of security in Europe in particular. Despite the ending of overt ideological competition between them, the historic sources of tension and insecurity between Russia and the neighboring states of Europe have not been significantly resolved by the passing of the Cold War—as was evident in the mid-1990s over the issue of NATO (see *North Atlantic Treaty Organization (NATO)*) expansion eastwards (see *Cold War*).

1. Historical Background

The East-West conflict had its roots in the uneasy relationship which existed in earlier centuries between the Russian Empire and the countries of Western and Central Europe. Even when Russia indisputably became a Great Power, its "Asiatic" and authoritarian character ensured that it was never accepted by the others as a full member of the European Great Power club. Such attitudes helped to stimulate Russian feelings of inferiority, insecurity and xenophobia. For their part, the Russians suffered physically as well as psychologically, repelling a series of invasions from the West over the centuries. The legacy of this relationship persisted to form the basis of East-West antagonism in the twentieth century: thus, during the Cold War the West typically regarded Soviet ways as less sophisticated than their own, while in the former Soviet Union there existed a strong desire to be recognized as equal to the economic and military power of the United States.

2. The Interwar Period

Before the Bolshevik Revolution in 1917, Western suspicions of the looming Empire in the East had been provoked by a variety of challenges: Russia's authoritarian political tradition, the size of the Russian military "steam roller," the assertiveness of Russia's "Orthodox" religion, the ambitions of pan-Slavism (see *Pan-Slavism*), the history of Czarist expansionism from the centre to the periphery of the Eurasian land mass, and the growth of nineteenth century territorial rivalries between Russia and other imperial powers in the Middle East and South Asia. There was also some ideological rivalry—on the one side Russian authoritarianism and messianism, and on the other Western democracy and Christianity—as well as the more traditional Great Power rivalries. After the Bolsheviks seized power, traditional Western suspicions of Russia were magnified by the revolutionary ideology espoused by the new leaders: "communism" promised (or, as seen in the West, threatened) not only to transform the backward state of Russia, but also to revolutionize international politics. The Bolsheviks welded Marxism to Russian populism and authoritarianism under an operational code largely established by Lenin. Thus Marxism-Leninism became the ideological banner of Stalin and his successors, and also the focal point for a new and more dangerous period in the old rivalry between Russia and the West.

Relations between the Western powers and the former Soviet Union were always difficult and often dangerous after 1917. The Western powers' hostility was manifest in their refusal to invite the new Bolshevik government in Moscow to be a founder member of the recently created League of Nations (see *League of Nations*), and in the unwillingness of the

United States government to extend diplomatic recognition to the new regime. On the Soviet side, hostility was channelled through the Comintern, an international organization dominated by Moscow and committed to undermining Western political systems by propaganda and subversion. At the same time, Western suspicions of the former Soviet Union were more than matched by Soviet mistrust of its capitalist and imperialist encircles—old Czarist fears were now magnified by the ideological framework of Marxism-Leninism. In the aftermath of the First World War, however, both sides had abundant domestic preoccupations. Thus despite mutual hostility the conflict was kept within limits: the West could not organize a coordinated and effective challenge to Bolshevism, while the limited power of the new Soviet state punctured hopes of a speedy "world revolution." The revolutionary ambitions and simplicities of the Bolsheviks had to be reshaped as a result of the need to rebuild the country and establish firm control following the terrible years of world war, revolution, foreign interventions and the civil war. Instead of fostering world revolution and the withering away of the state, Soviet foreign policy in the 1920s was forced to adjust to the international states system. Soviet power grew steadily, but in the 1930s Soviet extreme ambitions remained constrained by the massive but unfinished industrialization programs and the massive political purges seen as necessary to secure Stalin's version of "socialism in one country," and by the need to build up strength to meet the growing military threats posed by Nazi Germany and Imperial Japan.

For a short period in the late 1930s, Hitler succeeded in creating a common interest between East and West, where he was perceived as a common threat. Even so, mutual suspicion prevented the former Soviet Union and the Western democracies from making common cause; and at the last minute, in 1939, Stalin chose to buy breathing space by entering into a pact with Hitler. It lasted nearly two years. Hitler's attack on the former Soviet Union in June 1941, followed in December by his declaration of war against the United States, finally drove the Western powers and the former Soviet Union together. As a result of the victorious struggle which followed, Soviet power fully emerged onto the world stage as one of the "Big Three."

3. The Cold War: Interpretations

After defeating Hitler, the wartime partners—"the strange alliance"—broke up, and what was quickly dubbed the Cold War ensued. In light of the difficult relationship which had nearly always existed between the Eastern and Western powers, it is evident that it was their alliance rather than the Cold War which was the historical aberration. However, the phrase "Cold War" did give due recognition to the fact that in this case the mutual hostility was "deeper"—more paranoid—than that usually displayed by Great Powers. Hopes for a harmonious world rested on the relationship between the two dominant nations, now dubbed "superpowers." In the event there proved to be no cooperation between them, only hostility. The post-war world became characterized by a balance of terror rather than collective security, and by imposed order rather than positive peace.

The East-West conflict manifest itself as a heavily-armed Cold War between 1946 and 1963: that is to say, it was an intense political, ideological and economic confrontation, but the parties stopped short of using military force directly against each other. These years were further characterized by extreme bipolarity, rigid political and military alliances, arms racing, mutual paranoia, a simple 'two-camp' image of world politics and a zero-sum approach to the issues of the day. The "iron curtain" which was built across Europe divided two worlds: they had different political systems which were dominated by hostile superpowers; they were organized around military alliances which targeted each other and economic groupings which were in competition. The phrase "Cold War" implied a continuing struggle between East and West and the prospect of victory by one or the other, sooner or later—though in an era when the costs of hot war between industrial giants had risen beyond imagination, their struggle had to be pursued by other means. The Western concept of Cold War, as just described, had a rather more benign-sounding counterpart in the Soviet concept of "*peaceful* coexistence." This idea, which evolved from the Leninist period, stressed that the struggle between the two social systems was inevitable but that the means would not be military unless the imperialists struck first (see *Marxist-Leninist Concept of Peaceful Coexistence*). The constrained hostility of the superpowers in the nuclear age was succinctly expressed by the French sociologist Raymond Aron in 1947, when he said that war was improbable but that peace was impossible.

Debate in the West about the blame for the Cold War has been long and contentious, and it is still not settled. It has moved through three principal phases. First, for the decade and a half following the ending of the Second World War, Western writers blamed the former Soviet Union for the Cold War. From this viewpoint, it was Stalin who broke up the wartime alliance and ruined the prospects for peace in the post-war period. The case against him was based on his belligerent and suspicious behavior, his brutal incorporation of Eastern Europe into the Soviet camp, his apparent desire to communize Western Europe, his probing in some of the fluid situations left over by the war, and his non-cooperation in international institutions.

The second phase in the debate came during the 1960s and 1970s, when an American school of "revisionists" redirected the blame for the Cold War towards the United States. While there were various versions of the revisionist argument, the basic position asserted that the United States had pursued expansionist policies ever since the end of the nineteenth century in a political, commercial and cultural —if not necessarily a military—sense. Capitalism, it was argued, needed an ever-expanding market to survive. From this point of view, United States policy after 1945 was seen as a continuation (but with more power and vigor than ever before) of its traditional efforts to create an international situation in which US capitalism and democracy could succeed and dominate. The result of this US belligerence, according to the revisionists, was a Soviet backlash: an aggressive-defensive reaction on the part of Moscow, and the predictable domination of Soviet policymaking by hard-line Stalinists.

The third stage in the historiography of the Cold War was characterized by a liberal, middle-of-the-road interpretation of events. The lapse of time from the extreme anti-Soviet feelings which had characterized the height of the Cold War on the one hand, and from the anti-Americanism that had characterized the Vietnam War period on the other, now led to more critical distance on the part of historians and analysts. This perspective sees the Cold War as a particularly virulent form of the "normal" conflict which is apt to develop between Great Powers, exacerbated by the markedly bipolar setting of the post-war period. What has been called the "post-revisionist" interpretation of the Cold War stresses the unavoidable clash of interests between the two superpowers, their spiralling misperceptions in the unsettled conditions of the late 1940s, the action-reaction phenomenon and the impact of the dynamics of events. Rather than pointing the finger at one or the other side, this interpretation looks to the history of the interrelationship and the understandable Soviet desire for security arising from its traditional mistrust of the Western powers. Stalin therefore, like any Soviet leader,

wanted a weakened Germany and the creation of a defensive glacis of satellite states in Eastern Europe. However, the actions which the former Soviet Union took to enhance its security, together with exaggerated Western fears of Soviet military strength, led to inflated estimates of the Soviet threat to Western Europe. Meanwhile, Stalin greatly exaggerated the active military challenge posed to the Soviet Union by the Western powers—helped by the fact that US policy under President Truman (especially in comparison with the Roosevelt years) became appreciably tougher (see *Truman Doctrine*). These were also the brief years of the US atomic monopoly.

The Cold War gradually stabilized, though not without extreme anxiety. The alarms of the Berlin blockade and the Korean War were followed by a recognition that there was no rational alternative in the nuclear age but for East and West to coexist. Critical in this development was the Soviet acquisition of nuclear weapons after 1949, which for the first time made the United States homeland vulnerable to terrible destruction. In 1956 Nikita Khrushchev, Stalin's replacement as leader of the former Soviet Union, revised the old Leninist precept about the inevitability of war and declared that war between the two social systems was no longer fatalistically inevitable. This, he said, was the result of the strategic stalemate, not any radical change in the determinants of world politics. Despite the signs of thaw in the Cold War, East-West relations remained full of dangerous potential. Stable superpower relations were challenged in the second half of the 1950s by a series of developments: by the aggressive rhetoric of John Foster Dulles (see *Dulles, John Foster*), the United States Secretary of State under President Eisenhower, who threatened to "roll back" communism in Europe; by the challenges to Soviet authority in Hungary and Poland, which in 1956 led to an armed Soviet response; by the "delicate balance" of nuclear terror between the superpowers, at a time when surprise attacks were feared; and, perhaps most important of all, by the adventuristic foreign policy pursued by Khrushchev at the turn of the 1950s and 1960s. The most dangerous episode of these years was the 1962 Cuban missile crisis when, according to most sources, the world came closer to nuclear war than at any time before or since.

Having looked into the nuclear abyss, the superpowers pulled back. In the aftermath of the Cuban crisis the Partial Test Ban Treaty was signed in 1963 as a token of their desire to relax tension, and the hot-line was installed to facilitate communication in future crises. Other developments ameliorated the

Cold War and helped to break down the rigid bipolarity of the late 1940s and 1950s. The superpowers remained the dominant actors in world affairs, but in the 1960s their allies exhibited more independence: within NATO as well as the Warsaw Pact, "bloc fatigue," ideological relaxation and "polycentrism" became the order of the day. As the situation in Europe stabilized, the focus of the East-West conflict began to shift toward the developing nations, now made up of many newly independent states. This tendency was both increased and complicated by the emergence of a split between the People's Republic of China and the former Soviet Union. By the late 1960s the risks of war were greater between these communist giants than between the United States and the former Soviet Union: what was dubbed a "new Cold War" was an East-East affair.

4. Détente: Interpretations

As between the United States and former Soviet Union, there was a growing recognition through the 1960s of their mutual strategic interest in stabilizing the nuclear confrontation. This involved an attempt to develop secure second-strike nuclear systems, to replace the vulnerable ones originally deployed, and an acceptance of the need to engage in arms control (see *Nuclear Strategy*). The latter included an appreciation of the importance of limiting the spread of nuclear weapons to other countries, resulting in the Non-Proliferation Treaty (see *Non-Proliferation Treaty (NPT)*) of 1968. As a result of these efforts, the superpower relationship was being described as a "limited adversary" one; this signified the fact that while the superpowers remained competitors, they both accepted that they had a common interest in avoiding nuclear war. Such was the character of this "adversary partnership" that there was some early talk about "convergence" between the two systems. It was argued that industrialization and urbanization were creating a civilization common to all modern states, while nuclear weapons were imposing constraints on their competition. Shared interests were growing, with the former Soviet Union becoming less revolutionary and the United States becoming more planned. For the moment, world events discredited any further extension of the theory: their economic systems did not grow alike, nor did their conflicts of political interest disappear.

Despite the continuing conflicts of interest between the superpowers, after 1969 a deeper period of détente, or relaxation of tension, developed between them (see *Détente*). A major contributory cause was

the state of the Soviet economy, which led General Secretary Brezhnev to seek extensive trade agreements with the West; these required peaceful relations. On the Western side this was matched by the new strategy of President Nixon and his National Security Adviser, Henry Kissinger, which sought to entangle the former Soviet Union in a web of cooperative agreements. The United States, suffering because of the costly and inconclusive war in Vietnam, called for an "era of negotiations," to which the economically lame former Soviet Union responded. This new stage in East-West relations was greatly facilitated by the personalities directing the foreign policies of both superpowers.

The label "détente" which was attached to East-West relations during the 1970s was inadequately understood from the start. It was oversold, especially in the United States, and as a result, many people expected more out of the relationship than it was possible for the participants to deliver. The reasons for optimism were understandable, however, the early 1970s saw the signature of treaties which legitimized the post-war boundaries in Europe; there was President Nixon's visit to Moscow; and the signing took place of the first Strategic Arms Limitation Treaty, together with a bundle of other cooperative agreements. As a result of these developments, many in the West became disposed to believe that détente meant more than a relaxation of tension: that, in fact, it meant "live and let live," with more security and less defense expenditure. Détente never had such meanings in Soviet minds, and Soviet behavior in the mid-1970s quickly disillusioned any false hopes. The continuing Soviet arms build-up, obstructive behavior in subsequent rounds of the Strategic Arms Limitation Talks (SALT), "meddling" in the Middle East, internal repression, the abuse of human rights, "adventurism" in Angola and Ethiopia, the rejection of the spirit of the 1975 Helsinki Final Act, and eventually the Soviet military intervention in Afghanistan —all these actions fell short of what most Western opinion considered to be the proper standards of a détente relationship. As a result there was an abrupt change in Western (especially United States) thinking about détente in the mid-1970s: instead of welcoming détente, growing numbers of Americans came to think that it was a dangerous illusion deliberately fostered by the Soviet leaders in order to lull the United States into a false sense of security, while the former Soviet Union itself steadily continued upon its expansionist path.

The "lessons" of East-West relations in the 1970s were extensively discussed by policymakers and analysts. It became apparent, for example, that the former Soviet Union did not understand the extent to which its own behavior was seen in the West as inconsistent with a détente relationship; in particular, the former Soviet Union failed to appreciate that the West would see its active support for "national liberation movements" in Africa and elsewhere as being inconsistent with simultaneous protestations of a desire to relax tension. For their part, Soviet policy makers simply believed that their support for such movements was an internationalist duty during a period of "peaceful coexistence." While the West blamed the former Soviet Union for undermining détente, what was not always fully appreciated was the extent to which Soviet complaints about United States behavior closely mirrored Western complaints against itself. In this regard, Soviet commentators criticized the US arms build-up, its failure to follow through on the economic agreements it reached with the former Soviet Union in the early 1970s, its lack of seriousness about arms control, the unfriendly posture displayed toward the former Soviet Union through its attempt to improve relations with the People's Republic of China, its squeezing of the former Soviet Union out of Middle Eastern affairs, and its encouragement of Japanese militarization.

The old problems of mistrust cracked the façade of détente as the superpowers tried, in stumbling fashion, to establish ground rules for safe but self-interested behavior in the nuclear age. The culminating point of their efforts was the Basic Principles Agreement of 1972 and the Helsinki Final Act of 1975. But as the history of these agreements showed, it was one thing to choose forms of words to identify ground rules, and another entirely to have the superpowers apply them to each other's satisfaction through all the ups and downs of the unfolding international situation. The collapse of détente was marked, at the turn of 1979-80, by direct Soviet military intervention in Afghanistan and by the US decision not to ratify the SALT II Treaty. Détente ended—some would question whether serious mutual restraint ever really began—because of the interplay of subjective, objective and contingent factors: these included inherited mistrust, the competitive dynamics of bipolar confrontation, the pressures of innovation in military technology, the inherent difficulties of arms control, mutually inconsistent expectations about détente, and continuing competition for influence in the developing countries. At no point had the superpowers achieved a relationship of stable peace; rather, they were involved in the uncertain business of trying to work out safer means by which to carry on their competi-

tion for world influence. Détente was not an endpoint, but a process—and in the late 1970s it went out of fashion as the ruling groups of both superpowers entered a very conservative phase.

5. The Second Cold War

Relations between the superpowers deteriorated towards the end of the 1970s. Amongst other things, the Soviet intervention in Afghanistan seemed to suggest that the Kremlin leadership believed that the benefits of détente were limited and that they had little more to lose in their relationship with the US. This military move, in turn, seemed to confirm the warnings about Soviet ambitions from the New Right, who for several years had been setting the agenda in United States affairs. The chief manifestation of this trend was the election in 1980 of Ronald Reagan. The new President was a larger-than-life American patriot and anticommunist, dedicated to restoring the United States to primacy in world affairs after what he and his supporters saw as the dangerous and passive years associated with the "Vietnam syndrome." In his election campaign Reagan had prided himself on having opposed every arms control proposal to date. Not surprisingly, the first Reagan Administration adopted a deliberately belligerent posture toward the former Soviet Union, and backed it up with a defense program of historic dimensions. The former Soviet Union bristled in reaction, but still declared its commitment to détente. However, both Soviet words (which were not trusted) and Soviet actions (such as walking out of arms control negotiations, or shooting down of a Korean airliner) played into the hands of a White House determined to see the worst in what it called "The Evil Empire."

The death of détente was therefore followed by what some called a "new" or "second" Cold War, in which US-Soviet relations became worse than at any period since the Cuban missile crisis. The first half of the 1980s were dangerous years. There was name-calling, sabre-rattling, vigorous propaganda, tension over issues such as the deployment of new theatre nuclear weapons in Europe, sanctions, the breakdown of arms control negotiations, competition in developing countries, and an arms build-up on a massive scale. For the first time in twenty years, there was a real sense that war between the superpowers might, in some circumstances, be conceivable. Nevertheless, although powerful military-industrial and political interests in both superpowers sustained Cold War attitudes, the growing costs and risks of the new confrontation, together with a certain nostalgia for détente, led to the start of efforts on both sides to build a less dangerous relationship. In 1985 President Reagan, re-elected for a second term, seemed to want to replace his "trigger-happy" image for that of "peace-maker," but more importantly the new Soviet leader, Mikhail Gorbachev (see Nobel Peace Prize Laureates: *Mikhail S. Gorbachev*), appeared to want to play down the East-West confrontation in order to concentrate on domestic preoccupations.

6. The Gorbachev Revolution

During the latter half of the 1980s, the impact of Gorbachev's *novoe politicheskoe myshlenie* ("new political thinking") revolutionized Soviet political life in ways he did not foresee and brought about a radical improvement in East-West relations. Traditional Soviet thinking about foreign policy was characterized by an essentially zero-sum world view, in which there existed little or no potential for permanent improvement in relations with the West. By contrast, "new political thinking" introduced an approach to foreign policy planning in which mutual security was seen not only as feasible, but was embraced as a fundamental objective of relations between the former Soviet Union and other powers. Thereafter there occurred a calculated reassessment of Soviet policy across the spectrum of international affairs, including East-West relations, Eastern Europe and the communist world, arms control and intervention in the developing world. Soviet foreign policy shifted from confrontation to common security, arms racing to disarmament, and global rivalry to de-ideologizing world politics. Gorbachev became a more popular leader in the West than Reagan.

The intellectual justification behind this re-appraisal of traditional doctrines was set out by Gorbachev in *Perestroika: New Thinking for our Country and the World*, a book which popularized the concepts of *perestroika* ("restructuring") and *glasnost* ("openness") on both sides of the iron curtain (see *Glasnost and Perestroika*). Orthodox Marxism-Leninism had depicted the capitalist world as the principal threat to the survival of the Soviet state, and therefore as the main obstacle to the further spread of the international socialist cause. "New thinking" rejected this traditional approach to East-West relations, as the emptiness of Khrushchev's threat to "bury capitalism" one day became increasingly apparent during the 1970s and 1980s. Although they were faced by slowing economic growth, heightened awareness of the disparities in living standards between East and West, and the blatantly anti-Soviet rhetoric and policies of the Reagan

Administration, Soviet leaders in the early 1980s clung on to traditional policies of internal consolidation. Gorbachev's response to the same problems concentrated instead on proposals for radical economic and political reform. His insistence on the open scrutiny of established ideology stemmed from a recognition that Soviet socialism was increasingly failing to meet basic economic wants or solve the accumulated domestic social and political problems of the former Soviet Union and its eastern European allies, let alone fulfill its self-proclaimed role as the catalyst for world transformation.

Soviet relations with the Western world were a priority in Gorbachev's reforms, and "new thinking" transformed the superpower relationship, hitherto based on principles of power-balancing and "spheres of influence." Likewise, the substitution of class-struggle principles by concepts of "common security," "reasonable sufficiency" and "stable peace" signalled a fundamental change in the climate of East-West relations. The concept of "reasonable sufficiency" was inspired by the realization that as soon as nuclear capabilities cross the threshold required for mutual assured destruction (MAD), they have no extra threat value. One element of the revised notion of national security under Gorbachev was therefore that a huge reduction in the nuclear arsenals of the superpowers was necessary to ease psychological tensions and reduce the danger of accidental nuclear war. A second element comprised the concept of "common security." This included moving towards "defensive defense" rather than an offensive posture based on the contingency of having to fight and win World War III (see *Non-offensive Defense*). Such military restructuring was based on a recognition of the need for both sides in the East-West relationship to develop military postures that minimized or eliminated the potential for misunderstanding, by taking prior account of the likely impact of defense decisions upon each superpower's perceptions of the other's intentions.

The impact of "new thinking" was also apparent with regard to ongoing campaigns of Soviet involvement in the developing world. Traditionally, such foreign "adventurism" had served an important ideological purpose. Under the administrations of Khrushchev and Brezhnev, for example, the developing world was regarded as a supremely important area of international class struggle, holding enormous potential for the realignment of "the correlation of world forces" to the advantage of socialism. By the mid-1980s, this strategy of involvement had proved itself to be economically costly while exacerbating East-West tensions by feeding Western fears about

Soviet global intentions. "New thinking" reversed the priority attached to the developing world as a focus for Soviet expansionism and influence. Gorbachev soon initiated Soviet disengagement from various protracted and costly commitments in the Third World, and during the late 1980s and early 1990s the former Soviet Union withdrew from such "bleeding wounds" as Afghanistan, Angola, Cambodia and Ethiopia. But selective disengagement did not imply isolationism; instead foreign involvement shifted form to an attempt to build diplomatic and commercial influence with key countries in order to maximize Soviet economic and political interests.

7. The End of the Cold War

By far the most dramatic reforms associated with 'new thinking' took place in Eastern Europe (see *Eastern Europe, Transformation of*). The Brezhnev doctrine (see *Brezhnev Doctrine*) (which since 1968 had limited the sovereignty of the Soviet buffer-states through the threat of armed intervention by Moscow) gave way to what was called the Sinatra doctrine: By devolving political responsibility to the satellite states, Gorbachev shed a significant element of the Soviet empire's costly economic and military burden, leaving the socialist countries of Eastern Europe free to "do things their way" for the first time in over forty years. A key factor behind Gorbachev's thinking was the decision by the Soviet military establishment that it was no longer necessary (or desirable) to plan for the contingency of World War. This decision allowed a relaxation of established Soviet positions on arms control and the necessity to control Eastern Europe. During 1988, Gorbachev visited political leaders throughout the region, warning that henceforth they must assume responsibility for their internal affairs without the backing of the Red Army. The demise of the Brezhnev doctrine was one of the catalysts for the collapse of Soviet-style communism. For many East European citizens it had been the fear of Soviet tanks, rather than an earnest ideological commitment to their government's version of socialism, that had constrained the mobilization of their opposition to political authority. Nevertheless, when change came, it took everybody by surprise. This time, when people in Eastern Europe pushed, it was against an open door. In withdrawing Soviet military support to the regimes of Eastern Europe, Gorbachev opened the political flood-gates. "People-power" rose to topple a succession of regimes in a rapid chain-reaction that transformed the political face of Eastern Europe, and with it, the Cold War.

Around the globe, people looked on in astonishment as a "velvet revolution" swept away forty years of Soviet-style communism in a matter of weeks. In Poland, the legalization of the Solidarity union in April 1989 was consolidated by the defeat of the Polish communist party in the free elections in June. This set a precedent for the swift transitions from socialist rule that followed in Hungary, Bulgaria and Czechoslovakia. Gorbachev's visit to East Berlin during the 1989 October celebrations prompted near hysteria among the crowds there, and was followed by escalating demonstrations across the country in support of greater political freedom. Finally, on the evening of November 9, East Germans massed on the frontier with West Berlin, drawn by rumors that the border was soon to be re-opened. That night the Berlin Wall—which, since 1961, had stood as a defining symbol of the East-West conflict—was breached, paving the way for eventual German reunification in October 1990. Events moved more slowly in Romania, where the dictator Nicolae Ceausescu had made clear his opposition to democratic reform by ordering troops to open fire on protesters at a human rights rally in the city of Timisoara. Indignation at this atrocity led to widespread demonstrations against the regime, finally causing the army to mutiny. Captured while trying to flee the country, Ceausescu was executed, thus bringing to a bloody end a brief era of revolution which—in view of the enormity of the events themselves—had otherwise proved to be remarkably peaceful.

In Russia too, the reforms set in motion by Gorbachev finally escalated out of control, though the challenge to the established political order came not from the forces of democracy, as in Eastern Europe, but from conservative elements within the communist party itself. In August 1991, a group of high-ranking communist officials, army officers and members of the KGB staged a *coup d'état* in opposition to the increasing political and economic liberalization of "new thinking." With Gorbachev under house arrest and the Red Army converging on the Russian parliament building, Boris Yeltsin—a "democrat," political reformer and opponent of Gorbachev—successfully called upon the people to aid him in persuading the bewildered troops to disobey their mutinous superiors. Following the suppression of the *coup* and his popular election to power in June 1991, Yeltsin set about dismantling the communist party apparatus, establishing the political infrastructure of democratic government and implementing a program of drastic economic reforms. Finally, in December 1991, the Union of Soviet Socialist Republics was itself disbanded and replaced by the less formally integrated Commonwealth of Independent States (CIS).

8. The Future of East-West Relations

Across the Soviet bloc, which at its height had stretched from the Pacific in the East to the heart of Europe in the West, the familiar structures and symbols of communism fell as people turned to embrace the new ideologies of capitalism and democracy. In startling contrast to the 1980s, which had begun with superpower relations characterized by fear and hostility, the early 1990s saw the two former adversaries attempting to manage the demise of the Cold War system in partnership. New and previously quite unthinkable forms of cooperation developed between the former Cold War warriors—most notably during the 1991 Gulf War, when a combination of Russian-backed diplomacy and the US-led military force was used to liberate the small, oil-producing state of Kuwait from occupation by the Iraqi forces of Saddam Hussein. This unprecedented collaboration—all the more remarkable because of Iraq's Cold War alliance with the former Soviet Union—prompted US President George Bush to speak of a "new world order" replacing the former bipolar dynamic between East and West.

While speculation abounded that the historic East-West conflict was now finally at an end, the fall of communism was variously interpreted in the West as a precursor to renewed instability and conflict in Europe, as a triumph for the forces of liberal democracy that signalled "the end of history," and as an unmitigated geopolitical disaster for the United States and its economic interests. These differences of opinion about the Cold War, its end and the future of East-West relations reflect the fact that the years since the fall of communism have been complex and difficult. As familiar threats and patterns of interaction have faded, new dangers and uncertainties face people and politicians in both the East and West. Russian domestic politics has been characterized by turbulence rather than tranquillity, as Yeltsin steered a difficult course between the extreme demands of equally zealous political rivals in both the conservative and reformist camps. In their movement towards greater democracy and economic liberalism, the newly independent states of Europe (including Russia) experienced vastly increased levels of economic hardship, social dislocation and organized (frequently violent) crime, leaving many yearning for the apparent sense of order and stability that prevailed under the old regimes. Likewise among the states of Western Europe and North America, the removal of the old enemy served to expose the economic and social problems which accompanied the global triumph of capitalism. The 1990s witnessed escalating budget deficits, serious inflation in some countries, structural unemployment, poverty, increasing gaps between rich and poor (nationally and globally) as well as the frictions resulting from the effective alienation of entire sub-groups within society. All this tainted the claims of the triumphalists seeking to portray the collapse of communism as an unqualified endorsement of liberal democracy and free-market economics.

Most significantly, the problems of resurgent nationalism, and ethnic conflict within the former Soviet bloc, and uncertainty about the fate of the former Soviet Union's formidable nuclear and conventional forces have complicated the discussions about fundamental issues between East and West, notably the future security "architecture" in Europe and the place of the newly independent states within it. In March 1997, the US and Russian presidents, Bill Clinton and Boris Yeltsin, met in Helsinki to discuss the planned eastwards expansion of the NATO alliance, as well as other issues relating to arms control and the question of Russian economic reform. Western officials stated their determination to proceed with NATO expansion, citing it as a positive development that would enhance European security by incorporating a number of states formerly within the WTO (see *Security and Cooperation in Europe*). Moscow objected forcefully to the plan, however, claiming that it would leave hostile armies at its borders and contribute further to the strategic and economic isolation of Russia in the post-Cold War world. What these serious conflicts of interest reveal is that, despite the passing of the ideological competition between them and the new language of "partnership," "cooperation" and "reassurance" that now routinely pervades negotiations between Russia and the major states in the West, the historic insecurities between East and West have not been eliminated.

Bibliography

Arbatov G, Oltmans W 1983 *Cold War or Detente? The Soviet Viewpoint.* Zed, London

Booth K (ed.) 1998 Forthcoming *Statecraft and Security: The Cold War and After.* Cambridge University Press, Cambridge

Fleming D 1961 *The Cold War and Its Origins 1917-1960*, 2 vols. Doubleday, Garden City, New York

Fukuyama F 1992 *The End of History and the Last Man.* Hamish Hamilton, London

Gaddis J L 1972 *The United States and the Origins of the Cold War, 1941-1947.* Columbia University Press, New York

Garthoff R L 1985 *Detente and Confrontation: American-Soviet Relations from Nixon to Reagan.* Brookings Institution, Washington, DC

Gorbachev M S 1987 *Perestroika: New Thinking for Our Country and the World.* Collins, London

Kennan G F 1961 *Russia and the West under Lenin and Stalin.* Little Brown, Boston, Massachusetts

MccGwire M K 1991 *Perestroika and Soviet National Security.* Brookings Institution, Washington, DC

MccGwire M K 1997 NATO *Expansion in European Security.* London Defence Studies (No. 37) The Centre for Defence Sudies

Mearsheimer J J 1990 Back to the future: Instability in Europe after the cold war. *Int'l Security* 15(1). Cambridge, MA, MIT Press

Ponomaryov B, Gromyko A, Khvostov V (eds.) 1969 *History of Soviet Foreign Policy 1917-70.* Progress, Moscow

Ulam A B 1974 *Expansion and Coexistence: Soviet Foreign Policy 1917-73.* Praeger, New York

Yergin D 1978 *Shattered Peace: The Origins of the Cold War and the National Security State.* Houghton Mifflin, Boston, Massachusetts

KEN BOOTH; SIMON DAVIES

East-West Trade: Finland's Changing Role

The disappearance of "The Second World" and its transition to democracy and market economy in the Eastern part of Europe, has not left "The First World" untouched. Naturally the demise of the former Soviet Union and other socialist countries had varying effects on the outside world. Apart from reunified Germany, these changes probably had the greatest economic impact on Finland. The trade with the Council for Mutual Economic Assistance member countries was far more important to Finland than to any other OECD member country (cf. Table 1). The Finnish framework for trade relations with the socialist countries was also unique.

Finland's trade with the socialist countries, especially the former Soviet Union, was often described as a success story compared to the poor progress of other East-West trade and the distortions of intra-CMEA trade. Finland's exports to the former Soviet Union had experienced a slight decline since the mid-1980's and in 1991 it dropped by two thirds. This meant that Finnish-Soviet trade experienced an abrupt 'normalization' of trade right before the end of the former Soviet Union.

Although, among the Western countries affected by the transition's "shock treatment" Finland was the main recipient, however, Finland managed to quickly overcome the setback in East-West trade. In 1993, the growth rate of Finland's exports to the transition economies was higher than that of any other OECD member country. The explanation for this rapid recovery can be found in part by looking at a set of characteristics unique to Finland that led to the earlier successes and failures in Finnish-Soviet trade.

1. Trade with the Former Soviet Union

In the Second World War Finland was drawn because of the separate "Winter War" (1939-1940) with the Soviet Union. Although Finland belonged to the defeated, the country was not occupied by a foreign army or under foreign rule. Hence, after the war Finland was able to continue its development as a western democracy and market economy.

Finland's foreign trade and payments were gradually liberalized, after joining the IMF in 1948, and GATT in 1950. In 1958, the Finnish markka became freely convertible in commercial exchanges. Finland became a member of other international communities and organizations compatible with its outlook and policies. For example, Finland has participated in the cooperation of Nordic countries (Nordic Council 1951), in western European integration through the European Free Trade Association (from 1961), in the work of global organizations of developed market economies such as the OECD, and in 1995 Finland became a member of the European Union.

A central prerequisite for Finland's western orientation and neutral policy was formed by good and stable relations with the former Soviet Union. Since 1948 the basis for Finnish-Soviet political relations was established by the Treaty of Friendship, Cooperation and Mutual Assistance. A major requirement of the treaty was that Finland repel any attack on the former Soviet Union through Finnish territory. This treaty and the Soviet view of a linkage between its interests and Finland's policy had some restrictive effects on the latter. For example, Finland did not participate in the Marshall Program and could not proceed with Western integration at the same pace as its neighbors, Sweden and Norway.

The war reparation Finland had to pay during the years 1946-52 created the basis for exports to the former Soviet Union. Since 1951, when Finland and the Soviet Union initiated their mutual five-year trading agreements, the countries became important partners

Table 1 The significance of exports to the East (CMEA member countries) for the national economy measured by the share (%) of the exports to the East in total exports (1), and in gross domestic product (2)

	1970		1975		1985		1988		1989		1990	
	(1)	(2)	(1)	(2)	(1)	(2)	(1)	(2)	(1)	(2)	(1)	(2)
Finland	15.7	3.32	23.9	4.64	23.4	5.84	16.4	3.45	16.2	3.19	14.0	2.71
Austria	12.9	2.53	17.0	3.41	11.0	2.91	9.7	2.37	9.9	2.54	10.4	2.71
FRG	3.8	0.70	7.2	1.55	4.0	1.18	4.5	1.22	5.0	1.42	4.9	1.31
Sweden	5.0	1.01	6.3	1.51	2.5	0.77	2.2	0.61	2.4	0.65	2.3	0.59
France	3.6	0.45	5.0	0.76	3.0	0.55	2.2	0.38	2.1	0.38	1.9	0.33
Great Britain	3.2	0.50	3.0	0.55	1.5	0.34	1.6	0.27	1.6	0.29	1.4	0.27
OECD	2.9	0.30	4.6	0.62	2.7	0.39	2.5	0.36	2.7	0.40	2.6	0.39

Source: OECD Statistics

in mutual trade (cf. Table 2).

The high level of Finnish-Soviet trade can not be explained by the trading potential of Finland, which has a population of five million people, or even the geographical closeness of the two countries. The most important factors which led to the development of the special Finnish-Soviet trade relationship are outlined below.

Politics promotes trade. In the former Soviet Union foreign trade was a servant of foreign policy rather than of the economy. So it was in accordance with the former Soviet Union's striving for friendly and stable political relations with Finland that preferential treatment in trade was given. Finland's official policy also favored good political relations and promoted the utilization of the neighboring superpower's trading potential. This was expressed in Finland's trade policy. Imports from the former Soviet Union received the same treatment as the goods imported tariff-free from the EFTA member countries and also later from the European Community. The policy was to avoid any discrimination of the former Soviet Union in relation to Finland's western integration. Nevertheless Finland's trade with the former Soviet Union was not in contradiction to the embargo policy of COCOM, which Finland observed but did not join as a member because of the country's policy of neutrality.

The former Soviet Union's preferential policy towards Finland resulted in a special system of agreements and institutions, since effective tariffs did not exist in its centralized economy. The basis of the preferential position rested on a bilateral trading system until the year 1991, lasting twenty years longer than with any other developed western country. The main principle of bilateral trading was to keep the clearing account as balanced as possible. The balance was achieved primarily by adjusting trade flows. If Finland had a deficit Finnish companies increased their deliveries to the former Soviet Union. If Finland had a surplus it could be transferred from an interest-free clearing account to a special interest-bearing account as a credit. One common device used to adjust trade flows was crude oil trading from Russia to third countries by the Finnish company Neste. At the end of the 1980's, for example, oil trading covered about one fifth of Finland's exports to the former Soviet Union. At the same time, the share of payments in convertible currencies increased to one fifth of the total payments (Kajaste 1993 p. 116).

In addition to traditional commodity trade, other operations like industrial cooperation, construction projects, and joint ventures (since their approval in

Table 2 The development of Finnish-Soviet trade

Years	Total Soviet foreign trade	Share (%) of Finnish-Soviet trade in Western-Soviet foreign trade	Total Finnish foreign trade
1951-55	3.9	25.5	14.4
1956-60	3.1	18.1	16.4
1961-65	2.7	14.4	14.7
1966-70	2.6	12.2	14.2
1971-75	3.1	11.0	15.0
1976-80	3.5	11.2	13.6
1981-85	3.9	13.2	23.4
1986-90	2.9	11.5	14.1
1991	2.9	5.2	6.6

Source: Soviet and Finnish trade statistics

Table 3 Finland's special preconditions in competition with other Western countries for trade with the Soviet Union (Russia)*

	Under the old regime 1951-85	During Perestroika 1985-	In "New Europe" 1990-	Abolition of bilateral clearing 1991-	In Russia 1992-
Foreign policy	+++	++	+		
Trade policy	+++	++	++		
Institutions	++	+			
Experience	++	++	+	+	+
Geographical proximity	++	+++	++	++	++

* The number of plus-signs indicates the factor's positive impact on trade.

1987), played a role in Finnish-Soviet economic relations. In the 1970s and 1980s several big projects were realized by Finnish companies, mostly near the Finnish border, including hydroelectric plants, paper industry complexes, a mining complex, and hotels. The most significant Soviet projects in Finland were deliveries to two nuclear power stations and to the steel industry. Especially in the second half of the 1980s, operations other than traditional trade of goods and services increased considerably. However, their frequency remained low and the pattern differed from that in other markets. Activities, such as direct investments, requiring greater financial and managerial commitment were adopted more slowly in the Soviet market than elsewhere (Hirvensalo 1996).

A decline in trade between the former Soviet Union and Finland started in the mid 1980's (see Table 2). The reasons for the trade decline were primarily of Soviet origin. The changes in the economic and political system as well as in the economy and politics affected the entire Soviet foreign trade with the beginning of perestroika in 1985. The development of Finnish trade was not, however, solely attributable to general and common factors. In 1991, Soviet imports from Finland diminished by a whole 77 percent, compared to the decline of 38 percent in imports from Germany, 21 percent from France, and 10 percent from Italy, 73 percent drop in imports from ex-socialist Poland, 68 percent from Hungary, and 58 percent from Czechoslovakia (Foreign Trade, 4-5/1992).

There were also specific reasons for the decline of Finland's trade since 1985 and its total collapse in 1991. The favorable position of Finland compared to other western countries was gradually eroded when the revolutionary developments began in the former Soviet Union and Eastern Europe (see Table 3).

The final breakdown came in the beginning of 1991, when the bilateral trade system was abolished. Despite clear signals, there were authorities and enterprises in Finland as late as in the autumn of 1990 which did not expect that the bilateral system would be terminated so suddenly without a transition period.

2. The Rapid Recovery of Trade with Russia

During the Soviet regime the majority of Finland's trade with the former Soviet Union, approximately 80 percent, had its source or destination within the territory of the Russian Federation. In this respect, the situation did not change as Russia became the heir to the Soviet trade with Finland. In 1993 the value of Finnish exports to Russia grew by 100 percent and the Russians spent the same amount of money on purchases from Finland as the Americans: imports from Finland amounted to about 10 USD per capita. Despite of decline of Russia's GDP Finland's exports to Russia has grown continuously since 1993. In 1995 Finland was placed second after Germany in Russia's imports from EU member countries.

Finland's entry in the European Union at the beginning of 1995 gave it a new position as a member of a customs union. The trade policy of the EU concerning Russia was thus enforced in Finland. For example, Finland adopted immediately the Generalized System of Preferences (GSP) that applies to imports from Russia to the European Union.

Although the EU membership changes customs regulations and might affect the imports of some articles, the overall impact of the membership on Finland's trade with the East has been judged to be positive. After all, Finland now has its own markets as well as access to the huge EU markets to offer its trade partners both in the East and West.

Even as an EU member Finland has the option to continue the work of the Finnish-Russian economic commission. In addition, the special cooperation with the neighboring regions of Russia will be continued. This involves joint activities with the Russian regions on the

Finnish border, i.e., the province of Murmansk, the Republic of Carelia, St. Petersburg, and the province of Leningrad. Expectations have now been raised to link the cooperation of the neighboring regions to a wider international context covering the regions of the Baltic Sea and the Barents Sea. As a member of the EU, Finland can bind its mutual cooperation programs with the neighboring regions to its national contribution in the framework of the TACIS program of the EU.

3. Finland as a Gateway

Now that Russia is an emerging market economy a natural goal for Finland is to act as a mediating agent for Russia's internationalization. Finland therefore has an important role as a gateway between Russia and the outside world.

Among the developed western countries, only Finland offers the real advantage of a common border with Russia. Norway's importance as Russia's western neighbor is limited by the shortness of the common border in the arctic region as well as Norway's military commitment to NATO. Finland also has a special position among Russia's numerous neighbors. Finland has a well-developed infrastructure and economy, political stability and has no foreign policy problems with Russia. It is uniquely located at the mouth of the main route (Moscow-St. Petersburg) and the principal port of Russia (St.Petersburg). A new dimension is added by Finland's membership in the EU from the beginning of 1995, which brings the big powers of Europe in direct contact and gives Finland the role of linking the two. It is now possible to get from the EU to Russia with one step and vice versa.

3.1 Gate for Transportation

During the Soviet era Finland's position as a gate for transit traffic was at times significant. The railway system was facilitated by the same gauge in Finland and the former Soviet Union, which is different from that in the rest of Europe.

The disintegration of the former Soviet Union created a new situation in Russia and in the other former Soviet republics. As a result of the independence of the Baltic states, Belorussia and Ukraine, Russia was driven further apart from Western Europe than it had been for several centuries. The Baltic ports located in Estonia, Lithuania and Latvia are now in the hands of the newly independent states.

The main flow of transit deliveries is by sea transports via Finnish ports and the land transports between the ports and the Russian destinations. However, even air traffic receives a major source of

income from transit deliveries, currently representing 16 percent of Finnair's annual turnover (The Gateway Action Program, 1994). On the whole, the prospects of transit traffic in Finland are good.

3.2 Business Basement

Compared to operating as a transport gate between Russia and the outside world, it is a relatively new experience for Finland to act as a basement for business with Russia. This operation takes various forms. In some multinational corporations, Finnish subsidiaries are responsible for and Baltic markets and parts of the Russian market. So far, however, it has been more common to use other alternatives to participate in production processes in the Russian territory from a Finnish basement. In particular, the construction industry, transportation and forwarding, wholesale and retail trade, communications, consultancy and education have been involved in these operations. Juridical and accounting service companies are developing similar operations. Finnish companies such as insurance companies (Pohjola, Sampo), department store chains (Stockmann's), banks (Merita-Bank, OKO-Bank, PSP-Bank), and oil distributors (Neste) are acting actively in the Russian and Baltic markets.

Of course, traditional commodity trade may also involve gateway operations. It has been estimated that up to one third of Finnish exports to Russia now come from gateway operations. For example, bananas and other tropical fruit are refrigerated, ripened, stored and distributed by Finnish companies as they pass from the producers to Russian consumers. In 1995, the exports of bananas from Finland amounted to more than 300 million Finnish marks.

The Russians also use Finnish services to reach foreign markets. Investments in Finnish businesses and real estate, the new offices of some Russian banks in Finland, and the shopping tours of well-off Russian citizens in Finland signify the growing importance of the gateway in the East-West direction.

3.3 Acting as a Mediator between East and West

A traffic gateway denotes the movement of commodities and people including caring for them in stores and in hotels overnight. A business basement involves traffic and other business operations as well as auxiliary services required for their management. The next step is the most demanding one and involves efforts to minimize the negative effects of differences and borders between the various markets in business (Fable 4). The location decisions and the internal division of labor inside the production processes can then take place flexibly within the gateway and its

Table 4 The development of Finland's gateway functions

"Gate"	Transportation of goods and persons and caring for them in stores and at hotels
"Business Basement"	Auxiliary services and other inputs for various East-West business operations
"Mediator"	Flexible division of labor inside production processes in different markets

neighboring regions.

At this stage it is possible to flexibly locate and manage operations of wholesale and retail trade, banking, and other service businesses in Finland and in Russia or the Baltic states. The production processes with various manufacturing operations, subsidiaries, sub-contracting units, marketing agencies, etc., are located on either side of the Finnish and Russian or Estonian borders depending on logistical and economic considerations. This kind of operation would be greatly promoted by the cooperation of public authorities and officials in Finland, Russia and Estonia. It has been suggested, for instance, that the countries build common customs facilities and conduct passport and customs inspections on moving trains between Helsinki and St. Petersburg.

The gateway can act as a mediator that interlinks two economic areas with different constitutions in a way that minimizes the friction caused by the border-crossing activities. The differences between the areas would not disappear but their negative effects on business and trade are eliminated. The common gauge of Finnish and Russian railways would then truly symbolize the ease of crossing the borders between the countries.

The gateway is no honorary position that can be proclaimed by the EU, Russia or any other authority. Nor can Finland itself claim the right to the gateway position, however tempting it may be. Instead, there is an open competition to attract the gateway users not only to get the first deal but over and over again with each individual transaction.

The Finnish gateway will be successful only if foreign companies consider its services to be competitive and if the Russians accept Finland in this role. If companies operating in Russia do not know or appreciate Finnish services, the gateway has no basis to rely on. The Finnish gateway cannot end at the Russian border, which means that the cooperation with the Russians cannot be neglected. The Russians may dislike the Finnish gateway for reasons of prestige or the anticipated reductions of earnings and investments, especially in the St. Petersburg region. Although the competitive situation cannot be entirely denied, it should be remembered that the Finnish and Russian regions form the gateway together, with neither party alone being able to accomplish the required outcome.

4. Conclusions

Among the democratic market economies Finland had a special position in relation to the former Soviet Union. The rapid recovery of trade since 1993 after the decline in the Soviet era shows that Finland also managed to create and exploit a new kind of special position that is no longer based on the preferential treatment provided by political and trade policy privileges. The new position is based primarily on the utilization of neighborhood and acquaintance. Favorable economic relations based on the geographical closeness of Finland and Russia, the size of the Russian market, and the gateway position reinforced with Finland's membership in the EU can be expected to further increase trade between Finland and Russia.

The development of the market economy in Russia implies that it is now united with the Finnish economy although not integrated. The supply and demand conditions in Russia have a direct impact not only on commodity trade but also on production and the division of labor within the production processes. Because of large wage differences, Finland needs adaptation strategies for the national economy, industry branches and enterprises. Some uncompetitive parts of the production processes could be transferred to the East, which would reduce employment in Finland. If the competitiveness of the entire process is improved, however, the final impact on employment may turn out to be positive. Finland is thus in the forefront facing the problem that remains to be solved in the Europe as a whole: how to manage the all European redistribution of labor in a way that benefits all the parties involved, as should be the case in healthy trade relationships.

A related question to consider is Finland's position as a Gateway promoting matching and trade contacts between the former Soviet Union and the West. The Gateway is Finland's new strength, a potential for expanding trade relations with Russia and other successor states of the Soviet Union. Finland's role could be a solder between Russia and the European Union. Perhaps the new common border between these two big powers of Europe will help them find new economic domains of common interest.

See also: *Economic Integration; Interdependence, International; Nordic Political Cooperation; Nordic Security Problems; Glasnost and Perestroika*

Bibliography ─────────────────────────

Foreign Trade. 1992 No 4-5. Moscow

Gabrisch H 1985 *Finnish-Soviet Economic Relations.* The Vienna Institute for Comparative Studies. Forschungs-bertichte Nr 109. Vienna

Gateway toimenpideohjalma 1994 *Gateway Action Program.* The Finnish Ministry of Foreign Affairs. Helsinki

Hirvensalo I 1996 *Strategic Adaptation of Enterprises to Tur-bulent Transitionary Markets: Operative Strategies of Finnish Firms in Russia and the Baltic States during 1991-1995.* Helsinki School of Economics and Business Administration, Helsinki

Kajaste I 1993 Finland's trade with the Soviet Union: Its impact on the Finnish economy. *Economic Bulletin for Europe,* Vol. 44. Economic Commission for Europe, New York

URPO KIVIKARI

Economic Blockade

An economic blockade is an attempt to isolate a target country from economic and commercial contacts with the outside world. This isolation is achieved by the cessation of trade, financial, and aid contacts often combined with cessation of diplomatic, cultural, and sports contacts between the sender and target country. The economic blockade can be controlled by military and/or semimilitary means such as placing military vessels outside the target country's territorial waters with the purpose of hindering any trade from taking place with other countries.

There can be several reasons for a blockade. The main reason is that a blockade is introduced for national security reasons. The purpose is to give a sender nation additional freedom to act in foreign policy. In the case of the United States for example the reason is to assert leadership in world affairs. A blockade may also be introduced in order to (a) support military action, (b) as retaliation for failed policy or as punishment, (c) in order to strengthen economic or political dependence between sender and target, (d) enhance a commercial interest of the sender (Paul 1988).

Blockades used in support of military action were predominant before the Second World War. They are closely related to economic warfare or to "measures taken to facilitate the pursuance of the war by strengthening the economic defences or our own country and its allies and by weakening those of the enemy" (Einzig 1940 pp. 1-2). Economic warfare is still today an integrated element of warfare. Blockades introduced for peneological reasons concern the actions taken by the United States, the United Kingdom, the ex-Soviet Union and other global or dominant regional powers. A punishment may concern an isolated case like the shooting down of an airline or hostile or non-conformant policy action by a smaller nation. Geographic closeness has in several cases lead to economic dependence which has been used for political purposes. Especially the ex-Soviet Union introduces blockades against several of its neighbours. Regional punitive action can also be identified by the United States as well as by developing countries like India and Nigeria. Punitive economic action has also been introduced for purely commercial reasons relating to the price of global commodities like oil and copper.

Economic blockade is identified as a second level force or as economic coercion and pressure the first level being economic coercion. The main elements of economic blockade are (a) total embargo and boycott, (b) suspension from international bodies, (c) financial sanctions and (d) partial or total trade sanctions (Paul 1988).

Economic blockades are introduced by a nation state or an international organisation. Embargoes and boycott are introduced by other non-nation state organisations or even by companies.

Government-initiated action restricting trade is called an embargo. The terms "export embargo" and "import embargo" may be used to show the direction of the trade restrictions. A privately and collectively initiated trade restrictive action is called a boycott. To show the direction of the action the terms "export boycott" and "import boycott" are used. Boycott action can not be used in connection with the term economic blockade. Embargoes are the ingredients of economic blockades.

1. Historical Examples

Various more or less complete forms of total economic blockades can be identified. The most extreme cases have taken place during major international wars. Examples of economic blockades during war-time are the continental blockade during the Napoleonic wars and the economic blockades practiced during the First and Second World Wars. Other well documented cases of economic blockades are the League of Nations versus Italy (1935-36) and the United Nations versus Rhodesia (1965-79). Most other cases do not attempt a complete economic blockade. Usually the target country is allowed to trade with, or succeeds in trading with, at least some countries in the outside world. The trade restrictions are usually limited to either exports or imports. Both imports and exports are seldom restricted by the sender(s) simultaneously.

Even during extreme recorded cases of total economic blockades, trade and economic relations between sender country and target country are usually not cut completely. During the Continental Blockade, Napoleon traded through the neutral European countries. Trade was conducted during the Second World War between the United States and Nazi Germany (Higham 1984). Rhodesia was never isolated, in fact that country had a diversified foreign trade at the end of the 1970s (Losman 1979; Renwick 1981; Paul 1985). Special laws were initiated, for example the Byrd Amendment in the United States in order to import strategic minerals from Rhodesia. Various forms of limited economic blockades are well known to history. Both Thucydides and Aristophanes note Pericles' Magerian decree of 432 BC. Hufbauer and Schott (1985) observe it as the first celebrated occasion of limited economic blockades.

This first registered case was not a success as it was one of the main triggers of the Peloponnesian War. Limited economic blockades were used as foreign policy instruments both by the Romans and Renaissance popes.

Limited economic blockades were an unusual form of international interaction prior to 1914, as noted by Hufbauer and Schott (1985) and Hasse (1973). Hufbauer and Schott have identified 11 such cases between 1914-20. They have observed that all but two were linked to military action. Since 1945 the cases of limited economic blockades have mushroomed. Twelve new cases were observed during the 1940s and another 12 cases in the 1950s. In the 1960s over 20 new cases were documented, in the 1970s nearly 40 new cases and in the first half of the 1980s close to 30 new cases of limited economic blockades have been noted. The use of various levels of limited economic blockades have become a usual form of interaction between states in international relations. The principal senders have been the United States, the United Kingdom, the former Soviet Union, the League of Nations, and the United Nations. Another principal sender has been the Arab League. Most cases of limited economic blockades have taken place in developing countries. Several of the European countries have also been a sender or a target country of limited economic blockades (Hufbauer and Schott 1985).

2. The Uses of Economic Blockades

Economic blockades and limited economic blockades are used for various policy purposes. The main purposes are, according to Hufbauer and Schott: to disrupt military adventures or to complement a broader war effort, to impair the economic capability of the target country, thereby limiting its potential for military activity; and various other foreign policy goals mainly to destabilize the government of the target country. Hufbauer and Schott (1985) emphasize the military side of limited economic blockades. Other researchers on the subject have given more weight to the demonstrative function of economic blockades especially its limited forms (Nincic and Wallensteen 1983).

In some cases blockades are initiated in order to impose the sender's opinions on the target country in that the sender communicates signals with symbolic connotation to the target. In some cases this kind of an economic blockade may concern ideology like nazism, communism or racism. The symbols (economic blockade) carry two messages: one of ideological condemnation and secondly one of purpose—the act (economic blockade) is the message (Paul 1988). Symbolic economic blockades have been introduced especially by the United States against the ex-Soviet Union and by several nations and international bodies against parts of ex-Yugoslavia and some countries in Africa.

The emphasis in the 1980s is less on the military side and more on the demonstrative and signal-giving side of limited economic blockades. Nations seek means to show their views on issues like human rights, racial discrimination, and international terrorism. One such vehicle for showing one's opinion is through the limitation and even total cessation of economic contacts with the violators of such basic international codes of conduct. Examples of demonstrative signal-giving limited economic blockades are the ways in which the United Nations and many of its member countries including the European Community, and the Nordic countries have condemned apartheid in South Africa; the Dutch freezing of development aid credits to Suriname for human rights violations, and the United States actions against Paraguay, Nicaragua, Guatemala, and Argentina on the same issue during the 1970s.

Economic blockades are by their very nature collective and international. These aspects can be exemplified by the limited economic blockades and economic sanctions practiced by the United Nations, the European Community, the Arab League, and the

Council for Mutual Economic Assistance (COMECON).

Limited economic blockades are becoming more frequent, if not common, in international relations. Their function in international relations is also changing. From being an instrument of war they are possibly becoming and filling a function as an alternative to war. They can function as international security valves in situations of tension between states. Bearing in mind the risk of nuclear war they can maybe fill the role of alternatives to war. Paul (1985) has argued that various forms of limited economic blockades or economic sanctions may in the future be a substitute for war. Strong political and economic action can be taken without automatically triggering war. On the other hand, total economic blockade is in itself an act of war and therefore a supplement to military action. Total economic blockades have no role to play in relation to world peace and security. On the other hand limited economic blockades have their role to play in the quest for peace and security in the world. But even limited economic blockades are by their very nature instruments for an aggressive foreign policy and represent the first steps on an escalation ladder to war. In this respect they can not be seen, as such, and by their very nature, to be constructive instruments for enhancing world peace and security in general.

Bibliography

Einzig P 1940 *Economic Warfare*. Macmillan and Co. Ltd., London

Doxey M P 1971 *Economic International Enforcement*. Oxford University Press, London

Hasse R 1973 *Theorie und Politik des Embargos*. Institut für Wirtschaftspolitik an der Universität zu Köln, Cologne

Higham C 1984 *Trading with the Enemy*. Dell, New York

Hufbauer G C, Schott J J 1985 *Economic Sanctions Reconstructed: History and Current Policy*. Institute for International Economics, Washington, DC

Losman D 1979 *International Economic Sanctions: The Cases of Cuba, Israel and Rhodesia*. University of New Mexoco Press, Albuquerque, New Mexico

Nincic M, Wallensteen P (eds.) 1983 *Dilemmas of Economic Coercion*. Praeger, New York

Paul J-P 1985 *Ekonomiska Sanktioner som politiskt instrument international politik*. Helsinki

Paul J-P 1988 *Negative Economic Relations between States: A Case-Intensive Analysis*, An approach for describing the theory of long-term negative economic relations. Publications of the Swedish School of Economics and Business Administration, No 39, Helsingfors

Renwick R 1981 *Economic Sanctions*. Center for International Affairs, Harvard University, Cambridge, Massachusetts

JAN-PETER PAUL

Economic Integration

Economic integration can be defined as a process and as a state of affairs. Regarded as a process, it encompasses measures designed to abolish discrimination between economic units belonging to different national states; viewed as a state of affairs, it can be represented by the absence of various forms of discrimination between national economies. As defined here, then, economic integration can take several forms that represent varying degrees of integration. In a free-trade area (e.g., European Free Trade Association—EFTA, Council for Mutual Economic Assistance—CMEA or COMECON, Pacto Andino), tariffs (and quantitative restrictions) between the participating countries are abolished, but each country retains its own tariffs against nonmembers. Establishing a customs union (e.g., Switzerland and Liechtenstein on the basis of an agreement signed in 1923; India and Bhutan on the basis of an agreement signed in 1961) involves, besides the suppression of discrimination in the field of commodity movements within the union, the equalization of tariffs in trade with nonmember countries. A higher form of economic integration is attained in a common market (e.g., the European Economic Community), where not only trade restrictions but also restrictions on factor movements are abolished. An economic union (e.g., Belgium-Luxembourg), as distinct from a common market, combines the suppression of restrictions on commodity and factor movements with some degree of harmonization of national economic policies, in order to remove discrimination that was due to disparities in these policies. Finally, total economic integration (the final goal of the European Community) presupposes the unification of monetary, fiscal, social, and counter-cyclical policies and requires the setting-up of a supranational authority whose decisions are binding for the member states.

Economic integration is hardly new. The US Constitution of 1789, by abolishing the separate tariffs of the 13 states, created a customs union out of these federated entities. The nineteenth century unification of various German states into one nation was accompanied by customs union arrangements among sovereign states.

In the twentieth century no significant customs unions were formed until the end of the Second World War, although several attempts were made to integrate the economies of various European countries (e.g., Italy and France). Political obstacles can be singled out as the main causes for the failure of these projects to materialize. The post-Second World War period has seen an enormous increase in interest in problems of economic integration. In Europe there are examples of customs unions and later the economic union of the Benelux countries (Belgium, the Netherlands, and Luxembourg); the European Coal and Steel Community (ECSC) established in 1952 by the Benelux countries, France, the former Federal Republic of Germany and Italy; the European Economic Community (EEC, or the Common Market), established in 1958 by the countries of the ECSC; and the European Free Trade Association (EFTA), established in 1960 by Austria, Denmark, the United Kingdom, Norway, Portugal, Sweden, and Switzerland.

Although the European Community (see *European Union*) and EFTA are by far the most well-known of the economic integrations, they are by no means the only ones. The biggest geographically in the Western world has been the Latin American Free Trade Association (LAFTA), including Argentina, Brazil, Bolivia, Chile, Colombia, Ecuador, Mexico, Paraguay, Peru, Uruguay, and Venezuela. The guiding principle of this organization has been to allocate certain industries to certain countries, then to trade the resulting goods freely. But LAFTA's ambitions have been thwarted by political discord. Local interests supporting protectionism have proved very strong. The Andean Pact subgroup of LAFTA (Bolivia, Chile, Colombia, Ecuador, Peru, and Venezuela) at first had especially ambitious goals: they were to achieve a common external tariff in 1975, with completely free trade in the same year, and devised a plan for the integrated long-term allocation of industry. But all of these proposals have fallen through, and in the course of the in-fighting Chile withdrew from the pact.

Even so, LAFTA has had more success with industrial allocation than the Central American Common Market (CACM). After a promising start, CACM suffered severely from the short war between Honduras and El Salvador in 1969. This war effectively dismembered the CACM. Another two economic integrations have broken up completely: the West Indian Federation because of political hostility among the various island members, and the East African Union of Kenya, Tanzania, and Uganda largely because of

antipathy between Idi Amin, Uganda's ex-president, and the other two members.

The foreign ministers of Indonesia, Malaysia, the Philippines, Singapore, and Thailand signed on August 8, 1967 the Bangkok Declaration which provided for the legal basis of the formation of the ASEAN (see *Association of Southeast Asian Nations (ASEAN)*). Brunei became the sixth member in 1984, followed by Vietnam as the seventh member in 1996, and by Burma in 1997. Laos and Cambodia are waiting for their acceptance into the Association. It was the purpose of the organization to "foster regional economic, social, and political cooperation and to promote regional peace and stability."

The second ASEAN ministerial meeting was held in Jakarta in August 1968, and five priority areas of regional cooperation were identified: food production, communication, civil aviation, shipping and tourism. When the third ministerial meeting was held in December 1969 in Malaysia, the governments had agreed to set up a series of permanent committees on trade and tourism; food, agriculture, and forestry; transportation and communication; finance and banking; science and technology; mass media and cultural activities.

The Seventh Ministerial Meeting in Jakarta resulted in a reinforced feeling among the participants on the significance of economic collaboration and that more imperative action should be taken toward this end. The 1973 oil crisis was a motivation factor. The foreign ministers also agreed that cabinet members of ASEAN government responsible for economic planning would formulate guidelines for ASEAN to implement the recommendations of the UN especially in the area of industrial cooperation. The Eighth Ministerial Meeting took place in Kuala Lumpur on May 13-15, 1975 where the participants discussed economic cooperation and issued a mandate to the ASEAN permanent committees "to give high priority to projects that would enhance trade liberalization and industrial complementation." Also, a draft treaty of amity and cooperation was approved for consideration by member governments. The draft treaty was an attempt to embody in concrete form the ZOPFAN concept of Southeast Asia neutralization and also to leave an opening for possible adherence to the treaty of the Indochinese states and Burma. It is true that ASEAN was formed not for economic gains but for political and security reasons but there is much to this regional group formation than just economics, and that their regional economic cooperation is conditioned upon the existence of political will which presupposes political cooperation in the first place. By ensuring geo-political stability in the region, ASEAN has enabled the member nations to concentrate on their economic pursuits.

The fourth ASEAN summit meeting in Singapore on January 1992 marked a watershed. The ASEAN Free Trade Area (AFTA) was launched. It demonstrated a major new initiative with a 15-year timetable, beginning from January 1, 1993. AFTA's establishment represented a sense of crisis, reflecting a shift of foreign investment from ASEAN to China and Mexico. In the following economic ministers meeting in Manila, Philippines on October 22-23, 1993, the ministers agreed to implement a common effective preferential tariff (CEPT) mechanism on January 1993. This would then lead to tariff reductions on a range of manufactured and processed agricultural products traded within ASEAN and the eventual creation of an ASEAN free trade area in 2008.

While ASEAN's role in promoting a security dialogue at the Asia-Pacific level has attracted a good deal of publicity, the evolution of security measures at the intra-ASEAN level is equally crucial to the prospects of regional order in post-Cold War Southeast Asia. "But such a role would have to include more concrete and specific measures for greater security and defense cooperation within the grouping, as has been suggested during recent regional security debates."

Part of ASEAN's strategy is to include those beyond the PMC process to include all relevant actors in the Asia-Pacific that shape regional security, such as China and Russia. This has been the major rationale for creating the ASEAN Regional Forum (see *ASEAN Regional Forum*).

Most recently launched in 1989 in Australia, the Asia-Pacific Economic Cooperation (APEC) (see *Asia-Pacific Economic Cooperation (APEC)*) forum, is considered a profound innovation in the Pacific. The forum encompasses a mixture of states but, technically, what are claimed to be in the grouping are the economies. This claim underscores the fact that the APEC is purely economic in nature and any political and other non-economic issues are not treated as official items in the deliberations, although incidental talks among the summiters on such issues have not been prohibited. Until lately, the forum remains as a loose, consultative body made up of diverse members which are aiming at regional prosperity.

The APEC concept had been proposed in January 1989 by the Prime Minister of Australia, Bob Hawke, while on a visit to South Korea. The first ministerial meeting, which also inaugurated the Council, was held on November 6 and 7, 1989 where 23 ministers

from 12 countries attended. It tackled four major issues: world and regional economic development, global trade liberalization, opportunities for regional cooperation in specific areas; and future steps for Asia-Pacific economic cooperation. Although there was unanimity on the desirability of free trade, there was little agreement on the precise structure and membership of the new body.

The second ministerial meeting of the APEC group was held in Singapore on July 30-31, 1990. In a final statement issued at the close of the talks the group agreed to conduct an urgent review of the member countries' negotiating positions toward finding greater flexibility and facilitating a breakthrough at the deadlocked "Uruguay Round" of global trade talks launched in 1986.

Later, during the fourth APEC conference in Bangkok, the ministers of 15 countries made the significant move towards formalizing the loose APEC forum by approving the establishment of a permanent secretariat in Singapore, which would coordinate APEC activities, including research projects and work programs. A working group was established to prepare a plan for trade and investment cooperation in the Asia-Pacific region to the year 2000.

During the Seattle Summit of November 1993, APEC leaders put forward their statement which envisioned "a community of Asia-Pacific economies" and on the following year at the Bogor Summit, the members adopted the "APEC Economic Leaders' Declaration of Common Resolve," calling for the industrialized members to implement free and open trade and investment fully by the year 2010 and developing members by 2020. The Bogor Summit participants agreed on a two-step formula for freeing trade and investment as contained in the Bogor Declaration. Especially, the APEC leaders undertook to carry out the GATT Uruguay Round commitments fully and without delay and urged others to do the same.

The Osaka Summit began the process by adopting an action agenda setting out the principles, the menu of issues and the timetables through which APEC's political commitments would be translated into tangible results. The "Action Agenda" provided for the removal of the region's trade and investment barriers—by 2010 for developed countries and 2020 for developing countries. The agenda called for the members to begin implementing initial liberalization plans by January 1997, three years earlier than originally envisaged.

In APEC summit held in Manila and Subic, Philippines on November 21-24, 1996, the leaders of the 18 member-economies vowed to move "from vision to action" by further liberalizing trade and investments and strengthening economic and technical cooperation to bring about sustainable growth and equitable development "with a human face." A 26-point Leaders' Declaration adopting the Manila Action Plan for APEC (MAPA) was issued affirming a multilateral trading system, strengthening economic and technical cooperation, affirming the role of the business sector, and declaring a shared vision and deeper sense of community for APEC. MAPA is said "to contain the first steps of an evolutionary process of progressive and comprehensive trade and investment liberalization toward achieving (the) Bogor goals 2010-20, in accordance with the Osaka Action Agenda."

In the summit of APEC leaders held in Vancouver, Canada in November 1997, the leader committed themselves to the containment of the financial crisis that started to sweep the Southeast Asian economies up to Korea and Japan while mindful of the need to pursue liberalization in the 15 identified sectors.

The APEC summit in Malaysia in 1998 was held in the midst of the East Asian financial crisis, thus, not much has been agreed upon except the reaffirmation of the action plans.

Since 1985, extended negotiations have produced a series of bilateral trade pacts that have lowered trade barriers in the region and provided institutional underpinnings for the prospective North American economic alliance. The most important accord has been the Canada-US Free Trade Agreement (CUFTA), which set many useful precedents for the NAFTA (see *North American Free Trade Agreement (NAFTA)*). Beginning with the Canada-US Auto Pact in 1965, CUFTA was accomplished in January, 1989.

In addition, both the United States and Canada have concluded bilateral framework agreements on trade and investment in Mexico. The United States and Mexico signed three accords between 1985 and 1989. Canada-Mexico trade negotiations have proceeded on a parallel but slower track, reflecting the smaller level of direct economic transactions between those two countries.

On June 1990, US President George Bush and Mexican President Carlos Salinas de Gortari agreed to pursue the negotiation of a free trade agreement between the two countries. Exactly one year later, talks began with a third country, Canada, also taking a seat at the negotiating table.

The recession of the early 1990s reduced support for NAFTA within the USA and Canada, though the Mexican government seemed to be dependent more than ever before upon the ratification of NAFTA as a key element in its economic strategy.

On June 12, 1991, the three countries began formal negotiations for a North American free trade agreement. The leaders of the three countries announced the conclusion of the negotiations for an agreement on August 12, 1992. President Bush announced to the US Congress his intention to sign the trade agreement. Private sector advisory reports were also released. On December 17, 1992 the leaders of the three countries signed the North American free trade agreement in their respective capitals. The agreement covered market access, trade rules, services, investment, intellectual property, and trade remedies. On March 17, 1993 negotiations on supplemental agreements began. This agreements would cover labor issues, the environment, and import charges. By September, 1993 President Clinton had already submitted a bill to the US Congress and sought the body's approval of implementing the legislation in time for the implementation of the agreement effective January 1, 1994. In November 17, the US Congress ratified the Agreement and in November 20, the Senate ratified it, too.

The historical formation of NAFTA made it the largest economic and trade bloc with 360 million consumers in a market of $6,600 billion per year compared with the EC which had, at that time, 320 million consumers in a $6,000-billion market.

"The novelty of NAFTA is that this is the first time that fair trade provisions on labor and environmental standards have been built into a regional agreement, and may well presage similar future US demands in other forums. NAFTA is also unprecedented because of the extent of the disparities in income between the partners."

The NAFTA regime is broad in scope. "The issues covered include changes in restrictions on energy, automotive goods, steel, textiles and apparel, agriculture, transportation, financial services, investment, intellectual property, government procurement, technical standards, and the environment." The most relevant indicator of regime strength of NAFTA is the dispute settlement mechanism. The provisions of NAFTA cover a host of regulatory measures that should affect the ability of the participants to take unilateral and bilateral actions.

See also: *European Political Community; Integration Theories; Peace and Regional Integration; Regionalism in Asia Pacific, Organizational Forms of; Regionalism, Economic Security and Peace: the Asia-Pacific; Security Regimes: Focusing on Asia-Pacific*

Bibliography ────────────────

Balassa B 1969 *The Theory of Economic Integration.* Allen and Unwin, London

Fawcett L, Hurrell A (eds.) *Regionalism and World Economic Order.* Oxford University Press, New York

Hogenuurn J S, Brown W B 1979 *The New International Economics.* Addison-Wesley, Reading, Massachusetts

Vauluni N 1980 *L'Union douanière de la Communautè èconomique europèenne.* Brussels

BORIS GOMBAČ; PEDRO B. BERNALDEZ

Economics of Disarmament and Conversion

1. Introduction

Disarmament involves major reductions in Defense spending. It creates the associated challenge of successfully re-allocating resources from the military to the civil sectors of the economy. The prospects of a Peace Dividend arise from a reduction in so-called "unproductive" military activities allowing the resources released to produce more hospitals, schools or roads, or to lower taxation allowing greater private consumption (e.g., cars, videos, housing, etc.) (see *Disarmament and Development*). Attractive though this re-allocation appears, it is not without its problems. Questions arise as to whether such a change is socially desirable bearing in mind the time required and costs involved in adjusting to change, and whether the potential losers will be compensated or otherwise form major interest groups opposed to disarmament.

This article focuses on the problems of defining the Defense industrial base, the costs, benefits and prospects for conversion in both Defense industries and the Armed Forces, and the policy options. At the outset, consideration needs to be given to whether disarmament and conversion are special and unique problems and who are the likely gainers and losers from such changes.

1.1 Disarmament: Definitions, Concepts and Uniqueness

Disarmament involves major reductions in a nation's Defense spending. However, such reductions can take a variety of forms, each with different implications for arms races and arms control initiatives. For example, cuts can occur in aggregate Defense spending or in particular components such as Defense research and development (R&D), manpower or equipment; or in specific types of equipment, forces and numbers (e.g., chemical, biological or nuclear weapons; or delivery systems; or numbers of troops, etc.); or in the geographical distribution of Armed Forces (e.g., withdrawal from certain regions, such as Germany). This taxonomy is further complicated because cuts in Defense spending can be part of an international treaty between two or more nations or they can be unilateral voluntary initiatives.

Reduced Defense spending involves reductions in government expenditure and a supply-side release of resources for alternative uses. The task of finding alternative uses for the released resources represents the broad conversion challenge. In this sense, disarmament and conversion are about the economics of change and adjustment (see *Economics of Disarmament: Certain Premises*). Such problems are neither unique nor specific to Defense and disarmament. All dynamic economies are continuously adjusting to changing consumer demands, to new technologies and to the emergence of new sources of supply (e.g., newly-industrializing nations). Change means that firms and industries are subject to growth and decline. Examples include the decline of such UK industries as coal, shipbuilding, steel, textiles, tobacco, pedal cycles and motor cycles and the growth of the aerospace, computer, telecommunications and information technology sectors. Significantly, the declining UK industries are rarely the focus of conversion solutions. This raises the interesting question of what, if any, is "unique and special" about the Defense sector such that it often leads to demands for a conversion strategy to solve the adjustment problem.

In private enterprise economies, one obvious difference between Defense and other industries reflects the role of government. Within nation states, governments are the only buyer of military forces and the major, if not the only, buyer of Defense equipment. Governments can use the buying power of their Defense Ministries to determine the size of their Armed Forces and, through procurement policy, the size, structure, conduct and performance of their national Defense industries. In contrast, industries in the civil sector are affected by the demands of large numbers of individual consumers. For example, my decision to buy a Saab motorcar has an insignificant impact on both the losing UK car industry and the winning Swedish car company. But, if a government decides to reduce the size of its Army by 50percent or to award a major equipment contract to a foreign company, the effects are substantial and visible and can be seen to be the "responsibility" of government.

Fig. 1 outlines the economic impacts of disarmament, distinguishing between impacts on the Armed Forces and impacts on Defense industries. All too often, the focus is on Defense industries and their adjustment problems to the neglect of similar adjustment problems for the Armed Forces. There are also likely to be significant regional impacts of disarmament. Some towns and regions might be highly dependent on Defense companies as major employers (e.g., UK examples include Barrow, Plymouth and Yeovil). Similarly, military bases might be major sources of local spending in remote rural areas where there are few alternative employment opportunities. In such rural economies, the closure of a military base will have local multiplier effects reflected in reduced local spending (e.g., local suppliers of services to the base; sending in shops, garages, pubs and restaurants, etc.). The initial result will be a depressed local economy with fewer job opportunities, higher unemployment, outward migration and adverse impacts on the local housing market. Over time, recovery in the local economy will depend upon how well and how quickly local labor markets work.

Once the importance of government is recognized

as a distinctive feature of Defense and disarmament policy, there will be the inevitable emergence of interest and pressure groups seeking to influence public policy in their favor. Faced with the prospect of the closure of a major military base or Defense plant, there will be pressure for the government to "do something." Government as the buyer of Armed Forces and Defense equipment appears as the sole consumer able to change the fortunes of a local military base or Defense plant suddenly and unexpectedly. All markets are characterized by uncertainty, but the uncertainties in the Defense market result from the decisions of the government as its sole customer. These features increase the attractiveness of lobbying, since an interest group can easily identify the government as the agent to be influenced. All of which suggests the need for a model of the role of government in the political market place.

1.2 Disarmament and Public Choice Analysis

The economics of politics and public choice applies standard economic concepts of self-interest and exchange to analyze the political market place comprising voters, political parties, governments, bureaucracies and interest groups. In this model, voters allocate their votes to the party offering the greatest bene-

Figure 1
Impacts of disarmament

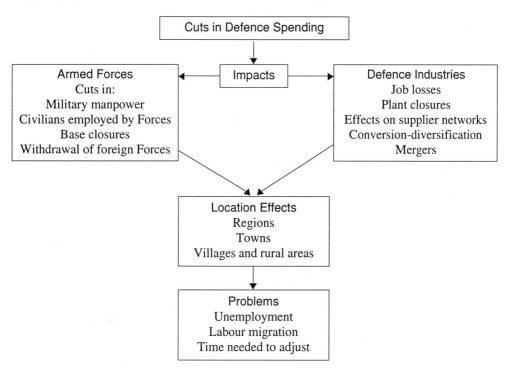

fits; political parties are assumed to be vote-maxi-mizers; governments seek reelection; bureaucracies are assumed to be budget-maximizers; and interest groups aim to create or preserve monopoly positions (rent-seeking).

A public choice approach to disarmament identifies some of the agents most likely to oppose policies to reduce Defense spending. It shows the types of arguments used by the Armed Forces and Defense Ministries to protect budgets and how domestic Defense contractors are likely to respond to cuts and the cancellation of major equipment programmes. For example, following the end of the Cold War, Defense Ministries and the Armed Forces have focused on out-of-area threats to national interests reflected in regional arms races in what is presented as an increasingly unstable and uncertain world, hence, the need to maintain "strong Defenses" to meet some future unknown and unknowable threats. At the same time, faced with cuts in Defense spending, the Armed Forces as major interest groups will seek to protect their traditional monopoly property rights (Armies protect the land, Navies the sea and Air Forces protect a nation's air space) and their prestige and high technology weapons projects. In return for accepting smaller Armed Forces, the emphasis will be on smaller but better equipped Forces (high technology equipment replacing personnel) offering flexibility and rapid reaction capable of operating anywhere in the world (including contributions to the UN peace-keeping missions). As a result, the Armed Forces will obtain a share of the Peace Dividend.

Disarmament means the cancellation of equipment projects, delays in ordering, the "stretching-out" of development programmes and smaller production orders. Defense contractors will become increasingly active in competing and lobbying for a smaller number of contracts. The possibility of awarding a Defense contract to a foreign firm will be greeted with howls of protest from domestic industry and threats of large-scale redundancies, plant closures, the loss of "vitally important" technologies and of a "key" part of a nation's Defense industrial base. Similarly, faced with threat of closure of a major military base, the local politicians and unions will lobby government to keep the base open; and governments seeking votes and re-election might be persuaded of the need to maintain such a base as a vital part of the nation's Defense infrastructure.

Public choice analysis provides a theoretical framework for analyzing the role of government and other groups in the political market place. It has already been suggested that the importance of gov-ernment makes Defense unique and different. Furthermore, through its spending power, including the award of contracts, government can allocate monopoly positions. For example, firms operating in protected national Defense markets and receiving cost-plus or cost-based contracts might pursue a "quiet life" characterized by organizational "slack," luxury offices for managers, high technology research programmes, the hoarding of valuable scientists and favorable terms and conditions of employment for the labor force. To such groups, disarmament is a threat to their vested interests. However, welfare economics suggests that for a change like disarmament to be socially desirable, the potential gainers must be able to compensate the potential losers and still be better-off: hence, the need to offer adequate compensation as a price for "buying-out" the monopoly powers of the losers from disarmament.

2. *Defining the Defense Industrial Base*

What is known; what is not known; and what is necessary to know, for sensible public choices about disarmament? As a starting point, information is needed on the size and importance of Defense industries in a nation's economy. Answers are needed to the following questions:

(a) What is the Defense Industrial Base (DIB)?

(b) How large is the DIB in terms of output and employment?

(c) Is the DIB a major exporter?

(d) Which are the Defense-dependent industries, firms, regions and local communities?

(e) Are contracts concentrated on a small number of large prime contractors?

(f) How does the performance of Defense industries compare with other industries in the economy?

The concept of the DIB has been the victim of various definitions. Consider the following examples:

(a) The DIB comprises the wide range of firms which supply the Ministry of Defense with the equipment and services it requires (16 p. 1).

(b) The DIB consists of those industrial assets which provide key elements of military power and national security: such assets demand special consideration by government (8 p. xxvii).

(c) "Superficially, the idea of the DIB is fairly straight-forward. It constitutes those companies which provide Defense and Defense-related equipment to the Ministry of Defense. But if we try to operationalize this definition, there are clearly many problems" (2).

(d) The DIB embraces industrial sectors that unequivocally manufacture military goods (e.g., artillery, missiles, submarines) as well as sectors which produce civil goods. Designation as a Defense industry depends upon the destination of the bulk of the industry's output: should most of it be earmarked for Defense markets, the industry is classified as a Defense industry (18 pp. 14-15).

(e) The DIB refers to "those sectors of a country's economy that can be called upon to generate goods, services and technology for ultimate consumption by the state's armed forces." A DIB has to fulfill two requirements: it must provide the "normal peacetime material requirements of the country's military; and it must be rapidly expansible to meet the increased demands of wartime or emergency situations" (5 pp. 1-2).

(f) For the USA, the DIB comprises prime contractors, sub-contractors and parts suppliers operating publicly and/or privately-owned facilities supplying air, land and sea systems. In addition to ensuring that the UAS is self-sufficient, the Defense industry is required to expand rapidly in times of national emergency (surge capability: (4 ch. 8)).

(g) A further US definition of the DIB applies the following rules:

   (i) select the top <u>n</u> industries ranked by Department of Defense dollar purchases (where <u>n</u> involves the selection of a threshold); and

   (ii) add to the list other industries considered vital to Defense production (12 p. 59). Examples include ball bearings and semiconductors.

(h) "The Defense industry is not defined in the usual way by its product; rather it consists of those firms from a number of different industries that sell to the Department of Defense. The nature of this governmental customer is the single most important determinant of the characteristics of the industry . . ." (13 p. 25).

(i) Defense contractors can be classified into four categories, namely, weapons systems firms (i.e., delivering a complete weapons system); subsystem firms providing major subsystems such as engines; parts firms which supply the tubes, gauges, valves etc., for subsystems; and the material makers which supply aluminum, titanium, etc., for weapons [3].

Firms in the DIB have a number of distinctive features:

(a) an emphasis on high technology and performance of equipment rather than costs;

(b) risks often borne by the government, which also supplies most of R&D funding;

(c) elaborate rules and regulations for contracts with the emphasis on public accountability;

(d) close personal relationships between major Defense contractors and the MOD (15 p. 58; 13 p. 26).

Inevitably, these various definitions have been criticized for being too broad, too vague, too arbitrary and subjective and for omitting some important firms and sectors (e.g., they emphasize equipment and exclude Defense-related services such as security, cleaning, etc.). Sometimes, the different definitions reflect the nature and purpose of studies of the DIB. Nor is any effort made to distinguish between industrial capabilities in R&D, in production and for in-service support and to identify those industrial capabilities which are Defense specific. For example, at one extreme, some Defense industries supply lethal equipment which can destroy, threaten or deter (e.g., combat aircraft, warships, tanks, missiles); whilst at the other extreme are products bought by the armed forces but which are also produced on a large-scale for the civilian population (dual-use items such as computers, food, motor cars).

   Data problems abound. For example, total employment cannot be estimated accurately without identifying all firms in the DIB, including the network of suppliers involved in subcontracting and the suppliers of materials, parts and components (i.e., the supply chain). Some suppliers might not be aware that they are involved in Defense production. For example, ball bearing manufacturers are unlikely to know whether their products are used in motor cars or main battle tanks. Even at the prime contractor level, it is difficult to obtain published data showing the proportion of the firm's labor force involved in Defense work. Often major Defense contractors are large conglomerates with a range of military and civil products (e.g., British Aerospace, GEC); and where company Defense sales data are published, they are usually report sales for a range of Defense products for both home and export sales. Elsewhere, firms might be involved in dual-use technologies. In addition to the firms directly and indirectly involved in Defense work, there are induced multiplier effects reflecting the spending of Defense workers in their local economies. As an indication of the extent of the UK DIB, the Ministry of Defense (MOD) Defense contractors list contained over 11,000 firms in 1991.

It is also misleading to refer to the DIB as a single, homogeneous entity. The supply side of the Defense market consists of varying numbers of small to large-sized firms, either publicly or privately-owned, with different degrees of specialization (e.g., in the UK, DERA and the Dockyards are publicly-owned; the rest of the UK DIB is privately owned). Indeed, it is misleading to refer to a single Defense market and industry. There are, in fact, a set of related markets for air, land and sea systems supplied by firms, some of which specialize in one sector or in a sub-sector (e.g., components) with different degrees of dependence of Defense sales. For example, the UK aerospace industry has aircraft, helicopter and guided weapons sectors and comprises firms supplying equipment, electronics and engines to final assemblers which might be building both military and civil aircraft. The efficiency with which a firm supplies equipment determines its unit costs and the quantity which can be bought from increasingly restricted Defense budgets. On this basis, Defense industries are a major element in national Defense. However, their efficiency can not be assessed independently of procurement policy since governments have created an administered and regulated market which departs substantially from the economists' competitive mode. This also raises the wider issue of whether governments should intervene to support their DIB either for military and/or wider economic benefits (jobs, technology, exports, etc.).

2.1 Developing a Definition of the Defense Industry: A UK Example

The various definitions reviewed above have their deficiencies:

(a) some are too vague and difficult to operationalize;

(b) they fail to distinguish the design, development, manufacturing, repair, servicing and support functions of Defense companies (a life cycle approach to defining the DIB);

(c) they often focus on the readily and easily identified elements of the DIB, namely, the prime contractors of specialized Defense equipment (e.g., aircraft, tanks, warships) to the neglect of (a) the supply chain and (b) the variety of suppliers of other goods and services to MOD and overseas Defense Ministries and overseas Defense industries;

(d) they focus on sales to the MOD and neglect the exports of UK Defense equipment and related services. Over the period 1990-93, exports of identified UK Defense equipment averaged some £3.5 billion per annum, representing 3.7 percent of UK visible exports over the same period.

2.2 A Taxonomy

A variety of frameworks can be used to define and classify the DIB. For example, distinctions might be made between lethal and non-lethal equipment; between equipment and services; or between the use of the products, their strategic significance, their technology and the dependence of the producers on military markets. An example is shown in Fig. 2 which distinguishes between dependence on Defense sales and the type of Defense equipment. In this Figure, firms in area X (high Defense dependency and Defense specific equipment) are clearly in the DIB,

Figure 2
Frameworks in which to classify the DIB

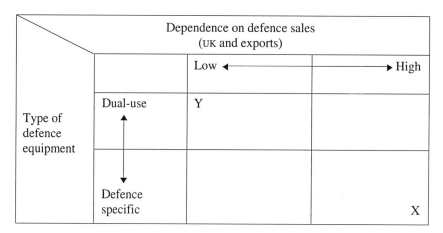

but the problems of classification arise with diagonal movements towards region Y. A further distinction might also be made between sales to MOD and sales to overseas Defense Ministries.

2.3 Some Solutions for the UK

Various solutions to defining and measuring the UK DIB could start from the available published data and definitions. These include MOD Defense expenditure in the UK by industry group; MOD estimates of UK employment dependent on Defense spending; and MOD major contractors. These various approaches to defining the DIB can be summarized as follows:

(a) Ministry of Defense expenditure in the UK by industry group. This shows UK industry annual sales to MOD. In 1993-94, the top six UK industries supplying MOD in terms of absolute sales were:

	£m (1993-94)
Aerospace	2,427
Electronics	1,309
Construction	1,208
Shipbuilding	1,202
Motor vehicles and parts	423
Ordinance, small arms	318
Total: all industries	10,355

The top six accounted for about 65% of MOD Defense expenditure in 1993-94. It can be seen that construction is included in the top six suggesting that this sector cannot be ignored in any broad interpretation of the UK Defense Industry (note: ordinance, small arms was in the top five in 1991-93).

(b) Ministry of Defense estimates of UK employment dependent on Defense expenditure. Data are provided for UK employment dependent on MOD expenditure on equipment and non-equipment (e.g., fuel, clothing) and on exports. The employment data show direct and indirect employment but not any induced multiplier effects.

(c) Ministry of Defense published list of UK-based contractors paid £5 million or more by MOD in a specific year. This list includes suppliers of food, fuels and services as well as equipment. It provides company data for sales to MOD in different sales bands (£5-10 million; £10-25 million, up to over £250 million). In 1994-95, companies paid £250 million or more by MOD comprised British Aerospace, the General Electric Company, Hunting, Rolls-Royce and VSEL/out of a total of 186 contractors paid £5 million or more by MOD.

(d) UK Defense exports need to be included in any def-inition of the UK DIB. For example, in 1993, UK Defense exports were some £2.97 billion, with aerospace exports accounting for 90percent of the total. Summary statistics for the UK DIB are shown in Table 1.

Table 1
UK defense industrial base, 1993

MOD defense expenditure in UK	£10,307 million
UK defense exports	£2,967 million
Total defense sales	£13,274 million
Defense industry employment	405,000

Source: UK Defense Statistics, 1995, HMSO, London.

3. Conversion: Definitions and Concepts

The immediate impact of disarmament is reduced Defense spending reflected in a reduced demand for resources in the Defense sector. The Armed Forces will require fewer personnel and will close some of its army, navy and air force bases. Similarly, smaller Defense industries will require fewer scientists, technologists and production workers, together with fewer R&D establishments and manufacturing plants. But releasing resources from the Defense sector is only the start of the adjustment process requiring a re-allocation of resources to alternative civilian uses.

Re-allocating resources from Defense to the civilian sector takes time and involves costs. Markets for labor, land, capital (e.g., factories) and entrepreneurship do not always adjust and clear instantly. Instead, adjustment takes time and costs arise in the form of unemployment and under-employment of labor, capital and other resources. As a result, disarmament resembles an investment process involving short to medium term costs to achieve long-run economic benefits in the form of a greater output of civil goods and services (the Peace Dividend).

To illustrate the concept of disarmament as an investment process, consider two contrasting scenarios, as shown in Fig. 3. First, a successful scenario (scenario 1) where disarmament occurs slowly and predictably in an expanding economy where governments intervene with policies to correct for major market failures, so assisting the adjustment process. Scenario I shows a successful investment with low costs incurred over a short period of time (e.g., months), followed by substantial economic benefits resulting in a high social rate of return from disarmament. Scenario II is a poor investment involving high

Figure 3
Disarmament as an investment process

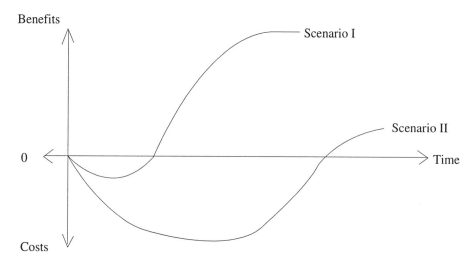

costs in the form of massive unemployment and a lengthy adjustment process (e.g., years) leading to a low or negative social rate of return from disarmament. In this scenario, the high costs might reflect disarmament occurring on a large scale, suddenly and unexpectedly, whilst an economy is in recession with the government leaving adjustment to market forces where markets are failing to work properly. The adjustment problems are likely to be even greater for economies which are experiencing both disarmament, and the transition from a centrally-planned, to a market system. Furthermore, disarmament in the 1990s is different in that it is occurring without a prior major war.

The re-allocation and adjustment process associated with disarmament forms the subject area of conversion which has at least two interpretations. First, there is the narrow definition which focuses on converting Defense plants into establishments manufacturing civil goods. Such direct conversion requires product substitution in which the same plant and workforce produce goods for civilian markets instead of military products. On this view, workers and factories would convert their production facilities at their existing locations from, say, warships to oil tankers, combat aircraft to airliners, missiles to microwave ovens. Similarly, scientists in military R&D establishments could be used to work on the myriad of challenging problems facing society in fields such as health, environment, poverty and space exploration. Such conversion appears attractive: it avoids wasting valuable physical and human capital through plant closure and unemployment and it uses the resources

for meeting society's needs (see *Arms Conversion*).

Second, there is a broader interpretation of conversion focusing on the process of reallocating resources from the Armed Forces and declining Defense industries to the expanding sectors and regions of the economy. This factor re-allocation process is occurring continuously in all dynamic economies and its success depends on the operation of the markets for labor, capital, land and entrepreneurship and on the general state of the economy (e.g., whether it is growing or in recession).

3.1 Direct Conversion: Myths and Reality

Although attractive, direct conversion (tanks to tractors) is not without its problems. Previous experience in market economies suggests that such conversion often represents the triumph of hope over experience: this is a field characterized more by failure than by success. Usually, advocates of direct conversion focus on the supply side completely ignoring the role of market demand and entrepreneurship. This approach resembles a centrally-planned economy where resources are allocated by command and not by market forces and unless the central planner has perfect information, the inevitable results are surpluses and shortages. But applying a centrally-planned approach to the conversion of Defense firms in a market economy encounters all the problems faced by the transitional economies.

There are sound economic reasons why direct conversion is difficult. Typically, Defense firms seeking to use their technology, resources and skills in new civilian markets have to identify potentially profitable civil markets. Identifying and entering new civil markets involves costs (e.g., retraining managers and workforce) and the new entrant has to compete against existing firms which have established reputations in the market. This raises particular problems for those Defense companies which have been highly dependent on Defense sales, relying on a single known customer, namely, the Defense Ministry, operating in a protected market with non-competitive, cost-based contracts, government-funded R&D and guaranteed profits. As a result, such Defense firms operate in a culture of dependency rather than an enterprise culture where entrepreneurship is required to search for market opportunities and where markets comprise large numbers of consumers.

Defense firms face further direct conversion problems if their resources of capital, technology and labor are highly specialized with few opportunities for transfer to the civilian economy. For example, some Defense plants and technologies have few, if any, direct civil applications such as plants for building ballistic missiles and nuclear powered submarines as well as armour and stealth technology. Other Defense firms and technologies have extensive civil applications such as aircraft plants which can build combat aircraft or civil airliners together with civil applications of radar, flight control systems and electronics. In these circumstances, and not surprisingly, some specialist Defense companies (e.g., prime contractors) have decided that their expertise and comparative advantage remains in the Defense field. Since they are good at Defense work, they have decided to remain in the Defense market and possibly seek a larger share of a declining market (e.g., via mergers and acquisitions creating large Defense contractors with a range of air, land and sea systems business, e.g., British Aerospace, GEC in the UK).

3.2 Conversion and the Armed Forces

Much of the debate about conversion focuses on Defense industries to the neglect of the conversion problems facing the Armed Forces. Disarmament results in base closures and redundancies for Armed Forces personnel raising questions about the marketability and transferability of military capital and military personnel.

Armed Forces are not-for-profit organizations so that they have not organized their bases and manpower on commercial, profit-maximizing principles (i.e., they operate in a different culture). Also in democracies when military bases are no longer needed, any alternative civilian use requires a transfer of ownership (its base commanders can not diversify into private civil-

ian markets). Nonetheless, experience shows that, following a transfer of ownership, there are alternative civilian uses for surplus military bases. For example, former military air bases have been converted into civil airports, into leisure facilities (e.g., gliding clubs; motor racing circuits), prisons, and industrial estates (see *Military Restructuring and Conversion*).

Questions also arise about the alternative use value of military manpower. Some military personnel acquire skills which are highly marketable and transferable to the civilian economy. Examples include computer operators, air traffic controllers, engineers, drivers and medical personnel. Other military human capital is highly specific and non-transferable such as missile operatives, paratroopers and tank gunners. For these groups with non-transferable skills, disarmament renders their human capital obsolescent.

3.3 The Environment Costs of Conversion

The environmental costs of disarmament and conversion are often neglected. However, closing military bases, Defense R&D establishments and Defense plants can involve substantial "clean-up" costs, some of which is needed before the bases and plants can be reused for civilian purposes. With military bases, the contamination of soil and groundwater can result from chemical and nuclear weapons storage and leakages from underground fuel tanks. Cleaning the site and restoring it for civilian use might involve additional clean-up costs from the demolition of buildings and the removal of debris. Clean-up is not cheap. US estimates indicate that the Department of Defense spent $11 billion on investigating, studying and cleaning-up contamination on American military bases over the period 1984-1994 and that finishing the job could cost as much as $30 billion.

4. The Role of Public Policy

Questions arise as to whether disarmament means that governments need "special" public policies aimed at the Defense sector and, if so, what might be the distinctive features of such "special" policies? At first sight, the case for "special" treatment seems convincing and persuasive. Governments are responsible for Defense spending so that they are inevitably involved in the adjustment process. Moreover, the impact of disarmament can be particularly severe for firms, industries, towns regions and rural economies which are dependent on Defense spending. Without appropriate public policies, the adjustment process for such Defense dependent sectors and regions might be long and painful. On this basis, public policies aimed at promoting efficient adjustment to disarmament can minimize both the time and costs involved in the transition. But efficiency and equity requires that such policies need to be part of a government general adjustment policy available to all sectors and regions vulnerable to plant closure and job losses (i.e., available to the civilian sector as well as the military-industrial sector). In other words, the appropriate solution requires a public policy towards assisting the re-allocation of highly specific and nontransferable resources throughout the economy, rather than focusing on the particular resource-specificity problems of Defense industries.

Disarmament creates both resource allocation and distributional issues (see *Human Security*). Welfare economics suggests that for a socially-desirable change, the potential gainers should be able to compensate the potential losers from the change and still be better off (the overcompensation test). Indeed, public choice analysis suggests that major interest groups in the military-industrial complex will oppose disarmament and lobby for specially-favorable policies to compensate them for their losses of rents. Here, though, there is a real danger of public policy being dominated by special interest groups and governments responding with policies favoring producers rather than consumers and taxpayers. The result could be subsidies and contracts being used to support jobs in Defense industries, thereby hindering the adjustment process needed to re-allocate resources out of Defense into alternative civilian activities.

Various policies are available for assisting an economy to adjust to disarmament and convert to civilian uses. Examples include manpower policy (e.g., training, retraining, mobility); capital policy (e.g., investing in new plant and equipment); technology policy (e.g., new civil R&D programmes); and regional policy (e.g., infrastructure, communications, enterprise zones). Throughout, the pursuit of efficiency and equity objectives requires public policies which assist the reallocation of resources from Defense to civilian sectors whilst offering incomedeficiency payments to compensate the losers from disarmament. In the final analysis, the Peace Dividend can not be obtained without a shift of resources from Defense to the civilian sector of the economy.

5. Conclusion: The Opportunities for Research

The economics of disarmament and conversion is an under-researched field and one which offers economists opportunities for applying both their theoretical and empirical tools and techniques. There are a variety of research questions:

(a) What are the effects of disarmament on labor markets as reflected in the employment and unemployment of redundant military personnel and Defense workers?

(b) What are the regional and local economic impacts of disarmament and which regions, towns and rural economies are vulnerable to reduced Defense spending?

(c) What is the experience of conversion of both Defense plants and military bases? Case studies are needed of successful and failed conversions and the reasons for success or failure.

(d) What are the lessons from previous disarmament efforts and from the experience of the civilian economy in adjusting to change?

(e) How successful is public policy in minimizing the adverse employment effects of disarmament and which policies are likely to be successful at the national, regional and local levels?

The economics profession has allocated substantial quantities of its human capital to addressing broad macro-economic issues such as inflation and unemployment, as well as more esoteric problems which give satisfaction to economists as producers. In contrast, the profession has allocated relatively few of its economists to study the theoretical, empirical and policy questions raised by Defense spending, disarmament, conversion and peace: issues which are important for the future of civilization. Perhaps the challenges of resource reallocation and conversion apply equally to the economics profession as well as to the military-industrial complex (see *Military Industrial-Complex*).

See also: *Arms Control, Evolution of; Social Progress and Human Survival; World Peace Order, Dimensions of; Future of Humanity*

Bibliography ────────────────────

CBO 1995 *Cleaning-up Defense Installations: Issues and Options.* Congressional Budget Office, Washington, DC
Dunne P 1995 The defense industrial base. In: Hartley K, Sandler T (eds.) *Handbook of Defense Economics.* North Holland, Amsterdam
Fox J R 1974 *Arming America.* Harvard University Press, Boston
Gansler J S 1989 *Affording Defense.* MIT Press, Cambridge, Massachusetts and London

Haglund D G (ed.) 1989 *The Defense Industrial Base and the West*. Routledge, London and New York

Hartley K 1991 *The Economics of Defense Policy*. Brassey's, London

Hartley K 1993 Aerospace the political economy of an industry. In: de Jong H W (ed.) *The Structure of European Industry*, 3rd edn. Kluwer, London

HCP 518 1986 *The Defense Implications of the Future of Westland PLC*. House of Commons, Defense Committee, HMSO, London

Hooper N, Hartley K 1993 UK Defense Contractors—Adjusting to Change. *Research Monograph* 3, Centre for Defense Economics, University of York

Latham A, Hooper N 1995 *The Future of the Defense Firm: New Challenges and New Directions*. Kluwer Academic Publishers, London

Mueller D C 1989 *Public Choice II*. Cambridge University Press, Cambridge

Ratner J, Thomas C 1990 The defense industrial base and foreign supply of defense goods. *Defense Economics* 2, 1

Reppy J 1983 The United States. In: N Ball, M Lichtenberg (eds.) *The Structure of the Defense Industry*. Croomhelm, London

Sandler T, Hartley K 1995 *The Economics of Defense, Surveys of Economic Literature*. Cambridge University Press, Cambridge

Southwood P 1991 *Disarming Military Industries*. Macmillan, London

Taylor T, Hayward K 1989 *The UK Defense Industrial Base*. Brassey's, London

UN 1993 *Economic Aspects of Disarmament: Disarmament as an Investment Process*. United Nations, New York

Todd D 1988 *Defense Industries: A Global Perspective*. Routledge, London

KEITH HARTLEY

Economics of Disarmament: Certain Premises

1. Introduction

Economics of armament is a "forward march" economy for the nation-states in war or stockpiling for war while the economics of disarmament is a "retreat march" economy from armament to civil economy and for human welfare. Economics of disarmament consists of the:

(a) conversion and transfer of military technology and capital to civil technology capital,

(b) transfer of the non-renewable and renewable raw materials to and for use in the civil sectors for human and material development,

(c) transfer of the military experts, personnel and human resources related to armament production and maintenance to the civil and social sector, in the interest of human development,

(d) transformation of the military and armament related jobs and services to civil or society-related jobs and services, and, finally,

(e) total transfer of the R&D in the military and armament technology to civil and social R&D.

Armament production, until now, used the most and the best of the basic non-renewable strategic raw materials and human resources in a very socially non-productive consumption and so became a burden on the society, because (a) the military products and service were and are non-usable for the society's maintenance and welfare and (b) the products and services do not create any values-in-use for human beings. Such types of social expenditure which do not create any value for the society and whose products and services do not enter into the society's consumption and development, can be characterized as inflation-inducive and inflation-creative expenditure for the society. The military and armament production and service-oriented inflation is consuming a good part of the cake, besides the cream of the society, leaving a needy mankind to look at it helplessly (see *Disarmament and Development*).

In order to understand the socio-economic needs and effectivity of disarmament, one has to understand the 'mal'-use and 'mis'-use as well as the 'mal'-effects of the material and human resources in the military and armament industries. The military and armament production-oriented use of the important energy resources like oil, gas, nuclear raw materials and metals, hard water, coal, etc., prevent their effective, productive and non-inflationable social use. An important part of chemical items and compounds are being 'mal'-used, directed to the chemical and bacteriological warfare materials for human and humanities destruction. Some important agricultural raw materials and animal products like corn, wheat, rice, potatoes, meat, eggs, fish, milk, etc., in huge quantities and of best qualities, are being used to feed and over-feed the military personnel during both war-time and peace-time war-preparedness.

And this happens when about half of the globe's people live at below basic needs-satisfaction level. Corn, potatoes and certain other cereals are being used to prepare alcoholic beverages for supplying and entertaining the military class of the world, described as means to stimulate. The supply also takes place at the state-subsidised low price for which the civilian population is taxed. Some other much socially-needed basic products like textiles and shoes of high quality, are also put at the consumption of the military class. The military class of each country is composed of the best physically well-built persons while the military and armament research, technology and development is composed of the best technical and scientific cadres of each country. It means that the military and armament sector drains the cream of each society's civil or social sector. It is nothing but the misuse of socially-needed human resources. The development of military technology and its expansion as well as extended use has been retarding the proper social use of industrial technology, since the latter is sacrificed for the former. The military use of basic and strategic raw materials generates both structural and class violence at the inter-nations and intra-nations levels (see *Militarism and Militarization*). This study will deal with certain basic problematic aspects of the economics of disarmament like the conversion of armament technology and means of production to civil/social technology and means; conversion of military personnel and research cadres to civilian personnel and civil technology research and development; alternative use of strategic and basic non-renewable and renewable raw materials, minerals and metals for human and social interests, and finally, the establishment of a correlation between human ecology and natural ecology which will contribute much to the happiness of humankind (see *Human Rights and Environmental Rights: Their Sustainable Development Compatibility*). In comparative perspectives, it will also examine the wasted aspects of the militarized human and natural resources and put forward alternative realistic solutions of the same for civil use.

2. Political Economy of Human and Natural Resources

By political economy of the human and natural resources one is to understand and put accent on:

(a) the economically productive and effective use of human and natural resources for the entire society's maintenance and progress, and

(b) the economic relations which bind social beings to the process and mode of production and the distributive aspects of socially-needed goods and services.

Human and material resources and sources used for human and social interests can be characterised as socially productive; and the same, if used for non-human and non-social interests can be termed as socially non-productive. The first type of use does contribute to human survival and development and the other type of use leads to material wastage (see *Peace and Social Development*). The factors and means of production related to economic and scientific activities and research-cum-development used for socially-needed goods and services do perform positive social functions. The factoral inputs and related economic activities in the process of armament production and maintenance, arms trade, research and development of the armament technology and maintenance of the armed and para-military forces and services are negative social functions, which constitute an unwanted and imposed burden on society. Table 1 shows (a) the volume of militarized human resources and (b) the value of militarized natural resources as well as the expenditure incurred on military capital and technology (in production, research and development).

The present number of the physically and mentally fit people in the world who are being used in the armed forces, armament production and maintenance, armament R&D, is around 150 million, which means that 3 percent of the cream of the human society is engaged in the socially non-productive sector of the army and the arms industry. The global armament production in 1981 was estimated to be worth US$ 1.7 trillion (at 1981 prices) which has gone up to US$ 2.9 trillion in 1990 (at 1990 prices). The military and para-military forces, the personnel engaged in arms production, the scientists and technicians engaged in military R&D, which constitutes the military class consume about 4 percent of the foodstuffs and beverages of the globe and also at subsidised prices. The military economy, known as the social-parasite economy, buys out the better socioeconomic and political privileges of the military elite, besides assuring it a high consumeristic living standard. The global military elite including those in armament production and maintenance in both the military and civil sectors, accounts for about 150 million, as stated earlier, whose creative talents, capacities and services, not only deprive the civil or social sector, but are also destined for use against the human sector and human-

Table 1

Types and values of militarized human and material resources in the army, armament production, military R&D and experiments: 1981 and 1990 (on global basis)

(Persons: in millions. Values: in US $)

Raw Materials	Human Resources	Capital	Technology
a) Minerals & Metals Aluminium: 1981: 6.3% 1990: 7.1%	a) Army Armed Forces: 1981: 35 mill. 1990: 39 mill.	a) Machinery Machinery: 1981: 5.5 trill. 1990: 8.4 trill.	a) R&D Res. & Dev. 1981: 35 bill. 1990: 64 bill.
Chromium: 1981: 3.9% 1990: 5.1%	b) Armament Prod. & Maintenance: 1981: 14.5 mill. 1990: 18.2 mill.	b) Financial: 1981: 140 bill. 1990: 290 bill.	b) Experiments: 1981: 3.5 bill. 1990: 6.2 bill.
Copper: 1981: 11.1% 1990: 14.7%			
Iron Ore: 1981: 5.1% 1990: 7.3%	c) Armament R&D 1981: 0.5 mill. 1990: 0.9 mill.		
Lead: 1981: 8.1% 1990: 11.2%			
Manganese: 1981: 2.1% 1990: 3.3%			
Mercury: 1981: 4.5% 1990: 6.2%			
Nickel: 1981: 6.3% 1990: 8.4%			
Platinum Group: 1981: 5.7% 1990: 7.2%			
Silver: 1981: 6.0% 1990: 8.4%			
Tungsten: 1981: 3.6% 1990: 5.1%			
Zinc: 1981: 6.0% 1990: 8.2%			

Notes: Mill.=Million US $ Bill.=Billion US $ Trill.=Trillion US $
    All the prices are current prices of the respective year
Sources: For the year 1981:
K. Subrahmanyam: *Strategic Analysis, Struggle for Disarmament* (Quoted from different sources and Disarmament Study Groups, Vol. VI, No. 1-2, April-May, 1982, Institute for Defence Studies and Analyses, New Delhi, pp. 50-52.
    For the year 1990:
    Data Bank of the Institute for Alternative Development Research, Oslo, Norway (Collected from different UN and official sources+objective estimations).
    SIPRI YEARBOOK 1991: World Armaments and Disarmaments, SIPRI, Pipers Väg 28, S-171 73 Solna, Sweden.
    The Military Balance: 1991-1992, The International Institute for Strategic Studies, 23, Tavistock St., London WC2E 7NQ, UK

ity. A good part of the basic and strategic non-renewable raw materials and metals are being swallowed up by the armament industry while millions of the globe's human beings are deprived of the fundamental socio-human needs. This very fact is shown in Table 1. It is a fact that most of the nuclear and advanced conventional arms producing and exporting nations do have import-dependency of the above strategic raw materials and they procure the same by exporting arms and ammunitions to the possessor countries. The surviving present superpower, until the emergence of the contesting new or newer ones, the United States did have an import-dependency of about 50 percent in certain important strategic non-renewable minerals and metals in 1975, which is expected to go up much towards the end of this century. An idea about this can be conceived from Table 2.

Since the United States is the only monopoly and superpower of the day and since she maintains both strategical and tactical superiority over the currently-disintegrated USSR, it can easily procure the above minerals and metals, in spite of competitiveness from other emerging nuclear powers, because of the following adopted and adoptable policies:

(a) stabilisation policy with neighbouring countries like Mexico and Canada, as sources of certain minerals and metals, and as markets for certain of her finished products and as bases of certain cheaper and labour-consuming industries with advantages of other economic factors and inputs,

(b) destabilisation policy towards those countries which do not follow a policy of friendliness towards the United States and the policy of law and order as desired by her, and

(c) taking advantage of the continuing depression and stagnancy trends in the international economy and binding the mineral and metal exporting peripheries to her orbit of the center in the desired terms, conditions and prices.

The global military expenditure in 1991 reached a volume of US $ 1.2 trillion which is about 10 percent of the world's Gross Domestic Product, as calculated by the Institute of Alternative Development Research in Oslo, on its own calculation basis. The combined armament investment, arms and military production, military and space R&D, defence budgets and civil

Table 2

The United States import-dependency of selected strategic and basic non-renewable minerals and metals and the sources of imports: 1975

Minerals and Metals	Import-Dependence (in %)	Major Sources of Imports
Manganese	100	Brazil, Gabon, South Africa, Zaire
Titanium	97	Australia, India
Chromium	91	USSR, Turkey, South Africa, The Philippines
Platinum	86	USSR, South Africa, Canada
Nickel	80	Canada, Norway, USSR
Aluminium	88	Jamaica, Surinam, Dominican Republic
Tantalum	88	Australia, Canada, Zaire, Brazil
Cobalt	98	Zaire, Finland, Norway, Canada
Tin	86	Malaysia, Thailand, Bolivia
Fluorinc	86	Mexico, Spain, Italy
Germanium-Indium	60	USSR, Canada, Japan
Beryllium	50	Brazil, South Africa, Uganda
Tungsten	60	Canada, Bolivia, Peru, Mexico
Zirconium	50	Australia, Canada, South Africa
Barite	40	Ireland, Peru, Mexico
Iron Ore	23	Canada, Venezuela, Brazil
Lead	21	Canada, Peru, Australia, Mexico
Copper	18	Canada, Peru, Chile, South Africa

Source: Richard Falk: Militarization and Human Rights in the Third World (quoted from The United States Military Posture for FY 1977), in *Problems of Contemporary Militarism*, Croom Helm, London, 1981, p. 214.

Table 3

Expenditure on armament production and military R&D in the overdeveloped and developed and less developed countries: 1955-1990 (in %)

World Zones:	1955	1980	1990
ODCS+DCS	96.7	83.9	81.3
LDCS	3.3	16.1	18.7
	100	100	100

Note: *) For 1990 Calculated by the author from the SIPRI Yearbook 1991, Stockholm, Sweden, and The Military Balance 1991-1992, IISS, London.

There a shift has taken place in the composition of the Overdeveloped and Developed countries in 1990 as compared to 1955 and 1980. For example, South Korea, Taiwan, Singapore, Saudi Arabia, The Arab Emirates, Kuwait, etc., are placed to the category of the ODCS and the DCS instead of the LDCS.

Sources: K. Subrahmanyam: *Strategic Analyses, IDSA*, New Delhi, Vol. VI, No. 2, 1982 (as quoted from the UN Report on the Relationship between Disarmament and Development).
SIPRI *Yearbook 1991* and *The Military Balance 1991-1992, as mentioned above.*

sectors put in service of the military sectors account for about 20 percent of the globe's social products and this amount may enable the production of sufficient food to feed about 1.5 billion half-fed and under-nourished inhabitants of the globe and assure free basic education to them. Chronic phenomena, for the liberated Third World countries during the last four decades have been: internal political and ethnic rivalry, power struggles, religious conflicts, secession wars, regional power games/wars and rivalries, mutual mistrust and destabilisation, disagreements over territorial boundaries, control over territories, imposition and maintenance of relationships of dominance, etc., and these have bound them to the import of the arms and ammunitions from the centre and export of raw materials to the centre. The LDCs should forget their old political arguments over colonial and neo-colonial exploitation and transfer of

surplus values to the metropoles, because there will never be any compensation (see *Maldevelopment*). They are to proceed towards sustainable and self-reliant development. In order to understand political economy and the implications of armament and disarmament one has to have a clear picture of the evolution of the expenditure on armaments in the economically Overdeveloped and Developed countries and in the Less Developed countries. Table 3 shows that:

It is worth knowing, for the purpose of comparison, the military expenditure of the USA and the USSR before disintegration, which is presented in the following table:

The global arms trade had, systematically and continuously been increasing, while more people of our earth are being thrown below the marginal line of nourishment. During the period 1986-90, compared

Table 4

USA and USSR official military, defence and defence-related energy expenditure (effected)

In billion US $, at current prices of each year.

Country	1989	1990	1991
USA	303.6	296.3	303.3
USSR (est)	247.4*)	225.4	238.0

Note: *) Calculated by the author

Sources: SIPRI *Yearbook 1991*, Stockholm International Peace Research Institute, Pipers Väg 28, S-171 73 Solna, Sweden, p. 117.
The Military Balance 1991-1992, The International Institute for Strategic Studies, 23 Tavistock Street, London WC2E 7NQ, UK, p. 36.

Table 5
World arms trade

Country	1965-70[1] (in %)	1970-76[2] (in %)	1986-90 (in %)	1970-76 (in Mill US $)	1986-90 (in Mill US $)
USA	49.0	38	32.57	12,303	53,811
USSR	29.2	34	36.79	11,057	60,799
France	4.4	9	8.34	2,953	13,783
China	3.3	2	4.65	537	7,684
UK	3.2	9	4.69	3,076	7,752
Czechoslovakia	1.9	0.3	1.46	87	2,408
Poland	1.9	0.1	*)	30	*)
West Germany	1.9	1.0	2.87	451	4,745
Canada	1.8	0.6	0.49	178	802
Italy		2.0	0.96	562	1,582
Netherlands		0.7	1.16	214	1,915
Spain		0.2	0.66	70	1,090
Australia		0.2	*)	60	*)
Sweden		0.2	1.10	54	1,813
Yugoslavia		0.1	*)	24	*)
Switzerland		0.1	*)	17	*)
New Zealand		0.04	*)	12	*)
Israel	*)	*)	0.66	*)	1,094
Brazil	*)	*)	0.72	*)	1,189
Egypt	*)	*)	0.40	*)	668
Others (includ: Japan,	3.4	2.46	2.48	742	4,097
Belgium, Ireland, and Third World Countries)					
Total	100	100	100	32,427	165,232

Notes: *) Amounts and percentages are included in "Others" of the respective period.
Percentages for the period 1986-90 are calculated by the author from the statistics presented in the *SIPRI Yearbook 1991*, SIPRI, Stockholm, Sweden, p. 198.
Sources: 1) Leslie H. Gelb: Arms Sales, *Foreign Policy*, No. 25, 1976-77, p. 9.
2) Signe Landgren-Backstr: *Arms Trade and Transfer of Technology to Third World Countries*, in the *Problem of Contemporary Militarism* (Asbj Eide & Marek Thee, ed.), Universitetsforlaget, 1980, pp. 232-34.
3) Aftenposten, Morning Number, Oslo, Norway, April 29, 1982.
4) *SIPRI Yearbook 1991*, SIPRI, Pipers Väg 28, S-171 73 Solna, Sweden, p. 198.

to that of 1976-80, arms trade increased five-fold, in which both the USSR and the USA enjoyed the great share. Table 5 demonstrates this.

Now let us come to the situation of the possession of nuclear arsenals and nuclear bomb-producing capacity of the nuclear and nuclearising nations of the globe. It is absolutely necessary to understand the importance of the economics of disarmament, besides the tremendous danger. Table 6 highlights this:

The expenditure on nuclear arsenal stockpiling, development of nuclear bombs, nuclear R&D in both the state and private sectors of the nuclearised and nuclearising countries is generally high and its socioeconomic and political consequences are even higher. But the land, water and atmospheric spread of nuclear wastes from both commercial and state plants does produce more negative consequences of the health, genetic and ecological, type on the earth's human and other bio-life, sea-life and atmosphere. There has not been any internationally accepted and binding programme of how to destroy the nuclear waste without

affecting, adversely, the bio-life, sea-life and atmosphere of the earth. Even a proper international public awareness regarding the mal-effects on the economy, ecology and health of the earth has not yet been aroused. The life span and potency of each Radioisotope, from the radioactive wastes is quite long. Each Radioisotope which consists of:

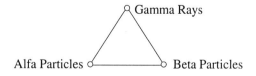

all of which cause harm to living tissues. The dangerous life-span of the Radioisotope from radioactive waste-spread has been calculated by the nuclear physicists, as:

(a) Radioisotope Plutonium 239 : Actively dangerous for 250,000 years

Table 6

Availability of plutonium, thorium and uranium 212 to the nuclear and nuclearising nations in 1980 and 1990 (from reloads of mixed plutonium and uranium oxide: MOX fuel)

Country:	Kg. of Pu (Plutonium) Holding 1980	Production capacity of Nuclear Bombs 1980	Production Capacity of Nuclear Bombs 1990**
Austria	400	46	65
Belgium	2,800	325	390
Brazil	500	58	126
F.R. Germany	11,700	1,357	2,400
India	360	42	140
Iran	3,200	371	125
Italy	2,100	244	345
Japan	9,000	1,044	2,295
South Korea	900	104	254
North Korea	. . .	. . .	50
Mexico	800	93	145
Netherlands	400	46	105
Philippines	1,000	116	180
Spain*)	5,600	650	1,050
Sweden	4,800	557	845
Switzerland	3,200	371	520
Taiwan*)	3,200	371	680
Yugoslavia	500	58	25
Egypt	700	81	101
USSR	. . .	. . .	2,800
USA	. . .	. . .	3,100
China	. . .	. . .	650
France	. . .	. . .	1,500
UK	. . .	. . .	1,400
Canada	. . .	. . .	850
Argentina	. . .	. . .	240
South Africa	. . .	. . .	845
Pakistan	. . .	. . .	65
Israel	. . .	. . .	255
Iraq	. . .	. . .	55
Libya	. . .	. . .	86
Australia	. . .	. . .	105
Algeria	. . .	. . .	42

Explanation: According to the *Generic Environmental Statement Mixed Oxide Fuel*, US Atomic Energy Commission, Vol. 3, August, 1974, p. IV, c-65: Assumed 580 kg per 1000 megawatt boiling water reactor reload and 770 kg. per 1000 megawatt pressurised water reactor reload, linear scaling for other reactor sizes (as quoted in source 1).

Certain countries do possess a nuclear arsenal, but it does not mean that they have proper technology or know-how or are willing to produce nuclear bombs.

   *) They produce nuclear energy (electricity) because of the insufficient volume of hydro or other types of traditional energy resources.

   **) The basis of calculation for 1990 is the same as in 1980.

The five UN veto-members: USA, former USSR, China, U.K. and France plus India are known nuclear bombs producing countries. Israel, South Africa and Pakistan are believed to have nuclear bombs and warheads. Argentina, Algeria, Brazil, Iraq, Iran, Libya, both the Koreas, Sweden and Taiwan are believed to have nuclear warhead development programmes.

The United Germany, Japan and Canada maintain a huge stock of nuclear arsenal.

Sources: Statistics for 1980:
   1) Albert Wohlsetter: "Spreading the Bomb without Quite Breaking the Rules," *Foreign Policy*, No. 25, 1975-76, New York, p. 153.
   Statistics for 1990:
   2) Data Bank, Institute for Alternative Development Research, Oslo, Norway.

(b) Radiosotope Uranium 235   : Actively dangerous
    (after decaying from   for 710,000 years
    Plutonium 239, in the
    course of time)

(c) Throium 230   : Actively dangerous
                        for 77,000 years.

Radium 226 and Radon 222 also, after decaying from the Thorium 230, are highly dangerous and have a long life-span.[1]

The reason for mentioning the above here is that the process of conversion from an armament economy to a disarmament economy during the coming years, in the domain of nuclear industry and technology, may accentuate the conversion from the military to the civil/social sector. But what types of measures are to be adopted for destroying or neutralising nuclear wastes? Nuclear electricity, after huge investment, may seem to be cheap, but to get rid of the irradiated fuel of the waste is not at all cheap. The technical options for their harmless and less-expensive eradication has not yet be found out. The Reprocessing Method of the chemical separation of the uranium and plutonium from the nuclear waste seems to be too expensive and maintains the danger of nuclear proliferation. The Conversion Method to shorter life-span isotopes through neuronic separation seem to be costly and technically yet uncertain. The Geological Burial (in granite-beds and mined repositories) and Sea-Bed Burial (in ocean sediments at high depth) Methods are considered to be a "for the time being" solution. Space Disposal and the Ice-Berg Burial in the Arctic and Antarctic Zones Methods can not be accepted because of insecurity in both the devices and effects. These methods will involve huge investment. The nuclear community consisting of the planners, scientists and economists of today, are to think of the remedial and preventive measures first before fuelling the nuclear arsenal. After the fall, disintegration and fragmentation of the former USSR, the United States remains the only superpower and centre today. Therefore, the risk of confrontation, war and fear of military imbalance is much reduced. If the United States now proceeds towards the disarmament and gradual conversion of the armament economy to the civil economy, the existing and emerging sub-superpowers will follow her course. The former dominant concepts of "parity," "balance," "power rivalry," "equal security" are becoming out-of-date concepts now. Civil defense should become the viable alternative defence for the nation-states in the coming decades (see *Civilian-Based Defense*). The practice of economic gains,

the concept of political and social prestige and ideological indoctrination of superiority of armament production and trade ought to disappear in the future and pave ways for civil welfare and standard of life, to be measured in correlated human and material satisfaction at equitable levels.

3. The Political Economy of Conversion and Alternatives

Considered from social utility, benefit and welfare, both the fixed and working capital in the armament industry can be considered as dead capital which does not need much explanation. The military R&D deprives the civil or social R&D considerably and swallows up a substantial part of a nation's budgetary cake and the GDP. The military industry, besides using the enormous volume of the globe's scarce raw materials, does also consume a significant proportion of global energy and energy resources. The estimated global average 9 percent official military expenditure in 1991 (1 percent of which is owed to the Gulf War of the year) can be characterized as an extra 9 percent inflationary burden on the global social economy (see *Economics of Disarmament and Conversion*).

The military technology and capital, and, the militarised human and material resources are lost civil or social opportunities, because their products and services do not enter into the consumption and benefit of humankind. The gradual disarmament and demilitarization process, on both the global macro- and national micro-levels and stages, will not only make the functional process of conversion, of the militarised use of the above to civil or social use, much easier and systematic, but will also release them from the militarised use of national income and national wealth. Certain realistic social sector development alternatives to military expenditure and development, calculated at the Institute for Alternative Development Research in Oslo, can be put forward as such:

4. Civil Development Alternative to Military Development

Military Domain	Civil Domain
	(a) Investment for two jobs in the civil sector
	(b) Creation of 50,000 jobs in an industrialised country, 100,000 jobs in the civil industrial sec-

i) Investment for one job in the military sector

ii) An expenditure of US $ 1 billion in the military sector

iii) Transfer of US $ one billon from the military sector

tor with appropriate technology and 150,000 jobs in the combined rural and industrial sector of a LDC.

(c) Creation of a tractor factory with a production capacity of 40,000 units per year, besides job creation.

(d) Sufficient to build 2 multi-purpose irrigation dams of high capacity or 4 of medium capacity.

(e) Effecting land reclamation of an area of 250,000 acres in order to convert uncultivable land to cultivable land.

(f) Construction of 40,000 apartments in urban areas or 120,000 in rural areas.

(g) Sufficient to finance the spinning and weaving looms to produce enough clothes for meeting the annual basic needs of a quarter million people.

(h) Enough to build 100 hospitals of medium size to meet both the curative and preventive sanitation and maternity needs of 50,000 patients a year.

(i) Sufficient to build 1000 schools for basic education with necessary teaching materials and tools for educating and training 30,000 pupils.

The above approach is the approach destined towards basic human needs satisfaction.

We conceive that 90 percent of the military technology can be converted to civil/socially-usable technology in a span of ten years and a transfer of US$ 1 billion from the military budget to the civil budget may enable the construction of 1,000 km asphalted roads in the LDC-rural areas for improving the intra-rural regional or intra-peripheral transport and communication system.

After abandoning chemical warfare, the highly-reactive chemical compounds can be used as preliminary and intermediate products for new and socially-usable synthetic products. It is expected that about 90 percent of the plants producing chemical compounds for warfare may, easily, be converted to civil chemical plants and production.

The diversion of investment-cum-expenditure from

the military production process to the civilian/social production process will function as an economic stimulant to the society, because it (a) will increase the social employment level and (b) will free the society from the worries of mal-effects of war (see *Arms Conversion*). Therefore one can find the economic solution and the welfare of converting the armament technology to civil technology, but what we need and miss much today is the political decision to effect it.

After the Second World War, the United States converted about 9 million armed personnel to civil personnel and the post-Second World period was the period of economic stabilisation and economic recovery for the United States. The 1992 budget-provisions of the United States foresees a cut of 100,000 personnel from the army because of the dismantling of the Warsaw Pact and, hence, the lack of fear from that rival part of the globe. Recently, the Russian Deputy Prime Minister Jagor Gaidar stated that the western countries had been spending yearly US$ 250 billion as defence expenditure for protection from the now-defunct USSR, which could now be diverted as aid to the economically distressed people of the Independent States of the former USSR.[2]

The conversion process from military industries, technology and personnel to civilian ones did already start in the non-disintegrated Soviet Union even before 1988. The former Soviet Premier Nicolai Ryzhkov admitted in 1988 that the share of civil-use products in the military industrial complexes in the then USSR accounted for around 40 percent[3] and it was expected that the process would speed up in the future. The industrial conversion of the military complexes in the former USSR included the following main areas: agricultural and food processing machineries, catering equipments, machine-building complexes, computers, electronics, medical equipment, consumer products, communication equipment, civilian and mercantile shipbuilding, civilian aircrafts, etc.[4]

The economics of armament is non-responsive to both economic cycles and social needs while the economics of disarmament can generate recovery and boomphases from recession and slump phases. It exerts positive effects on stabilising the social economy of a country.

5. Concluding Remarks

There can be found conservative and militaristic approaches which conceive that:

(a) the nuclearisation of arms industry and strengthening of the conventional arms and the army generate self-confidence for the nation-state concerned and produces stabilisation effects in the region or the neighbouring areas in the forms of (i) protective umbrella when the relationship is good, or (b) disciplined obedience when there is no way out because of helplessness for the weaker ones,

(b) both the nuclearisation and strengthening of the conventional armaments and strategies ensure internal social order and structural discipline within the country and the respective region, and

(c) social, economic and political order can be imposed at both the macro and micro levels through structured or structural type of military order.

But no structural military order can lead to the consciousness formation for social or civil order and the world's military elite consisting of only 4 percent of her population cannot be allowed to establish a structured social order and fix the destiny of 96 percent of the global inhabitants. The armament industry has not only been destroying the global economy and health, but global ecology too consisting of the human and natural ecology. Let us hope that the 21st century will become the century of disarmament economy which will establish a relational equilibrium between natural ecology and human ecology.

See also: *Alternative Defense; Military Restructuring and Conversion; Theoretical Traditions of Peace and Conflict Studies*

Notes

1. Nicholas Lenssen: "Nuclear Waste: The Problem That Won't Go Away," *World Watch Paper 106*, World Watch Institute, Washington, DC 20036, USA, p. 13.
2. *Dagbladet*, Oslo, Norway, January 2, 1992, p. 2.
3. *SIPRI Yearbook* 1991, SIPRI, Pipers Väg 28, S-171 73 Solna, Sweden, p. 150.
4. Idem.

Bibliography

Galtung J, Guha A et al., 1975 *Measuring World Development, Alternatives*, Part I in Vol. 1, Part II in Vol. 1. No. 4, New York, USA

Guha A 1985 *Conflict and Peace: Theory and Practice*. Institute for Alternative Development Research

Guha A, Vivekananda F 1991 *Development Alternative*, 2nd edn. 1985, 1st edn. Bethany Books, Stockholm, Sweden

Guha A, Khan S 1985 *Economics of the Militarized Human and Material Resources: Is there an Alternative?* Institute for Alternative Development Research, Norway

AMALENDU GUHA

Eco-technology

The creation of a humane civilization is a great challenge facing all mankind. In order to solve the problems of modern civilization, a completely new approach is required.

When we look at the long history of humankind from the viewpoint of mastery of the environment, we find that there are substantial differences between Japan and Europe because of their respective geographic and climatic conditions. The Japanese live close to, and with, nature; to Europeans nature is an object of conquest.

Modern technology has progressed on the basis of the methodology established by Galileo Galilei. And today, with a new leap forward in technology under way, there is increasing pressure to expand Galileo's methodology to all aspects of civilization. But the supremacy of technology can no longer go unchallenged. To prepare ourselves for the twenty-first century, technology has to come to terms with its "opposite," ecology. Such a convergence can be called "eco-technology."

The Honda Foundation, founded by Soichiro Honda has advocated "eco-technology" as a new concept of technology which does not pursue efficiency and profits alone but is geared toward harmony with the environment surrounding human activities. To establish and diffuse this concept the Honda Foundation established the Honda Prize in 1980. This prize is awarded annually to an individual or an organization, irrespective of nationality, for a distinguished contribution in the field of eco-technology.

1. Theoretical Background

The Old Testament says: "In the beginning was the word." However rich and excellent an image is, though, it will be imprisoned in the mind of the perceiver forever, lost to others, and unavailable to society, unless we have a means of expressing it in a concrete form. In this sense, technology is nothing short of the product of our perceptions. Therefore, when an image is born in the consciousness of a person who is in harmony with the natural order of the world (that is, its physical laws) it offers the potential of a variety of benefits to society as technology. If the image finds life in writing, music, or painting, the product will be a work of art appealing to the soul.

The Japanese have a proverb: "medicine is a benevolent art." This is understood to mean that medicine must not be practiced for profit. The proverb has its origin in the discourses of Confucius. In Ancient China the two important themes of human society were *mei* and *jin*. *Mei* means life; life is of absolute importance to humankind and all other living things. On the other hand, *jin* signifies the power to create heaven and earth and all other material things, and the ability to build upon them. Thus people in those days thought that it is in human society that *jin* is realized.

Confucius preached that profit should be considered only after we ensure *mei* and *jin*, the most basic needs of human beings. When we begin an action to obtain profit, it is important that we first take life and benevolence into consideration as the bases of our actions. The proverb "medicine is a benevolent art" thus invites us to learn from *jin* the vitality of nature to create and build, to invent technology to save the dying, and to recover the health of the sick.

As environmental problems have become more and more serious in recent years, the progress of technology has increasingly come to be regarded as the source of social evils. The main reason for this is that in the utilization of technology we have placed too great an emphasis on the economics of industry —that is, the pursuit of profit—while neglecting life and benevolence, the basic themes of human activities. What we must do now is to learn to create technology derived from essential human nature. Every technology should begin with our own image.

What we must do therefore is to help individuals develop images of perfection, to nurture new technology on the basis of these images and to give vitality to a sick civilization. These images should be transformed into benevolent art like the discoveries of previous people of genius. The inventions of Thomas Edison, for example, have contributed to the comfort of our lives.

If we turn our attention to automobiles, which are now a major cause of international economic friction, we find that the automobile industry in Japan started from the weaving machines invented by Sakichi Toyota, while that in the United States was pioneered by Henry Ford. It can be argued that Japanese automobile manufacturers inherited the delicate image of the first weaving machine, which was imbued with a more human factor, from the beginning.

It is important that the international community debate not only the ramifications of technology, but the image from which the technology derives—its cultural perspective. This may be a long way off, but we have to put it into practice at any cost as we enter the twenty-first century. The slogan of the activities of the Honda Foundation is the "Humane Use of Human Ideas." Eco-technology is the engineering concept created to apply this theme in practice.

The process of technological development seems to have three stages: research, development, and dissemination. In the first phase we conduct research to create something employing our unfettered, wide-ranging image. This is called *informe* in French, meaning the process of forming human thoughts and images into something concrete.

Technology is created, first of all, within a cultural context. It is born from the essence of culture which is created by human activities. On the other hand, what is science? According to one interpretation, it is the discovery and ordering of the inner essence of nature or ecology. Science was created when people began to express phenomena in nature as laws. Therefore it can be argued that science is the discovery and organization of nature's inner activities, while technology employs science to superimpose a human image.

The basis of technology is to make something using a set of rules formulated in accordance with natural laws. When we consider technology in society, people utilize laws at the research and development stages to formulate their objectives. Therefore what is needed now are new objectives incorporating additional cultural factors.

In particular, technological development is greatly affected by our social or national objectives. Technological development was initiated in Europe using a process of conceptual struggle, the so-called dialectical method. The form of this development comprises five basic ideas: analysis, synthesis, opposition, experience, and practice. The idea of opposition is particularly important; the objectives of technological development in Europe were influenced primarily by the desire to conquer nature. This in turn was deeply influenced by European culture, and has contributed to the great progress of European technology in harmony with its culture.

But now ecology must become the dominant concept in the dialectic. It will take some time before we can totally understand ecology as a system, but it has become possible to grasp certain relationships and to some extent develop analytical approaches. Thus it has become possible for us to consider the objective or rebuilding technology anew as the foundation of a new dialectical development. In this way the concept of eco-technology can be defined as the intention to develop new technologies.

2. *Stability of Compositions*

Modern technology contains a "fallacy of compositions." In other words, each individual technology is good and effective, but when technologies are combined the overall effect may be undesirable. On the other hand, ecology has a "stability of compositions." Although living things continue to compete violently with one another to survive, some eating others, the entire system develops in a positive direction, with a balance maintained. This balance is vague, and we may regard ecology as a vague system. It can be argued that Japanese culture is probably one of the least clearly defined cultures. In other words, Japan's cultural environment can probably admit every value and give it new life.

Modern civilization has three principal elements; raw materials, information, and energy, each of which gives rise to an industrial category—from raw materials the primary industries, from energy the secondary industries, and from information the tertiary industries. In areas related to information and energy, technology has made little progress. These areas may well become the foundation of civilization in the future, with industries based on ecology.

The voluntary behavior of groups is the basis of culture, or rather, the creation of a culture is the catalyst behind the actions of people. The understanding of these relationships is a major theme for eco-technology.

Modern automation technology was created in accordance with the principle that the products of technology should be shared fairly. In other words, in the beginning automation was intended to be the instrument for distributing the benefits of technology to the greatest possible number of people. Thus we can consider that the first stage in the development of technology, especially that of modern automation, is characterized by a fair distribution of the products of technology. In short, the intention to use technology to spread the benefits of civilization fairly acted in itself to advance technology. But as technology made progress, the concept of fair distribution was swallowed up by the waves of industrialization, and instead the idea of efficiency came to the fore in eco-

nomic growth. This was natural from the commercial viewpoint. As a result, when technology entered the dissemination phase, there was a movement toward humanization, the phase which we are now in. Humanization can be achieved at the individual and at the group level, but we should begin with humanization at the individual level. We should then proceed to the group level, at which stage we should ensure diversification, taking individual value systems into consideration.

When it comes to the question of individuals and groups, the Japanese mode of thought behavior appears to differ considerably from that of Europeans and Americans. Automation has achieved a greater success than expected in Japan; its rapid growth in industry has attracted global attention, and Japan offers the market an abundance of high quality automobiles and electronic equipment. This in turn helps to improve automation systems, resulting in the betterment of production technology. One reason for this is probably the fact that no definite contract exists between the individual and the group in Japan, and that even when a written contract is concluded between the two sides their recognition of the contract is vague.

In a Japanese firm the consciousness of the individual employee is in line with the objectives of the group and each employee is highly motivated; as a result, Japanese employees work very hard for their company even at the sacrifice of individual goals. They show an interest in the jobs of other workers and help these workers when the occasion requires. It may be said that automated systems, originally invented in the United States, were introduced to Japan because of these characteristics of Japanese culture. The behavior of individuals and groups, philosophies, and mechanisms differ completely from those in Europe and in the United States, and all are suited to modern automation.

In European and American societies it would be inconceivable for individual factory workers to know the underlying mechanism for the entire automation system in their factories and adapt to it. But in Japan workers want to understand the automation system in their plant in its entirety. In addition, workers use their own ideas to devise better systems by improving their workshops in step with automated operations. This naturally results in more productive technology, and is probably one big reason for the gap between Japanese and US industries.

Will these gaps continue to exist forever? No, because when unmanned factories appear a mere difference in culture will not allow Japan to attain superiority over the United States. At present Japan's cultural characteristics work well and help technological systems to advance in the right direction, but in the future such cultural influences will be reduced as the importance of technology grows.

Organization is the link between technology and culture, and therefore another major theme in eco-technology will be how to construct an effective organization establishing harmonious communications between technology and culture.

3. Concluding Remarks

In what fields should eco-technology be utilized? The theme has been widely discussed in connection with technology transfer, and problems are now being studied in various forms. For instance, "ecoscience" has as its main theme ecology, while "ecoeconomics" studies the relationships between culture, economy, and technology on the level of, for example, international organizations. In the United States debates are being held using the term "ecotopia."

All of these activities have the same root; the basis of their philosophy is that modern technology built on methodologies followed since Aristotle and Galileo. We should reconsider these methodologies and develop new technologies taking changes in the structure of industrial society into consideration.

Eco-technology should be able to make an internationally valuable contribution to the perceived need to establish anew some basic tenets of our present technological environment for world peace and security. As Galileo said, "there is no controlling power in the universe greater than the power that controls ourselves." Indeed, it requires much wisdom and courage for humanity to control the technology it has created.

An Eco-Technology Research Centre has been established at the Cranfield Institute of Technology, Cranfield, Bedford, United Kingdom.

Bibliography ─────────────

Aida S 1985 *A Concept of Eco-Technology; Technological Approaches to Complexity; The Science and Praxis of Complexity*. United Nations University, Tokyo
Aida S (ed.) 1983 *The Humane Use of Human Ideas—Discoveries Project and Eco-Technology*. Pergamon, Oxford
Aida S et al., 1985 *Culture and Automation*. Proc. IFAC Congr. 1984. Pergamon, Oxford
Sheridan T B, Vamos T, Aida S 1983 Adapting automation to man, culture and society. *Automatica* 19(6)

SHUHEI AIDA

Eden, Anthony

(Robert) Anthony Eden (1897-1977), British statesman, served as a Conservative Member of Parliament from 1923 until his retirement from public life in 1957. He was given a peerage as first Earl of Avon in 1961. An expert on foreign policy and diplomacy, Eden was noted for his deep interest in peacefully resolving conflicts whenever possible through discussion and negotiation. He was by no means a pacifist, however, and indeed fought on the Western Front as an infantry officer in the First World War.

After a brief stint as British Minister for League of Nations affairs, Eden was named Foreign Secretary of the British government in 1935. He resigned from this post early in 1938 though, out of frustration with the Chamberlain government's policy of "appeasing" the aggressive conduct of Mussolini and Hitler, a policy which he feared would lead to war. After war did indeed break out the following year he returned to government, serving as Foreign Secretary in the Churchill cabinet until the war's end in 1945.

Eden again became Foreign Secretary when the Conservatives returned to power in 1951. He was particularly well-regarded for his contributions to the peaceful solutions of the Trieste dispute between Italy and Yugoslavia, and of the French conflict in Indochina. Upon Churchill's retirement in 1955, Eden succeeded him as Prime Minister.

As Prime Minister, Eden continued his conscientious efforts to reduce East-West tensions, highlighted by his welcoming Soviet leaders Nikita Khrushchev and Nikolai Bulganin to Britain for a visit in the spring of 1956.

Ironically, the government of Anthony Eden, who was renowned as a man of peace and deliberation, began to come apart a few months later because his policies took a violently aggressive turn in the Middle East. In July 1956, Egyptian leader Gamal Abdal Nasser nationalized the Suez Canal, promising that the shareholders, of which the British government was the largest, would eventually be compensated. Eden was furious, not least because as Foreign Secretary he had been instrumental in negotiating the withdrawal of British troops from the canal zone in 1954, assuring critics of this move that it would lead to Anglo-Egyptian harmony.

A few months after Nasser seized the Suez Canal, Israel attacked Egypt. Though Eden denied British complicity in, or even foreknowledge of this attack, he swiftly took advantage of the situation, acting in concert with the French, by sending British and French troops to take the canal from Egypt on November 5, 1956. A worldwide storm of protest at this action, which frustrated United Nations attempts to negotiate a solution to the conflict, immediately followed. Even the government of Britain's closest ally, the United States, condemned Eden's policy. On December 22, Eden withdrew the British troops in favor of UN forces. Deeply humiliated, Eden resigned as Prime Minister and withdrew from public life in January 1957. Before his death, 20 years later, he published his memoirs in three volumes.

Bibliography —————————————————————

Barker E 1978 *Churchill and Eden at War*. St. Martins Press, New York
Campbell-Johnson A 1976 *Eden*. Greenwood Press, Westport, Connecticut
Carlton D 1981 *Anthony Eden: A Biography*. Lane, London
Eden R A 1939 *Foreign Affairs*. Faber and Faber, London
Eden R A 1960 *Full Circle*. Cassell, London
Eden R A 1962 *Facing the Dictators*. Cassell, London
Eden R A 1965 *The Reckoning*. Cassell, London

GARRETT L. MCAINSH

Education for Global Citizenship

Education for global citizenship has been present since time immemorial in the world's various philosophical and ethical teaching systems. Every culture has had traditions of learning which rise above the parochial or limited political interests of ruling elites, towards a transcendent humanism embracing all of humankind and nature in its field of concern. It is appropriate therefore to begin this article by surveying some of the contributions made towards current thinking by this enduring legacy.

1. Education for Global Citizenship in Antiquity

From their origins on the borderlands between Hellenic and Persian cultural zones, the classical philosophical schools from their inception evidenced a universalism which transcended the narrow interests of particular city states. Pythagoras (reputed coiner of the terms "philosophy," "cosmos" and "harmony") was suspect in the eyes of the tyrant of Samos and later the town mob of Crotona, for his synthesis of scientific and mystical doctrines which called students to be aware of their place as citizens of the cosmos. Socrates likewise, in calling his fellow Athenians to an awareness of wider ethical concerns than micro-political intrigues, paid the price with his life, but not before seeding the methodology of dialectical inquiry and the fearless pursuit of truth. His student Plato later formalised this legacy by instituting the Academy of Athens as an institution of higher education, open to citizens of the wider Hellenic world, instilling the idea of loyalty to spiritual ideals and ethical norms soaring beyond particular loyalties of clan, culture and religion. The most important early student of the Academy, Aristotle, continued to deepen this work by extending a broader scientific analysis of comparative political systems, and by subjecting ethical and metaphysical issues to a rigorous logical discussion, developing in the idea of the 10 categories a universal framework for ultimate truth questions. Subsequent to the Alexandrian expansion of Hellenism, the Stoic schools began to articulate a conscious doctrine of intellectual, spiritual and political loyalty owed by all thinking people to the "cosmopolis," and this "cosmopolitan doctrine" widely influenced thinking throughout the Mediterranean and Middle Eastern world, in famous educational centres such as Alexandria, Pergamon, Athens etc. Adopted by the Roman Republic and Empire as part of the blend of native Roman political and philosophical ideas with Hellenistic thought, Stoicism, with its doctrine of individual loyalties owed to the wider community and to the republic of mankind at large, became the bedrock of the Pax Romana which held sway throughout the Classical world for many centuries (see *Peace in the Ancient World*). Cicero in particular in his writings transmitted the ideals of personal responsibility before the wider civitas, and although republican and democratic ideals were eclipsed by the imperial sway, before long even Roman Emperors were consciously justifying their rule by appeal to the court of cosmic Reason, understood as the Logos governing right action in all communities irrespective of their racial or religious make up. Elsewhere, the ancient schools of Egypt had also developed religious teachings of universal co-responsibility and allegiance to divine wisdom, and Egypt acted as mentor and midwife to many of the classical movements of thought, and in the export of her Osirian and Isian mysteries inspired a philosophical eclecticism which influenced thinkers such as Apuleius, Plutarch and Iamblichus, in the golden afterglow of neo-Platonism. Interestingly, in Plutarch's telling of the Osirian legend, he makes out Osiris to have been a world teacher who travelled "throughout the whole known world teaching the arts of civilisation for the benefit of mankind at large, using only music and example, and eschewing violence, in his work for the moral education of mankind." Zoroastrian teachings (see *Zoroastrianism*) in Persia had meanwhile introduced a prophetic urgency to the quest for righteousness, setting the human life cycle and the quest for knowledge and education in the wider cosmological context of an eternal struggle between the forces of light and wisdom (led by Ahura Mazda, the Lord of Wisdom) and negativity and falsehood, in which human beings are called, through their self development, to aid the final victory of enlightenment over darkness. The wisdom teachings of the Middle Eastern civilisations of Sumeria, Babylonia, Canaan and Phoenicia had similarly channelled their ideals of global citizenship into largely religious formulae. It was out of this complex milieu that Judaism emerged with its own unique prophetic ideals of the global responsibility of mankind before a transcendent deity. In the writings of the Torah, especially in the prophetic books of Isaiah, Jeremiah and others, together with the Wisdom literature associated with the name of Solomon, Hebrew spirituality forged both an enduring vision of individual spiritual responsibility in the pursuit of righteousness, and a collective and social duty to build an ethical polity which could anchor and safeguard this message of universalism in a violent and troubling sea of rival imperialisms and competing religious traditions (see *Hebrew Bible and Peace*). Christianity proved the first major offshoot of this heritage, integrating the wisdom teachings of Rabbi Yeshua of Galilee, or Jesus Christ, with the Stoic ambience of Hellenism running throughout both the Gospels and the teachings of Paul, into a far-reaching educational lineage in which both individual and social elements were combined into a wider synthesis, which before long had become the ruling ideology of both the Roman (Catholic) and subsequently Byzantine (Orthodox) traditions (see *Christianity*). As in all the traditions being surveyed, a tension existed however, between the genuine strands of universalism and global consciousness (as in the various Christian-inspired "universal peace schemes"), and the particular exigencies of political imperium. Drawing on the imper-

ial legacies of Alexander and Caesar, the Roman Christian Empire, and the Byzantine world, and their successor states in the West, inherited this dual legacy: on the one hand the rhetoric of Christian spirituality and political theory envisaged a global polity bound in ecumenical unity and religious brotherhood, yet on the other hand, too often the realities of political intrigue and infighting led to the actual negation of the ideals professed. Often therefore it was the Gnostics or persecuted heretical groups (such as the Manichaeans) which actually attempted to live by global values beyond class or cultural boundaries. A further development of prophetic teaching saw the rise of Islam as a subsequent attempt to enunciate more clearly the world embracing universalism of monotheistic spirituality (see *Islam*). Education was vital to the spread of Islam, with the instruction of Mohammed that Muslims should "seek knowledge, even as far as China" leading to a busy eclecticism on the part of subsequent generations of Islamic scholars as they rapidly digested the scholarly traditions inherited from cultures as far afield as Greece, India, Central Asia, Persia, Egypt, Spain etc. Islamic mysticism (Sufism) particularly satisfied the restless intellects of generations of Muslim seekers as they sought to reconcile the apparent limitation of unique revelation with philosophic globalism. In India, the ancient teachings of forest sages (the Vedas and Upanishads) laid the foundations of Hindu contributions towards education for global citizenship, laying stress of the inner quest for the unity of cosmic and personal consciousness developed in the various schools of Yogic and Tantric thought. Out of these traditions, Buddhism also emerged as a unique agnostic ethical system, teaching personal responsibility and collective solidarity in the face of suffering, with compassion and wisdom as the twin pillars of its overarching ethical system, which soon spread through large parts of the Eastern Asia. Throughout Tibet, Mongolia, Japan, China, Korea, Sri Lanka and South East Asia, Buddhism eventually developed as a dominant belief system, active in many famous educational and monastic centres, which insisted on a cosmological context for the individual life experience, placing the imperative of enlightenment before the ethic of personal or tribal gratification (see *Buddhism*). Jainism (see *Jainism*), and later Sikhism, also arose out of the Indian subcontinent, as further spiritually based ethical systems which place loyalty towards holistic truth beyond egoistic awareness. More recently Gandhi, Tagore, Aurobindo and other spiritual teachers, have in their own unique ways continued to uphold the unique contribution of Indian spirituality to questions of global citizenship in the cosmic context. In China, the indigenous Taoist traditions echoed the insights of Indian Tantrism, perceiving reality as a dialectical flux of complimentary energies, awesome in their operation, enjoining humility and beneficence on their practitioners (see *Taoism*). While the school of the Chinese educator Mo Tsu echoed Christian and Stoic ideals of universal benevolence and love towards all beings as the aim of learning, it was the more academic and skeptical Confucius who stamped an enduring mark on China's educational heritage. Emerging at a time of confusion and violence (the "age of warring states") Confucius insisted that loyalty towards universal humanistic and cultural values should transcend one's particular political or personal advantage (see *Confucius*). He travelled tirelessly throughout China, crossing the then warring state frontiers, and developing a large following among the intelligentsia, working out in detail the practical ramifications of loyalty to philosophical principles and norms. Mencius (see *Mencius*) and later generations of Confucian thinkers further developed these ideas, such that not only did Confucianism act as China's primary educational tradition, but also throughout large parts of Eastern Asia (including Korea, Japan, Vietnam etc.) until partly replaced by Western (Christian and Marxist) ideas (see *Christian-Marxist Dialogue for Peace*).

It was not in the East, however, but in Europe, that the scientific enlightenment, accompanied simultaneously by the era of world exploration and expansive colonisation, truly began to usher in an era of globalisation whose effects are still being worked out today. Starting with the Mediaeval renaissance of the 12th century, and the rise of the Universities, when Western Christian thought was enriched by the reacquisition of Classical Greek and Roman models of cosmopolitan political thought (see *Cosmopolitanism*) (both through the intermediary of Islamic schools of translation and scholarship, and by refugees from a crumbling Byzantium), thinkers such as Marsilius of Padua expressed the ideal of a Christian world polity based on peace and justice and respect for both Divine and Natural law, whose collective interests transcended the selfish ambitions of particular reigning dynasties. Tragically, this ideal was split between advocates of the notion of the Holy Roman Empire, who saw in the Emperor the best guarantor for this transcendental justice, and those who looked to the Bishop of Rome, the Pope, as the mainstay of the system, particularly embodied in such farseeing Papal Statesmen as St. Gregory the Great, who envisaged a dynamic and interventionist role for the

Catholic Church as arbiter among nations on behalf of divine justice. Sadly, the conflict between these two approaches, created a moral confusion and a division of loyalties throughout Western Europe, which led, indirectly, to the emergence of the modern nation state as an outgrowth of this intractable tension of ideals. The Reformation and Counter reformations of the 16th and 17th centuries acted as a great stimulus to thinking, as rival schools of thought, be it Lutheran, or Calvinist or Jesuit, each in their own way, attempted to balance the tension of loyalties owed by citizens to their own immediate political leaders, to the religious community of believers which they professed, and to the wider shores of humanity. About the only thing which all these schools had in common was a great devotion to education as the means of transmitting value systems across generations, and of building up the "kingdom of God" on earth.

2. Modern Developments in Education for Global Citizenship

Following the first circumnavigation of the globe in the Renaissance era, and the opening up of regular sea routes to the Americas and across the Pacific, a train of events was set in motion which led directly to a renewed soul searching on the part of European intellectuals as to the relationship between particular or general political and ethical loyalties. Scientific skepticism, the Protestant insistence on direct spiritual verification, coupled with democratic republicanism and federalism, and a rejection of outmoded hierarchical worldviews, gave rise eventually to the ideals of the 18th century enlightenment, in which ancient religious dogmas were subjected to the rigorous tests of reason and found wanting. Instead, intellectuals (rediscovered the power of philosophy and science, and a loyalty to the "Republic of Letters," epitomised by such thinkers as Voltaire, Rousseau, Thomas Jefferson, Kant, Bentham, and Pestallozi, who each in their separate ways, sought to work out the configurations of ethical responsibility in the dawning era of global frontiers. The essential tool of the Enlightenment to effect change was understood to be education and the advances of the knowledge frontiers, such that developments in educational theory and practice mirrored the revolutionary changes underway in the political arena. Paradoxically, however, modernisation brought not only a growing awareness of universal values transcending cultural and religious particulars, but also unleashed the idea of nationalism (see *Nationalism*) and national militarism (see *Militarism and Militarization*), which in its more virulent forms in practice ran counter to the progressive ideals of universal liberty, quality and fraternity. The educational systems which arose during the course of the 19th century, with its long saga of rival European imperialism competing for world domination, were therefore tinged at root with this dual legacy—on the one hand they sought to impart the high ideals of scientific universalism, while on the other, they were subject to constraining influences of collective egoism and nationalist self promotion.

A further legacy of the 19th century towards education for global citizenship was the rise of liberal and socialist theory (see *Socialism and Peace*), which sought to promote the development of internationalism and peace (see *Internationalization*), yet which also left an ambiguous legacy to modernity, in that while most socialists were pragmatists who sought to advance the advent of a more equitable and just international society through democratic processes, in which education was to play a leading role (as in the work of the Fabian Society and their role in the foundation of the London School of Economics and Political Science at the University of London), the more militant Marxist-Leninist tradition which eventually emerged from the fires of World War One had its own brand of militant internationalism and model of global citizenship, promulgated through mass education programmes, which ended up in many quarters challenging nationalist, xenophobic and overtly racist educational programmes (e.g., in Nazism and Fascism) by equally militant and authoritarian models of internationalism constructed from enforced ideological blueprints, serviced by educational technocrats and ideologues, who opposed social injustice and capitalist militarism with versions of righteous class warfare and transposed Just War theories justifying the export of terrorist revolutionary struggles (see *Socialism, Scientific*).

3. 20th Century Developments in Education for Global Citizenship

The catastrophe of the First World War not only opened up the fissure between Marxist and non-Marxist spheres of influence, but it also dealt a severe blow to numerous international educational ventures which had been launched in the early 1900's to advance international intellectual and scientific collaboration, such as the American Fannie Andrews aborted effort to launch an international association of educators for world peace (due to take place in 1914), and the flurry of international intellectual congress

which had been launched in 1900, including the World Congress of Philosophy and the International Congress of Historians. Picking up the pieces after the war, the League of Nations promoted a series of strenuous efforts to counter nationalist propaganda in teaching by organising an International League for Intellectual Cooperation, which had the active support and involvement of leading thinkers of the day, including Henri Bergson, Albert Einstein, and Gilbert Murray. International efforts were also taken to reform history teaching to ensure that school textbooks avoided xenophobic approaches to the subject, while the development of international relations as a discipline in its own right was encouraged by the founding of Professorial chairs in the subject and by gatherings of experts in the field under the auspices of the League of Nations (see *League of Nations*). In the UK, the Royal Institute of International Affairs was established at this time, along with the Council on Foreign Affairs in the USA. Pioneers such as David Mitrany, Philip Noel-Baker and Quincy Wright (*A Study of War*) began to demand the methodical analysis of the causes of violence and conflict, and to work out the parameters of a peaceful and harmonious international system of power relations which could minimise catastrophe.

Such intellectual efforts at global consciousness were largely frustrated by the non-involvement of the revisionist Axis powers, and also by the non-participation in the League of Nations by the USA and the former Soviet Union. Japanese intellectual life also unfortunately underwent a growing hardening towards genuine internationalism, and instead a rigorous thought control was exerted through internal authoritarian educational structures which weeded out un-Japanese liberalism as subversive. With hindsight it is sad to reflect on the ineffectualness of the attempts of political scientists generally during the interwar period to think through those factors which advanced internationalism and globalism, with such work being carried on largely by creative thinkers not afraid to take risks in a general climate of appeasement, isolationism and polarisation. World War II, the tragedies of the holocaust against European Jewry and other "unacceptable aliens" and the unleashing of the Atomic bomb, came partly as a direct result of this failure of educators to impact sufficiently on the political realities of the situation and to influence them for the good.

World War II had a most profound impact on steeping up the thinking of educators on the need for providing educational solutions to war, racism and militaristic nationalism—to be summed up in the idea of global education, or education for global citizenship. During the course of the war, the Council for Education in World Citizenship was established in London in 1942 with senior support from many educational leaders and political figures, in order to campaign and educate for peace through international understanding, and to help reconstruct the world community intellectually after the war ended—and it has worked to this end ever since. At intergovernmental level, the Allied Ministers of Education convened a series of conferences to debate inter-governmental educational collaboration after the end of the war, many of the delegates being representatives of governments in exile, such as Poland, or Czechoslovakia, or the Free French. Sir Richard Livingstone (1880-1960) of Oxford University, published in 1943, *Education for a World Adrift* which urged that education for citizenship should not be seen merely as a question of knowledge in the abstract, but one tempered through the actual practice of civic virtues. He was one among many educators throughout the allied countries who were giving their thoughts over to the difficult tasks of reconstructing an ethical basis for civilisation.

With the formation of the United Nations Educational, Scientific and Cultural Organisation (UNESCO), initiated by the Allied Ministers of Education Conferences in London, a concrete structure was established which it was hoped would provide a forum for intellectual, scholarly and scientific exchange which would root out for ever the prejudices and xenophobia which had underlined the mass appeal of Nazism and Fascism.

Education was always seen as a key component of UNESCO's mission, even the overarching concept which gave substance to its work. A plethora of specialised academic and scholarly organisations were initiated under UNESCO's guidance in the first few years after World War II, dealing with aspects of the humanities and the social sciences, in an attempt to marshall academic aid, so to speak, towards the advantage of a war torn world. The International Bureau of Education, based in Geneva, and which had come into being in 1925, and acted as a major international co-ordinator of educational research and development on global issues and education for international understanding, worked closely with UNESCO, before being eventually formally incorporated into UNESCO in 1968. Its publications included an *Annual International Yearbook of Education*, and its large library was placed at the service of international scholars of education seeking a broader perspective than available parochially. Other intergovernmental organisations active in promoting education

for global citizenship included regional organisations such as the Commonwealth, and the Council of Europe (see *Council of Europe*), who placed emphasis on the questions of values education for their citizens within the wider world context.

During the decades following the end of World War II, the onset of the Cold War (see *Cold War*) and the associated ideological tension which arose between the hitherto allied power blocs of the USSR and the USA and Western European nations and others, also made it difficult for effective international projects and schemes to come to fruition around which all member states of the United Nations could agree. UNESCO became something of a battleground of competing ideological rivalries, as did much of the UN machinery, and instead the whole question of education became bound up with the race for competing models of development—socialist or capitalist—which rival systems peddled to their respective client states in the hope of gaining long term political and intellectual influence. Stalin's USSR had its own fear of liberal cosmopolitan internationalism, and most of the leading liberal Marxist intellectuals of the USSR were purged ruthlessly during this time, as Solzhenitsyn's work later documented for the world, based on his own personal experiences. As the Cold War intensified, the work of genuine education in global citizenship became suspect from both rival camps, who interpreted global education as meaning education and indoctrination in the models of society and culture which they themselves upheld. The tragedy is that many genuine idealistic people on both sides were caught up, so to speak, on opposite sides of the intellectual barricades, as the Iron Curtain hardened into the Berlin Wall.

The development of peace education (see *Peace Education*) also received a great stimulus from World War II, and as one of the component parts of education for global citizenship, it was often upheld by the educational wings of non-governmental organisations (see *Non-Governmental Organizations (NGOs)*), or of professional organisations who looked to education as the guarantor of a more peaceful future for mankind. War itself paradoxically also tends to act as a catalyst for global consciousness raising and education, with mass movements of troops and refugees throughout the globe occurring, leading to new stimuli and encounters (see *War*). As the Cold War (see *Cold War*) intensified into the Korean War in 1950-53, accompanied by the onset of the hydrogen bomb, and the nuclear arms race, a number of peace research institutes were established, in the USA and in Norway and Sweden particularly, to try to initiate a reasoned analysis of the problematic of war and violence, and the paths to peace and cooperative co-existence (see *Nordic Political Cooperation*), not through the traditional tools of defence and security studies, but from a different intellectual paradigm—that not only is it humanly possible to study peace, and through studying, to advance its realisation—but that it is a vital necessity, without which civilisation could perish altogether (see *Nonalignment*).

Non-aligned countries such as India and Yugoslavia, and newly independent former colonial countries, tended to see their educational needs as bound up both with educating the masses, and also as a way of asserting their newly acquired independence status. In India, the shadow of Gandhi and Tagore and other visionaries, in the hands of Nehru and his political heirs, created a model of such education for global citizenship by drawing on the traditional spiritual roots of Indian civilisation, along with the best of modern Western methods and ideas.

The Vietnam War, instead of being merely another neo-colonial conflict, had an even greater impact on discourse, in that it radicalised a generation of Western liberal scholars against the neo-imperialism of traditional models of educational submersion in favour of what Paulo Freire and others came to call education for empowerment, education for liberation. Eventually, along with many others, Kent State University in the USA, where protesting students had been shot, initiated its own peace studies programme, and these programmes, which now flourish in many American universities, have acted as a major leaven of education for global citizenship within the American academic context. Similar programmes have also developed in British, European, Asian and African centres of higher learning, and along with the work of several flourishing NGO's such as the International Peace Research Association, and the peace and conflict resolution sections of other professional academic bodies, have done much to focus minds on the future of the global polity. Much of this work was fuelled by anxiety over the nuclear arms race (see *Peace Studies*), responsible for diverting vast sums of money and precious human resources away from the constructive work of education—such that often in the past decades the work of peace education and education for global citizenship itself has been under resourced in comparison to the conventional military and defence related research bases. Such a problematique of course lies at the heart of the paradox of the work of education for global citizenship, since the fact remains that we still live in a world of nation states, with the United Nations as the court of last

appeal, so to speak, on the global international relations agenda —and in this sense genuine global citizenship remains as idealistic as ever. The uncertainties which have accompanied the ending of the Cold War—after the USSR was in effect bled to death, through the massive continuous diversion of its resources to militarisation, and the eventual realisation of its leadership that peace and nuclear disarmament were preferable to the *status quo*—have led both to intellectual euphoria (that the liberal Western model of reality has finally "won" so history can come back on course) and also to uncertainties and new anxieties, as in the recurrence of regional and resource wars, such as in the Gulf War, or in the Balkans. Often these contemporary conflicts have a religious, ethnic and nationalist dimensions to them, as in Israel/Palestine conflicts (see *Arab-Israeli Wars*), or in the wars which have waged in the Caucuses mountains, or they take a more underground form as terrorist conflicts, in which the line between politics and power and violence become uncomfortably blurred, as Northern Ireland.

Amidst the current climate education is being realised to be the most important strategy we have to genuinely deconstruct the long term ideological attitudes which lead to conflict and violence, and not surprisingly therefore the effort of educationists worldwide is being stepped up to inculcate global values and ideals into the citizens of planet earth (see *Peace and Peace Education: A Holistic View*). International literacy campaigns, for example, equipping people with the basic building blocks of formal education, have been prioritised with help from UNESCO and the International Bureau of Education. There are problems however in the very structure of the delivery systems of education, in that while national governments control the curricula of schooling, and also of higher education, the content of formal educational processes often lacks the needed global dimension. Another related problem concerns the fact that while global problems affecting the world community in the latter part of the 20th century are complex, multifaceted, issues, our education provision is too often concerned with producing specialised and technical knowledge to equip people for careers in advanced industrial societies. Specialist education alone however is insufficient to provide the sort of overall perspective which is needed to equip students with a global perspective. Fortunately, in many institutions of higher learning, there is a recognition of this, and courses are being developed which, for instance, give scientists, a general grounding in the humanities and social sciences, and vice versa. Interdisciplinarity of this sort, and the vision of a wholistic educational model, are a necessary counter balance to the specialist knowledge explosion which we are currently witnessing. Different specialised areas of learning can each contribute to the needed global perspective, and professionals in the various disciplines are fortunately, from their varying professional perspectives, contributing to an overall pattern of shared meanings. Let us consider next some of the ways in which this is taking place.

4. Education for Global Citizenship in Diverse Disciplines

Arts education is playing a critical role in raising global citizenship issues: the current wave of interest in world music among young people, for example, is a powerful way of creating awareness about the cultural inter-dependence of different peoples and civilizations. Drama, poetry, and the fine arts likewise, both at school and university level, have also taken on board something of the message of education for global citizenship in the cultural domain—although too often these are seen as extras to the core curriculum, rather than as central to the whole idea of civilized values.

Anthropology as a discipline has played a major role in deconstructing earlier mono-cultural interpretations of human culture by documenting the vast and complex array of cultural values and belief systems operative in every sort of society, including cultures which once might have been seen as primitive (see *Intercultural Relations and Peace Studies*). Indeed, the renaissance of respect and interest in the fate of indigenous cultures worldwide and the recognition of the importance of native peoples, has come to play an important role in the latest approaches to global education, and the work of anthropologists has made a significant contribution to this new found appreciation.

Philosophical education likewise, which is taught in some school systems, as well as continuing to play an important role in higher education worldwide, is flourishing with a more global outlook than ever before, with many new journals and professional educational association focusing on East-West philosophical encounter, on comparative philosophy, and global intellectual trends. Philosophers have also organised into professional organisations worldwide dealing with environmental ethics and the philosophy of peace, all of which adds richness and texture to the overall trends of education for global citizenship. The World Congress of Philosophy, meeting every five years, acts as a consistently high forum in which philosophers from throughout the globe can exchange

their approaches and pedagogical initiatives across frontiers and intellectual boundaries.

Psychologists and psychiatrists and other mental health professionals are also beginning to address profound questions of cultural diversity in questions of mental illness: comparative psychology and cross cultural psychology has become a major field of research and study among professional psychologists with number of associations organising research programmes in these questions (see *Psychology of Peace*). Jungian psychologists have traditionally always taken a profound interest in such matters, but other schools of thought are also now deeply involved in the discussion of whether there are global psychological patterns which are universally valid and active, or whether subtle states of feeling, mood, and the shifting boundaries between normality, madness and inspiration, are defined differently by different cultures and different times. Psychologists have begun to speak of the "anima mundi" (the soul of the world) and a growing number of thinkers and teachers have begun to argue that the outer material difficulties we are facing as a species today: problems of social organisation, of resource allocation, of conflict and violence, of environmental degradation—are in fact also psychological problems stemming from the way in which modern humanity views the world as essentially "soulless"—in which case, an urgent priority for education in global awareness is seen as helping students, families, citizens—to literally come to their senses and regain their soul awareness (see *Human Rights and Environmental Rights: Their Sustainable Development Compatibility*).

Language studies is another important area for global citizenship issues to surface, with translators, interpreters and linguists being ever more in demand, while the field of comparative languages and philology contributes greatly to the knowledge of other cultures and civilisations (see *Language and Peace*).

Geographers likewise through their professional associations have been working to broaden horizons through their unique ability to project the vision of a world community sharing finite resources on a complex, crowded globe. The role of travellers and professional geographical associations, such as the Royal Geographical Society, and the quest for adventure and sport in far flung areas of the world, often brought home to mass audiences via television—all of this has also increased our sense of belonging to a small, fragile, and wonderful planetary community, whose precious resources need marshalling and respecting for the benefit of all. Even those involved in educational aspects of the tourism industry are waking up to the need to foster a greater sense of global consciousness on the part of their clientele and workforce. One innovative project, for example, Airline Ambassadors, finds worthwhile charitable projects for travelling airline crews to do on their time off in distant locations throughout the world!

Libraries and museums continue, through travelling exhibitions, and increased exchange of data through advanced information technology, to widen the minds of students beyond the immediate framework of their environment (see *Peace Museums*).

Medical education has likewise assumed an increasingly global perspective, as doctors and medical researchers struggle to combat new forms of global illnesses, such as AIDS, and international organisations such as The World Health Organisation continue to play a lead role in this process. The WHO also managed, as a member of the UN family, to have the matter of the legality of nuclear weapons referred for judgement to the International Court of Justice in the Hague in 1994 as a matter of common medical concern affecting humanity (see *International Court of Justice*). So too the work of The Red Cross and similar medical organisations, such as Medecins sans Frontieres and MEDACT, with their campaigns against landmines, continue to raise awareness of global issues.

The scientific community in general, organised internationally through the various specialised associations within the International Council of Scientific Unions, and through professional non-governmental organisations, such as Scientists for Global Responsibility, and Pugwash (see *Pugwash Conferences on Science and World Affairs*), having contributed considerably to the ending of the Cold War through their documentation of the grave risks posed to humanity in the event of a general nuclear conflict, and continue to alert the public to the wider implications of global change.

5. Environmental Studies and Education for Global Citizenship

Environmental and ecological studies have become an increasingly important part of education for global citizenship, with a growing pressure for change through increased information, research and public awareness, of the negative impacts of advanced technology and industrialisation of natural resources and the cycles of the environment (see *Green Security*). The 1974 Stockholm conference on the environment gave an initial boost to such work, to be followed by the Vancouver Conference on Human Habits in 1976. The United Nations Conference on Environment and Development in Brazil, in 1992, likewise gave focus to the work of international educators interested in all aspects of ecology and development studies. This in turn has led to the worldwide Agenda 21 process, which is enabling local communities to organise around these themes on a local and regional basis. Organisations such as the Greening of Higher Education Council, and the World Wide Fund for Nature, have been campaigning for a more ecologically sensitive ethic to situate itself at the heart of higher education provision. Global issues therefore often stray onto the curriculum of both schools and universities in the discussion of environmental concerns. The sense that the planet as a community is in danger from over exploitation and resource depletion has been graphically brought home by the series of intense forest fires which have raged during 1997 in both Indonesia, Brazil and Australia: largely due to short term economic interests being placed ahead of the needs of either indigenous peoples or the long term environmental needs of the planet. Global warming and the effects of the increase of carbon monoxide levels due to industrialisation remain in the popular imagination as a further concern. Educational work around these and related issues, such as environmental policy studies and environmental mediation, has developed in recent years, enabling students to focus either on the technical aspects of environmental studies, or the political and social dimensions. Courses and educational institutes have also been developing which focus on the deeper questions of eco-ethics and environmental philosophy, questioning prevailing views of the philosophy of science, and arguing for an ethic of inter-connectedness which is embracing all life in its scope. The Gaia hypothesis of James Lovelock has become a useful starting point for debates in this field, and one which has stimulated a number of educational discussions. Economists have also begun grappling towards models which reflect the uncertainties and ethical dilemmas which we find ourselves in as a species: new sub-disciplines, such as green economics, or the economics of peace, which are not afraid to bring values questions into the discussions, have begun slowly to chip away at the observer model of more conventional economic paradigms (see *World Economy, Social Change and Peace*). In this sense economics may be paradoxically reverting to the initial insights of its founders, including Francois Quesnay, with his notion of physiocracy, or the primacy of nature as the source of value. Accidents such as the Chernobyl nuclear explosions in the Ukraine have similarly led in a graphic way to the realisation of our sense of community on a small planet, beyond arbitrary human political frontiers, and led to a plethora of educational initiatives on the part of both formal educational institutions and also NGOs like Greenpeace aimed at providing basic research to challenge traditional paradigms of "knowledge-as-power-over-others," and to develop an educational model of "knowledge-as-power-for-the-benefit-of-all-life." More grassroots educational initiatives have also been developing over many decades, with summer camps and direct woodcraft experience for young people enabling them to benefit from a living encounter with the natural world, learning about plants, trees, animals, natural rhythms and the beauties and challenges of nature. To experience the unveiling wonder of nature in this way is perhaps one of the best ways of arriving at the core of what it means to become a global citizen—for whereas citizenship implies an urban context linguistically, it is in fact in nature, where the parameters of the world run seamless, that the experience of true planetary awareness is often easiest achieved.

6. *World Order Studies and Education for Global Citizenship*

Another area of intellectual activity which has contributed greatly to the rise of education for global citizenship has been the post World War II phenomena of the rise of world federalism as a movement among intellectuals searching for an alternative to international anarchy or regional power blocs. Global citizenship as a political issue has been met head on by a number of organisations which were first launched from the late 1940's onwards, which looked forward to the time when mankind would literally form a global democratic political mechanism to enable world citizenship to become a reality in fact as well as in philosophical theory. The World Association of World Federalists (see *Federalism, World*) has been one of the leading organisations campaigning towards this end, stimulating a number of associated educational congresses and study projects. The Parliamentary Group for World Government and the One World Trust in the United Kingdom have likewise concentrated thinking over several decades as to the most feasible and desirable forms such a democratic world order could take. Some organisations have sought to work through United Nations reform and several research institutions have come into being which specialise in this area of study (including the Academic Council on the United Nations). Other groups such as the World

Citizens Assembly, The International Registry of World Citizens, Planetary Citizens (Planetary Initiative for the World We Choose), The Provisional World Parliament, and World Peace through World Law, have each in their diverse ways over recent decades sought to expand the sense of belonging from the immediate group of polity to the wider global community as a whole, through a whole series of educational initiatives. The World Order Models Project (WOMP) (see *World Order Models Project (WOMP)*) established by Richard Falk and Saul Mendlovitz has been one of the longest running of these educational endeavours, and has consistently organised educational events, research projects, and issued publications, opening for debate and inquiry the whole question of what sort of world community, what sort of international governance structures and political and economic frameworks, we would prefer to inhabit in the future.

7. *Human Rights, International Law and Education for Global Citizenship*

Closely related to all this have been parallel moves in professional legal education, where international law (see *International Laws*) and human rights education have become more and more important fields of study and research in recent decades (see *Human Right and Peace*). The tragedy of the holocaust during World War II, and the subsequent Nuremberg Trials, established certain principles in international law for the first time, namely that individuals can and must be held accountable to certain overall international ethical standards irrespective of the orders of particular governments. The Universal Declaration of Human Rights in 1948 (see *Declaration of the Rights of Man*) gave great impetus to educational work worldwide in the field of human rights, while the instruments created under the UN framework, for the monitoring and implementation of the Declaration, and its associated protocols, and the Declarations and mechanisms adopted by other international organisations, such as the Council of Europe, with its European Court of Human Rights: all these have contributed greatly to an increased awareness of one's duties as global citizens. The Peace Palace at the Hague, seat of the International Court of Justice, with its large and unique library of international law and human rights literature, also houses an international Academy devoted to the study of International Law to which scholars come from all over the world —and this and similar institutions worldwide (such as the Institute of Advanced Legal Studies at the University of London, or the Harvard Law School) continue to advance the frontiers of thinking in the area of our legal identity as global citizens. Difficulties abound in the field, of course, as the recent War Crimes tribunal at the Hague, in attempting to bring to justice perpetrators of crimes against humanity and crimes of genocide during the Bosnian war have shown: it is one thing to advance the theory of international law, it is another to advance the practice thereof (see *Nuremberg Principles*). Nevertheless, the fact that lines in the sand are being drawn, is itself of great importance, and cannot but help have long term impacts on the way we think and act one to another. One of the key questions raised here is whether human rights theory has been largely derived from secular or deist Western models, and then imposed on disparate cultures, who can appeal to other sources of law, for example, to different religions traditions, such as Islam, with their own independent approaches to the source of what defines good citizenship within the Islamic community, where other norms and practices of law may apply. Even here however, advanced scholars in the Islamic community are working to establish common frameworks of discourse and analysis, and to seek out common frameworks of jurisprudence and human rights law, transcending particular religious codes, by revealing the core values of universal human rights practice as situated within particular cultural and religious contexts. A further area of studies expanding significantly in recent times is that of mediation, which legal thinkers more and more recognise as a valuable alternative to formal legal procedures. Mediation has become a more widespread practice, active in all areas of conflict and dispute resolution, with its own professional networks and training organisations, all of which help to spread ideas of global citizenship and global responsibility (see *Mediation: A Tool for Peace Oriented Transformation; Mediation*). The Multifaith and Multicultural Mediation Service, is one such organisation, launched in 1996, which includes a strong educational dimension to its outlook, and offers mediation to tackle conflicts involving ethnic and or religious differences worldwide.

8. Development Studies and Global Citizenship Education

Development studies as an interdisciplinary academic field drawing on economics, sociology, technology, anthropology and the social science in general (see *Peace and Social Development*), has also played a significant role in shaping the content of modern education on issues of global awareness and citizenship. Academic institutions such as the Institute of Development Studies at the University of Sussex continue to grapple with the hard questions of global resource allocation, not just in terms of technology transfer or relative models of industrialisation, but also in terms of the transfer of knowledge, information and expertise, and the role of education in alleviating the conditions of a global "information underclass." Global NGOs such as Oxfam and Save the Children continue to raise hard political issues affecting the way that power and knowledge are controlled by global elites, for example multinational corporations, to their own economic advantage, rather than to the benefit of humanity as a whole. The United Nations Summit on Social Development in Copenhagen in 1996 raised these issues in a graphic way, with heads of nations and government ministers attending from over 140 countries worldwide to debate the issues of global unemployment, poverty and social exclusion, which are fracturing and dividing our communities in spite of the lessening of tensions in the aftermath of the end of the Cold War. At the Summit educational initiatives were recognised as crucial in tackling these enormous problems—in a world in which so many millions are still living in absolute poverty, and without access to work (see *Maldevelopment*). Education as empowerment, as essential to the rebuilding of self esteem, rather than merely skills provision or "training" for jobs in the careers sense, was seen to be a crucial ingredient in the pot of remedies adopted by general agreement among the representatives of the governments present. The challenge is on educators and educational administrators worldwide to help implement the basket of measures agreed at the Summit and to give them priority according to the details of their own particular national educational systems. Similarly, the work of global consciousness and fund raising initiatives such as Live Aid, which counts in effect as a sort of public initiative in education for global citizenship, which raised large amounts of money for famine relief in Ethiopia by enlisting the help of the world's rock musicians in a simultaneous live concert performed around the world, has demonstrated something of the way in which the global community can pull together in emergencies for the common good (see *Equitable Equality: Gandhian Concept*).

9. Religious Studies and Global Citizenship Education

Religious education continues to play a major role in

shaping the way that people understand their identities and their world perspectives (see *Religion and Peace*). The 20th century has seen a gradual rise in interfaith dialogue and exchanges, starting with the 1893 Parliament of the World Religions in Chicago, which event was repeated in 1993 in the centenary year, an event which brought together thousands of the leading proponents of interfaith dialogue to search together for common values. The World Congress of Faiths which has been going since the 1930's is another major longstanding contributor to this process, and has organised a large number of educational events. So too the World Conference on Religion and Peace, which was launched in 1970 to bring together men and women of religious and spiritual faith to discuss and study the key problems in the way of interfaith understanding and peace between divergent cultures and religions. Whilst previous centuries have seen considerable religious bigotry and the sense of religious mission has fuelled many acts of political conquest, on the whole, educators at the present time are emphasising the commonality of the spiritual vision bequeathed to humanity by the great religions of humanity, and scholars representative of these different traditions have begun engaging in an unprecedented level of dialogue and common educational work.

Within the Roman Catholic Church, figures like Thomas Merton, Father Bede Griffiths, Mother Theresa, and Karl Rahner have stimulated cross cultural dialogue in a way unprecedented before, and Vatican 2 ushered in a more sympathetic and respectful way of thinking about people of different faiths, a situation also reflected in the teaching programmes of Catholic schools and Universities around the world. The World Council of Churches (see *World Council of Churches (WCC)*) has likewise supported advanced global educational programmes designed to raise awareness of ethical issues and the search for common values through dialogue and interaction rather than confrontation and dogmatism. Buddhist schools of thought have likewise made considerable contributions to interfaith understanding, and a large number of refugee Tibetan Buddhist teachers have established successful teaching programmes and educational institutes worldwide, along with Zen and Theravadin educational centres, such that more knowledge is available about all aspects of Buddhist Studies, at all levels of the educational curriculum, than perhaps ever before. Hinduism likewise continues to develop its educational work, with ashrams and yoga teaching centres in many cities worldwide, not just in India, which emphasise the universality of the Hindu message of the eternal oneness of humanity before the Divine source. Islamic educa-

tion likewise continues to flourish worldwide with great vigour, as leading Islamic scholars grapple to reconcile traditional Koranic exegesis with the changing conditions of a world community. As is also the case with Judaism and most other religions, modern day religious communities could be said to be split into either fundamentalist camps, which insist on perceiving world affairs through the lens of their own particular tradition, and a more outward looking trend who emphasise the virtues of dialogue, encounter, uncertainty, flexibility and imagination when it comes to the educational transmission of spiritual ideals. It is a highly problematic area for education in global citizenship since some cultural and religious communities can feel threatened if they adopt a more universalising emphasis, necessitating much patient long term educational work, and the recognition that there are no short cuts to enlightenment, no easy routes to "cheap grace."

Some global educators have taken the root of emphasising the esoteric common core of human spiritual traditions as being the central thing to emphasise at this time. Robert Muller, for example, has devised a World Core Curriculum, based on his study of spiritual values across all belief systems. Organisations such as the Theosophical movement, the Anthroposophical Community, Findhorn, and the New Age community in general, continue to emphasise that the core part of the common curriculum of humanity at this time should address the unity of soul and spirit, mind and body, which alone gives common meaning to the fractured specialisms which otherwise would only confuse or endanger humanity. Never perhaps in human history has so much advanced esoteric teaching been available to humanity at large, in both written texts and oral transmissions from advanced teachers of all spiritual paths, and often, not surprisingly, one will find such schools deeply involved in advancing education for global citizenship.

10. Technology and Education for Global Citizenship

Perhaps no area of research and study is more important to the advancement of the idea of global citizenship than the developments underway in the field of information technology (see *Internet: A New Vehicle for Global Peace Efforts*). The development of the technology of communication, starting with the telegraph, then the telephone, and the radio, films and television—all these have graphically brought home to humanity, within a few decades, the sense of the shrinking of the size of the planet and the dawning of the idea of global citizenship. The use of radio, and then television, have been harnessed by educators with growing skill during the course of the 20th century for transmitting the ideals of global citizenship. The BBC and other major broadcasting corporations have a long trace record of programming aimed at schools and colleges, and with the advent of distant learning, educational organisations such as the Open University in the UK, and the Commonwealth of Learning (based in Vancouver, and responsible for distance learning provision throughout the 53 Commonwealth countries) continue to develop excellent programmes aimed at students sitting for formal degree courses from the comfort of their living rooms. The content of such programmes, partly governed by the facilities afforded by the technology utilised, are consistently broad and global in outlook. With the advent of personal computers, faxes, and now the internet, there is a rapid globalisation of communication possibilities, in which information and ideas can truly circle the globe at the speed of light. How this will all eventually impact on the social and cultural infrastructure of mankind remains to be seen, but certainly it brings enormously powerful tools of globalisation, and these are being utilised and explored by educators in a growing number of ways. Such distance learning technology has enabled a growing number of such efforts, now also utilising satellites, cable television, and videos and speaking cassettes to bring learning opportunities on a mass basis throughout the planet. Academics were among the first communities to be interlinked by the internet through their universities, and a growing number of international scholarly exchanges now take place through the medium of electronic mail, with enormous amounts of educational data being made available on the "Web." It may however present other problems and opportunities—that we are being bombarded with something of an information overload, such that the contribution of education as the crucial transmission of the faculty of discernment and evaluation—involving also the engagement of ethical criteria of selection and prioritisation—and the transmutation of mere information to knowledge and ultimately wisdom—has become more and not less critical. There are also profound issues involved concerning the political economy of knowledge and education, namely, whether it is right that the undoubted power of global information technology should be concentrated in relatively few corporate hands. In the 1970's UNESCO floated briefly the idea of tackling these issues, and announced that it was time to negotiate a New World Information Order, but this only led to the reassertion of dominance by the private corporate sector and the

cessation of Anglo-American involvement in UNESCO. The central issues involved however have not gone away. Too often information technology and the media remains under the control, either of narrow nationalist interests, often being used for blatant national propaganda purposes, or in commercial hands, where it is harnessed for spreading an ideology of commercialism and economic self interest, which may run counter to the ideals of genuine global citizenship. "Who controls the medium controls the message" remains unfortunately a truism, first pointed out by thinkers such as Gramsci and Marshall McLuhan. As yet it could be fairly stated that the mass media has not yet begun to live up to its potential as a medium for spreading the ideals of peace and global citizenship, instead feeding people with images of military heroism and violent adventure which creates a vicious downward spiral of ethical imagination and behaviour.

11. Gender Studies and Education for Global Citizenship

The rise of women's movements in modern times has made another significant contribution to the deepening awareness of global issues in the curriculum, with degree courses and modules available now in many universities which address the problematique of women's rights. While women comprise somewhere slightly over 50 percent of the world's population, they are far less advantaged in terms of their educational opportunities, and access to formal power in most institutional structures of the modern world. Intergovernmental organisations such as the United Nations, the Commonwealth and European Union and Council of Europe have, however, supported the development of significant educational initiatives aimed at redressing these problems. With the UN Beijing Conference on Women in 1995 and the ever-growing range of non-governmental educational networks focusing on women's rights in education, the issue has certainly been placed higher up the educational agenda than ever, if not yet resolved, since the issues go deep to the heart of our very definition of global citizenship and the real problems concerned with the gender politics of global political and ideological power (see *Feminism and Peace*).

12. Multiculturalism and Education for Global Citizenship

A further key area at the forefront of education for global citizenship concerns the work being done to address problems of racial prejudice and intercultural understanding by a wide number of agents and inter-governmental authorities worldwide. Whilst racism per se has received many formal condemnations, in the decades following the Second World War, which saw the blatant racist educational ideologies of Nazism and Fascism exposed and defeated, the deep-er prejudices and fears which different cultures hold against one another, often fuelled by religious and lin-guistic and general cultural considerations, remains an intransigent problem threatening to engulf humanity in a mass of internecine war and incidents of cultural terrorism and authoritarianism. Fortunately a large number of educational networks and organisations have come into being to marshall intellectual exper-tise to focus on tackling these problems, and collec-tively they are making a significant and growing con-tribution to the problems of racial exclusion and the persecution of ethnic minorities. Martin Luther King remains a towering example of a religious educator who stepped into the field of social activism, to chal-lenge the systematic abuse of power by entrenched cultural and racial interests, and his example has since been followed by many educators worldwide in dif-ferent cultural contexts (see *Cultural Roots of Peace*). While the formal ending of apartheid in South Africa has been achieved in the past decade, partly due to the concerted effort of the international community, the remaining xenophobic attitudes of different peoples to one another remains a major priority on the agenda of education for global citizenship. Nor is this an area with clear black and white ethical demarcations: too often, one form of racism can be replaced by a subtle form of inverse racism, in which rival codes of "polit-ical correctness" jostle for power: sadly, we are still some way from a genuine attainment of authentic global consciousness which alone can guarantee glob-al citizenship, such that the responsibility of global educators to work in this field remains greater than ever (see *Race and Racial Prejudice*).

Global Studies, Global Education and World Stud-ies as a complex (and variously named) academic field in its own right has also developed in recent decades, with its own specialist textbooks and school manuals. A number of innovative programmes are underway in different universities, trying to focus on the urgent need of raising the horizons of educators to address wider issues than found in the traditional curriculum. Too often however, such programmes remain outside the mainstream, or lack sufficient political and financial support to make a real impact, and one sometimes hears horror stories, such as the pulping in Australia of a whole series of excellent educational textbooks on peace and global education, produced and written under one administration, which were ordered to be pulped by an incoming administration with a different political agenda. Such stories highlight the perennial problem of educators trying to introduce a global dimensions into their educational work: for the most part, the world's for-mal educational structures remains funded and con-trolled by national or provincial political mecha-nisms, which too often act as if their own best inter-ests lie in minimising their interconnectedness with the world community at large, and think rather in terms of maximising their own immediate circle of particular interests. There remains much work to be done in the philosophy of education, and the rigorous analysis of the political economy of learning. The key word remains the achievement of balance: on the one hand, sensitivity to local interests and concerns, yet setting this within the wider context of global cit-izenship, and the shrinking size of global horizons.

13. The Role of Universities in Education for Glob-al Citizenship

In striking this balance the work of universities remains crucial. Ever since their rise in the mediaeval period of European history, when they stood as bas-tions of internationalism against the interests of regionalism, universities have struggled with a dual mandate, and twin masters: the advancement of truth in a transcendental academic sense on the one hand, and the advancement of the interests of particular religious or political groups on the other. This polari-ty remains an arena of active tension at the present time: are universities to act as servants of the nation state whose main purpose is to advance economic interests through the cultivation of intellectual capital —or are they guardians of genuine transnationalism (see *Transnationalism*), universalism and ecumenism, in which educators can operate in a genuine climate of academic freedom, to pursue their research and teaching mission on behalf of the global community as a whole? International organisations such as The International Association of Universities, and the International Association of University Presidents continue to work tirelessly to support educational ini-tiatives to enhance the latter aspect of their mission. The IAU endorsed the historic Talloires Declaration of 1988, which called on all universities to initiate programmes in peace and global studies, and the IAUP has been working for several years in association with the UN Department of Disarmament Affairs to make practical progress in introducing such courses in universities throughout the world.

In many countries, however, universities are still far too dependent on state support, and thus at the mercy of political fashions, and often academic freedom is itself threatened by economic and political power: organisations such as the World University Service and Amnesty International have therefore highlighted cases where academics have been persecuted, imprisoned, and even tortured and killed, to prevent them from exercising the high calling of their profession as independent witnesses to truth. Unless academic autonomy is safeguarded, the danger is that authentic education for global citizenship will be prevented from fulfilling its mission, either by the brutal silencing of dissident voices, or by the slow chipping away at independence by the gradual increase of reliance on commercial or politically motivated sources of funding from sources lacking the genuine breadth of outlook needed to guarantee autonomy. A further growing problem with the current university climate is the escalating cult of hyper-specialism, which militates against the sort of interdisciplinarity and breadth of outlook needed in education for global citizenship. Not surprisingly then, with leading edge educational work in global citizenship often of necessity being undertaken on the margins of formal academia, in association with advocacy groups or NGOs, it remains a matter of live contention as to whether the university as an institution can truly live up to its original calling to universalism in the modern era.

14. Conclusion

It is up to all of us involved in education, at whatever level, to ensure that the legacy of genuine concern for all humanity which has bequeathed to us from the eduational systems and wisdom traditions of the past, can be nurtured and transmitted on for the benefit of future generations, in new guises and structures appropriate to the needs of an ever increase sense of global inter-dependence. The work before us lies not only in the horizontal broadening of the curricula of the formal educational sector, by drawing out those elements of universalism and internationalism implicit in the content of formal academic disciplines, but also in terms of vertical depth and transcendence, by seeking to encourage students and teachers alike to ask deeper and deeper questions about the relationship of knowledge to life itself, by probing questions of meaning and not just appearance and form. In the classroom of global citizenship, we are all beginners, commissioned to the work of combining knowledge and humility, knowledge and love, knowledge and action. Only if we succeed, and lay behind us the curriculum of violence and cruelty which has been a hallmark, not only of this last century, but of so much of previous history, will we be able finally to graduate into a new intellectual millennium where different curricula can shape for future generations our authentic identities as citizens of the globe and of the cosmos.

Bibliography

Asbjorn E, Thee M 1983 *Frontiers of Human Rights Education*, Oslo

Barrow R, Milburn M 1990 (ed.) *A Critical Dictionary of Educational Concepts.*

Becher T 1989 *Academic Tribes & Territories*

Boulding E 1988 *Building a Global Civic Culture, Education for an Interdependent World*

CEWC *A History of the Council of Education in World Citizenship.* London

Connell W F 1980 *A History of Education in the 20th Century World*

Directory of Teaching Resources for Education in International Understanding, Cooperation and Peace, Marc Goldstein Memorial Trust, Institute of Education, University of London, 1993

Dunkin M (ed.) 1990 *International Encyclopedia of Teaching and Teacher Education*

Graves N 1984 *Teaching for International Understanding, Peace and Human Rights*

Husen T (ed.) *The International Encyclopedia of Education*

International Educational Bibliography. The International Bureau of Education

Kuehl W 1988 *Biographical Dictionary of Internationalists*

Lyons F S L *Internationalism in Europe 1815-1914*

Naish M 1992 (ed.) *Geography and Education: National and International Perspectives*

Reardon B 1988 (ed.) *Educating for Global Responsibility*

Selby D 1990 *Global Teacher, Global Learner*

T & M Klare 1990 *Peace and World Order Studies: A Curriculum Guide*

UNESCO (ed.) 1974 *Education for International Understanding, Cooperation and Peace*

THOMAS DAFFERN

Einstein, Albert[1]

Einstein's accomplishments in science were so daz-zling that they were bound to overshadow anything else he did, even though by the standards of ordinary mortals his attainments in several other fields would have been considered truly remarkable. Among these, the most outstanding were his political activi-ties, and in particular his ceaseless struggle for peace. Einstein considered himself a socialist and a pacifist, but he never joined an established political party. Although he lent his name to many a peace move-ment, he never followed a rigid pacifist line; indeed, for a time he was regarded as a traitor to the cause of pacifism. In his political activities, as in his scientific work, he was an individualist. He called himself "an incorrigible non-conformist." Since he did not follow an established line he was often criticized from both Left and Right. But throughout his life, he was moti-vated by love for humanity, reverence for life, esteem for culture, and respect for the intellect. Next to sci-ence, it was to these ideals that he devoted most of his time and energy.

The sanctity of life was the main reason for his abhorrence of war and the military machine. This comes through clearly in several of his statements:

> My pacifism is an instinctive feeling, a feeling that possesses me; the thought of murdering another human being is abhorrent to me. My attitude is not the result of an intellectual theory but is caused by a deep antipathy to every kind of cruelty and hatred . . . . (Nathan and Norden 1960 p. 98)

> To me the killing of any human being is murder; it is also murder when it takes place on a large scale as an instrument of state policy. (Nathan and Norden 1960 p. 93)

> . . . This brings me to the worst outgrowth of herd life, the military system which I abhor. I feel only con-tempt for those who can take pleasure marching in rank and file to the strains of a band. Surely, such men were given their great brain by mistake; the spinal cord would have amply sufficed. This shame-ful stain on civilization should be wiped out as soon as possible. Heroism on command, senseless—how passionately I despise them! How vile and con-temptible war seems to me! I would rather be torn limb from limb than take part in such an ugly busi-ness. (Nathan and Norden 1960 p. 111)

Apart from the destruction of life, war's debasing effect on culture was another reason for his pacifism:

> War constitutes the most formidable obstacle to the growth of international co-operation, especially in its effect upon culture. War destroys all those conditions which are indispensible to the intellectual if he is to work creatively . . . . Hence, he who cherishes the val-ues of culture cannot fail to be a pacifist. (Nathan and Norden 1960 p. 54)

This was not mere rhetoric: "I am not only a pacifist but a militant pacifist. I am willing to fight for peace" (Nathan and Norden 1960 p. 25).

The whole history of Einstein's life bears witness to his struggles to save humankind from self-destruc-tion, to eliminate cruelty and vulgarity and replace them by kindness and the enjoyment of intellectual achievements. The latter was natural to Einstein, who received exquisite joy from scientific work.

1. The First World War (1914-18)

Einstein's pacifist activities began at about the start of the First World War. Much earlier he had shown his dislike of the authoritarianism and militarism which had characterized prewar Germany by renouncing German citizenship at the age of 16 and becoming a Swiss citizen. (He claimed that he never became a German citizen again, although membership of the Prussian Academy of Sciences, which was conferred on him in 1913, automatically made him a Prussian citizen.)

The act which provoked him to come out into the open with his opposition to the war was a declaration issued in October 1914 by 93 major German intellec-tuals. Under the title "Manifesto to the Civilized World," the document attempted to whitewash the atrocities by the military, and in particular the viola-tion of Belgium's neutrality. But the declaration went further than this; it stated that if it were not for Ger-man militarism, German culture would have been wiped off the face of the earth. Within a few days of the publication of the Manifesto, a reply was issued under the title "Manifesto to Europe." Its main author was Georg Friedrich Nicolai (see *Nicolai, Georg Friedrich*), a professor of physiology of the Universi-ty of Berlin; Einstein was its coauthor, as well as one of only four signatories. In the highly charged nation-alist atmosphere in Germany in this period it required great courage to advocate opposition to war, a call for peace was equivalent to treason. It is evidence of Einstein's profound feelings that he should make such an audacious statement only shortly after accepting a professorship in the University of Berlin and directorship of the Kaiser Wilhelm Institute for Physics. Apart from being a retort to the Manifesto of the 93, this first public statement of Einstein's is noteworthy because it contained the foundations for his future political objectives: world government and peace based on international cooperation. In the achievement of these goals there lays an important role for intellectuals too:

> Never before has any war so completely disrupted cultural co-operation. It has done so at the very time when progress in technology and communications clearly suggest that we recognize the need for international relations which will necessarily move in the direction of a universal, world-wide civilization .... Technology has shrunk the world .... Travel is so widespread, international supply and demand are so interwoven, that Europe-one could almost say the whole world—is even now a single unit .... The struggle raging today can scarcely yield a "victor"; all nations that participate in it will, in all likelihood, pay an exceedingly high price. Hence it appears not only wise but imperative for men of education in all countries to exert their influence for the kind of peace treaty that will not carry the seeds of future wars, whatever the outcome of the present conflict may be. (Nathan and Norden 1960 p. 4)

Forty years later, in his last public statement, Einstein was to echo many of these sentiments, again calling on scientists to help humankind to avert destruction in another war in which there could be no victor.

Hard on the "Manifesto to Europe" Einstein cofounded a peace movement, the Bund Neues Vaterland (League of the New Fatherland). Its direct aim was to bring about an early and just peace, but it also had a long-term objective: the establishment of an international organization which would make future wars impossible. The Bund issued pamphlets, made public statements, distributed literature from British pacifists, and held meetings at which Einstein spoke. The group was harassed from the beginning, and in 1916 its further activities were banned. In spite of this, it continued a clandestine existence until it was able to come out into the open again, a few months before the end of the war. It was formally refounded on November 14, 1918 with Einstein as a member of its working committee.

2. *The League of Nations (1919-32)*

Einstein's conviction that the abolition of war required, as a first step, the setting up of a supranational organization, made him a natural and keen supporter of the League of Nations (see *League of Nations*). Born in 1920, the League of Nations

enjoyed Einstein's support for many years, although he was often angered and saddened by its ineffectiveness. Einstein's link with the League of Nations was maintained through his membership of its Committee of Intellectual Cooperation, which might be considered as the precursor of UNESCO. Together with Marie Curie and other eminent scholars, Einstein was invited to join the Committee in 1922; but his membership was not without difficulties. Although he was invited as an individual, and not as an official representative of Germany, the French gave expression to the strong anti-German feeling prevalent at the time by objecting to a "German" as a member. Some Germans objected to a "Swiss-Jew" representing them.

After serving on the committee for several months, Einstein resigned from it. The reason was characteristic: he resented the exclusion of German scientists from an international scientific congress which was to be held in Brussels. To him science was always international, and he could not tolerate the attitude of French and Belgian scientists who refused to sit down at a table with their erstwhile enemies. But he rejoined the Committee a year later.

During the next few years, Einstein was very active on the Committee of Intellectual Cooperation and attended most of its sessions. Although his objective was to bring into closer communication national cultures previously separated by language and tradition, he realized that a start could only be made with modest projects. These included the international organization of scientific reporting, the exchange of publications, the protection of literary property, and the exchange of professors and students among various countries. A more ambitious project was the establishment of an international university for the education of statespersons, diplomats, political writers, and professors of political science. Einstein was particularly conscious that history was often taught in a narrow way and that many textbooks contained offensive passages. As the Committee recorded his views:

> Historians are not sufficiently free of prejudice and it seemed impossible to attain impartiality. It was necessary to establish some kind of institution which should be entirely free and to appoint men according to their qualifications and without regard to their opinions. (Nathan and Norden 1960 p. 76)

However, despite lengthy discussions, few of Einstein's proposals were implemented; other members of the Committee were fearful of the interference with national sovereignty that they entailed.

Einstein's work in the League of Nations had the long-term objective of providing the basis for the peaceful coexistence of nations by creating more opportunities for collaboration and by fostering better understanding. At the same time, however, he was mindful of a short-term objective, which growing nationalist sentiment had made very urgent—namely, resistance to war. In the period 1925-32, Einstein became one of the most active leaders of the international antiwar movement.

Naturally, he sought to emphasize the role of science. He realized, however, that scientists alone would not be really effective in efforts to abolish war, and that their efforts must be supplemented by the direct action of members of the community in refusing to serve in a war. In a letter to the "No More War Movement" he said:

Science is a powerful instrument. How it is used, whether it is a blessing or a curse to man, depends on man himself and not on the instrument . . . . As long as human beings are systematically trained to commit crimes against mankind, the mentality thus created can only lead to catastrophe again and again. Our only hope lies in refusing any action that may serve the preparation or the purpose of war. (Nathan and Norden 1960 p. 104)

He amplified this by a solemn declaration about himself:

I would unconditionally refuse all war service, direct or indirect, and would seek to persuade my friends to adopt the same position, regardless of how I might feel about the causes of any particular war. (Nathan and Norden 1960 p. 95)

Having thus committed himself, he felt obliged to defend those who, having followed his appeal, found themselves in trouble by refusing to do military service. This meant that he had to intercede with the authorities of several countries on their behalf. But his main effort was to give active and moral support to the many international organizations for disarmament and against war. These organizations included the War Resisters' International, the Women's International League for Peace and Freedom, the People's Parliament for Disarmament, the World Peace League, the Joint Peace Council, the League of Nations Association, and the International Union for Antimilitarist Clergymen and Ministers. Whenever he could find the time he participated in their meetings; otherwise he sent letters of support and encouragement. But he exercised discretion in the causes he sponsored. Despite his often expressed keenness for unity among the various groups in the pacifist movement, he refused to support organizations which tended to exploit pacifism for ulterior motives. Thus he declined to attend the International Congress against Imperialist Wars held in 1932 in Amsterdam. In refusing to sign the appeal which was to be issued from the congress, he wrote: "Because of the glorification of Soviet Russia which it includes, I cannot bring myself to sign it" (Nathan and Norden 1960 p. 78). Later he explained his attitude to the Soviet Union as Follows:

I am a convinced democrat. It is for this reason that I do not go to Russia although I have received very cordial invitations . . . . I am an adversary of Bolshevism just as much as of Fascism. I am against all dictatorships. (Nathan and Norden 1960 p. 234)

3. The Nazi Menace (1933-39)

By 1932 Einstein was the acknowledged international champion of pacifism, the outstanding advocate of peaceful methods of settling disputes, and the staunchest opponent of war in all its ramifications. But all this changed radically in 1933. Within a short time Einstein reversed his pacifist stand and began to advocate military preparedness by the democratic countries of Europe.

The cause of this volte-face was the Nazis' seizure of power in Germany in January 1933. This event had momentous repercussions on his personal life: he left Germany for good and moved to the Institute for Advanced Studies in Princeton, United States, where he remained until the end of his life. The change of his political outlook was simply the result of his sober and realistic assessment of the situation. Einstein recognized the shape of things to come long before this had penetrated the minds of other leaders in the pacifist camp. Quite early on he arrived at the conclusion that the Hitler regime was aiming at the military conquest of Europe, that the war preparations were not a bluff, and that Europe's only hope of avoiding fascist tyranny lay in adopting a posture of military strength. Most pacifists failed to appreciate that the danger was real, or else dogmatically refused to deviate from their rigid pacifist principles under any circumstances. To them, Einstein became an apostate, a traitor to the cause of peace.

Even though he still supported people who refused to be conscripted into military service, he began to be attracted to the idea of securing world peace by setting up an international police force. With the advent of the Hitler regime, Einstein became increasingly convinced of the need for an organized military power to counteract the Nazi menace; but he insisted that the military organization must have an international character. And he was soon to revise his views about refusal of national military service. Thus he wrote in July 1933:

> ... I must confess freely that the time seems inauspicious for further advocacy of certain propositions of the radical pacifist movement. For example, is one justified in advising a Frenchman or a Belgian to refuse military service in the face of German rearmament? Ought one to campaign for such a policy? Frankly, I do not believe so. It seems to me that in the present situation we must support a supranational organization of force rather than advocate the abolition of all forces. Recent events have taught me a lesson in this respect .... (Nathan and Norden 1960 p. 229)

In a general statement issued before leaving for the United States, he said:

> My ideal remains the settlement of all international disputes by arbitration. Until a year and a half ago, I considered refusal to do military service one of the most effective steps to the achievement of that goal. At that time, throughout the civilized world there was not a single nation which actually intended to overwhelm any other nation by force. I remain wholeheartedly devoted to the idea that belligerent actions must be avoided and improved relations among nations must be accomplished.
>
> For that very reason I believe nothing should be done that is likely to weaken the organized power of those European countries which today represent the best hope of realizing that idea. (Nathan and Norden 1960 p. 232)

These explanations did not satisfy the pacifist leaders, who launched a bitter attack on him:

> ... At a very critical moment Einstein takes the part of militarism .... He now thinks he can save European civilization by means of fire bombs, poison gas and bacteria .... The apostasy of Einstein is a great victory for German National Socialism .... Einstein's action has done unutterable harm to the fight against militarism. (Nathan and Norden 1960 p. 232)

Einstein's comment was blunt:

> ... The antimilitarists attack me as being an evil renegade. These fellows wear blinders; they refuse to acknowledge their expulsion from "paradise." (Nathan and Norden 1960 p. 235)

During the following years, Einstein's public interventions became rarer; his gloom deepened as he observed his predictions about the Nazis' designs gradually coming true, with no measures being taken to counteract them. Increasingly, he resented the shortsightedness of his erstwhile fellow campaigners. In 1937 he wrote to the American League against War and Fascism:

It is, in principle, reassuring that a widespread organization, such as yours, exists to advocate the ideals of democracy and pacifism. On the other hand, it must be said that of late pacifists have harmed rather than helped the cause of democracy. This is especially obvious in England, where the pacifist influence has dangerously delayed the rearmament which has become necessary because of the military preparations in the Fascist countries.

It is quite true that any increase in military strength represents a danger to democracy. But if the democracies remain unarmed and defenceless in the face of the bellicose Fascist countries, the danger to democracy will be far greater.

In my view, this whole dilemma results from the rather shortsighted policies which pacifist organizations have pursued. The supreme goal of pacifists must be the avoidance of war through establishment of an international organization, and not the temporary avoidance of rearmament or involvement in international conflict .... The main goal of pacifist propaganda should be to support the strongest possible supranational authority for the settlement of international conflicts. But no support should be given to the concept of isolationism which today can only be characterized as the most shortsighted kind of selfishness. (Nathan and Norden 1960 p. 276)

In 1939, in another letter to the Queen Mother of Belgium, he expressed his premonition of impending catastrophe :

> ... I have been too troubled to write in good cheer. The moral decline we are compelled to witness and the suffering it engenders are so oppressive that one cannot ignore them for a moment. No matter how deeply one immerses oneself in work, a haunting feeling of inescapable tragedy persists. (Nathan and Norden 1960 p. 282)

Soon afterwards the tragedy commenced.

4. The Second World War (1939-45)

Einstein's role in initiating the work of nuclear weapons which eventually brought the war to an end, has been described in numerous publications, but it is still given a false gloss and he is often described as the father of the atom bomb. On the technological side, he has been given the credit for laying the foundations for it through his 1905 formula ($E = mc^2$) of the equivalence of mass and energy. On the political side, he is acknowledged as the person who gave the impetus to the United States government to start work on the bomb. In reality his contribution can hardly be described in these terms. Unlike his other pursuits, both in science and in politics, where he usually actively led the field, his role in the atom bomb project was passive. He himself never thought that the equivalence of mass and energy would find any practical application during his lifetime; he was greatly surprised when told of the possibility of a fission chain reaction leading to an unprecedented release of energy: "That never occurred to me," he is reported to have said. As for the initiative in starting the bomb project, this was a case of his great reputation being blatantly used by others—admittedly in a cause which Einstein willingly supported once the problem was outlined to him.

Einstein later deeply regretted his involvement with the atom bomb project:

> I have never taken part in work of military-technical nature and never done research having any bearing upon the production of the atomic bomb. My sole contribution in this field was that, in 1905, I established the relationship between mass and energy, a truth about the physical world of a very general nature, whose possible connection with the military potential was completely foreign to my thoughts. My only contribution with respect to the atomic bomb was that, in 1939, I signed a letter to President Roosevelt in which I called attention to the existing possibility of producing such a bomb and to the danger that the Germans might make use of that possibility. I considered this my duty because there were definite indications that the Germans were working on such a project. (Nathan and Norden 1960 p. 519)

How decisive was Einstein's initiative? It is quite possible that without Einstein's letter to Roosevelt the whole project might have been considerably delayed. On the other hand, independent work on the atom bomb had started in the United Kingdom, and it was here, indeed, that the feasibility of a nuclear explosive was established for the first time. It is believed that it was the transmission of this result to the Americans that finally convinced the United States government to start the project in earnest (Gowing 1964).

5. The Nuclear Age (1945-55)

The war over and fascism defeated, Einstein—at the age of 66—might have retired honorably from active political life. Instead he intensified his efforts, and the postwar years became a period of strenuous endeavors in the public arena. The reason for this was the new danger that arose as an aftermath of the war: the danger of complete annihilation in a nuclear war. The threat of such a war loomed large as the Cold War (see *Cold War*) deepened and the nuclear

arms race accelerated (see *Arms Race, Dynamics of*). The last ten years of Einstein's life were devoted to an incessant struggle to prevent a nuclear catastrophe. His age and state of health did not allow him to attend the many conferences and mass rallies that were convened on his initiative, but he sent messages of greetings, wrote articles in newspapers and journals, spoke on radio and television, and engaged in an enormous correspondence with many individuals and groups. He continued his public activities right up until his death.

As always he took the long view in assessing the new situation that had arisen from the development of nuclear weapons. The same perspective guided his attitude to the consequences of the growing divergence between the United States and the former Soviet Union—a divergence aggravated by the United States insistence on maintaining nuclear superiority. He came to the conclusion that no partial disarmament would be adequate, and that the only hope for the survival of humankind was through world government. The idea of a supranational authority, which he had advocated in the First World War, assumed much greater urgency after the Second World War and became the main focus of his activities.

Einstein was well-aware that the former Soviet Union was opposed to world government. He knew this even before the point was put to him explicitly in 1947 in a letter from four eminent Russian scientists, who maintained that world government would ensure world supremacy of the capitalist monopolies and that the call for it was prejudicial to the cause of peace which Einstein so warmly espoused. Einstein replied to the "benevolent attack" on him with a long article in which he analyzed the world situation and patiently explained why he had arrived at the idea of a world government as the only solution. The last part of his article reads:

> If we hold fast to the concept and practice of unlimited sovereignty of nations it only means that each country reserves the right for itself of pursuing its objectives through warlike means. Under the circumstances, every nation must be prepared for that possibility; this means it must try with all its might to be superior to anyone else.
>
> This objective will dominate more and more our entire public life and will poison our youth long before the catastrophe is itself actually upon us. We must not tolerate this, however, as long as we still retain a tiny bit of calm reasoning and human feelings.
>
> This alone is on my mind in supporting the idea of "World Government," without any regard to what other people may have in mind when working for the

same objective. I advocate world government because I am convinced that there is no other possible way of eliminating the most terrible danger in which man has ever found himself. The objective of avoiding total destruction must have priority over any other objective.

I am sure you are convinced that this letter is written with all the seriousness and honesty at my command; I trust you will accept it in the same spirit. (*Bulletin of the Atomic Scientists* 1947 p. 35)

Einstein realized that, in the prevailing climate, his logic would not be heeded—however persuasive it might be. But he considered that if other countries accepted the need for world government and began to take steps to implement it the then Soviet Union would come in sooner or later. In the early period after the war such ideas had a sympathetic response in the Western world, and the various organizations which worked toward this goal enjoyed considerable mass support. But political events such as the Korean War and the growing hysteria in the United States about "un-American" activities dampened enthusiasm and led to a decline in the campaigns for world government. Einstein met this with increasing gloom about the prospects of the survival of humankind.

Einstein was most interested in the role of scientists in tackling these issues and he gave strong support to the scientists' movements which sprung up after the war. In 1946 he became the chairman of the Emergency Committee of Atomic Scientists, a fund-raising and policy-making agency for several organizations of American scientists. The fund-raising campaign was very successful—the magic of Einstein's name always worked—and assisted the activities of the Federation of American Scientists and the publication of the *Bulletin of the Atomic Scientists*, a journal devoted to the ideals for which Einstein fought. The policy of the Emergency Committee was summarized in the following statement issued at its first conference in 1946:

These facts are accepted by all scientists:

(a) Atomic bombs can now be made cheaply and in large numbers. They will become more destructive.

(b) There is no military defence against the atomic bomb and none is to be expected.

(c) Other nations can rediscover our secret processes by themselves.

(d) Preparedness against atomic war is futile, and if attempted will ruin the structure of our social order.

(e) If war breaks out, atomic bombs will be used and they will surely destroy our civilization.

(f) There is no solution to this problem except international control of atomic energy and, ultimately, the elimination of war.

The program of the committee is to see that these truths become known to the public. The democratic determination of this nation's policy on atomic energy must ultimately rest on the understanding of its citizens. (Nathan and Norden 1960 p. 395)

The Emergency Committee endorsed Einstein's view about world government. Later however, it lost its impetus and was disbanded in 1951.

From time to time pacifist organizations advocated a kind of Hippocratic Oath for scientists, based upon a refusal to do any work of a military nature. Though he was always opposed to the use of science for military purposes, Einstein thought such ideas unrealistic. In a reply to call from scientists to support a cause he said:

. . . We must first ask ourselves: would any action by a group as small as the group assembled in Princeton have any decisive influence? Would the physicists and engineers necessarily follow our course of action? And assuming they would want to, would they be free to do so? To these questions my answer is "no," for the following reasons:

(a) Almost all scientists are economically completely dependent.

(b) The number of scientists who possess a sense of social responsibility is so small that their "non-participation" would have virtually no effect on the production of armaments.

For these reasons I do not believe that your proposal is, in any sense, practicable; indeed, it is doubtful whether anything of value could be achieved by forcing its adoption. (Nathan and Norden 1960 p. 465)

However, he was strongly in favor of scientists becoming actively involved in helping the community and governments to lessen the dangers arising from scientific progress. Almost the last act of his life was to endorse an appeal in this spirit.

The initiative came from Bertrand Russell (see *Russell, Bertrand*). Alarmed by the development of the H-bomb and the intensifying arms race, Russell conceived the idea that scientists ought to do something dramatic to bring home to the public and governments the magnitude of the disaster the might occur. In February 1955, he wrote to Einstein with the suggestion that a few eminent scientists, headed by Einstein, should issue a public statement to this effect. Russell felt that the signatories of the statement should be so diverse in their politics that any statement signed by all of them would be obviously free from procommunist bias. In an immediate reply, Einstein fully agreed with the proposal and suggested that Russell should draft the statement and assume leadership of the project. Russell prepared the draft and sent it to Einstein together with a suggested list of signatories. The letter was dated April 5, Russell recollects (see Russell 1969) that as he flew from Rome to Paris the pilot announced the news of Einstein's death. Russell felt shattered, not only for the obvious reasons, but because he saw the plan falling through without Einstein's support. But, on arrival at his Paris hotel, he found a letter from Einstein with his signature to the statement and agreement to the choice of proposed signatories. This was the last letter that Einstein signed.

The statement was issued at a large press conference in London on July 9, 1955. The full text is given below.

The Russell-Einstein Manifesto

In the tragic situation which confronts humanity, we feel that scientists should assemble in conference to appraise the perils that have arisen as a result of the development of weapons of mass destruction, and to discuss a resolution in the spirit of the appended draft.

We are speaking on this occasion, not as members of this or that nation, continent, or creed, but as human beings, members of the species Man, whose continued existence is in doubt. The world is full of conflicts; and, overshadowing all minor conflicts, the titanic struggle between Communism and anti-Communism.

Almost everybody who is politically conscious has strong feelings about one or more of these issues; but we want you, if you can, to set aside such feelings and consider yourselves only as members of a biological species which has had a remarkable history, and whose disappearance none of us can desire.

We shall try to say no single word which should appeal to one group rather than another. All, equally, are in peril, and, if the peril is understood, there is hope that they may collectively avert it.

We have to learn to think in a new way. We have to learn to ask ourselves, not what steps can be taken to give military victory to whatever group we prefer, for there are no longer such steps; the question we have to ask ourselves is: what steps can be taken to prevent a military contest of which the issue must be disastrous to all parties?

The general public, and even many men in position of authority, have not realized what would be involved in a war with nuclear bombs. The general public still thinks in terms of obliteration of cities. It is understood that the new bombs are more powerful than the old, and that, while one A-bomb could obliterate Hiroshima, one H-bomb could obliterate the largest cities, such as London, New York and Moscow.

No doubt in an H-bomb war great cities would be obliterated. But this is one of the minor disasters that would have to be faced. If everybody in London, New York and Moscow were exterminated, the world might, in the course of a few centuries, recover from the blow. But we know, especially since the Bikini test, that nuclear bombs can gradually spread destruction over a very much wider area than had been supposed.

It is stated on very good authority that a bomb can now be manufactured which will be 2,500 times as powerful as that which destroyed Hiroshima. Such a bomb, if exploded near the ground or under water, sends radioactive particles into the upper air. They sink gradually and reach the surface of the earth in the form of a deadly dust or rain. It was this dust which infected the Japanese fishermen and their catch of fish.

No one knows how widely such lethal radioactive particles might be diffused, but the best authorities are unanimous in saying that a war with H-bombs might quite possibly put an end to the human race. It is feared that if many H-bombs are used there will be universal death—sudden only for a minority but for the majority a slow torture of disease and disintegration.

Many warnings have been uttered by eminent men of science and by authorities in military strategy. None of them will say that the worst results are certain. What they do say is that these results are possible, and no one can be sure that they will not be realized. We have not yet found that the views of experts on this question depend in any degree upon their politics or prejudices. They depend only, so far as our researches have revealed, upon the extent of the particular expert's knowledge. We have found that the men who know most are the most gloomy.

Here, then, is the problem which we present to you, stark and dreadful and inescapable: shall we put an end to the human race; or shall mankind renounce war? People will not face this alternative because it is so difficult to abolish war.

The abolition of war will demand distasteful limitations of national sovereignty. But what perhaps impedes understanding of the situation more than anything else is that the term "mankind" feels vague and abstract. People scarcely realize in imagination that the danger is to themselves and their children and their grandchildren, and not only to a dimly apprehended humanity. They can scarcely bring themselves to grasp that they, individually, and those whom they love are in imminent danger of perishing agonizingly. And so they hope that perhaps war may be allowed to continue provided modern weapons are prohibited.

This hope is illusory. Whatever agreements not to use H-bombs had been reached in time of peace, they would no longer be considered binding in time of war, and both sides would set to work to manufacture H-bombs as soon as war broke out, for, if one side manufactured the bombs and the other did not, the side that manufactured them would inevitably be victorious.

Although an agreement to renounce nuclear weapons as part of a general reduction of armaments would not afford an ultimate solution, it would serve certain important purposes. First: any agreement between East and West is to the good insofar as it tends to diminish tension. Second: the abolition of thermo-nuclear weapons, if each side believed that the other had carried it out sincerely, would lessen the fear of a sudden attack in the style of Pearl Harbour, which at present keeps both sides in a state of nervous apprehension. We should, therefore, welcome such an agreement, though only as a first step.

Most of us are not neutral in feeling, but as human beings, we have to remember that, if the issues between East and West are to be decided in any manner that can give any possible satisfaction to anybody, whether Communist or anti-Communist, whether Asian or European or American, whether White or Black, then these issues must not be decided by war. We should wish this to be understood, both in the East and in the West.

There lies before us, if we choose, continual progress in happiness, knowledge, and wisdom. Shall we, instead, choose death, because we cannot forget our quarrels? We appeal, as human beings, to human beings: remember your humanity, and forget the rest. If you can do so, the way lies open to a new Paradise; if you cannot, there lies before you the risk of universal death.

Resolution

We invite this Congress, and through it the scientists of the world and the general public, to subscribe to the following resolution :

> In view of the fact that in any future world war nuclear weapons will certainly be employed, and that such weapons threaten the continued existence of mankind, we urge the Governments of the world to realize, and to acknowledge publicly, that their purpose cannot be furthered by a world war, and we urge them, consequently, to find peaceful means for the settlement of all matters of dispute between them.

Professor Max Born (Professor of Theoretical Physics at Berlin, Frankfurt, and Göttingen, and of Natural Philosophy, Edinburgh; Nobel Prize in physics)
Professor P. W. Bridgman (Professor of Physics, Harvard University; Nobel Prize in physics)
Professor Albert Einstein
Professor L. Infeld (Professor of Theoretical Physics, University of Warsaw)
Professor J. F. Joliot-Curie (Professor of Physics at the College de France; Nobel Prize in chemistry)
Professor H. J. Muller (Professor of Zoology at the University of Indiana; Nobel Prize in physiology and medicine)
Professor Linus Pauling (Professor of Chemistry, California Institute of Technology; Nobel Prize in chemistry)
Professor J. Rotblat (Professor of Physics, University of London; Medical College of St. Bartholomew's Hospital)
Bertrand Russell
Professor Hideki Yukawa (Professor of Theoretical Physics, Kyoto University; Nobel Prize in physics)

This statement, which became known as the Russell-Einstein Manifesto, was subsequently endorsed by thousands of scientists from many countries. It became the credo of the Pugwash Conferences on Science and World Affairs. The Pugwash Movement (see *Pugwash Movement*), which is the direct outcome of the Russell-Einstein Manifesto, carries out its activities in the spirit of the Manifesto to this day.

Thus, a quarter of a century after Einstein's death, the ideals for which he strove throughout his life are being cherished, promoted, and gradually implemented by an ever-increasing number of scientists.

Notes

1. The full text of this article originally appeared under the title "Einstein—the Pacifist Warrior" in Maurice Goldsmith, Alan Mackay, and James Woudhuysen (eds.) *Einstein: The First Hundred Years*, published by Pergamon Press in 1981. The edited text is reproduced by permission of Maurice Goldsmith and the International Science Policy Foundation.

Bibliography

Bulletin of the Atomic Scientists 4(2)

Gowing M 1964 *Britain and Atomic Energy*. Macmillan, London

Nathan O, Norden H 1960 *Einstein on Peace*. Simon and Schuster, New York

Rotblat J 1972 *Scientists in the Quest for Peace*. MIT Press, Boston, Massachusetts

Russell B 1969 *The Autobiography of Bertrand Russell*, Vol. 3. Allen and Unwin, London

JOSEPH ROTBLAT

Emergence of Global Community and the Establishment of New Global Ethics

The signs of an emerging global community first appeared, not in positive, but negative forms. They came into being as tangible threats to human survival and ecological integrity of the earth. These threats made us aware of the possibility of annihilation of humanity due to nuclear war which is the outcome of a combination of scientific-technological achievements with human arrogance and barbarism, or the irretrievable damage caused by human beings, to global environments. We are bound up in a common fate with our fellow beings, non-human beings, and other global existence. We human beings caused and asked for the present predicaments of the whole globe through our own irresponsible, inconsiderate behavior, as is shown in our egoistic pursuit of material goods and materialistic benefits. We, the human beings, have to confess our common sin and guilt, and share our common responsibility with one another. In this way, our global community, at least on a human level, emerged as an awareness of a community of guilt, in order to share problems and burdens of the past, for which we are responsible. Thus, we have to start our constructive efforts to work for a global community, with repentance for our own past mistakes and misdeeds.

When we talk of a 'global community,' 'community' may be understood first and foremost, as a peaceful and harmonious 'Life Together,' a 'Common Living,' or a 'Shared Life.' 'Global' means wholeness or wholesomeness of the entire earth, including relationships between nature and humanity, among individuals, groups and countries of the world. Accordingly, a global community means not only a global human community, but also a global ecological system or community.

A 'global ethics' is a system of norms and values to be applied and practiced for sustaining and strengthening a global community, or in a word, an ethics of a global community (see *Global Ethic*). The ethical actors of this ethics are human beings, but, it takes the whole globe in its scope. Global ethics is guidelines for moral conduct vis-à-vis the whole earth. Human beings are the only ethical subjects as they are endowed with reason and conscience, moral awareness of good and evil or moral aptitude for love and compassion. Global ethics has a global character in double sense. It claims to be an ethics globally, that is, universally acknowledged and observed by every one on earth, whether man or woman, young or old, religionist or nonreligionist, because the survival of humanity based on the sustainment of ecological integrity depends on it, it is binding globally. Secondly, it is an ethics which deals with problems of the world, in the context of the earth or the globe as a whole. Its concern and consideration is not limited to a mere individual's interests or national interests. Rather, it is motivated by the interests and welfare of all humanity and the rest of the earth.

Community, as the interrelationships of human beings and others, is characterized by three different types of interactions: conflict, competition and cooperation. These three patterns of interactions are to be found in any society or community relationships. Even in a most idealistic family, we may find these three types of interactions, as conflicts of interests and opinions among family members; competitions in terms of achievements; and cooperations in terms of role-taking, or the division of labor. To keep good relationships, we have to see to it that conflict should be resolved peacefully, competition be done with a spirit of fair play, and cooperation be made willingly in an atmosphere of love and compassion. The point I would like to make is that to continue good community relationships in the face of conflict, competition and cooperation, members of that community should keep at least minimal moral requirements for its peaceful and harmonious development. Then, the basis of global ethics which is required for global community will be the principles of peaceful, nonviolent resolution of conflicts, competition on the basis of fair deal and fair play, and cooperation for common aims with others of different faiths or ideologies. An emerging global community needs to be built upon and supported by necessary basis of global ethics and moral consciousness. Otherwise, the future of humanity and the globe will become dark and insecure.

As for 'Global Ethics,' we may refer to several experimental formulations which have been put forward so far. Around the time when the walls of Berlin were destroyed, there arose among theologians and religious thinkers of the world, a call for a 'global ethics' as an important sine qua non, or an indispensable prerequisite for the peace of the world and the survival of humanity and nature. The prophetic advocator of this idea, so far as I know, was Professor Hans Küng, a German theologian. In his book: *Weltethos* published in 1990, he starts his opening remarks with the following words: 'No survival without global ethics, no world peace without peace among religions. No peace among religions without dialogue among religions.' Thus, he urged the leaders of different religions to start dialogue on global ethics, as soon as possible. He emphasized 'the necessity of one ethics for the whole humanity.' Several consultations had been held on this urgent topic since 1989 among theologians of different religious backgrounds, under the guidance of Hans Küng. On the basis of these preparatory processes, the Parliament of the World's Religions, held in Chicago in 1993, with the participation of 6,500 people from every possible religion, on the occasion of the centennial of the World Parliament of Religions of 1983, publicized the 'Declaration Toward a Global Ethic,' as a fundamental ethical consensus needed for the present and future of humanity and the world. By the way, we should notice that the expression used here is not 'Global Ethics,' but 'a Global Ethic,' taking from 'Ethics.' Now, the name 'Global Ethic' has been accepted as a current term. I shall use that term hereafter.

In September 1994, there was an international consultation on 'Global Ethic in Education' in Nüremberg University, Germany and in November of the same year the 6th world assembly of the World Conference on Religion and Peace was held in Italy, where the subject of 'a common ethic' was taken up and developed. Hans Küng was among the main speakers in 1995, in a nation-wide annual study consultation sponsored by WCRP/Japan on inter-religious basis. 'Global Ethic' was adopted as the main theme of discussion. In this way, the problem of global ethics now came to be a focus of global concern, though the way to call it varies: Weltethos, a global ethic, a common ethic, an ethic of life-together, global responsibility and so on.

Another source of global ethics (see *Toward a New Global Ethic*) came from a commission established in 1992 composed of the world top-level, most distinguished leaders, in the belief that international development had created favourable circumstances for strengthening global cooperation to create a more peaceful, just and habitable world for all its people. It is called 'the Commission on Global Governance' chaired by co-chairpersons; Ingval Carlson (Prime Minister of Sweden and Shridath Ramphal (then Commonwealth Secretary General)). After having held energetically about a dozen meetings, it published recently a report entitled 'Our Global Neighbourhood.' It urges 'to practice tolerance and live together in peace with one another as good neighbours' (from the Charter of the United Nations) (see *United Nations Charter*). It pays attention to the growth of international civil society, in which the interdependence of nations and the role of people, not states, are becoming more important for the future of the world. It envisages the need for a common ethic in the following way: 'We also believe the world's arrangements for the conduct of its affairs must be underpinned by certain common values. Ultimately, no organization will work and no law will be upheld unless they rest on a foundation made strong by shared values. These values must be informed by a sense of common responsibility for both present and future generations. 'we believe that a global civic ethic to guide action within the global neighbourhood and leadership infused with that ethic are vital to the quality of global governance. We call for a common commitment to core values that all humanity could uphold; respect for life, liberty, justice and equity, mutual respect, caring, and integrity. We further believe humanity as a whole will be best served by recognition of a set of common rights and responsibilities.' In the above quotations, we see to some extent what constitutes the core values of a common ethic.

Another approach for 'Global Ethics' grew out of the recent world-wide concern about ecological crisis of the world. To overcome this crisis and to reestablish harmonious and sustainable relationships between nature and human beings, attempts have been made to work out the so-called 'environmental ethics' or *Umweltethik* in German. For example, in a background paper on 'Endangered Earth' of the 6th world assembly of the World Conference on Religion and Peace (WCRP) held in Italy, a new attempt was made to bridge 'environmental ethics' and the 'global ethic,' so that an idea of 'global environmental ethic' was introduced, this new concept implies double meaning (see *Global Environment and Peace*). On the one hand, it is a global ethic concerning environments. On the other, it is an ethic of global environments. It is an ethic to be applied and observed globally in order to save global environments. It points out an urgent task to restore appropriate relationships between nature and human beings. To do so two other problems are to be solved, which are inseparably related to each other, that is, the problems of North and South, and the present and future generations. Thus, global responsibility of doing justice to nature was combined with that of equitable sharing between rich and poor, or strong and weak. 'Environmental ethic' can be a part of 'global ethic', and the latter be enriched by the former.

Then, in a more concrete way, what is meant by a 'Global Ethic' and how is it to be formulated? As a preliminary step, we may refer to what Hans Küng and others have thought about it, especially in relation to religion. According to their understanding, a global ethic means neither a global ideology, nor a single unified global religion transcending all existing religions, nor a mixture of all religions. 'Nor does a global ethic seek to replace the high ethics of the individual religions with an ethical minimalism.' 'Global ethic seeks to work out what is already common to the religions of the world now despite all their differences over human conduct, moral values and basic moral convictions. In other words, a global ethic does not reduce the religions to an ethical minimalism but represents the minimum of what the religions of the world already have in common now in the ethical sphere. It is not directed against anyone, but invites all, believers and non-believers, to make this ethic their own and act in accordance with it.'

In this manner, what Prof, Küng and others have conceived under the name of a global ethic was a very modest attempt. Every religion has similar ethical precepts in common, such as 'do not kill,' 'do not steal,' 'do not lie,' et cetera, et cetera. Accordingly, the most urgent task is how to apply these ethical norms they have in common to the problems threatening human and ecological survival in the context of the global situation today. Thus, a global ethic may be said to be a minimal moral requirement, or an essential code of conducts for citizens of a global community. It is, in Hans Küng's words, 'a fundamental consensus on binding values, irrevocable standards, and personal attitudes.' We can not expect a new and better global order or community without a global ethic in this sense. As irrevocable directives of a global ethic, the Declaration of the Parliament of the World's Religions of 1993 pronounces four commitments.

They are;

(a) Commitment to a culture of non-violence and respect for life,

(b) Commitment to a culture of solidarity and a just economic order,

(c) Commitment to a culture of tolerance and a life of truthfulness,

(d) Commitment to a culture of equal rights and partnership between men and women.

This kind of definition and formulation of a global ethic is only a beginning of a valuable common striving for a new approach or a paradigm shift necessary for global common living or life together of the 21st century.

'Ethic(s)' means moral reflection as well as moral praxis. It is a matter or reason as well as will. To understand and to exercize a global ethic, the role of family and school as agents of education and training is extremely important Family is a most basic and universal unit of any society and a prototype of life together, where each individual learns to love and to be loved. It is ideally a community of persons, where every human being is treated humanely. A global ethic is best learned in family, if it is a life of love, communication and cooperation, sharing, giving and sacrificing.

A global ethic is acquired initially in family. Then it is amplified in the life of school, religion and society. Therefore, it is most urgent to review and renew our family life as a new life style of genuine partnership on the basis of human dignity and responsibility, getting rid of traditional authoritarian relationships of discrimination and subordination based on sex and age.

A global ethic of an emerging global community is a hope, a challenge, which kindles our heart. Let's learn to live it as a way of life of the 21st century.

See also: *New Morality for the Global Community*

Bibliography ─────────────────────────

David F W 1978 *Essays in Evangelical Social Ethics*
Endangered Earth (a background paper of the 6th WCRP World Assembly in Italy)
Küng H 1990 *Weltetnos* [*Global Responsibility*]
Küng H 1995 What do we need a global ethic for? A paper presented at the 6th WCRP World Assembly in Italy
Küng H, K-J Küschel (Hg) 1993 *Weltfrieden durch Relligions-*

frieden. Küng H, Karl-Joseph Küschel (ed.) *A Global Ethic: The Declararion of the Parliament of the World's Religions*

Lehmann P 1963 *Ethics in a Christian Context*

Plotkin A 1993 *The Ethics of World Religions*

Robra M 1994 *Oekumenische Sozialethik*

YOSHIAKI IISAKA

Emerging Tool Chest for Peacebuilders

1. A Peace "Tool Chest"

The basic premise of this paper is that we have learned much more about building peace in the twentieth century, through research and practice, than we normally tend to apply. Therefore, we will attempt an inventory of the available instruments for pursuing peace. Twenty-two peace "tools" will be presented—two that were inherited from the nineteenth century, and twenty that have been developed in this century. Applying the concept "tools" as a label for these twenty-two approaches can help to create a practical orientation toward their application. The enumeration of the tools in five rectangles in Fig. 1 can be viewed as five tool boxes. If they were stacked on top of each other, they would be familiar to the auto mechanic as five drawers in a mechanic's tool chest. If you told auto mechanics that five drawers of tools were indispensable to the peace "mechanic," both as a result of learning through practice and because the world is becoming increasingly complicated as a result of new technology, they would quickly understand. The tool chest of the auto mechanic has ever more drawers because new technology is making automobiles increasingly complicated.

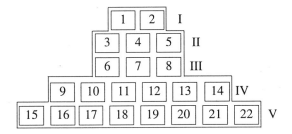

Figure 1
Peacebuilder's tool chest

We will present the tools in chronological order mainly to demonstrate that new tools arose out of experience that revealed the shortcomings of older tools. Practitioners of any trade or profession that employs tools can understand this—not only mechanics but also plumbers, carpenters, electricians, surgeons, etc. This is why they now have socket wrenches, electric drills, vice grips and lasers. Of course, it will be obvious that our chronological presentation is very simplified. Innovation in history is very complex. We are never completely certain when a new idea first arose. In some respects all ideas embedded in peace tools are very old. While we would assert that the learning process revealed in Fig. 2 certainly is reflected in the experience of some people, it is not based on intensive research on the deep historical origin of peace-related ideas. The basic purpose of the Fig. I, II is to offer an orderly context in which to learn about the 22 tools and the fact that they are functionally interrelated.

It must be understood that new tools do not necessarily make old tools useless or irrelevant. All 22 are presently perceived to be useful by *some*, for coping with at least some kinds of peace problems. Thus, the challenge for the peacebuilder is to analyze a specific threat to peace and to decide which set of tools might be relevant for that situation. Of course, this can only be done in the light of knowledge about (a) the historical and social context of a specific threat to peace, and (b) the strengths and weaknesses of *all* available tools. We certainly know that all tools, when employed inappropriately, can make things worse, and even do great damage.

2. Our Nineteenth Century Heritage

As we entered the twentieth century, the state system had already acquired significant experience with two peace tools. DIPLOMACY (1) is a significant human achievement that deserves much credit for the fact that most states have peaceful relations with most others most of the time. The system of embassies that each country has in the capitals of many other countries has developed over many centuries. Formerly consisting primarily of career diplomats representing their Foreign Ministry, now many embassies include representatives of other government departments responsible for health, labor, education, trade, environment, etc. Of course, this expansion of diplomatic representation reflects the impact of new technologies on relations between states (see *Ambassadors*).

Figure 2
The emergence of peace tool

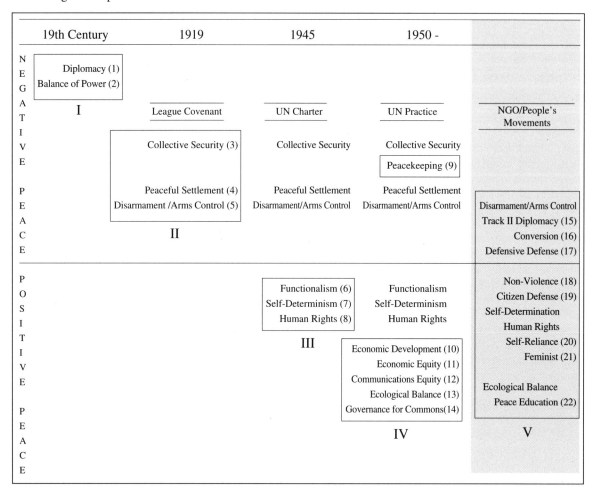

There are significant limitations in the capacity of the inter-state diplomatic system to permit sustained contact among all states. Large states have embassies in virtually all other states—some 185. And all of the smaller states tend to have embassies in the large states. But many smaller states cannot afford to have permanent embassies in all other states, and sometimes they may not really need permanent representation in distant small states. Instead, one embassy may be accredited to a number of states in a region. Thus, it is important to understand that there are limitations in the capacity of the diplomatic system to sustain linkage among all states.

Although we have emphasized that the inter-state diplomatic system preserves the peace most of the time, nevertheless disputes do arise and create situations in which states fear aggression by others. In such cases BALANCE OF POWER (2) may be used

to deter aggression. In the sense in which we are using the term, employment of balance of power means that a state attempts to acquire sufficient military and related capacity to deter aggression, or attempts to deter aggression by making alliances with other states. In some cases, when balance of power is employed as a deterrent it does indeed deter aggression. On the other hand, reciprocal application of balance of power does sometimes lead to arms races (see *Balance of Power*).

When State A fears the aggression of State B, they may not have an accurate estimate of B's military strength, so A tends to exceed the military competence of B just to play it safe. In turn, B tends to assume that A has aggressive intentions and feels a need to have a slight advantage over A. Thus begins an arms race that then spirals out of control as suspicion and distrust escalate. Although balance of power may sometimes preserve the peace, many believed that balance of power and accompanying arms races contributed significantly to the outbreak of World War I.

In the aftermath of World War I, states created the first world organization (members from Africa, Asia, Europe and North and South America) devoted to preserving the peace. As many as 63 states became members of this League of Nations, but there were never more than 58 members at any one time. Although the League only made modest contributions to restraining inter-state violence, as the first world "laboratory" devoted to inter-state peace, it made significant contributions toward the development of the United Nations in 1945.

3. The League of Nations Covenant

The League of Nations Covenant, which came into force in 1920, provided members with three main peace tools. First, COLLECTIVE SECURITY (3) was devised to overcome the weaknesses of balance of power as a deterrent to aggression. Collective Security obligated all who were members of the League to "undertake to respect and preserve as against external aggression the territorial integrity and existing political independence of all Members of the League." Those who advocated collective security believed that the pledge of *all* to resist aggression by *any* member would be such an overwhelming deterrent that none would have reasonable ground for fearing aggression (see *Collective Security and Collective Self-defense*). But the obvious common sense of collective security in the abstract ignores that *all* may not be able or willing to resist aggression by *any* other member. This may be explained by longstanding friendships and alliances and perhaps by fear of retribution by powerful neighbors. Also, when the aggressor is very powerful, the practice of collective security in the pursuit of peace may produce an even larger war than the initial aggression. For reasons such as these, collective security did not prevent aggression by Germany, Japan, and Italy that led to World War II.

The second main peace tool in the League Covenant was PEACEFUL SETTLEMENT (4), intended to prevent the outbreak of violence in those instances when routine diplomacy fails to do so. In cases where a dispute may "lead to a rupture" the Covenant requires states to "submit the matter either to arbitration or judicial settlement or to inquiry by the [League] Council." In other words, members involved in a dispute agree to involve certain "third parties" when they alone can not control escalating hostility. In employing third parties, states are drawing on human experience in a variety of other contexts: labor-management disputes, disputes between buyers and sellers, marital disputes, etc (see *Arbitration, International*). In giving third party approaches a place in the Covenant, the League obviously drew on earlier provisions for employment of third parties developed in the Hague Conferences of 1899 and 1907 (see *Intervention*).

The third main peace tool in the Covenant was DISARMAMENT/ARMS CONTROL (5). Some who believed that arms races had contributed to the outbreak of World War I thought that elimination, or at least reduction, of arms would enhance chances for peace. This was an effort to codify disarmament and arms control proposals that had been advanced in earlier times (see *Disarmament and Development*). Although Covenant provisions for disarmament/arms control never fulfilled the aspirations of advocates, they did provoke the negotiation of numerous arms control measures in the 1930s (see *Arms Control, Evolution of*). These provided valuable experience, and also a great deal of skepticism, for those who would again face similar circumstances after World War II.

4. The United Nations Charter

Following World War II the victorious states once again endeavored to create a world organization that would maintain the peace. When the United Nations Charter was drafted in San Francisco in 1945, it once again incorporated collective security, peaceful settlement and disarmament/arms control (see *United Nations Charter*). Experience under the Covenant led to strengthening of collective security by explicitly providing for procedures through which members would make armed forces available for collective security response and a Military Staff Committee that would plan for the use of these forces and advise and assist the Security Council in their employment. In some respects means for pacific settlement are more fully defined. Although disarmament/arms control is again made available, the Charter emphasizes it less than the Covenant.

But the most significant differences between the Covenant and the Charter consist of the addition of three peace tools. The first was FUNCTIONALISM (6) in which states cooperate in efforts to solve common economic and social problems that might disrupt normal relationships and even lead to violence (see *Functionalism*). Drafters of the Charter had in mind examples such as worldwide depression in the 1930s and the inability of states to collaborate in coping with this disaster. The depression led to strikes, extreme social unrest and violence in many countries and significantly contributed to the development of totalitarian governments and aggression in some cases. Emphasis on economic and social cooperation in the Charter is signified by the creation of the Economic and Social Council (ECOSOC) alongside the Security Council (responsible for collective security) which had been the only council in the League. ECOSOC was created "with a view to the creation of conditions of stability and well-being which are necessary for peaceful and friendly relations among nations . . . ." Its mission includes the achievement of higher standards of living, full employment, solutions of international economic, social, health and related problems and international cultural and educational cooperation. At the same time, ECOSOC has the responsibility of coordinating the activities of some 30 agencies in the UN system with responsibility for health, labor, education, development, environment, population, trade, atomic energy and a number of other global problems.

It is very important that we appreciate the degree to which the League "laboratory" provided the knowledge and experience that led to the significant place that economic and social cooperation is given in the UN Charter. Although the League Covenant gave relatively slight attention to economic and social activities, in practice, the League became significantly involved in a great number of economic and social issues. Indeed, as the days of the League drew to an end before World War II, proposals had already been made to create a League economic and social council.

The second peace tool added by the UN Charter was SELF-DETERMINATION (7). Here again the UN built on League experience. In granting independence to many nations formerly in the defeated Austro-Hungarian and Ottoman Empires, the World War I peace settlements recognized self-determination as a tool for building future peace (see *Self-determination*). In addition, parts of the former Ottoman Empire outside of Europe and other colonies of defeated states were placed under a Permanent Mandates Commission of the League of Nations, including Iraq, Syria, and Lebanon in the Middle East; Cameroons, Rwanda Urundi, Tanganyika, Togoland, Somaliland and Southwest Africa in Africa; and areas in the Pacific. These territories were administered by states who were members of the victorious coalition, with some attaining independence before World War II. It is very important that the Mandate system established reporting procedures through which administering powers were responsible to the members of the League. This laid the foundation for later growth in the belief that those governing colonies have some responsibilities to the rest of the world. In the UN Charter the Mandates were called Trusteeships, and placed under a third Council, the Trusteeship Council. But most important for self-determination in the Charter was inclusion of a "Declaration Regarding Non-Self-Governing Territories," which covered the many overseas colonies not under trusteeship. This Declaration asserts that those administering colonies are obligated "to develop self-government, . . . and to assist them in the progressive development of their free political institutions . . . ."

Eventually this Declaration provided the foundation for prodding the overseas colonial powers to begin relinquishing control of their colonies. This led to a strengthened Declaration by the General Assembly in 1960: "Declaration on the Granting of Independence to Colonial Countries and Peoples." Both the Trusteeship Council and the General Assembly played a very significant role in the largely peaceful dismantlement of overseas empires. In this respect, self-determination has proven to be a very useful peace tool. This remarkable transformation of the inter-state system more than doubled the number of independent states and the number of UN members.

Now the world confronts a new generation of self-determination demands by peoples in multi-nation states (as in Yugoslavia) and in multi-state nations (e.g., the Kurds). The UN system desperately needs to establish procedures whereby the legitimacy of these claims can be assessed—*before* severe disruption and violence occur. At the same time, those making self-determination claims deemed to be legitimate must guarantee the rights of minorities that are inevitably present in all political units. The numerous cases in which unscrupulous leaders employ self-determination strategies for personal gain is but one example of the fact that peace tools, as well as all other tools, can be used for both noble and depraved purposes.

The third peace tool added by the UN Charter was HUMAN RIGHTS (8). Although these words were never used in the League Covenant, human rights are mentioned seven times in the Charter, including the second sentence of the Preamble which announces determination "to reaffirm faith in fundamental human rights, in the dignity and worth of the human person, in the equal rights of men and women and of nations large and small." As in the case of economic and social cooperation, the Charter states that human rights shall be promoted in order to "create conditions and well-being which are necessary for peaceful and friendly relations among nations . . . ." Building on the brief references to human rights in the Charter, the UN General Assembly soon produced the Universal Declaration on Human Rights in 1947 which is now widely accepted as part of international common law and has even been applied by domestic courts in a number of states (see *Human Rights and Peace*).

In order to strengthen the legal status of the Declaration, its principles were in 1966 put in treaty form by the General Assembly, as the International Covenant on Civil and Political Rights and the International Covenant on Economic, Social and Cultural Rights. In addition, an array of more specialized treaties have been developed on genocide, racial discrimination, women's rights, children's rights, forced labor, cruel and inhumane punishment, rights of refugees and other human rights problems. All of these help to prevent the creation of unacceptable conditions of human depravity that may lead to severe unrest and even fighting.

Readers have noted that in Fig. 2 peace tools 1- 5 are placed in the category Negative Peace and tools 6-8 are in the category Positive Peace. Put in the simplest terms, Negative Peace is achieved by stopping violence. Positive Peace is achieved by building societies and inter-state relationships that do not generate conditions likely to precipitate violence or other causes of human suffering and deprivation. The first tends to depend largely on the expertise and activities of professional diplomatic and military people. The second draws on expertise in a diversity of professions coping with economic and social problems. The distinctive character of negative peace and positive peace cannot be pushed too far because they are intertwined. But it is important to understand that in this century practitioners learned that in applying tools that focused mainly on stopping the violence, or directly preventing it from breaking out, they often found themselves confronting overwhelming escalations of violence that could not be stopped. In other words, they learned that they were too late and realized that something should have been done earlier to cope with underlying causes of violence—before things got out of hand. This led to supplementing those peace tools employing a more negative peace emphasis with those more focused on positive peace.

Because the concept power (see *Power*), and power politics, superpower and world power are frequently used in works on international relations, it is useful to point out that our twentieth century journey in the quest for peace has greatly expanded the instruments through which power can be exercised. This concept has been frequently associated with one kind of power, military power. Kenneth Boulding insightfully drew our attention to "the three faces of power:" (1) threat power—the power to destroy, (2) economic power—the power to produce and exchange, and (3) integrative power—the power to create such relations as love, respect, friendship and legitimacy (Boulding, 1989). The "peace tools" invented in the twentieth century apply a diversity of forms of economic and integrative power. Thus, Self-determination employs the power of legitimacy in the quest for peace, and Functionalism employs a variety of kinds of integrative power. In other words, our quest for peace has revealed that power employed in problem-solving is often more effective than threat power.

5. United Nations Practice

The post-World War II context in which the United Nations emerged provided two severe challenges to those attempting to apply the six "peace tools" incorporated into the Charter. First, the East-West conflict escalated into confrontation between two military blocs: the North Atlantic Treaty Organization (NATO) (see *NATO*), led by former the United States and the Warsaw Pact, led by the Soviet Union. The Charter assumed that these states would collaborate in the Security Council in employing peaceful settlement and collective security in order to preserve the peace. But instead, the "policemen" threatened world war with each other and became indirectly involved in conflicts in Africa, Asia and the Middle East. There was particular danger that conflicts in the Middle East and the Congo (Zaire) would escalate into a world war. As a response, PEACEKEEPING (9) was invented. Although some variations have been employed, peacekeeping essentially involves a cease-fire, followed by creation of a demilitarized corridor on each side of a truce line. This neutral corridor is patrolled by a UN peacekeeping force.

Peacekeeping is fundamentally different from collective security in several respects. Peacekeeping forces require the permission of states on whose territory they are based (see *Peacekeeping Forces*). Although big powers have provided logistical support, until quite recently the troops normally come from smaller states deemed to be politically acceptable by the parties to the conflict. The troops normally only carry small arms that are used in self-defense. Their primary protection is the fact that their blue helmets, and the UN emblems on their jeeps, are given legitimacy by the members of the UN under whose authority they are acting. UN peacekeeping forces have successfully kept the peace in the Congo (Zaire), Middle East, Cyprus and other places for many years. But there has not been equal success in resolving the conflicts that have made them necessary.

The end of the Cold War has permitted rapid expansion of the number of peacekeeping forces, to Cambodia, the former Yugoslavia, the Iraq-Kuwait border, Somalia, and other places. In some instances, as in Somalia and the former Yugoslavia, UN forces have been employed without first acquiring a cease-fire, and in situations where there is no clear authority that could grant permission for entry of the UN force. These efforts tend to be referred to as "peace enforcement" i.e., limited use of arms toward the end of restoring peace. Whether "peace enforcement" will become a useful peace tool is still much in doubt because of the tendency of the use of even limited violence to result in escalation.

The second post-war challenge to the UN was the struggle for, and acquisition of self-determination by, overseas colonies of European-based empires. This not only transformed the inter-state system but also brought fundamental changes in the United Nations. There was rapid doubling of UN membership, largely by addition of new members from Africa, Asia, the Caribbean and Pacific Islands. Very significant has been widespread poverty in most of the new states, thus creating a deeper gulf between rich and poor UN members. Other terms applied to the two groups have been Developed Countries (DC) and Less Developed Countries (LDC). Also the term Third World has often been used for the poor countries of Africa, Asia and Latin America, as distinguished from the First World (free market industrialized countries) and Second World (former Soviet bloc).

The entry of so many Third World countries into the UN significantly affected the political context in which the three peace tools added to the UN Charter would be employed. First, Functionalism is most effectively employed as a peace strategy in instances where those collaborating have relatively similar economic and social levels. It is difficult to create collaborative exchange and cooperative arrangements between those who are very rich and have significant technological advancement and those who are poor and technologically less developed. In these situations the more advantaged partner will tend to dominate the weaker partner who will in turn fear domination. This does not provide good conditions for mutually beneficial collaboration.

Second, after Third World countries became independent, aspects of self-determination that were less conspicuous during the struggle for political independence became more apparent. On the one hand, increasing awareness developed that political independence did not necessarily lead to independence from economic and cultural domination by European centers. On the other hand, the degree to which the new states were creations of European colonial administrators became more apparent. For example, many African states were made up of a number of African peoples, and many African peoples were divided by arbitrary political boundaries. Thus, even after the granting of independence to colonially created states, it was apparent that a new generation of self-determination problems would be confronted in the future.

Third, the entry of so many Third World countries into the inter-state system, and into the UN, produced a stronger challenge to the human rights priorities of Western states. These states have a tendency to give priority to civil and political rights—voting, free speech, privacy, freedom of movement, organizing, freedom of religion, equality before the law, etc. On the other hand, Third World states tend to give priority to economic and social rights—right to education, equal pay for equal work, food, clothing, medical care, etc. Significantly, the Universal Declaration on Human Rights, approved by the UN General Assembly in 1948 tends to list civil and political rights first and economic and social rights next. The Western emphasis tends to be that "freedom" has priority before all other rights (see *Peace with Freedom*). But the Third World emphasis is that unless basic economic and social needs are acquired one has no capacity for enjoying opportunities provided by "freedom."

Prodded by the growing divide between the rich and the poor in the United Nations, three peace tools developed out of UN practice were largely a product of growing insight on the relevance of economic conditions and relationships for peace. ECONOMIC DEVELOPMENT (10) became a growing policy concern both within the UN and outside. The basic idea was that the rich-poor gap could be diminished if the rich countries provided development aid to the poor countries so that they could "take off" and become developed. It tended to be assumed that development in Third World countries should be patterned after the industrialized countries of Europe and North America. Emphasis was placed on heavy industry and economic infrastructure such as roads, railroads, airports and dams. In earlier efforts food and agriculture tended to be given low priority. Aid was primarily provided by special development loan

funds and technical assistance programs that emphasized the transfer of knowhow, often through providing technical experts and the tools they require. Economic development programs were established not
only by UN agencies and regional international governmental organizations but also by governments in
the industrialized countries. It was frequently argued
that the multilateral programs of the UN and other
international organizations were more fruitful
because they were more likely to be based on economic development criteria, but that bilateral programs tended to be less economically productive
because they tended to be more shaped by bilateral
political factors.

Many people would argue that both bilateral and
multilateral economic development programs have
often contributed to peace by diminishing poverty.
But overall they did not diminish the rich-poor gap in
the world (see *Maldevelopment*). Indeed, as economic development programs grew in the 1950s and
1960s, the rich-poor gap continued to grow. Critics
of these development programs began to argue that
the gap was growing because of the nature of the
economic relations between the developed countries
and the Third World. In other words, they attributed
the growth in the rich-poor gap to the international
economic structure in which countries in the Third
World were perceived to be dependent upon the
industrialized countries. From this perspective, it was
seen that the growth in the rich-poor gap would continue until this dependency relationship was overcome.

This led to Third World demands for INTERNA-
TIONAL ECONOMIC EQUITY (11). The Third
World movement for a more equitable international
economic system was centered in (a) the Non-
Aligned Movement, an organization of some 100
countries from all parts of the world that were neither
aligned with the NATO states nor the Warsaw Pact
states and in (b) the United Nations Conference on
Trade and Development (UNCTAD) (see *Nonalignment*). The latter began as a UN conference in 1964
and later became a permanent UN organization, with
headquarters in Geneva. The Third World caucus in
UNCTAD came to be known as the "Group of 77,"
although it eventually included some 120 states. In
these two organizations the Third World devised a
program for a New International Economic Order
(NIEO) (see *New International Economic Order*).
Among their demands were (a) stabilization of the
prices of Third World commodities (coffee, tea,
cocoa, etc.) in order to build a predictable economic
base for development programs, (b) pegging the

price of these commodities to the price of manufactured products which the Third World buys from
industrialized countries, (c) access of Third World
products to First World markets, (d) Third World
access to technology useful in their development programs, and (e) international regulation of the activities of transnational corporations in Third World
countries.

As revealed in the name of the new UN agency,
UNCTAD, the basic thrust of these demands were that
development aid would be less necessary in an
international economy structured so that the Third
World could "earn a living." Instead, it was asserted
that the international economy is structured so that
the benefits pile up in corporate headquarters and
banks in the industrialized countries, thus making it
necessary for Third World countries to seek aid.
Unfortunately, from a Third World perspective,
although an extensive campaign was waged in the UN
General Assembly for NIEO principles, for the most
part the industrialized countries were very unrespon-
sive. This has generated considerable animosity in
the Third World as the gap between the rich and the
poor continues to grow. At the same time, there was
puzzlement over the apparent inability of the Third
World to reach the people of the industrialized countries with the reasonableness of their appeal. For
example, there was a tendency for the press in the
United States to picture Third World demands in the
General Assembly as reckless demands for special
privileges by an "African-Asian-Latin American
horde" which was not grateful for all of the aid that
they had received.

Frustration over failure to convince people in
industrialized countries about the justness of their
NIEO appeal contributed to the demands of the Third
World for INTERNATIONAL COMMUNICA-
TIONS EQUITY (12). Observing that the headquarters of the world news agencies (United Press, Associated Press, Reuters, etc.) were in industrialized
countries, and citing examples of biased reporting on
the Third World, the Third world began to ask for a
New International Information and Communications
Order (NIICO). The demands for a NIICO was also
stimulated by technological change in communication, particularly the communications satellite that
makes it possible, using satellites in geostationery
orbit, for those having the technology to reach into
every country and virtually any village in the world.
Of course, this technology has been developed, and
is largely controlled, by giant communications corporations headquartered in the industrialized countries
(see *Communication: Key to World Peace*).

The struggle for a NIICO has been largely waged in the United Nations Educational, Scientific and Cultural Organization (UNESCO), with its headquarters in Paris. This dispute illuminates how technological change may transform the context in which a peace tool is applied and thereby generate conflict in its definition and use. The UNESCO Constitution, adopted in London in November 1945, asserted "that ignorance of each other's ways and lives has been a common cause . . . of that suspicion and mistrust between peoples of the world through which their differences have all too often broken into war." The Constitution asserted that these conditions could be overcome through education, pursuit of objective truth and "the free exchange of ideas and knowledge." The last would be employed "for the purposes of mutual understanding and a truer and more perfect knowledge of each other's lives." In practice, what was believed to be the essential spirit of these worlds was incorporated into the words "free flow of communication."

Those emphasizing free flow of communication as a prerequisite of peace in the aftermath of World War II tended to be thinking of totalitarian governments as the primary threat to its fulfillment. But as newly independent peoples in the Third World became increasingly sensitive to the quality of their recently won political independence, they developed growing awareness of the one-way international flow of news, radio and TV broadcasts, films, books and magazines. Indeed, some Third World cultures have been so deeply penetrated by media from industrialized countries that their survival is in jeopardy. Out of this dissatisfaction came a replacement for the earlier communications slogan "free and balanced flow of communication."

But how is "balance" to be achieved while still remaining "free." This is a virtually important peace issue that must be resolved through international dialogue and debate. On the one hand, the Western democracies fear that intrusions on "free flow" will lead to government interference that will prevent fulfillment of the essence of the UNESCO aspiration— unfettered possibility for people to obtain a "truer and more perfect knowledge of each other's lives." On the other hand, the Third World fears that "free flow" mediated by giant global communications corporations will be largely one-way flow, with content dictated by these corporations (see *Multinational Corporations and Peace*). Neither outcome is in the interest of people in any part of the world. Communications is a vital aspect of peaceful global relations. Ways must be found to structure communications in such a way that they foster peace rather than produce deeply felt animosity.

Although environmental issues have been a significant human problem at least since the Industrial Revolution in the late eighteenth century, ECOLOGICAL BALANCE (13) became a widely recognized problem in world relations as a result of the UN Environment Conference held in Stockholm in 1972. But at this time there was tendency for the industrialized countries to take the lead and for Third World countries to see it as a strategy to prevent them from industrializing too—thus as a way to keep them poor. But by the time of the UN Conference on Environment and Development (UNCED) in Rio de Janeiro in 1992 all parts of the world agreed that ecological balance is a problem confronted by all peoples. Furthermore, whereas in 1972 very few tended to see ecological balance as a dimension of peace, this perspective is now widely shared (see *Green Security*).

The relationship between ecological balance and peace can be viewed from at least two perspectives. One perspective achieved widespread visibility during the UNCED Conference when disputes erupted about (a) who is responsible for global pollution, (b) which ecological problems should receive priority and (c) who should pay "to clean up the mess?" In a context of growing pollution, and increasing sensitivity to the negative effects of pollution, these questions are likely to create increasing conflict in the future. Particularly acrimonious at the UNCED Conference was the debate between representatives of industrialized and Third World countries. The Third World drew attention to the fact that the industrialized countries are the primary polluters. From this they conclude that the industrialized countries should accept special responsibility for paying for programs to restore ecological balance. At the same time, Third World countries point out that these same countries have enjoyed the benefits of industrialization while polluting air, water and land. Therefore, if Third World countries are to be deprived of the opportunity to develop in the same way as the industrialized countries, but are to employ more costly approaches, the industrialized countries have an obligation to provide financial support for "sustainable development."

A second perspective on the peace-ecological balance relationship is that by disrupting normal relationships between specific human beings and their environment, pollution directly produces peacelessness for these people (see *Human Rights and Environmental Rights: Their Sustainable Development Compatibility*). In some cases, as with the destruction of the habitat of people in rain forests with bulldozers and explosives, it is as quick and devastating as war. Although not directly resulting in loss of human life, the total and irreversible destruction of habitat, culture and way of life can in some ways be more devastating than air bombardment of cities. In other cases, the result may be death, as in the case of poisoned air, water, earth and food. Although this form of death may be slower than war, it may be more painful. In many respects it shares some of the long-term characteristics of injuries of those wounded in war.

The rapidly growing intrusion of new technologies on the commons makes provisions for GOVERNANCE FOR THE COMMONS (14) an increasingly significant peace issue. By the commons we refer to areas outside the territorial boundaries of states that tend to be assumed to be spaces available to all, a term early associated with the village green in the center of small towns and also city parks. In the international context, the oceans and space are generally thought of as commons, and many would add Antarctica. We shall use the example of the oceans in our brief discussion, an exceedingly significant commons because it covers 70 percent of the surface of the globe. Before the days of more intrusive technology, the two main issues in the ocean commons tended to be establishing agreed upon borders of states, early set at a three mile limit, and insuring "freedom on the seas" in all of the rest of the oceans. But new technologies for ocean transit, fishing, drilling for gas and oil, mining minerals on the seabed and ocean research—as well as increased use of the oceans as dumping grounds for waste produced on land—has raised a host of new problems with respect to the ocean commons. Occasionally reports on these problems reach the headlines with reports on disputes over fishing rights and limits, oil spills in oil tanker collisions at sea and tankers running aground (see *Oceans: The Common Heritage*).

A historic step in building for positive peace was taken in 1982 with the completion of a comprehensive treaty for governance of the oceans, the United Nations Law of the Sea Treaty. Completed after 10 years of negotiation, a US negotiator, Elliott Richardson, called it the single most important development in international law since the drafting of the UN Charter. The treaty provides for a new organization in the UN system, the International Sea-Bed Authority, with its own Assembly, Council and Secretariat, as well as an International Tribunal for the Law of the Sea and a branch to oversee the mining of manganese nodules on the sea bed—the Enterprise. The treaty has already received more than the sixty ratifications required for its implementation.

Responsive to great technological change in the use of the oceans, the treaty extends the territorial limit of states to 12 miles, gives states with seacoasts right to exploit gas and oil off their coasts up to a 200 mile limit (and in some case 350 miles), provides rules so that the manganese nodules on the seabed are shared between the industrialized countries and the Third world and requires that industrialized countries sell mining technology to the Third World. Very significant here is the fact that the treaty has anticipated eventual conflict over the manganese nodules (containing nickle, cobalt and copper as well) after supplies on land are consumed. At the same time, the treaty builds on UN experience by providing new procedures for achieving consensus in the Assembly and Council of the Authority by providing for delays in final votes while the chairs of these bodies try to work out a consensus.

The treaty also offers new approaches for peaceful settlement of disputes. Not only are there provisions for getting quick decisions from the International Tribunal, but states involved in a dispute are offered five different options for working toward a settlement: the International Tribunal, the International Court of Justice, an arbitral tribunal provided for in the treaty and special arbitral tribunals consisting of experts in the issue under dispute (see *International Court of Justice*). In the latter course the parties to the conflict jointly pick the members of the tribunal. Thus, the treaty at the same time makes the options for peaceful settlement more obligatory and more concrete and offers new approaches that may offer parties to a conflict more confidence in the process. These provisions are clearly based on learning that has taken place in the UN "laboratory" since 1945.

6. Non-governmental Organizations and People's Movements

The final "drawer" in the "tool chest" outlined in Fig. 1 consists of non-governmental organizations and people's movements (see *Non-governmental Organization (NGOs)*). The term non-governmental organization (NGO) is a concept evolving out of international organization research and practice to distinguish inter-state organizations such as the UN that have governments of states as members from international organizations whose members consist of national associations or individuals that are not government officials. Prominent examples are organization such as the international professional associations (doctors, lawyers), international scholarly associations (political scientists and sociologists), international religious organizations (virtually all faiths and denominations), and international organizations focusing on specific issues, such as Greenpeace, Amnesty International and World Federation of Mental Health. NGOs made up of members from a number of countries are often refered to as International NGOs or INGOS. The more than 4,000 INGOS mirror virtually all those to be found within single countries. Many of these INGOS focus on peace issues but most do not. At the same time, movements arise to address specific peace issues such as disarmement, poverty, human rights and ecological balance. At times these movements are coalitions of already existing NGOs and INGOS but they may also include, and may be led by, others who become mobilized in response to a specific issue. Thus, because of considerable overlap, we combine NGOs, INGOS and peoples movements in our discussion.

People's organizations (PO) is a useful short title for the growing involvement of people outside of government in world affairs in general, and peace issues in particular. But before briefly describing their activities and contributions, we must recognize that the involvement of POs in the pursuit of peace is not something new. Peace movements have existed in a number of countries since the early nineteenth-century (see *European Peace Movements: Rises and Falls 1958-65, 1978-85 and 1990-98*). A striking example of an international movement was the gathering of social scientists from 20 countries in Paris in 1937 which urged coping with "the causes of war, by seeking to substitute for it peaceful methods of satisfying the profound need for change of which war is the expression and the instrument" (quoted by Chatfield 1984 p. 3).

POs have mobilized people for peace action by bringing pressure on governments to employ all of the peace tools that we have enumerated. For example, during the Cold War it was often peace movements that kept disarmament and arms control on the public agenda at times when governments of both of the superpowers seemed disinterested. Many organizations have had sustained involvement in movements advocating economic aid and adjustment in international economic practices. Many would assert that the towering achievements in drafting, and embryonic efforts at monitoring, international human rights standards have been attained largely because of sustained PO initiatives and pressure on individual states and UN organizations. At the same time, many would give POs considerable credit for placing environmental issues high on the global agenda. Reflections of this were the widely reported activities of the assembled POs from all over the world at the UNCED Conference in Rio de Janeiro in 1992.

POs have also been the inventors and advocates of at least eight new peace tools. It must be made clear that these do not replace tools already employed, but they do illuminate weaknesses of old tools, or the fact that there is no tool for coping with specific causes of peacelessness. SECOND TRACK DIPLOMACY (15) addresses the limitations of diplomacy and peaceful settlement by recognizing that negotiations stalled or broken off by governmental representatives may be revived by initiatives outside of government. Consisting at least in part of people outside of government, this approach offers a "second track" that may reach into alternative representatives of governments, often at a lower level. This approach has been advocated and employed largely by scholars, often including those who have had wide governmental experience (see *Track II Diplomacy*).

One form of second track diplomacy originated by an Australian official turned scholar, John Burton, is given the name "problem solving workshop." Burton is concerned that representatives of states often do not *resolve* conflicts, but tend instead to arrange *settlements* that "paper over" underlying grievances which will be the source of escalating conflict in the future. This is because representatives of states sometimes do not adequately represent the needs of all that will be affected by the settlement. To overcome this shortcoming, problem solving workshops assemble both governmental and non-governmental people who can widely represent the needs of all parties, including those not adequately represented by representatives of states. The workshops consist of meetings between these people and social scientists who help them to probe deeply into the basic roots of the conflict, stimulate dialogue between the parties in search of mutually acceptable solutions and introduce social science insights where they are deemed to be useful. Burton is particularly reluctant to have these social scientists pose solutions because he believes that viable solutions must come from the participants themselves. Not all practitioners of this approach share Burton's reluctance. This approach has been widely practiced in international disputes, including Cyprus, the Middle East, Northern Ireland and the Argentine-British war over the Malvinas/Falkland Islands.

The exceedingly slow progress in disarmament/arms control negotiations has provoked the development of four approaches that could in some instance be viewed as supplements to negotiations and in others as substitutes. These approaches sometimes diminish the need for specific kinds of weapons and at other times attempt to offer non-violent substitutes for weapons. CONVERSION (16) is targeted at the conversion of military production to that which satisfies civilian needs, such as housing, appliances, etc (see *Arms Conversion*). This approach tends to illuminate the domestic sources of arms races in that arms production is often advocated as a way to create jobs for factory workers, engineers and researchers. It follows that the communities in which those employed in arms development and production line come to depend on arms production to keep the local economy prosperous (see *Economics of Disarmament and Conversion*). But arms production as a means for providing employment may, of course, contribute to arms races by provoking other countries into responding by building more weapons. Conversion plans, drafted largely by POs in local communities, advocate ways in which more jobs can be created through investment in civilian production than through less labor-intensive military production.

In the twentieth century the explosive power and geographical reach of weapons has increased to the point where virtually any place on earth might be reached with a nuclear missile that might obliterate a large metropolitan area or make a rural area of similar size a desert. On the other hand, it is those who have this long-range destructive capacity that are most fearful that they may be destroyed. Why? Because Country A that has long-range nuclear weapons fears that Country B might destroy its weapons with their nuclear weapons. Why? Because Country B fears that Country A might make a "first strike" against its weapons (see *Deterrence*). To overcome the fact that those with the most powerful offensive weapons are least secure, some advocate DEFENSIVE DEFENSE (17), that is, defense employing weapons that are defensive in nature. This approach has largely been advocated by POs and scholars in Europe.

There is no doubt that it is sometimes difficult to distinguish between defensive arms and offensive arms. On the other hand, there is also no doubt that some arms, such as intercontinental missiles, aircraft carriers and long-range bombers have obvious offensive capacity. Other weapons, such as land mines and fixed shore batteries, can be employed in a strictly defensive capacity. In certain respects weapons between these extremes could be used for either offense or defense. But it cannot be denied that certain arms are essentially defensive, such as short range mechanized forces, interception aircraft and mobile anti-aircraft missiles (Fischer 1984 pp. 47-62).

Combined with other peace tools, efforts of State A to present a defensive posture to State B diminishes the fear of State B that A will be aggressive. This approach motivates states to acquire understanding, more than they often do, of how their weapons are perceived, and the consequences of this perception. At the same time, the defensive defense approach may stimulate arms designers to employ new technology in the design of weapons that are convincingly limited to defensive purposes (see *Non-offensive Defense*). Instead, it would seem that up to this point new technology has largely been directed toward bigger and bigger weapons with ever more distant reach.

NON-VIOLENCE (18), used by POs in the pursuit of social change, can be viewed as a substitute for the use of arms. Employment of non-violence diminishes the need for police, and military forces employed for internal security within a state, to use their weapons (see *Non-violence*). This can diminish the need for and employment of armed forces in countries where the military is expected to make a significant contribution to maintaining internal order. Indeed, much of the arms trade in the world is less motivated by the fear of neighboring states than by the fear of internal uprisings.

Presently there is a growing interest in non-violence throughout the world as an increasing number of people acquire first-hand knowledge of the failure of the employment of arms to bring peace. Significant is the way in which non-violence training gives those involved penetrating understanding of reasons for the often thoughtless impulse to respond with violence when provoked by others, and the long-term negative consequences of responding with violence. At the same time, they learn reasons why non-violent responses are more likely to receive non-violent responses in return. This restrains the launching of violence spirals which escalate into ever larger violent reactions (see *Social Conflicts and Peace*).

Unfortunately, many people still tend to wrongly perceive non-violent action as passive. Instead non-violence actively engages in conflict, but without inflicting violence on others and without violating its fundamental values. This strategy is based on the insight that social change created by violence may establish institutions of violence that outlast the revolution and may put in power people who habitually use violence. Those who advocate non-violence first try to reach opponents through petition, argument and discussion. If that fails, direct action such as non-cooperation with authorities, civil disobedience and fasting may be employed. But fundamental is the consistent recognition of opponents as fellow human beings. As stated by Ghandi in his campaign against British imperialism: "Whilst we may attack measures and systems, we may not, must not attack men. Imperfect ourselves, we must be tender towards others and slow to impute motives" (quoted by Ambler in Smoker, Davies, Munske p. 201).

Those who advocate non-violence are often confronted with the question: "But would you have employed it in resisting Hitler or Stalin?" No doubt some, who fervently believe that one should never violate one's own values, even under severe provocation, would answer yes. But this kind of question makes a fundamental mistake in assuming that a peace tool must be useful in *all* situations. The essential questions are whether it is useful in some situations and in identifying these situations. There is no doubt that Gandhi made fundamental contributions to the Indian struggle for independence; there is no doubt that Martin Luther King did the same for the struggle of African-Americans for their constitutional rights in the United States. At the same time, it is also certain that their non-violent leadership saved many lives by helping both countries to avoid cycles of violence that would likely have occurred had non-violent strategies not been employed.

CITIZEN DEFENSE (19) is closely related to non-violence employed for social change, but this tool employs non-violent techniques for national defense (see *Civilian-based Defense*). Citizen defense goes one step further than defensive defense by also eliminating defensive weapons. Fundamental to civilian defense is deterrence through convincing a potential invader that there would be no payoff from invasion. Instead there would be a struggle in which the invader would be continually challenged. Citizen defense requires large-scale, well-publicized organization and planning for massive refusal to cooperate with the invader's military government. Police would refuse to arrest local patriots, teachers would refuse to introduce the invader's propaganda, workers would use strikes and delays to obstruct the invaders from acquiring their needs. Politicians, civil servants and judges would ignore the invaders orders. Local plans would be made to maintain local media, schools and other local services.

This kind of resistance would have to be backed-up by underground broadcasting stations and presses, storage for food, medicine, water and fuel, and plans for dispersion of people to places where these facilities would be located. Gene Sharp, a strong civilian defense advocate and strategist asserts that "non-violent action resembles military war more than it does negotiation; it is a technique of struggle. As such,

non-violent action involves the use of power" (Sharp 1970 p. 21). At the same time it requires patriots with courage, ingenuity, tenacity and unusual creativity.

People who have lived their entire life in societies in which there is an unquestioned reflex in which violence is responded to with violence frequently have difficulty in accepting the fact that non-violent defense makes sense. But the argument for non-violent defense is persuasive enough that it must be included in any peacemakers "tool box." After all, there is always the possibility that military defense will be perceived as potentially aggressive.What often begins as truly defensive precautions may inadvertently involve a state in an arms race. At the same time, arms production and employment always takes resources that could be devoted to human needs. Furthermore, armed defense in modern war almost always results in the destruction of cities, their populations and the economic and social infrastructure. These costs and likely consequences of military defense impel us to approach with an open mind an alternative that does not in any way threaten neighbors and that is focused primarily on defense of life and social institutions.

Sharp reports that there have been many instances of effective non-violent defense, such as early resistance by American colonists, 1773-75; Hungarian passive resistance against Austrian rule, 1850-67; Finland's disobedience and noncooperation with the Russians, 1898-1905; and resistance in several Nazi-occupied countries, especially Norway, the Netherlands and Denmark (Sharp 1970 p. 20). Of course, civilian defense has never been employed in the way in which Sharp advocates, as a total substitute for military defense and with comprehensive governmental planning and training that reaches into every community. At the same time, there would have to be a comprehensive information program that communicated convincing evidence of this preparation to potential invaders. On the other hand, it would also seem feasible to combine certain elements of civilian defense, in tandem with very modest military preparations. Perhaps this would serve the security needs of some citizens without the provocative consequences that arise through total dependence on weapons for defense.

SELF-RELIANCE (20) emerged as a peace tool in the context of a dialogue focused primarily on the economic dimensions of peace which evolved from functionalism, to economic development, to international economic equity—each successive approach attempting to cope with limitations of that which had preceeded it. Some critics of the New International

Economic Order's approach to obtaining international economic equity are critical of its emphasis on creating a more equitable trading system. They observe that this would tend to increase the utilization of land in rural areas of the Third World for producing agricultural exports, thereby requiring those tilling small farms to become employees of large plantations. Thus, the rural masses would become dependent on trade in an international economic system in which profits would tend to gravitate to owners of agricultural industries, thereby increasing the gap between the rich and the poor. At the same time, rural people would become increasingly dependent on external sources for food and other necessities that had been produced at home. In making this argument, critics of the NIEO cite as examples African areas formerly self-sufficient in food production which now import food from abroad. Of course, the drastic change in local economies foreseen would also lead to equally dramatic changes in local culture which is intertwined with the local economy.

A very significant contribution of the self-reliance critique is that it shifts attention to the consequences of international economic relationships for the mass of individuals. It asks, what will be the impact of economic development and international economic equity strategies, which are designed and implemented by decisions in national capitals, on the mass of individuals who have not participated in making these decisions? By raising these questions insight is gained with respect to the fact that, although our discussions of peace tend to focus on relations between leaders of states and nations, the presence or absence of peace is most accurately measured by the degree to which the masses are experiencing peace in their daily lives (see *Peace and Social Development*).

Johan Galtung illuminates the meaning he gives to self-reliance and asserts its significance by making it a defining characteristic of development in two senses. First, he asserts that development should develop individual human beings, not things. Says Galtung, "development theory and practice have to be rooted in a theory of human needs that includes the five fundamental needs [food, clothes, habitat, health, education] but also goes beyond them, to such needs as freedom, work in the sense of creativity, politics, togetherness, joy, a sense of meaning of life." Second, Galtung declares that "development can only take place through autonomy, and a first step is to rely on your own forces and own factors, on your own creativity, your own land, raw materials, capital—however limited they are, at the individual level, the local level, the national level and the level of [regional] col-

lective self-reliance." Concretely, Galtung means that "one tries to produce things locally rather than to obtain them through exchange . . . ." The rationale for this is to reduce dependency on powerful external suppliers. Says Galtung, "most important in this connection is self-reliance in foodstuffs, in order not to get into a dependence that can be used by the food-rich to blackmail a country into submissiveness."

Emphasized is the fact that self-reliance does not mean self-sufficiency, or the absence of trade, but it does mean "reliance on oneself to the point that your own capabilities are so well developed that if a crisis should occur, then one could be self-sufficient." Galtung is particularly concerned when a local community, country or region does not make sufficient use of its own potential but submits to long-term economic exchange in which primary products are exchanged for manufactured goods. In this case, he sees that there is enduring acceptance of a long-term inferior position in which it will be difficult to satisfy the basic needs of local people (Galtung (no date) pp. 12-13).

Self-reliance is a useful example of the degree to which there are connections and overlaps between peace tools. We have already noted that self-reliance challenges development practices that might frustrate the full development of individual human potential and that might contribute to conflict produced by growing disparities in wealth. At the same time, self-reliance shares much with self-determination, although in this case it is not applied to nationality and ethnic groups but to the individual human being and a diversity of kind of economic units. Also, self-reliance, in its pursuit of human fulfillment, pursues some of the same goals as human rights, particularly those considered to be economic and social (see *Human Security*).

The FEMINIST (21) perspective is particularly useful in shedding light on the degree to which values associated with militarism and military organizations permeate societies and how this came to be (see *Feminism and Peace*). At the same time the feminist perspective provides a vision of alternative kinds of societies. It is necessary to consider the feminist perspective as a separate tool because women's perspectives and experiences have been largely omitted in most works on international relations and peace. One need not be a female in order to approach human behavior with a feminist perspective, but there is no doubt that the actual experiences of women has sharpened their perceptions and understanding of the roots of violence. This understanding is provoked by the violence experienced by women from the hands of men within societies, through rape and family violence. At the same time it is women, and their children, who suffer most extensively from militarization and war (see *Feminist Thought and Peace*). This includes not only the growing destruction of civilian societies by war but also the diversion of resources away from the needs of families into military weapons and organizations. Not insignificant is the fact that these military organizations are male-dominated and that they were created by political and military decisions made almost exclusively by men.

The feminist perspective takes note of male dependence on violence within societies, as a means for satisfaction of needs, for solving problems and for signaling individual significance and identity. Why are these attributes so prevalent in men and rare in women? Why are they much more prevalent in some cultures than in others? Why are they so prevalent in some men but not in others? In responding to these questions feminists conclude that the tendency to employ violence as a tool for coping with problems in human relationships is learned through early socialization of males in certain cultures. They are taught that to be a man you must be aggressive and respond to provocative frustrations with violence. Not to reply with violence is not to be in control and to deny one's "manhood." This form of socialization is then easily transferred in response to disappointments and frustrations in relations between gangs, between labor and management, and readily applied to questions of national and international peace and security.

Thus the fundamental contributions of the feminist perspective as a peace tool are (a) to question the inevitability of violence as a tool in the pursuit of peace and security, (b) to illuminate its negative consequences, and (c) to provoke thought about where the roots of the "violence habit" is to be found. Very significant is the fact that the last question directs our attention beyond arenas of inter-state conflict and into the daily life of individual societies—including our own.

The feminist perspective also offers a fourth contribution by providing visions of alternative ways for solving human problems. It is obvious that women also experience disappointments and frustrations and, like all normal human beings, engage in conflict in striving for personal goals. But, according to Betty Reardon, the "feminine view . . . emphasizes human relationships and how people behave to fulfill their human needs." Where the "masculine mode of thinking is that of a hierarchical organization . . . the feminine mode is based on a kinship model of less struc-

tured organization designed for the fulfillment of the needs of those in kinship networks. The values of such a mode tend to be familial, nurturant and inclusive. Whereas, the masculine values are more organizational, competitive and exclusive." From this it follows that "a feminist world security system would attempt to include all people and all nations based on a notion of extended kinship including the entire human family" (Reardon in Smoker et. al., pp. 138-139).

In other words, the feminist vision of a peaceful world tends to begin with family and kinship relations and then extends the quality of these mutually nurturing relationships to the world. It is less inclined to make unquestioned assumptions about the need for a state/military apparatus to oversee these world relationships. Of course, once again, we are encountering an overlap with peace tools already presented. In essence the feminist perspective offers insight into the need for positive peace tools. In this sense the feminist perspective confirms and supports the need for peace tools such as non-violence, self-reliance, economic equity and human rights. On the one hand, some have achieved their understanding of the need for these tools through experiences in the struggle for peace that revealed the shortcomings of negative peace tools, and of some positive peace tools as well. On the other hand, others (feminists) have reached the same insights by understanding coming out of the experiences of women—in times of war and "peace" —in everyday life. Of overwhelming importance is the fact that the feminist perspective not only illuminates the *need* for certain positive peace tools; feminine practice throughout the world also demonstrates that they work!

One professor of psychiatry discerns similarities between the trauma of "shellshock" experienced by soldiers in war and that experienced by women in civilian life: ". . . the psychological syndrome seen in survivors of rape, domestic battery and incest was essentially the same as the syndrome seen in survivors of war" (Chesler 1992 p. 11). This leads her to reach this challenging conclusion:

> The fate of this field of knowledge depends upon the fate of the same political movement that has inspired and sustained it over the last century. If in the late 19th century the goal of that movement was the establishment of secular democracy. In the early 20th century its goal was the abolition of war. In the last 20th century its goal was the liberation of women. All of these goals remain. All are, in the end, inseparably connected. (Herman 1992 quoted by Chesler p. 12)

PEACE EDUCATION (22) can be viewed as the obvious candidate to be the last tool to be presented because it obviously comprises all that has gone before. But it is certainly not last in importance. Indeed, the successful employment of all that we have learned about peacebuilding in the twentieth century is dependent on peace education (see *Peace Education*). Now broadened interdependence has directly involved *everybody* in a diversity of human enterprises that either contribute to or detract from peaceful human relations on a global scale. This is why it is now necessary that *all* begin to comprehend the peace potential generated in a diversity of "peace laboratories" in this century.

Over and over again in real-life "experiments" with an array of peace tools, practitioners have found the need to probe deeper and deeper into the causes of peacelessness. At the end of the quest a diversity of non-governmental/citizens movements were discerned to be a necessary "drawer" in the "peace tool chest" because the roots of peacelessness extend into domestic societies, local communities and even families. Thus, the seeds of peace must be planted, watered, nurtured and cultivated there. This means, of course, that *all* require peace education. Obviously it is not a subject essential only for present or future government leaders. Indeed, implementation of their peace plans requires the active support that only a citizenry with comprehensive peace education can provide. Furthermore, *comprehensive* peace education deepens insight on peace potential, particularly with respect to certain positive peace tools, and most specifically those requiring broad participation. It is obvious that the full extent of this potential has not yet been realized (see *Peace and Peace Education: A Holistic View*). Most people have not been challenged to join the quest for peace. This should be the purpose of peace education.

There are those who tend to limit peace education to what they call conflict management or conflict resolution. Sometimes these approaches focus on managing or resolving conflicts in the schools, between neighbors, between business enterprises and their customers, and between labor and management. There are many community programs that attempt to offer conflict resolution alternatives to the courts, thereby relieving overcrowded court agendas. These programs are very helpful, both in resolving conflicts and in educating those involved about ways for diminishing the social disruption, and violence potential, of human conflict. But obviously these approaches are only one aspect of peace education. We believe that peace studies must offer comprehen-

sive coverage of the diverse causes of peacelessness and their relationship. This encourages a long term perspective that illuminates strategies for removing the roots of disruptive peacelessness before they get out of control. History is replete with examples where conflict resolution approaches have offered too little, and too late. Even those practicing the employment of only one "peace tool," such as conflict resolution, need to understand where this "tool" fits in the full array of those available. After all, we would not prefer to have a personal surgeon who is not aware that some gallstones can now be eliminated by drugs and sound waves.

Finally, peace education with a comprehensive view is essential because it will probably be the only occasion in which young people are challenged to put into words their vision of a peaceful world. Because of the emphasis on extreme conflict and violence by the media, and because the academic study of international relations tends to emphasize the same phenomena, young people tend to assume that a world with widespread violence is inevitable. As a result, when students are asked to describe their personal vision of a peaceful world, they find it difficult to describe anything other than what they perceive the present world to be like. But peace education with a broad perspective cultivates the capacity of students to perceive widespread peace in the world, and significant achievements in efforts to diminish the scope of peacelessness. This enhancement of capacity to perceive peace potential makes it easier for students to employ their own values in envisioning their preferred peaceful world for the future.

Approaching peace education as a quest for ways through which one's personal vision of a peaceful world could be achieved is absolutely necessary if people in an interdependent world are to join the quest for peace. Students soon learn that pursuit of their vision requires two other kinds of knowledge. First, they must have an accurate picture of the present world. Second, they must have knowledge about how the present might be moved toward the preferred world. Since the achievement of significant goals always takes time, they must also think about what should be the first steps and what should follow. It should be obvious that this kind of peace education requires (a) very intensive study of the present state of human relations with a broad perspective. (b) It also requires systematic thinking about strategies for change based on knowledge about the past successes and failures of these strategies. And (c) it constantly challenges students to clarify and revise their preferred future. Did my first vision leave out the

Table 1
Summary of approaches to peace

Name		Instrument
DIPLOMACY		Inter-state communication
PEACEFUL SETTLEMENT		Good offices, conciliation, arbitration, judicial,
SECOND TRACK DIPLOMACY	I	Communication involving non-state actors, including problem-solving workshops
PEACEKEEPING		Cease-fire Patrol/Observation
BALANCE OF POWER		Military balance
COLLECTIVE SECURITY	II	Military superiority under system-wide authority
DISARMAMENT		No weapons
ARMS CONTROL		Reduce weapons
DEFENSIVE DEFENSE	III	Reduce military threat
CONVERSION		Convert to civilian production
NON-VIOLENT POLITICS		Diminish need for weapons as instruments for social change
CITIZEN DEFENSE	IV	Diminish need for weapons for national defense
SELF-DETERMINATION		Autonomy/Independence for identity groups
HUMAN RIGHTS	V	Legitimize transnational standards for economic, social, political, cultural rights
FUNCTIONALISM		Collaboration in solving common problems
DEVELOPMENT	VI	Overcome poverty/economic inequity
SELF-RELIANCE		Human development based on local definition of needs
INT'L ECONOMIC EQUITY		Overcome poverty/economic inequity produced by international economic system
INT'L COMMUNICATIONS EQUITY	VII	Overcome one-way international communication that inhibits mutual understanding and tends to overwhelm cultures
INT'L ECOLOGICAL BALANCE		Overcome destruction of habitat
GOVERNANCE FOR COMMONS		Collaborative problem-solving Sharing/equity in use of the commons
FEMINIST		Illuminating the roots of militarism and violence within societies
PEACE EDUCATION	VIII	Learning about the causes of peace; Learning about the diversity of peace strategies; Acquire a personal vision of peace
PEOPLE'S MOVEMENTS		Broaden opportunities for participation in definition of peace and in choice of peace strategies

special problems of the Third World? Was my proposal for a stronger world court too simplistic? Was my view of human rights too narrow? Why did I leave out the commons? Did I adequately recognize that, for many people, peace means more than stopping the shooting? Thus, having a personal vision of a peaceful world is absolutely necessary if peace education is to be meaningful. This makes possible a challenging dialogue between the world as it is and the world as it might be, mediated by theories

("tools") about how to get there (Galtung 1977 pp. 56-65).

7. Overview of Approaches to Peace

We have presented 22 "peace tools" in our survey of the quest for peace which has spread across the Nineteenth and Twentieth Centuries. The "tools" were somewhat arbitrarily gathered into five categories: nineteenth century, League Covenant (1919), UN

Charter (1945), UN Practice and NGO/Peoples Movements. Table 1 presents a complementary perspective in which the eight categories are based on the instrument, or means employed in the quest for peace.

Group I basically employs spoken and written *words*. The enduring significance of this approach was underlined by Jules Cambon 60 years ago: "The best instrument of a Government wishing to persuade another Government will always remain the spoken words of a decent man" (1931 p. 12). Fundamental is the worldwide system of embassies that has developed over many centuries. Very significant has been the development of procedures for widening the diplomatic dialogue to include a variety of kind of mediators, or "third parties." Another more recent innovation has been efforts to establish "second track" communication by bringing in additional government officials, former officials, representatives of private groups and social scientists. Peacekeeping is placed in this group primarily because it is a means for obtaining and maintaining a ceasefire so that negotiations can then be undertaken for coping with the conflict which precipitated the violence.

Group II basically employs *military power* as a deterrent to aggression, in the form of balance of power exercised through alliances and the exercise of military superiority through a system-wide collective security system.

Group III basically employs strategies for *eliminating* or *reducing* the number and power of weapons through disarmament, arms control, defensive defense and conversion.

Group IV basically attempts to *diminish* the *need for weapons* by providing alternative means for achieving social change (non-violent politics) and for national defense (citizen defense).

Group V basically employs *protection* of the *rights* of identity and self-determination for groups and protection of the human rights of individuals—economic, social, political and cultural.

Group VI basically employs *collaboration in solving common* economic and social *problems*. But in situations in which there are wide gaps between the rich and the poor, strategies are required to cope with poverty and economic inequity. Furthermore, strategies for overcoming these gaps require concern for the self-reliance of those who are the targets of development strategies.

Group VII basically employs approaches that seek to attain *equitable international economic, communications* and *ecological systems*. Inevitably this also requires collaborative problem-solving in governance for the global commons (oceans, space, Antarctica)

and equitable sharing in the use of the commons.

Group VIII basically requires the linkage of the population at large to the quest for peace, through *education and organized participation*. Feminist perspectives illuminate the roots of militarism and violence within societies. Peoples movements offer opportunities for people to participate in the building of more peaceful societies. Peace education prepares people for enlightened participation and at the same time stimulates them to acquire their own vision of a peaceful world toward which their personal participation is directed.

See also: *Peace Studies; Education for Global Citizenship; Global Environment and Peace; International Conflicts and Equilibria*

Bibliography ——————————————————

Alger C F 1995 Building peace: A global learning process. In: Merryfield M M, Remy R C (eds.) *Teaching About International Conflict and Peace*. State University of New York Press

Alger C F 1989 Peace studies at the crossroads: Where else? In: Lopez G (ed.) *Peace Studies: Past and Future, The Annals*. American Academy of Political and Social Sciences

Ambler R 1990 Ghandian Peacemaking. In: Smoker P, Davies R, Munske B (eds.) *A Reader in Peace Studies*. Pergamon Press, New York

Burton J 1990 *Conflict: Resolution and Prevention*. St. Martin's Press, New York

Cambon J 1931 *The Diplomatist*. Philip Allan, London

Chesler P 1992 The Shellshocked Woman. *The New York Times Book Review* 23 (August)

Chatfield C 1984 Concepts of Peace in History. *Conference on Peace Research in History*

Galtung J (no date) *Self-Reliance and Global Interdependence: Some Reflections on the 'New International Economic Order.'* University of Oslo

Galtung J 1977 *Methodology and Ideology: Theory and Methods of Social Research*, Vol. 1. Christian Eljers, Copenhagen

Herman J L 1992 *Trauma and Recovery*. Basic Books, New York

Reardon B R 1990 Feminist Concepts of Peace and Security. In: Smoker P, Davies R, Munske B (eds.) *A Reader in Peace Studies*. Pergamon Press, New York

Sharp G 1985 *National Security through Civilian-Backed Defense*. Association for Transarmament Studies, Omaha, Nebraska

Smoker P, Davies R, Munske B (eds.) 1990 *A Reader in Peace Studies*. Pergamon Press, New York

CHADWICK F. ALGER

Enduring Regional Conflicts and Nuclear Proliferation

1. Nuclear Proliferation: The New Dimensions

The end of the Cold War has brought nuclear proliferation to the central attention of policy makers and scholarly community alike, especially in the West. This has not been necessarily due to a sudden increase in the number of states that possess or intend to acquire nuclear weapons. In fact, there has been a decrease in the number of threshold states, those formerly suspected of harboring nuclear ambitions. South Africa, Argentina and Brazil are important cases of states that gave up their nuclear weapons programs in the 1990s. The decisions by the successor states of the former Soviet Union—namely, Ukraine, Belarus and Kazakhstan—to renounce nuclear weapons also happened contrary to expectations regarding their nuclear behavior. These developments belied predictions made in the 1960s and 70s of a nuclear-armed crowd of 15 to 25 states gate-crashing into the nuclear club. Yet, nuclear diffusion did occur among three major states outside the original five (India, Israel and Pakistan), and a small number of states (North Korea, Iraq, Iran, and Libya) are presumed to be making efforts to acquire them. The nuclear tests by India and Pakistan in May 1998 changed their status from undeclared nuclear states to declared nuclear states.

Scholarly work on nuclear proliferation during the last four decades has produced a number of mostly policy-relevant studies. Yet, the processes of nuclearization and denuclearization are still not fully understood (see *Nuclear Strategy*). There is also a theoretical debate on the virtues and perils of proliferation. These differences reflect a fundamental question as to whether deterrence is a universal construct, applicable to all conflicts similar to the East-West conflict (see *East-West Conflict*) during the Cold War (see *Cold War*) era, or not. Although some scholars believe that deterrence is possible in almost all situations because of the sheer uncertainty that nuclear possession produces deters even the most undeterrable states, others believe that the lack of effective command, control and communications and the urge to pre-empt might lead to nuclear use in a crisis situation involving newly nuclearized states. Opinion also differs as to whether deterrence is possible even when states pursue an opaque strategy by not proclaiming their capability and intentions or conducting open nuclear tests or declaring nuclear doctrines publicly.

Scholars and policy-makers alike are not completely in agreement on which strategies would prevent proliferation. The strategies often range from demand-side approaches like security guarantees, military and economic assistance, and promotion of nuclear free zones (see *Nuclear-Weapon-Free Zones: A History and Assessment*) and comprehensive test ban, to supply-side approaches like strengthening of IAEA (see *Comprehensive Nuclear Test Ban Treaty*) and bilateral safeguards systems, export controls on sensitive technologies and fuels, and coercive methods such as military and economic sanctions (see *Economic Blockade*).

Part of the difficulty in devising appropriate strategies is the lack of clarity on the incentive/disincentive structure of nuclear aspirants. Some pertinent questions that need answers are: under what conditions a state would nuclearize and under what conditions it would choose the opposite, i.e., declare itself non-nuclear? What role does the nuclear non-proliferation regime play in the choices that a state makes to acquire or forswear nuclear weapons? Are old approaches to non-proliferation still relevant or do new circumstances require new methods to deal with the few but important threshold and new nuclear states? Is global nuclear disarmament necessary to stop the spread of nuclear weapons? This chapter attempts to provide preliminary answers to some of these questions. I argue that a clearer analysis of the characteristics of states that are most likely to acquire nuclear capability is imperative to understand the dynamics of nuclear proliferation.

2. The Most Nuclear Proliferation-prone States

Half a century since the Hiroshima and Nagasaki attacks took place, it has become clear that not all states are equally prone to acquire nuclear weapons. I argue that states that are most likely to proliferate and least likely to denuclearize are those engaged in an ongoing protracted conflict or enduring rivalry. Simple security considerations are not enough for a state to nuclearize because such a choice involves tremendous costs for any medium/small state. Security considerations in an ongoing conflict may be the biggest incentive, especially if a state involved in such a conflict does not possess another source of deterrent or a political ally to rely upon (see *Nuclear Deterrence, Doctrine of*).

Enduring rivalries and protracted conflicts are characterized by competitive relationships over an issue of highest salience to two actors. The most potent issues that produce enduring rivalries are territory and ideology that by their very nature are exclusory. Scholars have identified the properties of these conflicts as: long duration, fluctuations in intensity, and deep rooted, intra-societal hostility. Often they are zero-sum conflicts in which states are extremely concerned about the relative gains that their opponents make (see *Conflict Impact Assessment (CIAS)*). Institutional mechanisms to regulate behavior do not exist and parties do not trust each other's intentions. Cooperation will be viewed as a sign of weakness and states tend to act as Grieco puts it, "defensive positionalists."

The cases include: US-Soviet, Sino-Soviet, US-China (until 1972), Arab-Israeli, India-Pakistan, India-China, South Korea-North Korea, and Taiwan-China rivalries. States that are engaged in these protracted conflicts/enduring rivalries have been most susceptible to nuclear acquisition because of existential fears and beliefs in the non-benign intentions of their adversaries. A critical question is to figure out how and when external and regional changes interact in proliferation decisions of enduring rivals. Has the end of the Cold War increased insecurity and thereby the proliferation propensity of states in protracted conflicts? What impact would the ending of a protracted conflict possibly have with respect to denuclearization? Under what conditions would states in these regions become fully non-nuclear?

Beyond the first-tier and second-tier nuclear nations, i.e., the superpowers and the three major powers, states with the most potent nuclear propensities are in three regions of the world: South Asia, the Middle East and East Asia. All three regions contain one or more enduring rivalries or protracted conflicts. These regions have few or no institutionalized security mechanisms to regulate conflict and confidence building measures have been largely absent. In South Asia, the enduring rivalries between India and Pakistan, and between India and China, have generated high levels of insecurity for the antagonists, especially for India and Pakistan. India has been pursuing a non-aligned policy (see *Nonalignment*) since independence which precluded an alliance relationship with a nuclear power sufficient to provide an extended deterrent. The friendship with the USSR in the 1970s never reached the level of a close-knit alliance. Although Pakistan had occasional alliance relationships with the US and China, they were not sufficient to provide a deterrent against its perceived rival, India. Although the arrival of the BJP-led nationalist government in New Delhi in March 1998 led to the decision to test nuclear weapons, the nature of the rivalries in South Asia is the crucial determining fac-

tor in the overt nuclearization choices of India and Pakistan. This is because, since the mid-1990s, governments controlled by different political parties including the Congress Party had maintained nuclear weapons ready to be tested. Similarly, Pakistan has been known to possess nuclear weapons since late 1980s, as otherwise, it was unlikely to be able to test six weapons within two weeks of India's tests. The Indian decision was also prompted by the increased collusion of China and Pakistan in the nuclear and missile areas.

In the Middle East, the Arab-Israeli enduring rivalry/protracted conflict (see *Arab-Israeli Conflict: Peace Plans and Proposals*) has engendered nuclear acquisition by Israel and the search for a countervailing capability by Syria, Iraq, Iran and Libya. The US alliance relationship with Israel does not include a nuclear guarantee and the Israelis have been loathe to leave their security to any other state. Although Egypt and Syria threatened nuclear spread, they have not done so. Egypt's peace agreement with Israel in 1975 removed a major incentive to acquire nuclear weapons. In addition, the Arab states have acquired other types of capability such as chemical weapons that could form sufficient deterrent in a limited war. They have also readjusted their strategies to limited aims (as evident in the 1973 War) and later on to guerrilla style operations which are not deterrable with nuclear weapons.

East Asia remains the third most volatile region with high proliferation propensity. The continuation of the Korean protracted conflict engenders the key incentive for nuclear acquisition by the parties and by states such as Japan. The US security umbrella helped to ease pressures on South Korea to nuclearize, while the end of the Cold War and the demise of the alliance support have increased the North Korean insecurity and thereby its nuclear acquisition propensity. In 1993-94, North Korea attempted the nuclear route by threatening to withdraw from the NPT, an act which generated strong opposition by other states, especially the US. Although the subsequent US-led diplomacy has achieved a suspension of the North Korean program, there is no fool-proof guarantee that North Korea's nuclear ambition has been permanently eradicated (see *North Korea's Nuclear Activities and US-North Korea Accord of 1994*). As long as the Korean division exists, the proliferation propensity is also likely to stay.

The nuclear intentions of Japan also remain unclear. Given the possibility of China emerging in the 21st century as a key hegemonic state with enhanced economic and military might, other states, especially Japan, may decide to acquire a countervailing capability. Tokyo's acquisition of a large amount of plutonium and the continuation of a fast-breeder reactor program have generated concerns especially among other Asian states of a latent Japanese intention to keep the nuclear weapons option open. The Chinese strategy so far does not provide much room for cooperative institutional arrangement in the security realm. The continuation of the US presence and the security umbrella could forestall Japan's potential nuclearization in the short and medium terms, but this might depend on the contours of US-Japan relations which remain unpredictable during the 21st century.

Current non-proliferation policies and theories of proliferation pay inadequate attention to security and deterrent efforts by parties in protracted conflicts. They assume such considerations are extraneous to proliferation decisions. Regional states do not need nuclear weapons as they are a class apart, reserved for the leading actors in the international system. If regional states acquire nuclear weapons, they are for prestige or irrational reasons and can be restrained through supply side restrictions or through carrots and sticks.

As stated, the theoretical and policy disagreement in this regard is most pronounced on the issue of the efficacy of deterrence among regional rivals. Some Western policy analysts have put forward weak arguments on the irrationality of regional states. These arguments do not convince regional actors who themselves are supposed to make decisions to renounce their nuclear ambitions. Supply side approaches are expected to prolong the lead time required for nuclear acquisition. Sanctions are a key source of dissuasive policy adopted by the US and its allies. However, sanctions have not always produced the desired end with respect to the states that are most proliferation prone, especially those in the protracted conflict/enduring rivalry zones. Nonetheless they, probably, have helped to slow down the pace of proliferation.

3. The Efficacy of Sanctions

Sanctions fall under the rubric of military and economic realm. The purpose behind sanctions is to reinforce international legal norms embodied in the nuclear non-proliferation regime and the Nuclear Non-proliferation Treaty (see *Non-Proliferation Treaty (NPT)*). Sanction-based policies assume that the proliferating state is likely to back down from weapons development given the costs of a nuclear program. If the potential for destruction in a military attack exists, the incentive structure could be altered as the econom-

ic and political costs of renewing the nuclear weapons program outweigh the benefits. Additionally, sanctions can buy time, and in the case of technology denial, the nuclearizing state would find the enterprise unworthy and costly while supplier states will not renew their supply of nuclear materials. For economic sanctions, it is often assumed that the target state values economic welfare as equally or higher than security objectives. Even if it does not value economic welfare, prolonged economic difficulties could force a state to alter behavior at a later date or the population will rise up in the face of hardships.

The three most prominent coercive instruments are coercive diplomacy, compellence, and preventive strikes. Under coercive diplomacy, military threats and diplomacy are combined. This indeed is a carrot and stick approach. The effort is to induce cooperation through diplomacy, but also to back it up with threat of punishment for non-compliance. The US strategy towards North Korea during 1993-94 falls under this category. Compellence is a second military based approach whereby the threat to use force is made until the target state adopts or changes policies desired by the compelling state. The US strategy towards Iraq before and after the Gulf War in order for Baghdad to give up its weapons of mass destruction program is an example of this strategy. Preventive attack is the next step in the hierarchy of military-based sanctions and this often involves destruction of a state's nuclear facilities through a surprise attack in an effort to arrest nuclear weapons development. The examples are the Israeli attack on Iraq's Osiraq reactor in 1981 and the UN Coalition attack on Iraqi nuclear facilities during the 1991 Gulf War.

Economic instruments include negative sanctions such as denial of technology, the cutting off of aid and trade privileges, imposition of tariffs and embargoes, freezing of assets, blacklisting etc. Positive sanctions comprise giving inducements such as arms and economic aid with the hope that the target state would halt its nuclear acquisition efforts. The US arms transfers to Pakistan, Israel, South Korea and Taiwan fall under this type of approach. Members of the London suppliers club have practised some of the negative sanctions in their transfer of nuclear materials vis-à-vis non-nuclear weapon states. These approaches have so far been applied to selected cases of states. The end result indicates a mixed pattern. For example, the economic and military inducements to Islamabad have not helped to rescind the nuclear program of Pakistan, while it probably helped in the case of Taiwan and South Korea. Negative sanctions or threat of sanctions toward North Korea and Iraq seem to have worked in the short-term, but it is not clear whether their nuclear appetite has been removed completely. The sanctions on India and Pakistan, imposed by the US and some of its allies after their 1998 nuclear tests, are unlikely to result in the rescinding of their nuclear programs.

Sanction-type coercive policies need not eradicate the incentives that in the first place resulted in efforts at nuclear acquisition. They need not remove security challenges to a state engaged in a protracted conflict. The sanctions could force a state to go for the clandestine route as Pakistan (until 1998) and Iraq have pursued their nuclear programs. As far as preventive attacks are concerned, the difficulty is that a one-shot attack may not alter the behavior of the state sufficiently. The state may have to be defeated decisively in a war and be transformed as happened in the cases of Germany and Japan. The Iraqi behavior after the Gulf war and the Osiraq attack attest to this contention. Iraq has continued its efforts to hide nuclear materials from international inspectors. Once sanctions end, and if Saddam Hussein stays in power, Iraq is likely to resurrect its nuclear program.

Military threats are not credible if the regional state holds military advantages in the theater, as in the case of North Korea. A military attack on North Korea was not credible given the geographical and strategic advantages it enjoys vis-à-vis South Korea, especially for a surprise attack, however, suicidal that may be. Pushing such a state into a corner could result in military backlash and may not reduce its proliferation propensity.

The strategy of denial of technology could increase a state's determination to develop nuclear capability indigenously. The Indian effort at national nuclear development attests to this pattern. Denial could however, slow down the process for technologically weak states and it may forestall the efforts altogether. The overall impact of sanctions has been mixed. Studies show that on national security issues, sanctions have been of limited impact. The immediate response of the population of the sanctioned state is to rally around the flag. Long-range changes could occur only if the target is a dependent state. The effects are unpredictable and can hurt the most vulnerable sections of a society. Carrots, or positive sanctions, are not equal to military security for a state engaged in an ongoing protracted conflict relationship. The US supply of F16s and other sophisticated conventional weaponry will not take away the utility of the great strategic equalizer that Pakistan is perceiving in the possession of nuclear weapons. They are not sufficient to compensate for denuclearization

by Pakistan, especially since its adversary, India possesses nuclear weapons.

The success of sanctions is context dependent. The targets against which sanctions are likely to succeed are: (a) a potential nuclear state that is not engaged in an intense protracted conflict, (b) States that give economic objectives high priority, (c) States that are democratizing or that are focusing on economic development while giving security considerations a back seat. The shift toward more benign foreign policy may result from democratization of a potential nuclear state. For example, the fear of sanctions could be underneath the decisions by the newly democratized Argentina and Brazil to forgo their nuclear weapons options and initiate regional nuclear rapprochement.

4. Time for New Approaches

The discussion so far suggests that sanctions and other tried out approaches may not be sufficient to deal with the proliferation problem in the long run. The key to non-proliferation rests in the resolution of regional conflicts. Efforts have to be made to resolve the protracted regional conflicts, the most likely source of nuclear acquisition. As long as the regional conflicts endure as zero-sum conflicts, the potential for nuclear proliferation remains, although temporary delays may be achievable with sanctions and other carrot and stick policies.

This discussion has clear relevance to the Korean peninsula, South Asia and the Middle East. In the latter two regions, proliferation has already occurred and current international approaches are unlikely to succeed. The major short-term objective would be to slow down the nuclear arms race and to create a stable deterrent relationship between parties than complete denuclearization. Active proliferation has not occurred in East Asia, therefore, the current approaches may buy time in this region. The establishment of a genuine nuclear free-zone in this region may be possible only when the protracted conflicts end and peaceful relationships develop among the regional states. For instance, the North Korean nuclear acquisition propensity is likely to remain as long as the protracted conflict with the South exists. Similarly, the US security guarantees that have provided the major disincentive for South Korea from exercising its nuclear option may be removed, if the guarantees end in some fashion. However, a peacefully reunified Korea could be a nuclear-free state as Germany became at the time of reunification. Similarly, in the case of the Middle East, a likely peace settlement between Israel and its neighbors could be the necessary requirement for Israeli denuclearization. The efforts to end protracted conflicts should therefore be given prominence in any successful non-proliferation policy along with other approaches.

Even if the new nuclear states are not fully denuclearized, at least ways could be developed to attain regional stability. This is most relevant in the South Asian and Middle East cases. India and Israel are unlikely to denuclearize for various reasons. As long as China remains a nuclear state and the Indian ambition to become a major power concomitant with its economic progress persists, the nuclear capacity will be maintained. Israel is unlikely to give up US nuclear weapons until its rivalry in the Middle East ends, but may keep them as a last resort weapon given the historical antagonism with its neighbors. Denuclearization of these two regions may require global nuclear disarmament. This is because the South Asian conflict is not dyadic, but involves three parties including a declared nuclear weapon state, i.e., China. As long as China retains nuclear weapons, India is likely to maintain the capability as well. In such a case, Pakistan will also maintain its covert program. The resolution of the Kashmir conflict and the end of the India-Pakistan protracted conflict could lead to denuclearization of Pakistan but it is unlikely in the Indian case because of the Chinese capability.

The major powers or the system leaders have been reluctant to adapt to changing realities. The five declared nuclear weapon states desire to hold on to their nuclear monopoly while denying the right to other states. Their unanimity of opinion in this respect has been evident at the NPT and CTBT negotiations and their response to the nuclear tests by India and Pakistan. The major powers, led by the US, pushed through the extension of NPT in perpetuity believing that their nuclear monopoly could be maintained for a long time to come, and that no power transitions will occur in the future. The major powers realize that with the advent of weapons of mass destruction, a fundamental shift in power has occurred. Rarely in history could the weak threaten the strong's territory. The weak's challenge always confined to their own territory where the strong first entered as colonizer or occupier. Yet, diffusion has not completely denied the power projection capability of the major powers. The key to the dominant states' capacity lies in their overwhelming military preponderance and technological superiority. Enhanced survivability of delivery systems could affect preventive and pre-emptive capability and power projection. Secondly, missile defense systems would make it difficult to penetrate major power territories. However, major-

minor power conflicts could become the low intensity variety and guerrilla tactics could emerge as a potent source of political opposition.

The current attempts at total denuclearization of regional actors may not succeed without concomitant efforts at global nuclear disarmament. The integration of new nuclear states, while continuing the attempts to prevent additional states from entering the arena, may become essential for medium-term stability of the regions. If not, these states are likely to continue their secret nuclear programs, creating uncertainty regarding intentions, capabilities and future policies. Additionally, the need to strengthen the norms against nuclear use—the tradition of non-use or "nuclear taboo," and the pledges of no-first use (see *No First Use of Nuclear Weapons*)—might reduce the incentives of some states.

The non-proliferation regime has to find a way to integrate the new nuclear states such as India, Pakistan, and Israel. Long-term possibilities of policy success rest with political options such as reduction of conflicts in the regional theaters and the implementation of time-bound global disarmament. Regional stability, arms control and confidence building measures need to be given a higher profile in international efforts at non-proliferation.

5. Other Short-term and Long-range Approaches

Short-term and long-term approaches to nuclear non-proliferation may be as follows:

(a) An effective comprehensive test ban that proscribes laboratory level testing as well. The recently concluded Comprehensive Test Ban Treaty (CTBT) is weak as it does very little to arrest vertical proliferation.

(b) Decoupling nuclear capability from great power status. This is achievable if two of the non-nuclear major powers, Japan and Germany, and a third rising power, India, were given their due role in international governance, such as granting of UN Security Council permanent membership.

(c) Effective no-first use declarations by all nuclear weapon states.

(d) Eventual delegitimization of nuclear weapons and the establishment of a universal regime similar to the chemical weapons convention.

The United Nations could be very instrumental in the creation of rules, norms and principles in the nuclear arena and their application in a non-discriminatory way. Global nuclear disarmament is likely to be achievable only when there is a fool-proof verification system and a compliance system monitored by the UN or a UN-affiliated agency. The current regime is often portrayed as not fully legitimate as there is a perception that the nuclear weapon states push through their agenda without regard for the genuine security concerns of the non-nuclear states. The creation of an effective non-proliferation regime could be on the agenda of the UN as the world enters the 21st century.

See also: *Disarmament and Development; Nuclear Deterrence, Doctrine of*

T. V. PAUL

Epistemological Foundations for Peace Research

Diverse methods can be used to conceptualize problems with conflict and violence, and test newly developed theories. Given the fact that earlier peace research identified prevention of war as a normative goal, many peace researchers have paid a great deal of attention to gathering date about war and other types of violence. Quantitative studies of arms races and formal decision making models have helped in understanding the behavior of decision makers. Scientific research on crisis decision making was originally aimed at predicting the occurrence of war.

Other peace researchers have attempted to find the sources of violence through a critical analysis of existing social, economic systems. Understanding the meaning of power in a hierarchical system is important in a critical peace research tradition. The analysis of structural sources of repression and exploitation is considered as the first step toward eliminating the root causes of violent conflict. Thus the emancipatory goal of peace research is associated with looking for obstacles to structural changes and exploring strategies to overcome them. Peace research has to serve the policy goal of transforming a world full of violence.

This paper discusses how a theory building process in peace research has been influenced by epistemological debates between the proponents of behavioralists and their critics in social science. In the first part, the author briefly explains the modes of inquiry for theory building. The majority of the chapter, however, looks at such issues as values, critical pedagogy, and holistic approaches in understanding the nature of peace and conflict.

1. The Emergence of Peace Research

Some argue that the history of peace studies has no geographic boundaries. It can be traced back hundreds and even thousands of years (see *Peace, Historical Views of*). Gold mines of ideas about peace were presented by philosophers in the early period of human civilization. Discussion about how to understand peace has been developed in various cultures. The study of peace and conflict in modern social science traditions originated in the 19th century. In Karl Marx's work, theoretical efforts were made to discover the structural sources of conflict in human history. Such sociologists as August Comte attempted to find general theories on social order and conflict. Social processes of conflict were understood in terms of organismic analogies. Max Weber analyzed the links between an individual actor's behavior and patterns of collective action.

The impulse for studying peace and conflict systematically was fomented in the early 20th century. The experiences of World War I led to the realization that given the enormous costs to human well-being, solutions have to be found to prevent war at both an intellectual and policy level. Research on the processes leading to an armed conflict was supported by efforts to examine socio-psychological and economic conditions. In addition, changes in the perceptions of political leaders were regarded as important in the transformation of an international system.

Peace research after World War II was influenced by the emergence of international relations as a new scientific endeavor to investigate problems between states. The course of peace research was also determined by possibilities of nuclear war along with fierce political, ideological and military confrontations between Soviet-led socialist bloc countries and Western alliances in the global arena as well as the devotion of resources to preparing for a war which would annihilate human civilization. The opposition to the Vietnam War generated critical thinking about national foreign policy agendas, and it expanded theoretical perspectives and research areas to be investigated.

The evolution of peace and conflict research since the 1970s has been characterized by inter-disciplinary understanding of violence and conflict at various social levels. Such social science and humanity fields as psychology, sociology, anthropology, political science, history, literature, linguistics, and geography brought new concepts and methodological innovations. It was essential to adopt experiential research methods as well as traditional scientific methods to explain the causes of violence at individual and group levels as well as international. The study of social phenomena is stimulated by intellectual challenges that derive from continuing and new sets of problems. The involvement of various disciplines in the development of peace research was inevitable with the realization that peace can not be achieved by one particular approach. Peace research has to rely on diverse methodological transitions given its disciplinary goals and the complexities of subject matters.

2. Modes of Social Inquiry

In a positivist mode of inquiry, social knowledge emerges from emulating the procedures of natural sciences. There is a clear distinction between facts and values. Efforts for new theoretical departures remain valid only if concrete empirical research programs are developed. A theory needs to be verified by the process of operationalizing and testing hypotheses. Research should be freed from non-empirical claims of individual conviction and conscience. In dealing with the complexity of empirical phenomena, theory ought to explain and predict the trend of events.

Contrary to that, hermeneutics is based on the analysis of the meanings which human beings attach to their actions. The study of mind is different from that of nature. Analysis should reveal social constraints and promote cultural understanding. The goal of research is enlightenment and emancipation. The values and priorities of goals tend to be diverse across social groups and classes. What is rational changes across time and space. Rationalities are intersubjective in the sense that they can only be really examined from within the experiences of social groups which are the object of research.

Critical theory methodology identifies forms of conflict and patterns of development which could lead to the transformation of a world order. There is no over-arching ahistorical structure. Explanation of the prospects for change requires analysis of the connections between modes of production and hierarchical political structures (Cox 1996). The scope of the inquiry also focuses on a distorted ideological account of social relations by a hegemonic class.

In a postmodern vein, problems in different social locations and histories are interpreted by multiple minds and knowledge rather than meta-narratives (Seidman 1994 p. 5). Speculation is the most open form of inquiry. Humanity cannot be studied through a legislative reason which is helpful in producing general theories. The social world is fragmented into a multitude of communities and cultural traditions. The role of a social analyst is to mediate between different social worlds and to interpret unfamiliar cultures (Seidman 1994 p. 14). Resolving major theoretical differences is not desirable nor feasible.

3. Scientific Approaches to Peace Research

The early endeavor to establish a peace science originates in mathematical modeling of dynamics of arms races (Richardson 1960). Quantitative studies of conflict behavior in the 1960s was affected by the revolution of behavioral sciences. Theoretical development was believed to be promoted by the collection of raw data, highly deductive propositions, and empirical verification. Formal models supported by statistical analysis were expected to explain both behavioral and structural characteristics of violent conflict.

The motivation behind scientific research was that ideas for creating a peaceful world would emerge from theories on human behavior and institutions verified by empirical methods. Hypothesis building would help researchers observe cooperative and conflictual patterns of behavior under different circumstances. Order in international relations could be analyzed in terms of such variables as distribution of power and patterns of interaction between political units (Kaplan 1957; Modelski 1978). Perceptions and cognition of decision makers and group processes are important variables in scientific approaches to research on war decision making. Regularities in human behavior were conceptualized and generalized in the studies of the Korean War decision making and the Cuban Missile Crisis (Allison 1971; Paige 1968).

4. The Critique of Behavior Sciences

The behavioralist traditions of peace research have been criticized for being too empiricist (Galtung 1975). Quantitative analysis is not able to reveal intentional aspects of behavior in a specific context. Developing peace research requires a framework for synthesis in integrating different sets of issues. While collecting data on manifest violence, arms races and military coups is critical to the development of empirical theories (SIPRI 1996), research design has to be guided by appropriate theoretical frameworks. The ability to think about and discuss key research questions stems from conceptual development of issues to be studied.

Ignoring normative questions would not help find alternative visions. Conditions for building peace are not dealt with in behavior research traditions. Statistical data and empirical findings themselves do not offer strategies for creating a peaceful world. The uncertainty of politics would not be removed by pure scientific analysis of human behavior. According to some observers in peace studies, the efforts to find regularities have been pursued "to the point of eliminating individual creativity and responsibility may well mire us in cyclic determinism." (Forcey 1989 p. 13) Critics of the positivist paradigm attribute the reductionist character of contemporary thought to the drive for control of nature.

The critique of behavioral sciences coincides with a "critique of conscience" in the academic community. Conscience dictates feelings, moral stances, and a concern for truth and justice. The desire for value explicit inquiry stems from the fact that human behavior would not be investigated without references to social collectivity in historical contexts. Overall, the normative starting point of peace research has to be anchored in the agreement that peace is the object of the quest (Broadhead 1997 p. 2). The utility of any research methods could be evaluated in terms of the way they are compatible with the general goal of a disciplinary focus.

5. Holistic Approaches

Some researchers suggest that peace studies should start from holism as the framework (Smoker and Groff 1996). Knowledge about general human experiences of conflict helps interpret specific events. Given their abstract nature, however, theories may not correspond with the facts and events which they seek to explain. The meanings of events are set up within a context of wholes. The intellectual transformation is necessary for developing a paradigm of peace. The achievement of peace should be a holistic goal of research.

Holistic versions of theories project the flow of alternative images of reality. There are different theoretical explanations about how and why to go to war. The plurality of theories ought not to be regarded as a preliminary stage of knowledge which will eventually lead to one true grand theory. Universally applicable knowledge is not produced by piecemeal theory building efforts. There seems to be consensus that peace research must not be limited to conventional empirical methods. Extended historical perspectives illustrate what is important in understand-

ing conditions for peace. The evaluation of research findings needs a yardstick for examining their relevance. The incorporation of emancipatory cognitive interest would help suggest theories for a peaceful world. More holistic approaches can be encouraged by hermeneutic philosophy of science.

Reasoning needs to be combined with experiences in understanding the holistic pictures of social relations. The outcome in the real world is not easily deduced from abstractly modeled relationships. In considering difficulties for justification of inducing wholes from parts, the ultimate validity of the big pictures is elusive. Theories which can be positively verifiable does not necessarily mean that they are true. Realities in peace and conflict do not last long enough to be subject to comprehensive, systematic and effective empirical assaults on them. Explanation can be based on intuitive understanding of long and varied experiences. There are various ways to observe the world, including historical interpretations. Different perceptions of social relationships result from the process of formation and transformation of images and symbols.

Peace studies may belong to the same category as history and critical sociology in terms of its methods to study an object. In contrast with economics, many factors related to structural violence such as political repression and economic exploitation cannot be easily understood without socio-historical contexts. Distinctions between independent and dependent variables are artificial. Understanding the outcome of an event would be enhanced by clarifying the specific goals of actors.

6. Emancipatory Projects

Direct criticism of sovereign state power may be based on questioning the mode of analysis to construct linear histories. Social and political boundaries cannot be imposed especially when truth and meanings are in doubt. Sovereign claims are used to shape human loyalties, but the forms of identities are not any more certain. Resolving differences of opinion about the legitimacy of state institutions is not possible within clearly defined and demarcated areas of research. Thus emancipatory projects oppose intellectual and social closure which does not tolerate diversity.

In a post-structural approach, language and discourse shape politics and social institutions (Bannet 1993). A normative social space is located in the process of assigning meanings to opposing phenomena. Binary opposition have contributed to the creation of linguistic and social hierarchies (Seidman 1994 p. 18). Post-structuralism aims to disturb the dominant binary meanings that function to perpetuate social and political hierarchies. Deconstructionism is the method to be deployed. This involves unsettling and displacing the binary hierarchies. The goal of a deconstructionist strategy is to create a social space which favors autonomy. This process is tolerant of difference and ambiguity (Seidman 1994 p. 19). The historically contingent origin and political role of binary hierarchies are uncovered by deconstructionism.

Instead of being instruments of bureaucratic social control, human studies should serve emancipatory aims. Society is imagined less as a material structure, organic order, or social system than as a construction rooted in historically specific discursive practices. Communities serve as texts whose symbols and meanings need to be translated. Interpretative knowledge promotes diversity, expands tolerance, and legitimates difference as well as fosters understanding and communication (Seidman 1994 pp. 14-5).

People's perceptions about the world rely on their social and cultural milieu. The goal of emancipation has nothing to do with science. Legitimation arises from their own linguistic practice and communicational interaction. As long as social science serves as the instrument of a disciplined society, truth is produced by power (Foucault 1967). All knowledge claims are moves in a power game. Social science can contribute to emancipation by widening and deepening our sense of community. If meanings rest with communities, knowledge can have a specific role in promoting human solidarity (Waever, Ole 1996 p. 171).

7. Value Issues

Even in a conventional mode of inquiry, values are not always considered separate from analysis. The accumulation of more data and testing hypotheses may reveal a trend in the arms race. However, the ultimate analytical goal should be not only explanatory but also prescriptive. The goals of peace research are defined in terms of broad human interests which are not dealt with by a state-centric paradigm. Human dimensions of security can be more easily understood in value paradigms. This paradigm shift requires a more focus on non-state centric actors, ranging from individuals to supranational institutions. The bias toward a more inclusive concept of global society as opposed to the exclusionary state can be justified in terms of a goal oriented research.

Each discipline is governed by certain sets of

assumptions and rules that determine its approaches to knowledge and acceptable methods (Forcey 1989 p. 11). Peace and conflict studies have been developed by value-guided research paradigms. Multidimensional concepts of security explain the importance of economic equity and ecological protection. Core theories have been established around negative and positive peace. Peace has become a more inclusive concept. The underlying assumptions of positive peace have value implications for the satisfaction of basic needs. Peaceful conditions include freedom from oppression and social justice beyond the absence of violence. The impact of poverty and economic exploitation on conflict can be empirically understood. However, their major form of inquiry ought to be dialectic. While peace and conflict studies need to be as objective as possible, it cannot succumb to the academic prejudice of total dissociation from the object of study. The starting point for peace research may be found in the ideals of social transformation through knowledge.

Efforts have been made to find a universal standard in Western societies which have a great deal of similarity in their cultural backgrounds. However, this standard may not apply to the non-Western societies because of their different value concepts. Therefore, it should be recognized that there is no universal value in the first place and that different values of peace exist in various parts of the world. We must conceptualize peace in terms of cultural expectations which various groups of people possess.

If normative pluralism is accepted, peace research must find the interactions between value expectations. It is also necessary to examine the role of different peace values in social change. The acceptance of diverse approaches to peace can co-exist with the recognition of common goals of peace research and education such as human development. Research ought to focus not only on different patterns of peacelessness prevailing in the world but also on the linkage which exists among them.

8. Participatory Research and Empowerment

Participatory projects are important in an organized effort of endogenous peace learning. It affects the sense of control over the world by the marginalized. Peace research can serve the survival needs specific to the grassroots level. Action research is part of a feedback process in learning those who are the object of study. The situations in local communities should be considered in terms of basic human need values.

The needs of people can be identified by integrating research and practice. Researchers should not arbitrarily define peace in their judgement but build an interactive relationship with those who are exposed to violence and are living under the condition of peacelessness. The mode of inquiries for empowerment maximizes the possibilities for reflection, creativity, and full participation of all engaged in the study. Action results from interpretations and assessments of choices.

If the overall intent of peace research is to develop the well-informed public, research should be incorporated into a personal, inward, and interactive process. Research and learning are a holistic process of integrating social experiences and knowledge. The task of peace research should be the analysis of the social process through which peace can be achieved.

9. Critical Pedagogy and Cultural Theory

Critical pedagogy deals with such issues as how knowledge can be used to change society. The Brazilian educator Paulo Freire criticizes a traditional method of learning which does not reflect local reality. He explains that the process of awakening people to the power of their own questioning (Freire 1996). It can be used to explore a model for transforming society (see *Peace Education and Human Rights: A Third World Critique*). Culture is not just a by-product of how a society organizes its social and productive relationships. It is a vital instrument for generating the insights and energy needed to transform those relationships (see *Cultural Roots of Peace*).

Cultural energy is a key element for mobilizing the social action that drives successful grassroots projects. It motivates social action among individuals, groups, communities, and even nations. It is generated by common people through everyday creative expression in work and entertainment. The presence or absence of cultural energy makes the difference in whether a project for social change can be launched, sustained, and expanded. Cultural energy is a powerful force in the creation and reinforcement of a group's solidarity, organizational efficiency, participation, and volunteer spirit.

This cultural theory has been applied to the explanation of a positive linkage between culture and development as well as between tradition and change. Generations of social and economic oppression and the concentration of power in a sovereign state system have made it difficult for many indigenous peoples in the Third World to survive on their own. Some found their survival strategy in the regeneration of their culture and identity. They attempt to achieve political and economic autonomy through culture-based development.

The culturally motivated development projects helped Indians in the Ecuador highland make impressive strides since the 1970s. For more than two decades streams of national and international organizations offered relief aid, but there were no prospects for change. Typically the outside assistance was organized by the representatives of white collar professionals whose social and cultural backgrounds are far removed from those of local people. Successful grassroots initiatives sprang from a group of individuals, many of whom were born in indigenous villages. They formed an Educational Fair to promote cultural revitalization and self-help efforts. The group encouraged community members to identify their difficulties and consider possible solutions. Two means for doing this were socio-dramas and puppet shows. This process produced a collective recognition of how the problem was rooted within the local reality.

Many of these communities have joined together to form federations that sponsored their own cultural revitalization efforts. Later they were integrated with training, production, health, and other development activities. By allowing them to examine their culture from within, participatory research provided the Sikunai Indians in Ecuador with a powerful tool for problem solving that unleashed the latent creativity in their own culture. Thus the community became a laboratory for discovering and multiplying locally available resources for development. In many indigenous communities, there is a common source of energy driving grassroots development. Cultural projects often began with local voices responding to local needs.

10. Goals of Peace Research

Peace research can be both a process of discovering knowledge about peace and a process of promoting peace. Research about peace helps define important issues in understanding conditions for peace. The potential for change can be increased by the realization of human capacity and value expectation. Thus it becomes important to identify the actors who could be either obstacles to or supporters of peace in various sectors of society. Peace research may focus on the different roles of various actors ranging from military industries and multi-national corporations of industrialized countries to peasants in the Third World villages. All of those actors are enclosed within a system of interdependency. The impact of these actors on political, economic, and cultural transformations, however, would be different.

Research for peace enhances a liberating experience that motivates an individual to seek changes for realizing peace. Research is a process whereby knowledge is created through a transformative experience. Therefore, the goal of peace studies is to develop alternative ways of promoting empowerment through action oriented research. For this purpose, peace research may include experiential learning which involves researchers directly in the phenomenon being studied. Field research, role plays, games, and participation in real events such as peace movements could be important methods of observation.

The goals of research are as equally important as or more important than the processes and methods of inquiry. Peace has been often breached under the name of peace. Thus the establishment of a normative paradigm has been critical in peace studies. The value concept affects the issues which peace research should deal with. It also has an impact on the method of selecting a subject and constructing a theory. The causes of violence can not be confirmed in an objective form unless a universally relevant measurement exists. Structural violence embedded in society may not be recognized at all by those who take only a negative peace approach (see *Structural Violence and the Definition of Conflict*). Therefore, the definition of peace can not be made without a value judgement on how people achieve their physical and spiritual well-being.

11. Conclusion

Efforts to study peace more systematically are ascribed to modern social science traditions. As political and ideological differences become a less significant element, peace research may need to shift its analysis more to human rights violations, political repression, unequal distribution of wealth, and other causes of human sufferings. Data gathering on repression and poverty still remains a very important task in peace research. However, too much emphasis on rigorous quantitative theory building efforts would not help find creative solutions to problems which humanity faces at the present time and in the future.

If peace research wishes to contribute to its original goal of emancipation and liberation, a holistic approach would be needed to integrate diverse human understanding and experiences. As a normative disciplinary field, peace research has a goal of achieving a peaceful society with peaceful means. Some of these ideas were recognized centuries ago.

Its global perspective and holistic approach would strengthen this tradition. A socio-cultural framework is desirable for integrating collective human experience into peace research.

See also: *Peace Studies; Words of Peace and War; Language and Peace; Psychology of Peace; Cultural Democracy; Peace Theory: An Introduction; Theoretical Tradition of Peace and Conflict Studies*

Bibliography ─────────────────────────────

Allison G 1971 *The Essence of Decision: Explaining the Cuban Missile Crisis*. Little, Brown, Boston
Bannet E T 1993 *Critical Theory after the Marxist Paradigm*. Paragon House, New York
Cox R 1996 *Approaches to Order*. Cambridge University Press, Cambridge
Dahl R 1976 *Modern Political Analysis*. Englewood Cliffs
Foucault M 1967 *Madness and Civilization: A History of Insanity in the Age of Reason*. Tavistock, London
Forcey L 1989 Introduction to peace studies. In: Forcey L (ed.) *Peace*
Freire P 1996 *Pedagogy of the Oppressed*, rev. edn. Penguin, London
Galtung J 1975 *Peace: Research, Education, and Action*. Christian Ejlers, Copenhagen
Guetzkow H S, Alger C F 1963 *Simulation in International Relations: Developments for Research and Teaching*. Prentice-Hall, Englewood Cliffs
Kaplan M 1957 *Systems and Process in International Politics*. John Wiley and Sons, New York
Modelski G 1978 The long cycle of global politics and the nation-state. *Comparative Studies in Society and History* 20 (April)
Paige G 1968 *The Korean Decision*. The Free Press, New York
Richardson L F 1960 *Strategies of Deadly Quarrels*. Quadrangle, Chicago
Seidman S 1994 'Introduction.' In: Seidman S (ed.) *The Postmodern Turn*. Cambridge University Press, Cambridge
Singer D, Small M 1972 *The Wages of War, 1816-1965: A Statistical Handbook*. Wiley, New York
Smoker P, Groff L 1996 Spirituality, Religion, and Peace. Int. *J. Peace Stud.* 1(1) (January)
Stockholm International Peace Research Institute (SIPRI) 1996 *SIPRI Yearbook 1996: Armaments, Disarmament and International Security*. Oxford University Press, Oxford
Waever O 1996 The rise and fall of the inter-paradigm debate. In: Smith S, Booth K, Zalewski M (eds.) *International Theory: Positivism and Beyond*. Cambridge Press, Cambridge

HO-WON JEONG

Equitable Equality: Gandhian Concept

1. Introduction

Equitable equality is a new concept in peace studies, which consists of (a) harmony of the heterogeneities, (b) uniformity of diversities, (c) equality with justice and (d) equity of equalities. The goal or end-result of the above is "homonoia" or union of hearts at the behavioral level in the society. Gandhi, in his mode of conviction and process life-long action, used justice or equity as value determinant and homonoia as the union of hearts in the human and social behavioral process. Gandhi was not against the Marxist goal of human equalization, but he differed in the means. The enforced homogenisation or equalization creates disorder and discontent at both the social formation and society's functional levels. Gandhi used non-violence as the best and most effective means of changing human mind, effecting revolution in human consciousness and uniting the human and social beings under the common platform of human progress and human feeling type of bondage. In his formation of ideology-cum-philosophy and process of action the following elements and actors functioned as such:

1.1 Violence:

(a) as negative to unity as method and means of human and social disorder and destabilisation,

(b) as method of dominance, suppression and subjugation leading to verticality in human and social relations, and

(c) as destruction of the human qualities and material values.

1.2 Non-Violence:

(a) as rational and positive to unity and uniformity,

(b) as method and means of human and social order and dynamic stabilisation,

(c) as means of generating human and social sustenance, by gradually destroying the verticality of the human and social relations, and

(d) as creative and productive for human qualities and socially-needed material values.

1.3 Human Marginalisation: as the mechanism of human inequality and human crime.

1.4 Homonoia: as the ideology and philosophy of the revolution of human and social conscience and consciousness.

1.5 Inequality: as the root of the formation of human and social class or strata relations which generate greed and over-consumption for some at the cost of deprivance and marginalisation of the others.

1.6 Equitable Equality: as the stable factor of social order and peace leading to human content.

1.7 Search for Truth: as the means for finding the meaning of humanity and human value-oriented life (Satyagraha) and life's goal.

1.8 Search for Human Integrity: as the means and ways of human bondage beyond the religions and fundamentalistic practice of certain religions, classes, strata, castes, creeds, origins and artificial human barricades, etc.

Gandhian concept of the positives is not the concept of the vertically added multiplied functional points of the qualities, it is the concept of the horizontally-added qualitative social and human values. These positives should not be counted as spiritual. These should be regarded as social and human ethic-based, social norms-based, verified and subjected to tri-dimensions of time, space and circumstances, under the process of continuity. These positives should not be regarded as absolute or static, but as relative, subjected to the transformations and changes as needed and demanded by the above tri-dimensions.

At the same time, the Gandhian concept of the negatives is not the concept of rejection. In logic, two negatives become affirmative. In Gandhian dialectics, the negatives are the roots just as the failures are regarded as the pillars of success. Negatives are the sources of creativity. Black sharpens and brightens the light. Similarly, the negatives provoke the thoughts for creation in the direction of change towards creative positivity Gandhi learnt the importance of non-violence from the negatives of violence. However, negatives become the rejections when the same are infiltrated to the human and social life and swallows up the human and social values as well as sicken them. When the negatives contribute to the mal-functioning of the body or organ, this needs dissection. Had the negatives not been present in the social body's functional mechanism, they should not have given birth to the need for discovery of the anti-biotic curative medicines or means.

The sense and essence of the Gandhian Equitable Equality, its theoretical contents and practical contexts are being discussed in this study with a view to establishing a conceptual framework of the same.

2. Equitable Equality: Premises, Elements and Concept

Gandhi refused to accept the Marxist-Maoist concept of the floor or scale type of homogenization. He included the element or space of justice in it and left the case of social and human acceptability to the social and human conscience and consciousness. Equity is the space between the floor and the ceiling and between the margin and justful comfort. The concept of marginality or enforced equality is the concept of reduction, staticity and non-progress. Peace and the process of peace and truth as well as march for truth cannot be marginalised through scale-cuts, because it does not keep pace for dynamicity and dynamic additions. His concept of village or rural socialism contains the labor-input and distribution of output in the following sense:

2.1 from each according to his wilful capacity, not to the extent of enforced capacity, and

2.2 to each according to his normal and basic needs—satisfiable necessities, not to scaled limit.

Can the equities be equals? Equity or Justice, in applicable sense, has to be equal towards and for all. But in the sense of its social and human needs, it is relative, depending on the degree, purpose and propensity. The crisis moments and the gravity of crisis determines the extents of relative difference between the (a) equity and equality and (b) equality and equity. Since both of these stages and states are possible and realizable only under the conditions and process of sustainable peace in the society and that also under no-violent environment, Gandhi opted for non-violence as the essential condition of social transformation and change, in which, the global marginal or the global periphery could be freed or emancipated. While the above two are the goal motivations of his standpoints he chose non-violence as the means of de-structuralisation of the society and de-marginalisation of the marginal section of the society. This is the human dimension of his concept and conceptual approach. He conceived that:

(a) A human being or individual cannot be marginalised by birth,

(b) A human being can be marginalised by denying education and attribution of environment and opportunities for creation and improvement of his physical and intellectual capabilities,

(c) An individual may be marginalised by being deprived of the means and ways of procuring and satisfying his fundamental basic needs, and

(d) A human being may be marginalised by being denied his right to use his utilities and performing functions.

He conceived that it is the structuralisation which caused the polarization of wealth, privileges, opportunities and power in the hands of a strata and forced the deprived section towards the social and economic periphery. In today's global structure, a marginal human being has been converted into a factor-input for production, i.e., labor and his social function has been kept out of evaluation (see *Structural Violence and the Definition of Conflict*). Therefore, Gandhi wanted the evaluation of the social values and potentials of every marginal social being and to integrate his creative values in the socio-economic system, process and functions of each community and society. The survival of the fittest approach, which lacks human dimension and approach, has given birth to social and counter-peace vices like: war, crime, torture, dominance, dependence, suppression, subjugation, social structuralisation, social and human marginalisation, etc.

If a society cannot use its: (a) Social Resources which is equal to social strength and (b) Social Sources which is equal to social potence and potentials; one can find the appearance of Social Destability, and Social Destability is a set-back stage which hinders the attainment of the society's equitable equality.

The casteless marginalised social community (which numbers around 120 million in today's modern India) is a product of the above negatives. In India, Gandhi termed the rightless casteless people in the plain lands of India as the Harijans or the Sons of God and those in the hills and mountains as the Girijans or the Sons of the Hills. Gandhi, through revolutionizing the human and social consciousness, wanted to effect a Global Social Order, which has and is to demarginalise this casteless community of India and the apartheid-ridden black people of Africa, where he started the first actions of his non-violent approach and revolution.

An equitable equality can be attained under the conditions of orderly human development and these conditions can be cited as such: a) Destructuralising the Structural Equality and b) Destructuralising the Structural Equity, because both the structured equality and the structured equity are imposed ones and any such imposed social order is an order of dependency on the structure.

According to Gandhi, truth which is the condition of human equity is not a professed belief. It is something that has to be lived and that has to be sustained for social and human continuity. As corollary to truth, Gandhi always opted for himself and for others not to have the non-necessities. If charity begins from neighbors and if somebody loves neighbors as himself, he cannot have the superfluities when others lack even the basic necessities of life. And this is the very content and inner essence of both the equal equity and equitable equality and in this very sense these are not contradictory, rather complementary.

Gandhi, besides practicing by himself, advised others to use "Samya-Yoga" or "Practice of Equality" in order to obtain the inner unity of man, whose very essence is based on "Love is One," which is based on unity. And this unity seeks to build an order of equal equity in which all the component humanistic elements will be in the right place. In the approach of achieving the best essence of the unity and diversity, human welfare can be considered as the most suitable one. Even if such welfare comes from the diversities, the same should not be destroyed.

The practice of equality is opposed to the practice of inequality, however, it is not opposite to the discrimination of the right. The practice of equality provides scope for development to every individual. Because of its very basis of inner unity it seeks for building a balanced order and a balanced order is an equitable and equal order.

As a conceptual clarification, Gandhi wrote that "the real implication of equal distribution is that man shall have the wherewithal to supply all his natural wants and no more. For example, if one man has a weak digestion and requires only quarter of a pound of flour for his bread and another needs a pound, both should be in a position to satisfy their wants. This is the concept of equity and ceiling. To bring this ideal into being the entire social order has got to be reconstructed. A society based on non-violence cannot nurture any other ideal."[1] And this is the sense of his equitable equity which intends to bring contentment to each social member. This concept can be explained as the ceiling concept. For effecting equal distribution in non-violent way Gandhian experiment

shows that an individual's wants have to be reduced to the minimum (see *Nonviolence, Philosophy and Politics of*). His means of having these bare necessities should be his earnings without dishonesty. There should be a self-restraint on desires, in every sphere of an individual's life, which contains the ecological motivation too, for not over-consuming the natural resources and for stealing the same from the mouth of the forthcoming generation by excessive use.

The rich accumulate the richness and wealth, by exploitation of, as well as, cooperation with the poor. This knowledge is to spread among the poor in order to strengthen them, but by adopting the means of non-violent non-cooperation they can crush the inequalities imposed on them by the rich (see *Nonviolence*).

A true human relation in a society ought to be achieved without conflicts and only through harmony and principles of mutual help and love. Such action reveals the very spirit of non-violent democracy. The democratic approach, which is the very basic way of realizing the equitable equality or equal equity, has to be based on the very essence that it should not be imposed on anybody, either by enforcement or artificially. The spirit and sensitivity of democracy is to come from within. Democracy is a practice and should not be considered as theory. The practice and behavior of democracy is to begin from and at home which, later on, extends to social level. It is the method of human accommodation in reciprocity. Its success depends on the negation of egoism. Proper functioning of equitable equity or democracy needs the observance of tolerance, patience and preparedness to accept other's views as well as impressing others with own viewpoints. The functional mechanism of democracy demands adjustability.

Two basic premises of the Gandhian Equitable Equality can be as such: a) Beside the tolerance of various religions and opinion, there should be sincere efforts for realization of their equality (see *Religion and Peace*). And under such conditions only the various communities and social groups can live in comity and amity as well as in mutual cooperation and understanding. The essence of such living process and understanding can generate the real Religion of Man and the spirit of Human Co-Living. b) Mankind should feel that "the world is one family" and this should be the goal of humanism. Therefore, peace and love should be the motto of all of our works and thoughts, instead of war.

As methods to materialize these two premises, Gandhi wanted a) the means and ends should match completely and both of these should be pure and true to each other, and b) Satyagraha or Search for Truth is the only and appropriate way of materializing this unity between the means and the ends and the very essence of Satyagraha contains the qualities of purity, humbleness and non-violence.

The concept of equitable equality or the equal equity needs a culture and its interaction, at the human level for obtaining positive values it is to have two types of approaches, namely, (a) sharing with and (b) accepting from. The fundamental human behavioral rule confirms that if the approach is positive, the result cannot be in the negative. The functional acceptability and strength of a culture depends on its depth and dynamicity of its character. The human and humanistic contents of a culture of a country or a society is influenced and affected by its geography, climate, important events and societal behavior in course of the process. Two or several cultures may mix together under the conditions of equitable equality, not on the basis of imposition from any of the partners, and such process can produce many positive and dynamic trends. The means of imposition destroys the very functional method of normal creative acceptability and, also, generates, conflicts and distrusts. The scientific approach to the culture of peace should be the effort to imbibe the social and human values and truth wherever or in which culture the same can be found (see *Cultural Roots of Peace*). The culture of peace demands the condition of balanced approach for avoiding negative outcome. In the absence of such an approach, the good can be turned to evil, positive to the negative, amity to enmity, understanding to misunderstanding, trust to distrust and love to hatred.

For the purpose of creating the conditions and spirit of equitable equality mankind is to be provided with the essentials of life. When the sufferings, starvation and inequality in a society are not shared by all and some take profit out of these social shortcomings or ills while others bear the burden, then the stage can be called as imbalance. In essence, it becomes a burden on the have-nots and on the principle and practice of equitable equality. Therefore, the abolition of social inequalities should be regarded as an essential condition for realizing equalization with equity. Human beings are primarily the beings of flesh and blood, but this dimension is not the supreme one for and about him. Human beings have minds and passions too. The development of these faculties is necessary not only for the qualitative and creative upliftment of humankind, but also for use as the means of social practice for bringing about a social change in the direction of equity and equality.

There are different social and human groups which cooperate mutually in different social functions. These social groups do have different identities and physionomical structures, habits and traditions, etc. In the course of their cooperation they assist each other reciprocally in preserving the conditions for survival and continuity. Force is incompatible to such cooperative social life (see *Social Progress and Human Survival*). But the efforts for establishing uniformity of all social groups and races will be dangerous. Because the differences between and among the social groups, races, nations, etc., are necessary for preserving the premises and conditions under which further and forthcoming development and promotion are possible. One important factor in the upper trend of human life is his intention and capacity for continuitive progression. In such process, he adopts, from conditions to conditions, climate to climate, mode and habit of life to mode and habit of life, culture to culture, thoughts to thoughts, etc. The diversities and distinctiveness among human communities are essential for the purpose of incentive and human spirit. A social group requires from another neighboring social group or groups something different which it does not possess, something distinctive which draws its attention, something which commands appreciation, etc. These elements enable us to understand the motives and needs for equitable social relation and behavior. Adjusted acceptance of these at different social groups and races can be characterized as the equitable equality. What is needed most essentially is the human approach to human problems (see *Human Security*). Human approaches to problems create scopes for adjustments as regards the means of attaining the principled goals.

As brain without heart is worse and more dangerous than heart without brain, so is equality without equity. And peace is the essential condition which guarantees equity. Because peace is not a negative state in which conflict is absent. In peace, conflicts are settled by negotiations, mediations, understanding and consensus. In the same way, the social inequality can also be settled by constitutional and democratic ways (see *Theoretical Traditions of Peace and Conflicts Studies*). The elements and feelings of fear and hatred need be avoided, and, instead, those of equity and equality are to be added. The state should try to create the conditions of the creative norms of equitable equality and implementation of the same during the time of peace. Inequality generates frustration, hatred, suspicion and fear. But the factors of inequalities of every sort needs proper attention for study towards finding out solutions. For removing inequalities and inequities at the human consciousness level, the following negatives ought to be eradicated: a) black and white racial feelings, b) religious enmity, c) repressive compulsions, d) respectlessness and insecurities, e) inferiority complex and compensatory cruelties, etc.

Tolstoy's *War and Peace* has been a journey from the destruction of war to the equity and rationality of peace, a journey from the universal violence of war to Gandhian non-violence of peace. A conscientious objector against the compulsory military service of our time, in Europe or elsewhere, is a product of revolution in his conscience between right and wrong, between irrationality and equity and between war and peace (see *Conscientious Objection*). Equity is a force of truth. Destructuralisation of the society is one of the basic premises of creating environment for social equity and non-violent equality. Only political equality cannot generate social and economic equity and equality. For realization of a total and equitable equality, one needs the social and economic equality based on equity, too. Otherwise, it will be incomplete and inconsistent to the total sense. Equity and Equality are the two inter-related aspects of human relation. A person should master both the aspects and the same is possible under the following conditions as conceived by both, Confucius and Gandhi:

Confucius: *Gandhi:*

a) Pu-hai (non-hurting) = a) Ahimsa (non-violence)

+   +

b) Jen (love of friendship) = b) Maitri (friendship
                              leading to love)

Equity

The conceptual meaning of Jen, as explained by Confucius, under different contexts, contain the following contents.[2]

(a) Reply to disciple Fan Chieh: Jen = Love for all people,

(b) Reply to disciple Yen Yuah: Jen = To subdue one's self and return to propriety,

(c) Reply to disciple Chung Kung: Jen = Not to do to others what one would not wish to himself,

(d) Reply to disciple Tzu Chang: Jen = Practising of five things, namely, Gravity, Generousity, Sincerity, Earnestness and Kindness.

The essence of the meanings of the aforesaid expla-

nations of Jen, as Confucius (see *Confucius*) gave, under different contexts, is justice or rightfulness. Later on, when Mencius (see *Mencius*), practised the above doctrine, in political sense, he explained as such: Jen = Benevolence; Ye = Righteousness to King Hui of the then Liang state in China. He, further, explained, on several occasions that Jen (Benevolence) is the tranquil habitation of man and Ye (Righteous) is his straight path.[3]

Lao-Tsu, the great social saint of China, perceived that "Tao is eternally inactive, yet it leaves nothing undone .... The simplicity of the nameless Tao brings about an absence of desire (see *Taoism*). The absence of desire gives tranquility."[4] By negation of desire or greed Lao-Tsu intended to mention the righteousness in a man, which symbolises the morality of equity. It means that Lao-Tsu's concept of equity was based, mostly, on non-violent social practice.

Mo-Tsu, another Chinese philosopher, maintained the similar mode of thinking like Gandhi, even during the period 500 BC-400 bc. Through the following negative arguments, like: "If all look upon others' houses as own house, who will steal? If all look upon others' bodies as his own body, who will murder? If all look upon others' families as his own family, who will exploit? .... Therefore, when all love each other there will be peace and when all hate each other , there will be chaos and calamity."[5]

Mo-Tsu was Buddha's contemporary. As Mo-Tsu had been developing the ideology of justful social behavior, Buddha had been developing his eight noble paths of Nirvana or Human Goal (see *Buddhism*). These very eight means and ways of justful behavior of a man of equity coincides with the Tri-Ratna or Three Jewels of Indian Hindu Jainism indicating the important elements of humanistic justice. To show their complementarities or value-resemblances, their value-elements are being put below:

These above functions of a person are and have to be performed within the social life and social process. Both Buddha and Mahavira Jaina believed in the process and doctrine of life in Karma or work and Samsara or Social Life (see *Jainism*). Both of them denied and did not take refuge in the Almighty and Omnipotent God or non-argumentable Absolutism. This metaphysical content is centered around the perception that one's zeal and effort could work out one's own salvation or reaching to the human goal. The principles of righteousness of both the religions had much impacts on the Gandhian concept of justice or equitable equality, in which he added two means, namely, Ahimsa or Non-Violence and Truth for attaining the same.

Jainism	*Buddhism*
Tri-Ratna (3-Jewels)	Nirvana (8-Noble Paths)
a) Samyag-Darsana (Just Conviction with the combination of faith and perception)	a) Samyag-Dristi (Just View)
b) Samyag-jnana (Just Knowledge)	b) Samyag-Samkalpa (Just Thinking)
c) Samyag-Charitra (Just Conduct)	c) Samyag-Bac (Just Speaking)
	d) Samyag-Karmanta (Just Conduct)
	e) Samyag-Ajiva (Just Living)
	f) Samyag-Vyayama (Just Effort)
	g) Samyag-Smriti (Just Remembrance)
	h) Samyag Samadhi (Just Meditation)

Equity is in contrast to wrong-doings and here, Confucius, Jesus Christ, Mohammed and Gandhi conceive and draw the essence as such:

(a) "What you do not want done to yourself, do not do to others." (Confucius, as quoted by Tan Yun shan in Ahimsa in Sino-Indian Culture Harijan, December 29, 1949)

(b) "Whatsoever ye would that man should do to you, do ye even so to them." (Jesus Christ in His Sermon on the Mount)

(c) "Followers of the right ways follow the correct ways for themselves and for the humankind." (Mohammed in Sura in the Hordes)

(d) "If I am a follower of Ahimsa (i.e., Nonviolence), I must love my enemy. I must apply the same rules to the wrong-doer who is my enemy or stranger to me, as a I would do to my wrong-doing father or son." (*Speeches and Writings of Mahatma Gandhi* p. 346)

The ethics of equity becomes a force when it is practiced at the social level and at this very stage it may attain social equality.

3. Testing the Validity of the Concept of Equitable Equality

Gandhi's concept of negation to violent realization of equality and equity is not one of negation, but of positive nature built up of self-denial and self-assertion. His doctrine and practice as well as political means of non-cooperation is not a negation. Enforced equalization efforts in the former East European socialism has failed because of the force used from above and, at the same time, excluding equity from its concept and action. The Scandinavian social democracy succeeded in obtaining both the equality and equity by balancing both in its goals and means, along with the rights and duties in the direction of satisfying the normal human needs. Under the present context, there does not exist any scope for violent revolution to establish equality in the society, in any part of the world, because such revolution ended with both the human and material destruction in this century and, by excluding equity in its concept and action, it lost the part and particles of human aspects (see *Revolution*).

The concept of the equitable equality has, so long, been a theoretical and intellectual concept as well as a concept for preaching and any concept cannot attain force unless practiced at the mass level. The use of the enforced equality has been proved to be a failure as seen in the collapse of Soviet type of Socialist System and introduction of the liberal socialism by China. At the same time, the equitably equal participation of different social and conflicting groups has produced positive results in problem-solution in the Palestine-Israel relation as well as North Ireland conflict. It has been showing also positive signals towards the resolution of the conflicting situation of Guatemala and unsolved relation between South and North Korea.

By his Non-Cooperation Movement and means Gandhi wanted to emphasize the non-cooperation with the wrong-doers and its analytical consequence is the positive justice or equity. Equity and Equitable equality cannot be achieved by using wrong means and right means only may ensure the achievement of an equitable or just end.

See also: *Conflict and Peace: Class versus Structural School; World Peace Order, Dimensions of a; Sustainable Peace; Gandhi, Mohandas Karamchand; India: Historical Concepts and Institutions of Peace*

Notes ————————————————————

1. *Harijan*, Vol. XVII, No. 6, Ahmedabad, April 11, 1953.
2. Tan Yun-shan " Ahimsa" in Sino-Indian Culture-I, *Harijan*, Vol. XIII, No. 41, Ahmedabad, Gujrat, India, December 11, 1949.
3. As cited by Tan Yun-shan in Sino-Indian Culture-II, *Harijan*, Vol. XIII, No. 41, Ahmedabad, Gujrat, India, December 18, 1949.
4. *Idem.*
5. *Idem*, as quoted from *"The Works of Mo-Tsu."*

AMALENDU GUHA

Erasmus, Desiderius

Desiderius Erasmus (c. 1466-1536) was one of the towering figures of Europe's Northern Renaissance. His sharp wit, elegant style, humane values, classical erudition, and painstaking scholarship caused him to be revered as "the prince of humanists" even during his own lifetime. Though born and raised in what is now the Netherlands, Erasmus should not be identified as belonging to any one country. His life was spent restlessly travelling throughout Europe, and he studied, taught, and lived for extended periods in England, France, the Low Countries, Germany, Italy, and Switzerland. Writing exclusively in Latin, then the universal language of scholars, his true home was the educated community of Europe, rather than any one geographic area or political unit.

Erasmus has an honored place in Western history as a scholar and educator, based on his superb Greek edition of the *New Testament* (1516), his sprightly Latin *Colloquies* (1519), and numerous works on the ancient classics. He is even better known, though, as a kindly but serious critic of his age. Erasmus struck out at many aspects of European society, using his matchless wit and satirical skill to attack injustice and irrationality wherever he found them. Academic pedantry, hypocrisy and corruption in the Church, people's boundless capacity for self-deception—all were skewered on the point of Erasmus's devastating pen. His concerns and his essentially humorous approach can best be seen in his most famous work, *The Praise of Folly* (1516).

A deeper side to Erasmus can be seen in such works as *The Handbook of the Christian Knight* (1503) and *The Education of a Christian Prince* (1516), in which he stressed that true Christianity was more a matter of behaving with kindness and compassion toward one's fellow humans here on earth than of seeking to win heaven through performing rituals. As was typical of the humanist movement, Erasmus was more concerned with ethics, and with human happiness and misery, than with abstract metaphysical or theological speculation.

Erasmus singled out war as one of the greatest causes of human unhappiness, something which brutalized and corrupted those who waged it even as it made them and their victims miserable. True Christians, he asserted, should seek to settle their differences through arbitration and compromise, rather than through "so destructive, so hideous, and so base" a thing as war. If attacked by an aggressor who scorned arbitration, said Erasmus, "I would have you bear the injury patiently ... and give up your right, be it what you will—such would be the conduct of a Christian hero."

Erasmus's views on war and peace can be found throughout his work, but are most fully developed in *The Complaint of Peace* (1517). Erasmus's pacifism is highly significant, since the tradition of Christian thought in his time was heavily weighted toward the acceptance of war. With very few exceptions, major Christian thinkers had been primarily concerned with defining the difference between a "just" and an "unjust" war, rather than with condemning war per se (see *Just War*). Erasmus, with his enormous prestige, put the idea of a much more thoroughgoing pacifism before the civilization of the Christian West. His thought had an enormous impact on such later Christian pacifists as the Anabaptists and Quakers (see *Quakerism*). Indeed, the entire modern pacifist tradition in the West, secular as well as religious, can look back on Erasmus as one of its founding fathers.

See also: *Pacifism*

Bibliography ————————————————————

Chapiro J 1950 *Erasmus and Our Struggle for Peace*. Beacon, Boston, Massachusetts
Erasmus D 1972 *The Complaint of Peace*. Garland, New York
Margolin J-C 1978 *Guerre et paix dans la pensée d'Erasme*. Paris
Phillips M M 1980 *Erasmus on his Times*. Cambridge University Press, Cambridge

GARRETT L. MCAINSH

Ethics in the Post-industrialized and Informationalized Society

1. Introduction: Emergence of a New Society

A silent revolution has been going on. A new society has been taking its shape in the latter half of the 20th century in the so-called modern industrialized countries. It came to be called a 'post-industrial society' or 'informationalized (information) society' or 'knowledge society.' Even though the nature and implication of this change is very radical and far-reaching, the process of change has not been recognized as such. In this sense, it is a silent revolution, it is silent, because it is not turbulent and dramatic. It is a revolution, because it is changing the quality of life of people and society. Even then, people are very slow to catch up with and adjust themselves to this drastic change of society.

The 'information(-alized) society,' which is well under way these days will bring with it, it is envisaged, a new way of life, thinking and communication to people, as well as new ways of management, maneuver and control to society. This pervasive and thoroughgoing change in society can not but raise ethical problems related to it, which deserves very serious consideration. This paper is an attempt to deal with this new change in society and the concomitant ethical problems. It is an attempt to search for a new life-style in a new society.

2. The Information Revolution?

When the modern industrial society was launched through the so-called industrial revolution, a dramatic and turbulent change was seen in the technology and organization of production. New technologies and inventions such as steam-engine of James Watt, power-loom of Edmund Cartwright, spinning jenny of James Hargreaves, water frame of Richard Arkwright, etc.; new systems of division of labor, which made production more efficient; discovery of new materials for production; development of capitalist mode combining capital, labor, market, etc. In the process of industrialization, one could see social upheaval and dislocation (see *Conflict and Peace: Class versus Structural School*).

In contradistinction to the industrial revolution, the present information revolution seems working below the surface, without any apparent social disturbance and confusion. It began at the core of highly developed, affluent society abundant in material production, where a third or service sector of industry was rapidly growing, where the pattern of mass-consumption became predominant and where centralized,

bureaucratic way of management and administration became preeminent in any large-scale organizations, whether business or governmental or non-governmental.

This information revolution, which gave birth to the informationalized (or information) society is said to be characterized by the technological revolution of the three C's, that is, Computation, Communication and Control. Computation revolution is seen in the development of computers and computer-related hard and soft technologies; communication revolution, in the development of various devices and media of communication, which transmit instantly information all over the world, or even to other planetary bodies; control revolution, in the development of ways and means of controlling systematically human, nonhuman and material resources by way of cybernetics, systems theory, game theory and other decision-(policy-) making theories, the formidable shift of power and influence occurs, when the methods of 'control' are developed on the basis of the combination of 'computation' and 'communication' technologies. In an information(-alized) society, the center of power and control shifts, as will be shown below. Anyhow, the information revolution is to the rise of the informationalized (or information) society, what the industrial revolution is to that of the industrial society.

3. What is the 'Information(-alized) Society'?

When we talk about the 'informationalized society,' the first thing we have to notice is that it is a theoretical concept, a conceptual model or in Weberian sense, an 'idealtypus' (ideal type). We should not confuse a theoretical construct with actual reality. Characteristics or elements which comprise the 'informationalized society' are, needless to say, taken up from reality, as it includes other characteristics or elements also. We abstract those elements which we think appropriate to form a theoretical construct, by discarding other elements which are unnecessary to our theoretical concern. For instance, even though Japan is deemed to belong to capitalist countries, Japanese economy as it is does maintain some feudalistic, or even socialist elements. Thus, to conceptualize capitalism, we cannot identify the total reality of Japanese economy with it. For that matter, there is no such thing as a society of pure capitalism, whether it is America or Britain. Of course, we may describe capitalism as a historical category, such as modern or ancient capitalism. But, capitalism as such is a conceptual model created through the process of abstraction, with a theoretical purpose to measure, criticize or assess reality by applying it. It is a tool of explanation and intellectual understanding, the 'informationalized society' is one of those theoretical constructs.

4. What are the Features of 'Information(-alized) Society'?

The concept of 'informationalized society' may be composed of certain characteristics to be enumerated below.

4.1 It is a Society of Excessive Information

Any society can not do without information. Human society has been suffering from lack of necessary information. One always depends upon necessary or available information to make decisions, actions and plans. One wants to share information to carry on business. 'Men shall not live on bread alone,' the Bible says. We may add, man will live on information that proceeds from society. In our present-day society, however, we are almost drowned in the sea of excessive information. Because of its excess, it is very hard to select necessary information from its pile. There are too many books which we ought to read, but cannot find time for it. Though, information is produced in a vast amount, only a part of it is effectively utilized. We are living in a society of mass-production, mass-consumption and 'organized obsolescence' of information. We are chronically suffering from indigestion of information. Sometimes, we prefer easy gossip and gag to serious news or academic information. Soap opera-like entertainment is better loved than debate on policy. Thus, a rule of economics to the effect that bad money expels good money applies also as a rule of information. How to collect and acquire necessary information is now becoming a professional discipline or a scientific methodology, which is not always available to ordinary people. One cannot be sure about the validity of news and information coming from mass media, and has no means to ascertain it.

Scientific information is short-lived and soon become obsolete or useless, thus has to be replaced and supplemented incessantly. Libraries have to complain about the lack of space for stocking books, films, CDs and other forms of information, while information service network of libraries has made much easier their reference services for the users. In this society of excessive information, the problem of how to deal with information will necessitate serious ethical reconsideration.

4.2 It is a Society Whose Economy Shows a Conspicuous Growth of 'Knowledge (or Information) Industry'

The knowledge industry is made up of the economic activities and services which are directly related to hardware and softwares of information, like computers of different types. TV sets, radios, video recorders, wordprocessors, tape-recorders, copying machines, printers, fax (facsimile), different kinds of players, portable telephone sets, records, CDs, tapes, to take just a few electronic gadgets which are familiar to our everyday life, occupies a large segment in our economy. Taken together, the category of knowledge industry will make the largest sector of industry. Special agents of production and dissemination of information, such as various data-base and data-bank services, broadcasting companies, newspapers, advertisement enterprises, press and publication agencies are thriving, credit card business is also related to information service, which has tremendous economic relevance. Economically speaking, even universities, seminars and conferences may be included in this category. Thus, the information(-alized) society is characterized in this category. Thus, the 'knowledge (information) industry.'

4.3 It is a Society Where the Capacities and Capabilities to Process and Manage Information Develop to an Extreme Degree

An operation or computation by high performance computers will be made in a split second, or one tenth of a billion. Capacity of memory and retrieval is also extraordinarily developed. It is far beyond human capability, and beyond our comprehension. The high capacity of computation combined with high-tech communication network will equip people who can possess and use it with unprecedented controlling power. With this new power in hand, people in management and administration, whether of a business or a state, make decisions and policies, which affect the lives of people and the world decisively. Here is completed a 'managerial revolution,' and there appears a trend of 'bureaucratic ascendancy' and the so-called 'administrative state.' In business, capital or the share-holders and labor, or the workers cannot match management, or the managers, because of their lack or uneven command of necessary information. In government, the legislative comes to depend upon the executive in its function of law-making, for lack of necessary information and knowhow on the part of the former. This means a shift in the center of power in society. Wherever information is unevenly distributed, and wherever information is practically monopolized and handled by the information technocrats, there is a difference in power and function of decision-making for a society, so that it can not help posing new problems and threats to democracy. In this way, the 'information (alized) society,' with its new power to control information presses us to check and reconsider the working and meaning of democracy.

Whether a recent development in the individual-based internet communication can be an effective antidote to the above mentioned new threats to democracy or not, is an open question yet to be answered.

4.4 It is a Society Which Effectuates Change in Values and Thinking, in the Course of Informationalization

In the 'information(-alized) society,' commodities are informationalized, i.e., acquired not only functional, material or utility values (this pair of shoes is made from good leather, sturdy—made for long use, and easy to wear.') but also information or symbolic values ('It is fashionable, looks nice, bears a famous brand.'). One's concern shifts more and more from material values to symbolic, image values. We do not hesitate to pay more for brands, designs and fashions. Advertisement or catalogue is a form of information-alization of commodities, while information is sold and bought as expensive commodities. When we buy newspapers, we are not concerned with paper as such, but with information printed in it. That is why we are willing to pay more than the cost of paper and ink.

As information build up a world of images, we tend to make decision on the basis of images, rather than reality. Information creates pseudo-reality of images and symbols, which lies between us and the objective world. New information devices give rise to a world of 'virtual reality,' which makes it more difficult for us to distinguish reality from image, or actuality from illusion. We tend to judge something or someone from his appearance, not from his intrinsic values, or his real features. Imagine, we buy tea. Even though the content is the same in quantity and quality, we are prone to prefer a handsome-looking container, or the one in a nicer box with better wrapping. We easily mistake the quality of tea for that of outer wrappings. In the same manner, to let people to think or decide, as we wish them to do, it will suffice

to change the images they hold, rather than to change reality itself. Information makes people subservient to power and authority. In international relations, usually propaganda war, which is fought by means of information such as images, rumors, ideologies and so on, precedes actual war. Espionage consists also of information-related activities. Information sometimes helps lead to the collapse of a regime or a government. That is why some governments hanged an iron or bamboo curtain to keep information off, or the people under them tried to smuggle inside information into other countries in such forms as 'samiz-dat' (secret books) and 'magnedat' (secret tapes). Governments, whether democratic, fascist or communist, cannot do without secret service, or any special professional agencies dealing with information, such as CIA, KGB and the like. They cost much. Secret money is drawn from the treasury and spent profusely to run them. The practice of stealing secret technological information among business enterprises is also quite prevalent.

In this way, the 'information(-alized) society' will bring change in our preference and understanding of values. Sometimes it adds to confusion of values. It creates new jobs and activities related to information.

5. Information and Personality

Control of individuals through information is extensively exercised by governments and mass media, advertisement agencies and other. They can manage personal data and control privacy. They can manipulate people through the techniques of what is called 'symbol manipulation,' 'brain-washing,' 'mind control,' 'subthreshold effects,' 'subliminal approach,' etc. People subconsciousness and desires are manipulated without any self-awareness. Sometimes, we are defenselessly carried away by these techniques. Or, the private information about ourselves is in the hands of governments. There is always a danger that our privacy is exposed, as our data are possessed and used by government and its agencies. How can we guard ourselves against this process of dehumanization, alienation or the possible loss of our identity and privacy?

Now, let's make some observation of personality structure and its relationship with information. In this context, Freudian theory of personality will be of great help. It says that in human personality three different systems are distinguished: the Id, the Ego and the Superego, respectively representing the instinctive, the rational and the moral part of Self. The Id operates on the 'pleasure principle,' which aims at avoiding pain and finding pleasure. The Ego operates on the 'reality principle,' which enables to think effectively to arrive at the objective truth, truth being defined as that which exists. The Ego distinguishes between phantasy and reality, which the Id is unable to do. The Superego, which is the moral or judicial branch of personality, is made up of the two subsystems: the ego-ideal and the conscience, enforcing its moral rules upon the ego by conferring rewards and punishments on it. The ego is held responsible for the occurrence of moral and immoral acts, because it controls over the actions of the person. Thus, each part of personality in Freudian sense has its distinctive and peculiar way to relate itself with information.

The Id is easily susceptible of being manipulated by information and symbols as it is unable to distinguish phantasy and reality. By its nature, the Id is dreamy and tends to be addicted to wishful thinking and daydream. To manipulate it, the unconscious part of human psyche becomes a suitable target. Information, which directly stimulates it without being noticed by consciousness, is manipulated by the so-called 'hidden persuaders' (Vance Paccard). In this way, our instinct and desire are addressed to directly or indirectly by depth-psychological techniques. That is why we are falling victim to the various commercial advertisement and political propaganda.

The Ego, the rational part of our personality is akin to rational information such as scientific knowledge, technical knowhow, factual data, computer-processed information and so on, which make the Ego cope with reality by accommodating to it or by asserting mastery over it. The Ego is the executive of the personality. It is rather easier for it to live a personal life according to the reality principle, but, it is far more difficult to exercise this function properly in a wider social setting, such as the state, or international society, because rational information is not always available to individuals. The Ego has not been trained and educated sufficiently in this field, and most of the necessary technical information is mainly owned or monopolized by the technocrats such as governmental bureaucrats and business managers. Here again, our rational part is managed by the technocrats and falls victim to a superior power who can command the flow of information. Both the Id and the Ego are passively manipulated and managed. Moreover, the Ego, when unable to master danger realistically, so often tends to use the so-called 'defense mechanisms of the Ego,' such as repression, projection, reaction formation, regression, fixation, etc., which deny, falsify, or distort reality, and accordingly impede the development of personality.

The Superego, the moral and judicial branch of personality, is said to develop in the child by assimilating its parents' moral standards of good and bad, and then internalize the moral authority of parents, thus forming the ego-ideal and the conscience, as mentioned above. But, unfortunately today, the moral standards of the parents are not always well established, and remain weak and ambiguous. The moral standards transmitted to or implanted in the child are also weak and ambiguous. Or, think of the case of the parents whose moral authority and standards are ideology-bound or fundamentalist-oriented. With this immature Superego, which so often falls victim to moral anarchy and looseness, or fundamentalist, dogmatic or ideological bigotry, how can the holder of this personality control the wanton Id, in cooperation with the Ego, which tends to be weakened by defense mechanisms.

In the present-day society, personality, with its three branches of the Id, the Ego, and the Superego, cannot cope with the flood of information, so as to deep the integrity of personality. In the 'information (-alized) society,' human person as such is menaced by the loss of humanity and identity. Thus, very urgent ethical problems arise, which demand our attention and solution.

6. *Ethics in the Context of the 'Information (-alized) Society'*

Our ethical and moral question is: How to remain human and behave humanly in the 'information (alized) society'? To answer it, we have to distinguish several facets of ethics in relation to this question.

First, on the level of each individual person, we have to reconsider the problem of how to be free from being a passive object of mass manipulation and social management. Without noticing it, we tend to be the target of manipulation in our instinctual drives and desires, which seek instant satisfaction in the 'consumption-oriented' society. We need to strengthen our power of self-control by establishing the 'inner-directedness' in the sense of David Riesmann's. We need to hold some transcendental ethical or religious belief-system, which gives us ethical directives and decisions in the context of new social situations. Lacking in some integrative faith or belief, whether religious or non-religious, we cannot participate in the work of making society humane, rejecting undue demands of pleasure-seeking desires. Also, we should not remain a silent beneficiary of the so-called 'democracy from above,' who becomes, to tell the truth, a mere object of social management.

Inflexible political ideology or dogmatic religious fundamentalism can not perform this task. How to train and nurture this kind of personality with the power of self-control is an urgent task of education.

We are assuming different social roles in society, our ethical judgement in organizations and groups naturally differ from that in our personal realm. For instance, we can be benevolent in our personal life, willing to sacrifice our interests for others. In social life, we can not so freely do that as we do in personal sphere, because, as a public person like a president of a business organization, or the state, we have to be responsible to the organizations to which we belong, and to seek the benefit of them even at the cost of others, as a responsible office-holder. The President of the USA can not be altruistic as to sacrifice American national interests for those of other state. The President is bound by an oath, as is defined in the Constitution. In this way, the moral standards in personal sphere can not be uniformly applied to social or public sphere, because one has to take the existence of institutions, organizations, groups and other social entities into consideration, when he or she behaves in or towards them. On the basis of this difference, often a distinction is made between the personal ethics and social ethics. It is, though, misleading sometimes, because it gives a wrong impression as if there is a double ethical standard, one for individuals and one for groups. It is not so. The distinction shows that one's ethical approach towards other individuals in personal sphere naturally different from that towards organizations and groups in social and public sphere. In the name of a business, you have to assert its own interests and fight or negotiate with others. It is incumbent for you to do so, as an 'organization man,' or as an 'office-bearer.' The social ethics means your ethical approach to social entities, or your ethical directive in social context. As Rheinhold Niebuhr's famous book shows, 'Moral Man in Immoral Society' is our social reality, which we can not deny. Thus, ordinary citizens, we have responsibilities in social and political life, while the politicians and the bureaucrats are responsible in a specific way as professionals. They have powers and authorities over the destiny of ordinary citizens. As Max Weber pointed out, the politician's responsibility is to be defined not in terms of 'Gesinnungsethik' (ethics justifying an act by its good motive), but 'Verantwortungsethik' (ethics responsible for the consequences of what has been done), that is, no excuse for the results. The special moral requirements for the politicians and the bureaucrats can be made legally bound upon them. Thus, in the sphere

of professional ethics and the ethical requirements for the social institutions and other entities, an ethical approach has to be combined with a legal approach to regulate the behaviors of social collectives effectively, while in personal sphere, the ethical and the legal are in contradistinction, because the former works spontaneously, and the latter compulsorily.

Anyhow, they, the technocrats of information (-alized) society have to be trained in the democratic and humanitarian values, so that they deal with people not as the objects of their manipulation and management, but as the subjects to be served, and to cooperate with.

7. Concluding Remarks

The development of information(-alized) society makes the world smaller and smaller. Life together among the peoples of the globe as well as between humans and nature is an unavoidable requirement for the peace of the world in the 21st century. For better or worse, the trend towards the information(-alized) society will be a predominant feature of the 21st century. Without becoming pessimists or optimist, we have to face the ongoing challenges of the 'information society' realistically, with hope, and hope is always with faith and love.

Bibliography

Bell D 1973 *The Coming of Post-Industrial Society*. Basic Books, NY

Brown J 1963 *Techniques of Persuasion: From Propaganda to Brainwashing*. Penguin Books, Baltimore

Fromm E 1977 *The Sane Society*. A paperback edition, Fawcett

Galbraith J K 1967 *The New Industrial State*. Boston, Houghton Mifflin,

Geenberger M (ed.) 1962 *Computers and the World of the Future*. MIT, Cambridge

Gould Jay M 1962 *The Technical Elite*. Augustus M. Kelley, NY

Hall S 1955 *A Primer of Freudian Psychology*. A Mentor Book, NY

Machlup F 196? *Knowledge Industry*. Princeton

Mount Jr E 1990 *Professional Ethics in Context*. Westminster/ John Knox Press

Packard V 1957 *The Hidden Persuaders*

Packard V 1977 *The People Shapers*

Playford, MacCoy 1967 *Apolitical Politics*

Riesman D 1950 *The Lonely Crowd: A Study of the Changing American Character*. Weber, Max, Politik also Beruf 1919

Iisaka Y 1968 *Perspective on the Contemporary Society*. NHK Books, Tokyo

Iisaka Y 1983 Information society and democracy. In: Iisaka et
al., (ed.) *Parliamentary Democracy*. Gakuyoushobou,
Tokyo

Iisaka Y 1987 Hyper-information society and democracy. In:
Iisaka et al., (ed.) *Information and Democracy*. Gakuy-

oushobou, Tokyo

Iisaka Y 1990 Management and democracy. In: *Management
and Democracy*

YOSHIAKI IISAKA

Ethnic Conflict and International Relations

One of the most striking features of contemporary global politics is the prevalence of bitter and protracted ethnic conflict. It has afflicted all types of regimes on all continents, though not with the same intensity. Gurr (1993) has estimated that 75 percent of the 127 largest states had at least one politicised minority at the start of this decade. Twenty-nine of these states were in sub-Saharan Africa, fifteen in Asia and five in the USSR and Eastern Europe. The political fragmentation in the Balkans and the former Soviet Union since 1991 has undoubtedly added to the total for the last of these regions. Gurr also reported in the same study that there are between 3,000 to 5,000 nations in the world and 575 potential nation states. As there are under 200 states at present there remains a very high possibility that ethnic conflict will continue to bedevil international politics for the foreseeable future.

Societies have always been influenced by ethnic factors in the way they relate to the world. Think, for example, of the city states of classical Greece, who had a clear sense of their own 'Greekness' and contrasted this with the 'barbarians' who lived around them. This ethnic factor exists when a group of people believe themselves to be a distinct community because of a unique culture (see *Jingoism*). Smith (1991 p. 21) argues that in addition to a distinct culture an 'ethnie' also requires a collective proper name, a myth of common ancestry, shared historical memories, an association with a specified homeland and a sense of solidarity for significant sectors of the population.

However, it was the emergence of the ideology of nationalism at the end of the eighteenth century which turned the fact of ethnic difference into the major political principle that all nations were entitled to self-determination. Indeed, against the pressures produced by the industrial revolution (Gellner 1983) and the impact of the French Revolution, the legitimacy of individual states was more and more judged against this ideal of national self-determination. Smith (1991 p. 74) has set out the core doctrine of nationalism: the world is divided into nations, each with its own individuality, history and destiny; the

nation is the source of all political and social power, and loyalty to the nation overrides all other allegiances; human beings must identify with the nation if they want to be free and realise themselves; nations must be free and secure if peace and justice are to prevail in the world (see *Nationalism*).

It was inevitable that this would have an impact on the conduct of international politics, since nationalism, which presented itself as a progressive doctrine, challenged the existing *status quo*. Concern about the destabilising impact of this new ideology was especially strong in the multi-national empires of Austria-Hungary and Russia, which formed a Holy Alliance in an unsuccessful bid to keep nationalist feelings in check. However it would be wrong to suggest that nationalism leads only to disintegration. It also inspired the unification of Italy and Germany. The reunification of Germany after the end of the Cold War and the ongoing debate about the future of divided Korea reminds us of the unifying aspect of nationalism.

Nationalism remained high on the agenda of international politics at the end of the first world war. National self-determination was embraced by both the liberal president of the US, Woodrow Wilson and the Marxist leader of post-revolutionary Russia, Lenin. This reveals what a promiscuous and accommodating idea national self-determination is. Although the peace treaties that ended this war tried to address nationalist demands all of the new states that emerged out of the defeated German, Austrian-Hungarian and Ottoman Empires contained significant minorities. As a result these states were also required to accept legally binding guarantees about the way that they would treat their national linguistic and religious minorities. The practice of these states was then monitored by a Minorities Section in the League of Nations Secretariat.

The issue of nationalism was not as important at the end of the second world war and most post-war studies of international relations ignored the role of ethnicity and nationalism in international politics. There were several reasons for this neglect. The first was that realism emerged after the Second World

War as the dominant theory of international relations. This emphasised the central role of states and was not unduly concerned about their internal cultural characteristics. The main challenge to the realist approach in mainstream international relations was based around the concepts of interdependence and supranationalism (see *Interdependence, International*). From this perspective ethnicity and nationalism were seen as problems to greater political integration and were, again, not seen as crucial aspects of international relations. Second, as the Second World War gave way to the Cold War the international political system divided into two competing ideological camps, each based around one of the two superpowers. Although we have noted how liberals and Marxists have both espoused nationalist ideas, neither ideology views national self-determination as an end in itself, rather it is viewed as a means to another end; either individual freedom or the victory of the proletariat. Both, in fact, downplay the significance of nationalism in human affairs.

A third factor was the general revulsion against nationalism because of the excesses of Nazism. Of course, Nazi ideology was only one variant of nationalist thinking, heavily impregnated with racist thinking and vulgar social Darwinist ideas about the survival of the fittest and natural selection. Nonetheless fascism also contributed to the sense that nationalism was a problem to be overcome. This blinded commentators to some of the more positive aspects of nationalism such as the defence of culture and the way it could mobilize people to seek liberation from oppressive foreign rule. We find this in the wave of anti-colonial struggles that emerged in the 1950s and 1960s.

The neglect of nationalism was also found at the United Nations, which decided early in its history that it was going to downplay the importance of minority rights and instead emphasise individual human rights. To this end the Organization deliberately excluded reference to the rights of minorities from its resolutions on human rights. It did establish a Sub-Commission on Prevention of Discrimination and Protection of Minorities in 1946, but this body was, on the whole, unable to further the cause of minority rights until quite recently. The one exception was the inclusion of Article 27 in the 1966 Covenant of Civil and Political rights. This was drafted by the Sub-commission and stated that in 'those states in which ethnic, religious or linguistic minorities exist, persons belonging to such minorities shall not be denied the right, in community with the other members of their group, to enjoy their own cul-

ture, to profess and practice their own religion, or to use their own language.'

As a result of all of these factors there was little interest in the relationship between ethnic conflict and international relations until the 1970s. The only major study of this topic during this period was written by Claude (1955). However, by the 1970s it became impossible to ignore the challenges that ethnic conflict presented to the inter-state system and from this date we have witnessed what seems to be an exponential growth of studies on ethnic conflict and international relations. This literature clearly identifies the main reasons why ethnic conflict has become an important factor in international relations.

The first challenge is presented by unstable multi-ethnic states that threaten to drag in surrounding states. This 'contagion effect' can be seen in the ethnic conflicts in Lebanon (Israeli and Syrian involvement), Cyprus (Greek and Turkish involvement) and Sri Lanka (India). In this way ethnic conflict can be internationalized (Midlarsky 1992). States and international organizations are also forced to make choices about the legitimacy of claims to statehood made by secessionist groups (see *Nonintervention and Noninterference*). During the Cold War the international norm was not to extend recognition to such movements because they would threaten the sovereignty and territorial integrity of a state and because an unrestricted right to self-determination would lead to 'balkanization' (see *Cold War*). Therefore, Bangladesh was the only secessionist state to obtain recognition of its statehood after Indian assistance allowed it to break away from Pakistan in 1971. Other secessionist movements failed after bitter civil wars (Katanga, Biafra) or violent conflict continued (Kurdistan, Sri Lanka). A general distrust of secessionist movements remains in international politics, but there has been some softening of the rigid anti-secessionist position in some conflicts. In the case of the former Yugoslavia, for example, states were willing to extend recognition to the successor states even when these secessionist movements were opposed by the rump state in Belgrade. Nevertheless numerous secessionist conflicts remain to trouble the international system. Examples include Chechnya in Russia, South Ossetia in Georgia, the Southern Sudan, the Kurdish areas of Turkey, several regions of Burma/Myanmar and the Punjab and Kashmir in India.

Where ethnic or nationalist groups are divided by international frontiers this 'ethnic overhang' can produce irredentism. It exists when members of an ethnic group in one state want to 'reclaim' members of the same group living across the frontier. If such irredentist claims are pursued in a vigorous manner it will threaten international peace and security. For example, a Somalian claim over the Ogaden region of Ethiopia led to war between these two states in 1976. Several commentators have expressed concern that irredentism will emerge as a significant issue in parts of the former Communist bloc. Hungary, for example, is sensitive to the treatment of ethnic Magyars in the surrounding states of Romania, Serbia and Slovenia. Millions of ethnic Russians are living outside of the borders of Russia in the so-called 'near abroad.' They make up over 20 percent of the population in Ukraine, 40 percent of the population in Kazakhstan and about 33 percent of the population in Estonia. The state of Armenia claims the enclave of Nagorno-Karabakh in neighbouring Azerbaijan and the conflict there has produced over one-million refugees. In Bosnia the potential for Serbian irredentism remains high despite (or perhaps because of) the Dayton Peace Accords.

Many terrorist movements, such as ETA and the IRA are also rooted in the frustrated claims of nationalists. The activities of such groups continues to disrupt normal life within states and occasionally has a dramatic impact at the global level. There are several state practices which also give rise to international concerns about human rights. These include forced assimilation (sometimes called cultural genocide), expulsion and genocide. Despite the UN Convention on the Prevention and Punishment of the Crime of Genocide (1948) genocidal activities aimed at cultural groups ('ethnocide') have been identified several times since the Holocaust. Cases include the Ibos in Nigeria (1966), the Cham in Kampuchea (1975-79), the Southern peoples in Sudan (1956-72), the Bubi tribe in Equatorial Guinea (1969-79), the Bengalis in East Pakistan (1971), the Ache Indians in Paraguay (1962-72), ethnic Chinese in Indonesia (1965-66), several ethnic groups in Uganda (1971-79), East Timor (1975-97), Bosnian Moslems (1992-95), the Hutus in Burundi (1965-73) and the Tutsis in Rwanda (1994).

Finally there is the challenge posed by the serious humanitarian problems caused by ethnic conflict. Ramsbotham and Woodhouse (1996) have pointed out that many of the most pressing humanitarian crises, including several that have led to 'forcible humanitarian intervention,' are rooted in ethnic conflict. The UN has for some time accepted responsibility for humanitarian problems encountered by refugees through the work of the High Commissioner for Refugees. Since the end of the Cold War the Security Council has also been prepared to designate a serious refugee problem as a threat to international peace and security in certain circumstances. This can then be used to justify external intervention in the internal affairs of the state according to Chapter 7 of the UN Charter (see *United Nations Peacekeeping*). This is what happened in Kurdish areas of Iraq in 1991.

Yet the apparent failures of international action in several of these 'complex emergencies' reminds us that creative and constructive international responses to ethnic conflict can be difficult to organise and implement. The cases of Bosnia and Rwanda have become prime examples of the weaknesses of the international system in this area (see *United Nations Reform: Historical and Contemporary Perspectives*). In fact it could be argued that the present structure of international politics, far from helping to ameliorate ethnic conflict actually encourages it. This is because of the way the international system legitimises the concepts of national self-determination and the nation-state and because the insecurities inherent in a sovereign state system (the so-called 'security dilemma') encourage a suspicious attitude to minorities who may be perceived as agents of outside powers (Ryan 1995). Often external intervention contributes to escalation because it is biased towards one or other side and is based on the self-interest of the intervening state rather than a general concern for the people caught up in ethnic conflict (see *Intervention*).

What then can be done? Some recent developments are worthy of note. One is the re-emergence of interest in minority rights and minority protection. In 1992 the General Assembly adopted the Declaration on the Rights of Persons Belonging to National or Ethnic, Religious and Linguistic Minorities. This is not a legally binding document, and its language is vague in places. Nonetheless it can be seen as an important step forward for the UN. In 1995 ECOSOC authorised the creation of a Working Group on Minorities. This is composed of five members of the Sub-Commission on Prevention of Discrimination and Protection of Minorities and it will attempt to promote the rights set out in the 1992 Declaration.

Another initiative in the area of minority protection is the creation by the UN of Ad Hoc War Crimes Tribunals for the former Yugoslavia and Rwanda. These are able to investigate breaches of the Genocide Convention and to put on trial persons suspected of genocide. After years of international inaction in the face of genocides around the world this is an encouraging development. However, it should also be noted than the proposal that a permanent War Crimes Tribunal should be created has not received the support of some influential members of the UN.

The Organization of Security and Co-operation in Europe has also undertaken initiatives in the area of minority protection. Most notably, in 1992, it appointed a High Commissioner for National Minorities, based at the Hague. The first High Commissioner, Max van der Stoel of Holland, has been involved in ethnic conflicts in many states of Europe, including Estonia, Latvia, Slovakia, Hungary, Romania, Albania, Ukraine, and Kazakhstan.

It is also interesting to note the increased attention that is being given by practitioners and researchers to the pre-violence and post-violence stages of ethnic conflict. There has been an enormous growth in recent years in the literature on conflict prevention, early warning and threat assessment. The OSCE's High Commissioner for national Minorities has been given an early warning function and is supposed to alert the OSCE of any dangerous situations that are likely to develop. This would allow efforts to solve ethnic conflicts to begin before the parties engaged in direct violence. In principle it should then be easier to deal with the conflicts of interest that divide the parties. However political problems remain. How can the appropriate bodies promote early action based on an early warning mechanism? Will states welcome international interference with aspects of their domestic policy? How will the resistance of states be overcome? Even if international action is possible the international community also needs more rapid reaction times when faced with complex humanitarian and political emergencies.

At the other end of the conflict cycle we are witnessing an increase in the number of states that are struggling to come out of ethnic violence. These include South Africa, Northern Ireland, Israel/Palestine, Bosnia, Lebanon, Angola and Liberia. In 1992 the strategy to deal with this was labelled post-conflict peacebuilding by Boutros-Ghali in *An Agenda for Peace*. This document points out that only sustained and cooperative work to deal with underlying economic, social, cultural and humanitarian problems can place peace on a solid foundation. One way the UN has started to address this problem is through 'second generation' peacekeeping in situations of internal conflict. This involves peacekeepers in more than just cease-fire supervision. Additional tasks performed include election monitoring, human rights monitoring and the supervision and training of local police forces. This has led to greater use of civilians and civilian police as peacekeepers (see *Peacekeeping Forces*).

The time may also have come for the international system to re-evaluate contemporary global attitudes to self-determination. There are two strands here. First there is the idea that the international system should be more liberal in the way it interprets the right of self-determination and should take certain secessionist claims more seriously if they meet certain criteria. One study has proposed that five criteria should be adopted when evaluating self-determination claims: the conduct of the ruling group; the choice of the people; the conduct of the self-determination movement; the potential for violent consequences; and the historical context (Halperin Scheffer and Small 1990), Secondly, there is an approach which argues that the right of self-determination need not lead to separation and that there are 'constructive alternatives to secession' for ethnic groups and states (Eide 1993). The best study on this theme has been written by Hannum (1990), who wants to see greater use of the concept of 'autonomy' in the way that individual states and the international system responds to ethnic issues.

Many of the developments identified here may seem inadequate when set against the continuing horrors of violent ethnic conflict. It is clear that much more has to be done if the international system is to develop appropriate mechanisms to deal with the ethnic challenge. Stronger cooperation between state, international organizations and NGOs is required to bring greater coordination and effectiveness to international responses to ethnic conflict. This will only be effective, however, if we move away from a state-centric approach to international politics and if the global society accepts that it has a responsibility for promoting good governance in multi-ethnic states. Although the 'CNN factor' can prick the global conscience in specific conflicts there is no evidence of a general willingness to undertake this challenging task.

See also: *Civilian-based Defense; Communication: Key to World Peace; Conflict: Inherent and Contingent Theories; Role of Europe in the Management of Global Problems*

Bibliography ————————————————

Brown M (ed.) 1993 *Ethnic Conflict and International Society*. Princeton University Press, Princeton, NJ

Claude Jr. Inis L 1955 *National Minorities: An International Problem*. Harvard University Press, Cambridge Mass

Gellner E 1983 *Nations and Nationalism*. Basil Blackwell, Oxford

Eide A 1993 In search of constructive alternatives to secession. In: Tomuschat C (ed.) *Modern Law of Self-Determination*. M. Nijhoff, Dordrecht

Gurr T R 1993 *Minorities at Risk*. US Institute of Peace, Washington

Gurr T R, Harff B *Ethnic Conflict in World Politics*. Westview, Boulder

Halperin M, Scheffer D J, Small P 1990 *Self-Determination in the New World Order*. Carnegie Endowment for International Peace, Washington

Hannum H 1990 *Autonomy, Sovereignty and Self-Determination*. University of Pennsylvania, Philadelphia

Mayall J 1990 *Nationalism and International Society*. Cambridge University Press, Cambridge

Midlarsky M I (ed.) 1992 *The Internationalization of Ethnic Conflict*. Routledge, London

Moynihan D P 1993 *Pandaemonium: Ethnicity in International Politics*. Oxford University Press, New York

Ramsbotham O, Woodhouse T 1996 *Humanitarian Intervention in Contemporary Conflict*. Polity, Cambridge

Ryan S 1995 *Ethnic Conflict and International Relations*, 2nd edn. Dartmouth, Aldershot

Smith A D 1991 *National Identity*. Penguin, Harmondsworth

STEPHEN RYAN

Ethnic-Religious Conflict, Nationalism and Tolerance

1. Introduction

Ethnic-Religious conflict can lead to narrow nationalism and also to international terrorism. The method and scale of the conflict/activity differs from incident to incident. A common denominator of all these conflicts is the destruction of the fabric of society and obstruction to world peace. At the threshold of the 21st century, the world is still suffering from the darkness of various conflicts and problems. The long shadows of conflict, strife and moral degeneration envelop us still. I sincerely hope that we will start a long and fruitful journey of concrete collaborations for peace and restoration of morality and humanity (see *Ethnic Conflict and International Relations*).

2. Ethnic-Religious Conflict and Nationalism

Ethnic conflict, religious conflict and nationalism are very often linked with each other, though not always. So, after defining each of them, I'll speak briefly of ethnic cleansing's history in connection with my topic.

2.1 Ethnic Conflict

Ethnicity refers to the communal identity of people who are classed together by common history, territory, social customs and physical traits.[1] An ethnic group is a group of people with characteristics in common that distinguish them from most of other people of the same society. Such people have ties of ancestry, culture, language, nationality, race, or religion, or a combination of these things.

Ethnic groups can bring variety and richness to a society by introducing their own ideas, culture and ways of life. But their clinging to their old values and customs too tightly can also threaten national unity.

When neighboring ethnic groups dislike and distrust one another, these feelings often lead to ethnic conflict, violence among groups and even full-scale war. Both World War I and II had started as local conflicts that "escalated" into global struggles.[2]

Ethnic conflict is a world phenomenon. For example, the recurrent hostilities in Northern Ireland, Chad and Lebanon; secessionist warfare in Iraq, Myanmar, Nigeria, the Philippines and Sudan; ethnic riots in India and Sri Lanka; and the terrible human tragedy in Rwanda and Bosnia; and, so on.[3]

Ethnic conflict is a recurrent phenomenon. It can be occasional by various circumstances. One of them is the international environment. Often overshadowed by international warfare and masked by wartime alliances, ethnic allegiances are usually revived by the wartime experience which could emerge again soon afterward, as they did after the First and Second World Wars. In their periodic reemergence, ethnic sentiments have been supported by the widespread diffusion of the doctrine of "national self-determination" (see *Self-determination*). The process was repeated after World War II, with the termination of colonial control in Asia and Africa.

In divided societies, ethnic conflict is at the center of politics. Ethnic divisions pose challenge to the cohesion of states and sometimes to peaceful relations amongst states. Ethnic conflict strains the bonds that sustain civility and is often at the root of violence that results in looting, killing, homelessness, and the flight of so many people.

2.2 Religious Conflict

The world's major religious conflict is between Christianity and Islam. It has caused political conflicts and wars on many occasions.

The conflicts between Christians and Muslims

have been going on for 1300 years. Let me describe some main conflicts.

From the 11th to the 13th century, the Crusaders attempted with temporary success to bring Christianity and Christian rule to the Holy Land.

From the 14th to the 17th century the Ottoman Turks reversed the balance and extended their sway over the Middle East and the Balkans.[4] In the 19th and the 20th centuries as the Ottoman power declined, Britain, France and Italy established Western control over most of North Africa and the Middle East. After World War II, the West began to retreat and the colonial empires disappeared.[5] Arab nationalism and Islamic fundamentalism manifested themselves. A number of military interactions have occurred since.

The core of those military interactions stems from religious conflict. Actually, Christians and Muslims acknowledge common roots, along with Jews, in the faith of Abraham, Sarah and Hagar. Both Christians and Muslims believe that God is ever inclined toward Humankind in mercy and justice (see *Christianity; Islam*). The two faiths have different doctrines, but they agree that the proper human response to the Almighty is a life of humble response, including repentance, faith and good works.[6] Distorted by the wrong teachings and misunderstandings, these proper human responses due less to the Almighty God than to temporal leaders reinforces the religious conflict. It is a tragedy that the religious conflicts led by temporal leaders are deeply rooted in many areas of the world. In many ways, religion has been a cover for greed and political corruption.[7] This also feels the religious conflict.

2.3 Nationalism

Nationalism can be defined as a people's sense of belonging together as a nation. It also includes such feelings as loyalty to the nation, pride in its culture and history, and desire for national independence (see *Nationalism*).

Since the mid-1700's nationalism has become an important force in international relations. It has helped change the map of Europe several times in the 1800's. It has also transformed Asia and Africa since the end of World War II by the Wilsonian espousal of the doctrine of national self-determination.

Effects of nationalism can be both good and bad. Nationalism gives people a sense of belonging and pride, and also a willingness to make sacrifices for their country. But it also produces rivalry, tension and strife between nation-states. Extreme nationalism may result in self narrowness, ethnic hatred and persecution of minority groups. As physical contact increases among peoples of different social, cultural and religious origins, misunderstandings and conflicts often break out into open hostilities and bloodshed. These circumstances distort nationalism and cause it to develop negatively.

2.4 Human Tragedy

When nationalism is so closely linked with ethnic-religious conflict, it usually approaches being a modern religion. It contains quasi-spiritual aspects that lend in "extremis" manifestations of a desire to "purify" the nation of "alien" groups.

There have been so many "ethnic cleansings" in the world. The worst case seems to be the fact that about six million European Jews were massacred by the Nazis between 1933 and 1945.

Unspeakably terrible scenes of ethnic cleansing happened in Bosnia. The Bosnian Serbian force's military operations against the Muslim civilians must come to an end. To help solve the tragedy in Bosnia, it is necessary for us to understand some part of the historical antecedents of the former Yugoslavia.

In 1941, Croatian nationalists carried out massacres of Serbian civilians in a Nazi puppet state comprising most of today's Croatia and Bosnia. Those nationalists regarded Croatia's more than 2 million Serbs as a threat to national integrity. In August 1941 in the small Bosnian town of Sanski Most, 2,000 local Serbs were killed in three days of execution. In other villages Serbians were rounded up and burned in their churches. Those trying to escape were gunned down.[8]

The extermination of Serbs was part of a wider campaign led by the Nazi government and its allies. It is estimated that they killed about 750,000 Serbs.[9]

When the Croatian army surrendered in May 1945, the British troops promptly turned over their prisoners to Marshal Josip Tito's partisans.

Some 5,000 Croatians were shot to death just within the borders of Slovenia. Over the next few days an additional 40,000 were killed by Serbians. Such was the Serbian revenge.[10]

Since March 1991, the violent clashes have been taking place again in the former Yugoslavia. Two axes began to emerge again, one dressed in the garb of Eastern Orthodoxy, one veiled in Islamic raiment. The two axes have been hardening as an ethnic and religious war in Bosnia.[11] Massive population transfers have swelled as fighting intensifies among Yugoslavia's various factions. For the past years some thousands of people including many civilians and children have been killed. The number of displaced persons and refugees has exceeded a few million.

It is estimated that 30,000-50,000 Muslim women were raped by Serbian troops who also killed so many other Muslim civilians in Bosnia. On July 1995, over 40,000 Bosnian Muslim women, children and old people were banished from the safe area of Srebrenica and young men of that area were taken away to unknown places by Serbian forces.

Discriminations and prejudices provide the thread that ties together the history of ethnic-religious conflict and ethnic cleansing.

In the former Yugoslavia, too, bigotry has fueled the fighting on all sides. While acknowledging that Croats have a higher standard of living, Serbs may dismiss them as a submissive people who willingly served strong Austrian or German masters. Likewise, Serbs may regard Bosnian Muslims as descendants of Slavic "turncoats" who converted to Islam under Turkish rule. In contrast, Serbs believe that they are a heroic, independent and virile race. They were among the first to throw off 400 years of Ottoman Turkish domination.[12] These historic feats and Serbia's well-established claims to statehood entitle it to lead the other Slavic peoples, who in turn regard the Serbs as domineering people seeking continually to impose their will and to infuse disgust into their relationships with other peoples.[13]

Surely, these kinds of discrimination, prejudice and bigotry have fueled the ethnic-religious violence in the former Yugoslavia. It is a terrible human tragedy. All possible concerted measures of international communities must be taken into action to end the violence in Bosnia as well as in other parts of the world.

3. Tolerance and Remedy

We, the members of the Global Village need to be continually educated and encouraged to be tolerant to differences of culture, custom, ways of life, religion and ethnicity. At the same time there should be no tolerance toward any kind of violence stemming from ethnic-religious conflict and other sources. There should be no tolerance towards any kind of religion that purposefully destroys the peace and fabric of our society.

Ethnic-Religious conflict, violence and narrow nationalism plague and cripple our morality and humanity. Continuance of such acts blights and ruins the whole democratic process.

The world's main religious conflict is between Muslims and Christians, as I said. The Koran teaches the Muslims the principles for righteous conduct and harmonious life in society (see *Islam*). You can find similar verses from the Bible. As believers of the two religions build their lives in the same general area, they are often affected by patterns of religious antagonism inherited form past disputes and misunderstandings between the two.[14]

The followers of all religions have to seek areas of mutual concern about how to live ethically, morally, and responsibly and to join in common struggles for peace and justice.

I do not mean that all religions should be united into one, but they should strive to gain appreciation of the traditions and good works of others. No matter what religion and ethnicity we might belong to, we should develop friendship with the people of other religions and other ethnic groups. This compels us to learn from each other and with each other. Then we are bound to increase our respect for the people of other religions and ethnic groups. And we will be able to engage with love, generosity and tolerance as we seek to raise all such relationships to the highest possible level of human fellowship and understanding.[15]

Religious persecution has been common in the history of civilization.[16] Policies and practices must insure the right of every religion to exercise its faith free,[17] so far as its doctrine and practices do not harm the law and peace of the society and nation where it exists. All kinds of anti-Semitic, anti-Islamic, anti-Hindu, anti-Buddhistic, anti-Christian and all other anti-religion's attitudes should be stopped and eliminated. We cannot restore morality and humanity so long as religions and ethnic groups stand against one another avoiding contact and mutually beneficial relationships.

I've met thousands of non-Christian individuals; Muslims, Jews, Buddhists, Hindus, Communists, Atheists, violent ex-criminals and so on in over 30 different countries which I've visited for the past 19 years. Many of them were very hostile to Christianity. But when I showed them my sincere desire to be a friend of theirs and told them about the Person of Jesus, not about Christian religion, they opened their hearts and we could call each other "friend."

By telling you a few Bible verses and one of my experiences, I'd like to suggest to you a practical strategy as a remedy to ethnic-religious conflict. Jesus said, "Love your enemies" (Matt. 5:44). "Greater love has no one than this, that one lay down his life for his friends. You are My friends, if you do what I command you" (John 15:13-14) (see *Christianity; Hebrew Bible and War*).

I've been working with "Worldwide Fellowship at Stanford" since 1987, after working for three years on the pastoral staff of Stanford University Church. "Worldwide Fellowship at Stanford" works for international students and visiting scholars at Stanford University, promoting friendship and building up understanding amongst the peoples of the world.

Religions, politics, diplomacy, human knowledge and formalized education alone cannot bring real peace to our world. The sparks of peace I offer can only be kindled through true friendship. This friendship can even develop into non-governmental diplomacy which might do far greater things than professional diplomats strive for in their dealings.

One of the main tasks which I've been involved with for over ten years is to arrange "get-togethers" over dinner combining seminars with various topics. I usually gather 40-150 international students and visiting scholars at Stanford University, who are from 30-50 different countries. I invite them one by one through phone callings, meetings and mobilizing my student staffers. The participants include Muslims from all countries in the Middle East and other parts of the world; Jews from Israel; Catholics from Europe and South America; Buddhists from Japan and other countries; Orthodox Christians from Russia and Ukraine; Protestant Christians from Korea, USA and other countries; and, so on. Usually several times a year I arrange such gatherings focusing on "friendship."

I arrange also "Inter-faith social dialogue" over dinner with Muslims and Christians, and with Hindus and Christians at Stanford University. It took over 6 months for me to obtain agreement from the Muslim student leaders, Ph.D. candidates at Stanford University for participation in this event with Christians. I had to meet them many times for negotiation. During and after such "Inter-faith social dialogue" and other ordinary fellowship gatherings over dinners, all the participants became so excited and were exhilarated by the fellowship with one another.

This kind of activity should be held as often as possible in universities, diplomats' communities and various international gatherings for us to promote friendship worldwide.

Generally speaking, the people of Azerbaijan and the people of Armenia do not have good relationship with each other. To be precise, many of them hate each other. I have known an Azerbaijan Muslim who has kept close friendship with an Armenian Christian friend for many years. One living in Baku, Azerbaijan and the other in Armenia were sharing friendship sincerely by visiting each other.

True friendship wins out over ethnic-religious conflict and narrow nationalism. True friendship begets tolerance toward the people of different religious persuasion, different ethnicity and different politics.

Regarding how to reduce or eliminate ethnic-religious conflict and narrow nationalism, there can be many excellent methods suggested by great scholars, experts and professional government officials.

However, I'd like to suggest that some effective non-governmental diplomatic bodies should be established, being fully supported in their international collaboration (see *Peacebuilding from Below*). In notable ways, this can be more effective and fruitful than governmental diplomatic bodies alone, eradicating the conflicts in our Global Village. Only the spread of international goodwill, transmuting fear to fair-mindedness, and international distrust to international cooperation, can brighten the hope for peace.[18]

Therefore, I urge and challenge that there should be international concerted actions to organize and support friendship movements to bring about genuine and lasting peace in the world.

4. Conclusion

Today, we are called to look beyond the limited and competing boundaries of nation-states to a larger and more inclusive community of persons.[19] This movement from narrow nationalism to global loyalties requires international law, international organizations[20] offering integrity and sincere collaboration to build the firm and peaceful Global Village we foresee.

If peace is to come in the midst of our Global Village, nation worship such as chauvinism and self-centered nationalism must be supplanted by the loyalty implicit in the declaration, "For God so loved the world" and the spirit of peaceful co-existence.

If you love your neighbors and your neighboring countries, that is more than wonderful. But international peace does not require the dimension that each man must love his neighbor; it requires only that we live together in mutual respect and tolerance, we submit our disputes to a just and peaceful settlement, and we direct our attention in collaboration to our common interests.

I think it is wrong, foolhardy and irresponsible for any democratic state to regard ethnic-religious conflict to be someone else's problem. It is an international threat which affects the whole Global Village. International communities must initiate and maintain concerted actions politically, diplomatically and economically to prevent and help rid ourselves of infamous acts of ethnic-religious conflicts (see *Global Neighborhood: New Security Principles*).

Peace and restoration of morality and humanity do not rest in charters and talks alone. They are on the shoulders of the people with visions, dreams and bold actions. This world needs doers, not talkers alone for peaceful co-existence to come into reality.

I believe that most international problems can be solved by our developing true friendship. True friendship is like a lever. Archimedes, a great mathematician and physicist of Greece said to his friends while explaining the principles of the lever about 2200 years ago, "Give me a fulcrum, a lever and a place where I can stand, and then I shall move this planet."

We should stand firmly on the soil of democracy clothed with moral and human integrity. We can get the fulcrum of finances in international concerted actions. And now, let us use the lever of friendship to move the world to a just and lasting peace.

Let us take our stand to go together hand in hand to bring the torch of peace around the world through true friendship.

See also: *Religion and Peace*

Notes ————————————————

1. Raimo Vayrynen, *Towards a Theory of Ethnic Conflicts and their Resolution*, University of Notre Dame, Indiana, 1994, p. 3
2. Wallace K. Ferguson and Geoffrey Brunn, *Survey of European Civilization*, Houghton Mifflin Co., Boston, 1969, p. 928

3. Donald L. Horovitz, "Ethnic Groups in Conflict," University of California Press, Ltd., London, 1985, p. 3
4. Samuel P. Huntington, "The Clash of Civilizations?" *Foreign Affairs*. The Council of Foreign Relations, Inc., New York, 1993, p. 31
5. *Ibid.*
6. The United Methodist Church Publishing House, *The Book of Resolutions of the United Methodist Church*, Nashville, 1992, p. 607
7. Edward Mnasfield & Jack Snyder, *Foreign Affairs*, May/ June 1995, Volume 74, Number 3, New York, 1995, p. 39
8. Standford University, *Peace Studies*, Spring Quarter 1993/1994, p. 116
9. *Ibid.*, p. 117
10. *Ibid.*
11. Edward Mansfield & Jack Snyder, *Foreign Affairs*, May/June 1995, Volume 74, Number 3, New York, 1995, pp. 102-103
12. Standford University, *Peace Studies*, Spring Quarter 1993/1994, p. 120
13. *Ibid.*
14. The United Methodist Church Publishing House, *The Book of Resolutions of the United Methodist Church*, Nashville, 1992. p. 608
15. *Ibid.*, p. 609
16. *Ibid.*
17. *Ibid.*
18. Wallace K. Ferguson & Geoffrey, *Survey of European Civilization*, Houghton Mifflin Co., Boston, 1969, p. 948.
19. The United Methodist Church Publishing House, *The Book of Resolutions of the United Methodist Church*, Nashville, 1992, p. 553
20. *Ibid.*

KI-SUNG KIM

European Peace Movements:
Rises and Falls 1958-65, 1978-85 and 1990-98

The reevaluation of the European peace movements, 1958-65, 1978-85, and 1990-98 highlights paradoxical "losses" as well as "gains," especially in the post cold-war period. In this article, parallels are drawn between the three periods where it is argued that the peace movements' achievements were matched by countervailing governmental responses. The progressive developments which offered grounds for optimism, are now off-set by the politico-economic globalisation problems, which create socio-environmental tensions, coinciding with destabilising reactive rises of religio-nationalist 'fundamentalism.' The greatest paradox is that the end of the super-power confrontation has fragmented the control of nuclear weapons, making nuclear conflict war more likely. Consequently, the post cold-war peace movements prophetic inspiration is needed more than ever.

1. The Rise and Fall of the Peace Movements 1958-65: Forty Years On

In the 1950's the world had never been more dangerous, yet never before had so many people joined together in the cause of peace. The mass-based protests were a modern psycho-political phenomenon involving virtually every capital and major city throughout the developed world.

1.1 The Rise

The first mass peace movement began in Holland in 1957, and by 1958, the Campaign for Nuclear Disarmament (CND) had formed in Great Britain (see *Campaign for Nuclear Disarmament (CND)*). Viewing the protest movement over the ensuing 20 years, Taylor and Pritchard found striking parallels between the

1958-65 period and the later reaction to the Reagan-Thatcher Axis 1978-88.

The emergence of mass protest evolved from linking three previously separate issues: (a) environmental concerns; (b) weapon technology; and (c) political deterioration of Superpower relationships.

The first two issues are still present, and indeed might be considered worse, as the end of the cold-war, has destabilised the former controls on nuclear weapons, which in response to a speeding convergence of environmental and economic pressures, has made war more not less likely (see *Militarism and Militarization*). In the 1950's, environmental anxieties focused upon the atmospheric testing of nuclear weapons. Forty years later, concerns centre on factors surrounding nuclear energy, and the plethora of western chemical 'ecological insults' added by the third world's 'dash for growth.' Garrett has noted earlier and increased rises in diseases of 'affluence' such as asthma and decline in human sperm counts in the western world; whilst Printchard and Evans showed that between 1963 and 1993, strong links emerged between increased population density and cancer deaths, whose rises are partly masked by more effective medical treatments. And of course, demographers are hoping that the world population will only double, not treble in the next 35 years (see *Future of Mankind*).

Weapon technology has changed since the 1950's but after the euphoria of the various arms limitations treaties, the entrenched vested interests of the international arms manufactures have developed their range of lethalities. This now embraces the developing world, to the detriment of their economics, increasing the tensions associated with conflict. Furthermore, there is the paradox of former USA 'Hawks,' favouring limits to nuclear weapons by their support of the Comprehensive Test Ban Treaty, yet opposed by the pacific India who mistrust the USA nuclear hegemony (see *CTBT in Indian Perception*). A new problem linked with technology is the spread of structural unemployment and its associated psycho-social insecurity, as the drive for profit gives a further twist to the spiral of ecological degradation, making millions of human beings 'redundant.' The extremes of this despair has been charted, seen in rises in young adult suicide throughout the Western world (see *Social Conflicts and Peace*).

Politically, unlike the 1950's, when the mass peace movements were triggered by Cold War rhetoric, belligerence between states such as in Africa, the former Yugoslavia and the inter-Islamic conflicts, means war has become regionalised. Consequently the strife is less focused, and fails to attract the moral-

political coalitions of yesteryear, evoking a sense of impotence amongst people of good will. Moreover, the hopes of the early 1990's following the collapse of the totalitarian Warsaw Pact states, the Israeli-Palestinian accord, the end of Apartheid, have been dented, not least by the unravelling of the Russian empire with the upsurge in ethnic, nationalist and fundamentalist fervour, now armed by western manufacturers eager to sustain their politico-economic influence (see *Global Neighborhood: New Security Principles*). Korton argued that 'when corporations rule the world,' democratic political accountability is eroded, giving a further twist to short term economic aspirations which can create serious social instability.

1.2 Lessons from the Fall 1958-65: Forty Years on

Examining the objectives of CND, it is clear that the first period of protest failed in its primary aims. Nuclear weapons and atomic strategies are still extant, even though apparently unusable in such conflicts as USA/UN-Iraqi war—but what might have happened if the allies had received a setback? The fact that the People's Republic of China, South Africa, Brazil, Israel, Pakistan and India now have nuclear weapons, indicates that the world is more dangerous than it was before, whilst the whereabouts of the former USSR weapons offer a potential for nuclear terrorism (see *Global Peace and Global Accountability*).

The reasons for the failure of the British-European peace movements have important lessons for the future: first, its inability to hold the disparate groups together upon the single issue of disarmament. Second, the protest being a moral one, necessarily had to become political, which alienated many of its apolitical supporters. Third, the moral impetus was dissipated by time and was overtaken by other events. Indeed in this post-Cold War period, there is little overt activity from the peace movements, whilst its heirs, with every justification, echo their 'protest maker' forbears in their ecological concerns.

Is it too soon to draw conclusions about the 1980's and 1990's? The question is will the earlier anxiety and activity be replaced by apathy and inertia as before, as the 'threat' to peace appears more diffuse, and the rising socio-economic insecurity, allied to disproportionate media influence of neo-liberal capitalism, makes protest far more difficult. This despite more overt security service violence, corruption and sleaze, which has seeped into public consciousness, but the stakes are high and the vested interests ever more persuasive, seen in their control of the public media. This success is graphically portrayed by the majority of USA citizens appearing to be unaware of the chronic human rights abuses in Latin America, yet expressing sincere concern about Asia. The political expertise, devoted to maintaining the citizen's "obedience to authority," is perhaps the key target for the peace movements and their natural allies, the 'Greens,' to demonstrate the inter-relationship of economic and environmental degradation, war, and human rights abuse (see *Green Security*). The many psycho-political pressures which block such awareness can be overcome, if the peace movements learn from their successes and the self-inflicted paradoxical defeats.

2. Peace Movements: Their Achievements and the Paradoxical Defeats

Whilst the macro-socioeconomic factors inherent in war are taken as self-evident, it is necessary to concentrate upon the psycho-political contributory causes. The first and most important lesson is that the many successes of the peace movements have been paralleled by reactive processes that have had paradoxical results. This action-reaction led to the first fundamental unintended paradoxical defeat; in pursuit of a moral objective, the peace movement appeared to question the political sovereignty of the state. Mass antinuclear movements, almost by definition, functioned outside the normal political channels. Consequently, they appealed directly to the citizen above the head of governments, challenging the state's notion of pro bono publica, what is best for the public good.

This article will examine, albeit schematically, ten of the major achievements of the peace movements and will show that most progressive achievement created its own counter process and opposition which need to be relearned in the post-Cold War period in order to continue to contribute to the moral leadership of an endangered world.

2.1 The Achievements

Perhaps the greatest achievement of the peace movements was raising public awareness of nuclear issues across international boundaries, cultures, and creeds. Thus, the CND symbol is recognizable in Red Square, Moscow, and Time Square, New York. Even today, young Europeans after unemployment, "rank Peace, Human Rights and Freedom of the Individual, top of their list of concerns" for the world.

The paradoxical effect has been, however, to create a counter-reaction from governments, and in order not to "lose face," have begun to erode civil freedoms.

The peace movements precipitated a fundamental

political debate. Previously, nuclear weapons were matters to be discussed by "experts," but governments are no longer immune from questions on defense. And whole generations, across the former superpower blocks, have never been more aware and cautious about matters nuclear.

The peace movements' breakthrough has, unfortunately, been matched by an improved ability of the state to deal with this perceived threat. As Pilger shows, governments control of the media has trivialized, and, at times, distorted evidence to influence public opinion. To some extent, western governments have used the existence of the "debate" to legitimize their fundamentally anti-peace stance, and governments, in undermining the peace movements' success, have contributed to the infringement of open communication, sometimes with quasi-illegal activities.

The peace movements activated the very best in humanitarian and liberal thought, uniting people across political and social divisions, quintessentially appealing to concepts of fraternity which unite our species, becoming associated with the progressive forces in every country.

This has had some unintended consequences. Skillful use of the psychopolitical backlash, as comfortable psychological norms were disturbed, aided governments of the Right. For example, the anti-Vietnam War movement destroyed Lyndon Johnson's presidency, leading to Richard Nixon; whilst the British Labour party's espousal of a non-nuclear defense policy, assisted Margaret Thatcher, and after initial gains, the portrayed 'excesses' of the Greens contributed to the success of the CDU in Germany.

The peace movements' brought about an upsurge in internationalism. This gave impetus to the appreciation of the North-South dilemma and for the first time, brought about the recognition that peace studies are a necessary and legitimate area of academic study.

The counter forces, however, have been quick to utilize the antithesis of internationalism, nationalism. Hence, the development of a French nuclear weapon and Gallic jingoism. Ronald Reagan, utilized the dormant nationalism, projecting his opponents as being insufficiently "patriotic," and soft on foreigners, with echoes reaching into the structure of the United Nations. All reflects the continued effectiveness of the aphorism "patriotism is the last refuge of the political scoundrel" (Samuel Johnson).

The peace movements have had a spate of imitatory mass protests which took democracy to the streets, bypassing the usual political structures. They led to a new style of politics which involved the individual in a collective way. They took Gandhian ideas of "passive disobedience" and developed them in the Western Culture, thus providing the West with a radical, nonviolent orientation, which sharply differentiated them from violent revolutionary movements.

Unfortunately, the unintended consequences was that they taught governments how to deflect mass protest by utilization of the media. In addition, the success of open protests led to imitatory movements concerned with a range of issues which whilst having merit, have facilitated the ability of governments to devalue mass demonstrations. The danger is that nonviolent direct action has become ritualized, giving further legitimization to governments, so that protests become a 'safety valve.' Moreover, by minimizing reporting, Governments have pushed protestors to greater ingenuity in order to gain attention and are forced to go closer to the margins of illegality which alienates the uncommitted, and undermining the morale of progressive spirits.

The difficulty is, however, to maintain public attention to the horrific, when their "instincts" would shun such ideas. The peace movements' initial successes can now be used against them as governments, like Julius Caesar, taunt, "The Ides of March have come." but they fail to hear, or suppress the rejoinder, "Aye, but the Ides of March have not yet gone."

The powerful vested interests that link arms and energy have been exposed by the peace movements, and the citizen increasingly understands Eisenhower's term "military-industrial complex" (See *Military Industrial Complex*). The peace movements have developed this awareness, but perhaps they themselves are not yet aware of the range of virulent antagonists who, with far greater resources at their disposal, are active in the protection of their vested interests.

The interdependency of ecosystems and the threat of a nuclear winter following a nuclear exchange, is one of the peace movements most lasting achievements. It gave tremendous impetus to the dissemination of such knowledge, proving invaluable to the environmentalist, as governments reluctantly have accepted the international scientific view that the devastation of the planet is feasible, not just through nuclear destruction, but damage to the climactic systems of the world. The most prodigious scientific body in the United States, the National Academy of Science confirmed the nuclear winter thesis, and that of global warming. However governments stood the argument on its head and asserted that the nuclear winter was another argument to support the deterrent case.

The important political progress aided by the peace movements must not be underestimated. There have

been major achievements by the Green Party, as seen in the former Federal Republic of Germany. Finland, and in Sweden where Party supporters have successfully limited the further growth of nuclear energy projects. Despite set-backs, the message of the Greens can play a crucial role in the development of a nuclear free zone in Europe (see *Nuclear Weapon Free Zones: A History and Assessment*). The peace movements have attracted stronger trade union and church support, and despite the traditionalist stance of the present Pope, his antinuclear war statements are not insignificant (New Year Message 1986). The successes continue and, in the case of the churches, the moral argument is accepted, though some continue to be concerned with what they see as illegal or violent side-effects of the protest movement. The range of authoritative lay and professional groups stimulated by the peace movements is impressive. Recently, the medical profession practically challenged governmental "civil defense" policy by demonstrating serious flaws in the notion of medical care after a nuclear exchange (see *Civilian-based Defense*). While the Special Sessions on Disarmament at the United Nations have been increasingly successful, they are nevertheless, an institutional counterweight to the vested military-industrial interests (see *Global Peace and Global Accountability*).

Perhaps, one of the most important achievements has been the unlooked-for fillip given to the peace movements by the women's movement. In the United Kingdom the courage of the women protesting at Greenham Common airbase was commented upon throughout Europe. The women's movement, with its distinct radical perspective, undoubtedly raises fundamental questions, particularly concerning defense. The extent of government anxiety was measured by the support given to the counter-women's movement, which had the bizarre image of a member of the British aristocracy leading "Families For Defence," urging the benefits of a nuclear defense, whose use over the British Isles guaranteed mass suicide. Governments throughout the West have decried the emergence of the women's movement by appealing to the worst forms of prejudice, not seen since the Establishment's response to the suffragettes at the turn of the century. It is not to be doubted that, if time permits, the progressive breakthrough could well be spearheaded by an aware and politically effective women's movement.

The second most significant achievement was the peace movements' moral strengthening of the United Nations, whose 'Universal Declaration of Human Rights' is no mere catalogue of passive rights but an active assertion for the pursuit of social justice (see

Declaration of the Rights of Man; Human Rights and Peace). The debate goes on and Goodstein has listed a range of international successes under the auspices of the UN on both environmental and peace issues (e.g., cooperation on ozone layers) and, the UN Prevention Deployment Force in Macedonia, and such ventures offer cause for optimism. It is on this international stage that issues of war, peace and the environment are being fought out.

The achievements of the peace movements are considerable, and the developments of the UN and the environmental and women's lobby are the most promising to date (see *Feminism and Peace*). Here, however, is a final paradox—because of their successes, there is a further degree of uncertainty in the power game equation and the peace movements have been criticized for potentially destabilizing a precarious balance. There is, therefore, a dangerous circularity in thesis and counter thesis between the peace movement supporters and their opponents. The peace movements have already taught important lessons, though some are still to be learned. The risk of a nuclear conflict is still considerable. Psychological, political, and economic barriers are almost insurmountable, and we may fail, but the goal is worth the struggle and the reward incalculable (see *Human Security*).

This article ends with a final paradox, as Hobsbawm looked at the age of extremes, registering an unprecedented century of devastation, yet the last fifty years saw leaders emerge who sacrificed power to the people; Ghandi, Pope John 23, Gorbachov, Nelson Mandela; thus progress is achievable. Furthermore, we need no new technology or science to resolve our human problems, only the political will. The structures, such as the United Nations, are there; what is required is the inherent majority for peace be mobilised, as all that evil requires to succeed is that people of good will do nothing (see *Global Neighborhood: New Security Principles*). Let the peace movements alert our fellow citizens to the opportunities for peace that the new millennium could truly bring.

See also: *Global Environment and Peace; Future of Humanity; Peace Building from Below; Peace and Democracy; Peace with Freedom*

Bibliography ─────────────────

Calvert P 1996 *Revolution & International Politics*. Cassell, London
Dorill S 1993 *The Silent Conspiracy*. Heinemann, London
Garrett L 1995 *The Coming Plague*. Virago Press, London
Goodstein E S 1995 *Economics & Environment*. Prentice Hall, Englewood Cliffs
Gorbachev M 1996 *Memoirs*. Doubleday, New York
Guillon M 1995 *Etrangers et immigres en ill de France*. L'Harmattan, Paris
Halloran P, Hollingsworth M 1995 *Thatcher's Gold*. Simon & Schuster, London
Hobsbawm E 1995 *Age of Extremes: The Shorter 20th Century 1914-91*. Abacus, London
Korton D C 1995 *When Corporations Rule the World*. Earthscan, London
McFate K, Lawson R, Wilson J 1995 *Poverty, Inequality & the Future of Social Policy—Western Sates in the New World Order*. Sage, New York
Pilger J 1998 *Hidden Agendas*. Vintage Press, London
Pritchard C 1995 *Suicide the Ultimate Rejection*. Open University Press, Buckingham
Pritchard C, Evans B 1997 Population density & cancer mortality in the Western world 1963-1993. *Public Health* 111. *J. Royal Society of Public Health*
Simpson J 1986 *The Independent Nuclear State: The United States and Britain and the Military Atom*. Macmillan, Basingstoke
Taylor R, Pritchard C 1982 *The Protest Makers: The British Anti-nuclear Movement—Twenty Years On*. Pergamon Press, Oxford
Taylor R 1988 *Against the Bomb*. Oxford University Press, Oxford
Wittner L S 1993 *One World or None: The Struggle Against the Bomb*, Vol 1. Stanford University Press, Stanford

COLIN PRITCHARD

European Political Community

The European Political Community (EPC) refers to the political cooperation between the member states of the European Community. This EPC system was intergovernmental and was to run in parallel with the treaty system. After the Treaty on European Union in Maastricht in December 1991, it has further evolved to a Common Foreign and Security Policy (CFSP).

Just as the creation of the United Nations was meant to prevent the collapse of international relations that could result in a new world war (Archer 1983), the European Community (EC) and European political cooperation after the Second World War aimed at realizing a new pattern of relationships between Western European countries and to contribute to the establishment of an area of peace in Europe.

The first attempt to create a European Political Community was made in the 1950s. The situation of Cold War (see *Cold War*) and confrontation between East and West in Europe after the partition of Germany into two states incited the six member states of the European Coal and Steel Community (ECSC) to sign the treaty for a European Defense Community (EDC) (May 27, 1952). The aim of the treaty was to integrate the armed forces of Western Europe into a European framework and especially to make the rearmament of the then Federal Republic of Germany acceptable to the Western European countries with whom it had been at war in 1914 and 1940. But an integrated European army was unthinkable without a political structure which should control, direct, and legitimize the EDC, Article 38 of the treaty called upon the Parliamentary Assembly of the ECSC to prepare a proposal for a European political entity. The plan for a European Political Community was presented to the six governments of the ECSC on March 9, 1953 and proposed to set up a European organization of the federal type with large competences in the fields of foreign affairs, defense, protection of human rights, and even in economic and social matters (Wallace 1984).

The plans for the two communities (EDC and EPC) were never realized because the French National Assembly rejected them on August 30, 1954. At a time when the tension between East and West was decreasing, France attached very little importance to the European Defense and Political Communities. In addition, both treaties implied the transfer of national authority to European organizations and that was the reason why France was unwilling to accept them.

After the signing of the Treaties of Rome (for the European Economic Community and the European Atomic Energy Community, March 1957), European political cooperation was once again on the agenda with the proposals for political union worked out by a French politician, Fouchet (November 1961). Because of the different views the "six" had on how the political cooperation between the EC members should function, they failed to reach an agreement (April 1962). The anti-Atlantic inspiration of the Fouchet plans backed by the French president de Gaulle and the fear that the political union, because of its intergovernmental character, would result in the dominance of the larger EC countries (France and the Federal Republic of Germany) over the smaller member states, were the most important reasons why the Benelux countries (Belgium, the Netherlands, and Luxembourg) broke off the negotiations.

A new impulse was given to political cooperation

at the summit meeting of Heads of State or Governments at The Hague (December 12, 1969) when the EC countries decided to appoint a special commission chaired by the head of the Belgian foreign ministry political department, Davignon, with the task of making new suggestions on the subject. In the light of the failures of the 1950s (Treaty of EDC and EPC) and the 1960s (Fouchet proposals) the Davignon Report of October 1970, formulated some modest steps toward European political cooperation. The report came forward with the idea of regular exchanges of information and consultation for the promotion of solidarity between member states and the harmonization of viewpoints on international problems.

Following a proposal of the report, the ministers of foreign affairs of the six countries agreed to set up a loose mechanism of political cooperation and consultation. It was decided that the ministers of foreign affairs and the officials of the foreign ministries should meet regularly to coordinate member states' policies and viewpoints. The main institutional novelty was the creation of a Political Committee composed of the heads of foreign ministry political departments.

Since the approval of the Davignon Report, the mechanism of political cooperation between the EC countries has constantly been improved upon and codified. The Copenhagen Report of July 1973 set up firstly a group of European Correspondents which had to fulfill the role of "secretary" for political cooperation and secondly, a special network of telex communication among the foreign ministries (COREU) to assure the permanent flow of information between the Western European capitals.

At the European Conference of Paris, December 1974, the Heads of State or Government approved the decision to meet three times a year as a European Council to discuss matters of political cooperation as well as specific issues of the European Community.

From 1970 until 1974, the basic institutional elements of political cooperation were developed and since then, different member states of the EC have taken the initiative of proposing ameliorations of its working. The report of the Belgian prime minister, Tindemans (December 1975), the London Report of October 1981, the initiative for a European Act by Gensher and Colombo, respectively ministers for foreign affairs of the former Federal Republic of Germany and Italy (November 1981), and the Solemn Declaration for European Union (Stuttgart, June 1983) were all attempts to stimulate the political construction of Western Europe. Even the European Parliament was concerned with the evolution of the European Community and political cooperation toward a Political Community. In February 1984, a draft treaty for European Union was adopted by the Assembly of Strasbourg. In its resolution, the European Parliament asked for the realization of a political union and reform of the institutional balance of the EC to enlarge the parliamentary role in the European construction. At the intergovernmental conference (Article 236 of the EEC treaty) in Luxembourg (September-December 1985), the 12 member states of the EC codified the mechanism of political cooperation as part of a new European treaty. However, the countries of the European Community are still at the stage of political cooperation only in the field of foreign policy and no concrete step has yet been made in the direction of a Political Community of a supranational or federative nature.

In comparison with the supranational character of the EC organizations, political cooperation is an intergovernmental mechanism of consultation and coordination. The institutional place of the European Council is not clear because it holds its sessions outside the framework of the Community, while at the same time it considers itself as the institution that should give new impetus to the EC at the highest level. The same ambiguity resides in the role of the Council of Foreign Ministers which is acting within the EC structure as well as under the agreements of political cooperation.

The Single European Act (SEA), which reforms the EEC Treaty, came into force in July 1987. Its objective was the completion of the frontier-free internal market by the end of 1992. The SEA reasserted the distinct juridical base of the EC and EPC systems. Under the SEA, EPC remains intergovernmental, and consequently subject to individual vetoes and, in case of blockage, unilateral actions. The organizational scheme confirmed the existing practice. A new advance was the establishment of a secretariat, based in Brussels, to 'assist the presidency in preparing and implementing the activities of European Political Cooperation and in administrative matters.' It should also be noted that EPC covered only the 'political and economic aspects of security,' not the military aspects.

European political cooperation took a step forward with the agreement of the Treaty on European Union in Maastricht in December 1991. The so-called Maastricht Treaty is to complete economic and monetary union and to introduce the single European currency by 1999 at the latest. The Maastricht Treaty, which came into force in November 1993, fixed as a Union objective 'the implementation of a Common Foreign and Security Policy (CFSP) including the eventual framing of a common defence policy.'

According to the Treaty, the objectives of a CFSP are: to safeguard the common values, fundamental interests and independence of the Union; to strengthen the security of the Union and its Member States in all ways; to preserve peace and strengthen international security, in accordance with the principles of the United Nations Charter as well as the principles of the Helsinki Final Act and the objectives of the Paris Charter; to promote international cooperation; to develop and consolidate democracy and the rule of law, and respect for human rights and fundamental freedoms. These were to be pursued by 'systematic cooperation between Member States' and the gradual implementation of 'joint action,' where the member states have common interests.

Decision making procedures are intergovernmental. It is the European Council of Heads of State or Government and the Council of Ministers which have overall control. The European Council defines the principles and general guidelines for CFSP, and all decisions in the Council are taken unanimously, except some about joint actions. However, the European Commission participates in all discussions, can make proposals, and has a right of initiative. The European Parliament is regularly consulted but has no direct powers. Once a common position has been defined by the Council, Member States must ensure that their national policies conform to it.

It is clear that the Treaty on European Union has taken EPC's 25 years of experience further by creating 'joint action' and 'common position' as new instruments. However, it does not guarantee that CFSP can work well as an effective mechanism for political cooperation. The remaining issue regarding the future of CFSP is whether there is an emergent identification of common political and security interests that guarantees unity. Effective institutions, alliances and policies in CFSP area require potent military capability, a working consensus on the conditions under which the capabilities should be used, and a credible willingness to act when agreed conditions exist (Nicoll W. et al., 1994).

Bibliography

Allen D, Reinhardt R, Wessels W (eds.) 1982 *European Political Cooperation: Towards a Foreign Policy for Western Europe*. Butterworth Scientific, London

Archer C 1983 *International Organizations. Key Concepts in International Relations*. Allen and Unwin, London

Hill C (ed.) 1983 *National Foreign Policies and European Political Cooperation*. Allen and Unwin, London

Nicoll W, Salmon T 1994 *Understanding the New European Community*. Harvester and Wheatsheaf, New York

Steps to European Unity. Community Progress to Date: A Chronology. 1983 European documentation series. Office for Official Publications of the European Communities, Luxembourg

Wallace H, Wallace W, Webb C (eds.) 1983 *Policy Making in the European Community*. Wiley, Chichester

Wallace W 1984 European defence cooperation: The reopening debate. *Survival* 26(6)

FILIP GOOSSENS

European Union

The European Union has a strong claim to be regarded as the world's most successful attempt at political and economic integration among states. Arising from the ashes of the Second World War, the Union has advanced much further than any other integration project involving groups of countries: it has a strong network of institutions; it has a broad and expanding range of policies; it is the world's largest trading bloc (accounting for over one fifth of world trade) and also has the world's highest level of intra-regional trade; its role as an international actor on the world stage (albeit so far mainly in the field of economic relations) is now well-established; most European countries outside the Union are keen to join it at the earliest possible opportunity (see *European Political Community*).

1. Membership and Distinctive Features

The Union currently has fifteen member countries, with a combined population of 371 million. The original six members of the European Economic Community (later the main component of the European Union) were France, West Germany, Italy, the Netherlands, Belgium and Luxembourg. These were joined by the United Kingdom, Denmark and Ireland in 1973; by Greece in 1981; by Spain and Portugal in 1986; and by Austria, Finland and Sweden in 1995. Any democratic European country can apply to join the Union, which could eventually comprise over thirty members.

The European Union is a unique formation and therefore comparisons with other political or economic organisations can be misleading. It is not a state: member countries retain their legal status as states and as actors in the international system. However, the Union is far more than an association of sovereign states, not least because it now has powerful institutional machinery which, in many policy areas, can override the wishes of individual member states.

The Union does not (yet) describe itself as a 'federation'—largely due to British objections to this terminology—and differs from a typical federal system in a number of respects: it does not have a written constitution, setting out the powers and responsibilities of federal and sub-federal institutions. The European Union's legal basis derives from treaties agreed between member states. Taken together, the treaties are the nearest thing the Union has to a constitution, although unlike most constitutional documents, they deal extensively with policy matters. In large measure, national governments retain control of their foreign and security policies. The Union does not have a criminal law. Although citizens of member states are now citizens of the Union, Union citizenship complements, but does not replace, national citizenship. Nevertheless, elements of federalism have been incorporated into the Union's institutional and policy developments: for example, the Union has a directly elected parliament (the European Parliament) and a court of justice (the European Court of Justice). It is to have a central bank (the European Central Bank) and a common currency (the 'Euro'). If the Union does develop into a federation—a 'United States of Europe'—then it will be of a unique type. The analogy with the United States of America is misleading, not least because member countries of the Union are fully-formed states, with their own distinctive national traditions, cultures and languages.

The Union has an extremely complex institutional structure, due to the mix of values which have influenced its creation. This is reflected in the tension between 'state-centric' and 'supranational' values, in particular between the conception of the Union as essentially a form of close intergovernmental cooperation between states and the conception of the Union as a project involving the transfer of state sovereignty to non-state institutions and policy making processes. In fact, both influences can be discerned in the Union's institutional machinery. The Union's goals, institutional structures and operating procedures have frequently been criticised for their lack of clarity. Even the term 'Union' is vague enough to allow for very different interpretations of the Union's nature, form and future direction. Tolerance of ambiguity, with regard to the interpretation of the Union's goals has possibly enabled the Union to develop at a faster pace than would otherwise have been the case.

2. Origins and Development

The European Union is essentially a by-product of the Second World War. The prevalent 'never again' mood in Western Europe at the end of the War gave a powerful boost to the search for solutions to several pressing problems: the need to find a permanent answer to the recurring problem of conflict between European countries (not least the historic enmity between France and Germany); the need to rebuild and regenerate Europe's shattered economies; and the need to restore Europe's position in the world.

The 'never again' mood also inspired a search for new solutions to the problems of inter-state conflict and economic regeneration. Conditioned by awareness of the horrors of fascism and extreme nationalism, this mood increased the receptiveness of West European leaders to ideas for closer co-operation between European countries. For example, the notion that building a community of interest between countries was the best insurance against future conflict received widespread support. Some ideas, springing from the European federalist movement which had been active in the interwar years and during the second world war, went beyond proposals for co-operation between sovereign states and embraced 'supranational' ideas for the merging of the sovereignties of European countries into a European federation.

Ideas for a European federation, involving the creation of a European government and parliament, however, proved to be too ambitious and were decisively rejected at the Hague Congress on the future of Europe in 1948. Far less radical plans for closer co-operation between governments—the intergovernmental approach—did, however, find a broad measure of support, amongst West European governments. A third approach to integration, known as the functionalist approach, is based on the idea that responsibility for certain functions should be transferred from national governments to 'supranational' agencies. These three approaches to European integration (i.e., 'intergovernmentalism,' 'federalism' and 'functionalism') have each contributed to the European Union's development, although by no means in equal measure.

The creation of the European Coal and Steel Community (ECSC), in the aftermath of WW II, was the first institutional stage in the Union's process of development. The aim was to establish a system of joint regulation over the coal and steel industries of member states, thereby, creating a *de facto* solidarity between the participants and rendering the prospect of war between them unthinkable. With the establishment of the ECSC in 1952, some responsibilities for coal and steel policy were transferred from national governments to a 'supranational' agency, the 'High Authority.' Although comprising only six countries (France, West Germany, Italy, the Netherlands, Belgium and Luxembourg) and with functions limited to two industrial sectors, the ECSC was viewed by its founders as a building bloc to further cooperation. It was influenced by functionalist ideas, although both intergovernmentalist and federalist strands of thought can also be discerned in its institutional structures. An attempt to extend the ECSC model of integration to the political sphere by creating a European Defence Community was abandoned in 1954 when the French National Assembly rejected this plan.

The perceived success of the ECSC experiment provided a stimulus for more ambitious plans for European integration. In June 1955, the foreign ministers of the six countries participating in the ECSC met in Messina to discuss proposals for further integration in the fields of trade and atomic energy. The resulting negotiations led to the signing of the European Economic Community (EEC) and Euratom Treaties in Rome in March 1957. The Rome treaties entered into force on 1 January 1958. The EEC Treaty provided the legal basis for a common market, a customs union and common policies in agriculture and transport. It established institutions and decisionmaking machinery to effectuate these policies. It also included the goal of 'an ever closer union amongst the peoples of Europe,' a political goal which was at the time overshadowed by the economic aspects of the Treaty. The Euratom Treaty provided for an Atomic Energy Community ('Euratom').

The Union's development has been a very uneven process, with periods of rapid growth and periods of inertia. The integration project which started with the formation of the ECSC has twice been 'relaunched': firstly with the Treaty of Rome and secondly with the Single European Market programme in the mid-1980s. Two factors seem to account for these periods of accelerated integration: firstly, they occur when governments become more receptive to the perceived benefits of further collaboration; secondly, there is perception of a common threat (of war in the early post-war years and of economic decline in the 1980s and 1990s). In the 1970s and early 1980s, the pace of

Community integration slowed down. The principal objective of the Treaty of Rome, to build a common market, was only partly achieved. Although customs duties on trade between member states were abolished by 1968, many impediments to cross-border trade remained. Numerous plans for deeper political and economic integration (including the ambitious Werner plan of 1970, for economic and monetary union within ten years) were not adopted.

The re-launching of the Community integration project in the mid-1980s was made possible by a combination of circumstances, perhaps most notably the growing perception amongst the governments of member states that the Community's economic performance was falling behind that of its major global competitors. The Single European Act (in force in July 1987) launched the Single European Market programme, which was designed to abolish all remaining impediments to the free movement of goods, services, capital and people across the borders of member states. The programme was formally completed in January 1993, although much remains to be achieved before all impediments to cross-border movement are achieved.

The Single European Market provided a further boost to deeper integration, by providing a stimulus and *raison d'être* for the Maastricht Treaty on European Union. The Treaty contains an ambitious and wide-ranging, if by no means always clear, blueprint for political and economic union. The Treaty was the result of two intergovernmental conferences ('IGCS') on economic and political union, the recommendations of which were considered by the European Council in Maastricht in December 1991. The Treaty contains provisions for monetary union and for the expansion and extension of Union responsibilities in many policy fields. The Treaty had to be ratified by all member states. Ratification proved to be unexpectedly troublesome in several countries and it was not until November 1993 that this process was finally complete, thereby allowing the Treaty to come into force. The Treaty included a clause allowing for its revision after five years. This led to the 1996-67 intergovernmental conference (IGC) on Union reform. The results of this IGC formed the basis of negotiations for an additional treaty, agreed by the European Council in Amsterdam in July 1997.

The Amsterdam Treaty, was signed in October 1997 (at the time of writing, it had still to be ratified). Disagreements between the governments of member states on a wide range of institutional reform issues within the 1996-67 IGC meant that the new treaty is less substantial than was once envisaged. It does,

however, address several key issues of crucial importance to the Union's development: the need to prepare the Union's decisionmaking structures for the accession of new members; the need to bring the Union closer to the people; the issue of unemployment; and the need to enhance the effectiveness of the Union's common foreign and security policy (widely thought to be one of the main failures of the Union after Maastricht). The Amsterdam Treaty contains some significant changes, such as extension of the powers of the European Parliament and of the authority of the European Court of Justice; new measures to strengthen the common foreign and security policy; new measures to ensure freedom of movement and to establish common rules on external border controls; plus additional commitments on employment, equality and human rights.

3. Structure

As a result of the Maastricht Treaty, the Union is comprised of a 'temple' structure, based on three 'pillars': the European Community (or first) pillar; the common foreign and security policy (the CFSP, or second) pillar and the Cooperation In Justice And Home Affairs (the JHA, or third) pillar. The second and third pillars in large measure involve collaboration between governments, due to the reluctance of some governments to allow the policy areas within these pillars to be subject to the Community's decision-making procedures. However, the Amsterdam Treaty, when ratified, will eventually allow a substantial area of justice and home affairs policy to be subject to Community procedures. Within the European Community pillar, there are three legally separate Communities: the European Economic Community (renamed the European Community in the Maastricht Treaty); the European Coal and Steel Community and Euratom. The European Community has the broadest scope of these Communities and embraces a very broad range of specific policies, such as trade, agriculture, transport, research and development and economic and monetary policy.

Unlike a state, the Union does not have a 'government' as such: governmental functions are spread between several interdependent institutions, none of which can function without the others. The principal institutions are the European Council, the Council of the European Union, the European Commission, the European Parliament ('EP'), the European Court of Justice ('ECJ'); the Court of Auditors and the European Investment Bank. The Community pillar governs the operation of the Council of the European

Union, the European Commission, and the EP; the ECJ, the European Court of Auditors and the European Investment Bank. The European Council constitutes the 'roof' of the temple, providing direction and guidance to the three pillars.

The following provides a brief description of these institutions:

3.1 The European Council is a meeting of heads of government or state of member countries, held at least twice a year. It has a guiding role and is often described as the 'brains' of the Union. European Councils are usually known by the specific place in which they are held (e.g., Maastricht, Corfu or Amsterdam). The Maastricht Treaty requires the European Council to provide the Union with the impetus for its development and to provide general political guidelines. It also pronounces on the broad guidelines of the economic policies of member states and defines the principles and guidelines of the common foreign and security policy. European Councils are heavyweight meetings, at which many decisions crucial to the Union's future are taken. Decisionmaking in the European Council is by consensus. The European Council is not a European Community institution and the EP has no power over it (although the president of the EP is allowed to explain the EP's views at the beginning of European Council meetings).

3.2 The Council of the European Union is the Union's main decision-taking body. It is comprised of ministerial representatives of the governments of member states. The composition of the Council derives from the subject area being discussed (for example, if it is transport, the transport ministers from the member states meet together as the Council). The Council's primary functions are to legislate, set political objectives, coordinate national policies and resolve differences between ministers or with other Union institutions. The Council used to be the sole legislative body of the Community. It now shares legislative power (although by no means on an equal basis) with the European Parliament. Together with the EP, it adopts the budget. It has responsibility for putting the European Council's guidelines into effect. It has responsibility for intergovernmental cooperation in relation to the CFSP and JHA pillars.

The Council presidency is held for six months by each member state in rotation. The Council uses three voting methods: *qualified majority voting* (QMV), where each state is given a number of votes, very roughly in relation to its population size; *simple majority* (each state has one vote) and unanimity. QMV now covers a very broad range of policy decisions; *unanimity* is used mainly in relation to common foreign and security policy, justice and home affairs and certain financial and constitutional matters. The Single European Act gave a strong boost to the use of majority voting and its use was further extended by the Maastricht and Amsterdam Treaties.

The Council is not all powerful. In most policy areas (the major exceptions being foreign and security policy and justice and home affairs), it can take decisions only after a proposal has been submitted by the Commission. It now shares decisionmaking power with the EP in many policy areas.

3.3 The European Commission is at the heart of the Union's policy and implementation processes and performs political, executive, legislative, administrative and monitoring roles. Chief among these are policy initiation and formulation: the drafting of legislative proposals for consideration by the Council of the European Union and by the EP; the development and presentation of ideas to these institutions and to the European Council; the role of 'guardian of the treaties'; the implementation of Community policies (meaning rulemaking, co-ordinating and monitoring rather than actually delivering policies); drafting the Community budget; and negotiating on behalf of the Union in dealings with non-Union countries in economic affairs and in discussions on enlargement (although the results of these negotiations are subject to approval by the Council and in some instances by the EP). It also acts as mediator and trouble-shooter between the Council of the European Union and the EP.

Although it performs 'bureaucratic' functions, the Commission is no mere bureaucracy. The twenty Commissioners, appointed by the governments of member states (but independent of them once appointed) tend to be professional politicians who have usually attained high political office in their own countries. The Commissioners are allocated policy portfolios by the Commission President. Each Commission has a term of office of five years. The Commission's power is limited by several factors: it is not directly elected and therefore lacks a clear democratic mandate. Its proposals can be rejected by the Council or EP. Policies are largely carried out by national, regional or local authorities, not by the Commission.

3.4 The European Parliament is the Union's only directly elected body. 626 MEPs are elected from the 15 member states, every five years. It has been agreed that future enlargement will increase the total of MEPs to a maximum of 700. The first elections to the EP were held in 1979 (before then, MEPs were appointed by the governments of member states). MEPs sit in Union-wide political groupings, not in national party groups. The EP's powers were once limited to provision of advice to the Council of the European Union and also scrutiny of the Commission. Its powers have advanced markedly, due primarily to provisions in the Single European Act, and the Maastricht and Amsterdam Treaties. It now shares decision-making power with the Council on many policy areas. It has the right to approve the appointment of the Commission. It can dismiss the Commission as a whole (although not individual commissioners). It has the right of assent over international treaties and over a range of institutional matters. It must approve applications for entry into the Union. It shares budgetary power with the Council.

The EP is, however, by no means all powerful. It is the governments of member states, not the EP, which choose the Commissioners. It has no control over the European Council. It has a minimal role in the CFSP and JHA pillars. Although it has a democratic mandate, this is muted by low turnouts for Euro-elections and by the lack of media interest in, and public awareness of, its role and functions.

3.5 The European Court of Justice is the judicial institution of the European Community charged with ensuring that Community law is observed. It adjudicates in cases involving European Community law. Cases are referred to it by Community institutions, governments, national courts, corporate bodies or individuals. Its judgements are binding. The Court comprises one judge from each member state. It has a heavy case load. The ECJ has played a crucial role in the development of the Union, by making binding judgements on cases arising from disputes about the interpretation of Community law. Its critics accuse it of a keenness to assert Community law over national law. Although powerful, the ECJ has limited jurisdiction. It can act only within its powers as defined by the treaties. Community law has not replaced national law (although if there is a conflict between them, Community law takes precedence).

3.6 Other Institutions. There are many other important Union institutions, chief among these being the European Investment Bank, which provides financial support in the form of loans for capital investment projects, mainly in the Union but also now to a limited degree in Central and Eastern Europe and the Third World; the European Court of Auditors, established in 1975 and operational by 1977, examines the finances of the Community; the European Monetary Institute (to be replaced by the European Central Bank); the Committee of the Regions (COR) and the European Environment Agency.

4. Union Policies and Policy Processes

The Union does not yet have a fully developed range of policies. Some policies, such as the common agricultural policy and the common commercial policy, are well-developed. Some policy areas, such as health, education, responsibility for pensions, taxation, domestic crime, external defence and foreign policy, are still largely in the hands of national governments. The budget to pay for Union policies is quite small, accounting for just over 1.2 percent of total Union Gross Domestic Product in 1997. About half the Union budget is still spent on the Common Agricultural Policy, although regional and social policy now accounts for around one fifth of expenditure.

The principal institutions involved in Community lawmaking are the Commission, the Council of the European Union, the EP and the European Court of Justice. The Commission develops proposals and is also responsible for carrying them out; the Council is, together with the EP, the decision-taker; the EP also performs scrutiny roles; the ECJ is responsible for adjudication. Broadly speaking, legislative procedures comprise the following: *co-decision*—introduced by the Maastricht Treaty (and extended in the Amsterdam Treaty) allows the EP to share decision-making power with the Council. It gives the EP the power, under certain circumstances and in certain policy fields, to block Council decisions. Co-decision is now applied to a wide range of policy areas within the European Community pillar; *consultation*—in policy areas of the Community pillar subject to unanimous voting in the Council, the Council is obliged to consult with the EP and in some cases the ESC and COR, but is under no obligation to accept their advice; the *assent* procedure gives the EP the right to approve important international agreements and agreements on the accession of new members.

Variations in the ability, and sometimes the will, of member states to implement policy remain a key problem. The principle of 'subsidiarity," introduced in the Maastricht Treaty, requires the European Community to act only when the objectives of the proposed action cannot be sufficiently achieved by the member states.

5. The Union as an International Actor

The Union is already well established as an international actor, although primarily in the field of economic relations, development aid and humanitarian assistance. Around 150 countries have diplomatic missions accredited to the EU. The Union has a vast range of protectionist and preferential trade agreements, thereby operating a pyramid of privileges in relation to access to Union markets. The Commission has observer status in many international fora. It has developed an elaborate network of relationships with non-Union countries and with groups of countries. It negotiates trade treaties on behalf of all member states, with individual countries and with groups of countries. The ability of the Commission to negotiate international agreements is complicated and in some cases weakened by the fact that its responsibilities in this area are shared (by no means always clearly) with member states.

The Union is a major provider of international aid, although only around 15 percent of aid emanating from member states is channelled through the Union institutions. The Lome Convention and the European Development Fund (EDF) are central to the Union's aid policy. The Convention is a formal, comprehensive and binding agreement between the Union and 70 Third World countries in Africa, the Caribbean and Pacific (the 'ACP' countries), committing the Union to a long-term programme of development aid. The EDF, financed directly by member states, channels aid to the Third World. The Union also has an extensive range of trade and aid relationships with the Third World outside the Lome mechanism.

The Union has special responsibility for co-ordinating Western aid for formerly communist Central and Eastern European countries (CEECs). The Union has considerable leverage in Central and Eastern Europe, not least because most CEECs are anxious to join the Union. The Union has preferred to develop bilateral links with the CEECs (there is no equivalent of the Lome Convention for Eastern Europe). The Union operates a pyramid of privileges in relation to the CEECs, based on types of agreement. Association agreements are the most generous and comprehensive, followed by preferential trade and cooperation agreements. CEECs with association agreements (also known as 'Europe' agreements) are likely to be offered membership of the EU, although the agreements do not specify a date. Each association agreement consists of market access, industrial and technical co-operation, financial assistance and a mechanism for political dialogue. Russia and the other former Soviet republics have signed Partnership and Co-operation agreements with the Union. These are wide-ranging agreements, but are less generous than association agreements and contain no reference to eventual membership of the EU.

The Union has developed an array of collaborative links with European countries outside its borders.

These developments are part of a trend towards the 'pan-Europeanisation' of European integration. It is likely that the Union and European countries outside it will become increasingly intermeshed in pan-European relationships, such as trans-European transport and energy networks and pan-European trade co-operation.

6. *The EU's Foreign and Security Policy (CFSP)*

Union member states have operated a very loose, *ad hoc*, form of co-operation in foreign policy since the 1970s (European Political Cooperation, or 'EPC'). EPC operated outside the Community's institutional framework and was rooted firmly in intergovernmental co-operation. The need for unanimity, varying degrees of commitment and poorly developed operating procedures limited its effectiveness. Such co-operation also lacked a treaty basis until it was given official recognition in the Single European Act, which stated that member states would seek to jointly develop and implement a European foreign policy. EPC resulted, according to its critics, in many public declarations, but little action. It had no defence element and little credibility.

The Maastricht Treaty formally established a Union CFSP, as one of the intergovernmental pillars of the Union. The objectives of the CFSP were set out in the Treaty:

(a) to safeguard the common values, fundamental interests and independence of the Union;

(b) to strengthen the security of the Union and its member states;

(c) to preserve peace and strengthen international security;

(d) to promote international co-operation;

(e) to develop and consolidate democracy and the rule of law, and respect for human rights and fundamental freedoms.

CFSP, unlike EPC, covers defence issues and strengthens the Union's commitment to joint action in foreign policy. The Treaty commits the Union to the eventual framing of a common defence policy, which might in time lead to a common defence. It requires member states to pursue these aims through systematic co-operation and joint action in areas where they have important common interests.

The end of the Cold War provided the Union with new opportunities to develop CFSP. It changed the geopolitical situation in Europe, and offered the Union the prospect of a more dynamic and influential role in

Eastern Europe (see *Security and Cooperation in Europe*). Union enlargement and the abolition of internal frontiers also require the Union to develop coherent external policies. CFSP remains unclear and undeveloped, not least because of the different degrees of enthusiasm amongst member states: there are maximalist and minimalist positions, with some countries favouring a unified foreign and defence policy, whereas others seeking only a greater degree of cooperation on external policies. Each country retains its capacity for unilateral action and therefore the Union has not been able to present a united front to the world. Although the majority of Union countries are members of NATO, the Union also includes non-aligned and neutral countries. The Union is still widely regarded as essentially a *civil power*. Its first big attempt to play a role in international crisis management—the civil war in ex-Yugoslavia—exposed the flaws in the Union's claim to have a credible CFSP. The Union organised several peace conferences and sent observers, but the results failed to prevent or stop the war. There were major differences of viewpoint between member states. Moreover, the Union did not have either the will or the muscle to exert much more than verbal and economic pressure on the belligerent parties. The United States and NATO played the decisive roles in bringing the war to an end. The key lesson which the Union must learn in relation to CFSP is that objectives and capabilities need to be brought into harmony.

The European Council defines the principles of, and general guidelines for, CFSP. The Council of the European Union (meeting as the Council of Foreign Ministers) takes decisions to define and implement CFSP on the basis of these principles and guidelines. The Presidency of the Council (held by each state in turn, for six months) plays a key role in managing CFSP. The Commission is fully associated with CFSP. It can initiate proposals for consideration by the Council, but shares this right with member states. Despite the EP's great interest in international developments, its substantive role in CFSP is very limited. It is kept informed about CFSP by the Commission and Council Presidency. It can ask questions and make recommendations.

Under provisions in the Maastricht Treaty, the Council, on the basis of guidelines from the European Council, decided that a matter should be the subject of joint action. Joint actions have included humanitarian aid for Bosnia; the administration of the Bosnian town of Mostar; the sending of observers to the elections in Russia; the stability pact for Central and Eastern Europe (1994); support for the democratic process in South Africa and for the Mid-dle East peace process and preparations for the Conference on the Non-Proliferation Treaty.

The Amsterdam Treaty seeks to enhance the effectiveness, coherence and credibility of CFSP. It states that the principles or strategies for joint action will be decided by the European Council on the basis of consensus, where member states have important common interests. The Council of the European Union will take steps to implement these common strategies, normally on the basis of majority vote. If a member state objects to a decision taken under this implementation procedure, it can invoke an 'emergency brake," involving referral to the European Council for discussion. The treaty allows for 'constructive abstention," meaning that member states can opt not to participate in a project, which they nevertheless will not oppose in principle. The treaty requires the Secretary General of the Council of the European Union to act as the High Representative of CFSP, thereby giving Union CFSP a clearer face. It also encourages member states to cooperate more closely in the field of armaments.

The Maastricht Treaty sought to give the Union a defence role. Central to this aim is the attempt to revive the West European Union (WEU), as a possible future defence arm of the European Union. The WEU, had its origins in the Brussels Treaty of 1948, signed by the UK, France, Belgium, Holland and Luxembourg, a defence treaty initially directed against the prospect of a resurgent Germany. The WEU, established in 1954, was in large measure set up as an expanded version of the Brussels Treaty. Until recently, it was widely regarded as a rather obscure body, overshadowed by NATO and with no clear purpose.

The WEU is not yet a Union institution. Although only member states of the Union are allowed to join the WEU as full members, only ten out of fifteen Union countries have full membership (the rest have observer status). Several central and east European countries are associate partners of the WEU. The Maastricht Treaty stated that the WEU is an integral part of the development of Union and is charged with the task of elaborating and implementing decisions and actions of the Union with defence implications. The Amsterdam Treaty seeks to encourage measures for closer relations between the WEU and the Union, with a view to the possibility of the WEU's integration into the Union. For example, all member states of the Union (including the WEU non-members) will be allowed to participate with the WEU in humanitarian, peacekeeping and peacemaking operations.

The WEU, unlike NATO, is an exclusively European organisation. Following much discussion between the governments of member states concerning the possible implications of the revival of the WEU for NATO (and in particular for the US role in Europe), it was agreed that the WEU's future development would not be at the expense of NATO, a principle confirmed in both the Maastricht and Amsterdam Treaties. In 1992, the foreign and defence ministers of member states issued the Petersberg Declaration, setting out the guidelines for the development of the WEU. It confirmed NATO's responsibility for collective self-defence and delineated its own roles as those of peacemaking, peacekeeping, crisis management and protection for humanitarian operations.

The WEU has helped to coordinate member states naval forces deployed in the Gulf. It helped to monitor the UN embargo on Serbia and Montenegro. It is involved in the Union administration of Mostar in Bosnia. It has established mechanisms for dialogue with East European countries on foreign and defence policy issues. It played a key role in launching the 'Stability in Europe' pact in 1995. However, it has yet to achieve credibility as a major force in European defence structures.

7. Enlargement

The enlargement, or widening, of the Union is inevitable. The Madrid European Council (December 1995) affirmed that enlargement was a political necessity and an historic opportunity. However, obtaining membership is no easy matter. There is no legal right to join. Prospective entrants must accept the commitments in the Union treaties. The Copenhagen European Council (June 1993) specified several factors which the Commission needed to consider when examining applications: democratic stability; a functioning market economy; assumption of the rights and obligations deriving from Community law; acceptance of the aims of political, economic and monetary union; and the Union's capacity to absorb new members whilst maintaining the momentum of integration. The Amsterdam Treaty states that membership of the Union is conditional on upholding the principles of liberty, democracy and respect for human rights.

There are several reasons why most European countries outside the Union wish to join it: for example, to gain full and certain access to Union markets; to participate in Union decisionmaking processes; to prevent isolation; to gain access to resource transfers from the budget; and to boost inward investment. Moreover, the end of the Cold War removed prohibitions on entry for CEECs (and also for Austria and Finland). What is not clear is how far enlargement

can proceed without affecting the effective functioning of the Union. For example, the Union's budget would require a major expansion to cope with the regional and social policy needs of CEEC entrants. The Common Agricultural Policy would not be viable, without a massive increase in the Union's budget, if the CEECs were admitted. Enlargement also has major institutional implications. It will increase the number of seats, and will change the weighting of votes in the Council; it will affect the composition of the Commission, the EP and ECJ.

The Union's strategy for enlargement centres on two key issues: conditions for membership and time scale for entry. It is clear that prospective candidates must adjust to the Union rather than the other way round. Members are likely to be admitted in waves rather than one at a time. The Union is seeking to coordinate implementation of its reform agenda with its strategy for entry of applicant countries. Applicants are required to take positive steps to prepare themselves for membership, such as measures to align their economies with the Single European Market. The entry prospects of aspirants varies considerably. Countries with association agreements with the Union stand the best chance of early entry. Some are currently too backward economically; others remain politically unstable; some have large populations. Some countries may well be offered closer formal relationships with the Union, instead of full membership.

8. Differentiated Integration

The increasingly diverse nature of the Union's membership, combined with differences between member states as to how far and fast Union integration should proceed, has given rise to ideas for 'differentiated integration,' embracing the notions of 'multispeed Europe' and 'Europe *a la carte*.' Multispeed concepts focus on the idea of variations in the *pace* of integration pursued by member states (for example, with regard to participation in the final stage of European monetary union). *A la carte* concepts accept that member states may be able to choose whether or not to participate in specific projects. Multispeed concepts assume that there is a common 'integration destination' for all member states whereas *a la carte* concepts do not. The multispeed idea has been generally accepted as a practical means of advancing the integration process, by providing a flexible framework for future integration. However, the idea of Europe *a la carte* remains controversial, because it would provide countries with opportunities to pick and choose from a menu of integration projects, a prospect hardly likely to add to the coherence of the Union. In reality, both multi-speed and *a la carte* forms of integration are discernible (although not always clearly so) in the Union's recent development. Moreover, the Amsterdam Treaty recognises that groups of Union countries may wish to pursue additional forms of co-operation in some policy fields. It therefore lays down conditions for such co-operation: for example, projects of this kind should involve a majority of, and be open to all, member states; they must serve the objectives of the Union and be compatible with the Union's treaties, institutional mechanisms and policies; and they should be used only as a last resort.

The value of differentiated integration is that it may provide a framework in which the diverse aspirations and capabilities of Union members *vis à vis* integration projects can be met, thereby holding the Union together and moving it forward. It may also provide a framework through which the aspirations of Central and East European countries for participation in Union integration projects can be at least partly satisfied. The danger inherent in differentiated integration, however, is that it is likely to exacerbate the Union's problems of institutional complexity, policy fragmentation and lack of coherence.

9. Conclusion

The Union is still evolving and many issues concerning its future form and direction are still to be decided. Although, for much of its history, it has often been viewed as primarily an economic formation, the Union has from its inception had political objectives. These objectives now embrace ambitious attempts to forge a strong and coherent common foreign and security policy and to equip the Union with a defence arm. Many questions remain about the current ability, and even the will, of member states to achieve these objectives.

The Union has many challenges ahead: the European integration project has yet to capture the hearts and minds of ordinary Europeans; the increasing size and diversity of the Union could place considerable strain on its ability to function effectively; the Union's efforts to become a heavy weight actor on the international scene, outside the field of economic relations, have so far had only limited success. However, the most fundamental original aim of European integration—the elimination of the prospect of war between the participant countries—has clearly been fulfilled, to the extent that this prospect is now unthinkable. The Union has justifiable claim to be regarded as the world's best example of how far a voluntary integration project, founded on the values of peace, democracy and freedom, can proceed. European countries with aspirations to join the Union are well aware that their prospects for entry depend upon respect for these values. Moreover, the ending of the cold-war division of Europe means that the European Union project should no longer be viewed as a purely West European enterprise. If this project remains 'a journey to an unknown destination,' the journey is set to include countries from all parts of Europe.

See also: *Federalism, World; European Political Community; Integration, Regional; Integration Theories; Peace and Regional Integration; Social Progress and Human Survival; Supranationalism*

Bibliography ————————————

Jones R A 1997 *The Politics and Economics of the European Union*. Edward Elgar, Cheltenham

Menon A, Howarth J 1997 *The European Union and National Defence Policy*. Routledge, London

Nugent N 1996 *The Government and Politics of the European Union*. Macmillan, London

Piening C 1997 *Global Europe: The European Union in World Affairs*. Lynne Rienner, London

Taylor P 1996 *The European Union in the 1990s*. Oxford University Press

Wallace H, Wallace W 1996 *Policy-Making in the European Union*. Oxford University Press

ROBERT A. JONES

Evolutionary Movement Toward Peace

Peace is often regarded as a condition solely related to human consciousness. This, however, is much too narrow a point of view. Peace, in many significant meanings, is something that is characteristic of the total evolutionary process, particularly of societal evolution, a great deal of which is unconscious.

The critical question is whether it is possible to divide the total activity of a system into two parts which might be called "peace" and "not peace." Even in the biological system, excluding humans and human artifacts, it is possible to distinguish between activities which are clearly conflictual and those which are not, conflict being defined as conscious interaction between two organisms involving "struggle," that is, conscious behavior on the part of each organism designed to improve its position at the expense of the other. Conflict in this sense is quite rare in biological systems, being almost confined to sexual selection, where one sex, usually the male, fights with another male for access to the female. This actually is a small part of biological activity, most of which is very peaceful (see *Human Nature Theories of War*).

There are three general relationships among organisms in an ecosystems. First, mutual competition, in which an increase in numbers of either of two species diminishes the number of the other. This rather rarely involves conscious conflict. There may be no interaction whatever between competing species. The second relationship is mutual cooperation, where an increase in numbers of either of two species increases numbers of the other. Sheep and dung beetles would be a good example. This type of relationship is by no means uncommon. The third relationship is that of predation, where an increase in predator numbers diminishes the prey, and an increase in prey numbers increases the predators. Actually this is ecologically a rather stable cooperative relationship, leading to the survival of both the predator and the prey. While there is something like conflict between individuals, there is not really conflict between the species. On the whole, therefore, one can say that the vast majority of biological behavior is peaceful (see *War: Environmental and Biological Theories*).

As we move into social systems and societal evolution, we begin to get the phenomenon of war, which is virtually unknown in purely biological interactions. This arises out of the capacity of the human race for very complex images and for communicating them through language to other humans. This opens the possibility for the organization of society through threat, in which the threatener says to the threatened, "You do something I want or I will do something you don't want." Institutions like slavery, taxation, and tribute follow when there is submission to a threat (see *Words of Peace and War*).

War results when there is defiance or counterthreat, which leads to the development of organized armed forces, paid for by taxation or tribute, and organized by propaganda, conscription, and internal threats toward their members. These are organizations specializing in the carrying out of threat through the destruction of human beings or human artifacts and property. The mutual carrying out of destruction by two armed forces is what is usually understood as war, though there is considerable variation in these operations (see *War*). There are wars of conquest, in which the controllers of a superior armed force try to establish control over other lands and peoples. Then there are wars of the breakdown of deterrence, in which threats are defied and an attempt is made, therefore, to carry them out in the face of counterthreat.

Human activities can be divided fairly sharply, therefore, into war-related and non-war-related. The latter might be called "inclusive peace." A rough estimate would be that war-related activities account for something in the order of 10 percent of human activity at the present time. Other conflict-related activities like law enforcement, policing, terrorism, and so on, might bring this up to about 15 percent, leaving from 85 to 90 percent for inclusive peace. This would include virtually all economic activity: the production of goods and services, running households, raising children, having fun, dancing, enjoying art, literature, and so on.

No estimate seems to have been made of the proportion of art and literature devoted to war and to peace. A rough estimate would perhaps put this at about 10 to 15 percent devoted to war and 85 to 90 percent devoted to peace: drama and the novel tend to have a higher percentage devoted to war; painting, sculpture, music, dance, and architecture on the whole tend to be devoted to peace. Because war tends to be more dramatic than peace, it tends to be overestimated in drama and history. Landscape and portrait painting are mostly of peaceful subjects. Music, of course, is usually devoted to harmony (see *Peace Museums*).

Over the course of human history the proportion of human activity devoted to war and to peace has certainly changed, but it is hard to get overall data on it. Because war has to be supported by peaceful activities, like producing food and making clothing for soldiers, the proportion of an economy which can be devoted to war depends very much on its general level of productivity and riches, and particularly on the efficiency with which the necessities of life can be produced. A society that has to devote 90 percent of its activity to producing enough food, housing, and clothing just to stay alive can only devote a small proportion of its activity to war. Improvements in food production, therefore may lead to a larger proportion of a society's activities devoted to war. Adam Smith (1937), for instance, wrote in 1776 in *The Wealth of Nations* that "Among the civilized nations of modern Europe, . . . not more than one hundredth part of the inhabitants of any country can be employed as soldiers, without ruin to the country which pays the expense of their service." In the Second World War the United States devoted something like 42 percent of its total product and employed some 12 percent of its labor force directly in the armed forces, and perhaps another 10 or 15 percent supplying them.

On the other hand, war also impoverishes. There is strong evidence that empire impoverishes the imperial power. From about 1860 on, for instance, the British and French Empires drained the imperial powers themselves, so that their economic development was much slower than a country, for instance, like Sweden, which devoted a larger proportion of its resources to its own increase in productivity and enrichment. There are many examples in history where wealth has created power and power has destroyed wealth (see *Arms Conversion*).

The interaction of war activity and peace activity over time is extremely complex. The naive assumption that the survival and success of a culture or society depends on its success in war, has very little evidence to support it, although there are undoubtedly some cases where this is relevant (see *Theoretical Traditions of Peace and Conflict Studies*). Spain's conquest of a great empire set back its economic development by almost 400 years. It was after the defeat of France by Germany in 1870 that Paris became the cultural capital of the world and Berlin stagnated. If we ask who won the Second World War economically, the answer is almost certainly Germany or Japan, who got rid of their military commitments and were able to devote their resources to enrichment. The United States and the former Soviet Union undoubtedly diminished their rate of overall development by the resources put into the war industry. It would be interesting to know the relative expectation of life of the armed and the unarmed in human history (see *Human Security*). One suspects that that of the unarmed is considerably higher.

The evolutionary pattern, therefore, is extraordinarily complex, but it suggests on the whole that war is an interruption of the evolutionary process and that most evolutionary processes take place in the peaceful sector (see *Social Progress and Human Survival*). This is because evolution primarily is a process in learning. This is true even of biological evolution, where mutation produces deoxyribonucleic acid (DNA) and genetic structures possessing increasing skill over the millennia. It is particularly noticeable in societal evolution, where the development of human knowledge and know-how on the whole has taken place in the peaceful sector. This is where we learned agriculture, most manufacturing, and, of course, science, the very success of which is due to the fact that it developed a subculture in which the principle that people should be persuaded by evidence and never by threat is fundamental. War and the threat system produced the inquisition and intellectual stagnation. It is the peaceful subculture that has produced science, even though science has also increased enormously the capacity for destruction and war.

One of the sources of hope is that societal evolution has produced increasing areas of stable peace, both internally within nations and among nations. Stable peace is a situation where independent nations have no plans to go to war with each other and the probability of war is virtually zero (see *Stability*). This was rare before the nineteenth century. After the Napoleonic Wars, however, it developed first in Scandinavia, then in North America, now in Western Europe, Australia, and Japan, so that we now have some 18 nations stretching in a great triangle from Australia to Japan, across North America, to Western Europe, who have no plans to go to war with each other. This has been a learning process, but to a surprising extent an unconscious process. The conscious peace movement has had very little to do with it. Stable peace arises out of the development of habit of mind on the part of national states, which leads to taking national boundaries off everybody's agenda and mutual legitimation of each other's internal sovereignty, which leads to disarmament of the frontiers. A world without war may well be the result of societal evolution, a process which may be speeded by consciousness, but which has proceeded hitherto largely at the unconscious level.

The global transformation that unfolded in 1985 and culminated in 1989, stretching to 1991 until to date has been showing great transcendence as a part of the evolutionary movement to peace. The dialectical change which caused the repudiation of socialism by democratic and liberal capitalism caused the implosion of the Soviet empire and the transformation of the former member-countries to liberal democracy and market economy. These societies are moving forward to a desired stage of evolution and change characterized by more individual freedom and social-civic rights and duties as well as personal property rights and economic entrepreneurship. This transformation seems to be leading toward a more peaceful world.

See also: *Conflict: Inherent and Contingent Theories; Peaceful Societies; War, Prediction of; Eastern Europe, Transformation of*

Bibliography ————————————————

Boulding K E 1961 *The Image: Knowledge in Life and Society.* University of Michigan Press, Ann Arbor, Michigan

Boulding K E 1962 *Conflict and Defense: A General Theory.* Harper and Row, New York

Boulding K E 1975 *Collected Papers,* Vol. 5: *International Systems: Peace, Conflict Resolution, and Politics.* Colorado Association University Press, Boulder, Colorado

Boulding K E 1977a The peace movement and the dynamics of peace. *Peace Progress* 1(4) (International Association of Educators for World Peace, Journal of Education)

Boulding K E 1977b The power of nonconflict. *J. Social Issues* 33(1)

Boulding K E 1977c Twelve friendly quarrels with Johan Galtung (Review of Johan Galtung, Essays in Peace Research) *J. Peace Res.* 14(1)

Boulding K E 1978a Future directions in conflict and peace studies. *J. Conflict Resolution* 22(2)

Boulding K E 1978b *Stable Peace.* University of Texas Press, Austin, Texas

Boulding K E 1980 The next one hundred years? *Science* 209

Boulding K E 1981 The evolution of peace. *Man, Environment, Space and Time* 1(2)

Boulding K E 1984a How do things go from bad to better? The contribution of economics. In: Boulding K E (ed.) 1984 *The Economics of Human Betterment.* Macmillan, London

Boulding K E 1984b Toward an evolutionary theology. In: Montagu A (ed.) 1984 *Science and Creationism.* Oxford University Press, New York

Smith A 1937 *The Wealth of Nations.* Random House, New York

KENNETH E. BOULDING; PEDRO B. BERNALDEZ

F

Fascism

Fascism is a peculiar type of totalitarian ideology which emerged in Europe after the First World War. The term also refers to the political system based on this ideology and also to a certain type of mentality or political attitude congenial to it. The word "fascism" was used first by Mussolini in Italy. It is believed to be derived from the Latin word, *fasces*, meaning a bundle of rods with an axe inside, which was symbolic of authority in Ancient Rome.

Italy, where fascism emerged first, was under its rule from 1922 to 1945. However, it spread quickly outside of Italy to other European countries, and came to power in some countries—most notably in Germany (in a variant form see *National Socialism*) and in other countries such as Croatia, Hungary, Romania, Spain, Portugal, and Norway. In most of the European countries, varieties of fascist party sprang up. Fascism also spread outside of Europe to Japan and to some of the Latin American countries, with inevitable adaptations to the political traditions and social conditions of the countries where it took its roots.

There are a set of easily discernible common characteristics in the variety of forms which fascism has taken in different countries: a political ideology of militant nationalism, proclaiming the state as paramount, the idolization of a particular leader or political leadership, a mechanism of totalitarian social control including the apparatus and techniques of mass manipulation, and the central control of economy and culture. Fascism should be distinguished from traditional right-wing authoritarianism in that it is based on the appeal to, and mobilization of, the masses and in that it strives after total control of society, allowing little freedom from state intervention in any sector of the society or the economy.

Fascist states have shared common characteristics with respect to economic and social background. Fascism prospers under situations of extreme social dislocation, resulting from economic depression, from war, or from great social upheavals such as rapid urbanization in which there occurs a large and sudden influx of rural population into urban areas, when the traditional political institutions and leadership are seen to be largely inadequate to cope with the pressing issues of the day. It also feeds on the international situation which fosters intense or embittered nationalist feelings. Fascist leaders actively encourage and play on the frustrated feelings of the masses that they are being victimized or that their legitimate demands are not being adequately met by other states. In consequence, fascism has tended to exalt war and to disdain the constraints of international law.

In times of social instability, fascism guarantees the restoration of law and order to the people who feel their status and interests are endangered and it promises sweeping changes to dissatisfied groups. It pledges itself to revolutionary changes in every aspect of life, leading ultimately toward a totally new society, a regenerated nation. In practice, however, it tends to perpetuate, after it comes into power, the existing conditions of society with its economic and social inequalities. What have tended to happen in fascist states are rather political and social changes—changes in the relationship between the society and the state or between the individual and authority. Economic and social gaps between the classes remain as they were.

The theoretical basis of fascism can be traced to a variety of sources. Its precursors are found in the theories of scholars such as Machiavelli, Fichte, Hegel, Nietzsche, Sorel, Le Bon, Gobineau, Mosca, and Pareto. In particular, the Hegelian connection to fascism has been a subject of some debate: while some—both in fascist and nonfascist camps—acknowledge Hegelian influence in fascism, others—again in both camps—emphatically deny that Hegelian philosophy has anything to do with fascism.

However, whatever the arguments may be, theory is not one of the strong points of fascism, although it has attracted quite a few serious intellectuals. As one of its typical slogans, "To believe, to obey, to combat," indicates, it is essentially a doctrine for action, and a reaction against liberalism and the mainstream of the moral and intellectual traditions of Western Europe, namely Christianity and rationalism in the modern age.

Theoretically it was not much more than an attempt at muddling through, a "from-hand-to-mouth" affair, basically tribalistic in nature. However, as it spread out, it assumed a pseudo-universalistic character. Thus Mussolini claimed in the mid 1930s that fascism had become "not merely an Italian phenomenon but a world phenomenon." Likewise Hitler proclaimed that Nazism was necessary not only for the Germans but also for the salvation of the whole of humankind. Such arguments served to justify the militarism and aggression of fascist states.

Interpretations of fascism as a historical phenomenon abound. Marxists hold to the orthodox view that fascism is the "final phase of bourgeois society," the stage reached by the capitalistic societies along the lines Marx had anticipated, in which the ruling classes resort to open repression in order to maintain their position. There are obvious difficulties in the Marxian analysis of fascism as it usually drew its mass support from the lower middle classes, workers, and peasants. That fascism emerged not only in industrialized but also in many underdeveloped countries, together with the facts of postfascist developments in some European and Asian countries add to the difficulties in maintaining a Marxist view with regard to fascism. However, it still remains not only viable but also the most important explanation of fascism. *Mutatis mutandis* it serves a useful function as a basis of rational interpretation of an important historical phenomenon as it is the most comprehensive and scientific explanation.

Some scholars see it as a phenomenon likely to emerge in the course of modernization. As Organski put it, fascism is part of the process of transition from a limited participation to a mass system, and is a last-ditch stand by the elites, both modern and traditional, "to prevent the expansion of the system over which they exercise hegemony." Organski thought that the changing balance in rural and urban populations carries a critical relevance in the analysis of fascism. According to him, there exists a zone of instability, a fertile ground for fascism, when nonagricultural employment is rising to 40 percent and continues until it reaches 55 percent. Beyond that point a society will have reached a substantially modernized state.

Another influential explanation of fascism is provided by the social-psychological approach. It regards the disorganized masses and their collective psychology as the ground of fascism. In the state of *anomie* the masses crave authoritarian leadership. For some scholars fascism is an expression of the defensive reaction of the state against disintegrative forces, corporate elements, and supranational ideologies, which work to undermine the authority of the state. Others tend to explain it away as something which is not basically amenable to rational explanation, as an atavistic eruption or even a bad dream. Still others view fascism as a phase in some of the worldwide trends in politics: a shift of power from the legislative to the executive or from elected politicians to the technocrats, the emergence of the masses and the importance of the techniques of their manipulation, corporatism, and so on.

Fascism collapsed as a major political force after the Second World War mainly because the major fascist countries were defeated militarily. Except for a few cases, fascism survives today only as a marginal political activity in some countries. But it is yet too early to say that its days are definitely over. Almost every society has the potential, whether exposed or hidden, for fascism. Some political movements with radically progressive slogans are said to be pervaded by fascist thinking. With the rapid development of science and technology there is a greater possibility today of the means of mass manipulation and of social control being concentrated in the hands of few. Nobody can categorically deny that if social and economic conditions turn to its favor, fascism might have another chance of seizing power, under whatever name it might be, even in places believed to be safest from its threat.

See also: *National Socialism*

Bibliography ————————————————————

Allardyce G (ed.) 1971 *The Place of Fascism in European History*. Prentice-Hall, New York
Carsten F L 1974 *The Rise of Fascism*. Methuen, London
Fromm E 1941 *Escape from Freedom*. Holt, New York
Green N (ed.) 1968 *Fascism: An Anthology*. Thomas Y. Crowell, New York
Gregor A J 1974 *The Fascist Persuasion in Radical Politics*. Princeton University Press, Princeton, New Jersey
Gregor A J 1974 *Interpretations of Fascism*. General Learning Press, Morristown, New Jersey
Hamilton A 1973 *The Appeal of Fascism*. Macmillan, New York
Hinsley F H 1973 *Nationalism and the International System*. Hodder and Stoughton, London
Laquer W (ed.) 1979 *Fascism: A Reader's Guide*. Penguin, Harmondsworth
Marcuse H 1964 *Reason and Revolution: Hegel and the Rise of Social Theory*. Beacon Press, Boston, Massachusetts

Nolte E 1966 *The Three Faces of Fascism.* Holt, Rinehart and Winston, New York

Rhodes A 1959 *The Poet as Superman: D'Anunzio.* Weidenfeld and Nicolson, London

Rogger H, Weber E 1965 *The European Right: A Historical Profile.* University of California Press, Berkeley, California

Wiskemann E 1970 *Fascism in Italy: Its Development and Influence.* Macmillan, London

Woolf S J (ed.) 1969 *The Nature of Fascism.* Vintage Books, New York

JONG-YIL RA

Faulkner, William

Born September 25, 1897 in New Albany, Mississippi, William Faulkner has achieved the status of one of America's foremost writers of fiction, as attested to by the number of awards he received: the American Academy's Howells Medal for Fiction, the Nobel Prize in Literature, the National Book Award for Fiction, the Pulitzer Prize, and the Gold Medal for Fiction of the National Institute of Arts and Letters. Since his death on July 6, 1962, Faulkner's reputation has continued to spread throughout the world. Although he wrote poetry during the early part of his career, and collaborated in various ways in writing films for Hollywood, Faulkner's reputation rests to a great extent on two substantial collections of short stories and such novels as *The Sound and the Fury* (1929), *As I Lay Dying* (1930), *Sanctuary* (1931), *Light in August* (1932), *Absalom, Absalom!* (1936), the Snopes Trilogy [*The Hamlet* (1940), *The Town* (1957), *The Mansion* (1959)], and *Go Down, Moses* (1942).

As a young boy growing up in north Mississippi, Faulkner learned the history and legends of the Civil War, including the experiences of his great grandfather, William Clark Faulkner, a Civil War veteran and author of a number of works including the well-known *The White Rose of Memphis.* Faulkner himself lived through two world wars but he never fought in any battle. In the summer of 1918 he did join the Royal Air Force and went through the basic training program in Toronto, Canada. In all, Faulkner spent 179 days in active service in the RAF, all of it in Canada. He did not travel overseas until 1925.

Never, strictly speaking, an activist for peace, Faulkner was keenly aware of the horrors of war and the inestimable value of peace. His most famous statement on this subject occurs in his 1950 Nobel Prize acceptance speech in Stockholm: "There are no longer problems of the spirit. There is only the question: When will I be blown up?" Humankind, and especially young writers, Faulkner noted, should realize that "the basest of all things is to be afraid" and that what counts are love, honor, piety, pride, compassion, sacrifice, and endurance. Man is "immortal, not because he alone among creatures has an inexhaustible voice, but because he has a soul, a spirit capable of compassion and sacrifice and endurance." Faulkner's rhetoric here is based on an abiding insight into humankind as a social and spiritual being, perhaps most notably seen in the character of Dilsey Gibson in *The Sound and the Fury*, a Black woman who serves the disintegrating Compson family and keeps the family going as best she can. Faulkner praised Dilsey when he wrote in the appendix to the novel, "They endured."

Though informed about the battles of both the Civil War and the First World War, Faulkner did not consider fiction a place to chronicle the history of warfare; rather he dramatized the plight of those affected by wars. *The Unvanquished* (1938) demonstrates well how Faulkner used the Civil War as part of his imaginative world. In this work, Bayard Sartoris, the narrator who relates events which take place throughout the seven stories which comprise the book, begins his recollections with 1863, the year of Lincoln's Emancipation Proclamation. Bayard and his friend Ringo are caught up in the reality of the war though in the first story, "Ambuscade," these two 12-year-old boys consider the battle of Vicksburg a game merely to fantasize about. They cannot comprehend at this stage in their lives what is happening as represented symbolically when they hide under Granny Rosa Millard's skirts when the Yankees approach. In "Retreat," however, the war becomes more vivid to the 13-year-old Bayard as he ventures from his home and senses soldiers on the move. In "Raid," which takes place a year later, Bayard witnesses first-hand the effects of serious fighting in the destruction of the railroad yard at Hawkhurst. For Bayard, Cousin Drusilla's evaluation of the war is shocking and forces Bayard to reflect on himself and Ringo: "Where could we have been at that moment? What could we have been doing, even a hundred miles away, not to have sensed, felt this, paused to look at one another, aghast and uplifted, while it was happening?" The Civil War had disrupted traditional values, most dramatically seen in the murder of Granny Millard and Bayard's subsequent revenge on Grumby—definitive evidence of Bayard's entrance into a cruel world. Drusilla, in contrast to some of the other women, is willing to help rebuild, and in doing so, exhibits strengths characteristic of both men and women. By the end of the book, Bayard has grown to a young man of 24 who seeks to avenge his father's death at the hand of B. J. Redmond, his father's political opponent. Yet by walking into Redmond's office unarmed, Bayard establishes a new code of conduct and shows the value of personal, human confrontation over empty chivalric gestures.

As *The Unvanquished* infers, the Civil War brought about many changes in the South but it did not inaugurate an era of lasting peace. Joanna Burden in *Light in August*, a hot-cold reformer, embodies within herself the Calvinistic burden of the South and the after-effects of the Civil War as she tries to educate Joe Christmas, a man who cannot resolve his racial identity. Likewise the Reverend Gail Hightower remains fixed on the past and cannot bring his theological training to help him grow into a changing present; he has lost his wife, been abandoned by most of his friends, and lives in the memory of his great grandfather who foolishly became involved in a raid stealing anchovies during the Civil War. Unlike both Joanna Burden and Gail Hightower, Lena Grove, a young woman searching for the father of her child, walks through the novel slowly, at peace with herself and her condition, and emerges with Byron Bunch, undoubtedly her future husband, in such a way that having drawn her strength from the earth and her natural environment she can create a future that will continue to focus on family, good friends, and loving card. Lena arrives at her inner peace not by avoiding difficulty and conflict, but by integrating whatever arrives in her life and dealing with it in a gracious and simple way. Lena represents something very positive in the Faulkner world; she knows her limitations, copes constantly with life's unsettling predicaments, and always keeps in motion. As Faulkner once put it, "The aim of every artist is to arrest motion, which is life, by artificial means and hold it fixed so that one hundred years later when a stranger looks at it, it moves again since it is life."

Undoubtedly, the work that embodies Faulkner's most comprehensive view of war and peace is *A Fable* (1954), which at one point in his life Faulkner considered his magnum opus. The story focuses not on Yoknapatawpha County, though scenes from the south are included, but on France during the First World War. Using the New Testament gospels as a background device, this novel is a retelling of the Christ story in modern garb as Faulkner asks an often-repeated question: if Jesus were to be reincar-

nated, how would he come back? Faulkner's dramatic response is portrayed in a French corporal who commits what amounts to mutiny by asking some German soldiers for a short truce; the corporal is then ordered executed by a French general who turns out to be his father. Subsequently, French soldiers searching for a body to place under the Arc de Triomphe discover the corporal's body, disgorged from its resting place by a rocket, and take it back to Paris where it ironically represents all the French who died during the war. Faulkner said of this novel:

> This is not a pacificist book. On the contrary, this writer holds almost as short a brief for pacificism as for the war itself, for the reason that pacificism does not work, cannot cope with the forces which produce the wars. In fact, if this book had any aim or moral . . . that to put an end to war, man must either find or invent something more powerful than war and man's aptitude for belligerence and his thirst for power at any cost, or use the fire itself to fight and destroy the fire with; that man may finally have to mobilize himself and arm himself with the implements of war; that the mistake we have constantly made is setting nation against nation or political ideology against political ideology to stop war . . . .

A Fable is not a treatise on war and peace, as Faulkner makes clear, but a dramatic portrayal of age-old conflicts; yet in this novel Faulkner was quite cognizant of the abstract principles he wished to embody in it.

In May 1918, the mutinous French soldiers return to Chaulnesmont where they are greeted by a tense and anxious citizenry. Will the ceasefire achieved temporarily by these soldiers turn into something more lasting? General Gragnon, the superior officer of this regiment, had in fact been willing to order these same men into a situation that would have been fatal to them. His superior, Bidet, sees the need to maintain order and preserve obedience as a value: "Let the whole vast moil and seethe of man confederate in stopping wars if they wish, so long as we can prevent them from learning that they have done so." A young pilot, Levine, learns of the duplicity committed by both the German and French officers who wish to continue the war; he realizes that blank ammunition is used when shooting at the plane bringing the German general to the French head-quarters. The breakdown of the moral code of warfare so affects Levine that he commits suicide. Ultimately, the old marshal determines the corporal's fate; he offers his son freedom provided the corporal recants, something he refuses to do: "We are two articulations . . . [of] two inimical conditions . . . . I champion of this mundane earth . . . you champion of an esoteric realm of man's baseless hopes and his infinite capacity—no passion—for unfact . . . ." The corporal accepts his death, and becomes an unwitting victim of peace. The last image of the novel is poignant: an illusive battalion runner appears at the old marshal's funeral and is beaten severely by the mob. Yet the runner has endured to this point; he has done this without either the support of the corporal or the old marshal. He says that he will never die.

If *A Fable* demonstrates anything about Faulkner's imagination, it shows that there are evil people in this world as well as idealistic ones who continue fighting at great odds to bring about a climate of peace. The corporal is a symbol of those trying to overcome evil; it should be noted, however, that the corporal himself is not successful. At the same time, his death does not conclude the novel—the enigmatic runner demonstrates Faulkner's belief that man may have to "arm himself with the implements of war to put an end to war." Personal peace, as Lucius Priest in *The Reivers* (1962) reveals in a very humanistic way, is a condition not achieved by wars, but by following a code of honorable conduct, of learning compassion and love, of seeking a family environment conducive to freedom and growth. Many of Faulkner's major characters are troubled by their inability to cope and thus change; those who do cope and use their wits, whether or not they are participants in a war, seem to be the ones capable of finding an inner peace.

Bibliography ————————————————

Bleikasten A 1973 *Faulkner's "As I Lay Dying."* Indiana University Press, Bloomington, Indiana

Bleikasten A 1976 *The Most Splendid Failure: Faulkner's "The Sound and the Fury."* Indiana University Press, Bloomington, Indiana

Brooks C 1963 *William Faulkner: The Yoknapatawpha Country.* Yale University Press, New Haven, Connecticut

Brooks C 1978 *Towards Yoknapatawpha and Beyond.* Yale University Press, New Haven, Connecticut

Falkner W C 1881 *The White Rose of Memphis.* Dillingham, New York

Faulkner W 1929 *The Sound and the Fury.* Cape and Smith, New York

Faulkner W 1931a *As I Lay Dying.* Cape and Smith, New York

Faulkner W 1931b *Sanctuary.* Cape and Smith, New York

Faulkner W 1932 *Light in August.* Smith and Haas, New York

Faulkner W 1936 *Absalom, Absalom!* Random House, New York

Faulkner W 1938 *The Unvanquished.* Random House, New York

Faulkner W 1940 *The Hamlet.* Random House, New York

Faulkner W 1942 *Go Down, Moses and Other Stories.* Random House, New York

Faulkner W 1954 *A Fable.* Random House, New York

Faulkner W 1957 *The Town.* Random House, New York

Faulkner W 1959 *The Mansion.* Random House, New York

Faulkner W 1962 *The Reivers.* Random House, New York

Matthews J 1982 *The Play of Faulkner's Language.* Cornell University Press, Ithaca, New York

Millgate M 1966 *The Achievement of William Faulkner.* Random House, New York

Pitavy F 1973 *Faulkner's "Light in August."* Indiana University Press, Bloomington, Indiana

Reed J 1973 *Faulkner's Narrative.* Yale University Press, New Haven, Connecticut

PATRICK SAMWAY

Federalism, World

The modern doctrine of world federalism has its roots in recent history, and today its heritage continues in what might be called the post-federalist ideal of global governance. The idea of creating a political union of states and peoples in order to abolish war may be traced back for centuries—back to Woodrow Wilson (see Nobel Peace Prize Laureates: *Woodrow Wilson*), Immanuel Kant (see *Kant, Immanuel; Perpetual Peace*), Abbe de Saint-Pierre, William Penn (see *Penn, William*), Henri IV and the duc de Sully (see *Henri IV*), and even Dante (see *Dante Alighieri*)— but until the collapse of the League of Nations in the 1930s most such proposals of international union were not strictly federalist. Kant, for instance, spoke only of a *confederation* of free and independent states.

The League of Nations (and its successor the United Nations) was the great realization of the dreams of a confederal system of nation states; for all its limitations, it was a triumph in the slow and painful progress of international law.

But the failure of the League to stem the course of international conflict before the Second World War, and then the untold sorrow of the war itself, caused many observers to search for the inadequacies in what had been achieved so far in international organization. Many argued, as did Clarence Streit in *Union Now* (1939), that the League failed not only because it never achieved universality in membership and because the *nations* had failed it, but also because the League had preserved the principle of the absolute national sovereignty of states, as reflected in the rule of unanimity for decisive action (see *League of Nations*). If international organization were to work effectively for the prevention of war, particularly at times of grave crisis when the defense of the majority was at stake, that principle had to be made less absolute by the division of sovereignty in accordance with the proven principle of federal government. That is, the nations would have to delegate certain sovereign powers (those relating to their general of common interests, such as peace) to the international organization, while retaining all others. They would have to create a constitutionally limited, federal world government, empowered to rule by law enacted under majority rule and reaching to individuals.

1. Confederation versus Federation

A confederation is a voluntary association, or a league, of sovereign states. States are said to be sovereign—though in fact by joining a league, as in entering into treaties and alliances, they accept limitations on their freedom of action—because, in accordance with international law, they retain the right to reject the league's recommendations, and because they enforce its decisions only by national law. There is no higher power, not even the union, that can compel a state to implement the decisions of the majority. Hence, a league is a very weak form of union.

Its weakness is vividly made manifest in the principle of collective security, the mode of enforcement contemplated under the League and now the United Nations (UN). Collective security was an advance on unbridled national adventurism and balance of power politics, but it is still the imposition of sanctions and ultimately war on the offending state itself (see *Collective Security and Collective Self-defense*). Such a measure is so indiscriminate that states, to protect themselves when joining a league, have insisted on a rule of unanimity or veto in the council that makes the enforcement decision. The veto vitiates the whole system. It prevents enforcement in the cases that really matter, when some nation is apparently launched on a course of aggression, and it establishes a psychological climate of inaction and powerlessness.

Historically, collective security has been exercised only three times: very inadequately by the League when applying economic sanctions against Italy after its invasion of Ethiopia in 1935; more severely by the United Nations when it deployed military forces against North Korea in 1950; and at a "defining moment" after the Cold War when the UN Security Council authorized the US-led Coalition to use force to repel Iraq from Kuwait in 1990. League sanctions against Italy were vitiated by British and French hopes that Mussolini might yet serve as a "balancer" against Hitler; UN armed action against North Korea was only possible because the Soviet Union (which possesses a veto) happened not to be sitting in the Security Council while boycotting the UN for its refusal to seat the People's Republic of China and because the United States was committed to a policy of resisting Communist expansion; and UN action to repulse Iraqi aggression came at a brief moment when it was widely hoped that the United Nations might finally be able to act regularly as originally designed in its Charter.

In the intervening years, UN "peacekeeping" forces (lightly armed for patrol and observation purposes only) had conducted thirteen valuable operations designed to stabilize cease-fire lines and to encourage negotiations by 1986, and as many new ones in the flurry of hopes for the UN after the Cold War (sixteen were current in 1997), but they have hardly had much impact on the 150 international wars that have occurred since 1945.

A federation, on the other hand, is a government of peoples. Since the system of states members and action on states has proved ineffective, federalists argue that a supranational, or world federal government, vested with powers to enact law binding on individuals must be created. Individuals would be made citizens of the world as well as national citizens. They would participate in the election of world representatives, and they would be subject to world laws just as to national laws. Three levels of government, then, are required in order to complete the rule of law: local, national, and world.

A world federation should be constituted, like democratic republics generally, with representative institutions—primarily a world legislature, plus a world executive and world judiciary—so that the people have a sense of participation in the making of the laws, and hence will obey them willingly as rules of action truly in the common interest. Constitutional safeguards, as well as continual public vigilance, will be required to prevent abuses of power. Special protections would have to be provided for human rights and the rights of minorities. Reliance would be placed on the rule of world law, enacted by the majority, as a greater protector of human equality than the present struggle for human rights in an anarchy of national states.

If this difficult, constantly readjusted political condition can be established, it should be possible to maintain world peace by court action on individuals accused of violating the world laws, instead of collective security action against states. Hence, the level of violence, threatened and actual, in modern life— and, incidentally the magnitude of government, even the world government, designed to protect people from violence—would be dramatically reduced. The idea is to bring mankind as a whole into a social contract: world federation would be established by a revolutionary exercise of the sovereignty of the people.

Thus, the rule of law would replace collective security as the means by which the human race would establish true peace. Peace, federalists say, is not merely the interim between wars, but is the presence of order, produced by law, in turn produced by government. Peace, they argue, is not the ultimate goal, but only the necessary condition for the fulfillment of human potential, for the good life. When peace is established, then will come the great achievements of science and religion, modern industry and development, social planning and free enterprise, liberal education and the arts. But the essential point is that these things are based on *law*. "Law," Mark Van Doren once explained, "is merely the thing that lets us live in peace with our neighbors without having to love them." It may not be so good a thing as religious consciousness or even maturity of character, and someday perhaps we may have no more need for government, but in politics, with men as they are, law is an indispensable minimum.

The world today seems very much in want of good laws above the national level. What people everywhere need to see is that the rule of world law, commonly enacted, would not be a loss of freedom, or a sacrifice of sovereignty, but would be an immense gain in order, in non-violent processes for the resolution of disputes and in more equitable planning for development. The rule of law on the national level is the actual basis of our freedoms; the rule of world law could produce the mutual confidence that would be the basis of an almost unimaginable material and spiritual world prosperity.

The great advantage of a *government* is that it permits orderly change, whereas a league tends to be a guardian of the status quo. The reason is that a government can enact law while a league cannot. Law is a rule of action or standard of conduct reaching to individuals, who are the persons that ultimately need government. The recommendations of a league, on the other hand, reach only to states, which retain the ultimate power to govern individuals and hence are not bound. The great difficulty for the rule of law on the world level is to vest a coercive power reaching

to individuals in the world federal government, but to do so in such a way that the rational power of the law generally obviates need for recourse to punishment. World law would require world police forces and even elite world military forces as part of its enforcement apparatus, but their function would be merely to overawe wrongdoers. No effective world law could rely to any appreciable degree on its power to punish violators, who would include national leaders; it must so manifestly represent the will of the world community, and be so deliberately formulated in the complex historical circumstances of our times, that the law would command universal respect and adherence *without* fear of punishment.

In brief, what humanity must do in order to establish a better ordered world, in the language of Hamilton and Madison in *The Federalist* (No. 20), is to abandon *violence* for *law*, to give up the "destructive *coercion* of the *sword*" for the "mild and salutary *coercion* of the *magistracy*."

If powers were granted to the federal world government to protect human rights and to regulate economic life, as probably would be necessary even to achieve peace and international security, the mild and salutary coercion of world law would be felt at all levels of every society, and most vividly at top levels of national government and economy. The rule of world law plainly implies interference in the domestic affairs of states, just as treaties do. The difference is that, under the latter, the highest legal recourse is to national courts, whereas, under the former, it is to new world courts.

The whole question of world federalism then becomes: Is humanity ready to accept the rule of world law?

2. *The Possibility of World Federalism*

World federalists argue that the global expansion of Western industrialization, finance, and economic techniques, the spread of European forms of liberal and socialist democracy, the counter-flow of non-Western cultural ideas from the post-colonial world, the shrinking of distances by modern transportation and communications, and in short the interdependence of civilized life today on the planet make the acceptance of world law possible. The world is already one, they say; only law and politics lag behind (see *Interdependence, International*).

Moreover, the global problems of nuclear war, traffic in armaments, erosion of human rights, the international debt crisis, worsening poverty in the underdeveloped world, international terrorism, overpopulation, environmental pollution, and the militarization of space—problems that can not be solved on a short-sighted nationalistic basis—make the acceptance of world law *necessary*. The traditional idea of national sovereignty, which seems to block all progress toward effectively solving our common problems, is a false freedom, if it compels people and their governments to live in constant fear of their neighbors in an anarchical society. Real freedom and prosperity will come when human beings join together under a common rule of law.

World federalists say that they, who wish to extend the rule of law, are the realists, while those who put their faith in a league of sovereign states or, worse, who suppose that peace can long be maintained by deterrence or competition in arms are the utopians.

The example of national federal systems, of which some twenty-two of various degrees of centralization have been formed since the founding of the United States, has always been prominent in the minds of world federalists. An extensive republic like the USA, with its numerous and disparate peoples, cultures, languages, and religions, or like the Russian Federation, which is also a federal republic, is an image in miniature of what a world federation would be like.

Federal world government would not mean the abolition of nations. Rather, the nations (sometimes themselves federal systems) would be preserved as subordinate authorities. Provincial, state, and urban authorities would, of course, also be preserved. Indeed, it is argued, world federalism is the most acceptable way, in an atomic age and in an interdependent world, by which nations and more local authorities *can* be preserved. They also *must* be preserved as sources of law better adapted to national and local circumstances, even if nations participate in a world federation for common security, regulation of the global economy, and other general purposes. World federation is the only acceptable form of international organization that is strong enough to abolish war, yet not so strong as to endanger the political and cultural diversity of mankind. "Unity and diversity" has been the watchword.

3. Proposals for World Federation

Two typical proposals of world federation are the *Preliminary Draft of a World Constitution* (1948), by Robert M. Hutchins, G.A. Borgese, and others in the University of Chicago's Committee to Frame a World Constitution, and *World Peace through World Law* (1958), by Grenville Clark and Louis B. Sohn.

These span the range between "maximal" and "minimal" proposals, respectively, that is, proposals that would vest the world government with powers to achieve peace and justice, and those that would limit it to powers to maintain international security. The whole spectrum of international organization, then, in the order of decreasing centralization of power, would look as follows:

> World empire;
> Maximal world federation (Chicago Committee);
> Minimal world federation (Clark and Sohn);
> League of sovereign states (United Nations);
> Balance of power (Western Alliance, bilateral
>   defense treaties);
> Anarchy of independent states, untempered even by
>   international law;

World empire, many people think, will be the way that the world is finally united. But judging by past attempts to unite the world by force (Philip II, Napoleon, Hitler), a new attempt by one nation to conquer the world would under modern conditions surely lead to nuclear war and hence to a breakdown of civilization even more chaotic than the last item of the list. World federalists are absolutely opposed to a bid for world empire. They resist the trend toward a Pax Americana or what used to be feared as a World Soviet Dictatorship. Use of force will destroy the respect for law and the viable national and local authorities on which a realistic world union depends. The only wise course, consistent with the best spirit of our times, is to follow the relatively nonviolent precedent for the establishment of most national federal systems.

There has been great variety in world federalist proposals. In addition to the Chicago Committee's draft of a world constitution and the Clark-Sohn plan, there have been well over fifty other model world constitutions. One of the most recent is the *Constitution for the Federation of Earth* (1977) by the group centered about Philip Isely. There have also been countless proposals of UN reform, though none quite on the scale of the Clark-Sohn plan. These include the Binding Triad proposal of Richard Hudson and proposals by the Campaign for UN Reform and the World Federalist Movement. A significant one outside the federalist tradition was the parting report of UN Joint Inspection Unit official Maurice Bertrand, *Some Reflections on the Reform of the United Nations* (1985) and his *A Third Generation World Organization* (1989). Another, strictly on European federation but very instructive for the world, was the "Spinelli Plan," *The Draft Treaty Establishing the*

European Union (European Parliament 1984), which provoked the much slower process negotiated in the Maastricht Treaty of 1992. These at least show that a lawful federation of the modern world is conceivable, and they could easily serve as draft negotiating documents for a realistic program of political action.

Many proposals have not been model world constitutions but political appeals to the public or to governments to assemble in a UN review conference or world constitutional convention, where official representatives would undertake to draft a new charter of union. The proposals of the US mainstream organization, United World Federalists, were largely such appeals. Its successor organization, the World Federalist Association, and the international organization, the World Association of World Federalists (now called the World Federalist Movement), have also, since about the time of the Korean War, emphasized strengthening the UN through Charter amendment and functional development of international law under the present Charter. A very large literature of commentary, criticism, and international education, reflected in this bibliography, has been produced in virtually every country of North America, Latin America, Europe, the former Soviet bloc, and in major countries of Africa, and Asia.

4. The World Federalist Movement since the Second World War

The political opportunity to undertake national policies leading to world federation was greatest, though still small, from about 1944 to 1950, that is, from the last year of the Second World War to the point when the Cold War was generally accepted as the dominant "reality" of international relations. The Soviet Union and the United States were allied in the war, of course, and this fact gave encouragement to those concerned with the structure of the peace. Many private persons and some with connections to the US government, like Grenville Clark, made formal proposals for limited, federal world government by 1944. But the United States was uninterested in anything stronger than a league of sovereign states, largely because of fear of Senate rejection as in 1920. The former Soviet Union was reluctant to submit even to a league after its disastrous experience with the League of Nations during the Munich crisis of 1938.

Nevertheless, the times did not permit a turning away from international organization. The great powers, as they guided the formation of the United Nations Organization at the Dumbarton Oaks confer-

ence (1944) and San Francisco conference (1945), permitted some relaxation of the principle of national sovereignty, since two-thirds majority rule was established for all organs, and unanimity was required only of the five permanent members of the Security Council, but the powers made the General Assembly only an advisory body of state representatives (one-nation, one-vote), and they granted the International Court of Justice no compulsory jurisdiction.

It was after the UN Charter was signed in June, 1945, that atomic bombs were first used in war. On August 6, 1945, the United States dropped an atomic bomb on the Japanese city of Hiroshima, followed by another in a few days on Nagasaki.

Mankind entered the atomic age. To many internationalists who had suffered through the war, the United Nations belonged to an *antiquus ordo seculorum*. It had not been vested with powers to govern states that had nuclear weapons at their disposal. Atomic fear emerged, particularly in the US, as the main motivation for immediately calling another international conference to establish a world federation. "One world or none!" was the rallying cry of atomic scientists and world federalists alike. They talked of world government in five years; if not achieved by 1950, when Russia probably would have developed atomic bombs, a general nuclear war would become inevitable. Continuation of the national pattern of recurrent warfare would lead to nuclear destruction of all civilization. Grenville Clark hosted the first Dublin conference of prominent internationalists in October, 1945; they issued a ringing call for immediately replacing the UN with limited, federal world government. But the Truman administration and the Senate deflected the call as mere obstructionism to the new United Nations.

Outside the United States, atomic fear was less of a motivation. In Europe and Russia, there was much more public concern about reconstruction after the war and about satisfying basic needs for food and shelter. A Polish peasant, when told about the dangers of atomic war, looked about him and asked, "Is it worse than this?" In the colonized territories of Africa and Asia, after British power had been humbled by Japan, humanity was on the move with demands for independence, economic assistance, and an end to racial discrimination. American appeals for world government to control atomic energy sounded suspiciously like attempts to fix the status quo under US domination. G.A. Borgese, an Italian émigré professor and secretary of the Chicago Committee to Frame a World Constitution, sensed this difference in values when he declared that *justice*, not mere abolition of war, was the universal object of world federation. "Peace and justice stand or fall together," the Committee declared in their draft world constitution. Borgese was not optimistic. Limited world government, he warned, was too strong for the United States, too weak for the rest of the world, including Russia.

Nevertheless, the movement for world federation made some notable progress. In the United States, twenty-two states passed resolutions recommending US participation in a world federal government. Resolutions were introduced in Congress, and there were hearings on world federation in the House in 1948 and 1949 and in the Senate in 1950. In Europe, the constitutions of France, Italy, West Germany, and the Netherlands were modified to permit limitations of sovereignty in order to participate in a European or world union. (Thirty-six national constitutions now have such provisions.) By 1950, the World Movement for World Federal Government had member organizations in twenty-two countries, with a total membership of 151,000 people.

But the movement was too small and too slow to form to influence policy or to bring about a new convention to draft a world constitution or to amend the UN Charter.

The United Nations soon proved inadequate to exert an effective mediating influence on the two great powers that emerged from the war. The United States did make an historic effort to establish the international control of atomic energy (the Baruch plan), which had implications for world federation, but the plan was not well thought out and negotiations were pressed in an atmosphere of atomic diplomacy (see *Baruch Plan*). By the end of 1946, when the Baruch plan was effectively defeated, both the United States and the then Soviet Union were accusing each other of Hitlerite ambitions. The US abandoned its foreign policy of cooperation with Russia and settled on the containment policy, which was announced in March, 1947 (see *Containment*).

Soviet policy apparently was more ambiguous, but the Truman Doctrine and the Marshall Plan provoked a strong reaction with the formation of the Cominform and the beginning of the ideological campaign against "rootless cosmopolitanism" (world government and friendliness with the West) later that year. Both countries, despite protestations of support for the UN, ceased to base their national security on the international security organization, and they returned openly to national programs of preparedness and military defense. The posture was one of war. It was called Cold War only when hostile operations like

those of World War II were not initiated (see *Cold War*).

5. Justice and World Federalism

G.A. Borgese viewed the Cold War as a struggle about the principle of *justice* on which the necessary world federation would be based. In an age of nations, Borgese argued, no nation could feel secure as long as any other possessed a threat to its existence. Hence, expansion has been a strategic necessity for both sides. Ultimately, the security interest of states will lead to a world political union, achieved by force or consent. The course of national history, from a broad perspective, was clearly toward union, as is shown by attempts in recent centuries to unite the feuding nations by force. But the nations of Europe gradually wore themselves out with their wars, and, by the end of the last general war (the ninth by some reckonings), only two great, sovereign powers remained, Russia and America.

They found themselves the bearers of the two great traditions of Western democracy—liberalism and socialism. America was the champion of liberty; Russia, of equality of condition. If the world had to be united, one would make it over by creating a world government of minimal powers in order to preserve popular freedoms, including freedom of business enterprise. The other would create a world government of maximal powers in order to bring the protection of the state to the people against concentrations of private industrial and financial power. It was a small difference in valuations, perhaps, for America recognized the principle of equality before the law; and Russia, freedom from class exploitation. It was a difference rather like that in past ages about whether salvation came by faith or by works. In the mid-twentieth century, it was very nearly enough to plunge the world in fire.

The "victory of the West" in the Cold War may seem to have decided the question in favor of liberty and capitalism, but the issue of justice has hardly been settled. World federalists still offer a solution to this modern political difficulty. The purpose of their model world constitutions is to demonstrate that the two main strands of justice are sufficiently shared to make possible a union by consent between East and West, North and South. A mixed capitalist-socialist system is usually proposed. It could be democratic yet contain a strong central authority. Protections could be provided for political and economic freedoms, for liberal as well as civil, economic, social, and cultural human rights, for private as well as socialist enterprises. Procedures in the world legislature could permit maximum representation of diverse peoples and interests, but, when all processes for the protection of minorities were satisfied, enactments would have the force of law. The world legislature is usually made unicameral precisely to avoid the paralysis that democratic assemblies are liable to.

Federalists argue that the political struggle formerly between capitalism and communism, and now between the developed and underdeveloped worlds, can at least conceivably be brought under one world legal order, much as has been done under national governments for the struggle between capital and labor. Moreover, apart from national ideologies—made rigid by the military necessity that they serve to prepare the people for war—all nations now in fact have mixed systems, part public, part private. What is needed are peaceful processes for the settlement of disputes, which would obviate the need for claiming a right to recourse to arms.

Grenville Clark and Louis B. Sohn (1958), for instance, carefully provided that the UN Economic and Social Council be reconstituted to give representation to the twelve nations with the highest gross national products; then they proposed that a World Development Authority, under the Council, be established with powers to make grants in aid or interest-free loans to governments or organizations for economic and social projects considered necessary for the "creation of conditions of stability and well-being." The Chicago Committee, more radically, provided for an extensive bill of rights and duties, a broad grant of powers, a world planning agency, and a clause permitting public purchase of business that had acquired the "extension and character of a transnational monopoly."

6. Major Problems in Constructing World Federation

There are four major problems for world federalism: membership, representation, powers, and approaches.

6.1 Membership

On membership, virtually all world federalists are agreed that universality is the ultimate goal; most hold that it is the immediate goal. Universality is the great achievement of the United Nations. Every weakness in the UN has been tolerated rather than tamper with the principle of universal membership, and every attempt to evict one country (the then Soviet Union in the early days and in recent years South Africa or Israel) has been rejected as a threat to the peace. Nevertheless, a minority of federalists

argue in favor of a partial union first—notably Clarence Streit and his followers, who have proposed starting with an Atlantic union of liberal democracies. One would also have to include among those who would only start with democracies Winston Churchill, Robert Schuman, Jean Monnet, and all those, mostly under Monnet's inspiration, who have toiled for European union.

6.2 Representation

In a universal world federation, representation is the most vexed problem. Should representation be proportional to population, which is the strictly democratic principle, but which would give predominance to poorer, more populous, and less "politically experienced" countries like India? Or could representation be "weighted" somehow to make active participation more attractive to the great powers? Grenville Clark and Louis B. Sohn proposed that the UN General Assembly be reorganized according to a system (subject to periodic amendment) of weighted representation cleverly scaled with respect to population, wealth, education, and traditional great power ranking: the US, Russia, China, and India would each be allocated 30 votes; mid-sized powers like Britain and France, former West Germany and Japan, 16; smaller nations, 8; and so on for a total of 625 world representatives. Clark and Sohn urged that the representatives be elected by the people wherever possible, so that representatives develop a sense of responsibility to the people instead of to national governments; elsewhere, appointment by parliaments, national monarchs, or communist parties would have to be tolerated.

The Chicago Committee earlier proposed an ingenious alternative scheme of regional popular elections and nine electoral colleges, which eliminated the invidious weighting scheme. But it had the same effect, since the nine regions (nicely coincident with the world civilizations that world historian Arnold Toynbee distinguished) had different populations. These representatives were to be finally elected by all the electoral colleges in plenary session, so each representative would in principle represent the whole world. There were to be 99 of them. Little has come of such schemes because of opposition by national officials, who are unconvinced that such popularly representative institutions could be relied upon to provide security or fair regulation of international business, and by poorer, populous countries, who resent the implied slight to their people.

6.3 Powers

The powers to be delegated to a world federation

could range all the way from the minimum necessary to preserve the peace to the maximum desirable to promote justice throughout the world. Grenville Clark argued that only minimal powers were acceptable for delegation by the nations at present; amendment could provide for gradual expansion of powers as the world federation proved trustworthy. This was the doctrine of "minimalism." G. A. Borgese and the Chicago Committee, at the other extreme ("maximalism"), contended that a mere security government would be a world police state; the federation had to start with powers to achieve justice, for injustice was at the root of the crisis of modern civilization. Hence, in addition to powers to preserve the peace, the world federation would have to have powers to regulate world commerce, supervise world communications and transportation, lay world taxes, issue world money and control world finance, prepare plans for equitable economic development, regulate emigration and immigration, and supervise the rectification of borders and the creation of new states. Streit was a maximalist within his democratic Atlantic union.

There has never been open resolution of this contentious issue, but as the UN has entered the economic development field and peace workers everywhere have turned to development projects since political progress toward federation seems so slow, virtually all federalists are now maximalists. So are virtually all internationalists.

6.4 Approaches

The greatest problem of world federalism is the political transition. Most federalists have argued that the only practical course is to conduct a campaign of public education to persuade people that it is in their own self-interest, particularly in peace, to reach an international agreement for the non-violent establishment of world federal government. Federalists have always resisted talk and hints of preventive war, use of force, and a national bid for empire. The preferred method is to convene a general review conference for the reform of the United Nations, as provided for in Article 109 of the Charter, or to convene a new world constitutional convention, like that in San Francisco in 1945. This is commonly known as the approach of UN reform. The approach is official, legal, and "realistic." Appeal is made not to moral sentiments or to the sense of human brotherhood, but to national interests. The politics of UN reform has consisted largely of lobbying with legislators and high executive officials to produce a resolution or other national initiative for a new conference. United World Federalists saw its purpose almost entirely as lobbying in

Congress for a world federalist resolution. Its successor, the World Federalist Association conducts a broader educational program but still attempts to influence Congress.

A variant on this official approach is the "parliamentary" approach, in which national parliamentarians, including members of the US Congress, would introduce the federalist resolution themselves. The British Parliamentary Group for World Government began this approach. It is carried on, with more political "realism," by Parliamentarians for World Order (now Parliamentarians for Global Action).

A minority of federalists have argued that national governments are natural enemies of a project that would reduce national sovereignty, so an appeal must be made directly to the people in order to produce a wholly new social contract. They propose to hold popular elections of delegates to a world constitutional convention, using state electoral machinery wherever possible; these delegates, legitimated by their election, would then assemble in convention to draft the world constitution. This is the peoples' convention approach. It is unofficial, revolutionary, and "utopian." Most proponents see it as an educational device to bring greater grassroots popular pressure to bear on officials, in order to move them to undertake UN reform. Henry Usborne, a British Member of Parliament, led a difficult campaign to hold such a peoples' convention in Geneva in 1950.

Still another approach would be to form a transnational political party aimed at winning national offices for the purpose of carrying out a program of establishing world federation. A more modest variant would be to form an advisory committee of leaders of national political parties and trade unions on the model of Jean Monnet's Action Committee for a United States of Europe.

Actually, all federalist approaches are revolutionary, in the sense that they all aim to create favorable political conditions for the transfer of sovereign powers from nations to a higher governing authority. What is proposed is no less than the dissolution of the external sovereignty of nations. But federalists argue that—since sovereignty is really the right of the people to institute new government, laying its foundations on such principles and organizing its powers in such form as to them shall seem most likely to effect their safety and happiness—there can never be a "sacrifice" or dissolution of sovereignty. Rather, sovereignty is *strengthened* by uniting governments. Far from being a loss, establishing federal world government would be a gain of immense powers of social cooperation, analogous to what has been achieved under the US federal Constitution, which was bitterly opposed at first.

Even the provision in Article 109 that each of the Big Five must ratify any amendments to the Charter need not be a barrier, if there were overwhelming popular demand for a stronger United Nations. Delegates to a UN Charter review conference could provide that the new Charter should go into effect when ratified by some large majority of states plus, say, three or four of the five "permanent members," just as the delegates to the Philadelphia convention of 1787 provided that the new US government should go into operation when the Constitution was ratified by nine of the thirteen states, and not unanimously, as required by the Articles of Confederation.

World federalists say that the times themselves are revolutionary. We are witnessing the rise of the working classes to power in the West, and the awakening of the impoverished masses in Latin America, Africa, and Asia. These events reduce even the Cold War between Russia and America to a mere wave on the tide of history. Revolutionary times call for a revolutionary response.

7. Criticism of World Federalism

Critics of world federalism have tended to bridle at the arguments of world law and to examine its root assumptions, particularly those of world community and world democracy. There has been much searching for alternatives short of a challenge to national sovereignty in the present period when nationalism remains stronger than ever.

Critics such as Reinhold Niebuhr (1949), who withdrew early from the Chicago Committee, immediately sensed that a precondition for the popular acceptance of world law was a shared sense of values, of world community. Law cannot work merely by virtue of the penalty attached; there must be respect for the law and voluntary obedience. In the world today, Niebuhr observed, there was hardly enough sense of belonging to a common community of humanity to provide that ready obedience to the rule of world law. Dean Acheson once observed that government simply does not work where five percent of the population refuse to obey the law, as Truman was finding out with the coal strikers of 1946 or the British with the situations in India or Palestine. World community must precede world government.

G.A. Borgese and the rest of the Committee replied that government helps to *create* community, as the history of the US federal government shows. A world government would begin to create the habits of

submitting to a higher law by which the power of national traditions can be broken. He and others argued, mostly from world literature and ordinary people's demand for peace, that world community existed sufficiently for a beginning. There is no gradual way to peace. The problem of war must be rooted out by a decisive act, as at Philadelphia in 1787. It is a problem of *will*. Hence, world community and world government will develop together.

There has been extensive debate on this point, and much of the argument amounts basically to an assertion that there does not exist the will to begin to establish world law, or that there does. The balance of opinion, however, in the early days went decidedly toward Niebuhr. Today, it is shifting to the view that world community is steadily forming. Federalists continue to maintain that law and community are interlinked parts of one process and evolve together.

The former Soviet Union was unable to distinguish proposals of world federation, which had been made mainly by American private citizens, from the foreign policy of the United States. World federalism, Russian writers used to say, is a mere front for Wall Street imperialism. This identification was a mistake, but that it was even made indicates how difficult it will be, after many years of Cold War, to bring the political struggle between developed, transitional, and developing countries into a representative world legislature, courts, or conciliation tribunals, where it would be allowed, by either the United States or other members of the Group of Eight, to reach decisive conclusions. Most countries now claim to believe in "democracy," but there remain deep divisions in our times between the concepts of liberal and social democracies. Until the slow reconciliation of these concepts is accomplished, there can be no establishment of a working, world democracy.

Federalists reply that the real difficulty is not the concept of democracy, but the posture of war, which destroys the trust essential to the working of any government. Communist governments, which as social democracies were relatively alike, were several times at war against one another or on the verge of it, most notably the former Soviet Union and the People's Republic of China. After the Cold War and the abandonment of its ideological struggles, there is still no peace. What is essential for world federalism is that all nations renounce the right to wage war. Against all conventional wisdom, the former Soviet Union unilaterally went far in this direction under Mikhail Gorbachev's leadership, as the Communist Party voluntarily relinquished its monopoly on national power and permitted the Warsaw Pact to dissolve. Georgi Shakhnazarov's

Pravda article, "The World Community is Amenable to Government" (1988) marked the divide.

The United States has yet to respond to the historic opportunity thus opened up to create a fundamentally nonmilitary foreign policy for the 21st century. When the US renounces its role as the world's "sole remaining superpower," which new economic and political forces are making increasingly irrelevant, it may be possible for the country of Washington and Madison, Hamilton and Jefferson to turn again to building the rule of law throughout the whole world. Although the cultural difficulties are immense, there seems no fundamental reason why Americans and Russians, with other peoples, can not participate in a limited, federal world government, just as they have begun to do in the United Nations, and as communists and other democrats have learned to do in such European countries as Italy and France.

8. Alternatives to World Federalism

Many critics have shown that the proper analogy for world federation is not the Thirteen States of 1787, but the British Commonwealth or historic Europe. The Commonwealth has developed gradually and is still not bound together by law; in Europe, national fears and differences are much more typical for the world at large. The attempt to unite Europe, then, has much more significance for the world than Philadelphia. The "Communities," as Walter Hallstein and Jean Monnet describe them, are a new form of international organization—neither confederations nor federations. The Spinelli plan for European Union, passed by the European Parliament in 1984, is certainly the most significant recent draft constitution for the practical federation of modern states. The council-commission-summit structure of the Communities has been cited by Maurice Bertrand as a new model for the reform of the United Nations.

Functionalism, a theory of closer international relations first propounded by David Mitrany in 1943, has proved to be the most successful of all alternatives to world federation. Mitrany rejected schemes to change constitutions or to merge sovereignties. Instead, he urged support for international organizations like the International Labour Organization and other programmes and specialized agencies that have since been incorporated into the United Nations system. These organizations, some of which have been created by simple executive agreements without formal enactment in law, perform services ("functions") for citizens of national states. Over time, as they perform necessary functions beyond the ability of nation states

in an interdependent world, the people of those nations will gradually develop loyalty to the new supranational institutions. Mitrany called the process "federalism by installments" (see *Functionalism*). Its success can be seen most clearly in the Third World, whose Group of 77 (now actually 124) is sometimes seen, with other groups of states with common interests, as typical of emerging transnational political parties.

Over the years, there has been much quiet progress in the United Nations, despite an atmosphere, as the Secretary-General warns, of a retreat from multilateralism. A typical achievement was the signing of the Law of the Sea in 1982 by 119 nations. The requisite sixty ratified it by 1995; even the US, which has not ratified it, is observing it as "customary international law." By 1998, there were no less than 25 binding multilateral treaties on human rights on deposit with the Secretary-General, of 95 instruments throughout the world. It seems that humanity will have an international bill of rights before there is a world government to enforce it. The current conventional wisdom at the UN is that substantive Charter amendment is impracticable, given the deep divisions between North and South, East and West. But much could be accomplished through interpretation of the Charter, as in the case of peacekeeping, which is entirely based on a loose construction of Chapters VI and VII, or as in the relationship of the specialized agencies to the Secretariat, which is technically an administrative matter.

Quite a bit of work has been done in the last twenty years on the alternative of "world order" to traditional power politics by the group at the World Policy Institute centered around Saul Mendlovitz (1975) and Richard A. Falk (1975) (see *World Order*). Six volumes of the World Order Models Project have now been completed (see *World Order Models Project (WOMP)*). These virtually describe a world ordered by law but avoid the clear concepts of federation.

9. Global Governance

By the 1980s, there was some renewed interest in world federal government by writers groping for a solution to the problem of nuclear war. Jonathan Schell (1982) and Freeman Dyson have raised the idea only to reject it. The US Catholic bishops, in their Pastoral Letter of 1983, come close to advocating world government as a long-term political solution to the problem. Many of the arguments have the ring of atomic fear, similar to arguments of Americans in the 1940s. Less is heard of arguments about the positive promise of world federation, as G.A.

Borgese used to make.

Thinkers as widely separated in recent times as Arnold Toynbee (1948), Andrei Sakharov (1968), and Saul Mendlovitz (1975) have predicted world government by the year 2000, but world federalists have been unable to found an influential institute of world federal law or a world university to guide the historical processes tending in such a direction.

Nevertheless, the end of the Cold War has brought back many of the notions of world federalism in the guise of "global governance." As used by Shridath Ramphal and the authors of Our Global Neighborhood (1995), "Governance is the sum of the many ways individuals and institutions, public and private, manage their common affairs" (p. 2). But they later admit that "Good governance requires good government" (p. 61), and they often emphasize that global governance "will strive to subject the rule of arbitrary power—economic, political, or military—to the rule of law within global society" (pp. 5, 150). The sense seems to be that, at the end of the Cold War, what Madison, Hamilton, and Jay in *The Federalist* called the "necessity of government" is recognized, but the management of affairs that we now find in international relations as well as in civil society is broader and more diverse than the old vesting of sovereign powers in a constitutional government. Something new is happening in world politics. Hence, "global governance."

In a survey of mine of the literature produced mostly since the end of the Cold War and focusing on U.N. reform (1995), most writers seem to see three general directions for the future of the United Nations, analogous to the three fundamental bases of international politics—balance of power, collective security, and rule of law:

(a) Cautious development of the state system, utilizing the UN as at present only when bilateral diplomacy must avail itself of the services of multilateral diplomacy.

(b) A non-hierarchical system of perhaps one hundred international organizations, including a much more effective United Nations empowered to achieve the purposes in its Charter.

(c) A world federal government, preserving the nation-states but providing a higher level of legislative, executive, and judicial authority, probably on the model of the emerging European Union.

A non-hierarchical system (alternative 2) is now overwhelmingly preferred, not only because statesmen (and women) are reluctant to part with national

power, but also because the peoples of the states are fearful, after over forty years of the Cold War, to centralize power in a world state, even if it could be designed as a federal system with such checks and balances as not to become a threat to liberty. The present world situation appears to be a period of political creativity no less inferior to that at the founding of the United States, and the emerging world political order promises to be as different from any of the twenty-two historical federations as the US federal government looked from the confederation and colonial governments that preceded it.

Consider the following facts replete in the literature of UN reform:

(a) US hegemony since 1973, like British hegemony after 1918, has been declining.

(b) The absolute sovereignty of states, enshrined in the UN Charter's Article 2(7), no longer preserves states from war, economic disruption, or, now, humanitarian intervention.

(c) International war is decreasing in incidence, while domestic and ethnic conflict affecting international peace and security is increasing. The UN, which was designed to stop Hitlerite aggression across borders, is now increasingly charged with maintaining the peace among individuals, as if it were a world state.

(d) Common security is supplanting national security as the first interest of states, and economic power is increasingly recognized as more of a reality than military power.

(e) Nuclear weapons, which their most optimistic champions claimed undermined Realpolitik, are unusable.

(f) Increasingly, consensus, rather than consent of every state willing to be bound, is recognized as the basis of international obligation laid down in the recommendations, or enactments, of the General Assembly.

(g) The individual is being recognized as a "subject" of international law, particularly under the Nuremberg principles and now under some ninety-five human rights instruments.

When the *individual* is protected by international human rights law, has a role via non-governmental organizations accredited to the UN in the making of treaties and the hardening of customs, and has standing before world courts and international tribunals, have we not crossed the line from an association of sovereign states to a government of states and peoples?

What, then, is the relevance of world federalism to the search for peace? Its primary contribution is an adequate conception of the goal. Peace is not the interim between wars; it is a positive thing, an active social condition, chosen deliberately and consciously maintained. Peace is the presence of justice, that is, of order, of law, and of government. World peace will require *institutional* change in order to provide for the regular, orderly resolution of international disputes and for international cooperation in the common interest. Federalists argue that structural change— UN reform—may precede "trust," and indeed will help to create it. If peoples and governments already trusted one another, cooperating and competing without violence, there would be no need for world government, or for the United Nations for that matter. The UN is weak today because it has not been structured to reach decisions that seem fair or can be enforced, even in matters about which there are not great East-West differences, like the civil war in Bosnia. World federalists express the need for stronger international institutions in the familiar language of federal government, but no doubt new and unprecedented institutions will have to be created, for the whole human race is far more diverse than any community yet united under a federal system. Europe is probably the best model.

The achievement of the rule of world law will largely depend on new, enlightened national leadership. Jean Monnet used to say that, for the hard work of uniting sovereignties, people act only when faced by a crisis. The world now is faced by a massive crisis, symbolized by the threat of nuclear war. At the moment, it is only a crisis of the mind. To bring about an agreement to establish a stronger form of international organization, we need now not more arguments based on atomic fear, for they move people not toward world federation but toward more ready expedients like deterrence. We need a new positive vision of peace. What federalists are really calling for is a new kind of world political wisdom.

See also: *Cosmopolitanism; Federation; Global Integration; Integration Theories; Justice and Peace; Nationalism; Supranationalism; United Nations Governance; United Nations Reform: Historical and Contemporary Perspectives*

Bibliography ⎯⎯⎯⎯⎯⎯⎯⎯⎯⎯⎯⎯⎯

Baratta J P 1995 *The United Nations System: Meeting the World Constitutional Crisis.* ABC-Clio, Oxford, England; Transaction Press, New Brunswick, New Jersey

Bertrand M 1985 Some Reflections on the Reform of the United Nations. United Nations A/40/988

Bertrand M 1989 *A Third Generation World Organization.* Nijhoff, Dordrecht, The Netherlands

Childers E, Urquhart B 1994 Renewing the United Nations system. *Development Dialogue* 1, Ford Foundation

Clark G, Sohn L B 1958 *World Peace through World Law.* Harvard University Press, Cambridge, Massachusetts

Commission on Global Governance 1995 *Our Global Neighborhood.* Oxford University Press, Oxford, England

Commission to Study the Organization of Peace 1975 *Building Peace: Reports of the Commission to Study the Organization of Peace, 1939-1972*, 2 vols. Scarecrow, Metuchen, New Jersey

Committee to Frame a World Constitution 1948 Preliminary Draft of a World Constitution, *Common Cause*, 1. Reprinted in 1965 as *A Constitution for the World.* Center for the Study of Democratic Institutions, Santa Barbara, California

Falk R A 1975 *A Study of Future Worlds.* Free Press, New York

Falk R A, Johansen R C, Kim S S (eds.) 1993 *The Constitutional Foundations of World Peace.* State University of New York Press, New York

Glossop R J 1993 *World Federation: A Critical Analysis of Federal World Government.* McFarland, Jefferson, North Carolina

Gorbachev M S 1988 Address to the General Assembly of the United Nations. *General Assembly Official Records.* Plenary, 43rd sess., 7 December 1988

Hamilton A, Madison J, Jay J 1787-88 *The Federalist Papers.* Modern Library, New York. Nos. 9, 10, 15, 16, 17, 21, 23, 39, 46, 51

Isley P et al., 1977 *A Constitution for the Federation of Earth.* World Constitution and Parliament Association, Lakewood, Colorado

Johansen R C 1978 *Toward Dependable Peace: A Proposal for an Appropriate Security System.* Institute for World Order, New York

John XXIII, Pope 1963 *Pacem in Terris* (Encyclical Letter Addressed to all Humankind, Rome, April 11, 1963). St. Paul Editions, Boston, Massachusetts

Laszlo E et al., 1977 *Goals for Mankind: A Fifth Report to the Club of Rome on the New Horizons of Global Community.* Dutton, New York

Mendlovitz S H (ed.) 1975 *On the Creation of a Just World Order: Preferred Worlds for the 1990s.* Free Press, New York

Mitrany D 1966 *A Working Peace System*, rev.edn. Quadrangle, Chicago

Monnet J 1978 *Memoirs.* Doubleday, New York

Nathan O, Norden H (eds.) 1960 *Einstein on Peace.* Shocken, New York

National Conference of Catholic Bishops 1983 *The Challenge* of Peace: God's Promise and Our Response. US Catholic Conference, Boston, Massachusetts

Newcombe H 1983 *Design for a Better World*. University Press of America, Lanham, Maryland

Niebuhr R 1949 The illusion of world government. *Foreign Affairs* 27

Palme Commission 1982 *Common Security: Blueprint for Survival*. Report of the Independent Commission on Disarmament and Security Issues. Simon and Schuster, New York

Reves E 1945 *The Anatomy of Peace*. Harper, New York

Sakharov A D 1968 *Thoughts on Progress, Peaceful Coexistence, and Intellectual Freedom*. Norton, New York

Schell J 1982 *The Fate of the Earth*. Knopf, New York

Shakhnazarov G 1988a The world community is amenable to government [upravlyayemo]. *Pravda* 15 (January)

Shakhnazarov G 1988b Governability of the world. *Int'l Affairs* (Moscow) 34, 3

Stimson H L 1947 The challenge to Americans. *Foreign Affairs* 26

Streit C K 1939 *Union Now: A Proposal for a Federal Union of the Leading Democracies of the North Atlantic*. Harper, New York

Stromberg R N 1978 Collective security. In: Deconde A (ed.) 1978 *The Encyclopedia of American Foreign Policy: Studies of the Principal Movements and Ideas*, Vol. 1. Scribners, New York

Toynbee A 1948 *Civilisation on Trial*. Oxford University Press, New York

Wells H G 1920 *The Outline of History*, 2 vols. Macmillan, New York

White E B 1946 *The Wild Flag*. Houghton Mifflin, Boston, Massachusetts

JOSEPH P. BARATTA

Federation

Recent commentators have avoided offering a precise definition of federation. The term, however, is commonly used to describe the system of government prevailing in the following countries: Canada, Mexico, the United States, Argentina, Brazil, Venezuela, the Germany, Switzerland, Austria, Czechoslovakia, Nigeria, Sudan, Tanzania, India, Malaysia, and Australia. The Union of South Africa (1910) which became a republic with a new constitution in 1961, substantially amended in 1983, has also been considered as showing the attributes of a federation.

The vast disparity in the actual practice of the so-called principles of federation in these states effectively makes any all-encompassing definition so wide that it would cover almost every existing state. Generally, in a federal system, there is a central authority for the whole state, which controls the external affairs of that state together with such internal matters which are agreed to be a common interest of the constituent parts of the whole state. There are also provincial or local authorities (sometimes described as "state" authorities if the federation is made up of a number of different states), which have powers of legislation within their own spheres of administration, usually specified in the constitution.

A federation has commonly been formed when a number of states come together to form a new one, but in such a way as to reconcile a national unity within the new state with the continuation of the rights of the previous states in certain areas. Sometimes this has been considered a device to maintain the rights of minority racial, tribal, or cultural groups and to preserve their identity within the new larger grouping. Such federations sometimes move towards a decentralized system. There are instances, however, of the central authority increasing its control over the different units in an attempt to maintain the national unity of the whole state, and thus moving towards greater centralization. In the end, in most federations, a conflict has developed between local autonomy and central control. The doctrinaire preaching of the political system called "federation" is known as "federalism:" P. J. Proudhon (see *Proudhon, Pierre-Joseph*) was one of its earliest exponents. A federation is also distinct from a "confederation"; in the latter the central government is not sovereign, but holds its authority by the consent of the constituent units. Various models of federation are surveyed below.

1. United States and Switzerland

Modern ideas of federation largely derive from the political system that evolved in the United States. The American Constitution of 1787 does not mention the word "federation," but it is widely regarded as outlining the principal example of federal government. The American system is based upon the supremacy of the constitution: "This constitution and the laws of the USA, which shall be made in pursuance thereof ... shall be the supreme law of the land, and the judges in every state shall be bound thereby, anything in the constitution or laws of any state to the contrary notwithstanding."

The United States constitution establishes a division of powers between the general (central) government, and the governments of the associated states. The central government has supreme authority within its particular sphere, but that sphere is defined—albeit in somewhat contradictory and ambiguous terms—and limited. Under the 10th amendment of 1791, "the powers not delegated to the United States by the Constitution, nor prohibited by it to the states, are reserved to the states respectively or to the people." This means, in effect, that within their particular spheres, the individual states are coequal with, and in no way subordinate to, the central authority. This principle of distinct and coordinate governments was finally established by a constitutional amendment of 1913 which made the election of senators a matter for the people of the states and not for their legislatures. The central government's power to make treaties and to conduct foreign affairs, is, as a general rule, not limited by the powers reserved to the states.

The Swiss constitution of 1848 reflected aspects of that of the United States. A principal safeguard of the federal structure is the device of the referendum: under the Swiss constitution, if either eight of the cantons or 30,000 voters demand it, a law passed by the Federal Assembly must be submitted to the voters as a whole for approval.

2. Canada

The British North America Act of 1867 conferred on Canada a "federal" constitution. That, and the subsequent amending acts, divided the powers between the legislatures in the provinces and the central government by giving the provinces exclusive control over a list of subjects, and Ottawa control over the rest. The powers of the government of Canada were defined, but it was understood that this was not a complete list. Neither the provincial nor the central government had the power to change the distribution of powers specified in the constitution. To safeguard the rights of the then minority of French speakers, that power was reserved for the British parliament.

In 1982 Prime Minister Pierre Trudeau, faced since 1976 with a Quebec controlled by the separatist Parti Québecois under René Lévesque, and with objections from the western provinces to the preponderance of central Canada in the federation, secured a revision of the whole federal structure. In January 1982 the British parliament repealed the British North America Act, and on April 17, 1982 Queen Elizabeth II of Canada proclaimed the Constitution Act of 1982 which provided for an amending process wholly within Canada. The principal procedure of the new amending formula requires resolutions of the Senate and House of Commons, and the concurrence of two-thirds of the provinces representing at least 50 percent of the people of Canada. Parliamentary supremacy was preserved, however, on the issue of the new Charter of Rights and Freedoms. The provinces' control of natural resources within their boundaries was strengthened, and the federal government was committed to make equalization payments to the provinces to enable them to provide comparable levels of public services across Canada.

3. Australia, South Africa, Former Soviet Union, and the Former Federal Republic of Germany

The Constitution of the Commonwealth of Australia enacted in 1900, specifically stated that the people of the associating colonies were to form a "federal Commonwealth." Before modified by amendments, the Constitution Act of Australia provided that the powers of the Commonwealth and state parliaments were to be limited, but not by each other; though coordinated with each other, they were to be subordinated to the constitution. The constitution of the Union of South Africa in 1910, however, provided specifically for the subordination of the provincial governments to the central government. The Republic of South Africa Constitution Act of 1983 abolished the Westminster-style parliamentary system, strengthened the power of the president, and provided for a new three-chamber parliament representing the white, Asian, and mixed-race communities. Under Article 30 the legislative power was specifically vested in "the State President and the Parliament of the Republic, which as the sovereign legislative authority in and over the Republic, shall have full power to make laws for the peace, order and good government of the Republic."

The Constitution of the Soviet Union of 1936 was similar to the South African constitution in that although there was a division of powers between the All-Union government and those of the constituent republics, in effect the Supreme Soviet controlled finance and, under Article 14, the All-Union legislature had such comprehensive powers that if it chose to exercise them, little would be left to the constituent republics. Although amendments in 1944 gave the constituent republics certain powers over military affairs and foreign relations, in effect the central government could continue to exercise its supremacy in these fields.

Similarly, the Basic Law of the former Federal Republic of Germany (1949), though it allowed the regions to administer the law, reserved for the federal government in the exclusive list, and potentially in the concurrent list, the most vital areas. The regions were also represented in the upper house, the *Bundesrat* which had the power of veto over constitutional amendments.

4. India and Pakistan

After 1945 federation was used as a constitutional device in some of the newly independent states of the Commonwealth. On January 26, 1950 the written constitution of the Republic of India came into force: it divided powers between the Union and the "states." The Union parliament was given exclusive power to legislate on 18 items concerned principally with citizenship, foreign affairs, and defense, which in effect conferred on its legislative and executive power over the whole field of external sovereignty. The parliaments of the states have exclusive sovereignty over some subordinate issues, and the division between the two can only be changed if both the Union parliament and the parliaments of not less than one-half of the states agree. But articles 249, 352-60, and 371 provide for emergency provisions enabling the Union government to change the union into a unitary state if the situation seems to make this necessary: the President of India can, if he or she considers the security of India to be threatened either by war, external aggression, or internal disturbance, proclaim a state of emergency which effectively allows the executive of the Union to control the executives of the states, and the parliament of the Union power to legislate on issues normally reserved to the states. Under the premiership of Indira Gandhi (1969-77, 1980-84) centralization was emphasized, as separatist movements, particularly the Sikhs in the Punjab, grew in strength.

Until April 10, 1971, when Bangladesh (formerly East Pakistan) declared itself a sovereign independent republic, Pakistan was a federation of two states separated by 1,000 miles of Indian territory. President Ayub, on March 1, 1962, promulgated a constitution which stated that Pakistan was a federal state with two provinces, East and West Pakistan. The central government was given legislative power over trade and commerce between the provinces and with other countries, and over national economic planning. In effect the West Pakistanis had the economic power and the East suffered.

5. Rhodesia and Nyasaland

On August 1, 1953 the Federation of Rhodesia and Nyasaland came into being. This was an attempt by the British government, following the visit of the Labour Secretary of State for Commonwealth Relations, Patrick Gordon Walker, to Southern Africa in 1951, to widen the gulf between Southern Rhodesia and South Africa, and to prevent South Africa's influence from spreading through the settler white populations in East and Central Africa. There was a danger that these settlers could throw in their lot with South Africa resulting in the oppression of millions of blacks and terrible wars "between a white-ruled Eastern Africa and a black-ruled Western Africa." In November 1951 the Conservative government in Britain decided that the "Central African Federation" was the only effective means of resisting Afrikaner pressure on Southern Rhodesia and Northern Rhodesia. South Africa was economically dominant, and the Nationalist rulers had expansionist aims: a British bloc of territories in Central Africa was necessary to counter this. The federal parliament had considerable powers, but "native" policy was left in the hands of the three territories. The blacks were finally disillusioned with the provisions for reform of the federal franchise in 1957 which effectively reduced black representation. In 1960 Hastings Banda led Nyasaland out of the federation, and towards independence as Malawi. Kenneth Kaunda did the same in Northern Rhodesia which joined the Commonwealth as the independent state of Zambia. On November 11, 1965 Ian Smith and his cabinet signed a Proclamation of Independence for Southern Rhodesia which became Rhodesia, later to become Zimbabwe.

6. West Indies and Malaysia

The Federation of the West Indies came into existence in January 1958. But the mainland territories refused to join. The small islands had little in common with the larger ones. Jamaica and Trinidad which comprised over 80 percent of the federation's area, contained 70 percent of its population, and about that percentage of its wealth, but were separated by 1,000 miles of sea. There were fears in Jamaica that a common market would ruin its industries, and, following a referendum, Jamaica withdrew, followed by Trinidad. On May 31, 1962 the federation was officially dissolved.

A similar policy was attempted in former British Southeast Asia with the creation of the Federation of Malaysia in 1963 comprising Malaya, Singapore, North Borneo, and Sarawak, but fears of oppression of the Chinese by the Malay majority led Singapore, under Lee Kuan Yew, to secede on August 9, 1965.

7. Nigeria

During the 1950s Britain moved Nigeria towards independence under a federal system: theorists thought that this might enable a country of vastly different tribal groupings whose boundaries had been arbitrarily drawn during the age of imperialism to continue as an independent state. On October 1, 1960 the Federation of Nigeria was proclaimed. In 1966 Major-General Johnson Aguiya-Ironsi abolished all political parties and tribal associations, replaced the "regions" with "provinces" and changed the name to the "Republic of Nigeria." On September 1, 1966 Lieutenant-Colonel Jakubu Gowon restored the federal system of government, but the next year Lieutenant-Colonel Ojukwu announced the secession of Biafra and this rebellion lasted until January 1970. Nigeria has experienced several coups since then.

8. Conclusion

"Federation" is a term that has been used to cover such widely different systems of government that it is impossible to generalize about its contribution to peace, stability, and security. Prior to 1945 states commonly described as federations such as the United States, Canada, Australia, and Switzerland, appeared to have shown that a reconciliation was possible between the needs of the newly created entity and the continued identities of the units comprising it. When these principles were applied to what became known as the Third World, however, practical experience seemed to confirm the difficulty of exporting "First World" constitutional practices to developing countries. In these newly independent countries, therefore, the adoption of federative systems of government has not resolved the problems of an imperial legacy.

See also: *Federalism, World*

Bibliography ———————————————

Appadori I 1981 *The domestic Roots of India's Foreign Policy 1947-1972.* Oxford University Press, Delhi
Dawson R MacG, Ward N 1963 *The Government of Canada.* University of Toronto Press, Toronto
Hodson H V (ed.) 1983-85 *The Annual Register 1982, 1983, 1984.* Longman, London
King P 1982 *Federalism and Federation.* Croom Helm, London
Lapping B 1985 *End of Empire.* Grenada, London
Morrison S E, Commager H S, Leuchtenburg W E 1977 *A Concise History of the American Republic.* Oxford University Press, New York
Ovendale R 1983 The South African policy of the British Labour Government, 1947-51. *International Affairs* 59
Wheare K C 1963 *Federal Government*, 4th edn. Oxford University Press, London

RITCHIE OVENDALE

Feminism and Peace

1. A Feminist Critique of the Peace Concept

What feminist peace researchers have brought to the fields of peace, development and human rights studies is a clear linking of the micro with the macro in the analysis of direct violence as well as indirect violence (Brock-Utne 1997; Gierycs 1997; Reardon 1997). Although some few male researchers, in parts of their writing, have also made this linking, the main development in the analysis of peace, human rights and development through micro-macro linkages has come from feminist scholarship.

I have elsewhere (Brock-Utne 1989) shown how the peace concept itself will be changed and more complete when seen from a feminist perspective. In my discussion I have made use of the well-known splitting up of the peace concept in "negative" and "positive" peace (see *Positive versus Negative Peace*). This splitting up of the peace concept has been with the peace research field since its very beginning and we find it already in the editorial of the first issue of the *Journal for Peace Research* written by Johan Galtung (1964).

In a chapter on linking the micro and macro in peace and development studies I have referred to feminist scholarship linking unorganized direct violence on the micro-level to organized structural violence on the macro level (Brock-Utne 1997).

The first of the final documents from the four UN Women Decade conferences (Mexico 1975, Copenhagen 1980, Nairobi 1985, Beijing 1995) which stresses the feminist insight of linking micro violence with macro violence and stating that there is no peace as long as women are being beaten and mutilated is the Nairobi document (Brock-Utne 1988).

Development theories, which are dealing with structural violence, have hardly paid any attention to women and have done little to link the structural violence at the micro level to the structural violence at the macro level. If women are mentioned, it is only as a variable in research. These standard theories also tend to view the household as a "black box" and a basic unit of analysis. My chapter on linking the micro and macro in peace and development studies shows that gender is not just a research variable. It is a central theoretical concept.

Gender blindness of development planners and experts has not made them realize that development projects which introduce an intervention which increases women's work load while giving the returns to their husbands may easily prove detrimental to the nutritional status of children and women in the family. Within a setting where structural violence is committed against whole countries there may also be structural violence going on at the micro level. Without a study of the mechanisms responsible for direct and structural violence at the micro-level within the household (the black box in most social science research including peace and development studies), we shall be unable to understand the structural and direct violence taking place at the macrolevel.

2. Feminist Peace Education

A feminist peace educator does not talk about the way children are raised, but the way boys and girls are raised. A feminist peace educator tries to do away with rigid sex role socialization and the training into feminity or masculinity (Brock-Utne 1989, p. 153). S/he sees to it that women's work for and writings on peace are made visible. A feminist peace educator tries to draw lessons for all humankind from the way women work for peace.

Even though many of the questions that feminist peace educators ask today already were asked sixty years ago by Virgina Woolf (1938) in her beautiful novel "Three Guineas," they were not made part of the agenda of peace education and research before the last decade. In the novel "Three Guineas" Virgina Woolf asks how women can help men achieve peace when they are so oppressed themselves, when they have little education and the education they get is not of the holistic kind enabling them really to understand peace issues and teaching them to cooperate. Rather it is an education for war since it is an education teaching them to compete and giving them a compartmentalized knowledge where social and human questions are divorced from the technical ones.

Yet even after the publication of this book, the field of peace education continued to be looked at as a gender-neutral field (see for instance Rôhrs, 1983 as typical for this approach), a field where sexism was a non-issue. It was only when feminist scholars started to combine peace education with their knowledge of sexism and with the field of gender role socialization, that certain gender-specific questions were asked within the academic fields of peace research and peace education (Reardon 1985, Reardon 1988, Brock-Utne 1985, Brock-Utne 1989) Questions like: Do we educate boys for war and girls for peace? Are girls more socialized in empathy than boys are? What are the consequences of having that sex which is less socialized in empathy and most in aggressive behavior rule the world? What will applying feminist theories to the field of peace studies, including disarmament, human rights and development mean for the field of peace studies? (Brock-Utne 1985, 1989). What is the relationship between militarism and sexism? (Easlea 1983, Reardon 1985).

3. The Invisibility of the Works of Women on Peace

Peace education from a feminist perspective also means making the works of women on peace visible. An evaluation of the content of eight books in peace education written in Swedish and currently in use in Swedish schools from pre-school through high-school showed that a feminist perspective is still very much lacking in peace education (Brock-Utne 1992). The high school text is an anthology with excerpts from the works on peace from 23 authors. Among those there are two women, the one as a co-author with a man. Among the 17 one-authored articles only one is written by a woman. That makes six percent of the articles in a book which on its front-page defines peace as justice! In *Educating for Peace—a Feminist Perspective* (Brock-Utne 1985) many illustrations of the attempts to silence women working for peace and making their work invisible are given.

If such attempts do not succeed, then the next mechanism which will be used against her will be that of ridicule. After her death the mechanism of invisibility will again be used, making sure that she will be "forgotten" in the history books. The famous pacifist novel "Die Waffen nieder" (Down With Arms) by the Austrian peace heroine Bertha von Suttner (1889) (see Nobel Peace Prize Laureates: *Bertha von Suttner*) was such a work which the establishment at her time did not succeed in silencing (see *Die Waffen nieder*). Instead she was ridiculed. And now her works and herself are "forgotten" in history books. The Swedish project gives another example to add to the list of attempts at making the work of women invisible, to "forget" that women have written some of the most penetrating works in the field. And this is done in a country where well-known women like Frederika Bremer, Ellen Key and recently Alva Myrdal, Inga Thorsson and Maj-Britt Theorin have been leading figures in the struggle for global disarmament.

Some of the most penetrating works on global questions concerning peace in the wide definition of the word have been written by women. One of the earliest critics of the way we destroy this planet was the Swedish author Elin Wägner (1941). Later followed Rachel Carson (1964) with *The Silent Spring*, then Carolyn Merchant (1980) with *The Death of Nature*, Rosalie Bertell (1985) with *No Immediate Danger?* When it comes to works on Human Rights, Katarina Tomasevski's (1989) book is especially valuable as she is able to see human rights in a wide perspective. By stressing economic rights as much as the more commonly mentioned civil rights, she also lets the fate of the poor people of the world, especially women, since they are the poorest of the poor, be the main concern of her book. The structural violence committed by us in the so-called First World towards the peoples of the Third World is dealt with brilliantly by Susan George (1976) in her books: *How the Other Half Dies, A Fate Worse Than Debt* (George 1988) and *Faith and Credit* (George 1994). The arms race and collective direct violence is dealt with intelligently and thoroughly by Helen Caldicott (1986) in her book: *Missile Envy*. There are strong psychological mechanisms at work against these women and their writings. The strongest of them all is trying to silence them and to make their works invisible.

4. Peace Education within Women's Peace Groups

The author has often been invited as a discussant to local groups of the Nordic Women for Peace both in Norway, Sweden and Finland. The discussions going on in these groups are impressive and can be looked at as the best application one can find of the pedagogic principles which peace educators as well as feminist educators and adult educators want to adhere to. The atmosphere is one of sharing, of learning from each other.

An analysis of the way women work for peace in this world brought out three main characteristics:

(a) Women working for peace make use of a varied set of non-violent techniques, acts and strategies.

(b) Women take as their point of departure the concern for and ultimate value of life, especially the life of children, but also the life of all human beings and of nature.

(c) Women's work for peace is transpolitical, often transnational, aimed at reaching women and sometimes also men and state leaders in the opposite camp. (Brock-Utne 1985 p. 37-70)

Often women working for peace try to envision a new world, a pragmatopia where the power is divided evenly between women and men, everyone has satisfied the basic necessities of life and conflicts are solved non-violently (Pietilä 1986; Brock-Utne 1992a).

5. Are Boys Educated for War and Girls for Peace?

There is an enormous pressure on mothers who would like to give their sons an education which is more in line with feminist ideas. An education where the sons are taught to cooperate, care, show tender emotions, share household chores rather than to compete and be tough (Arcana 1983; Klein 1985; Forcey 1987; Brock-Utne 1991). In an in-depth study, twenty feminist mothers of sons and twenty more traditional mothers of sons were interviewed. It was found that most of the mothers, no matter what category they had been placed in, wanted to give their son a different education from the one most boys get in our societies (Brock-Utne 1991). Neither of the groups felt that they had succeeded in raising their sons the way they had wanted.

The only clear difference which could be detected between the two groups of mothers was found in the way they explained their lack of success. The traditional mothers put the blame on the genes: "Boys will be boys," while the feminist mothers put the blame more on environmental factors, including themselves—their lack of time as well as the absent fathers, the influence of the sport coaches, the influence of the fathers of the friends of their son, of television, videos and games.

See also: *Feminist Thought and Peace; Theoretical Traditions of Peace and Conflict Studies; Peace Education*

Bibliography

Arcana J 1983 *Every Mother's Son: The Role of Mothers in the Making of Men.* The Women's Press, London

Bertell R 1985 *No Immediate Danger? Prognosis for a*

Radioactive Earth. The Women's Press, London

Brock-Utne B 1985 *Educating for Peace. A Feminist Perspective*. Pergamon Press, New York/Oxford/Toronto/Sydney/Paris/Frankfurt. Reprinted in 1987 and in 1989. A Korean edition in 1986. A Norwegian edition in 1987, an Italian edition in 1989.

Brock-Utne B 1988 The development of peace and peace education concepts through three UN women decade conferences. In: Alger C, Stohl M (eds.) *A Just Peace through Transformation*. Boulder, Westview Press, Colorado and London

Brock-Utne B 1989 *Feminist Perspectives on Peace and Peace Education*. Pergamon Press, New York/Oxford/Toronto/Sydney/Paris/ Frankfurt

Brock-Utne B 1991 The raising of a peaceful boy. In: *Peace Education Miniprints* 8 (January) 1991. Lärarhögskolan i Malmö, Malmö, Sweden

Brock-Utne B 1992a The feminist experience and social change in Europe and Africa. In: Boulding E (ed.) *New Agendas for Peace Research. Conflict and Security Reexamined*. Boulder & London, Lynne Rienne Publishers

Brock-Utne B 1992b Evaluering av undervisningsmateriell til bruk i fredsundervisningen. [Evaluation of teaching material to be used in peace education] Malmö: Institutionen för pedagogik och sp eci almetodik. In: *Särtryck och småtryck* 739 (March) 1992

Brock-Utne B 1997 Linking the micro and macro in peace and development studies. In: Turpin J, Kurtz L R (eds.) 1997 *The Web of Violence*. University of Illinois Press, Chicago

Caldicott H 1986 *Missile Envy. The Arms Race and Nuclear War*. Bantam Books, Toronto/London/New York

Carson R 1964 *The Silent Spring*. Penguin Books, London

Easlea B 1983 *Fathering the Unthinkable. Masculinity, Scientists and the Nuclear Arms Race*. Pluto Press, London

Eisler R 1997 Human rights and violence. In: Turpin J, Kurtz, LR (eds.) *The Web of Violence*. University of Illinois Press, Chicago

Forcey L R 1987 *Mothers of Sons. Toward an Understanding of Responsibility*. Praeger, New York

Galtung J 1964 "Editorial." *J. Peace Research* (1)

George S 1976 *How the Other Half Dies*. Penguin Books, Harmondsworth

George S 1988 *A Fate worse than Debt. A Radical New Analysis of the Third World Debt Crisis*. Penguin Books, Harmondsworth

George S 1994 *Faith and Credit*. Penguin Books, Harmondsworth

Gierycs D 1997 Education on the human rights of women as a vehicle for change. In: Andreopoulos G, R P Claude (eds.) *Human Rights Education for the Twenty-First Century*. University of Pennsylvania Press, Philadelphia

Klein C 1985 *Mothers and Sons*. G.K.Hall & Co, Boston

Merchant C 1980 *The Death of Nature*. Harper & Row, San Fransisco

Pietilä H 1986 Women's peace movement as an innovative proponent of the peace movement as a whole. *Peaceletter*. No. 2, Helsinki

Reardon B 1985 *Militarism and Sexism*. Teachers College Press, New York

Reardon B 1988 *Comprehensive Peace Education. Educating for Global Responsibility*. Teachers College Press, New York

Röhrs H 1983 *Frieden—Eine Pädagogische Aufgabe. Idee und Realität der Friedenspädagogik*. [Peace—An Educational Task. Ideas and Reality in Peace Education.] Agentur Pedersen, Braunschweig

Suttner B von 1889 *Die Waffen nieder* [Lay Down Your Arms]. E. Pierson, Dresden

Tomasevski K 1989 *Development Aid and Human Rights*. Pinter Publishers, London

Woolf V 1938 *Three Guineas*. The Hogarth Press, London

Wägner E 1941 (New Edition 1978) *Väckerklocka*. (Alarm clock) Delfin, Stockholm

BIRGIT BROCK-UTNE

Feminist Literature and Pacifism in the First World War

In *England's Hour* the British writer Vera Brittain (1893-1970), looking back at almost a quarter of a century of feminist and pacifist activity, expressed her frustration in these words: "Over and over again, since this second Great War of my lifetime began, I have asked myself why the eager, well-meaning peace movement of the nineteen-twenties failed so completely to shape the course of international policies. Why I failed." The only answer she offers to her question occurs in the next paragraph: "We failed because we were too easily satisfied"(pp. 81-82). Instead of celebrating when British membership in

the League of Nations Union (a real influence for peace in its early days) reached a quarter of a million, Brittain claims that the peace campaigners should have worried that a quarter of a million is only a two-hundredth part of a population of fifty million. She accuses herself and other pacifists of complacency.

Brittain's question is more significant than her answer. She was hardly complacent. If she occasionally overestimated what had been achieved, she continued to fight actively for women's issues and for peace all her life. Nor does her answer address the heart of her question, still relevant in the United

Kingdom and elsewhere some 50 years and several wars later: why did the strong women's peace movement of the early twentieth century fail to influence a large enough number of people to sway international policies? It is this formulation of the question that will be addressed in this article.

But of whom to ask the question? The most obvious answer is to ask the women themselves, but since in most cases this is no longer possible, the next best thing—though a very different thing—to be done is to question the work they produced. There is a great deal of this work in all literary forms. Many feminist writers of the period wrote about the women's struggle for peace. The problem is, of course, that much of the literature has either been forgotten or has disappeared. We may have read Virginia Woolf, but have we read Phyllis Bentley, Sylvia Townsend Warner, Rebecca West, Storm Jameson, Winifred Holtby, or indeed Vera Brittain? We may have heard of Jane Addams, but do we know Ellen Key, Bertha von Suttner, Dora Russell, Lida Gustava Heymann, Rosika Schwimmer?

It is not surprising that Vera Brittain's daughter, the English politician Shirley Williams, thinks her mother's *Testament of Youth* is the only book about the First World War written by a woman. It is certainly one of the very few available today. Yet William Matthews' annotated *Bibliography of British Autobiographies* lists 72 other published autobiographies by women which deal at least in part with the First World War. Seventy-two is just the starting figure, of course. What about countries other than the United Kingdom? What about those written but not published? What about those Matthews missed? Despite the efforts of such publishing houses as Virago and the Feminist Press to reissue lost literature by women of this period and the efforts of such feminist critics as Dale Spender, Jane Marcus, Elaine Showalter, and Sandra Gilbert to bring it to our attention, there is clearly a treasure trove of modern material still to be rediscovered. So in reading women's writing of the first part of the twentieth century to discover why the feminist efforts for peace failed, we must always bear in mind the possibility of other evidence from those buried works we must be missing.

The literature we have suggests that, although there was a strong pacifist/feminist tradition that preceded the First World War, the war itself made pacifists out of many women and men who had not previously been so. The key to this conversion was the actual experience of seeing the effects of war at close quarters in contrast to the *dulce et decorum est* propaganda which was current in the United Kingdom at

least for the first few years of the war. The antiwar sentiments in the better known poetry of such male poets as Wilfred Owen and Siegfried Sassoon are echoed in the autobiographies, fiction, and poetry of the women who went to war. Vera Brittain's *Testament of Youth* can be read as an account of the birth of a pacifist. It begins with Vera as an unthinking Edwardian young woman declaring the first day of the war to be the "most thrilling"of her life, describes the deaths of her fiance Roland, her brother Edward, and two other close friends, recounts her nursing experiences in France and Malta, and leaves her determined to devote her energies to working for peace. The causes of her pacifism are the two most frequently reflected in literature.

The first is the horror of battle itself, or rather its results, the waste of life, the suffering of the wounded. Nowhere are these horrors more graphically portrayed than in a little known autobiographical work of Helen Zenna smith called *Stepdaughters of War*. Smith contrasts the realities of ambulance driving on the front line in France with the competitive, unthinking patriotism of her mother and her mother's friends in England.

Wartime and postwar fiction by women portrays the results of war atrocities in some often repeated characters. The soldier returns from the war physically damaged, dying of tuberculosis like Ted in Winifred Holtby's *Land of Green Ginger* or Giles in G. B. Stern's *A Deputy Was King*, or psychologically damaged, suffering from shell shock, like Francis in Britain's *Account Rendered* or Septimus Warren Smith in Woolf's *Mrs. Dalloway*, or suffering from amnesia like Chris on Rebecca West's *The Return of the Soldier*. Female protagonists, like Sarah Burton in Holtby's *South Riding* or Virginia Dennison on Brittain's *The Dark Tide*, often lost finances in the trenches. The dead lover becomes the embodiment of all sexual passion; a lost, more intense world which is never recaptured in the postwar marriages many of these characters eventually make. In Brittain's *Born 1925* and *Honorable Estate*, as in her own life, and in Ruth Holland's *The Lost Generation*, for example, these second relationships are companionable, perhaps equal, partnerships in ways the first were not, but emotionally flat. If it is true, as Jane Addams (see Nobel Peace Prize Laureates: *Jane Addams*) among others claimed, that enthusiasm for continuing the war was fueled on both sides among civilians by stories of enemy atrocities, it is also true that the actual experience of these atrocities was more likely to make pacifists out of those who lived to tell about them.

The second motivation towards pacifism most frequently described in literature is an awareness of internationalism, a sometimes sudden realization that the British soldier and the German soldier shared a common humanity. The ordinary soldier is portrayed as a peaceloving man, at war only because of patriarchal conditioning and government propaganda. When she is nursing wounded Germans in France, Vera Brittain is struck with a sense of internationalism which finally forces her to see the futility of war. In *Testament of Youth* she conveys the irony of nursing the very men her brother is trying to kill. Bombarded by war propaganda which persuaded whole nations that their enemies were inhuman monsters, soldiers and nurses who actually encountered the enemy were all the more surprised to find them just like themselves. In the work of Jane Addams, Vera Brittain, Winifred Holtby, and many others, this sense of internationalism which had initially made them converts to pacifism became their most powerful argument to convert others.

These two causes of pacifism among women who experienced the war correspond to two different pacifist philosophies which Carolyn Stephenson (1982) describes as "negative" and "positive" approaches to peace. This is essentially the same distinction that Jane Addams made in *Newer Ideals of Peace*, where she called the first approach "dovelike," the second "active and dynamic." Stephenson explains the difference in this way: "Briefly stated, one can conceive of peace primarily as the absence of war or social violence, or one can view peace as the presence of justice in society (see *Positive versus Negative Peace*)." These two pacifist attitudes are intertwined to some extent in the work of virtually every pacifist writer, but they relate to feminism in very different ways, ways which have important implications for the success or failure of both the peace movement and the women's movement.

The "negative" approach to peace depends, for feminists, on the idea that war is a male institution. This is sometimes presented as a biological argument that men are innately predisposed towards violence, that we can see this in the "natural" aggressiveness of little boys. It is also presented as the result of conditioning, as a sociological argument that men are socialized into the acceptance of this view and reproduce the behavior associated with it. War is also defined as a male institution on the grounds that since only men have ever had political power, only men have been in the position to wage war. As Virginia Woolf points out in *Three Guineas*, "Scarcely a human being in the course of history has fallen to a woman's rifle; the vast majority of birds and beasts

have been killed by you, not by us" (p. 6).

At first hearing, this argument may have a certain attraction for feminists, but what does it really imply about women? The pacifist women at the 1915 Hague Peace Conference certainly accepted the view that if women rather than men had had political power the First World War would never have taken place. They saw women's suffrage as the key to peace, the central demand upon which all others depended. But what are the real implications of this idea? Marielouise Janssen-Jurreit's (1982) comment on women's work for peace in this period provides the answer: "Behind it was the foregone conclusion that women, because of a biological capacity to produce life, have more immediate interest than men in the settlement of conflict by peaceful means" (p. 137). It is the "motherhood" argument; it claims that because women give birth they are naturally more humanitarian, more nurturing. It is a notion which has appeared in literature by both men and women probably since tales were first told. It had a large revival in the nineteenth century which has continued into our own. Here is Olive Schreiner in 1911: "No woman who is a woman says of a human body, 'it is nothing'"; and Rosika Schwimmer in 1914: "We are united by the motherhood instinct." Here, too, is Ellen Key in 1916: "If the motherliness of woman is not so incensed by this war that it causes a mass rising against the injustice of woman's position, then I don't know from what source we may expect salvation." And here is the Canadian novelist Margaret Laurence addressing an antinuclear rally in the 1980s: "To me, the disarmament issue is a true motherhood issue." Interestingly Laurence defines all women as "mothers," innately more concerned with human life than men: "As women, whether we've borne children or not, we've got to think of a time when there is no more birth, only death, then nothing."

This author does not wish for a moment to undervalue the women's peace activities that have been fought under this banner. It certainly has the power to bring together women who would not rally for other women's issues. The women's Strike for Peace in 1962 and its attack on the House Un-American Activities Committee is an excellent example of how powerful politically the motherhood concept can be under certain circumstances. However, it is important that we be aware of its dangers. There are some obvious political dangers. First, it can be used for prowar as well as antiwar purposes; a woman called upon to respond to the emotion of her mothering may be as susceptible to the so-called patriotic arguments as to the pacifist ones. In a 1930 letter to the feminist publication *Time and Tide*, Vera Brittain said: "We heard a great deal about the tears of the mothers which were supposed to inspire our men to inflict smashing blows on the enemy—though since there were just as many mothers on the other side, and, therefore, presumably, just as many tears, it might have been supposed that the galvanizing effects of these lamentations would have cancelled each other out."

Second, the motherhood argument can easily be used to argue that women are primarily mothers, that they should not do anything—work, for example—that is detrimental or dangerous to this chief female function. Vera Brittain's 1953 attack on this argument in *Lady into Woman* testifies to its prevalence in postwar Britain. She points out that the figures for the number of women dying each year in childbirth made motherhood as an occupation a little more dangerous than mining. She points out too the inconsistency in the arguments of those who use motherhood against women workers. Describing the charges of unwomanliness, competitiveness, neurosis brought by antifeminists, she says "no modern psychologist would have entrusted children to women described by the anti-feminist males who nevertheless regarded childbearing and rearing as their main function" (pp. 41-42).

The motherhood argument is usually linked to the notion of innate biological differences in male and female characters and thus to the idea of the natural division of labor. In *Girls Growing up in Late Victorian and Edwardian England*, Carol Dyhouse (1981) traces the ways in which the biological argument was used to keep women in their traditional place. She makes the case that throughout this period work outside the home is seen as fundamentally incompatible with marriage and motherhood for middle-class women, and that education for women is primarily directed at their future influence on their sons. So-called "scientific" arguments used to justify the division of labor, such as the claim that women who "overtaxed" their brains through too much intellectual activity would be unable to bear children or the idea of a distinction between "active" male cells and "passive" female ones, persisted well into the twentieth century (pp. 152-54). Although the idea of innate female characteristics as the basis of a new female value system can be used politically for feminist goals, as it has been by several writers of feminist utopias. It has some built-in dangers which may well weaken its force.

The second type of pacifism, the positive or "active and dynamic" pacifism as Jane Addams called it, is linked to the idea of internationalism. The recogni-

tion that the enemy as an individual is "just like me" pits the notion of the importance of the individual, particularly the individual's right to self-determination, against institutionalized mass thinking, the state, the "they" who make the decisions. By 1916 the sense that those fighting the war were the impotent victims of politicians of another generation was widespread. It was the old men's war. The message of Woolf's *Jacob's Room and Mrs. Dalloway*, of Britain's "indictment of a civilisation," *Testament of Youth,* of Margery Laurence's poem addressed to "You who sat safe at home/And let us die," is summed up in the title of a 1928 novel by Charles Harrison, *Generals Die in Bed.*

Pacifism seen as opposition to the oppression of individuals is organically linked to feminism and to the struggle of any oppressed group, whether defined by gender, class, race, or religion. Carolyn Stephenson (1982) claims "The central commonality between feminists and pacifists is their opposition to oppression, whether that oppression be sexism, racism, or any other oppression. This opposition to oppression is based, in both cases, on the empowerment of the individual, on power which is constructive rather than destructive." In the work of many of the feminist pacifist writers in the early twentieth century this connection is fundamental. So we find, for example, that Winifred Holtby was a feminist and a pacifist but also devoted much of her energy to the liberation of black South Africans. Sylvia Pankhurst working with poor women in the East End of London and Jane Addams working with immigrants in Chicago saw pacifism and feminism as part of the larger struggle for social justice.

Woolf's *Three Guineas* demonstrates that money given to provide education for women and to help them enter the professions is money given to help stop war: "The three guineas, you will observe, though given to three different treasurers are all given to the same cause. For the causes are the same and inseparable." This cause is "the rights of all—all men and women—to the respect in their persons of the great principles of Justice and Equality and Liberty" (pp. 143-44).

To read the pacifist literature of the early part of this century is as depressing as to read the feminist. Like the feminist statements, the pacifist ones have an eerie contemporary ring to them. The Swedish pacifist Ellen Key (1916) commented on the First World War: "Each one of the great powers might have preserved the peace, had it so desired . . . . But as they had expended all their energy in preparing for war, the outbreak of war, in a moment of high tension, became inevitable" (p. 19).

We might perhaps disagree over how successful feminism has been in this century; despite the failure of the Equal Rights Amendment in the United States and the backlash which followed the two world wars, some gains have been made. But we could hardly argue over women's efforts for peace; they have been, as Vera Brittain knew, a conspicuous failure.

Asking the same question more than 50 years and several wars later seems to be no easier to answer. Did the problem lie in the fact that many women thought they had something to gain from war, that feminists were split from the beginning? It is a split which remains with the women's movement today. Emmeline Pankhurst, who threw her influence behind the war effort in 1914 believing that women would prove themselves as good as men in war work and thus earn the vote, is merely one in a long tradition of feminists who have devoted their energies to competing in the male world on male terms. Who can oppose the idea that women have the right to work, but how many of the gains in women's employment were already beginning and would have happened, albeit more slowly, without the First World War? In support of this view Vera Brittain points to the Scandinavian countries, where women advanced more rapidly than anywhere else in Europe despite the fact that, until the Nazi invasion of 1940, Norway, Sweden, and Denmark had avoided war for more than a century.

Did feminist pacifism fail because feminists misjudged the effects of female suffrage? Did voting women advance the cause of either feminism or pacifism? Undoubtedly there were some gains in laws for social reform which can be attributed to the women's vote. But on the whole the women's vote tended to be conservative, as did the women elected to positions of political power. Sheila Rowbotham (1973, 1976) claims that in the United Kingdom "The feminists, like the Labour men and women, were let into parliament and put on committees. Once inside the constitution, they forgot that they had sought admission because they believed the world should be made anew" (p. 162).

Rowbotham argues that not only did women get coopted, but that the theoretical links between feminism and such other movements against oppression as socialism and pacifism were lost. The postwar feminists in the United Kingdom concentrated on achieving specific changes in the laws and no longer had the sense of that prewar feminist consciousness which extended "beyond the reform of the vote into an attack on male dominated culture as a whole" (p. 162). Is this the primary reason why feminist pacifism failed? In forgetting its theoretical base, its links

with other movements, did feminism lose its power to influence the world for peace? Young women who had not experienced the prewar struggles were likely to dismiss feminism as a limited movement whose aims had essentially been achieved.

Is what we need then a return to a sense of the organic bonds between feminism, pacifism, and other radical movements? This is all very well in theory, but in practice feminist issues tend to get subsumed in the dominant male culture. Vera Brittain, who worked throughout the 1920s for the League of Nations, says the League was dominated by male values from the beginning despite the efforts of the feminists who worked within it.

Virginia Woolf suggests a compromise position which may point to a solution. Addressing a man who has asked her to join his society to promote peace, she said, "We can best help you to prevent war not by joining your society but by remaining outside your society but in cooperation with its aim. That aim is the same for both" (p. 143). Woolf called her new society the Outsider's Society. It was to be a society without offices, committees, secretaries, conferences, meetings, oaths, or ceremonies. In other words, Woolf recognized a fundamental problem in organizing the opposition to oppression, that any organization, however good its aims, tends by its very nature as an institution to become oppressive itself.

If a way can be found to keep the women's movement sufficiently flexible not to be oppressive, in cooperation with other movements but not subsumed by them, is it likely to be a stronger influence for peace? Perhaps. But we must still deal with the fact that the strongest argument for a separate women's pacifist movement has always been the biological one. More women will work for peace under the banner of motherhood, but, as stated earlier, this argument can all too easily be used against feminist aims. Men are, after all, conditioned to reject their mothers and bond with their fathers; in the last resort mothers, as mothers, are not to be taken seriously.

How are we to make those arguments which cannot be turned against us forceful enough to stop war? This author has no fully satisfactory answer to this anymore than to Vera Brittain's question about the failure of feminist pacifism in this century. It is suggested, though, that part of the answer to her question may lie in the fact that so much work by women has disappeared from view even in the past 70 years, when we were looking, as it were. At least 72 published records of the First World War vanished even before such potentially receptive readers as Vera

Brittain could find them. If every generation of women is not doomed to repeat the experiences of its mothers and grandmothers, some way must be found not only of retrieving women's literature but of preventing its future disappearance. Only then can we hope that the feminist pacifist arguments against oppression will in both quantity and persuasiveness be sufficient to change a world in which women are eager to adopt the term "postfeminist" and men can call nuclear weapons "peacekeepers."

See also: *Feminist Thought and Peace; Pacifism;* Nobel Peace Prize Laureates: *Bertha von Suttner; Jane Addams*

Bibliography

Brittain V 1953 *Lady into Woman*. Andrew Dakers, London
Brittain V 1978 *Testament of Youth*. Virago, London
Brittain V 1981 *England's Hour*. Futura, London
Dyhouse C 1981 *Girls Growing Up in Late Victorian and Edwardian England*. Routledge and Kegan Paul, London
Gilbert S Soldier's heart: Literary men, literary women, and the Great War. *Signs* 8(3)
Huston N 1985 The matrix of war. *Poetics Today* 6(1/2)
Janssen-Jurreit M 1982 *Sexism: The Male Monopoly on History and Thought*. Farrar, Straus, Giroux, New York
Key E 1916 *War, Peace and the Future*. Putnam, London
Rowbotham S 1973, 1976 *Hidden from History*. Vintage, London
Stephenson C M 1982 Feminism, pacifism, nationalism and the United Nations Decade for Women. *Women's Studies International Forum* 5(3/4)
Woolf V 1938 *Three Guineas*. Harcourt, Brace, and World, London

JEAN E. KENNARD

Feminist Thought and Peace

In the nuclear age, the question of why men seem incapable of living in peace is an issue not only of academic interest but also of survival (see *Human Security*). Because wars have been fought by men, it has sometimes been said that men are "naturally" warlike. That men's warlikeness is not genetic is evidenced by the fact that there are peaceful men. And while it has been said that women are "naturally" peaceful, there are women—for instance, Indira Gandhi or Margaret Thatcher—who have seemed to bend over backward to prove they were not too "soft" or "feminine" when they assumed roles traditionally assigned to men.

Nonetheless, throughout recorded history women have been associated with nonviolence. Aristophanes' famous play *Lysistrata* reports how in classical Greek antiquity women peace activists barred their husbands from their beds until they put down their arms (see *Aristophanes*). And in modern times women have continued to play a major role in the peace movement. However, in contrast to the past, when women were essentially reduced to pleading with men to stop their wars, women as both activists and theorists are increasingly taking independent action to bring about peace.

Already in the late nineteenth and early twentieth centuries, a number of unconventional women were prominent antimilitarists. For example, in the United States, Jane Addams was President of the Women's Peace Party (later renamed the Women's International League for Peace and Freedom) (see Nobel Peace Prize Laureates: *Jane Addams*). More recent examples of women who have made a dramatic break with women's traditional "auxiliary" role in the international peace movement are Dr. Helen Caldicott, the Australian-born founder of Women's Action for Nuclear Disarmament (WAND) and Physicians for Social Responsibility, Eva Nordland of Norway, founder of Nordic Women for Peace (see *Peace Movement in Nordic Countries*), who organized peace marches on Paris, Moscow, and Washington, DC, and Randall Forsberg, founder of the Massachusetts-based Institute for Defense and Disarmament Studies, a major force in launching the American nuclear freeze movement.

Women in various countries have also begun to build new political blocs committed to the more "feminine" values of ecological responsibility, sexual equality, and peace. Some examples from the West are the German "Greens" party founded by Petra Kelly, the candidacy of Sonia Johnson for the US presidency on the Citizens' Party ticket, and organizations such as the Women's International League for Peace and Freedom (WILPF) headquartered in Switzerland, and Women's Environment and Development Organization (WEDO) headquartered in New York.

Moreover, in contrast to the past, when men controlled the pen as well as the sword, today many of the most forceful antiwar writings, such as Nobel Peace Prize winner Alva Myrdal's *The Game of Dis-*

armament (see Nobel Peace Prize Laureates: *Alva Myrdal*) and Caldicott's *Nuclear Madness*, are the works of women.

Underlying these differences between present and past is a fundamental perceptual shift largely pioneered by feminist writers and researchers. In essence, these feminist theoreticians assert that our mounting global crises—the threat of nuclear holocaust and its interlinking with the global population explosion, environmental pollution, and the widening gap between rich and poor—are inherent in the prevailing androcratic or male-dominated paradigm, and thus cannot be solved within it.

For example, in *The Female World*, sociologist Jessie Bernard (1981) describes how in male-dominated systems there are two separate and not equal worlds: the main or man's world and a subsidiary, also male-controlled, female world. These worlds have in the course of time developed two different sets of governing values, which Bernard terms the "male ethos" of competition/power and the "female ethos" of love/duty. In today's world, Bernard notes, "the power-driven male, operating on a never ending one-upmanship basis, who has to be victorious over all others no matter what, may be analogous to the stag with maladaptive horns" (p. 538).

Bernard's analysis is roughly paralleled by Harvard psychologist Carol Gilligan's work (1982) on the differences between female and male conceptions of morality. The way men have learned to conceptualize morality, Gilligan found, is in far more abstract or impersonal terms than women. For most men, morality is "playing by the rules." For women, however, morality generally tends to impose an affirmative duty to act in a caring or compassionate way that varies from situation to situation. In other words, the conventional male morality seems to be more a morality of noninterference with other individuals' established rights—and thus one tending to maintain the status quo. In contrast, women's view of morality is more that of a positive obligation or duty to care for other, particularly for those not in an equal position or those in need.

Another body of work examining how the sexual stereotypes developed to maintain male-dominated systems shape differentially women's and men's attitudes and behaviors is that of psychiatrist Jean Baker Miller (1982), director of Wellesley's Stone Center for Developmental Services and Studies. Of particular interest is Miller's analysis of the contrasting way women and men conceptualize power. The conventional or male definition of power means "power over"—the power to control or limit the actions of others. By contrast, the way women tend to view their own power is as "power to"—the kind of actualizing power mothers have over their children. Miller notes how the "masculine" view of power is an outgrowth of an essentially confrontational worldview equating masculinity with conquest or dominance. She also notes how male-centered systems have historically been exploitive not only of women, but also of other men.

The questions posed by these types of studies directly relate to the question of what kinds of societies will be peaceful and what kinds will be warlike. A 1985 study conducted by the authors as co-directors of the Institute for Futures Forecasters addressed this question. Since then one of the authors (Eisler) has conducted a multidisciplinary study indicating that there are, in systems terms, structural correlations between male dominance, a generally hierarchic and authoritarian social structure, and a high degree of institutionalized social violence, including warfare.

Eisler's study has focused on a fundamental, but generally ignored issue: how is the overall structure of a social system affected by the way it structures the roles and relationships between the female and male halves of humanity?

Reexamining social systems and social history taking into account new discoveries in both the natural and social sciences—notably the works of Prigogine, von Bertalanffy, Wiener, Laszlo, Csanyi, Gould, and Eldredge, as well as the new research of feminist scholars—Eisler has developed the method of inquiry she calls the study of relational dynamics for the investigation of war and peace in terms of two contrasting models of social organization. (Findings from this study are reported in Eisler's books, *The Chalice and the Blade* and *Sacred Pleasure* and in Eisler and Loye's *The Partnership Way*.)

One is the dominator model. A key characteristic of this model is the ranking of one half of humanity over the other. This can be either a patriarchy or matriarchy.

The other is the partnership model of social organization. A key characteristic of this model is the equal partnership of the female and male halves of humanity, and with this, the incorporation into social policy of traits stereotypically considered feminine, such as nonviolence and nurturance.

Since a patriarchal form of dominator organization has prevailed for most of recorded history, the dominator model has been believed to be either divinely or naturally ordained. However, analysis of new data from archaeology, anthropology, religious history, and myth indicates that the original direction for human cultural evolution appears to have been in the direction of a partnership rather than a dominator model.

This type of organization is today beginning to emerge. It is most closely approximated by the Scandinavian nations, where a higher status of women and an emphasis on policies promoting stereotypically "feminine" values such as caretaking and nonviolence go together. It has also been found in some more peaceful tribal societies, such as the Tiruray, Kung, and BaMbuti. The primitive level of technology of these societies earlier led to the view that only the most technologically simple societies are sexually equalitarian, and that "civilization" requires male dominance. This is what Marx and Engels incorrectly deduced from nineteenth century anthropology and archaeology, which led them, following the lead of Morgan and others, to assert that male dominance ushered in a "higher" stage of civilization.

However, the latest archaeological data indicate that this is not an accurate model of social evolution, that the evolutionary thrust in the mainstream of early Western civilization seems to have been toward a partnership model. (Eisler's *The Chalice and the Blade* listed in the Bibliography is a good source here. *The Chalice and the Blade in Chinese Culture*, edited by Professor Min Jiayin of the Chinese Academy of Social Sciences, indicates a similar thrust in early Eastern civilization.)

These data also indicate that the supreme deity was originally seen as female. However, they do not support the belief that in early societies women dominated men. Contrary to the 19th century view that, not being patriarchies, these societies were matriarchies, these discoveries reveal a sexually equalitarian and generally more nonhierarchic social organization.

As British archaeologist James Mellaart (1967) writes of Catal Huyuk, the largest Neolithic site ever found, there is no evidence in the excavations of any marked differences in status or wealth. Mellaart, whose excavations of Catal Huyuk have advanced our knowledge of prehistory, also remarks on the extraordinary cultural continuity between the first agricultural (or Neolithic) civilizations and the earlier Paleolithic or Stone Age era.

Post-Second World War excavations, not only in Turkey but also in the Balkans and Asia Minor, indicate that the first cradles of civilization were not the male-dominated, warlike, and generally hierarchic ones of the later Fertile Crescent. There were much earlier Neolithic societies, which are now known to have been far more advanced than was formerly believed. It has been ascertained that out of these highly creative earlier societies came most of the major technological breakthroughs upon which civilization is based: not only agriculture, but also organized religion, government, manufacturing, trade, architecture, and even a rudimentary form of writing.

As archaeologist Marija Gimbutas writes, the social organization of these societies was very different from those that followed. Although matrifocal and matrilinear, they were sexually equalitarian, with a belief system "focused on the agricultural cycle of birth, death, and regeneration, embodied in the feminine principle, a Mother Creatrix" (Gimbutas 1977 p. 281). They were also, as already noted, generally equalitarian. And there is strong evidence indicating that for thousands of years these societies, whose art shows that the male as warrior was not idealized, were generally peaceful.

The destruction of these societies by male-dominant nomadic pastoral hordes coming from the fringe areas of our globe who, as Gimbutas writes, "worshipped the lethal power of the sharp blade" (p. 281), ushered in what we are taught was the beginning of Western civilization. But it was in fact the end of an earlier era. As the noted Greek archaeologist Nicolas Platon writes of Minoan Crete—the remarkable Bronze Age civilization where the earlier type of social organization survived into historic times—these were societies where "the important part played by women is discernible in every sphere." And they were also societies marked not only by a "ubiquitous joy of living" but also by a remarkable "love of peace" (Platon 1966 pp. 148-49).

Also documenting the relationship between violence in interpersonal and intergroup relations and the domination of half of humanity over the other are cross-cultural studies. For instance, a cross-cultural study by McConahay (1977) indicates that the more rigidly male-dominated a society is, the more heavily it will rely on violence in both interpersonal and intergroup relations. Historical studies show a similar pattern. A dramatic modern example is Nazi Germany, where the reimposition of rigid male dominance went hand in hand with the militarization that culminated in the Second World War.

Drawing upon these types of data, Eisler's study extends feminist theory by positing that our social history has been shaped by, and is best understood in terms of, the interaction between the dominator paradigm that has prevailed through most of recorded history and the earlier partnership view of human organization that periodically resurges. Examples of such resurgences are the early Christian movement, the Medieval Troubadour movement, the "Flower Children" of the 1960s, and the more recent emergence of a social movement combining pacifism, feminism, and ecological responsibility. But until now, these periods have always been followed by regressions to both male dominance and warlikeness, which are structurally interrelated.

Examining the critical issue of war or peace from this perspective not only sheds new light on women's traditional association with work for peace; it also suggests that to a far greater extent than is generally realized the attainment of global peace hinges on the success or failure of the global women's movement in helping bring about a fundamental social systems transformation. There is much concern, for example, about how the increasingly suicidal expenditure of material and human resources on technologies of destruction can be replaced with a higher valuing of technologies that sustain and enhance life. Eisler's Cultural Transformation Theory indicates that this would be a realistic possibility in a society no longer in need of sexually stereotyped socialization—a socialization where women (the subordinate or "second" sex) are taught to be caring, compassionate, and nonviolent, while men are from infancy handed toy swords and guns and taught to associate "real" masculinity with domination and conquest.

Similarly, the entry of substantial numbers of women into leadership roles now monopolized by men would be an important step toward reducing international tensions. No longer being merely occasional or token leaders, who must constantly prove they are not too "soft" or "feminine," women could bring what Bernard calls the female ethos of love/duty into key positions.

This dynamic can be seen in developments in the Scandinavian nations during the 1970s when the rising status of women (and more women entering politics) and an emphasis by government policy on stereotypically "feminine" activities such as caring for children and the elderly, keeping all members of the family healthy, environmental housekeeping, and the establishment of peace academies teaching nonviolence went hand in hand.

In sum, the rise in status of women worldwide would bring with it a higher valuation of values still primarily associated with women and "femininity" such as empathy and nonviolence not only in women but also in men. These are systems dynamics that would in turn accelerate the transformation of values that futurist reports like the Global 2000 and the Club of Rome studies assert are essential for social systems survival. In the words of the second Club of Rome study, this would be a shift to a system of values "balancing competition with cooperation," governed by a "concern for future generations" and a real "global partnership" or, in terms of Eisler's study, a partnership model of social organization.

See also: *Feminism and Peace; Population Pressure, Women's Roles, and Peace; Sexual Equality and Peace; Global 2000 Reports; Peaceful Societies*

Bibliography ————————————————

Bernard J 1981 *The Female World.* Free Press, New York

Dinnerstein D 1976 *The Mermaid and the Minotaur.* Harper, London

Eisler R 1981 Gylany: The balanced future. *Futures* 13 (6)

Eisler R 1984 Violence and male dominance: The ticking time bomb. *Humanities in Society* 7 (1,2)

Eisler R 1987 *The Chalice and the Blade: Our History, Our Future.* Harper and Row, San Francisco, California

Eisler R 1995 *Sacred Pleasure: Sex, Myth, and the Politics of the Body.* Harper, San Francisco, California

Eisler R, Loye D 1983 The "failure" of liberalism: A reassessment of ideology from a new feminine-masculine perspective. *Political Psychology* 4 (1)

Eisler R, Loye D 1990 *The Partnership Way: New Tools for Living and Learning.* Harper Collins, San Francisco, California

Eisler R, Loye D, Norgaard K 1995 *Women, Men, and the Global Quality of Life.* Center for Partnership Studies, Pacific Grove, California

Eldredge N, Gould S 1972 Punctuated equilibria: An alternative to phyletic gradualism. In: Schopf (ed.) 1972 *Models in Paleobiology.* Freeman, Cooper, San Francisco, California

Enloe C 1983 *Does Khaki Become You?* South End Press, Boston, Massachusetts

Gilligan C 1982 *In a Different Voice.* Harvard University Press, Cambridge, Massachusetts

Gimbutas M 1977 The first wave of Eurasian Steppe pastoralists into Copper Age Europe. *J. Indo-European Studies* 5(4)

Gimbutas M 1982 *The Goddesses and Gods of Old Europe.* University of California Press, Berkeley, California

Laszlo E 1984 Cybernetics in an evolving social system, *Kybernetes* 13

McAllister P (ed.) 1982 *Reweaving the Web of Life: Feminism and Nonviolence.* New Society, Philadelphia, Pennsylvania

McConahay D, McConahay J 1977 Sexual permissiveness, sex-role rigidity, and violence across cultures. *J. Social Issues* 33(2)

Mellaart J 1967 *Catal Huyuk.* McGraw-Hill, New York

Mesarovic M, Pestel E 1974 *Mankind at the Turning Point: The*

Second Report to the Club of Rome. Dutton, New York

Miller J B 1982 Women and power. In: *Work in Progress.* Stone Center for Developmental Services and Studies, Wellesley, Massachusetts

Platon N 1966 *Crete*. Nagel, Geneva

Prigogine I, Stengers I 1984 *Order Out of Chaos*. Bantam, New York

Reardon B 1985 *Sexism and the War System*. World Policy Institute, New York

RIANE EISLER; DAVID LOYE

Field Diplomacy: A New Conflict Paradigm

1. A World in Crisis

One of the most important challenges facing the global community in the next decade, is the prevention of destructive conflicts. Listening to the discourse in the United Nations and other governmental and non-governmental organizations this may sound like kicking in wide open doors[1]. But the failure of conflict prevention and the high number of conflict zones, indicates that we still have a long way to go. A global survey of contemporary conflicts counts 22 high-intensity and 39 lower intensity conflicts, and 40 serious disputes[2]. In 1995 five groups were victims of genocides or politicides. The risks of future victimization of 47 communities in different parts of the world are assessed as high or very high[3]. The growth of nationalist feelings at the end of the Cold War is only the beginning of more suffering. More conflicts are expected, with old and new causes, such as the unequal or unfair trade balances between North and South, unemployment in the North, the environmental pollution, fundamentalism, mass immigration and the growing number of failed states. These problems which could hurt people so much that they would be prepared to fight for them.

Most of today's efforts are of a reactive nature. *Proactive conflict prevention* refers to measures taken before the conflict escalates; reactive conflict prevention to measures taken after the conflict has escalated. The aim of the latter is to contain and reduce the intensity, duration and geographic spillover of the violence. When one has failed to prevent a conflict from crossing the threshold of violence it becomes much more difficult and costly to manage a conflict. Not only does one have to settle the dispute(s) which originated the conflict, but in addition one needs to end fighting, and keep and rebuild the peace.

The costs of destruction of war and of peace rebuilding are very high. It is practically impossible to find an accurate and complete accounting of those costs. A complete assessment of the costs should not only include the human and economic costs, but also the social, political, ecological, cultural, psychological and spiritual destruction. These eight dimensions of war destruction give us an idea of the size and complexity of peace rebuilding. Despite the fact that proactive conflict prevention is a more cost effective way of handling conflicts, the international community has difficulty to get rid of its propensity to respond to conflicts in a reactive manner. The fault for the latest violent spasm in Liberia rests mostly with the warlords. The international community refused to adequately finance a disarmament effort by the United Nations and the West African peace-keeping force that has been in Liberia since 1990. All of this would cost more than $20 million. But in the past six years Washington has poured almost half a billion dollars of humanitarian aid into the country, not including the cost of the evacuation—the third such operation since 1989.[4]

2. Preventive Diplomacy?

How does one account for the failure of conflict prevention? Several explanations can be listed: lack of interest; lack of foresight; propensity to react; traditional diplomacy; lack of consensus; cumbersome decision-making, inadequate infrastructure, lack of know-how and the complexity of the conflicts[5]. The three most important causes on this list are : (a) inadequate prognosis; (b) the absence of perceived vital

Figure 1
Proactive and reactive conflict prevention

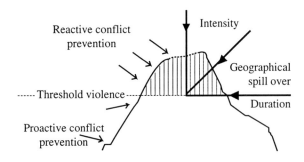

interest at stake, and (c) the lack of conflict transformation skill.

Inadequate foresight or warning systems have turned diplomacy into a chronic crisis management operation. Despite the recent efforts made by the great international organizations—the UN, OSCE, NATO, the EC and WEU—and by the academic institutions to improve their diagnostic and prognostic tools, much more will have to be done to achieve a better in- and foresight of conflict dynamics. A great deal of attention has been paid to early warning systems of worst case developments, such as threats or the possibility of violent escalation. Practically nothing has been done to develop warning systems indicating opportunities to intervene. The genocides in Yugoslavia, Rwanda, Burundi, are to a great extent histories of missed opportunities. There is also an urgent need to develop a system for conflict impact assessment (CIAS). This is necessary because today's conflict prevention policies look like (a) compilations of uni-dimensional approaches and (b) do not account for the possible negative externalities of the well-intentioned efforts. The peacekeepers in Bosnia became an obstacle for effective peace reinforcement. The Khmer Rouge of Cambodia parasitized on the refugee camps in Thailand. The threat with a war crimes tribunal can under certain circumstances protract a violent conflict. Democratization pressures could be a blessing, but could also enhance centrifugal forces, and lead to anarchy and end up in a dictatorial system. The development of an effective system for conflict prevention will require a systematic assessment of the positive and/or negative impact of different measures on the conflict dynamics.

The second major cause of today's inadequate conflict prevention system, is the *lack of perceived interests.* Africa is full of alarm bells and flashing lights. But as long as major countries or their international organizations do not perceive their vital interest at stake, proactive conflict prevention will remain a pipe dream. Moral or humanitarian concerns do not seem to guarantee effective conflict prevention measures. This leads to paradoxical results. Instead of more cost-effective proactive efforts, justified by enlightened self-interests, we see costly reactive measures, triggered by moral considerations. It will take a great effort to convince the international community that in a complex interdependent world conflict prevention is of vital interest. To that extent, efforts could be made (a) to help the decision-makers to better assess the costs of alternative conflict strategies, and (b) to oblige them to account for the war destruction. It would help if conflicts were embedded

in a democratic environment, or if decisionmakers would have to justify their war activities before something like an International Accounting Office. Today it is practically impossible to get reliable information about the costs and benefits of violent conflicts. The available data tend to be partial, incomplete and not very trustworthy. It is high time to break down the taboos surrounding this black accounting. This would allow a more objective analysis of the huge costs of conflict prevention failures, and validate the thesis that proactive conflict prevention efforts are more cost-effective than the reactive ones.

The third major cause of the failure of conflict prevention is *the lack of conflict expertise.* For the most serious problems in the world one finds research and training programs. Medical doctors are required to study during seven years; lawyers and civil engineers five, economists and psychologist five . . . etc. For dealing with large scale violence no comprehensive academic is provided. Until recently international conflict management was training considered the exclusive domain of diplomats and soldiers. The training was provided in the military academy or on the job.

The conflicts they handled were predominantly interstate conflicts. These traditional approaches of conflict prove to be of limited relevance for coping with the most dominant type of post WW II conflicts: the Low Intensity Conflict (LICs)[6]. Several characteristics of traditional diplomacy tend to inhibit an effective prevention of the escalation of ethnic or nationalist disputes. There is for example the tendency to draw a sharp distinction between civil wars, in which no external power is supposed to interfere, international wars which are the concern of all states. Civil war will only pose a threat when it spills over the boundaries or when major powers become involved. For them the right approach is to isolate or quarantine the war zone. This is the logic of 'real politic.' Related to the real politics, is the preference given to the raison d'état or to the national interests; the sovereignty of the people comes in second. Traditional diplomacy also tends to be elitist and to reduce conflict prevention to the employment of the familiar methods of peacemaking (negotiation including promises and threats) and/or peacemaking and enforcement. The handling of the new types of conflicts requires a more sophisticated analysis of conflict dynamics and a better acquaintance with the available battery of conflict prevention instruments.

According to the agenda for peace of Boutros Boutros-Ghali, it requires not only skills in peace making and peace keeping, but also in peace (re) building. As newest addition to the diplomatic vocabulary, peace-building tends to be loosely defined. Peace building refers to the creation of an objective and subjective context which enhances a constructive transformation of conflicts and leads to a sustainable peace. A sustainable peace is a legitimate peace, supported by the people involved. Such a peace is built on the concept of conflict transformation, underscoring the goal of moving a given population from the status of extreme vulnerability and dependency to that of self-sufficiency and well being. In the more specific terms of conflict progression, transformation is the movement from latent conflict to confrontation to negotiation to the peaceful relationships of a security community[7] (Fig. 2). (see *Conflict Resolution, Process of*)

Peace-building requires two sets of efforts relating to: (re)construction and (re)conciliation. The most visible efforts are the structural measures which are meant to improve the life conditions, to reduce discrimination and to provide ways and means for settling disputes. A great deal of the peace agreements include structural measures of a political, economic, legal, educational, military and humanitarian nature. All of this translates into efforts to organize and supervise elections; to rebuild the economy; to strengthen the legal system and stop impunity; to rebuild the educational infrastructure; to resettle refugees and to implement an effective arms control system.

Less visible, but as crucial, are the (re)conciliation efforts. These efforts intend to create a new moral-political climate in which people are committed to the restoration of ruptured relationships and to the construction of a new future. This implies not only reconciliation with the present (a peace agreement settling particular disputes); but also reconciliation with the past (healing psycho-historical wounds can take a great deal of time); and reconciliation with the future. A reconciliation with the past, present and the future, is necessary for achieving a sustainable peace. Another essential part of the new moral political climate is the (re)conciliation of contradictory but in fact interdependent values and forces (such as the search for truth, peace, justice, welfare, and mercy), which will help the conflicting groups to heal the wounds of the past and to envision a common interdependent future. Truth is the longing for acknowledgment of wrong and painful loss and experiences; it is disposed to get a better understanding of the causes of the violence, and to avoid misperception and misunderstanding. Mercy articulates a benign attitude, a disposition to show kindness or compas-

Figure 2

Progressive transformation of conflicts

Inspired by Adam Curle, *Making peace*, 1971,
Tavistock Publication, London.

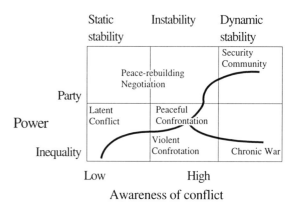

sion; a need for acceptance, letting go, new start. Peace underscores the need for security and harmonious relationships devoid of violence or oppression. Welfare reflects the longing for having adequate material or financial resources; for prosperity and well-being. Justice represents the need for the maintenance of what is just especially by the impartial adjustment of conflicting claims or the assignment of merited rewards or punishments. Those and other values are played out as political concepts with their own constituencies. In several post conflict situations we have frequently a fierce competition between the proponents of a 'War Crimes Tribunal'; a 'Truth and Reconciliation Commission,' and 'amnesty.' Reconciliation creates the possibility and the social space were all those values or needs are validated, rather than a framework that suggests that some must win out over the others.[8]

3. The Rise of Unofficial Diplomacy

The diplomatic overload and the growing complexity of the international environment has led to an increasing involvement of "outsiders" in relations within and between countries. At a conference organized by the Institute at Bellagio, in 1973, there developed a consensus that the role of non-officials in international peace making had been far too neglected and that their importance would increase[9]. Since then we have seen a near exponential growth of peace activities rendered by non-governmental actors. The peace services range from enhancing communication, improving mutual understanding, disapproving violence, mediation, reconciliation, to interpositionary peacekeeping. Non-governmental actors have developed a whole series of practical tools for peacemaking, peacekeeping and peacebuilding (see *Track II Diplomacy*).

One of the better known tools of the peace making approach is the problem-solving workshop, which brings together representatives of conflicting parties for direct interaction in an unofficial, private context, with a panel of social scientists acting as facilitators[10]. Workshops are designed to encourage an analytic approach to joint problem solving of a conflict that will be conducive to the emergence of a creative 'win-win' outcome satisfying the basic needs of both parties. Other methods of peacemaking can be found under such headings as 'unofficial, track II, parallel- and multi-track diplomacy.'

A great deal of creativity is also found with respect to keeping the peace[11]. Four different methods for separating the parties in a conflict are distinguished: buffer zones, peace zones, interpositionary peace-keeping, and intercessionary peacekeeping. Buffer-zones are demilitarized and unpatrolled areas. Peace zones are civilian-occupied spaces where no fighting takes place. In the Philippines, civilians successfully created peace zones as demilitarized spaces for alternative development and consensus building in several communities[12]. Interpositionary peacekeeping is based on the idea of placing themselves physically between groups engaged in violent conflict in an impartial stance toward all parties. There are several examples of civilian interpositioning. The first project of the Peace Brigades International (PBI) was in Nicaragua along the border with the Honduras in 1981. A PBI team, later joined by Witnesses For Peace (WFP) volunteers, interpositioned between Nicaraguan civilians and contras based in Honduras. This human shield was deployed to prohibit the imminent invasion by US "and contra" forces and to monitor events in the area. While interpositioning maintains equal distance between hostile parties, many civilian peacekeeping groups use intercessionary peacekeeping which maintains unequal distance between the parties. Intercessionary peacekeepers hope to deter violence by accompanying certain individuals or groups in danger or being a presence in a threatened community. In addition to the clearly dissociate aspects of peacekeeping, there are also other activities conducted by peace keepers, such as observing/documenting/monitoring, alerting the international community, showing solidarity, and facilitating communication.

Finally a great deal of the peace efforts of NGO's are *peacebuilding activities* (see *Non-governmental Organizations (NGOs)*). They address structural violence and prevent destructive conflicts from occurring or recurring. Boutros-Ghali identifies peacebuilding as attempts to identify and support structures which will tend to strengthen and solidify peace in order to avoid a relapse into conflict[13]. Peacebuilding refers to efforts to strengthen and support democratization and electoral processes, economic development projects, humanitarian relief efforts, the legal system, the educational infrastructure, and the implementation of arms control measures.

The unofficial or track II diplomacy distinguishes itself from the traditional diplomacy not only by the way civilian diplomats intervene in conflicts or the tools they use, but also by the conceptual and normative approach of conflicts. The diplomatic thinking of traditional diplomats and Track II diplomats differs in several ways.

A first difference relates to their respective *worldview*. The international landscape of the traditional diplomats is an Hobbesian environment in which nation-states struggle for power and pursue their national interests. It is perceived as a very competetive and potentially insecure place. Their main interlocutors are key political and military leaders in the conflict. They are persons who either represent themselves, and/or the highest representative leaders of the governments and opposition movements in an internal struggle. Track II diplomats on the other hand pay much more attention to the civilian space in international relations. They search for common ground and look for the development of win-win relations.

Differences are also found in their analytic style. Traditional diplomacy defines peace as the absence of war and as the result of particular distributions of power (hegemonic—bipolar—multipolar) and arms control. Track II diplomats assume that one cannot resolve conflicts and thus make peace unless the root causes of the conflicts are identified and dealt with. The implication of this is that for conflicts to be resolved, one must look beyond surface issues and address the substantive and emotional issues as well as the parties' needs and interests that are at the root of the conflicts[14].

A third set of differences between traditional and track II diplomats concerns their preferred world order. Both the traditional and track II diplomats want peace. For the traditional diplomats this means the absence of military violence; for the track II diplomats it implies equally the absence of structural, psychological and cultural violence. For track II diplomats a sustainable peace has to be a legitimate peace.

Finally, there are also differences in their strategic approach. Official diplomacy makes use of the conventional diplomatic, legal, military and economic instruments. They tend to approach peace from the top-down and assume a trickle down effect. Track II diplomats, on the other hand, stress the importance of building peace bottom-up. They assume that one cannot impose an external or elitist peace formula on a conflict; that the conflict belongs to the society in which it is taking place and the resolution has to come from within that society[15].

Figure 4
Three generations of diplomacy

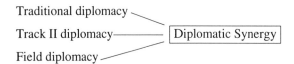

Traditional diplomacy
Track II diplomacy — Diplomatic Synergy
Field diplomacy

4. Field Diplomacy: A New Paradigm for Conflict Prevention ?

One of the most recent developments in the area of non-governmental diplomacy is field diplomacy. A couple of years ago, this term was coined by R. Moreels, past president of the Médicins sans frontières in Belgium. While working as a surgeon in conflict-zones he became aware of the near absence of official and unofficial peacemakers in the field, where peace services were also urgently needed[16]. Field diplomacy is not considered an alternative to the traditional and the parallel diplomacy, but as a necessary complement.

The assumptions or the paradigm underlying the praxis of field diplomacy has been informed by people with peacemaking experience in conflict zones. Field diplomacy (FD) is characterized by a credible presence in the field; a serious commitment to conflict transformation; its multi-level approach; the illicitive engagement; a wide time perspective; the attention for the deeper layers of the conflict; preference for an integrative conflict prevention policy; and the recognition of the interdependency between seemingly different conflicts (see Fig. 5).

4.1 A Credible Presence in the Field

A first characteristic of field diplomacy is the requirement of a credible presence in the field. Field diplomats assume that one has to be in the conflict zone to get a better insight into the dynamics of the conflict

and to facilitate the transformation of the conflict more effectively. This contrasts clearly with the official and parallel diplomatic activities which mostly operate within the capitals or from abroad. The building of a trustbank or a network of people who can rely on each other is essential to elicit measures to prevent a destructive transformation of the conflict. Building trust takes a great deal of time and effort, when a conflict erupts it is too late.

4.2 A Serious Commitment

A second attribute of field diplomacy is a serious commitment to a constructive transformation of the conflict. Using a metaphor, a conflict should be adopted. As a child, one cannot adopt it for a week or a month; it is a long term commitment. The efforts need to be credible. Conflict prevention and reconciliation is likely to be a long-term and difficult journey. Peacemaking can be a very stressful and risky activity. An appropriate motivation and adequate backup is necessary to keep a peace team productive.

4.3 A Multi-level Engagement

A sustainable peace is a legitimate peace, that needs to be supported by the people. Therefore not only the highest, but also the middle and grass-root levels of the conflicting groups need to be involved in the peace making, peace keeping and peace building. Not only the elites, but also the people should be made stakeholders in the peace process. In addition to the top leadership, also the middle range and grassroots leadership should be involved. In the middle range are persons who are highly respected and/or occupy formal positions of leadership in sectors like education, business, agriculture or health. Their position is not necessarily connected to or controlled by the formal governmental or major oppositional movement authority or structures[17]. They are located in a position where they are likely to be known by and know the top leadership, yet they are connected to both the top and the grassroots levels. Their position is not based on political nor military power, nor are they indicating to have ambition for such power. They tend to have important pre-existing relationships with counterparts that cut across the lines of conflict within the setting. Finally they are more numerous than the top level and have connection as networks to many significant people across the physical and human divides of the conflict. They are ideal actors to be involved in problem solving workshops, in training for conflict resolution, peace

Figure 5
Field diplomacy

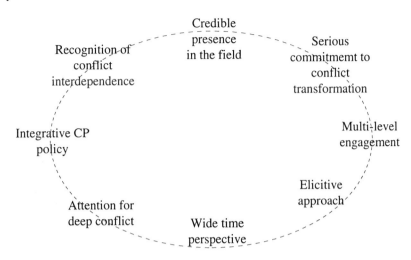

commissions and insider-partial teams. The grass-roots leaderships is situated at the base of the society. In settings of protracted conflict and war this base is characterized by a survival mentality; people are involved in a day by day effort to find ways of meeting the basic needs of food, water, shelter and safety. The leadership is faced with the overwhelming task of dealing with the crisis at a day to day level. Leaders here include people who are not involved in local communities, indigenous NGO's carrying out relief tasks for the local populations, health officials, and refugee camp leaders. These are people who have a thorough understanding of the suffering and fear under which the majority of the population may live, who understand intimately the politics of a given locale, and know on a face to face basis the local leaders of the government and opposition movement[18]. They could be involved in local peace commissions, grassroots training, the elimination of mental walls and prejudices, and psycho-social work in post-war trauma healing.

4.4 Elicitive Approach

The fourth characteristic of field diplomacy is its elicitive approach. This approach contrasts with the prescriptive approach which underscores the centrality of the trainer's models and knowledge. The elicitive approach is process-oriented and gives people a chance to participate in the way the conflict is handled. Both approaches empower the people, but do so in a different way. The prescriptive approach empowers participants in as much as they learn and master

new ways, techniques, and strategies for coping with conflict. The elicitive approach pursues empowerment as validating and building from resources that are present in the setting[19]. This approach requires listening, learning, and an understanding of the culture(s) within which the conflict is embedded. The aim is to catalyze an indigenous self sustainable peace process. This approach of course does not exclude criticizing the aspects of the conflict culture which are inhibiting a constructive transformation of the conflict. But in any case it takes local will to make outside help work. One of the most important tasks is to identify and to empower indigenous field diplomats or community mediators and peace initiatives.

4.5 A Wide Time Perspective

A fifth aspect of the conflict paradigm of field diplomats is that peace building is perceived in a wide time perspective: forwards and backwards. A sustainable peace requires a (re)conciliation of the present, the past and the future. A peace agreement, settling "here and now" disputes, is not enough. Equally important is a (re)conciliation about the past and the future. Historical wounds which are left unhealed tend to mortgage the future cooperation. The joint expectation of mutual benefits of cooperation will not only help living with the past, but is also the creation of a sustainable peace. The development of a new conflict culture in which competing values, such as peace, truth, mercy, welfare and justice, are reconciled, is part and parcel of the reconciliation process.

4.6 Attention for the Deep Conflict

A sixth element of the conflict paradigm of field diplomacy is the attention for the deeper layers of the conflict. The atmosphere of conflict may seem hard, tough and pragmatic and so in one sense it is; the conduct of the campaigns is planned with ruthlessness and precision. But, writes Adam Curle, when we consider the underlying layer of motives, apprehensions and often ideology, we enter the realm of chaotic emotional unreason. War engenders a mental environment of desperation in which fear, resentment, jealousy and rage predominate.[20] Consequently building peace requires not only attention for the hard layers of the conflict (the political-diplomatic, military, legal, economic, ecological), but also to the softer layers of the "deep conflict." A publicly signed peace agreement does not guarantee a sustainable peace. Peace also requires reconciliation at the psychological and emotional levels. Also very important is the spiritual level. At this level peace making and peace building means transforming despair into hope, hate into love, nihilism into meaningfulness, condemnation into forgiveness, and alienation into understanding. In the social sciences those levels of the conflict tend to be neglected.

4.7 An Integrative Conflict Prevention Policy

A seventh characteristic of the peace thinking of field diplomats is that they do not consider their activities as an alternative to the peace efforts of the official and parallel diplomacy. Instead they plead for a better coordination of governmental and non-governmental activities. Today's conflict prevention policy is low on coordination and coherence. There is the beginning of a coordination between governmental and non-governmental activities, but there is a long way to go. Most conflict prevention packages are not only incomplete, but also basically compilations of uni-dimensional measures. Reconstruction gets more attention than reconciliation. Not enough attention is given to the interdependence or the negative externalities of such measures as the organization of elections, peace keeping, humanitarian aid, economic reconstruction, legal reinforcement, and the rebuilding of the educational system. This is not a plea for developing a master plan controlled by a peace authority, but for a more comprehensive and creative approach in which the different components are validated and integrated into a more effective search for peace (see *Conflict Impact Assessment (CIAS)*).

4.8 Recognition of Conflict Interdependence

Finally, field diplomats recognize the complex interdependence between seemingly different conflicts. Problematic in the transformation of conflicts is not only the artificial legal distinction between internal and external conflicts, but also the propensity to conceptually isolate or quarantine closely interwoven conflicts. There is for example a linkage between internal and international democracy, but in the North the promotion of the first has become part and parcel of foreign policy; the latter however remains a taboo. Most of the conflicts in the Two Thirds World cannot be reduced to pure internal conflicts. They are or were at one time or another influenced by conflicts at a regional or global level. Consequently a peace policy in Rwanda or Burundi implies not only efforts for dealing with the conflicts within the boundaries, but equally peace efforts at the sub-regional, the Euro-African, and at the global level.

During the Summer of 1995 a seminar was held in Harrisonburg, Virginia about the philosophy and praxis of conflict prevention and conciliation. Most of the participants had a rich experience with peace making in the field: in Sudan, Liberia, Sierra Leone, Rwanda, and Nicaragua. There was a consensus that the prevailing theories for coping with conflicts were not doing the job and that there was a need for another way of thinking about conflict transformation. Field diplomacy is a new paradigm distilled from the experience of people providing peace services in the field. It is more than a set of techniques with respect to communication, mediation and conciliation; it is a new philosophy. A more effective development and organization of field diplomacy will require a great effort from all who want to get rid of destructive conflicts in the world. A very important contribution could be the systematic analysis and evaluation of the peace services provided in the field. In the last few years there is a growing interest in field diplomacy. There is however also a great deal of resistance and skepticism. Some question if this new approach is not too idealistic. The answer is yes, as much, as the idea of a European Union in the thirties.

See also: *Conflict Resolution, History of; Arbitration, International; Negotiations, Direct; Democracy and Foreign Policy; Diplomatic Recognition*

Notes

1. W. Bauwens & L. Reychler, *The Art of Conflict Prevention*, (Brassey's: London, 1994).

2. PIOOM *Newsletter and Progress Report,* Vol.7, Winter 1995.

3. PIOOM, 'Newsletter'.

4. Goldberg Jeffrey, 'How to rescue Liberia ? Disarm the Warlords', in *International Herald Tribune*, April 17,1996.

5. Bauwens & Reychler, *op. cit.*

6. Martin van Creveld, *The Transformation of War,* 1991, (The Free Press, New York).

7. John Paul Lederach, *Building Peace: Sustainable Reconciliation in Divided Societies,* (UN University, Tokyo, Japan), January 1994.

8. John Paul Lederach, *Beyond Prescription*, op cit.

9. Maureen Berman and Joseph Johnson (eds.), 1977, Columbia University Press, New York.

10. Herbert Kelman, *Interactive problem solving,* in V.Volkan, J. Montville, D. Julius (eds.) *The Psychodynamics of International Relationships ; Unofficial Diplomacy at Work,* Vol II, 1991, (Lexington Books, Lexington).

11. Lisa Schirch, *Keeping the peace,* Research report, (Life and Peace Institute, Uppsala, October 1995).

12. Gaston Ortegas Peace Institute, *Peace Zone Primer,* (Ateneo de Manila University, in Lisa Schirch), *op cit.*

13. Boutros-Ghaili, *An Agenda for Peace,* (1992, United Nations Press, New York).

14. Hizkias Assefa, *Peace and reconciliation as a paradigm: a philosophy of peace and its implications on conflict, governance, and economic growth in Africa,* (1993, Nairobi Peace Initiative, Kenya).

15. Eftihia Voutira and Shaun Whishaw Brown, *Conflict Resolution; a cautionary tale, Studies on emergencies and disaster relief, Report* No 4, 1995, Nordiska Afrikainstitutet.

16. R. Moreels and Luc Reychler, *De agressie voorbij : terrein diplomatie* (Beyond agression: field diplomacy), (1995, Roularta, Zellik).

17. J.P. Lederach, *Building Peace,* pp. 42-46.

18. J.P. Lederach, *op cit.*

19. J.P. Lederach, Beyond prescription: perspectives on conflict, culture and training, (Final draft, Syracuse University Press, April, 1994).

20. Adam Curle, *Tools for transformation: a personal study,* (Hawthorne Press, United Kingdom,1990).

LUC REYCHLER

Flaubert

Born in Rouen on 12 December 1821, Gustave Flaubert studied at the Collège Royal in his native town, where, while he was still in his teens, some of his *récits* and stories appeared in local periodicals. Receiving his *baccalauréat* in 1840, he enrolled at the University of Paris Law School from 1841 to 1843 but did not do well there. A nervous crisis in January 1844 led his parents to decide that he should abandon his legal studies. Thereafter he would devote himself to writing. At the same time he traveled a great deal and kept journals, published after his death, of his various trips. One of the more memorable of these trips was in the summer of 1847 with Maxime Du Camp, whom he had met in Paris in 1843. Mostly on foot, the two friends visited Anjou, Brittany, and Normandy. Another one, again with Du Camp, was more ambitious and took him to the Near East and, as he returned home, to Greece and Italy (November 1849 to June 1851). From the trip Flaubert returned a mature man, with a much more realistic view of the world about him. There were excursions to the Pyrenees Mountains, Corsica, Switzerland, Germany, and England as well.

Due in some measure to the epileptic seizures he experienced from 1844 onward, Flaubert never became too seriously involved with women. At a discreet distance he adored Mme Maurice Schlésinger, whom he first saw on the beach at Trouville in 1836. There were also the English sisters, Harriet (Henriette) and Gertrude Collier, whom he met, in France, while on vacation one summer. With the poetess

Louise Colet, whom he encountered in Paris in June 1846, he was to have a sensual relationship that lasted until August 1848 and that resumed when he returned from the Near East in 1851. Punctuated with demands, accusations, and recriminations, it came to a decided halt in March 1855. There was also Juliet Herbert, his niece's English governess. There were several others, less important. Flaubert got along better with women when he was their friend than when he or they expected him to be their lover. Jeanne de Tourbey, Mlle Leroy de Chantepie, Mme Roger des Genettes, George Sand, and Princess Mathilde were women with whom he felt at ease and whom he genuinely liked. Probably his deepest attachments, though, were with other men. In time, the one with Maxime Du Camp palled, but his relations with such friends as Ernest Chevalier, Ernest Feydeau, and the poet-dramatist Louis Bouilhet were durable and rewarding. The deepest relationship he ever experienced was the one with his boyhood companion Alfred Le Poittevin, who died young in 1848. It was to him that Flaubert dedicated his *Mémoires d'un fou* and the final *Tentation de Saint Antoine*.

Even as an adolescent Flaubert appears to have sensed, if indeed he did not know, that he was destined to become a prose writer. At thirteen and fourteen he was already turning out, in a Romantic vein, some promising narratives and dramatic sketches that, given the period's artistic norms, bear comparison with what the mature Romantic writers were producing. Several, including "Bibliomania" and "Une

Leçon d'histoire naturelle," came out in a Rouen newspaper in 1837. Among his notable early compositions should be mentioned *Mémoires d'un fou* (1838), dedicated, as pointed out above, to Le Poittevin; *Smarh* (1839), with which he explored a form he would use in the *Tentation de Saint Antoine*; and the tale *Novembre* (1840-42). In 1843, while in law school, he began the first *Education sentimentale*, completed two years later. This novel treats the theme of disillusionment. Still basically Romantic in inspiration and tone, it nevertheless ends on a realistic note. Henry Gosselin, its main character, comes to Paris to continue his studies. There he meets, woos, and elopes with a married woman, but circumstances eventually separate the lovers, and the woman returns to her husband. Their love little by little dies in spite of efforts to keep it alive through correspondence. Similarly, Henry drifts away from his closest friend Jules, to whom he had once been deeply attached. Their lives, which they once were convinced would be so exceptional, turn out to be as humdrum as those of everyone else. In this novel, which Flaubert would never publish (the public did not see it until 1910), the author sounded the nihilistic themes that he was to orchestrate over and over again: existence is sterile; the human condition, especially among the mediocre, is absurd; man's noblest impulses lead nowhere; genuine life is unattainable and its baser substitutes are unrewarding; even friendship perishes with time. From this Flaubert would soon conclude that there is little worth pursuing except art, and to this he would in short order dedicate himself unreservedly. With the first *Education sentimentale* Flaubert would not strike his artistic stride, but his essential pessimism had not only taken shape but had been given written expression. Moreover, he had produced a work that was autobiographical, which would be more or less true with all of his other writings. It was while the novel was being written that he and his parents learned he was prone to epileptic seizures and that it was decided he should not return to law school. The novice author was now free to devote himself to his real vocation and to hone his talent.

Next Flaubert turned his attention to the *Tentation de Saint Antoine*. He started work on it on 24 May 1848, completing an initial version 12 September 1849. As had been true with the first *Education sentimentale*, he was not wholly satisfied with it, nor were the close friends to whom he read it. After his return from the Near East, he considered publishing extracts in Maxime Du Camp's *Revue de Paris* but decided against the idea. Reworking it in 1856, he still did

not make it public, although fragments appeared in *L'Artiste* in December 1856 and in January and February 1857.

Meanwhile he had conceived and begun writing *Madame Bovary*, the novel that not only would make him famous but would also establish Realism, in prose fiction, as the western world's dominant new literary school, with himself as its chief oracle. Flaubert labored over the novel for several years. Implicit in it is his credo. For the most part, people are mediocre or stupid, he believed. They are tedious and petty and inclined to be dishonest, callous, even cruel. The world in which they move about, with its cares and events, is ugly. To escape it, the sensitive intellectual must seek a haven in art. Escaping into art, however, need not mean turning one's back upon reality's dreariness. Reproducing that sordid exterior world in a splendid piece of writing can be a great artistic achievement. Creating art is a hard but rewarding task. To achieve it in fiction writing, as Flaubert understood it, called for close observation, precise documentation, psychological accuracy, attention to detail, always using "the exact word," and, on the author's part, an esthetic distance based theoretically on the most complete objectivity. In actual practice, this impersonal stance was more likely to be a mocking irony toward one's characters and the situations in which they find themselves. Flaubert began writing the novel on 19 September 1851 and concluded it on 30 April 1856.

Flaubert's heroine, if that is what she is, had a model in Delphine Couturier, a provincial girl who married and deceived an obscure smalltown doctor, Eugène Delamare, and whose life, along with that of her husband, ended in suicide. Flaubert's chief character is Emma Rouault, a peasant farmer's daughter who has received a finishing school education that, given her romantic propensities, has ill prepared her to be the wife of the kind but dull village physician, Dr. Charles Bovary, who adores her. Far from being the dashing intellectual she had taken him to be, Charles, she soon discovers, is an incompetent bore, and she becomes disillusioned. What could she do to fill the emotional void that marriage, to him, brought with it? For Emma, being a wife and mother, playing her piano, participating in provincial social activities, going to church were not the solution. Reading Romantic novels, where heroes and heroines always pair off in what appears to be an ideal world, only deepens her inarticulate frustration. Several adulterous love affairs, ultimately unsatisfactory, lead her to immoderate spending and precipitate a crisis. When she is unable to extricate herself from it, this dilemma, along with her accumulated disappointments, prompts her to commit suicide. Charles never recovers from the shock. Prostrate but uncomprehending, he eventually discovers some of her lovers' correspondence with her and dies of a broken heart. His and Emma's little daughter is sent to live with two successive relatives and soon has to go to work in a cotton mill. There are no momentous events in the novel, there is little in it save the inexorable wearisome triviality of life in a hamlet where nothing ever happens.

Madame Bovary, after appearing in installments in the *Revue de Paris* (with some deletions) from 1 October to 15 December 1856, came out in book form in April 1857. In January and February, accused of immorality, Flaubert and the *Revue de Paris* were prosecuted but were acquitted. Realism had won. Flaubert was famous and soon would be at work on his next novel, *Salammbô*, which takes place at the time of the first Punic War, when Carthage was locked in a fierce struggle with her mercenaries.

As had been true of *Madame Bovary*, writing it was slow, even painful. Flaubert's insistence upon accurate documentation took the writer to North Africa from April to June 1858. Completed in April 1862, the novel was published the following November. In it the events had historical importance, but, as Flaubert presented them, the characters' motivations and deeds show the Carthaginians and their adversaries to have been no better than provincial Frenchmen living in the nineteenth century. Like *Madame Bovary*, *Salammbô* set off a controversy, but this time the author found himself pitted against an archeologist rather than the law. The novel, difficult to read, was and has remained much less successful than its predecessor.

Again, it was not long before Flaubert was working on another novel. Once more, it was an historical novel, but this time it dealt with a rather recent period. It was the second *Education sentimentale*. Just as young Gustave Flaubert had seen and fallen in love with Mme Schlésinger on Trouville Beach years earlier, so now his protagonist, Frédéric Moreau, is overwhelmed when, on a riverboat, he sees Marie (Mme Jacques) Arnoux, wife of a quixotic businessman. Arnoux deceives his beautiful, patient wife with a succession of unworthy rivals, especially Rosanette Bron, "la Maréchale." Serving as a backdrop for the action is the Revolution of 1848 and the political turmoil that led up to, accompanied, and followed it. In Paris, Frédéric discovers, as Flaubert discovered, that he has no interest in or talent for law, which he has come to the capital to study. With an inheritance that

soon comes his way, he drops his law studies. Tenderly, he loves Mme Arnoux at a respectful distance but has involvements with various other women, including the unlettered courtesan Mlle Bron and the cold Comtesse Dambreuse, whom he almost marries. His artistic inclinations and ambitions, such as they were, come to naught; the long-suffering Marie Arnoux eludes him; and he eventually settles down to the doldrums of a placid, uneventful existence in the capital. Only when it is too late does he learn that Marie, aware of his love, may have shared it in her virtuous way. Perhaps Flaubert's best novel, the *Education sentimentale* reflects the novelist's continued pessimism and his absolute lack of faith in human nature. Few of the characters have any enduring principles. Among the novel's memorable portraits is that of Sénécal, a rabid republican who nevertheless goes to work as a policeman under a new, conservative government and cynically shoots republicans. Likewise, there is Mlle Vatnaz, a vehement feminist whose convictions do not keep her from acting as Jacques' Arnoux's procuress. Flaubert completed the *Education sentimentale* on 16 May 1869 and published it on 17 November.

Flaubert now resumed work on the *Tentation de Saint Antoine*, the third version, finishing it on 20 June 1872. However, it did not come out until nearly two years later, on 31 March 1874. Flaubert had a predilection for this work, and, as we have seen, had toiled on versions of it since 1848, returning to it over and over. This ultimate version, perhaps more polished, is at least as speculative as the preceding ones. St. Anthony, a monk given to epileptic seizures, is exposed in a series of hallucinations and visions to a host of attractive sins as well as to other religions and sects that are not without their appeal. Anthony is tempted but remains faithful to his own orthodox Christian commitments. As usual, Flaubert tried to be objective in the work, holding that no religion offered its believers absolute truth. More or less, all were alike. Despite the care lavished on it, the book had but little interest for most readers. One notes that Flaubert, with his own epileptic propensities, created a character here who was subject to them also and who experienced visions during the attacks.

Over the next few years Flaubert spent his time on several projects. One was the novel *Bouvard et Pécuchet*, outlined in 1863, worked on in 1872, resumed in 1877, but all the same left unfinished. It was published in 1880 and 1881, after the author's death. As elsewhere, the writer declaimed in it against the silliness and vice that he detected in most people.

1877 saw the publication, as a volume, of *Trois contes*, consisting of the *Légende de Saint Julien l'Hospitalier*, written in 1875 and 1876 and published in *Le Bien public* in Paris 1877; *Hérodias*, composed in 1876 and 1877 and first appearing in *Le Moniteur* in April 1877; and *Un Coeur simple*, dating from 1876. These three tales, which are novelettes rather than the short stories their title would lead one to expect, represent some of Flaubert's best work. *Hérodias* and *Saint Julien l'Hospitalier* reveal the author's deft handling of traditional religious narratives, adding to them new interpretations and new dimensions, particularly from the standpoint of motivation. Nowhere is the author's psychological acumen displayed to better advantage than in *Un Coeur simple*.

Like so many writers, Flaubert occasionally tried a genre for which he had a less marked talent than in the one where he excelled. Perhaps urged on by Louis Bouilhet's example, he liked and dabbled in the theatre. Only two experiments need be mentioned here. *Le Candidat*, written in 1873, probably deserved a better reception than it for when it was preformed at the Vaudeville the next year. When Flaubert died on 8 May 1880 in Paris, staging *Le Château des coeurs*, written in collaboration with Bouilhet and Charles d'Osmoy in 1862 and 1863, was being considered. Would it have been a success?

With his dedication to a lofty artistic ideal, with his disdain for ordinary mortels and the minuscule concerns that claim their attention, and, above all, with his delicate health, Flaubert was not predisposed to meditate about peace or war. As a student, he was exempted from military service in 1842. In April 1848, however, he was enrolled for a time in the National Guard. Both the *Education sentimentale* and *Bouvard et Pécuchet* ridicule the masses and the masses' civil unrest at the time of the Revolution of 1848. *Salammbô* (1862) shows war in all its unspeakable horror, yet, concerning it, the author's attitude remains one of basic detachment. Nevertheless, he was distressed and apprehensive when the Franco-Prussian War broke out in the summer of 1870. To Jeanne de Tourbey, now Comtesse de Loynes, he wrote that, in addition to his personal problems (health and money), he was worried about "public" matters. "I experience immense distaste at seeing humankind's irremediable savagery. How sad it is, and how stupid! I think of the rivers of tears that are going to flow, of all those ruins that are going to be created! ... The war is bothering me. I am beside myself as a result of it. I am having trouble pulling myself together .... What an abominable year, dear friend!" Unwittingly, he was all too prophetic in adding, ironically, "And the winter coming on, probably, will be very nice indeed!" Still, he could not foresee that, a month or so later, he would be personally involved in the hostilities. In September, with the war going very badly for France, he would accept a lieutenantship in the National Guard. Soon he would become bellicose, cordially wishing the German invaders to the devil. During the months of December and January, his and his mother's home in Croisset (Normandy) would be occupied by German soldiers, which did nothing to appease his angry frustration. Even had there been no other reasons, the invasion and occupation prevented his becoming a peace advocate, and on its appearance he applauded the *Soirées de Medan*, the short stories that, just before his death, Zola, Maupassant, and others published in 1880 on the recent war.

Bibliography

Bardèche M 1988 *Flaubert*. La Table Ronde, Paris
Bart B 1967 *Flaubert*. Syracuse University Press, Syracuse
Chessex J 1991 *Flaubert ou le désert en abîme*. Grasset, Paris
Robert M 1982 *En haine du roman. Etude sur Flaubert,* Paris
Sartre J P 1971 *L'Idiot de la famille*. Gallimard, 3 vols, Paris
Thibaudet A 1935 *Gustave Flaubert*. Gallimard, Paris
Troyat H 1988 *Flaubert*. Flammarion, Paris

HARRY REDMAN, JR.

Food Insecurity and the Role of Targeted Food Aid

At a time when sufficient food is produced at a global level to meet the needs of every individual alive, an estimated 800 million people in developing countries suffer chronic undernutrition, and 2 billion people worldwide lack essential micronutrients (FAO 1995a). 1.6 billion people (29 percent of the world's population) are at risk of iodine deficiency and over 2 billion people are affected by iron deficiency to which women and children are particularly prone (WHO/UNICEF/ICCIDD 1993; FAO/WHO 1992a). 190 million children are underweight and 230 million children have stunted growth as a result of an inadequate diet (WHO 1995).

Whilst world population growth is projected to continue to slow over the next 15 years, 94 percent of the estimated 1.8 billion increase will take place in developing countries. There is an urgent need to ensure that today's hunger is addressed today, not left for tomorrow when its severity and impact may be compounded.

1. Food Security: An Evolving Concept

Food security can be defined as the access of all people to the food needed for a healthy life at all times (FAO/WHO 1992). The conceptual framework of food security has evolved considerably over the last three decades. Until the mid-1970s food insecurity, and its principal manifestation hunger, were largely regarded as arising out of deficient agricultural production. The emphasis was on solving global food insecurity by increasing agricultural productivity and output. The world food crisis in the mid-1970s demonstrated the importance for food security at a national level, of both the availability of basic food commodities, especially cereals, and of the stability of supply. These concerns were predominant in discussions and undertakings as part of the World Food Conference in 1974. The emphasis was on both increasing production to keep up with population growth and the maintenance of supply stability through national and international grain stocks that would avoid large fluctuations in international grain prices.

However, ensuring an adequate and stable supply of basic food commodities at a national level, or even a regional level within individual countries, does not automatically rule out hunger for everyone. Even in places where there are well stocked markets nearby and commodities are reasonably priced, some households are food insecure because they do not have enough purchasing power to buy sufficient food. Household food insecurity is also present where markets have been disrupted and availability is not assured or is highly fluctuating. For households, and individual members of households, to be food secure, each must have assured access to sufficient food. The ultimate objective of world food security should be to ensure that all people at all times have both physical and economic access to the basic food they need. The International Conference on Nutrition (ICN), held in 1992, added a nutrition dimension, expressing the objective that "all people at all times have access to safe and nutritious food to maintain a healthy and active life" (FAO/WHO 1992b).

Food insecurity also has a temporal dimension. It can be chronic, seasonal or acute. Acute food insecurity refers to a rapidly deteriorating situation leading to starvation or death, typically caused by natural disaster or war. Chronic food insecurity, by contrast, is

a consequence of diets persistently inadequate in terms of quantity and/or quality, resulting from household poverty. Seasonal insecurity is related to cycles of food growing and harvesting.

There are, therefore, three principal conditions to achieving this objective of food security: sufficient availability (supply) of basic food commodities, stability of supply, and access to food at the household level (see *Social Progress and Human Survival*).

2. Acute Food Insecurity

Acute food insecurity arises from absolute shortages of food, often due to climatic vagaries or other natural disasters; or to inaccessibility of food because of armed conflict, or massive collapse in purchasing power associated with disruptions in labor or food markets. Problems of food insecurity are compounded by displacement associated with conflict, the immediate cause of most crises since the early 1990s. In these so-called "complex emergencies" many people are often uprooted from their home, lose most of their possessions and face months, perhaps years, of misery and sometimes death. To these people, survival supersedes any thoughts of long-term development.

The number of "complex emergencies" has grown sharply in recent years. In the mid-1990s, there were at least 50 serious armed conflicts ongoing in the world, with an increasing concentration of frequency and destructiveness in poorer developing countries (Sivard 1994; Hansch 1995). These crises are "complex" not so much in their manifestation of human suffering (which may differ little from suffering during other emergencies), but in their scale (often regional rather than national), and the complexity of their causes and potential resolutions, which often have political and military dimensions.

As conflict has taken over from drought and floods as the primary cause of famine and human displacement, the numbers of refugees, internally displaced persons and non-displaced but asset-stripped households has grown sharply, particularly in Africa. The total number of refugees has doubled approximately every six years since the mid-1970s. By 1994, the number of refugees had reached approximately 25 million, of whom roughly one third were in Africa (UNHCR 1995; UNECOSOC 1995) (see *Ethnic Conflict and International Relations*). In addition, the number of Internally Displaced Persons reached an estimated 25-30 million in 1995, as many as 60 percent of them in Africa (United Nations 1995; UNHCR 1995). The global total of people uprooted by conflict or political disturbance has reached roughly 50 million—an average of 1 million people for every conflict.

What is more, the impact of hunger due to conflict and population displacement is not limited to the individuals involved. Host communities, typically as poor as the displaced people coming to them for help, are drawn into the dislocation. The hosts are affected as commodity prices rise, labor markets are disrupted, local or national development activities are curtailed, and widespread natural resource damage results from new concentrations of displaced people needing land and fuel to survive. The recent growth in numbers of refugees and internally displaced people shows no signs of abating (see *World Peace Order, Dimensions of*).

Chronic food insecurity is prevalent amongst households with low and variable incomes, limited assets, few marketable skills, and few powerful advocates to act on their behalf—the chronically poor. These include many smallholder farmers, landless and/or daily laborers, livestock herders, and the unskilled unemployed. Numbering hundreds of millions, these people earn less than US$1 a day, of which roughly 70 percent tends to be spent on food consumption, and they subsist in an abject poverty that never rules out hunger (WFP 1995; FAO 1995b).

Food insecurity is not just a manifestation of poverty, it perpetuates poverty. Persistent food insecurity, largely found in low-income food-deficit countries, is a stumbling block to efforts aimed at eliminating poverty, and is thereby self-perpetuating. It is part of a vicious cycle of low productivity and earnings, ill-health, indebtedness and malnutrition. Past investments made by vulnerable households are eroded and future incomes are compromised. Hungry children cannot derive full benefits from their education, even if they manage to gain access to formal education. Poor women cannot invest sufficiently in their own, or their children's future, since they are fully preoccupied by the multiple problems associated with current hunger (see *Peace and Social Development*).

Women are disproportionately represented amongst the chronically hungry. In addition their development is often constrained by a series of inequalities. Whilst women often bear the greatest part of the responsibility for ensuring food for the whole family, they most often do not have equal access to productive resources, employment, markets and trade. A lack of access to savings mechanisms and institutions constrains investment possibilities and longer term growth in productivity. Such inequalities both constrain women's own development and also restricts their potential contribution to food security for all.

Vulnerability is increased at critical times in the life-cycle, such as for babies in the womb, the new-born and young child-bearing/lactating women. Those yet to be born suffer a deficiency of nutrients if their mothers are themselves malnourished since the "programming" of chronic diseases among adults starts with malnutrition among women during pregnancy (Hoet 1995). The dangers of premature birth, low birth-weight at normal partum, and growth retardation due to nutrient deficiencies or health problems are major constraints to normal childhood development (see *Population Pressure, Women's Role and Peace*).

Even if children survive severe malnutrition early on, they are likely to become disadvantaged adults and are more likely to be victims of future emergencies. They will be less productive and thus be faced with the chronic burdens of poverty. Mothers will face harder pregnancies and give birth to nutritionally-compromised children, and both men and women will face health and productivity constraints.

3. The Geography of Food Insecurity

No place is immune to food insecurity if conditions lend themselves to massive failures in nutrition and health. Recent tragedies in eastern Europe and former Soviet republics have underlined this fact. That said, certain people in certain places are more at risk than others. For example, acute food security that can lead to famine tends not to be found in cities (unless they are placed under siege or devastated by conflict), or in regions of high agricultural output. Widespread acute food insecurity and hunger have not been prevalent in temperate climates in the absence of war or policies that restrict access to adequate food for 150 years. They tend not to be found where transactions costs for food marketing are low.

Hunger is predominant in regions where economic returns to agriculture tend to be low and in which there are high transactions costs due to deficient infrastructure and inefficient markets. This combination of factors is characteristic of the poorest countries of the world, particularly low-income, food-deficit countries located in the semi-arid, warm sub-humid and cool tropics (Sharma et al., 1995; Rosegrant et al., 1995). Additional nutrition problems are to be found among impoverished households in urban slums worldwide. The latter are often attributable to insanitary living conditions and certain micronutrient deficiencies that may not be best tackled through food assistance.

Currently, Asia contains the largest number of people facing food deficiencies. The number of people not eating a minimum diet in southern and eastern

Asia is estimated to be over 500 million, equivalent to 18 percent of the population of the region (ACC/SCN 1993; FAO 1995b).

In South Asia, more than two-thirds of the food insecure are to be found in the driest agroecological zones of the warm tropics (Broca and Oram 1991). Their diet is dominated by coarse grains such as millet and sorghum (with other cereals and cassava acting as important complements). The driest areas of the sub-region benefitted relatively less from productivity gains as a result of technological improvements than did the moister tropics and sub-tropics.

Food insecurity and poverty increased in parts of Latin America and the Caribbean during the economic structural adjustments of the 1980s. The number of chronically undernourished is estimated to have grown from 46 million in 1980 to over 60 million in the early 1990s; this amounts to 14 percent of the population (FAO 1995b). Considerable improvements are anticipated in malnutrition rates in this region during coming decades, as it is relatively less poor than sub-Saharan Africa and South Asia and market and institutional infrastructures are more developed.

Sub-Saharan Africa shows the most cause for concern, characterized as it is by a decline in domestic per capita production, high fertility rates, natural disasters and the growing problem of emergencies displacing huge numbers of people. Over 200 million, more than 40 percent, of the region's population are chronically malnourished (FAO 1995b). Africa is also the only region to have suffered a fall in per capita food supply for direct human consumption compared with the early 1970s. Roughly 50 percent of Africa's poor inhabit semi-arid regions and therefore depend on low and variable rainfall for food production (Broca and Oram 1991). As a result, local diets are dominated by low-yielding coarse grains (traditional maize, millet and sorghum) and roots and tubers that have so far shown limited potential for productivity increases.

4. The Role of Targeted Food Aid

Food aid needs will nearly double over the next decade even with reasonably optimistic assumptions about recipient countries' ability to produce or have the financial capacity to import food commercially. Total food aid needs to maintain consumption and meet emergency needs for refugees are projected to be 27 million tons by 2005 and very possibly more (USDA 1995). But food aid flows have in fact dropped dramatically, from over 15 million tons of cereals in 1992/93 to around 8 million tons in 1995/96.

Food aid is a keystone of the international community's attempts to uphold fundamental human rights relating to life and food security. Any genuinely human-focused development can not ignore the problem of food insecurity. The guiding principle of food aid must be to reach people who need it most, primarily in food-deficit countries, at times when they need it most, and in ways that achieve lasting impact as well as short term help. Thus, the first claim on scarce food aid resources has to be targeted actions that address one or other of the major dimensions of current food insecurity.

The World Food Programme (WFP), the food aid organization of the United Nations, provides assistance in the form of food commodities. This targeted food aid is typically distributed directly to the most food insecure. Of course, food aid is not the answer to all food insecurity in the world. Some conditions are more appropriately tackled through interventions based on the targeted delivery of cash or other resources. Nevertheless, there are three priority areas in which targeted food aid should play a principal role in coming years.

4.1 Saving lives in emergencies. The right to life is enshrined in the Charter of the United Nations. Saving people whose ability to gain access to food has been curtailed is the first principle of humanitarian intervention. People have to survive before they can benefit from, and contribute to, sustainable development (see *Human Security*).

Food is a fundamental resource for saving life. Where acute food insecurity is a result of natural disasters, actions need to be swift to assist people in their home areas in order to protect their livelihoods. Without a swift response, loss of life and productive assets, through farm and livestock sales and seed consumption for survival, can result in a long-term erosion of development potential for whole regions. For example, the international response to exceptional drought in southern Africa in 1991/2 was successful in preventing widespread mortality. Yet, the scale of the drought was such that countless households lost many of their productive assets and had to use up income reserves in order to survive the crisis.

The rise in "complex emergencies" has meant that acute food insecurity is increasingly found in the presence of political instability which compounds inadequate past investments, infrastructure deficiencies, rapid population growth and environmental limitations to increased productivity. All of this makes the task of tackling hunger more difficult. The compounding of constraints to the attainment of food security is all too apparent in sub-Saharan Africa.

There is a need at local, national and international levels for better preparedness against crises, and more attention must be paid to the needs of disaster affected people once emergencies have passed—the rehabilitation phase should lay a solid foundation for development (see *Crisis*). Better interaction is also needed between development and relief professionals to ensure investments that reduce household vulnerability to disasters. In all of this, food aid has a major role to play.

The human damage caused by severe hunger is only a part of the overall problem. A depletion of resources caused by large-scale hunger, or the creation of refugee camps, carries the implications of food insecurity far beyond the realm of a discrete event. Once a disaster has passed, even a natural disaster, the process of household-, and nation-rebuilding can be severely impeded by the loss of people, community integration, livestock, savings and even the government's capacity to tax and invest. Thus, once conditions have stabilized and minimal food consumption has been established among affected people, food aid must be used in varied ways to help enhance human skills and economic assets through nutrition and other training programs, as well as through community, infrastructure and agricultural development activities.

The first task is to prevent people whose lives have been saved from slipping back into severe hunger again. This may involve supplementary feeding for still-vulnerable groups combined with a carefully phased reduction in the scale and size of more general distribution activities. The second task is to help regain or rebuild the asset base and productive capacities of people and the local economy. Roads and markets, schools and clinics often need to be rebuilt in war-torn countries such as Mozambique, Cambodia and Ethiopia. The use of local private sector capabilities for the transport of food through private traders also contributes to a reestablishment and strengthening of markets. Increasing amounts of food aid are being used to support programs to demobilize thousands of combatants, to de-mine once productive farmland, to resettle long-term refugees, and, importantly, to rebuild, through food-for-work schemes, the roads, bridges, and market-places upon which secure agricultural growth and economic recovery will depend. Emergency operations can leave lasting results beyond saving life.

4.2 Supporting food security at critical times of an individual's life is a pre-investment in future health and productivity. People cannot eat retroactively. It is extremely difficult to make up for the damage inflicted by inadequate nutrition in the first five years of life. The nutritional welfare of mothers and infants is vital. If it is inadequate, the damage is both lasting and far broader than the individuals and families involved. Society as a whole suffers when children cannot learn, when poor health restricts energy and productivity, when hungry women give birth to a new generation that is malnourished. What is at stake is the productive potential of enormous numbers of affected individuals. Failing to harness this potential allows the perpetuation of hunger and poverty.

Given its inter-generational reach, the longer food insecurity persists the harder it becomes to resolve. Actions to address the current hunger of mothers and infants have significant benefits for long-term food security. Investing in people, not just in their productive assets (such as land, tools, and crops), represents a 'pre-investment' in food security.

Addressing micronutrient deficiencies is a relatively inexpensive and cost effective exercise, particularly when compared to the scale of emergency interventions needed to respond to widespread nutritional failure. Ignoring mild symptoms of malnutrition today can lead to acute symptoms tomorrow.

Since its foundation in 1962, WFP has invested US$1.5 billion in projects providing ante-natal, pregnancy, infant and maternal health and nutrition care, largely under the umbrella of Maternal and Child Health or Vulnerable Group Feeding projects. Such interventions often provide an income incentive, as a security that permits women the time to pursue important activities other than finding food, including child-care, income generation and health care activities. Food aid provided as wages or as incentives can reach women in food insecure households which are often "crowded-out" of projects offering technical assistance or cash (WFP 1996b).

4.3 The key role of women in food security. Women are a key part of the solution to hunger (Quisumbing et al., 1995). They shoulder a major share of the responsibilities for household food security, and experience has shown that resources in the hands of women often have a greater nutritional benefit to children than the same resources controlled by men. They are more likely than men to spend a given income on food for the family (Pena, Webb and Haddad 1994). Thus, resources for women represent resources for food security. Successful development for women does not stop at the individual, it benefits whole households and communities. Reducing gender disparities by enhancing the human and physical resources commanded by women leads to growth in household agricultural productivity, greater income and better food and nutrition security for all (Quisumbing et al., 1995) (see *Feminism and Peace*).

4.4 Addressing chronic food insecurity. The chronically food insecure are typically by-passed by mainstream development initiatives and are unable to benefit fully from the market. To attain sustainable food security they require better access to productive resources, credit, social services, market outlets, and decision-making authority. But before they can reach that point their current hunger has to be tackled. Food aid can compensate for inadequacies in both endowments and markets by giving people the chance to sustain themselves and enhance their capabilities to participate in the marketplace.

The case for food aid is strongest where chronic undernutrition co-exists with weak markets that are characterized by insufficient and erratic supply and wide price fluctuations. Food aid can be provided through labor-intensive works programs (including food-for-work). Such activities simultaneously address weaknesses in household productivity and deficiencies in purchasing power. Food aid can also support development projects such as stabilization of shifting dunes, the establishment of tree and shrub nurseries, the building of small-scale irrigation infrastructure, or the creation of village-level grain and seed banks. The marketing of food produce can also be improved by the construction of feeder roads and bridges.

5. Tasks Ahead

Above all food security is about people. It is about a life free from the risk and fear of malnutrition or starvation. In the battle against food insecurity attention is needed both to long-term goals of raising agricultural productivity and world food supplies, and to the immediate problem of hundreds of millions of individuals who go hungry today. The attainment of food security therefore involves eliminating current hunger and reducing the risks of future food insecurity.

Food insecurity needs to be treated as a mainstream development problem. This requires closer partnerships in the use of food and non-food resources. Recent efforts to better integrate food aid into recipient country food security' nutrition strategies and safety-net programs have to be broadened and strengthened. The planning of food assistance on the basis of country-specific strategies and its integration with other instruments of assistance is essential.

Efforts aimed at raising agricultural productivity and output in food-deficit countries as well as the purchasing power of hungry people need to be intensified. But, neither increased food production nor complementary financial transfers will alone be sufficient to tackle the problems of food insecurity, particularly among the millions facing hunger in more remote regions in developing countries. While food deficits related to 'permanent' emergencies, weak markets, inappropriate economic policies and armed conflict continue to cripple growth in many countries, there will be a crucial role to be played by food aid that is targeted on the world's hungriest people.

See also: *Food Weapon; Human Nature Theories of War; Declaration of the Rights of Man; Future of Humanity; Human Security; Peaceful Societies; World Economy, Social Change and Peace*

Bibliography —————————————————————

ACC/SCN (Administrative Committee on Coordination-Subcommittee on Nutrition) 1993 *Second Report on the World Nutrition Situation*, Vol. I. ACC/SCN, Geneva

Broca S, P Oram 1991 *Study on the Location of the Poor.* International Food Policy Research Institute, Mimeo

FAO (Food and Agriculture Organization of the United Nations) 1992 *Improving Household Food Security.* Theme paper No. 1. In: *Major Issues for Nutrition Strategies.* International Conference on Nutrition, Rome

FAO 1995a *Elements for Policy Inclusion in a Draft Policy Document and Plan of Action on Universal Food Security.* Document CL 108/12 for the 108th Session of the Council, Rome

FAO 1995b *Food Agriculture and Food Security: The Global Dimension. Historical Development Present Situation Future Prospects.* Document WFS 96/Tech/1 prepared for the World Food Summit. FAO, Rome

FAO/WHO (World Health Organization) 1992a *Nutrition and Development—A Global Assessment.* International Conference on Nutrition. FAO, Rome

FAO/WHO 1992b *Major Issues for Nutrition Strategies.* ICN/92/INF/7. FAO, Rome

Hansch S 1995 An explosion of complex humanitarian emergencies. In: *Countries in Crisis: Hunger 1996.* Sixth Annual Report on the State of World Hunger. Bread for the World Institute, Washington, DC

Hoet J J 1995 *Role of Foetal and Infant Growth and Nutrition in Causality of CVD and Diabetes in Later Life.* WHO Collaborating Centre. Louvain University, Belgium

Pena C, P Webb, L Haddad 1994 *Women's Economic Advancement through Agricultural Change: A Review of Donor Experience.* International Food Policy Research Institute, Mimeo, Washington, DC

Quisumbing A R, L R Brown, H S Feldstein, L Haddad, C

Pena 1995 *Women: The Key to Food Security*. Food Policy Report. International Food Policy Research Institute, Washington, DC

Rosegrant M, M Agcaoili-Sombilla, N D Perez 1995 *Global Food Projections to 2020: Implications for Investment*. Food Agriculture and the Environment Discussion Paper. International Food Policy Research Institute, Washington, DC

Sharma M, L Brown, A Qureshi, M Garcia 1995 *An Ecoregional Perspective on Malnutrition*. 2020 Vision Brief 14. International Food Policy Research Institute, Washington, DC

Sivard R L 1994 *World Military and Social Expenditure 1994*. Washington, DC

United Nations 1995 *Strengthening of the Coordination of Emergency Humanitarian Assistance of the United Nations*. Document A/50/50/Rev. 1. Report of the Secretary-General to the General Assembly, Fiftieth session, Item 20 (a). New York, NY

UNECOSOC (Economic and Social Council of the United Nations) 1995 *Summary of the Survey of Economic and Social Conditions in Africa, 1994*. Report E/1995/42 to the Substantive Session of 1995, Geneva, 26 June-28 July 1995

UNHCR (United Nations High Commission for Refugees) 1995 *Refugees at a Glance*. Information Brief: UNHCR Liaison Office. New York

USDA (United States Department of Agriculture) 1995 *Food Aid Needs and Availabilities: Projection for 2005*. Economic Research Service Report. Washington, DC

WFP (World Food Programme) 1995 WFP Mission Statement. WFP, Rome

WFP 1996a *Tackling Hunger in a World Full of Food: Tasks Ahead for Food Aid*. WFP, Rome

WFP 1996 *Ending the Inheritance of Hunger: Food Aid for Human Growth*. WFP, Rome

WHO (World Health Organization) 1995 *Global Database on Child Growth*. Geneva

WHO/UNICEF (United Nations Children's Fund) ICCIDD (International Council for Control of Iodine Deficiency Disorders) 1993 *Global Prevalence of Iodine Deficiency Disorders*. Micronutrient Deficiency Information System Working Paper No. 1. Geneva

CATHERINE BERTINI

Food Weapon

The term "food weapon" was a polemical slogan discussed intensively in the United States following a 1974 Central Intelligence Agency (CIA) report suggesting that the agricultural abundance of North America should be seen as an arsenal of power in world politics. Synonyms for this concept include "food power," "agri-power," "food as a political tool."

"Food weapon" means in general that countries which are exporting a large amount of food are therefore in a powerful position in relation to other countries which need imports to feed their population, in particular developing nations. The countries with surplus could use food as a political instrument, offering it as a carrot, denying it as a stick. Food-importing governments would thus be exposed to strong political interference.

The United States, the European Union, Canada, Australia, and Argentina provide more than 90 percent of the world exports of grain. The United States not only provide more than half of the world exports, but are also the largest producer by far. Not surprisingly, the issue of "food weapon" is mostly discussed with reference to the United States as the leading agricultural power, although in principle the other large exporters are concerned as well.

The above-mentioned CIA report, although secret, was published shortly before the World Food Confer-

ence in Rome was opened in 1974 (see *World Food Conference*); the study concluded that increasing worldwide grain shortages caused by worsening meteorological conditions would give the United States a measure of power it had never had before. As custodian of the bulk of the world's exportable grain, it might regain the primacy in world affairs that it held in the period immediately following the Second World War. The report considered as well the possible outcome of such an extraordinary economic and political dominance by stating (this being often quoted out of context) that "Washington would acquire virtual life and death power over the fate of the multitudes of the needy," if there were not enough food supplies available in bad harvest years. It also added that not only the poor less developed countries, but also the major powers would be at least partially dependent on United States food. Former agricultural secretary of state Earl Butz was widely quoted as saying at the World Food Conference, "Food is a weapon. It is one of the principal tools in our negotiating kit." In spite of these official declarations and similar ones by United States proponents of food power, which suggest that this may be the "ultimate weapon" in world politics, the idea of food weapon seems to be a bit deceptive.

It is not a new idea that food is power; the idea of

withholding food from the political enemy is as old as warfare and the scorched-earth policy. Since the Second World War, United States governments have often made policy concerning food export and food assistance to advance their own political designs. When the war was ended, food supplies from the United States helped to stabilize the social and political situation in Europe. Food aid under Public Law 480 (see *Agricultural Trade Development and Assistance Act of 1954 (United States)*), the United States legislation on food assistance of 1954, was used for diplomatic and political purposes to relieve the misery of friendly nations, to spare their governments the cost of buying food on the open market, to help them to keep popular discontent within politically manageable bounds, to help them to lower urban food prices, to show off American productivity and generosity, and to bargain for other benefits. Being primarily budgetary support, food aid was never distributed as mere humanitarian assistance; except for emergency relief, food was always allocated by political and strategical criteria.

However, even this United States food assistance legislation was initially not established as a "weapon" but was adopted with little thought of the lasting political consequences. It was a program the government devised to get some political and economic use out of food that was accumulating anyway for domestic political reasons. The international result was that the United States became the world's residual supplier of agricultural commodities, the one place to turn to in emergencies. The American agricultural dominance was acquired more by accident than by political planning. In the early 1970s, United States farm exports reduced the deficit in the balance of payments. In fact, American food policy is primarily formulated to serve the domestic interests of farmers and grain companies, though at the same time it benefits financial policy.

The influence of the "farm bloc" and the course of United States farm policy determine the possibilities and the constraints of foreign food policy at least as much as state department strategists. With regard to a global strategy, it is an open question whether it is the role of United States diplomacy simply to support domestic agriculture, or if there can be any discretionary use of food for political purposes. In principle, the same can be said about the European Union and the other large producers. The commercial disadvantages of a political restriction on food exports are forceful as can be seen in the case of the wheat embargo against the former Soviet Union. Furthermore, a "food weapon" could be used in the opposite

direction as well by very poor countries: they might exercise a "power" over the rich exporting countries, allowing thousands of children to be shown starving on television; public opinion then would not allow mere political considerations of giving aid or not.

Already restricted in political terms for domestic reasons, the use of food as a weapon in world affairs is not an instrument which is easy to handle. While countries in difficulties may appreciate Western food largesse, they tend to react strongly against the overt use of food as a political weapon. In the 1970s there were two main incidents where food power was discussed or exercised. For diplomats focusing on improving United States-Soviet relations, food trade had been just another element to bolster détente; after the Afghanistan invasion however, it was decided that the former Soviet Union should be punished by an embargo on American wheat. The effects of this exercise of the food weapon are still being controverted but were at least not too impressive; in any case, the former Soviet Union was able to buy grain elsewhere in the free market. In spite of their position as leading oligopolist, the United States cannot impose a total embargo against any country which is able to mobilize enough purchasing power.

The second incident occurred in 1973 when food embargoes were used to put political pressure on the Organization of Petroleum Exporting Countries (OPEC); additionally, it was suggested that by reducing food aid to poorer developing countries the latter would be forced to intervene with OPEC to lower oil prices again ("food for crude"). Although this was not realized, some United States politicians hoped that an "Agri-OPEC" might be formed suggesting that the United States might found a cartel of food-exporting countries. However, this was never likely to work as was possible in the case of oil, because of both the structure of production and the kind of product. The above-mentioned domestic interests would not allow to stop export production, even if this were as easy as turning off the oil tap. Oil power is based on nonrenewable resources, in contrast to food. Importers could circumvent long-term food export embargoes by substitution and, mainly, by raising their own production.

Food is a short-term political weapon and works only under certain circumstances: the country applying for food has to have a serious food problem and to be rather short of foreign exchange; other food aid, for example from the United Nations system, must not be available. Regimes which are anyhow dependent on foreign assistance to survive politically may be much more easily exposed to pressure by food power than those which are more independent, with a political and economic basis of their own. Food power may be an element of an embargo strategy against an isolated regime if there is any support of the United Nations and the international public for a policy threatening life and health of the people. This worked partially after the second gulf war; both the economic sanctions against Iraq and the limited oil for food exchange authorized by resolutions of the Security Council of the UN actually exercise a kind of food power—but in a much more sophisticated way than the above-mentioned CIA report had suggested.

In short, "food weapon" is a partially false term. Food as a weapon is only capable of exerting a small international influence. There is no specific advantage in principle over other forms of political leverage provided in the form of development assistance, foreign policy, or international trade in general. As a short-term policy, it may be capable of deflecting attention from the structural problems which essentially make pressure by food at all possible. If there is food power, it is a matter of structural power, and if there is influence by food, it is primarily economic and commercial influence.

The main reason for the possibility of large exporters using food power as a political weapon is the fact that many developing countries, especially the poorer ones, have neglected the development of their own agriculture over the last decades. This neglect also arises as a result of earlier food aid not being properly integrated in a reasonable development design. In this sense, food as a political tool doubtless helped to create long-term dependence, although this may not have been intended consciously, coming about as a result of mere commercial interests. It is necessary to stress that food policy is not only made by governments but also by banks, stockbrokers, grain companies, the price mechanism, and so on.

In principle, for most of the food-importing countries without large foreign exchange purchasing power there is just one "defensive weapon" to answer the "food weapon" in the long run: they should question the benefits of "interdependence" with regard to the basic food supply and carry through a policy of determined autarky in agriculture to reach "food self-reliance."

See also: *Autarky; Self-reliance; Economic Blockade*

Bibliography ───────────────────

Central Intelligence Agency (CIA) 1974 *Potential Implications of Trends in World Population, Food Production, and Climate*. Washington, DC
Postel S 1996 *Dividing the Waters: Food Security, Ecosystem Health, and the New Politics of Scarcity*. Washington, DC
Rosenfeld S S 1974 The Politics of Food. *Foreign Policy* 14
Seshagiri N 1979 *The Food Weapon*. New Delhi
Simon J L 1996 *The Ultimate Ressource* 2. Princeton
Solkoff J 1985 *The Politics of Food*. San Francisco
Uvin P 1994 *The International Organization of Hunger*. London/New York
Wallerstein M B 1980 *Food for War, Food for Peace: United States Food Aid in a Global Context*. Cambridge, Mass.

REINHARD WESEL

Franklin, Benjamin

Benjamin Franklin (1706-90), publisher, inventor, scientist, philosopher, and diplomat, stands high on the list of the founding fathers of the United States of America. Born in colonial Boston into the large family of a soapmaker, Franklin learned the printer's trade after being apprenticed to his older brother in 1717. Self-educated through wide reading, he soon became known as a trenchant and penetrating writer on a number of subjects. In 1723 he moved to Philadelphia, in the colony of Pennsylvania, to further his career as a printer and publisher. That city, except for long periods of diplomatic missions to England and France, would be his home for the rest of his life. By 1730 Franklin had his own printing firm, which proved so successful that he was able to retire from business a wealthy man in 1748.

Franklin was a great believer in the idea of men of good will getting together to form associations to deal with common problems. He was instrumental in helping to form or energize organizations which promoted reforms in government, science, and other concerns of the people of Philadelphia. At one point, he played a key role in getting the Pennsylvanians to overcome their pacifist Quaker dislike of armed force enough to establish a militia to protect the colony against attacks from pirates and Indians.

Science was a particular interest of Franklin's, and he made several significant contributions in this field. In particular, his pioneering work on electricity, published in 1751, made him famous in educated circles throughout Europe, as well as in America. He also won renown for developing the Franklin stove, a heating device of unprecedented efficiency.

As the relations between Great Britain's thirteen American colonies and the mother country worsened, Franklin became drawn more and more deeply into politics. No visionary advocate of independence, Franklin admired Britain enormously. In fact, he concentrated his efforts on preventing a violent breach between the colonies and the mother country. Between 1757 and 1775 he spent most of his time in London as the representative of Pennsylvania and other colonies, arguing passionately against the repressive measures which the British government was adopting in the colonies. He left the British capital only when it had become overwhelmingly obvious that he had failed, and that war was inevitable.

On his return to Philadelphia, Franklin helped to draft America's Declaration of Independence, then left for France in 1776 to attempt to secure French aid for the American cause. Franklin's writings had made him a much-admired figure in France, and his warmth, wit, and boundless affability made him many more friends there after his arrival. He handled the crucial negotiations with skill, playing on French resentment of Britain, and concluded an alliance in February 1778. French aid and support thereafter were instrumental in the success of the American Revolution.

Franklin returned home in 1785, after the United States had won its independence. He played a role in drafting the new republic's constitution, but for the most part withdrew from public life in those years and lived quietly until his death in 1790. Franklin's good humor, common sense, wit, and charm, as well as his considerable accomplishments, have made him one of the most affectionately remembered figures in American history.

Franklin despised war as destructive, wasteful, and dehumanizing. His interest in helping to bring about a more peaceful world can be seen in his decision, in 1782, to publish Pierre Andre Gargaz's *Project of Universal and Perpetual Peace*. Even though the author was an obscure French convict who could not pay to have his impassioned plea for peace published, Franklin did the job for free in the hope that the work might contribute to making the world a more peaceful place.

For all his sincere detestation of wary, though, Franklin could never bring himself to join the ranks of the doctrinaire pacifists. While he was fond of making statements like, "in my opinion there never was a good war, or a bad peace," he felt that aggression and injustice must be resisted—by armed force if need be. Like so many other Western thinkers, Franklin drew a sharp distinction between just and unjust wars. While condemning the latter as "nothing less than murder," he recognized the morality of fighting to defend a just cause. Liberty, he argued, was well worth risking one's life to defend. "Those who would give up essential liberty to purchase a little temporary safety," he tartly reminded an English friend, "deserve neither liberty nor safety."

Franklin hoped that the new American republic, a land of peace-loving farmers, would set an example to the world of a great nation which eschewed warfare and conquest. Nonetheless, he was appalled by the naïveté of many Americans, who argued that once Britain had recognized its independence, the new nation should simply disarm and forget its alliance with France, withdrawing into a pure and peaceful isolation from the power struggles of the world. Franklin warned them that the world was a dangerous place, where peace and freedom, to survive, had to be well-defended. "If we do not convince the world that we are to be depended on for fidelity in treaties," he wrote, "our reputation and all the strength it is capable of procuring will be lost .... Let us therefore beware ... of neglect in military exercises and discipline, and in providing stores of arms and munitions of war, [for] the expenses required to prevent a war are much lighter than those [required to fight one that is] not prevented."

While advocating a realistic acceptance of the fact that war is sometimes unavoidable, Franklin urged that statesmen do all that they could to combat the causes of wars, so that at least war's frequency could be diminished. He advocated free trade as a measure which would help to eliminate the economic causes of war. He also campaigned for peace settlements which truly settled the issues involved, with no loose ends to cause further conflict over the same question. Similarly, he sought to mitigate the suffering of war and the hatred and bitterness which such suffering inevitably produced, by urging that noncombatants be left undisturbed in time of warfare. "I would have nobody fought with but those who are paid for fighting," he urged. "This once established, that encouragement to war which arises from the spirit of rapine would be taken away, and peace therefore more likely to continue and be lasting."

Franklin, the negotiator of the United States' first alliance, was in many ways the founder and shaper of the American diplomatic tradition. His belief in his own country's virtue, his hatred of offensive war, and his realistic and undogmatic approach to international relations are among the cornerstones on which American diplomacy has rested.

Bibliography ————————————————

Clark R W 1983 *Benjamin Franklin: A Biography.* Random House, New York
Gargaz P A 1973 *A Project of Universal and Perpetual Peace.* Garland, New York
Ketcham R L (ed.) 1965 *The Political Thought of Benjamin Franklin.* Indianapolis, Indiana
Stourzh G 1954 *Benjamin Franklin and American Foreign Policy.* University of Chicago Press, Chicago, Illinois
Van Doren C 1938 *Benjamin Franklin.* Viking Press, New York

GARRETT L. McAINSH

Freud, Sigmund

Sigmund Freud, the founder of psychoanalysis, was born in Moravia in 1856. His family moved to Vienna three years later. It was here that he would spend most of the rest of his life and it was here that he would undertake the studies which made him world renowned. In 1938 he was forced into exile by the German occupation of Austria. He died a year later in London.

Freud developed an early interest in the natural sciences, eventually setting on the field of neurology, but he never completely abandoned a concern for literature and the arts. After studies at the University of Vienna he traveled to Paris where he worked with the French neurologist J. M. Charcot, who had successfully used hypnosis in the treatment of patients suffering from hysteria. Upon his return to Vienna, Freud collaborated with Josef Breuer in the research which culminated in their *Studies in Hysteria* (1895), which argued that hysteric symptoms may be treated by bringing patients to recall traumatic experiences which had been repressed from consciousness. In pursuing this line of inquiry, Freud discovered that these traumatic experiences were typically sexual in content and typically occurred during early childhood. He came, however, to question whether the traumatic experiences recalled by patients had an actual basis in historical fact and argued that what was crucial was not the actual existence of such events, but rather the ways in which patients responded to events, either real or fantasized. Advancing his controversial theory of "infantile sexuality" (which received its fullest explanation in his *Three Essays on the Theory of Sexuality* (1905)). Freud argued that the child is a sexual being, dominated by drives which may or may not be channeled into those sexual practices which are acceptable in adult society. On the basis of these observations and in concert with a series of now-classic case studies, Freud articulated an ambitious theory which sought to explain a wide range of phenomena in terms of the subject's never completely successful attempt to gain mastery over unconscious impulses.

Freud elaborated his concept of the unconscious in a series of groundbreaking works (*The Interpretation of Dreams* (1900), *The Psychopathology of Everyday Life* (1901), *Jokes and their Relation to the Unconscious* (1905)) which sought to illuminate the functioning of unconscious impulses through an examination of everyday experiences. These works were followed by an attempt to give a more systematic form to his inquiries in lectures—the most accessible being his *Introductory Lectures in Psychoanalysis* (1916)—and technical papers on metapsychological issues. In the course of writing these papers Freud found it necessary to make a number of important modifications in his initial theory. He reformulated his initial model of psychological processes into the now-famous trio of "ego," "id," and "superego," postulating and even greater role for unconscious impulses by stressing that even parts of the "ego" were unconscious. He also reorganized his theory of the impulses around a new dichotomy between erotic impulses—which bind individuals together and further the life of the species as a whole—and aggressive impulses—which resist anything which thwarts the organism's path to its own extinction. His most important works from this period are *Beyond the Pleasure Principle* (1920), *Group Psychology and the Analysis of the Ego* (1921), and *The Ego and the Id* (1923). In the last decade of his life, Freud produced some of his most controversial writings: *The Future of an Illusion* (1927), *Civilization and Its Discontents* (1930), and *Moses and Monotheism* (1939). In these works he argued that modern civilization, resting as it did on the repression and sublimation of erotic and aggressive drives, made demands which the individual could not possibly fulfill.

1. War and Aggression

The problem of human aggressivity occupied a central place in these last reflections and the problem of war was addressed directly by Freud on at least two occasions. As early as his 1915 paper "Thoughts for the times on war and death," Freud argued that the recurrent brutality of war shows that "there is no such thing as 'eradicating' evil tendencies." Human aggression has its origins in elemental instincts which may be partially directed towards socially acceptable ends but which can never be completely eliminated. Hence civilized society exists only because "a great many people . . . are not . . . following the dictates of their own natures." Because primitive aggressive drives are only repressed and not eradicated, a regression which would unleash their full fury always remains possible. War provides such an opportunity and thus permits modern men to be what they always were in their unconscious: "a gang of murderers."

Freud reiterated this position a decade and a half later in an exchange with Albert Einstein entitled *Why War?* (1983). Here he agreed with Einstein that there must be "an instinct for hatred and destruction . . . which goes halfway to meet the efforts of the warmongers." Such an instinct has as its ultimate end the reduction of all life to inanimate matter: "Thus it quite seriously deserves to be called a death instinct." Freud saw no hope of eliminating the death instinct— it is as basic to the species as the erotic drive towards preservation and unification—but he did believe in the prospect of "*indirect* methods of combating war." Since war is the product of the death instinct, the most promising strategy for opposing it is to bring the opposing erotic instinct into play. "Anything that encourages the growth of emotional ties between men must operate against war."

2. Freud's Significance

While there is much in Freud's discussion of war which is quite suggestive, in the end his account leaves a good deal to be desired. An appeal to a "death drive" as an explanation for human aggressivity does little to account for the recurrent fact of war. War is an organized social activity requiring considerable coordination and planning; it is not a simple reactive response. To say that there is an instinct which goes "half-way" toward explaining the outbreak of war is to provide an explanation which is at best partial. The positing of such an instinct does little to illuminate the causes of particular conflicts. Nor does it provide help in the task of discerning the general patterns associated with interstate violence.

It should, however, be stressed that Freud never intended his discussions of war to serve as complete and self-sufficient explanations of the causes of international violence. His concern here, as elsewhere, was to show the degree to which irrational and unconscious factors influence conscious human activity. Freud was fond of likening the impact of his work to that of Galileo and Darwin. Just as Galileo had shown that man did not stand at the center of the universe, and just as Darwin showed that man was a relatively late creation in the animal kingdom, so too psychoanalysis offered yet another insult to the pretensions of humanity: the conscious subject was not even the master of its own domain, since it must constantly struggle to overcome primitive unconscious forces. Those who are charged with the formulation of those policies on which the question of war or peace ultimately hangs are by no means immune to the forces Freud analyzed, as Lasswell (1930, 1935) has shown. Nor can the loyalty of populations to their rulers be fully explained in terms of their own rational self-interest, a theme first extensively explored in Adorno et al., (1950).

See also: *Aggression*

Bibliography ————————————————

Adorno T et al., 1950 *The Authoritarian Personality*. Harper, New York

Freud S 1915 Zeitgemässes über Krieg und Tod. *Imago* 4 (1) [1957 Thoughts for the times on war and death. In: Strachey J (ed.) 1957 *The Standard Edition of the Complete Psychological Works of Sigmund Freud*, Vol. 14. Hogarth Press, London]

Freud S 1933 *Warum Krieg?* Internationales Institut für Geistige Zusammenarbeit, Paris [1964 Why war? In: Strachey J (ed.) 1964 *The Standard Edition of the Complete Psychological Works of Sigmund Freud*, Vol. 22. Hogarth Press, London]

Lasswell H 1930 *Psychopathology and Politics*. University of Chicago Press, Chicago, Illinois

Lasswell H 1935 *World Politics and Personal Insecurity*. McGraw Hill, New York

JAMES W. SCHMIDT

From Morality to Ethic: Toward an Ideal Community

It is perhaps now more necessary than ever to draw a distinction between Morality, that prescribes a certain number of behaviors determining what an individual or a society in its whole must aim at, that in one word is patterned upon a *prescriptive logic*, and Ethic that, on the other hand, refers to the equilibrium and to the mutual relativisation of the different values holding together a given set of individuals (for example a group, a community, a Nation, a people, etc.).

Ethic is first of all an expression of the global and unsuppressible vitalism. It expresses the responsibility of this given set of people for its own continuity. In this respect it can hardly be formalized. We could metaphorically compare Ethic to what Medicine defines as *Koenestesy*, the inner sensation of surrounding environment and motion at the same time. We could make an abstraction and claim that collective Ethic is the experimented sense of Statics and Dynamics forming a society as such.

In a time when, because of the use of political representations, many are those who pretend to be moral guides (and Nietzsche ironically calls theirs a *shallow morality*), it could be worth reminding that the worst tyrannies have always been established in the name of the moral *devoir-être*, and that the soft totalitarian of present day bureaucracy owes much to it.

On the other hand it would be hard to deny that many of the attitudes we commonly qualify as immoral often stem from an undeniable generosity. Thus Morality often turns out to be the inspirer of the social status quo.

On the other hand, Ethic shows itself either in the start of a time of effervescences which although seemingly accepting any different moral imposition (particularly concerning sex and labour rules) finds out countless shifts to express the stubborn vitalism of sociality. We could say about what a shrewd reader said about Arsène Lupin: it's his will-power that makes him achieve the unachievable, "for he has the reality of the unreal and the truth of the fault. Aberration recognized as such, becomes a truth."[1]

Now that a narrow rationalism has had its day, we are realizing the effectiveness of the unreal, of the symbolic, of the imaginary for the *social game*. As far as the fault is concerned, science has proved its fertility. It is certain that what I called "aesthetical immoralism" of the mass has preserved along the times, in a tricky and stubborn way, a wide range of attitudes that are considered to be *anomical* by the common morality.[2]

Besides, this common morality should be made humbler because of the fact that, quite often, what today is anomical has been yesterday's truth, or will be tomorrow's. If the word say that the Anomical is also the truth of reality. What ever it is "Lupinism" is perhaps a dow of the mass that in its "perspective

conservativism" preserves, against the rule of morality, what it needs to go on. We too often forget this evidence, which makes Anomy the mover of every society. In this sense we could be one of aberrations: it may also be the quintessence of any aberration.

In this sense we could consider it as the depository of this "virtu" that according to Machiavelli allows a people to feel as such, despite all the vicissitudes and historical oppositions (see *Machiavelli, Nicollò*).

It certainly was with a due consideration that vilified Pareto to assert, a classical and rigorously sociologize, and did not hesitate to get bitterly angry with the "virtuist myth," and to remark, by virtue of his deep knowledge, that the great civilizations of the past owed much to libertinism, and also to most part of the abhorrent practices.

Pareto's brilliant and keen analysis is of a great sociological interest, and from this point of view we may remind the detractors of enjoyment and the devotees of the *"devoir-être"*—the urgency of the Sensual, which remains the basis of any popular ethic. What I elsewhere called orgiasm, in its paralytical modulations as well as in everyday experience, stresses the gaiety of the "carpe dime" and lays on a side the economical and political *project*. This orgiasm overtly shows the ineffectiveness of "virtuist ideologies," which means to keep under control, to accustom, to rationalize what can not but escape them: the game of passions.

Among all the explanations given by Pareto in order to show the interest of what I call ethical immoralism, we should keep at least two. We can briefly remark that, as a matter of fact, the dynamism, we of a given society owes nothing to moralism. On the contrary, "It is impossible to assume that good habits . . . have ever assured a people any victory."[3]

Pareto's historical references support his lapidary remark.

Furthermore, from a more strictly methodological point of view, "traditions, legends, folk songs, are very useful for studies on sociology, but they are also quite obscene."[4] These two remarks are not matched here by chance. In fact they delimit the proper field of orgiasm or anomy, or at least what makes it relevant to a sociologue. A town, a people, a more or less limited group of individuals, who cannot get to express all together their madness, as their fancy, are bound to a quick destructuration and, as Spinoza remarked, deserve "the name of solitude."

Except a few cases of collective sublimation—whose successful examples are quite scarce in history, and most part of which ended up in a carnage or in self-destruction—a society needs to stake disorder of passions, in order to recognize itself as such. Then anomy to this triviality, which imprints a deep mark to every moment of our existence by forming the core of the social structure. The unbridled, coloured, noisy structure of society owes much to sensualism.

From children's morbid games to the genuine lubricity of folk festivals, through the sophisticated mysteries of love intrigues, the range of the games of passion is very wide, so that we can find the mark of it at any level in professional life.

Thus it isn't worth wondering that such a matter of facts leave so deep marks in every representation of the civilizations that followed one upon another. It seems to be necessary to lay on a side any normative evaluation and to question ourselves on such a slightly obscene constancy. This constant deserves as much regard as it has been, with no less constancy, strongly fought, stifled, or denied. In such a configuration, anomy is, to a certain extent, a "Form"[5] which allows us to understand a wide range of situations that, although less marked, mostly escape to moral rules.

We can regularly find in the course of human history different ways of usage accustoming. Of course this accustoming has been quite well modelled in our civilization starting from the Middle Age but, just to make a typical example. Dionysos' myth shows that his devotees weren't necessarily welcome in ancient towns.

We could believe that such a disciplinary effort was, and still is, aiming at this uncontrollable side, this "natural" side, at this shady side that has always been scaring, and which can hardly be bent to the principle of reality or, in a wider sense, to a *mise au travail*. This is the only reason why morality is tyrannical. We have made a remark on bourgeoisie which could easily fit quite different ages: we said that "It has no morality, but it exploits a morality." In that case we were aiming at the "bourgeoisisme," that is to say that peculiar attitude one can find in capitalism as well as in every soft of communism, judging anything by the standard of utility.

This attitude cannot accept whatever is linked to the idea of "loss," the unproductive life; what Beatille call social "expense." Nevertheless, while "energeticism" is being catched, canalized, while (like Heidegger would say) nature is *led to reason*," we can observe a more or less evident persistence of "deepening," of loss, and the stressing of the instant.

Exceeding morality reinforces the ethical tie by virtue of its own peculiarity, as it allows the expression of imaginary, of ludism, of phantasms. Theatricality of disorder evokes the point of "being together." Usage accustoming makes people forget that

effervescence is vital for any social structure.

There is perhaps an aesthetics of *unbridlement*, which is not only a characteristic of dropouts and of "not-yet-integrated youth," referring to that "shady side" which has been haunting society and each individual from time immemorial. We have to mean the word "aesthetics" in its widest sense, which refers to sensations and sensuality shared by people. Orgiasm has always been a way to keep this *unbridlement* alive and to integrate it to the complexity of social and individual body. More in detail, orgiasm allows sharing of the tragic, which forms, more or less consciously, the basis of any wordly situation.

In fact, against "economical" morality, which always looks towards the morrow (may it be religious or profane) by a careful management of its affective or material belongings, enjoyment of the present devours everything at once. The tragic, which is cause and effect of this attitude, needs to be shared. Exuberance under its various forms can be analyzed as an expression of an overload of incorporated tragic. In love, in the unbridlement of senses, in the social expression of gaiety, the bitter taste of finiteness is always lurking. Unruly Dionysos is, let's not forget it, at the same time the god of death.

A typical expression of tragic, which characterizes the "sense of life," is this gift of oneself. From the ancient *hieroduly* to the present erratic sexuality, and maybe also in some forms of classical prostitution, we can find a complete expression of self, a way of getting lost in the collective sexual stream, which reinforces a universal sympathy that refers to the solid organicity of people and things. According to Baudelaire (see *Baudelaire*), "the more prostituted being, the being by excellence, is God."

In fact, in several religious traditions, it is just Him who gives each and everybody all his love. Prototype and Model at the same time, this Supreme Prostitute expresses in a paroxystical form the ethical tie of *sociality*, which then will be able to free itself in different ways. What could appear as shocking or paradoxical in the name of an "economical" vision of Self, is on the contrary absolutely proper in the name of a mysterious tie running through social structures.

If we analyze these "rules of hospitality" (Klossowski) lucidly and without any false shame, they will necessarily lead us to those minuscule everyday situations that then assume a totally new meaning. I said "ethical *immoralism*." This slightly provocative expression means to point out collective body's solid and underground self-consciousness.

This expression points out the sense of responsibility one could feel towards existence, although it sometimes has to be shown through acts which could be judged as anomical. The idea of equilibrium of things (which we can find in the writings by above mentioned Pareto) is the leading one of this way of thinking. Moralism, despite its very praiseworthy intentions, is based upon one or several connected values so that, by subsequent exclusions, it necessarily ends into a deadly vulgarization.

Ethic, in its respect, integrates every different value and, by making them interact gets the greatest *social* benefit. This is the ethic we find in the communitary structure, which puts into effect an undeniable tolerance in any community of men. This also explains the charm of the "deviant" or, in religious terms, of the "sinner." It is actually shocking to observe that common morality is unceasingly diverted by several practices. All this expresses a powerful popular relativism "who knows" that there are irrepressible *pulsions* that, in the end, directly or indirectly contribute to a global well-being.

A community, in every political or religious *representation*, is basically pagan, in the sense that it feels as indispensable the plurality of its idols as *archetypical expressions* of its own features. Ethic is nothing but an almost intentional layout of these different figures into a solid organicity. This process is well known. As far as we are here concerned, I may say that it allows us to understand the shift from a logic of identity to a logic of identification.

The former is mainly individualistic, but the latter is much more collective. Therefore ethic is a consequence of attraction. We join together because of chance and wishes. An objective chance prevails. Yet values, admiration, "hobbies," taste shared by people become an endeavor, are the bearers of ethic. To be more precise, I define ethic as a morality "with neither obligations nor sanctions": with no other obliga-

tion than joining together, than being part of a collective body, with no other sanction than being excluded if the interest (*inter esse*) that ties me up to the group[6] should cease.

This is what founds the ethic of communitary sharing inside something that is *a factor of socialization*. This is, in the end, what is going to characterize more and more the tribal logic that is about to take shape under our eyes, and which is likely to become the main feature of the future *sociality*.

See also: *Global Ethic; Restoration of Morality, Tolerance and Humanity*

Notes

1. See, F. George, *La loi et le phénomène*, éd. Christian Bourgeois, 1978, p. 65.
2. See, M. Maffesoli, *La Conquète du Present*, Paris. PU 1979, et *L'ombre de Dyonisos* (1982). Paris. Le Livre de Poche 1991. (Trad. anglaise: *The Shadow of Dionysos*. SUNY New York 1993).
3. V. Pareto, *Le Mythe vertuiste et la litterature immorale* oeuvres complètes, dir. G. Busino, T. XV, Droz 1971, pp. 127 131.
4. Ibid.
5. Besides its ordinary sense, this noun, as it is used in more specific way, refers to G. Simmel's meaning. It comes than close to Weber's "ideal type."
It is necessary to create an analysis outline that aims to take to evidence the smallest details of social life, preserving their own dynamics. "Formalism" becomes here a way to approach everyday triviality.
For more details refer to: M. Maffesoli, *La Connaissance Ordinaire*. Paris. Méridiens. Klincksieck 1985 (English translation *Ordinary Knowledge*, London, Polity 1996).
6. See, M. Maffesoli, *Le temps des tribus* (1988). Paris, Le Livre de Poche 1991. (Eng, translation: *The Time of Tribes* London, Sage 1996).

MICHEL MAFFESOLI

Fromm, Erich

As a psychoanalyst and social philosopher, Erich Fromm (1900-80) explored basic psychological issues underlying war and peace, free societies, and social institutions. He was greatly concerned with the development of international harmony in the nuclear age. He applied psychoanalytic principles to developing a "sane society" based on human needs and potentials and became one of the most influential and popular psychoanalysts in the United States. His interdisciplinary writings on human nature, ethics, and love have contributed to the study of peace and attracted social scientists as well as a general readership.

As a boy, Erich was an intensive student of the Old Testament, being especially fascinated by Biblical prophets such as Isaiah, Amos, and Hosea who promised universal peace. The First World War, however, caused him to question and reconsider his sympathy for these messianic visions of nations harmoniously coexisting. As his concern for international peace and understanding became more impassioned and his distrust of national ideologies increased, he focused his attention on understanding war and the irrationality of human mass behavior.

In Germany, during his twenties, he studied psychology, philosophy, and sociology and received psychoanalytic training. He concentrated his studies on the work of Karl Marx and Sigmund Freud (see *Freud, Sigmund*), and on the writings of D. T. Suzuki. Much of Fromm's considerable writing and research after that time was directed toward the synthesis and reformulation of their various insights. He became particularly concerned with understanding human fulfillment and the relationship between the individual and society.

Fromm left Germany in 1934 as Nazi power began to surge. He settled in the United States, where he held several academic positions and became a controversial lecturer. He was not welcomed in orthodox Freudian psychoanalytic circles because of his assertion that cultural training rather than instinct is the primary shaper of social character.

Seeking to understand the widespread appeal of fascist propaganda, Fromm studied the character structures receptive to these fascist influences. This investigation culminated in his first major book, *Escape From Freedom* (1941). This book was a landmark study in authoritarianism and became influential in political philosophy as well as psychology. It traced how the influence of the Reformation and the rise of capitalism over several centuries had created circumstances that left people with greater freedom than ever before. As Western men and women gained this freedom, however, they also became more responsible for their actions and choices. Ultimately this freedom brought an increasing sense of aloneness, estrangement, and helplessness. Many individuals fled from these anxiety-provoking and frightening circumstances and chose not to engage in the battle; they chose to "escape from freedom," to become overconformists to society and submissive to authoritarian rulers. The "mechanisms of escape" from this struggle were not only unproductive to the individual but also did not serve society well. A favorable congruence between social character and social system was necessary to achieve peace and national stability.

Fromm saw human freedom as a lifelong struggle for each person to realize his or her unique human potentials. This major idea was the unifying theme of his prolific writings. In this endless struggle, individuals are unavoidably caught between instinctual animal drives and restrictive social forces. They are in the existential dilemmas of being both animal and human, both individual and social.

Thus Fromm regarded himself as a "dialectic humanist," advocating the necessity of an unceasing struggle for human dignity and freedom. As soon as a person gains freedom from one form of enslavement it is inevitable that he or she becomes vulnerable to a new higher level of bondage. No sooner than the young adolescent, for example, breaks the restraints of parents, he or she becomes subject to peer group control, and the struggle for freedom begins anew. Tragically, as people grow older and adjust to alienated lifestyles, they often loose awareness of their own humanness by conducting themselves in ceremonial gestures that are out of touch with any real inner feelings and capabilities they may have.

Fromm did, however, offer constructive alternatives to this alienation in several later books such as *Man for Himself* (1947), *The Sane Society* (1955), *The Art of Loving* (1956), and *The Revolution of Hope* (1968). He believed that it is basic human nature to strive for personal "wholeness," self-expressiveness, self-awareness, and self-realization, yet he saw many aspects of society working against these human potentials. Thus he advocated new social systems that would be responsive to the necessity of developing human beings who were capable of loving genuinely and satisfying human needs. The solution to the endless existential struggle was the attainment of "productive character." While every person has the potential to conquer greed, selfishness, and loneliness and become a productive character, few people have the stamina or required will.

In the late 1950s and 1960s Fromm saw tremendous danger in widespread technology and he warned of the possibilities of an increasingly mechanized population of human beings who could become virtual robots. He focused his attention on the essential question of whether humanity can become master of its material creations, or whether it will be at their mercy and perish in an overtechnicized industrial world. Addressing this question, Fromm wrote *The Revolution of Hope: Toward a Humanized Technology* (1968) and other books on politics, nuclear armaments, and the peace movement. In *May Man Prevail* (1961) he argued that political beliefs often verged on pathology. People are the victims of "projective" thinking in which all the evil that they feel in themselves is projected onto the enemy, who then appears as the embodiment of all evil.

In order to explain war and peace through studying the origins and causes of aggression, Fromm wrote *The Anatomy of Human Destructiveness* (1973). In this book he described the peaceful nature of preliterate hunting and gathering tribes as a basis for his ideas about how destructiveness increases with civilization. In this book Fromm uses case studies of Stalin, Himmler, and Hitler to argue his theory.

In addition to his extensive writings on subjects

related to war and peace, Fromm was actively involved in the American and international peace movement of the 1960s. He saw the present historical situation as being a critical juncture in determining whether humanity would take a rational hold of its destiny or fall victim to destruction through nuclear war. With efforts toward peace as his strongest political interest, he helped to organize the National Committee for a Sane Nuclear Policy (SANE) in 1957—the name being taken from his book *The Sane Society*. His work on behalf of peace advocate Senator Eugene McCarthy during the US 1968 campaign for the Democratic presidential nomination was his last political activity.

When Fromm was in his seventies it was said that his greatest contribution was his own humanism as he lived it. He highly valued friendship and genuineness, and he expected others to be both authentic and sincere. While being personally warm and friendly he maintained a sense of private personal space. He had a vast intellectual curiosity, read widely, and continued to study and take courses in his seventies. He remained a disciplined worker. Every day he engaged in self-analysis and practiced Tai Chi, a series of Chinese exercises developed as an aid to meditation and self-defense. While working on a treatise about psychotherapy, he died in Switzerland on March 18, 1980, a few days before his eightieth birthday.

See also: *Aggression; Psychology of Peace*

Bibliography ———————————————

Elkind D 1981 Erich Fromm (1900-1980). *Am. Psychol.* 34
Evans R 1966 *Dialogue with Erich Fromm*. Harper, New York
Fromm E 1941 *Escape From Freedom*. Holt, Rinehart and Winston, New York
Fromm E 1947 *Man for Himself: An Inquiry into the Psychology of Ethics*. Holt, Rinehart and Winston, New York
Fromm E 1955 *The Sane Society*. Holt, Rinehart and Winston, New York
Fromm E 1956 *The Art of Loving*. Harper, New York
Fromm E 1960a The prophetic concept of peace. *The Dogma of Christ and Other Essays on Religion, Psychology and Culture*. Holt, Rinehart and Winston, New York
Fromm E 1960b Psychoanalysis and Zen Buddhism. In: Fromm E, Suzuki D T, DeMartino R (eds.) 1960 *Zen Buddhism and Psychoanalysis*. Harper and Row, New York
Fromm E 1961 *May Man Prevail? An Inquiry into the Facts and Fictions of Foreign Policy*. Doubleday, Garden City, New York
From E 1963 *War Within Man*. American Friends Service Committee, New York
Fromm E 1966 A global philosophy of man. *The Humanist* 26
Fromm E 1968 *The Revolution of Hope: Toward a Humanized Technology*. Harper and Row, New York
Fromm E 1973 *The Anatomy of Human Destructiveness*. Holt, Rinehart and Winston, New York
Funk R 1982 *Erich Fromm: The Courage to be Human*. Continuum Press, New York
Hausdorf D 1972 *Erich Fromm*. Twayne, New York
Sobel D 1980 Erich Fromm dies in Switzerland. *New York Times* (March 19)

ROBERT CHARLES SMITH; STEVI LISCHIN

Functionalism

The Covenant of the League of Nations, which was signed at the Paris Peace Conference in 1919, established the first worldwide intergovernmental forum for political debate and action. The League was considered by many to be an answer to plans for peace that had been proposed for several centuries. But the League failed to prevent World War II and some of the wars that led up to the cataclysm of 1939-1945, and many observers analyzed the failure of the League with a view to designing an institution with greater potential for peace. World federalism, an arrangement whereby independent countries would surrender their sovereignty to a single supranational world state, was one suggestion, but few believed that world federalist proposals would become a reality (see *Federalism, World*).

With a vision of designing a more practicable path-

way to peace, David Mitrany wrote *A Working Peace System* in 1943 (see Mitrany 1943). Mitrany argued that a skeletal framework of institutions for peace-making already existed, namely, technical international organizations in such fields as communications and health. Mitrany noted that decisions made in these organizations were shaped by technical experts, and the result was that the world interest prevailed over petty national interests. Since political leaders would never surrender the sovereignty of their nations in one full swoop, a multiplication of technical international organizations in diverse fields had considerable potential for integrating the world into a framework of law that would grow, steadily and unobtrusively. In other words, sovereignty could be shared; it did not have to be surrendered to achieve peace. Ultimately, Mitrany speculated, there would be universality in legally binding rules of law covering all possible fields of endeavor. Political leaders would be unable to declare war, as the entire fabric of world civilization could not so lightly be placed in jeopardy. Because Mitrany's analysis placed primary attention on specific areas of technical expertise, it has been called the functional approach to peace. The view that the proper pathway to peace is through the development of technical international organizations is called functionalism. Whereas world federalism is comprehensive in design, the advantage of a functionalist pathway to peace is that it can be built incrementally, as the advances in globalizing policy in one technical area spill over into another.

The first technical intergovernmental organization (IGO), the Rhine Commission, came in 1815. The first worldwide technical IGO, the International Telegraphic Union, emerged in 1865. By 1914, more than thirty functional organizations had been formed (Walters 1960 p. 7), and they continued to thrive even while the League of Nations failed.

After the formation of the United Nations at the San Francisco Conference of 1945, a series of breakthroughs in functional cooperation began to occur in Europe. In September 1944, Belgium, Luxembourg, and the Netherlands signed a customs convention; known as Benelux, the arrangement came into effect on January 1, 1948. Although the original idea was for a complete economic union between the three countries by a later date, the target date of January 1, 1950, was postponed while another development was underway. This second breakthrough came in 1952, with the unification of a single industry under an intergovernmental organization, the European Coal and Steel Community (ECSC), in which the Benelux countries joined along with France, Italy, and West Germany. Five years later, the six countries signed agreements to form the European Economic Community (EEC), popularly known as the European Common Market, and the European Atomic Energy Community (EURATOM), both of which came into force in 1958. The three communities—ECSC, EEC, and EURATOM—merged in 1967 into a single organization called the European Community, which in turn was superseded by the European Union in 1992.

For a decade after World War II, Mitrany's predictions appeared to be coming true, as the new organizations of Western Europe included countries that had been on opposite sides of World Wars I and II, and these countries were not fighting wars against one another. But an analysis of ECSC by Ernst B. Haas in *The Uniting of Europe* (1958) provided cautionary qualifications to Mitrany's analysis. As

developed further in his examination of the International Labor Organization, published under the title *Beyond the Nation State* (1964), Haas formulated a theory that he called neofunctionalism. His argument was based on the fact that technical organizations can only be effective if they are intergovernmental, rather than nongovernmental, and he noted that functional institutions expand the scope of their technical operations only when political leaders provide a high degree of support. Political support for task spillover, in turn, is based on the success of the technical bodies in fulfilling national objectives. Mitrany argued that technical institutions would expand due to their success, but he did not specify the means by which the expected increase in technical scope would come to pass; his arguments were at a normative level. Since Haas documented his findings with the experience of two actual cases, his conclusions were more generally accepted.

Theories of functionalism and neofunctionalism were developed by experts in European politics, so they could be challenged as Eurocentric. Indeed, Ernst Haas and Philippe Schmitter (1966) found that conditions in Latin America could sustain neither functional nor neofunctional pathways to peace, a point on which other scholars agreed (e.g., Hansen 1969). Subsequent developments in Europe also began to cast doubt on the optimistic predictions of the functional and neofunctional pathways to peace. While Haas stressed the need for political leadership in the growth of tasks assumed by the European Community in its earlier years, his students Leon Lindberg and Stuart Scheingold (1970) provided a detailed analysis of the role of political leaders in first mobilizing coalitions of support for the growth of European functionalism in particular economic sectors and then in blocking subsequent progress in those same economic sectors. In *Europe's Would-Be Polity*, they demonstrated that a coalition of interests, once formed, tends to oppose further arrangements in the same economic sector, because that means redistributing rewards within coalition partners and thus negates the logic of the coalition's formation in the first place. Other negative assessments of the European Community also began to appear in the late 1960s and 1970s. In *The European Community: A Superpower in the Making* (1973), Johan Galtung argued that the European Community had become an instrument of economic imperialism; his analysis focused on how the Common Market had become "more than a 'market,'" since it was engaged in a "struggle for power, world power for Western Europe" (p. 17). As Mitrany (1966 p. 212) later reflected, Europe's technical organizations had become exclusivist, "drifting back onto the political track" and thus missing "the way to possible universality." Noting that European institutions had become ossified, Ernst Haas (1976) argued that functional and neofunctional theories had become "obsolescent" (though not "obsolete"), and he turned his theoretical efforts to other foci.

Accordingly, a new interest emerged in international regimes, that is, issue-areas in which nations may cooperate, whether or not through institutions. The prevailing explanation for successful international regimes, known as hegemony theory, argued that effective global cooperation requires enforcement by a dominant world power. With the decline of American power in the world, an alternative theory, based on rational choice axioms, suggested that regimes are stable and viable when they appeal to the economic self-interest of all parties. Since the two approaches revived an earlier debate between realism (which insists on the primacy of power in world politics) and liberalism (which claims the primacy of economic self-interest), the new debate was identified as one between neorealism and neoliberalism (Keohane 1984; Baldwin 1993).

While the enthusiasm for neofunctionalism was tempered by the experience of European and Latin American regionalism, such pessimism ignored progress in another part of the world, namely, Asia. Analyzing the development of regional institutions in Asia, James Schubert (1978) and Michael Haas (1989) found that functional international organizations grew in number and in task expansion throughout the 1960s and 1970s, while political forums in Asia tended to collapse. Thus, they argued, Mitrany's functionalism explained progress in regional cooperation in Asia more than Ernst Haas's neofunctionalism.

On February 7, 1992, countries of the European Community signed the Treaty of Maastricht, thereby agreeing to rename the organization the European Union. The most prominent aspects of the document are an agreement to establish a common currency through a European Central Bank by 1999 and the establishment of a European citizenship, though the treaty also encourages harmonization of policies in many other areas, including crime control, defense, and foreign affairs. Since the proposal could be traced to a spillover in the activities of the European Community, the neofunctionalist logic appears to have been vindicated once again.

See also: *European Political Community; Integration Theories; Integration, Regional; Supranationalism; Association of Southeast Asian Nations (ASEAN)*

Bibliography

Baldwin D A (ed.) 1993 *Neorealism and Neoliberalism: The Contemporary Debate.* Columbia University Press, New York
Galtung J 1973 *The European Community: A Superpower in the Making.* Allen and Unwin, London
Haas E B 1958 *The Uniting of Europe.* Stanford University Press, Stanford, California
Haas E B 1964 *Beyond the Nation State.* Stanford University Press, Stanford, California
Haas E B 1976 Turbulent fields and the theory of regional integration. *Int'l Organization* 30 (2)
Haas E B, Schmitter P C 1966 Economics and differential patterns of political integration: Projections about unity in Latin America. In: Etzioni A (ed.) *International Political Communities.* Doubleday, Garden City, New York
Haas M 1989 *The Asian Way to Peace: A Story of Regional Cooperation.* Praeger, New York
Hansen R D 1969 Regional integration: Reflections on a decade of theoretical efforts. *World Politics* 21 (2)
Keohane R O (ed.) 1984 *After Hegemony: Cooperation and Discord in the World Political Economy.* Princeton University Press, Princeton, New Jersey
Lindberg L N, Scheingold S A 1970 *Europe's Would-Be Polity.* Prentice-Hall, Englewood Cliffs, New Jersey
Mitrany D 1943 *A Working Peace System.* Quadrangle Books, Chicago, Illinois, reprinted 1966 Schubert J N 1978 "Toward a 'working peace system' in Asia: Organizational growth and state participation in Asian regionalism." *Int'l Organization* 22 (2)
Walters F P 1960 *A History of the League of Nations.* Oxford University Press, London

MICHAEL HAAS

Future of Humanity

Aristotle's theory of cause and effect suggests that the future is simply the outgrowth of the present. This means that, given an understanding of the present, we can project possible future developments as the world moves quickly into the vast outer space.

Until recently there was always another place on

the earth's surface to explore. As a result, humans have climbed the highest mountains, sailed through the North and South Poles, and conquered the ocean floors. At present, our major concern is fully concentrated on discovering the mysteries of outer space, an effort which took us to the moon in 1969. Such a concentrated effort has already enabled humans to study the earth and our solar systems from space itself. Hence, the space benefits derived so far cannot be taken lightly.

1. Current Space Benefits

As a result of intensive space exploration in recent decades, we can list some evidences of space benefits in areas of medicine, environment, weather forecasting, communications, and world peace.

1.1 Medicine

Foreseeable health problems of astronauts traveling in space are manifold. In this regard, medical experts conducted deep research to counteract such problems. As a result, we are witnessing a rapid scientific medical development that is proving beneficial to the whole of the humanity. Since the space age started, medical techniques, diagnostic and treatment systems have improved considerably. To quote a few instances:

1.1.1 Sensors developed for astronaut monitoring are finding many uses. An infant can wear at her neck a tiny sensor and radio transmitter that sounds an alarm if she experiences breathing difficulty. The device had been used initially on an experimental basis at Children's Hospital Medical Center of Northern California in Oakland and elsewhere. Its success was highly encouraging.

1.1.2 A NASA-developed system, originally designated to monitor an astronaut's heart action, offers a very important aid to cardiac patients and physicians. In this system, electrodes are sprayed on a patient's body so that heart signals can be radioed via a telemetry system to the hospital from the moving ambulance. Reading the electrocardiogram at the hospital console, the doctor has advance knowledge of the patient's condition before the ambulance arrives.

1.1.3 A night switch, which was developed for activating switches in the spacecraft by a mere movement of the astronaut's eye, has now been adapted to aid paralyzed people. The sight switch can manipu-

late wheel chairs and activate callboards. The system has undergone testing and evaluation at the Rancho Los Amigos Hospital in Downey, California with positive results.

1.1.4 Hundreds of major operations were performed by surgeons wearing a garment that was first developed for space research. Such a garment prevented 7 percent to 8 percent of infections that usually accompany long-exposure surgery.

1.1.5 A pressure transducer used to measure Apollo impact during drop tests has been used as a standard for checking hospital instruments and for fitting artificial limbs. In addition, a telemetry unit designed for cardiac monitoring of astronauts has been modified for use in intensive care units of hospitals.

1.2 Environment

Through space every element of our environment—oceans, rivers, mountains, valleys, earth resources and urban involvement—is carefully observed. The benefit of the entire planet is given priority over the benefit of a particular global locality. As a result, the day will come when we will see cleaner air and water, better management of waste, and a kind of technological equipment that will help harvest the abundant undersea resources.[1]

In addition, critical ecology problems will be better pinpointed and examined, new natural resources of universal interest will be located, and minority groups will have all the business and training opportunities needed with every kind of prejudice eliminated.

At this dawn of the space age era we are already witnessing environmental benefits and facilities. To mention some:

1.2.1 NASA's Langley Research Center has developed a system to reuse water from urine or wash water on space missions. This device promises future application for earth-bound uses.

1.2.2 Remote monitoring systems, perfected in the space program, are being utilized in cleaning up our air. This system is presently used in New York City and is aimed at evaluating various roadway configurations for air pollution potential.

1.2.3 Life support systems originally developed to enable the human being to survive in space are now being used to help this same human being survive in underwater habitats of the Tektite program. One of the purposes of this program is to determine our capability to perform underwater scientific missions while continuously living on the ocean floor with saturated diving conditions for long periods of time.

1.2.4 The Earth Resources Satellite in orbit will make repetitive observations of the earth from space and it will greatly aid us in assessing and understanding the changes taking place in our environment. These observations can aid the farmer by telling him when to plant and when to harvest and even to spot crop diseases for him. The space era will enable us not to look away from earth but toward it so that we may enable ourselves to live better than previously right here on earth.

1.2.5 A television camera system designed to detect hydrogen leaks in a rocket engine will enable geologists to detect oil and mineral deposits from orbit in global areas where humans never had the opportunity to notice before. This will enable us to discover the rich resources of our earthly potential for the greater benefit of all people around the world without exception.

1.3 Weather Forecasting

In quite a few instances, newspapers all over the world covered their front pages with headlines about global disasters that resulted from unpredicted weather patterns. The space program has developed devices that can save lives and protect crops by a fairly accurate prediction of storms. In this regard, we may consider the following:

1.3.1 The meteorological satellites launched in the 1960's have given us more information about our atmosphere and its complex weather-making mechanisms than had been learned since human beings first began the study of the weather hundreds of years ago.

1.3.2 Instruments from space are indicating wind directions and speeds, atmospheric temperatures and humidity as well as other various previously unavailable information.

1.3.3 Weather satellites have detected and tracked every tropical storm over the past several years, allowing time for threatened areas to receive warnings well in advance of the impact of a storm. Official estimates indicated that many thousands of lives and many millions of dollars on property have been saved as a result of satellite information about such storms.

1.3.4 It is predicted by meteorological scientists that future scientific space developments will enable us to make reliable, accurate weather predictions at least two weeks in advance.

1.3.5 The increased understanding of the global weather mechanism as studied from space, will actually help to develop full weather control to the benefit of the entire human race in the blooming space age of the 21st century.[2]

1.4 Communications

General Mark Clark, in a speech he gave in California quite a few years ago, quoted Athenian General Pericles as saying: *If a person cannot communicate the knowledge he claims to have, he should, for all practical purposes, be considered as not having the claimed knowledge at all.*

Every conflict and war that developed in history could be traced to lack of communication in some way or another. The emerging space age will provide us with solutions for communication-problems that were never before even possible to conceive. The recently born space age will tie the world together by both voice and picture. A new educational surge will bring teaching to remote global areas previously difficult to reach. Initial evidence of this could be outlined briefly:

1.4.1 International live television via satellite for education, entertainments and information is now routine because of the space program's communication satellites.

1.4.2 Through space satellites, mass education is now possible to remote areas of India, Brazil, and areas of other nations previously unreached.

1.4.3 A newly developed space device, known as a tertometer, which is immune to interception and jamming, offers many possible applications in industry, at sea and in air-sea rescue operations.

1.4.4 Computerized learning and educational television are influencing entire global areas simultaneously. Space exploration has already broken through the barriers of culture that hitherto created a hindrance to intercommunication in various global areas.

1.4.5 Within few years, educators will make it a habit attending international congresses by remaining in their own country. Through satellite networks they can see each other simultaneously and discuss items of significant importance even though they may be several thousand miles apart.

1.5 World Peace

Many highly educated people think that peace cannot be achieved for the simple reason that human beings do not really want it. This is certainly a rather broad statement. During the course of history, people from various walks of life toiled incessantly for the establishment of peace within the family, the community, the nation and the world at large. Lack of knowledge, suspicion, fear of the unknown, prejudice and feeling of insecurity were, and still are, major stumbling blocks to world peace.

With the birth of the space age, the road to a united global community came into perspective. This could be illustrated from the following data:

1.5.1 The European Space Research Organization (ESRO) and the United States National Aeronautics and Space Administration (NASA) have already affirmed a mutual desire to undertake a cooperative program of space research by means of satellites.

1.5.2 The International Astronautical Federation, which is made up of over 60,000 engineers and scientists from organizations in 35 countries including Russia, have united their efforts to develop astronautics for peaceful purposes on an international basis.

1.5.3 US-Russia cooperation on specific space programs has covered such things as mutual exchange of lunar surface samples; establishment procedures for expansion of combined future space research; and data exchanges of weather monitoring information, to mention a few instances.

2. Looking into the Future

The destiny of future generations is largely in the hands of today's adult generation in power. This adult generation that runs the destiny of present nations, has already made it clear that the search for

the unknown in space is already on and it will be carried on.[3]

During the last few decades, both the USA and Russia stressed the importance of continued space ventures. If space exploration is used for peaceful purposes, as it was intended from the outset, the human race will continue to benefit immensely as we have already experienced. On the other hand, if such space ventures will be used for military purposes, unfortunately the human race will be embarking on a risky course which may make life as we know it today obsolete.

At this stage of history, human beings have witnessed the turning point of a new era—the space age. It is hoped that the scientific and technological developments that lay ahead in the future space investigations may eventually enable us to solve properly problems previously believed impossible even to approach.

See also: *Eco-technology; Human Security*

Bibliography

Boutros-Ghali B 1994 *Building Peace and Development: Annual Report on the World of the Organization.* Department of Public Information, United Nations, New York, NY

Ferencz B 1994 *New Legal Foundations for Global Survival Security through the Security Council.* Oceana Publications, Inc., Dobbs Ferry, NY

Olson R D 1995 *Toward a Social Technology of Peace: A Sociology of Conflict Resolution.* Oxford, Ohio

Prasad S N, Shukla S (ed.) 1995 *Democracy Education and Peace.* The Associated Publishers, Ambala Cantt, India

Raskin M G 1992 *Abolishing the War System.* Aletheia Press, Narthampton, MA

Singh S K (ed.) 1994 *World Conference on Unity of Man.* Unity of Man, Austria

Sri Chinmoy 1995 *The Garland of Nations: Complete Talks at the United Nations.* Health Communications, Inc., Deerfield Beach, FL

The Report on the Commission on Global Governance 1995 *Our Global Neighborhood.* Oxford University Press, Oxford

CHARLES MERCIECA

G

Game Theory

The original impetus to the development of game theory came from mathematical analysis of so-called games of strategy, of which chess, go, bridge, and poker are well-known examples. Games of strategy differ from games of pure chance, such as dice or roulette, in that they involve skills in anticipating outcomes of decisions, including those made by other players. Thus, a chess player contemplating the choice of a move might be guided by the following considerations: "If I move the knight to this square, my adversary will have the following options . . . of these, this is his best move, and if he chooses it, then I shall have the following options . . ." and so on.

In a game as complex as chess, to follow a chain of reasoning of this sort to the end of the game is far beyond human capacity. It is possible, however, to conceive such a chain. It would include specifications of every choice of available options that could possibly occur in the course of the game. Such a schedule of specifications is called a strategy. In a game in which the rules ensure that the number of moves is finite, the number of strategies available to each player, although it may be extremely large, must also be finite.

A game of this sort, involving two players (a two-person game) can in principle be represented in the form of a matrix, where the rows represent the strategies available to one player (called "Row") and the columns those available to the other (called "Column"). A play of the game in this representation consists of a single choice of a strategy made independently by each of the players. In view of the way a strategy is defined (providing for all situations that can arise), this choice completely determines the course and the outcome of the game.

The definition of a two-person game represented in this manner is completed by specifying a pair of payoffs, one to each player, associated with each of the possible outcomes. These are entered in each cell of the game matrix as a pair of numbers, representing the gains or losses of Row and Column respectively.

1. Two-Person Zero-Sum Games

The first games to be analyzed in this manner were those where the gains of one player are always equal to the losses of the other. These are called two-person zero-sum games, referring to the fact that the sum of the payoffs in each cell of the game matrix is zero.

Since in a two-person zero-sum game the payoffs of one player are always equal to those of the other but with opposite sign, it suffices to enter the payoffs of one player into the game matrix. By convention, these are Row's payoffs. An example is shown in Fig. 1.

Figure 1

A two-person zero-sum game matrix with a saddle point in row U_1, column T_2

	S_2	T_2	U_2	V_2
S_1	-4	-2	8	0
T_1	0	-8	7	-6
U_1	5	-1	0	2

Here Row has three available strategies, Column has four. For instance, if Row chooses strategy T_1 and Column strategy V_2, Row loses 6 units, and, since the game is zero-sum, Column wins 6.

The solution of such a game is a prescription of a strategy to each of the players that can be regarded as optimal. An optimal strategy is one that accords the player the largest payoff obtainable under the constraints of the situation. The constraints stem from the circumstance that both players, assumed to be rational, are attempting to obtain the largest possible payoff. A rational player in this context is one who also ascribes rationality to his or her adversary.

The simplest two-person zero-sum games are those that possess a saddle point, that is, an entry in the game matrix that is both minimal in its row and maximal in its column. In Fig. 1, the entry in row U_1, column T_2 is such an entry. It can be shown that if such an entry exists, the strategies that intersect in it are optimal for each player. To see this, observe that if Row chooses S_1, the worst payoff he or she can expect is (–4): if he or she chooses T_1, the worst possible payoff would be (–8); if U_1, the worst possible payoff (–1) would be the best of the three worst payoffs. A strategy such as U_1 is called a maximin strategy (containing the maximum of the minimal). In a game with a saddle point, the best strategy against the opponent's maximin strategy is also a maximin strategy. Thus, in a game with a saddle point, maximin strategies represent a sort of balance of power between rational adversaries.

In games without saddle points, the situation is more complex. Reasoning in terms of maximin strategies leads to a vicious cycle ("He thinks that I think that he thinks . . ."). A major achievement of game theory has been the introduction of the concept of mixed strategy, that is, a strategy determined by a random device, the player's choice being the determination of the probabilities governing the operation of the device. With this enlargement of the concept of strategy, it has become possible to prescribe optimal strategies ("pure" or mixed) to both players in all two-person games representable in matrix form, with or without saddle points.

Although algorithms for finding such optimal strategies have been developed, the significance of this fundamental result has remained theoretical rather than practical. Real-life situations involving conflicts of interest are not usually defined sufficiently sharply to permit realistic representations as formal two-person zero-sum games. Games of strategy, being defined by exact rules, can be so represented, but the number of strategies in those worth playing is generally far too large to permit complete analysis. On the other hand, the conceptual value of the theory of the two-person zero-sum game is considerable. The definitive solution concept, applicable to all such games, suggests that the theory of rational decision can be extended to include situations where several rational decision makers with conflicting interests are involved. Such situations are of obvious interest in fields of activity where success in competition is a dominant value. The worlds of competitive business, competitive politics, and war come to mind. It is not surprising, therefore, that when a highly sophisticated treatise on game theory appeared toward the end of the Second World War (von Neumann and Morgenstern 1944), it attracted a great deal of attention, especially in circles where imperatives of competi-

tion or military strategic considerations are the primary determinants of rational decisions.

Since conflicts generated by divergence of interests are pervasive in all social life, hopes were raised that game theory would provide useful models of social behavior and thus extend important mathematical methods of theory construction to the social sciences. It soon became clear, however, that social conflict situations differed fundamentally from conflict situations represented by two-person zero-sum games. First, the number of participants, representing various interests, generally exceeds two. Second, even in situations with only two conflicting parties, the interests of the parties are not usually completely opposed, as they must be in a zero-sum game, where the more one player wins, the more the other must lose. In most real-life cases, the interests of conflicting parties partly diverge and partly converge. An obvious example was the conflict between the superpowers. On many counts, their interests were conceived to be diametrically opposed, but it was also said to be in the interest of both powers to avoid a nuclear war.

Attempts to extend game theory to situations with only partly diverging interests have met with serious difficulties. These are not of a technical but of a conceptual nature and so can be quite instructive if they lead to reexamination of the fundamental concepts underlying game theory, including the concept of rationality.

2. Non-Zero-Sum Games

Consider the game represented by the matrix in Fig. 2. This is an example of a non-zero-sum game. Since the payoffs of one player do not determine those of the other, both payoffs must be shown in each cell of the matrix. The first is Row's payoff, the second, Column's. The convergence of interests is reflected in the fact that both players prefer outcome C_1C_2 to D_1D_2. However, if Row chooses C_1, it is rational for Column to choose D_2, since the outcome C_1D_2 gives Column more (+10) than C_1C_2 (+1). Also if Row chooses D_1, it is rational for Column to choose D_2, since in outcome D_1D_2 the loss is smaller (–1) than in D_1D_2 (–10). Consequently, it is rational for Column to choose D_2 regardless of how Row chooses. By the symmetry of the players' situations, it is rational for Row to choose D_1 regardless of how Column chooses. If each player chooses "rationally," outcome D_1D_2 results, which is worse for both players than outcome C_1C_2.

The paradox can be resolved if a distinction is

Figure 2

"Prisoner's Dilemma" game matrix

	C_2	D_2
C_1	1,1	−10,10
D_1	10,−10	−1,−1

made between individual and collective rationality. In the above example, it is individually rational for each player to choose D but collectively rational for them to choose C.

The game represented by Fig. 2 is known in the literature of game theory as "Prisoner's Dilemma" (see Luce and Raiffa 1957). It is an example of a large class of games in which, if every player acts "rationally" in his or her individual interest, everyone is worse off than if each acts in the collective interest.

Many situations of this sort are observed in real life. Disarmament may be in the common interest of two powers locked in an arms race, yet, each continues to escalate the race in pursuit of its own interest (that is, to be ahead in the race). When a bank is threatened with failure, it is in each depositor's individual interest to withdraw his or her deposits. But if everyone acts in this way, the bank may actually fail, entailing losses for everyone. It is in the interest of each country engaged in commercial fishing to maximize the size of the catch, but if every country does this, the fish population may be depleted, and the fishing industry may be ruined. The prototype of such situations has been called "Tragedy of the Commons" (see Hardin 1968).

3. Cooperative Games

Collective rationality can be served if parties with partly conflicting, partly identical interests form coalitions to pursue their collective interest. Such coalitions entail binding agreements on the choice of strategies. For instance, in the Prisoner's Dilemma (see Fig. 2), if Row and Column make a binding agreement to choose C_1 and C_2 respectively, they avoid the individually rational but collectively irrational outcome D_1D_2.

In situations depicted by games with more than two players (*n*-person games), subsets of the set of players may form coalitions. The theory of *n*-person (*n*>2) cooperative games deals with situations of this sort. "Cooperative" refers to the possibility of forming binding agreements in choices of strategies.

In *n*-person cooperative games, the focus of interest is no longer on rational choices of strategies. It is simply assumed that each player and each coalition of players will choose strategies that guarantee the best possible payoff (or joint payoff in the case of a coalition) under the constraints of the situation. Of central interest now is the question of how this largest attainable payoff is to be apportioned among the members of a coalition. If a coalition represents a cooperative enterprise the problem may be that of allocating costs as well as gains.

Solutions to such problems depend on the sort of principles that are chosen to be the basis of the rules of apportionment. These rules may be based on the relative bargaining positions of the players, for example, their potential value to each possible coalition; or, perhaps, on certain standards of equity of fairness. Mathematical rigor, characterizing all aspects of game theory, demands that these principles be precisely spelled out and that the solutions based on them be purely logical consequences of the rules derived from these principles. If, for any reason, the solutions are deemed on intuitive grounds to be unsatisfactory, they can be replaced by other solutions only in consequence of specific revisions of the underlying principles. In this way, attention is directed to specific assumptions that underlie any conception of rationality or fairness, and to the necessity of making these assumptions explicit and hence subject to scrutiny and analysis.

4. Evolution of Cooperation

Since the 1980's increasing use was made of game-theoretic models to show how cooperation could evolve in a population of "egotists" in the course of natural selection. Aggressive encounters between conspecifics, e.g., competing for mates or territory are simulated by computer programmers, mostly of an iterated Prisoner's Dilemma game, whereby the "Players" were characterized by different strategies of combat, and the payoffs accruing in the course of encounters with others in a population of such players were transformed into reproduction rates. Although the more aggressive strategies have a short-term advantage against more cooperative ones, the latter eventually outstrip them in the "struggle for existence" since encounters between pairs of aggressive strategies reduces the payoffs accruing to both, hence the reproduction rate of both. Eventually, the cooperators become the predominant "genotypes" in the population. The simulation constitutes an elementary demonstration of how the world may be "inherited" by the meek rather than by the fierce.

5. Intellectualization of War

In the light of these developments it can be said that emphasis in game theory has shifted away from the problem of finding rational strategic decisions in conflict situations to that of examining the consequences of applying different principles of conflict resolution (see Rapopor 1974). This shift, it would seem, enhances the value of game theory as a conceptual tool in the social sciences. It does not, however, enhance the value of game theory as a tool of strategic thinking in situations of pure conflict, that is, those where the interests of conflicting parties are diametrically opposed, so that conflict resolution cannot benefit both sides. Strictly speaking, the only situations of this sort are those that can be modeled by two-person zero-sum games. It is not surprising, therefore, that in military circles, interest in the applications of game theory has been confined to that branch of the theory. In fact, in a conference on game theory sponsored by the North Atlantic Treaty Organization (NATO) in 1964, all except one of the papers presented dealt exclusively with the two-person zero-sum game (Mensch 1966).

For the most part, military applications of game theory deal with textbook problems, which are gross simplifications of tactical or strategic situations and therefore have, at most, heuristic value. However, one branch of game theory holds out a much greater promise to designers of military strategy and of weaponry, namely the theory of differential games. Consider the problems faced respectively by a designer of an intercontinental ballistic missile and a designer of an antiballistic missile. It is in the interest of the former to have the missile get as near to its target as possible and in the interest of the latter to have the missile intercepted as far from the target as possible. Clearly, the interests are diametrically opposed. Solutions to "games" of this sort present considerable challenges to mathematicians: the realization in hardware to the designers of missiles that must be equipped respectively with "evasion" and "pursuit" strategies. Games of pursuit and evasion are a class of so-called differential games (Isaacs 1965).

This challenge illustrates the radical transformation of the mentality ordinarily associated with militarism. Traditionally, dedicated members of the military profession counted bravery, loyalty, and perhaps self-sacrifice among the military virtues. To someone unsympathetic to military values, the warrior may have appeared cruel or slavishly obedient. These images have virtually disappeared and technical virtuosity is now the predominant military virtue. War itself has become a contest between weapons systems of rapidly increasing complexity and sophistication. The development of game theory has been an important factor in making activities associated with the preparation for and conduct of war intellectually attractive. This is demonstrated by the high caliber of the mathematicians and scientists working at institutions devoted to military research; in fact, most of the important developments of game theory have taken place at these institutions.

As game theory became a household phrase both positive and negative attitudes toward it developed in the general public. Some decried the representation of war as a game of strategy in which people and cities played the part of chess pieces or poker chips. Others, concerned primarily with success in competitive business or with prospects of victory in a future war, welcomed what they believed to be a new sort of know-how supposedly conferred by expertise in game theory. One has only to observe the increasing popularity of board games simulating business competition, geopolitics, and war for evidence of this.

The relevance of these games to the exercise of strategic skills derives from the fact that they are all zero-sum: the winnings of some are balanced by the losses of others. The two-person zero-sum paradigm is also dominant in military thinking. A well-known maxim of military rationality is "not the intentions and not the preferences of the adversary but his capabilities ought to be the point of departure in the design of strategy." This principle applies with full force in determining optimal strategies in a two-person zero-sum game, where a rational opponent seeking to maximize his or her gains must necessarily seek to maximize the opponent's losses. In other words, what can possibly be done to harm us will be done by a rational opponent. Moreover, the existence of an adversary is indispensable if the military (zero-sum) conception of rationality is to be of relevance to rational decision making in conflict situations. This creates psychological pressures to find an adversary and to seek reinforcing evidence that he or she is, in fact, an adversary. This image is fixated by well-known mechanisms of mutually reinforcing hostility.

The prestige attained by defense establishments, especially of the Superpowers, in the course of the Cold War has contributed to the spread of the zero-sum mentality from military to political conventional wisdom. Briefly, this mentality is embodied in the assumption that what is best for "them" is necessarily worst for "us." This preoccupation with diametrically opposed interests and the consequent neglect of common interests by the Superpowers has created a formidable obstacle in the way of peaceful resolution of the conflict which threatens to engulf humanity in an omnicidal war.

6. Pitfalls and Promises

To the extent that game theory, by encouraging the intellectualization of war, has contributed to this impasse, its historical role can be regarded as negative. However, game-theoretic analysis of situations beyond the zero-sum paradigm has provided far-reaching insights into the intricacies of rationality, has suggested logically consistent and conceptually lucid models of conflict resolution and, above all, has exposed the severe limitations of strategic thinking, and has thus made a potentially significant contribution to the maturation of the human intellect and to the building of bridges between intellectual and ethical concerns. To what extent this potential contribution can be utilized depends on how widely the sig-nificance of game theory as a sophisticated approach to problems generated by conflicts is understood.

See also: *Conflict Resolution, History of; Peace, Systems View of*

Bibliography

Hardin G 1968 The tragedy of the commons. *Science* 162

Isaacs R 1965 *Differential Games*. Wiley, New York

Luce R D, Raiffa H 1957 *Games and Decisions*. Wiley, New York

Mensch A 1966 *Theory of Games: Techniques and Applications*. English Universities Press, London

Rapoport A 1974 *Game Theory as a Theory of Conflict Resolution*. Reidel, Dordrecht

von Neumann J, Morgenstern O 1944 *Theory of Games and Economic Behavior*. Princeton University Press, Princeton, New Jersey

ANATOL RAPOPORT

Gandhi, Mohandas Karamchand

Mohandas Karamchand Gandhi was born on October 2, 1869, at Porbunder, Gujarat, probably the ancient city of Sudamapuri associated with the legends of Sri Krishna. Gandhi's father and grandfather had been prime ministers in the native system of government loosely articulated with (and completely subordinated to) British rule, then in its second century in that part of India. Both men had been known for their probity and courage. His mother, Putlibai, was unusually devout, even by the standards of Hindu womanhood. Both parents played a major role in shaping him.

Another influence was his childhood nurse, who taught him the use of a *mantram* (Divine Name) as a talisman against his obsessive fearfulness, a Hindu practice he would come to consider the "staff of his life" and devote to its promotion one of his most useful little books (Gandhi 1949). Another inestimable influence on Gandhi to come was his "spiritual reference book," the *Bhagavad Gita*, which opened its pages to him through the translation of Sir Edwin Arnold during the difficult "exile" period of his student days in London. Shortly after his return to India Gandhi met a wealthy Jain jeweller in Bombay named Raychandbhai whose religious devotion and inward detachment from business affairs impressed him tremendously. Nonetheless he could not quite, as he says with characteristic candor, "enthrone him in my heart as my guru," a throne which "remained vacant" despite a lifetime of serious seeking for guidance from the sincere practitioners of any faith.

The achievements of the future mahatma ("greatsouled one") are hard to discern in Gandhi's unpromising childhood and youth, which to outward appearances were in some respects the exact opposite: he was not only "sluggish" of intellect and a "mediocre" student but extraordinarily timid and shy (Gandhi 1957 p. 6). One early characteristic, though, which proved to be important was his extremely serious concern for truthfulness in everything he said or did. In a sense the secret of Gandhi is the secret of how he developed this apparently modest and unremarkable capacity into a tool for personal transformation.

In accordance with a then-prevalent Hindu custom (which in later life Gandhi himself would have a major influence in changing), Gandhi was married at the age of 13 to a beautiful girl, Kasturba, of the same age. It was in this relationship that Gandhi was forced by honesty to conduct his first experiments with nonviolence and self-sacrifice, experiments which were to be of such moment for the modern world. Through many storms, man and wife became passionately devoted to one another and to the causes to which they were to devote themselves with such effect. Schools, clinics, and other institutions in India today bear Kasturba's name. It is often misunderstood, especially by Western observers, that the personal and later social demands which the mature Gandhi made of his wife were an expression of his love for her and a testimony to the relationship which was to grow in beauty and significance for more than half a century.

At the age of 18, his father having passed away, Gandhi was sent by his family to England for higher education in law, as a way of improving their fortunes. It was 1888. His mother had him take a vow before her that he would abstain from women, wine, and meat eating, a vow which he kept. Nonetheless, the journey caused a break with the orthodox community, who disapproved strongly of a Hindu voyaging to a foreign and not very religious culture, a break he would repair on his return to India. These two facts together show something of the individualistic but serious religiosity that would characterize the whole of Gandhi's "experiments with truth" (the subtitle of his autobiography).

When in England, Gandhi at first tried to imitate Western manners, even going so far as to try to learn the violin and the foxtrot, but shortly gave this up as a hopeless failure. From here on his openness to other ways and ideas would never lead to imitation or a departure from his own. Although Gandhi was called to the Bar (not a great scholastic achievement by the peculiar standards of the times), made some important friendships both among British and resident Indians, reacquainted himself with the *Gita* and threw himself into vegetarianism, this early period in England, in the greatest possible contrast to his triumphal return as sole representative of India's unheeded masses in 1931, was a torment of shyness and disorientation. The day after enrolling as barrister in the High Court in London, June 11, 1891, found him on board a ship for India.

What awaited him was the tragic news of his mother's death and the rapid discovery that despite his London training and the expectations of his extended family he was a complete failure at law practice. His childhood shyness was so strong that he literally ran out of the court at his first opportunity to present a brief, in a minor case. Then destiny, so to speak, intervened. He was offered a job representing a Moslem client in a complex law suit in Natal, in what is now South Africa, where racial prejudice was far more openly and humiliatingly practiced than in other portions of the Empire.

It was in South Africa that the real Gandhi was born. As is well-known, he was forcibly ejected from a first-class railway coach at the mountain station of Pietermaritzburg, capital of Natal, and this and similar events broke the shell of the old, inhibited person

he had thought himself to be. The crisis forced him to discover undreamed of potentialities which, he would always insist, lurk unsuspected in every one of us. The only difference is that he developed them scientifically for the rest of his long and intensely active life.

Why in the case of one man, and not a brave one at that, this insult which was and is offered daily to millions of men and women around the world caused such a revolution is something of a mystery. Gandhi was, it is true, unusually sensitive to respect and insult; yet, as explained elsewhere (Easwaran 1978), the explanation has to be at a deeper level: that he did not feel the insult only for himself. He felt in it the evil from which all humanity was groaning, insulted and insulters alike. His oft-quoted comment on this period runs, "It has always been a mystery to me how men can feel themselves honoured by the humiliation of their fellow beings." Where self-interest failed utterly to awaken him, this challenge and the dawning recognition that his life must have a much higher purpose evoked new resources within him and launched him on his inimitable path of lifelong discovery.

Gandhi's first move was to convene a meeting of the whole Indian community of Pretoria and place before them a fourfold program: to observe truth scrupulously, even in business, to be sanitary, to submerge religious and caste differences, and to learn English (Fischer 1950 p. 51). Quite a few features would remain typical of his way of operating for the rest of his long career (Gandhi was 24):

(a) operating publicly and within the law (though he is better known for crossing the barriers of law when it conflicted with natural justice);

(b) small beginnings (though he is of course better known for the giant scale on which some of these small beginnings would evolve);

(c) dogged patience;

(d) a comprehensive package of projects, some of which seem quite irrelevant to the casual observer; and finally,

(e) entirely practical measures (although most Gandhian activists today try to rely on measures that are only symbolic).

Gandhi's efforts to uplift the Indian community soon brought them into conflict with the European government, which then as now brought prison and various forms of severe repression. Out of this crucible was forged the weapon which perhaps is now the only weapon the modern world can use: *satyagraha* (see *Satyagraha*). The story is told in the second and last full-length book Gandhi was ever to have time to write, and in many ways his most important, possibly one of the most important political testimonies to be written in our century: *Satyagraha in South Africa* (Gandhi 1928). The doctrine of *satyagraha* is perhaps its central statement, drawing on the comprehensive significance of the Sanskrit concept of *satya*, meaning "truth," "reality" (that which is), and "good" (Gandhi 1928 p. 433; see also for this period, Easwaran 1978 pp. 41-54):

> The world rests upon the bedrock of satya or truth. Asatya meaning untruth also means non-existent, and satya or truth also means that which is. If untruth does not so much as exist, its victory is out of the question. And truth being that which can never be destroyed. This is the doctrine of satyagraha in a nutshell.

Truth remained the continuous thread behind everything for which Gandhi strove. He felt himself to be nothing more nor less than "a humble seeker after truth," and subtitles the autobiography of his early phase, as mentioned, a "Story of my Experiments with Truth." It was when his growing awareness of truth reached a certain stage that he found nonviolence (*ahimsa*) to be the highest law of all life, and the highest norm to be sought in all relationships for the human being, thus echoing the discovery Hindu sages have made and verified over thousands of years: *ahimsa paramo dharma*, "Non-injury is the highest law" (or "the supreme religion").

Roughly 50 years were spent in the cruel laboratory of oppression forging this principle into an effective instrument of social action under modern conditions. In the words of Martin Luther King Jr. (see Nobel Peace Prize Laureates: *Martin Luther King Jr.*), Gandhi "was the first person in history to lift the love ethic of Jesus above mere interaction between individuals to a powerful and effective social force on a large scale" (King 1958 p. 78; incidentally, Gandhi himself might have objected to "mere" interaction between individuals; for him, nothing took precedence over the individual and his or her relationships). Gandhi was to the science of nonviolence what his great admirer Einstein was to modern physics. While *satyagraha* is sometimes used to denote active nonviolent resistance specifically, it can also be extended to mean the entire comprehensive program of strenuous changes at the individual, social, and national level without which such resistance would have lacked in effect. For Gandhi had

the almost inconceivable ambition not only to liberate India from British rule but to do so in such a way that the entire status of conflict, not only of imperial domination, in the world would be affected; and that meant putting most of the emphasis not on resistance proper but upon what came to be called *sarvodaya*, "uplift of all." It is still little realized how much he gave to religion, economics, education, the position of women, health (where he tinkered endlessly), ecology (his spinning wheel was its unsung inspiration), theory of and relations with labor, race relations and other aspects of communal harmony, political science, and the theory of world order (for some assessments, see Sharp 1979, Agarwal 1970, Ramachandran and Mahadevan 1967, Schumacher 1973; for religion it is best to consult the collections of his own statements, e.g., in *My Religion* or *Hindu Dharma*). Many legacies of his genius and personal power have hardly been tapped by the modern world. His *Constructive Program* (1941) lists some 15 operations for the uplift of India which he devised and directed, putting into many of them the creative energy ordinary mortals devote to a career. Trusts, educational and other institutions, newspapers, and projects for human uplift "fell like plate from his pockets" during the mature phase of his career, much of which was spent on far-flung lecture tours or in prison.

The political career of *satyagraha* and the Constructive Program which unfolded in India after the 20-year incubation in South Africa is, while not universally appreciated in its larger significance, tolerably well-known, due to the public nature of Gandhi's life and the devoted attention of many capable biographers (Tendulkar 1953; Pyarelal 1956, 1968; Fischer 1950), who can draw on Gandhi's own voluminous writings (92 volumes in the Government of India series) and the diaries of his devoted secretary, Mahadev Desai (Desai 1968) as well as the public record. The highlights of this career have also now been popularized by the film by Richard Attenborough.

Periodically, in the decades-long struggle against its colonial domination India waged under his guidance, there were dramatic confrontations which, while not as important as the relatively unheeded constructive interludes, brought the true colors of oppression to the surface and have become almost a part of sacred history for modern India and parts of the modern world. Examples of these confrontations are: the nationwide *hartal* ("stoppage") of March 1919 against the Rawlatt Act, which Gandhi called off in April because of violence committed in his own ranks but which subsequently produced the infamous massacre of unarmed men, women, and children in the Jallianwalla Bagh, Amritsar, galvanizing the country into unending resistance; the great fasts; the "epic march" from his Sabarmati ashram (spiritual community) to the sea to make illegal salt, March-April 1930, and the brave advance into lathi beatings carried out by the volunteers at the Dharamsala salt pans, producing for probably the first time in history an invitation for one of His Majesty's political prisoners to leave jail and attend the Round Table Conference in London, 1931; the " Quit India" campaign of 1942 and the tragic falling-out of Moslem and Hindu communities (which is now known to have been largely the result of machinations by certain sections in the Imperial Government—see Lapping 1985); independence for a divided India; and Gandhi's own assassination on January 30, 1948.

These events are, as mentioned, sufficiently well-known not to require detailing here. They have been well-analyzed from the political and philosophical perspective (Bondurant 1958; Iyer 1983; Naess 1974). Yet the phenomenon of the man remains elusive: as Nehru said, one had to be Gandhi in order to judge him.

Gandhi left scant hints about the intense spiritual disciplines he must have followed to create himself in this way, but the following is one clue to the source of his amazing energy: "I have learnt through bitter experience the one supreme lesson to conserve my anger, and as heat conserved is transmuted into energy, even so our anger controlled can be transmuted into a power which can move the world" (Easwaran 1978 p. 74).

Anger controlled in the way practiced by Gandhi (not to be confused in any way with repression) becomes its positive counterpart, compassion, or love. All of Gandhi's co-workers bore testimony to the extraordinary and universal power of his love. It accounts for the tremendous trust and enthusiastic support he won from literally millions of Indian villagers, businessmen, and maharajahs—even those who did not have any personal contact with him: as one woman follower said, "You felt as though he were blessing you constantly with his eyes." Western observers too have given eloquent testimony to the effect that Gandhi had (Shirer 1979; Sheean 1949). A kind of self-sacrificing love, then, attained by an uncompromising search for truth and fueled by the incessant conversion of negative energies like anger and selfish desire, might define the secret of Gandhi's power over events and persons.

Naturally one effect of Gandhi's own transformation, sometimes considered the most remarkable effect, was his ability to help others transform themselves. Many British allies were won over to his cause, including former opponents and others who became, like Madeleine Slade and the Reverend Charlie Andrews, among his most devoted and important co-workers. But the most spectacular transformation occurred among the "wild Pathans" of the Northwest Frontier Province, some 100,000 of whom formed history's first nonviolent army, the Servants of God (*Khudai Khidmatgars*) under the leadership of the "Frontier Gandhi," Abdul Ghaffar Khan (Easwaran 1984) (see *Khan, Abdul Ghaffar*).

There has been controversy over whether or not Gandhi was a saint. For Indians the issue seems exaggerated, since there need not be a hard-and-fast difference between spiritual attainment and work in the world, though there usually is. Gandhi himself responded to a British prelate who had the temerity to say that they were both, after all, men of God: "You are a politician disguised as a man of God; I am a man of God disguised as a politician." In his view, "politics without religion are mere dirt."

From a Hindu point of view, there is no doubt that Gandhi was a "man of God" squarely in the ancient tradition of its sages and spiritual teachers. There are four paths to God, suiting four types of personality, in Hindu belief down the milennia: *bhakti*, or "devotion," *jnana*, or "spiritual wisdom," *karma*, or "selfless action," and *raja yoga*, or "the royal road" to God, a combination of all three, based on the practice of meditation. While Gandhi shows obvious traces of all four (they are not mutually exclusive in practice), he was primarily and quite obviously a karma yogi—in fact, *the* karma yogi who arose to awaken this immemorial tradition for modern man. Even before his return to India he was working 15 hours a day, seven days a week; while writing *Hind Swaraj* during the return voyage from England in 1909 (reprinted almost without revision in 1938), when his right hand grew tired he switched to his left.

More telling than the sheer rate and pace of Gandhi's activities—secular workaholics have been known to do as much, especially in the United States—all this energy was devoted to the welfare of others. Equally significant, he was not "driven" but did this titanic work with relative ease and personal detachment; in a word, joyfully. When asked by John Gunther, "Gandhi, don't you want a vacation?" he is said to have snapped back, "John, I'm always on vacation!"

Village India heard of him not so much from newspapers or the radio, where he was depicted, rightly, as a great political leader, the emerging

Father of the Nation, but from the lips of wandering *sadhus* (holy men) singing devotional songs like *Gandhi, parama sannyasi*—the "great saint," or in more Indian terms, the "supreme renunciate." Millions of Indians intuitively regarded him as not only the savior of the nation but one of the great reformers of India's religious culture. When he spun, they spun; when he fasted, they felt it was a sin to eat.

India as well as the West has been slow to recognize, however, that along with this went a great intellectual gift, which Gandhi himself seems to have carefully concealed. This is seen in his uncanny political shrewdness and the remarkable creative genius of his programs, as well as the cogency of almost everything he said and wrote. He claimed to be a "practical idealist," and it is said that he prayed, "Give me devotion, give me wisdom, but never take away my common sense."

For all these reasons Gandhi has had a tremendous if sometimes unseen influence on the peace movement, on liberation struggles, human rights, and the slow development of world consciousness, all of which we are slowly becoming aware of under the pressure of universal nuclear threat.

Why was Gandhi never given the Nobel Peace Prize? Mainly because peace has been so poorly understood. The word "peace" is publicly used with such contradictory meanings that acts of war and preparation for war are easily passed off in its name. Virtually no campuses or research institutions exist to remedy this basic lack, though some are starting to awaken to the challenge. Therefore because Gandhi did not publicly stop an open war between two countries his relevance to the peace process went unnoticed during his lifetime. It is only recently that violence, not war, has come to be recognized as the opposite of peace. This recognition is as yet confined largely to scholarly circles, although such Peace Prize awards as those to Mother Teresa of Calcutta (see Nobel Peace Prize Laureates: *Mother Teresa*) and Bishop Tutu of South Africa (see Nobel Peace Prize Laureates: *Desmond Tutu*) come closer to acknowledging that peace is a comprehensive process involving the uplift of human consciousness and building of human community at all levels. When this is widely understood the world will recognize that Gandhi did more for peace than any person in living memory. In his words, "non-violence is not merely a personal virtue. It is a social virtue to be cultivated like the other virtues . . . . What I ask for is an extension of it on a larger, national and international scale" (Prabhu and Rao 1967 p. 130).

How is this "extension" to be accomplished? Gan-

dhi's mighty task lay in the liberation of a great country from its colonial imprisonment. The British would not allow him to organize civilian-based resistance against the feared Japanese assault of 1942-44 (which would have shorn them of imperial purpose), and so his theories on nonviolent defense were never tested (Tendulkar 1953 Vol. 6). Even his close followers had difficulty understanding how the force of love could be mobilized against the force of an invading army. It is left to us to work out how to apply his principles in our own conflict situations, especially in the crucial issue of national defense.

Yet the essence of Gandhi's work was peace, and he did more than raise a general desire for it: he also laid the groundwork for a specific peacekeeping institution, the *Shanti Sena* ("Peace Army"), which 40 years later was very effective in containing the Chinese incursion into Tibet as well as in other conflicts (Walker 1981 p. 73; Gandhi 1982 pp. 93-96). It has been the parent of the World Peace Guard and other peace brigades such as the Witness for Peace movement which has been furnishing extremely effective nonviolent protection against terrorism in Central America. He also proposed, in essentials, the concept of civilian-based defense which is now being much studied, particularly in Western and Northern Europe (Sharp 1985). This is considered by many, including military strategists, as the best hope to prevent nuclear catastrophe, for it is the only form of defense which neither threatens the attacking party, thus provoking them into attack, nor calls for the militarization of society.

British domination in India was only the last phase of a war that had been lost militarily 200 years earlier, just as race prejudice within Hindu society was the seed of the eternal war of man against woman and man. Gandhi had not the slightest doubt that nonviolence was not the best way, as he once put it, but the only way to rid ourselves of the scourge, in all its forms. (For his collected thoughts on defense, see Gandhi 1959.)

It is sometimes claimed that nonviolence has failed; but this puzzles followers of Gandhi who know that it cannot have failed since it has hardly been tried. At the 1985 "Beyond War" award ceremony the Prime Minister of India, Rajiv Gandhi, said that in the long travail of history only "the nonviolence philosophy of Jesus, Buddha, and Mahatma Gandhi" has survived. Gandhians of today feel that humankind cannot survive by standing still. We must make a great leap forward, which can only be by turning this philosophy into a living personal and social truth. That was the only homage Gandhi ever accepted: to follow the way of nonviolence and truth. Only thus will we not only please his spirit but, in the immortal words of Jawaharlal Nehru, "give solace to innumerable hearts" who must live on in this violence-stained world.

See also: *Civilian-based Defense; Nonviolence*

Bibliography ——————————————————————

Agarwal S N 1970 *Relevance of Gandhian Economics.* Navajivan, Ahmedabad

Bondurant J V 1958 *Conquest of Violence: The Gandhian Philosophy of Conflict.* Princeton University Press, Princeton, New Jersey

Brown J M 1972 *Gandhi's Rise to Power.* Cambridge University Press, Cambridge

Brown J M 1977 *Gandhi and Civil Disobedience.* Cambridge University Press, Cambridge

Chatterjee M 1985 *Gandhi's Religious Thought.* Macmillan, London

Desai M 1968 *Day-to-Day with Gandhi.* Sarva Seva Sangh Prakashan, Rajghat, Varanasi [Benaras]

Diwaker R R 1974 *Mohandas Karamchand Gandhi: A Bibliography.* Sujit Mukherjee, Delhi

Easwaran E 1978 *Gandhi, the Man.* Nilgiri Press, Petaluma, California

Easwaran E 1984 *A Man to Match His Mountains: Badshah Khan, Nonviolent Soldier of Islam.* Nilgiri Press, Petaluma, California

Erikson E H 1970 *Gandhi's Truth.* Faber, London

Fischer L 1950 *The Life of Mahatma Gandhi.* Collier, New York

Gandhi M K 1928 *Satyagraha in South Africa.* Navajivan, Ahmedabad

Gandhi M K 1949 *Ramanama.* Navajivan, Ahmedabad

Gandhi M K 1957 *An Autobiography: The Story of My Experiments with Truth.* Beacon, Boston, Massachusetts

Gandhi M K 1959 *Nonviolent Way to World Peace.* Navajivan, Ahmedabad

Gandhi M K 1982 *The Words of Gandhi.* Newmarket, New York

Iyer R N 1983 *The Moral and Political Thought of Mahatma Gandhi,* 2nd rev. edn. Concord Grove, Santa Barbara, California

King M L Jr 1958 *Stride Toward Freedom.* Harper and Row, New York

Lapping B 1985 *End of Empire.* Granada, London

Naess A 1974 *Gandhi and Group Conflict: An Exploration of Satyagraha.* Universitetsforlaget, Oslo

Prabhu R K, Rao U R 1967 *The Mind of Mahatma Gandhi.* Navajivan, Ahmedabad

Pyarelal N 1956/1968 *Mahatma Gandhi: The Early Phase/ Mahatma Gandhi: The Last Phase.* Navajivan, Ahmedabad

Ramachandran G, Mahadevan T K (eds.) 1967 *Gandhi: His Relevance for Our Times.* Gandhi Peace Foundation, New Delhi

Schumacher E F 1973 *Small is Beautiful: Economics as if People Mattered.* Harper and Row, New York

Sharp G 1979 *Gandhi as a Political Strategist.* Porter Sargent, Boston, Massachusetts

Sharp G 1985 *National Security Through Civilian-Based Defense.* Association for Transarmament Studies, Omaha, Nebraska

Sheean V 1949 *Lead, Kindly Light.* Random House, New York

Shirer W L 1979 *Gandhi: A Memoir.* Simon and Schuster, New York

Tendulkar D G 1953 *Mahatma: Life of Mohandas Karamchand Gandhi,* 8 vols. Government of India Publications Division, New Delhi

Walker C C 1981 *A World Peace Guard: An Unarmed Agency for Peacekeeping.* Academy of Gandhian Studies, Hyderabad

EKNATH EASWARAN

Gautier, Theophile

Théophile Gautier, due to the almost incredible variety of his interests, is one of the best representatives of nineteenth century France. He was born in Tarbes on 30 August 1811. Three years later his father, a tax official, was sent to Paris, and it was there, with his two sisters, that he grew up. He was precocious, acquiring at an early age an interest in the Greek and Latin classics as well as a knowledge, as deep as it was broad, of French literature. When he was ten, he was sent to the Collège Louis le Grand as a boarder but did not like the school and was permitted to withdraw after a few months. The following October, as

an *externe*, he entered the Collège Charlemagne, where he remained until he had completed his studies. During this period he took time to learn swimming at the Ecole Petit and, encouraged by tolerant parents, studied painting in the studio of Louis Edouard Rioult. He would have been an artist had he not, in 1829, come across Victor Hugo's *Les Orientales* and decided to become a poet instead. At the Collège Charlemagne he had struck up a friendship with Gérard de Nerval, who, with Pétrus Borel, introduced him, on 27 June 1829, to the author himself. Before long, Hugo had moved next door to the Gautiers, and the acquaintance soon developed into cordial friendship.

Meantime, Hugo's daring drama *Hernani* was staged at the Comédie Française on 25 February 1830. The initial performance was tempestuous, pitting the enthusiastic young Romantics against the proponents of Classical tradition. The Romantics won the day, holding the stage for thirteen years until the public, tired of their excesses, drove them from it in 1843. Recruited to cheer the play, the adolescent Gautier, decked out in a crimson waistcoat, was one of those who clamored the loudest in his admiration, thus assuring the play's success. For a time Gautier would subscribe to the Romantic ideal and, late in life, he would even be the movement's historian. A member of the Petit Cénacle, he would have Romantic artists and writers as his closest friends and, even later, when he had put a certain distance between the school and himself, he would have nothing but kind words for such important Romantic figures as Nerval and Balzac. But in 1833 he was nonetheless ready to deride the movement's excesses in a volume of tales, *Les Jeunes-France*. With *Emaux et camées*, a volume of poems published in 1852, the break was consummated. Gautier's ideal was art, and he believed that the Romantics, with their implausible situations and their verbose pathos and posturing, overshot the artistic mark. As for later writers, a number of them such as Baudelaire, Flaubert, and the Goncourt brothers would be his friends.

Gautier was an inveterate traveller. Alone or with friends he visited England, Spain, Belgium, Italy, Germany, Scandinavia, Russia, and the Near East. Many of these trips inspired accounts that, even today, make for fascinating reading.

Gautier never married. A relationship with Eugénie Fort, never quite severed, produced a son, Théophile Gautier, Jr., in 1836. The contralto Ernesta Grisi became the author's mistress in 1844 and remained his common-law wife until a few years before he died. Gautier and Mme Grisi had two daughters, Judith and Estelle, and it was Judith's short, unwise marriage to Catulle Mandès, which Gautier opposed and Mme Grisi promoted, that ended the liaison in 1866. Gautier had other mistresses, but his great passion, destined to remain an essentially spiritual one, was centered around Ernesta Grisi's sister, the dancer Carlotta Grisi, whom he used to visit constantly at her villa in Switzerland, near Geneva.

During the Second Empire Gautier was one of the numerous artists and writers that Napoleon III's cousin, Princess Mathilde Bonaparte, gathered about her in her home on Paris' Rue de Courcelles and at her country estate. Gautier was one of the Princess' favorites, and late in 1868 she named him her librarian. The Franco-Prussian War, which led to the Second Empire's overthrow, saddened Gautier, although his patriotism as a Frenchman remained untouched. He died of a heart condition on 23 October 1872 and was buried two days later in Montmartre Cemetery.

Gautier was one of those rare geniuses with a talent for almost every genre. He wrote rapidly, turning out, in quick succession, poems, short stories, novels, plays, travel literature, criticism. It was with a volume of verse, *Poésies*, that, not yet nineteen, he broke into print. *Albertus* (1832) and *La Comédie de la mort* (1838) followed. With *Emaux et camées* (1852) and its famous "L'Art" (added in the 1858 edition), he renounced facile Romantic verse and announced his doctrine that creating exquisite, durable poems demands tireless, persistent, concentrated labor. His *Poésies nouvelles* came out in 1863, and 1869 saw the publication of two sonnet collections. Initially his short stories and novellas appeared in newspapers or magazines, then collections of them would be published in book form. The first collection was *Les Jeunes-France* (1833). *Nouvelles*, in 1845, included such well-known tales as "Omphale," "La Morte amoureuse," "Fortunio," "Une Nuit de Cléopâtre," "La Toison d'or," and "Le Roi Candaule." "Militona" was included in *Trio de romans* in 1852. Along with other short pieces, *Romans et contes* (1863) contains "Le Club des Haschichins," "Le Pavillon sur l'eau," and "Jettatura." With Charles Nodier and Prosper Mérimée, Gautier was one of the principal French writers of his time to exploit the supernatural in his work. "La Morte amoureuse," first published in the *Chronique de Paris* in 1836, is an early example, just as "Spirite, nouvelle fantastique," which came out in the *Moniteur universel* in 1865, is a late one. "Spirite" deserves special comment. Dedicated to Carlotta Grisi, it appeared in book form in 1866. It tells the story of a young man, Guy de Malivert, who, when he looks in his mirror, sees a beautiful girl there. She comes to life and explains that, when she was on earth, she had loved him. He never saw her, and she had died in a convent. When Malivert is killed during a trip to Greece, the two are at last united in Heaven, where they can be seen as two brilliant spots in the sky.

In book form, Gautier's first novel, *Mademoiselle de Maupin*, appeared late in 1835. Satirizing newspapers and their materialistic aims and methods, the preface, a brilliant statement of the Art for Art's Sake credo, was hailed as a manifesto by writers, painters, and musicians who, whether they subscribed to his position on other matters or not, agreed with the author that art should never be utilitarian and that it ought to serve no purpose whatever except an esthetic one, that of creating beauty. "That which is useful is ugly," Gautier boldly declared in it. As for the novel itself, it set off a scandal with its depiction, at once lyrical and vigorous, of mores that, at the time, seemed questionable. The novel takes place in seventeenth century France, where Mlle de Maupin—young, rich, and independent—decides to find out for herself what a man's life is really like. Disguised, she embarks on a series of adventures, inspiring in the process a violent passion on the part of a certain Rosette but finally falling in love with Albert, a deserving young man who discovers her true sex. Another novel, *Le Roman de la momie*, was serialized in the *Moniteur universel* in 1857 and came out as a volume the following year. Archeologically, Gautier had taken great pains with his story. Using ancient Egypt as its decor, the novel narrates two impossible loves. Tahoser, orphaned daughter of a high priest, loves a Jew, Poeri, who is married. Meanwhile, Pharaoh loves Tahoser and promises her whatever she wishes if she will marry him. She declines until, out of pity, she agrees when his eldest son dies because of his refusal to allow the Hebrews to leave the country. When he at last allows them to do so, then, changing his mind, drowns as he pursues them. Tahoser becomes the nation's sole ruler, but only for a short time. She dies, and her embalmed body gives the novel its title.

Among Gautier's novels *Le Capitaine Fracasse* is a special case. Planned in 1835 and announced in 1836 and again in 1846 as being in preparation, it was put aside and perhaps worked on sporadically over a period of several decades, finally appearing in installments in the *Revue nationale et étrangère* from December 1861 to October 1863. As a volume, it was published in October 1863. The period is the Louis XIII era, the characters are an itinerant troupe of actors rather like those in Scarron's *Roman comique*. The young Baron de Sigognac, poor and living on his family's isolated Gascon estate, receives an unexpected visit from the actors, who ask to spend the night in his château. Delighted with his guests and the life they lead, the baron joins the troupe. After innumerable adventures, he marries one of the actresses, Isabelle, and, thanks to the timely discovery of a treasure hidden in his château, lives happily ever after. Into the incredible, complicated plot the author inserted great many digressions, many of them personal in nature, helping to explain why this novel is considered Gautier's most appealing

one, despite the deep pessimism that pervades it.

Gautier wrote the scenarios for five ballets. The most brilliant of these are *Giselle*, first performed on 28 June, 1841, and *La Péri*, initially danced on 17 July, 1843. Both of these had as their leading ballerina Carlotta Grisi. In addition to his ballets, Gautier tried his hand, generally in collaboration with someone else, at pure theatre, the genre for which he had the least talent. Among his plays are *Un Voyage en Espagne* (1843), *Le Tricorne enchanté* (1845), *La Juive de Constantine* (1846), *Pierrot posthume* (1847), *Regardez, mais ne touchez pas* (1847). A collection of his plays, *Le Théâtre en poche*, appeared in 1855. Just before his death in 1872 a more complete collection came out under the title *Théâtre: mystère, comédies, et ballets*. Extraordinarily varied in tone, the plays reflect Gautier's multitudinous interests, but, reading them, it is not hard to see why the author's literary reputation rests upon other, more durable foundations. Yet, in 1867, Gautier considered writing a tragedy that, he hoped, would clinch his election to the Académie Française. He abandoned the idea. His failing to write the tragedy had nothing to do with it, no doubt, but he was never elected to membership.

Despite true successes as a poet and as a prose author, Gautier earned his real livelihood with a far more mundane kind of writing. As early as 1834 he had been turning out literary criticism for *La France littéraire*. In 1836 he began writing for Emile de Girardin's *La Presse*, where he remained until 1855. Joining the staff of the government newspaper, the *Moniteur universel*, in the latter year, he wrote for it until 1868. When the *Moniteur* was restructured, Gautier began writing for its successor, the *Journal officiel*. Meanwhile, he had written for various other periodicals and had published a number of his poems and stories in them. For the most part, Gautier's journalism had to do with criticism of painting, sculpture, music, drama, and literature. In all of these he had splendid insights. His literary criticism, perhaps his best, began in January 1834 with a series of articles in *La France littéraire* on Villon, Théophile de Viau, St-Amant, Cyrano de Bergerac, and others and was later published, with the addition of a chapter on Scarron, as *Les Grotesques* (1844). The *Histoire de l'art dramatique en France depuis vingt-cinq ans* (1858-59) is a compendium of drama and opera reviews written for *La Presse* between 1837 and 1852. The *Histoire du romantisme*, which began appearing in *Le Bien public* in 1872, came out later that year, after Gautier's death, in book form. A second volume was added in 1874.

Gautier's travel literature includes *Constantinople*, written during a trip to the Near East in 1852 and consisting of articles sent back to *La Presse*. The book appeared in 1853. Apart from the creative works it produced, a trip to Spain in 1840 resulted, in 1843, in *Voyage en Espagne*, which had likewise been a series of articles. *Voyage en Italie* (1852) narrates Gautier's travels in Italy in 1850, while *Voyage en Russie* (1867) chronicles a visit to Russia in 1858 and 1859.

When the Franco-Prussian War broke out on 15 July 1870, Gautier was visiting Princess Mathilde at her estate at St-Gratien. Learning that war had been declared, he wrote Carlotta Grisi that he was apprehensive and that he had a horror of war but noted that all those around him were exhilerated. Soon exhileration turned to anxiety and then depression as the French lost ground and as, eventually, France was invaded. Quickly the Third Republic seized power. Back in Paris, Gautier watched and waited as the German armies approached. Having already surrounded it for months and cut off its supplies, on 1 March, 1871 the invaders entered the city. Soon the Commune sprang into being, adding to the hardships and political tension. The Third Republic's new government retired to Versailles and blockaded Paris, and a two-month civil war was on. Until the domestic trouble was over, Gautier moved to Versailles. On 10 May the Treaty of Frankfurt, ratified thirteen days later, ended the war with Prussia, and on 28 May the Commune was subdued. Gautier returned to Paris and was appalled as he viewed the ruins and rubble the dreaded *pétroleuses*, the Commune's zealot arsonists, had left, especially the Tuileries Palace, which had been burned. He was glad that Mérimée, who had died on 23 September 1870, had not lived to see what had happened to his valuable library, likewise burned. For all we know, Gautier's precious masterpieces, unpublished, may have gone up in flames. In Paris, the civil war with its destruction had been as terrible as the invasion.

Due to age and a serious heart ailment, Gautier could not, unlike Flaubert, don a National Guard uniform. Instead, from September 1870 to October 1871, he wrote a series of articles for the *Journal officiel* that he published as a book *Tableaux de siège*, late in 1871. Recording what life was like in and near the capital during the period, the articles have a gripping immediacy that stems from the first-hand observation that went into their composition. Gautier was devoted to his pets, and there is an article dealing with Paris' domestic animals, which had had to learn that, with food having become scarce,

humans that might otherwise have been regarded as friends must now be looked upon with caution, even avoided. As for wild animals, Gautier overheard a little boy at the zoo asking his mother if she would eat certain ones he saw there. Other aspects of the ordeal commanded Gautier's attention as well. At the Comédie Française, which was being used as a hospital station, he watched classical performances punctuated now and then when an actor or actress recited patriotic verse to audiences composed not only of the usual kind of theatregoers but also wounded soldiers. Gautier was interested in noting that, in the midst of all the hardship, bloodshed, and disasters, the arts were managing to survive. Some artists had been killed. Others, such as Gustave Doré, were seeking inspiration in the war and its horrors and were producing works that would commemorate France's dreadful experience. Irreplaceable paintings had been shipped to the coast so that, should the need arise, they could be hustled abroad. Statues, harder to evacuate, had been wrapped and left where they were, although the Venus de Milo, hidden in an oak box, had been secreted in a Préfecture de Police basement. At the Cour des Comptes, Gautier was anxious to see what was left of Chassériau's enormous twin murals, *War* and *Peace*, painted in the 1840s. Carlotta Grisi had posed for one of the figures in *Peace*. Badly damaged by smoke and heat, *Peace* was still recognizable, but *War*, Gautier thought, had been irretrievably ruined.[1]

When he saw what invasion and civil war could do, Gautier was aghast. Modern civilization, of which people are so proud, merely concealed mankind's essentially barbarous nature, he decided. "After so many centuries, we would have thought the savage beast that lies deep within man better tamed" (*Tableaux* pp. 324-325). Paris, Gautier believed, was "the heart of France" and "the brain of the universe." It also represented, in his view, what was best in the French nation. He had nothing but praise for the Parisians, who, in spite of their ordeal, endured it all with simple, patient, robust heroism. "France's heart was beating in the skinny chest of starving Paris," he declared (*Tableaux* p. 371). Without reservation he admired the French soldiers, and, when the wounded were brought in, he was heartened to see the speed with which they were attended to. If pain allowed them to sleep, he hoped, patriotically, that they would dream of victory (*Tableaux* p. 123). For the German invaders, on the other hand, he had harsh words. Their presence was "odious," and when he looked at them in the midst of the destruction they had caused, he experienced an aversion that circumstances did not permit him to translate into deeds, an "unfortunately impotent hatred." He liked to think that Heinrich Heine, the German poet who had spent so much of his life in Paris, would have condemned "these Kantian and Hegelian hords" (*Tableaux* pp. 225, 350).

Notes

1. Théophile Gautier, *Tableaux de siège* (Paris: Charpentier, 1886), p. 331. Portions of both murals, which had been commissioned in 1840 and completed in 1844, survived the war. Gautier would have been pleased to know that, starting in 1898, fragments of both were transferred to canvas and taken to the Louvre.

Bibliography

Grant R B 1975 *Théophile Gautier*. Twayne Publishers, Boston

Richardson J 1959 *Théophile Gautier, His Life and Times*. Coward-McCann, New York

Savalle J *Travestis, métamorphoses, dédoublements. Essai sur l'oeuvre romanesque de Théophile Gautier*. Paris

Schapira M C 1984 *Le Regard de Narcisse. Romans et nouvelles de Théophile Gautier*. Presses Universitaires de Lyon, Lyon

Spoelberch de Lovenjoul C de 1987 *Histoire des oeuvres de Théophile Gautier*. Charpentier, Paris, 2 vols

Tild J 1951 *Théophile Gautier et ses amis*. Albin Michel, Paris

Ubersfeld A 1992 *Théophile Gautier*. Stock, Paris

HARRY REDMAN, JR.

General Agreement on Tariffs and Trade (GATT)

From the vantage point of the globalised international economy of the late 1990s, it is difficult to imagine a world in which the number of foreign products available in any given market is pre-determined by politicians, where tariffs are instruments of statecraft the value of which is manipulated to reward allies and to punish adversaries, and where international trade relations are conducted largely in an atmosphere of suspicion, with a tendency to degenerate into trade wars. Yet, this depiction characterises the international trading system of several hundred years prior to the establishment of the General Agreement on Tariffs and Trade (GATT) only fifty years ago. Spurred in particular by the wish of the international community to avoid a repetition of the competitive tariff increases and preferential trading zones that characterised much of the 1930s, the GATT was signed in 1947 as part of the Bretton Woods agreements following the Second World War to construct a predictable, and peaceful, liberal international economy.

The relationship between liberal international trade and peaceful international relations has a long heritage. As John Stuart Mill (1912) remarked, "It is commerce which is rapidly rendering war obsolete, by strengthening and multiplying the personal interests which act in natural opposition to it." Such a sentiment was echoed by one of the main post-war planners of the liberal trade regime, United States Secretary of State Cordell Hull (1948), who proclaimed that, "unhampered trade dovetails with peace . . . if we could get a freer flow of trade . . . so that one country would not be deadly jealous of another and the living standards of all countries might rise, we might

have a reasonable chance of a lasting peace" (see *Emerging Tool Chest for Peacebuilders*).

The GATT sought to accomplish this by regularising international trade by bringing under international supervision such instruments as quantitative restrictions, tariffs, and subsidies; and to depoliticise the formulation of trade policy through the articulation of norms, standards of conduct, and decision-making procedures. The GATT has been largely successful in fulfilling this mandate, notwithstanding the fact that the disagreements between its member states, known as Contracting Parties, during multilateral trade negotiations (MTNs) conducted under its auspices often are dramatised by the media. Negotiations that involve money are usually power-games; the GATT has transformed these into poker-games in which each state vies for the best hand, but, as with all games that promise rewards, the players are unlikely to leave the table. Nowhere has the attachment to the GATT for its normative and practical value been illustrated more explicitly than in the Uruguay Round, the eight successful MTN, which brought under the purview of the institution new issues of trade, created a strengthened dispute-settlement procedure, and inaugurated a new umbrella organisation for this enhanced mandate, the World Trade Organisation (see *World Trade Organization (WTO)*).

1. Law, Agreement, Regime, or Institution?

Almost from its inception, the legal and institutional personality of the GATT was unsettled. The GATT originally was intended to be an interim agreement until the more ambitious and comprehensive International Trade Organisation (ITO) negotiated under the Havana Charter could be ratified by state governments (Wilcox 1947; Brown 1950). Due in part to the United States Congress' fear of losing sovereignty over trade matters, the ITO never came into being, and the "General Agreement," which was composed mainly of statements of principle, continued to operate as an executive agreement. Indeed, it was not until 1968 that the US Congress granted permanent authorisation for contributions to the GATT secretariat, which it referred to as "the executive agreement known as the General Agreement on Tariffs and Trade." As such, although the GATT existed formally under the Bretton Woods Agreements, the executive Agreement did not have the formal personality of an organisation (Dam 1969).

Whether the GATT was, or was not, an international organisation such that its Articles constituted international law in the formal sense has been the subject of much debate (Hudec 1978; Jackson 1992). Notwithstanding, international agreement on the fundamental norms on which the GATT rested in itself marked a watershed in interstate commercial relations. The fundamental norms are that liberalisation and an open, multilateral level playing-field are beneficial to the international community. These norms gave expression to more specific principles, primarily of unconditional most-favoured nation treatment (MFN, Article I), of non-discrimination (Article II), and of national treatment (Article III). Together, these norms and principles—along with more specific rules for their actualisation—are said to constitute an "international regime" whose normative-coercive power is greater than the sum total of its regulations (Finlayson and Zacher 1983).

Indeed, the politics of international commercial diplomacy were conditioned by the GATT, for its principles legitimised certain actions and proscribed others, thereby providing contracting parties with a standard upon which to evaluate and criticise the policies of each other. The GATT thereby provided a basis on which to discuss, and to settle disputes. The GATT also assisted cooperation. Positive reciprocity—that is, the expectation of greater market-access—and the demand on the part of governments for predictable trade policies underpinned the system. The expectation of real material gains over time kept states at the negotiating table, even at times when their policies were being challenged. In the words of Robert Hudec (1978 p. 33): "The key to GATT regulatory pressure has always been the coercive power of normative standards defined in the rules and the power of

authoritative third-party rulings on the issue of compliance with those rules." Alongside the normative power of the GATT was an—albeit imperfect—dispute-settlement and enforcement mechanism. A contracting party could redress its grievances if it believed that its access to a market which it had been promised became nullified or impaired by an action or policy of another contracting party.

The GATT, as a binding international agreement, also performed the critical function of altering the domestic trade politics within the member states. After the GATT entered into force, governments could utilise the fact that they were bound to the liberalisation process and that certain remedies against foreign competition were legally proscribed in order to circumscribe the power of protectionist special interest groups. Moreover, each successive round of the GATT afforded governments a mechanism to counterbalance protectionist forces by providing a focal-point around which to cultivate lobbies that favoured liberalisation by holding out the reward of increased exports. Hence, the GATT process has been likened to a bicycle—so long as the momentum behind the rounds continued, the edifice of liberalisation would not falter (Destler 1986).

Through the General Agreement, the Contracting Parties agreed to prohibit quantitative restrictions, to bind initially the level of their tariffs, and to reduce these progressively over time. Thus was established the GATT process of regular MTNs, or "rounds" of negotiations, designed to liberalise gradually international trade; the slow, yet progressive nature of which was as much a function of the desire to mitigate the dislocations to employment and industry that abrupt liberalisation can entail in order to maintain domestic political support behind the project as it was of the desire to avoid disruptions that a wholesale dismantling of preferential trading arrangements could cause (Ruggie 1983; Wiener 1995).

To enhance further the positive aspects of liberalism, whilst abating its potentially harsh social consequences, the general commitments were qualified by safeguards and escape-clauses to which contracting parties could have recourse, for instance in the case of balance-of-payments difficulties or import surges. Moreover, for governments to justify politically at home the lowering of tariffs in an international forum, the MTNs were conducted on the basis of granting and receiving "concessions" (i.e., lower tariff levels) on a reciprocal basis.

Thus, the GATT performed a crucial political function. It was the expression at the international level of the norms that underpin a liberal trading system, yet an expression tempered to maintain social legitimacy. It served as the focal point for the discipline of government policies; the GATT changed previously sovereign instruments into internationally controlled devices, and changed state autonomy into a right to mutual scrutiny.

2. From Optimism to the Dark Era of GATT

The GATT system of multilateral commercial diplomacy was relatively straightforward when its membership was small (there were 23 initial signatories to the Agreement), and the issues were relatively clear: the GATT applied mainly to the tariff levels applied to industrial manufactures. Immediately following the Second World War, average tariff levels were high (approximately 40 percent), thus providing a certain leeway to tariff cutting. Also, the early rounds of negotiations—Geneva in 1947, Annecy in 1949, Torquay in 1951, Geneva in 1956, the "Dillon Round" from 1960-62, and the "Kennedy Round" from 1963-67 were characterised by a consensus on growth and liberalisation.

However, as the rounds progressed and the average value of tariffs decreased (to approximately 4.7 percent, on average after the full implementation of the Tokyo round Agreements), further tariff cutting became difficult; remaining tariffs related to socially sensitive industries. Moreover, by the 1970s, the international economy suffered the effects of competition from newly-industrialised countries, oil shocks, recession, and stagflation, which culminated in heightened demands for protectionism in industrialised countries. Governments resorted increasingly to "grey area" measures, such as non-tariff barriers (NTBS) and orderly marketing arrangements (OMAS), which were not proscribed under the letter of the GATT, but which did challenge the spirit of liberalisation, non-discrimination and multilateralism. The "new protectionism" grew such that a study group initiated during the Tokyo round from 1973-79 identified over 450 government policies that were used as non-tariff barriers to trade.

Also, for a time it appeared that governments were disillusioned with the GATT dispute settlement mechanism. In short, the panels operated such that the respondent in a proceeding was able to block a panel's recommendations. This, coupled with an increase in trade disputes during the 1970s and 1980s over a range of issues, prompted some states to resort to unilateral sanctions, such as the infamous "Section 301" of the 1974 United States Trade Act. The sum total of extra-legal trade barriers, bilateral trade arrangements,

and coercive unilateralism, it was feared, would erode political commitment to the GATT and the credibility of the multilateral regime.

3. The Uruguay Round: Genesis of the WTO

Yet, the GATT did not falter. This was due mainly to the realisation by governments that their increasing interdependence required the maintenance of an international regulatory forum and that this forum was in need of modernisation to encompass the newest sectors of growth in the international economy. In 1986, the Contracting Parties initiated the latest MTN, the Uruguay round—a project that would increase the relevance of the GATT and at the same time stimulate new pro-liberal interests in the domestic context to countervail protectionist forces.

The Uruguay round was the longest and most complex set of multilateral trade negotiations ever conducted. Its agenda was the widest in the history of the post-war trade institution, and its Agreements, contained in the 20,000 pages of Marakesh Protocols, encompass wholly new areas of trade in services, agriculture, trade-related investment measures (TRIMS), and trade-related intellectual property rights (TRIPS), not to mention the new institutional structures and arbitration procedures to accommodate these. Due to the difficulties raised by these new issues, the negotiations lasted from 1984-94, concluding four years after the scheduled date for completion.

3.1 Agriculture

Agriculture was included formally in the General Agreement in 1947. However, several measures subsequently removed agriculture from the regime's oversight, instigated primarily by the United States' waiver from agricultural commitments in 1955 to safeguard aspects of its Agricultural Adjustment Act. The precedent had been set for the ability of states to use price-support mechanisms to safeguard the income of farmers.

While agricultural trade had been on the agenda of several previous MTNs, little progress was made in this socially sensitive sector. However, several factors in the early 1980s raised the issue to the foreground of the trade agenda. These owed mainly to oversupply generated by production-related support payments which became so great that the US began to convert military bases into food storage facilities. The consequent decline in world prices caused the worst farm-debt crisis in the United States since the depression, and drained seriously the public budgets for agricultural support. For instance, the European Community's Common Agricultural Policy (CAP) absorbed 60 percent of the total European Community budget in the mid-1980s.

The negotiations were difficult for a variety of reasons, the most important of which was the difficulty for governments to alter the domestic bargain with farmers. However, the Uruguay round achieved a commitment to eliminate progressively price-support payments, to replace non-tariff barriers to trade with tariffs (tarrification) and to reduce the latter by 36 percent over 6 years, and to reduce by 36 percent the value and 21 percent the volume of export subsidies over 6 years.

3.2 Services

It has been estimated that service industries in the industrialised (or, post-industrialised) states accounts for up to 70 percent of employment, and that over 25 percent of world trade is in services. The major service industries, such as financial services (banking and insurance), telecommunications, and professional services (law, accounting, consulting) were among the largest business enterprises not to benefit from market-access opportunities negotiated in the GATT, and in many cases, they were larger than those that did. Thus, industrialised states sought to extend the coverage of the GATT to include services.

The negotiations involved a considerable amount of institutional learning in studying services, and the manner in which GATT principles could be extended to them. Four "modes of supply" were articulated: the movement of the consumer to the location of the service supplier; a cross-border supply; the temporary movement of a service provider to a market; and the commercial establishment of a service provider in a market. In all cases, what was at issue were not border measures to access a market, but complex sets of other measures affecting the trade of services, such as "laws, regulations, rules, procedures, decisions, or administrative actions or take other forms (GATS, Article XXVIII(9) (a)) that extended—and some argued, strained—the traditional competence of the GATT. Certain services required the discussions to extend further into issues of investment, such as for common telecommunications carriers, which may require an investment in wires and packet-switching devices to be able to provide their communications service.

To accommodate services, the General Agreement on Trade in Services (GATS) was drafted which shares much of its language with the GATT, but which interprets general GATT obligations in a specific manner. Quantitative restrictions are not prohibited under GATT. Unconditional MFN does not apply to services; rather each member grants national treatment to the service providers of other members on the basis of specific reciprocity for a limited number of service industries specified in each member's schedule of commitments. Non-discrimination is expressed in terms of national treatment, which means foreign service providers are to be treated the same as national service providers. This differs from the traditional GATT meaning in that different national regulatory regimes may apply to the same service industry in different member states, thus rendering objective evaluations of reciprocity difficult.

3.3 Trade-Related Investment Measures

To gain the most from a foreign investment, many governments, though mainly in the Third World, impose conditions on the investor in return for the right to a commercial presence on their territory. The industrialised countries argued during the Uruguay Round (which had issue-linkages to the services negotiations) that such investment measures are trade distorting. A notable example of this is local content requirements, which require a foreign manufacturer to utilise a certain percentage of locally produced goods as inputs to the final product in order to stimulate national industries, which may interfere with the logic of the free market. Other examples of TRIMS are: local equity requirements, which require a certain share of the investment to be held by nationals so that some of the profits (at least in theory) remain within the country; local hiring targets to stimulate employment; national participation in management so that nationals gain managerial skills; and various technology transfers to local industries. As a result of the Uruguay Round, governments have agreed to curb some TRIMS, and work is continuing.

3.4 Trade-Related Intellectual Property Rights

Negotiations to promote the international respect for intellectual property—which includes copyrights, industrial patents, and trademarks—date from the International Convention for the Protection of Intellectual Property (1883). There existed since then a loose international regime composed of the Paris Convention on Industrial Property, the Patent Cooperation treaty, and the Berne Convention on Copyright (1886) administered by the World Intellectual Property Rights Organization (WIPO), as well as the Universal Copyright Convention (UCC, 1952) administered by UNESCO. However, none of the international arrangements prior to the TRIPS Agreement were coercive, in that a state could not activate retaliatory measures against another state for its failure to provide adequate protection for intellectual property. Under TRIPS, however, intellectual property issues fall to be arbitrated under the WTO dispute settlement mechanisms which provides for coercive remedies in some circumstances (see below).

The issue of intellectual property was introduced into the GATT following the Tokyo Round when the United States initiated an Agreement on Measures to Discourage the Importation of Counterfeit Goods, which allows for the confiscation of counterfeit goods at the border. Subsequent studies revealed that industrialised countries suffered a loss of revenue from a range of goods being counterfeit and sold in third markets—most notably in the pharmaceutical, electronics, and entertainment industries—which distorted trade patterns.

After much acrimonious negotiation, the TRIPS Agreement succeeded in securing agreement on a range of patentable matter, without discrimination against any type of invention, whether relating to a product or process, or any field of technology. The term of patents was agreed to be 20 years from the date that patent protection is sought, or 17 years from the date that the patent is granted. The TRIPS Agreement also recognises that the importation of a good is sufficient grounds on which to gain patent protection, rather than requiring that the patent be produced, or "worked" nationally. Thus, the agreement prohibits discrimination on the grounds of the place of invention, that is whether the product is imported or domestically produced. Moreover, in the event that a government requires that a compulsory licence be granted to a manufacturer within its territory to exploit a patent, the TRIPS Agreement requires the payment of adequate remuneration to the patent holder.

3.5 The WTO: Institutional Structure and Arbitration

The World Trade Organisation is the executive organ of the new trade regime, under whose auspices the member states meet in bi-annual Ministerial Conferences and in the General Council which meets more regularly to govern the day-to-day functioning of the Organisation. The WTO is also an umbrella organisation which incorporates the GATT, GATS, TRIPS and TRIMS working groups, and a new dispute-settlement mechanism.

The new dispute-settlement mechanism offers many avenues through which parties to a dispute can resolve their differences, such as through good offices, conciliation, mediation, or consultation. The main achievement of the new mechanism is that it is more automatic and coercive than its predecessor. Failing a satisfactory resolution through other means, a complaining party may request the formation of a Panel to consider the matter. The Dispute-Settlement Body (DSB)—which is a special session of the General Council—is required to form a Panel, unless it decides by consensus not to do so. The report of the Panel is automatically adopted by the DSB, unless it rejects it by consensus. Consensus is defined in terms of inverted decision-making; that is, decisions are adopted automatically unless the members of the DSB decide by consensus *not* to adopt them. Thus, a respondent can no longer delay or block the process, as was the case previously. The decisions of Panels and of the Appellate Body (a quasi appeals mechanism) are binding and coercive. That is, a member can be released from the concessions granted previously to the respondent as a sanctioning device.

4. Conclusion

Over the past fifty years, the GATT has transformed from an entity whose institutional personality was debated into an organisation in both functional and legal respects, with a growing political role commensurate to its enhanced mandate. That mandate is growing. Even before the Marakesh Protocols were opened for signature, the Organisation began to study such issues as regional integration, the environment, and workers rights.

The Uruguay round demonstrated a number of things. The first is that fears of new protectionism, bilateralism and unilateralism undermining the political commitment of member states to the organisation have been overstated. That a liberalising agreement was reached in agriculture, a socially sensitive area, is testament to the continued priority that governments place on stability through international agreement. That an agreement was reached during a situation of crisis in this sector while previous attempts had failed attests to the willingness of governments to exercise political leadership at home for the sake of gaining such international stability.

The second is that the international trade regime is evolving, and its principles are adapting. Notwithstanding the practical difficulties involved in accommodating services into the GATT—to say nothing of the political ones—the fact that the GATS has been established, along with a schedule for working groups and further negotiations bodes well for adapting the regime to the new realities of the international trade system (Wiener 1996).

The third is the success in the area of TRIMS in

gaining a recognition that the conceptual line between trade and investment has become blurred in an era where foreign direct investment is a greater engine of growth for the international economy than is trade. At a time when concerns about fortress "trade-blocs" has given way to concerns about discriminatory "investment zones," even the recognition in principle that investment measures require serious attention in the multilateral context is an achievement.

Finally, the Uruguay Round created a World Trade Organisation that may be evolving a decentralised monopoly of force. The enforcement mechanism still operates on the basis of self-help. Although it would be straining the argument to suggest that the WTO is evolving a system akin to that which pertains under the Chapter VII enforcement mechanisms for collective security in the UN Security Council, it nevertheless can be viewed as a form of collective economic security, with a diffuse monopoly of force.

See also: *Global Integration; Globalization; Internationalization; Interdependence, International; International Law; Treaties of the Modern Era*

Bibliography ———————————

Brown W A 1950 *The United States and the Restoration of World Trade: An Analysis and Appraisal of the ITO and the General Agreement on Tariffs and Trade.* Brookings Institution, Washington, DC

Dam K 1969 *The GATT: Law and International Economic Organisation.* University of Chicago Press, Chicago

Destler I M 1986 *American Trade Politics: System under Stress.* Institute for International Economics, Washington, DC

Finlayson J A, Zacher M W 1983 The GATT and the regulation of trade barriers: Regime dynamics and functions. In: S D Krasner (ed.) *International Regimes.* Cornell University Press, Ithaca

Hudec R E 1978 *Adjucation of International Trade Disputes.* Trade Policy Research Centre, London

Hull C 1948 *Memoirs of Cordell Hull*, Vol.1. Hodder & Stoughton, London

Jackson J 1992 *The World Trading System: Law and Policy of International Economic Relations.* MIT Press, Cambridge, MA

Mill J S 1912 *On Liberty.* Oxford UP, Oxford

Ruggie J G 1983 International regimes, transactions, and change: Embedded liberalism in the postwar economic order. In: S Krasner (ed.) *International Regimes.* Cornell University Press, Ithaca

Wiener J 1995 *Making Rules in the Uruguay Round of the GATT: A Study of International Leadership.* Dartmouth, Aldershot

Wiener J 1996 Transatlantic trade: economic security, agriculture, and the politics of technology. In: J Wiener (ed.) *The Transatlantic Relationship.* Macmillan, London

Wilcox C 1949 *A Charter for World Trade.* Macmillan, New York

JARROD WIENER

Geneva, Spirit of

Geneva is a small city but, almost absent-mindedly, it has become the international capital of the world. It is unique, and that uniqueness has arisen through a special mix of geography and history—a mingling of people in special situations and a fertilizing of ideas and ideals in a setting that has been at once self-reliant, even isolated, yet open to the currents of world thinking. If one has to sum up what Robert de Traz called "the spirit of Geneva" in a few words, those that come to mind might include such descriptors as independence, refuge, detachment, morality, discretion, free inquiry—and peace.

How can such diverse qualities of work, place, and folk become blended into a single essence? The answer has to begin with two aspects of Geneva's geographical position: its immediate physical setting, vital to its early development; and its global siting, a commanding factor of today. As to the physical site, the city is located in a basin, bounded to north, west, and south by the high ridges of the Jura and Salève. It occupies a small hill between the junction of the rivers Arve and Rhône and the southwestern end of Lake Geneva where the lake empties into the Rhône. This site has been settled at least since Neolithic and probably since Paleolithic times. It affords a passage where the Rhône can be crossed by bridge and it commands the meeting of routes to north, west, south, and east.

Geneva's rise to its present unique identity follows a complex historical pattern. In 58 BC the troops of Julius Caesar occupied the site and erected not only a bridge but an outpost of empire, a fortified *oppidum*. Later the city became successively the King of Burgundy's capital; a territory ruled by prince-bishops of the Holy Roman Empire; the focal point of the Swiss Reformation under Jean Calvin; part of Napoleon's France; and, since 1815, a member canton of the Swiss Confederation. For much of the time Geneva was striving, by treaties or by struggle, to protect its independent identity against the machinations of envious neighbours like the counts and dukes of Savoy. From around 1200 until 1850 it gradually became a heavily fortified citadel by land and water, with its great oval of "dog-toothed" barricades exceeding the inhabited area within, while from the thirteenth to the fifteenth century its great fairs made Geneva a magnet for the exchange of goods and ideas.

It was not until 1536, with the adoption of the Protestant faith under the influence of Guillaume Farel and the arrival of the young Jean Calvin, that the modern image of Geneva began to take shape. After some hesitation the city became a southern bastion of the Reformation, the "Rome of Protestantism," attracting large numbers of people from England, France, Italy, Spain, and other countries who were fleeing from persecution. Its great publishing enterprise was turned to the production of the new "Geneva Bible," largely in English and French. Calvin's Geneva became virtually a religious dictatorship, with public entertainment banned, and dress, eating, and life generally being rigidly controlled under surveillance and threat of imprisonment. What had been a gay, ribald community was turned into a bulwark for the propagation of a stern holiness that was meant to achieve the salvation of the world.

This Calvinist legacy produced a lasting tincture in Genevan life. Many of its influential families first arrived during the Reformation. Max Weber and R.H. Tawney have traced the effects of Calvinism in producing a "Protestant work ethic" and the rise of capitalism. In the seventeenth century there arose a sharp dichotomy—later to polarize in a short-lived revolution, *l'Egalité Genevoise* of 1792-98— between the legacy of Calvin, as seen in the haughty, austere governing families of the upper town, who were to produce its bankers, personalities in the sciences, philosophy, and other disciplines, and the freer, more boisterous and liberal watchmakers, goldsmiths, craftsmen, and artists of the less-exalted lower-town districts around the lake shore.

Into this stratified climate, in 1712, was born Jean-Jacques Rousseau, the son of a watchmaker, whose forebears had arrived during the Reformation. Rousseau has left a profound impression as a citizen of Geneva who both shocked and fascinated the eighteenth century world and whose legacy in political theory, education, and literature was to sow the seeds of the French Revolution of 1789 (see *Rousseau, Jean-Jacques*). It is still a thrilling sight to view the pages of "The Social Contract," in Rousseau's hand-

writing, in a small museum attached to the University, with its opening sentence: "Man is born free, yet everywhere he is in chains." Voltaire, who arrived in 1755, also contributed greatly to the intellectual life of Geneva, shocking and enthralling his illustrious contemporaries and emerging as a major figure in the new wave of rationalism that was to leave its mark on an evolving society (see *Voltaire*).

By the mid-nineteenth century Geneva's fame, fortune, intellectual renown, and natural beauty had become a magnet for the worlds of science, letters, political debate, music—and revolution. Everyone— from Bakunin to Byron, Stendhal to Sismondi, Ruskin to Wagner—had to live there or absorb its atmosphere. The city-republic had been opened up to modernity, was prosperous, welcoming to refugees, and—as part of the Swiss Confederation—highly democratic and politically neutral. And, following from the teachings of Théodore de Bèze in Calvin's Geneva, the idea of pursuing world peace was coming to the fore. The Abbé de Saint-Pierre's far-sighted project for "perpetual peace" (1715) was publicized in a work by Rousseau, and in 1771 the idea of a League of Nations was suggested, as it was again in 1830 when J.J. de Sellon organized a Peace Society in Geneva.

Two notable events were to confirm Geneva's destiny as an international centre. The first, following Henry Dunant's pamphlet on the horrors he had witnessed at the battle of Solferino, was the establishment of the International Red Cross. This was achieved in 1864 by a committee of national delegates, following a private initiative by Dunant, General Dufour, and three other Geneva notables that had been arranged a year earlier. The first of a series of Geneva Conventions on the conduct of war and the treatment of wounded, prisoners, and noncombatants was signed at the Conference, and henceforth armed conflict began to be somewhat restricted by humanitarian principles (see Nobel Peace Prize Laureates: *Henry Dunant; International Red Cross*).

The Franco-Prussian war of 1870-71 was the first in which the Red Cross was to function in practice, and it was Geneva's exercise of neutrality in that conflict that clinched the republic's standing as a future international capital. A room in Geneva's Town Hall now called the "Alabama" room was chosen as the venue for the first exercise in impartial international arbitration, that between Great Britain and the United States in 1872, in respect of the frigate *Alabama*, a vessel built in the former country which had inflicted heavy Confederate damage on the Union forces during the American Civil War. It is difficult to imagine such a case being resolved at all, much less in such an objective way, under today's escalating conditions of confrontation.

It was the vital field work of the Red Cross, plus its instruments of international humanitarian law, that were to carry the Geneva torch throughout the First World War which erupted 42 years later. The neutral mission that inspired the Red Cross, because it ensured that aid is extended impartially to all combatants, was to bring a new conception to warfare, and it also set the scene for the consummation of Geneva's world role when the Great War ended.

1. The League of Nations

Throughout the obscene miseries of the First World War, redeemed only by the humane presence of the Red Cross, the question of what was to follow the conflict was foremost in some people's minds. The writer H.G. Wells, who coined the phrase "the war to end war," whose efforts were aimed at giving a sensible content to the eventual peace, and who was to play a far greater part in the peace of 1945, was one of those who visualized and worked for a League of Nations when the war ended. Such a League was finally brought into being in 1919 as part of the peace treaties (see *League of Nations*). Here it is important to note how its creation was entwined in the story of Geneva, and what lessons it has to offer for the development of world order through such international machinery as has evolved from the Geneva spirit.

Already, in December 1918, Lord Robert Cecil, one of the key figures in the League's creation, had said that the new organization's headquarters ought to be based in a city of a neutral country that was not a state capital. For this and other reasons he proposed that Geneva, with its cosmopolitan background, was well-suited to the purpose. Under the chairmanship of US President Woodrow Wilson, a Commission to draft the League of Nations Covenant met in Paris in April 1919. Geneva was duly selected as the League's headquarters with the support of a former Swiss President of the International Committee of the Red Cross, Gustave Ador, and of the Swiss observer Professor William Rappard, who played a notable part in Geneva's affairs over a long period. Wilson and others of the US delegation also advocated Geneva. In the ensuing Swiss national referendum on the subject, although well over 80 per cent of Geneva voters were in favour, the vote was only narrowly confirmed.

At that time Geneva was not well served by communications or endowed with suitable premises for large-scale meetings. The League's first Secretary-General, Sir Eric Drummond, arrived from London with some of his Secretariat late in 1920 and set up temporary offices in the lakeside building since called the Palais Wilson. In November the League of Nations Assembly met for the first time in the Salle de la Réformation, a relatively small hall, now demolished. The problems of accommodating a major world gathering in this hall must have been considerable, even with the use of the adjoining Hotel Victoria for supporting services. Not until 1929 was the foundation stone laid for the future Palais des Nations, a permanent site of the League in years to come.

While the League's Council met four or more times a year, sometimes in other cities, the annual meetings of the Assembly became great public occasions in Geneva. As well as offering events of wide public interest, with the world's leaders assembled to resolve weighty political problems, the sessions created social occasions at which it was the one thing to be seen. Among familiar names of the League days were Edouard Bènes, Léon Bourgeois, Aristide Briand, Lord Cecil, Anthony Eden, Arthur Henderson, Edouard Herriot, and others like Litvinov and Stresemann. As well as visitors and the members of the international Secretariat, around 40 countries retained permanent missions in the city while many international nongovernmental organizations maintained their headquarters there.

The League's deliberations became earnest affairs. As André Maurois observed, they appeared more like religious services than parliamentary debates. However, it should be noted here that this was, and is today, what outsiders must see. There is always a seeming paradox in that, even on technical matters, representatives sent from ministries run by calculating politicians, as well as following their brief for political stand taking, often debate earnestly and on a high moral plane of commitment simply because they personally may be genuinely concerned, as experts, to help arrive at a fruitful solution.

The fact is that much of the League's work, pioneering as it was and carried on by a highly efficient Secretariat, was surprisingly fruitful so that, for the first decade or so, even its political efforts augured well for the future. The League's Covenant, most of it drafted by Lord Robert Cecil and Woodrow Wilson, was by present-day standards ambitious but entirely suited to a community of nations sincerely wishing to avoid war. Its Articles 10-16 provided for ". . . reduction of national armaments to the lowest point consistent with national safety and the enforcement by common action of international obligations." They provided for sanctions and even for armed intervention where necessary. War against a member state meant war against all. "It shall be the duty of the Council in such a case to recommend to the several Governments concerned what effective military, naval or air force the members of the League shall severally contribute to the armed forces to be used to protect the covenants of the League" (Article 16, paragraph 2).

From the first Geneva Assembly in November 1920 the League's development was rapid with regard to both technical, social, and economic agreements and measures to preserve peace. In 1921 an International Conference on Traffic in Women and Children was held and a convention for its suppression adopted. By 1923 a series of international conventions covering maritime ports, railways, simplification of customs formalities, and cross-frontier aspects of electric power transfer and development had all been drawn up and approved. A Protocol for Pacific Settlement of International Disputes was opened for signature in 1924 and others relating to the financial reconstruction of Hungary were signed. The first Opium Conference was held, preparing the way for an international Opium Convention that was adopted a year later.

The year 1925 was notable in various ways, first for the registering of the agreements of the Locarno Conference between five West European states which in effect guaranteed European frontiers. In the same year there was a Conference on Traffic in Arms, while at Singapore, following a Health Conference there, an Eastern Epidemiological Bureau was opened. Two important agreements were reached: one prohibiting use of gases and bacteriological methods of warfare; and the other covering supervision of the international trade in arms.

In Geneva this rate of progress was essentially maintained until 1932. In 1926 Germany was admitted to permanent Council membership, a Preparatory Disarmament Commission met and an important Slavery Convention was adopted. By 1928 the Assembly had adopted a General Act for Peaceful Settlement of International Disputes, which came into force the following year. In 1929 the Statute of the Permanent Court of International Justice was revised (see *International Court of Justice*).

In the following year, the Nansen International Office for Refugees was created, while a Commission of Enquiry for European Union held its opening session (see Nobel Peace Prize Laureates: *Fridtjof Nansen and the Nansen Office*).

Developments continued at a similar pace in 1931. The Assembly adopted a General Convention on means of preventing war, there was a European Conference on Road Traffic, and following another on limiting manufacture and distribution of narcotic drugs, a Convention was adopted also on that subject.

It was in 1932, and despite the opening of the League's Wireless Station, that clear cracks began to appear in the League's edifice. A Conference on Reduction and Limitation of Armaments opened in Geneva but Germany announced its decision to withdraw from it. In the following year, despite the acceptance of a Convention on the International Status of Refugees, both Germany and Japan announced their intention to resign from the League itself. The Armaments Conference was also adjourned, though another meeting did take place in 1934, when the Soviet Union became a permanent League member. In 1935 the Council decided that the Saar Territory should be reunited with Germany, and that country took over its government. The year 1936 saw the Secretariat's move into its new headquarters, the Palais des Nations, the enormous building above the lake that, further extended, still serves today as Geneva's main focus of international effort.

But the League's end was in sight. Germany denounced the Locarno Treaty, Italy proclaimed its sovereignty over Ethiopia, and three Latin American states announced their withdrawal. A year later Italy too announced its resignation from the League and the International Labour Organization. While some useful work continued, and a nonaggression treaty was signed between Afghanistan, Iran, Iraq, and Turkey, the League had become impotent in its main peacekeeping role. The obligations it laid on member states had been broken by Japan in respect of Manchuria. Germany rearmed its side of the Rhine, Italy invaded Ethiopia, while other events, like the Spanish Civil War, were bypassing the League's authority and various members were looking to their own supposed interests to the exclusion of those of the League of Nations.

Today we are learning afresh that the world contains a great many weak-headed or obdurate but strongly motivated people, some of them fanatical extremists whose devotion to irrational causes may know no limit, and others functioning as influential politicians. The League's disunity and reluctance to act according to its rules could be, and was, exploited by such single-minded zealots and adventurers—those Nazis, fascists, and despots who brought about the Second World War.

The League held its last meeting on December 11, 1939, its staff and organizations dispersed throughout the war period, and the Assembly did not meet again until 1946, when it convened to wind up the organization and turn over its headquarters and its functions to the new United Nations body. Among those present who, like Philip Noel-Baker, had been active at the birth of the League of Nations was Lord Robert Cecil, one of its prime movers. He announced: "The League is dead; long live the United Nations!"

2. The United Nations

Throughout the Second World War, the question of what was to follow was once more a matter of concern. With war aims again in mind, H.G. Wells created the first World Declaration of Human Rights and Duties in 1940-42, and this was widely disseminated throughout the old and new worlds (see *Human Rights and Peace*). In 1942, following an "Atlantic Charter" drawn up by Winston Churchill (see *Churchill, Winston*) and Franklin Roosevelt the year before, a "Declaration of United Nations" was accepted by 26 countries. In 1945 a UN Conference on International Organization met at San Francisco to draw up the UN Charter, working on the basis of proposals drafted by China, the then Soviet Union, the United Kingdom, and the United States a year earlier. The organization duly came into existence on October 24, 1945.

While the new body built considerably on the League of Nations pattern, it was also in a position to reap the fruits of wisdom born of bitter experience. In particular, the Charter already laid much stress on a new concept—that of human rights and duties. The International Bill of Human Rights became a basis for United Nations work (see *International Bill of Human Rights*).

Though it has a roughly similar purpose to the League's Covenant, the functions assigned in the UN Charter to its three main organs—the General Assembly, the Security Council, and the Economic and Social Council—are couched in milder and somewhat less ambitious terms. In the Security Council there is a distinction between permanent and nonpermanent members, and its peacekeeping role also is broadly similar. It was presumably felt that a common interest in peace would have a stronger effect in the future than in the past.

But what is created by politicians must reflect the weaknesses inherent in their calling. There was a curious parallel between the fact that Franklin Roosevelt, a prime mover in planning the UN, was to die in 1945, just as Woodrow Wilson had faded from the

international scene in 1920. In any event, foreseeable pressures mounted and in the process the need for a neutral seat was ignored and New York chosen as the official UN headquarters. For various reasons—which history has amply confirmed—this was a major blunder by the world community.

From 1942 or before, though at first covertly, the host country had maintained a sustained antagonism against a leading member state; is the only country to have used the atomic weapon, six weeks after signing the UN Charter; maintains a major financial deficit and an unstable currency; and is assigned 25 per cent of the UN budget but, as a matter of policy, has deliberately withheld large contractual payments. In addition, New York can be seen to be geographically unsuited to such a role. If we seek to determine the centre of the earth's inhabited land surface—that is, fix the pole of a hemisphere containing the maximum inhabited land area (nearly 94 percent), we find that such a point falls near Nantes, in western France, some 330 kilometres from Paris and 470 kilometres from London. If, as we should, we seek a *neutral* city that is nearest to the centre of the earth's inhabited land area, then that city is Geneva, about 570 kilometres from the theoretical centre and thus an optimal point for delegates to attend international meetings. By contrast, New York is nearly 80 degrees of longitude distant and more awkward for many to reach.

What, then, of Geneva's international role with the United Nations? In the variety and intensity of its activities the Palais des Nations, and various UN agency headquarters that have blossomed around the original Red Cross building, have maintained the city's place as the world's effective international capital. Over 7,200 meetings a year, varying from major conferences to short technical gatherings, are held at the Palais des Nations, involving member states, observer groups, accredited NGOs and specialised agencies. Some 9,000 people are at work within the entire United Nations system of organizations, although the budget for the UN itself, for the biennium 1994-95, is equal only to that for public works spending of the Canton of Geneva. Moreover, nearly five per cent of total spending should, in fact, be recouped from revenue-producing activities such as sale of publications and 150,000 visitors per annum. Of the total number of member states (185) 142 maintain Permanent Missions to the UN Office at Geneva. When we look at the comprehensive coverage of global and international activities, it can be seen that the late-nineties furors about UN cost-cutting has been little more than a self-interested ideological ploy, part of a post-Cold War drive for politi-

cal and commercial hegemony by a major protagonist. This is a field where a hidden global conflict
now looms. To further human aspirations that still
struggle to emerge, it is high time to replace an outdated world free-for-all that stifles all cooperation in
favour of one that can allow ever more vital common
ends and interests to be pursued.

The range of international work that goes on in
Geneva—the conferences, expert meetings, basic
research, gathering of common statistics, drafting of
conventions and international agreements—as well as
the spread of subjects covered offers a conspectus of
those matters that a loose global control organ and a
world civil service will have to encompass if and
when it comes into being through ad hoc reductions of
sovereignty and the creation of a standing world body.

What, then, is the present-day coverage of Geneva's historical and world-oriented role? First, it is a
home base for the UN High Commissioner for Human
Rights and the UN Centre for Human Rights (see
Declaration of the Rights of Man). This major field
of activity covers also monitoring bodies for Covenants
and Conventions dealing with civil and political
rights, economic, social and cultural rights, torture,
racial discrimination, the rights of the child and innumerable other rights questions, including, e.g., the
rights of women and environmental rights.

Other Geneva centres include the standing UN Conference on Trade and Development, the Economic
Commission for Europe, disaster relief and prevention activities of the Department of Humanitarian
Affairs, the UN Compensation Commission plus UN
Research Institutes for Social Development, Training
and Research, Disarmament Research, the UN Volunteer Programme, the standing Conference on Disarmament and a Geneva Branch of the Centre for Disarmament Affairs. The International Law Commission also convenes there.

Of innumerable international, intergovernmental
and non-governmental bodies that have become part
of a "Geneva Spirit" should be mentioned the
International Labour Organization, the World Health
Organization, the International Telecommunications
Union, the World Intellectual Property Organization,
the World Meteorological Organization, the UN High
Commissioner for Refugees and a new World Trade
Organization. The UN Environment Programme and
most of the other UN institutions maintain offices at
Geneva. The Intergovernmental Conference on the
former Yugoslavia has, of course, been sited there.

Environmental concerns figure increasingly in the
Geneva Spirit. As well as a Geneva office for the UN
Environment Programme, such special initiatives are

sited there as the Framework Convention on Climate
Change and the UN Convention to Combat Desertifi-
cation, as well as offices for Sustainable Development, the UN Population Fund, Centre for Human
Settlements, World Food Programme, The Food and
Agriculture Organization and UNESCO, the UN Scientific, Educational and Cultural Organization. During
1997 an original lakeside site of the League of
Nations, facing Mount Blanc, should finally be converted to form an international environmental centre.

Of Geneva's many international bodies that lie outside the UN family, CERN, the European Centre for
Nuclear Research, merits special mention. Major discoveries about the fundamental nature of sub-atomic
particles, the near-ultimate constituents of matter, are
currently being made there.

What does all this mean in terms of assisting global development? Today's work on health, environment, labour, refugees, narcotic drugs, international
law, European transport and much else represents a
major extension of former League activities. The
WHO field of effort is now enormous, embracing
research and assistance spanning all the main diseases and maladies affecting the developing and
"developed" worlds. It currently incorporates a mam-
moth programme to achieve health for all by the year
2,000. In the same way, assistance to and resettle-
ment of refugees and displaced persons, swollen in
numbers to some 50 million by endless civil wars,
conventional conflicts, and invasions, as well as by
environmental decay and famine, poses an ever more
urgent problem. The same applies to other phenomena like natural disasters which afflict burgeoning
populations, a social decline that stimulates drug taking, alcoholism, and crime, and the continuing
expansion of economic malaise in developing and
"developed" states alike.

In other words, the seemingly overbureaucratic
structures of international life do tackle real needs. If
the accuracy of weather forecasting is now improving, this is because coordinated global programmes
of observation and research, undertaken by direct
cooperation of the world's meteorological services
through the WMO, are making this possible. World
and regional investigations like the Global Weather
Experiment, begun in 1979, have disclosed results
for overall development of weather systems and
offers a foundation for the continuing World Weather
Watch to the year 2000.

The Economic Commission for Europe, which
embraces some 80 percent of global economic activity and which dates from 1947, is one of the world's
five regional economic commissions. Its research and

operational activities on energy, industry and technology, environment, trade, transport, statistics, agriculture, timber, and economic analysis cover virtually all international aspects of economic life. One of the many practical consequences of its work is the Convention on Long-range Transboundary Air Pollution signed in 1979 by 35 countries—an activity leading to further environmental agreements.

This is not to ignore the perennial issue of disarmament. The 40-member Conference on Disarmament is the world's only multilateral body for arms negotiation, and thus carries on Geneva's tradition as the rightful place for seeking peace (see *Disarmament and Development*). A tiny group of countries hampers active results from discussions that cover fundamental aspects of the question. In a complex history some basic UN agreements have followed from past work pursued in Geneva since the early 1960s. These began with one in 1962 on a direct "hot-line" link between the two largest nuclear powers, this being followed by another that led to the treaty of 1963 banning nuclear tests in the atmosphere, outer space, and under water. Five years later a further major treaty was concluded—that on nonproliferation of nuclear weapons to non-nuclear states.

The next arms treaty that followed from work pursued at Geneva was one, opened for signature in 1971, prohibiting planting of nuclear and similar weapons on the sea bed. This was followed by a convention prohibiting warfare through use of bacteriological and toxin weapons (1972) (see *Biological Weapons Convention: An Overview*) and another, opened for signature in Geneva in 1977, that prohibits military use of techniques to modify the environment and is known as ENMOD. Another agreement in the arms field, reached in 1981, outlaws or limits any use of conventional weapons found excessively injurious or indiscriminate in their effects. Over the ensuing years discussions have produced an agreement on chemical weapons, while means of monitoring nuclear tests have been brought to a state of near-completion.

A further Geneva preoccupation of primary importance is that with human rights and duties (see *Human Rights and Peace*). Many basic standard-setting international instruments have been drafted there, including more recently the Convention on Torture and the Declaration on Elimination of Intolerance and Discrimination based on Religion or Belief—the latter after more than 18 years of discussion. Efforts continue to reduce the toll of torture, "disappearances," and other human rights violations that today affect virtually the entire world. More recent human rights instruments now in force include Conventions on the Rights of the Child and increased stress on problems raised by Discrimination Against Women.

There is room here only to mention some main aims of the UN Environment Programme, e.g., to coordinate a Global Environment Monitoring System, an ambitious scheme to measure environmental changes worldwide, aspects of which are handled at Geneva. In 1985 a Convention was adopted, after eight years' work, on the protection of the Ozone Layer—a belt of rarefied gas between 10 and 50 km above the Earth's surface that shields all life from the sun's ultraviolet radiation. Discussions to produce this agreement also went on in Geneva.

So-called "summit" meetings, as well as major conferences, have tended to be held in the same city. Among the largest gatherings of a special nature was the Conference on Application of Science and Technology for the Benefit of Less-developed Areas of 1963, at which over 2,000 scientific papers, covering every aspect of the subject, were considered by 1,665 participants. This conference led to the creation of a UN programme on the use of science and technology for development. Of comparable size were other conferences on peaceful use of atomic energy. The first of these was fateful indeed, since it let loose the proselytizing pioneers of nuclear energy on an unsuspecting world that has only slowly learnt better as knowledge has grown. Nuclear power has proved both completely uneconomic yet unknowingly costly to decommission. It poses a lasting question-mark that overshadows the whole of human development.

Since the international Maritime Conference of 1948, which led to the establishment of the International Maritime Organization, some major gatherings have been held at Geneva on the Law of the Sea. This too is a major exercise. Some fundamental agreements on the freedom of the seas and on their conservation have already been reached, but the keystone, the final inception of an international authority to control commercial exploitation of the sea bed and ocean floor, remains a project for the future (see *Oceans: The Common Heritage*).

So-called "summit" meetings and peace conferences are by now a familiar feature of Geneva life. The latter have included meetings on Korea, Indochina and Laos, a peace conference on the Middle East and the "Big Four" discussions of 1955 between leaders Bulganin, Eden, Eisenhower, and Faure. More recently, efforts have been made to resolve conflicts in a range of areas, including Georgia, Abkhazia, East Timor, Liberia and protracted negotiations on the former Yugoslavia.

If the Alabama Room in Geneva's Old Town had

been chosen as the location for the latest talks we would have come back full circle to the Arbitration Tribunal of 1872. But international life has changed greatly in the interval, so that the dominant personalities of the past have become submerged in a vast bureaucratic treadmill. The "Geneva Spirit" can triumph in the years ahead, but only if it can produce a standing global body to supersede mere *ad hoc* nationalism. This must be the real destiny of that small city that grew up on a hill between the Arve, the Rhône, and the Lake of Geneva.

Bibliography ———————————————

Dilloway A J 1986 *Is World Order Evolving? An Adventure into Human Potential*. Pergamon, Oxford

League of Nations (Information Section) 1938 *Essential Facts about the League of Nations*. League of Nations, Geneva

Palthey G 1964 Geneva and the international organizations. In: Laederer B (ed.) *Geneva: Crossroad of the Nations*. Editions Générales, Geneva

Reverdin O 1964 Geneva: A distinctive destiny. In: Laederer B (ed.) *Geneva: Crossroad of the Nations*. Editions Générales, Geneva

Spinelli P P 1964 *Geneva and the International World*. CPII, Geneva

United Nations 1992 *Basic Facts about the United Nations*. United Nations, New York

JAMES DILLOWAY

German Eastern Policy after Unification

1. Continuity and Change in German Eastern Policy

For about 20 years the term "Ostpolitik" was internationally used to describe the policy of the then Federal Republic of Germany towards the then Soviet Union and the socialist governments of Eastern Europe (see *Ostpolitik*). It was initiated by the social-liberal administration under Chancellor Willy Brandt in the years of 1969-1973 and was continued by all following governments irregardless of their political orientation. As its heart, "Ostpolitik" combined the attempt to promote normalization and détente with the long-term goal of preserving the prospect of a reunification of the two German states. In 1990 the principal objectives of this policy were achieved: the then Soviet Union and all other Eastern neighbor states not only agreed to the unification of Germany, but even accepted the integration of the former German Democratic Republic into the western alliance, NATO (see *NATO*). This historical event was one of the most significant symbols for the end of the Cold War (see *Cold War*).

Until today, however, there is no consensus among German political elites as to how and to which degree the specific approach of the "Ostpolitik" really contributed to the dissolution of the eastern block and the consequent German unification. Many experts are convinced that it was the "Ostpolitik's" motto "change by convergence" ("Wandel durch Annäherung"), which significantly contributed to the peaceful ending of the Cold War and the fall of the Berlin wall; nonetheless there remain some skeptical voices. The latter argue that it was mainly western economic aid to the socialist countries—accorded in the context of the "Ostpolitik"—that for a long time had helped to stabil-

ize regimes that were almost bankrupt and thus to artificially strengthen their international renommé. From this point of view, a more offensive approach towards the former Soviet Union and its allies would have precipitated political change in these countries and, in consequence, allowed German unification to be achieved earlier and at lower cost.

Whereas this retrospective discussion remains somehow speculative and of limited historical interest, the following question seems more relevant and intriguing: how should the German "Ostpolitik" be (re)defined under the new conditions of unification and unlimited national sovereignty? For not only has the former German Democratic Republic, once the main focus of the "Ostpolitik," disappeared. The opening of the Iron Curtain towards Eastern Europe and the disintegration of the Warsaw Pact Organisation have entailed even more serious consequences for Germany's role in European and world politics. The revolutionary changes within the former socialist block have not only affected Germany, of course. The end of the bipolar world order has brought about serious changes in the international agenda of the entire Atlantic Alliance as well as of each of its member states. In comparison to its western partners, however, the German foreign policy of the 1990s faces an even more fundamental task. This is not only due to the geographical situation of the country in the relative heart of the European continent, often referred to as "the east of the west and the west of the east." What is still more important is that, unlike all other members of the western alliance, the unified Germany not only has to react to changes taking place in its international environment; it is itself one of the major agents of this change. In consequence, the development of neighborly relations with the eastern European countries must be considered in the much wider context of the unified Germany's new foreign policy (see *Eastern Europe, Transformation of*).

2. Fundamental Challenges to and Risks for German Foreign Policy since Unification

When the international conditions of German unification were settled in the Two+Four Treaty between the two German states, the United States, the former Soviet Union, Great Britain and France in the Summer of 1990, the curtain opened on a new phase of German foreign policy. The restoration of Germany's unlimited national sovereignty guaranteed by this treaty considerably augmented its foreign policy duties in European and even in world politics. With its central location on the European continent, a population of approximately 80 million people, one of the largest national armies in Europe, and with a Gross National Product equal to almost one third of the economic output of the entire European Union (EU), the unified Germany is clearly perceived—outside of its borders at least—as "the most powerful country in Europe" (Ash: 67). Even if German politicians have repeatedly qualified this perception as being largely exaggerated, there can be no doubt that Germany's scope for international action has widened remarkably since 1990. Perhaps it is still too early to judge how the country is coping with its growing international influence, which engenders new opportunities and new difficulties at the same time.

There is general agreement that—in comparison to all other western European countries—Germany has profited the most from the end of the Cold War. Besides the unexpected boon of a peaceful and rapid unification, the altered international atmosphere has also decisively improved Germany's security status while offering almost unlimited economic advantages. From the former frontier state of the western alliance that ran the highest risk of military confrontation within its territory, Germany has now advanced to play the role of central European link bringing together the former enemies in peaceful communication and cooperation. It is hardly surprising that Germany is by far the most important western trade partner of all central and eastern European states. Accordingly, the political elites and people of these countries have placed high expectations in German financial and moral help on the stony path to economic recovery and political stabilization. Thus, geographic proximity to and close economic ties with the transition states of the former socialist block entail not only profitable cooperation opportunities; they could suddenly be perceived as a very heavy burden as well. As German President Roman Herzog concisely stated in a speech delivered to the country's foreign policy elite in 1995: "If we do not succeed in stabilizing the East, the East will destabilize us."

This "special relationship" between Germany and its direct and indirect Eastern neighbors has provoked a wide range of reactions in these countries as well as from Germany's partners within the EU and the Atlantic Alliance. Whereas all sides take it for granted that the unified Germany will necessarily form the cornerstone of the emerging post-Cold War European political architecture, there remain several reservations as to how this role should be realized. All these preoccupations have a common source: the fear of being dominated by German national interests. The traumatic historical experience with a Germany that imposed its will on the whole continent in the first half of the 20th century is still very alive in the collective mind of all Europeans. The concern that Germany "has again become the giant that holds the destiny of Central Europe in its hands"(Willenz: 67), if not always explicitly stated, can nevertheless be easily traced in the behavior of Germany's western and eastern neighbors.

Western fears of a Germany trying to dominate its partners in the EU by virtue of its continuing economic and increasing political strength were clearly articulated in December of 1991, for example. Without waiting for a consensus among the EU countries and the United States as to a common reaction to the Croatian and Slovenian secession from the Yugoslavian Federation, Germany recognized the national sovereignty of these two republics, thus forcing its western allies to follow suit. The temporary irritations in German-Polish relations stemming from Germany's hesitance to officially recognize Poland's western border caused even more serious inquietude in many European capitals. For mainly domestic reasons, the West German Government was loath to guarantee the inalianability of the "Oder-Neiße-Line" until after unification. Despite the fact that this dispute was quickly settled by the ratification of a border-treaty in November of 1990, many old fears had been revived.

These few examples clearly illuminate the difficulties German politicians have in adapting to the new conditions of the country's foreign policy. Due to the fast pace of international change at the beginning of the 1990s, there was in fact little time to deliberate on the theory of the matter. Whereas the classical

"Ostpolitik" of the 1970s was the outcome of long-term conceptual considerations, the new "Ostpolitik" —like the foreign policy of the unified Germany as a whole—has mainly followed the principle of "learning by doing" or "muddling through." Consequently, this policy can best be described as a pragmatic combination of holding on to traditional features while cautiously exploring new terrain. Following the successful example of the Federal Republic in the decades prior to unification, the larger German state has taken particular care to continue a strategy of consistent multilateralism. This unconditional integration of the national foreign policy into the structures and decision-making processes of the European Union and NATO is the best way of appeasing still subsisting suspicions in the West and East as to a possible German predominance in Europe. At the same time this policy can be understood as an attempt at financial and moral burden-sharing in order to cope with the multitude and magnitude of problems to be solved in post-Cold War Europe in the years to come. Whereas the multilateral level clearly dominates German relations towards Eastern Europe, bilateral contacts have also considerably increased since the opening of the Iron Curtain.

3. The Bilateral Level of German Eastern Policy

Immediately after unification Germany made it clear that some of the basic principles of the "Ostpolitik" should continue to shape its relations towards eastern Europe. It therefore concluded a series of so-called "neighborhood treaties" which in content and spirit followed in the tradition of the treaties signed in the early 1970s. As then, the first agreement to be negotiated was with the former Soviet Union. On the 9th November of 1990, the treaty "on good neighborly relations, partnership and cooperation" was signed by the German Chancellor and the Soviet President. It consists of 22 articles stating among other things a mutual renunciation of force, arms control measures and the establishment of regular bilateral consultations on the level of foreign and defense ministers. After the demise of the Soviet Union in December of 1991, the Russian Federation assumed the obligations of the accord. Until today, Germany has extended this treaty by declaring its intent to bilaterally assist and cooperate with almost all Soviet successor states, such as the Ukraine (a common declaration "on the foundation of mutual relations" was signed in June of 1993). There can be no doubt, however, that Russia is perceived as Germany's most important partner in this region.

The priority of close and friendly ties to Russia

derives from the dominant role this huge country necessarily plays in all aspects of East-West relations. In addition to this, Russia can profit from the "gratitude factor" (Woyke: 19) resulting from Soviet consent to German unification, which still positively influences Germany's attitude towards its biggest eastern neighbor. A very important item in this context has been the withdrawal of all Soviet/Russian troops from German territory as agreed to in the Two+Four Treaty. The fact that this proceeded without incident—the last contingent already leaving in August of 1994 some months ahead of schedule— was mainly due to Germany's massive financial assistance of approximately 16 billion DM, including a vast housing program and several training and retraining initiatives (Höhmann et al., 21f).

This sum only represents a relatively small part of the total of direct and indirect German financial assistance afforded to Russia and, to a much lesser extent, to other Soviet successor states as a means of supporting their economic reforms and stabilizing their domestic political situation. This active assistance has also been inspired by the hope that it will contribute to the creation of a reliable and profitable economic partnership in the long run, opening the Russian market to German products and investments while securing important supplies of Russian raw materials and energy resources for the German economy. Another important motive for the generous German financial assistance to Russia can be seen in the attempt to improve the living conditions of about two million ethnic Germans still living in Russia and thus discourage their mass immigration to Germany.

The concern for the fate of German minorities is also a considerable factor within the second area of Germany's new "Ostpolitik," including its direct neighbors in central Eastern Europe. In the two years following unification, Germany concluded bilateral treaties with Poland (14.11.90/17.6.91), Bulgaria (9.10.91), Hungary (6.2.92), Czechoslovakia (27.2.92; the agreement was accepted by both successor states) and Romania (21.4.92). With the exception of some minor variations, mostly concerning historical particularities, all these agreements have a common objective: they reinforce the principles of friendly neighborly relations and peaceful cooperation that—at least with Poland and Czechoslovakia—had already been agreed upon in the original treaties of 1970 and 1973. A very important new aspect, however, is the explicit emphasis on the European dimension of the bilateral relations. Thus, Article 8 of the German-Polish Treaty of 1991 even postulates Germany's determination to "foster to the best of its ability Poland's efforts at entering the European Community" (see *European Political Community*).

In order to follow up these general statements of intent with actions, a great number of additional agreements has since been concluded with several eastern European countries on various issues, such as traffic, social policy, cultural and youth exchange programs, etc. The prolonged and intense public disputes preceding the ratification of the "German-Czech Declaration on Mutual Relations," finally signed in January of 1997, demonstrates how difficult and painful it can be to transform some aspects of the solemnly declared partnership into everyday diplomacy. The declaration aimed at the final settlement of all questions concerning the consequences of German occupation during the Second World War and the subsequent expulsion of the German minority from Czechoslovakia. It took almost five years to reach a compromise in this matter offering a realistic perspective of mutual reconciliation.

4. The Multilateral Context of German Eastern Policy

The multilateral approach which has always played an important role in German foreign policy has become even more predominant since unification (see *Multilateralism*). There exists a general consensus within Germany's political elite that the country's current "Ostpolitik" can only succeed if it is conceived and implemented within the framework of the European Union and the Atlantic Alliance. German politicians have repeatedly expressed the conviction that their particular contribution to this European Eastern policy lies in its role as intercessor for the interests of the countries situated beyond the former Iron Curtain. As mentioned above, this self-imposed commitment has even been explicitly laid down in a number of bilateral agreements, such as the German-Polish Treaty of 1991.

Consequently, Germany is counted among the most fervent supporters of the EU's enlargement to the East (see *European Union*). As it will obviously take a relatively long time until even the most successful new democracies in central Eastern Europe will be able to meet the economic criteria for full membership, Germany in the mean time is actively participating in the efforts to strengthen the ties between the EU and the aspiring members. The first EU cooperation agreements with Poland and Hungary were signed as early as December of 1991. Since then, all central Eastern European countries, including the Baltic states, have not only concluded similar cooperation agreements, but even formally asked for full membership. Different forms of interim agreements have also been negotiated with Russia, the Ukraine and other former Soviet republics, as well as with Albania. Besides the attempt to intensify economic exchange between western and eastern Europe, all these agreements have a common political objective. The institutionalization of different commissions and forums, such as the so called "structured dialog" at the ministerial level is meant to create an atmosphere of regular and intense partnership and thus to build a common European identity beyond the present-day borders of the European Union (Weidenfeld: 99f).

The second major item to be dealt with on a multilateral level concerns the question of how to establish a stable and inclusive security architecture stretching —to use General de Gaulles famous phrase—"from the Atlantic to the Urals" or even beyond. In security matters, the principal subsumation of Germany's national policy to that of the Atlantic Alliance has never been an issue of serious domestic debate. The palpable increase in Germany's influence within the Organization for Security and Cooperation in Europe (OSCE, former CSCE) and NATO subsequent to unification and the complete restoration of national sovereignty has been consistently used to encourage the strategic reorientation of these organizations.

In November of 1990 the heads of state of all CSCE-members solemnly proclaimed the end of the Cold War and engaged themselves in building up a new common European security system including the former western and eastern blocs. The disastrous experience of the civil war in the former Yugoslavia that could neither be prevented nor suppressed by the European Union or the CSCE—despite of innumerable diplomatic efforts—made it painfully clear, however, that NATO remains the most reliable security structure in Europe. At the same time, in accordance with the new atmosphere of rapprochement and cooperation among the former adversaries of the Cold War, NATO not only established the Cooperation Council (NACC) in 1991 as a means of institutionalizing the contacts to the Eastern European states, but also invited them to join the "Partnership for Peace Program," consisting of a wide range of diplomatic and military cooperation (see *Security and Cooperation in Europe*).

Germany actively encouraged these initiatives and has tried to spur them on even further. Parallel to its positive attitude towards EU-enlargement, it has thus propagated the accession of all willing central Eastern European countries to NATO. At the same time German officials have tried to overcome the Russian opposition to this idea by emphasizing the purely defensive character of the alliance. This German position was only partly shared by other NATO-partners. It took some measure of discussion within the organization to find a common strategy in this matter. In May of 1997, a bilateral charter was signed with Russia creating a new form of "security partnership." On the basis of this agreement, at least a partial NATO-enlargement could be envisioned probably including Poland, Hungary and the Czech Republic.

The growing activism of German foreign policy has also led to military engagement beyond Germany's borders. Whereas this had been an absolute taboo for evident historical reasons until the 1990s, the united Germany decided to participate in peace-keeping operations in the Balkans—inasmuch as these were carried out under the auspices of the UN and NATO. This fact most clearly illustrates the country's concurrent desire to take on new international responsibilities, particularly in the East, while remaining true to long-term multilateral commitments towards its Western partners.

Bibliography —————————————————

Ash T G 1994 Germany's choice. In: *Foreign Affairs* 73(4)

Bingen D 1996 Ostverträge. In: Weidenfeld, Werner/Korte, Karl-Rudolf (ed.) *Handbuch zur deutschen Einheit*. Neuausgabe, Bonn

Höhmann H H, Meier C, Timmermann H 1997 *Russia and Germany in Europe: Recent Trends of Political and Economic Relations*. Berichte des Bundesinstituts für ost-wissenschaftliche und internationale Studien 38

Kaiser K, Maull H W (ed.) 1995 *Deutschlands neue Außenpolitik*, Vol. 2. Herausforderungen, München

Knapp M 1996 Die Außenpolitik der Bundesrepublik Deutschland. In: Knapp M, Krell G (ed.) *Einführung in die internationale Politik*. München

Maull H W 1997 Quo vadis, Germania? Außenpolitik in einer Welt des Wandels. In: *Blätter für Deutsche und Internationale Politik* 42

Paulsen T 1996 Außenpolitik. In: Weidenfeld W, Korte K R (ed.) *Handbuch zur Deutschen Einheit*. Neuausgabe, Bonn

Pradetto A, Alamir F M 1997 Deutschlands Rolle in Mittel- und Osteuropa. In: *Politische Bildung* 30

Reiter E 1997 Die NATO-Reform entscheidet die eurasische Sicherheitsordnung. In: *Österreichische Militärzeitschrift* 35(4)

Timmermann H 1996 Partnerschaft mit Rußland. Chancen und Probleme der EU-Anbindungsstrategie. *Berichte des Bundesinstituts für ostwissenschaftliche und internationale Studien* 43

Timmermann H 1995 Rußland und Deutschland. Ihre Beziehungen als integraler Bestandteil gesamteuropäischer Kooperation. *Berichte des Bundesinstituts für ostwissenschaftliche und internationale Studien* 39

Weidenfeld W 1997 (ed.) *Neue Ostpolitik—Strategie für eine gesamteuropäische Entwicklung*. Gütersloh

Willenz E 1993 Germany and Mitteleuropa: Retrospect and Prospect. In: *German Politics and Society* 28 (Spring)

Woyke W 1997 Von der Orientierungslosigkeit zur Konzeption—die Außenpolitik des vereinten Deutschland. In: *Politische Bildung* 30(1)

SILVIA VON STEINSDORFF

German Peace Movement [*Friedensbewegung*]

1. Introduction

The story of the German Peace Movement [*Friedensbewegung*] is an honourable one, falling into three periods; that of the late 1960s in response to the 'first cold war' epitomised by the Berlin blockade; second in the 1980s following the revival of the Reagan-Thatcher vs Brezhnev confrontation; and lastly in the post unification and break-up of the USSR period of the 1990s where we identify the reasons for its apparent decline, and potential metamorphosis into a new politico-moral alliance in a revived new peace-environmental campaign.

2. The Politics

Noack argued that the "new" peace movement which formed after 1979, followed the tradition of antimilitarist opposition and pacifist aspirations which flourished around the turn of the century from 1880 to the First World War and in the Weimar Republic until 1933. Up to and after the First World War the idea of peace was championed predominantly by the liberal bourgeois, being strongly influenced by religious, pacifist, socialist, youth, and women's organisations. During this period, however, the peace movement was limited to intellectual circles, hardly touching a mass consciousness.

The main innovation in Germany following the First World War was the emergence of the Marxist world revolutionary peace perspective, alongside those of primarily liberal, bourgeois origin, and western world progressive Christian pacifists, whose German branches were finally disbanded by the Third Reich. The period of National Socialism (see *National Socialism*), from 1933 to 1945, totally dislocated what had gone before. Even so argues Noack, there were always inherent divisions between the "international law" pacifists, who wished to end the political causes of war, and those pacifists of an ethical and religious persuasion who sought the application of Ghandian and Christian principals of non-violent politics.

The Federal Republic of Germany was founded in 1949, partly as a bulwark against the perceived threat of 'advancing communism,' and at first the question of its potential military contribution was controversial, but impelled by superpower rivalries, it was not only granted sovereignty in 1955, but became a member of the North Atlantic Treaty Organisation (NATO) (see *NATO*). This inevitably tied the German Democratic Republic firmly to the Warsaw Pact, with powerful emotional ramifications for a country now divided. Talk of war had particular relevance to people who had recently experienced and could see over their eastern boarder, the horrors of human oppression associated with a totalitarian system.

The early and encouraging policies of detente (see *Détente*) in the early 1970's, led to the 'Strategic Arms Limitation Treaties' I and II (1972-79). However, the Mutual and Balanced Force Reductions talks, in which the Federal Republic had played an important role through the signing of treaties with the Soviet Union (1970), Poland (1970), Czechoslovakia (1973), and the German Democratic Republic (1972), were ostensibly brought to an end by the Soviet intervention in Afghanistan in 1979. In the United States however, the policy of detente had become domestically untenable, not least because of the widespread feeling of national weakness and humiliation in the wake of the Vietnam War defeat, combined with the oil crises of 1973-74 and the Iran débâcle at the beginning of 1979. There began a swing back to superpower confrontation politics which resulted in a considerable feeling of insecurity in Western Europe, caused above all by the election of US President Ronald Reagan in November 1980, coinciding with his ideological muse, Prime Minister Thatcher in a reactionary Britain, who together revitalised their country's armaments industries. The industrial-military complex, with an improved international situation which had faced questions of why expend so much national wealth on armaments, now had their external enemy to justify the vast increases from which the Right found subsequent political benefits from grateful employees and happy share-holders.

In Germany of course, every significant change in superpower relations immediately affected the Federal Republic in its pivotal position between blocs. Whereas the policy of détente in the 1970's had absorbed and redirected large sections of the peace movement of the 1950's and 1960's, the "new Cold War" at the beginning of the 1980's called a new peace movement into being.

2.1 The Rise

The principles of the new Cold War were challenged by large sections of the German public with the passing of the NATO double-track Brussels decision of December 1979, independent of the security crises which had long been brewing in the Western alliance. Experts had long since been predicting the breakdown of the peace based on nuclear deterrence by new weapons systems and their corresponding strategies. Apart from a brief burst of public outrage over the plans to introduce the neutron bomb, no area of foreign and security policy had more effect on the political landscape of the Federal Republic, or caused such a deep cleavage in public opinion, as the Brussels "Armaments Decision."

The irony was that the instigator of the NATO double-track decision, the former Federal Chancellor Helmet Schmidt, initiated the Brussels decision with his London speech of 1977 on the growing threat of Soviet medium-range missiles. This speech was supposed to be a contribution to the consolidation of the US nuclear guarantee to Western Europe and the further development of NATO. Instead, it summoned into existence vigorous extra-parliamentary protest movements, not only in the Federal Republic of Germany, but in the DDR and in many other European countries, which sprang up surprisingly quickly.

Between 1979 and 1983, when the stationing of the nuclear warheads were being prepared, West Germany witnessed growing demonstrations. The Hamburg Protestant church conference *(Kirchentag)* in 1981 was attended by 80,000 people and a demonstration took place summoned by the motto: "Beware, nuclear death threatens us all." A few months later, on October 10th, the communist newspaper *Unsere Zeit* wrote on the front page of a special edition: "Bonn sees the largest peace action in its history," after more than 250,000 people with prominent people like Noble prize winner Heinrich Böll had gathered in the *Hofgarten*. At the same time, in numerous other cities, like-minded actions took place. Nearly half a million people met in Bonn in June 1982 to protest at the NATO summit. Attending the Easter Marches was by far the most common form of peace demonstration, and in 1982 around 200,000 people of all ages took part, with feelings of solidarity to similar events in Britain and France. The following year, 600,000 people were counted at the Easter Marches. In October 1983 more than one million people gathered at different meetings in West Berlin, Bonn, Hamburg and Ulm.

This astronomic success of the *Friedensbewegung* however ended suddenly, first by the stationing of the nuclear missiles, which created a sense of impotence, and fuelled a degree of apathy as the apocalypse did not occur. Year after year, less people joined the Easter Marches. It remained, however, an impressive institution with some 200,000 people in 1987.

How did this happen? The SDI-utopias from Ronald Reagan 1983/84 onwards had been kept in check by progressive and productive talks with Mikhail Gorbachev, Brezhnev's successor as the General Secretary of the Soviet Communist Party. Parallel to their talks in Reykjavik around 200,000 people met on October 11, 1986, at one of the main bases for the nuclear missiles in the West German Hasselbach. To considerable world astonishment, Reagan and Gorbachev managed to sign the INF Treaty in December, to abolish intermediate-range nuclear missiles step by step. The arms race was not only stopped, it even seemed possible to reverse it, the *raison d'être* for the peace movements appeared to be gone overnight, and of course the removal of the Berlin Wall and the reunification of Germany gave continued impetus to this increased sense of security.

Up until 1983, the *Friedensbewegung* could hardly be written as anything but a history of success as it maximised the opportunities of the mass media to reach a mass audience and at the same time, raise questions which touched the core fears of those living in Europe who began to realise that in any conflagration, they were in the target area, and an atomic defence guaranteed mutual destruction—physical as well as political *selbstmord* suicide.

The last demonstration in Bonn took place in June 1987, with some 100,000 people. Since then, the number of Easter marchers has fallen continually, to approximately 50,000 in recent years, more in commemoration than real fear for any immediate future superpower confrontation. Only the Gulf War in 1990 provided renewed motivation for some 100,000 people, largely by high school pupils, college and university students to protest in various forms. Neither the civil war in Yugoslavia (1991-96) nor the genocide in Rwanda (1996) gave reason for any comparable action.

2.2 Appraisal

Noack argued that in considering the peace move-

ment's significance for the Federal Republic, it is important to distinguish between potential and actual effects. In an international context, it appears that not only were hopes raised in Moscow, but also fears in Paris, London and Washington—with special reference to the concept of neutrality newly awakened by the peace movement—who overestimated the movement's political consequence.

This was also true in the case of appraisal from within, which is characterised by two extremes: there is no question of the movement being a permanent established factor, or even jeopardising the state; equally invalid was the euphoric picture of the peace movement as "liberating men, women and children from their fear of war in a new epoch in the labour movement." At the same time it is certain that, through its function and activities as a "super citizens' action group" the peace movement has made no small contribution to a discussion which resulted in the armament and security question becoming a matter of public concern.

It is true that the peace movement has not been in a position to present a concept of security politics beyond its rejection of general and specific armaments. Yet its stimulating effect on sections of society such as the churches and labour unions and the women's movements cannot be denied. The government, political parties, political and military experts, and scientific institutions have come under pressure to justify their concept of security more vigorously than ever before. It can generally be asserted, however, that the broad-based emotional approval of the peace movement's goals has by no means led to an equally broad-based political approval of those goals, for example, the neutrality concept falls largely on deaf ears.

As a social movement which consciously sought to avoid rigid organisation, the peace movement was subject to a constant process of transformation. A sustained repetition of the mass demonstrations at the start of the 1980's, with their mobilising effect, was not possible. Apart from this, the movement has failed to achieve its goal of preventing the stationing of American medium-range missiles, and it is unclear whether the resulting stagnation will lead to the final disintegration of a unified peace movement, or whether the impetus that brought the coalitions together may merge into another unifying force.

2.3 Organizational Impact

A chronological history is no substitute for an analysis of the impact and strength or weakness of the

Friedensbewegung. Even today, there is an obvious discrepancy between myth-generating suppositions and satisfactory, comprehensive empirical studies on the rise and fall of the organised peace movement. In particular, work on its impact on government policy is missing. One difficulty is that we do not possess a theory on 'New Social Movements' as a broader social basis. Equally unsolved is the question of what the *Friedensbewegung* actually was and is, and where the differences are in concept and social structure, compared to other well-known movements like the 'Environmental Movement,' the 'Third World Movement,' the 'Anti-Nuclear Power Movement' or the 'Women's Movement.' The civil rights groups such as the Committee for Civil Rights and Democracy (*Komitee für Grundrechte und Demokratie*-KGD) founded in 1980 or the social democratic Gustav Heinemann initiative (1978) or the influential Federal Society of the Civil Initiatives for Protection of the Environment (*Bundesverband Bürgerinitiativen Umweltschutz*) of 1972 out of the 'Environment Movement' also considered themselves explicitly as peace groups. This strong connection of topics from various directions seems to be even stronger in groups in the German Democratic Republic, where some peace groups, human rights groups or environmental groups, were founded in the early 1980's. The Initiative for Freedom and Human Rights (*Initiative für Frieden und Menschenrechte*) was one of the brave outstanding groups in East Germany after 1985. The transformation of the DDR in the final phase of 1989/90 was not possible without even more institutionalised groups like *Bündnis 90* (Union 90), *Neues Forum* (New Forum) or *Demokratie Jetzt* (Democracy Now).

The internal structure of the West German *Friedensbewegung* must therefore be seen as multidimensional which was both its strength—uniting diverse groups, and a weakness because centrifugal forces made them inherently unstable one-cause alliances. Some particular peace groups existed such as KOFAZ, Committee for Peace, Arms Reduction and Co-operation *(Komitee für Frieden, Abrüstung und Zusammenarbeit)*, the Krefelder Appeal (*Krefelder Appell*), the International Co-operation and Security (*Internationalen Ausgleich und Sicherheit*), the Co-ordination Bureau for Civil Disobedience (*Koordinationsstelle Ziviler Ungehorsam KOZU*) or the initially influential *DFG-VK* (German Peace Society—United Opponents of Military Service—*Deutsche Friedensgesellschaft-Vereinigte Kriegsdienstgegner*), founded in 1892, as well as other large numbers of local peace groups. In addition, parts of established organisations, societies, church groups or parties took part in

the debate and showed themselves sympathetic. In the mobilising phase between 1979 and 1983, peace became an integration ideology and thus an "imagined community."

Looking at the internal organisational networking and at the connection between traditional socio-cultural structures, one can talk about the self-styled picture of a grassroots movement only with restrictions, there were, of course, groups who saw themselves as independent from already existing larger organisations such as the Federal Conference of Independent Peace Groups [*Bundeskonferenz Unabhängiger Friedensgruppen] (BUF)*, the already mentioned Co-ordination Bureau Civil for Disobedience or the Federation of Non-Violent Action Groups (FÖGA) and various urban groups. Two thirds of the peace group organisers, however, were party members and a considerable number of activists came from member organisations linked to parties.

The *Friedensbewegung* fed on the human, financial, intellectual and public relations resources of the SPD (German Social Democrats), its two youth groups *Jusos* and *Falken*, the SPD-near Association of Social Democratic Women *(Arbeitsgemeinschaft sozialdemokratischer Frauen)*, the Initiative for Freedom, International Agreement and Security of the Trade Union Federation (DGB), the two main churches with the connected *Aktion Sühnezeichen*, Living Without Armament (*Ohne Rüstung Leben*) and Pax Christi, the SDAJ (Socialist German Workers Youth) and the German Communist Party *DKP*.

A special and much discussed problem is posed by the last party, as the DKP was supported and financed in many ways from East Berlin and Moscow. This fact often threatened to discredit the peace movement and has been actively used by its opponent in every western country. When considered carefully, one will not grant too much influence to the DKP then or during the Gulf War, when the peace movement saw its last rise. The DKP had ceased to have any political influence and the affiliated student organisations MSB and SHB had ceased to exist, which mirrors, almost exactly, its fate in Britain, France and Holland.

An even more influential level of institutionalisation was marked by the *Green Party,* founded in 1979. The Green Party programme was centred around 'peace,' and the party had grown enough in those years to enter the *Bundestag* in 1982 by passing the necessary five percent share of the voters in the general election. In addition, the *Koordinationsausschub* (co-ordination committee), which had become a "clearing house for the *Friedensbewegung*" whose influence in the years after 1981 cannot be overestimated, had reached such a level of organisation and institutionalisation that the *Friedensbewegung* was now called a "movement organisation." The old attributes in portrayals of the *Friedensbewegung* such as informality, autonomy, self-regulation, spontaneity, emotionality and revolutionary anarchy, as opposed to programme, strategy, routine and reflexivity, were discarded as useless.

Regarding the *Friedensbewegung* less from an organisational and more from a socio-cultural viewpoint, one social group is especially conspicuous: the Christians, especially the non-episcopalians. Besides a strong personal and organisational position of Christian groups, the *Friedensbewegung* was characterised by Christian symbols. The writing on the wall was formed with the apocalyptic vision of the Book of Revelations, while the ideal of a peaceful society was taken from the Sermon on the Mount. Token signs such as the dove of peace and the cross of death, and slogans like *"swords into ploughshares"* were part of a Christian tradition, as were silent marches, periods of fasting, candle-lit processions and the hymns. And so a politicisation of church was accompanied by a sacralisation of society, particularly at the Church conferences *(Kirchentage)* which also played a role in the dismantling of the DDR.

First and foremost, the West German *Friedensbewegung* was typically western and modern, and specific German aspects were of only secondary importance. Its recruitment basis consisted of younger people, with a large proportion of women, most of whom, if of working age, worked in customer-oriented service jobs, typical of 'protest makers' in Britain. The *Friedensbewegung*, therefore corresponded to modern service society. Their ideological positions did not conform to traditional class differences. A moral principle, oriented conservatism, however, became fundamental, which then fed itself into important parties and social groups. Traditional social demarcation lines were softened in a push of individualisation typical for a late capitalist "risk society."

The most important specifically German focus in peace-political thought was and is the Nazi period, with its mass extermination and war atrocities. The division of Germany, on the other hand, did not play an important role mentally in the late seventies—it had become an almost normal situation, but the unification supported the idea that nuclear war in Europe was no longer a likelihood. Furthermore the value of military symbolism had been lost with the Second World War. Hence German rearmament in 1956, based on male conscription, did nothing to reactivate fears about a new militarism, indeed, West Germany saw itself as being responsible for those crimes against humanity committed in the name of Germany. This responsibility was honourably acknowledged in the West German constitution, the *Grundgesetz* (Article 26), and merits the highest commendation, for after all, where are all the apologies for crimes against humanity from the former colonial powers of Britain, France, Italy and Spain?

2.4 The Decline

The reasons and causes for the ever decreasing influence of the organised peace movement are still not clear, though appear to be similar to what occurred in Britain, and can only be tentatively approached:

(a) The example of the DFG-VK between 1985 and 1987 shows that stagnation in campaigning (ritualised forms of action; ideological trench warfare) and planning are damaging for the movement.

(b) Some groups found themselves in an economic crisis or were overtaxed by the workload they faced: they had problems maintaining the level of mobilisation.

(c) The meltdown in the nuclear power plant of Chernobyl in April 1986 eclipsed the *angst* connected with missiles and guns, so fundamental for the *Friedensbewegung*. Although peace organisations tried to incorporate the nuclear accident in Chernobyl in their platforms, the worries of large portions of the population shifted to the dangers of nuclear power embodied in Chernobyl, rather than in nuclear weapons, mainly perceived as a pure ecological problem. This new primary threat was a successful symbolic competition. Besides Chernobyl the so called *Waldsternden* (dying of the forests) had become a main focus of public concern as an emotional mass phenomenon.

(d) A further weakening occurred when the peace movement tried to distance itself organisationally from the anti-nuclear power movement. This phenomenon was not accidental, but rather due to the statement inherent in the peace movement to explain and fight against each and every social problem (arms race, environmental destruction, unemployment, exploitation of the third world, poverty, social inequality).

(e) The *Friedensbewegung* was based on spectacular actions, the drive of which was due to the rules of mass psychology. This secured a large media coverage, but also made it dependent on the media, with inadvertent consequences. The perception of threat as depicted by the mass media was a condition for the ordinary people to become involved. This was easily done in Germany as here the most dense storing of ABC-weapon arsenals in the world was to be found. Furthermore, Germany would be the central theatre of war in the case of conflict. After the stationing, however, the media was encouraged to turn to other areas with large emotional impact.

(f) The *Friedensbewegung* never managed to free itself from the timetables set by the government or NATO policy. Success was connected with the prevention of the stationing, and because of its self-limitation to a more or less single issue movement, it was fatally weakened by the arrival of the weapon systems.

(g) Although the *Friedensbewegung* had managed to gain self-discipline through much training and asceticism, it lacked the staying power to face the *fait accompli* of the step-by-step stationing. A fair share of *naiveté* regarding the influence of the extra-parliamentary movement on politics also played a role.

(h) One important factor, unrecognised by many inside the movement: the scope of action of the German state was limited by the remnants of Allied occupation law and the NATO treaties. Equally unrecognised remained the fact that while a democratic state allows a large variety of protest, this state, however, legitimate as it is through elections, was also less vulnerable to pressure from grassroots activities.

(i) The dualism of two different systems of state and society, which were elevated by Ronald Reagan into a Manichean black and white, provoked a simple world view with easy explanations and solutions. In times of detente and even more so after the end of the Cold War, when Habermas' concept of the *Neue Unübersichtlichkeit*, i.e., incalculability of social and political problems became apparent, such a simple model of and for peace was no longer attractive and lacked the power to integrate.

(j) The *Friedensbewegung* has been changed fundamentally since the Gulf War and then irreversibly since the civil war in former Yugoslavia. There is no innocent refuge in a neutral position anymore, as suggested by parts of the peace movement, if the life of civilians are directly at stake. Moreover, no *a priori* defined position to the question of military intervention can claim moral justice

anymore, every threat to humanity needs to be analyzed carefully before pursuing actions of any kind. This devalues various experts, at the expense of masses of lay people. On the other hand after the unification treaty of 1990 between the two German governments and the Allies, the decision for military intervention lays more in the hands of the German government and the Western European Union (WEU) than before and has therefore been broader legitimised by the people themselves. Thus 'world peace' will remain a public issue.

Having said all this, it would not be justified to speak of a failure of the *Friedensbewegung* in Germany or indeed in any of the western European countries because there are achievement and subtle influences which can be demonstrated. For example, there appear to be lasting influences on the political culture in Germany, mainly in expanding democracy, broadened forms of political participation, as German jurisdiction had to deal with it, as with the paradigmatic case of the sit-ins at the gates of army barracks as a form of passive resistance, the German Supreme Court has only recently acknowledged these forms of protest, but they are now case law. The *Friedensbewegung* has achieved a certain status in some parties and in education, and was institutionalised in various smaller local forms. The civil war in Yugoslavia became the pivotal question for the pacifist core of the *Friedensbewegung*, whether the ways parted. However, numerous forms of local help were pursued but largely ignored by the media: humanitarian aid was organised privately or asylum for deserters was given.

To do justice to the *Friedensbewegung*, future studies will have to concentrate on peace culture studies and will have to leave the old organisational sociology behind. Only in this way, can the *Friedensbewegung* be understood as a part of the 'New Social Movement,' where the so-called 'left post-materialist' sets the tone. With the help of Inglehardt's "Change of Values" studies it will be better understood how the *Friedensbewegung* was accepted far into conservative circles. The most symbolic example of this acceptance is the speech from the former president Richard von Weizsäcker, member of the governing conservative CDU, which was given on May 8th, 1985, at the 40th anniversary of the end of the war in Europe. In this speech, he talked about the peace initiatives in Germany, which he saw as having a promising lesson from the unsurpassed atrocities of the Second World War caused by Germany.

But perhaps the peace movement's greatest influence, was that it gave birth to the 'Greens,' who saw at the core of their protest, that the intelligent human search for peace was being threatened by an unintelligent response to the environment (see *Green Security*). As peace and environmental issues increasingly come together the *Friedensbewegung* endowment to world peace, is epitomised by Goethe's prophetic words which are resonant for peace and environmental crusades of the next millennium:

"This was the medicine but the patient died
and no one asked who was cured?
This hellish nostrum in these valleys and hills has
ravaged more deadly than the plague.
I myself have given the poison to thousands,
and I must hear the impudent murder praised."

"Hier war die Arzenei, die Patienten starben,
Und niemand fragte: wer genas?
So haben wir mit höllischen Latwergen
In Diesen Tälern, diesen Berggen
Weit Schlimmer als die Pest getobt.
Ich habe selbst den Gift an Tausende gegeben:
Sie welkten hin, Ich muß erleben,
Daß man die frechen Mörder lobt."

Goethe Faust Pt 1

See also: *European Peace Movements: Rises and Falls 1958-65, 1978-85 and 1990-98*

Bibliography

Beck U 1986 *Risikogesellschaft: Auf dem Weg in eine andere Moderne.* Suhrkamp, Frankfurt a. M

Gress D 1985 *Peace and Survival: West Germany, the Peace Movement, and European Security.* Hoover Institution, Stanford, California

Holmes K R 1984 *The West German Peace Movement and the National Question.* Foreign Policy Report Series. Institute for Foreign Policy Analysis, Cambridge, Massachusetts

Leif T 1990 *Die strategische (Ohn-) Macht der Friedensbewegung: Kommunikations-und Entscheidungsstrukturen in den achtziger Jahren.* Westdeutscher Verlag, Opladen

Mushaben J M 1985 Cycles of peace protest in West Germany: Experiences from three decades. *West European Politics* 8(1)

Noack P 1970 *Friedensforschung-ein signal der Hoffnung?* Lutzeyer, Freudenstadt

Noack P, Staude M 1986 *Peace movement in the Federal Republic of Germany.* In: Pauling L, Laslo E, Yoo J Y (eds.) *World Encyclopedia of Peace,* Vol 1. Pergamon Press, New York

Pilger J 1998 *Hidden Agendas.* Vintage Press, London

Pritchard C 1986 European peace movements 1958-65 and 1978-85: Hopes for the future? *J. Peace Studies* 5

Pritchard C, Evans B 1997 Population density & cancer mortality in England, Wales & the Western World. *The Society of Public Health—Public Health* 111

Schmitt R 1990 *Die Friedensbewegung in der Bundesrepublik Deutschland.* Studien zur Sozialwissenschaft, Westdeutscher Verlag, Opladen, Frankfurt

Steinweg R (ed.) 1982 *Die Neue Friedensbewegung, Analysen aus der Friedensforschung.* Friedensanalysen 16, Suhrkamp

Taylor R K S, Pritchard C 1982 *The Protest Makers: The British Anti-Nuclear Campaign 1958-65 Twenty Years On.* Pergamon Press, Oxford

KENAN H. IRMAK; COLIN PRITCHARD

Gide, André

André Gide (1869-1951), the French writer, was one of the most eminent men of letters of his time. He was born into the prosperous bourgeoisie in Paris, where his father was professor of law at the Sorbonne. After erratic early schooling, he finished his *lycée* degree and for the rest of his long life devoted himself to writing. Paris was his headquarters, but he was a great traveler, and also spent much of his time on his wife's estate in Normandy. Among his most famous works are *L'Immoraliste* (1902), *La Porte étroite* (1909), *Les Caves du Vatican* (1914), and *Les Faux-Monnayeurs* (1926). He is also known for other novels, plays, critical and personal essays, and his *Journal*; for his role in molding French literary values, partly through his influential work with *La Nouvelle Revue Française*; and for encouraging other writers. He was

an outstanding craftsman and stylist but was also considered a moralist in the French sense, that is, a commentator on mores and human character who, by revealing people to themselves, tried to direct them toward improvement of their behavior, but without didacticism. His fiction, essays, and diary are thus very psychologically oriented. In this sense, he belongs to the great classical tradition of French prose writers, being both introspective and concerned with manners. Among the major themes of his work are art itself, religion, freedom, the family, and homosexuality. He was an early advocate of recognition of homosexuality as a natural phenomenon which should not entail a denial of individual rights.

If Gide had lived in a time of less social change and political disruption, he might have remained throughout his career concerned only with literary values and psychological insight, for he was devoted to his writing and to the problem of the individual person as to nothing else. Circumstances, however, ultimately forced him to consider questions which went beyond the literary and psychological realms, and it is here that he has some importance as a spokesman on war and peace.

Early in his career, Gide was concerned with international literary relations: for instance, he lectured in Belgium and his works were translated into German; he was himself a translator of English literature into French; and he maintained literary relationships in a number of countries. Unlike many of his contemporaries before and after 1914, he had no personal dislike of Germans and indeed admired German culture, Goethe being one of his favorite writers. Though he considered himself as a representative of French writers and was indeed typically French in many ways, he also recognized the existence of a European culture, to which many nations had contributed and which could be shared by all. He was not, however, a pacifist, and his reactions to the First World War were as patriotic as any. During the war he did volunteer work with Belgian refugees at the Foyer Franco-Belge in Paris. After 1918, when his fame was widespread, he published a number of essays on the question of European peace and stability (see his *Incidences*). In these he advocated a Franco-German intellectual rapprochement and argued that a spirit of revenge against Germany would be counterproductive and contrary to the ideal of culture for which he stood. He insisted that henceforth Europe would be courting ruin if it continued its petty nationalist competitions. Without advocating an internationalized Europe, he prompted, through his personal activity and writings, literary exchanges which would contribute to cultural understanding and political stability.

In 1925 Gide undertook a long journey through parts of Black Africa. Previous sojourns on that continent had been made for personal reasons and had been limited to North Africa, but this trip turned into a discovery of some of the evils of colonialism—not so much the evils of the entire system as particular abuses—and came to be almost a political trip as well as a personal one. Upon his return he denounced the abuses in two documentary works, *Voyage au Congo* and *Retour du Tchad*. These works did have some practical effects in Paris; the texts were cited in ministerial investigations. The experience also contributed to Gide's growing enthusiasm for Soviet communism, leading to a sort of political conversion.

His *Nouvelles Nourritures terrestres* express in lyrical terms this new enthusiasm. During his communist period (approximately 1930-36), he never showed great admiration for Marxist economic theories—in general he was not interested in political and economic theory—and was not a Party member. What attracted him in Russia, he said, was not Marx but Christ—that is, the ideal of brotherhood and the hope of remedying social inequity. Like many other intellectuals who were fellow travelers, he was very active in social and cultural movements organized by the Third International and their sympathizers. On several occasions he spoke at congresses of socialist writers; he signed petitions; and traveling to Germany, he intervened, with Malraux (see *Malraux, André*), on behalf of the arrested communist leader Dimitroff. These activities are all related to the question of peace, since Marxism proclaimed itself the one movement that would bring about world peace, after the overthrow of nationalist governments, and communism was widely considered to be the one European bulwark against fascism and its aggressions. Moreover, the connection between French socialism and pacifism was an old one. Gide was so well-known and respected that the communists were happy to have him participate in their undertakings. His speeches and other texts dating from this period were collected as *Littérature engagée*.

In 1936, Gide was invited to tour Soviet Russia with a number of other French writers. His rather naive view of Soviet communism (especially his insistence that it was not irreconcilable with individualism) was so greatly changed by this visit that upon his return he wrote two volumes to indicate his disappointment. What had displeased him was not always what might have disturbed another observer, and, although he was aware of the Moscow Trials, he did not become immediately cognizant of the extent of political persecutions in the then Soviet Union. However, he did realize that no social or political utopia had yet appeared in Russia. In the Spanish Civil War, he favored the Republican side and supported French intervention, but did not campaign actively for it. Like many of his generation, and especially his rather pacifist friend Roger Martin du Gard, he had retained from the First World War a horror of conflict, and was inclined to think at times that peace was to be maintained at any cost. However, as the 1930s drew to a close he ultimately recognized that peace and stability in a Europe dominated by Hitler were impossible, and that appeasement should not be prolonged. When the Munich pact was signed in 1938, he was temporarily relieved, not realizing that it was more to the advantage of Germany than France and England. (His reflections on the approaching conflict can be found especially in his correspondence with Martin du Gard.)

Gide published no major text dealing with the issues of the Second World War, but his ideas on the conflict can be found in his diary and correspondence. His positions have been criticized as ambivalent and not so clearly anti-German as his critics would have wished. It was not a question of his collaborating actively with the Nazis, or even of praising their military accomplishments or the Vichy government; the fact was that he considered the latter to be the established authority of France, even if he did not admire it. Under the occupation, he temporarily collaborated with the *Nouvelle Revue Française*, probably without realizing the political implications. Moreover, like many others, he was critical of pre1939 France for its lack of moral values, its political divisions, and its military weaknesses, and he implied that French character might have been at fault. After spending the first years of the war in Paris, from 1942 on he lived in Tunis. After the war he busied himself with writing and with his friends and family. In 1947 he was awarded the Nobel Prize for Literature.

Gide was a brilliant literary theorist; his essays and remarks on such topics as classicism, romanticism, the theater, and the novel are fully rationalized and extremely perceptive and original statements. Likewise, his practical criticism, on such writers as Montaigne (see *Montaigne*) and Dostoyevsky, seen in his essays and diary, was very astute. As a social thinker, he was neither systematic, consistent, nor brilliant, but he is an interesting example of a man of letters of the upper bourgeoisie, eminently suited to the life of the mind, on whom contemporary events impinged so that he was forced to take note of them and adopt a position. His statements on colonialism, social injustice in Europe, Fascism, the French political scene in the 1930s, and the two world wars contained little, if anything, that was original. However, they carried considerable weight, or at least drew a great deal of attention, because of the prestige associated with his name. It is in that sense only then, that he should be considered an important spokesman for social justice and peace.

Bibliography ——————————————————

Brée G 1953 *André Gide. L'insaisissable Protée*. Belles Lettres, Paris

Gide A 1902 *L'Immoraliste*. Mercure de France, Paris [1930 *The Immoralist*. Knopf, New York]

Gide A 1909 *La Porte étroite*. Mercure de France, Paris [1924 *Strait is the Gate*. Harrolds, London]

Gide A 1914 *Les Caves du Vatican*. Gallimard, Paris [1925 *The Vatican Cellars*. Knopf, New York]

Gide A 1926 *Les Faux-Monnayeurs*. Gallimard, Paris [1927 *The Counterfeiters*. Knopf, New York]

Gide A 1927 *Voyage au Congo*. Gallimard, Paris [1929 *Travels in the Congo*. Knopf, New York]

Gide A 1928 *Retour du Tchad*. Gallimard, Paris [1929 *Travels in the Congo*. Knopf, New York]

Gide A 1935 *Les Nouvelles Nourritures*. Gallimard, Paris [1949 *Fruits of the Earth*. Knopf, New York]

Ireland G W 1970 *André Gide: A Study of His Creative Writings*. Clarendon Press, Oxford

O'Brien J 1977 *Portrait of André Gide*. Octagon Books, New York

CATHARINE SAVAGE BROSMAN

Gladstone, William Ewart

William Ewart Gladstone (1809-98), who was four times prime minister of Great Britain and perhaps the greatest of all liberal statesmen by virtue of the length of his career in high office and his national and international fame, is of significance to the study of peace chiefly for his evolving political vision of what constituted a peaceful and ordered world, and for the policies he pursued to achieve this (see *World Order*). Here we shall examine Gladstone's background and character, the nature of nineteenth century British liberalism which he both adopted and helped to mold, and his approach to foreign policy, war and armaments, the peaceful settlement of disputes, national self-determination, and human rights, as well as assess the relevance of his ideas and outlook to the world of today.

Born the son of a prosperous Liverpool merchant and West Indies slave-owner, Gladstone entered the House of Commons as a Tory in 1832 and first held cabinet office under Peel in 1843. When Peel broke with the majority of his party over the repeal of the Corn Laws in 1846, Gladstone followed him into an intermediate position between the Tories and the Whigs, but drew closer to the latter as, with the growing influence of the Victorian middle class, they evolved into the Liberal Party in the 1850s. After serving as Chancellor of the Exchequer under Aberdeen, Palmerston, and Russell, Gladstone became leader of the Liberal Party in 1867. From then almost until his death in 1898 he was a dominating force in British politics, whether as prime minister (in 1868-74, 1880-85, 1886, and 1892-94) or in opposition.

Gladstone's social background helps to explain his moral character and political outlook. He was a product of the rising commercial class and reflected its ethos and values including the strongly pious evangelical Christianity to which many of its members were attracted. Gladstone's faith penetrated deeply into his being and revealed itself both in his absolute personal integrity as is apparent in the detailed "confessional" diaries he kept for 70 years, and in his belief that he was held to politics to make "Christian responses" to political challenges.

Such a man could hardly have achieved the power and influence he did had not the time been ripe, but in early Victorian England the old aristocratic culture was slowly succumbing to new social and economic forces. Amongst these were rapid urbanization, a vast increase in manufacturing and trade, and the growth of a middle class dedicated to moral and material progress. Such developments had their political repercussions: protection gave way to free trade, and the agricultural to the industrial interest. At the same time, and associated with these changes, there was growing opposition to the aristocratic dominance of the army, to the traditional foreign policy of preserving the balance of power in Europe, and to the wars which were fought as part of that policy. The emerging liberal spirit found its focus in the Great Exhibition of 1851, a striking demonstration of international progress in the arts of peace, and of Great Britain's supremacy in this field.

Gladstone, although he did not exemplify this new commercial spirit in as marked a degree as did Cobden (see *Cobden, Richard*), Bright, and others of the "Manchester School," was nevertheless sufficiently touched by it to develop an outlook upon the international world very different from that of aristocrats like Castlereagh, Palmerston, and Salisbury, or of one who, although born an outsider, came to identify himself with aristocratic England: his chief parliamentary rival, Benjamin Disraeli.

These, like that other great conservative realist, Bismarck, saw Europe as an arena in which states preserved their independence and enhanced their influence by the skillful and relentless pursuit of power politics, whereas Gladstone, although he could on occasion take firm unilateral action (as when, on the outbreak of the Franco-Prussian War, he secured from both Bismarck and Napoleon III a promise to respect Belgian neutrality, or in 1885 raised a credit of £11

million to resist a Russian threat to Afghanistan), had an instinctive and characteristically liberal preference for the concerted action of the powers; the good order of Europe, he believed, should be a shared responsibility. Indeed, his approach to foreign crises may be said to prefigure the idea of the Security Council as the role of that body was originally conceived, although, like the founders of the League of Nations (see *League of Nations*) and the United Nations (see *Status and Role of the United Nations*), he tended to assume a greater degree of international consensus than in fact usually obtained. One instance of this may suffice. Gladstone, a Christian traditionalist, saw Europe still as a Christian Commonwealth. It was an archaic view and one with which Bismarck (who spoke of "Professor" Gladstone) had little patience. Several times Gladstone attempted to get concerted European action over the iniquities or failings of the Ottoman government, but when, in 1880, to force the Sultan to conform to the terms of the Treaty of Berlin, he proposed the despatch of an international force to seize Smyrna, Bismarck responded that his prayers would accompany the expedition.

His advocacy of armed intervention (see *Intervention*) in this matter shows that Gladstone was far from being a pacifist, but even here the object was to secure the Sultan's compliance "with the least risk to peace," (Morley 1903) and in general he abhorred war both as a moralist and as an economist. But even more central to his outlook was the maintenance of "the public law of Europe" and because he believed that Russia had flouted this law, he supported the Crimean War and to the end of his life believed that it had been just. When, however, early in 1855, Russia made concessions which Gladstone felt provided a basis for peace, he argued strenuously, in the face of the growing bellicosity of public opinion, for a cessation of hostilities. This brought him much unpopularity, but threw him into closer association with Cobden and Bright, both radical pacifists, and thus completed his transformation from Peelite Tory into Liberal.

Gladstone's dislike of war was paralleled by a suspicion of great armaments and defenses and an abhorrence of their cost. He reduced from £9 million to £5 million Palmerston's expenditure on coastal forts during the "war scare" with France in 1860. In 1853 he proposed the reduction of British forces in the Pacific, but failed to carry the cabinet. A similar failure marked the end of his official career. When, in 1893-94, the invention of cordite for naval guns seemed to threaten Britain's naval supremacy, the

Admiralty urged the Government to undertake an extensive battleship-building program. This Gladstone opposed, unconvinced by the arguments and appalled at the size of the estimates, but the cabinet backed the Admiralty, and Gladstone, virtually isolated, finally resigned from the premiership. In such matters he was increasingly out of step with the times as the Great Powers embarked upon those rivalries which were to culminate in the First World War (of which Gladstone, watching the parade of German naval might at the opening of the Kiel Canal in 1895, had a premonition) (see *Militarism and Militarization*).

A great believer in the rule of law, Gladstone was an important influence in the settlement of the *Alabama* Claims. These arose from the career of a steam sloop, the *Alabama*, which shortly after her launch at Birkenhead in 1862, was secretly transformed into a Confederate commerce raider in the American Civil War, thereafter taking an immense toll of Northern shipping. The failure of the British Government to prevent the vessel from sailing infringed the principle of neutrality, and after the war the United States claimed against Great Britain for the heavy losses incurred. The issue dragged on until Gladstone's first government took it in hand by negotiating the Washington Treaty of 1871 which both provided for the arbitration of the dispute and sought to establish rules of maritime neutrality (see *Negotiations, Direct*). The matter was finally resolved in 1872 by a mixed panel of arbitrators meeting at Geneva. The award against Great Britain was assessed at over £3 million, about one-third of the original American claim (see *International Judicial Settlement; International Law; Pacific Settlement of International Disputes*). Although condemned by some sections of British opinion, the settlement not only greatly advanced the cause of international arbitration (see *Arbitration, International*) but also marked the beginning of a steady and long-term improvement in Anglo-American relations. John Morley (1903) wrote:

> The treaty of Washington and the Geneva arbitration stand out as the most notable victory in the nineteenth century of the noble art of preventive diplomacy . . . [Mr Gladstone's] association with this high act of national policy is one of the things that gives its brightest lustre to his fame.

Gladstone's instinct for removing the causes of social conflict, together with his belief in freedom, lay behind his championship of national self-determination. Early in the American Civil War this sentiment seemed to extend even to the Confederacy although

he detested slavery and regretted the break-up of the Union. In a speech at Newcastle he declared:

> Jefferson Davis and other leaders of the South have made an army; they are making, it appears, a navy; and they have made what is more than either, they have made a nation.

His feeling that if a desire for independence was expressed vigorously enough by a people then it had better be conceded, certainly colored his view of imperialism. He was against the "forward" policies of Disraeli in South Africa and Afghanistan, and in colonial annexations saw only future trouble (see *Colonialism; Imperialism*). Thus he opposed the acquisition of Cyprus and the Transvaal and in his great Midlothian campaign of 1879 fulminated against a policy inseparable from human suffering. "Remember," he exclaimed, "that the sanctity of life in the hill villages of Afghanistan . . . is as inviolable in the eye of Almighty God as can be your own," and, respecting another colonial conflict, inflamed his hearers with "the record of ten thousand Zulus slain for no other offense than their attempt to defend against our artillery with their naked bodies their hearths and homes, their wives and families." When, shortly after he came to power for the second time, he sought to reverse Conservative policies, conceding after the Boer victory at Majuba Hill virtual independence to the Transvaal in 1881, and withdrawing from Afghanistan the same year. It was Gladstone's unwillingness to take on further imperial responsibilities that lay behind his curious dilatoriness over rescuing Gordon, besieged by the Mahdi in Khartoum for eight months in 1884-85. He had sent Gordon out to evacuate the Sudan, not to become the excuse for seizing it.

The one great exception to these anti-imperialist policies was the establishment of virtual British control over Egypt. But here the necessity of preserving order and legitimate authority proved paramount, for a nationalist rising in 1882 had led to the massacre of a number of Europeans, endangered the life and throne of the Khedive, and threatened the financial order the powers had imposed upon a bankrupt country. Gladstone's government had wished to act in conjunction with France, but the French withdrew and the British were obliged to put down the rebels alone. Yet such a policy went against the Liberal grain: the occupation was assumed to be temporary as indicated by the refusal to declare an annexation or protectorate as foreign opinion widely expected. Instead the government maintained Khedival rule with all its obligations to the other powers, a decision which was to cause endless trouble for the future.

The most notable of Gladstone's attempts to give effect to national self-determination (see *Self-determination*) lay in his prolonged parliamentary struggle to achieve Home Rule for Ireland. It was very much a personal campaign and dominated his last years and his last two administrations. The rise of an Irish Nationalist Party committed to this cause (the Fenians, in contrast, employing terrorist methods, wanted an independent republic) convinced Gladstone that Ireland had to be given self-government in the interests both of herself and of the United Kingdom as a whole. His first attempt to achieve this, in 1886, split his party and failed in the House of Commons. His second, in 1893, succeeded in the Commons, but was overwhelmingly defeated in the House of Lords. Yet the Home Rule movement, once launched, could not be stayed, and for better or worse helped determine the fate of Ireland in the decades to come.

Gladstone's Irish policy was part of a wider political philosophy: his belief in the rights of peoples and of individuals. He was first awoken to what nowadays would be called the "human rights" question when in 1850 he visited political prisoners, liberals like himself, chained and fettered in the filthy dungeons of the King of Naples. This experience—"the negation of God erected into a system of government"—made him an advocate of Italian liberty and unity. The state of things in the Ottoman Empire had a similar effect. Their often savage treatment of the Armenians and of their other Christian subjects—as in the "Bulgarian atrocities" of 1876—roused him to passionate denunciations of the Turks and formed the chief theme of his extraordinary Midlothian campaigns. For him and his followers there could be no question thenceforth of supporting Turkey as a counterweight and buffer to an expanding and ambitious Russia. The Turks should clear out "bag and baggage . . . from the provinces they have desolated and profaned." A massacre of 6,000 Armenians in Constantinople in 1896 brought him, in his 87th year, to make his last great public speech, in which he urged unilateral intervention (see *Words of Peace and War*) by Great Britain against Ottoman misrule.

Gladstone's career thus ends on a note of contradiction. For the opponent of an expanded navy was advocating on behalf of humanity and justice a course of action which might well have embroiled his country with other European powers, none of which at that time was particularly friendly to it. It was the sort of dilemma which the liberal or radical to this day finds difficult to resolve; he is generally antipathetic to war and armaments and yet frequently deems it his country's duty to put an end to intolerable abuses abroad.

Has the Gladstonian example any relevance to the cause of peace in the late twentieth century? As a man molded by the culture, ideas, and conscience of the early, even pre-Victorian world, Gladstone was something of an anachronism even before the close of his own career. History, however, has a way of coming to full circle, and few would now deny that his misgivings about imperialism have, in many instances, been borne out by events. Yet much of what has succeeded the colonial empires, at least in those parts now subject to tyranny, corruption, and brutality every bit as bad as the Turkish misgovernment against which Gladstone inveighed, would have filled him with anger and disgust. Compared, however, with the nineteenth century liberal conscience, the twentieth century liberal conscience has been numbed—or rather, largely through the influence of the Third World itself, has been conditioned into thinking that imperialism and racism rather than tyranny, oppression, and even genocide, are the greatest evils and threats to peace. Gladstone, High Victorian that he was, believed above all in civilized values and the rule of law, and these he did not see as being incompatible with national independence. Perhaps today he would have done, and have continually drawn attention to, denounced, and demanded action against, those states and regimes whose contempt for human rights and the rule of law is so marked a feature of the contemporary scene (see *Global Ethics, Human Rights Laws and Democratic Governance*).

In two further respects the Gladstonian outlook and example would seem to be pertinent to the world of today. He always set high store by the shared responsibility of the powers for maintaining international peace and order, and would have bent every effort towards making the cooperation of the "community of power" a reality. And, given his integrity rooted in his Christian faith, he would have abhorred not only as unspeakably evil, but as inconsistent with a peaceful and ordered world, that practice of some contemporary democracies to employ in support of their foreign policies means, and to enlist as allies regimes, of a character flagrantly incompatible with the values they purport to uphold.

Bibliography

Feuchtwanger E J 1975 *Gladstone*. Allen Lane, London

Gladstone W E 1971 *Midlothian Speeches, 1879*. Leicester University Press, Leicester

Hammond J Le B 1938 *Gladstone and the Irish Nation*. Longmans, London

Jenkins R 1995 *Gladstone*. Macmillan, London

Knaplund P 1927 *Gladstone and Britain's Imperial Policy*. Allen and Unwin, London

Knaplund P 1935 *Gladstone's Foreign Policy*. Harper, New York

Magnus P 1954 *Gladstone: A Biography*. Murray, London

Matthew H C G 1986 *Gladstone 1809-1874.*, 1995 *Gladstone 1875-1898.*, Clarendon Press, Oxford

Medlicott W N 1956 *Bismarck, Gladstone and the Concert of Europe*. Athlone Press, London

Morley J 1903 *The Life of William Ewart Gladstone*. Macmillan, London

Shannon R 1963 *Gladstone and the Bulgarian Agitation 1876*. Nelson, London

Shannon R 1982 *Gladstone*, Vol. 1: *1809-1865*. Hamish Hamilton, London

BRIAN E. PORTER

Glasnost and Perestroika

These two concepts have become an essential part of our political vocabulary. The feelings towards them are different. However, it is difficult to find a person who would deny the fact that perestroika and glasnost have opened a completely new stage in the history of the former Soviet Union, that they have had a profound influence on international development, as well as on socio-political processes everywhere.

Perestroika was born as a result of urgent and critical internal problems of the then Soviet Union. By the end of 1970s, the long-standing, but hidden crisis of our country had reached an extremely dangerous limit. We could not leave things as they had been for many decades—it would have meant having an imminent collapse of the whole country in the near future. Economic stagnation and social inflexibility were an evidence of the exhausted resources of the internal policy, that were based on principles, that were securely fixed since Stalin's time. Foreign policy was dictated by the same principles, and it condemned us to participate in nuclear and conventional arms races, that by that time had already reached the point, where the whole world could have been hurled into an abyss at any moment (see *Cold War*).

In certain scientific and ruling political circles, that were breaking through dogmas of ideological mentality, an understanding was reached that the former Soviet State had found itself to be in almost complete isolation from the cardinal reforms taking place in the world, as well as from the modern technological and industrial processes; an understanding that the time had come for a new period in the world's history, where the laws of confrontation were becoming harmful for all of humankind, and where the former USSR was set up to hopelessly lag behind, and its people were doomed to have a permanently impoverished existence.

Starting from March-April of 1985, we began to form a new political course. From the very beginning we adopted a tendency for improving and perfecting the existing system by accelerating economic and social development. However, two years later, it became clear that the system did not want to yield to repairs. That's why, at the final stages of perestroika we were not talking about the improvement of the old, but rather about a transition to a new economic system, where the law and order ruled and human rights were the first priority.

The transition turned out to be extremely difficult and complicated. Much more complicated than it seemed in the beginning. First of all, it was because the totalitarian system had literally infiltrated the very pores of the society, and had accumulated great inertia for resistance. It was the resistance of the ruling Party and government structures. It was the resistance of nomenclature—the army of bureaucrats, Party officials, ideologists of all ranks, the people, who owed their careers, their social and economic position to the old regime. It was also the resistance of the habits, deeply-rooted rules, and the whole lifestyle and behavior of millions of people. The mass psychology of dependence on government, that had been cultivated for many years, caused a general lack of ability and desire for becoming responsible for one's own life and having the order in a society.

The whole period of perestroika was filled with the struggle to involve as many people as possible in the process of change. We had to do it in the midst of open antagonism towards the reforms, that was hidden in the beginning, and on a certain stage, there was opposition even from those, who had welcomed and supported the changes in the beginning.

In Soviet times, the consciousness of the majority of people had deep-rooted memories of Stalin's horrid dictatorship; in spite of the 20th Convention of the Communist Party of the then Soviet Union, and timid attempts to make reforms during Khrushchev's time and even at the beginning of Brezhnev's rule, neostalinist laws still governed, so the fundamental transformation of the society could have been started and carried through only "from the top," through the initiating actions of the administration of the ruling Party.

Of course, nothing could have been achieved, if the initiative "from the top" wasn't supported by at least the most active part of society, and if the ideas of perestroika were not understood and accepted by the people. And this, in turn, would have been impossible without breaking the Party's monopoly on the mass media, when people still feared to openly express their opinions, and criticize the existing system.

Glasnost was supposed to serve this very purpose. Glasnost, as well as perestroika, had to pave its way with great difficulties. Old structures, that regarded top secrecy to be monopoly's guarantee for power, did everything to prevent the "opening" of politics to people. Even the most sincere supporters of perestroika followed the long-lasting traditions of making everything a secret. In spite of all that, glasnost, being democratic in its very essence, received a great response from the society. It woke people up from the slumber of the stagnation period; it helped them to overcome their past inactivity, and indifference towards public work; it helped them to feel involved in the reforms. Glasnost created an atmosphere of adjusting to changes, understanding the new political course, creating one's own opinions of the events that were happening. Without the policy of glasnost none of perestroika's achievements could have taken place.

Glasnost did not just create favorable conditions for the realization of reforms, it also tried to prevent any attempts at sabotage, including violent acts. If perestroika became a peaceful process, it was mostly due to glasnost.

Glasnost ensured the beginning of the deepest psychological breakthrough ever. Although in Russia some people even now are sympathetic towards Stalinism and feel nostalgic towards the past, the absolute majority of the citizens are firmly set in the direction of democracy, freedom, and any further affirmation of humanistic values within the civilization of Russia. This was one of the deciding guarantees of the reforms' irreversibility.

Glasnost was first intended to be a way to bring the idea of perestroika to the attention of the people, and include people into specific changes; to be a mechanism that had direct and reverse connections between the initiators of reforms and the citizens; but then, in a short period of time, glasnost acquired its own logic of development and started to turn into a real FREEDOM of SPEECH. It became the biggest and most

decisive victory of perestroika, by the way, and its most solid victory against encroachment from the left and right.

Perestroika proved once again that normal, democratic development of a society excludes having total secrecy, and mystery, as a method of government rule—it suggests glasnost, in one word—openness, the total capacity of having freedom of information for the citizens, and freedom of people expressing their political views, their views of the world, and their other opinions and convictions, including the freedom of expressing criticism.

What exactly did we manage to achieve during six years of perestroika? During this comparatively short time—in six years only—we managed to do a lot. The main problems of perestroika were mostly solved or started to be solved.

We eliminated the totalitarian system, the monopoly of the Communist Party on governing power, on being in charge and managing the property of the whole country; Party's monopoly on ideology, which became a national obligation, and was no longer a subject to be disputed under a threat of repression.

We started deep democratic reforms. We introduced the practice of free elections to Parliament and other organs of power. We established the freedom of press, religious freedoms, the multi-party system, the freedom of secession from the country with the right to return. Real constitutional bodies of power were formed, and first steps towards the division of power were made. Human rights were recognized as the absolute principle of nation's functioning.

We started the movement towards mixed economy, towards the equality of different forms of ownership. Economic freedom was legalized. Entrepreneurship started to gain force; the stock system and the system of privatization was established. In the framework of the land legal code, peasant economy started a comeback and farming began. Millions of hectares of land were given into the hands of people from the countryside and from the cities. Private banks were making their first steps.

We posed a question of changing the USSR from an actual unitarian state into a real multi-national federation. We came to the threshold of making a new Treaty of Alliance, which would ensure the sovereignty of each republic, while preserving the economic, social, informational and legal space that is necessary for everyone in the framework of the governing state.

All changes suggest, first of all, a totally new outlook on things in the minds of the people, who are connected in some way to these changes. It is the obvious truth. Perestroika here is no exception. And in order to decide to go ahead with it, we needed a critical reevaluation of all the Soviet experience, rejection of dogmas and false stereotypes, that have been deeply rooted in our minds, starting from school days; a whole new knowledge was required, a knowledge that would go around ideological bans, including real (and not altered to fit propaganda) knowledge of the world, surrounding us, and of the already changed role and place of one's own country in this world.

In short, we needed NEW THINKING. First signs of it were seen far in advance, even before the governing power was transferred into the hands of reformists' wing in the administration of the Communist Party of the then Soviet Union. The initial idea for the New Thinking came from an understanding of the growing mutual connection and interdependence of the parts that compose the modern world, and of the harmfulness of the world's "class" confrontation for the humankind.

People usually connect the New Thinking only with the foreign policy during perestroika. It is not quite correct. Of course, in its aspect that is related to the international affairs, there was a certain set of ideas and principles of its own: each country's freedom to choose its social system; balance of interests instead of balance of power and confrontation; non-application of weapons and refusal to use weapons as a political threat towards other countries; equality, regardless of size and development level of different countries; tendency towards disarmament; priority of the international law over internal jurisdiction, etc.

As a whole, the New Thinking is a political philosophy, based on universal values of democracy and freedom. In that quality, it determined domestic policy of perestroika, taking place of communist dogmatism and class ideology.

The main political achievements of the New Thinking in the international sphere are: liquidation of the "cold war," as a result of mutual efforts with the politicians of the West; termination of the nuclear arms race and the start of reduction of nuclear armaments, as well as conventional arms; transformation of dialogues between the leaders of different nations, as well as all types of negotiations, into a decisive and preferable method of conducting international affairs; stressing the importance of using political methods to dismiss any arguments and disagreements; first practices of mutual regulation of regional conflicts.

During perestroika years, and up to now, its initiators were reproached for the absence of "clear plan" of the reforms, a kind of "schedule of events." However, the events of those years, as well as the years that followed, showed that in times of deep, substantial changes in the principles of society's development, it is not only impossible, but also counterproductive to offer some previously constructed scheme and detailed schedule of reforms. It is important, though, to have a clear goal of reforms, a concept of their general tendency.

Such clear goal, such concept, was inside and out of the perestroika's policy: Deep democratization of the social life style, the rise of economy and people's well-being based on the new principles of development, including the principles of demilitarisation of the national economy; taking a step away from confrontations of foreign policy and achieving significant improvement of the international scene, which would eliminate the threat of a World War. While we were moving towards our goals, we had to change the specific estimates more than once, set new stages, constantly look for new solutions. And, in spite of the fact that some mistakes and miscalculations were made, the main goals of perestroika—through such policy—were achieved.

Since 1992, the government of Russia had several times announced the start of specific programs, but none of those was carried through. There were many reasons for those failures. An important role was played by the fact that the general goal of reforms in Russia, after it took over the USSR, was never really defined. It was no accident that the president of Russia, four years after the Russian Federation was founded, had to entrust a group of scientists to come up with some "national idea" instead of such a goal.

Phenomenon of perestroika raised, under a modern angle of vision, one of so-called "timeless" questions of history—a question on the relationship between revolution and evolution, on the role of reforms in development of a society. In its very essence, perestroika, of course, was a revolution. In its form, it was a revolutionary process, political and ideological reformation.

Probably, it would be better if perestroika in the USSR was started earlier. But it would be a tragedy, if it were late, say, by 10-15 years. Then, a social explosion of tremendous destructive force could have happened, that would have had countless international consequences. Later, historians, if they were to survive, would have called it a revolution. Most likely, it would have been a catastrophe due to a criminal delay of the imminent reforms.

The course towards a gradual and, most importantly, peaceful realization of the reforms, was taken from the very beginning. We failed to carry it through without a bloodshed, though. But it was uncomparable with what happened later, for example, in Chechnya. Mainly, those were provocations of perestroika's enemies. As a whole, the change of the system went peacefully. And evolutionally.

The actions, that were taken in Russia starting from 1992, so-called "shock reforms," proved that evolutional, peaceful methods are undoubtedly better than rushed ones, especially those that used force and violence (like the shooting of the Parliament). The growing hostility among the majority of citizens, social fever in the country, periodic crises at the top, strikes, manifestations, hunger strikes, road blocks, etc.—all that was the price we paid for incompetence and improvisation, which were harmful to the interests of the people; the price for the factual absence of government regulations of the processes.

Today, looking through the prism of all the years gone by, and considering the established tendencies of the world's development, the lessons and conclusions of perestroika's efforts appear to be of great interest. Not only what had been done, but also what we could not achieve and why.

First of all, we could not ensure the harmony of political and economic transformations.

Dialectics of perestroika's process had very soon shown the impossibility of a serious change in economic sphere, without freeing the society from political and ideological tangles, without the "oxygen of freedom," in other words—without the total breakdown of totalitarian structures. And it was done.

However, during the political reform, its irregular nature in different directions turned out to be a serious flaw. Democratization of the social life style had quickly overtook the process of forming new structures of administration, which replaced the previously existing and quickly decaying Party and government apparatus. The much-needed decentralization of the government happended significantly faster than the possibility to carry out, in the short period of time, all the deep reforms of the Union's Federal mechanism.

That lack of coordination, and those differences in the developing processes, were used by reactionary, vindictive forces, ideological enemies of perestroika, the nationalist-separatist forces in the republics, and extremely ambitious new echelon of political activists, who used the new democratic rules to break through to the top of the power.

The difficult economic situation of the country provided a favorable environment for the destructive activities of all these forces; it was inevitable, partly because of the transitional period, and partly because it was one of the consequences of economical reforms, that were lagging behind, and our many errors in conducting them. As a result, the social situation was aggravated. The material welfare of the people became visibly worse. Hostility grew.

It was growing, in spite of the fact that the policy of perestroika, in its very essence and through its clearly-defined goals, had provided for the primary attention to be paid to social problems, and the improvement of all the welfare system.

On top of all that, a number of random events took place, which made it easy for a group of people, occupying the key government posts, to go through with a shady deal—to organize the coup on August 17-22, 1991. The coup failed shamefully, which was the best prove of the historical justification of perestroika, as well as the fact that during its process, the democratic changes had reached a rather high level of irreversibility.

In spite of that, the coup pulled a trigger and set off the explosive mechanisms of our country's disintegration, which was still possible to prevent by signing the Treaty of Alliance, that was scheduled to take place in Moscow on August 19th. After the coup, the intrigues and ambitions of different politics took over this negative process, and in the end managed to destroy the unified state. That was actually the end of perestroika.

However, the input of perestroika in the history of Russia, in its whole ancient history, is enormous and can not be eliminated from its democratic future.

See also: *Gorbachev's Perestroika: From Idea in 1985 to Ideology in 1995*

MIKHAIL S. GORBACHEV

Global 2000 Reports

In 1977 President Jimmy Carter sent an environmental message to the United States Congress in which he wrote:

Environmental problems do not stop at national boundaries. In the past decade, we and other nations have come to recognize the urgency of international efforts to protect our common environment. As part of this process, I am directing the Council on Environmental Quality and the Department of State, working in cooperation with the Environmental Protection Agency, the National Science Foundation, the National Oceanic and Atmospheric Administration, and other appropriate agencies, to make a one-year study of the probable changes in the world's population, natural resources, and environment through the end of the century. This study will serve as a foundation of our longer-term planning.

To build the foundation called for by the President, about 30 of the United States government's top professional experts drew together the best data and models available anywhere in the government. Approximately one million dollars were spent on the work. There were also certain political problems encountered in releasing the report (Barney 1980). The resulting report, *The Global 2000 Report to the President*, was published in the fall of 1980. The primary parts of the report are available in English, German, Japanese, Spanish, Chinese, Italian, and French.

The primary conclusions of the report are as follows:

If the present trends continue, the world in 2000 will be more crowded, more polluted, less stable ecologically, and more vulnerable to disruption than the world we live in now. Serious stresses involving population, resources, and environment are clearly visible ahead. Despite greater material output, the world's people will be poorer in many ways than they are today.

For hundreds of millions of the desperately poor, the outlook for food and other necessities of life will be no better. For many it will be worse. Barring revolutionary advances in technology, life for most people on earth will be more precarious in 2000 than it is now—unless the nations of the world act decisively to alter current trends.

This, in essence, is the picture emerging from the US Government's projections of probable changes in world population, resources, and environment by the end of the century, as presented in the Global 2000 Study. They do not predict what will occur. Rather, they depict conditions that are likely to develop if there are no changes in public policies, institutions, or rates of technological advance, and if there are no wars or other major disruptions. A keener awareness of the nature of the current trends, however, may induce changes that will alter these trends and the projected outcome . . . .

The needed changes go far beyond the capability and responsibility of this or any other single nation. An era of unprecedented cooperation and commitment is essential . . . .

To meet the challenges described in this Study, the United States must improve its ability to identify emerging problems and assess alternative responses. In using and evaluating the Government's present capability for long-term global analysis, the Study found serious inconsistencies in the methods and assumptions employed by the various agencies in making their projections. The Study itself made a start toward resolving these inadequacies. It represents the Government's first attempt to produce an interrelated set of population, resource, and environmental projections, and it has brought forth the most consistent set of global projections yet achieved by US agencies. Nevertheless, the projections still contain serious gaps and contradictions that must be corrected if the Government's analytic capability is to be improved. Put simply, the evaluation showed that the federal agencies of the US Government are not now capable of presenting the President with internally consistent projections of world trends in population, resources, and the environment for the next two decades.

With its limitations and rough approximations, the Global 2000 Study may be seen as no more than a reconnaissance of the future; nonetheless its conclusions are reinforced by similar findings of other recent global studies . . . . All these studies are in general agreement on the nature of the problems and on the threats they pose to the future welfare of human-kind. The available evidence leaves no doubt that the world—including this Nation—faces enormous, urgent, and complex problems in the decades immediately ahead. Prompt and vigorous changes in public policy around the world are needed to avoid or minimize these problems before they become unmanageable. Long lead times are required for effective action. If decisions are delayed until the problems become worse, options for effective actions will be severely reduced.

At the time of the release of the report, President Carter appointed a five-member task force to make recommendations on the issues addressed by the report. Unfortunately the government's experts, who wrote the *Global 2000 Report*, were not permitted to participate significantly in the preparation of the recommendations, and the resulting document, *Global Future—Time to Act* (Speth 1981), became so highly politicized that three of the five members of the President's task force refused to sign it when it appeared in the final weeks of the Carter Administration.

The peace and security of nations around the world are very much dependent on resolving the issues discussed in the *Global 2000 Report*. It is increasingly apparent that "prompt and vigorous changes in public policy around the world" are needed if the problems associated with these issues are not to become "unmanageable."

Responses to the report have varied from country to country. In the United States, the government changed shortly after the publication of the *Global 2000 Report*. The Reagan Administration limited its follow-up to an analysis of the uses that private business make of global data (Train 1984). A few hearings were held in the Congress, and the Office of Technology Assessment prepared a thoughtful analysis of the use of global analysis and its relevance to public policy (Mills 1982). Most of the United States follow-up work, however, was done outside of government by private, independent organizations. The Global Tomorrow Coalition was founded to bring together approximately 100 nongovernmental groups to address global issues. The right-wing Heritage Foundation criticized the work (see Kahn and Simon 1984). The Year 2000 Committee lobbied Congress for the establishment of an Office of Foresight in the executive branch. The Creative Initiative Foundation produced several educational films on global issues. Zero Population Growth prepared an extensive package of educational materials.

The *Global 2000 Report* has been compared with several other reports including some Club of Rome reports (Meadows et al., 1974, Mesarovic and Pestel 1974) and the Brandt Commission reports (Brandt Commission 1980, 1983). The Global 2000 work neither confirms nor refutes the Club of Rome work because the Global 2000 projections stop at the year 2000 whereas the Club of Rome projections extend to the year 2100. As far as they go, however, the United States government's projections are not inconsistent with the Club of Rome projections. The Brandt Commission reports do not have detailed analyses to support their many recommendations. The *Global 2000 Report* provides analysis to support some but not all of the Brandt Commission's recommendations.

The *Global 2000 Report* has attracted much attention in the then Federal Republic of Germany where there have been several discussions of the report in the Bundestag. The Bundestag commissioned a detailed review (von Bülow 1982) by German government ministries and German scientific institutions. The review concluded that, "the basic thesis of the American global analysis is shared in principle even by critics" and argued that the global tendencies presented in the United States report "represent key problems for the future of humanity." It observed that a widening gap between the rich and poor "can lead to great tensions in the world."

The German review headed by Andreas von Bülow, Minister of Science and Technology, noted that the problems facing the world cannot be solved "through German efforts alone," and that cooperation among nations will be required. In pursuit of the needed cooperation the Germans participated in an international consultation in late 1980 about the *Global 2000 Report*. This consultative effort came to nothing, Bonn reported, because the international consultation on the *Global 2000 Report* "is no longer sought" by the United States government.

In Italy, the Italian Senate held a full day of hearings on the *Global 2000 Report*. The transcript of these hearings was published as an Italian Senate report, *Previsioni Circa lo Sviluppo nei Prossimi Decanni*.

The Canadian Government commissioned a study of the implications of the *Global 2000 Report* for the future of Canada. The resulting book was published under the title *Global 2000: Implications for Canada* (Barney et al., 1981).

The Government of the People's Republic of China initiated a *China in the Year 2000* study for Premier Zhao Ziyang. This study was modeled in part on the Global 2000 study. It is an extensive report of approximately 300 pages that has involved hundreds of institutions throughout China.

National year 2000 studies that are patterned in part on the *Global 2000 Report* are in progress in Iceland, Mexico, and the Republic of Korea. Similar studies are under consideration for Brazil, Taiwan, and Senegal.

The inquiries and studies stimulated by the *Global 2000 Report* continue, and will receive support and encouragement in the future. The Rockefeller Brothers Fund has provided initial funding to a new nonprofit, nongovernmental organization, the Global Studies Center, to provide technical assistance and training for such efforts.

A prerequisite of a peaceful world is a world secure in health, prosperity, and justice. The Global 2000 studies provide new tools for understanding how the security of all nations—and ultimately the peace of the world—can be increased.

Bibliography

Barney G O 1980 *The Global 2000 Report to the President*. Government Printing Office, Washington, DC

Barney G O, Freeman P H, Ulinski C A 1981 *Global 2000: Implications for Canada*. Pergamon, Oxford

Brandt Commission 1980 *North-South: A Program for Survival*. MIT Press, Cambridge, Massachusetts

Brandt Commission 1983 *Common Crisis*. Pan Books, London

Carter J 1977 *Environmental Message to the Congress.* Government Printing Office, Washington, DC

China in the Year 2000. (Available in Chinese only from Institute for Technological Information of China)

Dearborn N 1983 Global 2000: Radar for the ship of state. *Futures* (April)

Kahn H, Simon J 1984 *The Resourceful Earth.* Basil Blackwell, Oxford

Meadows D H et al., 1972 *The Limits to Growth.* Universe, New York

Mesarovic M, Pestel E 1974 *Mankind at the Turning Point.* Dutton, New York

Mills W 1982 *Global Models, World Futures, and Public Policy: A Critique.* Government Printing Office, Washington, DC

Speth G 1981 *Global Future: Time to Act.* Government Printing Office, Washington, DC

Train R E 1984 *Corporate Use of Information Regarding Natural Resources and Environmental Quality.* World Wildlife Fund, Washington, DC

von Bülow A 1982 *Bericht der Bundesregierung zu "Global 2000."* Der Bundesminister für Forschung und Technologie, Bonn

GERALD O. BARNEY

Global Common Society (GCS)

The world atmosphere of today characterized by globalization, democratization, scientification, humanization, and welfarization are serving as centripetal motions toward integration. These centripetal tendencies are the signs of the advent of the Regional Cooperation Society (RCS), and Global Cooperation Society (GCS) and of the transformation from the RCS into GCS. The regional associations of nations such as APEC, NAFTA, and ASEAN we see today are the examples of the initial stage of the transformation from the RCS into the GCS.

The establishment of world community will be probably developed through the following series of stages: Regional Cooperation Society (RCS)→Regional Common Society (RCS)→Regional Integrated Society (RIS)→Global Cooperation Society (GCS)→Global Common Society (GCS)→Global Confederate States (GCS).

1. GCS in Political Philosophy

Throughout history, the design for peace and mutual prosperity of mankind has been nurtured by the sufferings and complications of wars among races, tribes, and nations. Both Oriental and Occidental political philosophies have long emphasized the need for a world community to bring peace and coprosperity to the human beings. The idea of unity and brotherhood of mankind in the ancient Chinese political philosophy and homonoia and cosmopolitanism of the ancient Occident can fall under the idea of world community. This ancient ideal of a harmonious world has captured the minds of many philosophers ever since and has been developed into a variety of thoughts and theories such as Dante's 'Monarchia' and Kant's 'Zum Ewigen Frieden' (Perpetual Peace).

2. Conditions and Necessity of GCS

However, it took many centuries of great historical changes to create an objective environment which could realize the idealism of the world community not as a fantasy but as a practicable alternative. The conditions for creating the world community had not become mature till we passed through the modern age. It is certain that the modern age has produced the favorable conditions for the construction of the world community in the organic relationships among nation state, capitalism, and democracy.

As we live in the age of industrialization, democratization and information revolution we are inextricably building up the dense networks of interdependence involving all of us on the earth. Due to the spread of democratic spirit, mutual respect for human rights, and ever increasing international exchange and cooperation, everyone in the world has the opportunity to enjoy the same quality of life.

Especially in the late 20th century, thanks to the scientific-technological revolution and the revolutionary compression of time and space, the world as a global village is becoming a 'space of simultaneous life' rather than a 'space of one-day life.' And due to the development of transportation, communication, and industrial technology, the people and the nations of the world are deepening their interdependent relationship though mutual exchange and cooperation. Thus, all the people on earth are tending to become members of one single global community or one human family, not adversaries or strangers, though they may use different languages and possess different citizenship. In the face of the problems of global scale such a environmental degradation, pollution, population, foods shortage, violation of human rights, narcotics, international crimes, terrorism, and danger of nuclear and bio-chemical weapons and of the emergence of Cyber Space through the Internet all the peoples of the world belong to one single community of a common fate.

3. GCS and Pax UN

It is very opportune that we should establish a global common society in which all the peoples in the world live together as members of one family in a global village. In spite of this great demand of our times, there are still some countries which are pursuing to be a 'Strong Nation' but not a 'Great Nation' which would take the initiative and exert the leadership for the co-prosperity of all mankind. A 'Great Nation' is not the one designed to control over the world as in the 'Pax Romana' but the one intended to play a leading role in creating a global common society in which the same rights of all states and freedom, equality, and co-prosperity of all mankind as shown in the UN Charter, can be guaranteed.

As we are facing a transnational and borderless global society through deepening international exchanges and cooperation we have to reorient our thinking and behavior to match the rapid changes in world atmosphere. In the same context, the UN should be transformed into the Pax UN system in which it will not be either a lady-in-waiting just for the superpowers any more or merely an organization for passing any resolution simply by the majority in the UN.

> The UN has been the venue for the member states to discuss and resolve impending agendas for the security and welfare of mankind. But the new UN for all mankind, that is to say, the Pax UN under its vision for the GCS should be not only a venue for discussion of its member states but a strengthened world organization having its own view and goal on the future of mankind to actively execute and manage the resolutions made by member states. (Young Seek Choue 1984 p. 18)

> The Pax UN will be totally different from the system such as Pax Romana in which international security and world order are controlled by a nation or a couple of superpowers. In Pax UN system, the UN will and should represent all the sovereign states and will do its due functions to realize the goal of universal sovereignty of all states and people. (Young Seek Choue 1996 p. 26)

The RCS has appeared in various corners of the world today. It should and will be developed into the so-called Regional Integrated Society which will be the former stage of the GCS and then of the Global Integrated Society—a UN-centered global union of nations. The Pax UN should take the initiative and responsibility of creating a Global Common Society in which all mankind will live together as members of one family.

Since it is not only desirable but inevitable for us to live together, it is now urgent for us to establish a set of global ethical norms and common goals based on the universal sense of goodness and righteousness. In so doing, it is imperative for us to institute a Pax UN based on the universal sovereignty of all peoples and all nations.

In the future, we will not be able to take sides with either spiritual culture or material civilization. We will have to harmonize and coordinate these two aspects of civilization in the name of humancentrism so that we can make science, technology, institutions, and organizations serve human beings in order to usher in a 'Humanistic Human Society' 'Cultural Welfare Society', and 'Universal Democratic Society.'

Only when we will have achieved such a society— that is, 'globally confederated states' under Pax UN, can we peacefully co-exist and co-prosper. We have to construct the GCS under the Pax UN system to guarantee permanent world peace and co-prosperity.

4. Prospects of GCS

We should realize that it is no longer possible for each nation to think in terms of its own exclusive interests and to seek unilaterally its own wealth and power. Therefore, it is now time for us to construct a grand vision of human society for the next millennium in order to make further progress in human history. And we must reconstruct human society in order both to make it suitable to the spirit and the trend of our times and to transform the world into a cultural world.

As our history has developed by recurring integration and disintegration, we should not overlook some factors that may fragmentize the world. However it is obvious that the world today is heading for a united society, and it is more widely recognized now ever in international society that human beings should belong to one society with the same fate by creating a peaceful atmosphere.

Now the world is changing from the age of exclusive nationalism, ethnic racism, imperialistic militarism and ideological class struggle into the age of democracy for reconciliation and cooperation in order to help one another internationally. In other words, the world is moving toward a transnational society, a cross-cultural society and a borderless society. In this age of great transformation we must extend the dimension of our thinking to a global one for all human beings by reformulating our conceptual construct. Thus, we must create the world community in which all nations can live and prosper together peacefully.

Since the world community has just started to sprout, it may be a little too soon at present to have an optimistic view about our future. Nevertheless, Barraclough helps us cherish a hope for the vision of the world community with his comment: "The civilization of the future will continue to develop into a worldwide one in which all the continents would play their own role."

Bibliography ————————————

Barraclough G 1977 *An Introduction is Contemporary History.* Penguin Books

Choue Y S 1981 *Oughtopia.* Pergamon Press, Oxford/New York

Choue Y S 1984 *World Peace through Pax UN.* Kyung Hee University Press, Korea

Choue Y S 1987 *Peace in the Global Village.* Kyung Hee University Press, Korea

Choue Y S 1995 A Grand Design of Human Society toward the Next Millennium. Keynote Speech at the 1995 World Youth Leaders Conference, held in Seoul, Korea, on May 31-June 2, 1995

Choue Y S 1996 Peace Strategies for a Global Common Society and the Role of the United Nations in the 21st Century. Keynote Speech at the Commemorative Ceremony and International Peace Conference for the 10th Anniversary of the UN International Year of Peace and the 15th Anniversary of the UN International Day of Peace, held from September 17 to 19, 1996

Choue Y S 1997 The Realities of Human Society and Vision for the Forthcoming Millennium. Keynote Speech at the Commemorative Ceremony and International Day of Peace, held from September 1 to 3, 1997

Dante A 1949 *On World-Government or De Monarchia.* (Translated by H W Schneider) Liberal Art Press, New York

Kant I 1984 *Zum Ewigen Frieden* (1795). Reclan, Stuttgart

Song B R 1998 The vision for the world community in the European thought. *The Journal of Contemporary European Studies* 7

BYUNG-ROK SONG

Global Economic Interdependence: Why Crisis?

Economic interdependence, both at the structural and functional levels as well as at the territorial and human developmental levels, provided it is based on the complementary and cooperative advantages instead of the competitive and comparative advantages, can be regarded as the optimum choice for (a) human development and (b) economic development through (i) rationalised utilisation of both the human and natural resources, (ii) alternative utilisation of the existing and emerging resources and potentials, in both the human and economic interests. A genuine economic interdependence between and among nation-states may take place under the following conditions and perspectives:

(a) when the exchange of the use-values of the commodities and materials are equal,

(b) when the values-in-exchange and values-in-use are at par, and

(c) when the terms of trade and exchange between the raw materials and finished goods and services are based on the combination of the intrinsic values of the raw materials, the labour-input values and the social/individual utility values.

The concept of the Global Economic Interdependence is expected to be the concept of the economically equitable equity for the nations-states. But, in order to understand this concept one is to understand the concepts of the Structural Economic Interdependence like:

(a) Interdependence of centre and periphery levels, or Enforced Interdependence, of Vertical Interdependence, which is the result of imperfect competition,

(b) Interdependence of the Global Centres or Interdependence of Power/Control Adjustments, which, generally, takes place under the condition of perfect competition,

(c) Interdependence of the Peripheries or Interdependence of the Dependency Adjustments, which result from the quasi-perfect and quasi-imperfect competition, and

(d) Interdependence of the Independencies or Horizontal Interdependence which takes place under the conditions of complementarities and non-competition.

Some of these concepts lead to (i) dependent type of interdependencies or vertical type of correlation while some others create (ii) the independent type of interdependencies on the basis of mutual benefits or horizontal type of exchange relations.

Again, the heterogeneities in development models and efforts, the outcome of the indigenous or relevant and sustainable development concepts are also to be taken into account for creation and promotion of the Global Economic Interdependence of equitable equality. Otherwise, the establishment of the interdependence of the economies of the same or similar development levels will generate the structured type of interdependence, e.g.,

(a) interdependency of the overdeveloped and developed economies or the centres at the top level,

(b) interdependency of the medium-developed economies or the sub-centres at the middle level, and

(c) interdependency of the underdeveloped economies or the peripheries at the bottom level.

The danger of the above lies in the fact that such level-type of interdependence may generate development-homogenization at different development levels, failing to enable the cross and multi-type of interactions and embodiment of the experiences of the diverse types of experiments and modes.

According to the functional procedure and mechanism the economic interdependencies may be of two types, namely,

(a) inter-nations or cross-national type with the motivations of reciprocities of actions and obligations, and

(b) inter-factorial and actoral type with the motivations and actions of complementarities between and among the input-and output-generating factors as well as actors.

For the purpose of obtaining a just economic interdependence for the entire globe certain adjustments of terms and conditions between the economically overdeveloped and developed North and the economically underdeveloped South and the former East Europe are to be effected. The South and the former East Europe opt for (a) the labour-cost approach besides the proper evaluation of the intrinsic value approach of the raw materials while the West pleads for (b) the value-added and the marketing factor approach in determination of the foundation of the economic relations and commercial exchangeability.

The inherent meaning of the global economic interdependence is the establishment of the global economic order by avoiding the inequality and inequity in the mutual economic relations between the rich and the poor nations. It is the fact that the dominant actor, the capital+technology of the rich nations has still been playing the determinant role over the dependent actor, the raw materials and labour of the poor nations.

1. Problems and Confrontations on the Way of Materialization of the Global Economic Interdependence

Today's economic reality is that (a) the economically underdeveloped countries have been struggling for equal footing with the economically rich countries, for the purpose of achieving a horizontal and equitable economic order. But (b) the economically overdeveloped and developed nations intend to maintain the ongoing economic order of verticality with certain concessional adjustments instead of effecting radical changes. Two counter-arguing approaches have been dominating the economic ideology and means of achieving the international economic interdependence. The barter-type or the system approach for exchange of equal use-values (or intrinsic values), is mostly based on the labour input-cost+material input-cost (or use-values)+normal semi-processing and processing costs, and the poor nations which push forward this approach believe that this ought to be the normal basis of economic relations with the rich nations. The other approach or the approach of the industrialised nations centre around the exchange value system, which includes the value-added elements or the tertiary elements to the use-value creation of the former. The value-added approach of the North has got two different types of arguments, namely, (i) the supply-side arguments and (ii) the demand-side arguments. The Supply or the Sales-side arguments include (a) the technology+capital input costs, the results of the past in semi-processing and processing of the commodities and services for exchange or exports and production of capital goods on the ground that the same contribute to the addition to the normal intrinsic and use-values of the primary raw materials and qualitative improvement of the labour-input in the developing countries. The tertiary service cost is considered to be an important factor in the value-addition process in the supply-side approach of the value-added theory with the argument that it makes the much-needed capital, technology, commodities and services available to the dependent partner. The Demand-side arguments of the value-addition approach hold that:

(a) the value-in-use of a particular commodity or service as well as of capital and technology differs in time, space and circumstances as well as from an individual to the society,

(b) the value-in-use also depends on the possession of purchasing power or income, propensity to consume, propensity to spend and choice variations, and

(c) the value-in-use, in modern time, depends also much on the tertiary or service sector as related to the placement in time, space and to the user/consumer under the respective needed circumstances.

It ought to be remembered that in the international economic relations of interdependence only the national surplus products are not put for exchange or for parting with. Sometimes, the import priorities of raw materials and cheaper labour in case of the developed economies and most of the times, the import priorities of the capital and technology in case of the developing economies do determine the nature and volume of the capital and technology as well as the commodities and labour forces which are put to the exchange relationship. In case of the developed economies it is the choice variations while in case of the developing economies the enforced or created surplus of certain processed and semi-processed products to be parted with, which play the behavioral role. In the international economic relations there always exists a contradiction between the surplus values of commodities and services of the rich nations and the below-worth values of the raw materials and labour of the poor nations.

The following actors and actions can be regarded as the barriers to the materialisation of the horizontal, complementary and cooperative type of global economic interdependence:

(a) when the developed economies, due to their monopoly ownership and control over the tertiary economic sector and means, bind the developing economies into their orbital chronic dependency,

(b) when the developed economies make buffer stocks of certain strategic and basic non-renewable raw minerals, metals and materials, for several years, in order to press the developing economies to cut down the prices at much below level of the worth value and thus attain substan-

tial price-differential gains,

(c) when the developed economies become self-sufficient and stockpile cereal products and certain other agricultural raw materials due to technological superiority and improved measures and, consequently, generate diminishing trends in demand of the same from the market of the developing economies,

(d) when the developed economies develop alternative synthetic raw materials to compete and reduce the import of the natural raw materials of the developing economies,

(e) when the developed economies generate and exercise the vertically negative price trend in the world commodity market for certain commodities of the developing economies and cause the abandonment of their production, and

(f) when the Multi-National Corporations of the developed economies generate "created demand" of certain non-basic needs-based consumer products in the developing economies through window displays and burden the latter economy to these products, at the cost and serious burden of and on the national economy.

In order to remove the above barriers, the implementation of the causal-conditional type of the Generalised System of Preference, shortly known as the GSP, with the motivation of favouring imports by the developed economies from the developing ones, was and is still much being talked. The arguments shown in its favour are as such:

(a) increase in the import-earnings of the developing economies due to either elimination or substantial reduction, by the developed economies, of import duties on several import items from the developing economies,

(b) increase in the demand in the developed economies of the imported items from the developing economies because of their lower market prices, caused through import-duties reduction or elimination,

(c) increase in export sales, causing inducement to incentives for investment facilities in the export-oriented industries of the developing economies, and

(d) increase in the export-earnings of the developing economies besides the growth in the productivity and employment as well as increased income for the employees in the export-oriented industrial branch.

The above chained arguments are theoretically valid, but, in practice seemed to be a failure, because there appeared several times, in very short cyclical order and span of time, world-wide economic crisis which affected mostly the developing economies compelling them to re-introduce protectionism.

The arguments of the (i) comparative advantages and (ii) competitive advantages are very often advocated while structuralising the world economic order of interdependence.

The global economic dependence, in contrast to the global economic independence, is still based on the Ricardian Model of Comparative Advantages, in both of its classical and neo-classical forms, which can be traced as such:

(a) the classical form: where demand becomes the determinant of the equilibrium terms of trade, and

(b) the neo-classical form: where the comparative advantage or proportions of factors of production become more important determinant than the techniques of production.

It negates the Marxist labour theory of value-determination in international exchange.

The neo-classical economists like Samuelson and others hold that when the techniques of production of two countries are identical and the factor-inputs are different, there is scope for gains. Finally, the differences in demand patterns may also give rise to differences in pre-trade price ratios even if the techniques and factor-inputs remain identical. Hence their prediction is that if the division of labour is extended, in the trilectical dimensions of time, space and circumstances with consumers' preferences and producers' techno-potential conditions (for the effective play and game of demand and supply) the potential gain of all countries at international level will increase. But these are not valid in realities. Two of the factors of production, raw material and labour are underrated while the other two, capital and technology, are overrated in the neo-market production structure and as consequence the owner of capital and technology, the centre, can easily subordinate the owner of raw materials and labour, the periphery. The contemporary imperfect market condition, in which labour depends heavily on capital and technology, is to be altered to the situation of perfect competition which may lead to true specialisation, undo the mal-functions of comparative advantages and generate economic welfare both at the centre and the periphery, the developed economies and the developing economies. The global economic interdependence of the mutuality of exchange values cannot take place as long as there will remain the transfer of capital from the underdeveloped economies to the developed ones through unequal exchange and terms of trade. Such transfer always takes place in the name of comparative advantages, but the comparative advantages need be redefined. There are two types of comparative advantages, namely,

(a) the comparative natural advantages consisting of the:

(i) possession of certain types of raw materials,

(ii) possession of good climactic and soil conditions facilitating the growth of certain agricultural raw materials like food-stuffs and cash crops,

(iii) possession of human forces necessary to effect production and to serve as potential market for consumption of the products and services, and

(b) the man-created comparative advantages like capital and technology, the result of the past and present labour and based on surplus value produced by the labour and used for maximising the surplus values, used as the means of penetration, bargaining and finally, exploitation. But the surplus values may also be explained as accumulation from the past to the future via the present for assuring the economic process and growth.

2. How to Develop Global Economic Interdependence

For achieving a realistic and balanced global economic interdependence the focus is to be made on the (a) development of the trade of commodities and services, not on the (b) trade of the development means. The goal of the Global Economic Interdependence being the materialisation of a real and objective economic order between the developed and the developing economies, there arises the question about the means and conditions of achieving the same. Some of these conditions are as such:

(a) when the exchange takes place at equivalence or par, which is to be determined in terms of materials and not money, in terms of raw materials and labour-input contents and not only of technological and tertiary sectoral contents, in terms of broad social utility values and not in terms of the individual or strata utility values,

(b) when the processed goods of the developing

economies are exchanged with the processed goods of the developed economies,

(c) when the raw materials and the semi-processed goods of the developing economies are exchanged with the same of the developed economies,

(d) when the theories and practices of the comparative and competitive advantages are replaced by the theories and practices of the complementary and cooperative benefits between both the developed and the developing economies,

(e) when the command and structuring of the division of labour is shifted from the centre to the peripheries, from polarisation to the surface-extension, from verticalization to the horizontalization, from the centre of capital and technology to the zones of raw materials and labour, etc.

An uneven interdependence between the developed and the developing economies may cause economic power for the former at the cost of the latter. The post-Second World War development concepts, which constituted the foundation of the global interdependency behaviour since the fifties cannot be regarded as having strong economic argumental validity because of the facts that:

(a) the developing economies are to reproduce the models and patterns of development of the developed economies in order to undo their underdevelopment,

(b) the technical assistance, economic aid and trade concessions from the developed economies can quicken the abolition of underdevelopment,

(c) the industrialization of a developing economy will reduce the wide gap and disparities in income and social benefit distribution in the respective developing economy,

(d) the economic development is to be growth-oriented and the creation of the needs-satisfaction is to be backed by the existing purchasing power, etc.

These concepts with the confused and incorrect ideas and appreciations misled the developing economies very much and instead of enabling them to adopt the relevant and sustained development measures, most of the developing economies adhered to the high and expensive technology-oriented development models and patterns of the centre or core economies and achieved, to certain degree, affluent

material development at the cost of the appropriate human values. The approach of catching the development level of the developed economies from behind by the peripheral economies, and the centre's plea for the open door policy for the centre's investment in the developing economies through MNCs and TNCs will produce the dependent type of interdependence, but cannot undo the problems of the underdevelopment.

The industrialization of the contemporary developed economies has now been leading towards a high degree of consumerism and adoption of the same by the developing economies has been inducing the consumerism ideology-based industrialization in the developing territories too.

3. Concept of Global Economic Interdependence

In order to understand the global economic interdependence one is to understand the interaction and interrelation of the same at the territorial, structural and economic functional levels. Its typological equivalence is presented in the following diagram:

The concept and functionality of interdependence at International and Intra-national level is completely different. In the first case it is a relationship of (a) two or more nation-states of the globe, or (b) centre-subcentre structure, or (c) global whole and national constituent part of the global, while in the second instance it is the interdependence within each nation-state, national structure and national economic functional mechanism.

There may take place interdependence between the centre+sub-centre and the semi-periphery+periphery+sub-periphery, provided the developing economies adopt open door policy at all levels to the developed economies, as also desired by the World Bank.

Table 1

Interdependence relationship—typology at spatial, structural and economic functional levels

Nature	Type	Spatial	Structural	Economic Functional
Inter-National	Mega Macro	World National	Global Sub-Centre	Global National
Intra-National	Medi	National Regional	Semi-Periphery	Economic Sectoral
	Mini	National District	Periphery	Economic Sub-Sectoral
	Micro	Commune/ Village	Sub-Periphery	Economic Unit

Now, let the interdependence be explained at different conceptually interpretative and functional systems and stages.

(a) Structural Economic Interdependence

(i) At Power Level through Ownership: Inter-linkages of the Multi-National Corporations (MNCs) (see *Multi-National Cooperation (MNC)*) and the Trans-National Corporations (TNCs) of the developed economies with their subsidiaries, collaborating partners and firms under deals in the developing economies, through the bindings of ownership and contracts of capital+technology and service deals. This can be interpreted as the interdependence of the dependency type.

(ii) At Factorial Inputs Level: The input-ratio of each of the factors of production like raw materials, white and blue-collared manpower, capital, technology, entrepreneurship and that of the tertiary factors like terms of trade, insurance, means of production, marketing and placement to the consumers, etc., and the ownership+control of the majority of the factorial actors determine the interdependency relation and concession between the stronger and the weaker groups in terms of economic values.

(iii) At Output Level: The economic contents and market-demand actors of the processed, semi-processed and primary products and the value+control of the same determine the nature and type of interdependence relationship of the economies involved, in either plus or minus terms.

(iv) At Distribution Level: The ownership and control over the distribution and marketability of the products and services do determine the interdependency and dependency relationship of the positive and negative reciprocity type between and among the economies.

(v) At Purchasing Power (Income) Distribution Level: The income distribution or the distribution of the purchasing power system determines the propensity to consume of the people in each of the developed and the developing economies, which, in consequence, exercises influence over the trends or patterns of consumption, and hence the development and availability of the consumers' goods and services at and for the purchasing power-strata in both the developed and the developing economies.

(b) Interdependence of Dependencies

When one economy is more of:

(i) Vertical Type: When one economy is more dependent on another or other economies, in economic value terms, the relationship between the stronger and the weaker economies are of vertical nature with polarisation effects of the surplus on one end and the deficit on the other.

(ii) Horizontal Type: When two or more economies are dependent on each other or others on equal terms it can be termed as the interdependency of the horizontality or mutuality. Here the exchange value is determined on the basis of the use-values of the commodities and services of each of the partner economies.

(c) Interdependence of the Independencies: When two independent economies, whether at the level of the developed economies or at the level of underdeveloped economies conclude agreements and effect exchanges on the terms of (i) equality and reciprocity and (ii) equity or justice, such actions can be characterised as the actions of the interdependence of independencies, generating mutual value-receipts and value-transfers.

But (a) the price behaviour, and (b) the control of demand over the supply, and (c) control of supply over the demand determine the behaviour of the degree of interdependence and dependence. This is being traced in the above diagram.

Figure 1

Price behaviour of the Normal Demand+Induced Demand and the Normal Supply+Induced Supply in determining interdependence

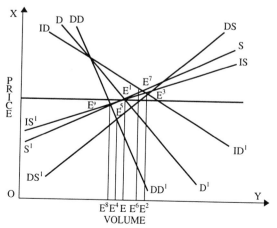

Observations and explanations:

(a) At Normal Demand (D-D^1) and Normal Supply (S-S^1) stages the price and volume interdependency is achieved at the Equilibrium (E-E^1) level.

(b) At Induced Demand (ID-ID^1), indicated by price and Induced Supply (IS-IS^1), the price is determined at the the the E^2-E^3) level, which is higher than the E-E^1 level because of the higher demand and less supply effects.

(c) At Dumped Demand (DD-DD^1) and Dumped Supply (DS^1-DS) stage the volume of supply and the price is determined at the interaction point of E^4 and the level is represented by E^4-E^5.

(d) At Induced Demand (ID-ID^1) and Dumped Supply (DE-DS) the volume of supply and the price interact at the point E^7 and the volume of supply is represented by E^6-E^7 level.

(e) At Dumped Demand (DD-DD^1) and Induced Supply (IS-IS^1) stage the price and the volume of supply interact at E^9 stage where the price is determined and the supply level is represented by E^8-E^9.

The above diagram represents the practical economic exchange behaviour which guides and determines the mode of interdependence and dependence in exchange relations at both the regional and the global levels.

The Global Economic Interdependence guides and influences the Global Development Interdependence. Economic development leads to the creation of goods and services for the humankind. The North has accumulated and developed both the capital and technology and is in need of raw materials while the South is in possession of raw minerals and materials but needs capital and technology. Their needs to obtain and develop the capacity+potentials to supply or part with, are explained in the following diagram:

Fugure 2

North-South interdependence of development means (capital+technology vs raw minerals+materials)

SOUTH (DEVELOPING ECONOMIES)

NORTH (DEVELOPED ECONOMIES)

Interpretations:

CT-CT^1=Development (Production+Marketability) level of Capital and Technology of the Developed Economies (the North)

RM-RM^1=Development (Exploration+Supply) level of Raw Minerals and Materials of the Developing Economies (the South)

CT=Capital+Technology used in the own economy

E-E^1=Development Elasticity (Underdevelopment, Development and Overdevelopment, based on Needs and Capacities)

A=Development Level of Capital and Technology at Underdevelopment Stage in the Developed Economies

CT-U=Underdevelopment of Capital and Technology at Underdevelopment Stage in the Developed Economies

C=Overdevelopment Level of Capital and Technology at Overdevelopment Stage in the Developed Economies

CT-S=Surplus of Capital and Technology at the Overdevelopment Stage in the Developed Economies

OX=Development Level of Capital and Technology matched by the Development Level of Indigenous Production of Raw Minerals and Materials in the Developed Economies

B=Development Level of Raw Minerals and Materials at Underdevelopment Stage in the Developing Economies

RM-U=Underdevelopment of Raw Minerals and Materials at Underdevelopment Stage in the Developing Economies

D=Overdevelopment level of Raw Minerals and Materials at the Overdevelopment Stage in the Developing Economies

RM-S=Surplus of Raw Minerals and Materials at the Overdevelopment Stage in the Developing Economies

OX=Development Level of Raw Minerals and Materials matched by the Development Level of Indigenous Production of Capital and Technology in the Developing Economies

Observations and explanations:

(a) Both the Technology+Capital and Raw Minerals+Materials find at the equilibrium level of development (OX or OX^1) for both the Developed and the Developing Economies, which mean that their development level in the real and saturity level is O.

(b) CT at the A level is situated at the under-utility (CT-U) level and finds itself at the import-dependency level of the RM

(c) CT^1 at the C level finds itself at the surplus (CT-S) level or overdevelopment stage, or export-dependency level of the CT

(d) RM at the B level is situated at the under-utility (RM-U) level and finds itself at the import-dependency level of the CT

(e) RM^1 at the D level finds itself at the surplus stage of exploration and production or overdevelopment or export-dependency of the same, necessitating the import of the CT

The conclusions which can be drawn from the above diagram, which represents the inter-and counter-actions of opposite directions, may be drawn as such:

(a) the developed economies having the export-dependency of the surplus capital+technology should adopt the measures of exporting the same to the developing economies needing these most for their genuine relevant and sustainable development, and

(b) the developing economies having the export-dependency of the surplus raw minerals and materials should adopt the policy of exporting the same to the developed economies for having the appropriate and indigenously absorbable capital+technology which they need most.

Such type of interdependence of the development means and development materials between the developed and the developing economies may open the much desired perspective of the equitable horizontalization of the development levels.

The most important factor which determines and influences the type as well as the extent of the global economic interdependence is the cost-benefit aspect. While the cost aspect is economic and the capacity-cum-propensity of an economy to spare with, the benefit is measured by the use or utility values of the same economy derived by the cost. Both the neo-market economies of the developed countries and the sustenance-seeking underdeveloped economies are now centred on the following steps of economic efficiency-measures while determining their interrelations at both the macro-and micro-economic aspects, though the micro-measures are getting the preference today, namely,

(a) the direct value-creation and addition by each transaction or project for each year,

(b) the indirect value-creation and addition because of the differential action of trialectics of time, space and conditions, and

(c) incremental-cum-extra value-creation or addition, or (decremental effects in reverse case) obtainable by comparing a project dependent on international collaboration or dependency and a project of indigenous resources and implementation of non-external dependency.

The above approach of cost-effect apprehension or cost-benefit analysis would become the model and approach of determining the interdependency relation between the developed and the developing economies, specially at the micro or project level. Because under the conditions of the current neo-market economy there will take place very few macro-level projects of economic interdependency between the developed and the developing economies, while, instead, there will appear many micro-interdependency projects which will be based on the economic efficiency in preference to the social proficiency of the macro collaborative economy. The reasons for the promotive success of the micro-collaborative economic projects are the following:

(a) value of the indigenously produced inputs,

(b) value of the imported inputs from abroad, and

(c) value additions in the forms of salaries and wages, state taxes, interests on financial capital and credit, entrepreneurial and management profits, etc.

4. Functioning of the Global Economic Interdependence

Generally there take place three types and levels of international economic exchanges or interdependence relations, namely,

(a) North-North Economic Interdependence,

(b) South-South Economic Interdependence, and

(c) North-South Economic Interdependence.

Because of the present economic development level and structure the former East European economies may be identified with and included in the category of the developing economies of the South. Their collaborative or interdependable characteristics may be explained as such:

(a) North-North: Covers mostly the capital+technology and is more engaged in the deals of the processed or finished products

(i) More competitive in the market,

(ii) More comparative in the production cost+ marketing price levels,

(iii) Less complementary in nature.

(b) South-South: Covers mostly the regionally-needed processed and semi-processed products, certain regionally-produced capital means of production, certain types of raw materials, etc.

(i) More complementary in the market,

(ii) Less competitive and comparative because of the similar labour and capital inputs.

(c) North-South: Covers mostly the capital and technology of the North and Raw Minerals and Materials of the South

(i) Less competitive because of the less bargaining power of the South against the dictum and terms of trade of the North,

(ii) Less complementary in nature.

When it is the talk of relevant or appropriate development in the economies of the South, based on the indigenous values and needs the South-South economic interdependence of a part of the means and ends seem to be more practical. But when its own means are not sufficient to meet the ends it is obliged to import the same from the North. The developed and continuously improving and sophisticating economies of the North have been trying and practicing, since long, to get rid of their second-grade technology, second-hand machinery capital and a good part of the old or out-dated consumer products like motor vehicles, tram cars, etc., and their export to the developing South. It is of no doubt that the South gets the economic benefit of the same. But unfortunately, by such import the negative environmental effects of the same like air pollution, more use of energy, deterioration of the local environment and values do also take place in the developing economies. Therefore, such dependency is the dependency of the helpless "have-nots" on the mighty "haves." The North-North economic interdependence is the interdependence of filling up the gaps of each other in their own economies. The essence of economic interdependence of the forthcoming century is expected to reduce the gap between the economically rich and the poor countries. And in order to effect the same the local economies of the South should strengthen their own economic foundations in order to reach the stage of adjustments and complementarity.

An equal and equitable economic interdependence between two economies expects the correlative function of the perfect competition and when the same is related between the developed North and the developing South one presupposes the existence of the same or similar bargaining power of raw minerals and materials of the South towards the capital and technology of the North.

By moving from the theory to the empiri one may observe that

(a) the share of economic exchange between and among the developed economies has been experiencing an increasing trend, in terms of both the volume and the amount,

(b) the share of the economic exchange between and among the developing countries on one hand and between the developed and the developing countries, on the other hand show a diminishing trend, in monetary volume.

While the machineries, consumer products and the armaments constitute the main transaction items of the developed economies, oil and gas become the important items of exports of some developing economies. Most of the big developing economies like China, India, Indonesia, Brazil, Mexico, etc., do possess strong domestic economies and they, rather, have more intra-national economic interdepencies than the inter-national economic interdependencies.

5. Crisis in Global Interdependence Relationship

There has not yet appeared, both in the economic theory and practice, any ethical concept or correlationship of global economic interdependence. The contrast or contradiction in the practical approach between the developed and the developing economies is the contrast and contradiction of (i) profit for the entrepreneurs and (ii) benefits accrued for the masses, as result of the interdependency relationship. Such contrast between both the economies may be traced as such:

Developed Economies: *Developing Economies:*
Cost of Production   Cost of Exploration+Exploitation
and Profit   +Cultivations and Benefits for
                               the National Economy+Masses

The relationship between the two may shift from the relationship of plus and minus to that of equivalance.

See also: *Interdependence, International; Globalization; Global Integration; Economic Integration; World Economy, Social Change and Peace*

Bibliography ————————————————

Guha A 1978/79 Towards an alternative economic order. *The Korean Journal of International Studies* 10(1), KIIS, Seoul

Guha A 1983 The new international economic order: For the rich or for the poor nations? *Gandhi Marg* 5(2), New Delhi

Guha A 1989 Interacting and counteracting characteristics of the emerging international order. Mimeo, Institute for Alternative Development Research, Oslo

Guha A, Vivekananda F 1985 *Development Alternative.*

Bethany Books, Stockholm, Sweden

AMALENDU GUHA

Global Environment and Peace

The precipitant and preconditional determinants of peace are multiple. Ever since philosophers in antiquity first began to contemplate the sources of peace, they have progressively expanded awareness of its many roots, and identified an increasingly large number of factors that are potentially correlated with, and causes of, its preservation. As knowledge of the origins of peace has grown, so has recognition of the complexity and variety of its pillars, as well as the circumstantial and contextual foundations on which inherently fragile international peace are contingent.

In the rather elusive quest for greater understanding of viable paths to *lasting* peace, it is remarkable how recent has been consideration of environmental factors in peace theory. Indeed, it would not be hyperbole to assert that until the past quarter century the linkage between the global environment and peace was almost totally ignored. Although, to be sure, the pioneers in the creation of the formal study of environmental politics made a cogent case on behalf of the importance of ecological issues in the equation that accounts for global stability, nonetheless peace researchers and students of international politics generally did not pay heed to these arguments. Until the mid-1970s, the nexus between the global environment and peace was largely treated as exogenous—outside the explanatory frameworks that were evolving.

Before explaining why this characterization fortunately is no longer accurate, it is useful, as a preface, to comment on the primary reasons *why* attention to the relationship between environmentalism and international peace was so overlooked and delayed. Four primary influences may be identified which account for the failure to treat ecopolitics as a dimension of peace studies for so long a period.

First, since the advent of the Second World War, the field of world politics was dominated by the world view of realism. This paradigm approached the problem of war and peace by placing extraordinary emphasis on the distribution of military power, and changes in it, as the key element in international security. Neorealist or structural realist theories especially stressed that the shifting balance of power globally was decisive. As a consequence, realism and neorealism ignored or dismissed as unimportant the non-military underpinnings of global stability. The realpolitik school of thought in its variant constructions blocked from view the impact of environmental and ecological factors, and underestimated the capacity for the international community to manage conflict and promote change through collective cooperation.

Second, a state-centric perspective prevailed in the study of international affairs. This exaggerated the importance of national borders, and perpetuated the myth of national sovereignty and the state's autonomous independence. The result was a failure to conceptually recognize the interdependence of all humans in a shrinking planet and their dependence on a sustainable natural environment for survival.

Third, an environmental vision did not gain acceptance until the degradation of nature and its resources began to reach crisis proportions. Only after the dangers of resource depletion and scarcities became readily apparent, and concerns began to mount during the OPEC-induced oil crisis in the 1970s about the eruption of conflict and wars over access to and allocation of energy and other resources, did it become imperative to begin to treat the environmental threats to national and international security as a public policy issue on the global agenda. This attention accelerated with growing public awareness in the same period of many alarming environmental disturbances caused by the deterioration of the ozone, global warming, pollution and contamination of the global commons (see *Future of Humanity*). As environmental dangers became too severe to neglect, "environmentalism" and grassroots movements to limit the damage inflicted by humanity and technology on nature arose to challenge the orthodox approaches of realist and liberal theories of the bases of peace.

Fourth, the Cold War operated as an intellectual obstacle to investigation in peace studies of the relationship between the global environment and peace. That fifty-year hegemonic struggle had equated international security with nuclear deterrence, in order to prevent mass annihilation. While it lasted, the Cold War interfered with the effort of environmentalists to broaden the public's definition of security to enable global citizens to better appreciate the non-military threats to their preservation. It was not until the Cold War's abrupt termination in 1989 and the precedent-setting disarmament agreements (such as START) that followed in its wake, that the environmentalists' message began to fall on receptive ears. Liberated from the paralyzing grip that East-West confrontation and unrestrained arm races had exerted, the international community at last could begin to frame a conception of international "security" that returned it to its root psychological meaning—freedom from fear. It was then that ecopolitics began to be incorporated in conceptions of what peace fundamentally means. The accommodating reformulation built "peace of mind" into the definition by explicitly tying protection of the environment to the preservation of life, in order to take cognizance of humanity's need for confidence—a sense of security—about human destiny and the prospects for the planetary habitat's future. In this reconstruction, the inherently synonymous concepts of peace and environmental balance as common properties of harmonious interrelatedness were integrated in a way that paved the way for a broadened definition of peace.

1. "Environmental Peace": Paradigmatic Preliminaries

To capture the essential properties of the emergent ecological-peace perspective, some definitional caveats are in order. Environmentalism, like peace itself, is an elusive concept. It means different things to different people, and there is no clear consensus even among scholars and activists who associate themselves with the environmental peace movement as to the proper boundaries of the field, the questions to be asked, the methodological principles that should govern inquiry, or the most promising policy prescriptions to be pursued. Environmental peace is an incipient paradigm, still in search of agreement about approach and purpose. It has not yet cohered into a unified school of thought. Instead, debate about the very definition of the emerging field remains intense, with various internecine controversies exhibited about the ways the causes, characteristics and consequences of environmental problems and their relationship to underlying patterns of peace and war should best be studied.

Having said that, there nonetheless exist some common denominators that make ecological peace a distinct intellectual movement. Those working within its evolving confines embrace a common set of premises. Among them are the propositions that (a) the protection of the global environment is a critically important item on the global agenda; (b) the survival of the human species is contingent upon the

successful management of the diverse threats exacerbated by the population explosion, the depletion of non-renewable resources, the demise of the earth's carrying capacity, and the ecological disturbances caused by "growth" and "development"; (c) effective strategies necessitate accepting a holistic and transdisciplinary conception of the global ecological system that recognizes the symbiotic relationships that operate among the multiple biological, climactic, atmospheric, and economic and political processes and subsystems that collectively shape outcomes; (d) environmental degradation is a transnational problem that can only be addressed through multilateral channels, in an interdependent and integrated planetary ecosystem—unilateral national programs are destined to fail; (e) an effective response to the regulation of global environment problems necessitates the voluntary surrender of national sovereignty and the substitution for it of shared or "pooled" sovereignty; (f) because maintenance of the balance of the planetary habitat's constituent subsystems is necessitated to prevent ecological entropy, an ethic of collective responsibility is needed that is based on the conviction that a threat to the environment anywhere is a threat everywhere; (g) the coordinated management of the global commons requires a rejection of "free riding" and autarchy and a redefinition of global citizenship—there no longer can exist a contradiction between patriotism and concern for the entire world; (h) purely technological solutions to protect the environment are doomed to fail, and therefore supranational international institutions (such as the United Nations) and international regimes (such as the Rio Declaration on Environment and Development, Agenda 21, and the U.N. Framework Convention on Climate Change) need to be strengthened, with global acceptance of norms permitting the authoritative enforcement of regulatory rules; (i) the accelerating "globalization" of international relations exerts increased pressure for the involvement of subnational grassroots environmental protection movements, political parties such as the Greens, and non-governmental organizations (NGOs) to construct a worldwide strategy to meet the dangers, committed to and driven by a "think globally, act locally" philosophy; and (j) because historically peace has broken down whenever states have sought by imperialism and force to acquire from abroad resources unavailable at home, the just and equitable distribution of the earth's natural resources is indispensable to the preservation of world peace (see *Green Security*).

Corollary propositions within this paradigmatic movement include the beliefs that the world cannot have economic and military security without environmental security; no state can have a healthy economy in a polluted global commons because everyone is downwind or downstream from everybody; the world can control earth-degrading and earth-depleting manufacturing processes, products, and businesses into earth-sustaining ones by using economic incentives and penalties; anticipating and preventing problems is cheaper and more effective than reacting to and trying to cure them; and humanity's survival, life quality, and economics are totally dependent on the earth—earth can get along without people, but people cannot get along without the earth.

This crystallizing environmental peace paradigm or ideological *weltanschauung* has set the stage for the emergence of a new consensus about the relationship between environmental issues and peace. This ideology, still in the process of formation, has expanded public awareness of the linkage, and created incentives for rethinking the ways the global environment can be built into the mainstream of peace studies.

The incentives to create a reconstructed peace paradigm that links the environment to the human quest for peace are provided by the kinds of evidence that has accumulated in the past three decades about the magnitude of the planetary environmental problemmatique. Space technology has also enabled the world to see from afar uncomfortable images—of atmospheric poisons that encircle the globe; of massive holes in the ozone shield which protects humans from dangerous ultraviolet rays; of dwindling water supplies; of vanishing forests and widening deserts; of diminishing supplies of oil, coal, and other nonrenewable resources on which humankind depends for welfare.

Technology has made ecological dangers visible from afar, allowing the world to witness the earth as a living, breathing, unified whole, absent of political boundaries and borders. Ironically, however, technology has also contributed to the growing problem, because, as conventional wisdom has it, "whatever humankind makes unmakes humankind." It is a paradox that the very science and technology that have increased prosperity and peoples' average life spans has also contributed to humans' ability to overly exploit natural resources, so that depletion and degradation threaten to significantly reduce humans' capacity to meet their future needs.

Ecopolitics—the intersection of ecology with the politics of peace—has begun to gain a wide following in large measure because of the recurrent and refutable evidence that the global environment is under extraordinary stress. Many people are suffering from acute shortages of water, forests, and fertile land, and their safety has been put at risk. The globe's *carrying* capacity—the maximum population that the earth can support over a given period of time—is much in doubt, especially in light of projections that the earth's 6 billion inhabitants is likely to double in the twenty-first century.

Ecology deals with the interactions of living organisms with one another and with their nonliving environment and the impact of human activity on the environment. Politics is concerned with the exercise of power. Ecopolitics, then, centers on how political actors influence perceptions of, and responses to, their environments. Ecopolitics or the environmental preconditions for peace have become central to the effort to broaden prevailing conceptions of global security at both the national and global levels. The reasons stem from the growing recognition that national and international security—freedom from fear—means much more than escaping from the fear of a holocaust caused by the use of weapons of mass destruction. It also means freedom from the risk and danger of the degradation and destruction of the global environment.

2. The Two Faces of "Environmental Peace"

How best to think about the nexus between environmentalism and peace? Researchers are divided about the most useful means of broadening the picture of peace to accommodate threats to international security which do not entail the use of force. But most positions can be subsumed, dichotomously, under two basic but contradictory categories of contemporary theorizing.

The first "face" of contemporary approaches stresses global environmental threats as a *cause* of conflict. It sees the increasing magnitude of resource scarcities and environmental despoliation as trends likely to precipitate acts of aggression within and between states. Proponents arguing from this position take as their point of departure the propensity of environmental problems to produce friction and bloodshed, and conclude that in the absence of the meaningful management of the global ecology conflict over increasingly scarce resources will inevitably escalate to wars or, just as apocalyptically, to the destruction of the natural processes that sustain life. In short, the prompt development of an environmental peace perspective is seen as imperative as *the* next focal point in peace research, given the many ways ecological disruptions can and demonstrably do generate international conflict.

A second "face" of pre-theoretical effort also

springs from concerns about ecological dangers, but it draws a different conclusion. This perspective sees environmental problems less as a cause of conflict and more as a helpful *catalyst* to reconstruct a revised peace studies theory that brings ecopolitics into its discourse as a complement to previous and newer rival paradigms. In accordance with the adage that things must get worse before humanity becomes willing to mobilize efforts to make them better, ecological dangers are seen as motivating forces behind the contemporary global endeavor to engineer change through transnational cooperation: like the advent of nuclear weapons, ecological deterioration changes all the answers and all the questions, and makes necessary fresh thinking and new approaches. Unless the eco-system is preserved, the annihilation of the human species is possible, and without survivors only the dead will experience permanent peace. Thus, the irony of ecological dangers is that they are energizing the search for solutions, breeding, not conflict, but collaborative efforts to medicinally control the threats and, in so doing, avoid warfare.

Hence, peace studies exhibit paradoxical impulses, in response to the propensity for environmental problems to simultaneously create both conflict and cooperation. Environmental challenges as a consequence may be interpreted to be driving the theoretical discourse in a direction that must incorporate the issue-area in the explanatory equation, and distinguish the conflicts they threaten to foment from the opportunities for remedial responses through cooperation that those challenges are also fomenting. The dysfunctional and functional dual character of environmental dangers seem to be working hand in hand; both prompt peace studies to more systematically treat the policy, ethical, and political dimensions of these variables, and to intensify the attention given to strategies for protecting the global environmental order that can reduce the incentives for nations to wage war.

Observe that the current efforts to reconstruct the study of peace stimulated by these twin properties do not rest the entire theoretical reconstruction endeavor on the premise that environmental politics and peace can or should be studied in isolation from other more traditional approaches. True, most advocates call for putting ecopolitics on an equal footing with geopolitics and geoeconomics. But rare are those who recommend substituting the latter for the former. Most participants in the quest for a revised peace studies paradigm instead are seeking to find common ground between divergent approaches. A fusion or merger is needed, the logic of this argument concludes; trends in the global environment push for the conceptual

reformulation of peace studies, while not necessarily calling for the jettison of previous approaches to peace in favor of a new one in the absence of a convincing demonstration of the inferiority of the old ones and the superiority of a new ecopolitical paradigm. Most advocates of a redirection of peace studies thus recommend eclecticism in the search for a compelling model of the relationship of the global environment to peace.

3. The Ecology of Global Peace: Environmental Degradation and the Making of an Environmental Peace Paradigm

"Environmental peace" that seeks to push thinking beyond borders seems destined to rise as sub-paradigm in peace research. Focusing on the transboundary character of challenges to preserving the global environment, it operates from the belief that threats to global life systems such as global warming, stratospheric ozone depletion, the loss of agricultural land, tropical forests, marine habitats, biodiversity, endangered species, and the pollution of surface water and groundwater are just as important to the future of humankind as the threat of nuclear catastrophe. Environmental degradation challenges states by undercutting economic well-being and the quality of life all of them presumably seek for their citizens.

This emergent paradigmatic perspective, it should be noted, is less akin to the perspective of realists than to that of liberal theorists; the latter look not to the state but to international organizations and nongovernmental actors as vehicles of interstate cooperation to cope with environmental challenges. Because the efforts of proponents of ecological politics to redefine peace beyond its state-centric moorings challenge prevailing realist and conceptions of world politics (which remain highly popular), the recent theoretical reformulation enterprise is understandably controversial.

Global environmental issues also pose to peace researchers other controversies. Salient is the debate that engages the contending perspectives of "cornucopians" and "neo-Malthusians." Cornucopians believe that if free market economic principles are followed, the marketplace will right ecological imbalances that threaten humankind. For them, prices are the key adjustment mechanism by which the greatest good for the greatest number can be provided. Neo-Malthusians disagree vehemently with this interpretation. For them, an unrestrained laissez-faire marketplace has clearly failed to curtail the costs of excessive exploitation of both renewable and nonrenewable resources. The dominant conventional wisdom which maintain that the free market will always maximize social welfare, and that not only is an infinite supply of natural resources available but also adequate and safe sinks for disposing the wastes produced by the exploitation of those resources, are predicated on fantasies. To neo-Malthusians, it is unrealistic to assume that as long as technology is given free rein and prices are allowed to fluctuate freely to stimulate the search for substitutes, absolute scarcity can be postponed to the indefinite future.

The dominant cornucopian paradigm is now under harsh attack by environmentalists and other activists in many national political settings. It is also under attack internationally. *"Sustainability,"* a concept which enjoys widespread support among governments and a broad range of international nongovernmental organizations particularly active in shaping the global environmental agenda, is now perceived as an alternative to unlimited growth (see *Human Rights and Environmental Rights: Their Sustainable Development Compatibility*). Its heritage is traceable to *Our Common Future*, the 1987 report of the World Commission on Environment and Development popularly known as the Brundtland Commission after the Norwegian prime minister who chaired it. The commission concluded that the world cannot sustain the growth required to meet the needs and aspirations of the world's projected population unless it adopts radically different approaches to basic issues of economic expansion, equity, resource management, energy efficiency, and the like. Rejecting the "limits of growth" maxim popular among neo-Malthusians during the 1970s, it emphasized instead "the growth of limits." The commission defined a "sustainable society" as one that "meets the needs of the present without compromising the ability of future generations to meet their own needs."

The Brundtland Commission report is an important landmark in the rapid emergence of environmental issues as global concerns. The process began in earnest in 1972, when the UN General Assembly convened the first United Nations Conference on the Human Environment in Stockholm. Conferences have since been held on a wide range of environmental topics, with scores of environmental treaties negotiated and new international agencies put into place to promote cooperation and monitor environmental developments. Together they attest to the challenges to the dominant paradigms in peace research that have intensified during the past three decades.

A second milestone in the development of global environmental consciousness was the *Earth Summit*, which took place in Rio de Janeiro, Brazil, in 1992—the twentieth anniversary of the Stockholm conference on the environment. Formally known as the United Nations Conference on Environment and Development (UNCED), the meeting brought together more than 150 states, fourteen hundred nongovernmental organizations, and some eight thousand journalists. A program of action agreed on at Rio, *Agenda 21*, embodied a political commitment to a broad range of environmental and development goals. Prior to the Earth Summit, the environment and development had been treated separately—and were often regarded as in conflict with each other, as development frequently imperils and degrades the environment. But at this turning point, the concept of *sustainability* galvanized support for the simultaneous treatment of environmental and development issues. Recognition of the interrelatedness of global welfare issues continued at the 1994 Cairo International Conference on Population and Development (ICED), where population and development were also now placed on the same track.

Because sustainability means living off the earth's interest without encroaching on its capital, it had drawn attention to meeting the current needs of this generation without depriving future generations of the resources necessary for their own survival, and without generating the kinds of pressures that will lead to wars fought over scarce resources. Literally hundreds of books and articles have asked in one way or another how this ambitious goal can be achieved. A common thread throughout them is that sustainability cannot be realized without dramatic changes in the social, economic, and political fabric of the world as we now know it and without intervention to regulate the abuses inherent in laissez-faire anarchy.

Proponents of a reconstructed peace paradigm urge people to ask if that is possible. Are individuals willing to sacrifice personal welfare for the common good? Will they sacrifice now to enrich their heirs? The well-known *tragedy of commons* metaphor (the tendency for rational self-interested behavior by individuals to lead to the destruction for the collectivity of shared or common ecological systems) provides little basis for optimism, whether applied to individuals or states. Add to this the anarchical structure of international system—which discourages states from cooperating with one another out of fear that some will gain more than others—and the gravity of the situation becomes clear. While environmental issues and challenges often transcend national boundaries, at present they remain hostage to a global political system ill-equipped to manage environmental threats to global security. Even though some headway towards global environmental policies and treaties recently has been made, it must be acknowledged, however, that environmental diplomacy continues to move painfully slow—environmental treaties remain relatively weak and difficult to monitor, and substantial progress in supranational regulation is hard to observe.

In the political climate foreseeable on the horizon, we can grasp why traditional views of peace, which seek to deter the outbreak of wars, are likely to look increasingly anachronistic and are already beginning to be seriously questioned. In response, a departure from conventional approaches has begun. The environmental peace paradigm emerging rivets its attention on the environmental factors underlying potentially violent conflicts and the impact of global environmental deterioration on the well-being of societies and economies. Environmental degradation is now increasingly seen as a security issue in itself because it is a cause of violent conflict and because it speaks directly to the root definition of national security as tied to feelings of safety and survivability.

In pursuing the origins of fresh thinking about environmental peace, it would be mistaken to claim that this recently reconfigured cognizance of the relationship between environmental degradation and global peace is altogether unprecedented. As noted above, scholars and policy makers sounded the alarm in the early stages of the evidence that there has been serious degradation of natural resources (freshwater, soils, forests, fisheries, and biological diversity) and vital life-support systems (the ozone layer, climate system, oceans, and atmosphere). Nonetheless, the recent acceleration of global economic transactions and the ecological threats they have wrought have expanded awareness of the probability that these are likely to foment aggression between competitive states in the absence of international regulation to arrest the dangers (particularly in failing and fragmenting states experiencing chronic problems and massive flights of refugees because of environmental stress). The probability that these risks are likely to

further increase has raised the sense of alarm to a new level. If peace is to prevail, the international community will need to listen even more attentively to the voices issuing the warnings. The challenge for peace researchers will be to refine and develop an environmental peace paradigm that is couched in a vocabulary that will be heard throughout all quarters of the global environment.

See also: *Human Security; Eco-technology; Global Neighborhood: New Security Principles*

Bibliography ———————————————

Bissell R E 1996 The resource dimension of international conflict. In: C A Crocker, F O Hampson, P Aall (eds.) *Managing Global Chaos: Sources of and Responses to International Conflict*. United States Institute of Peace Press, Washington, DC

Choucri N (ed.) 1993 *Global Accord: Environmental Challenges and International Responses*. MIT Press, Cambridge, Mass

Gore A 1992 *Earth in the Balance: Ecology and the Human Spirit*. Houghton Mifflin, Boston

Homer-Dixon T F 1994 Environmental scarcities and violent conflict. *International Security* 19(1) (Summer)

Kegley C W 1995 *Controversies in International Relations Theory: Realism and the Neoliberal Challenge*. St. Martin's, New York

Porter G 1995 Environmental security as a national security issue. *Current History* 94(May)

Porter G, Brown J W 1996 *Global Environmental Politics*, 2nd edn. Westview, Boulder, Co

Suhrke A 1996 Environmental change, migration, and conflict: A lethal feedback dynamic? In: C A Crocker, F O Hampson, P Aall (eds.) *Managing Global Chaos: Sources of and Responses to International Conflict*. United States Institute of Peace Press, Washington, DC

Westing A H (ed.) 1986 *Global Resources and International Conflict: Environmental Factors in Strategic Policy and Action*. Oxford University Press, New York

CHARLES W. KEGLEY, JR.; GEOFFREY G. KEGLEY

Global Ethic

1. Basic Idea

A period of the world which has been shaped more than any before it by world politics, world economy, world technology, world communication, and world civilization needs a global ethic (Weltethos). That

means: a *fundamental consensus* concerning binding values, irrevocable standards, and personal attitudes. Without a basic consensus over ethics any small or large community is threatened sooner or later by disorder, chaos or even dictatorship—even so the world community. There can be no better global order without a global ethic. The conception and development of the idea of global ethic is based on the following basic principles:

(a) No peace among the nations without peace among the religions,

(b) No peace among the religions without a dialogue between the religions,

(c) No dialogue between the religions without basic research in religions.

With these basic principles the "Project Global Ethic" wants to express that the religions of the world can only contribute to peace of mankind if they reflect on those aspects of ethic which they already have in common, i.e., on a basic consensus of their values and norms which can be supported by believers and non-believers (see *Religion and Peace*).

2. Global Ethic and World Religions

Global ethic means neither a global ideology, nor a single unified global religion transcending all existing religions, nor a mixture of all religions. Humanity is weary of unified ideologies, and in any case the religions of the world are so different in their views of faith and "dogmas," their symbols and rites, that a "unification" of them would be meaningless, a distasteful syncretistic cocktail. Nor does a global ethic intend to replace the high ethics of the individual religions with an ethical minimalism. The Torah of the Jews, the Christians' Sermon on the Mount, the Muslims' Koran, the Hindus' Bhagavadgita, the Discourses of the Buddha, the Sayings of Confucius— for hundreds and millions of men and women all these remain the foundation for faith and life, thought and action.

A global ethic seeks to work out what is already common to the religions of the world now despite all their differences over human conduct, moral values and basic moral convictions. In other words: A global ethic does not reduce the religions to an ethical minimalism but represents the minimum of what the religions of the world already have in common now in the ethical sphere. It is not directed against anyone, but invites all, believers and non-believers, to make this ethic their own and act in accordance with it (see *Intercultural Relations and Peace*).

After two world wars and the end of the Cold War, the collapse of fascism and nazism and the shaking to

the foundations of communism and colonialism, humanity has entered a new phase of its history. Today mankind possesses sufficient economic, cultural, and spiritual resources to introduce a better global order. However old and new ethnic, national, social, economic, and religious tensions threaten the peaceful building of a better world. We have experienced greater scientific and technical progress than ever before; yet we see that world-wide poverty, hunger, death of children, unemployment, misery, and the destruction of nature have not diminished but rather have increased. Many peoples are threatened with economic ruin, social disarray, political marginalization, ecological catastrophe, and national collapse (see *Global Neighborhood: New Security Principles*).

In such a fundamental global crisis humanity does not only need political programs and actions. Humanity needs a *vision of peoples living peacefully together*, or ethnic and ethical groupings and of religions sharing responsibility for the care of Earth (see *Future of Humanity*). A vision rests on hopes, goals, ideals, standards. But all over the world these seem to have slipped from our hands. However, the religions in particular, despite their frequent abuses and historical failures, bear a responsibility to demonstrate that such hopes, aims, ideals, and standards can be guarded, grounded and lived.

The conception of global ethic is based on the idea that an ethic already exists which can counter those disastrous global developments. Of course this ethic provides no direct solution for all the immense problems of the world, but it does supply the moral foundation for a better individual and global order. There is already a consensus among the religions which can be the basis for a global ethic: a minimal *fundamental consensus* concerning binding values, irrevocable standards, and fundamental moral attitudes (see *Moral Development and Peace*). This basic consensus can be affirmed by all people, religious or non-religious.

This idea has been formulated, programmatically developed and presented to a wider public by *Hans Küng* in his book "Projekt Weltethos" in 1990 (Engl.: Global Responsibility 1991). All experiences with the problems of a global ethic, above all at an UNESCO symposium in Paris in 1989 with the topic "No world peace without peace among the religions" and furthermore at the World Economic Forum in Davos in 1990, had come together in this book, and in it the need for a global ethic in the context of the world religions and the world economy could be already discussed.

3. Declaration toward a Global Ethic

3.1 Structure and Hermeneutics

For the first time in the history of religions, the Council of the Parliament of the World's Religions, which met in Chicago from August 28 to September 4, 1993, and in which 6,500 people from every possible religion took part, ventured to work out and present a "Declaration Toward a Global Ethic." As was only to be expected, this declaration provoked vigorous discussion during the Parliament. However, the welcome thing is that at a time when so many religions are entangled in political conflicts, indeed in bloody wars, representatives of very different religions, great and small, endorsed this Declaration with their signatures on behalf of countless believers on this earth.

To clarify questions of hermeneutics and methods were important for style and content of the declaration on a global ethic. For the first steps toward a conception we were confronted with the following considerations: On the one hand, there were no historical models; for the first time in the history of the religions a declaration on an ethic was to be worked out which was to be acceptable to the adherents of all religions. But, on the other hand, for a long time the necessary intuition of the declaration as a whole was missing, the perspective form which it should be written and the kind of language it should use. For the declaration that was envisaged had to be all of a piece, with no dry paragraph work, no colourful bouquet of quotations, no academic discourse, no diplomatic communiqué, none of those compromise products which usually emerge from committee work. It was clear: though a declaration on a global ethic of course could not do without the "input" of a great many heads, it needed a concept and a program for developing the material. Finally as a result of them, in succession I gained three essential insights:

First, it was indispensable—against the background of today's world-horizon—to make a clear distinction between the ethical level and the purely legal or political level and at the same time to give a precise definition of the term "global ethic."

Second, the fundamental ethical demand on all men and women and all human societies or institutions should be a basic principle, which is theoretically evident, but practically not at all evident: "Every human being must be treated humanely." Every human being can easily describe what "in-human" is. However, it is not easy to describe in a positive way what "humane," "truly humane" is. Helpful is the "Golden Rule" which

can be demonstrated in all the great religions and ethic traditions: "Do not do to another what you would not want to be done to you."

Third, these fundamental demands can be made concrete in four ancient directives which can also be found in all the great religions: "Do not kill, do not steal, do not lie, do not commit sexual immorality."

So much the central pillars of the declaration on a global ethic have been already erected (see *Global Ethics, Human Rights Laws and Democratic Governance*). However, it is necessary to describe their content in more detail. First, some hermeneutical considerations must be outlined.

For a better understanding and for showing its relevance it is important to know what the declaration on a global ethic wants to be and can be and what it cannot be. The declaration is:

(a) *No reduplication of the Declaration of Human Rights*: If religions essentially only repeated statements from the UN Declaration of Human Rights, one could do without such a declaration; however, an ethic is more than rights. Certainly, a declaration on a global ethic should provide ethical support for the UN Declaration of Human Rights, which is so often ignored, violated and evaded. Treaties, laws, agreements are observed only if there is an underlying ethical will really to observe them (see *International Bill of Human Rights*).

(b) *No political declaration*: If religions made concrete statements on questions which were directly related to world politics or economics like the Middle Eäst conflict or the resolution of the debt crisis, the difference between the political and the ethical levels would not be observed and the declaration on a global ethic would immediately be drawn into the maelstrom of world-political discussions and confrontations; it would deepen the political dissent rather than bridge it. So no specific modern Western theory of the state or society can form the basis of such a declaration. Furthermore, the declaration on a global ethic is neither a casuistic moral sermon nor a philosophical treatise nor an enthusiastic religious proclamation.

Along with these negative demarcations came some positive pointers. In positive terms, what should a declaration on a global ethic contain? Programmatically, such a declaration must penetrate to a deeper *ethical level*, the level of *binding values irrevocable criteria* and *inner basic attitudes*—and not remain stuck at the legal level of laws, codified rights and paragraphs with which issue might be taken, but also not at the political level of proposing concrete political solutions Despite all its consequences for specific areas, an ethic is primarily concerned with the inner realm of a person, the forum internum, the sphere of the conscience, of the "heart," which is not directly exposed to sanctions that can be imposed by political power (the power of the state, the courts, the police). Briefly: The declaration on a global ethic must be capable of securing a *consensus, self-critical, related to reality*, and *generally comprehensible.*

Even if all men and women are to be addressed, including those who are not religious, it should be made plain that for religions, an ethic has a religious foundation. For those with a religious motivation, an ethic has to do with trust (quite rational trust) in an ultimate supreme reality, whatever name this may be given and no matter what the dispute over its nature may be among the different religions.

The declaration has the name "Declaration Toward a Global Ethic" (Welt-Ethos), not "Global Ethics" (Welt-Ethik). "Ethic" means a basic human moral attitude, whereas "ethics" denotes the philosophical or theological theory of moral attitudes, values and norms.

4. Contents of a Declaration on a Global Ethic

The declaration on a global ethic is convinced that all human beings have a responsibility for a better global order, that our involvement for the sake of human rights, freedom, justice, peace, and the preservation of Earth is absolutely necessary.

Our different religions and cultural traditions must not prevent our common involvement in opposing all forms of inhumanity and working for greater humaneness. The principles expressed in this global ethic can be affirmed by all persons with ethical convictions, whether religiously grounded or not.

The declaration on a global ethic recalls explicitly the 1948 Universal Declaration of Human Rights of the United Nations (see *Declaration of the Rights of Man*). What it formally proclaimed on the level of rights we wish to confirm and deepen here from the perspective of an ethic: the full realization of the intrinsic dignity of the human person, the inalienable freedom, the equality in principle of all humans and the necessary solidarity and interdependence of all humans with each other. On the basis of personal experiences and the burdensome history of our planet we have learned that a better global order cannot be created or enforced by laws, prescriptions, and conventions alone; that the realization of peace, justice, and the protection of earth depends on the insight and

readiness of men and women to act justly; that action in favour of rights and freedoms presumes a consciousness of responsibility and duty, and that therefore both the minds and hearts of women and men must be addressed; that the rights without morality cannot long endure, and that there will be no better global order without a global ethic.

It is a fundamental demand of the declaration toward a global ethic that every human being must be treated humanely. We all are fallible, imperfect men and women with limitations and defects. We know the reality of evil. Precisely because of this, we feel compelled for the sake of global welfare to express what the fundamental elements of a global ethic should be—for individuals as well as for communities and organizations, for states as well as for the religions themselves. We trust that our often millenia-old religious and ethical traditions provide enough elements of an ethic which is convincing and practical for all women and men of good will, religious and non-religious. At the same time we know that our various religions and ethical traditions often offer very different bases of what is helpful and what is unhelpful for men and women, what is right and what is wrong, what is good and what is evil. We do not wish to gloss over or ignore the serious differences among the individual religions. However, they should not hinder us from proclaiming publicly those things which religions already hold in common and which we jointly affirm, each on the basis of our own religious or ethical grounds.

Now as before, women and men are treated inhumanely all over the world. They are robbed of their opportunities and their freedom; their human rights are trampled underfoot; their dignity is disregarded. But might does not make right! In the face of all inhumanity our religious and ethical convictions demand: Every human being must be treated humanely! This means that every human being without distinction of age, sex, race, skin colour, physical or mental ability, language, religion, political view, or national or social origin possesses an inalienable and untouchable dignity. And everyone, the individual as well as the state, is therefore obliged to honour this dignity and protect it. In economics, politics and media, in research institutes, and industrial corporations—humans must always be the subjects of rights, must be ends, never mere means, never objects of commercialization and industrialization.

There is a *Golden Rule* which is found and has persisted in many religious and ethical traditions of humankind for thousands of years: *What you do not wish done to yourself, do not do to others!* Or in positive terms: *What you wish done to yourself, do to others!* This should be the irrevocable, unconditional norm for all areas of life, for families and communities, for races, nations and religions (see *Conflict Resolution, Process of*).

"Four Irrevocable Directives" arise from this basic principle:

First, commitment to a *culture of non-violence* and *respect for life.* This commitment is based on the directive: *You shall not kill!* Or in positive terms: *Have respect for life!* The consequences of this ancient directive are: All people have a right to life, safety, and the free development of personality in so far as they do not injure the rights of others. No one has the right physically or psychologically to torture, injure, much less kill, any other human being. And no people, no state, no race, no religion has the right to discriminate against, to "cleanse," to exile, much less to liquidate a "foreign" minority which is different in behavior or holds different beliefs.

Second, commitment to a culture of solidarity and a just economic order—based on the directive: *You shall not steal!* Or in positive terms: *Deal honestly and fairly!* The consequences of this ancient directive are: No one has the right to rob or dispossess in any way whatsoever any other person or the commonweal. Further, no one has the right to use her or his possessions without concern for the needs of society and Earth.

Third, commitment to a culture of tolerance and a life of truthfulness. Which is based on the directive: *You shall not lie!* Or in positive terms: *Speak and act truthfully!* The consequence of this directive is: No woman or man, no institution, no state or church or religious community has the right to speak lies to other humans.

Fourth, commitment to a culture of equal rights and partnership between men and women. This commitment is based on the directive: *You shall not commit sexual immorality!* Or in positive terms: *Respect and love one another!* The consequences that follow are: No one has the right to degrade others to mere sex objects, to lead them into or hold them in sexual dependency.

The declaration toward a global ethic closes with a fourth chapter with the headline: *transformation of consciousness.* It refers to the historical experience of mankind which demonstrates the following: Earth cannot be changed for the better unless we achieve a transformation in the consciousness of individuals and in public life. The possibilities for transformation have already been glimpsed in areas such as war and peace, economy or ecology, partnership between

men and women, where in recent decades fundamental changes have taken place. This transformation must also be achieved in the area of ethics. Every individual has intrinsic dignity and inalienable rights, and each also has an inescapable responsibility for what she or he does and does not do. All our decisions and deeds, even our omissions and failures, have consequences (see *Peace, Historical Views of*).

Keeping this sense of responsibility alive, deepening it and passing it on to future generations, is the special task of religions. We are realistic about what we have achieved in this consensus, and so we urge that the following be observed:

First, that the basic principles developed in the global ethic will give the chance and possibility to find the right answers and solutions on many disputed questions and problems (birth control, abortion, homosexuality, euthanasia, gene-technology etc.). However, we have to consider that a universal consensus on many disputed ethical questions (from bio- and sexual ethics through mass media and scientific ethics to economic and political ethics) will be difficult to attain.

Second, a new consciousness of ethical responsibility should be institutionalized. Therefore as many professions as possible, such as physicians, scientists, business people, journalists, and politicians should develop up-to-date codes of ethics which could provide specific guidelines for the vexing questions of these particular professions.

Third, above all, the various communities of faith are urged to formulate their very specific ethic: what does each faith tradition have to say, for example, about the meaning of life and death, the enduring of suffering and the forgiveness of guilt, about selfless sacrifice and the necessity of renunciation, about compassion and joy. These will deepen, and make more specific and concrete, the already discernible global ethic.

5. Consequence and Reception

The Declaration Toward a Global Ethic forms the basis for an extensive process of discussion and acceptance which has been sparked off in all religions. The men and women who signed the Declaration Toward a Global Ethic are aware that religions cannot solve the environmental, economic, political, and social problems of Earth. However, they can provide what obviously cannot be attained by economic plans, political programs or legal regulations alone: a change in the inner orientation, the whole mentality, the "hearts" of people, and a "conversion" from a false path to a new orientation for life. Humankind needs social and ecological reforms, but it needs spiritual renewal just as urgently. The Declaration Toward a Global Ethic is infused with the idea that the spiritual powers of the religions can offer a fundamental sense of trust, a ground of meaning, ultimate standards, and a spiritual home.

The Declaration Toward a Global Ethic is not an end but a beginning. That was clear from the start, and it was expressed clearly again at the end of the Parliament when this declaration was termed an "Initial Declaration Toward a Global Ethic." It is the hope that this document may set off a process which changes the behavior of men and women in the religions in the direction of understanding, respect and cooperation.

The idea of a global ethic has already received approval from all over the world and from all areas of public life. Numerous representatives of political, cultural, religious and scientific worlds have supported different statements of the "Global Ethic"; documented in the book "Ja zum Weltethos." Taken together these varied voices give impressive evidence that there is already a change in consciousness concerning global ethic. These voices and comments have this in common: Make sure that humankind can live together peacefully as community (in "multicultural" and "multireligious" cities) as well as on the global level; through world communication, world economy, world ecology and world politics consciousness of a common ethic for all people is more important than ever.

Not only individuals but world organizations now underline explicitly the necessity of a global ethic. As recent as 1990 when "Projekt Weltethos" was published there were no international documents that spoke of a global ethic. Certainly, there were already declarations concerning human rights—in a basic way the 1948 UN Declaration of Human Rights—but no comparable declarations on the responsibility of mankind. Since 1990 some important international documents not only support human rights but speak explicitly of human responsibilities; yes, they even call for a "global ethic" and they try to make it more concrete.

First, the UN issued the report of the *Commission on Global Governance*, titled "Our Global Neighbourhood." In its second chapter this report refers to the question of "Values of Neighbourhood in the One World." Considering the increasing strains in all areas of neighbourhood it calls for an *Ethic of Neighbourhood*" (see *Global Peace and Global Accountability*).

Secondly, the UN and UNESCO published the report of the *World Commission on Culture and Develop-*

ment, titled: "Our Creative Diversity." It contains a first chapter on "global ethic" which underlines common ground instead of the differences of humankind.

Third, the *Interaction Council* of former Presidents of States and Prime Ministers, chaired by Helmut Schmidt, published the "*Universal Declaration of Human Responsibilities*." The declaration was supported by a group of experts and officially presented for adoption to the United Nations on September 1, 1997. This document, "Declaration of Human Responsibilities" was intended to complement and to strengthen the 1948 "Universal Declaration of Human Rights," to underline the equal importance of rights and responsibilities, and to bring freedom and responsibility into balance.

6. Perspectives

The "Global Ethic" expresses the hope that there are enough people on earth who believe in change and in the power of religions to influence the hearts of many toward the good.

Can religions be expected to accept such a declaration? Are such hopes realistic or an illusion? We would say to skeptics and pessimists: No one will deny that within the space of two or three decades it has been proved possible to bring about worldwide universal change in awareness about economics and ecology, about world peace and disarmament, and about the partnership between men and women. The Declaration Toward a Global Ethic was written and has been approved in the hope that such a change in awareness may take place in a basic ethic, common to humankind, that is, a global ethic. It is up to the religions of this earth and to people all over the world in a quite practical way, wherever they are, to make sure that this Declaration remains more than paper, that it is filled with life, that it inspires people to a life of mutual respect, understanding and cooperation.

Success depends on the international community itself—by its organ, the United Nations, to fill the gap (desideratum) which was expressed in the debate on human rights during the French Revolution: to add to the already established Universal Declaration of Human Rights ("les droits de l'homme"), a Universal Declaration of Human Responsibilities ("les devoirs de l'homme")—as suggested by Interaction Council—and to do everything possible to transform this declaration into the consciousness of mankind.

7. Stiftung Weltethos (Foundation "Global Ethic")

The "Stiftung Weltethos" was founded in 1995 thanks

to *Graf K.K. von der Groeben* who was encouraged and motivated by the book *"Projekt Weltethos"* (Engl.: "Global Responsibility"). According to the founder the Foundation "Global Ethic" should "demonstrate to the people that there are more satisfying values than material pleasure and that it should be a delight to work for a higher goal. We must free ourselves from 'self-fulfilment' and from thinking only of affluence and make clear to people that we need high ethical norms to achieve commonality in peace and freedom." The investments of this foundation make the work of Hans Küng possible who leads a small research team. This support makes a long-term perspective on global ethic possible.

The foundation will support other initiatives and projects with the same goal and purpose of the foundation. The programmatic basis of the work of the foundation is the "Declaration Toward a Global Ethic" of the Parliament of the World's Religions.

The three central purposes of the foundation are: realization and support of intercultural and interreligious research; encouragement and realization of intercultural and inter-religious education; support of intercultural and inter-religious meetings, necessary for research work and education.

See also: *Emergence of Global Community and the Establishment of New Global Ethics; From Morality to Ethic: Toward an Ideal Community; Toward a New Global Ethic*

Bibliography ───────────────

Küng H 1990 *Projekt Weltethos*. München [engl.: Global Responsibility. 1991 In Search of a New World Ethic. London]

Küng H, Kuschel K J (eds.) 1993 *Erklärung zum Weltethos*. Die Deklaration des Parlamentes der Weltreligionen, München

Küng H 1991 *Das Judentum*. München

Küng H 1994 *Das Christentum*. Wesen und Geschichte, München

Küng H *Der Islam* (in preparation)

Küng H, Kuschel K J (eds.) 1993 *Weltfrieden durch Religionsfrienden*. Antowrten aus den Weltreligionen, München

Küng H (ed.) 1995 *Ja zum Weltethos*. Perspektiven für die Suche nach Orientierung, München

Kuschel K J 1994 *Streit um Abraham. Was Juden, Christen und Muslime trennt—und was sie eint*. München

Kuschel K J (ed.) *Weltethos und Wissenschaften*. Beiträge aus Philosophie und Theologie, Wirtschafts-, Sozial- und Kulturwissenschaften (in preparation)

Lähnemann J (ed.) 1994 "Das Projekt Weltethos" in der Erziehung. Referate und Ergebnisse des Nürnberger Forums 1995 Hamburg

Rehn J (ed.) 1994 Verantwortlich leben in der Weltgemeinschaft. Zur Auseinandersetzung um das "Projekt Weltethos." Gütersloh

A Draft of a Universal Declaration of Human Responsibilities, proposed by the Interaction Council, September 1, 1997 (manuscript)

HANS KÜNG

Global Ethics, Human Rights Laws and Democratic Governance

In an era extolling the values of diversity, pluralism and multiculturalism, there is a tendency for cultural relativism to become the principal source of moral guidance (see *Cultural Roots of Peace*). Thus, notwithstanding a steadily shrinking globe—economically, politically and socially—it is still not very fashionable to consider issues pertaining to universal or global ethics. Some of these issues are as old as recorded civilization; others are new and urgent, plaguing those witnessing the end of the 20th century and the dawn of the 21st century. The massive atrocities and fatalities of World Wars I and II and over 150 regional wars since 1945, not to mention the Holocaust and the ongoing genocidal war in Bosnia-Herzegovina, Rwanda and elsewhere, underscore the urgent need for a consensually-validated and effective global ethics (see *Global Ethic*).

1. Ancient and Modern Principles

Scholars as diverse as theologians, philosophers, and political scientists have sought to articulate universal standards of morality. In ancient times we have the proclamation of two well-known universal standards: the Decalogue and the Golden Rule (see *Peace in the Ancient World; Peace in the Middle Ages*). In modern times we have Kant's categorical imperative (see *Kant, Immanuel*).

1.1 Decalogue

The Decalogue or Ten Commandments, although traditionally traced to Moses and first appeared in the Old Testament (Exodus and Deuteronomy), have been incorporated in Christian catechetical practices and worship (see *Christianity*). In Islam, they are less prominent but are implied in much of Muhammad's teachings. The Ten Commandments may be grouped as follows:

(a) Commandments 1-3: God's self-identification, prohibition against the worship of other gods, idolatry and misuse of the divine name,

(b) Commandments 4-5: Positive commandments to observe the Sabbath and to honor parents,

(c) Commandments 6-7: Prohibition of killing and adultery,

(d) Commandments 8-10: Prohibition of stealing, testifying falsely and hankering after life and goods of neighbors.

Leaving aside the theological concerns of Commandments 1-3, Commandments 4-10 enunciate transcultural obligations and morals, which have had an enormous impact on the lives of people in many societies. They have been the focus of moral and religious education—the substance of moral socialization efforts in many societies (see *Religion and Peace*). In addition, some of these commandments have been incorporated in the criminal laws of many countries. By institutionalizing or reinstitutionalizing these moral principles, with the aid of the legal system, the socialization process is strengthened and the level of compliance is thereby increased (Bohannan 1968; Evan 1990). That all socialization efforts, in all societies, fail to some degree to achieve their normative objectives, is an idea Durkheim first advanced in his work, *The Rules of Sociological Method*.

It is noteworthy that Commandment 4, observing the Sabbath, has been a source of secular concern to organized labor for well over a century. In Western capitalist countries, trade unions have struggled for a five-day week and were instrumental in persuading the International Labor Organization to incorporate this practice in their international labor standards. In the absence of an organized labor movement, this Commandment is still honored in the breach in many countries around the world.

Commandment 6, thou shalt not kill, deserves special attention in view of the recurrence of wars and the high rate of homicides. Instead of interpreting this commandment literally, several religions have taken the liberty of interpreting it liberally, developing various "just war" theories. Huston Smith, the comparative religion scholar, tellingly observes:

> In the realm of *ethics*, the Decalogue pretty much tells the cross-cultural story. We should avoid mur-

der, thieving, lying and adultery. These are minimum guidelines . . . but they are not nothing, as we reflect on how much better the world would be if they were universally honored (Smith 1991 p. 387).

1.2 Golden Rule

A principle of great antiquity, the golden rule is a component of the moral teachings of many cultures and religions (Donagan 1977 pp. 57-60). "Every religion has some version of the Golden Rule" (Smith 1991 p. 385). It can be traced back to Confucius, the Talmud and the New Testament (St. Matthew and St. Luke) (see *Peace According to the New Testament*). In positive form, this principle is commonly formulated as "Do unto others as you would have others do unto you"; in the negative form it is, "Do not do unto others what you would not have others do unto you." Some philosophers have criticized this principle on the ground that it does not provide a precise guide to action; others have objected that it could require people to act irrationally (Singer 1992 p. 406). Notwithstanding these and other criticisms, this moral principle has the virtue of generality and universality.

1.3 Categorical Imperative

Of all modern philosophers, I shall single out Kant because of the striking universality of his ethical theory. The keystone of his theory of ethics is the principle of the categorical imperative which, as it happens, has been linked to the Golden Rule (Hirst 1934). Moral principles for Kant are principles of duty that are universalizable. One version of the categorical imperative is as follows: "Act only on the maxim through which you can at the same time will that it be a universal law" (Singer 1991 p. 177). Another version of the categorical imperative relates to the ethics of means and ends. "So act as to treat humanity, whether in their own person or in that of another, in any case as an end withal, never as a means only" (Hirst 1934 p. 330). This ethical formula derives from Kant's view of the individual as an end "in himself," a conception with profound implications for interpersonal relations, human rights laws, and democratic governance.

2. Three Recent Formulations of Global Ethics

The problem of developing a theory of global ethics has not been confined to the work of professional philosophers. In recent years the work of non-philosophers in this area has been more provocative than that of ethicists. I shall single out three recent contributions: (a) the work of an international legal scholar, Richard Falk, 2) a declaration by a group of theologians and 3) Podgórecki's theory.

(a) *World Order Models Project*. Immersed in the international legal tradition of Hugo Grotius and keenly aware that international law is in need of a basic restructuring to meet the challenge of the nuclear age, Richard Falk embarked on a collaborative research inquiry called the "World Order Models Project" (Falk 1975) (see *Grotius, Hugo*). The task of this project was to analyze several alternative systems of international order on the assumption that the world would eventually survive the superpower nuclear confrontation. Falk identified five alternative world order systems: 1) a Westphalian nation-state system, 2) a concert of great powers, 3) a concert of multinational corporations, 4) a world government, and 5) a humane world community. Falk and his colleagues (Kothari 1974; Johansen 1980), reject alternatives 1-4 and accept alternative 5, a humane world community because it alone has a high profile on four global humanistic values: peace, economic well being, social justice and ecological balance. Falk expresses these four central values in terms of potential variables in the following manner: (1) the minimization of large-scale collective violence; (2) the maximization of social and economic well-being; (3) the realization of fundamental human rights and conditions of political justice; and (4) the rehabilitation and maintenance of environmental quality, including the conservation of resources. (Falk 1975 p. 11).

These four World Order Model Project values deserve to be considered candidates for a theory of global ethics (see *World Order Models Projects (WOMP)*).

(b) *A Declaration by a Group of Theologians*. The Parliament for the World's Religions, held in Chicago in September 1993, was a centennial conference to succeed the previous convocation held in September 1893. Approximately 6,000 individuals from around the world every major and minor religious group were in attendance. A variety of sessions and workshops were organized, some under the auspices of the Assembly of Religious and Spiritual Leaders. One of the tasks of this assembly was to review a statement entitled "A Global Ethic," prepared by The Rev. Dr. Küng (Council for a Parliament of the World's Religions). After some deliberation, the assembly changed the title of the document to "Towards a Global Ethic, an Initial Declaration," indicating that it is but one step in an ongoing search for the creation of a multi-religious consensus on principles and issues to be included in a global ethic.

Among the principles enunciated in this document are the following:

2.1 No New Global Order without a New Global Ethic

Our different religious and cultural traditions must not prevent our common involvement in opposing all forms of inhumanity and working for greater humaneness.

The principles expressed in this Global Ethic can be affirmed by all persons with ethical convictions, whether religiously grounded or not (p. 3).

2.2 A Fundamental Demand: Every Human Being Must be Treated Humanely

This means that every human being without distinction of age, sex, race, skin color, physical or mental ability, language, religion, political view, or national or social origin possesses an inalienable and untouchable dignity. And everyone, the individual as well as the state, is therefore obliged to honor this dignity and protect it. Humans must always be the subjects of rights, must be ends, never mere means, never objects of commercialization and industrialization in economics, politics and media, in research institutes, and industrial corporations (p. 4).

There is a principle which is found and has persisted in many religious and ethical traditions of humankind for thousands of years: *What you do not wish done to yourself, do not do to others!* This should be the irrevocable unconditional norm for all areas of life, for families and communities, for races, nations, and religions (p. 5).

3. Irrevocable Directives

3.1 Commitment to a Culture of Non-violence and Respect for Life

In the great ancient religious and ethical traditions of humankind we find the directive: You shall not kill! Or in positive terms: Have respect for life! Let us reflect anew on the consequences of this ancient directive: All people have a right to life, safety, and the free development of personality insofar as they do not injure the rights of others. No one has the right physically or psychically to torture, injure, much less kill, another human being. And no people, no state, no race, no religion has the right to hate, to discriminate against, to "cleanse," to exile much less to liquidate a "foreign" minority which is different in behavior or holds different beliefs (p. 5) (see *Nonviolence*).

3.2 Commitment to a Culture of Solidarity and a Just Economic Order

In the great ancient religious and ethical traditions of humankind we find the directives: *You shall not steal!* Or in positive terms: *Deal honestly and fairly!* Let us reflect anew on the consequences of this ancient directive: No one has the right to rob or dispossess in any way whatsoever any other person or the common weal. Further, no one has the right to use her or his possessions without concern for the needs of society and Earth (p. 6) (see *Global Environment and Peace*).

3.3 Commitment to a Culture of Tolerance and a Life of Truthfulness

In the great ancient religious and ethical traditions of humankind we find the directive: *You shall not lie!* Or in positive terms: *Speak and act truthfully!* Let us reflect anew on the consequences of this ancient directive: No woman or man, no institution, no state or church or religious community has the right to speak lies to other humans (p. 7).

3.4 Commitment to a Culture of Equal Rights and Partnership Between Men and Women

In the great ancient religious and ethical traditions of humankind we find the directive: *You shall not commit sexual immorality!* Or in positive terms: *Respect and love one another!* Let us reflect anew on the consequences of this ancient directive: No one has the right to degrade others to mere sex objects, to lead them into or hold them in sexual dependency.

We condemn sexual exploitation and sexual discrimination as one of the worst forms of human degradation. We have the duty to resist wherever the domination of one sex over the other is preached-even in the name of religious conviction; wherever sexual exploitation is tolerated, wherever prostitution is fostered or children are misused. Let no one be deceived: There is no authentic humaneness without a living together in partnership (p. 8).

4. A Transformation of Consciousness

Historical experience demonstrates the following: Earth cannot be changed for the better unless we achieve a transformation in the consciousness of individuals and in public life. The possibilities for transformation have already been glimpsed in areas such as war and peace, economy, and ecology, where in recent decades fundamental changes have taken place. This transformation must also be achieved in the area of ethics and values! . . . .

> Therefore we commit ourselves to a common global ethic, to better mutual understanding, as well as to socially beneficial peace-fostering, and Earth-friendly ways of life (p. 9).

It is noteworthy that this declaration of ethical principles draws upon one or another of the principles of the Decalogue, the golden rule, Kant's categorical imperative and the four central values of the World Order Models Project. To the extent that these overlaps occur, it points to some consensual elements of an emerging global ethic.

4.1 Podgórecki's Theory

A sociologist, steeped in law and philosophy and a man of letters, to boot, Podgórecki has had a long-standing concern with problems of ethics. In one of his formulations, Podgórecki takes as his point of departure the concept of neighbor or fellow creature. He posits three stages of development or "moral styles of life": individually-oriented ethics, socially-oriented ethics, and global ethics (see *Moral Development and Peace*).

By individually-oriented ethics, Podgórecki refers to a set of norms regulating behavior in small groups. "Generally speaking, individual ethics condemn thieves, murderers, forgers, people who commit adultery, people who give false evidence and so on. Thus we can say that generally—if we accept the point of view of individually-oriented ethics—we condemn people who harm other people in the narrow scope of the relationships between them in 'face-to-face' situations" (Podgórecki and Loś 1979 p. 321).

For this reason, Podgórecki thinks that the ethics of the Decalogue protects interactions in small groups. In large groups and organizations requiring the performance of institutionalized roles, relationships between people tend to become impersonal and reified, generating anomie and alienation. This situation is conducive to the emergence of socially-oriented ethics.

Given the diversity of social and political systems with divergent organizations and institutions (see *Intercultural Relations and Peace Studies*), there is a need for a set of transcending moral standards, which Podgórecki refers to as "global ethics." This ethical orientation involves enlarging the concept of neighbor as well as the scope of responsibility to encompass *all* living creatures. In his multi-volume portrait of a Chinese thinker, he calls Si-tien, Podgórecki sums up his theory of global ethics with the following five propositions:

(a) "All living creatures should unite,"

(b) Global ethics indicates that the higher someone's position on the planet, the larger the scope of responsibilities attached to his position,

(c) Those who belong to the category of human beings have a duty to be reliable sponsors for all other living creatures,

(d) All living creatures are responsible for the whole environment and universe (including the most remote galaxies) which they share,

(e) Global ethics clearly show that certain ideologies or religious beliefs are outdated, having been formulated when the problem of global destruction was not recognized as the potential result of accumulated individual actions. According to global ethics a human being is not the "lord of other living creatures" but a cohabitant on the same planet. Human beings have a double responsibility because of their ability to diagnose the present and forecast the process of decomposition and destruction. (Podgórecki 1994 pp. 77-79)

Podgórecki's theory appears to be inspired by the ethical teachings of Buddhism, which prohibits acts of violence against all fellow human beings as well as all fellow creatures (see *Buddhism*). The antidote to violence and hostility, according to Buddha, are four sublime states that can be cultivated through meditation: loving kindness, compassion, sympathy and even-mindedness (McFarlane 1986 p. 98). Clearly, Podgórecki's theory of global ethics, although compatible with the ethical presuppositions of the World Order Models Project and the Declaration of the Parliament for the World's Religions, is more global and demanding than either of them. All three theories, however, have direct implications for a legal system of human rights and a political system of democratic governance, both of which I shall now consider.

4.2 From Ethical Injunctions to Human Rights Laws

All global ethical theories, explicitly or implicitly, support the proposition that all human beings, *qua* human beings, have rights which should be respected. But they are ambiguous as to which human rights merit respect and how they shall be protected. Protect-

ing rights is clearly the province of law; and making a transition from the realm of ethical prescription to law is a complicated process, involving a process of reinstitutionalization (Gorecki 1987; Bohannan 1968).

With the founding of the United Nations in 1945, there was a great impetus to develop an "international bill of rights" (Henkin 1981 p. ix) (see *International Bill of Human Rights*). The task of drawing up the first instrument to protect human rights was assumed by the Human Rights Commission, a subordinate component of the Economic and Social Council of the United Nations. After three years of successive drafts and numerous controversies the Human Rights Commission produced the Universal Declaration of Human Rights (see *Declaration of the Rights of Man*), which the General Assembly adopted in 1948 as "a common standard of achievement for all peoples and all nations" (United Nations 1980 p. 9).

The 30 articles comprising this historic document are a blend of philosophical and legal norms of an individual and collective character. Articles 1-3 are statements of ideals: right to life, liberty, equality, and security of persons. Articles 4-27 set forth civil and political rights for everyone, such as freedom from slavery and servitude, freedom from torture, right to an effective judicial remedy, freedom of movement, right to asylum, and so on. Article 22 introduces Articles 23-27 pertaining to economic, social, and cultural rights, viz., entitlements as a "member of society," such as the right to work, right to rest and leisure, right to education, etc. The concluding Articles 28-30 underscore that everyone is entitled to an international and social order in which all human rights can be fully realized.

Although the Universal Declaration of Human Rights is not legally binding of the member states of the United Nations, its impact—legal, moral, and symbolic—has been extensive (Humphrey 1979; United Nations 1980) (see *Human Rights and Peace*). The resolutions of the General Assembly, the treaties of regional communities, the constitutions of many nation-states, and the decisions of the International Court of Justice, all reflect the influence of the Universal Declaration of Human Rights. In addition, and of considerable import, it paved the way for the drafting of two legally-binding covenants: the International Covenant of Civil and Political Rights and the International Covenant of Economic, Social, and Cultural Rights.

These two controversial covenants, along with the Optional Protocol to the Covenant on Civil and Political Rights—permitting individual citizens whose rights have been violated to send a written communication to the Human Rights Committee—were submitted to a vote in the General Assembly in 1966. Although adopted by the General Assembly in 1966, it took 10 years before the requisite number of ratifications brought them into force.

While these human rights laws were being fashioned, other significant multilateral treaties in the field of human rights were being created, notably, the Genocide Convention, the Convention on the Elimination of all Forms of Racial Discrimination, the Convention on the Political Rights of Women, the European Convention on Human Rights, etc. (Bilder 1978). Clearly, the process of universalizing human rights norms has been a continuous challenge from the time of the founding of the United Nations to the present.

Of considerable potential impact on the evolution of human rights is the Declaration adopted by the World Conference on Human Rights convened in Vienna in 1993 (United Nations 1993). One of its basic propositions is that

> All human rights are universal, indivisible and interdependent and interrelated. The international community must treat human rights globally in a fair and equal manner, on the same footing, and with the same emphasis. While the significance of national and regional particularities and various historical, cultural and religious backgrounds must be borne in mind, it is the duty of States, regardless of their political, economic and cultural systems, to promote and protect all human rights and fundamental freedoms. (United Nations 1993 p. 30)

This proposition was tellingly reinforced by a prefatory statement by UN Secretary General Boutros Boutros-Ghali:

> "... human rights constitute the common language of humanity. Adopting this language allows all peoples to understand others and to be the authors of their own history." (United Nations 1993 p. 8)

In order to strengthen the United Nations' monitoring capacity of compliance with human rights laws, the Declaration recommends that the General Assembly establish a United Nations High Commissioner for Human Rights and provide additional resources for the Centre for Human Rights. In addition, the Declaration urges the speedy ratification of various human rights standards, e.g., Convention on the Rights of the Child, Convention against Torture and Other Cruel, Inhuman or Degrading Treatment or Punishment, and Convention on the Elimination of all forms of Discrimination against Women.

Notwithstanding these important provisions of the Vienna Declaration, political opposition to such

noble legal norms is bound to arise in a world comprised of sovereign states—jealous of their sovereignty and struggling to maintain themselves in power against threats from within as well as from without.

The barriers to implementing human rights laws pose a serious dilemma for international law (see *International Law*). If a sovereign state chooses to violate a legally binding norm pertaining to human rights, ostensibly in order to protect and promote its self-interest, what recourse is there within the community of sovereign states, as it is presently constituted, to bring pressure on the transgressor? The answer, clearly, is relatively little. Apart from moral suasion, trade sanctions can be imposed and resolutions deploring the action of the transgressor can be passed. These sanctions, however, are likely to have limited effectiveness. Given the transcendent principle of national sovereignty, no effective system of enforcement is likely to emerge. Short of transforming the present international system in the direction of a transnational or a supranational system of world order, the problem appears to be insoluble (Evan 1962; Kothari 1974; Falk 1975). To promote the transformation of the international system, international nongovernmental organizations, especially but not exclusively in the field of human rights, can perform a salutary function (Evan 1981; Scoble and Wiseberg 1981). Apart from publicizing human rights violations, international nongovernmental organizations such as Amnesty International can develop knowledge-based proposals for institutional innovations. As regards human rights violations, a creative proposal, for example, advanced by a number of scholars and groups as long ago as 1954, deals with the establishment of an international court of criminal justice (Gross 1973; Murphy 1974; Woetzel 1974) (see *International Criminal Law*).

Yet another strategy to counter the tendency of nation-states—in the name of sovereignty—to violate human rights is political in nature. As the Vienna Declaration makes plain, democracy and democratization are functional prerequisites for the implementation of human rights laws.

4.3 Democratic Governance

The Vienna Declaration posits a link between democracy, economic development and human rights. "The international community should support the strengthening and promoting of democracy, development and respect for human rights and fundamental freedoms in the entire world" (United Nations 1933 p. 31). In his introductory statement to the Vienna Declaration, Secretary General Boutros Boutros-Ghali underscores this crucial relationship: "Only democracy, within States and within the community of States, can truly guarantee human rights .... The process of democratization cannot be separated, in my view, from the protection of human rights (see *Democratization, An Agenda for*). More precisely, democracy is the political framework in which human rights can best be safeguarded" (United Nations 1933 p. 10, 17).

Of the 180 member states of the United Nations only a small fraction are democracies, largely in Western Europe, North and South America, and parts of Asia (Lijphart 1994). Among the developing countries, we are witnessing an ongoing process of democratization accompanied by an increasing incidence of ethnic conflicts which, of course, involve systematic violation of human rights. Democratizing countries have a choice of a majoritarian electoral system and a proportional representational system or a consensus form of democracy (Lijphart 1994). To protect the rights of ethnic minorities, new democracies would be well advised to opt for a system of proportional representation. However, this institutional choice may prove ineffective in countries plagued by long-standing and embittered ethnic conflicts that have given rise to secessionist movements, as in the case of the Tamils in Sri Lanka and the Kurds in Turkey. To stem the violence associated with secessionist movements such countries may have to consider a confederal democratic solution on the model of Switzerland.

New democracies, if they are to be accorded legitimacy by their own citizens as well as by the international community, will have to acknowledge what the international legal scholar, Thomas French, refers to as "the emerging right to democratic governance" (French 1992). French claims that since the middle of the 1980s we are witnessing the evolution of an international rule system that defines the minimal requisites of a democratic process capable of legitimating the exercise of power by national governments as well as by the international community. The evolution of a normative entitlement to democracy in international law has occurred in three phases: "First came the normative entitlement to self-determination. Then came the normative entitlement to free expression as a human right. Now we see the emergence of a normative entitlement to a participatory electoral process" (French 1992 p. 90). Older democracies, says French, should volunteer to be monitored concerning their compliance with democratic norms and thus facilitate the establishment of an inter-

national monitoring service. Eventually, all other nations will acknowledge it as their duty to avail themselves of the monitoring service (see *Global Peace and Global Accountability*).

If French's assessment about the recent evolution of international law is correct, it bodes well for the eventual emergence of a global ethic and for the eventual implementation of human rights laws.

4.4 Towards a Multi-Disciplinary Theory of Global Ethics

In this brief discussion of three broad and complex issues—global ethics, human rights and democratic governance—I have necessarily touched on many ideas. Is there any way to integrate these ideas? I shall seek to do this by setting forth, albeit in skeletal form—a multi-disciplinary theory of global ethics (See Table 1)[*]. Judging from the observations by Ferrari and Velicogna (1993), Treves would find this effort intellectually congenial, for in his last published essay he considers human rights as "instruments of protection of the individual from state power" (Ferrari and Velicogna 1993 p. 213).

In Table 1, I have listed five disciplines from which I seek to identify concepts and correlative propositions for an integrative theory of global ethics. I do not wish to imply that this is an inclusive listing of disciplines. Upon further reflection, other disciplines, such as psychology and anthropology, might be added. Nor do I wish to imply that the concepts and propositions derived from each discipline are exhaustive. They are clearly illustrative only. But the five disciplines selected will serve my purpose in sketching an integrative theory of global ethics.

From theology, I select the concept of duty, which has a religious foundation although it can be interpreted in a secular manner as well. The Decalogue, as the corresponding propositions, are in fact secular in nature, except for the first three commandments. The other concepts I have derived from theology is empathy and compassion, for without these concepts, it is not evident how the interpersonal proposition of the golden rule can be formulated.

The field of philosophy is obviously an immensely broad area of inquiry. Taking a Kantian perspective, I posit the concept of individual autonomy which, in turn, relates to the two formulations of Kant's categorical imperative discussed in the text.

Sociology has concerned itself with the evolution of citizenship rights (Marshall 1950) of a political, economic and social nature. For several decades there has been some further analysis of this concept

Table 1

Towards a multi-disciplinary theory of global ethics

Discipline	Core Concepts	Propositions
Theology	Duties	Decalogue
	Empathy/Compassion	Golden Rule
Philosophy	Individual Autonomy	Categorical Imperative
Sociology	Citizenship Rights	Univesal Citizenship Status
Political Science	Legitimacy of State	Democratic Governance
International Law	Human Rights	Universal Declaration of Human Rights
		International Covenant of Civil and Political Rights
		International Covenant of Economic, Social and Cultural Rights
		Vienna Declaration Adopted by the World Conference on Human Rights Rule of Law

within and beyond the boundaries of the nation-state (Bendix 1964; Pranger 1968; Turner 1986). As the international community becomes increasingly institutionalized, there is a growing need for a new status, viz., universal citizenship, which would complement national citizenship (Dahrendorf 1994; Falk 1994; van Steenbergen 1994). In other words, all human beings would have two statuses: national and international.

As regards political science, one may posit legitimacy of the state as a fundamental concept. If the source of legitimacy of a state is derived from the governed, it paves the way for a system of democratic governance based on such normative entitlements as free expression and a participatory electoral process.

Finally, public international law consists of a large body of customary and statutory concepts. I have selected human rights as especially crucial for a thesis of global ethics. Correlative propositions are those embodied in the International Bill of Rights, viz., the Universal Declaration of Human Rights, the International Covenant of Civil and Political Rights, the International Covenant of Economic, Social and Cultural Rights and some of the salient propositions enunciated in the Vienna Declaration adopted by the World Conference on Human Rights. Underlying all of these propositions is the overarching constitutional principle of rule of law.

Admittedly, this integrative theory of global ethics is incomplete and preliminary in nature. For one thing, I have not addressed a crucial question of the logical and substantive linkages among the propositions derived from the five disciplines. For example, if one were to begin with the Golden Rule, as a basic proposition, would not the Decalogue and Categorical Imperative follow logically? Likewise, given a system of democratic governance, human rights such

as those institutionalized through the United Nations would seem to be corollaries and merit adoption and implementation. In addition, a system of democratic governance would be compatible with the establishment of a rule of law in the international community which, in turn, would eventually encourage the adoption of universal citizenship status (see *World Citizenship*).

Underlying this cluster of propositions is an implicit theory of normative universalism which rejects the theory of cultural relativism. Associated with a theory of universalism is a theory of natural law (see *Natural Rights*). A secular theory of natural law, based on the needs and values of individuals, has been advanced by philosophers as a justification for human rights since the eighteenth century (Evan 1990; Beyleveld and Brownsword 1986).

Clearly, the principal purpose of the multi-disciplinary theory of global ethics presented in this paper is to stimulate other scholars to extend, modify and improve the structure of a theory of global ethics.

See also: *World Peace Order, Dimensions of a*

Bibliography —————————

Bendix R 1964 *Nation-Building and Citizenship.* University of California Press, Berkeley, Calif

Beyleveld D, Brownsword R 1986 *Law as Moral Judgement.* Sweet and Maxwell Ltd, London

Bilder R B 1978 The Status of International Human Rights Law: An Overview. In: J C Tuttle (ed.) *International Human Rights: Law and Practice.* American Bar Association, Philadelphia

Bohannan P 1968 Law and legal institutions. In: *International Encyclopedia of the Social Sciences*, Vol. 9. Macmillan, Free Press, New York

Council for a Parliament of the World's Religions 1993 *A Global Ethic*. Parliament of the World's Religions, Chicago

Dahrendorf R 1994 The changing quality of citizenship. In: B van Steenbergen (ed.) *The Condition of Citizenship*. Sage Publications, London

Donagan A 1977 *The Theory of Morality*. University Press, Chicago

Evan W M 1962 Transnational Forums for Peace. In: Q Wright, W M Evan, M Deutsch (eds.) *Preventing World War III*. Simon and Shuster, New York

Evan W M (ed.) 1981 *Knowledge and Power in a Global Society*. Beverly Hills, Sage Publications, CA

Evan W M 1990 *Social Structure and Law*. Sage Publications, Newbury Park, CA

Falk R A 1975 *A Study of Future Worlds*. Free Press, New York

Falk R A 1994 Making of Global Citizenship. In: B van Steenbergen (ed.) *The Condition of Citizenship*. Sage Publications, London

Ferrari V, Velicogna N G 1993 Philosophy and Sociology of Law in the Work of Renato Treves. *Ratio Juris* 6

French T M 1992 The Emerging Right to Democratic Governance. *Am. J. Int'l Law* 86

Gorecki J 1987 Human Rights: Explaining the Power of a Moral and Legal Idea. *Am. J.* 32

Gross L 1973 International Terrorism and International Criminal Jurisdiction. *Am. J. Int'l Law* 67

Henkin L 1981 Preface and introduction. In: L Henkin (ed.) *The International Bill of Rights*, IX-31. Columbia University Press, New York

Hirst E W 1934 The categorical imperative and the golden Rule. *Philosophy* 9

Humphrey J P 1979 The Universal Declaration of Human Rights: Its history, impact and judicial character. In: B G Ramcharan (ed.) *Human Rights: Thirty Years after the Universal Declaration*. Martinus Nijhoff, The Hague

Kothari R 1974 *Footsteps into the Future*. Free Press, New York

Johansen R C 1980 *The National Interest and the Human Interest*. Princeton University Press, Princeton, NJ

Lijphart A 1994 Democracies: Forms, performance and constitutional engineering. *European J. Political Res.* 25

Marshall T H 1950 *Citizenship and Social Class*. Cambridge University Press, Cambridge

McFarlane S 1986 Buddhism. *World Encyclopedia of Peace*, Vol. 1. Pergamon Press, New York

Murphy J F 1974 Professor Gross' comments on international criminal jurisdiction. *Am. J. Int'l Law* 68

Podgórecki A, Loś M 1979 *Multi-dimensional Sociology*. Routledge and Kegan Paul, London

Podgórecki A 1993 *The Trivia of Si-Tien and Si-Tien: The Unknown Chinese Thinker*. Carleton University, Ottawa

Pranger R J 1968 *The Eclipse of Citizenship, Power and Participation in Contemporary Politics*. Holt, Rinehart & Winston, New York

Reath A 1989 The Categorical Imperative and Kant's Concept of Practical Rationality. *The Monist* 72

Scoble H M, L S Wiseberg 1981 Problems and Comparative Research on Human Rights. In: V P Nanda, J R Scarritt, G W Shepherd Jr. (eds.) *Global Human Rights: Public Policies. Comparative Measures and NGO Strategies*. Western Press, Boulder, CO

Singer P (ed.) 1991 *A Companion to Ethics*. Basil Blackwell, Cambridge, MA

Singer M G 1992 Golden Rule. In: L C Becker, C B Becker (eds.) *Encyclopedia of Ethics*. Garland Publishing, Inc., New York

Smith H 1991 *The World's Religions*, rev. edn. Harper San Francisco, A Division of Harper Collins Publisher, New York

Steenbergen B van (ed.) 1994 Towards a Global Ecological Citizen. In: B van Steenbergen (ed.) *The Condition of Citizenship*. Sage Publications, London

United Nations 1980 *United Nation Action in the Field of Human Rights*. United Nations, New York

United Nations 1993 *World Conference of Human Rights: The Vienna Declaration and Programme of Action*. June 1993. United Nations, New York

Woetzel R K 1974 Professor John F. Murphy's letter on Professor Gross' comments on international terrorism and international criminal jurisdiction. *Am. J. Int'l Law* 68

WILLIAM M. EVAN

Global Familism

Global familism is a concept which promotes a new belief that all human beings on earth are members of a global family. Regardless of race, color, religion, and sex, human beings are equal partners jointly responsible for the prosperity and peace of the world. Each individual is equal in dignity and importance. Human beings, as individuals and as a group, are more valuable than any political, economic, social, or religious organization. Operationally, global familism means institutional reformation and philosophical evolution. "Institutional reformation" proposes political relativism, gradual military disarmament, global economic and educational integration, and cultural entropy through supranational cooperation. "Philosophical evolution" advocates that global identity and "humancentrism" be adopted as a global norm and that humankind repel the logical and moral fallacy that a group of human beings may kill other groups in order to save their own lives.

On this ever-shrinking planet, under the nuclear threat of genocide, many concerned intellectuals have expressed the view that the exclusive norms of the present political, social, and economic order, such as nationalism and regionalism, must be replaced with a new norm strengthening global coexistence, global cooperation, global coprosperity, and lasting global peace. The World Order Models Project that has been promoted largely by Saul Mendlovitz (1975) is the most visible advocacy of such a goal (see *World Order Models Project (WOMP)*). Richard Falk's conception of reform of the present world political system into a monistic world government constitutes a particular challenge to concerned intellectuals. The planetary government proposed by Donald Keys is also a notable effort toward world unity as are the concepts of a "global society" presented by Choue (1981). Other research projects include the "world citizenship" project of the Center for the Reconstruction of Human Society, in the Republic of Korea (Choue 1975) and the work of the International Association of University Presidents.

No less notable than these efforts is the Russell-Einstein Manifesto of July 1955 (see *Einstein, Albert* for text of manifesto). In an appeal to scientists for prevention of nuclear war, the signatories spoke "not as members of this or that nation, continent, or creed, but as human beings, members of the species Man . . . ." They go further: "We appeal, as human beings, to human beings: remember your humanity and forget the rest. If you can do so, the way lies open to a new Paradise: if you cannot, there lies before you the risk of universal death." This humane appeal to human beings as natural beings, and not as national citizens compartmentalized by territorial borders, has a latent implication for freeing human beings from nationalism. For lasting world peace and human prosperity, national citizens must be transformed into planetary citizens. In view of this essential requirement, Lester R. Brown (1972) has proposed a world without borders. A world without borders, in turn, dictates global familism, a sense and feeling that all the human beings on earth are brothers and sisters and are in the same boat.

In the age of "Sci-Tech" (science and technology), the revolutionary advancement of science and technology has converted the world into a small global village whose villagers are multiple interdependent in terms of culture, economy, politics, behavioral psychology, and even fashion. Peoples of different nationality, race, color, religion, and social status all watch or listen to the same news and events through a television set or a radio. Through this simultaneous exposure to the same world news and cultural artifacts, they develop identical emotions and feelings. They laugh together and mourn together over the same news and stories at the same time. The US intervention in the Vietnam War sparked off an antiwar public opinion around the world. The apartheid policy of South Africa has caused worldwide protests by human rights groups. The shooting down of a Korea Air passenger aircraft by Soviet interceptor aircraft incited the anger of the world. An American TV series, "The Rich and The Poor," has attracted the attention of and impressed many people throughout the world. The decision of the headquarters of a multinational corporation in an industrialized country, let us say the United States, France, or Japan, affects the economy of all those nations housing its branch offices. The political chaos in oil-producing nations creates energy crises in many oil-importing countries such as the Germany and Japan. During the political revolts against the Pahlevi kingdom in Iran, for example, the United States was planning to ration gasoline.

As the present author has pointed out elsewhere (Yoo 1980):

> Satellite communications, rapid air and maritime transportation systems, ever increasing volume of international trade, mushrooming international associations and international organizations, growing multinational corporations, international public opinion, globalizing travel and tourism, and even migrations have made enormous contributions to making the world a global village. Furthermore, biogeographical and ecological limitations have taken part in this new trend.

In this age of the global village, nationalism and regionalism can no longer be a guiding norm. Even internationalism does not provide us with a satisfactory philosophical and behavioral basis of truly global coexistence, cooperation, coprosperity, and peace. Nationalism is a politico-cultural ideology pertinent to the post-feudal and pre-nuclear age. In the post-industrial era, when all the nations of the world are multiple interdependent, it must make way for a political principle of global dimensions (i.e., global familism) in tune with the global configurations of interest and power relations. The cult of the nation and exclusive patriotism to the nation, which is now constituted as a political and militaristic Leviathan, poses the biggest ideological obstacle to the establishment of a global society and world peace. Various conflicts between and among nations over border questions, over relative political influences, over ideological issues, and over racial antagonism and oppression still create tensions threatening the outbreak of nuclear war.

Nationalism was born with a noble sentiment to embody attachment to a cause wider than that of oneself or one's family, to embody the pride of the cultural and political achievements of one's own nation, and to embody one's love for the eufunctional plot of earth on which one was born. Paradoxically, however, the noble sentiment has been over-ridden by patriotic scoundrels and by expansive jingoism.

The first paradox is a moral one. Nationalism, in its revised form, has become a dogma demanding an absolute, exclusive devotion to one's nation at the sacrifice and ignorance of individuals and other countries. It refuses to recognize the common bond of humanity, the individual's rights and freedom. It has been corrupted into an "antithesis to the Christian concept of the brotherhood of all men." Every nationalist lives the principle: "My country first, right or wrong."

The second paradox is a political one. The rise of nationalism was based upon humanity's earnest search for the individual liberties and self-government characteristic of the development of England in the seventeenth century and of the United States in the late eighteenth century. It was also closely linked with the decline of older religious, tribal, clannish, or feudal loyalties. The ideologies of the French Revolution, the Frankfurt Parliament of 1848, Mazzini, and Woodrow Wilson, among others, provided nationalism with the libertarian impulses and moral fervor which supported all nations that wanted to be free and to establish a state of their own. However, libertarian nationalism was rapidly harnessed to the purposes of power and fashioned to the political and military tools of victory by the likes of Napoleon, Cavour, Bismarck, and Clemenceau. This transformation of nationalism has created a large potential for two types of international conflict: hostilities between a nationality and an alien master, and confrontations between nations over the delimitation of their respective boundaries.

A third paradox is modern nationalism's exclusive and ethnocentric world view. After the First World War whole populations have been systematically indoctrinated with the tenets that all human beings owe their first and last duty to their nationality, that nationality is the ideal unit of political organization and of the actual embodiment of cultural distinction, and that all other human loyalties must be subordinate to the nation-state, that is, to national patriotism.

A nation-state, through patriotic education, the national army, and the mass media, inculcates in its citizens the fantasy that they are a world by themselves, that they are the only chosen people for the promised land, and that they have to build up the pride of national glory even at the expense of sacrifice of others.

The fourth paradox of nationalism is its warring mentality. Modern nationalism focuses popular attention upon war and preparedness for war. To achieve national liberation, nationalists had to fight against colonial masters. After independence they had to fight against other power contenders to secure political legitimacy. In the process of nation building they were forced to fight territorial or ideological wars against their neighboring countries. The Second World War and the Cold War following it magnified this paradox both qualitatively and quantitatively. Almost all nation-states of the world are spending large portions of their governmental budgets on the accumulation of weapons. Iran, Saudi Arabia, Israel, Egypt, and the People's Republic of China, among others, are purchasing weapons in large quantity. In Indochina and in Ethiopia, Angola, and many other African countries careful preparations are being made for or against wars. This warring mentality argues against the original ideals of nationalism.

Practically, what we need for enduring world peace and global cooperation is more than simple mitigation of nationalism as Carlton J. H. Hayes (1926, 1960) once advocated. A whole new outlook on the future of humankind has to be brought in to guide national behaviors and intellectual activism. This new outlook should be more than internationalism or cosmopolitanism. It must be global familism which is inclusive of internationalism and cosmopolitanism. Ancient philosophers and eighteenth century rationalists understood cosmopolitanism as a decrying of local and national distinctions and of patriotism: the individual or the social class would be the essential unit of its world-state, and not the nationality or the nation-state. Internationalism recognizes a primary loyalty of the individual to his or her nation and observance of his or her national language and cultural traditions; politically it aims to build the world with national groups. In the technetronic age, to quote Zbigniew Brzezinski, and in the post-industrial society, to refer to Daniel Bell, neither internationalism nor cosmopolitanism is sufficient to develop and promote fully the new outlook of humankind and of the world. Global familism, what we may call true globalism, can provide a better solution to our problems.

See also: *Federalism, World; Global Integration; Interdependence, International; Nationalism; Transnationalism; World Order; World Order Models Project*

Bibliography

Braunthal J 1946 *The Paradox of Nationalism*. St Botolph publishing, London
Brown L R 1972 *World Without Borders*. Vintage Books, New York
Choue Y S 1975 *Reconstruction of Human Society*. Kyung Hee University Press, Seoul
Choue Y S 1981 *Oughtopia*. Pergamon, New York
Hayes C J H 1926 *Essays on Nationalism*. Macmillan, New York
Hayes C J H 1960 *Nationalism: A Religion*. Macmillan, New York
Mendlovitz S H 1975 *On the Creation of a Just World Order*. Free Press, New York
Pauling L 1983 *No More War*. Dodd, Mead and Co, New York
Yoo J Y 1976 The open society: Toward a humanistic world federation. *Unified World* 1
Yoo J Y 1980 Global familism. *Phil. Forum* 16

JONG YOUL YOO

Global Integration

Global integration is the process whereby the world is gradually developing into a single economic and financial, communications, social, cultural, and political unit. Seen in that way global integration has a large number of different aspects, which may all contribute to the same end: a more united and peaceful world. But although such part-integration processes are a precondition of global peace, durable peace is not a necessary consequence of such processes. Global integration requires indeed the growth of different kinds of interdependencies across national boundaries on a worldwide scale, but such interdependencies may as well lead to conflict in themselves, and even to violence, as to more peaceful conduct (see *Interdependence, International*). In fact, when interdependencies grow, the chances for conflict grow too. States can be interdependent as enemies and as friends. Global integration therefore must also imply a pacification process, the development of institutions and procedures which can guarantee the peaceful settlement of conflicts at the world level (see *Pacific Settlement of International Disputes*).

If the pacification function is then regarded as essential to integration processes, these can be defined in a more analytical manner as the formation of increasingly large—in terms of territory and population—attack and defense units out of previously existing smaller units. Global integration then is the process whereby functional equivalents to the central monopoly of violence of the state—and other monopoly functions—develop at the world level. Globalization processes my help the development of such functional equivalents, for example, in the monetary field. They may also include states which are dependent on global financial and economic network to take more account of each other and thus prevent serious conflicts between them.

This perspective thus implies a definition. Global integration is seen as the development toward a more durably peaceful world, a world order, whereas the different kinds of increasing interdependencies on a world scale will be called processes of globalization. There is no necessary sequence from globalization processes to global integration, but the former are a precondition for the latter.

In order to better understand the process of integration at the world level, it is necessary to first examine the previous phase and level of the integration process: the formation of nation-states. What precisely is the difference between states and other forms of social organization, such as business corporations, trade unions, political parties, local communities, universities, and so on? As soon as a further question is asked, that is, why banks or trade unions usually do not maintain private armies to fight other banks or to wage the class struggle, the difference becomes clear. If such organizations did so, the police—and when needed the army—would intervene and the responsible leaders at least would be sent to prison. Banks or trade unions usually have no need to resort to violence, because in most states there are institutional means available—courts and bargaining procedures—to settle their conflicts.

States are thus distinguished from other kinds of social organization in the sense that their institutions effectively claim the monopoly of the legally recognized right to use violence and physical coercion to maintain the peace (law and order) and to enforce their rules and decrees within their boundaries, whereas nobody else within their territory is allowed to use violence or threaten to use it (see *State, Theory of the*). Peace within the state is the peace of the state. And similarly peace in the world must be the peace of a world state or of a functional equivalent to it.

States are survival units for which the control of

the use of violence within, and the preparation for the use of violence toward other such units is crucial. That is the reason why states, as is true of all other survival or attack and defense units, are the units which people refer to as the society or the social whole. Despite processes of globalization, the world is not yet perceived by the vast majority of people as the social whole. States and specifically nation-states still are the primary units of "we-identification."

Contemporary nation-states are the latest phase in a long line of survival units, such as bands of hunter-gatherers; nomadic bands or clans; sedentary or nomadic tribes; fortified villages or towns (cities); military-bureaucratic empires; feudal-warrior units, large and small; dynastic states and others. The primary function of such units or "integrations" is to protect its members against attacks from other such units that is, from conquest, domination, or plunder, or to prepare themselves for similar activities. Defense and attack functions can therefore not be separated from each other, except in the case of the smallest and weakest units.

In earlier phases networks of survival units in different parts of the world, say China, Africa, the Americas, or Europe, existed quite separately from each other. Now there is indeed only one such network that covers the world as a whole: a world of states. Both the size of survival units and the geographic scope of their reach and interests have grown continually.

In the development of survival units the pacification of larger and larger territories goes together with an increasingly specialized organization of the potential use of violence against other such units. This process, however, has not always been continuous. Empires were formed in the past by military conquest but their size often made it impossible to control transport, taxation, administration, and military techniques from their center. They could therefore not be kept together for very long. Only the Chinese empire survived for more than 20 centuries, though it too had its periods of disintegration. Charlemagne did not succeed in durably reviving the Roman Empire: his realm disintegrated after his death. The feudal period itself was the outcome of disintegration processes: centrifugal forces became stronger . . . centripetal forces. Vassal became autonomous lords. These processes clarify the nature of the relationship between integration processes and the growth of interdependencies. In order for larger units of integration to develop, a certain minimum level of interdependencies is required at each stage.

Only because of the expansion of trade and trans-port, the rise of towns, the birth of a money economy, and the development of military techniques (gunpowder), did durable control over larger territories become possible in the late Middle Ages. This can be seen in retrospect, but it was not the driving force as such behind the formation of dynastic states. Nobody planned or willed the development of states; it was the outcome of coercive rivalry, of Fichte's simple rule that those who do not become stronger when others do, in fact become weaker. Territorial states ruled by dynastic monarchs thus emerged from centuries of armed struggles between feudal houses. In competitive processes there is always a strong tendency toward the monopolization of power.

State formation as the process of the monopolization of the means of violence in the hands of a single ruler or dynasty has been a violent elimination struggle. In 1500, Western Europe was still made up of about 500 independent political entities, whereas in 1900 no more than 20 remained. Colonial empires also forcefully integrated previously autonomous tribal peoples into the larger units that became independent states. Neither the former Soviet Union nor Yugoslavia was able to withstand the centrifugal forces that emerged together with the erosion of communism. Long before, monarchs and princes were able to expand and intensify their control over the territories which they ruled, only because of the continuation of rivalry on the higher level of integration between states. To maintain a standing army requires a sufficient money supply. And that in turn requires an increasingly elaborate and permanent organization of tax collection. Thus the two basic central monopolies of states, the monopolies of control over the means of violence and taxation, had to develop in interplay. They each formed a necessary condition for the development of the other. Durable taxation monopolies could only be consolidated during long periods of war, such as the Hundred Years' War (1339-1453) between the territorial units which roughly became present-day France and Britain.

Only after the large territories that became the states as we now know them were pacified by royal forces of order, could the marked distinction develop between domestic peace and interstate war and between domestic politics and foreign policy. The world of states became the next level of the global integration process. Modern international politics developed as the continuation on a higher level of integration of the competition between feudal lords and other forms of survival units.

States soon became aware of the fact that if they only pursued their narrow immediate interests without regard for the development of the larger whole of which they formed a part, they would hurt themselves. On that basis, so-called balance of power policies could develop (see *Balance of Power*). Prince Metternich, for example, wrote in the early nineteenth century:

> What characterizes the modern world and distinguishes it from the ancient is the tendency of states to draw near each other and to form the kind of social body based on the same principle as human society.

These balance of power policies led to the Concert of Europe, which, in turn, gave rise to the League of Nations (see *League of Nations*) and later to the United Nations (see *United Nations: Achievements and Agenda*). Also, from the end of the nineteenth century onwards, a number of the more specialized functions of regulating and coordinating international transactions and communications have been entrusted to functionally specific international organizations. The more technical these functions are—postal, telegraph, health—the more smooth these organizations can work. The more they touch on vital interests of states, the more difficult, if not impossible their regulation through international organization becomes. There the absence of a monopoly of violence at the international level still conditions the perspectives and conduct of states.

However, some functional equivalents to the monopoly functions of the state developed in the guise of Great Powers. When the Dutch claimed the *mare liberum* as their legal back-up to fighting the Portuguese and Spanish trade monopolies and succeeded, it was the beginning of unhampered long-distance trade for the members of all states, even though some were able to use the new opportunities better than others. When England maintained the principle of freedom of the seas and used its navy not only for establishing its own overseas power but also for eliminating piracy and the "Pax Britannica," this further secured free long-distance trade among nations. These monopoly functions then are quite similar to those of dynastic monarchs which pacified their own, more limited territories and created the conditions for the emergence of national economies. In the same way, a global economy could only develop in the wake of the British navy. The great seapowers pacified the transport and trade routes that linked the continents. On that basis a world economy—admittedly centered on Europe and unevenly developing—could emerge. It could not have developed but for the monopoly functions of the Great Powers. The pacification of the seas and the development of

maritime law were important preconditions for it. Later especially the monetary functions of Great Powers has been crucial. The gold standard can be seen as the first substitute (or functional equivalent) of an international standard currency. Without such a standard currency international trade can rapidly break down, as was the case after the Great Crash of 1929.

A global balance of power also gradually developed, dependent on but not determined by the development of a global economy. In the seventeenth century, Britain still had two foreign secretaries, one for the Northern balance of power and one for the central European balance. These two balances were at that time still relatively autonomous from each other; relatively, because the fact that Britain was interested in both shows that the two balances became interconnected. An overarching European power balance developed only gradually with the expanding size and composition of trade and financial exchange networks, with the improvement of means of transport, in sum with the increasing interdependencies between all parts of Europe and the world at large at the same time. But latent changes in the degree of interconnectedness of the power relations in Europe only became manifest after Napoleon's attempts to make France into the hegemonic power on the European Continent. After his final defeat in 1815, the idea of the Concert of Europe marked the development toward the higher level of integration of one, single European power balance. That did not exclude local balances (for example within Germany until 1866, or in the Balkans) but these then became part of a hierarchy rather than separate balances in their own right as before. At the same time a similar integration process occurred at the world level. Before the expansion of Western Europe autonomous power balances existed in different parts of the world. The great wars leading to the unification of China in the period of the Warring States, from the fifth to the second century BC, remained completely unaffected by the rivalries of Greek states at the same time and vice versa. But through conquest and pacification the European powers gradually eliminated nearly all autonomous power balances in other parts of the world. That was a precondition for the globalization of Great Power rivalry and the emergence of one overarching global power balance.

The great seapowers—Portugal, the United Provinces of the Netherlands, Great Britain, and the United States—were the principal intermediaries between Europeanization and globalization of Great Power rivalry. Especially England and later the United States held the balance in Europe and could thereby expand their global influence, whether by acquiring colonies, economic dominance, or political and military bases. That Great Power rivalry which began to extend outside Europe was first demonstrated by the support of France for the American War of Independence. An even more significant harbinger of globalization was the war between Russia and Japan in 1905, the more so because Russia lost. Its victory was not only a further spur to Japan's ambitions, but it also stimulated other nationalist movements in the Asian colonies.

How strongly interconnected the world had become manifest during the Great War between 1914 and 1918, which has gone into history as the First World War. The entry of the United States into the war indeed marked the end of European self-reliance: European Great Powers could no longer settle the conflict and make peace by themselves. But though it had worldwide repercussions, the First World War was still primarily a European conflict: it had its origins in Europe and the principal theater of the war was still in Europe. But in the meantime Japan became an aspiring Great Power. And though the Second World War again began in Europe, Japan's attack on Pearl Harbor opened a second theater of war in Asia, so that it developed into the first really global war. Japan's rising industrial and military power had unintentionally drawn the world together in a similar way as the rise of Prussia had integrated Europe in the eighteenth century.

The first global war meant the end of the Eurocentric world. Great power rivalry had become globalized. With the exception of the former Soviet Union as a successor state of the Russian Empire, no European state remained a Great Power any longer. After 1945 only the United States and the former Soviet Union could stay in the race. The European powers had eliminated themselves from Great Power competition by the two world wars. After 1945 Great Power rivalry became global and will remain so, if it will return again—after the peaceful ending of the hegemonic rivalry between the former Soviet Union and the United States. That has shown quite clearly that great nuclear powers cannot even allow a serious crisis between them. Great power rivalry has become subject to strong limitations.

Is there now a possibility that global integration will move to a next level, given the intensified globalization processes and the dampening influence of nuclear research? Great wars—global wars—have become excluded. Wars between states have became infrequent—the last one was the attack of Iraq on Kuwait—but wars within states have increased.

The leading states in the UN and other international organization appear to more and more see it their duty, at least to relieve humanitarian problems. The debate about the universality of human rights is also implicitly a debate about global integration. But they also represent the resistance against globalizing processes of nationalist and fundamentalist movements. Whether globalization processes will lead to a next phase of global integration is still uncertain (see *Globalization*).

See also: *Federalism, World; Integration Theories; World Order; New World Order and New State-Nations*

Bibliography

Bartlett C J 1984 *The Global Conflict 1880-1970: The International Rivalry of the Great Powers.* Longman, London

Claude I L 1964 *Swords into Ploughshares: The Problems and Progress of International Organization*, 3rd edn. Random House, New York

Cohen B J 1977 *Organising the World's Money: The Political Economy of International Relations.* Macmillan, London

Elias N 1982 *The Civilizing Process*, Vol. 2: *State Formation and Civilization.* Basil Blackwell, Oxford

Haas E B 1964 *Beyond the Nation-State.* Stanford University Press, Stanford, California

Hinsley F H 1963 *Power and the Pursuit of Peace, Theory and Practice in the Relations between States.* Cambridge University Press, Cambridge

McNeill W 1963 *The Rise of the West: A History of the Human Community.* University of Chicago Press, Chicago, Illinois

Mandelbaum M 1981 *The Nuclear Revolution.* Cambridge University Press, Cambridge

Tilly C (ed.) 1975 *The Formation of National States in Western Europe.* Princeton University Press, Princeton, New Jersey

de Vree J K 1972 *Political Integration: The Formation of Theory and its Problems.* Nijhoff, The Hague

Wallerstein I 1980 *The Modern World System*, Vol. 2: *Mercantilism and the Consolidation of the European World Economy 1600-1750.* Academic Press, New York

G. VAN BENTHEM VAN DEN BERGH

Global Models, Computerized

A model is a simplified, generalized image of a perceived reality created to serve a specified purpose. Three common types are mental models, physical models, and mathematical models. With the advent of the computer, modeling has gained a powerful tool which permits great elaboration of mathematical models.

Computerized global modeling is computer modeling done to investigate social questions or problems of global scale (Meadows et al., 1982 pp 7, 13). Modeling of global problems is hardly new. Lewis F. Richardson's (see *Richardson, Lewis Fry*) mathematical theory of war was developed over a period of some 34 years, from 1919 to 1953 (Rapoport 1957). Today the term global modeling usually refers to work begun by Jay Forrester (1971) at the Massachusetts Institute of Technology (MIT). With a background in electrical engineering, Forrester saw the potential of that discipline's system dynamics in applications far beyond those of his field. In 1961 he published *Industrial Dynamics*, a study of a firm using system dynamics. This was followed by *Urban Dynamics* and finally a global system dynamics model in *World Dynamics* (1971). Forrester's guiding principle was that

> All systems that change through time can be represented by using only levels and rates. The two kinds of variables are necessary but at the same time sufficient for representing any system. (Forrester 1971 p. 18)

In his global model, Forrester used five "levels:" population, pollution, natural resources, capital investment, and fraction of capital devoted to agriculture. A typical equation looks like this:

$$P_k = P_j + (DT) (BR_{jk} - DR_{jk})$$

where the level of world population P at time k is calculated from the level of population P at the preceding time j and the birth rate BR and death rate DR in the intervening period jk which is of length DT. The equations are adjusted using a base period, 1900-70, so that the computer run, beginning in 1900 and proceeding in increments of DT, replicates the historical data up to 1970. It then continues to run into the future to the year 2100. A critical assumption is that the relationships determining the 1900-70 behavior remain valid to 2100. Typical conclusions of *World Dynamics* are that (a) growth will cease—the question is when and how, not whether; (b) we may be living in a golden age, at an apex in the quality of life. The Club of Rome, a private advocacy group

with members from many countries, decided to support this approach to examine the world problematique, and commissioned a group of Forrester's MIT proteges to produce a model based on that of Forrester. The resulting popular book, *The Limits to Growth* (Meadows et al., 1972), sold more than three million copies and was translated into 23 different languages. It admirably fulfilled the aim of the Club of Rome to trigger a worldwide discussion of the global future and raise the awareness of politicians and the educated public to the "predicament of mankind." The model forecast global collapses of population, pollution disasters and industrial catastrophes for the twenty-first century (see *Future of Humanity*).

Computer modelers analyzed the Meadows work and produced both critiques and more detailed modeling studies (several supported by the Club of Rome). Mesarovic and Pestel (1974) made several major changes in the computer model: (a) dividing the world into 10 regions rather than treating it as a single unit; (b) limiting the model runs to 50 rather than 130 years (i.e., to 2025); (c) using a hierarchical structure for each of the regional submodels. The work did not use the Forrester system dynamics directly but could be portrayed in the same notation. The principal results were that: (a) cooperation is better than confrontation; and (b) delays in addressing the critical issues can be disastrous. Like the model of Meadows et al., this model viewed the world with alarm and issued a clarion call for prompt action. Computerized global modeling rapidly became a cottage industry. There followed the Bariloche model of the Fundacion Bariloche in Argentina, designed to show that a world liberated from underdevelopment and misery was possible by 2060. The Free University of Amsterdam's Hans Linnemann pursued the MOIRA model to test international relations in agriculture. Six symposia on global modeling were conducted at the International Institute for Applied Systems Analysis (IIASA) in Laxenburg, Austria, from 1974 to 1978. The first decade of global modeling as reflected in these gatherings has been entertainingly described and summarized in *Groping in the Dark* (Meadows et al., 1982).

Specific criticism of global modeling began with Cole et al., in *Models of Doom* (1973). One can strike directly at the unconditional Forrester claim quoted earlier as being incredibly naive. One can point to the fact that the assumed constancy of the model structure is totally unrealistic: human beings do change their social systems when crises loom. Another point is made by Berlinski:

> The most effective mathematical modeling starts simply and uses to the fullest the resources of theory. It is this prescription taken neatly in reverse that characterizes *World Dynamics* and *The Limits to Growth*; there the prevailing pedagogical maxim has been: pile up an imposingly complex system of equations and then subject them to an analysis of ineffable innocence . . . . [Another lesson:] It is not always necessary to subject an analytically intractable system to simulation in order to understand it qualitatively; . . . qualitative insights are at greater depth than partially quantitative results. (Berlinski 1976 pp. 83-84)

Furthermore, Hoos writes:

> Futurists engage in solemn methodological discourse . . . . Uninhibited by time or space, they indulge in simulations that range from the presumptuous to the ludicrous . . . . They posit a supranational model in which nations will behave more rationally than the people who populate them . . . . The design of the future 'one world' demonstrates . . . the gap between the perfection of the system dreamed up by the international jet set intellectuals and the imperfections which are the down-to-earth realities. The more ambitious the model, the more likely is the fraternity of futurists to ignore fatal flaws and defer to it as a landmark. (Hoos 1972 pp. 235-36)

Herbert Simon points out:

> The fundamental conclusion drawn from the model —that exponential growth cannot be sustained indefinitely—is entirely true, has enormous impact for public policy, and could have been inferred from textbook treatments of linear dynamic systems without any computation . . . . There may even be actual harm in carrying out such a modeling exercise . . . . It may give skeptics entirely too much ammunition for questioning even those conclusions that can be validly drawn from the model. (Simon 1988)

Global modeling can serve as a useful stimulant for thinking about the future, but it must not be taken too literally as a replication of the global system for predictive purposes.

Since the mid-1980s the development of "complexity science," particularly at the Santa Fe Institute, also underscores the weakness of these models. They can suggest basic megatrends but they ignore the unstable, chaotic phases that accompany the catastrophes the models project and consequently their inherent unpredictability. Complexity science has been opening up entirely new paths through the use of the computer as a laboratory tool to study complex, non-linear dynamic systems. In particular, it is becoming

an effective methodology to deepen our understanding of systems whose elements are adaptive, such as sociotechnical systems (see *Peace, Systems View of*) (Axelrod 1997).

One of the most promising approaches is the use of computer simulation to "grow" complex nonlinear dynamic systems from the bottom up (Casti 1997; Epstein and Axtell 1996). New worlds are created that are miniatures of the real world or true silicon worlds. The computer makes it feasible to analyze systems that consist of more than a few interacting variables and are not in the range of the huge numbers that could be treated statistically (as, for example, the particles in a gas). The system elements, or agents, are intelligent and adaptive in the sense that they make decisions on the basis of simple rules, can modify the rules, or create new ones. No single agent has access to what all the other agents are doing, that is he/she has local, but not global, information. The creation of such electronic worlds can provide remarkable insights, such as emergent behaviors resulting from the interaction of these agents. Microlevel interactions between individual agents and global, aggregate-level patterns and behaviors mutually reinforce each other. This bottom-up simulation approach has already been used successfully to model a variety of systems:

(a) the traffic in Albuquerque, encompassing 200,000 households, 400,000 daily travelers, and 30,000 road segments—showing the appearance and disappearance of traffic jams;

(b) genetic regulatory networks, involving a network of the 100,000 genes in a human body cell that switch each other on and off — exhibiting a powerful tendency to self-organization and indicating that a cell type is a stable recurrent pattern of gene expression;

(c) biological systems, starting with a simple stick figure which mutates in accordance with a simple set of rules, creating a set of offspring each determined by a single mutation; the striking result is that highly complex forms evolve, including look-alikes of real primitive plants;

(d) social systems involving primitive exchange-type economies that can test the efficient market hypothesis—with the surprising result that if the agents are at least a little bit human in their behavior, there is no reason to assume markets will perform the way economic textbooks tell us they should. (Casti p. 174)

The last of these models, *Sugarscape*, should be of

particular interest to forecasters. A relevant question, raised by the developers of this model, is the effect of foresight on the agents. Trading sugar and spice, they initially make their decisions based on their current holdings. If agent behavior is modified so that they can look ahead a certain number of time intervals, one finds that

> clearly, some foresight is better than none in this society since the long run average foresight becomes approximately stable at a nonzero level. However, large amounts of foresight . . . are less "fit" than modest amounts. (Epstein and Axtell p. 129)

Another potential capability is the introduction of technological innovations into *Sugarscape* as substitutes for diminishing resources and determining how they affect the economies of the traders.

Linstone (1984) sees the need to apply multiple perspectives in viewing systems problems which go beyond pure technology. Global modeling is in the nature of a "technical" perspective. Also needed are "organizational" (or societal) and "personal" (or individual) perspectives. These are not unique; for a given problem several organizational and personal perspectives usually have to be considered. Each perspective illuminates certain parts of the problem and provides insights not attainable with the others. The three types use different paradigms (e.g., different discount rates, different ethical bases). Used together, they help to bridge the chasm between the ivory-tower analyst and the real-world decision maker. Botez and Celac (1983) have noted that it is totally unreasonable for East and West to "see" a single global model to represent the world. Inevitably they will "see" through the filter of differing organizational perspectives. It is the participative modeling process which can contribute to better mutual understanding and thus enhanced prospects for world peace.

See also: *World Order Models Project*

Bibliography

Axelrod R 1997 Advancing the art of simulation in the social sciences. *Complexity* 3(2)

Berlinski P 1976 *On Systems Analysis.* MIT Press, Cambridge, Massachusetts

Botez M C, Celac M 1983 Global modelling . . . without models? *Technological Forecasting and Social Change* 23

Casti J 1997 *Would-Be Worlds.* John Wiley & Sons, Inc., New York

Cole H S D et al., 1973 *Models of Doom.* Universe Books, New York

Epstein J M, Axtell R 1996 *Growing Artificial Societies.* The Brookings Institution, Washington, DC; The MIT Press, Cambridge, Massachusetts

Forrester J W 1971 *World Dynamics.* Wright-Allen Press, Cambridge, Massachusetts

Hoos I 1972 *Systems Analysis in Public Policy: A Critique.* University of California Press, Berkeley, California

Linstone H A 1984 *Multiple Perspectives for Decision Making.* North-Holland, New York. Revised edition to be published 1999 by Artech House Inc.

Meadows D et al., 1972 *The Limits to Growth.* Potomac Associates, New York

Meadows D et al., 1982 *Grouping in the Dark.* Wiley, Chichester

Mesarovic M, Pestel E 1974 *Mankind at the Turning Point.* Dutton/Reader's Digest Press, New York

Rapoport A 1957 Lewis F. Richardson's mathematical theory of war. *J. Conflict Resolution* 1(3)

Simon H 1988 Prediction and Prescription in Systems Modeling, Speech at the IIASA Conference on Perspectives and Futures, Laxenburg, Austria, June 14-15, 1988

HAROLD A. LINSTONE

Global Neighbourhood: New Security Principles

A heightened concern with the interests of people is a prominent feature of the concept of the global neighbourhood that the independent Commission on Global Governance (see *Commission on Global Governance*) advanced in its report, issued in 1995. In giving the title 'Our Global Neighbourhood' to the report, the Commission signalled its conviction both that the world had become smaller and more interdependent and that people, as the neighbourhood's citizens, deserved attention as much as the states that dominate the international stage. This concern with

people strongly influenced the Commission's approach to global security, with its emphasis on the need to move away from exclusive preoccupation with the interests of states. "Global security must be broadened from its traditional focus on the security of states to include the security of people and the planet," in the words of the Commission's report.

The protection of the nation-state, shielded by the armour of sovereignty, has conventionally been the defining aim of international security policy. The concept of security as the protection of the state from external aggression has been a foundational principle of the international system. Firmly linked to this central tenet have been other important norms: that the boundaries of a sovereign state are inviolable and that a state may not interfere in the internal affairs of another. It was the Commission's view that while these norms had served to hold down the incidence of aggression among states and contributed to global stability and peace, there had also been, specially in recent decades, other, less wholesome consequences for people from exclusive concern with the sanctity of states. The concept of state sovereignty in security matters had, in its words, "provided the rationale for creating powerful national military systems, justified budgetary policies that emphasize defence over domestic welfare, and encouraged measures that severely restrict citizens' rights and freedoms."

Sovereignty is a power to be exercised on behalf of the people of a state, but rulers exercising this power have often abused their position and arrogated to themselves the benefits that should flow from it. Despotic rulers violating the rights of their people have used sovereignty—and the related principle of non-intervention—as shields to protect themselves and to secure immunity from international censure. Some regimes have not been above using the need to preserve the security of a state as an excuse for policies that gravely undermined the security of its own people and protected only those in power. In the light of these factors, if the concept of security is confined to the protection of states, it could lead to the right to security of people—who form the citizens of states and in whose name states claim sovereignty—being severely compromised.

Nation-states continue to be the principal units of the international system which, in order to preserve global stability and peace, must continue to offer protection to states against external attack. It is time, however, for that function to cease being the only aim of global security policy. The protection offered to states against predators has undoubtedly helped to make attacks against states less frequent but it is doubtful if people's sense of security worldwide has necessarily been enhanced. There is reason to believe that, the greater security of states notwithstanding, people in many parts of the world feel distinctly insecure. While the fear of attack from outside has diminished, there have been other factors of domestic origin giving rise to insecurity, often on a large scale. Over thirty civil wars of varying ferocity and duration have been going on at any time in recent years in the world, and it has been the general pattern that these conflicts cause more casualties among civilians than among those directly involved in them as combatants (see *Civil Wars: Dynamics and Consequences*).

Afghanistan, Bosnia, Cambodia, Rwanda, Somalia are only the more egregious in the list of killing-fields that testify to the massive violations of human security that have occurred without interstate war having been the cause (see *Ethnic Conflict and International Relations*).

The threat of violent conflict as a pervasive source of insecurity is given a more menacing edge by some features of the contemporary world. These include the wide availability of conventional weapons, the unrestrained activity of the arms bazaar, and the failure to bring to an end the production of weapons of mass destruction—nuclear, biological and chemical. To these may be added the continuing presence, if on a somewhat reduced scale, of authoritarian and even brutally despotic rulers. The recent surge of democracy has swept away many such regimes but it may be premature to conclude that they are close to being made extinct; in Sierra Leone there was an attempt to reimpose a military dictatorship in June 1997, just one year after democracy had been restored after a long period of military rule.

1. A Wider Concept of Security

The Commission on Global Governance, in elaborating its ideas for security in the global neighbourhood, was keen that security should be considered in its widest dimensions. Security is conventionally viewed as protection from the physical violence associated with war. This is indeed a cardinal dimension of security, but security is essentially a sense of wellbeing which, as the Commission pointed out, can be assailed by factors, such as poverty and deprivation, that are unrelated to physical violence. Acute poverty continues to blight the lives of a significant proportion of the world's people. That world economic growth has bypassed such a large number of people and failed to lift them from destitution has tended to be obscured by the dramatic advances made recently by several developing countries, especially in East Asia, whose people were also poor not so long ago. The sobering fact is that, as United Nations estimates show, the number—if not the proportion—of people condemned to live in conditions of what the World Bank has termed absolute poverty—on incomes of roughly a dollar a day or less—has continued to rise. People having to exist at this level of poverty are clearly leading lives of pronounced insecurity and vulnerability, never far from hunger, prone to infection and disease, and sentenced to low life expectancy. It is therefore important that economic factors as they impinge on the security of people should not be left out of global security considerations.

The concept of security has additionally to take account today of threats posed to the integrity of ecosystems that sustain life on earth. People's security has to embrace the security of the planet as well. The most worrying ecological hazards are well known; they include the emission of gases, mainly carbon dioxide, that contribute to global warming, reductions in the ozone layer exposing people to the risks of ultraviolet radiation, loss of biological diversity through the extinction of species, and the leeching of toxic chemicals into soils and water. The continuing presence of thousands of nuclear weapons, large stocks of fissionable material and many nuclear reactors, with the risk of radiation they present, is a further source of anxiety. Scientists may not be unanimous in assessing the extent or urgency of environmental dangers but there has been an enlarging consensus within the scientific community that we face unprecedented circumstances that, coupled with the accelerated increase in human numbers, could test the capacity of the planet to support the human population. (see *Human Rights and Environmental Rights: Their Sustainable Development Compatibility*)

2. Norms for Global Security

These various considerations led the Commission to put forward a set of principles to guide security in the global neighbourhood as the world approached the end of the twentieth century:

All people, no less than all states, have a right to a secure existence, and all states have an obligation to protect those rights.

The primary goals of global security policy should be to prevent conflict and war and to maintain the integrity of the planet's life-support systems by eliminating the economic, social, environmental, political and military conditions that generate threats to the security of people and the planet, and by anticipating and managing crises before they escalate into armed conflicts.

Military force is not a legitimate political instrument, except in self-defence or under UN auspices.

The development of military capabilities beyond that required for national defence and support of UN action is a potential threat to the security of people.

Weapons of mass destruction are not legitimate instruments of national defence.

The production and trade in arms should be controlled by the international community.

The Commission thought that acceptance of these norms would go a long way towards meeting the twenty-first century's most pressing security challenges, which it described as: "preserving and extending the progress made in securing states against the threat of war while finding ways to safeguard people against domestic threats of brutalization and gross deprivation and ensuring the integrity and viability of the life-support systems on which all life depends." It put forward a series of suggestions for improving global arrangements for enhancing security in all its dimensions (see *Future of Humanity*).

3. A Duty to Intervene

When the United Nations Charter was drawn up and the United Nations was formed as an organisation in 1945, the world was just emerging from the enormous devastation caused by World War II. The first objective of the UN's founders understandably was to set in place arrangements to maintain international peace and security and to prevent a recurrence of war. Breaches of the peace were envisaged as resulting only from external aggression, and the aim was to have disputes or situations that might lead to war between nations settled peacefully and to prevent or suppress acts of aggression. The Charter gave the UN Security Council the authority to take action when there was a threat to international security. It was not intended that the UN should concern itself with internally generated threats to—or actual violations of—the security of people. The Charter included express provision barring UN intervention in matters of states domestic jurisdiction (article 2.7) besides requiring UN members not to threaten or use force against "the territorial integrity or political independence of any state" (Article 2.4) (see *Intervention*). It is prudent to believe that the large number of countries that emerged as independent states and became members of the UN in the decades after the UN was formed were encouraged and reassured by these provisions. Most of them small countries that would be hard put to defend themselves against predators, and all anxious to preserve their newly gained—or regained—independence, they derived from these provisions of the UN Charter a measure of security, and it is likely that at least in the early years rulers and people would both have unreservedly welcomed the protection the Charter offered.

Circumstances are no longer the same. Though

there is no certainty that the days of predatory behaviour by states are over, the incidence and possibilities of aggression by one state against another have been distinctly lowered. But threats to peace and people's security from internal causes—ethnic conflict, secessionist movements, insurgencies, extremist groups, repressive regimes—have multiplied. The violation of the security of people in numerous countries, often on an extensive scale, has given rise to growing public disquiet worldwide and to demands that the international community should intervene on behalf of people at risk. The prohibition against interference in matters of domestic jurisdiction notwithstanding, there has been a feeling that the United Nations should have not just the right—but the obligation also—to go to the aid of people when their right to life is extensively violated.

In articulating a similar position the Commission on Global Governance was not contending that the principle of non-intervention in domestic affairs should be abandoned. It was asserting that circumstances in the global neighbourhood justify some qualification of this principle so that the world community may legitimately act to ensure the security of people whose lives are threatened but whose states are unwilling or unable to protect them. Even with international law as it is, the United Nations has in practice intervened on a few occasions in what were, strictly, internal situations, as in Somalia or Rwanda. But there must be unease that in doing so, the Security Council is stretching provisions of the UN Charter intended to deal with interstate conflicts in order to respond to purely intrastate situations. There is therefore a strong case for revising the Charter to give the Security Council explicit authority for intervening when there is gross abuse of the security of people. A Charter amendment would have the virtue of putting intervention on a legal basis—and also of defining the circumstances in which it may take place, thereby both licensing and circumscribing it. It is desirable that in the global neighbourhood there should be international action to stop gross abuses of people's security; it is also desirable that there should at the same time be safeguards to ensure that intervention takes place only in specific circumstances and is not arbitrary.

In proposing that the UN should be armed with the power to intervene in domestic situations, the Commission on Global Governance said that while the line separating what was a purely domestic affair from one that is of legitimate global concern "cannot be drawn in the sand," it was convinced that "in practice virtually all will know when it has been crossed."

It suggested the following as a litmus-test question: "Given the sustained importance of the principles of sovereignty and non-interference in internal affairs, has the situation deteriorated to the point where the security of people has been violated so severely that it requires an international response on humanitarian grounds?"

The Commission feared that the world community might have to ask that question frequently in the future, and concluded: If the global neighbourhood is to be tolerable home for all its people, it has to be kept peaceful. And keeping the peace has to be a collective responsibility. The common security of its people depends on that responsibility being shouldered.

4. A Council for Petitions

While the maintenance of security in the global neighbourhood requires that the international community should be ready to consider the use of force to protect people, it is desirable that it should also take measures to prevent situations from reaching the point when such action become necessary. This consideration lies behind the suggestion that a Council for Petitions should be established within the United Nations to which civil society organisations could make representations when they sense that an emerging situation could put people's security at risk on a large scale. In making this proposal, the Commission was mindful that governments themselves are generally not eager to be seen to be interfering in the affairs of other governments, particularly before a situation assumes crisis proportions and exhibits obviously offensive features. It was also aware that there could be voluntary bodies that both have good access to information on the ground and would be less inhibited than a state's neighbours about drawing public attention to situations that could endanger people's security.

Both the measures discussed—a UN Charter provision signalling that sovereignty can no longer be a shield against UN intervention in cases of gross abuse and a Council for Petitions with the authority to inquire into petitions from people's organisations anticipating such abuse—can be expected to have a significant deterrent effect and enhance the security of people in the global neighbourhood.

5. Preventing Violent Conflict

Interstate conflicts have become less frequent, but it is salutary to recall that this century has seen two world wars and been the bloodiest in human history.

Iraq's grab for Kuwait was a reminder that aggression is not an extinct phenomenon. Moreover, in many parts of the world there are unresolved disputes that mar relations between neighbouring states and could ignite conflicts between them. Some of these states have large military establishments and those that do not feel pushed to enlarge theirs. It is therefore essential that governance in the global neighbourhood should include an improved capacity to deal with threats to peace and security, whether from internal or external causes, and to promote non-violent approaches to resolving disputes.

In discussing the United Nations' role in the maintenance of peace and security, the Commission on Global Governance placed an emphasis on the preventive approach, underlining the value of strengthening its capacity to anticipate and resolve crises before they degenerate into violence and also to respond early to outbreaks of violence (see *Field Diplomacy: A New Conflict Paradigm*). The UN's system for gathering information on situations and trends that may lead to violent conflict or humanitarian tragedies needs to be upgraded. Member governments should feel it their duty to share such information with the UN; clearly there are several states with well-established information-gathering capacities that could assist the UN in this area. It is desirable that there should also be arrangements for the UN to benefit from information available to non-governmental organizations working at grassroots level which may be able to complement information gathered in capitals. The better collection and analysis of information should be combined, where appropriate, with missions despatched by the UN Secretary-General to potential trouble spots. Besides sifting and assessing information, such emissaries could explore possibilities for resolving disputes and their very presence could in some circumstances be a catalyst in promoting contact between contending parties.

It should also be an aim of security policy in the global neighbourhood to work for the maximum use of peaceful means for resolving disputes. The UN Charter's Chapter VI addresses the pacific settlement of disputes and enjoins parties to any dispute likely to endanger international peace and security to seek a solution through peaceful means. It sets out the various means that may be employed: "negotiation, enquiry, mediation, conciliation, arbitration, judicial settlement, resort to regional agencies or arrangements or other peaceful means." Article 33 of the Charter further says that "the Security Council shall, when it deems necessary, call upon the parties to settle their dispute by such means." It is clearly desirable that more use should be made of this provision. While the Charter envisaged its use when there was a risk of international conflict, in current circumstances in the global neighbourhood, there would be value in resort to such methods even in internal disputes, when their continuance threatens people's security.

6. A UN Volunteer Force

There has been evidence from UN experience in dealing with violent conflicts in the past decade to support the argument that the UN should be able to act more promptly to prevent a threatened descent into violence or to contain an outbreak of violence before it spreads. The fact that the UN has to depend on ad hoc contributions of troops from different countries, with different military cultures and command systems, inevitably means delay. Security in the global neighbourhood would be well served by equipping the United Nations with a modest military force of its own. First suggested by Trygve Lie (see UN Secretaries-General: *Trygve Lie*), the first UN Secretary-General, the idea of a UN force has been revived since the Security Council was freed from the virtual paralysis induced by Cold War tensions.

In expressing strong support for the idea, the Commission on Global Governance came out in favour of a well-trained Volunteer Force with a maximum strength of 10,000, to be available for deployment under the exclusive authority of the Security Council. This force would not take the place of traditional peacekeeping forces or of forces required for large-scale enforcement operations, as in the Gulf action against Iraq. The Commission envisaged it "giving the Security Council the ability to back up preventive diplomacy with a measure of immediate and convincing deployment on the ground. It would provide the immediate spearhead and reconnaissance element for a later, much larger operation, should that prove necessary." The very availability of such a force for immediate deployment could have a deterrent influence. In presenting the case for a UN force, the Commission quoted the remarks made by President Roosevelt in 1944 in arguing for the creation of the United Nations: "A policeman would not be a very effective policeman if, when he saw a felon break into a house, he had to go to the town hall and call a meeting to issue a warrant before the felon could be arrested."

7. Removing the Threat of Mass Destruction

A principal aim of security policy in the global neighbourhood should be to remove the threat of mass destruction that now hangs over all who live in it. Efforts to bring about the elimination of weapons of mass destruction—nuclear, chemical and biological—have therefore to remain high on the world security agenda (see *Disarmament and Development*). Progress has been made on several fronts, not least the ending of confrontation between two biggest nuclear powers, but awesome dangers remain. The main responsibility falls on the acknowledged nuclear powers; their failure to honour the promise made in Article VI of the Nuclear Non-Proliferation Treaty to pursue nuclear disarmament has been a disservice to the world community. But the threshold nuclear states cannot avoid a share of responsibility. The report of the Commission on Global Governance put forward a number of recommendations for moving towards the goal of a world free of nuclear and other weapons of mass destruction.

Another important goal of security policy must be demilitarization. The arms race between the two superpowers is a thing of the past, and the upward trend in global military expenditure has been checked. But the sums spent in aggregate on armies and armaments remain obscenely large. Furthermore, arms spending continues to climb in some parts of the world. Arms exports have also declined, but part of this decline could be the result of importing countries expanding their own production, and all the major powers continue to peddle their lethal products in the world arms bazaar. Even a ban on the export of landmines, many of whose victims are innocent civilians, has proved difficult to achieve. In the interests of peace and security in the global neighbourhood, there needs to be a stronger commitment to reducing levels of militarization and international action to curtail the arms trade.

8. Towards Economic Security

With the security of people demanding to be seen in all its dimensions, including that of economic security, a key proposal of the Commission on Global Governance urged the establishment of an Economic Security Council (ESC) within the United Nations to give policy leadership in the economic, social and environmental fields. The Council was intended to fill a gap in the structures of global governance, and to be more representative than the Group of 7 leading industrial countries and more effective than the UN's Economic and Social Council. It was to function at the same level as the UN Security Council. The Commission envisaged the ESC's tasks would include the following:

(a) continuously assess the overall state of the world economy and the interaction between major policy areas,

(b) provide a long-term strategic policy framework in order to promote stable, balanced and sustainable development,

(c) secure consistency between the policy goals of the major international organizations, particularly the Bretton Woods bodies and the World Trade Organization, and

(d) give political leadership and promote consensus on international economic issues.

9. Reforming the Security Council

The Security Council is the most powerful organ of the United Nations and is charged with responsibility for maintaining world peace and security. It acts on behalf of the community of nations that are members of the United Nations. It is therefore crucially important that it should be representative of that community lest it lose credibility and legitimacy (see *United Nations Reform: Historical and Contemporary Perspectives*). The case for some enlargement of the Council to include a few countries that have emerged as major powers and to make it more representative of developing nations and of the different continents is incontestable. It was well argued in the report of the Commission on Global Governance which put forward a set of proposals for reforming the Council. These envisage its enlargement as well as action, in two stages, to eliminate both permanent membership and the veto.

The reform of the Security Council, coupled with action to legitimise its intervention on behalf of people in prescribed circumstances, and the creation of an apex body to promote global economic security would bring about a significant improvement in the institutional arrangements for ensuring security in the global neighbourhood.

See also: *Human Security; Future of Humanity; Global Ethic; Democracy and Peace; Comprehensive Security; Social Progress and Human Survival; Alternative Dispute Resolution; Global Ethics, Human Rights Laws and Democratic Governance*

Sir Shridath Ramphal

Global Peace and Global Accountability

Attempting to secure regional or global peace largely by maintaining military balances of power against potential aggressors is a shallow and ultimately futile strategy. But so is the attempt to achieve international peace primarily through enhancing the collective security capabilities of the United Nations or regional organizations. As with efforts by "law-and-order" elements *within* countries to maintain peace by providing themselves with fighting forces superior to the forces of the "outlaw" elements, efforts to sustain peace *among* countries through deterrence or victory in battle will prove to be dangerously unstable unless genuine political community can be created among the otherwise warring peoples.

A realistic strategy for a durable peace must be essentially a strategy for building community—a community of voluntary consent, not coercion. This is no less true for the world as a whole than it is true for the maintenance of domestic and regional peace (see *Peace and Democracy*).

But isn't the proposition "community first, *then* peace" a counsel of despair? For the nations of the world seem no closer to constituting themselves as a genuine global community than they did when this bloody century began. Indeed, the years since the Cold War have featured the *dis*integration of political communities more than their integration.

The "globalization" resulting from the increasing mobility of goods, people, and information is evident largely in the realm of the economy, and hardly at all in the polity (except for some institutional growth in the European Union). Looking at the world as a whole, markets are getting larger and stronger—including, ominously, the markets in lethal weapons and dangerous substances—while national governments are becoming more impotent and frustrated in their capacity to hold the big players in the global economy accountable for the impact they have on people's lives.

The authority of national governments is also being challenged and undermined from below, so to speak, by the reassertion around the world of primary identifications and intra-community loyalties that were suppressed in the imperial colonial and Cold War systems (see *Ethnic Conflict and International Relations*). Emotionally alienated from the dominant communities of the political jurisdictions into which they were forced by war and great-power diplomacy, many of these primordial ethnic and religious communities (utilizing the new technologies of communication and transportation) are now playing havoc with the state-sovereignty system—demanding autonomy, even national statehood for themselves, and re-establishing political bonds with their "brothers and sisters" across established international borders.

This growing incongruence between (a) the global economy, (b) many of the world's identity-communities, and (c) the territorial jurisdiction of the state-sovereignty system is a basic structural source of the delegitimation of government authority and the outbreak of anarchic violence in many areas of the post-Cold War, post-colonial world (see *World Economy, Social Change and Peace*). The public order crisis threatens to get much worse—and we can look forward to a century of civil war, transnational war, even planetary holocaust—unless we can achieve a substantial degree of congruence between the most intensive areas of human interaction and the reach and authority of political community.

1. Accountability as the Foundation of Political Community

The realization that global political community is a precondition for durable global peace need not be cause for despair if the diverse, and often antagonistic, communities of the world can come to understand that the global community which is required for world peace is a community of *processes*, more than a community of shared substantive values. We don't have to embrace Samuel Huntington's atavistic "clash of civilizations" (Huntington 1996) to concede that at the level of some of the most basic cultural norms (including the respective rights and duties of individuals, families, and religious and political communities; the respective roles of men and women; the range of personal choice and what is prescribed by the community; and the separation, if any, between private and public spheres of morality), the human species remains as resistant as ever to homogenization. Indeed, many of us (cosmopolitans and communitarians alike), for whom the world's cultural heterogeneity is a high value, applaud this resistance.

There is no reason why a global political community designed to discourage conflicts from exploding into war cannot be compatible with the cultural-pluralist realities of world society (see *Intercultural Relations and Peace Studies*). And there is certainly no necessity for this kind of global political community to maintain a Leviathan-like worldwide monopoly of coercive power.

There is, however, an indispensable foundational

requirement of a basically peaceable world community: *global accountability*. No political system (domestic or international) deserves to be regarded as a community if its members are not accountable to one another for upholding at least a set of minimal legal and moral principles. The larger and more diverse the community, the smaller will be the set of legal and moral principles to which its constituents can be held accountable (Walzer 1994). Even though the normative regime operating globally must therefore be expected to be relatively "thin" (as compared with the normative consensus prevailing in most domestic polities), it should not be too much to demand broad international acceptance of the accountability principle itself. With this much agreed, we can proceed with building global political community on its most crucial foundation, and the nations of the world can be more patient with one another—and mutually respectful of their differences—as they work to construct a thicker consensus and institutional scaffolding for the evolving global community.

The basic accountability principle can be stated simply: *Those who (can) substantially affect the security or well-being of others—especially by inflicting harm—are accountable to those whom they (can) affect*. This principle should apply both "horizontally" (among countries or among other organized communities and groups) and "vertically" (within countries and other organizations, between governing agencies and their constituents; and between non-governmental entities, such as multinational enterprises, and the socioeconomic groups whose standard of living and human rights may be at the mercy of decisions made in executive boardrooms) (Johansen 1994).

The accountability arrangements can exhibit a wide spectrum of obligations and a variety of forms (Brown 1995; Brown 1996).

Minimally, the people potentially hurt by an action, will be at least informed about what is being (or will be) done to them, in time for them to voice objections. More substantially, if harm is inflicted by accident or despite prior objections, the perpetrators will be obligated to provide appropriate compensation. Maximally, projects would not be able to go forward without prior approval by populations expecting to suffer substantial harm.

The extent of institutionalization can also vary widely—ranging from ad hoc meetings only among the parties affected by a specific project, to permanently-sitting legislative, administrative, and judicial bodies with responsibility for allocating rights and responsibilities and costs and benefits in particular sectors or (more ambitiously) across interdependent sectors of activity.

The effort to achieve global accountability thus raises complex and controversial ethical, legal, and political questions. Few answers can be derived directly from the core accountability principle or from other standard principles of political or legal philosophy. As with similar accountability issues in domestic political systems, many of the arrangements will have to be worked out through practical bargaining among the groups that set up and participate in particular regimes.

2. Enhancing and Elaborating upon Existing Accountability Arrangements

Rudimentary global accountability regimes already exist in the fields of arms control, transportation and communication, the economy and the environment, and human rights (see *Treaties of the Modern Era*). They provide a scaffolding on which thicker and inter-related networks of accountability can be built congruent with the emergent interdependencies of peoples—networks of accountability that when functioning can provide the sinews of global political community required for durable world peace.

2.1 Arms Control

Some of the most innovative international accountability arrangements are the legacy of the Cold War fears of the United States and the former Soviet Union that without agreeing to certain restrictions on their vulnerable and provocative military forces they could stumble into a nuclear war that would devastate both countries. In the negotiations initiated in the 1970s with the Strategic Arms Limitation Talks (SALT), and continuing into the 1980s and the early 1990s with the Treaty on Intermediate Nuclear Forces (INF) and the Strategic Arms Reduction Treaty (START) and its follow-on accords, the two nuclear superpowers jointly defined crucial limits on the types, numbers, and deployment sites of the nuclear weapons in their respective arsenals, and instituted monitoring and surveillance arrangements to assure each other that they were adhering to the agreed limits. By so doing, Washington and Moscow conceded to a degree of mutual accountability for their respective national security policies unprecedented in international relations.

Parallel with their efforts to control and build mutual accountability into their bilateral strategic relationship, the United States and Russia have been cooperating to reinforce the global accountability provisions of the Nuclear Nonproliferation Treaty

(NPT) (see *Non-Proliferation Treaty (NPT)*).

Consistent with their shared interest in keeping the nuclear-weapons club as small as possible, The United States and the then Soviet Union in the late 1960s pressured most of the non-nuclear weapons states to agree not to acquire nuclear weapons, either via transfers from the nuclear powers or by developing a capacity themselves to make them, and to grant the International Atomic Energy Agency (IAEA) the right to monitor their nuclear energy facilities to assure that no materials were being diverted into weapons programs.

The nuclear nonproliferation regime is, of course, still fragile, incomplete, and operationally weak. Once any of the three "undeclared" nuclear weapons states (Israel, India, and Pakistan) openly admits to having a nuclear arsenal, some of the parties to the NPT are likely to exercise their legal right to withdraw from the treaty. Also, the IAEA "safeguards" system is quite loose and subject to leaks: countries must give prior approval to the inspection of particular facilities; and the on-site inspections are typically of records rather than of the physical equipment itself. (In reaction to the recent problems with Iraq and North Korea, arms control specialists have been formulating proposals to strengthen IAEA monitoring capabilities in the direction of providing the agency with surprise "full-scope" inspection rights to nuclear facilities of member states; but most governments are still resistant to giving any global agency this degree of supranational authority.)

The accountability problem is compounded by the increasing commercialization of the transnational transfers of nuclear materials and reactor components. This has been one of the glaring holes in the NPT, and efforts to plug it by the formation of a voluntary association of nuclear materials exporters (the "London Suppliers Group," now comprising some 30 countries) has thus far been unable to effectively stanch the flow, in large measure due to the lack of a multilateral supplier-monitoring regime. The parallel need to restrict the commercialization of trade in weapons capable of carrying nuclear warheads was part of the impetus for the formation in the late 1980s of a voluntary Missile Technology Control Regime (MTCR) in the late 1980s. Although more than 30 governments profess adherence to the MTCR, it has proven to be a notoriously weak accountability arrangement, since it has no inter-governmental monitoring or verification capabilities and, increasingly, the trade in technologies usable in missiles is conducted by privately-owned multinational corporations (Vam Ham 1994).

Moreover, the continued accountability of today's non-nuclear weapons states to their co-signatories of the Nuclear Non-proliferation Treaty will depend upon the seriousness with which the existing nuclear weapons states—especially the United States and Russia—demonstrate *their* accountability with respect to the NPT obligation (in Article VI) "to pursue negotiations in good faith on effective measures relating to . . . nuclear disarmament, and on a treaty on general and complete disarmament under strict and effective international control" (United Nations 1968).

A feasible way for the United States and Russia to take the lead in implementing this NPT obligation was proposed in December 1996 by the former head of the US Strategic Air Command, General Lee Butler and the former Supreme Allied Commander in Europe (SACEUR), General Andrew Goodpaster. Endorsed by retired military leaders of similarly high rank from countries all around the globe (from Russia to France to Japan), the Butler-Goodpaster initiative recommends that the United States and Russia begin immediately to reduce their strategic nuclear arsenals to 1000 to 1500 warheads each (which they could do without either of them jeopardizing their security), while committing themselves to, and negotiating subsequent reductions—down to hundreds on each side, then to tens, and finally to complete elimination of the nuclear weapons. Along the way the three other nuclear weapons countries and the threshold countries would be drawn into the process. As explained in a detailed backup study by the Henry L. Stimson Center in Washington, this "evolutionary" process of nuclear disarmament

> would be achieved in four phases, with each phase corresponding to a new strategic environment and involving changes in nuclear roles, in the operational status and size of nuclear forces, and in arms control arrangements . . . .
>
> Progress toward the elimination of all weapons of mass destruction would require stringent national and international verification regimes; companion regimes for biological and chemical weapons would be essential. (Stimson Center 1995)

The proponents of this disarmament process are fully aware that "Under current political conditions, the elimination of nuclear weapons is infeasible," and that the objective can only be achieved "after far-reaching changes occur in the principles that guide state policies and actions." But they insist that it is not too early to begin the process (Stimson Center 1995).

2.2 Transportation and Communication

The need for countries to negotiate with one another over their shared use of the world's media for transportation and communication has a long tradition. Disputes over the use rights of these resources have produced an impressive corpus of international treaties that is now being reformulated to deal with the burgeoning congestion crises in the transportation and communication fields. It is no mere coincidence that the father of international law, Hugo Grotius (1583-1645) (see *Grotius, Hugo*), concentrated primarily on conflicts among users of the oceans and rivers. For it was on the world's waterways that those who ventured beyond their national borders have been most likely to get in each other's way and come to blows.

The congestion-management and resource-use imperatives brought on by the contemporary revolutions in transportation and communication, however, are stimulating rethinking of the inherited rules for using international navigational routes and media and how they should be enforced. The open-access, free-use regimes that traditionally prevailed on such routes and media have become counterproductive if not dangerous. In response to the new realities, the cognizant international organizations—such as the International Maritime Organization (for international shipping and navigation), the International Civil Aviation Organization (for air traffic), and the International Telecommunication Union (for electronic broadcasting)—are today preoccupied with devising globally standardized "rules of the road" and with how to induce national governments and industry groups to organize and fund the necessary enforcement.

Innovative accountability arrangements are increasingly needed for peacefully handling conflicts among different *types* of users of an international "highway" who are getting in each other's way: navies vs. ocean shippers vs. fishing fleets vs. recreational coastal interests; military reconnaissance satellites vs. orbiting telecommunications platforms, vs. meteorological and other scientific laboratories deployed in outer space.

2.3 The Economy and the Environment

The thickest institutionalization thus far of global accountability arrangements exists in the fields of trade and monetary affairs. This institutionalization was an outgrowth of the perception prominent in the 1940s among American and British officials that

World War II was at least indirectly a result of the protectionist and beggar-thy-neighbor economic policies pursued by the major countries in the 1920s and early 1930s. The premier global economic institutions established at the end of the war—the General Agreement on Tariffs and Trade (GATT) (see *General Agreement on Tariffs and Trade*), which was folded into the World Trade Organization (WTO) (see *World Trade Organization*) in 1994, the International Monetary Fund (IMF), and the World Bank—were all supposed to work in tandem (a) to assure that the leading economic powers avoided the unilateralist tariff wars and monetary devaluations that brought on the Great Depression, and (b) to stimulate the evolution of an integrated global free market. These are still their primary missions.

Paradoxically, it has been the most transnationally active entrepreneurs in the private sector (who in domestic markets normally *oppose* regulation) that have emerged as the prominent champions of these institutions of global economic accountability. The paradox is explained by the fact that the WTO, the IMF, and the World Bank, while fostering "horizontal" accountability among the governments, multinational corporations, and financial networks who dominate the world economy, are even further removed from "vertical" (democratic) accountability than are the economic policy-making institutions of the nation-states.

The WTO is the principal institutional locus of two types of accountability processes: It hosts inter-governmental negotiations to induce countries to reciprocally eliminate most of their tariffs and non-tariff barriers to international commerce. And it appoints dispute-settlement panels from which member governments are obligated to seek prior authorization before applying trade-restricting sanctions against countries alleged to be violating the free-trade accords already in existence.

The IMF is an essential complementary institution to the WTO, for the latter's regulation and reduction of barriers to trade could be easily subverted if countries could unilaterally alter the international exchange values of their currencies at will. Simply by "devaluing" its currency relative to foreign currencies, a country can raise the price its citizens must pay for imported goods—the equivalent of a tariff. To avoid such trade-restricting devaluations, the monetary regime founded by the United States and its (non-Communist) allies for the post-World War II world provided that all countries would "peg" their currencies to the US dollar at non-fluctuating rates of exchange, and that the value of the dollar would remain stable in relation to an ounce of gold. Alterations in the international exchange rates of national currencies would have to be approved by the IMF. This "fixed-rate" regime has been loosened in recent decades to accommodate to unilateral fiscal policy and market-driven changes in the actual purchasing power of national currencies. Although still accountable to the IMF system for major currency-value alterations, countries under the present "flexible" rules may act unilaterally within certain multilaterally-approved bands or stipulated ranges.

The IMF also has the role of providing temporary financial help to softening the economic impact of export-import imbalances that countries suffer from time to time in the competitive global market. When a country's poor international competitiveness is deemed by IMF experts to be the product of more fundamental structural problems, the IMF may offer a longer-term and more substantial financial aid package; but it has made such structural assistance conditional on the recipient government's adoption of IMF-mandated policies (usually designed to reduce the role of the state in the economy, provide an encouraging climate for multinational corporate investments, and stimulate export-led growth). Many Third World countries, desperately in need of the financial assistance, are particularly resentful of this facet of the global accountability system, regarding the IMF "conditionality" policies as violations of their national sovereignty (Grieder 1997).

Even the World Bank, whose primary mission has become to assist the economic development of poorer countries, has been conditioning its loans on recipient's adherence to the market-oriented structural adjustment policies favored by the IMF. Third world governments, in reaction, are urging that they be accorded a greater say in IMF and World Bank decisions than they now have under voting arrangements heavily weighted in favor of the donors, so as to make the loan criteria responsive to their unique circumstances and cultural traditions—in effect, making the world's financial institutions reciprocally accountable to their clients.

In negotiations over the care of the global environment, the Third World countries have been relatively more successful in obtaining some adjustments in the international accountability arrangements that they perceive to be asymmetrically stacked against them than they have been in most of the other international arenas (see *Global Environment and Peace; Green Security*). Clearly, this is attributable primarily to the realization on the part of the affluent industrial countries that their own well-being *requires* the cooperation of developing countries who are contributing to the destruction of the planet's ecological commons. The developing countries have been insisting that the industrial countries be accountable to *them*—accountable for the globally skewed levels of economic well-being, North and South, which are at least partially traceable to the colonial system, and which the poorer South cannot afford to rectify in the environmentally-sound way the North wants without substantial subsidies from the affluent North (see *North-South Conflict*).

The results of this somewhat more symmetrical bargaining relationship concerning accountability for harm done to the global environment are seen in the equity provisions in the accords for protecting the ozone layer and in various of the covenants and agreements produced at the 1992 Earth Summit and its follow-up negotiations. Thus the 1990 London Revisions to the Montreal Protocol on Substances that Deplete the Ozone Layer allowed an extension in the deadline for phasing out the offending substances to countries that would suffer economic hardship from a total phaseout, and a multilateral fund was established by which the affluent parties would finance the acquisition of appropriate technologies by developing countries to help them convert to ozone-safe industries and products (Benedik 1991). Similarly, the Framework Convention on Climate Change approved at Rio in 1992 made a start toward dealing with the predicaments of the late-industrializing South by establishing funding mechanisms that, if adequately provisioned by the affluent countries, could subsidize the adoption of more efficient energy systems by the poor countries (Porter and Brown 1996).

In short, in the economics of global environmental protection, at least the *principle* of mutual accountability is now widely accepted. Its implementation, however, will require concrete and durable commitments from the United States and the other advanced industrialized countries, which as yet have not been sufficiently forthcoming.

2.4 Human Rights

A government that has signed and ratified the major human rights covenants has, by so doing, subscribed to the norm that governments are accountable to their citizenry and to the international community at large for how they treat the people within their jurisdictions. And a majority of countries have now formally acceded to most of the core human rights covenants, often called the "International Bill of Rights" (see *International Bill of Human Rights*): the International

Covenant on Civil and Political Rights; the International Covenant on Economic, Social, and Cultural Rights; the International Covenant on the Elimination of All Forms of Racial Discrimination; the Convention on the Elimination of All Forms of Discrimination Against Women; the Convention on the Rights of the Child; and the Convention Against Torture and Other Cruel, Inhuman, or Degrading Treatment or Punishment. While it is true that most governments are still reluctant to call one another to account in international forums except for egregious violations that have already become a cause celebre, the burden of justification has shifted in recent decades to those governments still insisting on sovereign immunity from international accountability for their human rights behavior.

Some governments—China, Singapore, Saudi Arabia, Turkey, and Cuba, for example—are holdouts for the traditional view that the burden of justification falls on those who would undermine the norm of non-interference by states in one another's domestic affairs (see *Nonintervention and Noninterference*). But the statist hardliners are finding that a poor human rights record, despite their efforts to suppress the information, is likely to translate into considerable diplomatic friction, let alone embarrassing exposures by influential non-governmental organizations, with countries who have embraced the human rights ethos. Countries with poor human rights records may be denied full membership in regional and specialized international organizations with stringent human rights criteria. Such countries may also find themselves the targets of boycotts organized by transnational non-governmental organizations.

There is no going back to the older system in which how national governments treat the people within their jurisdictions is no one else's business. A system of international and transnational accountability is evolving. Driven not only by material forces but by competing ideas about justice—often bitterly, even violently contested—the state-sovereignty system is in the process of gestation into the embryo of a yet-to-be-born world community. The sage British scholar, R. J. Vincent, had his eye on the essentials when he speculated a few years ago that the global

system is on the verge of experiencing "a transformation from international relations to world politics as significant as that which established the society of states, and for which the idea of human rights is a kind of midwife" (Vincent 1986).

See also: *Global Economic Interdependence: Why Crisis?; Global Integration; Globalization; Global Neighborhood: New Security Principles; World Order: Gandhi's Concepts and Contributions*

Bibliography

Benedik R E 1991 *Ozone Diplomacy: New Directions in Safeguarding the Planet.* Harvard, Cambridge

Brown S 1995 *International Relations in a Changing Global System: Toward a Theory of the World Polity.* Westview, Boulder

Brown S 1994 *New Forces, Old Forces, and the Future of World Politics.* Harper Collins, New York

Greider W 1997 *One World, Ready or Not: The Manic Logic of Global Capitalism.* Simon & Schuster, New York

Huntington S P 1996 *The Clash of Civilizations and the Making of World Order.* Simon & Schuster, New York

Johansen R C 1994 Building world security: The need for strengthened international institutions. In: Klare M T, Thomas D C *World Security: Challenges for a New Century.* St. Martin's, New York

Porter G, Brown J W 1996 *Global Environmental Politics.* Westview, Boulder

Stimson Center 1995 *An Evolving Nuclear Posture: Second Report of the Steering Committee on Eliminating Weapons of Mass Destruction.* Henry L. Stimson Center, Washington, DC

United Nations 1968 *Treaty on the Non-Proliferation of Nuclear Weapons.* 729 U.N.T.S 161, United Nations

Van Ham P 1994 *Non-Proliferation Regimes in the 1990s: Power, Politics, and Policies.* Council on Foreign Relations, New York

Vincent R J 1986 *Human Rights and International Relations.* Cambridge University Press, New York

Walzer M 1994 *Thick and Thin: Moral Argument at Home and Abroad.* Notre Dame University Press, Notre Dame

SEYOM BROWN

Global Visions for the Next Millennium

When former New York Senator Robert F. Kennedy was campaigning to become president of the United States, he made the following statement shortly before his assassination in California. He said: "Every

event which takes place in history starts with an idea, with a vision, or with a dream. Our actions are always performed in relation to a conceived idea, a vision, or a dream. In other words, our positive thinking generates positive actions while our negative thinking evolves into negative actions."

1. Historical Perspective of Society

Before setting up positive global visions toward the next millennium, we need to have a good historical perspective of society. The books of world history are all centered on regional and global wars. The great positive contributions that human beings made throughout history are all reported by historians as mere marginal events. The traditional political slogan: *Si vis pacem para bellum*—if you want peace prepare for war, has proven to be fallacious. A careful study of the past 6,000 years of recorded history reveals the opposite of this slogan to be true: *Si vis bellum para bellum*—if you want war prepare for war . . . *si vis pacem para pacem*—if you want peace prepare for peace.

If we had the power to perform magic in the sense that we could make things happen once we seriously decide we want them, what would we try to make happen? Whatever we wish it must be constructive and positive. It must be in the best interest of all people without exception. This would lead to genuine permanent peace. It cannot be to promote the interest of one group to the exclusion of others for this, as we have witnessed century after century unto this very day, would lead to mutual disrespect and mistrust as well as to inevitable conflict, struggle and war. Let us keep in mind the words of Pope Pius XII which he uttered to both the British and the Germans on the eve of World War II. He warned these two great nations saying: In a war everyone is a loser and no one is a winner.

The Pope's words proved to be prophetic. Germany lost the war and its economy collapsed. Unemployment and poverty became rampant. On the other hand, Great Britain won the war and its economy equally collapsed. Unemployment and poverty flourished and the great British Empire collapsed. The political contention that a strong military build-up guarantees the security of a nation has constantly proved to be fallacious to say the least and to be disastrous to say the most.

2. Positive Visions of the Future

Since the beginning of times, human beings have learned to live at peace on a permanent basis individually and collectively. The means which lead to such an end should be viewed as our *de facto* global visions toward the next millennium. Such global visions may be listed as follows:

2.1 Adequate Nourishment

For people to survive they must have adequate nourishment. Countless millions of people are dying daily due to malnutrition. They either do not have enough food or the food they eat is contaminated with pesticides and other poisonous elements. Besides, several countries have enough food for the population but they do not have the ability of food preservation because they lack canning industry.

2.2 Clean Air and Pure Water

The weapons industry, in particular, has contaminated our arable land and the very same water we drink from our lakes and rivers with toxic wastes. As a result, we have endangered human life and the life of every species one may imagine. Numerous people, including several celebrities, have died of cancer as a result in the midst of their youthfulness. Ironically, the weapons industry claims that it exists to save our lives when the contrary has been experienced.

2.3 Good Health Care System

Since people are the backbone of the nation, every government should put top priority on a good health care system, which should be provided free for all citizens. Healthy people tend to think straight. They demonstrate greater ability in concentration and, as a result, they tend to achieve great and positive results in anything they undertake. Besides, it always remains true that healthy people create a healthy nation.

2.4 Sound Education

Through a sound education we are capable of developing our rich human resources to solve properly and effectively every problem we may encounter. Since our students may be viewed as the future pillars of our society, they are entitled to have a free education from the cradle to the grave. The financial burden which our society has put on our citizens have forced many to disregard their tremendously rich potential to the detriment of the nation itself.

2.5 Individual Spiritual Revival

Ascetics describe humans as being partly animals and partly angels. With animals we share the five senses along with such necessities as eating, drinking, and sleeping. With the angels we share such properties as thinking, reasoning, planning and the practice of virtue which may include kindness, prudence, charity, patience, and courage, among others.

These are spiritual qualities which should be cultivated so as to produce what may be termed as the ideal citizen.

2.6 Safeguard of Human Rights

Although the UN Declaration on Human Rights has been signed by every single country, yet the vast majority of nations tend to ignore such a document. People have a right not only to lead a healthy life and to secure a sound education, but also to travel freely and to settle anywhere they want. Besides, both men and women are individually free to marry or to remain single. Also, they have a right to form their own individual independent state or nation.

2.7 Protection of Women and Children

Women have always proved themselves to be as capable as men in getting things done. Yet, the predominantly patriarchal society has always tended to treat women as inferior. In Africa, for example, women are viewed as man's property or merely as a piece of furniture. On the other hand, children have been greatly abused in making them work like adults and in recruiting them as soldiers while trained to kill mercilessly other human beings.

2.8 Elimination of Organized Crime

Every great power in history has collapsed mostly due to organized crime which ultimately brought corruption in the government itself. In organized crime we have an elite of people who try to advance in life at the expense of others and through the exploitation of people. As a result, many problems arise which may include dishonesty, recession, unemployment, blackmailing, cheating, confiscation of property, unlawful imprisonment, and murder.

2.9 Promotion of World Citizenship

In the year 42 AD, Roman philosopher Seneca made the following statement. There will be world peace only after we educate our children to look at the world and say with realization: *"Omnis orbis terrarum patria mea est—the whole world is my native land."* To be a world citizen one should instill greater pride than just to be merely a citizen of this or that country. If Seneca's philosophy is taken seriously we are bound to have peace throughout the next millennium.

2.10 World Government in Operation

The structure of the USA may be viewed as a miniature type of world government. Every state has its own government but without the existence of a state

military. The United Nations could be restructured to function the same way. While every nation would remain sovereign flying its own flag and developing its civilian economy, no nation would keep its own military. This way no nation would ever dream of waging a war against another nation.

If there is one big lesson we should learn from the recorded history of the past 6,000 years it should be this. Any kind of problem the world faces can never be solved on a permanent basis through military means. A careful study of the world history reveals that the military has contributed more to the creation of problems than to their solution. The means used by the military, supposedly to solve problems, has been always the same: weapons of destruction which contributed systematically to the destruction of culture, the environment, numerous species, and of human life itself.

It is difficult to conceive war without the military or the other way round. The two of them go hand in hand. They are like two legs of the same person. What is ironic is evidenced by the fact that a substantial number of people of nations, which were viewed as strong militarily, have suffered immensely from malnutrition, adequate health facilities, good education, drug abuse, organized crime, apathy, lethargy, spiritual atrophy, insecurity and nervous breakdown.

These elements can be observed today in countries which have put top priority on the military as a means of security. That will include both Russia and the United States. On the other hand, those nations in history which downgraded the importance of the military and put, instead, top priority on the health care and education of the people succeeded to have numerous problems solved overnight. Among such countries we find Costa Rica, Malta, New Zealand, Switzerland, and the Scandinavian countries whose people are enjoying a kind of life that is healthier, more hopeful and more peaceful.

There is no need for us to live another fifty, hundred, or more years to see what the world would look like in the future. The world will be exactly what we are preparing it to be by the kind of actions we are taking today individually and collectively, regionally and globally. Nothing more and nothing less!

3. Beyond Modern Civilization

Modern civilization has been greatly influenced by the industrial revolution in the economic sphere, religious evolution on a global scale, various trends in cultural integration, and space age technology which forced all nations into becoming totally interdependent.

Although the industrial revolution enabled human beings to travel from one global area to another fairly fast, it also brought with it a considerable amount of air and water pollution. Such elements have become increasingly a hazard to our environment and to our very own survival. The success and failure of the next millennium will depend on how we are going to deal with the problem of pollution today.

The religious evolution we are experiencing on a global scale cannot be taken lightly. It is a very positive element for it uplifts the human spirit to a higher level of existence in a way that most of our present priorities are bound to be straightened for the better. After all, we are essentially what we may be described to be as spiritual beings whose psychology and philosophy are exclusive properties of the human spirit.

As time passes, the trend for cultural integration is becoming more imminently felt. In countries with diversified cultures, people are given the opportunity to learn how to live together in mutual respect, peace, and harmony. Diversity among human beings has made our world more enriched and more colorful. People have the opportunity to inspire each other continuously in the hope of creating a better future for the third millennium.

Last but not least, space age technology has brought the people of the world closer together than ever before. Seneca's philosophy of peace—*omnis orbs terrarum patria mea est*—the world is my native land, is felt more than ever before. The satellite system is enabling us to watch what people are doing in every global area instantaneously. Our computers we are allowing us to have a rapid access to numerous libraries, schools, businesses, and homes all over the world. Our primary task is to make the stated global visions a tangible reality. This would be our best and greatest legacy for the next millennium.

CHARLES MERCIECA

Global War, Alternatives to

Alternatives to global war are those political and social processes and institutions that can substitute for the positive functions of a global war while circumventing its negative consequences, particularly those that are lethal. In order to avoid a future global war, alternatives to it need to be found and/or invented.

The concept of alternatives to global war is narrower and more sharply focused than the broader concept of alternatives or equivalents to all war. It implies two ideas: (a) that war performs functions that can, under certain circumstances, be performed through alternative social arrangements and mechanisms; and (b) that "global war" is a separate class of war for which specific alternative mechanisms can be designed.

1. Alternatives

In the literature of peace and international relations there exists a significant tradition that relies on functional analysis for exploring the problem of controlling warfare. The first to suggest such an approach, in a famous essay entitled "The moral equivalent of war" and written on the eve of the First World War, was William James (1910), the pragmatist philosopher. James argued that war was an opportunity for the display and exercise of such positive "martial virtues" as the "ideas of honor" and "standards of efficiency," and that peace could be achieved by finding alternatives to war that were equally "moral," such as community labor.

A substantial and progressive reworking of the James thesis was Walter Lippman's essay "The political equivalent of war" (1928). For Lippmann war was a process of political decision making, "one of the ways by which great human decisions are made" that could indeed be supplanted if alternative ways of taking decisions were put in place in the world political system. For him, however, world government (see *World Government*) was the only real alternative mechanism of political decision-making that he could envisage. He argued that "war will not be abolished . . . unless there is an international government strong enough to preserve order and wise enough to welcome changes in that order."

At about the same time, too, international attention was accruing to Mahatma Gandhi's campaign of nonviolent resistance to British rule in India (see *Gandhi, Mohandas Caramchand; World Order: Gandhi's Concepts and Contributions*). This was an attempt to substitute a nonlethal equivalent for what might otherwise have become a war of national resistance, and attracted widespread support as a model of violence-free political action.

Since 1945 much thought has been given to the possibility of abstention from the use of violence, much of it centered on the concept of "civilian-based defense" (see *Civilian-based Defense*). Writers such as Sharp (1965, 1980), Roberts (1967), and Fischer (in Weston

1984 pp. 504-31) drew on the experience of Second World War resistance movements, the lessons of Czechoslovakia in 1968-69, and the Swiss experience. For them, the legitimate functions of war were defensive, and that is why a functional alternative to war had to provide for a country's defense or even deterrence (see *Deterrence*) by such means as nonviolent resistance, noncooperation with the invaders (see *Conscientious Objection; Nonviolence*), or a "nonprovocative defense policy" (see *Alternative Defense*).

In the 1980s the problem of alternatives has attracted renewed attention. These were, of course, no more than untested hypotheses spun out by "alternative theorists," but according to at least one observer, "as military strategies have so long and systematically planned for war, so these thinkers are beginning to plan for peace. Working in isolation from one another, and largely without financial resources, these researchers have been sketching strikingly similar designs for their peaceable worlds and the likely transitions to them" (Sommer 1986). One survey of such alternatives may be found in the collection edited by Weston (1984).

All of these approaches to the question of alternatives share a basic premise of functional analysis that Merton (1968 p. 135) formulated as follows: "Any attempt to eliminate an existing social structure without providing adequate alternative structures for fulfilling the functions previously filled by the abolished organization is doomed to failure (see *Conflict and Peace: Class versus Structural School*)."

2. Global Wars

The other premise underlying this discussion has been the view that the structure to be abolished is war itself, viewed as a universal human institution. That implies rather a sweeping program of change. Such a broad conception of war also implies diverse views of the functions that war in general might fill and for which a substitute is to be provided. For the task of abolishing all war is, of course, one of considerable magnitude and one that, like that of curing all disease, must be approached with considerable circumspection.

This article adopts a narrower perspective and favors a more precisely focused strategy. If it is agreed that the priority problem is that of the next global war because global war is the only type of war that is probable to take the form of nuclear war, then the search for substitutes may appear to be a more tractable problem. Global war is a phase of world politics that in the experience of the past several centuries of the modern

era has alternated with periods of general (or systemic) peace (see *Global Wars; War*). During the period 1815 to 1914, for instance, the world at large was at peace even if civil, local and regional wars were quite a common occurrence at various times and in diverse regions of the globe. In the experience of the modern world system since 1494, five generation-long periods of global war have in fact been followed by much longer intervals of such general peace (see *Peace, Systems View of*). The most recent period of global war was the era of the First and Second World Wars viewed as one prolonged incident of worldwide warfare. The result of these past global wars has been to install world powers in a position of global leadership, and to decide on system-wide policies and innovations.

3. Nuclear Deterrence as Alternative to Global War

In the years since 1945 it has been argued that nuclear deterrence—that is, the capacity to inflict devastating retaliation, and the policy based upon such capacity—might be viewed as a principal instrument for maintaining general peace. Deterrence was widely credited with preventing major war by making it unavoidably intolerable for all the participants. More particularly, the general peace in the years since 1945 was widely thought to have been maintained by nuclear deterrence (see *Nuclear Deterrence, Doctrine of*). Yet scholars who have looked at this problem find it hard to demonstrate that nuclear deterrence has in fact worked in that way (Kugler 1984). "Long-cycle" theorists do not find it surprising that general peace has prevailed since the end of the Second World War because the post-global-war phase is in fact least likely to conduce to major hostilities (Modelski and Morgan 1985 p. 408, 410).

In the light of concern over the possibility of nuclear annihilation in the event of a deterrence failure and in the context of the possible use of nuclear weapons, the broader concept of "alternative security systems" has been gaining ground. "Since nuclear deterrence contains the last resort of mutually-assured destruction. There must be a search for alternatives of a nonnuclear kind" (Newman, in Newman and Dando 1982 p. 234; see also Stephenson 1983). Among such alternatives, disarmament and world government are prominently mentioned (Johansen 1983).

One problem has been what Burns Weston (1985) has described as "our collective inability to perceive workable alternatives." He lists ten of what he regards as viable options (even though they all presuppose a nuclear-free world); they range from Jonathan

Schell's concept of a "weaponless nuclear deterrence" (1982, 1984), through reliance on conventional and defensive forces, and noncoercive inducements, to reforming the United Nations, and peace education. But none of these alternatives are intended as "an escape from that ultimate creative initiative that would rule out war itself as a means of settling differences between nations," and that raises basic questions of "system transformation."

Does the existence of rival nuclear arsenals impede "system transformation?" It might be argued that the parity in nuclear weapons that is at the basis of nuclear deterrence in fact creates a stalemate and that is the precise object of deterrence. The condition of stalemate hinders, or tends to hamper, structural shifts that inevitably occur in the world system, and forestalls the possibility of systemic decisions on basic issues such as leadership, and solutions to global problems that need to be made at certain long, but definite, intervals. Most generally, to believe that nuclear deterrence can go on "indefinitely without major disaster requires an optimism unjustified by any historical or political perspective" (Freedman 1983 p. 399). A major change in the world did occur in 1989/91 and since the dissolution of the former Soviet Union the role of nuclear deterrence has receded into the background but the nuclear arsenals, while reduced, have not been disarmed, and nuclear proliferation remains a major problem.

4. Democracy, Free Trade, World Opinion, and Peace

A most important "system transformation" underway in the world system is democratization that may be defined as the world-wide spread of democracy (see *Peace and Democracy*). Over the past two centuries, a steadily rising proportion of the earth's population has been living in democratic societies. At the end of the 19th century, a dozen countries, accounting for some 10-12 percent of the world's peoples, could be described as democratic. At the close of the 20th century, several dozen countries, with over 50 percent, that is, a majority, of the world's population, could be so regarded. In that time, the number of people living in democracies has grown from about 200 million, to over three billion. In another century, most of the world might be democratic. The nation-state no longer is at the center of democratic practice and thought; the focus is now on the world (Held 1995).

This matters because "democracies do not go to war with each other." Recent work in International Relations (cf. Russett 1993) has established by

empirical research "the fact of democratic peace." That is, democracies have been shown to be unlikely to engage in disputes that escalate into violence, and rarely to fight each other even at low levels of violence, let alone war (see *Democracy and Foreign Policy*). On the other hand, democracies have not been inherently less bellicose toward non-democracies, and have fought successful global wars. Over time, the spread of democracy creates a steadily expanding "zone of peace," a space within which peace prevails.

"Democratic peace" prevails because democracies form a community within which decisions are made, and problems are resolved by democratic (that is, non-warlike) procedures. The norm of "democratic peace" is observed in that community and gains additional strength from such common institutions as NATO (North Atlantic Treaty Organization) (see *North Atlantic Treaty Organization (NATO)*), OECD (Organization for Economic Cooperation and Development), and European Union (see *European Union*), and from the support of major democratic powers.

The "democratic peace" is laying the foundations of a global civil society and it is strengthened by two other aspects of globalization (see *Globalization*): economic interdependence (see *Economic Interdependence*), and the rise of world opinion. Interdependence is the product of world-wide economic growth and of trade and investment that is increasingly free. The early advocates of free trade, and Richard Cobden (104-1865) in particular, have been emphatic in their belief that free trade is the foundation of peace. Since 1945 the growth of world trade has been most significant. In turn, the Information Revolution, powered by world-wide diffusion of electronic media is creating the technical infrastructure of global interdependence. It makes it possible for informed world opinion, aware of the nuclear threat, to be brought to bear on crucial questions of war and peace.

These developments give substance to the idea of "system transformation," and vindicate Immanuel Kant's famous conjecture, penned in 1795, that "Perpetual Peace" (see *Perpetual Peace; Kant, Immanuel*) will be the product of a "natural" process, mediated by the proliferation of (democratic) republics, joined in a (democratic) community, while engaged in free commerce.

5. Alternatives to the Next Global War

Democratization, together with free trade and the information revolution, create the context within which alternatives to the next global war become conceivable (see *Ethics in the Post-Industrialized and Informationalized Society*). The "zone of democratic peace" might grow so large and gain such strength that those left outside it might not be able to muster the forces required for issuing the challenges that might lead to global war. More positively, the democratic community will hopefully devise, within its own bounds, democratic forms of "macrodecision," that is, will find ways of choosing global leadership and deciding upon global priorities, without global war. The question is how, when, and by whom might such alternatives be devised.

We know that in the absence of a nuclear-free world, and short of ruling out all war, sustained attention needs to be given to the question of preventing just one war, another global war. Since 1494 global wars have regularly reordered the world system by giving it new political leadership, and this makes it necessary to think about the possibility that, in some not too distant, and not unforeseeable, future, world politics could move once again into a period of sustained tension and major crises (deconcentration and coalition-building), in which the major powers arrange themselves, in a multipolar configuration, into rival coalitions. A series of confontations between such coalitions could (but also need not), (ca.2030?) bring about a global war and such a war would likely be a nuclear war.

As on several previous occasions, a powerful continental challenger might arise in a manner not unlike that observed in previous cycles in relation to Germany, France, or Spain. Those problems arose in the context of European territorial, political, and ideological controversies and were resolved only through prolonged warfare. Even if all of Europe were to become a zone of peace, East Asia might become the scene of global-scale confrontations in the 21st century.

To forestall such a possibility alternative political designs short of world government and disarmament need to be explored in good time. Returning to Lippmann (1928), the search will be on for alternative means of making those "great human decisions" of world politics. The search will be on for sets of democratic procedures that might function as substitute mechanisms of macrodecision for the selection of new leadership and new policies. We know from experience that elections and parties are essential elements of collective decisions in democratic societies. Critical elections are known to have mediated major structural changes in national societies, and elections and parties have arguably become the effective substitutes for civil war (Goldman 1983).

Little is known whether, or in what manner, elec-

tions and parties, possibly evolving in relation to the United Nations (see *Status and Role of the United Nations*), could function as a substitute mechanism for global war because that will be the result of political innovation that will be substantial though short of "systemic transformation." It could, conceivably, assume the form of simulated combat, or some other kind of competition, which is what an election is in any event. But the innovative effort is likely to be considerable and will require more than a generation to gain acceptance, and for testing and implementing in the practice of world politics. The long-cycle phase of deconcentration/coalition-building that global politics will be entering after the year 2000 is likely to become such a testing period for innovations that in the context of new institutional arrangements will select new leadership and decide upon global priorities for the 21st century (see *Global Neighborhood: New Security Principles*).

See also: *Deterrence; Transnationalism; War, Prediction of; Construction of the Principle of Toleration and Its Implications for Contemporary Democratic States*

Bibliography

Freedman L 1983 *The Evolution of Nuclear Strategy*. St Martin's Press, New York

Goldman R M 1983 Achieving domestic arms control in England and Mexico: Political parties as an alternative to war. In: Goldman (ed.) *Transnational Parties*. University of America Press, Lanham, MD

Held D 1995 Cosmopolitan Democracy and the Global Order. *Alternatives* 20

James W 1910 The moral equivalent of war. *International Conciliation* 27 (February)

Johansen R 1983 Toward an alternative security system. *World Policy Paper* No. 24. World Policy Institute, New York

Kugler J 1984 Terror without deterrence: Reassessing the role of nuclear weapons. *J. Conflict Resolution*

Lippmann W 1928 The political equivalent of war. *Atlantic Monthly* 142

Modelski G 1987 *Long Cycles in World Politics*. Macmillan, London

Modelski G, Morgan P M 1985 Understanding global war. *J. Conflict Resolution*

Merton R K 1968 *Social Theory and Social Structure*. rev. edn. Free Press. New York

Newman B, Dando M (eds.) 1982 *Nuclear Deterrence*. Castle House, Tunbridge Wells

Roberts A (ed.) 1967 *The Strategy of Civilian Defence*. Faber and Faber, London

Russett B 1993 *Grasping the Democratic Peace*. Princeton

University Press, Princeton, NJ

Sharp G 1965 The political equivalent of war: Civilian defence. *International Conciliation* 555 (November)

Sharp G 1980 *Social Power and Political Freedom*. Porter Sargent, Boston, Massachusetts

Schell J 1982 *The Fate of the Earth*. Knopf, New York

Schell J 1984 *The Abolition*. Knopf, New York

Sommer M 1986 Beyond the bomb: Imagining a non-nuclear defense. *Nuclear Times* (March-April), New York

Stephenson C (ed.) 1983 *Alternative Methods for International Security*. University Press of America, Washington, DC

Weston B H (ed.) 1984 *Toward Nuclear Disarmament and Global Security: A Search for Alternatives*. Westview Press, Boulder, Co

Weston B H 1985 Lawyers and the search for alternatives to nuclear deterrence. *University of Cincinnati Law Rev.* 54(2)

GEORGE MODELSKI

Global Wars

Global war has been, in the experience of modern world politics, a war for global leadership. In the past half-millennium, it occurred, in a pattern of major regularity, about once every century, forming a distinct, generation-long, phase of global politics. That phase might be called one of "macrodecision" because it was then that by a process of collective decision in a coalition war one power was selected to a leading position in the global system. The three other phases ("agenda-setting," "coalition-building," as well as "execution" that follows upon "macrodecision") might then, by contrast, be regarded as a period of general peace. General (or systemic) peace is compatible with regional or local wars (see *Peace, Systems View of*), such as the Franco-German war of 1870-1 in the nineteenth century, or the Korean war, or the Iran-Iraq war in the era since 1945 because such regional wars did not disturb the peace of the world as a whole or raise issues of global leadership (see *Local Wars Since 1945*).

That makes the concept of global war theory-specific, that is, one whose meaning is dependent on the theory of which it forms a part. Global war as "macro-decision" is seen as a concept in an evolutionary paradigm of global politics (Modelski 1987,1996). That theory proposes that the evolution of the global political system over the past 500 years can be seen as driven by a competition for global leadership, in which the rise of successive world powers can be conceptualized as a series of several 120-year, four-phase, long learning cycles of which global war constituted the "macrodecision" phase, the selection mechanism of the entire process. But, the selection mechanism is itself subject to change in that arrangements other than global war can be deployed to bring about a "macrodecision."

1. The Universe of Global Wars

The universe of global wars considered here consists

of the following five cases (Modelski 1987; Thompson 1988).

(a) Wars of Italy and the Indian Ocean Wars (1494-1516). These were wars fought by Spain against France principally in Italy and for the control of Italy at that time the hub of the Mediterranean-European system that centered on Venice. But this Franco-Spanish conflict was closely related to the naval campaigns Portugal mounted after 1500 in the Indian Ocean and that reached as far as Malacca and the Spice Islands and that put in place the outlines of the first global political system. The partnership of Portugal and Spain was the winning coalition of these wars.

(b) The Spanish-Dutch wars stemmed from the assertion of the independence by the United Provinces of the Netherlands (1579-81), and Spain's seizure of Portugal and its global network (1580), and continued through the war of the Armada with England, the wars in France, and the Dutch attack on the Spice Islands, until the Truce of Antwerp (1609). The Dutch-English-French coalition, based *inter alia* on religious ties, was the key to this protracted struggle that gave a key role to the Dutch Republic.

(c) The wars of the Grand Alliance against Louis XIV of France (1688-1713). These two major coalition wars, also known as the War of the League of Augsburg, and the War of Spanish Succession, were both organized under the leadership of William of Orange who ascended the English throne in 1689. The two maritime powers, Britain and the Netherlands, were the core of the winning team of that far-flung conflict as the result of which Britain came for the first time to "rule the waves."

(d) The wars of the French Revolution and of Napoleon (1792-1815). These were waged by a series of coalitions under British leadership and culminated in the victory of the Quadruple Alliance in 1814-15. A Concert of Europe (see *Council of Europe*) to coordinate Great Power policies in Europe; outside Europe and on the high seas Britain's global leadership was renewed for a second term.

(e) First and Second World Wars (1914-45) may be viewed as one long period of intense political combat and armed struggle in which the principal challenger was Germany and in which the core element of the World War II alliance of the "United Nations" was the special relationship between Britain and the United States. The United Nations was established as the general international organization of the post-1945 period, while the United States assumed a position of global leadership in the global political system (see *Status and Role of the United Nations*).

2. Related Concepts

Being theory-specific, the concept of global war is therefore not identical with, but is nevertheless related to, such other concepts as that of "general war," "hegemonic war," and "world war" and partakes with them of much of the relevant information (see also Levy 1985; Thompson 1985).

Quincy Wright (see *Wright, Quincy*) (1942 Appendix XX) defined a general war, quite broadly, as one that is participated in by all of the Great Powers. Jack Levy (1983 pp. 74-75; 1985 p. 369) viewed a general war as one involving "most" of the Great Powers in a conflict marked by particularly high levels of destructiveness. Arnold Toynbee (1954 p. 234f) on the other

hand, saw general war, more particularly, as an aspect of the operation of the balance of power (see *Balance of Power*), and one phase of a "war-peace cycle" that has repeated itself at intervals of approximately one century in "modern and postmodern Western history."

Relevant, too, is Robert Gilpin's (1981 pp. 197-98) concept of hegemonic war: a war that determines which state or states will be dominant in, and govern, the international system. If hegemony is interpreted broadly as leadership (see *Hegemony*), then global war is a leadership war in Gilpin's sense, but his definition is also cast in universal terms applicable to all history; "global wars," on the other hand, concern only the modern period since 1494. Paul Kennedy's (1987) coalition wars carry much the same connotations.

Reference might also be made to Immanuel Wallerstein's (1984 ch. 4) use of the concept of "world war" in his account of the evolution of the capitalist world economy. He, too, links it to the emergence of "hegemony" but espouses a more limited, economic, conception of it.

Table 1 shows global wars as compared with general, hegemonic, and world wars, and how these several concepts identify the known major wars of the past five centuries. It demonstrates that at least among these five scholarly approaches there is considerable convergence; there is unanimity on designating the two most recent, and therefore the two cases of greatest significance for practical purposes, as wars of this special type. The consensus lessens the further back we go but remains considerable for the cases of the wars of the Grand Alliance, and those of Spain and the Netherlands. The Thirty Years' War alone remains a case of contention, even though it ought to be regarded as the regional war of

Table 1
Global wars compared with general, hegemonic, and world wars

	Global war	Toynbee's general war	Wallerstein's world war	Gilpin's hegemonic war	Levy's general war
Italian and Indian Ocean Wars	yes	yes			
Dutch-Spanish Wars	yes	yes			yes
Thirty Years' War 1618-48			yes	yes	yes
Dutch War 1672-78		yes		yes	yes
Wars of the Grand Alliance	yes	yes		yes	yes
War of the Austrian Succession 1739-48					yes
Seven Years' War 1756-63					yes
French Revolutionary and Napoleonic Wars	yes	yes	yes	yes	yes
First and Second World Wars	yes	yes	yes	yes	yes

special import to Germany that it was. Overall, there is an almost perfect fit between the "global wars" of this analysis and Toynbee's general wars, except that Toynbee's theory does not provide for the concept of leadership, or explores the question of alternatives to global war.

3. Characteristics of Global Wars

Each of the five wars singled out as global wars for this analysis has all of the following characteristics.

3.1 Participants

Each global war was, in its basic thrust, a contest for global leadership, principally involving an aspiring world power, and a challenger. The world powers were those that successfully led the war-time coalition, and displayed such other necessary characteristics as powerful forces of global reach including navies, successful economies with leading sectors, free and open societies that were responsive to priority global problems. Those rising to global leadership also did so on on the basis of a policy agenda that forwarded the evolution of the global system. The challengers, by contrast, deployed large continental armies that threatened and alarmed their neighbors but had trouble organizing coalitions; they maintained arbitrary and absolute rule, closed their societies and commanded large but less advanced economies.

3.2 Duration

Each lasted between 25 and 30 years, that is, for the life-time of one generation, creating what is known as a generational experience. A sequence of armed contests was usually involved, each past global war being composed of at least two major wars, each setting off related and minor combats of its own. Each such sequence may however be viewed as one war because in each case the identity of the principal contestants, and the character of the issues at stake, remained the same throughout.

3.3 Global Scope

Each such global war was a conflict of global scope and participation, and crucial to the constitution and functioning of the global political system. Prior to 1494 there were, of course, no global wars because there was no global political system in place, even though the campaigns of the Mongols did create, by about 1280, a Eurasian continental world empire, that

in its turn was destroyed by rebellion in China, and by Timur (by 1400). An oceanic, and truly global political system was put in place principally by Portugal and in concert with Spain (Treaty of Tordesillas 1494) (see *Conciliar Movement*).

Each global war involved fighting on several continents; each was significantly an oceanic war and featured decisive naval battles. Each involved the navies of all the global powers (that is states with major forces of global reach in the form of sea and more recently, air, power). Each ended with the monopoly of forces of global reach vested in the leader of the winning coalition (Modelski and Thompson 1988). In that sense each was a general systemic war.

3.4 Causes

A global war is the result of a structural crisis in the global political system, a product of the decay of leadership and of rivalry among ascending powers competing for leadership. In this general sense, each global war resulted from loss of legitimacy, that is delegitimation, and subsequent deconcentration, that brought about a search for new leadership. That led to the formation of new coalitions, that serving the function of "resolving the pre-war ambiguities in the hierarchical leadership structure of the system" (Thompson 1983:159). For that reason, every global war might be said to have the same set of necessary (but not sufficient) conditions. What is more, every such conflagration might also be regarded as a product of a deterrent failure, triggered by threats to the stability of a critical region of the world system: Italy in the first instance, then the Low Countries, more recently Western Europe as a whole and, in the future possibly including East Asia.

3.5 Consequences

Each global war was a test of strength that brought about a new leadership structure for the system and in that sense also constituted a hegemonic war. The Indian Ocean campaigns directly, and the Italian wars indirectly (via curbing Venice) gave the global role to Portugal. The Spanish wars established the Netherlands in a lead position. The wars of Louis XIV transferred leadership to Britain in a process that should be described as one of cooptation (of Britain to that role). In 1815 Britain's position was reaffirmed in even stronger terms. The two world wars of the twentieth century placed the United States in a role of global leadership. In that perspective every global war had at least one important consequence (and performed at least one distinct function): it served as a systemic decision process by means of which leadership was selected for the global polity for a period of up to four generations.

3.6 Lethality

The systematic study of the intensity of war was pioneered by Wright (1942: Appendix XVII) and by Richardson (1960) and their work has helped to highlight the statistical singularity of global wars in the universe of all wars. Analysis of the data now available makes it possible to estimate in an aggregate fashion the battle deaths attributable to the five global wars discussed in this article. Table 2 shows that in the period 1494-1945 our five global wars accounted for close to four-fifths of all battle fatalities in the interstate wars of the modern Great Power system. Even though such wars comprised only about one-quarter of the total time, they were responsible for the bulk of the loss of life. In particular, the First and Second World Wars made up 95 percent of interstate war fatalities in the 130 years prior to 1945, and the entire general peace period between 1815 and 1945 produced only five percent.

Two other noteworthy points emerge from Table 2. The lethality of global wars, as of all wars, has steadily risen over the past five centuries. Secondly, the weight of global wars in the entire picture of interstate wars has also grown significantly and ominously over the same period. Global wars were by far the most lethal kind of interstate conflict.

3.7 Global Wars and Ideology

Viewed even at the most superficial level, all five global wars carried strong ideological elements. In the first three cases these were religious in character. Portugal was carried into the Indian Ocean War as an extension of its crusading warfare against the Moors in Iberia and North Africa and in a search for Christian allies. The Dutch-Spanish wars were at the heart of the wars of religion that issued from the era of the Reformation and whose reverberations continued right into the age of Louis XIV (whose revocation of the Edict of Nantes and expulsion of the Huguenots in 1685 powerfully aided the formation of a counter-coalition "in the Protestant interest"). But the Treaties of Utrecht that settled the Wars of the Grand Alliance also proclaimed the principle of the Balance of Power, and the two most recent global wars fuelled conflicts of a more secular but no less powerful character, still having to do with the organization of society. The wars of the French Revolution were fought under the banner of liberty, fraternity and equality but Napoleon dispensed with representative institutions and substituted for them his own absolute rule; his opponents restored legitimacy, and democracy first took shaped in the aftermath of these wars. The First and Second World Wars ended as a crusade for freedom and democracy. But at a more profound level these ideological characterizations and justifications stood as responses to urgent global-systemic problems that the wars helped to resolve.

3.8 Global Wars, Development, and Technology

Recent research by Rasler and Thompson (1983, 1994) has afforded a systematic look at the relationship between global wars and political and economic development via an examination of statistical time series since 1700 for such variables as gross national product (GNP) growth, budgetary expenditures, and defense costs. They have found that global (rather than inter-

Table 2
Global war battle deaths[a]

Global war	Battle deaths (million)	As percent of battle deaths
Italian and Indian Ocean Wars	0.1	
Dutch-Spanish Wars	0.2	1517-1609: 20
Wars of the Grand Alliance	2.0	1610-1713: 37
French Revolutionary and Napoleonic Wars	2.5	1714-1815: 40
First and Second World Wars	20.7	1816-1945: 95
Five global wars	25.5	1494-1945: 79
Interstate wars 1494-1945	32-2	

a Source: Modelski 1986, calculated from data in Levy 1983 pp. 88-92 state) wars must be considered as one of the most important sources for the growth and expansion of the modern state and that such wars have been directly responsible for the creation of and, through imitation, the eventual diffusion of, modern public credit systems.

More generally appreciated is the fact that global wars have tended to crystallize and institutionalize rapid changes in military technology. The entire modern age might aptly be described as the era of artillery, opened as it was by the French invasion of Italy, spearheaded by the first mobile artillery comma-pains, and by Portugal's launch into the Indian Ocean, to seize command of the sea by naval artillery. It then continued through five centuries right up to the heavily-gunned and finally nuclear armies and navies of the Second World War. As a rule, technological and other innovation that commonly germinated in periods of general peace (as science as a whole surged in the nineteenth century) found prompt application in the global war to follow (as in the First and Second World Wars).

3.9 Evolutionary Characteristics

Viewed as a series, each global war was more complex and more highly organized not only in technology but also as an aspect of world politics. Each of the peace settlements following these wars (such as the Treaties of Utrecht, or the post-1945 order) ushered in a more elaborate structure of international institutions.

3.10 Recurrence

The average period of general peace, that is, the time elapsed between the ending of one global war and the start of the next one, has been, in the four intervals between the five global wars just described, about 80 years. The last complete period of general peace, however, extended over nearly one hundred years. If these cases serve as valid precedents for extrapolation into the future, then the possibility of an outbreak of a sixth global war does not arise until some time in the third of fourth decade of the 21st century.

4. Global War and Nuclear War

As just mentioned, all five global wars have been notable for the prompt use of the most advanced techniques of warfare and destruction. The only belligerent use of nuclear weapons to this date has been in the closing days of the last global war, over Japan in August 1945. How likely is it that the next global war might be fought with nuclear weapons? Given the pattern of recurrence for global wars noted above, there is no need to invoke nuclear deterrence as the crucial factor in the preservation of general peace in the past 40 years (see *Nuclear Strategy*). Nor can nuclear deterrence be regarded, both on theoretical and on practical grounds, as anything more than an interim solution to the problem of avoiding nuclear war (Modelski and Morgan 1985) (see *Nuclear Deterrence, Doctrine of*).

Students of strategy estimate the likelihood of a future war—use of nuclear weapons as some function of the following factors: (a) contagion from local or regional war; (b) escalation of crisis between major powers; (c) surprise attack; (d) terrorist attack; and (e) nuclear accident. Each of these carries some positive probability that nuclear weapons might be employed at any time.

But if these probabilities are additive then it is the circumstances surrounding the approach of another global war that appear to be particularly dangerous. If global wars are indeed caused by a structural crisis, the decay of the leadership structure, then they are also anticipated by a variety of conditions in which an event or a combination of events might trigger a nuclear exchange. At the origins of the First World War, for instance, was a crisis stemming from Britain's declining ability to shoulder its leadership functions. When that condition was combined with a set of triggering conditions: contagion from a regional conflict (Serbia versus Austria), crisis escalation between major powers (involving Russia, Germany, France, and Britain), a terrorist attack (assassination of the Austrian Archduke), and even a sort of surprise attack, on Belgium, the system broke down into a major conflagration. Taken together, all these events and developments made the onrush of a great war irresistible, and could conceivably occur again in a major crisis.

Since the dissolution of the former Soviet Union and the Soviet bloc in 1989-91, the arms race has abated and significant reductions have been effected in the nuclear arsenals of the major powers. The total abolition of nuclear weapons remains a more distant goal and the risk of nuclear war continues to be an element of world politics (see *Nuclear Weapons Abolition*).

5. Alternatives

A global war is, above all, a "macrodecision" phase of a political process to which, as noted already, specific outcomes may be attributed. However, that political process is also subject to evolutionary learning because leadership selection is not an inherently war-generating process, and macrodecision can take forms other than those of a global war, and leaves open the possibilities of innovation, especially promising in the context of the evolutionary processes of democratization and globalization (see *Evolutionary Movement Toward Peace*).

If the selection to global leadership, and the organization of global political institutions were to be accomplished by other means (see *Global War, Alternatives to*), then the pressures for a violent resolution of a future structural crisis would likely be dramatically reduced.

Bibliography

Chase-Dunn C 1981 Interstate system and capitalist world-economy. *Int. Stud. Q.* 25(2)
Chase-Dunn C, V Bornschier 1998 *The Future of Hegemonic Rivalry.* Sage Studies in International Sociology, Beverly Hills, CA
Gilpin R 1981 *War and Change in World Politics.* Cambridge University Press, Cambridge
Kennedy P M 1987 *Rise and Fall of the Great Powers 1500-2000.* Random House, New York
Levy J S 1983 *War in the Modern Great Power System 1495-1975.* University Press of Kentucky, Lexington, Kentucky
Levy J S 1985 Theories of general war. *World Politics* 37(3)
Modelski G 1985 Global wars and world leadership succession. Paper Presented to the Second World Peace Science Congress. Rotterdam, June
Modelski G 1987 *Long Cycles in World Politics.* Macmillan, London
Modelski G 1986 Evolutionary paradigm for global politics. *Int. Stud. Q.* (September)
Modelski G, Morgan P M 1985 Understanding global war. *J. Conflict Resolution* 29(3)
Modelski, G, W R Thompson 1988 *Sea Power in Global Politics 1494-1993.* Macmillan, London
Modelski G, W R Thompson 1989 Long cycles and global war. In: M Midlarsky (ed.) *Handbook of War Studies.* Hyman, Boston
Rasler K, Thompson W R 1983 Global wars, public debts, and the long cycle. *World Politics* 35(4)
Rasler K, W R Thompson 1994 *The Great Powers and Global Struggle 1490-1990.* University Press of Kentucky, Lexington
Richardson L F 1960 *Statistics of Deadly Quarrels.* Boxwood Press, Pacific Grove, CA
Thompson W R (ed.) 1983 *Contending Approaches to World System Analysis.* Sage, Beverly Hills, California
Thompson W R 1988 *On Global War: Historical-Structural Approaches to World Politics.* University of South Carolina Press, Columbia
Toynbee A 1954 *A Study of History*, Vol. 9. Oxford University Press, London
Wallerstein I 1984 *The Politics of the World Economy.* Cambridge University Press, Cambridge
Wright Q 1942 *A Study of War.* Chicago University Press, Chicago, Illinois

GEORGE MODELSKI

Globalization

Globalization is the process that forms global institutions. Global institutions are those that operate as though the world were in fact a single place; they must be distinguished from others that function at the regional, national, and local level, each of which presupposes a distinct spatial scope, and also a separate set of social relationships.

A primary example of a global institution is the world market. But that is quite a general concept; more often the reference is to world markets for particular products or services, such as gold, computers, or banking. Examples of global institutions of recent and contemporary importance include financial markets, such as those for the principal currencies; inter-governmental organizations such as the United Nations; professional and humanitarian bodies such as International Political Science Association, or Amnesty International, and media services such as the Cable News Network (CNN). Examples from earlier times include the far-flung enterprises of the Dutch East Indies Company (VOC) (1600-1797), or the activities of International Red Cross, founded in 1865. Yet other such institutions, possibly even more numerous and diverse will likely arise in the 21st century.

This means that the process of global institutional change has been underway for some considerable time, and is likely to continue, albeit not necessarily in a straight line. While its sources go back for as long as a millennium, the process has become particularly prominent in the latter half of the 20th century, and interest in it has come to be centered on the concept of globalization.

The present article examines that concept, and its recent formulations, primarily by drawing attention to its complexity. By portraying globalization as having four dimensions, it points to its wide ramifications, and cautions against an excessively economic interpretation.

1. The Concept of Globalization

Defined as the modern way of global institutional change, globalization is a process that has already been underway for a number of centuries, say the best part of the millennium now closing, and is likely to continue in that mode well into the future, beyond even the 21st century. Global institutional change has passed through three periods in the past millennium. The first one, opening about 1000 years ago in Sung China on the basis of a flourishing market economy and learning society (McNeill 1982; Modelski & Thompson 1996) culminated in the Mongols' failed attempt at erecting a world empire on the basis of the Silk Roads, the trade artery that served as the backbone of the classical world system. In the second period, from before 1500, the West Europeans built a system of sovereign states as the nucleus, and an oceanic trading system as the alternative framework, for the world system (Modelski 1972 ch. 3). The period since about 1850 might be called that of global organization because that is when world-wide institutions increasingly began to take shape within that framework, and globalization became apparent in a direct fashion.

In recent discourse the concept of globalization first attracted notice in relation to transnational corporate activities (see *Transnationalism*). Students of these activities began to draw attention to the rise of global corporations, those that saw the entire world market as their field of activities (Modelski 1978; Hout et al., 1982; Levitt 1983). Those firms that recognized this were likely to be growing faster and more profitably. Advertisers, for instance, claimed that enterprises could reap significant economies by conducting world-wide campaigns for their products that found a global customer base, such as Sony Walkman, Nike or Windows 95. In turn, critics of corporate power saw globalization as a new stage of capitalism, and laid blame for whatever they saw as failures of the system on globalization (see *Multinational Corporation and Peace*).

The present article portrays globalization not just as an economic process, or a process whose sole impact of interest arises out of the relations between the power of the market, and the competence of the nation-state. Globalization is a complex concept and to make it more tractable it will be portrayed here as multidimensional, as a spectrum of four interdependent processes, of (a) economic globalization (that is, building the global economy); (b) democratization; (c) formation of world opinion; and (d) political globalization (that is, constructing global political institutions).

Each of these is an evolutionary process of distinct shape and period that has increasingly acquired an especial character all its own. All four might be seen as co-acting, and jointly marking the course of globalization. That course can be bumpy and rugged, with frequent ups-and-downs, but it is capable of being charted, and better understood.

2. Economic Globalization

Economic globalization is, at bottom, the institutionalization of free trade. Trade is of course, as old as civilization and probably older. But the traditional condition of economic exchange has been a high degree of political control over access to protected markets. Even over short distances, especially overland, encumbrances to commercial transactions would usually be high, and even the inauguration of long-distance oceanic voyages ca. 1500 was accompanied by the imposition of new commercial monopolies by Portugal and Spain.

The principle of "freedom of the seas" formulated by Grotius (see *Grotius, Hugo*), the founder of modern international law in 1609, and implemented in the Truce of Antwerp (Modelski & Modelski 1988: Pt.3) was the first step on the road to freer trade. The next was Adam Smith's influential analysis of "Systems of Political Economy" (1776: Book V) and his criticism of mercantilism and of restraints upon imports. But it was not until mid-19th century that the doctrine of free trade took hold in British trade policies (the signal event being the abolition of the Corn Laws in 1846), and began to spread with the help of major innovations in sea and land transportation (railroads and steamships) even as Friedrich List formulated his criticisms of free trade in "The National System of Political Economy" (1841).

The era up to 1914 saw the first great expansion of world trade, and the beginnings of multinational corporate activity, but the two World Wars of the 20th century set back that process. It was after 1950 that the world settled into another period of trade expansion that has continued at a strong pace since. One spectacular feature of the decades of the 1980s and 1990s has been the emergence of the foreign currency market as "in many ways the only truly global market" with a daily volume of transactions estimated at $US1.3 trillion in 1995 (Sassen 1996 p. 40). Another such feature has been the rise of global corporations that operate in all the major economies and produce for, and sell to, a global customer base. A third has been the consolidation of international regimes governing trade, both at the global level, in the World Trade Organization (see

World Trade Organization (WTO)), and in regional customs unions such as the European Common Market (see *European Community*).

At the turn to the 21st century trade is freer than it was only a few decades ago but it is far from being totally free. The contemporary expansion in global exchanges is led by the Information Revolution that has created an economy in which economically relevant knowledge now disseminates world-wide at amazing speeds and at little cost. Three K-waves have driven these transformations in the global economy since 1850 (Modelski and Thompson 1996). First came the launching of industrial sectors based on scientific research and development: the chemical industry, the electric power industry, telegraph and telephony. Then came, in the next wave after 1914, electronics, including radio and television, together with autos and aviation. Since the 1970s leadership in the global economy has begun to shift to the information industries, a set of industries based on the computer but including also communications, cable, media and entertainment. This shift, whose take-off stage will move into a high-growth phase after 2000, is set to raise "electronic space" to a central role in the economy and lead to "the virtualization of economic activity" (Sassen 1996 p. 21). The process of building a global economy has been much advanced by these developments but it is hardly complete, and it is likely to continue for a long time to come (see *Internet: A New Vehicle for Global Peace Efforts*).

3. Democratization

If economic globalization requires increased competitiveness in the production of goods and services, then democratization means greater competition among alternative forms of social organization. Democracy might be defined as a technology of cooperation and as such might be contrasted, and might be seen as competing with, non-democratic, authoritarian, and totalitarian prescriptions for social cooperation. That contest has been underway for some time, and is likely to continue into the 21st century.

The underlying process is the spread of democracy around the globe. The base for that process was laid earlier in the modern era in a series of trial-and-error experiments that, drawing on classical models, included reform movements in Sung China, republican regimes in Renaissance Italy, and the development of representative institutions in several parts of Europe. The first breakthrough was that achieved, in an alliance with England, by the Dutch Republic. Britain, in turn, also in alliance with the Dutch,

evolved a model liberal society that by mid-19th century, and conjointly with the then rising United States became the base upon which democracy took off as a global process. By the end of the 19th century, the fraction-democratic (percentage of the world's population living in democracies) exceeded ten per cent; at the end of the 20th century, the fraction-democratic exceed fifty per cent. For the first time in the history of the world, the democracies constitute a world majority.

In other words, the innovative practices embodied in democratic social organization and in representative institutions (that is the practices of indirect, large-scale rather than only direct, and small-scale democracy) have been spreading to all parts of the globe, and have become a world-wide standard. The trend toward the globalization of democracy observed so far obeys the law of diffusion of innovations (Modelski & Perry 1991), and can be projected into the near future, to the effect that by the end of the 21st century most of the world's peoples will live in democracies (see *Peace and Democracy*).

4. Rise of World Opinion

The third major evolutionary trend is the rise of an informed world public, based on an incipient global culture. World opinion is the product of competing visions of social reality and consequently of global problems that need to be attended to. These visions of reality are mediated by an emerging global culture of common symbolic systems and media of communication within which such visions and agendas of problems can be constructively discussed and evaluated. Within that culture, some visions and some definitions will for a time attain the status of a global consensus. An example of such a consensus might be the rejection of nuclear weapons, and nuclear weapons tests.

The rise of world opinion is aided by the Information Revolution in the global economy, and by advancing democratization. Both of which trends make it more likely that broadly-based public opinion will be of increasing importance for defining global problems (see *Communication: Key to World Peace*).

Since the 1970s, global opinion has come to attach increasingly high priority to problems of global integration, that is to giving expression to new forms of global community, and to strengthening links of solidarity, especially among democracies. These tendencies have contrasted with those, fundamentalists and others, who have resisted the possibility of more inclusive relationships. It is on the basis of such ongoing integration and community formation that problems of global organization will enter the agendas of world opinion in the next century, and may lead to the solution of problems of controlling weapons of mass destruction.

The rise of world opinion does not mean the waning of regional distinctions, national cultures or local identities. All it does is making possible a dialog based on mutual understanding among those wishing to advance global problems in ways that do not infringe upon vital interests at the other levels.

5. Political Globalization

Political globalization is a response to the search for better ways of responding to global problems. It brings in train increased competitiveness to the arena of public policies and to the production of public goods for the global system.

The classical response to the attempt to "order" the world has been imperial (see *Imperial*) but the desire to rule over the "four corners" of the world could never be implemented. Only about a thousand years ago did the prospect of a world empire acquire greater reality. In Sung China, after 1000, conditions of population growth and economic expansion made such a vision more nearly attainable. The Sung exercised what they claimed to be the Mandate of Heaven in a rather mild manner but it was the Mongols who put the idea to a test and between 1200 and 1300 came close to conquering Eurasia. But their attempt at global organization on an inner-continental basis failed, and so did Timur's bid, ca. 1400, even more decisively (see *Colonization*).

What might now be recognized as the nucleus of global organization based on oceanic linkages first begun to accrete, on a regional basis, in Renaissance Italy and surrounding areas and from the 16th century onward, in Western Europe, around issues of global leadership. In the 17th and 18th centuries it focused on the cooperation of the two "maritime powers," the Dutch Republic, and Britain, and their confrontations with Spain, France, and finally Germany. The high points of diplomatic organization were the major European peace settlements including Truce of Antwerp (1609), the Treaties of Westphalia (1648), the Peace of Utrecht (1713-4), and the Congress of Vienna (1814-5). In the 19th century, the Concert of Europe, a committee of the Great Powers, attended to the international crises of the continent (see *Treaties of the Modern Era*).

Since mid-19th century however, what has been primarily a set of European arrangements began to assume a global character. The United Nations, created in 1945 on the initiative of the United States and British cooperation continued, in the Security Council, the nuclear element of a committee of Great Powers, but now with wider representation that included China (see *United Nations Governance*). But in the General Assembly it also acquired a universal component that has come to be representative of all of the world's national governments. A number of specialized international organizations with global functions were also created, including the two important financial institutions, the World Bank and the World Fund, as well as, in the 1990s, the World Trade Organization (see *World Trade Organization (WTO)*). Europe itself has developed a special set of regional institutions centering on the European Union.

Thus at the turn to the 21th century, a certain number of global functions are being routinely performed by global as well as regional organizations. Among these are the collection of information on global conditions, economic and other assistance to national governments, dispute settlement, and peacekeeping. But the vital center of world politics remains with the major powers (and with the United States in particular) and with their initiatives (and lack of initiatives). As the global system is certain to continue undergoing crises, these will also require the exercise of global leadership.

Since 1850, the "technical" basis for world organization has been put in place, both in the positive sense of communication and information supplied by global networks of all kinds and, negatively, in the possibilities of destruction of previously unimaginable scope. More recently, ca. 1970, a second cycle has begun, one whose principal global problem centers on community, that is on laying the "social" foundations of global organization. Such a foundation of civil society for the global system is likely to be provided by democratization. It is only then, when the social foundations have been laid, several decades into the 21st century, that global organization might acquire a fuller "political" framework of a federalist character. That is why the structure of politics of the 21st century, while globalizing, will continue to give a prominent though not exclusive place to global leadership, exercised within the context of an emerging democratic community.

6. Effects of Globalization

This article has shown globalization to be the development of a world-wide layer of intensified interactions, substantial enough to support continuous and diversified institutionalization. This long-range process, gaining increasing momentum since the mid-19th century, has also been of varying scope and intensity, but has attracted special attention in the 1970s when the term was first coined.

While in a broad sense it might be seen as the ingathering of the human family, in its actual working globalization has led, because of greater mobility, and a general intensification of relations, to greater competitiveness, and hence also to greater opportunities for conflict.

As a general rule, globalization, via such mechanisms as free trade, and greater democracy, increases the efficiency of social cooperation, and yields substantial benefits to those engaged in it. But it also stimulates competition in all its aspects, as in the classical case of free trade, when established monopolies loose their protected niches and face the cold winds of the world market, or when employees of abandoned enterprises lose employment. A contemporary example is that of the national telephone monopolies now entering the era global competition among long-distance carriers. Another is the impact of globalization even upon the defense industry, so far securely protected by "national security" exceptions. The pressure of competition is particularly palpable on erstwhile leading sectors such as textiles, steel, or electronics.

Another widely noted consequence of globalization is the effect on the nation-state. States have had to adjust their functions to the expanding roles of financial and capital markets (Cerny 1995). In particular, governments have found it more difficult to set rates for their currencies, and in some celebrated cases the pressure of currency markets has forced devaluations. Governments, too, might have to react to the increased mobility of capital and of skilled labor by altering their tax policies, e.g., by shifting the tax base from income toward consumption and property.

But those claiming to see in these tendencies the approach of an "end to the nation-state" in "a borderless world" (Ohmae 1991) are surely overstating the problem of the reallocation of the functions of the state. States are far from "losing control." Those blaming "globalization" for the plethora of difficulties that states face in meeting their budget obligations cannot be quite right either. The critical approach to globalization is understandable (see e.g., Kofman and Youngs 1995; Mittelman 1996) in a situation of much painful structural readjustment, but it needs to be kept in a long-range perspective.

While globalization enlarges the areas of competi-

tion and reduces the power of entrenched monopolies, both economic, political and social, it also sets in motion processes that tend to civilize and smooth that competition and create new opportunities for cooperation. In effect, some of the consequences of the processes of globalization tend to be offset by other such processes. While the pressure of world markets seems unstoppable, and the power of global corporations overwhelming, such other trends as democratization and the rise of world opinion serve as counterweights and provide avenues for corrective measures. If economic forces and the information industries seem to be speeding up globalization, then democratization, and global politics might slow it down. The Information Revolution is cutting the costs of communication world-wide, and new international regimes put in place some elements of global governance.

See also: *Global Integration; Global Familism; Integration Theories; Interdependence, International; Internationalization; Multilateralism; World Order; World Government*

Bibliography

Amin S 1996 The challenge of globalization. *Review of International Political Economy* 3

Cerny P G 1995 Globalization and the changing logic of collective action. *Int'l Organization* (August)

Hout T, Porter M E, Rudden E 1982 How global corporations win out. *Harvard Business Review*, September-October

Jones B R J 1995 *Globalization and Interdependence in the International Political Economy: Rhetoric and Reality.* Pinter, London

Kofman E, Youngs G (eds.) 1996 *Globalization: Theory and Practice.* Pinter, London

Levitt T 1983 The globalization of markets. *Harvard Business Review* (May-June)

List F 1904 (1841) *The National System of Political Economy.* Longmans, London

McNeill W 1982 *The Pursuit of Power.* Chicago University Press, Chicago

Mittelman J H (ed.) 1996 *Globalization: Critical Reflections.* Lynne Rienner, Boulder

Modelski G 1972 *Principles of World Politics.* The Free Press, New York

Modelski G (ed.) 1979 *Transnational Corporations and World Order.* W.H. Freeman, San Francisco

Modelski G, Sylvia Modelski (eds.) 1988 *Documenting Global Leadership.* Macmillan, London

Modelski G, Perry III G 1991 Democratization in long perspective. *Technological Forecasting and Social Change*. March-April

Modelski G, R. Thompson W R 1996 *Leading Sectors and World Powers: The Coevolution of Global Economics and Politics*. University of South Carolina Press, Columbia

Ohmae K 1990 *The Borderless World: Management Lessons in the New Logic of the Global Marketplace*. Harper Business, New York

Porter M E 1990 *The Competitive Advantage of States*. The Free Press, New York

Reich R E 1991 *The Work of Nations: Preparing Ourselves for 21st Century*. Knopf, New York

Sassen S 1991 *The Global City*. Princeton University Press, Princeton

Sassen S 1996 *Losing Control: Sovereignty in the Age of Globalization*. Columbia University Press, New York

Smith A 1937 (1776) *The Wealth of Nations*. The Modern Library, New York

GEORGE MODELSKI

Globalization and Regional Challenges: The Case of Central Europe

1. Introduction

After decades of isolation the transition economies of Central Europe are re-entering the global economy. In 1990 Central Europe faced the break-down of economic ties dominant during the previous four decades and a complete fiasco of the so-called socialist integration model operating within the framework of CMEA (Council of Mutual Economic Assistance) dissolved finally in June 1991.

The goal of reforms undertaken in these countries after revolutions is the integration with the global economy. International integration is vital for successful reintegration and reconstruction of Central European countries economies (see *Global Integration*). The successful integration of the transition economies brings also benefits for the world economy. Economic success in the Central European countries could foster prosperity throughout the continent.

The fall of socialism in Central Europe has national, regional and global dimension. The collapse of the socialist bloc has initiated far-reaching changes in the international, political and economic system. Communism's demise destroyed the political barriers dividing Europe and shattered Central European countries economic structure. In order to fill political, strategic and economic vacuums created in that region, after the fall of the Soviet bloc, they need to be integrated with European Union structure. A call for "return to Europe" became a strategic goal of transformation process. This process is not an easy one and requires many years of structural adjustments (see *Eastern Europe, Transformation of*).

Former centrally planned economies have implemented market oriented reforms, liberalized trade and foreign investment and opened their markets. Imports help to make their markets more competitive and exports provide sources of growth. Foreign direct investment is the way of acquiring modern organizational system and technology as well as markets and capital.

The six years experience reveals that comprehensive liberalizations combined with financial discipline and institutional reforms shortens the transitions period and lowers the cost of the reform. Countries that have pursued radical stabilization and reform programs have been rewarded by the resumptions of vigorous growth in last years, expanding trade, declining unemployment, and falling inflation. They are also able to attract more and more of foreign direct investment.[1]

Central European countries joined many global economic institutions as the World Trade Organization (WTO), Organization for Economic Cooperation and Development (OECD) as well as several regional trade agreements (CEFTA). These should enhance market access and strengthen a liberal trade and movement of capital in transition economies.

In order to face the challenges of globalization (see *Globalization*) the Central European countries want to get benefits associated with regional and sub-regional integration. Strong affinities among neighboring countries—regionalization—provide the context for across border linkages and higher degree of international integration. There is no conflict between the concepts of internationalization and regionalization of the economies in Central Europe. These processes are complementary and can influence each other in this region as they prepare for European Union membership.

The economies of Central Europe as well as European Union need some time. The first group has to develop administrative and organizational structures to implement and enforce the rules of the Union. The European Union has to go through the process of reforming its institutions to be prepared for new era of globalization, before being ready to accept new members (see *European Union*).

Central Europe is trying to define its international

identity in an unusually complex and rapidly changing international environment. They are going at the
same time through three types of interrelated processes: process of transition, process of developing regional and subregional ties, and process of responding to
globalization.

2. The Main Goals of Sub-regional Economic Cooperation in Central Europe—Visegrad Group

The fall of the USSR and unification of Germany created a political and geostrategic void in Central
Europe. The collapse of centrally planned economy
led to destruction of most of the traditional economic
links in East-Central Europe and disintegration of
trade and economic relations among Central and
Eastern European countries.

After the 1990 revolutions Central European countries have faced similar challenges arising from systemic transformations. Geographic proximity, comparable level of social and economic development
and stages of economic transformation should lead
them in a natural manner toward cooperation. There
were many obstacles to economic integration (see
Integration, Regional) in this region.[2]

The difficult process of political and economic cooperation based on new political and economic principle
was initiated by four countries of Central Europe:
Poland, Hungary, Czech and Slovak Republics (Visegrad Group). In the course of recent years they have
been implementing programs connected with the creation of the free market area.

In February 1991 during the meeting in Visegrad
(Hungary), Polish, Hungarian and Czechoslovak
leaders stated that their "aspirations are to coura-
geously meet the tasks confronting our nations and in
con-formity with historic heritage and European traditions as well as processes of development to do the
utmost for peace, security and well-being of our
nations."

The "Declaration of Cooperation Between Poland,
Hungary and Czechoslovakia Leading to European
Integration" described the model of cooperation in
various areas: political, economic, cultural as well as
in the field of systemic transformations. Visegrad
Group wanted to create conditions for cooperation
between its members without, however, setting up
some formal organizational structures. During the
next meeting of the Presidents of these countries on
October 15, 1991 in Cracow "The Cracow Declaration" was adopted. It defined concepts of sub-regional cooperation during the process of negotiations on
integration with the European Union as well as their

participation in other international organizations—
NATO, EFTA, CSCE (Conference on Security and Cooperation in Europe) (see *Organization for Security and
Cooperation in Europe (OSCE)*). It also points out to
the need for liberalization of mutual trade and agreements for most speedy liberalization of trade.

Leaders stress in the Declaration that the main goal
of these nations is to "return to Europe." The re-join-
ing Europe after almost 50 years of separation from
the all-European mainstream of changes needs basic
transformations in political and economic systems of
Central European countries. Cooperation among the
countries of Visegrad Group could be an important
factor in their efforts for integration with the European Union.

It was stressed, however, that such cooperation
cannot be an alternative to European integration—
which for members of Visegrad Group is a strategic
goal—but only the means to achieve this goal.

The Visegrad Group possesses a large economic
potential and there are the most advanced in market-
oriented reforms. They have a total population of
some 65 mln (Poland—38.5 mln, Hungary—10.5
mln, Czech Republic—10.3 mln, Slovak Republic—
5.4 mln). In 1994 their combined GDP was about 183
billion dollars and trade turnover 106.4 billion dollars.

The main goals of Visegrad Group cooperation are
the following:

(a) to strengthen their bargaining power in negotiations with European Union and to get the best
possible conditions for joining that organization;

(b) to invigorate economic activity and to increase
competitiveness of the economies of these countries;

(c) to enhance specialization and technological
cooperation within various industrial branches
and to restructure manufacturing systems;

(d) to harmonize systemic transformations and to
come closer to the European Union standards
and requirements;

(e) to develop cooperation in ecology, transport and
tourism.

Cooperation covers many areas which these countries can solve through common efforts with benefits
for the whole region and financial help for these
goals from the European Union. Specific programs
are being approved during meetings of the Presidents, Prime Ministers and Foreign Ministers of the
member states.

3. *Central European Free Trade Agreement—* CEFTA.

The countries of Visegrad Group signed on December 21, 1992 an agreement on the establishment of a new regional economic organization: Central European Free Trade Area—CEFTA, which came into effect on March 1, 1993. This agreement provides for gradual reduction of custom duties (tariffs) and non-tariff limits in trade with industrial products among these countries in next five to eight years until there will be fully free trade in the year 2002. Tariffs reduction will be diversified for three groups of commodities:

(a) group A includes industrial goods of low manufacturing level, half-products and raw materials (these constitute 63 percent of Polish industrial exports to Hungary and 67 percent to Czech and Slovak Republics). Tariffs in this group (about 40 percent of industrial goods) were abolished as of March 1, 1993;

(b) group B includes industrial goods of "low sensitivity" and for these the reduction of tariffs is to start in 1995 to be lowered by 1/3 annually so that in 1997 the trade in this group should be free of tariffs;

(c) group C includes goods "most sensitive" to international competition such as textiles, leather goods, steel products, television sets—and for these the tariff reduction is planned for a longer period of time—from 1995 to 2001;

(d) the concessions for liberalization of agricultural products are limited. It was decided only to lower import quotas for meats, vegetables, dairy products and alcohol.

Despite many obstacles the last three years show that the sub-regional cooperation within the Visegrad Group picks up its momentum. It is illustrated by growing scope of cooperation, acceleration in lowering of tariffs and rapid growth of trade.

The list of CEFTA accomplishments to date could include:

(a) shortening of time to eliminate tariffs. In August 1995 CEFTA members decided to accelerate the process of lowering the tariffs for many industrial products of "middle sensitivity" before January 1, 1996 so that in 1997 (one year earlier than planned) tariffs for some "most sensitive" goods (textiles and steel products) will be abolished. About 80 percent of industrial goods are traded free. Tariffs for few scores of most sensitive goods which constitute 3 percent of trade, such as cars, should be eliminated by the year 2002.

(b) acceleration of liberalization of trade in agricultural products beginning with 1996. The timetable was presented in September 1995.

(c) decision to open CEFTA to other countries. In 1995 a new article 39 A was introduced and it stipulates that this is an "agreement of free trade open to other participants." Future members should meet three conditions: belong to the World Trade Organization, have the status of the country associated with the European Union and to sign bilateral trade agreements with all members of CEFTA. During the summit meeting of CEFTA in Brno (Czech Republic) in September 1995 a new country—Slovenia—was admitted since it met all required conditions. In the future Romania, Bulgaria and Baltic states could join CEFTA.

(d) striving for expansion of future cooperation in terms of the area and forms. As of now CEFTA is concerned only with trade. There are many signs of growing willingness to start negotiations also on the subject of free flow of capital, labor force and services in the near future.

(e) accepting principles regarding the origin of goods coherent with those of the European Union (50percent).

(f) increasing trade among members of Visegrad Group. During the last three years foreign trade of the countries of Central Europe has had a dynamic growth (50 percent from 1992 to 1995).

Sub-regional cooperation could play very important role in modernization of economies and in improving their competitiveness while they strive to integrate with the European Union. Visegrad Group, partially in accordance with the Union suggestions and also in connection with their own need to strengthen economic position, has undertaken a program for closer mutual economic cooperation. The Group was viewed initially as a "foyer leading to the European Union," its purpose being to facilitate and accelerate integration with the Union which—in turn —supported all efforts for closer cooperation of these countries.

Today it seems that skeptics who did not augur well for the new group were not right. Although it is still difficult to foresee Visegrad Group's future, one could see however, even now, that it plays a stabilizing role and invigorates economic activities in the region. Sub-regional cooperation among the Visegrad countries performs a constructive supplementary function in relation to the strategic goal of preparing for full membership in the EU.

4. Integration of Visegrad Group Countries with the European Union

The Visegrad Group in its Cracow Declaration stated that its strategic goal is the complete access to the European political, economic and security system.

The fact is that the European Union did not always take a clear stand on the issue of Central and East European countries admission. In 1991 three countries: Poland, Hungary and Czechoslovakia (since 1993 separated into Czech and Slovak Republics) were proposed the status of so called associated members. In 1992 similar status was granted to Bulgaria and Romania. The commercial part of the agreement with Poland became effective in the field of foreign trade on March 1, 1992 .

The "European Agreement" went into effect on February 1, 1994 and it provided a broad framework for economic and political cooperation. It regulates the framework of economic cooperation and the ongoing political dialogue between these countries and the Union and it opens the road to membership.

"European Agreement" aims at:

(a) establishment of an appropriate framework for political dialogue contributing to development of close political relations between the parties;

(b) supporting the development of trade and stable economic relations between the parties in order to facilitate dynamic growth;

(c) providing financial and technical assistance;

(d) providing framework for gradual integration with the European Communities;

(e) help to lock Central European countries into the open trade system;

(f) create incentives for European companies to engage in closer cooperation.

The Agreements provide for regulations concerning trade liberalization and give a better access to the EU markets as well as regulations in services, capital flow and labor movement. It contains specific regulations for mutual reduction of custom duties and other trade instruments in the period lasting ten years. In the first stage it will result in the creation of a free trade area in industrial goods in 1997. Due to considerable differences in level of development, liberalization follows the principle of asymmetry—the EU has embarked earlier on reduction of tariffs and other barriers to imports from Visegrad Group countries. The scope for liberalization of trade in agricultural

products has been limited. Chances for further liberalization of agricultural trade will depend on assessment to be made by the Association Council.

The common stand of the European Union has been presented in the document of European Commission at the end of November 1994.[3] It states "ability of the Union to admit new members with simultaneous continuation of the European integration process maintaining its internal coherence and basic principles has to be preserved both in the interest of Union members and of the candidates."

Both, the Union and the candidates for membership, have to be prepared for this. To implement pre-integration strategy it is necessary to establish close relations between countries of Eastern and Central Europe and Union institutions. In addition to continuous political dialogue consultations on matters of energy, environment, transport, science and technology, are being proposed. Various forms of cooperation of parliaments as well as government representatives will be worked out.

The document lists short and long range actions for the increase of competitiveness of associated countries' economies so that they could reach the ability to undertake economic competition in European market. "White Book on Internal Market" has been prepared describing steps those countries have to take in various sectors to create conditions for a unified market.

First of all it applies to legislative and regulatory systems as well as to standards to be compatible with the Union. Proposals have been also prepared dealing with agricultural issues, promotion of investments, common foreign and security policies, actions to preserve the natural environment, transport, culture, education, information, financial cooperation and internal cooperation among associated countries.

European Union leaders at the Copenhagen Conference in 1993 made its first commitment to the Central European countries accession. They approved during their summit in Essen in December 1994 the strategy of integration of associated countries. This strategy should prepare them to full Union membership. At the Madrid Summit in 1995 it was stated that six months after conclusion of Masstricht II, the European Union will start negotiation with new members.

Realization of the quick admission to the Union of Central European countries will result in considerable costs. It became one of the main arguments against it. To apply presently operating in the Union programs to associated countries (who have considerably lower level of development than the average one in the Union—per capita GDP in the Union is about 18 thousand dollars while in the Central Europe it is below 4 thousand), would require considerable expenditures. Projected costs of admission to Visegrad Group (Poland, Hungary, Czech and Slovak Republics) would, according to the London Center for Economic Policy Research, increase Union annual expenditures by 64 billion ECU and this in turn would require an increase of membership contributions by almost 60 percent.[4]

The Union intends in the immediate future to assign more means to support transformation processes and for adjustment programs which are preparing countries of Eastern and Central Europe for full membership (program PHARE). Projected assistance for these countries will come to 5.5 billion ECU in 1995-99 while in 1990-94 it was 3.3 billion ECU.

It seems that the debates in the Union concentrate mainly on the issue of costs and too little attention is given to benefits which inclusion of Central and Eastern European markets into all-European system would bring. Measurable economic benefits include doubling in last year's Union exports to Central European markets as well as profitable foreign investments.

Membership in the European Union will give Central European countries a new opportunity as well as a challenge. Because of considerable development gap dividing them from members of the Union, the integration process calls for difficult and costly reforms. Adjustment to the conditions already existing in the EU requires far reaching changes in the economies of these countries.

This will affect many sectors, but particularly that of agriculture which in many of these countries is inefficient. Far reaching structural changes in the industry are called for so that its products could measure up to the competition on European market. Legislative changes and stable macro-economic policy are absolutely necessary to facilitate meeting of Maastricht criteria. Some countries of Visegrad Group already today are meeting these standards better than some Union members.

Why is the access to the EU of such importance for Central Europeans? Membership in the Union could permit them to create stable ties with market system and with democratic institutions giving thus a chance to make the whole transformation successful. Proper course of its process depends on the ability of the society to bear its costs. Perspective of speedy admission to the Union makes present sacrifices more acceptable. The future of these countries, their security and stable, growing ability to develop can be securely anchored only in the unified Europe.

The process of integration of the Central European countries with the European Union markets has been very successful (rapidly growing trade and capital flows). Their full membership in the EU depends to a large extent on the way the process of restructuring of their economies will develop and if they will measure up to membership requirements.

It will also depend on the measure the Union itself will reform its structures under Maastricht II. Present institutions of EU were created for the market of six countries only, today they have to meet the demands and requirements of fifteen and in the future the membership could grow to twenty seven.

The reforms which started in 1996 may last for more than a year. Till now no specific dates for admission of the Central European countries to the Union were presented, but it was stated during the meeting in Madrid in 1996 that the negotiations will begin 6 months after the completion of Masstricht II.

At the Luxembourg summit on 12-13 December 1997 the European Union agreed to start negotiations on March 1998 with first-group countries—Poland, Hungary, Czech Republic, Slovenia and Estonia; this leaves five applicants in waiting: Bulgaria, Latvia, Lithuania, Romania and Slovenia.

5. *Conclusion*

Central Europe is trying to define its international identity in an unusually complex and rapidly changing global economy.

Post-Cold War climate helped to create favorable conditions for new forms of regional cooperation. Pro-market reforms and opening of economies brought economic systems in the region closer together. To enlarge the market economy facilitates better understanding between political elites who are similar in their acceptance of the challenges of development arising from the globalization and need to make their economy more effective and competitive.

CEFTA countries' economies are increasingly integrated with the European Union which is their main trading partner, one of the main sources of foreign direct investment and technical assistance.

Acknowledging that joining European Union and other Western institutions like NATO is the primary goal of the Central European countries, these countries have treated CEFTA as a transitory form of their cooperation. CEFTA was used as a pre-accession instrument, to some degree similar to the European Agreement to achieve these goal.

Bringing Central European Countries into the EU will be a difficult operations for both sides. Neither has done anything like it.

The applicant countries themselves are working to

meet the EU demands for memberships. Eventually they will be expected to adopt all EU laws and regulations. They need to improve the efficiency of existing institutions of market economy. A considerable amount of economic reform remains before they will meet the EU criteria for membership. The European Union is determined to help applicant countries along the road to reform.

It is not just the applicant countries that need to modernize to make a success of enlargement. The European Union must reform and change its institutions. They were created in 1957 for 6 members, now they serve 15 members and in future they might serve 25 members. Agenda 2000 goes on to tackle the highly sensitive topics of the next EU budget settlements and reforms of the Common Agricultural Policy and EU structural funds. It calls for the budget to remain at its 1.27 percent of the EU total GNP and hopes that the economic growth will provide enough additional resources to settle the differences between EU countries and leaving some money over to give to poor applicants.

The single currency remains top priority in the EU. Eleven countries joined the European Monetary Union which began in January 1999 with the launch of the euro. Euro will at once become the world's second currency, it may challenge the American dollar's supremacy. The effects of EMU on the world economy will depend on the external spillovers from its effects on economic performance in Europe and the extent to which the euro is used in international transactions. The latter will be influenced by the strength and stability of new currency. It will be a great challenge for Central European economies to meet all necessary obligation for joining the European Monetary Union in future.

Several questions remain to be answered: when and under what conditions the enlargement of the EU will take place? What kind of European Union will accept the candidates as new members?

Notes

1. Stock of FDI in 1995 was in Hungary about 10.7 billion dollars. Poland 6.8, Czech Republic 5.8, Slovenia 1.5 and Slovakia 0.7

2. Beside these favorable factors there were many others hampering the co-operation. They were the results mainly of bad past experiences and of competition in the race for European Union membership. See G. Kolankiewicz. Consensus and Competition in the Eastern Enlargement of the European Union. *International Affairs*. 1994, No. 3

3. Strategy for the Integration of the Associated Countries. Brussels 1994.

4. R. E. Baldwin, *Towards and Integrated Europe*, Center for Economic Policy Research (CEPR). London February 1994.

BARBARA LIBERSKA

Gorbachev's Perestroika: From Idea in 1985 to Ideology in 1995

1. Introduction

Gorbachev's idea of Perestroika (see *Glasnost and Perestroika*) on Soviet Union's economic reform of 1985 was becoming a Perestroika Ideology in 1995, after a decade. Its transformation from idea to an ideology was being tested in tri-dimensional perspectives of (a) time, (b) space and (c) conditionality, in the former Soviet Union and the present Commonwealth of Independent States (CIS). The Gorbachevian Glasnost, i.e., openness through horizontal or egalitarian and humanistic or equity-oriented democracy, was a complementary addition to his ideological concept of Perestroika. The CIS and the world intellectuals perceived this concept, but it needed practical application, because a theory or an ideology gets its momentum and practicable strength when it is tested in the above-mentioned three dimensionalities.

The determinants and dimensions of Gorbachev's Perestroika were based on tri-dimensions, namely, the former Soviet Union or the present CIS nation-states (not only the Russian Federation's) people's (a) Human/ Social Needs, (b) Human/Social Rights and (c) Human/Social Duties. These three determinants are like (i) time, (ii) space and (iii) circumstances (conditions), mentioned above. The real and successful interaction of these two models can contribute to the creative solution of the transitional heterogeneous and hetero-directional approaches which had and have been flourishing in the monolithic societies of the former USSR and other East European societies. The ideology of the never-realised communism has been proved to be a utopia until now because of the uncovered gap between (a) the change in the human consciousness and (b) the inclination towards the aptitude for material consciousness. The applicative diameter of communism was based on the socio-equalistic ideology of egalitarianism as goals and means to the enforced homogenization which was chosen as the mechanism instead of the consensus and equitable harmonization. Enforcement (a) obstructs the creative initiative of an individual or a community, on the one hand, and (b) destroys the values of equity or justice, on the other hand.

The retrospective analysis of the time, space and circumstances show that the individuals as a separate entity, or a part of the collectivity, both at the individual and collective levels, do not still prefer the stage and state of establishing the norm of floor, but instead prefer the level of ceiling, which means the option for desire after meeting the norm and level of basic needs. Gorbachev's Perestroika ideology consisted of the following components and interacting elements:

(a) mobilisation/inclination to duties (thesis);

(b) participation/right to democracy (antithesis);

(c) openness/right to expression and impression (conthesis);

(d) realisation/satisfaction of the human/social needs (synthesis); etc.

Perestroika was started as the social and economic charter and philosophy for the Soviet Society, but the social and human consciousness of the then Soviet Union was not prepared for it. During the period of transition, the state apparatus engaged itself more in the solution of the immediate or short-run problems and inconveniences instead of concentrating on the long-run and complex problems of the society and the economy. But the Perestroika after a decade, contains newer values, newer dimensions and newer perspectives. While the Perestroika can be regarded as the socio-economic and political revolution for the present Russian and East European societies, with peaceful means and ends, it can also be regarded as the ideal and acceptable solution for humanizing and socializing the bureaucratised and state sector-dominated economies and societies.

The modern definition of philosophy or ideology differs from that of the past. The philosophy and philosophical ideology of today can be defined as the cosmic essence of the ideas, approaches and theories with humanistic or social aspects of verification under the conditions of time, space and circumstances. The sense and sensitivity tests are the other two aspects which the Perestroika ideology is to undergo, for the purpose of making it a vital ideology.

This study will deal with two important theoretical aspects, namely, the Perestroika's social and scientific determinants and dimensions in the present and future perspectives, and the historical destiny of the Perestroica's economic reforms.

2. Perestroika's Social and Scientific Determinants and Dimensions: Present Prospects and Future Perspectives

Gorbachev's Perestroika is a combination of both the socioeconomic philosophy and human psychology motivated towards the democratised liberalization of the Russian and the CIS nations' economic, social and political life; the harmonized and relevant development of the individuals of the Commonwealth of the Independent States on the basis of their fundamental social and economic needs as well as political and cultural behaviors, ecological possibilities and potentials, human and social values, mode of life, cultural heritages and attitudes; etc., and above all, the federalised consensus of the goals, means (production) and ends (distribution) for implementing the time, space and conditions-bound social human needs.

Perestroika's social, economic, political, cultural and ecological prospects and perspectives were not or could not be assessed and evaluated during the Gorbachev's presidential period. That is why it remained as a socio-economic philosophy of emancipation for the centralised and dogmatised socioeconomic system and its being in the Eastern European regions. The post-Gorbachev period is the period of transitional experiments which experienced the anarchic co-existence of the different ideological and political manifestations and expressions without proper solution for the just or equitable as well as humanistic solution for the former Soviet Union or the present CIS.

Gorbachev opened the political perspectives, without a drop of bloodshed, in the ex-Soviet republics, but its economic perspectives could not even be experimented or tried to generate the effects during his presidential and political lime-light period. There are arguments that Eastern Europe needed and preferred economic emancipation to political emancipation for the overall triumph of the Perestroika ideology. Because the political and social emancipation in empty stomach or long-cherished desire for economic emancipation created a vacuum between the human/social desire and the enforced long-run deprivation. Mao Tse-dung's ideology of "Let hundred thoughts contend and hundred flowers bloom" which was never given a trial-chance in China either in the Mao-Chou era or in the Teng-Li Peng era, was, unknowingly, tried in the Gorbachev era in the age-long weakened economic structure of the Soviet societies. Now, arises a question: will the Gorbachevian Perestroika ideology fail in the historical perspectives, i.e., in the process of the humanity's, society's and civilization's continuity and dynamic stability? Certainly YES, as long as the problem of verticality of relation between:

(a) the structured power and the deprived section of the ruled or dominated masses,

(b) the social top-dogs (social elite) and the social underdogs (the pauperised),

(c) the social and human relations between the "previligentsia" and the "depriventsia,"

(d) between and among the communities of the peoples, cultures, religions, beliefs, etc.,

(e) the haves and have-nots,

(f) the heterogenities and the enforced homegenities, etc.

will exist and will not be solved.

The Gorbachevian Perestroika's future depends on the realistic or objective assessment of the present-day problematics. The Gorbachevian Perestroika devoids off the populistic policies of short-term range of Yeltsin and Jerenovski. There is a theoretical and practical difference between the populistic and humanistic popular policies. While a populistic policy produces short term benefits and lasts short, the popular policy is human-oriented and contains the premises and perspectives of long-term orientation.

Now let us make the socio-scientific assessment and evaluation of Gorbachev's Perestroika in social, economic, political, cultural and ecological dimensions, under the trialectical conditions and perspectives of time, space and circumstances. The time determinants and dimensions contain the temporal aspects, the space determinants and dimensions contain the territorial aspects while the circumstances determinants and dimensions consist of the existing and continuing conditionalities. Before proceeding to the theoretical and practical explanation of the above determinants and dimensions let us explain the theoretical (a) concept, (b) content and (c) context of the Trialectics or Tri-dimensional operationalities of the concept. The Kant-Hegel-Marx-Engels concept of dialectics proceeds with the dialectical approach of the contradicting/contrasting/contrary/confronting arguments of the thesis (the positives) and antithesis (the negatives) which run in the counter-distinctively and never-meeting horizontally parallel direction, in which they never Meet, Argue, Contradict, Confront

and Contrast directly. But there exists an independent, separate identity, self-propelled and self value-dimensioned actor which can be termed as conthesis (the author's own terminology), which is independent of both the thesis and antithesis. The tri-dimensional interaction of the (a) thesis, (b) antithesis and (c) conthesis can produce the desired (i) goals (thesis), (ii) means (antithesis) and (iii) adjustable regenerative functional actor (conthesis) to generate the ends-effects or results to satisfy the needs of the humankind (synthesis). The Conthesis is both the determinant and dimension which, through its coordinating centripetal and centrifugal action, exercises action/influence over the actors of (a) Thesis and (b) Antithesis for direct contradiction, contrast and confrontation in order to produce a result through Interaction among (a) Thesis (Positive), (b) Antithesis (Negative) and (c) Conthesis (Neutrality for bringing both the Thesis and Antithesis in the front of the consensus functional behavior).

Let us explain here the determinants and dimensions in the present assessment and future determinants and dimensional prospects of the Gorbachevian Perestroika (in the humanistic and historical perspectives).

The validity, longivity, viability and effectivity of any ideology of our time has not only to be interdisciplinary in character and multi-dimensional in sphere, but has also to be tested in social systems and sub-systems, human conditions, territorial specificities and boundaries, economic structures and possibilities, political superstructures and modes, cultural/religious/linguistic varieties+specificities, modes of living/heritages/thinking patterns, ecological/ecosophical behaviors, etc. Such type of testing can, by no means, be mechanical, its very contents consist of the social acceptability and social creativity. Perestroica's survival, success and superiority will depend on its capability to create consciousness of the combined action of social equity and soluble means of sustainability from the level of economic chaos and poverty, effective correlation of social mobilisation and participation, etc.

3. Historical Destiny of the Perestroica:

The philosophical and economic as well as the abstract essence and concrete sense of the Perestroika centre around the premises and action of the following: (a) tested, (b) testing, and (c) testable troica of the (i) Static or Conservative (thesis), (ii) Dynamic or Radical (antithesis) and (iii) Dynamic Stability or Dynamically Stable (conthesis) actors. Ideologically,

Figure 1

Interaction model of Gorbachev's Perestroika at social, economic, political, cultural and ecological determinants and dimensions levels.

(a) Social Dimension:

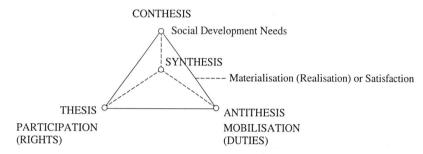

Explanation: The needs are the very basics of the humankind's life and livelihood. The human/social needs entail both the social/human duties and responsibilities (mobilisation) and social/human rights (participation) for its satisfaction at both the social/ human levels.

(b) Economic Dimension:

(i) On Needs-Assessment Basis:

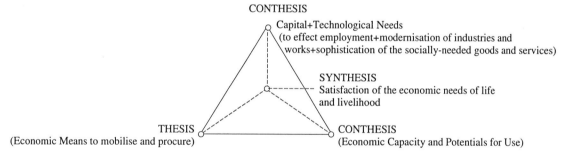

Explanation: The assessment of the capital+technology needs of all CIS countries, besides their raw materials and minerals as well as the potentials are necessary for the macro, medi and micro development projections. The internal economic means for production+procurable means are also to be assessed objectively, to match the usable capacity and potentials, permissible by the reimbursible capacity.

(c) Political Dimension:

The political needs, duties and rights known as the prime determinants of the Perestroika's political dimension, have to undergo the actoral interaction of the actors like (i) equality or homogenization, (ii) equity or justice and (iii) consensus or adjustment. Such actoral interaction is value-motivated and is expected to produce the desired political goal of a balanced National and Global Citizen. The interactive pattern of functionability of the model can be put as such:

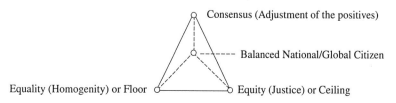

(d) Means-Ends Dimension:

Any ideology and its operativity and validity are to undergo the tests of ends-oriented means and means-based ends, in both the inductive and deductive ways. Perestroika of the last decade of this century and the forthcoming decades of the 21st century shows an inclination towards the social-democratic nature of both the combined human-material development orientation. The means-ends interaction with motivational goal is being traced as such:

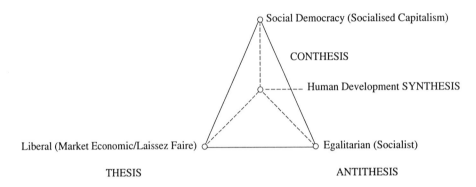

The human development is the emerging means-ends oriented action and the concept for the globe's humankind and Gorbachev's Perestroika-mission is inclusive and conclusive of this very vision.

(e) Functional Dimension:

The functional success of an ideology like Perestroica needs a cognitive-recognitive verification, which can be termed as functional dimension. The interacting actoral pattern of the same can be put as such:

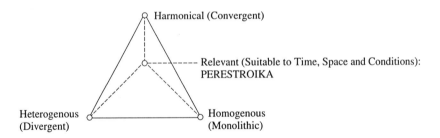

In its functional process, the Perestroika is to accept the adaptability, adjustability, accomodability and adherence through dynamic and revolutionary counter- and inter-action and on the very basis and sphere of the same it can generate the much-needed Relevant Development for the Russian and the CIS territories which can throw lights for such relevant development to conform the people's values, modes of life, culture, ecology, thinking patterns or beliefs and needs-based demands of each and every corner of the globe in the forthcoming decades.

Perestroika started with the local socio-economic and politico-ideological perception (for, of and under the former USSR conditions), but its present Concept and Contents can be extended to the global, regional and local Contexts, because of its functional viability and validity.

(f) Cultural Dimension:

Cultural identities on the basis of the cultural values do constitute the very basis of modern social and cultural formation and the Gorbachevian Perestroika, in its reformist retrospectives and perspectives, inherently contains the following interacting actors, which, in synthetised form, will generate the Relevant Identity. The actoral interactive sketch can be drawn as such:

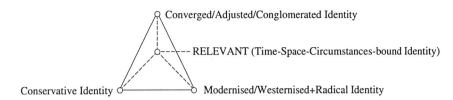

Converged/Adjusted/Conglomerated Identity

RELEVANT (Time-Space-Circumstances-bound Identity)

Conservative Identity

Modernised/Westernised+Radical Identity

Consciousness formation and the identity of consciousness are the two outstanding features in the dimension of the cultural identity. While the (i) inheritance of the positives from conservative cultural identity and (ii) the acceptance of the dynamics from the emerging determinants and values, can be considered as the most essential in the process of the newer cultural formation and identities, (iii) the converging identity of both as conthesis functions as the correlational actor in order to pave the way for and towards proceeding to the synthesised result or effect of the (iv) time-space-circumstances bound agreeable/passing or relevant identity.

Conservation of the conservative ideology may lead to neo-nationalism/neo-fascism/neo-tzarism, while anarchic radicalism with the western modernisation may lead to the loss of the nation's cultural identity. The adjusted or positively-converged identity may ensure the emergence of the relevantly acceptable identity, and the features and actors, of which Gorbachev is aware. That is why he opts for a balancedly acceptable cultural identity as the policy for the reformed Perestroica.

(g) Ecological Dimension:

The ecological dimension of the Perestroika is based on the human and natural values which tries to ensure an ecological human development at both the national and global levels. Eco-dimension is more sensitive and senseful. The following is the sketch of interaction of the co-functioning actors:

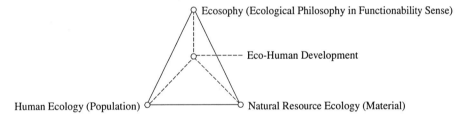

Ecosophy (Ecological Philosophy in Functionability Sense)

Eco-Human Development

Human Ecology (Population)

Natural Resource Ecology (Material)

theoretically and politically these troica can be explained as such:

(a) Staticity=Conservatism or Non-Changeability;

(b) Dynamicity=Radicalism or Fast Transformation without correlating the time-space-circumstantial functional mechanism and procedure; and

(c) Dynamic Stability=Social Democratic Evo-Revolution with establishing and maintaining dynamicity within stability.

Now let us explain the essence of the Gorbachevian think-piece of the dynamic stability.

It is an interacting connection between:

(a) the disappearing and the emerging,

(b) the staticity and the dynamicity,

(c) the structure and the superstructure,

(d) the old and the new,

(e) the preceding and the succeeding,

(f) the diminishing and the creating, etc.

Finally, the Perestroika is a dynamic concept which guarantees stability and progress, security and continuity, safety and assurance, etc. It is a concept of the effective social democracy which combines and ensures stability and progress, economic growth and social welfare, market economy and social well-being, prosperity and assurance of the distribution-generated equity, etc.

The Perestroika of 1985 has been put into the test-trials of empiris, in all the five important directions like economic, political, social, cultural and ecological. The following is the (a) triangular and (b) trialectical intra-actable and inter-actable approaches, of both the (i) theoretical and (ii) practical tests and (1) strategical and (2) tactical verifications:

Development Needs

Domains:	Spheres:
Economic	Areas to be based on Assessments (of
Social	all the 47 constituting states of the
Cultural	Russian Federation)
Ecological	

These actors of the development needs necessitate both types of the quantitative and qualitative interaction in order to materialise the goals of the societies and satisfy the demands.

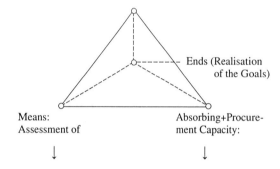

Means:
Assessment of

↓

a) Indigenous+Procurable
        from Abroad
b) Social/Economic/Political
        Mobilisation

Ends (Realisation of the Goals)

Absorbing+Procurement Capacity:

↓

a) Usable Capacity+
        Repayment Potentials
b) Social/Economic/
        Political Participation

At functional level the development needs may be assessed as follows:

Assessment and Coordination Function:

Sphere:/ Domain:	Macro level	Medi level	Micro level
Space	All the 47 territories	Urban	Rural
Economic	Constituting republics/ National	Economic sector	Economic unit
Time	Past	Present	Future
Social	Centre	Sub-centre	Peripheries
Circumstances	Disappearing	Existing	Emerging
Political	Needs	Rights	Duties

The destiny of the Gorbachevian Perestroika ideology or its future applicability or success depends on the assessment, combination and interaction of all the determinants, dimensions, actors and measurements, as shown above.

How can the Perestroika generate (a) employment/income/purchasing power, (b) production of the needful goods and services and (c) supply/distribution of needful goods and services on the basis of distributed income/purchasing power and propensity to use the same? How far and to what extent can Perestroica combine effectively the functional mechanism of the market economy and the social democratic welfare economy, at optimum level, to become the destiny-deciding factor of its validity, vitality and the social democratic welfare economy, at optimum level, will become the destiny-deciding factor of its validity, vitality and continuity? Again, the neglected (a) tertiary (service+marketing and marketability functions), (b) primary (agricultural and raw mineral exploration sector with worn-out+primitive technology), and (c) outdated secondary (processing and semi-processing) sectors do need modernization with relevant values and modes-based appropriate technology, suitable to the mode of life, tradition and heritage, culture and human-cum-material ecology of each of the constituting 47 republics of the unionistic federalised Russia (at intra-level) and other CIS states (at inter-level) as Mikhail Sergeyvich Gorbachev dreamt of. The Gorbachevian Perestroika pre-supposes and supposes the inclusitivity and continuitive conclusitivity of the positive and humanistic means and values of other systems, societies and cultures which, either identically or/and similarly, be adjusted, integrated, incorporated and regenerated in the socio-economic-political stage and state of each of the constituting state. The Perestroica ideology opens the front of culture, mode of life, acceptance of values and positive as well as the adjustable and integrative-cum-promotive values from other cultures, systems, nation-states and value-centres, which may contribute, in the future, to:

(a) internationalisation of each of the constitutive Russian states and the CIS state,

(b) the impression and expression of the values, modes of life and the thinking patterns in both directions, and

(c) the acceptability, adjustability and incorporability of the human/social positive elements.

4. Concluding Remarks

In reality, Gorbachev's Perestroika is the reform in quest for solution of the economic problem of the component states of the Russian federation and the Commonwealth of Independent States and in this respect it opts for proper and optimum coordination of the inputs of the factors of production like (a) Raw Materials+Substitutes, (b) Blue+White-Collar Human Resources or Human Capital and (c) Capital+ Technology or Past Labour. The proper and correlated optimum interacted processing in course of the production function, can assure the desired optimum output. Of course, the market economic management will help the achievement of the efficient/optimum output, necessary for meeting the market and social needs. At the same time the economic reform is to materialise without much dislocation of employment.

See also: *Eastern Europe, Transformation of; World Economy, Social Change and Peace; Social Progress and Human Survival*

Notes

Conthesis is the terminology used here to represent a determinant, dimension and actor, which was coined and introduced by the author in the domain of philosophy and ideological clarification. In Latin, "con" means "with" and, scientifically, it is a criteria of connection and coordination. By virtue of its own entity and identity it functions as an independent actor which can exercise its own power of co-action over the inter-and counter-actors.

Bibliography

Guha A 1989 *From Dialectics to Trialectics: New Process and Method for Social Research*. Institute for Alternative Development Research, Oslo

Galtung J *Measuring World Development*, Part I & Part II

Guha A et al., *Alternatives*. December, 1974 and March, 1975 issues, New York

AMALENDU GUHA

Graduate Institute of Peace Studies (GIP)

1. Purpose of the Graduate Institute of Peace Studies (GIP)

The GIP, one of the two laureates of the 1993 UNESCO Prize for Peace Education (see *UNESCO Prize for Peace Education*), was established in September, 1984 to play a role in the creation of a global community which is spiritually beautiful, materially affluent, and humanly rewarding—a society of 'ought-to-be.' "Its purpose is to educate and foster able and peace-oriented international leaders for the future of mankind." This is the ideal of GIP as stressed by Dr. Young Seek Choue, Founder and Chancellor of Kyung Hee University System in Korea.

The GIP is a unique educational institution for peace-centered learning designed to meet the peace leader's demands, both domestic and international, of the 21st century envisaged to be more diversified and more specialized than the present one. Aware of the societal needs of a country and the radical changes in the international community, the GIP is committed to the task of effectively coping with the anticipated trends in the development of human civilization. Thus, the academic program is intended to develop students into well-rounded leaders equipped with general knowledge and specific skills to meet the new challenges of the 21st century; to anticipate not only the problems and discriminate the issues, but also to search for opportunities for making the world an ideal one. Accordingly, the Institute's program is intended for students with ambitions of pursuing an academic or practical career which requires an interdisciplinary understanding of the changing national and international realities. In the over-all view of peace education, the curriculum of GIP is geared towards the development of peace-loving and peace-promoting individuals who shall be prepared to face the challenges of leadership in the coming century.

2. Special Characteristics

The role of educating future leaders for the 21st Century makes GIP meritorious and distinct from other institutes of higher learning. Whereas the general trend in contemporary education emphasizes theoretical aspects, the GIP believes that the great leader can only be brought up through total personality education fostering character development and leadership skills.

2.1 Full Scholarship

To accomplish this educational mission effectively, all students are required to stay in the dormitory and undergo various co-curricular activities to augment the academic program. Considering the economic constraints to the acquisition of requisite education, the GIP provides full scholarship covering tuition fees, living expenses and necessary books for two and a half academic years.

2.2 Leadership Training Programs

As a unique characteristic of the Institute, it conducts regularly leadership training programs which are attended by all students, professors and staffs for about three days and three nights. Seminars and discussions and visits to vital industries, government offices and various public facilities are conducted to provide the students with opportunity to broaden their perspectives by gaining insight into contemporary international and domestic developments, problems and solutions.

2.3 Lectures in English

In principle, courses in the GIP are taught in English except those which deal specifically with Korean studies. Classroom activities vary depending on the nature of courses and the needs of the students. Included are lectures, colloquia, seminars, field researches, simulations, informal discussions, and the like. The use of English language in classroom activities, examinations, research and thesis writing is to be mandatory since the Institute believes that the future leader should be equipped with functional skills and high proficiency in the use of English as an international language. Hence the students in their first year undergo intensive course in English Language Skills Development at the language laboratory which is equipped with modern gadgets.

2.4 Honor System and the Student Body

The student body, which is led by the chairman, controls all student activities. It comprises several student committees in areas of general affairs, academics, publication, library, athletics, etc. Every student participates as a working member of any of such committees. The committee on general affairs is mainly in charge of early morning student activities including group meditation, discussion, physical exercise and cleaning the dormitory and surrounding area. The committee on academics holds the nationwide English speech contest for international peace every Spring semester and the UN student membership seminar every Fall semester for promoting peace-loving ideas to the youth. The committee on publication issues every semester *Peace Forum*, the English periodical of the Institute containing articles written by students and professors as it has been done since the establishment of the GIP. Library services are provided through honor system as coordinated by the committee on library which takes charge of lending and reaccessioning of library materials. The committee on athletics manages athletic events which are periodically done. A main feature of the committee's activities is special training in oriental swordsmanship.

2.5 Mock Sessions and Internship

The mock UN General Assembly, simulated Korean cabinet meeting and National Assembly are held in turn every semester to allow students to obtain the capability of analyzing and understanding contemporary international and domestic trends and issues.

After completing the four-semester in-campus program, the students undergo on-the-job internship during which they also write their thesis. Through this internship students are able to apply theoretical knowledge to the field thereby acquiring ideas on the differences between theory and practice. For at least once a month special lectures are held to help students broaden their knowledge. Since the 21st Century will be characterized by technological advance the Institute offers courses in computer science regularly. Thus the students can write research papers and graduate thesis using computer facilities as well as learn with ease database, statistics, and word-processing.

2.6 Students' Communal Life

The Institute aspires to provide the students with an environment that is conducive to their total personality development as embodied in the statement of its goals. Maximum opportunity for education is provided through curricular and co-curricular activities in which all students are enjoined to participate.

Community living is a distinct feature of the Institute where students are encouraged to manage their own lives with a modicum of guidance from a professor designated for the purpose. Housed in a modern dormitory, the students learn to live with others in an atmosphere of brotherhood and camaraderie. Certain rules of the house are set by the students themselves with suggestions from and concurrence of the administration. Being self-reliant, the students form committees to manage their affairs and some responsibilities are shared through individual or group charges.

Upon admission to the Institute, for the first two years the students are required to reside in the campus dormitory for developing ability to live communally. The dormitory is called "Sam-jong-so-hon," which is the birthplace of the 21st Century leader and the cradle of total-personality education. "Sam-jong-so-hon" is derived from "Sam-Jong-Haeng," which means "three virtuous deeds," namely "Jong-Ji": right knowledge, "Jong-Pan": right judgement, "Jong-Haeng:' right action. "Sam-Jong-Haeng" is the principle and the code of conduct of dormitory life as well as of future leadership. Dormitory life is guided by Honor System based on the spirit of "Sam-Jong-Haeng." All students are familiar with the principle of autonomy, self-reliance and self-independence.

Daily life at the dormitory starts at 6 o'clock in the morning. Just after waking up the students meditate for 15 minutes and discuss the day's schedule. Thereafter they perform calisthenics and go on jogging for about 3 kilometers. Then they clean their living quarters as charged while simultaneously clearing up their minds and spirit. After breakfast they do independent study, after which they attend the formal classes which last till about 5 o'clock in the afternoon. Just before dinner they are free to choose between independent study and physical exercise at the gymnasium. After dinner they conduct group activities according to personal interest, such as 'Love Meeting,' Christian prayer-discussion session, 'Peace Studies' discussion, 'English Discussion' and so on.

Dormitory life is governed by certain rules which provide an honor system that controls student behaviors. The guidance counsellor provides advise for further development of skills in dealing with life problems. Any violations carry demerits which when accumulated deserve disciplinary actions by faculty committee upon recommendation of the student body. Remedial measures are taken to check behavioral problems.

2.7 Uniqueness in the Procedures of Admission

The GIP recruits a limited number of freshmen with the view that particularized and intensive education of the chosen few can promote quality education. Three examinations for admission are given during a week period which include English language skills examination, essay writing, and interviews, and physical examination and medical evaluation. During the interview the Examination Committee makes a comprehensive assessment not only of the applicant's study plan and general knowledge of the field he applies for but also of his character, personality and understanding of the problems and issues on contemporary societies and his proposed measures for resolving such problems. Physical and medical evaluation insures that the applicant possesses the proper condition to undergo rigorous activities of a leader.

The Institute offers open-door service to the students from all over the world for realizing international peace. The GIP has had students form the United States, China, Iran, New Zealand, Norway, Belgium, Uzbekistan, Taiwan, Thailand, and the Philippines who after graduating have gone back to their homelands and are now working in various fields such as diplomacy, journalism, education and international business.

See also: *Peace and Peace Education: A Holistic View; Education for Global Citizenship; World Citizenship; Peace Education*

JAE-SHIK SOHN

Graham, Billy

By far the most significant personality in twentieth century evangelical Protestantism in the United States is William F. (Billy) Graham (born 1918). His impact as an evangelist and preacher is unparalleled, because modern communications and transportation technology have permitted him to proclaim the Christian gospel to all parts of the globe in a manner no individual before him has been able to do.

The son of a small dairy farmer in North Carolina, Graham was converted as a teenager in a revival meeting, received a minimal theological education, and eventually became a Youth for Christ evangelist and president of a small fundamentalist Bible college. He was catapulted to national fame through a remarkably successful campaign in Los Angeles in 1949, and after this he devoted all his effort to evan-

gelism. In the next decade he held large meetings ("crusades") across the United States and then in Europe, Asia, and Africa. He built up a large organization, the Billy Graham Evangelistic Association, which administered the crusades, produced radio and television programs and (through a subsidiary) motion pictures, distributed his books and printed sermons, and sponsored smaller meetings by other team members, called "associate evangelists."

Beginning in the 1960s, in addition to his crusades Graham organized congresses on evangelism in various parts of the world and introduced a major ecumenical thrust into evangelical Christianity. He also contributed a scholarly element by funding the journal *Christianity Today* and the Billy Graham Center at Wheaton College in Illinois. He met regularly with statesmen and business leaders around the world and was the confidant of several United States presidents. Although in the early years established religious leaders and reputable theologians looked down upon him, Graham gradually came to be accepted by most of them, and by the 1980s he was a prominent figure on the ecumenical scene and even had cordial relations with Pope John Paul II.

Because of his stature as a Christian minister, Graham's views on war and peace attracted far more attention than normally would have been the case. During his long career his position evolved from a narrow anticommunism and Americanism to a balanced, globalist understanding of international relations and the importance of arms control. As early as 1947 he had sounded the alarm against communist expansion into two halves, a Christian-based West and a godless communist realm inspired and directed by the Devil. In the early 1950s he saw the world locked in a life-and-death struggle between Christianity and the "disciple of Lucifer." He fully agreed with the efforts to ferret out native communists in the United States and lamented that the country was rapidly becoming a second-rate power. The best defense against communism, he said in 1954, was old-fast-ironed Americanism, conservative and evangelical Christianity, prayer, the personal acceptance of Jesus Christianity, prayer, the personal spiritual renewal. With the communist barbarians beating at the gates, American national survival was incumbent on its people turning to God.

Graham wholeheartedly supported the Korean War, even to the point of publicly praying for "victory for our troops," and was outraged by the dismissal of General Douglas MacArthur. He visited the American men in Korea at Christmas in 1952 and praised their valor, and he denounced the standstill peace. He later urged that French Indochina "be held at any cost" (1954), supported the rearmament of the Federal Republic of Germany as a deterrent to war (1954), castigated the Soviet suppression of the Hungarian uprising as a "massacre" that "would make even Hitler and Mussolini blush" (1956), blamed communists for smuggling drugs into the United States to hasten its downfall (1962), and said history would condemn "the country for not aiding the 'Cuban freedom fighters' at the Bay of Pigs (1961)." Thus one naturally expected that he would support the widening American involvement in Vietnam.

In the initial stages of the imbroglio Graham indeed was supportive, but he was maturing in his political outlook and was careful not to make the extreme statements that had characterized his youth.

He did not affirm it as a crusade for righteousness but in 1965 made serval comments that were widely interpreted as endorsing President Lyndon B. Johnson's actions in the war, such as a prayer breakfast speech where he portrayed Christ as a "firesetter" and "sword wielder." Moreover, he visited the American forces in Vietnam at Christmas 1966 and 1968 and returned home lauding their morale and courage. Although he had begun to doubt whether his country could achieve the objective of eradicating communism from Southeast Asia, he was careful not to criticize the President's handling of the conflict or to identify in any way with peace protesters. He funcioned as the principal spiritual adviser of both Presidents Johnson and Richard M. Nixon, and there is no evidence that he recommended to either that the United States pull out of Vietnam. Certainly by the time of the Cambodian invasion in 1970 he had wanted to see the war halted, but this would have to be by negotiation, not an American defeat.

When Nixon resumed the bombing of North Vietnam in late 1972, Graham was under intense pressure from fellow clergymen to condemn the action, but he demurred, insisting that he was a New Testament evangelist, not an Old Testament prophet, a proclaimer of God's message of love and grace and the necessity for repentance, not a social reformer and political activist. At the same time, he declared he had never advocated war and in fact deplored it, and was "praying for every responsible effort which seeks true peace in our time." Also he repeatedly maintained that Christians were on both sides of the question, and it was too complicated for him to understand and speak out on.

In the early 1970s a distinct shift in Graham's outlook on political matters had become evident. He backed off from his earlier nationalism and declared on several occasions that he had erred in identifying the gospel with Americanism. At the Lausanne Congress on World Evangelism in 1974 he proclaimed that now he went forth "as an ambassador for the Kingdom of God—not America." The same was true with his anticommunism. He announced that communists did a better job of living up to the demands and discipline of their ethic than Christians did, dropped negative comments about the ideology from his sermons, and emphasized the opportunities for spreading the gospel in the bloc countries. In 1977 and 1978 he preached in Hungary and Poland for the first time and was deeply impressed by how Christianity survived under the regimes there and the longings for peace among their populations. Moreover, in 1973 he had served notice that he would speak out on matters where he felt a "definite moral issue" was involved, and for him the threat of a nuclear holocaust was becoming such a question.

In 1979 Graham came out publicly for nuclear disarmament in an interview on CBS television news and in *Sojourners* magazine, and reiterated his views on numerous occasions thereafter. He did not advocate unilateral disarmament per se nor did he identify with pacifism, but he did strongly endorse the idea of a negotiated reduction in armaments. Graham's stance was that East-West differences were not worth a nuclear war, God did not want resources that could be used for alleviating human suffering and hunger to be diverted to massive armaments, and the SALT II arms limitation treaty was a step in the right direction. He admitted that his change of heart had been "a rather late conviction of mine," and a "sort of pilgrimage over the last few years." It came from conversations with leaders in many countries who were concerned about the nuclear arms race, assistance from other Christians sensitive to the matter, and a restudying of what the Bible had to say about our responsibility as peacemakers.

Graham's most dramatic move in behalf of peace was his appearance at a conference of "Religious Workers for Saving the Sacred Gift of Life from Nuclear Catastrophe" which was hosted by the Orthodox Patriarch of Moscow in May 1982. Although he was heavily criticized by the American Right for going and the White House was uneasy about the visit, he made a forceful and prophetic speech that declared the nuclear arms race to be a "moral and spiritual issue." He maintained that the current highly politicized and individualistic way of thinking had failed and they were tied to the kind of technology that could lead to a nuclear Armageddon. In subsequent trips to the German Democratic Republic and Czechoslovakia he continued to point out the moral implications of the arms competition, and in a 12-day preaching mission in the Soviet Union in September 1984 he repeated his theses about the danger of nuclear war and the possibility for world peace and better relations between the Superpowers. In 1982 he endorsed the so-called "freeze" on the testing, production, and deployment of nuclear arms, but then edged away from his position after a meeting with President Ronald Reagan, with whom he had developed a cordial relationship.

In 1985 he went to Romania and Hungary where he addressed huge crowds and reiterated the themes of peace, greater religious freedom, and reduction of church-state tensions. As another part of the leavening process in the Communist bloc lands, the Graham

organization in 1988 donated $50,000 to assist earthquake victims in Soviet Armenia. That same year he met Mikhail Gorbachev at the White House during his visit to the United States, which led eventually to another invitation to the former Soviet Union in 1991 for a five-day school of evangelism and lengthy talks with the Russian leaders and then a full-fledged crusade in Moscow's Lenin Stadium in 1992.

Two elements have informed Graham's peace emphasis. One is his belief that peace is a spiritual problem, and it will be achieved primarily by the use of spiritual means—prayer, preaching the gospel, and the work of the Holy Spirit in changing the lives of individuals. As he said when laying a wreath at the Leningrad war memorial in 1984: "The ultimate problem is within man's heart. Without a change of heart and a change of mind there will be no lasting solution to the problem of war." The second is premillennial eschatology, to which he subscribes. Most versions of this hold that conditions in the world will grow steadily worse until Christ returns to earth, but Graham himself feels that Christians as stewards of God's creation are expected to work to preserve and care for the world he has made. In that respect they will be found faithful at Christ's coming. Giving the logic of religious individualism and apocalyptic premillennialism, as well as the multitude of evangelical supporters he has in the United States who view their country as a divinely chosen nation and oppose any peace initiative that might compromise its preeminent position in the world, Graham's adoption of such a strong stance on behalf of nuclear disarmament, world peace, and Superpower coexistence is most remarkable.

See also: *Religion and Peace; Christianity*

Bibliography —————————————————

Frady M 1979 *Billy Graham: A Parable of American Righteousness.* Harper and Row, New York

Graham B 1997 *Just As I Am: The Autobiography of Billy Graham.* Harper, San Francisco

Martin W 1991 *A Prophet with Honor: The Billy Graham Story.* William Morrow, New York

McLoughlin W G 1960 *Billy Graham: Revivalist in a Secular Age.* Ronald Press, New York

Pierard R V 1980a Billy Graham: A study in survival. *Reformed Journal* 30

Pierard R V 1980b Billy Graham and the US presidency. *Journal of Church and State* 22

Pierard R V 1980c Billy Graham and Vietnam: From cold warrior to peacemaker. *Christian Scholar's Review* 10

Pierard R V 1983 From evangelical exclusivism to ecumenical openness: Billy Graham and sociopolitical issue. *Journal of Ecumenical Studies* 20

Pierard R V 1984 Billy Graham: Will he stay the course for peace? *Covenant Quarterly* 42

Pollock J 1966 *Billy Graham: The Authorized Biography.* McGraw Hill, New York

Pollock J 1966 *Crusades: 20 Years with Billy Graham.* World Wide, Minneapolis, Minnesota

Pollock J 1979 *Billy Graham: Evangelist to the World.* Harper and Row, New York

Pollock J 1985 *To All the Nations: The Billy Graham Story.* Harper and Row, New York

Streiker L D, Strober G S 1972 *Religion and the New Majority: Billy Graham, Middle America and the Politics of the 70s.* Association Press, New York

RICHARD V. PIERARD

Green Security

1. Security Discourse in a Globalizing World

As regards the political content of security, it means those tasks of a state which attempt to ensure the security of its citizens against outside threats. It is in this form that it is connected with the real or imaginary security provided by weapons. This approach also connects security and defense in national policies.

The determination of the content of the concept meshes seamlessly with the development of nation-states and with competition between states, which has generally been taken for granted at least in the realist paradigm in the field of international studies. As the state began to be perceived as a sovereign actor in relation to other international actors, it assumed a new function of ensuring the integrity of the territory and the socio-political organization of the state. This development took place as late as the 17th and 18th centuries.

In other words the concept of security is closely connected to the history of the modern state and the 'anarchic' nature of the international system (see *Anarchy, International*). There is no reason to speak of security as a collective good provided by states for their citizens before the emergence of modern states. In principle, borders have been protected to ward off a physical threat to the citizens, but in practice human sacrifices have been accepted in order to save the state.

Since the 16th century in the modern international system security has been organized by nation states. However, this has become much more complicated in a global system. According to traditional security discourse, several important elements of national security are outside the national borders in a global world. Industrial welfare society of the developed world is based on non-renewable resources which in many cases cannot be found inside the national borders or the realm of national sovereignty (see *World Peace Order, Dimensions of a*). It is possible to say

that since the 16th century the industrialized world connected the whole world into one network which allowed the utilization of other's resources (see for instance Roberts 1996 p. 506). Therefore states have an interest to control resources beyond their borders (see Käkönen 1988 pp. 147-59). This is one of the reasons which have led to a situation where traditional concept of security is not enough anymore (see *Comprehensive Security*).

There is also another element to be mentioned in connection with this. Industrial society is also based on cheap means of existence. This is the major reason why European nations began to import on a mass scale basic foodstuffs at the same time as the growing industry required labor force on a mass scale (Weatherford 1990 p. 59-78). Since that time, one of the major concerns in political discourse has been finding cheap means for the subsistence of the labor force. Therefore food producers have low incomes, and in order to improve their own situation and to keep food prices down they have to overexploit nature. This is one connection where internal stability, growth oriented economy and environmental degradation are interlinked.

In the modernization approach security has traditionally been strictly connected to nation states. In a globalized system the essence of security has changed. Already during the Cold War there emerged a discussion about common security which also expanded the scope of the concept of security (Käkönen 1992). However, during the Cold War the hostile bipolarity made it impossible to establish any kind of common security system. After the Cold War it has been possible to imagine that western democracy combined with market economy will be the only existing socio-economic system for the time being (see *Cold War*). Therefore the world will almost share common values which should make it possible to accept an understanding of common security.

2. Security and Environment

Not only globalization and the end of the Cold War but also environmental concern has changed the understanding of security (see *Global Environment and Peace*). Issues closely connected in environment were brought into international studies in the 1970s. For the Stockholm International Peace Research Institute (SIPRI) Arthur Westing (1976; 1977 and 1980) conducted research on how wars and use of weapons had affected the environment. This orientation gave information about how violent conflicts caused degradation of the environment which further increased human losses. It was also made clear that in violent conflicts the environment was destroyed consciously. In fact ancient Egyptian norms tell that destroying of the environment was already then a method to fight the enemy. However, according to Egyptian norms, polluting of wells was forbidden. However, in the 1970s environmental issues were not connected to security and the concept of security was strictly defined as security provided by specific state institutions.

In this connection it is worth referring to the point that the environment as a material space for societies has in practical human history always been closely related to human and social security. Material conditions for social spaces were already for the traditional societies the base for human reproduction. Therefore the relation between the territory as a space and population in an organized society was important. This relation could be changed by following means: by expanding the territory by wars; by population control or by advancing technology. When food species became scarce the hunting societies expanded their hunting grounds. The Agrarian societies increased productivity by more intensive production methods or by expanding the area under cultivation; i.e., by changing the environment (see Harris 1982; Roberts 1996 p. 501 or Ponting 1993 pp. 161-223).

Increasing population and the scarcity of resources for existence has always been a cause for insecurity. Technological advances and economic growth since the 16th century has led us to forget the traditional wisdom. However, the population growth and globalization have brought back the old problems and issues. It is difficult to believe that improvement of productive technology can help to maintain the balance in the relation between the space and population forever (see *Eco-technology*). Therefore environment and environmental changes are gaining a place also in the security agenda.

Already in the 1980s, environmental issues were connected to security. Barry Buzan (1983) began this discourse in the early 1980s. In his work Buzan made it clear that human individual security and the security of a state are not at all the same (see *Peace and Social Development*). Also the threats faced by people and states were different. Therefore scholars began to talk about economic, environmental and ecological security in connection with traditional national and armed security. Development was also connected to international security (see for instance Hettne 1984a; Gleditsch 1994 and Dalby 1994).

As regards the change and expansion of the concept, it is important that many international expert bodies redefined security as far back as the late 1970s and in the 1980s. The following expert bodies should be mentioned in particular: the commission on North-South relations under the direction of Willy Brandt, late Federal Chancellor of the Federal Republic of Germany; the commission on international disarmament and security under the direction of Olof Palme, late Prime Minister of Sweden; the commission on development and armament under the direction of Inga Thorson, a Swedish minister for disarmament; and the commission on environmental questions under the direction of Gro Harlem Brundtland, Prime Minister of Norway (Hettne 1984b).

Regarding the problem under discussion, all these reports have in common the connection of armament to poverty and hunger in the world (see *Economics of Disarmament: Certain Premises*). Both phenomena, according to the reports, increase the probability of conflicts, which maintains the need for armament. The problems form a vicious circle, in which they feed each other while the increase in the amount of weapons ultimately adds to insecurity in the international community. In other words, armed security works against its own original goal, so that, armament has become a central source of insecurity—a threat to humankind.

It is quite evident that the definition of the concept of security in solely military terms is highly problematic in the era of globalizing world (see *Globalization; Global Integration*). Concentration on the military element easily transforms economy into a strategic element. This leads to a situation where the guaranteeing of economic security becomes a military problem and it is no longer a political or purely economic one. This transforms distant economic interests such as Persian Gulf oil into elements of national security for states depending on oil import. Trade is likely to lose its original essence as an instrument moving economic values between societies and states. Finally, economic interdependence or distant security threats in economy will get military solutions (Käkönen 1987 pp. 115-9). This development is one important reason for defining the concept of security in a broader sense than has traditionally been the case.

Security is not connected only to the states but also involves people. We have moved towards the expansion of the concept of security on a variety of activity levels. In the minds of citizens the concept has expanded in the face of new threat images, like AIDS. Modern communication has made many of the new threat images everyday reality to all people. Among researchers the concept has also acquired new content. It is visible in research analyses connected with the traditional theory of international politics. Many representatives of the realist school consider new aspects of security together with armed security; the most prominent of these is possibly environmental security (see Buzan 1989). Environment is also an important sector in international relations (see Thomas 1992). Environmental issues are climbing up from the margin into the sphere of the so called high politics.

3. Environmental Security

The adaptation of the concept of environmental security is one result of attempting to widen the scope of traditional state and political system centric discourse on security. In the post-Cold War period the discussion about environmental security gave a chance to ask how the massive financial resources devoted for national or international security in the bipolar world should be used after the tension disappeared. It also gave a good base to raise the question of whether it is important to discuss national security or societal security. Already Buzan (1983) made it clear that the threats faced by traditional nation states and by societies of ordinary people were not at all the same.

Almost simultaneously with the process of the withering away of the Cold War, the international community of scholars opened a discussion about the essence of the concept of security. The discussion about the extended essence of the concept of security opened a dialogue between peace researchers and the traditional security establishment. In a sense, it is possible to call it a struggle over the hegemony to define security. However, at the same time it has been a struggle over the resources; i.e., how in the post-Cold War era to use the resources traditionally devoted to armed security. Has it been wise to connect environmental problems to traditional security is another issue. For instance, Gleditsch (1994) and Finger (1994) have pointed out that the means for

providing national security in a traditional sense are different than the means for providing environmental security in a case where the entire existence of nature and human beings are threatened.

After the Cold War the huge military costs are not justified anymore. Simultaneously, there are not enough resources to take care of the environmental problems which also threaten the existence of people. In this respect environmental security discourse made it acceptable to say that even during the period of declining public resources there were resources in the military security sector which could be transferred into the field of societal security. This argumentation followed very much the logic of post-World War II peace movements. These movements seldom aimed to change socio-economic structures of existing societies. They simply wanted to move resources from a threatening military sector to more civilian purposes.

The new security discourse also raised public concern about much wider security issues than traditional national security. It became gradually clear that modernity has caused many threats which are common for the whole of human kind. First of all environmental threats were taken as a security risk in the cases like the Chernobyl nuclear power plant accident. And in a much wider perspective, people understood that airborne pollution does not respect any borders. Therefore, there is a common concern that many threats on societal security have to be dealt on a wider political arena than nation-state.

Traditional state centric security policy concentrated on the threats coming from outside. Today many problems related to environmental changes can affect the social systems. Erosion of fertile soil; exhaustion of fish stocks or drought can cause the collapse of a social system (cf. Storey & Smith 1995; Lyck 1994). These threats can not be dealt by traditional defense policy means since they come from inside. In these kind of situations the consequences are local although causes are related to global environmental problems which do not respect state borders.

In this connection it is good to go a bit further and ask what are the current threat images and the most likely future conflicts. After the Cold War there are few if any scholars who estimate a global nuclear war or any kind of a world war to be a realistic possibility. Current statistics does not give high probability even for inter-state wars. In the post-Cold War period intra-state wars have become the most likely alternative. On the other hand, if we look at current literature, the most likely security threats states will face are: international nuclear terrorism; international terrorism related to fundamentalism; international

Figure 1
Causal relations in environmental security

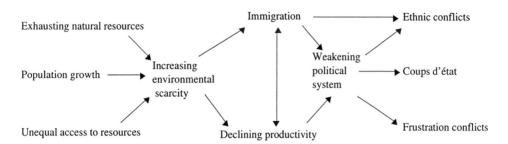

Sources of Environmental Scarcity   Social Consequences

drug trade and violence connected to it; international crime and illegal immigration (see *Crime Trends and Crime Prevention Strategies*). All these different aspects are connected to immigration the European and US security discourses (see Bigo 1996).

Today there is also a growing pile of studies which indicate that environmental change is one of the causes for conflicts. Therefore it is possible to begin to talk about environmental conflicts. A Belgian research institute uses the concept 'Green Conflicts.' In the 1990s the research group of the Belgian institute has found altogether 71 green conflicts which they have categorized in the following way: forest conflicts; fishery conflicts; water conflicts; conflicts for arable land and conflicts caused by environmental refugees (Schmitz 1992 pp. 63-89 and the annex). However, there is no direct connection between environmental changes and conflicts. Environmental changes in weak socio-economic systems are combinations for manifest conflicts since weak societies do not have resources to deal with the consequences (Bächler et al., 1996 p. 55, 66). Homer-Dixon (1994 p. 31) has come more or less to the same conclusion.

4. Militarization of Environment

There is a potential trap in securitising environmental issues although the environmental problems might cause violent conflicts. Securitisation easily connects normal societal problems into traditional security and defense which again leads to militarization of the problems. In the discourse on environmental or comprehensive security there are conflicting interests. First, we have to understand that even national armies are just organizations which will defend their interests; i.e., to receive their financial resources. For instance this can bee seen in NATO's attempt to renew

itself in the post-Cold War period. The same can be found in the new tasks the US Army has taken for itself (see Butts 1994). After the Cold War it was possible to believe that armies will loose their resources. The threat of a global war disappeared and it became justified to ask how much of the resources used for national security are needed after the Cold War. In fact the global military spending has been reduced by about 20 percent since the end of the Cold War which has been a threat to the military industry, first of all to the US military industry.

Today it is possible to say that there was a high risk in accepting the concept of environmental security. In this discourse the peace movement or peace researchers were not necessarily the winners. Though there has been a reduction in military spending, the resources have not been transferred for solving environmental problems, for instance. The reduction in military consumption is more related to the economic decline than to the end of the Cold War. In this situation the discussion about environmental security which connects environment to traditional security gave a good chance for the armies to find a new justification for their existence and for the resources devoted to the armies (see for instance, Butts 1994). National armies have experience to deal with the threats and they also have the means for instance to monitor the state of the environment and the state of the world seas. For instance, the satellites for national security can be used for monitoring the global environment. This was a good argument for the military to defend their position in a changing world. However, this raises questions about the militarization of environmental problems.

There is now doubt about how the armies can be used for protecting the environment. According to historical evidence, the US Army was used to protect the Yellowstone national park against local people who in their interests for subsistence violated the peace of the park (Byers 1994). In this kind of context it is possible to argue that the army or military was protecting the biodiversity of the nature. Biodiversity was also maintained in many army-owned areas which were not used but remained as natural reservations (see Butts 1994). But we also have evidence and cases about how the armies have destroyed nature even in their peace-time exercises (Heininen 1994). However, today the US army is training other national armies for protecting important national parks for instance in Africa (Butts 1994). And it is extremely difficult to say that the defense of the parks would not protect the survival of many scarce species. However, this does not mean that the armed protection of parks is the correct way of saving species.

The Yellowstone example begs the question why securitising of environmental issues is not the correct way to deal with the problem. In this case the poor people were not eager to lose a part of their living. Therefore they violated regulations which prevented hunting or cutting wood in the national park. Instead of sending the army to protect the park the correct way to deal with the problem would have been to compensate the losses for the local population. In this sense the problem is not security or safety but social or economic equality. In a wider perspective the problem could be presented also in another way. Hunting is a means for subsistence as long as there is demand for furs and meat. In establishing national parks for maintaining the biodiversity, attention should also be directed to demand or consumption rather than to some few peoples' living conditions.

From a positive perspective armies have an experience in cleaning the environment. For instance in the USA the army has cleaned several seriously affected military bases (Butts 1994). Therefore it has become a slogan to say that army is good for environment. However, it is never said in connection with why armies have to clean their own waste. The military reflects the wider society in a modern world. The military is not only an actor which protects the modern nation state but it is also an aspect of the modern. Therefore it is possible to say that modern industrial society can not live without waste. As a reflection of the modern, the military produces its own waste which often is hazardous to human beings and nature. One important element here is that the aim of many military operations has been to destroy not only human life but also preconditions for life (see Westing 1976, 1980). This was clearly the case in Vietnam where the US army used several different polluting chemicals against nature. In order to reach national goals, armies have according to Finger (1994) a right to destroy nature and even people. The environmental problems caused by the Soviet Army in Estonia during the Cold War is good evidence about how armies even in the peace time behave for national safety.

In this respect the collapse of the former Soviet Union was a good phenomenon. It gave to the world a chance to find out how the armies pollute the environment. In this connection we should not give any relevance to the point that the former Soviet Union was a socialist country. More important is that the former Soviet Union was a version of modern society. The material welfare in a socialist as well as in a capitalist society has been based on exploitation of man and nature (Adler-Karlsson 1990). The former GDR as well as Estonia are good cases to learn about what was done to the environment during the Cold War in the name of global stability created by the nuclear balance. In both cases we know now how the Soviet army polluted the soil in and around its military bases (see Vares & Lassinantti 1995). In Estonia the military damage on environment has been well documented by the Estonian authorities (see EcpPro 1995; see also Lootus 1996).

The Estonian case also provides a clear picture that the cleaning of the Cold War military waste of a foreign army is too expensive for a small nation. However, we should not stop here. It is possible to go further. It should be justified to say that the modern is maybe too expensive for all societies with the waste associated with the modern. This argument can be supported also with facts from the USA. According to Butts (1994) the US Department of Defense uses about 9 billion US dollars annually for cleaning up its own facilities. The recent US official estimation tells us that in the following 75 years the US authorities have to spend from 200 to 350 billion dollars to clean the sites related to Cold War military security (Karvonen 1995 C1). And it is most likely that the final bill will be even higher.

5. Greening of Security?

Above I have emphasized that the adaptation of the concept of environmental security easily leads to militarization of environment. However, there is also a slight chance to understand the potential outcome of the discourse differently. The end of the Cold War raised hopes that the role of armed security would decline, and other even more common threats to social and human security would be dealt with more seriously. Since environmental problems have gained a visible position in discussions about security, it has become possible to discuss the greening of security. Is there a chance to convert the military organization into a civilian organization?

Byers (1994) has supported this interpretation of the concept of environmental security. He would like to allow the military to protect the environment in order to transform the military into a paramilitary and further into a non-military organization. This was one option after the Cold War. But there is a danger that a militarist approach to deal with environmental issues leads to the militarization of the society as Finger (1994) has stressed and I have pointed out above. The military has taken seriously the challenge raised by environmental problems. It has integrated the environment into the traditional security, and therefore it is to be feared that the environmental issues will be militarized. The point here is that national security can function well without any concern for global environmental problems (Finger 1994).

However, ecological changes and environmental threats are undoubtedly related to traditional national security issues. In limited issues there is a direct connection between nature and national security. Butts (1994) points out that ecological changes might cause social instability and therefore environmental concern is an aspect of national security. Funke (1994) has taken up the same connection by arguing that the degradation of nature leads to a decline in the national economy which also affects the national security. Both of these arguments get support from the conclusions made by Homer-Dixon's (1994) and Bächler's (1996) projects to which I have referred earlier.

Here we come to the point why environmental issues and specifically environmental conflicts belong to the core of peace research. At the same time it becomes clear why it is problematic to securities environmental problems. People do not meet environmental problems equally. Environmental changes put people, both globally and locally, in different positions which reminds very much the situation Johan Galtung long time ago called structural violence (see *Peace Theory: An Introduction*). The existence of structural violence is always a potential source for conflicts. This conclusion has been supported by John Burton (1990 pp. 36-7) who has argued that in case where the social and the legal systems do not allow some people to satisfy their needs these people are ready to use illegal means, i.e., vio-

lence, in order to reach their goals. Therefore, economic stability and equality are preconditions for environmental security. However, if economic stability is based on the exploitation of natural resources exceeding the limits of nature, we are facing a cul-de-sac. This is a dilemma which might be impossible to solve within the existing paradigm.

The arguments above explain why, after the end of the Cold War, there has been reorientation in peace research though SIPRI took environmental issues into its agenda already earlier (see also Conca 1994). For peace researchers this reorientation was also an attempt to influence the redefinition of the concept of security as mentioned above. The stress on environmental issues was an effort to direct funds from armed security to civic security in order to contribute to the possible post-Cold War conversion, as argued for instance by Funke (1994). Today we can say that the battle between the two different security approaches has, at least for the time being, been lost by peace researchers which means that the military won and they have been able to adapt themselves into the field of environmental issues as argued earlier.

The concept of security is historically so closely connected to nation states and armed forces that it is difficult to change its essence. This means that peace research has to deal with environmental issues from its own point of view. There are several linkages between the hard core of peace research as peace, war, conflict, structural violence, or conflict resolution and environmental problems. To my mind maybe the most interesting aspect of peace research is peaceful transformation. It is evident that environmental changes cause social changes and social changes easily create potential for conflicts. Peace research should find ways to avoid the conflicts and manage changes through peaceful means by increasing equality simultaneously.

Above I have already referred to environmental conflicts on a more general level. In this connection it is necessary to go a bit further into the details. therefore I will briefly discuss two different water conflicts: the Israel-Palestine conflict and the Nile case. The Israel-Palestine conflict can be understood as a conflict over the control of water. Already in 1916 and 1919 the leaders of the international Zionist movement determined that the forthcoming Jewish state's borders have to be in the Litan river, on the Golan heights and in the Jordan river. These borders would give a Jewish state a possibility to control the water within the territory. In the wars which followed the establishment of the state of Israel it has expanded to the borders demanded in 1919. At the same time, Palestinians have lost the control of water even in the West Bank and they have to pay six times more for the water than the Jewish colonies do (see more about the conflict in Lindholm 1992 and Lowi 1993). In this case the conflict is related to a scarce renewable resource and the control of this resource changes the position of two different groups vis-á-vis each other. This has further led to a situation where it has become difficult for the Palestinians to satisfy their needs (see *Arab-Israeli Conflict: Plans and Proposals*).

In the Nile valley we came across the problem who has the right to use the water. Egypt is a riparian state, the last one, in the Nile valley. 80 per cent of Egypt's water comes from the Nile. On the other hand 80 per cent of the sources of the Nile are in Ethiopia. As a sovereign state Ethiopia has a responsibility and the right to improve the standard of living of its own citizens. This can be done by developing agriculture which requires proper irrigation systems. As Ethiopia develops its agriculture there will be much less water for both Sudan and Egypt. As a national security issue this situation could lead Egypt into a war with Ethiopia as once indicated by Boutros Boutros-Ghali (Schmitz 1992 p. 68). Again in this case the use of a renewable resource could change the position of people in different countries vis-á-vis each other. It is difficult to see how the problem could be solved peacefully by means of traditional security. A completely different approach is needed for a peaceful conflict resolution.

6. Environmental Problems and Security

During the history of humankind, environmental changes have affected both states and the power relations between states. And the reactions to changes of this kind have often been the use of force (see Harris 1982; Pointing 1993). As traditional security-political thinking maintains its ruling status, it is not difficult to imagine that states would still today try to solve problems caused by environmental changes by resorting to force. Environmental conflicts are even more complicated than expressed by the cases above. Many of the environmental conflicts will have a global character. The consequences of the global climate change are unequally divided. The pollution of environment has created material wealth in the developed world. However, the most serious costs for environmental degradation will be paid by the least developed countries and most marginalized people since they do not have resources to face these problems (Dossier 1996 p. 7, 9, 10; Bächler et al., 1996 p.

62). In the case of an environmental conflict in the developing world this means that the conflict partners do not have a chance to affect the industrialized world where most of the causes for environmental changes, and thus for conflicts, originate.

As regards the use of resources, environmental problems offer perhaps the best example of the difference between traditional security-political thinking and comprehensive security-political thinking. Even now, environmental changes affect the relations between people, social groups, ethnic groups and states. In the arid areas of the earth people even now have to resolve the conflict between different modes of production, for example, in relation to the right to use water as indicated above (see also Mohamed Salih 1994 or Sarmela 1988 pp. 129-33). This kind of conflicts often arises between ethnic communities and it therefore also leads to ethnic conflicts (Mohamed Salih 1994; Moorehead 1994). Therefore violent environmental conflicts are mostly internal conflicts with a potential to expand into international ones (Bächler 1996 p. 56). In this regard environmental changes are also becoming a factor which will in the future possibly cause the greatest numbers of refugees.

Environmental changes and the degradation of environment have already forced people to leave their traditional lands and homes; environmental refugees are already a fact and they have been a source even for violent conflicts (Homer-Dixon & Percival 1996 pp. 8-9; see also Butts 1994; Dalby 1994). In some cases environmental refugees have increased stress on the environment and first of all on arable land and available water resources. This again has caused conflicts between displaced people and the local ones, for instance, in Ethiopia and India (Arsano 1989; Homer-Dixon & Percival 1996 pp. 14-6). In the latter case people in Bangladesh were displaced and moved over the border into India. In this case the conflict had also an international character.

In this connection it is good to understand that climate change and greenhouse effect are factors which create potential for conflicts and refugees. It has been estimated that the greenhouse effect will raise the sea level by one meter for example in the Indian Ocean after the year 2000. This would mean that for instance the Maldive Islands would be left under water. This would not be a great problem because of the small population of the islands. A real problem would be created by Bangladesh, which is flooded yearly and in which maybe a couple of hundred million people would be left homeless. These people have to be settled somewhere, and one alternative to their migration is a resort to arms if the traditional security approach is applied.

To my mind it is important to realize that the perspective constructed above is not necessarily a worst case scenario or a doomsday utopia. There seems to be evidence enough that natural hazards, like hurricanes, floods, droughts and forest fires have increased in the 1980s and the 1990s has been a real period of natural catastrophes (Dossier 1996 p. 7; Cutter 1996 p. 526). Natural catastrophes have affected most seriously marginalized areas of the world where the poor people live. And these catastrophes have produced environmental refugees (Cutter 1996 p. 534).

To me it is clear that in environmental conflicts we have problems which can not be dealt with by means of traditional security or defense policy. The solution is to go to the roots of the problems; i.e., the essence of the modern society. However, instead of seriously dealing with the causes of environmental problems, experts are very much interested to find ways to protect own nations. For instance, an effective decrease of green house gases would lower the risk of the rise of the sea level. But many experts concentrate on how to protect people of rich countries, for instance, by constructing dams against the rising sea level according to the Netherlands' model.[1] This approach is closely related to traditional security thinking and it means the management but not solving of the problem (Finger 1994). In an ultimate case, rich countries do have resources even to construct shelters against increasing ultra-violet radiation and make the 'sci-fi' visions a reality.

These kinds of arguments give some evidence that it may have been a mistake to expand the traditional scope of the concept of security beyond its national reach. The military has been capable to take over the comprehensive concept of security and to preserve its own position. The connecting of environment and security has also given a possibility to militarize environmental issues or to deal with the issues in a way that some people will be protected and other people will be left outside. How the global environmental changes will affect many of the people of the world is not the concern of the rich world in cases where the problems are securitised. This approach has also given a chance for military to maintain most of their Cold War resources while the civilian organizations like Green Peace have to rely on private donations in taking care of global environmental threats. The transformation of resources from the military sector into civilian sectors has not been realized.

We can hardly deny that environmental threats often are transboundary by nature. This corresponds closely to the traditional threat images. Therefore, it is easy to connect environmental threats to traditional national security policies. However, they are also an issue in peace research as indicated above. This dualism is reflected in this article. In a sense there are two different approaches and frameworks to deal with environmental changes and security. On the other hand it seems to be clear that beyond the environmental security discourse there is also a discourse on local and global inequality. Therefore, to deal with the global and local inequalities is the correct way instead of securitising the problems introduced above. This transfers the security issue into more normal social and political issues.

The armed national security model also causes another kind of problem. In the context of current post-Cold War international politics it is easy to imagine situations where armed force would be used against a state which is a source of pollution or toxic waste. It is even possible that the UN will establish an environmental security council (Langlais 1995 p. 330) which would ask international forces; i.e., NATO, to force a state to follow international environmental regulations. This kind of reasoning gives a chance for NATO to change its image instead of questioning its relevance as a military alliance in the post-Cold War period. The use of force is of course the extreme case in addition to sanctions and international boycotts. This model is approached already by Finger (1994) and it is not difficult to buy it after we have seen the UN authorized so-called humanitarian interventions in the post-Cold War period.

The Somalian and Yugoslavian cases show quite clearly that there are hardly any real military solutions to current political and economic problems not to talk about environmental threats. Dalby (1994) and Funke (1994) have pointed out that the use of force does not solve the real problems, but only deals with some aspects of them. On the other hand, the use of military force is destructive to the environment as argued earlier and Westing's studies give hard evidence for this. One possible solution to the dilemma between environmental security and national security seems promising. In environmental issues international cooperation has to be stressed as well as our common security which is not bound to any single state. And this gives a chance to go from military alliances over to environmental alliances as indicated by Michael Renner (1989 p. 64).

7. Conclusion

As this article indicates, peace researchers and the military have common arguments in talking about security and the environment. But there is also a conflict between the two different approaches. Therefore, it is correct to talk either about the militarization of environmental issues or about green security which would partly mean demilitarization of security issues. The same can be expressed by saying that there is a struggle over the resources for defense connected to military and civilian ways of dealing with inequality. The military has already taken over many environmental issues. But where are the civilian forces capable of disarming the national defenses and to transforming the military into a civilian environmental task force?

It is evident that there are contradictory arguments in the field this article has been discussing. I have tried to present arguments from two different camps. The solutions have to be found in social and political discourses and decisions. The aim of the contradictory argumentation in this article is to help us to understand how complex the relation between nature and organized modern society is. Social and political interest groups do not share common values. Different connections between the nation-state system, economic growth, national security and environmental problems challenge us to ask whether the problems have to be solved in the frames of totally new paradigms.

I have chosen this mode of examination to demonstrate that the traditional emphasis on national security is maybe an outdated conception. We have to be able to move from national security to global security, where the starting-point is not the survival of separate states and political systems but the survival of the human species and the environment it needs. Hopes of a change of this kind are included in the international politics of our time.

When this problem is approached from another direction, we may come to the conclusion that a secure world is a world where one need not feel the fears connected in the system. This again means that security is increased by making the relations between people more equal and rendering decision-making in the international community more democratic. As to the realization of these comprehensive objectives of humankind, it is maintained that the resources created by humankind are not used for weapons but on the environment for creating security within the global system.

New and forthcoming security threats are inevitably connected in inequality and environmental changes. Over-exploitation of natural resources and environmental degradation have become the issues in global security (Bächler et al., 1996 p. 55). However, traditional security policy does not have means to deal with the problems. Therefore, security policy has to come close to economic and social policies. We have a

chance to talk about normalization of security. From an environmental point of view a policy for sustainable development on a global scale will became an issue for security. This is the legitimation for talk of talks about green security.

Without any serious doubts it is possible to say that sustainable development will be the necessary precondition for the future peace in the world (Dossier 1996 p. 15). Therefore international cooperation on the level of civil societies for true sustainable development is a must for humankind. And, finally, it is possible to say that sustainable development and green security require:

(a) Equal distribution of material values;

(b) Equal distribution of values between existing and forthcoming generations, and

(c) Preservation of the nature (Dossier 1996 p. 16).

Therefore, it is worthwhile to abandon the state centric concept of security which has a negative connotation. In this context, negative security means dealing with the threat. Sustainable development in connection with green security is associated with positive security. Positive security means the elimination of the factors which cause threats to people (see Langlais 1995). In this sense it is understandable that green security most likely requires a new social paradigm.

See also: *Human Security; Economics of Disarmament and Conversion; Human Rights and Environmental Rights: Their Sustainable Development Compatibility; Future of Humanity*

Bibliography ————————————————

Adler-Karlsson G 1990 *90-luvun Oppikirja*. Art House, Helsinki

Bächler G, Klötzli S, Libiszewski S, Spillmann K R 1996 Umweltzerstörung, eine Konfliktursache. *W&F Wissenschaft und Frieden* 14(3)

Bigo D 1996 Internal Security in the EU. A presentation in the seminar 'Immigration, Security, and Identity' at the University of San Diego

Burton J 1990 *Conflict: Resolution and Prevention*. Macmillan Press, Basingstoke

Butts K H 1994 Why the military is good for the environment. In: J Käkönen (ed.) *Green Security or Militarized Environment*. Aldershot, Dartmouth

Buzan B 1983 *Peoples, States, Fear: The National Security Problem in the International Relations*. Wheatshelf Books, Brighton

Buzan B 1989 The Systemic Context of European Security. *Working Papers* 5. Centre for Peace and Conflict Research, Copenhagen

Byers B A 1994 Armed forces and the conservation of biological diversity. In: J Käkönen (ed.) *Green Security or Militarized Environment*. Aldershot, Dartmouth

Conca K 1994 In the name of sustainability: Peace studies and environmental discourse. In: J Käkönen (ed.) *Green Security or Militarized Environment*. Dartmouth, Aldershot

Cutter S 1996 Societal responses to environmental hazards. *Int'l Social Science J.* 150

Dalby S 1994 The politics of environmental security. In: J Käkönen (ed.) *Green Security or Militarized Environment*. Aldershot, Dartmouth

Dossier 1996 Energiekonflikte. Kann die Menscheit das Energieproblem friedlich lösen? Interdisiplinäre Arbeitsgruppe Naturwissenchaf, Technik und Sicherheit (IANUS) an der T H Darmstadt. Dossier Nr. 22. Wissenschaft und Frieden

EcoPro 1995 Endise NSV Liidu sojaväe poolt Eesti keskkonnale tekitatud kahjude hindamise koondaruanne. A/S EcoPro, Tallinn

Finger M 1994 Global environmental degradation and the military. In: J Käkönen (ed.) *Green Security or Militarized Environment*. Aldershot, Dartmouth

Funke O 1994 Environmental dimensions of national security: The end of the Cold War. In: J Käkönen (ed.) *Green Security or Militarized Environment*. Dartmouth, Aldershot

Gleditsch N P 1994 Conversion and the environment. In: J Käkönen (ed.) *Green Security or Militarized Environment*. Aldershot, Dartmouth

Harris M 1982 *Kulttuurien Synty*. Kirjayhtymä, Vaasa

Heininen L 1994 The military and the arctic environment. In: J Käkönen (ed.) *Green Security or Militarized Environment*. Aldershot, Dartmouth

Hettne B 1984a Development theory and the third world. *Sarec Report* R 2, Helsingborg

Hettne B 1984b Approaches to the Study of Peace and Development. A State of the Art Report. EADI, *Working Paper* 6, August 1984

Homer-Dixon T F 1994 Environmental scarcities and violent conflicts: Evidence from cases. *Int'l Security* 19(1)

Homer-Dixon T, Parcival V 1996 *Environmental Scarcity and Violent Conflict: Briefing Book*. American Association for the Advancement of Science and University College, University of Toronto, Washington

Käkönen J 1987 The politics of scarcity in the changing world system: Implications for Europe. In: V Harle (ed.) *Challenges and Responses in European Security*. Avebury, Aldershot

Käkönen J 1988 *Natural Resources and Conflicts in the Changing International System. Three Studies on Imperialism*. Gower Publishing Company, Aldershot

Käkönen J 1992 The concept of security—From limited to comprehensive. In: Jyrki Käkönen (ed.) *Perspectives on Environmental Conflict and International Politics*. Pinter Publishers, London & New York

Karvonen K 1995 Kylmän sodan ydinasejätteiden siivouksesta jättilasku USA:lle. Helsingin Sanomat 5. huhtikuuta 1995

Langlais R 1995 Reformulating Security. A Case Study from the Arctic Canada. Humanekologiska Skrifter No. 13. Göteborg

Lindholm H 1992 Water and the Arab-Israel conflict. In: L Ohlsson (ed.) *Regional Case Studies of Water Conflicts*. Padrigu, Göteborg

Lootus H 1996 Military Activities and the Environment: The Soviet Army in Estonia 1939-1994. Unpublished MA thesis at the University of Tampere

Lowi M M 1993 Bridging the divide. Transboundary resource disputes and the case of West Bank Water. *Int'l Security* 18(1)

Lyck L 1994 Färöerne-et samfund i dryb krise på vej mod opplösning. *Nordrevy* (2/3)

Mohamed Salih M A 1992 Environmental conflicts in African arid lands: Cases from the Sudan and Niger. In: J Käkönen (ed.) *Perspectives on Environmental Conflict and International Politics*. Pinter Publishers, London & New York

Moorehead R 1992 The land tenure and environmental conflict: The case of the Inland Delta Mali. In: J Käkönen (ed.) *Perspectives on Environmental Conflict and International Politics*. Pinter Publishers, London & New York

Pointing C 1993 *A Green History of the World. The Environment and the Collapse of Great Civilizations*. Penguin Books, New York

Renner M 1989 National security: The economic and environmental dimensions. *Worldwatch Paper* 89 (May)

Roberts N 1996 The human transformation of the earth's surface. *Int'l Social Science J.* (150)

Sarmela M 1988 Paikalliskulttuurin rakennemuutos. Karisto Oy, Hämeenlinna

Schmitz M 1992 Les "conflits verts:" Apercu général sur la menace de l'an 2000. In: M Schmitz (ed.) *Les Conflits Verts. La détérioration de l'environnement, source de tensions majeures*. GRIP, Bruxelles

Storey K, Smith B 1995 Collapse in the Newfoundland groundfish fishery: Responses, constrains and opportunities. In: Johansen STF (ed.) *Nordiske fiskersamfund i fremtiden*, Vol. 1. Fiskeri og fiskersamfund. Tema Nord 1995: 585. Köbenhavn

Thomas C 1992 *The Environment in International Relations*. The Royal Institute of International Affairs, London

Vares P, Lassinantti G (ed.) 1995 *Ecological Security of the Baltic States, Nordic Countries and North-West Russia*. The Institute of International and Social Studies, Estonian Academy of Sciences and The Olof Palme International Center, Tallinn

Weatherford J 1990 *The Indian Givers. How the Indians of the*

Americas Transformed the World. Fawcett Columbine, New York

Westing A H 1976 *Ecological Consequences of the Second Indochina War.* SIPRI, Almqvist & Wiksell, Stockholm

Westing A H 1977 *Weapons of Mass Destruction and the Environment.* SIPRI, Taylor & Francis, London

Westing A H 1980 *Warfare in a Fragile Environment. Military Impact on the Human Environment.* Taylor & Francis, London

JYRKI KÄKÖNEN

Grotius, Hugo

Hugo Grotius (1583-1645), Dutch jurist, scholar and diplomat, is often cited as "the father of international law." After taking a law degree in France in 1598, Grotius began to practice law in his native Netherlands. He soon became active in political affairs, and in 1613 was sent on a diplomatic mission to England. The Dutch and the English were great naval rivals at this time, and Grotius had already won renown with a seminal essay on the freedom of the seas which had appeared in 1609.

He was forced to flee his native land in 1621 because of the violent religious conflicts there, and spent the next decade in France. After a brief return to the Netherlands in the early 1630s, he was once again forced to leave by his enemies. He made his way to Stockholm, where he was made Swedish ambassador to France in 1634, a post which he held until a few months before his death 11 years later.

Grotius's claim to be the father of international law is based largely upon the enormous impact of his book *De Jure Belli ac Pacis* (On the Law of War and Peace), which was published in 1625. Grotius saw clearly that the Reformation and the rise of the sovereign nation-state had totally shattered the ideal of Christian unity which had been so attractive to Dante (see *Dante Alighieri*) and other medieval thinkers. Neither the Pope nor the Holy Roman Emperor had the power to impose any meaningful order on Europe, and it did not appear that anyone could possibly gain such power in the foreseeable future. Rulers were acting from naked self-interest, attacking one another whenever they thought that they could gain some advantage thereby.

As a sensitive humanist, Grotius hated such violent turmoil, but he was realist enough to see that war could not simply be wished or argued out of existence. In the absence of any authority strong enough to prevent war, Grotius sought to find some principle which could at least place some limitations on the waging of war. He found this principle in the concept of natural law, the idea that the world is governed by immutable, rational moral principles which are inherent in nature itself. The human sub-ject, in consequence, as a rational creature, must try to make his or her behavior conform to the dictates of this law of nature. Since this natural law was the same for all people, and thus all nations, it furnished an unshakeable foundation on which the conduct of all states—even non-Christian states—toward one another could be based. The relations between sovereign states, in other words, have a genuine moral foundation; they are not simply whatever the whims and interests of the rulers of those states choose to make them.

Natural law enjoined honesty upon all men, from which Grotius concluded that the legitimate basis of relations between sovereign states lay in the concept that treaties and agreements, once made, must be faithfully adhered to. In the Latin phrase which his work made famous, *pacta sunt servanda*. Grotius here recognized that no sovereign state could in practice be bound by any rules which it did not agree to. Thus he urged that it should be the voluntary agreements into which they freely entered which should regulate their conduct toward one another and produce a framework of order for Europe's chaotic international environment. He stressed that even wars should be limited by international agreements. The combatants should keep their actions within the framework of existing international agreements, by recognizing the rights of neutrals and the freedom of the seas, for example.

Grotius also believed that, even if there was no treaty to the contrary, a state should not go to war every time its ruler thought that there was something to be gained at another's expense. Natural law, insisted Grotius, was rational, and thus favored peace over the bloodshed and destruction of war. He argued at length in his treatise that only a "just war" could morally be waged. To Grotius, a war was "just" if it was fought to repel an invasion or to deter an imminent attack; if its goal was to recover something which had been wrongfully taken away; or if it was to avenge a wrongful act. Even though Grotius's political thought was highly authoritarian, denying subjects the right to revolt against their rulers under any circumstances, he insisted that the subjects of a ruler who has embarked upon an "unjust" war have a perfect right to refuse to cooperate with that ruler in any way.

By insisting upon the sanctity of treaties and upon limiting both the occasions for war and the way in which war should be waged, Grotius had a profound impact on the direction of Western thought about the relations between states. Indeed, such achievements as the Permanent Court of Arbitration at the Hague, the League of Nations, and the United Nations owe much to Grotius's thought.

See also: *International Law; Just War; Treaties of the Modern Era*

Bibliography

Edwards C S 1982 *Hugo Grotius: A Study in Political and Legal Thought*. Nelson-Hall, Chicago, Illinois
Grotius H 1972 *The Freedom of the Seas*. Ayer, Salem, New Hampshire
Grotius H 1980 *The Rights of War and Peace, Including the Law of Nature and of Nations*. Hyperion Press, Westport, Connecticut
Knight W S M 1925 *The Life and Works of Hugo Grotius*. London
Lauterpacht H 1946 The Grotian tradition in international law. *Br. Yearb. of Int.l Law* XXIII

GARRETT L. MCAINSH

Guevara, Ernesto (Che)

Ernesto (Che) Guevara (1928-67) was one of the most important communist theoreticians of guerrilla warfare. He was also one of the best-known guerrilla fighters of the twentieth century. Guevara was born on June 14, 1928 in Rosario, Argentina into a privileged family of Spanish and Irish descent. In 1946 the Guevara family moved to Buenos Aires where Che (a Latin American nickname for Argentinians) started his medical studies. In 1952 he interrupted his studies and toured the continent of South America.

In 1953 he returned to Argentina to resume his studies and graduated with the degree of doctor of medicine and surgery the same year. Two months later he left for Central America. In December 1953 he was in Guatemala where he later held a minor post as an inspector with the agrarian reform movement in the government of the Leftist president Jacobo Arbenz Guzman. In June 1954, when the Arbenz regime was overthrown by Colonel Carlos Castillo Armas, Guevara joined the resistance. The resistance was unsuccessful and he stayed at the Argentinian Embassy in Guatemala for two months for his own protection. Afterwards he went to Mexico where he met Fidel Castro and his brother Raul. He joined their revolutionary "26th of July" movement, acting as a physician when needed, becoming chief of personnel for Castro's expeditionary force, and helping to train Cuban guerrilla forces.

In December 1956 Guevara participated in Castro's ill-fated invasion attempt on the south coast of Cuba's Oriente Province and was one of the 12 survivors of the original force of some 80 men. In 1958, he conducted the military campaign that culminated in the abdication and flight of dictator Fulgencio Batista.

His forces swept through Comaguey and Las Villas provinces and fought the decisive battle of Santa Clara. In January 1959, as Castro assumed control of the Cuban government, Guevara took command of La Cabana fortress overlooking Havana harbor.

In 1960 Guevara wrote a training manual *Guerrilla Warfare*, his only full-length book. It was fundamentally a text on how to conduct guerrilla warfare and has become not only a bible for revolutionaries but also the antibible of some counterinsurgency forces. The book contains comments and directions on tactics, techniques, weapons, training, structure of the forces, propaganda, the moral, physical, and mental qualities needed by the guerrilla, and the role of women. Guevara's most important teaching was that the Cuban Revolution contributed three fundamental lessons to the conduct of revolutionary movements in the Americas: (a) popular forces can win a war against the army; (b) it is not necessary to wait until all conditions for making revolution exist—the insurrection can create them; and (c) in underdeveloped America the countryside is the basic area for armed fighting.

According to Hodges (1977):

Each of these precepts contradicted an established guideline of communist parties in Latin America. The first challenged the belief that a revolutionary vanguard must establish political democracy and win a popular victory at the polls prior to a showdown with the military-bureaucratic apparatus. The second thesis challenged the dogma that revolutionaries must wait for the leadership of a Marxist-Leninist party and for all the conditions of a revolutionary situation to be in existence before seizing arms and launching an armed struggle. The third thesis challenged the view that the most favorable terrain for waging an armed struggle lies in the cities where the proletariat is concentrated. Arguing that the revolutionary vanguard is least vulnerable in rural areas in rugged country comparatively inaccessible to the regular army, Che concentrated on mobilizing the peasantry rather than the proletariat, through a program of agrarian reform. (Hodges 1977 pp. 21-22)

According to Walter Laqueur (1976):

Guevara's three basic tenents are fundamentally opposed to the teachings of Marxist-Leninism and, to a certain extent, even to Maoism. For he regarded the armed insurrection not as the final, crowning phase of the political struggle but expected, on the contrary, that the armed conflict would trigger off, or at least give decisive impetus to, the political campaign. (Laqueur 1976 p. 330)

Another important concept was the insurrectional *foco*, a concept developed most fully by French journalist Regis Debray, based on his analysis of the writings and personal testimony of Guevara and Castro (Debray 1967). The *foco* is a nucleus of armed fighters, a revolutionary commune for living and fighting together. In Debray's terms, "The guerrilla force (or *foco*) is the party in embryo .... The people's army will be the nucleus of the party not vice versa" (Debray 1967 pp. 106-116).

In 1962 Guevara published an article entitled "Guerrilla Warfare: A Method" in *Cuba Socialista*. In this article he concisely described how a guerrilla campaign can be started and carried out. According to Jay Mallin this article is considered the most important of Guevara's theoretical writings. It not only provided instructions on the conduct of guerrilla warfare but also set forth Guevara's belief that this type of combat could be utilized for the conquest of nations throughout the Western hemisphere. Guevara foresaw guerrilla uprisings in Latin America as being part of an overall continental campaign rather than purely local affairs in each country.

Between 1959 and 1965 Che became increasingly dissatisfied with his roles as administrator and diplomat for the new Cuban government. He traveled widely, representing Cuba at many international conferences, and by 1965 his aggressive advocacy of revolutionary solutions to the poverty of developing nations was proving embarrassing to the Cuban government. Close to an open break with Castro, in 1966 Guevara led more than 100 revolutionary fighters from the Sierra Maestra days on an expedition to aid a Leftist government involved in civil war in the Congo

(now Zaire). After nine months of relative failure they returned to Cuba. Soon thereafter Guevara assumed leadership of a smaller revolutionary expedition to Bolivia, where he arrived in November 1966. The group, a mixed force of Cubans and Bolivians which numbered 60 at its maximum, carried out a few ambushes from its rugged, virtually unpopulated base area in southeastern Bolivia, but was gradually worn down through disease, lack of supplies, and military pressure. The remnants were ambushed by an army patrol on October 7, 1967, and two days later the wounded Guevara was summarily executed.

During the 1960s, Guevarism had a major influence on the younger generation of the established communist parties, on Latin American Trotskyists, and on dissident cadres of the Left-wing socialist parties. In most of Latin America the followers of Guevara's theories broke away from the orthodox communist parties. Following Guevara's death in October 1967 the Guatemalan Fuerzas Armadas Rebeldes (FAR) reiterated its allegiance to him. Uruguay's Tupamaros also accepted the Guevarist strategy of the insurrectional *foco* but adapted it to an urban environment. Chile's Movimiento de Izquierda Revolucionaria (MIR) was likewise influenced by Guevarism.

While the myth of Guevara has continued to influence revolutionaries throughout the world, his strategy for revolution in Latin America is widely regarded as a failure. As of 1976 Chailland identified some 30 instances of serious rural guerrilla activity in 15 Latin American countries which were inspired by Guevara's writings and personal example. None of these revolutionary movements had succeeded in overthrowing governments, and only in Venezuela, Guatemala, and Colombia did they persist for a significant length of time. Urban guerrilla movements in Uruguay and Brazil were no more successful. In Chailland's view the basic weakness of guerrilla movements based on the *foco* doctrine "has been their political inability to give rise to a disciplined organizational apparatus connected to a nationwide support structure" (Chailland 1977 p. 49). Nowhere was this more evident than in the Bolivian expedition organized and led by Guevara. The Bolivian *foco* failed to attract any support from peasants, who already had benefited from land reform after the 1952 revolution in that country, or to build support among urban groups. In an analysis of the Bolivian campaign Bell attributes its defeat less to flaws in the doctrine itself than to Guevara's repeated failure to abide by his own teachings (Bell 1971 pp. 238-40).

The 1979 success of the Sandinistas in Nicaragua in defeating the Somoza regime, however, may be regarded as a belated vindication of some of Guevara's insights. In this instance several crucial conditions were present: there were no democratic illusions about prospects for peaceful change, and the Sandinista succeeded in building broad-based support in cities as well as in the rural areas where the Sandinista fighting units operated. The crucial failure of Guevara's doctrine, therefore, may be that it was overoptimistic about the prospects for creating the conditions of successful revolution. The greater part of these conditions may have to be present before an insurrection can create the remainder.

See also: *Revolution*

Bibliography ————————————————

Bell J B 1971 *The Myth of the Guerrilla: Revolutionary Theory and Malpractice.* Knopf, New York

Chailland G 1971 *Revolution in the Third World: Myths and Prospects.* Viking Press, New York

Current Biography Yearbook 1963 Wilson, New York

Debray R 1967 *Revolution in the Revolution? Armed Struggle and Political Struggle in Latin America.* Grove Press, New York

Guevara E 1963 *Guerrilla Warfare.* Vintage Books, New York

Guevara E 1963 *The Diary of Che Guevara: Bolivia; November 7, 1966-October 7, 1967.* Bantam Books, New York

Hodges C 1977 *The Legacy of Che Guevara: A Documentary Study.* Thames and Hudson, London

Laqueur W 1976 *Guerrilla: A Historical and Critical Study.* Little, Brown, Boston, Massachusetts

Mallin J 1973 *Ernesto "Che" Guevara: Modern Revolutionary, Guerrilla Theorist.* SamHar Press, Charlotteville, New York

Sinclair A 1970 *Guevara.* Collins, London

TED ROBERT GURR; JEFFREY IAN ROSS

Gulf Conflict: Domestic Protest and Political Terrorism

1. Introduction[1]

The Persian Gulf Crisis and War, hereafter referred to as the Gulf Conflict, is one of the most complicated relatively recent events to analyze. Given the complex nature of the cultural, economic, political, and social structure of the Middle East, there are diverse issues that can be addressed in analyzing the Gulf Conflict. Perhaps the most anomalous issue connected to the Conflict was the threat and reality of oppositional political terrorism.[2]

Almost from the beginning of the Conflict, Saddam Hussein, as well as leaders and representatives of various terrorist groups throughout the world, warned us that they would engage in and/or sponsor terrorist activities if the United States and its coalition, also known as allied forces, attacked Iraq or Iraq's forces in Kuwait.[3] Threats of terrorism became a reality in many countries. Between 104 (Ross 1993a) and 275 (United States 1992) terrorist incidents, in connection with the Conflict, were carried out between August 1, 1990 (the day the Iraqi tanks rolled over the Kuwaiti border) and March 10, 1991 (the signing of the peace accord between Iraq and the coalition forces).[4]

The study of terrorism connected to the Gulf Conflict is important for four principle reasons, which are from least to most important: (a) it is a unique phenomenon, (b) rarely do states (or their allies) publicly threaten to engage in state-sponsored terrorism,[5] (c) it allows us to test some recently formulated hypotheses connected to the structural causes of terrorism, and (d) we might be able to prevent similar acts of terrorism in the future and thereby prevent needless destruction, injuries and deaths.

Approximately twelve general research hypotheses, dealing with perpetrators and targets, can be formulated and tested in connection with the relationship between terrorism and the Gulf Conflict (Ross 1993a).[6] This article, however, only concerns itself with eight related hypotheses from this research effort, focusing on the relationship between political unrest and terrorism.

2. Literature Review and Outline of Research Hypotheses to be Tested

A number of authors have articulated a series of psychological and structural factors considered to be important causes of terrorism (e.g., Crenshaw 1984; Gross 1972; Ross 1993b). Few authors, however, have empirically tested the relative importance of these factors.[7] Extrapolating from Ross' (1993b) structural model of terrorism, ten separate causes are identified including modernization level, geographical location, type of political system, presence of other forms of political unrest, historical and cultural facilitation, anti-terrorist organization failure, organizational split and development, availability of weapons and explosives, support, and grievances. One of the most easily testable of the previously outlined factors is the presence of other forms of violent or non-violent political unrest, which may legitimize the violence, and act as a catalyst for terrorism. These types of unrest include civil disobedience, protests, demonstrations (e.g., Monti 1980), strikes, riots, guerrilla warfare, revolution, war, or other individuals' or groups' terrorist actions. Although the criminological literature has identified a relationship between international war and domestic homicide rates both cross-nationally (Archer and Gartner 1976; 1984) and in selected countries and contexts (e.g., Fishman 1983; Kleck 1987; Landau and Pfefferman 1988) as well as between capital punishment and homicide rates (Bowers and Pierce 1980; Gartner 1990), it is relatively silent about political crime of a violent nature.

In general, unrest can interchangeably provide learning opportunities, increase the legitimacy of violent actions, heighten grievances, and ultimately motivate individuals and terrorist organizations to engage in terrorism. More specifically, unrest both inside and outside a state's borders may influence individuals and groups to commit terrorism (i.e., contagion). Generally, the closer, geographically, the unrest, the greater the likelihood of it being a catalyst to those predisposed to engage in terrorist events in that country. Presence of other forms of unrest is also heightened when there is a communication mechanism that relays this information (i.e., the mass media) (e.g., Midlarsky, Crenshaw, and Yoshida 1980). [8]

It is argued that among the various forms of political unrest, those which are conflict-based would be most predictive of terrorism (Ross 1992). Thus, protest against American and coalition participation in the Gulf Conflict should be highly associated with terrorism associated with the Conflict.

A number of case studies examining, in whole or in part, demonstration connected to the Gulf Conflict have been written. Elbaum (1991) reviews the "grassroots-based anti-war movement" in the United States, including its membership, impetus, and impact. He also documents protests against intervention by people who had family in the military, and the refusal to serve by some of the military called up for mobilization. Cohen (1991) examines the Israeli Peace Movement's response to the Gulf Conflict, particularly in relationship to their country's treatment of Palestinians in the occupied territories/West Bank. Hamarneh (1991) discusses, in part, the Jordanian people's support of Iraq's invasion of Kuwait and protest against the deployment of allied forces to the Gulf. Cierra (1991) examines the anti-war move-

ment in Western European countries. He states that "[t]his movement . . . is characterized by great diversity, corresponding to different political situations, and to each country's position in the economic, political and strategic structures of Europe" (p. 281). Finally, Rahman and Baker (1991) review the Pakistani public's response and support for Iraq.[9]

Although providing excellent descriptive and analytical accounts of these movements, this literature does not consider the violent nature of these protests, the problem of terrorism, the development or testing of hypotheses, the creation of theory, nor does it provide quantitative analyses for such events. In an effort to correct this imbalance, this author outlines and tests a series of hypotheses connected to demonstration and terrorism.

To begin with, two types of terrorism took place during the Conflict: those acts connected to the Crisis and those independent or tangential to it. For purposes of this study, those terrorist incidents related to the Conflict were called Gulf-Related Terrorism (GRT) and served as this researcher's dependent variable.

In order to test the importance of protest, eight hypotheses were derived. First, the higher the number of protests that states experience by their own citizens against committing troops to the Gulf (PROCTOG), the greater the amount of GRT they should experience. This hypothesis assumes that individuals and groups will become frustrated with their governments' lack of attention to their policy demands motivating the more committed to engage in terrorism or support individuals predisposed to commit this type of political and criminal violence. Thus:

Hypothesis 1: The higher the number of PROCTOG, the greater the GRT.

Second, the higher the amount of terrorism unconnected to the Gulf Conflict (NONGRT), the higher the amount of terrorism connected to the Gulf Conflict (GRT). Here NONGRT serves as a potent reminder to individuals and groups opposed to the Gulf crisis that they can resort to terrorism to reinforce their policy demands.

Hypothesis 2: The higher the NONGRT, the greater the GRT.

Third, closely connected to Hypothesis 1 and based on the assumption that demonstration alone is not as important as the nature and characteristics of the protest, the higher the intensity (I) of PROCTOG operationalized in terms of presence of violence (PREVIOLE) and number of protesters (NUOFPROT), the greater the possibility of GRT. Consequently:

Hypothesis 3: The greater the PREVIOLE, the greater the GRT.

Hypothesis 4: The greater the NUOFPROT, the greater the GRT.

Hypothesis 5: The greater the intensity (I) of PROC-TOG, the greater the GRT.

Six, the previous hypotheses are probably dependent on the length of time that allied troops were stationed or active in the Gulf. That is, citizens opposed to the Conflict probably became increasingly frustrated at the foreign armed forces present in the Gulf the longer they were there. Consequently, the longer the time the troops are in the Gulf, or Time in Gulf (DAYINTO), the greater the I, and thus the possibility of GRT (Fig. 1). Therefore:

Figure 1

Model of the connection between protest and oppositional political terrorism in connection to the Gulf Conflict

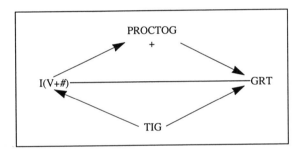

Hypothesis 6: The greater the DAYINTO, the higher the I.

Seven, there is a chance that the presence of violent protest (PREVIOLE), the greater the day into the Conflict (DAYINTO), the greater the number of protesters (NUOFPROT), and the greater the number of Gulf-related protests (PROCTOG) jointly contribute to the amount of Gulf-related terrorism (GRT).

Hypothesis 7: The greater the PREVIOLE, the greater the DAYINTO, the greater the NUOFPROT, and the greater the PROCTOG, the greater the probability of GRT.

Finally, the progress of the Conflict, beyond simple number of days coalition troops were stationed in the Gulf, should have an effect on GRT. In other words the greater the threat of war, the higher the GRT. Thus, the data should be categorized into three periods: (1) when the Iraqi tanks crossed the Kuwaiti border (August 1, 1990) until the United Nations deadline demanding Iraq's withdrawal from Kuwait (January 15); (2) the start of operation Desert Storm (the bombing raids) (January 16) until just before the ground war into Kuwait (February 23, 1991);[10] and (3) the start of the coalition's ground war (February 24, 1991) into Kuwait and the signing of the cease-fire agreement (March 10, 1991). Thus:

Hypothesis 8: The number of PROCTOG and GRT should be greater in the last period of the Conflict.

3. Methodology

Achieving a comprehensive picture of the nature of terrorism and protest in connection with the Gulf Conflict from public sources is difficult. First, there are a plethora of materials from which to choose. Second, much information is perceived to be biased. Third, and most important, the majority of source material is not readily accessible for events database construction. Keeping these cautions in mind, two data sets were constructed. These data sets were then analyzed to test the aforementioned hypotheses. First, the dependent variable, GRT, was obtained from a data set built from the ITERATE IV (version 3) chronology (Mickolus 1993),[11] and other sources.[12] This investigator coded the incidents on fourteen variables: day, month, and year into the Conflict that terrorism took place, type of terrorism, country where event occurred, country targeted, city where terrorism took place, whether terrorism was connected to the Conflict, perpetrator, type of victim, number injured, number killed, and number of protesters arrested.[13]

Second, a database was constructed and later coded as a subset of the first, to analyze the demonstration hypotheses. A compilation of protest events called Protest Connected to Gulf Crisis (PROCTOG) was prepared by this author covering the same time period as GRT. First, a chronology of demonstrations, protests, and riots connected to Gulf Conflict, PROCTOG, was assembled.[14] All incidents in this chronology were coded on twelve variables including: day, month, and year into crisis protest took place, type of demonstration, presence of violence in protest, country where protest took place, city where demonstration occurred, type of victim involved in protest, number injured in demonstration, number killed in protest, and number arrested in protest.[15]

These data sets cover the period from the Iraqi invasion (i.e., August 1, 1990) to the signing of the cease-fire/peace accord (i.e., March 10, 1991).

Table 1

Month when protest and terrorist events took place

| | Protest | | Terrorism | |
	Frequency	Percent	Frequency	Percent
August	5	4.4	0	0.0
September	2	1.8	3	2.9
October	24	21.2	3	2.9
November	1	.9	2	1.9
December	3	2.7	1	1.0
January	63	55.8	55	52.9
February	15	13.3	37	35.6
March	0	0.0	3	2.9
TOTAL	113	100.0	104	100.000

Descriptive and inferential statistics were performed on the data and the previously articulated hypotheses were tested.

4. Selected Results

A total of 113 demonstrations against the allied participation in the Gulf Conflict were reported by PROC-TOG. The greatest concentration of demonstrations in terms of frequency, occurred during the month of January which corresponds with the coalition bombing (Desert Storm) and the beginning of the land campaign (see Table 1 and Fig. 2).

Protests took place in a total of twenty-four countries. Although the advanced industrialized countries experienced the bulk of these protests, over half of them took place in Canada and the United States.[16] More interesting is the finding that many of the countries (e.g., twenty-three, especially those making up the coalition) did not experience any protests. Lack of protests in allied countries may be explained by either the apathy of citizens, satisfaction with their country's actions, or the quality of the data (see Table 4). Terrorism took place in thirty-six countries. Eleven countries in which protests took place did not experience Gulf-Related Terrorism. In sum, when the number of protests in each country is compared with the terrorism experienced by that country we discover that out of a total of forty-six incidents where either terrorism and/or demonstrations occurred, only thirteen countries experienced both terrorism and protest.

For the majority of protests across the countries, 84.1 percent (95), the researcher was unable to determine if they were violent or not (of the remaining 15.9 percent (18), only 11.5 percent (13) involved violence and 4.4 percent (5) were nonviolent). In cases where people were injured, it was mainly the protesters with no injurious consequences to either authorities or passersby. Pakistan was the only country where three pro-Iraqi protesters were killed. In terms of arrests, the largest number of people apprehended was 500 in two

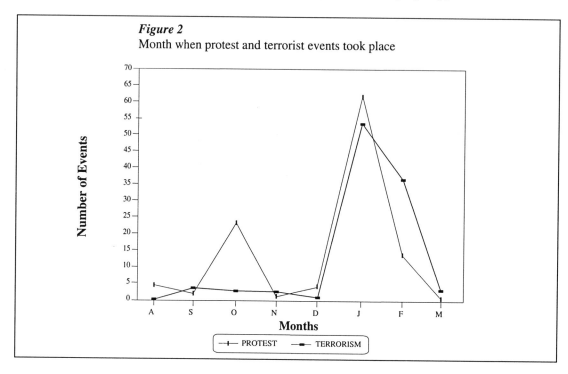

Figure 2
Month when protest and terrorist events took place

Number of Events

Months

PROTEST   TERRORISM

Table 2
State where protest and terrorism occurred

Country where incident took place	Freq.	Protest Percent	Terrorism Freq.	Percent
Turkey	1	.9	11	10.6
Chile	0	.0	10	9.6
Peru	0	.0	9	8.7
Philippines	0	.0	9	8.7
Germany	7	6.2	7	6.7
Egypt	2	1.8	5	4.8
Lebanon	0	.0	5	4.8
Iran	0	.0	4	3.8
Italy	2	1.8	3	2.9
Jordan	6	5.3	3	2.9
Yemen	1	.9	3	2.9
USA	37	32.7	3	2.9
Australia	0	.0	2	1.9
Colombia	0	.0	2	1.9
France	5	4.4	2	1.9
Greece	0	.0	2	1.9
Nigeria	0	.0	2	1.9
Thailand	0	.0	2	1.9
Tunisia	2	1.8	2	1.9
Venezuela	0	.0	2	1.9
Algeria	0	.0	1	1.0
Bolivia	0	.0	1	1.0
Brazil	0	.0	1	1.0
Cyprus	0	.0	1	1.0
Dubai	0	.0	1	1.0
Guatemala	0	.0	1	1.0
Haiti	0	.0	1	1.0
Hungary	0	.0	1	1.0
Iraq	2	1.8	1	1.0
Morocco	1	.9	1	1.0
Netherlands	0	.0	1	1.0
Puerto Rico	0	.0	1	1.0
Saudi Arabia	0	.0	1	1.0
Spain	1	.9	1	1.0
Sweden	1	.9	1	1.0
Uganda	0	.0	1	1.0
Bangladesh	1	.9	0	.0
Canada	30	26.5	0	.0
Israel	2	1.8	0	.0
India	1	.9	0	.0
Japan	1	.9	0	.0
Libya	1	.9	0	.0
Norway	1	.9	0	.0
Panama	1	.9	0	.0
Pakistan	3	2.9	0	.0
United Kingdom	3	2.7	0	.0
Missing	1	.9	0	.0
TOTAL	113	100.00	104	100.00

Table 3
Presence of violence in protest

	Frequency	Percent
Yes	13	11.5
No	5	4.4
Unknown	95	84.1
TOTAL	113	100.0

Table 4
Number of protesters who attended demonstration

Size of Crowd	Frequency	Percent
1[*]	1	0.9
40	1	0.9
50	1	0.9
100	4	3.5
125	1	0.9
200	2	1.8
300	4	3.5
400	1	0.9
500	1	0.9
700	1	0.9
1000	7	6.2
2000	1	0.9
3000	9	8
4000	1	0.9
5000	1	0.9
8000	1	0.9
10000	2	1.8
15000	2	1.8
20000	1	0.9
40000	1	0.9
50000	1	0.9
127000	1	0.9
137500	1	0.9
150000	1	0.9
300000	1	0.9
Missing	65	57.5
TOTAL	113	100

separate events which took place in Canada.

For approximately half of the protests, the number of protesters per demonstration was missing. Nevertheless, the median number of protests was 3,000 with the highest reaching 300,000 for one protest. In general, the number of protesters per demonstration increased as the United Nations mandated January 15 pull-out deadline approached and even more so as the date of the start of the land campaign neared (see Table 4).

Table 5 shows simple correlations for the previously articulated hypotheses 1 through 6. There is a significant perfect negative relationship between PROCTOG and GRT; the relationship between NONGRT and GRT is a negative and significant $r=-.56$, $p <.0001$. Hypotheses 3 to 6 are not significant, $p > .05$.

To determine if there is a relationship among VIO-LENCE (violent protests), DAYINTO (day of conflict), and NUOFPROT (number of protesters), a multiple regression was computed with GRT (number of Gulf-related terrorist incidents) as the dependent variable (hypothesis 7). PROCTOG, however, was omitted from the analysis due to multicollinearity. The variables were forced into the equation. Table 6 shows the results of this analysis. Results suggested that there was a significant linear relationship, $r = .37$, $F (3,213) = 11.56$, $p < .0001$.

Only one of the independent variables, DAYINTO, contributes significantly to the prediction of GRT with $Sr2 = .12$, $F (3,213) = 29.58$, $p < .0001$. The contributions of number protesters and violent protests are nonsignificant. The three independent variables in combination contributed only .01 in shared variability. Altogether, 14 percent (13 percent adjusted) of the variability in number of GRT was predicted by knowing the scores on these three variables.

To test the relationship between periods of Conflict and GRT (hypothesis 8), a Chi-square analysis was performed. The results suggest that there is an association between periods (3) and type of political behavior (i.e., PROCTOG and GRT), Chi-square (2) = 49.18, $p < .005$. In the first period (Aug. 1-Jan. 15), there was more PROC-TOG (29 percent) than GRT (9 percent). The relationship was reversed for the third period (Feb. 24-March 10), in which there was more GRT (63 percent) than PROCTOG (17 percent). In the second period (Jan. 16-Feb. 23), there was also more PROCTOG (54 percent) than GRT (29 percent). This period had also more GRT and PROCTOG than period 1 (9 percent and 29 percent, respectively). In the main, the majority of GRT occurred in the third period, but more than half (54 percent) of PROCTOG took place in the second period. Thus the decline of PROCTOG toward the end of the Conflict is accompanied by an increase in GRT during this same period.

5. Summary and Conclusion

In general, Gulf Conflict-related protests (PROCTOG) and non-Gulf-related terrorism (NONGRT) are related to Gulf-related Terrorism (GRT). In other words, the presence of other types of political unrest are related to terrorism. The weaker relationship is between NONGRT and GRT ($r = -.56$), which partially supports

Table 5

Pearson product-moment correlations for hypotheses 1 to 6

Hypothesis	r	P
1. Relationship between PROCTOG and GRT	-1.00	.0001
2. Relationship between NONGRT and GRT	-.56	.0001
3. Relationship between PREVIOLE and GRT	-.14	*.74
4. Relationship between NUOFPROT and GRT	-.05	*.74
5. Relationship between I (NUOFPROT +PREVIOLE) and GRT	-.21	*.62
6. Relationship between DAYINTO and I	.42	*.30

*nonsignificant at p>.05.

Table 6

Standard multiple regression of violent protests, day into conflict, and number of protestors on the number of Gulf-related terrorist incidents.

Variables	GRT	VIOLENCE	DAYINTO	NUOFPROT	B	Beta	Sr2 (unique)
VIOLENCE	-0.4	-	-0.09	-0.09	-0.22	-0.06	0.01
DAYINTO	0.35	-0.09	-	-0.12	0	0.35	0.12
NUOFPROT	-0.01	-0.09	0.12	-	-1.17	-0.06	0
				Intercept	-.157		
Means	0.48	0.0	8189.73	19037.06			
StdD	0.5	0.27	49.08	25023.49			
						R2=.14a	
						Adjusted R2 = .13	

a Unique variability = .13, Shares variability = .01

a contagion effect. Thus the initial hypothesis which motivated this research is supported. Moreover, the number of GRT events is moderately predicted by DAYINTO, NUOFPROT, and VIOLENCE. However, by themselves these variables are not significantly related to GRT.

At first glance, the finding of a perfect negative correlation between PROCTOG and GRT is counterintuitive. However, when we look at the relationship between PROCTOG and GRT categorized into three of the dominant periods of the Conflict the relationship becomes clear. While GRT increased in each period and peaked in the third, PROCTOG was highest only in middle period. In other words, during the first period of the crisis demonstration was high and terrorism was low, by the 3rd period, the reverse was true, that is, there were less incidents of protest but considerably more incidents of GRT.

Since the results of this study suggest that, at least in the Gulf Conflict, types of political unrest such as protests and non-Gulf-related terrorism are related to Gulf-specific terrorism, a useful avenue of future research might be to explore the relationships among other forms of political unrest (e.g., strikes, riots, guerrilla warfare, etc.), including protests and non-specific terrorism, and other structural causal variables and context-specific terrorism. Until this type of work is performed the causal relationships underlying oppositional political terrorism will remain an elusive phenomenon.

See also: *Structural Causes of Oppositional Political Terrorism: Towards a Causal Model; Psychological Causes of Oppositional Political Terrorism: A Model; Contemporary International Terrorism, Nature of*

Notes

1. See Ross (1993b) for an introduction to this research agenda.

2. The researcher uses a modified version of Schmid's definition (1983). See, for example, Ross (1991) for an example of this modification. Additionally, all future references to terrorism should be interpreted to refer to oppositional political terrorism.

3. See, for example, Joel Brinkley, "Israelis Assert Palestinians Plan Terror Attacks for Iraq," *New York Times*, August 18, 1990, p. 5; Alan Cowell, "Egypt Raises its Guard Against Iraqi

Terrorism," *New York Times*, Monday September 17,1990, p. A12; *Globe and Mail*, January 15, 1991, p. A7. On the other hand, see, for example, Edward N. Lutwak, *New York Times*, January 13, 1991, IV, 19:1, who suggested that the threat of terrorism to U.S. troops in the Persian Gulf, to Israel and to Western cities was exaggerated.

4. According to the State Department (1992), "Most of these attacks ... were sporadic, uncoordinated, and low-level incidents. Only a small percentage resulted in deaths, significant injuries, or property damage" (p. 1). They "were minor incidents, resulting only in property damage. War-related attacks brought the total number of international terrorist incidents in 1991 to 557, up from 456 in 1990. Fully half the incidents in 1991 occurred during January and February, while Operation Desert Storm was underway. After the war, however, the number of terrorist incidents dropped sharply and actually fell below 1990 levels" (p. 1).

5. Most states that engage in state-sponsored terrorism like to conceal their responsibility.

6. These hypotheses build upon those outlined by Bueno De Mesquita (1981); Levy (1981); Organski and Kugler (1980); Starr and Most (1976; 1978) in their quantitative research on war.

7. See, for example, Hamilton (1978) for an exception.

8. Other forms of political unrest can also heighten grievances and lead to organizational splits and development which have also been identified as causes of terrorism.

9. For a more general analysis of protest amongst Islamic Fundamentalist groups in the Middle East see Piscatori (1992).

10. For chronologies of the events see, for example, *Journal of Palestine Studies*, 20, 202-232; and Appendices in Darwish and Alexander (1990); and Bulloch and Morris (1991).

11. A widely recognized data set which lists acts of international terrorism throughout the world. See, however, Ross (1988) for a criticism of the ITERATE data sets. See Ross (1993c) for a review of ITERATE IV. GRT was identified through such things as letters written to authorities or reliable sources, past history of a group to support Iraq, nature of the target and the the nature of the perpetrator.

12. The State Department does not provide detailed chronologies of terrorist events to the public nor academic researchers.

13. Of the 487 acts of terrorism that took place during this time period, 44.6% (217) were linked to the Gulf Crisis, 34,3% (167) were not, and in 21.1% (103) of the cases it was not possible to distinguish the connection. Further iterations could test six months before and six months after the Iraqi invasion of Kuwait.

14. These included New York Times Index (August 1990-March 1991), Times of London Index (August 1900-March 1991), Canadian News Index (August, 1990-March 1991), and Journal of Palestine Studies. Given that close to 75 subdivisions are listed under the term "demonstrations" in the New York Times Index, this researcher turned to the classification called Middle East instead and found most of the citations there. The Times of London did not list one single "demonstration" connected to the Gulf. and the Canadian News Index, on the other hand, catalogued demonstrations under demonstrations. Demonstrations of military personnel opposed to the allied presence in the Gulf and those supportive of the presence of foreign troops were excluded. For a general outline of the methodology for this type of events data analysis, see, for example, Ross (1988b).

15. As PROCTOG is dependent on newspaper coverage, it suffers from the same general problems for which these type of data sets are criticized. Thus a considerable amount of informa-

tion may very well be missing. For example, noticeably absent was information on the fate of protesters, counter-demonstrators, and the police, who sometimes intervened.

16. Jordan was not opposed to Iraq's invasion.

Bibliography

Archer D, Gartner R 1976 Violent acts and violent times: A comparative approach to postwar homicide rates. *Am. Sociol. Rev.* 41

Archer D, Gartner R 1984 *Violence and Crime in Cross-national Perspective.* Yale University Press, New Haven

Bowers W H, Pierce G L 1980 Deterrence or brutalization: What is the effect of executions? *Crime and Delinquency* 26

Bueno de Mesquita B 1981 *The War Trap.* Yale University Press, New Haven

Bulloch J, Morris H 1991 *Saddam's War.* Faber and Faber, London

Cirera D 1991 Lost illusions: Europe's peace movement. In: P Bennis, M Moushabeck (eds.) *Beyond the Storm: A Gulf Crisis Reader.* Olive Branch Press, New York

Cohen S 1991 From the sealed room: Israel's peace movement during the Gulf war. In: P Bennis, M Moushabeck (eds.) *Beyond the Storm: A Gulf Crisis Reader.* Olive Branch Press, New York

Crenshaw M 1984 The causes of terrorism. *Comparative Politics* 13

Crenshaw M 1986 The psychology of political terrorism. In: M G Herman (ed.) *The Political Psychology of Contemporary Problems and Issues.* Jossey-Bass, San Francisco

Darwish A, G Alexander 1991 *Unholy Babylon.* St. Martin's Press, New York

Elbaum M 1991 The storm at home. In: P Bennis, M Moushabeck (eds.) *Beyond the Storm: A Gulf Crisis Reader.* Olive Branch Press, New York

Fishman G 1983 On war and crime. In: S Breznitz (ed.) *Stress in Israel.* Van Nostrand Reinvold Co, New York

Gartner R 1990 The victims of homicide: A temporal and cross-national comparison. *Am. Sociol. Rev.* 55

Gross F 1972 *Violence in Politics: Terror and Political Assassination in Eastern Europe and Russia.* Mouton, The Hague

Hamarneh M 1991 Jordan responds to the Gulf crisis. In: P Bennis, M Moushabeck (eds.) *Beyond the Storm: A Gulf Crisis Reader.* Olive Branch Press, New York

Hamilton L 1978 *Ecology of Terrorism: A Historical and Statistical Study.* Ph. D. Dissertation. University of Colorado, Boulder

Kleck G 1987 America's foreign wars and the legitimization of domestic violence. *Sociological Inquiry* 57

Landau S F, Pfefferman D 1988 A time series analysis of violent crime and its relation to prolonged states of warfare: The Israeli case. *Criminology* 26

Levy J S 1981 Alliance formation and war behavior: An analysis of the great powers, 1945-1975. *J. Conflict Resolution* 25

Mickolus E 1993 *Chronology of Terrorism, 1988-1991*. Greenwood Press, Westport, CT

Midlarsky M et al., 1980 Why violence spreads: The contagion of international terrorism. *Int'l Studies Q.* 24

Monti D J 1980 The relation between terrorism and domestic civil disorders. *Terrorism: An International Journal* 4

Organski A F K, Kugler J 1980 *The War Ledger*. University of Chicago Press, Chicago

Piscatori J (ed.) 1992 *Islamic Fundamentalisms and the Gulf Crisis*. American Academy of Arts and Sciences, Chicago

Rahman T, Baker L 1991 South Asia in the wake of the Gulf war: The Pakistan example. In: P Bennis, M Moushabeck (eds.) *Beyond the Storm: A Gulf Crisis Reader*. Olive Branch Press, New York

Ross J I 1988a An events data base on political terrorism in Canada: Some conceptual and methodological problems. *Conflict Quarterly* 8

Ross J I 1988b Attributes of domestic political terrorism in Canada, 1960-1985. *Terrorism: An International Journal* 11

Ross J I 1991 The nature of contemporary international terrorism. In: D Charters (ed.) *Democratic Responses to International Terrorism*. Transnational Publishers, Ardsley-on-Hudson, NY

Ross J I 1992 Attacking terrorist attacks: Initial tests of contagion between domestic and international terrorism in Canada. *Low Intensity Conflict and Law Enforcement* 1

Ross J I 1993a *Research hypotheses in connection with the threat and reality of oppositional political terrorism during the Gulf conflict*. Paper presented at the Annual Meetings of the Canadian Political Science Association, Ottawa. June

Ross J I 1993b Structural causes of oppositional political terrorism: Towards a causal model. *J. Peace Research* 30

Ross J I 1993c Review of E. Mickolus, Terrorism, 1988-1991. In: *Terrorism and Political Violence* 5

Schmid A P 1983 *Political Terrorism: A Research Guide to Concepts, Theories, Data Bases and Literature*. Transaction Books, New Brunswick, NJ

Starr H, Most B 1976 The substance and study of borders in international relations research. *International Studies Quarterly* 20

Starr H, Most B 1978 A return journey: Richardson, 'Frontiers' and wars in the 1946-1965 era. *J. Conflict Resolution* 22

United States. Department of State 1992 *Patterns of Global Terrorism: 1991*

JEFFREY IAN ROSS

H

Hague Conferences

1. The Conference of 1899

The first Hague Conference originated in August 1898 when Czar Nicholas II invited all those Powers with diplomatic representation at St. Petersburg to send delegates to a convention to discuss the reduction of armaments as well as ways of avoiding war. The proposal caused astonishment and not a little suspicion, coming as it did from an autocrat possessed of the world's largest army. All those invited accepted, however, except two Latin American states—one, Brazil, on the grounds that she had no permanent army worth mentioning. Thus twenty-six Powers were represented: the twenty European states, including Turkey, together with the United States, Mexico, Persia, China, Japan and Siam. Montenegro, although accepting, asked Russia to act on her behalf.

The explanation of the Russian ruler's initiative lay in the state of the Russian economy, just as it did ninety years later when Gorbachev proposed strategic arms limitation talks. The dismissal of Bismarck in 1890 had removed from the European states-system the last great guarantor of conservative restraint and in the next few years the major European Powers began to move towards the alliances and alignments which eventually led to the First World War, and to rearm accordingly. Russia, the least developed of the Great Powers, and already under heavy economic strain through an extensive programme of railway building and other industrial projects, found herself unable to keep up with the arms race, particularly in artillery (new German field guns could fire at six times the rate of Russian ones). To re-equip her army would require yet more crippling loans from France, a solution which Count Witte, the Finance Minister, was desperate to avoid. That a possible way out of these financial difficulties might be by an international agreement to reduce armaments was put to his chief, Count Muraviev, and so the Czar, by a Foreign Ministry official, M. Vasili, who as consul in Budapest in 1896 had seen the subject discussed at a confer-

ence there of the Inter-Parliamentary Union. Count Witte's own proposal to the Czar was that the Great Powers should suspend additions to their armaments for ten years.

These suggestions formed the basis for the initial invitation to consider the reduction of armaments, but because of the suspicions aroused, Count Muraviev in January 1899 widened the scope of the forthcoming Conference to include the prohibition or limitation of certain weapons, improvement in the laws of war, and the furtherance of such means of peaceful settlement as good offices, mediation and arbitration. The Czar was concerned that the Conference should not be held in the capital of a Great Power lest political interests should impede progress, and so The Hague was chosen. The Conference opened on May 18, the Czar's birthday, under the honorary presidency of Queen Wilhelmina of the Netherlands, and lasted until 31 July. The twenty-six participating countries sent 100 delegates, most of them 'wordy or simply ornamental old men' (Hayes), but also more considerable figures from the ranks of diplomats, jurists, and military and naval experts. Amongst the few sincerely committed to international peace were Sir Julian Pauncefote, who had negotiated an Anglo-American arbitration treaty, the Frenchman, Baron D'Estournelles, and the international lawyers de Martens from Russia, and Andrew D. White from the United States. And among the military and naval experts were the German, Colonel Schwarzhoff, Britain's dynamic naval reformer, Admiral Sir John Fisher, and the distinguished American historian and sea-power theorist, Captain Mahan.

The delegates were divided into three committees, the first dealing with armaments, the second with the laws of war, and the third with the peaceful settlement of disputes. In the matter of arms limitation, the primary purpose of the Conference, no progress was made. Germany, now a rival to Russia in European power-politics, had no desire to limit her military or naval strength when she could outspend her potential enemies, a point most congently argued by her delegate, Colonel Schwarzhoff. But in any case, the Czar and his advisers seem to have had no conception of the complexities and technical difficulties involved, far greater than could be overcome in a few weeks' discussions. Moreover it was unrealistic to approach the subject without considering political questions, and these were specifically excluded from the agenda of the Conference. Some advance, however, was made in the laws of war. Belligerency was defined, the Red Cross Convention of 1864 was extended to naval warfare, and better treatment for prisoners of war and the wounded was laid down. The use of soft-nosed or 'dum-dum' bullets was outlawed, as it remains to this day. Fisher made his assent to a ban on the use of asphyxiating gas-shells at sea conditional upon unanimity—and Mahan opposed the ban. Ironically, considering that Coventry, Dresden and Hiroshima lay less than five decades away, the dropping of projectiles and explosives from balloons, 'or by other new methods of a similar nature,' was prohibited for five years (the time limit, instead of permanence, inserted by the American delegate).

In contrast to these meagre, though useful, achievements, a notable step was taken in the field of the peaceful settlement of disputes with the setting up of the Permanent Court of Arbitration. The term 'Court' was misleading, for its essence was simply a panel of arbitrators, but there was established at The Hague a secretariat to regulate procedure, keep the archives, and receive applications, thus providing a necessary framework for *ad hoc* tribunals. Arbitration, despite its being voluntary, and excluding cases likely to affect vital interests or honour, was in consequence greatly encouraged, and in the years before the establishment of the Permanent Court of International Justice in 1920 (also at the Hague) not infrequently resorted to (see *Arbitration, International*).

It can hardly be said that the first Hague Conference came up to the expectations of those idealists who hoped that it would mark a new era in international relations. To the parties of pacifists who assiduously lobbied the delegates the results were intensely disappointing, but to some of the world's political leaders they were only to be expected. Lord Salisbury, the British prime minister, thought the Conference should not be taken 'too seriously,' and the German Kaiser dismissed it as 'utopian.' Yet in retrospect it can be seen as representing in some of its concerns, and through certain of its delegates, a sort of undertow to the rising tide of nationalism and militarism that was flowing in a contrary direction above it. That undercurrent was not checked in 1899; it re-emerged in the second Hague Conference and other initiatives, and during the First World War came into

its own in all the influences and ideas that gave birth to the League of Nations.

2. *The Conference of 1907*

Although the first Hague Conference made no provision for a successor, many assumed that there would in time be one. The initiative for calling another conference was taken by the Inter-Parliamentary Union, meeting at St. Louis in 1904. This petitioned President Theodore Roosevelt to act as convenor, but after a delay due to the Russo-Japanese War, the President deferred to the Czar, who once more issued invitations to the Hague.

The second Hague Conference was more truly a world conference than the first. In 1899 twenty-six of the world's fifty-nine states had attended; in 1907 it was to be forty-four of the fifty-seven (the two Boer Republics having been annexed by Great Britain) sending 256 delegates. The great difference in numbers was owing to the participation, at the insistence of the United States, of the Latin American countries; for the first time at a major political conference the European states were in a minority. The non-European majority would have been larger, had not Abyssinia, Costa Rica and Honduras declined to come, and the participation of Korea, although anxious to attend, been successfully opposed by Japan.

The conference met on June 15, 1907, a second delay of almost a year having been caused by the holding of the 1906 Geneva Convention, as well as by a conference of South American states. This time there was no attempt to regulate armaments. The British, seeing the expanding German navy as a threat to their security, favoured a halt to further warship building but to any such suggestion the Germans were vehemently opposed. On April 30, von Bülow, the German Chancellor, announced Germany's veto on any proposals for disarmament. The Conference therefore concentrated on further refining the laws of war, especially at sea, and developing additional means of judicial settlement.

In the juridical sphere the outcome was as disappointing as in that of arms limitation. Two courts were to be established at The Hague: an International Prize Court, and a Permanent Court of International Justice; but the first fell through over a failure to agree on principles and the second over a technicality: the objections of the smaller powers, mainly Latin American, to the method of appointing the judges. The imposing Peace Palace which Andrew Carnegie provided for these new courts, as well as for the Permanent Court of Arbitration, its registry, library and archives, had its foundation stone laid during the 1907 Conference, but it was not until 1920 that a world court proper (the Permanent Court of International Justice), created that year along with the League of Nations (see *League of Nations*), was to sit there.

Great hopes had been placed in the second Hague Peace Conference by idealists the world over, but before it ended after four months' work, on 18 October, little of substance had been achieved. Perhaps its most significant act was to resolve that a third Conference would meet at The Hague in 1915, without the need for an invitation by the Czar or anyone else, and that a preparatory committee should start work on the agenda two years earlier. But the 1915 Conference never met. Like many of the measures agreed at The Hague to limit the practice and effects of war (such as the ban, renewed to the next Conference, on bombing from the air), it was swept aside by the catastrophe of 1914. Yet if the two Hague Conferences, especially the second, looked like failures at the time, this was largely because the epoch in which they were held was singularly unpropitious for their success. In retrospect it can be seen that they established a valuable precedent: the meeting, in time of peace, of representatives of the world's Powers to discuss measures of humanitarian concern, embody them in conventions and declarations, and then submit them to their governments for ratification. Little of this was done before the first Hague Conference; it is an ongoing practice today.

Yet the final verdict on the Hague Peace Conferences must be that they demonstrate a bleak, Hobbesian truth: law does not constrain power (see *Power*), except in marginal ways; it reflects it. The Conferences of 1899 and 1907, largely because the rivalries and suspicions of the Powers were manifested there as elsewhere, failed to impede the arms race and therefore the headlong rush of the nations towards the First World War; indeed in the second Conference the deliberations seem to have been conducted on the assumption of its inevitability. And when that war began, much of the positive work the Conferences did do, the carefully contrived measures to render the means of fighting less cruel, and to protect civilians, was quickly disregarded. Similar ineffectualness owing to the political climate of the decade dogged the League of Nations and the general Disarmament Conference in the 1930s. The descent into the next World War was inexorable, and the techniques of waging war, without regard to any major distinction between combatants and civilians, had, by the end of it, and in the form of nuclear weapons, become unprecedented in their cruelty and lethality. Attempts to lessen by international legislation human suffering caused by war have had their successes—and notably in the treatment of prisoners of war—but are always liable to be overborne by political and strategical imperatives as well as overtaken by advances in the technology of human destruction.

Bibliography

Beales A C F 1931 *The History of Peace: A Short Account of the Organized Movements for International Peace*. Bell, London

Choate J H 1913 *The Two Hague Conferences*. Princeton University Press, Princeton

Hale O J 1971 *The Great Illusion 1900-1914*. Harper, New York, Chap I, iii

Hayes C J H 1941 *A Generation of Materialism 1871-1900*. Harper, New York, Chap VIII, vi

Higgins A P 1909 *The Hague Peace Conferences*. Cambridge University Press, Cambridge

Hinsley F H 1963 *Power and the Pursuit of Peace*. Cambridge University Press, Cambridge

Holls F W 1900 *The Peace Conference at the Hague*. Macmillan, New York

Hull W I 1908 *The Two Hague Conferences and their Contributions to International Law*. Ginn, Boston

Mackay R F 1973 *Fisher of Kilverstone*. Clarendon Press, Oxford, Chap 6

Scott J B 1909 *The Hague Peace Conferences of 1899 and 1907*, 2 vols. Johns Hopkins Press, Baltimore

Scott J B (ed.) 1918 *The Hague Conventions and Declarations of 1899 and 1907 Accompanied by Tables of Signatures etc.*, 3rd edn. Oxford University Press, New York

BRIAN E. PORTER

Hanseatic League

1. Introduction

The Hanseatic League was originally a private international organization which later became public, and which flourished in Northern Europe from the second half of the twelfth to the latter part of the seventeenth century. It was essentially a commercial institution of German merchants and German towns which these merchants dominated for five centuries. It provided trade concessions for its members, regulated trade, provided protection against pirates, instituted compulsory arbitration for its members, and even waged war on their behalf. Like the United Nations, the League was concerned with nonpayment of assessments and the ministate (minitown) problem. The League spanned sufficient time to witness not only the modification of the international systems, but its transformation from the Middle Ages to modern times. In fact, this transformation accounts for the decline of the League. The study of the League by the Hanseatic Historical Society has undergone significant development; before 1920 research had stressed institutions, but after this date it focused increasingly upon the common culture and the social forces which molded the members of the League. The study of international organizations has witnessed a similar transition, but both approaches persist.

The term *hansa* or *hanse* designates a merchant guild or a merchant association. The first of these was an association of German merchants founded in 1160 in Gotland (Visby), an island now belonging to Sweden. Traders from various German towns at first lived with the Swedes, but later they separated to form their own Kontor ("factory"). They elected their own aldermen who had jurisdiction over the membership and who represented it to outside powers.

2. Establishment and Development

As early as the beginning of the 13th century, German merchants who had settled at the island of Gotland in the Baltic created a mercantile association which focused on Cologne and 29 other towns. This association secured important trading privileges abroad, in particular, England, Flanders, and Russia. In 1241, the town of Lubeck, a competitor, entered into a treaty agreement with Hamburg which provided control of the route between the Baltic and North Seas. Consequentially, the influence of the Gotland association diminished.

The Lubeck-Hamburg association gained tremendous strength when in 1252 commercial treaties were established with the Flanders. Rostock and Wismar concluded an alliance with Lubeck in 1259 for common action in 1259 to combat piracy and banditry. Encouraged by the growing influence of the Lubeck-Hamburg union, other northern German towns became affiliated with the organization. Very soon a federation was formed and it was designated as the Hansa in 1343, which consisted of 85 towns.

It is customary to speak of 77 members, but this number refers to fully fledged members which took part in decision making and paid assessments. There were a number of associate members which did neither, but the merchants of these towns were also beneficiaries of the League's activities. Usually the towns concerned were small. The League thus solved the minitown problem in a forthright manner on the basis of inequality, a procedure in accord with the ideas of the time.

3. Structure

The crucial local organization in the League structure was the Kontor. It was the enclave, located abroad, which exercised jurisdiction over the expatriate merchants, conducted negotiations with local authorities, and served as a source of information and enforcement for the Hansetag after the latter had expanded its authority. The most obvious technique used to further the purposes of the League and the merchants it served was the trading privilege wrung from local authorities by enticement, threat or force. It was usually won by the local Kontor for the common benefit of hansa members at the expense of prospective foreign, and sometimes domestic, merchants. Privileged markets were thus obtained, but not on the basis of reciprocity or mutual concessions. Aside from Bruges, the Kontore were established in primary producing areas, possessed no merchant marine, no indigenous trading class, and little capital. The trading privileges obtained were an exception to, or reduction in, local duties; the right to reexport goods duty free; exceptions from local laws regulating flotsam and jetsam; regulations guaranteeing the security of the expatriate merchants and their merchandise; and the recognition of ordinances which created the extraterritorial rights of the Kontore. The League also provided the means for the compulsory arbitration of disputes among the members. If the parties could not reach a settlement by mutual agreement, they were to submit the matter to the Hansetag for a binding decision. A body of maritime regulations was established, and procedures were established for the arrest, trial, and execution of revolutionaries. Boycotts were imposed to accomplish League objectives and even war.

All of the members of the League were city states, except for the Grand Master of the Teutonic Knights. This assertion refers to the period after 1356, the year in which the organization became public, when it converted from an association of merchants to one of cities. That year marked the first meeting of the Hansetag, the diet of the hansa of the towns. The occasion for the meeting was a dispute which involved German merchants of the Kontor of Bruges. The towns, characteristically led by Lübeck, judged the dispute to be of such import that they had the Hansetag send a diplomatic delegation to attend to the matter. This was the first time that the central authority of the towns embodied in the Hansetag spread out to include the other Kontors as well. While still a private organization, merchants became members by being accepted by the aldermen of a Kontor. There was ready acceptance of applicants who were natives of North German towns or residents of any of the Kontore. After 1356, admission of towns was by the Hansetag. Membership was terminated by expulsion or withdrawal. Expulsions were rare, but they occurred as sanctions for having violated the principles or orders of the League, and more often, after a successful revolution had deposed the merchant ruling class.

The hansa of the merchants succeeded in dominating the trade routes of the North Sea and the Baltic, along a line which stretched from London and Bruges through the Holstein Peninsula to Reval and Novgorod. Later, the Holstein Peninsula was avoided in favor of the all-water route which necessitated a detour around Denmark through the sound. Raw materials and foodfurs, wax, wood, and grain were obtained in the East; finished products and salt in the West. The hansa of the merchants succeeded in carving out this empire and bequeathing it to the hansa of the towns. By the thirteenth century the towns and the League itself were under the control of the rentier mercantile patriciate, a class which owned local real estate and dominated long-distance commerce. This class dominated east and west of the Elbe; in the East the German prevailed over the Slav. The cohesion of this class was further enhanced by intermarriage. This cohesion helps explain the transition from the hansa of the merchants to the hansa of the towns and also the regulation of 1418 directed against revolutionaries. Lubeck, the "supertown"of the League provided the dialect used as the official language of the organization for 150 years.

4. Power and Influence

The first major political action taken by the league was in 1362 when it declared war on Denmark in retaliation against the seizure of Visby, a Gotland town. Victory over Denmark was gained which resulted in the latter being compelled to grant indemnities, strategic territories and other concessions. This tremendously increased the power of the league. The following century was a period of great prosperity for the association. They created new centers of trade and civilization in northern Europe, integrated the trade and commerce of the region, developed agriculture and industrial arts,

perfected a system of weight and measures, and constructed canals and highways. Concerned with the naval establishment by the association, many rulers in Europe built alliances with the league.

The league attempted to protect its ship convoys and caravans by quelling pirates and brigands, and it fostered safe navigation by building lighthouses and training pilots. Most importantly, it sought to organize and control trade throughout northern Europe by winning commercial privileges and monopolies and by establishing trading bases overseas.

The League's aggressively protectionist trading practices often aroused opposition from foreign merchants. It used gifts and loans to foreign political leaders to protect its commercial privileges, and when this proved inadequate, it threatened to withdraw its trade and occasionally involved in embargoes and blockades.

In the 14th century the Hanseatic League had a membership of 100 towns, mostly German. Though basically a mercantile rather than a political organization, the League tried to ensure peace and order at home; warfare between towns, civic strife within towns, and robbery on the roads were all suppressed as far as possible.

5. Disintegration

Systemic factors seem to account to a great extent for the rise and the demise of the League. The Kontor was the local focus which housed the merchants and whose officials looked after their interests. Each year the merchants gathered to elect its officials, called aldermen. From 1356 on, the Kontore were subject to the authority of the Hansetag, the central organ which usually assembled in Lubeck. It made decisions on crucial matters affecting the institutional missions, expulsions, economic regulations, ratification of treaties, sanctions, and war. Regulations called upon it to meet every year; actually it met more often. The burgomeister of Lubeck served as its presiding officer. Only the representatives of the towns had the right to vote, and the decisions were made by majority vote. They were binding upon the membership. Sanctions used included expulsion with loss of trading privileges, the embargo, and even war. The League managed until its last days with a minimum of structure and resources at the central level. The Hansetag which met in 1557 decided to change this by imposing annual assessments on the towns, in accord with their wealth. This was met by much resistance, and the central treasury was never well-stocked. In 1556 the League instituted the office of Syndic, an office similar to that of a contemporary secretary general. Prior to this date, executive administrative tasks were carried on by officials of Lubeck.

The process of disintegration, which began towards the close of the 15th century, was accelerated by a variety of factors. Most significant of which were the rise and consolidation of other sovereign states in other parts of Europe, the discoveries of America and a new route to India, and the growth of Dutch and English sea power. Increasing friction between the league and England culminated in 1589 in the English seizure of 61 Hanseatic vessels.

The League died down because it lacked central power with which to withstand the new and more powerful nation-states forming on its borders. Lithuania and Poland were united in 1386; Denmark, Sweden and Norway formed a union in 1397; and Ivan III of Moscow closed the Hanseatic trading settlement at Novgorod in 1494. The Dutch were growing in mercantile and industrial strength, and in the 15th century they were able to oust German traders from Dutch domestic markets and the North sea region as a whole. New maritime connections between the Baltic and Mediterranean seas and between the Old World and the Americas caused a gradual diversion of trade westward to the great Atlantic ports.

The last meeting of the Hansetag, which occurred in 1669 can be regarded as the death date of the League. But it had declined before then, the victim of what today is termed systemic influences. The fate of the League was very much tied to that of the North German town, prospering with it and sharing in its decline. From the tenth century onward the North German town prospered materially and intellectually; later German migrants and merchants turned to the East. Lubeck emerged as the most populous and prosperous in Northern Europe. The North German town freed itself from territorial rulers. The rise of the League was also aided by technology, by the development of the cog, a ship which could carry eight to ten times more than its competitors. And the decline of the League can be traced in part to ship technology as well. In 1595 the Dutch launched a new, fast ship called the fluite. It could make twice as many trips as its predecessors. By the end of the sixteenth century, the Dutch had more tonnage afloat than the combined fleets of all of the Hanseatic cities. The North German town was eclipsed by the new international actors which were being fashioned by monarchs who favored their own nationals over "foreign" merchants. The "sovereign" North German city could not compete in the emerging state system. The great discoveries expanded enterprise beyond the thinking of the medieval hansas. The Reformation compromised previous religious homogeneity with the patriciate class remaining Catholic and the guilds sympathizing with the reformers. The Thirty Years' War (1608-48) administered the coup de grace to the League.

By 1630 the League consisted of only Lubeck, Bremen and Hamburg. This weakened union endured for 39 years but the three cities retained nominal political independence and the traditional designation of the Hansa towns until the revocation of these privileges in 1934 by the Nationalist government of Adolf Hitler.

See also: *Peace in the Middle Ages*

Bibliography ——————————————————

Encarta 1998 Hanseatic League. *Encarta Concise Encyclopedia.* http://encarta.msn.com/index/concise/0vol11/020360000.asp

Gotland 1998 The Hanseatic League. http://gotland.luma.com/Hanse.html

HANSA Consortium 1997 Hanseatic League. http://www.effedue.com/hansa/league.html

UCSB Department of Black Studies 1998 The Hanseatic League. http://www.ssfc.ucsb.deu/blac/antillians/hanseatic.html

FREDERICK H. GAREAU; PEDRO B. BERNALDEZ

Hebrew Bible and Peace

The usual definition of peace as the absence of conflict and strife is not adequate to capture the fullness of the Hebrew word *shalom* (*šalom*, coming from the verb "to be complete, whole"). The concept must be related to a cluster of terms which we would call "theological;" these ideas are central to the self-understanding of the ancient Hebrews and their descendants, the Jewish people. Virtually all of Western civilization has been influenced by the Hebrew Bible or Old Testament, albeit in a variety of ways, so we find resonances of this mentality woven into the fabric of even modern social and political thought (see *Christianity*).

1. Peace in Hebrew Thought

The nomadic and semi-nomadic existence of the ancient Hebrews gave them a concrete experience of the solidarity that should underlie life in society. Every member has a responsibility toward all others, offering an active cooperation in matters of mutual concern (procuring water, rights, defense, etc.). There is a dynamic interchange between the individual and the group; leaders (patriarchs, kings, nobility, and priests) embody the entire community as they make decisions. This principle of "embodiment" led many to believe that a later generation would suffer for the misdeeds of ancestors, a perception that could be abused (Jeremiah 31: 29-30; Ezekiel 18) (see Robinson 1980).

Two human relationships provided the Hebrews with analogies to describe aspects of the mystery of the divine and their association with God: the treaty between nations and marriage.

The societies of the ancient Near East defined their relations in terms of treaties (usually imposed by an emperor on vassal states) and legal responsibilities that flowed from them. The great emperor was depicted as a benefactor whose gracious attitude would continue and called for a response of service. The bilateral treaty was a basis for peace and harmony throughout the region. Transgression of the commandments which the vassal had accepted was the occasion for a court case and punishment. Genesis 15 describes a unilateral covenant whereby God committed himself irrevocably to Abraham and his descendants, but other covenant experiences were bilateral, involving responsibilities on both sides. Thus Exodus 19-20 depicts the Sinai covenant as the formation of a people who are promised a land wherein they will be free—to serve the one God and him alone (Exodus 19: 4-6).

The covenant is a pure gift, flowing from divine initiative and graciousness, an expression of steadfast love (*hesed*) which is multifaceted and integral to the very name of God (the name manifesting the person-Exodus 3: 14; 34: 6-7). The response to this gift is called *hesed* as well, translated "loyalty, devotion," made explicit through keeping the commandments.

The goal to which the covenant community moves is union with God, bringing wholeness, tranquility, and harmony to the people and eventually to all creation. This peace (*šalom*) is a divine gift, but it requires a response: Everyone within the covenant is challenged to be a peacemaker.

The most intimate human experience of mutual sharing and openness to *šalom* is marriage. The prophets Hosea (1-3), Jeremiah (3: 1-5), and Ezekiel (16) used the images of marriage and adultery to teach the unique nature of Israel's union with God and the implications of failure to keep the command-

ments. The harmonious couple and their family are a source of inspiration and joy for the entire community (Psalm: 127, 128; Ecclesiasticus 26: 1-4).

2. The Relationships Governed by the Commandments

Both the individual human being and every society are able to survive only in relation to other realities. The Bible records the Hebrew conviction that there are four relationships; the individual and the community touch God, neighbor, self, and nature, either to foster peace or discord (Finkel 1982).

2.1 God

The Hebrew esteem for the human person is crystallized in the doctrinal insight that every human being is created in God's image and likeness. Both male and female are collaborators with God in procreation and in subduing the rest of creation, that is, ordering it toward perfection (Genesis 1: 26-28). This exalted understanding of the human being lays an onus on the person in the moral order. One is to imitate God (Leviticus 19: 2) and the divine attributes (listed in Exodus 34: 6-7) in the practical details of everyday life (caring for the poor, the widow, the orphan, the stranger, the sick, etc.).

Šalom is one of the divine names (Judges 6: 24), so those who desire to live according to the divine will must foster well-being and harmony in all their endeavors. To take time for self-evaluation concerning the effectiveness of one's imitation of God is one of the reasons for the sabbath observance (Exodus 20: 8-11; Deuteronomy 5: 12-15). A day of rest on a regular basis provides the community and its members with a perspective on the use of time and talents. Moreover, the commandment imposed the obligation on an owner to allow like rest for his slaves and beasts of burden. War and even the carrying of weapons was forbidden.

2.2 Neighbor

Relations with neighbors must be governed by principles fostering peace. "Depart from evil and do good; seek peace and pursue it" (Psalm 34: 14). The decalogue focuses on the family, first with the life-long obligation of honoring one' parents (esteeming them as cooperators with God in sharing life and imaging the divine to their children) and providing for them in time of need, and secondly prohibiting sexual relations that would transgress a commitment to another person.

The basic rights to life, reputation, and property

are protected by other commandments of the decalogue (Exodus 20: 13-17). Even the desire for persons or things belonging to another must be controlled. The simple form of these commandments
may derive from teachings within the family, long
before the time of Moses. When the clan becomes a
people at Sinai, the sanctions are attached to the laws
(Exodus 21-23) and complex cases are dealt with in
casuistic form. When transgressions might escape
detection, the members of the community place
themselves under a curse should they commit such
crimes (Deuteronomy 27: 15-26).

Concern for others is seen as imitation of God; just
as God is merciful to all his creatures, so should the
Israelite be, even with regard to his enemy (Exodus
23: 4-5). The pursuit of peace is also linked with the
search for justice (*sedeqah*) and right judgment
(*mišpat*) in society. These activities are an imitation
of the righteousness or integrity (*sedeqah*) of God,
who calls for norms of goodness and honesty in the
legislative and judicial orders (Exodus 23: 1-3).

In the early days of Israel in the desert, Moses
learned to delegate the authority he had to judge the
people. First, he taught them the statutes and decisions; then he chose able, trustworthy, and God-fear-
ing men to take the cases of given groups of the community. He reserved the difficult cases to himself.
Thus was peace to be achieved in the nation that had
departed from Egypt (Exodus 18: 13-27). In ancient
Israel, the judge was told: "You shall not pervert
judgment (*mišpat*) . . . Justice, justice (*sedeq*) shall
you pursue . . ." (Deuteronomy 16:18-20).

A basic principle in Deuteronomic legislation is
"There will be no poor among you" (15:4), because
the land is God's gift to the entire people. The rhythm
of seven applied not only to the week with a day of
rest for all, but also to the use of the land. Every seventh year the fields were to lie fallow, and all the
people were to have equal access to any produce that
might spring up. Moreover, debts were remitted at
this time, and slaves were released (Deuteronomy
15:7-18). The priestly code took this a step further
with the institution of the jubilee year after seven
sabbaticals. In the fiftieth year, all alienated land was
to be returned to its original owner (Leviticus 25:8-
55) (see North 1954).

2.3 Self

Individuals are expected to be concerned about their
own selves. The Hebrews rooted self-esteem in the
realization that the human being is "little less than
God, crowned with glory and honor" (Psalm 8:6).
This must not pit one person against others. "You

shall not take vengeance or bear any grudge against
the children of your own people, but you shall love
your neighbor as yourself: I am the Lord" (Leviticus
19:18). If this commandment is limited to relations
among Israelites, one reads further to find: "When a
stranger sojourns with you in your land, you shall do
him no wrong . . . you shall love him as yourself, for
you were strangers in the land of Egypt" (19:33-34).

2.4 Nature

Most "primitive" people have a deep sense of closeness
to the earth and to all the forms of life that sustain
them. In the ancient Near East, the completion of each
harvest was the occasion for a thanksgiving festival.
The Hebrews built on these rhythms of nature with the
three great pilgrimage feasts (Deuteronomy 16:1-17).
The fruits of the earth were offered, but within the context of a celebration for the ways that God had guided
their history. The legislation shows a special concern
for various groups of the poor or disadvantaged.

Everyone had to develop a special concern for
domestic animals (Exodus 20:10; 23:4-5; Deuteronomy 22:1-4). Even the wild bird and its offspring were
protected, so that the line would not be obliterated; it
was forbidden to take the mother with the young
(Deuteronomy 22:6-7). Destruction of trees, especially fruit trees, was likewise prohibited (Deuteronomy
20:19-20).

The biblical tradition recognizes that all creation is
a gift of God, to be used for the enhancement of
human life but to be treated with respect and to be
shared with others, especially those incapable of taking proper care of themselves.

3. Pilgrimage as an Experience of Peace

In many cultures it is commonplace to regard life as
a journey, with specific goals involving a sense of
purpose and commitment. Pilgrimage is a particular
type of journey; the pilgrim joins others in an experience that manifests the sacred meaning of life,
growth, and transformation.

The typical pilgrimage consists of four elements: a
separation from one's home, work, and ordinary
activities; a nonstructured group of people set out for
a sacred place; a specific purpose is enunciated (forgiveness of sins, purification for a new task, etc.);
and hardships and rigors are accepted.

After the Temple was built in Jerusalem, this "city
of peace" (as popular etymology explained the name)
became the goal for Israelite pilgrimages (see
Deuteronomy 16:16-17; Psalms 15, 24) and experienced their solidarity in a special way (see Psalms

122, 125, 127, 128, 133). Ideally, this event would have a continuing impact on their daily lives and orient them toward the age of universal peace promised through the prophets (see Frizzell 1982).

This future era of peace is associated with the descendant of David who would be God's Anointed One *par excellence* (*Messiah* in Hebrew, *Christos* in Greek). Just as God had given David victory over his enemies and allowed the people of Israel to dwell undisturbed, so would he establish the royal dynasty of David forever (2 Samuel 7:8-16). The successor to David, Solomon (Shlomo, "man of peace") became the sign of this hope for a just reign that would endure (see Psalm 72, attributed to Solomon, and Psalm 132).

The prophets of later periods referred back to the reign of David and Solomon and Nathan's oracle (2 Samuel 7) and expressed hope for the future. The messianic ruler would be called "Prince of Peace" and he would govern the kingdom with justice and righteousness (Isaiah 9:6-7); guided by gifts of God's Spirit he would bring a harmony that would spread eventually to all creation (Isaiah 11:1-9).

The threat of Nebuchadnezzar's army hung over the Kingdom of Judah from 604 to 587 BC, when Jerusalem was destroyed and most of the people were taken into exile. Both Jeremiah (23:1-6) and Ezekiel (34:1-31) proclaimed that the Davidic Messiah would establish security for the entire people by ruling with justice and righteousness. Ezekiel sees this as a covenant of peace with freedom from fear of wild beasts and marauding armies (Ezekiel 34:25-31; 37:24-28). As a reciprocal relationship between God and his people, the covenant provided the framework for an ever-deepening experience of the divine presence, the unique source of the life and blessings associated with peace. This will have a universal impact. "Then the nations will know that I the Lord sanctify Israel, when my Temple is in their midst forevermore" (Ezekiel 37:28).

Isaiah (2:1-5) and Micah (4:1-4) record a vision that the Temple of Jerusalem would become the only place of pilgrimage for all the nations. There they would learn the teachings of the one God and accept him as their judge. The weapons would be made into agricultural instruments and war would not be studied anymore.

"The central vision of world history in the Bible is that all of creation is one, every creature in community with every other creature" (Brueggemann 1982 p. 15). Although our world is much larger and more complex than any ancient culture ever dreamed of, human nature has not changed. We cannot afford to ignore the insights harvested from the collective wisdom of the millennia.

See also: *Religion and Peace*

Bibliography ──────────────────

Batto B F 1987 The covenant of peace: A neglected Ancient Near East motif. *Catholic Biblical Quarterly* 49

Brueggemann W 1982 *Living Towards a Vision*. United Church Press, Philadelphia, Pennsylvania

Chester A 1989 The concept of peace in the Old Testament. *Theology* 92

Comblin J 1963 *Theologies de la Paix*, 2 vols. Editions Universitaries, Paris

Cox D 1989 Peace and peacemakers in the "writings" of the Old Testament. *Studia Missionalia* 38

Durham J I 1970 Šalom and the presence of God. In: Durham J I, Porter J R (eds.) *Proclamation and Presence* (for G W. Davis)

Enz J I 1972 *The Christian and Warfare: Roots of Pacifism in the Old Testament*. Herald Press, Scottsdale, Pennsylvania

Finkel A 1982 Aging: The Jewish perspective. In: Tiso F (ed.) *Spiritual Perspectives on Aging*. Sunday Publications, Lake Worth, Florida

Finkel A 1984 Jerusalem in biblical and theological tradition: A Jewish perspective. In: Tanenbaum M H (ed.) 1984 *Evangelicals and Jews in an Age of Pluralism*. Baker House, Grand Rapids, Michigan

Frizzell L 1982 Pilgrimage: A study in the biblical experience. *Jeevadhara* 12

Frizzell L 1984 Elijah the peacemaker: Jewish and early Christian interpretations of Malachi 3. *SIDIC* 17(2)

Good E M 1962 Peace. *Interpreter's Dictionary of the Bible*, Vol. 3. Abingdon, Nashville, Tennessee

Gross H 1956 Die Idee des ewigen und allgemeinen Weltfriedens im Alten Orient und im Alten Testament. Trier

Hanson P D 1984 War and peace in the Hebrew Bible. *Interpretation* 38

Harrelson W 1980 *The Ten Commandments and Human Rights*. Fortress Press, Philadelphia, Pennsylvania

Healy J P 1992 Peace: Old Testament. *Anchor Bible Dictionary*, Vol.5. Doubleday, Garden City

Heschel A J 1951 *The Sabbath*. Farrar, Strauss and Giroux, New York

Hirsch R G 1974 *The Most Precious Gift—Peace in the Jewish Tradition*. New York

Homolka W, Friedlander A H 1994 *The Gate to Perfection: The Idea of Peace in Jewish Thought*. Continuum, New York

Jacobs L 1972 Peace. *Encyclopedia Judaica*, Vol.13. Keter, Jerusalem

Klassen W 1984 *Love of Enemies: The Way to Peace*. Fortress Press, Philadelphia, Pennsylvania

Levine Etan 1974 The Hebrew Treatise on Peace. *Augustinianum* 14

MacQuarrie J 1973 *The Concept of Peace.* SCM, London

North R 1954 *Sociology of the Biblical Jubilee.* Pontifical Biblical Institute, Rome

Patrick D 1985 *Old Testament Law.* John Knox Press, Atlanta, Georgia

Pedersen J 1964 *Israel: Its Life and Culture.* Oxford University Press, Oxford

Robinson H-W 1980 *Corporate Personality in Ancient Israel.* Fortress Press, Philadelphia, Pennsylvania

Rouner L 1990 *Celebrating Peace.* University of Notre Dame Press, Notre Dame, Indiana

Ruble R T 1989 The gift of shalom in the Old Testament. In: Parker T, Fraser B (eds.) *Peace, War and God's Justice.*

Schwarzschild S et al., *Roots of Jewish Nonviolence.* Jewish Peace Fellowship, Nyack, New York

Sisson J P 1986 Jeremiah and the Jerusalem conception of peace. *J. Biblical Literature* 105

Stamm J J, Bietenhard H 1959 Die Weltfriede in Alten und Neuen Testament

Steck O H 1972 *Friedensvorstellungen im alten Jerusalem.* Zurich

Tamez E 1982 *Bible of the Oppressed.* Orbis Books, Maryknoll

Von Rad G 1964 Eirēnē. *Theological Dictionary of the New Testament,* Vol. 2. Eerdmans, Grand Rapids, Michigan

Westermann C 1969 Der Frieden (Shalom) im Alten Testament. In: Picht G, Todt H E (ed.) 1969 *Studien zur Friedensforschung,* Band 1, Ernst Klett, Stuttgart

Westermann C 1974 *Gesammelte Studien.* Kaiser, Munich

Yoder P 1987 *Shalom: The Bible's World for Salvation, Justice and Peace.* Faith and Life, Newton, Kansas

Yoder P, Swartley W (eds.) 1992 *The Meaning of Peace.* Westminster/ John Knox, Louisville, Kentucky

Zampaglione G 1973 *The Idea of Peace in Antiquity.* Notre Dame University Press, Notre Dame, Indiana

LAWRENCE FRIZZELL

Hegel, Georg Wilhelm Friedrich

Georg Wilhelm Friedrich Hegel (1770-1831) is best known for his influential philosophy of history. After growing up in a sedate Protestant area in southern Germany, Hegel spent his young manhood as a student and teacher of philosophy, tossed about from place to place in the upheavals of a Germany convulsed by the wars of the Napoleonic era. Finally, with the restoration of peace he was given a chair at the University of Berlin in 1818, where he remained until his death some fourteen years later. There his renown, which had been growing since the publication of his first major work, *The Phenomenology of Mind* (1807), became enormous. Students came to Berlin from all over Germany expressly to hear his lectures.

Hegel argued that history is basically an account of human spiritual and moral progress. It is best understood through the operation of the dialectic—the clash of opposing ideas (thesis and antithesis) out of which comes a synthesis which incorporates the best of both thesis and antithesis. The synthesis becomes the thesis of a new historical era, provoking a new antithesis, which gives rise to a new synthesis and yet another era. Thus history has progressed in the human climb toward knowledge of absolute truth, or God.

Hegel tended to minimize the role of individuals in achieving historical progress. Rather, to him the nation-state was the real moving force which shapes culture, morality, and behavior. Individual minds, he argued, are simply variants of the *Volksgeist*, or "spirit of the people" of a particular nation at a particular time.

In *The Philosophy of Right* (1821), his major work on politics, Hegel argued that the individual is, in fact, rightly subordinate to the nation-state. The human being's highest need, he asserted, is to participate in causes larger than his or her own trifling concerns. Only through the nation-state can an individual participate meaningfully in history. Therefore, the nation-state has a just claim on the loyalty and obedience of its citizens. Hegel had little sympathy for the liberal idea that government derives its just power from the consent of the governed. For him, the state stands above the individuals who comprise it.

Hegel saw the state as totally sovereign, morally able to operate in complete freedom. Thus, he rejected the idea of international law as something which tried to place limitations on this freedom. Even treaties freely entered into were not regarded as binding by Hegel, on the grounds that the state's sovereignty cannot be limited, even by the state itself.

For Hegel, then, states are completely free to make war or peace as they wish. Indeed, he argued that the ability to make war is the conclusive test of their sovereignty. Hegel regarded war as inevitable in a world of sovereign states, and even as desirable. War, he insisted, gives the citizens a sense of unity and strengthens their determination to maintain their independence. History, he declared, unfolds itself through war and conquest. War can be seen as a clash of thesis and antithesis which produces a synthesis superior to either. The alternative to war, he believed, was not peace but stagnation.

Hegel's impact on nineteenth century Germany was enormous. Through his writings and even more through his lectures at the University of Berlin, his thought helped to shape the outlook of the leaders of German society, particularly of Prussian society. His views on the state's claim to the loyalty and service of the citizen, and on the historical necessity of war became integral parts of the intellectual atmosphere within which the German elite moved.

See also: *State, Theory of the*

Bibliography ————————————

Avineri S 1972 *Hegel's Theory of the Modern State*. Cambridge University Press, London

Friedrich C J (ed.) 1953 *The Philosophy of Hegel*. Modern Library, New York

Kaufmann W A 1978 *Hegel: A Reinterpretation*. University of Notre Dame Press, Notre Dame, Indiana

Mure G R G 1982 *An Introduction to Hegel*. Greenwood Press, Westport, Connecticut

Rosenzweig F 1920 *Hegel und der Staat*. Oldenburg

GARRETT L. MCAINSH

Hegemony

Hegemony is a concept derived from the Greek word *hegemonia* which meant "high command," "kingship," and "leading position of a state," especially the dominance of one state within an alliance of states, for example "the hegemony of Sparta." In international relations the concept of hegemony has since come to mean the supremacy of a particular state in a group of interdependent, rival states.

Most European states, for example, emerged from the struggle of two or more large feudal houses (noble families) for hegemony in a particular territory. The victorious house, having established its hegemony could then become the ruling dynasty of the larger entity of a state. In all competitive processes we can observe a strong tendency toward such an establishment of hegemonial positions, a tendency towards the monopolization of power chances. As Elias (1982) has formulated this "monopoly mechanism":

If in a larger social unit many smaller units which through their interdependence from the larger one, have relatively equal strength and are thus able to compete freely—unhampered by previously existing monopolies—for the chances to acquire social power, ..., then there is a very high probability that some will win and others submit. As a consequence gradually fewer and fewer units will control more and more power chances, so that more and more units will be eliminated from the competition and will become directly or indirectly dependent upon an ever decreasing number.

In all rivalries between survival units such as dynasties or nation-states there is thus a built-in tendency toward hegemony. At the interstate level the competition for territory, armaments, and other power resources has indeed led to the emergence of the so-called Great Powers—now often called Superpowers. Great Powers, however, are not as such to be equated with hegemonial powers. They may have had hegemony within the alliances formed around them, such as the North Atlantic Treaty Organization (NATO) (see *North Atlantic Treaty Organization (NATO)*) or the Warsaw Pact. The former Soviet Union and the United States were clearly the hegemonial powers within their respective alliances (see *Alliance*). But Great Powers are precisely those states that struggle for hegemony in a larger state system. In the past such competitive state systems were limited in geographical scope to, for example, China; the Indian subcontinent; the Near East including Greece; and in the Roman period, the Mediterranean region including large parts of Western Europe. Now one state system covers the world as a whole.

In certain cases interstate competition did in fact lead to the hegemony of one state and later to the formation of an imperial state, such as the Chinese and Roman Empires. Most of these empires, however, in the past disintegrated again. The conditions for the establishment of military hegemony of a state are not the same as the conditions for the establishment of durable central rule over the same large territories. The only exception has been the Chinese Empire which, founded after the ch'in state, had managed to subdue the other four competing states at the end of the so-called Warring States period (476-221 BC).

In other competitive state systems, especially in Western Europe, a relatively successful device against hegemony has been established in the form of so-called balance of power policies (see *Balance of Power*). The classical conception of the balance of power as it developed among the dynastic states in Western Europe is expressed very well in a passage from the pamphlet *Europe's Catechism*, published in 1741:

> Catechist: Hold my pretty child—one Word more. You have been asked concerning the Balance of power—Tell me what is it?
>
> Europe: It is such an equal Distribution of power among the princes of Europe, as makes it impracticable for the one to disturb the repose of the other.
>
> Catechist: When any Potentate has arrived to an exorbitant Share of Power, ought not the rest to league together in order to reduce him to his due proportion of it?
>
> Europe: Yes, certainly—otherwise there is but one Potentate, and the others are only a Kind of Vassals to him.

In other words, if one of the Great Powers would seek more than its "due proportion" of power, the others would form a coalition against it to prevent it from acquiring hegemony (see *Collective Security and Collective Self-defense*). The conditions for balance of power policies are quite stringent. The most important is indeed a more or less even distribution of power between the Great Powers, which should also number at least three. But such an even distribution is not a durable given. Power relations change all the time. Some states become richer and militarily stronger than others. An even power balance therefore has to be maintained by continual combination and recombination, that is to say by flexibility in forming alliances. When a balance threatens to break down or is in the process of breaking down—for example when first the French Revolutionary and then the Napoleonic armies overran great parts of Europe—the other Great Powers have to form an emergency coalition against the aspiring hegemonist, even when they were hostile to each other before.

Though war is therefore an indispensible instrument to preserve or restore a balance of power and prevent hegemony, it should never aim at destroying an enemy state, not even an aspiring hegemonist, because that would harm or destroy the balance between the others. As the Abbe de Pradt wrote in the eighteenth century: "The preservation and the integrity of Prussia are important not only to the Empire, to Sweden, Denmark, Turkey, England and above all to France . . . ; but it is further important to the powers that seem to menace it: because each should prefer its actual state to the excessive expansion of the other, and consequently is interested in its preservation."

Balance of power policies as such, however, cannot easily contain large shifts in the power ratios between the member states. The *levee en masse*—the introduction of conscription (see *Conscription*) in revolutionary France—which gave France superior military power and later led to the attempt by Napoleon to make France the hegemonial power in Europe, demonstrated the fragility of the classical balance of power. A balance will break down when an increasingly powerful state neither recognizes the balance as such nor respects its rules any longer.

When the grand coalition of Russia, Great Britain, Austria, and Prussia had defeated Napoleon, however, the European balance was restored. France was immediately admitted again as one of the members of the "concert" of the Great Powers. The coalition had expressed in its formative treaties as its aim: "To put an end to Europe's sorrows and secure its future peace through the restoration of a just balance of power" and "a redivision of their respective forces suitable to assure this equilibrium." The Congress of Vienna indeed restored a reasonably even balance which lasted until 1914 and secured a relatively peaceful nineteenth century for Europe. Outside Europe competition went on. In the same scramble for Africa took place, which all colonial powers extended the scope and intensity of their role.

At the end of the century, however, the unification of Germany and to a lesser extent that of Italy began to undermine the balance of power in Europe. After 1890 Germany withdrew from the careful balancing policies of Chancellor Bismarck and embarked on a more competitive course. Its building up of military strength—especially its naval power—could only be interpreted by Great Britain and France as the beginning of a bid for hegemony. That was one of the constitutive elements in the formation of two rather rigid alliances in Europe—the Triple Alliance and the Great Entente—which turned out to be one of the most important preconditions for the outbreak of the First World War.

It was the first time that Great Britain joined a Continental alliance. Before the beginning of the twentieth century, Great Britain had always acted as a balancer of the power relations on the continent. It would always throw its weight in such a manner that no continental power could acquire hegemony. As Great Britain had embroiled itself so completely in the First World War, another external balancer was required to resolve the inter-European conflict. The United States then for the first time took that role upon itself. But the United States withdrew again immediately after the war and did not join the League of Nations (see *League of Nations*). No stable balance in Western Europe could then again be established.

After 1933, Nazi Germany began another attempt to acquire hegemony in Europe. This attempt foundered for two reasons: the German army did not succeed in defeating the former Soviet Union, and the United States again entered the war in the role of external balancer. At the same time Japan made a bid for regional hegemony on Eastern and Southeast Asia, as expressed clearly in its purported aim to establish a "greater East Asian coprosperity sphere" in Asia. The wartime coalition between the former Soviet Union and the United States defeated the two aspiring hegemonists, but when the war was over these two Great Powers found themselves in the position of the only two remaining contestants in the struggle for hegemony at the world level.

It is often asked what the real conflict was between the two hegemonic rivals, the United States and the former Soviet Union. Because it is difficult to give an answer to that question in terms of specific interests or issues of such importance that no compromise could be possible, the conclusion may then follow that the conflict is not really about anything but ideology and perception. The relationship between the former Soviet Union and the United States, however, was not simply a conflict: it was a persistent rivalry. Its stake was not even to acquire global hegemony, but to prevent the opponent from acquiring such a position. To preclude the opponent from achieving hegemony both Superpowers had taken measures which made it appear that hegemony was being sought. It is for this reason that the rivalry between the United States and the former Soviet Union had assumed such a coercive and global character. In hindsight, it can be seen as the last of a long line of elimination struggles, which contrary to its predecessors ended peacefully because the shadow of nuclear war precluded the use of any kind of violence between them.

The possibility of mutual destruction through their respective invulnerable second-strike nuclear capabilities deprived the rivals of any hope to submit each other. On the contrary, the danger of nuclear war made for restrained conduct in all crisis situations between them (see *Crisis; Crisis Management*). All political crises between nuclear powers since the Cuban Missile Crisis of 1962 have been managed below the level of nuclear alerts. What was expected to be a 'winning weapon' in the early postwar years, turned into a device for impotence and political stalemate. Instead of working to obtain hegemony, the two nuclear rivals were forced to observe an unprecedented degree of restraint.

The nuclear weapons became irrelevant after 1989, as is often claimed. It seems rather that their effects on great power conduct have widened to all the five recognized nuclear powers in the NPT (see *Non-Proliferation Treaty (NPT)*): the United States, Britain, France, Russia and China. They all possess invulnerable second strike capabilities, which implies an assured destruction capability. They are all condemned to eschew any use of violence and to pursue crisis avoidance in their mutual relations. That leads to the very important conclusion that great or global powers are no longer possible. It also means that a struggle for global hegemony remains excluded. If China and the United States would start to really compete for world leadership, they could only rely on political and economic power resources, and perhaps even to some extent conventional capabilities. But their rivalry would have to be and remain peaceful. If we include in the analysis of the limitation of the great power rivalry the consequences of rapid financial and economic globalization, not just great powers, but all states benefiting from these processes will restrain themselves and take the interests of other states more into account than in the past. The search for hegemony may then turn into a search for means of multilateral cooperation, that can effectively deal with both common interests and the self-interests of states. This may still be utopian, but the irrelevance of hegemony is not.

Bibliography

Bergh G vd 1992 *The Nuclear Revolution and the End of the Cold War: Forced Restraint*. Macmillan Basungstate

Bousquet N 1980 From hegemony to competition: Cycles of the core? In: Hopkins T K, Wallerstein I (eds.) 1980 *Processes of the World System*. Sage, Beverly Hills, California

Bull H 1977 *The Anarchical Society: A Study of World Order*. Macmillan, London

Claude I L 1962 *Power and International Relations*. Random House, New York

Cox R W 1983 Gramsci, hegemony and international relations: An essay on method. *Millenium: Journal of International Studies* 12 (2)

Diamond A S 1951 *The Evolution of Law and Order*. Greenwood Press. London

Elias N 1982 *State Formation and Civilization*. Blackwell, Oxford

Gilpin R 1981 *War and Change in World Politics*. Cambridge University Press. Cambridge

Gulick E V 1982 *Europe's Classical Balance of Power*. Greenwood Press, London

Keohane R O 1984 *After Hegemony: Cooperation and Discord in the World Political Economy*. Princeton University Press, Princeton, New Jersey

Seabury P (ed.) 1965 *The Balance of Power*. San Francisco, California

G. Van Benthem Van Den Bergh

Heinemann, Gustav

Gustav Heinemann (1899-1976) was an attorney, mining director, Minister of Justice of the Federal Land of Nordrhein Westfalen, Federal Minister of the Interior, founder of the Emergency Pool for Peace in Europe and of the All-German People's Party (GVP), Federal Minister of Justice, and Federal President.

Heinemann was perhaps the most important political opponent of German rearmament during the Cold War period (see *Cold War*). At that time he was the leading advocate and spokesman for an alternative foreign policy. Chancellor Adenauer's foreign policy favored the integration of the then Federal Republic of Germany into the North Atlantic Treaty Organization (NATO) (see *North Atlantic Treaty Organization (NATO)*) but Heinemann proposed the preservation of peace in Europe through the reunification of the two Germanies on a democratic foundation.

Raised in a republican-democratic environment Heinemann chose to become a lawyer. He rose rapidly from the position of legal adviser to a member of the executive board of the Rhine steelworks in Essen. During the Nazi era he was one of the organizers of the ecclesiastical resistance of the "Bekennende Kirche" (an anti-Nazi group within the Protestant church). Following the Second World War he was a founder member of the Christian Democratic Union (CDU), the party of Adenauer, and he soon became chief *bürgermeister* of Essen and Minister of Justice of the Federal Land of Nordrhein-Westfalen. In 1949 Adenauer appointed Heinemann—as a representative of Protestantism—Minister of the Interior in his first Cabinet. Critical of Adenauer's unconditional Western orientation in foreign policy, Heinemann offered his resignation in August 1950 as soon as he learnt of Adenauer's intentions concerning rearmament.

Following his retreat from political life in Bonn, Heinemann organized part of the resistance to the rearmament program. Immediately prior to the second election to the Federal Parliament a party was formed from a circle of Christian individuals, among them a bishop and a famous Catholic writer, which attempted to prevent German rearmament. Heinemann was a leading figure in both organizations. Although the All-German People's Party (GVP) was unsuccessful in the elections to the Federal Parliament, Heinemann remained a popular and provocative public speaker and writer. However, his unremitting campaign could not prevent rearmament and the Federal Republic's membership of NATO. From 1957, as a Member of the Federal Parliament and of the Social Democratic Party (SPD)—which in the meantime had moved closer to his conceptions of foreign policy—he clashed with his principal opponent in this matter, Konrad Adenauer, in the forum of Parliament. Heinemann's speech of January 23, 1958, in which he exposed the planned armament of the Federal Republic with nuclear weapons as a further indication of the fundamental tendency of the foreign policy of Adenauer to cement the division of Germany, was a landmark in the history of the Federal Diet. In the same speech he vehemently opposed the GDU's ideological conception of the age as one of controversy between Christianity (meaning the Western democracies) and Marxism (meaning the Soviet Union). After the punishment of the devastating defeat in the Second World War, Heinemann argued it should be the policy of the Federal Republic to ensure that Germany was a land of absolute peace: a "house of an infectious recovery, of an extending peace for neighboring peoples" (Johannes Jänicke).

But Heinemann could not prevent the nuclear armament of the Federal Armed Forces. Despite this setback, he became a central figure in the continued extraparliamentary campaign against nuclear armament, primarily as a speaker at mass demonstrations. His involvement in the "Fight Nuclear Death" movement confirmed his position as one of the most important and influential personalities within the leading opposition party, the SPD. Among his former followers, Johannes Rau, Diether Posser, and Erhard Eppler gained increasing influence within the SPD. Yet Heinemann was neither an apparatchik nor a political manager. He was admired for his skill in political debate, his dedication and sincerity. The combination of these civic virtues with his combative opposition in the first decade of the Federal Republic made him the ideal social democratic candidate for the highest public office, the office of the Federal President, in 1969. His election, on a slim majority with the help of the liberal Free Democratic Party (FDP), although highly controversial was correctly interpreted by Heinemann as a significant shift in power (*Machtwechsel*). Heinemann did not regard his election simply as the replacement of one political elite by another; rather, he saw the collapse of the "CDU state" as a victory for the political forces which were working toward the reduction of bloc confrontation between East and West and thereby the elimination of the danger of war in Central Europe through a policy of *Entspannung* (détente) leading to treaties between the then Federal Republic of Germany and the then German Democratic Republic. In the light of the student rebellion which had erupted in 1967, he also hoped his election would contribute to "internal reconciliation in the Federal Republic."

In the course of his term of office, which lasted until 1974, Heinemann promoted efforts for mutual disarmament and for the scientific analysis of the causes of war and the roots of peace. Having fought unswervingly for his political ideals as a political outsider in the 1950s, he now adopted, in the office of Federal President, the role of initiator and critic, standing above party political differences. He was required to play the part of an integrator and representative of the Federal Republic but he retained his convictions which he continued to advocate in a non-controversial manner. His influence upon the young generation should not be underestimated, and the peace movement which emerged in the late 1970s was indeed indebted to his example.

Bibliography

Baring A 1982 *Machtwechsel: Die Ära Brandt-Scheel*
Gollwitzer H 1977 *Politik an den Grenzen des Bürgertums: Evangelische Theologie*
Heinemann G W 1975-77 *Reden und Schriften*, 3 vols
Koch D 1972 *Heinemann und die Deutschlandfrage*

HANS KARL RUPP

Helsinki Process

Helsinki, the capital of Finland, became synonymous in international politics in the last quarter of the twentieth century with the Final Act of the Conference on Security and Cooperation in Europe (CSCE) (see *Organization for Security and Cooperation in Europe (OSCE)*). The Final Act was signed there on 1 August 1975 by the 35 participating states; these comprised 33 European countries (all except Albania, the United States and Canada). The CSCE was generally thought to be the major achievement of the detente relationship which grew between East and West in the late 1960s and early 1970s. It was hoped that the Final Act would be a step toward a further relaxation of tension on Europe. In the short-term the optimism was not justified, and a new round in the Cold War began not long afterwards. In the longer term, however, "Helsinki" played a role in the eventual ending of the Cold War, and created a framework for security cooperation in Europe (see *Security and Cooperation in Europe*) that some have thought transferable to other troubled regions in the world.

The Helsinki Final Act, the outcome of a conference beginning in July 1973, was an understanding (a non-binding agreement to implement) rather than a legally binding commitment. It was hoped that the document would provide a framework to make detente a continuing process; the Soviet leader Brezhnev announced that "international detente is being increasingly invested with specific material content." But the competitive dimension of detente, which had been well in evidence during the CSCE negotiations, came even more into the open after the signing of the Final Act. This was evident in the Helsinki review conferences in Belgrade (1977), Madrid (1980-83), and Ottawa (1985) and in the Conference on Disarmament in Europe (CDE) which began in Stockholm in 1984 to further the military dimensions of the process. The competitive dimension was only to be expected, as the CSCE had its origins in the depths of the Cold War, and in particular in the desire of the former Soviet Union through the 1950s and 1960s to have its hegemony over eastern Europe legitimised in a "European Security Conference." This had been long opposed by Western states, for the very reason why it was so important for the former Soviet Union. The ambitions of the latter in this regard, however, were such that it eventually agreed to participate in a process broadened to include a more comprehensive conception of security (including human rights, economic and environmental issues), and also the participation of the non-European states of Canada and the United States. The competitive Cold War (see *Cold War*) and unpromising origins of the Helsinki process is an important reminder to those who are critical of the idea that Helsinki offers a useful and comprehensive framework for security in other parts of the world, on the grounds that the conditions are not right. If they were, such a process would scarcely be necessary.

1. The Four "Baskets"

The aim of the Final Act, which for some was a "surrogate peace treaty" for the Second World War, was "to improve and intensify" relations between the participating states, and "to contribute in Europe to peace, security, justice and cooperation as well as to rapprochement among themselves and with other States of the world." The document was divided into four sections or "baskets" (reflecting the way the negotiations were organized).

Basket One consisted of two main parts. The first was a declaration of 10 principles which the participating states agreed to observe in their international relations. These were such norms as the "inviolability of frontiers" and the renunciation of actions "making each other's territory the object of military occupation." The second part was concerned with military security issues. Here the participants agreed to certain "confidence-building measures" designed to remove some of the secrecy surrounding military activities, and general pledges about the importance of arms control and disarmament.

Basket Two concerned economic, scientific, technological and environmental cooperation. Basket Three dealt with humanitarian cooperation, including the free flow of information, ideas and people among the participants (such as marriages between different nationals, and the improvement of working conditions for journalists). Basket Three and Principal Seven of Basket One (respect for human rights and fundamental freedoms, including the freedom of thought, conscience, religion or belief) were the major human right provisions of the Final Act. It has been in this area, arguably, where the Helsinki process has had its major impact. Basket Four gave provision for a follow-up conference. The latter was especially important for the small nations who formed a majority of the CSCE and who saw the Helsinki process as a platform for furthering their own positions on international issues.

2. Tensions Between the Superpowers

The history of the CSCE process leading to the signing of the Helsinki Final Act was full of ironies. Four aspects are worth noting. First, the Final Act itself, with all its cooperative principles and expectations, was signed at just the time that the detente relationship which had made it possible, and which it was designed to strengthen, was undergoing serious decline—especially at the superpower level. Second, a marked change occurred in the former Soviet Union's relationship with the idea of a European security process. Since the mid-1950s the idea of a European security conference had been periodically mooted by the former Soviet Union, with the primary aim of securing formal recognition of the post-1945 territorial status quo, notably the division of Germany, Poland's new frontiers, and the gains made by the former Soviet Union itself. However, during the Helsinki conference and subsequently, rather than have its position legitimised, it proved to be the former Soviet Union that suffered most embarrassment from the process—diplomatically, domestically, in intra-bloc affairs, and in terms of East-West propaganda (see *East-West Conflict*). This was the result of Western, domestic and eastern European criticism of Soviet failures to live up to their human rights commitments. Criticism of Soviet bloc regimes on human rights grounds *from within* became increasingly significant and salient.

Third, there was an equal but opposite change of opinion on the part of the United States government. Originally, Washington had not been keen on the idea of a European security conference, seeing it as a Soviet ploy to strengthen its role in European affairs. In the event, United States administrations came to use the Helsinki process as an effective arena for attacking the former Soviet Union. Finally, an early Soviet objective in promoting the idea of a European security conference had been to split Western Europe and the United States, by preventing US participation. This would have helped establish the idea that the former Soviet Union was the only superpower with legitimate interests in Europe. In the course of the negotiations Western unity held, and the former Soviet Union was obliged to accept United States (and Canadian) participation in CSCE, an outcome that helped to legitimize North American involvement in European affairs.

In August 1985, following a half-decade of the intense US-Soviet rivalry which became dubbed the 'new Cold War' (see *Cold War*), the time came to mark the tenth anniversary of the Final Act. Not surprisingly most delegates felt that they had little to celebrate. For many, the anniversary of the Final Act offered only an opportunity to record a catalogue of failures. The Reagan Administration maintained its confrontational posture towards the former Soviet Union, with Secretary of State George Shultz declaring that "the most important promises of a decade ago have not been kept." There were some differences of tone, however. The Western Europeans were generally more upbeat, following the slight easing of tension with the accession earlier in the year of Gorbachev (see Nobel Peace Prize Laureates: *Mikhail S. Gorbachev*) as new Soviet leader. As will be seen, the results of the Helsinki process were more complex than Schultz's verdict suggests; beneath the surface, developments of a profound nature for the future of security in Europe were taking place—developments which were encouraged by the Final Act.

After ten years the Helsinki process was battered, but not beaten. Without doubt, the record in the different baskets had been patchy and the whole process had obviously been subject to the vagaries of superpower relations (often affected by factors other than issues in European security). Neither superpower wanted to take responsibility for terminating the process, while the smaller powers for the most part were anxious that it be upheld. Detente *within* Europe was always healthier, and the desire to maintain it always stronger, than was the case between the superpowers. This was reflected in different attitudes towards the Helsinki process.

In 1975 there had been some unrealistic expectations about Helsinki. The Final Act could not alone change the dominating features of postwar European affairs, such as the East-West divide or the desire of governments to avoid external interference in their domestic affairs. Nor was it likely to change the balance of power between two massively armed alliances (see *Balance of Power*). But if the Final Act's contribution to "European security" was limited in the short term, it was not insignificant. On the positive side Helsinki provided a framework for the regulation of European security affairs, and the acceptance of norms of a Europe based on such principles as sovereignty, equality of status, and a relaxation of tension between countries. Equally, although the obligations undertaken were not legally binding, they were as much as could be agreed at that point. On human rights Helsinki was not without early effect. If the former Soviet Union wanted recognition as a full member of the European community of states—a historic Russian aim—it had to meet certain requirements in the way it treated its citizens. The Helsinki process both established a standard in this respect and legitimized international interest in the matter. It provided 'soft law.' By 1985 the new Soviet leader, Gorbachev, appreciated this.

3. The Human Rights Issue

Both during the 1973-75 negotiations at Helsinki and subsequently, it was the Basket Three provisions which were the source of most interest, contention, and cynicism. The reason for this was the former Soviet Union's acceptance, in the Final Act, of undertakings which no communist government had hitherto agreed, and which no Western government confidently expected the former Soviet Union to follow through. In the years following, the Helsinki process was typically characterized by Soviet attempts to divert attention away from the human rights provisions, while the West and the United States in particular, gave them particular prominence.

Politics were at the heart of the human rights issue. For the Soviet leadership, the main aim of the process was to further their ascendancy over eastern Europe as had been declared unilaterally in the 1968 Brezhnev Doctrine (see *Brezhnev Doctrine*). In contrast, the Western governments hoped that they could use the human rights issue to embarrass the former Soviet Union within its own sphere of influence in eastern Europe, as well as internationally, while at the same time preventing the legitimizing of Soviet ascendency in Eastern Europe. Consequently, while the Western countries sought to use Basket Three as way of undermining Soviet authority in eastern Europe, Soviet representatives emphasized the traditional principle of non-intervention (see *Nonintervention and Noninterference*) in matters of domestic jurisdiction (conveniently setting aside their own Brezhnev Doctrine—the doctrine of limited sovereignty—in this regard). For its part the United States has not been an enthusiastic proponent of Basket Three issues in the early 1970s. Under the influence of Kissingerian realism the US position tended towards the traditional belief that human rights were internal matters and in any case irrelevant to the high political concerns of foreign policy. At the same time Kissingerian pessimism about the former Soviet Union led him to think that the Helsinki process was flawed because it would result in a geopolitical success for the former Soviet Union—getting its ascendancy over the region legitimised—with no comparable benefits for the West. It was the desire of certain Western European governments to promote human rights and humanitarian principles via the CSCE process that helped tip the balance of the argument in favour of Basket Three.

The United States strictly monitored the human rights implementation of the Final Act by the former Soviet Union and its eastern European allies, largely to provide ammunition for criticizing the Soviet record in subsequent review conferences. Despite its initial hesitation on Basket Three, therefore, the United States took up a leading role in the review conferences. And as US-Soviet relations deteriorated at the end of the 1970s, the West as a whole took on a more unified stance. In addition to government-level interest, the implementation of the Final Act within the Soviet bloc was also the focus of attention for several independent "Helsinki monitoring groups" which were set up in the east. By the early 1980s they were being strongly repressed (in the former Soviet Union individual members were imprisoned, forced to emigrate, or sent into internal exile). Such harsh treatment was not unrelated to the role human rights had come to play in the Western propaganda campaign against the former Soviet Union. President Carter's first communication with Moscow, for example, had not been to the former Soviet government, but rather to a Helsinki monitoring group. By the time of the tenth anniversary of the Final Act, it was widely believed that human rights in the former Soviet Union, and its humanitarian contacts with the outside world, had not improved over the period and in important ways were worse. For its part, the Soviet government tried to defend its human rights record, while criticizing aspects of the Western record. In particular, it attacked Western violations of social and economic rights, including racial discrimination in the United States. Despite the criticism they had to face, the Soviet leaders did not want the greater diplomatic opprobrium which would come if they had unilaterally rejected the whole Helsinki process, having been so instrumental in its origins.

Despite many early disappointments on the human rights front, there were some achievements. Shortly after the Final Act there was relaxation on the Soviet side, and this resulted in large-scale Jewish emigration; this led both to greater individual freedom and many reunited families. Eastern European "dissidents" varied in their attitudes to Helsinki. Some called on the West to abandon the process. Having failed to get their governments to live up to their undertakings, and having been repressed for it, they wanted the West to end what they saw as a charade. They argued that the Final Act did nothing for human rights in Eastern Europe, while it formalized Soviet territorial domination of the area. But most dissidents argued that Helsinki was an important human rights symbol, which produced some positive results, though these were sometimes at heavy personal cost. The clamping down on the monitoring groups was especially harsh on individuals in Czechoslovakia and the former Soviet Union itself. Nevertheless, these very violations of agreements entered into by governments only served to draw attention to the issue, and raised the political visibility of internation-

ally accepted standards of behaviour with respect to human rights. The publication of the Helsinki Final Act, together with the review conferences, played a part in making the governments of the Soviet bloc accountable on human rights questions. In particular, by stimulating the growth of the monitoring groups armed with their government's open commitment to the principle of "the right of the individual to know and act upon" human rights—Helsinki helped to put these countries on the road to becoming what they called 'normal countries' (in a Western European sense) by the end of the 1980s.

4. Cooperation and Review Conferences

The other Baskets of the Final Act attracted nothing like the same attention as Basket Three. This was particularly the case with Basket Two, the provisions regarding economic and other forms of technical cooperation. As it was, these provisions merely codified something which had already been taking place, to a greater or lesser degree. Expanding such contacts had always been a major Soviet objective in its detente policy, though one about which it became disillusioned as superpower relations deteriorated in the second half of the 1970s. Nor did the former Soviet Union find any solace in Basket Four. As indicated above the subsequent review conferences turned out to be awkward occasions. The US representatives made hard-hitting attacks on human rights violations in the East, and other Western countries joined in.

When the review conferences moved from assessing the Final Act's implementation to the discussion of new proposals, progress proved to be difficult. This was particularly the case with Basket One, which concerned sensitive military security issues. The arrival of Gorbachev as Soviet leader, with his commitment to openness (glasnost) and winding down the military confrontation, began to change this.

5. Confidence-building Measures

Among the main principles listed in Basket One was an undertaking to refrain from the threat or use of force. Basket One also contained a section on confidence-building measures (CBMs). The rather limited CBMs arising out of the Final Act included a binding provision to notify participants of major manoeuvres (involving more than 25,000 troops) and then a voluntary agreement to provide notification of small scale manoeuvres, and to invite observers to these. At subsequent review conferences the Western powers tried to strengthen the military provisions of Basket

One. An agreement for a Conference on Confidence-and Security-Building Measures and Disarmament in Europe (CDE) was eventually agreed, and began in Stockholm in 1984. The first phase of CDE was concerned with confidence-and security-building measures (CSBMs) to reduce the risk of military confrontation in Europe; and in the second phase, it was envisaged that the conference might take up actual disarmament measures. The first proposals of the NATO powers at the CDE consisted of a familiar package requiring the parties to exchange data on forces, to provide notification on major military movements, and to accept onsite inspection. The proposals of the Warsaw Pact forces were equally familiar, including a "no first use" declaration (see *Nuclear Weapons, No First Use of*), a nonaggression pact, a chemical weapon free zone, a nuclear weapon free zone (see *Nuclear Weapon Free Zones: A History and Assessment*), limits on defense budgets, and the notification of manoeuvres. The NATO members considered that the Warsaw Pact proposals were too dependent on voluntary declarations rather than on concrete agreements, while the Warsaw Pact criticized the NATO proposals as being too narrow. Following the breakdown of the Strategic Arms Reduction Talks (START) and the INF talks as a result of the serious deterioration of superpower relations in the previous year, the CDE at the start of 1984 became the only set of arms negotiations in which the superpowers were still talking to each other (see *Nuclear Weapons Abolition*). As such CDE was able in 1986 to be a barometer of the first signs of improving Soviet-US relations following the start of the implementation of Gorbachev's "new political thinking" (see *Glasnost and Perestroika*). Over the next few years, until the dismantling of the Berlin Wall, progress in arms control and disarmament accelerated more quickly than could be accommodated by any of the established forums.

6. The CSCE and the End of the Cold War

The Helsinki process, by the mid-1980s, had shown elements of competition and cooperation, failure and achievement. At the height of the second Cold War, in the first half of the 1980s, it appeared to be going nowhere. In the event, however, it must be identified as one of the causal factors in bringing a peaceful end to the Cold War. The process helped the countries primarily responsible for security in Europe to develop a dialogue of cooperation; it offered a useful framework in the areas of confidence-building and disarmament; and above all it had a significant impact on relations between the countries of Eastern Europe and

Moscow. The diplomatic arena which Helsinki provided for the socialist regimes of the east was important in improving their room for manoeuvre, but even more significant was the support that the process gave to the dissidents, monitoring groups, and developing civil societies in the countries of the Soviet bloc. By empowering civil society in the east of the continent, and helping them reconceive what it meant to live in a "normal country" (especially in terms of human rights). Helsinki played a part in establishing new norms of behaviour—norms which led to the domestic delegitimization of the regimes resting on Moscow's military power. Gorbachev and his supporters recognized and accepted this change. These norms were eventually embraced by the reform regimes that took over in eastern Europe after 1989, namely multiparty democracy, an independent judiciary, political pluralism, the separation of state and political parties and protection for minorities. By its role in helping to socialize the governments and peoples of the Soviet bloc into widely accepted norms of political behaviour and human rights, the Helsinki process undoubtedly played an important—albeit unexpected—role in the ending of the Cold War.

7. From CSCE to OSCE

Whatever the achievements of the Helsinki process, they were secured without the presence of permanent institutions. Those who had attempted to belittle it during the Cold War always dismissed it as merely a 'talking shop' and asked what its telephone and fax number were, and the whereabouts of its troops. From the Paris Summit of 1990 onwards, one of the symbolic markers of "the end of the Cold War," there was therefore an attempt to give this (rather successful) talking shop some institutional flesh, and this was marked by a change in its name. It became the Organization for Security and Cooperation in Europe (OSCE) at the Summit of Heads of States in Budapest in December 1994. As a result of the multiplication of states in a Europe widely defined as stretching from "Vancouver to Vladivostock," the membership of the process became 54 (until it was reduced by one as a result of the suspension of 'Yugoslavia').

Post-Cold War CSCE/OSCE developed the idea of common security that had tenuously grown during the Helsinki process. It worked in three "baskets:" questions relating to security in Europe; cooperation in economics, science and technology, and the environment; and cooperation in humanitarian and other fields. According to the Charter of Paris: "Security is indivisible and the security of every participating State is inseparably linked to that of all the others . . . . We are determined to enhance political consultation and to widen cooperation to solve economic, social, environmental, cultural and humanitarian problems."

The organizational flesh of the expanded Helsinki process grew quickly after 1990. At the highest level are *Summits* between heads of states or governments, to provide overviews of the whole process, every two or possibly three years. Meeting with the same purpose, but at least once a year, is the *Ministerial Council* at the level of Foreign Ministers. This Council constitutes the main decision-making body of the OSCE. Under it, meeting more frequently, and dealing with budgetary planning and current issues is the *Senior Council* (in Prague) which meets once a year as the *Economic Forum*. A *Permanent Council* meets weekly (in Vienna) for regular consultation and decision-making. A Secretary General and Secretariat were set up to support the work of the *Chairman-in-Office*, the rotating political head of OSCE.

In addition to these organizational developments, the period since the Paris Summit has seen the setting up of a number of structures designed to further the common security aims. The most notable are as follows: the *Conflict Prevention Centre* (CPC), based in Prague, with the aim of cooperating and consulting on unusual military activities; the *Forum for Security Cooperation* (FSC), based in Budapest, concerned with the traditional arms control agenda of verification, information-sharing and so on; the *Office of Free Elections* (OFE), based in Warsaw, created to help the democratic process in eastern Europe (which soon became the *Office for Democratic Institutions and Human Rights* (ODIHR) developed to monitor elections, help democracy-building, strengthen civil societies and coordinate with non-governmental organizations); the *High Commission on National Minorities* (HCNM), based in the Hague, to identify and promote the early resolution of tensions that might endanger peace; the *High Level Planning Group* (HLPG), established as part of OSCE's interest in the controversial area of peacekeeping; and finally, a *Parliamentary Assembly* was established as part of an attempt to give the process a more democratic dimension.

As might have been expected, the early fortunes of these new organizations during the turbulent years of the 1990s was mixed. The highest hopes of CSCE/OSCE enthusiasts could not be realistically met, given the complexity of some of the issues, the limited resources at the OSCE's disposal, and the limited experience and embryonic structures of its various bodies. A preliminary balance sheet would identify

the CPC as having contributed to military confidence-building in the region, though not developing very far a 'prevention' infrastructure; the FSC has worked well with other bodies involved in the region's security to further arms control initiatives; ODIHR has been active in monitoring elections (in Bosnia for example) and in developing links with the Permanent Council, allowing early warning of crises (as in its reports on the situation in Belarus); the HCNM has played a part in forestalling potential trouble, in Kazakhstan and Kyrgystan, as well as operating in a range of other countries and quickly proving its relevance for a crucial aspect of the OSCE's future work; the HLPG, operating in one of the most difficult and sensitive areas, that of peacekeeping, has at least identified the parameters of the problem, if not yet advanced effective responses to what in the short-term are insoluble problems; and the Parliamentary Assembly has become increasingly involved in the OSCE's activities. By the mid 1990s the OSCE had organised nine missions in trouble-spots within its region, mostly in eastern Europe and the former Soviet Union, undertaking tasks such as mediation, fact-finding, organising contact-points between parties and establishing language training for minorities. In 1992 it was agreed that the CSCE would act as a regional arrangement under Chapter VIII of the UN Charter, and would act in the region in the front-line tasks of early warning, conflict prevention and crisis management. Not every OSCE initiative met with success; this was most publicly the case during the wars within former Yugoslavia, but it must be added that no other organization's efforts were able to bring that violent imbroglio to a satisfactory conclusion either. Nevertheless, the working framework and missions of the OSCE helped establish a promising—albeit limited—foundation for preventive diplomacy and confidence-building for the vast and varied region stretching from Vancouver to Vladivostok.

8. Assessment

The history of the Helsinki Process, from CSCE to its metamorphosis into OSCE, is one of ironies, inflated hopes, cynicism, unexpected outcomes, false dawns and real achievements. Despite the criticisms of the Helsinki process (and subsequently OSCE) as merely a "talking-shop," without enforcement mechanisms and significant resources, it undoubtedly played a part in the ending of the Cold War. Furthermore, in its OSCE form, it offers a comprehensive approach—because of its broad membership, its common security approach, its various organizational mandates, its links with other international bodies, and its potential flexibility—to dealing with security issues in Europe (both widely defined). The OSCE's task is huge, but if there is one lesson to be learned from the Cold War Helsinki process, it is the desirability of not judging too quickly, or having unrealistic expectations in relation to the size of the task. One undoubted failure remains the 'democratic deficit' of OSCE. It is very much an organization of states. The Helsinki Citizens Assembly was set up as a pan-European dialogue of non-state groups, but its impact through the 1990s has been minimal. Its aim of creating a trans-European civil society and ensuring that a peoples' agenda is heard in the highest councils, and that integration takes place 'from below' must necessarily be long-term.

One indicator of the success of the Helsinki process has been the interest shown by people in other regions of the world in translating its comprehensive common security approach to their own troubled situations. There has been talk, at the diplomatic level, of adopting the Helsinki process, which began in Cold War Europe and metamorphosed into a post-Cold War instrument, as a model. Today's security issues across the world are multiple and serious, and they cannot always be dealt with successfully in the short term. What is certain is that a successful strategy for dealing with them will require the comprehensive agenda (dealing with the environment as well as arms control and the breakdown of peace) the multi-level approach (dealing with minorities as well as states), the adaptive style (from CSCE to OSCE) and the common security approach (developing habits of cooperation) that characterised the complex evolution of the Helsinki process from its unpromising origins during the Cold War.

See also: *Collective Security and Collective Self-defence; Role of Europe in the Management of Global Problems*

Bibliography ————————————————

Flanagan S 1979 The CSCE and the development of detente. In: Leebaert D (ed.) 1979 *European Security: Prospects for the 1980s*. Health, Lexington, Massachusetts

Flynn G A 1976 The content of European detente. *Orbis* 20

Garthoff R L 1985 *Detente and Confrontation: American-Soviet Relations from Nixon to Reagan*. Brookings Institution, Washington, DC

Goodby J 1985 Security for Europe: Stockholm revisited. *NATO Rev.* 33(5)

Holst J J 1983 Confidence-building measures: A conceptual framework. *Survival* 15(1)

Kemp W A 1996 *The OSCE in a new context. European Security Towards the Twenty-first Century*. Royal Institute of International Affairs, Discussion Paper, London

Luxmore J 1986 *The Helsinki Agreement: Dialogue or Delusion?* Institute for European Defence and Strategic Studies, Occasional Paper No 20, London

Mastny V (ed.) 1986 *Helsinki, Human Rights and European Security*. Duke University Press, Durham, North Carolina

Mersesca J J 1985 *To Helsinki: The Conference on Security and Cooperation in Europe, 1973-1975*. Duke University Press, Durham, North Carolina

Medvedev R 1980 *On Soviet Dissent*. Columbia University Press, New York

KEN BOOTH

Henri IV

Henri IV (1553-1610), first Bourbon king of France, promulgated one of the earliest plans for achieving perpetual peace in Europe. His rise to the French throne took place during the Wars of Religion, a series of bloody civil conflicts which racked France almost continuously between 1562 and 1598. One by one, during these wars, the males of the ruling Valois dynasty died without heirs, until in 1584 only the childless Henry III remained. This development left the head of the related Bourbon family, the future Henri IV, the heir apparent to the French throne.

The Bourbon Henri's situation was complicated, however, by the fact that he had been raised in the Protestant faith. His royal blood, his enormous wealth, and his ability combined to make him the natural leader of the Protestant faction in the wars which were convulsing predominantly Catholic France. The prospect of this heretic taking the throne intensified the wars, as Catholic extremists formed a Holy League dedicated to blocking his ascension at any price. As the French monarchy was being torn apart in the struggle between the Protestants and the League, Henri III was assassinated by a partisan of the League in 1589.

This murder made Henri IV the nominal king of France, but the League, with Spanish backing, refused to recognize his legitimacy. The Wars of Religion ground pitilessly on. Even after Henri sought to conciliate Catholic opinion by publicly abandoning his Protestant faith and converting to Catholicism in

1593, diehard resistance remained. Not until 1598 did the wars finally come to an end, as the last of the Leaguers reluctantly made their peace with Henri IV.

Intelligent, affable, witty, and easygoing, Henri is the most fondly remembered of all France's kings. His rule featured substantial tolerance of religious diversity and attempts to improve the standard of living of France's wretched peasants. In addition, he largely ended the disorder which had made life in France so terrifying and dangerous for so many years. Henri IV did a great deal to restore the prestige and authority of France's battered crown, beginning the process of taming its turbulent, violence-prone aristocracy.

Henri IV is also remembered, not altogether accurately, as a king who preferred peaceful progress to the glory of war and conquest. One reason for this reputation is the the fact that after achieving power in 1598 he kept France out of war for the next twelve years. His peaceful foreign policy, however, appears to have been due more to his recognition of the fact that France needed a period of rest and recovery than to any commitment to peace for its own sake. Indeed, Henri never ceased to plot against the power of the rival house of Hapsburg in Europe. His apologists frequently overlook the fact that in 1610 he actually declared war on the Hapsburgs. Only his death at the hands of a fanatical Catholic assassin a few weeks later prevented a conflict which would have shattered the peace of Europe.

Henri's reputation as a man of peace also rests upon a remarkable plan ascribed to him posthumously by his chief minister, the Duc de Sully. After Henri's death, Sully, in retirement, published a memoir of the reign. In his work he asserted that Henri had had a "grand design" for establishing perpetual peace in Europe once the house of Hapsburg had been humbled. While scholars have concluded that this plan was more the work of Sully himself than of Henri, it still stands out as a fascinating attempt to come to grips with the international violence then endemic to Europe.

The grand design entailed refashioning Europe into a "Christian Commonwealth" composed of 15 states. Most of the existing major European states would continue to exist, but would do so with altered boundaries. According to the grand design, Henri favored boundaries based on language, so that all English-speaking people would live under the king of England, all French-speaking people under himself, all Czechs in a new Czech state, and so on. While this plan seems to anticipate the rise of the modern nation-state, critics have pointed out that the main beneficiary of such a redrawing of boundaries in the early seventeenth century would have been Henri himself. Conversely, those who would have lost the most territory and power would have been Henri's rivals, the Hapsburgs.

The grand design further proposed that these 15 states form an international assembly composed of 66 representatives, apportioned among them on the basis of population. These representatives would serve for three year terms. They would deliberate on the problems facing Europe, and would arbitrate all disputes between the 15 states. They would thus provide a forum in which the rulers of Europe could redress their grievances without going to war.

This grand design first appeared in a rather disorganized form with the publication of Sully's memoirs in 1638, at a time when Europe was in the grip of the devastating Thirty Years War. It quickly became famous, as the idea that a king as prestigious as Henri IV had come up with a plausible scheme for the elimination of such wars caught the imagination of people weary of endless strife. Republished in a more organized and accessible form in 1745, and appearing in English translation in 1756, the scheme continued to exercise the imagination of people in the eighteenth century. Indeed, the famous French philosopher Jean-Jacques Rousseau (see *Rousseau, Jean Jacques*) used it as a starting point for his own examination of the problem of peace. Even down to our own century the influence of the grand design has been felt. When Robert Cecil was writing the charter of the League of Nations after the First World War, he stressed that this seventeenth century scheme of Henri IV and Sully was one of the inspirations behind his own efforts.

See also: *League of Nations*

Bibliography —————————————————

Andrieux M 1954 *Henri IV dans ses années pacifiques*. Paris
Butler G 1920 *Studies in Statecraft*. Cambridge
Cook B W (ed.) 1972 *Peace Projects of the Seventeenth Century*. Garland, New York
Lenox C 1819 *Memoirs of Maximilian de Bethune, Duc of Sully*. Edinburgh
Pfister C 1894 Les "Economies Royales" de Sully et le Grand Dessein de Henri Quatre. *Revue Historique*
York E 1919 *Leagues of Nations: Ancient, Mediaeval, and Modern*. Swarthmore Press, London

GARRETT L. McAINSH

Hugo, Victor

Victor Marie Hugo, France's greatest poet, was born at Besançon on February 26, 1802. He had two older brothers, Abel and Eugène. Their father, Léopold Hugo, was an army colonel, later becoming a general. Until his marriage irrevocably disintegrated, Léopold enjoyed having his wife and children near him, with the result that the future poet, as a boy, traveled extensively, developing in the process a taste for the exotic that would characterize much of his work and gaining a decidedly international outlook.

Victor's mother, Sophie Hugo, was a Bourbonist, and Victor, who lived with her, initially shared her political convictions. Soon he was sprinkling those convictions into poems and, with them, was winning attention, prizes, and a small pension. With Abel he founded his first newspaper, the *Conservateur littéraire* (1819-21). His *Odes et poésies diverses,* soon to become *Odes et ballades,* appeared in 1822. He was in love, and his new success, plus the pension, allowed him to marry Adèle Foucher. From this point on, Hugo was an established man of letters. His play *Hernani,* first performed to a tumultuous audience on February 25, 1830 was an enormous success, thus assuring the triumph of French Romantic drama. Five months later came the July Revolution and with it a new king, Louis Philippe d'Orléans. Hugo switched political loyalties, courted the heir and heiress to the throne, and fared even better than he had done under the Bourbons. The new regime censored some of his plays, to be sure, but so had the previous one. The year 1841 saw his election to the Académie Française, and in 1845 he was made a Peer of France. When the July Monarch fell in 1848, he made speeches to save it. The speeches fell on deaf ears, and the Second Republic was proclaimed. Hugo then did what his conscience or his ambition dictated and discovered that he was a republican. There is even reason to believe that he entertained serious hopes of becoming the Second Republic's president. Failing that, he hoped to play a major role in the new government's executive branch. Like Chateaubriand and Lamartine, he coveted such a role more than he would have admitted. Unlike them, he never attained it even temporarily.

With his sons and two or three associates, he headed another newspaper, *L'Evénement,* socialistic in tone. Returning from exile in the United Kingdom, Louis Napoleon Bonaparte easily won the presidency when elections were held in December. For a moment, Hugo's optimism soared. But when the new president offered him no position he considered commensurate with his abilities, he petulantly hurled himself into the innocuous but noisy opposition. At first he attacked the new chief executive in his newspaper. *L'Evénement* assailed the Prince-President's policies and was banned. Several of the newspaper's staff members, including the author's two sons, were tried, fined, and sentenced to short prison terms. With his paper silenced, the circumvented author raised his voice elsewhere, belaboring the Prince-President in the National Assembly. He was in an anomalous position, however. He had made a speech in the Chamber of Peers in 1847 favoring permitting the Bonapartes to return to France. Perhaps more than any other individual writer, he had created the Napoleonic "legend" and now he found himself irrevocably at odds with the head of the Bonaparte family. He tried to make his stance credible by drawing a distinction between "Napoleon the Great" and "Napoleon the Little," but his position was hardly tenable. Sensing that the nation approved, the Prince-President moved on December 2, 1851, to extend his powers. A plebiscite endorsed his action, and in short order he was proclaimed Napoleon III. The nation had expressed its will, but the thwarted poet screamed that it had been betrayed, made shrill, incendiary declarations, issued proclamations, and scuttled away into exile.

On several occasions he declined to return, declaring that he would come back when freedom did. From 1859 onward he was free to return whenever he wished, and eventually his wife and sons did so. Except for those attacking the government, his books continued to be published, sold, and read in France, and he lived comfortably on their income. At first he resided in Brussels, then settled on the island of Jersey. While there he lent his name to a vehement protest when Queen Victoria paid a state visit to Napoleon III, and he was expelled (1855). He then moved to Guernsey, where he lived for the remainder of his "exile." During these years he made appeals on behalf of liberal causes (John Brown, Garibaldi) and experimented with the occult. Meanwhile, he impotently flayed the Emperor with *Histoire d'un crime* (1852) and *Napoléon le petit* (1852) in prose and, in verse, with *Les Châtiments* (1853). When the disastrous, Franco-Prussian War led to the Second Empire's overthrow and the proclamation of the Third Republic, he rushed back to Paris and the center of the political arena. As usual, his dream of wielding supreme, even dictatorial, power was urging him on, as his intimate writings make clear. As usual also, the chief role eluded him, and he succeeded only in getting elected to the National Assembly, where he sat with the radicals. He seemed out of place, made speeches that were considered absurd, and resigned. Disgruntled and not much happier with the Third Republic than he had been with the Empire, he went back to Guernsey, but unable to accept viewing events from this distance, returned to Paris on July 30, 1873. Three years later he was elected to the Senate.

Hugo's last years, as productive as the earlier ones had been, saw the publication of new novels, verse, drama, orations. The writer died a deist, without the Catholic Church's final ministrations and rites, on May 22, 1885. The state funeral that the government awarded him was an international event, and he was interred, in Paris, in the Pantheon.

Like his parents before him, Hugo had a problematical married life. To his children he was a devoted father, but he proved to be a difficult husband. Egocentric in the extreme, he was hard to live with. At one point his friend, the literary critic Sainte-Beuve, fell in love with Adèle Hugo, whose physical intimacy with her husband had already ceased. Eventually the romance, which lasted until 1837, ended the two men's friendship. Hugo thus had a made-to-order pretext for giving free rein to his extramarital amorous propensities. The actress Juliette Drouet, whom he met in 1833, could be described as his official mistress, and the liaison lasted until her death in 1883. There were countless other mistresses, however, including Juliette's maid. When Adèle Hugo left Guernsey in 1865, Juliette moved into Hauteville House, the poet's residence on the island, as lady of the manor.

Misfortune also struck the poet's household in other ways. Several times, for example, a strain of mental disorder in the family manifested itself in his lifetime. In addition, both of Hugo's sons died before their father. Hugo's greatest heartbreak, though, came when his favorite child, Léopoldine, not long after her marriage, drowned with her husband in 1843.

Hugo was the center of his world, not a rare phenomenon among individuals who crave unlimited power. Politically he was incompetent, but he did not know this nor would he have believed it, and he continued to hunger for vast authority, at the same time vituperating against those who did. In short, he was as uncompromising in his political beliefs, especially during the last 35 years of his life, as his foes were. Yet, when he chose to do so, he could display a generous attitude toward those who took positions contrary to his own. The compassionate "A Henri V" (L'Année terrible, 1872) is addressed to the Comet de Chambord, the Bourbon pretender to a lost throne. Likewise, he called for amnesty, in a Senate speech, for individuals who had been active in the Commune, a short, fanatical rebellion against the Third Republic in the spring of 1871. His plea came too late, though, the purge having virtually spent itself. His humanitarianism, sometimes misdirected, was nonetheless sincere, and he seldom hesitated to champion a cause he believed in. He had a very real artistic talent as well, and sometimes used it to express his deep humanitarian commitments. Reversing the usual trend, as he grew older he became ever more liberal, ever more radical. He died a militant anticlerical.

The public, by and large, had little interests in his political stances or in his causes but nevertheless read his books. If his character and deeds are marked by reversal and antitheses, so is his work. It is also characterized by exuberance, robust imagination, and facility, not to mention a flair for exoticism noted earlier. If on the whole his psychology is superficial, his undeniable power to bewitch his readers with sheer verbal skill almost compensates for the flaw and even makes one willing to overlook his philosophical pretentiousness and visionary absurdities as well. Essentially he remained a Romantic to the end.

Hugo's vast literary output embraces nearly every genre and expresses the author's ideas on a plethora of topics, reflecting his inconsistencies and, in some cases, his very real evolution. Extraordinarily unequal in quality, it has more breadth than depth. Among the prose works there are short stories such as the admirable "Claude Gueux" (1834), which foreshadows episodes in the later Les Misérables. Considered as a whole, the novels are their author's weakest title to fame. Among them should be mentioned Nôtre-Dame de Paris (1831), which consecrated French Romanticist's penchant for the Middle Ages and, in the person of Quasimodo, gave readers an unforgettable example of the sublime and the grotesque, a noble heart encased in a hideous body. Les Misérables (1862), a better move in spite of its length and the tedious, overworked pathos, treated innocent love, social injustice, and revolution. Quatre-vingt-treize (1874) presents the novelist's concept of the French Revolution and affirms his contention that, whatever its methods, its aims were ultimately noble and that whatever had to be done to realize them was thus not only permissible but even laudable.

Hugo's best plays are superior to the novels. Cromwell (1827), too long to be staged, was published with a preface that came to be looked upon as a Romantic manifesto, expounding the writer's doctrine that to the three ages of humankind's development corresponded the lyric, the epic, and the *drama* and that the *drame*, as modern literature's most appropriate expression, must break with French Classicism and achieve true "realism." by mixing the comic and the serious, the "grotesque" and the "sublime" *Hernani* (1830) and *Ruy Blas* (1838), set in Spain in the early sixteenth and late seventeenth centuries, are the best examples of their writer's dramatic art, although there is much to be said for the considerably later *Torquemada* (1869, publ. 1882) and the posthumous *Théâtre en liberté* (1886). There were others as well, most of them brimming over with love complications, poison, plots, and violence. While it was *Hernani*, interestingly enough, that had secured the stage for Romanticism in 1830, it was another Hugo play that was destined to drive Romanticism from it. Filled with the author's stock devices and excesses, *Les Burgraves*, performed at the Comédie Française in March 1843, was more than the weary theatergoing public could take, and it reacted. Amid loud booing, the play was withdrawn.

But Hugo's real achievement lies in poetry. What Balzac did for the French novel, Hugo did for verse. Not even the author's exaggerated posturing or his solemn contention that poets, himself in particular, are priests ("La Function du poète") immunizes a reader against the lines' magic spell. Starting with the *Odes* in 1822, numerous collections of verse flowed from his pen, each new volume revealing an increased mastery of the art of versification, manifested especially in the poet's progressive liberation of the Alexandrine and in a heightened, more compelling lyricism. There were *Les Orientales* (1829), *Les Feuilles d'automne* (1831), *Les Chants du crépuscule* (1835), *Les Voix intérieures* (1837), *Les Rayons et les ombres* (1840), *Les Contemplations* (1856), *Les Chansons des rues et des bois* (1865), *L'Art d'être grand-père* (1877), *La Légende des siècles* (1859, 1877, 1883), to posthumous *Toute la lyre* (1888, 1893), to name the most important. Faced with having to select one masterpiece, most readers would choose *Les Contemplations*.

Hugo admired his father, General Hugo, and referred to him as "that hero with the smile so gentle," praising his magnanimous behavior even to an unchivalrous enemy ("Aprés la bataille"). It was General Hugo's name that he gave to the child that was to become his favorite, Léopoldine. Hugo's uncle, Louis Hugo, was also a general. While not interested in a professional military career, Hugo was

a member of the National Guard at the time of the Revolution of 1830. His exaltation of heroic warriors in *La Légende des siècles* and elsewhere and the unstinted hatred he came to feel for the Germans who occupied France in 1870 and 1871 would preclude his automatically being considered a champion of peace. Yet there were moments when a yearning for peace appeared to take possession of him. In such poems such as "Depuis six mille ans la guerre" (*Chansons des rues et des bois*), he could be moved by the sight of mothers and their children and inveigh against war, wondering how, as one contemplates nature at dawn, one could consider marching away to annihilate one's fellow man:

Et l'aube est là sur la plaine!
Oh! j'admire, en vérité,
Qu'on puisse avoir de la haine
Quad l'alouette a chanté.

Similarly, as the Crimean War ended in 1856, Hugo seemed to be calling for a new era of universal peace, declaring that the poet, taking Peace as his muse, must put an end to war:

La muse est aujourd'hui la Paix, ayant les reins
Sans cuirasse et le front sous les épis sereins;
Le poète à la Mort dit: Meurs, guerre, omber, envie!
Et chasse doucement les hommes vers la vie . . . .

As early as the preface to *Les Burgraves* (1843), Hugo had declared that nations are all made of the same stuff and have identical goals. Poets have all countries, indeed have the whole of civilization, as their homeland. In time, the writer hoped, all people would be like poets and the entire world as their domain.

Several years later an International Peace Conference met in Paris, convening on August 21, 1849. Hugo was elected its president. His opening speech, which received a certain amount of press attention, he published with the simple title "Discours d'ouverture" although to some it is known as "The United States of Europe." Excerpts from it have been published in recent times in Marcel Merle's anthology, *Pacificisme et internationalisme* (1966) (see *Peace and Regional Integration; Internationalization*), and a truncated, misleading version appeared in Albert Fua's *La Voix de Victor Hugo dans la Guerre Mondiale* (1920). The complete text is to be found in Hugo's *Avant l'exil*. To the assembled delegates Hugo stated that universal peace is a "religious thought" emanating from God, whose law is peace not war. Deploring the immense sums nations squander, as he saw it, on armaments, he urged that, on the contrary, these sums be devoted to trade and research, agriculture, science, and arts. With the advent of universal peace would necessarily come universal happiness, universal prosperity. He predicted that the time would come when wars between nations would be as inconceivable as wars between Boston and Philadelphia, and when cannon, having become obsolete, would be relegated to museums. The only battlefields then would be "markets opening up to commerce and minds opening up to ideas." When this happens, bullets and bombs will be replaced by votes, and one senate will govern all of Europe (see *Peace and Democracy*). The United States of America and the United States of Europe, joining hands across the sea, will collaborate to bring about the common good. Carried away by his enthusiasm, the orator did not take Asia and Africa into account, except to affirm, vaguely, that "Africa would be restored to mankind" and that "Asia would be restored to civilization." Three days later the conference adjourned. As it did so, Hugo again addressed the delegates, urging them to replace vengeance, fanaticism, and war with reconciliation, tolerance, and peace (see *Tolerance in an Age of Conflict*). He concluded by expressing the hope that August 24, 1849 would mark the end of strife and the beginning of world concord and peace. Both speeches brought resounding cheers. Théodore Ruyssen has described the opening address as being "perhaps the finest page in all of pacifist literature."

With a final section called "Déclaration de paix," Hugo's *Paris*, which the author dated May 1867, was released as the Paris Exposition was opening its doors. The war between Prussia and Austria had ended, and the writer liked to think that the nations participating were doing so in a spirit of concord. All railroads, he pointed out, were headed in the same direction, toward peace. The world's future lies not in hatred but in agreement, he told his readers. Nations must lay down their arms and unite. Nothing can reduce the momentum of the forces bringing this about. Hugo stressed what he took to be the spiritual closeness linking France and Germany. Two years later he would attend another peace conference, this one held in Lausanne, Switzerland. Meanwhile, on July 14, 1868, he planted in his garden a tree that he called the United States of Europe tree.

But the poet's thinking was soon to undergo a serious alteration. The change came about when Prussia and its allies prostrated his country. Once war became an immediate, personal experience involving France, the poet's attitude veered dramatically. In *L'Année terrible* (1872) he could in principle extol peace and deplore "horrible" war ("L'Avenir"), but at the same time he exhorted his countrymen to continue to fight and not accept a dishonorable peace. "We have to fight," he reminded them ("Juin II"), and he called upon God not to allow France to fall into what he called the "abyss," his view of the peace terms the Germans were offering ("Avast la conclusion du traité").

On the floor of the National Assembly he delivered a fiery yet visionary speech on war (March 1, 1871). In it he asserted that France would rise again and that the world would see it, sword in hand, repossessing Alsatia and Lorraine and then seizing the entire left bank of the Rhine River. That done, France would be magnanimous. There would be peace, boundaries would be erased, and the United States of Europe would spring into being. It does not seem to have occurred to the speaker that Germany might demur at France's incorporating it into a United States of Europe, having abolished its boundaries.

When the 1874 International Peace Conference was held in Geneva, Hugo was invited but did not attend. Understandably, he was less exuberant about peace than he had been in 1849, when the only territories occupied by foreign powers were at a distance. Now Germany had gone to war with France, had defeated it, and had annexed two French provinces. Hugo sent the Peace Conference a message. Significantly, he called it "La Question de la paix remplacée par la question de la guerre." Admittedly, he told the delegates, he now had reservations about peace. "A crime against France has been committed," he informed them. The loss of French land was unacceptable, and war must result. Not until the wrong had been redressed would there be brotherhood and peace. Again, however, the poet predicted an ultimate United States of Europe. The message was included in *Depuis l'exil*, as was another message the following year, when the poet wrote the delegates that his hopes for peace would have to be "postponed."

See also: *Peace Movements of the Nineteenth Century; Just War; Just War Theory*

Bibliography ————————————

Barny R 1994 "L'Evolution idéologique de Hugo vue à travers les thèmes de l'Europe, de la paix et de la guerre" and "Guerre et paix dans *Les Misérables.*" *Annales littéraires de l'Université de Besançon*, No. 539

Baudouin C 1972 *Psychanalyse de Victor Hugo*. Armand Colin, Paris

Fua A 1920 *La Voix de Victor Hugo dans la Guerre Mondiale.* Delagrave, Paris

Hugo V 1843 Préface, *Les Burgraves. Théâtre, II.* Gallimard, Paris

Hugo V 1849-74 *Actes et paroles: Avant l'exil, après l'exil.* Nelson, Paris

Hugo V 1867 *Littérature et philosophie mêlées.* Nelson, Paris

Hugo V 1972 *The United States of Europe.* Garland, New York

Juin H 1980-84 *Victor Hugo*, 2 vols. Flammarion, Paris

Kahn J F 1984 *L'Extraordinaire métamorphose ou 5 ans de la vie de Victor Hugo 1847-1851*

Maurois A 1956 *Victor Hugo.* Cape, London

Merle M 1966 *Pacifisme et internationalisme.*

Richardson J 1976 *Victor Hugo.* St Martin's Press, New York

Saurat D 1948 *Victor Hugo et les dieux du peuple.* Editions du Vieux Colombier, Paris

HARRY REDMAN, JR.

Human Nature Theories of War

Is war natural?—This is the basic question that human nature theories of war address. They investigate whether there is something particular about human beings that compels them to act aggressively towards other human beings, that dictates social groups to live in conflict with other social groups, and that forces states to wage war against other states. And since the question of causality is intimately linked to the question of prevention, these theories also ask whether aggression, conflict and war are necessary, inevitable and ineradicable, or whether there is hope to cure these ills by changing human nature, placing violent instincts under restraints, or providing more acceptable and less damaging outlets for innate aggression (see *War*).

1. The Argument

The causes of war can be analysed on different levels of social complexity. Introducing three images to the study of international politics, Kenneth Waltz (1959) found explanations for the existence of war "within man, within the structure of the separate states, (and) within the state system." Although one might easily imagine more levels of analysis, this scheme is a useful tool to systematise the major causes of international conflict.

First-image theories localise the primary causes of war in the nature and behaviour of man. Wars result from egoism, aggressiveness and stupidity, be it on the individual level of certain decision makers or on the general level of humankind (see *War: Environmental and Biological Theories*). The former is analysed by decision making theories, the latter by human nature theories of war. Other causes, both approaches argue, are secondary and have to be interpreted in light of these more basic factors. Even if, the argument goes, humans lived in other social forms than states and even if the international system was not anarchic, there would still be war since it originates from the ineradicable defects of mankind (see *Anarchy, International*).

Although adherents to this kind of theory agree on the identification of root causes, they disagree about the political consequences they draw. Optimists argue that if the primary causes of war are on the individual level, the elimination of war can be achieved through enlightening humans or rearranging their psycho-social order. Pessimists on the other hand, while accepting the optimists' idea in principle, reject the possibility of achieving it. War can not be abolished, they maintain, because human nature can not be changed.

Leo Tolstoy, who regarded human warfare as an inevitable necessity, represents the pessimistic standpoint. In an article published in 1868, he concluded that people kill each other in war because they have to fulfil "an elemental zoological law which bees fulfil when they kill each other in autumn, and which causes male animals to destroy one another" (Tolstoy 1966). In a similar vein, psychologist William James (1911) traced the existence of war to "the rooted bellicosity of human nature" and its "innate pugnacity." Yet contrary to Tolstoy, William was an optimist and saw a way to a more peaceful world in establishing a "moral equivalent of war." This would require the "military conscription of the whole youthful population" for a certain number of years during which the draftees would be forced to dig mines, wash dishes, build roads, and construct skyscrapers. Physical labour, James believed, would work as cathartic experience and the young men would return "into society with healthier sympathies and soberer ideas."

Optimism and pessimism are a matter of degree, of course. Yet they point to the fact that adopting a human-nature theory of war may lead to agreement over the causes of war, but may spark disagreement over their interpretation and even prompt contradictory policy conclusions.

2. The Tradition

The argument that the causes of war lay in human nature is neither modern nor European in origin. Instead, it has a long tradition in various cultural spheres (see *Cultural Roots of Peace*).

Most often, however, it is attributed to the Christian doctrine of original sin. St. Augustine (1948) taught that man's "love of so many vain and hurtful things" as quarrels, murders and wars stems from his fallenness from God. Since man is part of the evil empire, his mind and body are inherently defective (see *Peace in the Middle Ages*). "For though there have never been wanting . . . hostile nations beyond the empire, against whom wars have been and are waged, yet, supposing there were no such nations, the very extent of the empire itself has produced wars of a more obnoxious description." Until today the belief that human sinfulness is the root cause of war is a powerful idea that has influenced many political theorists of the realist school (Niebuhr 1953; Morgenthau 1954) (see *Religion and Peace*).

Beyond this line of thought a similar argument has been elaborated in the philosophy of Spinoza. For Spinoza, however, it is not sin but the dualism of passion and reason that is the source of political ills. Whereas human beings guided by reason live in harmony and cooperation, humans led by passion are drawn into conflict. According to Spinoza (1951), reason may moderate passion, but who thinks that man "can ever be induced to live according to the bare dictate of reason, must be dreaming of the poetic golden age, or of a stage-play."

While Spinoza hoped for the improvement of politics through the prevalence of reason, Thomas Hobbes regarded a strong government, the Leviathan, as the only chance to guard human desires. Having established three principal causes of quarrel in the human nature—competition, diffidence, and glory—Hobbes identified the state of nature as a state of war: "Hereby it is manifest, that during the time men live without a common Power to keep them all in awe, they are in that condition which is called War; and such a War, as is of every man, against every man" (Hobbes 1985) (see *Power*). Although Hobbes does not refer to international war in this context, his philosophy has informed many theories of international politics and interstate conflict.

That this line of thought is not only an occidental tradition, however, is evidenced by Confucius who taught that "there is deceit and cunning and from these wars arise." After all, the ubiquity of this idea seems to indicate that attributing the causes of war to human nature is in itself an obvious if not a natural assumption.

3. The Theories

With the development of modern science, various academic disciplines have taken up this tradition of thought. They have further elaborated the idea of human pugnacity and have turned it into scientific theories. In this respect, the most important disciplines for the study of war and peace are psychology, biology, and anthropology.

3.1 Psychology

When Sigmund Freud, the founder of psychoanalysis, first took up the issue of war in 1915, he did so in a pessimistic mood. War, he found, is a "natural thing" with a "good biological basis." That is the reason why war "can not be abolished" (Freud 1957a). By 1932, however, Freud had changed his position gradually. Though he still regarded war "in practice to be scarcely avoidable," he now hoped that "human aggressive impulses" and the "instinct for hatred and destruction" could be diverted or displaced by civilization so that "they need not find expression in war" (Freud 1957b) (see *Psychology of Peace*).

The reason for this change of opinion is the development of Freud's theory of drives (Trieblehre). In 1915, Freud hesitated to acknowledge the existence of an autonomous aggressive instinct, since this would have invalidated the basic dualism on which many of his ideas were founded. In 1920, however, Freud contrived the drive of regression (Regressionstrieb) which he claimed to consist of two opposing elements: the life drive, or Eros, and the death drive, later called Thanatos. While the life drive seeks to preserve and to unite, the death drive aims to end all longing and tension by death. Theses drives do not exist in isolation, but interact and modify each other. So the death drive can be redirected from the inside where it is about to destroy the individual to the outside. Overt aggression is thus the result of inward aggression being redirected toward others. It took ten years until Freud used—reluctantly, it seems—this theory to explain international conflict. In a letter to Albert Einstein he attributed war to the deep-seated unconscious death drive and remained ambivalent about the question of prevention. While in principle it might be possible to suppress human aggressiveness, this could also direct the impulse inwards again and lead to self destruction.

Many psychologist writing in the psychoanalytical tradition have stressed this dilemma. War may be dreadful, but it serves as an outlet for individual aggression; peace may be desirable, but it threatens the individual's mental balance. This tragic element in the psychological perception of human aggressiveness justifies the conceptualisation of war as a "paranoid elaboration or mourning" (Fornari 1975).

3.2 Biology

Within the discipline of biology, ethologists study the behaviour of animals. Some ethologists have drawn analogies between animal behaviour and human behaviour arguing that man is the product of two million years of biological evolution. Strictly speaking, humans are nothing but intelligent animals and have to be analysed with the same scientific methods. Theories explaining animal aggression, therefore, also explain human aggression (Eibl-Eiblsfeld 1979).

For Konrad Lorenz (1966) the concept of aggression refers to intra-specific fighting, rather than to the killing of animals of other species for food. Aggression, Lorenz argues, is a biological instinct that ensures not only the survival of the individual but, more importantly, the survival of the species. Aggression has four main functions: (i) it keeps a balance between population and resources like territory and food; (ii) it aids to defend the young; (iii) it contributes to the survival of the fittest through sexual selection; (iv) it stabilises social relations through the creation of dominant-subordinate systems.

Aggression among animals is highly ritualised and rarely leads to killing. Aggression among human beings, however, lacks the mechanisms preventing slaughter. Lorenz identifies man as the only species that habitually kills his own kind (see *Aggression*). He argues that ". . . it is more than probable that the destructive intensity of the aggression drive . . . is the consequence of a process of intra-specific selection which worked on our forefathers for roughly forty thousand years, that is, throughout the Early Stone Age. When man had reached the stage of having weapons, clothing, and social organisation, so overcoming the dangers of starving, freezing and being eaten by wild animals, and these dangers ceased to be the essential factors influencing selection, an evil intra-specific selection must have set in. The factor influencing selection was now the wars waged between hostile neighbouring tribes" (Lorenz 1966).

Thus, in the ethologist's view, aggression is an innate drive for which man must seek release, but "for which in the social order of today he finds no adequate outlet." It is futile, Lorenz maintains, to suppress the instinct by prohibition or punishment, but it is possible to find substitutes like sport and other measures which can soften the impulse. While there is

disagreement whether aggression needs an external stimulus to be released or whether it can discharge spontaneously, ethologists agree that the main source of aggression is internal and that human warfare is the product of the biological evolution of humankind.

3.3 Anthropology

Anthropologists have questioned the assumptions of both psychologists and biologists. They argue that war is not the product of biological, but rather cultural evolution. Nevertheless, war is still regarded as natural in the sense that it is genuinely linked to humans as society-building creatures (Fox 1992/93).

For quite some time anthropologists have studied peoples, like the Eskimos or the Bushmen, who never go to war (Thomas 1959). Margaret Mead (1964) concluded from this that war is not a natural instinct, but a social invention. Peoples "go to war if they have the invention, just as peoples who have the custom of dueling will have dueling and peoples who have the patterns of vendetta will indulge in vendetta." Thus, Mead denies that war is a natural necessity. But the problem is, that "once an invention is made which proves congruent with human needs or social forms, it tends to persist." Consequently, war can only be abolished if a new institution is invented that substitutes the valued function war has performed so far.

For anthropologists the key to the explanation of war is the change in the social and cultural environment after the agrarian revolution. Richard Leaky (1981) argues that "as soon as people commit themselves to agricultural food production as against nomadic food gathering . . . they commit themselves to defending the land they farm." War, then, is the result of a new stage of social development that made the ability to fight mandatory. This in turn required large communities, strong political organisations, efficient taxation systems, and powerful military organisations. Thus, the agrarian revolution and the military revolution reinforced each other producing ever more powerful and militant societies.

This development, however, is not necessarily doomed to end in catastrophe. Ernest Gellner (1991) argues that while in the first stage of human development violence was contingent and optional, in the second stage violence indeed became pervasive, mandatory and normative. Today, however, humankind may be entering a third stage where "violence becomes once again optional, counter-productive, and probably fatal."

4. The Critique

While each theory outlined above can be criticised

individually for both the soundness of their methods and the validity of their results, some general remarks on possible lines of criticism must suffice at this point.

4.1 Feminism

Adherents of human nature theories of war agree that the primary causes of war originate in the nature of man (see *Feminism and Peace*). From a feminist standpoint the question arises how this applies to women. For it is evident, as Virginia Woolf (1938) put it, that "scarcely a human being in the course of history has fallen to a woman's rifle; the vast majority of birds and beasts have been killed by you, not by us." Thus, human nature theories of war can be criticised for not differentiating between man and woman, for falsely identifying masculine aggressiveness with human pugnacity, and for disregarding the more peaceful nature of women (Harris/ King 1989). Even feminists, however, have questioned the assumption that women are innately pacifist and more peaceable by nature than men (Enloe 1983).

4.2 Political Science

Human nature theories claim to be able to explain war; but what about peace? If it were true that war derives from the innate aggressiveness that is part of the nature of mankind, then warfare should be the permanent state of affairs. Yet war, conflict and aggression are not constant in space and time. Critics from the field of political science have argued, therefore, that the argument is flawed since it does not meet the falsifiability criterion of scientific theories. While human nature may play a role in bringing about war, "it cannot by itself explain both war and peace, except by the simple statement that man's nature is such that sometimes he fights and sometimes he does not" (Waltz 1959).

Even if we assume that there is a natural impulse of aggression, other critics add, we cannot easily extrapolate from that impulse to social conflict and international war (see *International Relations and Peace Studies*). What is missing in most human nature theories of war, then, is the differentiation between aggressiveness, conflict and war, that is, of discord and violence on different levels of social complexity. Unless these levels are thoroughly investigated in their own right and then analytically interrelated, the equations of aggressiveness and war remain "simple analogies between one level and another (that) tell us little or nothing about causation" (Hinde 1993).

4.3 History

War, as treated by human nature theories of war, is a static unchanging event. Yet wars are heterogeneous. Major wars and small wars, ethnic conflict and border clashes need different explanations. Moreover, historians argue, war has changed considerably over time and cannot simply be analysed as a social constant. Especially modern warfare has become an institution with rules and norms prescribing 'appropriate' behaviour and confining individual aggressiveness.

Hence, military historians have repudiated the premise of human nature theories of war that war between states is the result of irrational and emotive actors following their dark drives. "Men have fought (during the past two hundred years) neither because they are aggressive nor because they are acquisitive animals, but because they are reasoning ones" (Howard 1984). There is hardly a war that is not the result of "conscious and reasoned decisions based on the calculations, made by both parties, that they can achieve more by going to war than by remaining at peace" (see *Militarism and Militarization*).

5. Conclusion

Despite this criticism that challenges core assumptions, human nature theories of war still provide some insights into the conditions of peace. The exact degree to which human nature contributes to war may never be measured; and the dispute whether war is a social invention or a natural phenomenon may never be decided—if only because our concept of 'nature' is a social construction. This notwithstanding, human nature theories of war remind us that peace once achieved cannot be taken for granted, for international organizations and state institutions are no fool-proof protection against the uncalculable sides of human nature. Peace therefore has to be reestablished and reaffirmed in practice day by day.

See also: *Conflict: Inherent and Contingent Theories*

Bibliography

Augustine St 1948 *The City of God.* Hafner Publ., New York, 2 vols

Eibl-Eiblsfeld I 1979 *The Biology of Peace and War.* Thames & Hudson, London

Enloe C 1983 *Does Khaki Become You? The Militarisation of Women's Lives.* Pluto, London

Fornari F 1975 *The Psychoanalysis of War.* Indiana University Press, Bloomington, London

Fox R 1992/93 Fatal attraction. War and human nature. In: *The National Interest* 30

Freud S 1975a Thoughts for the times on war and death (1915). In: *The Standard Edition of the Complete Psychological Works.* (ed.) & Tr. J Strachey, Hogarth, London, Vol. 14

Freud S 1975b Why War? (1932) In: *Standard Edition* Vol. 22

Gellner E 1991 An anthropological view of war and violence. In: Hinde R A (ed.) *The Institution of War*. Macmillan, Houndmills, London

Harris A, King Y (eds.) 1989 *Rocking the Ship of State: Towards a Feminist Peace Politics*. Westview, San Francisco, London

Hinde R A 1993 Aggression and war: Individuals, groups, and states. In: Tetlock P E et al., (eds.) *Behavior, Society and International Conflict*. Oxford University Press, New York, London

Hobbes Th 1985 *Leviathan* (1651). Penguin, London

Howard M 1983 *The Causes of Wars*, 2nd edn. Harvard University Press, Cambridge

James W 1911 *Memory and Studies*. Longmans, Green, New York

Leaky R 1981 *The Making of Mankind*. Dutton, New York

Lorenz K 1966 *On Aggression*. Bantam, New York

Mead M 1964 Warfare is only an invention—Not a biological necessity. In: Bramson L, Goethals G W (eds.) *War: Studies from Psychology, Sociology, Anthropology*. Basic Books, New York

Morgenthau H J 1954 *Politics among Nations*, 2nd edn. Knopf, New York

Niebuhr R 1953 *Christian Realism and Political Problems*. Charles Scribner's Sons, New York

Spinoza B Theologico—Political Treatise

Thomas E 1959 *The Harmless People*. Knopf, New York

Tolstoy L 1966 *War and Peace*. Norton, New York

Waltz K N 1959 *Man, the State and War*. Columbia University Press, New York

Woolf V 1982 *Three Guineas (1938)*. Penguin, Harmondsworth

CHRISTOPHER DAASE

Human Rights and Environmental Rights: Their Sustainable Development Compatibility

1. Introduction

The most powerful claim an individual can make is when he uses the term "right." The term "right" describes our highest, strongest, most compelling and inviolable claims we make against others, the sovereign, or any other entity. Some rights are considered entitlements so that others including the state cannot interfere with. For example, the right to life means that individuals possess the right not to have their life taken away (that is the right not to be killed) by others. Of course, unless there are actions undertaken by such individuals that under due process, their life is put to an end. Our most revered rights are called fundamental rights and freedoms such as right to life, right to liberty, freedom of speech, freedom of religion, freedom of association, freedom of thought, etc (see *Peace and Democracy*).

Sometimes, it becomes necessary for government to enact certain laws so as to protect individuals from discrimination by others or by public and private institutions. These laws are called "Human Rights Laws" which include the fundamental freedoms as well as protection for political, social and legal rights and privileges (see *International Bill of Human Rights*). For example, a human rights code will generally provide for freedom from discrimination on the ground of certain characteristics such as race, colour, creed, religion, sex, ethnic origin, etc. The code also describes what rights and freedoms are protected, what the limits to those rights and freedoms are, how they are to be enforced, and to whom those rights and freedoms apply. It is obvious that rights and freedoms of one person or group of persons may conflict with those of others; then the role of government is to balance such rights and freedoms as provided for in the law of the land (see *Human Rights and Peace*). Rights and freedoms are ideals that each government is morally and to a great extent legally obligated to strive for. If there are any human rights abuses anywhere, such governments are immediately accused and domestic as well as international pressures are brought to bear upon such entity. But environmental abuses go on unnoticed and uncared for.

Rights and freedoms have been granted to individual human beings; and in some countries their rights are guarded with utmost care. However, such a care is not shown with respect to the environment. Can the present generation ruin the environment to satisfy its own greed without caring for the rights of future generations? Does the environment need protection and has it any specific rights? Do other species also have the right to life which is considered an absolute right for humans? For example, if there is an evidence of genocide, international law (based on the UN Charter of Human Rights) is invoked; but an ecocide continues on without much international action. Today, the concept of human rights is based on the fundamental principle that all human beings are entitled to life, liberty, and dignity of life. Should not all species be given some if not the same right to survive and develop? Should not our preoccupation with protecting human beings alone be challenged? Do animals, plants, other species, and the environment have no other existence but to serve humans? These challenges have wider implications for the present and future of humanity and the universe (see *Green Security*).

Should the concept of environmental rights be based on the human rights paradigm? If human rights codes are created to prevent discrimination and abuses against individuals, could we not have environmental rights which provide for (a) prevention of the ecological disaster, (b) mitigation and reduction of environmental risks, (c) government preparedness to respond to any environmental emergency (such as the case of Bhopal crisis), and (d) rehabilitation actions taken by the local and national authorities to reestablish the damaged area or biosphere? But most importantly, when we talk about the scope of environmental rights, do we include only individuals or group of people, or nations, or the entire Creation? Should we not include future generations, animals, and inanimate objects? Also, should we consider that the right to a clean, healthy and appropriate environment is a collective right? Is not the right of a group superior to the right of an individual? If human rights are the moral entitlements for individuals, should not then the environmental rights be the moral entitlements of groups, communities, nations, and the universe? These and related questions require our immediate attention.

2. Sustainable Development and Environmental Rights

What are the specific environmental rights and responsibilities so that we may have sustainable development? Before we list these, it is important that we define the term sustainable development. Or, can there be a sustainable development framework for human rights, or can one use the human rights framework to protect environmental rights? In 1995, Aaron Sachs writing for the Worldwatch Institute stated that among other things, the Universal Declaration of Human Rights should include a provision for a secure, healthy and ecologically sound environment.[1]

2.1 The Concept and Definition of Sustainable Development

The Brundtland Commission report, *Our Common Future*, defined the term as "development that meets the needs of the present without compromising the ability of future generations to meet their own needs."[2] The definition contains two key concepts: (a) the concept of needs, in particular the essential needs of the world's poor, to which overriding priority should be given; and (b) limitations imposed by the state of technology and social organization on the

environment's ability to meet present and future needs. But it is not clear who—North or South—is going to determine the "needs" of present generations; and how are we going to ascertain the "ability" of future generations? If one wishes to seek answers from the rich and industrialized North, their suggestion will be to create a global environmental policy which has some conditionality attached for poor nations. On the other hand, in an answer to the same question, the South would be more likely to emphasize both poverty alleviation and the provision of basic needs with appropriate financial assistance, rather than insisting on quality management of the environment. Of course, the concept of sustainable development has fundamentally changed the nature and scope of debate about the environment and its relationship to development. It has actually subsumed the entire notion of economic development within its orbit; as such, pursuit of economic growth is no longer the main core value. Rather, it is a part of the larger picture, the central theme of which is how to integrate economic and environmental concerns in a development strategy. As the World Commission on Environment and Development has stated: "We have in the past been concerned about the impacts of economic growth upon the environment. We are now forced to concern ourselves with the impacts of ecological stress . . . upon our economic prospects."[3] However, in order to make this definition sufficiently comprehensive, the author suggests the following formulation: *sustainable development obligates humanity to use, develop, manage, and care for the environment and planetary resources in such a manner that supports the stewardship of Creation (including all natural resources, biodiversity, and the welfare of all living beings), and the continuity of cultural and spiritual heritage of each community, as well as the maintenance of harmony between people and nature for present and future generations.*[4] In essence, as this definition suggests, sustainable development, as a general principle, ought to ensure that it is the recognized duty of all people and their governments to protect, conserve, preserve, and finally pass on to future generations nature's heritage, while at the same time preventing all deliberate measures and acts (of individuals and states) which harm or threaten our Nature's heritage.

The concept of sustainable development implies a fusion of two imperatives: the right to develop, and the right to have environmental quality. What it means is that any future development ought to be achieved in a sustainable and equitable manner. Thus the concept denotes a balance, "so that 'sustainable' brings environmental concepts into the development process, while 'equitable' inserts developmental matters into international environmental protection efforts."[5] Furthermore, the concept implies intra-generational equity (between the rich North and poor South), so that the needs of all people are taken into account, especially through the transfer of resources to developing nations (see *Equitable Equality: Gandhian Concept*). However, we have to consider how these needs are going to be taken into account if one portion of humanity keeps squandering natural resources in the name of sustaining their own version of quality of life while the majority of the world population continues its onslaught on natural resources in the name of hunger and poverty. It is here that we see the need for the concept of sustainable development to be linked with the ethics of environmental stewardship (see *Peace and Social Development*). As discussed below, unless we bring these two concepts together and operationalize them through our governing institutions as well as through our personal commitment, the crises that we are facing now will not disappear. We, as human beings, are the ecologically dominant species in the ecosystem that we inhabit. Although we have the same need for heat, light, water, and food that other species have, we alone possess the specific attributes which give us dominance over other living species. Furthermore, we have been able to manipulate natural forces in the ecosystem with an intensity unsurpassed by any other living being. This manipulation has given rise to the breakdown of the natural self-protective and self-perpetuating mechanisms built into nature—a situation made even worse by our belief that we have the right to use the natural environment solely for our own ends, without consideration for the consequences of our actions on the system. This human tendency has shaped our views and has been used in turn as justification for our attitude towards nature and the ecosystem. That tendency has also influenced our thinking about the environment and its rights.

2.2 Environmental Rights

Although some believe that it was the 1960s when a world-wide concern for the environment arose. However, in many spiritual traditions and cultures, exhortations have been used to protect the environment. For example, the Greek and Roman civilizations believed that animals possessed some inherent or natural rights which were independent of human civilization and its government; the principle was referred to as *jus animalium*. Aboriginal people had an appropriate understanding of nature's rights; they

would hunt not for sports or pleasure but only for sustenance. Eastern religions such as Hinduism, Buddhism, Jainism, and Taoism told their believers to respect God's Creation, and to practice non-violence not only with respect to other human beings but also in regard to animals and others. However, it was in the late 1960s and early 1970s that the recognition of a right to a safe and healthy environment was advocated more forcefully.

In an article entitled "Planetary Rights," Edith Brown Weiss examines a link between human rights and the earth. She identifies this link as planetary rights, and these are defined as intergenerational rights, duties and obligations associated with international duties of use.[6] Her use of the term, "planetary rights," includes the rights of nature to exist, with the focus on community rights rather than individual rights. This is an important distinction because where as human rights are directed towards protecting an individual from something while the community dimension is placed either at a subordinate status or in a weaker position. On the other hand, the rights of nature or planetary rights are intertemporal, and focused towards community or groups, nevertheless, individuals rights do get an appropriate place. It is in this context that we should examine the nature and scope of environmental rights, as detailed below:

(a) All forms of life have equal right to exist and survive;

(b) All human beings have the fundamental right to an environment adequate for their well-being;

(c) The right to health, freedom from hunger, and an adequate standard of living;

(d) A universal responsibility to protect the environment;

(e) The right to development is an inalienable human right which should correspond to meeting the development and environmental needs of present and future generations;

(f) Intergenerational equity and responsibility;

(g) A just and equitable international economic order;

(h) Poverty as a major cause of global environmental degradation should be recognized as a constraint for human development;

(i) Safety of food, water and living environment for all;

(j) Protection and preservation of bio-diversity,

biospheres, ecosystems health, and the commons (such as oceans, lakes, rivers, atmosphere, etc.); and

(k) Sustenance of traditional form of life for indigenous people.[7]

For the above listed rights to work, it is important that the foundation on which these rights are based, the sanctity of life principle, should be appropriately understood. The principle requires that we as human-beings (i) should not attach 'degrees of relative worth' or 'pragmatic utility' as a yardstick for determining or measuring the sanctity of life of other human beings or even other species; (ii) although there are laws to prevent human life from being destroyed, there ought to exist equally comprehensive laws to protect nature from the further destruction or any radical changes; (iii) humans must extend the sanctity of life principle to the environment because if not done so its rejection may endanger the entire human life; and (iv) the wilful destruction of the environment, called ecocide, is as critical for the survival of civilization as is genocide.

3. Genocide and Ecocide

Genocide, as a term, is used to describe the deliberate attempt to exterminate a race of people (such as the Nazis attempted against the Jews during World War II); similarly, the term *ecocide* is used to describe the wilful destruction of the environment, and includes such human activities as wanton destruction of agricultural crops, defoliation of forests by the use of herbicides and chemicals, massive aerial bombardment, and a systematic destruction of any wild species. The term 'ecocide' was first used during the Vietnam war.[8] However, the scope of this term was later expanded to include the assault of one nation against the other nation's people, their culture and biological fabric including the environment.[9] While the term ecocide is rooted in wartime activities, in this paper, the use of this term is wider and does not restrict to only the destruction and the large scale disruption of the environment for military purposes but includes industrial activities which cause sufferings to the individuals, their culture, as well as the biological fabric of their surroundings; thus the peacetime activities are also included in this definition. Most recently, Richard A. Falk and others have formulated an International Convention on the Crime of Ecocide which they want the United Nations to adopt. The suggested code considers the following acts as a part of ecocide: (a) the use of weapons of mass destruc-

tion including bacteriological and chemicals; (b) the use of chemical herbicides to defoliate forests for military purposes; (c) aerial bombardment of an area which destroys the quality of soil; (d) destruction of large tracts of forests or cropland for military purposes; (e) the use of techniques designed to increase or decrease rainfall or otherwise modify weather as a weapon of war; and (f) the forcible removal of human and animal population from their natural habitat to other areas in order to expedite the pursuit of military or industrial objectives.[10] In the case of weather modification, iodine is used over a period of hours on a specific cloud formation causing high levels of precipitation resulting in floods.

But how is the term 'ecocide' related to 'genocide'? Human rights abuse were recognized by the United Nations when it adopted the Universal Declaration of Human Rights in 1948 (see *Declaration of the Rights of Man*). The objective of this Declaration is to ensure that all nations comply to the universal principle of treating every individual in a fair and humane way; however, if these rights are systematically denied (in the form of ethnic cleansing, systematic extermination or destruction of entire people or a group belonging to a specific nation or creed, etc.) to any group of people, the UN Security Council may take an appropriate action. For example, in the case of the Gulf War, President George Bush used the term 'eco-terrorism' to describe Iraq's policies of oil-well burning and dumping of oil in the sea. As is the case of a regular warfare, environmental warfare (that is, the intentional destruction of the environment for military or even industrial purposes) is ecocide. But unlike the UN Universal Declaration of Human Rights, the environmental rights are yet to be adopted by the UN. Even in 1972, during the first UN Conference on the Human Environment, no guarantee to environmental rights was proposed. Principle 21 stated that "States had . . . the sovereign right to exploit their own resources pursuant to their own environmental policies, and the responsibility to ensure that activities within their jurisdiction or control did not cause damage to the environment of other states or of areas beyond the limits of national jurisdiction."[11] It was no wonder that many countries then assumed that they were free to do whatever they wanted with the environment inside their territory. It was much later, specially when the Brundtland Commission report, *Our Common Future*, came out in 1987 that concerted international effort was made to consider environmental rights. The Report suggested that there was an intimate linkage between environmental stress, poverty and security; and environmental threats to security were emerging on a global scale.[12] The report formulated certain principles such as: (a) "All human beings have the fundamental right to an environment adequate for their health and well-being"; (b) "States shall conserve and use the environment and natural resources for the benefit of present and future generations"; and (c) "States shall settle environmental disputes by peaceful means."[13] There is no doubt that the Brundtland Commission was able to generate a world-wide international interest on the plight of the environment; one such result was that the Earth Summit of 1992 could induce enough interest among the numbers of states to consider an Earth Charter. However, this Earth Charter remains an ineffective document because it does not have the same credibility as is the case with the UN charter on human rights.

3.1 Ecocide in Vietnam War

The Vietnam war was different from any other war fought by the Americans because the battle did not take place in any major fronts; instead it was primarily an insurgency movement within South Vietnam. When in 1960, the National Liberation Front (NLF) was created by the North Vietnam and the Ho Chi Minh Trail was used by insurgents. In order to locate insurgents and to cut off the supply routes from North Vietnam, the US military decided to engage in a counter-insurgency war. To accomplish its aim, the US military initiated a plan of defoliation so that a clear aerial view was available. Four methods were used: (a) forests were sprayed with specific herbicides; (b) Rome plows (very large bulldozers) were used to clear all vegetation along with the top soil; (c) Napalm was of used to burn certain target areas; and (d) heavy aerial and artillery bombing was used around the clock to destroy any thing that the herbicides, Rome plows or Napalm could not do.[14] The clear objective was to destroy every inch of the environment which was strategic important to the US operations. It was for the first time in human history that such a rigorous force and destructive capabilities of a superpower were used. In addition, one million bombs, 22 million artillery shells, and 10 million (40 millimetre) grenades were left unexploded.[15] During the Vietnam war, 28 million tons of bombs in total were dropped.[16]

Herbicide was the most effective and cheapest weapon to be used in the Vietnam war; among these herbicides there were three main ones: Agents Blue, White and Green employed between 1961 and 1971, although majority of the spraying occurred in 1967 and 1968; as a matter of fact, by 1969, 43 percent of all arable land and 44 percent of the total forest area of Vietnam had been sprayed (and out of that total 34 percent was sprayed more than twice).[17] Agent Orange, the most deadliest one, has dioxin (with 2,4,5-T) concentration of 1.98 parts per million (ppm) while the permissible concentration for use in North America is supposed to be only two parts per billion.[18] Thus the level of toxicity was a thousand times more than the permissible limit. It was not until 1970 that the use of Agent Orange was banned in Vietnam. The loss of cropland, forest cover, loss of timber, destruction of mangroves, destruction of many species was enormous.

Just as genocide became associated with the World War II, ecocide is associated with the Vietnam War. However, unlike the Nuremberg and Japanese trials, no tribunals were set and thus no trials for ecocide were ever held because in the 1970s, after the Vietnam War, the US was not held accountable; similarly, after the Gulf War, Iraq was not held accountable for either burning oil wells or dumping oil in the sea. Unless ecocide is included as a crime against humanity, ecocidal practices will continue.

3.2 Ecocide during the Gulf War

Unlike the Vietnam war which lasted for several years, the Gulf war was a short phenomenon. While the Vietnam war took place in a tropical zone with forests providing shelter to insurgents, the Gulf war created another ecocide when 210 oil wells were set on fire by the Iraqis.[19] Approximately three million barrels of oil were burning each day which resulted in enormous amount of the release of 10,200 tons of sulphur dioxide, 25,000 tons of nitrogen oxide, and 285,600 tons of carbon dioxide per day.[20] In addition, other chemicals were released due to the burning of oil. The worst impact of the oil burning was soot which affected many countries; for example, Kashmir (India), Turkey and parts of Afghanistan suffered from a black rain that year. In addition to the burning, oil leakage was equally enormous. About 100 wells (releasing 6 million barrels a day) created 240 huge oil lakes.[21] In addition to the burning of oil wells, Iraqis dumped 2.5 million barrels of oil in the coastal areas.[22] It seems that Iraqis used the environment as a weapon to damage the economy of Kuwait and neighbouring countries. It is difficult to assess the impact of the Gulf war on the environment, it seems that ecocide remains a strategy of warfare.

These two case studies have demonstrated that ecocide causes a circular process of destruction whereby when the environment gets destroyed, its inhabitants (humans as well as other species) suffer. While humans become environmental refugees, other species become extinct or rare.

4. Concluding Observations

It is humanity which has created the global environmental crisis; it is also the same humanity which keeps on destroying the very habitat that it depends on; and it is the same humanity which has developed a hierarchy of human rights to protect its own progeny but is reticent to extend the same privileges to the environment and other species. While individual rights have been given universal legal status, collective rights (in the form of the right, clean, healthy, and otherwise appropriate environment) is yet to receive the same national and international approval. Those who question who would be authorized to possess the environmental rights and how such rights would be exercised, perhaps forget that no children, the unborn (fetus), the insane, people in comas, and others have received such privileges. There is no reason why environmental rights could not be accorded a similar status.

The environmental and human rights movements have valuable contributions to make to each other because while the environmentalism can contribute to the greening of human rights by impelling the human rights movement to recognize that humans are a part, not apart from, of nature, and that the right to a safe, healthy and environmentally sustainable development is a universal need; while the human rights movement can contribute to the protection of the environment by supporting the extension to the environmental movement of certain concepts such as the rule of law, due process of law, presence of a strong system of legal remedies, political participation, and vigilance over any infringement of such rights which may deal with the environment. For example, creating an effective rule of law for all areas of human endeavour including its interaction with nature might help the cause of environmental rights. At a minimum, environmental rights and human rights issues must not be separated because in the final analysis human being will not be able to survive without the environment; mainly because the nonhuman nature has its own integrity that defies human arrogance and demand human respect. Environmental rights remind us that every life form has the right to exist on its own, and that the days of human hegemony over the nature are over. Instead, there is a need to bring both humans and nature closer to each other so that the integrity and sustainability of the environment is linked with human dignity, for the benefit of both the present and future generations.

See also: *Social Progress and Human Survival;
Future of Humanity*

Notes

1. Aaron Sachs, *Eco-justice: Linking Human Rights and the Environment* Washington DC: Worldwatch Institute, 1995, p. 53.

2. World Commission on Environment and Development, *Our Common Future*, New York: Oxford University Press, 1987, p. 43.

3. World Commission on Environment and Development, *Our Common Future*, p. 5.

4. This definition and the discussion in this section has been drawn from this author's book, *India's Environmental Policies, Programmes and Stewardship*, London: Macmillan Press, 1997, pp. 27-29.

5. IUCN, Commission on Environmental Law of IUCN, *International Covenant on Environment and Development*, (Draft), Gland, Switzerland: IUCN, March 1995, p. 42.

6. Edith Brown Weiss, "Planetary Rights", in Richard Pierre Claude and Brns H. Weston, eds., *Human Rights in the World Community: Issues and Action*, (second edition), Philadelphia: University of Pennsylvania Press, 1992, pp. 187.

7. Based on an Environmental Code of Conduct and Guidelines by O.P. Dwivedi in *Environmental Ethics: Our Dharma to the Environment*, New Delhi: Sanchar Publishing House, 1994, pp. 133(c)138. See also, Barbara Rose Johnston, "Human Rights and the Environment", *Human Ecology*, Vol. 23, no. 2, 1995, pp. 111-123.

8. Arthur W. Galston used this term to describe how mangrove forests and other forested areas of Vietnam were being destroyed by the US aerial bombing. He described the term as the "wilful destruction of the environment". See editorial, *New York Times*, 26 February 1970. He reasoned that the Vietnam war was causing permanent damage to the environment, and that the United States government should take full responsibility for it.

9. Barry Weisberg, ed. *Ecocide in Indochina: The Ecology of War*, San Francisco, USA: Canfield Press, 1970, p. 4.

10. Richard A. Falk, "Environmental Warfare and Ecocide—Facts, Appraisal, and Proposals", in *Revue Belge de Droit International*, Vol. 9, 1973, p. 93.

11. UN, Declaration of the UN Conference on the Human Environment, 1972, *Yearbook of the United Nations*, Vol. 26, 1972, p. 321.

12. World Commission on Environment and Development, *Our Common Future*, New York: Oxford University Press, 1987, pp. 290(c) 294.

13. WCED, Our Common Future, (Principles 1, 2, and 22) pp. 348-351.

14. Vo Quy, "The Wounds of War: Vietnam Struggles to Erase the Scars of 30 Violent Years", *Ceres*, Vol. 134, March/April 1992, p. 13.

15. Earl S. Martin and Murray Hiebert, "Explosive Remnants of the Second Indochina War in Vietnam and Laos", in *Explosive Remnants of War, Mitigating the Environmental Effects*, edited by Arther H. Westing, London: Taylor and Francis, 1985, p. 10.

16. E.W. Pfeiffer, "Degreening Vietnam", *Natural History*, Vol. 34, 1990, p. 38.

17. Orville Schell and Barry Weisberg, "Ecocide in Indochina", in *Ecocide in Indochina: The Ecology of War*, edited by Barry Weisberg, San Francisco, CA: Canfield Press, 1970, p. 19.

18. F.L. McEwen and G.R. Stephenson, *The Use and Significance of Pesticides in the Environment*, Toronto: John Wiley, 1979, p. 278.

19. Frank Barnaby, "The Environmental Impact of the Gulf War", *The Ecologist*, Vol. 21, no. 4, 1991, p. 168.

20. Barnaby, p. 168.

21. Laura Edgerton, "Eco-Terrorist Acts During the Persian Gulf War: Is International Law Sufficient to Hold Iraq Liable?", *Georgia Journal of International and Comparative Law*, Vol. 2, no. 1, 1992, p. 153.

22. Barnaby, p. 170.

O. P. DWIVEDI

Human Rights and Peace

In parallel with the evolution of society, an idea we know today as the "rights of man" has been evolving slowly over the past seven hundred and eighty years—in fact since its first recorded stirrings in 1215 when *Magna Carta*, the Great Charter, was signed by King John of England to create a Common Law and a "community of the realm." Familiar milestones on this path toward a common code of rights and duties included, first, further steps to circumscribe the "divine right of Kings," culminating in the Bill of Rights that sealed the English Revolution of 1689; then the Declaration of Independence proclaimed by the thirteen North American colonies in 1776; and next a Declaration of the Rights of Man that heralded the French Revolution of 1789.

For the modern conception, embracing a worldwide code of human rights and duties, we have to wait until the year 1940, when the writer H.G. Wells, who in a series of books had been calling for a global awareness to match the new conditions imposed by modern communications and productive technique, wrote two letters to *The Times* on war aims, following up with a draft World Declaration of the Rights of Man (see *Declaration of the Rights of Man*). Such was the unparalleled world prestige of Wells at this time that the Declaration, after being refined by an eminent committee and a long debate in the national press, was translated into ten languages, dropped by microfilm to the Resistance in occupied Europe, and distributed worldwide to three hundred editors in forty-eight countries. The final version of this World Declaration was the forerunner of that massive effort by the United Nations to implement a world code of rights and duties that has occupied the UN over the ensuing four decades, and which it is the purpose of this article to examine.

First, however, a word on the related concept of peace. Being an animal uniquely ranged against its own species, the genus Homo has punctuated the rise of cities, nation-states, and empires with a spreading range and destructiveness of armed conflict as well as a parallel search for means to prevent war. Perhaps the first recorded scheme for a Universal Peace Organization was that drafted by the King of Bohemia in 1462. From this time on, principles of international law came to be perceived, under the doctrine of Grotius (see *Grotius, Hugo*), to rest on the idea of justice and therefore on a need for grievances to be aired through peaceful arbitration. In line with this new trend, several schemes for international organization emerged in seventeenth—and eighteenth—century Europe, of which a project for "perpetual peace," drafted by the Abbé de Saint-Pierre in 1715 and providing for a general assembly, an international secretariat, and standing armed forces, is perhaps the best known and the most imaginative. Although peace societies and congresses abounded throughout the nineteenth century and beyond, culminating in that of 1919 which led to the founding of the League of Nations (see *League of Nations*), the Abbé de Saint-Pierre's farsighted scheme remains unattained to this very day.

In our own time a vast speeding-up of economic and technical change, plus ever-widening horizons spread by new knowledge, movement, and information, have both sharpened the scope for animosity and multiplied the sources of overt strife. Most of the sixty-odd main conflicts since 1945 have occurred in the developing world and have been civil wars in which only a minority of the casualties, around twenty million in all, have occurred among the armed forces. Political coups, regional separatist struggles, religious fanaticism, and harsh ill-treatment of indigenous populations have in total increased, often being exacerbated or engineered through Great Power intervention to secure business or political interests or to remove governments which seek to follow an independent line (see *Local Wars Since 1945*). Though the main forms of human rights abuse differ widely between so-called "developed" and "developing" states, they persist nonetheless in most of the world's administrations.

Moreover, instability itself breeds human rights abuse. As counter-revolution and separatist ethnic or religious disputes have become polarized, mainly at the intermediate stage of economic development, torture, involuntary disappearances, and extrajudicial executions have come to be met by counteracting guerrilla action, hostage taking, and indiscriminate terrorism. Entrenched business-cum-political interests and uncontrolled arms exports have thus fanned a worldwide climate of terror that has confounded the simpler vision of those who drafted the United Nations Charter (see *United Nations Charter*) at the end of the Second World War. While idealism still finds expression through the United Nations, its sources and its emphasis have changed because any move toward an overseeing supranational control has been evaded. To understand fully the links between human rights and world peace, one must first look in more detail at how the entire concept of human rights and duties has evolved in the postwar world.

1. Human Rights Development in its First Five Decades

As first put together in London in 1940-42, H.G. Wells' pioneer Declaration of the Rights and Duties of the World Citizen comprised a brilliant preamble and 11 articles, which may be listed as follows:

(a) The Right to Live;

(b) Protection of Minors;

(c) Duty to the Community;

(d) Right to Knowledge;

(e) Freedom of Thought and Worship;

(f) Right to Work;

(g) Right to Personal Property;

(h) Freedom of Movement;

(i) Personal Liberty;

(j) Freedom from Violence;

(k) Right of Law Making.

The first article included the idea that everyone, as "joint inheritor" of the natural resources, powers, inventions, and possibilities so far accumulated, is entitled, within their measure, to various specified means to realize his or her full possibilities of physical and mental development from birth to death. This article contained the germ of a "Right to Development" discussed below. Other articles were equally revolutionary in conception.

The impact of the Declaration (Dilloway 1986) was decisive. Its direct successor, the Universal Declaration of Human Rights that was drafted and finally adopted by the newly created United Nations Organization on December 10, 1948, two years after the death of Wells, embodied nearly all the content of its predecessor, with a few exceptions that remain unattainable to this day. While the International Bill of Human Rights, which includes the Universal Declaration, is discussed in a separate article (see *International Bill of Human Rights*), the latter's main provisions must be stated here because they underlie all that follows.

In its thirty articles, the Universal Declaration of Human Rights defines those principles intended to offer a "common standard of achievement for all peoples and all nations." Its first three articles proclaim that all human beings are born free and equal in dignity and rights, are endowed with reason and conscience, should act toward one another in a spirit of brotherhood, and are entitled to all rights and freedoms without any kind of distinction. Everyone has the right to life, liberty, and security of person.

From here Articles 4 to 21 set out various civil and political rights, including those to freedom from slavery; from torture or cruel, inhuman, or degrading treatment or punishment; the right to recognition as a person before the law and to equal protection by the law against abuse of rights; to freedom from arbitrary arrest, detention, or exile; the right to a fair public hearing before an independent and impartial tribunal; and the right to be presumed innocent until proved guilty. Other civil rights include freedom from arbitrary interference with privacy, family, or correspondence; freedom of movement and residence; the right to a nationality, and of asylum; the right to marry and found a family; to own property; to freedom of thought, conscience, religion, opinion, and expression; the right to peaceful assembly and association—but equally that of not belonging to an association; and the right to take part in the government of one's country and of equal access to its public service. Finally, "the will of the people shall be the basis of the authority of government," which shall be expressed in periodic election by universal suffrage and secret or free voting procedures.

Article 22 introduces a second group of articles defining various economic, social, and cultural rights—those to which everyone is entitled by virtue of his or her membership of society. Such rights, though indispensable for human dignity and free development of personality, rest on national and international effort within the limits of the organization and resources of each state. These rights, comprised in Articles 22 to 27, thus include the right to social security; to work, under just and equitable conditions; to equal pay for equal work; to rest and leisure; to a standard of life adequate for health and well-being; and the right to education, under defined conditions, and to participate in the cultural life of the community. The concluding Articles (28 to 30) proclaim that everyone is entitled to a social and international order in which the Declaration's rights and freedoms may be fully realized. Conversely, since everyone has duties to the community, the exercise of such rights and freedoms shall be limited only by laws designed solely to secure recognition and respect for the rights of others and to meet requirements of public order and the general welfare in a democratic society. No state, group, or individual may claim the right to destroy any right contained in the Declaration.

These, then, in outline, are the first principles of human rights and duties that have inspired international cooperation during the first fifty years of United Nations action. These principles have been expanded and given legal force in two basic covenants—those on civil and political rights, and on economic, social, and cultural rights respectively (see *Cultural Roots of Peace*).

Experience has shown that agreement on elementary rules for civilized living does not suffice to curb the barbarism of states or individuals, however sophisticated. Without counting nine separate Declarations of the UN General Assembly stating norms to promote peace and a similar number of arms control agreements, plus others on peaceful use of outer space and the Geneva Conventions of the International Red Cross (see Nobel Peace Prize Laureates: *International Red Cross*) covering rules for the protection of victims of war, well over fifty international instruments covering specific human rights have entered into use over the last five decades.

These conventions and declarations seek to counter a wide range of abuses of rights or duties that arise or persist in the contemporary world, and some relevant areas of study can be grouped by subject broadly as follows:

(a) The International Bill of Human Rights;

(b) War crimes and varied forms of crimes against humanity;

(c) Slavery, forced labour and similar practices;

(d) Protection of persons subject to detection or imprisonment;

(e) Racial discrimination;

(f) Nationality, statelessness, and displaced persons;

(g) Marriage, the rights of the child, discrimination against women, and youth;

(h) Social welfare and development;

(i) Harmful traditional practices affecting the health of women and children;

(j) Cultural development;

(k) Rights of indigenous peoples;

(l) Freedom of information;

(m) Freedom of association;

(n) Housing rights and problems of extreme poverty;

(o) Problems of democratic society;

(p) Rights to a sound environment;

(q) Conscientious objection to military service.

To go into more detail, a selection from some major United Nations instruments within these groups is set out below, together with year of adoption. The texts and full titles of over 50 such instruments are contained in *Human Rights: A Compilation of International Instruments* (UN 1992):

(a) (1) Universal Declaration of Human Rights (1948);
    (2) International Covenant on Civil and Political Rights (1966);
    (3) International Covenant on Economic, Social, and Cultural Rights (1966);
    (4) First Optional Protocol to Item 2 (1966) concerning communications from individuals;
    (5) Second Optional Protocol concerning abolition of the death penalty (1989);

(b) (6) Convention on the Elimination of All Forms of Racial Discrimination (1965);
    (7) Convention Against Discrimination in Education (UNESCO 1960);
    (8) Convention on the Elimination of All Forms of Discrimination Against Women (1979);
    (9) Declaration on the Elimination of Intolerance or Discrimination Based on Religion or Belief (1981);
    (10) Convention on the Political Rights of Women (1952);

(c) (11) Convention on the Prevention and Punishment of Genocide (1948);
    (12) Convention on the Non-applicability of Statutory Limitations to War Crimes (1968);
    (13) International Convention Against the Taking of Hostages (1979);

(d) (14) Slavery Convention (1926);

(15) Protocol Amending Item (13) (1953);
(16) Supplementary Convention on the Aboli-
    tion of Slavery and Similar Practices (1956);

(e) (17) Standard Minimum Rules for Treatment of
    Prisoners (1957, 1977);
(18) Convention Against Torture (1984);

(f) (19) Convention on the Status of Refugees (1951);
(20) Protocol Relating to the Status of Refugees
    (1966);
(21) Convention on the Reduction of Stateless-
    ness (1961);

(g) (22) Convention on the Nationality of Married
    Women (1957);
(23) Convention on Consent, Minimum Age,
    and Registration of Marriages (1962);
(24) Convention on the Rights of the Child (1990);
(25) Declaration on Protection of Women and
    Children in Emergencies, and so on (1974);
(26) Declaration on Promotion Among Youth of
    Ideals of Peace and Understanding, and so
    on (1965);

(h) (27) Declaration on Social Progress and Devel-
    opment (1969);
(28) Universal Declaration on Eradication of
    Hunger and Malnutrition (1974);
(29) Declaration on the Use of Scientific Progress
    in the Interests of Peace, and so on (1975);
(30) Declaration on the Right to Development
    (1986);
(31) Declaration of Principles of International
    Cultural Cooperation (UNESCO 1966).

This list omits some further questions, and of
course certain matters of current concern still under
consideration in 1997, but even so the vast output of
standard-setting instruments defining human rights
and duties still needs to be supplemented by several
types of protective, remedial, or promotional action.
Every year special situations in around fifteen states
are examined by the UN Commission on Human
Rights and its Subcommission of experts. In addition,
special groups or rapporteurs investigate thousands
of alleged cases of torture, disappearances, arbitrary
executions, slavery, or other types of discrimination.
For some basic conventions special machinery exists
for periodic review of the way states are exercising
the obligations they have chosen to assume. Beyond
this again there is often a need for the education and
informing of special groups—prison staff, civil

administrators, police, military officers, and even citizens—in the exercise of their rights and duties.

Since 1947 United Nations machinery has existed
to further the role of rights and duties in human
affairs. In addition to the parent body—a Commission
on Human Rights—a Sub-Commission on Prevention
of Discrimination and Protection of Minorities is a
body of individual experts that formulates proposals
and conducts research. Since 1946 a Commission on
the Status of Women has been concerned with questions of women's rights. To monitor national performance under the two basic Covenants and various
conventions, bodies established for this purpose
include a Committee on the Elimination of Racial
Discrimination (1970), the Human Rights Committee
(1977) and others covering Economic, Social and
Cultural Rights (1985), the Elimination of Discrimination Against Women (1982) and Torture (1987).

2. Peace and the Human Rights Prospect

Despite the lack so far of any sort of supranational
control, a moral pressure to respect human rights
standards is having some overall success, though it is
a success hard gained in a world where the tacitly
approved model of conduct—a whole climate produced by an obsolete economic frame—is at once
combative and self-seeking at a time when interdependence, and the interrelatedness of all human and
nonhuman phenomena, are daily being disclosed by
every new discovery. Further, while economic life
releases and converts ever more inanimate energy, it
fails more and more completely to absorb the excess
energy of youth.

The United Nations General Assembly Resolution
32/130 of 1977 states that all human rights and fundamental freedoms are indivisible and interrelated, and
the same can be said of human rights, peace, and disarmament. Both linkages are well displayed by new
work in the human rights field still going on in 1997.

Since the late eighties, and though disapproved of
by some rich market-economy states, a Declaration
on the Right to Development has grown in stature as
an expression of the aspirations of developing countries. This idea implies two things: first, a right of
each state to equitable treatment in developing its
resources within a world community for the good of
its citizens; and, second, the rights of each individual
within the state to life, food, education, and the
means to develop individual uniqueness for his or her
own and the common good (see *Global Ethics, Human
Rights Laws and Democratic Governance*). If the
ultimate test of a right's existence is that it does not

restrict the same or another right of other individuals, the same criterion must be equally valid where the interdependence of states is concerned. To enter into the full implications of the Declaration on the Right to Development would go beyond the scope of this article but an analysis of its wide-ranging international effects can be found in Dilloway (1986) and United Nations (1979).

Along with ethnic divisions, two archaic sources of conflict—authoritarian religion and free market political economy—play an increasing part in the new post-Cold War chaos of global disarray. Since both embrace the antitheses of that very essence of cooperation that is the condition on which humanness itself depends, our new valueless free-for-all has produced a fresh decline in human rights observance that coincides with an attempted broadening of UN programmes. In part this is because international effort has earlier avoided facing up to the fact that rights and duties clash with prevailing economic dogma in respect of collective as well as individual relations. A new, if belated, stress on economic, social and cultural rights must help to redress an earlier imbalance that favoured civil and political relations as against those that impinged on the economic domain.

Some general conclusions on the role of human rights relative to world peace can now be summed up as follows: First, the quality of humanness being a social product, society rests on the interdependence of unique personalities cooperating to meet their common needs and individual wants within a consensual frame of common interest. This in turn means that economic society is, or should be, an essential part of the total frame of mutuality and not, as market theory teaches, something apart and combative that obeys its own rules.

The true function of a code of human rights and duties is thus to mark out the acceptable shape and relationships of a just society—including, today, a peaceful world community. At our new stage of development, that community must allow, in its present policies, for the rights of future citizens. This in turn means that it should at least possess a loose standing body of high authority to oversee world development. It has, too, to embrace the full gamut of essential rights and duties—individual and collective—which ramify increasingly into every sphere of activity and into all international agreements.

What is needed to complete our neutral view of human rights and duties is a positive concept of cooperative interdependence in diversity that can supplant the long-outmoded dogma of competitive market economy and politics. Adversarial distinctions—religious, ethnic and political—receive a false legitimacy through an economic insistence on competition that is two centuries out of date.

With this proviso, the final justification for a code of rights is, first, that it defines the conditions in which human potential can develop peacefully in an interdependent milieu; and, second, that such a code, whether for the individual or for interstate relations, offers the *only* frame of common ideas that can span the diversity of cultures, religions, living standards, and political and economic systems to create a common nexus of humane practice for an emergent world community.

See also: *From Morality to Ethic: Toward an Ideal Community*

Bibliography

Boutros-Ghali B 1992 *An Agenda for Peace*. United Nations, New York

Daes E I A 1990 *Freedom of the Individual under Law: An Analysis of Article 29 of the Universal Declaration of Human Rights*. Centre for Human Rights, Geneva (Study Series No. 3). United Nations, New York

Dilloway A J 1986 *Is World Order Evolving? An Adventure into Human Potential*. Pergamon, Oxford

Dilloway A J 1983 *Human Rights and World Order*. H G Wells Society, London

United Nations 1979 *The International Dimension of the Right to Development as a Human Right in Relation with Other Human Rights Based on International Cooperation, Including the Right to Peace* (E.CN.4/13 34). United Nations, Geneva

United Nations 1987 *Human Rights Machinery*. Fact Sheet No. 1. United Nations, New York

United Nations 1988 *United Nations Action: The Field of Human Rights*. United Nations, New York

United Nations 1994 *Human Rights. A Compilation of International Instruments*. United Nations, New York

United Nations 1994 *Human Rights. Status of International Instruments*. United Nations, New York

United Nations 1993 *United Nations Peacekeeping*. United Nations, New York

United Nations 1996 *The High Commissioner for Human Rights: An Introduction*. United Nations, New York/ Geneva

JAMES DILLOWAY

Human Security

Human Security is both a vision and an agenda. It is a projected picture of a finer world and a goal to be pursued via cooperation among states and peoples. The idea of "human security" entered into the vocabulary of contemporary International Relations with the publication of the United Nations Development Programme's (UNDP) *Human Development Report 1993.* "New concepts of human security," the UNDP said,

> must stress the security of people, not only of nations . . . . The concept of security must change—from an exclusive stress on national security to a much greater stress on people's security from security through armaments to security through human development, from territorial security to food, employment and environmental security.

For the authors of the *Human Development Report*, human security concerned people and not necessarily states. It differed from the conventional notion of security as *national* security, which traditionally has had to do with securing states and governments against threats to national territory and national interests. By contrast, human security pertained to the condition of people's lives, and it meant freedom from all manner of threats to their well-being. Since 1993, the idea of human security has become a subject of academic reflection aimed at clarifying its meaning. But it has also become the object of political debates because it is not universally accepted as a goal of international public policy (see *Comprehensive Security*).

At minimum, people may be considered secure if they are protected from the threat of the physical destruction of their lives or property as a result of assault from hostile neighbors. Here, human security and national security partly overlap in meaning. But, at maximum, the condition of human security can be imagined to be a totally threat-free environment where people are protected against all manner of agents and forces that could result in the degradation of their lives, property or values. To place or leave human beings in environments which deny them adequate food, shelter, clean air, clean water, privacy, liberty, autonomy, information and other values and conditions that required for human flourishing, is to jeopardize their security. In this more encompassing sense, human security obviously means much more than national security.

A substantial majority of people living in the world today exist in environments that lack even the minimal conditions of human security. Many are threatened by their neighbors, who may live next door or across some near or distant political frontier. Many people are also threatened by their own governments, who may for political or ideological reasons deny them dignity, justice, freedom or sustenance. Today, many millions of people are threatened by poverty and the ruined health and spiritual despair that are its typical accompaniments. Millions perhaps are also threatened by ignorance which comes from being denied education and therein the basic tools for acquiring knowledge and realizing their rational capacities as human beings. A significant proportion of the human race is also jeopardized by the destruction of our planet's natural environment, and projections reveal that environmental despoliation is likely to become an ever increasing threat to human security in the foreseeable future. The very young and the elderly are particularly insecure in today's world, as are women in some societies, ethnic, linguistic and racial minorities in others, rural dwellers in many places and millions of refugees forced from their homes by wars, famines, unemployment and failing ecosystems. Because human insecurity runs so rampant today, human security remains much more an aspiration than a fact (see *Stability; Peace and Social Development*).

While some see introducing the notion of human security into contemporary discourse as rhetorically pouring the old conceptual wine called "development" into a new conceptual bottle called "human security," the reconceptualization is useful because it emphasizes the psychological end state of development instead of the more mechanical processes of developing. Enhancing human security is surely what development is all about. But, when the end result of development is explicitly defined as heightening human security, the yardstick for assessing development's progress changes. Development becomes a quality evidenced by diminished anxiety and despair instead of simply a quantity registered in economic indicators. When development equals enhanced human security it involves much more than increasing gross domestic product, privatizing, marketizing, industrializing or otherwise altering the economic—and social—statistical profiles of societies. Development defined as enhanced human security becomes real when anxiety lessens, misery subsides, despair diminishes, hope blossoms and contentment grows among the majority of people in the majority of societies (see *Development: Cultural Dimensions*).

There is of course a correlation between material welfare and human security, but it is partial at best, and it is certainly not linear because high levels of human anxiety and spiritual malaise also typify many wealthy societies. Human insecurity is by no means limited to the poorer countries. Qualities of life and varieties of living consonant with human security may well differ from community to community, and therefore so too may visions of development differ. What remains constant is contentment as an end state.

The UNDP assigns to international organizations the task of elevating the quality of security in human environments. This, the authors of the *Human Development Report* say, should be the overriding and unifying goal of international cooperation. Notably, pursuing human security as a goal bridges the traditional bifurcation of international organizational agendas where "war and peace" questions have been rather strictly segregated and separated from "economic and social" issues. This, for example, has been very much the case with the United Nations, where, structurally, programmatically and practically, the "peace and security" side of the organization has had little to do with the "social and economic development" side. Dealing with problems of peacekeeping and collective security has been the legislative responsibility of the Security Council and the executive task of specialized departments within the Secretariat. Welfare and development issues, on the other hand, have formed the agenda of the Economic and Social Council; implementing programs here has been the task of the Secretariat's Department of Economic and Social Affairs and its Department of Humanitarian Affairs as well as that of several of the UN's specialized agencies. Such a division of international organizational labor has certainly made sense bureaucratically, but conceptually as well as practically it has made the United Nations into two rather loosely connected organizations—i.e., one that attends to peace and security and another that promotes social and economic development. If there has been any conceptual linkage at all between the two "sides" of the UN, it has been in the Charter's affirmation that peace is not possible as long as inequality among states and misery and ignorance among peoples continue to cause wars (see *United Nations: Achievements and Agenda*).

Advocates of the pursuit of human security, however, assign to the United Nations and affiliated international organizations a set of goals even more ambitious than promoting and procuring peace. Establishing peace between states and within societies, need not be an ultimate end; it can rather be one means for enhancing human security. Peace is unquestionably an attribute of a humanly secure environment: threats of attack, bombardment and violent death are surely sources of great anxiety to

many people. Yet peace is only one attribute of human security. What the United Nations advocates of human security would have the United Nations aspire toward in its economic, social and humanitarian activities is to foster the rest of the attributes of a humanly secure environment around the world. Therefore, when the primary mission of the United Nations is defined as enhancing human security, military peacekeeping and economic and social development cease to be disjointed undertakings, and instead become two sets of complementary instrumentalities employed in pursuit of a unified, transcendent goal—the elimination of anxiety and despair.

Supporters of the concept of human security say that what the United Nations must have, is not only "an agenda for peace," but also "an agenda beyond peace." UN thinking—though not necessarily the thinking of all member states—could be evolving toward such a new agenda. In his 1992 report entitled *An Agenda for Peace*, Secretary-General Boutros Boutros-Ghali ventured beyond establishing peace and devoted a disproportionate amount of space to discussing United Nations responsibilities in post-conflict situations. He called for programs that would foster social integration within countries, and that would strengthen civil societies, instill democracy and protect human rights. The United Nations, he reasoned, should not only help to establish peace, but it should also help people to maximally benefit from it. *The Agenda for Peace* was later supplemented by an *Agenda for Development*, which might have closed the conceptual circle by welding peacekeeping to social development to economic development to human rights. But, this development credo mostly voiced conventional themes concerning the obligations of rich and poor countries and thus fell short of a human security synthesis (see *Human Rights and Environmental Rights: Their Sustainable Development Compatibility*).

Conceptualizing the international organizational mission as one of comprehensively promoting human security frees the policy imagination to contemplate the nature and variety of threats in individuals' environments, to consider how such threats may be removed, and to wonder how international organizations might contribute to removing such threats. Achieving peace is always a required first step. But enhancing human security also centers the UN in the field of human rights. Or, perhaps better stated, it centers human rights in the UN. It makes the United Nations into a vehicle of democratization, and it makes the world organization a main provider of material well-being. The UN's mission becomes not merely obtaining peace, but raising the quality of the peace obtained.

What is perhaps most significant, but also most controversial, in the notion of human security is that it focuses international organizational attention directly on individuals and their circumstances. This implies that the appropriate role for international organizations, and the prescribed role for the UN, should henceforth be to relate immediately to people, and to serve them directly in such ways as to enhance the quality of their lives. Here the UN is no longer conceived as primarily an instrument of governments that primarily serves their interests. The role of the UN implicit in the notion of human security is to make people more secure, not to make governments more comfortable, legitimate, autonomous, wealthy or powerful. This is a revolutionary idea indeed.

Ultimately, the idea of human security comes to constitute a challenge to state sovereignty. To make *people* psychologically secure under some conceivable circumstances, may be the antithesis of making *states* politically and ideologically secure, especially when states themselves are the perpetrators of individuals' insecurities (see *Psychology of Peace; Peace with Freedom*). Conceivably in some cases, the appropriate role for international organizations that are promoting human security would be to intervene to protect people from governments, or otherwise to empower people against governmental neglect and abuse. Pressing international organizations into the service of individually-focused human security could therefore constitute an incremental step toward circumventing or marginalizing states and legitimizing supranational governance.

It is not surprising then that the UNDP's advocacy of human security as the UN's main mission has not been universally well-received. Numerous governments, sensitive about sovereignty, opposed to supranationality and wary about international intervention into their affairs, have voiced objections. Some of these have been outspokenly harsh. The idea of international organizations relating directly to people, frontally assaults almost everything traditionally associated with traditional conceptions of the state, and this is naturally discomforting to many governments. Yet, in human history, innovative ideas usually march out in front of reality. But good ideas have a way of becoming reality. Many students of the world affairs today accept that the comprehensive pursuit of human security is surely a good idea, and there is increasing evidence to suggest that its time may be coming, if indeed it has not already arrived.

See also: *Positive versus Negative Peace; Social Progress and Human Survival; World Peace Order, Dimensions of a*

Bibliography

An Agenda for Peace 1992 Report of the Secretary-General, United Nations, Department of Public Information

Choue Y S 1991 *White Paper on World Peace.* Kyung Hee University Press, Seoul, Korea

Evans G 1993 *Cooperating for Peace.* Allen & Unwin, Australia

Human Development Report 1993, 1993 UN Development Programme. Oxford University Press, New York

Our Global Neighborhood 1995 The Report of the Commission on Global Governance. Oxford University Press, New York

DONALD J. PUCHALA

Human Value and Materialistic Civilization

1. Introduction

Materialism has triumphed at the cultural level. We believe that physical well-being and material prosperity are the highest values. Capitalism is a more strident materialism than Communism ever was.

The ethical position consonant with materialism is utilitarianism and its social science is economics. Economic utilitarianism is the dominant ethical position today. It is founded on a mistaken metaphysics.

The Metaphysical Question:

Metaphysics deals with the fundamental assumptions about the nature of reality. Beyond the distinction between matter and spirit is the metaphysic of the incarnation of spirit in matter. This is the Christian position. The mathematical laws of physics and biology, as well as the emergence of consciousness from the phylogenetic system, show that there is a consciousness present from before the beginning of the process, which provides the laws by which the process guides itself. The emergence of consciousness is the system gone to self-consciousness and self-criticism.

The Meta-ethical Question:

Meta-ethics deals with the fundamental convictions about the nature of human nature in terms of which we promulgate our ethical guidelines.

If the phylogenetic system can intervene in itself to

correct itself what shall guide this activity? Some notion of the goal or purpose of the whole. What is this goal? It is the perfection of humanity. Human being, the historical manifestation of the consciousness endemic in the phylogenetic system, is intuitively aware of the purpose and goal of the system, namely the perfection of human being: and the perfect human being is an eternal paradigm like a mathematical law, that has been present since before time, in the mind of God, and has from the beginning been guiding the process of the system towards itself as a goal (This is not a holdover from Platonism, but a new conclusion based on mathematical physics). The prime ethical directive in the metaphysical system is the perfection of humanity.

The Ethical Question:

The ethical correlative of this is responsibility. We should act to fulfill the prime phylogenetic directive, to perfect humanity.

The Religious Question:

Since we act not only to fulfill but also to frustrate this prime ethical directive religions should instruct people in its fulfillment. The "Golden Rule" is a good summary of the directive.

2. Materialistic Civilization

The demise of the materialist Marxist systems in the West does not mean the demise of materialism. The end of Communism might be seen as the triumph of a much more efficient materialism than Marx ever imagined, a materialism untempered by the curbs on greed and self-assertion that socialism attempted. Capitalist materialism is the unfettered pursuit of material gain limited only by competition and scarcity. It originated, if Max Weber is correct, in a morally severe cultural context and was originally controlled by the moral sanctions of Protestantism. This Protestant ethic in capitalism has given way before an ethic of relentless consumption and shameless self-aggrandizement. Materialism has triumphed at the cultural level.

The real values of capitalism are mercantile and monetary. As Jeremy Bentham (see *Bentham, Jeremy*) said in the nineteenth century, one must assign a monetary value to everything because only in monetary terms can the value of things be compared. In this spirit we have the cost-benefit analyses of the once "dismal" now glorious science of economics, and I have heard "cost-benefit" presentations on the subject of nuclear defense systems that assign monetary value to human lives—under a million casualties and it is not cost-effective to build a $100 billion anti-missile system. This kind of analysis is endemic to the utilitarian ethic that is the corollary of mercantile materialism, and it displays the challenge to ethical thought in our time.

The dominant ethical reason in our time is utilitarian, and the dominant social science is economics, because the dominant metaphysical assumption of our time is materialist. If humanity and morality are to be renewed we must either find resources of moral renewal within materialist utilitarianism or challenge the materialist metaphysic with a more adequate account of reality.

It is not to be assumed that because a system is metaphysically materialist or agnostic it cannot warrant an ethics that deserve admiration. Materialist metaphysics can warrant an altruistic, responsible ethics. Adam Smith was a professor of moral philosophy and wrote *The Wealth of Nations* as a contribution to ethics. Rule utilitarianism and enlightened self-interest warrant an ethics that is for the most part praiseworthy. Therefore, I do not wish to suggest that materialism is bound to issue in immorality, because that is not true; and in any case idealism has caused as much if not more horror. Rather I want to criticize the metaphysical assumption of materialism in metaphysical terms rather than from an ethical point of view. There is a link between metaphysics and morality, but it is not one of logical entailment. Nevertheless, an accurate metaphysic is more likely to inspire an adequate ethic.

The logical alternative to materialism is some form of spiritism or "idealism," as it is called in Western philosophy. If human being is not only a material entity but also a spiritual being then advantages are to be sought not only in the material realm but also in the spiritual, and since, in the usual form of this alternative, the spiritual endures while the material obviously decays, the greater advantages are to be found in the realm of the spirit. A spiritual metaphysic does not, however, guarantee a humane ethic. On the contrary, the assumption that spiritual benefits far outweigh material benefits has sanctioned torture in this world to secure bliss in the next, as the logic of the Spanish Inquisition held. The deprivation of the body, whether self inflicted or inflicted by others, benefits the soul. This is a dangerous metaphysical position because it warrants the meta-ethical idea that life in this material world is insignificant compared to life in the spiritual world, and thus justifies carelessness about human and natural life in this world.

There are, historically, two kinds of response to a spiritual metaphysic, libertinism and asceticism. Both are ways of showing contempt for matter, one abuses material being because it is of no consequence the other shuns it because it is evil. Both of these responses were present in the Gnostic religions of the late classical period in the West when Christian orthodoxy was establishing itself. Christian orthodoxy found a way between these two extremes with the help of the doctrine of the incarnation of the divine (see *Christianity*).

In Christ the spirit enters into and bonds with matter without confusion, without change, without division, and without separation (*asungchutos, atreptos, adiairetos, achoristos*) as the four famous adverbs of the Chalcedonian definition say. It was the heretics who sought to maintain a separation and a division between spirit and matter in the person of Christ. Christ as the seamless union of matter and spirit is the key to a proper understanding of matter and spirit. They are in fact inseparable and indivisible.

The dichotomy between matter and spirit, body and soul is highly problematic not only from a theological but also from a scientific point of view, and any constructive criticism of materialism must begin with a critique of this dualism.

I shall argue for a third way based neither on a materialist nor a spiritualist metaphysic but on the idea of the incarnation of the divine, the materialization of the spirit or the spiritualization of matter, symbolized, and for some of us realized, in the birth of Jesus from a virgin and the resurrection of Jesus from the dead. These two "events" in the history of Jesus entail the transformation of the normal processes of nature by the divine and the limitation of the normal properties of the divine by nature. I am aware that these are the two least acceptable gospel "events" according to the standards of materialist judgment. In this view matter is not susceptible to influence by spirit, in fact, there is no such thing as spirit except as an epiphenomenon of matter. Therefore, these gospel stories cannot be literally true; they are either symbols of the aspirations of the mind or signs of its susceptibility to wishful thinking. I submit that they are literally true.

A materialist explanation of the occurrence of such stories must invoke the category of mind, because the stories exist and they must be caused. Mind is the word for the cause of such things, but on a materialist view mind does not have an ontological status apart from the brain. Mind is the function of the brain; a materialist judgment with which paradoxically I concur. My third way, of the incarnation of the divine, does not need to draw a line of separation between the brain and the mind. Mind is in fact a function of matter; but what sort of a thing is matter that can produce such a thing as mind? If mind comes from mat-

ter can we reverse the equation and say the mind influences matter; is there a reciprocity of any kind in this relationship?

Now I know that a lot of nonsense is spoken and believed under the rubric, "Mind over matter," but abuse does not exclude proper use, and in any case there is some perfectly respectable evidence to suggest that the question of the relative primacy of mind and matter should be left open, that the question might be undecidable. Quantum theory, for instance, shows that at the sub-atomic level matter is susceptible to the influence of mind. When observed, sub-atomic units behave sometimes as particles and sometimes as waves. What they are, when not observed, is unknown. The account of sub-atomic particles begins only when observer and observed come upon the scene together; there can be no going back before this dyad. Thus the question of the relationship between matter and mind is open again, if only a crack, although this opening does not warrant a general skepticism about the findings of the empirical sciences, and a general credulity about the power of the mind. The laws of nature might be merely statistical but they are nevertheless firm enough for the purposes of technology, and we have been very successful using those laws.

My argument is, in its broad outline, not new; it owes much to Teilhard de Chardin, Alfred North Whitehead, and their recent interpreters, amongst whom is Paul Davies, professor of mathematical physics at the University of Adelaide, Australia, and winner of Templeton Prize for Progress in Religion.[1] The argument is not a re-presentation of their views but my own appropriation of some of their insights.

3. Human Values

3.1 The Metaphysical Question

There is no necessary congruence between metaphysics and morals. One does not have to act consistently with what one believes about the nature of the world and the nature of human nature, but such integrity seems to me to be desirable, and so I shall try to show what a third alternative to, on the one hand, a utilitarian ethic based on an economic meta-ethic and a materialist metaphysic, and, on the other hand, an absolutist ethic based on a mystical meta-ethic and a spiritual/idealist metaphysic, might look like.

I do not use the term "metaphysics" in the old sense of a rational inquiry into the nature of being but rather in the pragmatic sense of a reflection on the presuppositions of the hypotheses we frame about the world.

The modern period was inaugurated by Descartes at the beginning of the 17th century with his methodological principle *de omnibus dubitandum est* (every appearance must be subjected to critical doubt) and his consequent division of the things of the world into the *res cogitans* (the things that occur to thought) and the *res extensa* (the things that occur to sense perception). The relationship between these two categories was problematic then and became more so with the passage of time. Some attempted to reduce the *res extensa* to the *res cogitans*, as in idealism, while others reduced the *res cogitans* to the *res extensa*, as in materialism. The first move failed, the second succeeded, and produced the world we know as modern. The beginning of modernism was the firm distinction between the material and the spiritual, which led to the demise of the spiritual. The moral consequences of modernism are the plight we find ourselves in at present and which this conference has been called to address. The reduction of human being to a *res extensa* has provided the ethical foundation for a manipulation of nature and humanity that threatens destruction at the same time as it promises wonderful benefits.

I want to emphasize that I do appreciate the benefits of our pragmatic materialism; I am glad we do not live in a religiously dominated world, which would be even more susceptible to superstition and tyranny than our present world. I am glad that there was an Enlightenment in the West. As a result there is a modicum of objectivity in our world and wonderful progress has been made in science and technology, especially in the field of medicine where it impinges vividly on most of us. This science and technology is the greatest contribution of the West to world civilization; it has transformed the ancient cultures of Asia, and it came to pass as a result of the demystification of the world by the scientific turn to materialism. Therefore, the scientific turn to materialism must be celebrated at the same time as it is criticized.

There is a dark side to science and technology, which is especially evident in the ecological crisis we seem to be entering because of over-population and a wasteful exploitation of natural resources, both made possible by scientific and technological advances. The challenges I wish, however, to highlight, are those that come from advances in the biological sciences. I began with a passing reference to quantum physics in my introduction, now I shall take up the most important source of metaphysical concern to me, namely biology.

The dominant metaphysical paradigm in the field of human nature is evolution by natural selection. This is what is taught in our universities. Human being is the product of a phylogenetic process that proceeds in an entirely random way. There is no guiding intelligence; natural selection is a matter of chance. The only discernible direction in the process is towards survival of the species, and that takes place not through individual consciousness but through the gene. The basic drive of all living things, including human beings, is to pass their genes on to the next generation under the most favorable circumstances. Consciousness is an epiphenomenon of this process.

I shall discuss the meta-ethical consequences of this model later. At present I want to point out that there are good grounds for modifying this understanding of phylogenetic evolution. The process may appear once to have been random but now it is trying to introduce rational control into itself. My standing here and reflecting on the process is itself a function of the process itself. In Charles Darwin, the phylogenetic process came to self-consciousness and from that point was able to reflect critically upon itself. In the mathematics of Paul Davies, the Templeton prize winner, the process comes to understand the laws that guide its physical development. Right now, through us, the phylogenetic process has come to self-consciousness and is reflecting critically on itself. The biologist is the gene gone to self-consciousness, the physicist is the atom gone to self-consciousness, and through each of them the system is intervening in itself to discover and impose rational order and conscious control.

Science and technology is, therefore, the way the process of being seeks to improve itself. If this is the case then consciousness is not an epiphenomenon, but rather a fundamental transformation of the phylogenetic system which enables it to intervene in itself. This has been recognized for some time by those who speak of co-evolution in the sense of evolution running on the two tracks of nature and culture. Culture influences biology in fundamental ways, and the old question of the primacy of nature or nurture, biology or culture, has been obsolete in the realm of biological science for at least twenty years. We know now that cultural changes, for instance changes in the hierarchical status of male cichlids (Fernauld), cause changes in the patterning on their brains which in turn cause changes in their sexual organs. A change in social status is accompanied by a change in physiology. If this is the case then consciousness in its form of culture and society is an important factor in the development of the phylogenetic system.

A once apparently random system is now trying to discover the laws that underlie the apparent randomness and to impose order on itself, this much seems beyond dispute. The next step, which I am prepared to take, is open to dispute, namely that consciousness was present in the system from the beginning. This does not necessarily entail that therefore nothing in the history of the system was ever random, because it is possible for there to be consciousness that does not have control, consciousness that has desires it is unable to realize. Davies' guiding laws are evidence of the presence of consciousness from before the beginning of the process, from before time, since with St. Augustine (see *St. Augustine*) we now know that time and space came into being along with matter, in the "Big Bang." The universe did not come into being in time and space but in nothing, and in that nothingness there were the laws in terms of which it was constituted and would change. This change is time, and it takes place according to the timeless laws of the consciousness that was there when there was no time and space, according to the mind of God.

With the emergence of historical being in humanity the system is able to separate itself from itself and criticize and seek to improve itself, by gradually gaining control over more and more of itself. This is the metaphysical meaning of science and technology, and of the incarnation of the divine. At this point of the exposition, we can say that the divine is the consciousness that was always present in the system and now emerges in human being and through human science and technology gradually gains control over the system. This is not all that might be said of the divine but all that should be said at this point.

3.2 The Meta-ethical Question

This understanding of the incarnation of the divine in matter has consequences for the understanding of the nature of human nature. This understanding is a meta-ethical understanding. By meta-ethics, I mean the guiding convictions about the nature of human nature in terms of which we frame our (ethical) hypotheses about human behavior. Let me begin with an example. We have recently demonstrated that the implantation of fetal brain tissue in a diseased brain can offset the effects of Parkinson's disease. This disease is caused by the deterioration of a relatively small number of neurons that have been identified and located. Fetal tissue has been shown to replace those damaged neurons, the implanted tissue bonding with the native tissue quite satisfactorily. This was demonstrated in a human being who died of other causes, shortly after receiving the implantation treatment for Parkinson's. An autopsy showed the satis-

factory bonding of the implanted tissue. The same thing has been demonstrated in the neurons that control circadian rhythms in mice. We now face the question of whether human fetal brain tissue should be made available commercially to treat Parkinson's disease, or the failure of circadian rhythms.

I can think of several levels on which to answer the question, but any answer must begin with a recognition of the feeling of reluctance, most of us have at the thought of the commercial exploitation of human fetuses. Instinctively, we feel that this course of action violates a conviction we have about our own dignity. We intuitively value ourselves more than this course of action takes into account. There is more than one explanation for this intuition, but the explanation I favor is based on the assumption that human being, the historical manifestation of the consciousness endemic in the phylogenetic process, is intuitively aware of the purpose and goal of the system, namely, the perfection of human being; and that perfect human being is an eternal paradigm like a mathematical law, that has been present since before time, in the mind of God, and has from the beginning been guiding the process of the system towards itself as a goal. In theological terms this is the image of God in which we are made, and the perfection of Christ manifest in the life, death and, especially, the Resurrection of Jesus. The intuition of that goal is the prime ethical directive in the system and in the human consciousness that is the hitherto most sophisticated form of the system. In this way the meta-ethical imperatives arise out of the metaphysical indicatives.

3.3 The Ethical Question

In the light of these meta-ethics, that the prime ethical directive is the perfection of human being, what secondary directives shall we derive? Let me take another example.

Recently 80 plus religious leaders in the USA signed a document objecting to the patenting of biological organisms. It is not clear to me what their objection is, whether it is against the manufacture of such organisms at all or merely against their commercial exploitation. In any case, it is not theologically or ethically sufficient to say that since living organisms are created by God they can not be appropriated for private profit. The meaning of the term "created" in this context is too vague to bear the weight of the ethical stricture. "Creation" in this case can only mean that God inspired human beings with the ability to create the organisms in question, because there is no denying that they were made by human beings. So the question becomes, if divine creation operates through human creation, who is entitled to dispose over the results of that creation?

It seems to me that the same logic as divine creation through human agency should control the answer to the ethical question, who shall decide about the disposition of the results; human beings as necessary agents of the divine shall decide. But what principles shall guide this decision? The principles derived from our metaphysical and meta-ethical discussion so far; and in this case they are: the divine purpose as discerned through our understanding of the phylogenetic process; and that purpose is that we should intervene in the system to reduce its cruelty and wastefulness, to reduce human suffering and promote human perfection.

The fact that we have the power to intervene in our own on-going creation highlights the category of responsibility. Human being, human intellect, and human judgment are increasingly responsible for the future course of the phylogenetic process, for the future of creation. Instead of obfuscating this fact by appealing to an element of obscurity they call God, the religious leaders should have emphasized human responsibility, and the transparency of the divine within the experience of responsibility. This is a form of the Kantian argument for the existence of God from the phenomenology of moral reason. The first commandment in the Bible is the commandment to be co-creators with God, completely responsible for the process of creation (Gen 1: 26-27—God made us in the divine image and commanded us to be fruitful and multiply and take responsibility for the creation. Our original mandate is to pro-create images of the divine).

Responsibility is the primary moral category to be derived from the metaphysics and meta-ethics I have outlined. Responsibility implies something or someone to respond to. In this case, of general responsibility, I believe that the "other" of responsibility is the divine within the system, and if this is the case there must be some way to know the purposes of the divine so that we can respond to them and so collaborate in realizing them. I believe that we have intuitions of these purposes and I have summarized them in the somewhat vague phrase as the perfection of humanity. This might be construed as an inflated version of the natural imperative to survival, but I think that the advent of mind makes it more than that. In any case, the moral traditions of the great religions, which all converge on some version of the Golden Rule, preserve this fundamental moral intuition, and it is contrary to the simple drive for survival.

The Golden Rule, treat others as you would like them to treat you, is firstly a prohibition on revenge,

which treats others exactly as they treat you. Revenge is a survival drive arising from the phylogenetic system and so this fundamental moral insight is a prime instance of the system criticizing itself.

Now, I take this moral insight to be a testimony to the divine existence and purpose that was hidden in the system from the beginning and that began to emerge as the system developed the capacity to recognize it, namely consciousness. The divine is, therefore, not the same as consciousness but is nevertheless inseparable from it. A utilitarian would argue that it is not necessary to posit the existence of the divine to explain the emergence of the Golden Rule; it is merely enlightened self-interest, a rule that in the long run benefits everyone and so enhances the survivability of every individual. This is a cogent argument that gains power from its conformity with the parsimony of Occam's razor. I do not intend to discuss it here, except to say that parsimony is not a necessary requirement for an adequate explanation. H.L.Mencken had it right when he said that for every complex question there is usually a simple answer— that is wrong! Some complex phenomena demand more than parsimony.

The theological assumptions of the religious leaders who condemned the patenting of biological organisms is an instance of the kind of unbalanced appeal to one side of the Cartesian dualism that has led to the triumph of materialism. They claim that living organisms are related to the spiritual in such a way as to make it inappropriate to include them in the conventions of commerce. These organisms are not human and so do not raise the questions that the commercial exploitation of human fetuses does. I can see no reason why, under the ethical norm of responsibility they should not be patented.

The ethical challenge is so important because just as science and technology enable a benign and helpful intervention in the process of creation so they enable a destructive and deforming intervention. As the phylogenetic process comes to self-consciousness, divine and human action converge and diverge. At some points they are identical and compassion enters the system through human action; at other points they are anti-antithetical and pain and destruction enter through human action. Human consciousness has, therefore, a measure of freedom against the imperatives of the system. We can recognize and realize or recognize and reject the divine purpose.

3.4 The Religious Question

Religions display this same ambiguity of creation and destruction compassion and cruelty, therefore moral education and exhortation is an essential part of religious life. This moral exhortation should in my opinion not set the spiritual over against the material, construct a Manichean or Modern dichotomy between matter and spirit. Rather it should inculcate responsibility and the obligations responsibility entails, to care for the creation, respect all living things, and honor the incarnation of the divine while responding to the transcendent possibility of the next, new and challenging stages in the development of creation. In this spirit humanity will not be an increasing burden on the system dragging it down to collapse, but rather a powerful energy in its progression towards fullness of bliss and perfection for all existing things. That will be what the Christians call the second coming of Christ, because for us Christ revealed the culmination of the process as eternal life, by his resurrection from the dead in a totally transformed and unprecedented form of matter, his resurrection body.

These are of course matters of Christian faith and I do not ask everyone to share my belief in them, but only to observe that they do fit into a coherent and not unlikely account of the natural and human world as we understand it.

4. Conclusion

We are far from a full understanding and must, therefore, keep our minds open to growth and change. It is surely the case that none of the great religions gives a final account of the nature of things, and neither do secular sciences and philosophies. We are, happily I would say, all living in the question, all enlivened by the quest and the controversy. For this reason I have spoken only of questions—the metaphysical question, the meta-ethical question, the ethical question and the religious question. I love questions because they open up a future and give energy to my curiosity. I do not want answers before my death, because to have the answer is indeed to reach that quiescence that is most akin to death. I believe that on that day we shall have our answers, and be at peace, but we shall not be able to rob those still living in the question of the joy of the quest.

See also: *Religion and Peace; Education for Global Citizenship*

Notes

1. His acceptance speech is a convincing exposition of the view that the process of creation, from the physical to the organic to the living to the conscious stages, is still going on, and that it is guided by transcendental laws. These transcendental laws, which are described by mathematics, indicate the presence of a transcendental lawgiver. This is a fine new version of the classic teleological argument for the existence of God. Paul Davies, 'Physics and the Mind of God; The Templeton Prize Address," *First Things* 55 (August-September, 1995) pp. 31-35.

ROBERT HAMERTON-KELLY

Humancenterism

Humancenterism is a thought that regards man as "a spiritual being who is neither God, nor an animal" and puts particular emphasis on the "dignity of man." It reaffirms that human being should be the center of human history and civilization and humanity must be valued above everything else.

1. Humanism and Humancenterism

Pico della Mirandola (1463-94), a representative humanist in the 15th century, remarks in his work, *De Dignitate Hominis*:

Having created man and put him at the center of the universe, God told man, "Adam, I would not have conferred your place, shape, and role; this is because I want you to define your place, figure, and responsibility according to your own wish, will, and decision. All the other creatures have been formed by the universal law. However, you, as a man, is not restricted in any sense. To you I delegate the power that you form your own appearance to your own will.

God conferred free will to man, thereupon he could decide his own fate. This is a typical position of humanism. Humancenterism is clearly distinct from the concept of Humanism. Humanism is a beneficiary concept from the omnipotent God, which differentiates the object from the subject. Hence it originates from the concept of Goddism. On the other hand, humancenterism does not recognize the difference between the subject and the object, only emphasizing the uniqueness and independence of human beings. Young Seek Choue put it this way:

Humancenterism is a viewpoint different from the "anthropocentrism" or the similar ones such as the belief of the Chondoism that "human being is the Heaven" and the belief of the Hinduism that "You are the Universe." Strictly speaking, these thoughts equally treat man as God .... Humancenterism, as man is man, no more and no less, can neither elevate himself to the level of divinity, nor debase himself to the level of animality. Humancenterism teaches the value of humanity and human dignity, by emphasizing that man is a spiritual being, not just the son of God or an animal (Young Seek Choue 1996 p. 76).

Human beings have their own unique values: personality, subjectivity, and humanity. Because of these unique features, man can be a "harmonized personality" and to be of the highest value in the universal order. This is the dictation of humancenterism.

2. The Essence of Humancenterism

The Medieval Age was characterized as the spirit-dominated era. Material well-being was deemphasized in favor of spiritual and religious life. On the other hand, modern era, especially since the Industrial Revolution, witnesses excessive obedience to material well-being. The cult of materialism has enhanced the development of Science and Technology. Digital Revolution, the impact of information glut, life science, and genetic-engineering technologies are progressing at an extreme pace. The digital telecommunication revolution has turned the planet Earth into a global village. Scientists can manipulate the brain to produce sensations of happiness and mastery and rearrange the genetic code. Science and technology are progressing in every field at an extremely fast pace, with no signs of slowing down. Yet, people in this "brave new world" seem to be more uneasy, anxious and restless, like the one continually haunted by "something." Change and development have been so rapid that we have lost our sense of direction. Furthermore, man is faced with the threat of genocidal nuclear and other types of holocaust.

The philosophy of humancenterism, therefore, dictates that all the worldly affairs—material, institution, science, ideology, etc.,—should be designed in such a way that human dignity is respected to its maximum. Not only that, even religious affairs are rejected unfairly to interfere with human life. Many people have been persecuted purely for religious reasons. Man is for man himself. Material and institution are also for man. So are science and technologies, for no more and for no less.

3. Humancenterism and Science & Technology

We are living in a turning point society: Daily innovating computer and network technologies, application softwares, artificial intelligence, genetic engineering technologies. Science and technology advances at its own way with an uncontrollable pace. Its advancement may lead to the bottom of fortune's wheel.

Where are we rushing in? Are we making a dash for a suicidal attack? The important thing is to brake the blinded rush of science and technology which is threatening to the existence of culture, civilization, and nature. The important thing is to reduce speed to hold the explosion off. We need to make a metarmorphic change to survive. We need to be headed for a different future. We need to shift our paradigms to prepare for a new era.

A new realm called Cyberspace has emerged and rapidly replacing some parts of the Newtonian physical space. In that space, tremendous amounts of information, opinions and values are already interacting. People find numerous information, knowledge, and values; some of them even lead a life in that space. The more this virtual space becomes important and substantial for human life, *the moral system* of our society will be more chaotic. Also, the issues of artificial intelligence and human clones are appallingly warning that "man is an organic life in itself" and if this "nature of life" will not be taken care of, the very fabric of human society would be fundamentally falling apart. The modern society, in which technology deeply permeates every sphere of our life, desperately requires humancenterism, which contains "humanity" and the "spirit of life."

4. Humancenterism and Oughtopia

The philosophy of humancenterism is the most essential element of Oughtopia, the concept originally proposed by Young Seek Choue in his original work, *Oughtopia* (Oxford: Pergamon Press, 1979). The name "Oughtopia" is composed of two words, i.e., "ought (must be)" and "topia (place)," and aims at realizing a society which is spiritually beautiful, materially affluent, and humanely rewarding (Jong Youl Yoo 1980 p. 353).

Humancenterism should be one of the key ingredients for an Oughtopia society. Humancenterism, a recognition for an original human value, seeks to liberate the distorting structures of man's true nature, thereby places "dignity of man" to be of the highest value in the worldly order. It is a movement to retrieve mankind's personality. And it is a philosophical necessity to rearrange the priority among the goal and instruments. Human life as an existing being, human society and scientific civilization—these are all means, not the goal for human being.

Humancenterism is not given but made. It is the role and responsibility of the whole human being to judiciously select and implement the information technologies relevant to the vision of the future society. Our future society should be the one where the human value and human dignity are most respected. But only when we could spontaneously and sensibly respond to the new social waves and global trends, the materially affluent, spiritually beautiful, and humanely rewarding, the Oughtopia society will become a reality.

Bibliography

Bell D 1989 Communication Technology: For Better or for Worse? In: Salvaggio, J L (ed.) *The Information Society: Economic, Social & Structural Issues*. Lawrence Erlbaum Associates, Hillsdale, New Jersey

Busuttil S et al., (eds.) 1990 *Our Responsibilities to Future Generations*. Foundation for International Studies, Malta

Cater D 1981 Human value in information society. In: Rochell C C (ed.) *An Information Agenda for the 1980s*. American Library Association, Chicago

Choue Y S 1979 *Oughtopia*. Pergamon Press, Oxford, UK

Choue Y S 1982 *On Peace*. Bubmunsa, Korea

Choue Y S 1987 *Peace in the Global Village*. Kyung Hee University Press, Korea

Kennedy P 1993 *Preparing for the Twenty-first Century*. Random House, New York

Kwon G H 1995 The Vision, Goals and Tasks for the Human-centered Information Society. Paper delivered in International Conference, Kyung Hee University, Korea

Kwon G H 1997 *The Logic of Information Society*. Nanam, Korea

Morin E, Kern A B 1993 *Terre-Patrie*. Moonye Publishing, Korea

Winpisinger W W 1989 *Reclaiming Our Future*. Westview Press, Boulder

Yoo J Y 1980 An Experimental Model of Oughtopia: A Future of Our Making. In: Kim K H (ed.) *21st Century: Prospects and Problems*. Kyung Hee University Press, Korea

GI HEON KWON

Humanistic Values for the 21st Century

The 21st century promises to be a time of scientific and technological growth at a level never before experienced in human history. This growth will either trigger chaos, disruption, war, starvation and disease or will introduce a period of humanistic cooperation, development, progress and peace.[1] What emerges will depend upon what values are embraced, taught, encouraged and legislated. The value choices, which must be deliberately chosen and not left to chance, must be secular, global and familial. The accepted values must be embraced, taught, encouraged and supported internationally, nationally, locally and personally.

What is proposed here represents some of the value choices, the ethical building blocks, that will enable a world of peace and harmony to come into existence—a world in which human diversity is respected and tolerated and, at the same time, a world in which each individual will be enabled and encouraged to maximize his or her potential, without discrimination and in an atmosphere of freedom.[2] What is required to bring about this idealized world is a democratic, pluralistic society which recognizes the human rights of each individual and in which no man or woman or class of men or women shall be demeaned and treated as mere slaves existing only to fulfill the desires of those who would be their masters; a world in which no man or woman or class of men or women shall be used as tools for the lusts of others,[3] or for the ambitions of others or for the greed of others;[4] a world in which the life of every man and woman and child shall be recognized and esteemed as a unique and ultimate statement of the evolutionary process and therefore of inestimable value.[5] To achieve and make real this concept of a world of peace for the 21st century the following humanistic values provide the basic essentials.

1. Humanistic Values for the 21st Century must be Secular, Democratic and Pluralistic

The values must be of the people, for the people and by the people. They must embrace common moral decencies such as altruism, integrity, freedom, justice, honesty, truthfulness, responsibility, compassion and must reflect the normative standards human beings discover and develop through living together. Value development must draw upon reason, science, the arts, and must express concern for justice and fairness and concern for the physical and mental well-being of every human being in an effort to maximize individual freedom without limiting the freedom of others.[6]

Humanistic values espouse cooperation and peaceful living and reject the use of violence to settle problems whether the problems be international, national, local or familial. Humanistic values recognize cultural or religious diversity and individual creativity while rejecting the validity of declarations made by any group alleging spiritual superiority or political autonomy over others. Humanistic values incorporate many of the moral and ethical values espoused by the world's religions, but seek to move beyond particularistic religious belief systems (which often foster separatism) and beyond political agendas (which tend to be local or too narrow) to focus on the full humanity of the person or persons. Obviously, some humanistic values will receive support from religious and political organizations; others will not. For example, the great religions have preached universal brotherhood but, unfortunately, intolerance of other faiths and a spirit of divisiveness have made the implementation of the brotherhood ideal impossible. Narrow, parochial doctrines of salvation have barred those outside of the faith system from fellowship with those within. Humanistic values for the 21st century cannot be so contained and must not be limited by theologies or by deontological ethics that have, over the centuries, encouraged divisiveness and produced violence.

Nor can nationalistic or ethnic teachings and pronouncements that encourage divisiveness and produce violence be permitted to thwart the promulgation of humanistic values. It is clear that the development and emergence of nation-states have freed citizens from foreign domination and have encouraged ethnic and national self-determination. There is no reason why national governments should not play constructive roles in achieving a peaceful world by maintaining systems of law and order that encourage cultural growth and economic prosperity conducive to achieving conditions of internal harmony and enrichment of the lives of those living within their jurisdiction. Unfortunately, some nation-states have violated the rights of their citizens and have engaged in violence to achieve goals.[7] Economic rivalries between nation-states have led to bloodshed and wars. Such battles will not cease until humanistic values are recognized and expressed in world law that is accepted and respected by all countries and supported and enforced on a transnational level.

2. Humanistic Values for the 21st Century must be Global[8]

As the first generation in human history to have viewed our planet from outer space, we have been made conscious of the uniqueness of this fragment of cosmic matter which we call "earth" that circles a

rather small star (our sun) in an immense universe.[9] So far as we know at this moment, we humans are the only intelligent, rational beings existing anywhere in the cosmos. Statistical estimates suggest that elsewhere planets circling stars may have produced other intelligent life forms, but at this moment we know nothing of these other life forms, despite the claims of those who say they have encountered extra-terrestrial beings. To the best of our knowledge, we are utterly alone in the universe and we are bound together by our habitation on this planet. Our value system must extend beyond national, ethnic, religious, territorial and racial boundaries. Only a global ethic, a global humanistic value system that embraces the entire world will suffice for the 21st century.

There have been some efforts at regional economic and political cooperation. Pacts and treaties between nations governed by rules of civilized behavior are in existence. But these do not go far enough and balance-of-power politics, economic exploitation, racial strife and religious bigotry have fostered feelings of hatred and produced violence. The time is at hand for a new vision that will enable the development of political, economic, social and cultural institutions that will foster peaceful coexistence and cooperation on a world-wide basis. This vision can only become reality through the recognition of a global ethic that acknowledges both responsibilities and duties to the world community.

Because humanistic values are pluralistic, a spirit of tolerance is primary. However, tolerance does not signify the ignoring of patterns of behavior that violate or infringe upon the rights and freedoms of others. Tolerance marks the recognition of the wide variety of human expression and patterns of living; it does not mean closing the eyes to injustice, cruelty or the dehumanization of persons.

3. Humanistic Values for the 21st Century must be Based on a Familial Ethic

Anthropological and mitochondrial DNA researches[10] have made clear our evolutionary heritage. As one of the many life forms that have evolved over the millennia, human beings have developed from very simple origins to become the most complex life pattern among all living creatures.

Our best research informs us that human life originated in Africa and from Africa moved to other continents to become the multicultural people we are today. We are all brothers and sisters—children of the same parents. Differences in skin coloration, hair, eye form, and so forth represent the kinds of variations one finds in any family where no two offspring are exactly the same or develop in exactly the same way. Nevertheless, so close are we to one another that blood from one race can be transfused to save the life of someone of a different race. Our body structures, despite minor discrepancies, are the same. Body parts such as heart, lungs, kidneys, liver and so forth can be transposed between humans without regard to race, nationality, ethnic origins or other sub-categories of the human family. Therefore, as members of a single family, we must embrace humanistic family values that supersede boundaries, of nation, race, religion, ethnic origin, sexual differences, sexual preferences and so forth. We must move beyond the outmoded nationalism and separatism that have been taught for centuries and that only serve to breed tension in the human family.[11] The implication that, by belonging to one nation or race or group of people or by embracing a faith system with its particular beliefs, rules and regulations, somehow separates an individual from or elevates a person above others, cannot provide a basis for global familial values. Such membership provides identity solely on the basis of a limited group association which negates responsibility and caring for those outside of the group. Separatism based on ethnicity, nationalism and religion has bred disaster. The humanistic family ethic, while tolerating and understanding differences in customs, beliefs and social agendas, embraces an inclusiveness that seeks to rise above religious and political animosities and tensions to emphasize what unites human beings rather than that which separates them. Wherever and whenever ancient moral and separative principles are taught they must be recognized and incorporated as subsections of the broader humanistic family values.[12]

A 21st century humanistic ethic requires that the scientific basis for the oneness of the human family be accepted and taught internationally, nationally and locally in classrooms, in families, in religious and secular institutions. Moreover, the factual basis for this teaching must supersede all creationist mythologies of human origins generated by earlier non-scientific generations.

At the core of this familial ethic is support for the universal declarations of human rights (see *Declaration of the Rights of Man*) that embrace all human beings.

4. Humanistic Global Familial Values for the 21st Century must Embrace a Survival Ethic

To preserve and honor and revere the small blue planet "earth" which is our home all humans must recognize and support an ecological ethic that evolves out of a global family concept. Our view of the earth from space plus research into the inter-relationship of ecological factors makes clear that our planet is an independent globe with a single life-support system. There is not one life-support system for Asia and another for the Americas and still another for Africa or Europe—all planet earth life-support systems are the same. There are no national boundaries to our ecosphere. We are one and the earth is our home.

Only fools trash their own homes. Nevertheless, some members of our human family suffer from short-term vision. Their lust for wealth and power expresses little or no concern for human well-being. These persons, and the corporations they represent, are indifferent to what the rape, desecration and despoiling of forests, land and waters and the destruction of non-human life forms can mean to the health and security of present and future generations. They trash our home, the earth.[13] In addition, the naive and ill-informed also despoil our environment. Acting on the basis of non-scientific superstitions, ignorant people kill endangered animals for bones, horns, tusks, penises and other body parts that are supposed to have magical power to enhance sexuality, cure disease or prolong life. No matter what excuses are given for ecological indifference, international, national and local education, laws, and counter-controls must be developed as part of a conservation ethic. Individuals or groups of individuals must not be permitted to trash our home, the earth. Those who do must be brought to account before courts of law and punished so that their actions become so unprofitable that they will be abandoned.

We are now at a point in history where the establishment of an international environmental monitoring agency is urgently needed. Appropriate standards for the disposal of industrial waste and for the control of toxic emissions must be developed not only to protect the earth's precious resources, but also to preserve a healthy environment for future generations.

5. Humanistic Global Survival Values for the 21st Century Require that We Treat One Another as Members of a Family, Which Means that We must Look out for and Care about One Another's Welfare

To honor and protect the lives of family members requires commitment to producing a world free from violence, conflict and power struggles. Statements and pronouncements about the importance and value of human life are not enough. In the words of the ancient Romans, we require: facta non verba: deeds not words—pronouncements must be supported by action.

On an international basis, war and all forms of violent territorial battles and power struggles must be finally and completely outlawed. War has been recognized by military leaders,[14] scientists,[15] philosophers,[16] religious leaders[17] and others as an obsolete way of settling problems. Pacts and treaties promising peace must be supported with the potential for active intervention when agreements are violated and war is threatened. The employment of counter-controls[18] make the use of violence unprofitable and unsuccessful. In this respect, the United Nations has sometimes been effective but, on the other hand, has failed over and over again.

The experiences of World War II taught us the folly of trying to appease or negotiate with power-hungry sociopaths. In 1938, Neville Chamberlain, after seeking to appease Adolph Hitler at the Munich Conference, devised the slogan "Peace in Our Time." The emptiness of Hitler's commitment to peace soon became apparent. There were no counter-controls in place and World War II erupted. Indeed, recent studies have indicated that lack of controls encouraged so-called "neutral" nations, even as they provided shelter for fleeing Jews, to provide Germany with materials essential for maintaining war machinery without which the Germans could not have produced warplanes, submarines, tanks and other armaments. If ethical counter-controls had been established, and these nations had been encouraged to put aside greed for money and refuse to help Germany, it is estimated that the war in Europe could have been ended months, even years, earlier.[19] Today, the conflict in Bosnia, which could have been contained at its start, was permitted to escalate because the counter-controls that were in hand were not immediately employed. NATO and the United Nations failed to live up to their promise of deterring genocide. Time and again after NATO threatened but failed to deliver, the Serbs ignored the threats and continued to slaughter. We know that only when effective counter-controls are put into action immediately that conflict will be contained thereby compelling negotiations. This fact was made clear after the Persian Gulf conflict. When Saddam Hussein's military efforts and radar were unable to locate and repel the American F-117A Stealth Fighters, his efforts to annex Kuwait failed. Later, in October 1994, he once again threatened to move on Kuwait. The deployment of both Stealth Fighters and Stealth Bombers persuaded him to change his plans.

Sociopathic, power-hungry people usually prove to be moral cowards and social failures who fear exposure. Counter-controls compel them to observe human rights and conform to international peace efforts.

The detonation of nuclear bombs in the deserts of Pakistan and India in 1998 have destroyed the facade of non-proliferation and security that the world had hoped was provided when, in 1996, 168 nations endorsed and signed The Comprehensive Test Ban Treaty (see *Comprehensive Test Ban Treaty (CTBT)*). Perhaps both Pakistan and India will be deterred from military engagements out of respect for one another's military arsenal. It is doubtful that the imposition of sanctions against the two countries will have any immediate political impact beyond reducing the poor in each nation to levels of near starvation and death by diseases that could ordinarily be kept in check (which has been the result of sanctions in Iraq). In seeking to deter any conflict, the long-lasting tensions between the two neighbors that have resulted in three wars need to be respected. It is important that the armaments in both countries be stabilized and the mounting of nuclear warheads on missiles be discouraged or prevented. Now, both countries must be admitted to the circle of nations possessing nuclear armaments and both Pakistan and India must be urged to sign the Comprehensive Test Ban Treaty. International efforts designed to help India and Pakistan develop safeguards against any accidental launching of missiles are also important control factors. At the time of writing, there have been no reactions or responses from neighboring China.

As a further counter-control, war criminals—those who violate human rights and engage in international conflict—must be brought to trial before the United Nations War Crimes Tribunal and held responsible for their crimes against humanity (see *Nuremberg Principles*).[20] When those who employ violence and terrorism discover that the pay-off for their actions will be a demeaning trial in a criminal court, this counter-control serves as a deterrent. The establishment of the International Criminal Court in 1998 is, therefore, a giant stride in this context.

Counter-controls must be employed nationally—only then will the disruptive and peace threatening efforts of sociopathic terrorists and paramilitary groups be contained. The presence of such controls in America became apparent following the New York Trade Center bombing and the Oklahoma bombing. Those responsible for the violence were quickly apprehended. The perpetrators were recognized, not as heroes but as villains. Counter-controls are also in effect in

Japan as revealed in the actions following the subway bombings by members of the Aum Supreme Truth sect.[21] Being caught, tried and punished makes terrorism unprofitable. Apart from the naive who become the instruments of terrorist groups and who envision themselves as heroes who die for a cause, most terrorists do not want to die (see *Terrorism*). They want to live and bask in the glory of their destructiveness. Counter-controls that pre-doom them to failure through exposure and containment are the most effective barriers to the growth and success of anti-social groups. Therefore each nation must establish counter-control units that cooperate with counter-control groups in other nations to protect citizens from terrorists.

On a familial and personal level it becomes incumbent upon every citizen of planet earth to embrace, teach and practice values that reject violence as a way of solving human problems.[22] Family members must protect one another and protection can only develop out of a caring response. When familial disputes arise, violence can never be accepted as a way to resolve the problems. We must begin within the individual family units to re-educate the human family and to redirect aggressive instincts. Child abuse, child abandonment, spouse abuse and elder abuse are on the rise world-wide. Whether the abuse be verbal, physical, psychological, neglect or abandonment, those responsible must be held accountable. Through exposure, those who prey upon others or who abuse others lose the security of anonymity and become symbols of human depravity, thereby discouraging others from engaging in such behavior. Places of refuge, where the abused can obtain counseling, shelter, food and support, must be established and maintained until the people of the world become educated to non-violent ways of settling problems.

6. Humanistic Global Family Values must Express Concern for the Health and Well-being of All Members of the Human Family

The first steps have been taken with the introduction of national health insurance programs in all first world countries except the United States and South Africa. Health protection must be extended worldwide. Epidemics can no longer be viewed as local problems but must be seen as menacing all members of the human family. Wars, crop failure, drought, earthquake and storm damage that affect the health and lives of members of the world family in one part of the globe affect us all and call for compassionate and supportive response from family members world-wide. We are one family and in the words of the 17th century British poet, John Donne we need to remember that:

> No man is an iland, intire of itself; every man is a piece of the Continent, a part of the maine; if a Clod bee washed away by the sea, Europe is the lesse, as well as if a Promontorie were, as well as if a Mannor of thy friends or of thine own were, any man's death diminishes me, because I am involved in Mankind: And therefore never send to know for whom the bell tolls, it tolls for thee. (*Devotions XVII*)

The first steps have been taken. For example, South Korea set aside past rivalries and memories of war to reach out to family members of North Korea with shipments of food. United Nations peace-keeping forces regularly respond to cries for food and medicine in ravaged countries (see *United Nations Peacekeeping Operations*). Feelings of concern for the well-being of our human family members prompt many of us to respond personally to human need. Such patterns of compassionate family outreach must be part of the value system for the 21st century.[23]

What is equally important are the efforts to close the gaps in international family relationships occasioned by inhumane behavior in the past. For example, President Jacques Chirac has publicly acknowledged and apologized for the actions of the Vichy government which, with considerable citizen support, turned Jews over to Germany for deportation to the death camps during World War II. Some 800 Germans went to Holland to apologize to the Dutch for the Nazi invasions. Pope John Paul II apologized for the Roman Catholic Church's complicity in the slave trade and the exploitation of native people throughout the Americas.[24] The Evangelical Lutheran Church in America has repudiated the 1543 anti-Semitic ravings of their founder Martin Luther and acknowledged his contribution to the Slaughter of Jews in Nazi Germany. In June, 1995, the Southern Baptist Convention, which came into being during a North-South split over slavery, issued a repudiation of "historic acts of evil" and an apology "to all African-Americans for condoning and/or perpetuating individual and systematic racism in our lifetime." Japanese Prime Minister, Tomichi Murayama, has issued two apologies: the first was to women forced into prostitution to serve Japan's armed forces before and during World War II, and the second was for his nation's deeds during World War II.[25] These acknowledgments and apologies are important recognitions of past inhumane behavior, but something more is needed. What is needed is an accompanying commitment to the present and the future that never again will the nation or the faith system become involved in any behavior or activities or attitudes that violate the civil rights or the human rights of other persons or peoples. Apologies for the past are important polite gestures; commitment to compassionate behavior in the present and in the future is essential.

7. Humanistic Global Family Values Demand Familial Responsibility as We Face the Problem of Population Control

We have learned from the past and the present what tragedies can develop when population exceeds the ability of a nation to provide food, housing, health care, nurturing and education for all of its members.

It has been estimated that more than 35,000 children die needlessly every day from starvation, malnutrition and diseases that could easily be controlled. These children are born into families unable to provide the food, clothing, shelter, health needs, comfort and help required for a meaningful life. Because of where and when they are born, they are the unwanted. Should they mature into adolescence or adulthood, their futures promise to be like those of their parents—characterized by poverty, lack of food, medicines, clothing, shelter and the necessities for a dignified and purposeful life. We no longer need to breed like animals to assure our survival; our concern must be with quality of life (see *Human Security*). It is immoral to breed children whose existence will be characterized by want, suffering, and lack of hope.[26]

As we look to future population growth, we know that we are at a point in human history when limits must be placed on the size and growth of our human family. The necessity for these limits must be taught, accepted and practiced internationally, nationally, locally and individually. To bring children into the human family without the ability or means or intent to support their health, growth and development is a desecration of family values. Every child should be a wanted child. Nor can there be discrimination on the basis of sex. A female child must be as welcome and acceptable as a male child. Presently, where efforts at population control are legislated, as in the Republic of China, there is good evidence that infant girls are abandoned, or exposed and permitted to die, or are killed, because a male child is preferred.[27] Ancient values based on sex are no longer acceptable.[28] Males and females are of equal worth and cultural or religious patterns of discrimination must be made obsolete through education and through counter-controls.

Even as we emphasize equality of the sexes it is important to realize that, despite the implications in the Universal Declaration of Human Rights (which needs to be updated to avoid sexist language), all human life is not of equal value. The declaration states that

> All human beings are born free and equal in dignity and rights. They are endowed with reason and conscience and should act towards one another in a spirit of brotherhood.

This statement is acceptable in a general sense, but it is not accurate. All human beings are not endowed with reason and conscience. Anacephalic infants are born with only functioning lower brain stems which enable them to breathe and their hearts to beat but they lack all cognitive functions and are unable to live beyond a few days. Anacephalic newborns cannot be considered "endowed with reason and conscience," nor should such an infant be considered to be of equal worth to children not so incapacitated. Similarly, a person who has entered a persistent vegetative state has lost the ability to reason and is without conscience. The PVS person cannot be accorded rights equal to those who have the ability to reason and evaluate consequences.[29] In both cases—that of the anacephalic infant and that of the person in a persistent vegetative state—these individuals will never function fully or cognitively as human beings and will forever be completely dependent on others to make life and death decisions. Nevertheless, they are still members of the human family and must be recognized as such. In the language of the Universal Declaration of Human Rights they are to be treated with dignity and accorded whatever rights are in keeping with their needs and dependency situation. Such "acting toward" might not include efforts to prolong their existence. With permission from next-of-kin, guardians, attorneys for health-care or if the PVS patient has signed an advanced directive, "acting toward" might involve the termination of these lives with a lethal injection and, under proper safeguards and with proper permissions, include the utilization of body parts for the saving of lives of others.[30] By such action, persons who do not have or who have lost the power of reason and conscience can be enabled to make valuable contributions to the welfare of the human family. In all cases and situations, the lives of family members must be honored and protected against abuse.

8. Humanistic Values must be Taught

It is one thing to propose values, but how are they to

become known and adopted? One way is through education. The word "education" comes from the Latin root *educare* which means "to lead out." As an educator, it is my task to "lead out" (*e-duco*: I lead out). "Leading out" involves the dismantling of barriers which impede humanistic ethical growth, while bringing others to a place where new ethical horizons can be seen, recognized, appreciated and approached. Eduction calls for belief in what is to be shared, commitment to the ideals embraced by humanistic values, and hope for the future (see *Education for Global Citizenship*). So many are disillusioned and without any belief in the possibility for change. The educational program, which can be instituted as part of curricula in classes ranging from kindergarten to university and also through the public media should include the following:[31]

(a) entitlement of all to rights and freedoms without discrimination based on sex, race, language, religion, politics, creed, national or social origin, prosperity, or birth;

(b) the right to personal security and protection:

(c) the right to personal liberty which includes;

- freedom from involuntary servitude or slavery;
- freedom from harassment;
- freedom of thought and conscience;
- freedom of speech and expression;
- moral freedom to express one's values and pursue one's lifestyle so long as it does not harm others or prevent others from exercising their rights;

(d) the right to privacy which calls for respect for the rights of others concerning:

- confidentiality;
- control of one's own body;
- sexual preference and orientation;
- life-stance;
- reproductive freedom within the boundaries proposed by point 7 (above);
- health care based on informed consent;
- the desire to die with dignity;

(e) the right to intellectual and cultural freedom which requires a spirit of toleration and understanding with regard to:

- the freedom to inquire and engage in research;
- the right to adequate education;
- the right to cultural enrichment;
- the right to express and publish one's views;

(f) the right to adequate health care (see point 6, above);

(g) freedom from want which means that society must guarantee:

- the right and opportunity to work;
- the satisfaction of basic needs when individuals are unable to provide for themselves;
- care for the elderly;
- care for the handicapped;
- the right to adequate leisure and relaxation;

(h) economic freedom including:

- the right to own property;
- the right to organize;
- protection from fraud;

(i) moral equality, which entails equal opportunity and equal access;

(j) equal protection under the law which is vital of a free, democratic society and includes:

- the right to a fair trial;
- the right to protection from arbitrary arrest or unusual punishment;
- the right to humane treatment;

(k) the right to democratic participation in government which includes:

- the right to vote;
- the right to assembly and association;
- the right to hold religious beliefs or not to hold religious beliefs;

(l) the rights of marriage and the family which includes:

- the right to marry or cohabit;
- the right to divorce;
- family planning;
- the right to bear and the responsibility to raise wanted children;
- child care;
- the right of children and each family member to be protected from abuse and physical or cultural deprivation.

9. Humanistic Global Family Values must be Concerned with Providing each Member of the Human Family with the Means to Become Involved in Meaningful Work, Employment or Efforts Designed to Promote the Well-being of the Entire Human Family

A meaning-filled life is more than mere existence; it involves purpose, direction and a sense of belonging. Humanistic family values embrace individual rights to autonomy, dignity, free choice, liberty, fraternity, the pursuit of happiness and security. Our human family has devised a multitude of different ways to accomplish these goals through law, education, role modeling, as well as through words, acts and symbols of encouragement and support. Each positive effort must be appreciated and inherent differences tolerated. To establish such values and the ethical standards that protect all human beings for the 21st century, we must be prepared to learn from the past, evaluate the present and project the highest and best that we know into our aspirations for the future. We must examine our values on the basis of international, national and personal commitments.

What we do now in these sessions is important. We must, each one of us, pledge ourselves to action in helping to move humankind towards a way of living where the humanistic family ethic overlays the nationalistic, linguistic, religious and ethnic differences that separate us. We work toward the time when the world will be at peace and human energy will be focused on the needs and well-being of all members of a single family, a time when we will enjoy and celebrate our unique differences while exalting the importance of our human similarities, a time when we will acknowledge the basic human needs that unite us including our mutual concerns for the futures of our children, our grand-children and our great-grand-children who constitute the future.

For the world of the 21st century, humanistic values must project the vision of a peaceful world in which no man, woman or child, or class of men, women or children shall live as servants or slaves existing simply to fulfill the whims and wishes and desires of others, a world in which no man or woman or child shall be used as a tool to satisfy the lusts or greed or ambitions of others, a world in which every human life, the life of every man, woman and child shall be a wanted, welcomed and esteemed member of one human family.

Notes

1. It is not my intent to discuss the "meaning of peace." Instead I will draw from the radio broadcast by a fellow Humanist Laureate and member of the Academy of Humanism, Johan Galtung of Norway, titled: "Solidarity in a Global Perspective" (WQXR, Jan. 27, 1987) who pointed out: Peace is not merely survival; it is not merely absentia bellum, Peace is, of course, peace with freedom . . . peace with well being . . . peace with identity . . . peace with ecological balance.

2. The importance of this concept was noted by Young Seek Choue, *White Paper on World Peace.* Seoul: Kyung Hee University Press, 1991, p. 193.

3. For example, in India young girls have been virtually enslaved as prostitutes: In the Bosnia-Serbia conflict young girls have been raped and brutalized.

4. In Los Angeles, California, Thai women, brought into the United States illegally, were enslaved and imprisoned in a building fenced with razor-wire and forced to work up to 15-hour days to produce clothing for a lucrative garment industry. The women were paid less than 25% of the prevailing minimum wage and their earnings were seized to pay for their being smuggled into the United States. In Pakistan, pre-teen-aged children were taken out of school by their parents and forced to work long hours to prepare athletic equipment for companies like Adidas.

5. This phrasing is dependent, in part, on the words of Felix Adler, the founder of the Ethical Culture Societies, *Life and Destiny,* New York: McClure, Phillips & Co, 1903, pp. 140-141.

6. A full statement of Humanist Affirmations has been published under the title: *The Affirmations of Humanism: A Statement of Principles and Values* by *Free Inquiry,* Buffalo, New York.

7. For example, Turkey has routinely sought to suppress free speech. Some 74 Turkish journalists were in prison in December, 1994, for violating laws against free expression and, according to Amnesty International, at least 26 people have "disappeared" and 11 journalists and distributors of a pro-Kurdish newspaper have been slain since 1992. So oppressive is the government that Aliza Marcus, an American correspondent for Reuters News Service, was put on trial in October, 1995, for "provoking enmity and hatred by displaying racism or regionalism." What Marcus actually did was investigate Turkish military efforts to undermine Kurdish guerrillas by destruction of Kurdish villages. "Rights Watch," *Los Angeles Times,* October 15, 1995.

8. The global village concept was emphasized by Dr. Young Seek Choue, *In Search of a New International Order Towards World Community.* Seoul: Institute of International Peace Studies, Kyung Hee University, 1991, p. 45.

9. Russell Schweicker, who was Lunar Module Pilot for the Apollo 9 earth orbital flight in March 1969, wrote of seeing "the Earth as a small thing out there" and of realizing that "on that small spot, that little blue and white thing, is everything that means anything to you—all of history and music and poetry and art and death and birth and love, tears, joy, games, all of it on that little spot out there" in "No Frames, No Boundaries" in *Beyond War, Selected Resources.* Palo Alto, CA 1985, p. 17.

10. See, Brian Fagan, "All About Eve." *Archaeology,* November-December, 1992, pp. 18-24; Robert Lee Hotz, "Genetic Study Says All Men Have a Common Ancestor." *Los Angeles Times,* May 26, 1995, pp. Al, A43; S. Päbo, "The Y Chromosome and the Origin of All of Us (Men)" *Science,* Vol. 268, May, 1995, pp. 1141-1142; R.L. Dorit, H. Akashi, W. Grant, "Absence of Polymorphism at the ZYF Locus on the Human Y Chromosome" *Science,* Vol. 268, May, 1995, pp. 1183-1185.

11. "The Age of Nations is past. The task before us now, if we would not perish, is to shake off our ancient prejudices and to build the earth." Pierre Teilharde Chardin, 1936, quoted in *Beyond War, Selected Resources,* 1985, p. 30.

12. Historian Henry Steele Commager noted in *Atlantic,* 1982 that "Every major problem that confronts us is global. Even to mitigate the problems requires the cooperation of statesmen, scientists, moral philosophers in every country."

13. The evidence of trashing ranges from the accident at the Union Carbide's plant in Bhopal, India, to the disaster at Chernobyl, Russia, to the deforestation of the tropical forests of the

Amazon in Brazil. It is estimated that there are presently between 5 and 10 million different species of life on earth and that by the end of this century we will probably have lost close to one million of these life forms.

14. In a speech delivered in July, 1957, President Dwight D. Eisenhower stated:

War in our time has become an anachronism. Whatever the case in the past war in the future can serve no useful purpose. A war which becomes general, as any limited action might, could only result in the virtual destruction of mankind.

In 1961, General Douglas MacArthur said:

The very triumph of scientific annihilation (the atom bomb) has destroyed the possibility of war's being a medium for the practical settlement of international differences. Global war has become a Frankenstein to destroy both sides. If you lose, you are annihilated. If you win, you stand only to lose (War) contains only the germs of double suicide. (Abolishing war) is the one issue upon which both sides will profit equally. It is the one issue—and the only decisive one—in which the interests are completely parallel. It is the one issue which, if settled, might settle all others.

15. In 1946 Albert Einstein declared, "The unleashed power of the atom has changed everything save our modes of thinking and we thus drift toward unparalleled catastrophe." (Quoted in "Introduction," *Beyond War: A New Way of Thinking*, Palo Alto, CA, 1985, p. 1.

16. Karl Jaspers, the German philosopher who was awarded the German Peace Prize in 1958, stated, "The threat of the atom bomb cannot be met by removing the bomb alone. It can only be met by removing war, by establishing world peace. If a new war comes, atom bombs are sure to fall. If an atomic holocaust is to be averted, no world war must break out. Every little war threatens to set off a world war. So there must be no more war." From *The Future of Mankind*, quoted in *Beyond War: Selected Resources*, p. 1.

17. The statements range from the December 24, 1967, words of Martin Luther King, Jr. "One day somebody should remind us that, even though there may be political and ideological differences between us, the Vietnamese are our brothers, the Russians are our brothers; and one day we've got to sit down together at the table of brotherhood." to what Pope John Paul II said in a speech at Hiroshima in February, 1981: "In the past, it was possible to destroy a village, a town, a region, even a country. Now it is the whole planet that has come under threat. This fact should compel everyone to face a basic moral consideration; from now on, it is only through a conscious choice and then deliberate policy that humanity can survive." (Quotations from *Beyond War: Selected Resources* Palo Alto, CA, 1985, pp. 16, 20.

18. For a discussion of the relevance of counter-controls in curbing violations of policy, see, B. F Skinner, *Cumulative Record: A Selection of Papers* (Third Edition). New York: Appleton Century-Crofts, 1972, pp. 3-38, 283-291.

19. Norman Kempster, "Neutral Nations Kept Nazi Forces Going, U.S. Says," *The Los Angeles Times*, June 3, 1998, pp. A1, A8. The materials supplied included industrial diamonds, platinum, cork and foodstuffs from Portugal; tungsten, iron ore, industrial diamonds, platinum, from Spain; iron ore, ball bearings, wood products from Sweden; chromite from Turkey; and food, arms and industrial products from Switzerland. In addition Spain provided the Blue Division that aided Germany on the Eastern Front, Sweden provided the Germans with naval escorts through the Baltic Sea and allowed transfer of arms and troops through its territory; Turkey gave Germany access to the Dardenelles; and Switzerland financed the German war machine and allowed transfer of goods, arms and troops.

20. The 1995 observation of the 50th anniversary of the Nuremberg war-crimes courts serves as a reminder of the effectiveness of that court in bringing to trial many of the brutal Nazi violators of human rights. In October, President Clinton gave his personal support to establishing a permanent standing court and observed that bringing war criminals to justice is the best way to lift collective guilt and rebuild war-torn societies. A permanent court, he noted, would be "the ultimate tribute to the people who did such important work at Nuremberg." Paul Richter, "Clinton Supports Permanent U.N. Tribunal on War Crimes," *Los Angeles Times*, October 6, 1995, p. B8.

21. Reactions to the Aum Supreme Truth sect's attacks prompted public outcry for a crackdown on religious groups and the Japanese government has responded by seeking to revise the Religious Corporation Law, shifting jurisdiction over the nation's 185,000 non-profit religious corporations from local authorities to the central government, placing it under the jurisdiction of the Education Ministry. Such a change would make it possible to ask why a religious organization, like the Aum Supreme Truth group, would need a helicopter and two pilotless drone aircraft of the type designed for delivery of biological weapons. At the same time, there is fear of recurrence of the kind of religious oppression experienced in Japan prior to World War II. Teresa Watanabe and Hilary E. MaGregor, "Control of Religions Ignite Rift in Japan," *Los Angeles Times*, October 16, 1995, pp. A3, A8.

22. Children can be taught simple formulae for peace from an early age. For example, they can recite: "I will resolve conflict. I will not use violence. I will maintain a spirit of good will. I will not preoccupy myself with destructive and hateful thoughts. I will work together with others to build a world of peace." Slogans can become commitments. (Adapted from *Beyond War: A New Way of Thinking*, p. 26. In Ankara, Turkey, Professor Joanna Kuçuradi spends time visiting orphanages where she teaches children philosophy and ethics. In Turkey and elsewhere throughout the world, first steps toward a humane and ethical future are being taken.

23. The efforts of groups like Médecins Sans Frontières (known in English as "Doctors Without Borders"), which is headquartered in Paris, France, provides a model of humanistic outreach devoid of any religious or political agenda. M.S.F. is the world's largest independent, voluntary, emergency medical assistance and relief organization. In 1954, M.S.F. sent 3,000 volunteers of 45 nationalities on medical missions to 72 countries, despite risks, to try to bring health and healing to the men, women and children refugees—victims of war and tragedy.

24. On the other hand, the Roman Catholic Church has not faced up to its silence, or as some would say, its "compliance," in the role played by Father Christian von Wernich in the so-called "dirty war" in Argentina during the 1970s (see, for example, William R. Long, "A Church Wrestles With Its Conscience Over Dirty War," *Los Angeles Times*, July 4, 1995, pp. A1, A2.

25. Sam Jameson, "Japan Apologizes to WWII Sex Slaves," *Los Angeles Times*, July 19, 1995. On August 13, 1995, Prime Minister Tomuchi Murayama issued the clearest apology yet for his nation's World War II deeds, noting that its "colonial rule and aggression caused tremendous damage and suffering." He went on to say, "In the hopes that no such mistake be made in the future, I regard in a spirit of deep humility these irrefutable facts of history and express here once again my feel-

ings of deep remorse and state my heartfelt apology." (*Los Angeles Times*, August 13, 1995, pp. A3, A21). What is lacking is a strong commitment (rather than a "hope") to guarantee Japan's commitment to peace and to humanitarian principles in the future.

26. In 1984, Jonas Salk, the creator of the vaccine that promised to eradicate polio, observed, "I see now that the major shift in human evolution is from behaving like an animal struggling to survive to behaving like an animal choosing to evolve. In fact, in order to survive, man has to evolve. And to evolve, we need a new kind of thinking and a new kind of behavior, a new ethic and a new morality. It will be that of the evolution of everyone rather than the survival of the fittest. We are driven both by survival and by evolutionary instinct. The evolutionary instinct compels us to bring out the best in ourselves and in each other, to recognize our interconnectedness with everyone else." Arianna Stassinopoulos, "Courage. Love. Forgiveness. Dr. Jonas Salk's Formula for the Future" *Beyond War, Selected Resources*, pp. 18-19.

27. The need for population control in China cannot be denied. However, there are brutal and inhuman overtones in the present situation. The abandonment of infant girls to orphanages, some of which are so poorly equipped that 85% of the infants die, has been documented and was presented on the C.B.S. television program "Eye to Eye" on August 17, 1995. The exposure of new-born girls and the aborting of female fetuses further underscores the preference for male offspring.

28. The United Nations Fourth World Congress on Women, meeting in Beijïng, China, in 1995, called attention to the plight of young women from East Asia, particularly Pakistan, Bangladesh, Sri Lanka and the Philippines, who have taken jobs as domestics in oil-rich Persian Gulf states. Not only are these vulnerable women preyed upon by recruiters who extract large shares of first-year earnings in exchange for a job and a passport, but also from employers who exert absolute control by withholding passports, salaries and food and also by subjecting these women to beatings, rape and other forms of sexual harassment and physical abuse. Exempt from many Persian Gulf government labor laws, any form of reprisal by the women (such as stabbing the rapist) results in court trials and punishment which go unreported as part of a conspiracy of silence. Irene Natividad, "End the Conspiracy of Silence," *Los Angeles Times*, October 3, 1995, p. B9.

29. For a discussion see Peter Singer, *Rethinking Life and Death: The Collapse of our Traditional Ethics*. New York: St. Martin's Press, 1994.

30. Baby Theresa Ann Campo Pearson, born anacephalic, without a skull and only enough brain stem to regulate reflexive breathing and a heartbeat, is a case in point. When her parents sought to make her organs available to other infants before Theresa died, permission was denied because under the laws of the state of Florida (and every other state) Baby Theresa could not be accepted as a viable candidate for organ donation. She lived for only nine days. Mike Clary, "Baby Theresa's Gift: Debate Over Organ-Harvesting Laws," *Los Angeles Times*, April 16, 1992, p. A5.

31. The issues presented are drawn from *A Declaration of Interdependence: A New Global Ethics* endorsed by the Board of Directors of the International Humanist and Ethical Union and the Tenth World Congress of the International Humanist and Ethical Union meeting July 10 to August 4, 1988, at the State University of New York at Buffalo. The declaration was signed by a number of Humanist Laureates, including myself.

GERALD A. LARUE